More praise for
THE BLIND SIDE

"Yet another triumph . . . [*The Blind Side*] is about much more than college football recruitment . . . it is actually about the American dream itself." —A. G. Gancarski, *Washington Times*

"Lewis has such a gift for storytelling . . . he writes as lucidly for sports fans as for those who read him for other reasons." —Janet Maslin, *New York Times*

"Grabs hold of you." —Allen Barra, *Washington Post*

"[Lewis] is advancing a new genre of journalism." —George F. Will, *New York Times Book Review*

"Lewis has perfected the art of analyzing interesting changes inside American institutions—the bond market, Major League Baseball—and then decorating the scene with personalities behind the statistics." —Jay Hancock, *Baltimore Sun*

"No reader with even a passing interest in the current state of our games should fail to read it." —Bill Littlefield, *Boston Globe*

"In *The Blind Side*, Michael Lewis provides a compelling book . . . explaining how this subtle and brutal game has changed as the balance of power has shifted between talented athletes and clever, devoted coaches." —*The Economist*

"Lewis knows how to put the reader on the field. . . . *The Blind Side* displays all of Lewis' particular writing strengths: the ability to drive a story forward, the eye for both the big picture and telling detail, shrewd wit, and an unerring instinct for discerning social complexity. . . . You'll be tempted to stand up and cheer as you read." —Susan Larson, *Times-Picayune*, New Orleans

"Lewis is a terrific reporter and a gifted prose stylist. He absorbs the vibrations of the world he immerses himself in without getting carried away. So as the book progresses, he never loses track of Michael Oher." —John Freeman, *Houston Chronicle*

"Entertaining and illuminating . . . about racial division, sporting tactics and financial arbitrage." —John Gapper, *Financial Times*

"Combining a tour de force of sports analysis with a piquant ethnography of the South's pigskin mania, Lewis probes the fascinating question of whether football is a matter of brute force or subtle intellect." —*Publishers Weekly*, starred review

"Lewis delivers a thunderous hit." —Bryan French, *Fort Worth Star-Telegram*

"As he has done before, Lewis brilliantly deconstructs a culture." —Sherryl Connelly, *New York Daily News*

"A penetrating tale . . . an engrossing, if anguished, story of serendipity and salvation." —Mark Hyman, *BusinessWeek*

"Grippingly told." —*Library Journal*, starred review

"[Lewis has] a gift for narrative pace, for sly wit, for the telling detail, for the clarity and verve of his sentences." —George W. Hunt, *America* magazine

"[*The Blind Side*] works on three levels. First as a shrewd analysis of the NFL; second, as an exposé of the insanity of big-time college football recruiting; and, third, as a moving portrait of the positive effect that love, family, and education can have in reversing the path of a life that was destined to be lived unhappily and, most likely, end badly." —Wes Lukowsky, *Booklist*, starred review

"A book about idiosyncratic idealism—but with a hopeful ending." —Jacob Weisberg, *Slate*

"It's the sort of book that one might understandably categorize as just another (true) story about football . . . but Lewis goes much deeper." —Brian Cook, *Sky* magazine

"In my recent reading of Michael Lewis's outstanding *The Blind Side*, I cried any number of times, such was the powerful effect of that story." —Robert Birnbaum, *The Morning News*

"[A] superbly written and exhaustively interviewed tale." —Steven Goode, *Vindicator*

"As good a portrait of contemporary American society [. . .] as anything that Tom Wolfe produced in his prime." —Brian Zabcik, *Corporate Counsel*

"A gripping tour through the world of college recruiting, professional football strategy, and the volatile mix of faith and sports." —*Christianity Today*

"An extraordinary and moving story of a young man who will one day be among the most highly paid athletes in the NFL." —*The Octavian*

"A look at the strategy, the underpinnings, the personalities of modern football, told personally and clearly in the form of one young player." —*Blue Ridge Business Journal*

"Lewis effortlessly moves back and forth between subtle football tactics and major social issues." —John Lawson III, *Tampa Tribune*

"A brilliant investigation of what determines success in American football and, separately, in American society."
—Mike Steib, *Void* magazine

THE BLIND SIDE

ALSO BY

MICHAEL LEWIS

Liar's Poker
The Money Culture
Pacific Rift
Losers
The New New Thing
Next
Moneyball
Coach

THE **BLIND SIDE**

Evolution of a Game

—

MICHAEL LEWIS

W. W. NORTON & COMPANY

New York London

Copyright © 2007, 2006 by Michael Lewis

All rights reserved
Printed in the United States of America
First published as a Norton paperback 2007

For information about permission to reproduce selections from this book,
write to Permissions, W. W. Norton & Company, Inc.,
500 Fifth Avenue, New York, NY 10110

Manufacturing by RR Donnelley, Bloomsburg
Paperback book design by Barbara Bachman and Devon Zahn
Production manager: Devon Zahn

Library of Congress Cataloging-in-Publication Data

Lewis, Michael (Michael M.)
The blind side : evolution of a game / Michael Lewis. — 1st ed.
p. cm.
ISBN-13: 978-0-393-06123-9 (hardcover)
ISBN-10: 0-393-06123-X (hardcover)
1. Oher, Michael. 2. Football players—United States—Biography.
3. University of Mississippi—Football. 4. College sports—United States.
I. Title.
GV939.O44L49 2006
796.332092—dc22
[B]
2006023509

ISBN 978-0-393-33047-2 pbk.

W. W. Norton & Company, Inc.
500 Fifth Avenue, New York, N.Y. 10110
www.wwnorton.com

W. W. Norton & Company Ltd.
Castle House, 75/76 Wells Street, London W1T 3QT

1 2 3 4 5 6 7 8 9 0

For Starling Lawrence

Underpaid guardian of the author's blind side.

CONTENTS

———

THE BLIND SIDE

—

BACK STORY

FROM THE SNAP of the ball to the snap of the first bone is closer to four seconds than to five. One Mississippi: The quarterback of the Washington Redskins, Joe Theismann, turns and hands the ball to running back John Riggins. He watches Riggins run two steps forward, turn, and flip the ball back to him. It's what most people know as a "flea-flicker," but the Redskins call it a "throw back special." Two Mississippi: Theismann searches for a receiver but instead sees Harry Carson coming straight at him. It's a runing down—the start of the second quarter, first and 10 at midfield, with the score tied 7–7—and the New York Giants' linebacker has been so completely suckered by the fake that he's deep in the Redskins' backfield. Carson thinks he's come to tackle Riggins but Riggins is long gone, so Carson just keeps running, toward Theismann. Three Mississippi: Carson now sees that Theismann has the ball. Theismann notices Carson coming straight at him, and so he has time to avoid him. He steps up and to the side and Carson flies right on by and out of the play. The play is now 3.5 seconds old.

Until this moment it has been defined by what the quarterback can see. Now it—and he—is at the mercy of what he can't see.

You don't think of fear as a factor in professional football. You assume that the sort of people who make it to the NFL are immune to the emotion. Perhaps they don't mind being hit, or maybe they just don't get scared; but the idea of pro football players sweating and shaking and staring at the ceiling at night worrying about the next day's violence seems preposterous. The head coach of the Giants, Bill Parcells, didn't think it preposterous, however. Parcells, whose passion is the football defense, believed that fear played a big role in the game. So did his players. They'd witnessed up close the response of opposing players to their own Lawrence Taylor.

The tackle who had just quit the Philadelphia Eagles, for instance. Jerry Sisemore had played tackle in the NFL for eight years when, in 1981, Taylor arrived. Sisemore played on the right side of the offensive line and Taylor usually came off the other end, but Sisemore still had to worry about the few times Taylor lined up across from him. Their teams were in the same NFL division and met twice each regular season. The week leading up to those games, Sisemore confessed, unnerved him. "Towards the middle of the week something would come over you and you'd just start sweating," he told the *New York Times*. "My last year in the league, opening day, he immediately got past me. . . . He just looked at me and laughed. Right there I thought I had to get out of this game." And after that season, 1984, he did.

The feelings of those assigned to prevent Taylor from hurting quarterbacks were trivial compared to those of the quarterbacks he wanted to hurt. In Taylor's first season in the NFL, no official records were kept of quarterback sacks. In 1982, after Taylor had transformed the quarterback sack into the turning point of a football game, a new official NFL statistic was born. The record books defined the sack as tackling the quarterback behind the line of scrimmage as he attempts to pass. Taylor offered his own definition: "A sack is when you run up behind somebody who's not watching, he doesn't see you, and you really put your helmet into him. The ball goes fluttering everywhere and the coach comes out and asks the quarterback, 'Are you all right?' That's a sack." After his first NFL season Taylor became the only rookie ever named the league's most valuable defensive player, and he published a treatise on his art. "I don't like to just wrap the quarterback," he explained. "I really try to make him see seven fingers when they hold up three. I'll drive my helmet into him, or, if I can, I'll bring my arm up over my head and try to axe the sonuvabitch in two. So long as the guy is holding the ball, I intend to hurt him. . . . If I hit the guy right, I'll hit a nerve and he'll feel electrocuted, ne'll forget for a few seconds that he's on a football field."

The game of football evolved and here was one cause of its evolution, a new kind of athlete doing a new kind of thing. All by himself, Lawrence Taylor altered the environment and forced opposing coaches and players to adapt. After Taylor joined the team, the Giants went from the second worst defense in the NFL to the third best. The year before his debut they gave up 425 points; his first year they gave up 257 points. They had been one of the weakest teams in the NFL and were now, overnight, a contender. Of course, Taylor wasn't the only change in the New York Giants between 1980 and 1981. There was one other important newcomer, Bill Parcells, hired first to coach the Giants' defense and then the entire team. Parcells became a connoisseur of the central nervous system of opposing quarterbacks. The symptoms induced by his sack-happy linebacker included, but were not restricted to: "intimidation, lack of confidence, quick throws, nervous feet, concentration lapses, wanting to know where Lawrence is all the time." The players on the Giants' defense picked up the same signals. As defensive back Beasley Reece told the *New York Times*, "I've seen quarterbacks look at Lawrence and forget the snap count." One opposing quarterback, finding himself under the center before the snap and unable to locate Taylor, called a time-out rather than run the play—only to find Taylor standing on the sidelines. "I think I saw it more with the quarterbacks in our division," says Giants linebacker Harry Carson. "They knew enough to be afraid. But every quarterback had a certain amount of fear when he played us."

By his fourth pro season Taylor was not just feeding these fears but feeding off them. "They come to the line of scrimmage and the first thing they do is start looking for me," he said. "I know, and they know. When they'd find me they'd start screaming: *56 left! 56 left!* [Taylor wore No. 56.] So there's this thing I did. After the play was over I'd come up behind them and whisper: *don't worry where I am. I'll tell you when I get there.*"

A new force in pro football, Taylor demanded not just a tactical response but an explanation. Many people pointed to his unusual combination of size and speed. As one of the Redskins' linemen put it, "No human being should be six four, two forty-five, and run a four-five forty." Bill Parcells thought Taylor's size and speed were closer to the beginning than to the end of the explanation. New York Giants' scouts were scouring the country for young men six three or taller, 240 pounds or heavier, with speed. They could be found. In that pool of physical specimens what was precious—far more precious than an inch, or ten pounds, or one tenth of a second—was Taylor's peculiar energy and mind: relentless, manic, with grandiose ambitions and private standards of performance. Parcells believed that even in the NFL a lot of players were more concerned with seeming to want to win than with actually winning, and that many of them did not know the difference. What they wanted, deep down, was to keep their jobs, make their money, and go home. Lawrence Taylor wanted to win. He expected more of himself on the field than a coach would dare to ask of any player.

Parcells accumulated lots of anecdotal evidence in support of his view of Taylor's football character. One of his favorites involved these very same Washington Redskins. "Joe Gibbs in a game in

Giants Stadium basically decided that Taylor wasn't going to make any plays," said Parcells. "He put two tight ends on Taylor's side— along with the left tackle—and two wide receivers in the slot away from Taylor." This was extreme. An NFL football field is a tightly strung economy. Everything on it comes at a price. Take away from one place and you give to another. Three men blocking Taylor meant two Giants with no one to block them. Taylor's effect on the game, which the Giants won, was not obvious but it was nonethe- less great. "But after the game," Parcells continued:

The press sees that Lawrence doesn't have a sack and hasn't made a tackle and they're all asking me "what's the matter with Taylor?" The next week we go out to San Diego to play the Chargers. Dan Henning is the coach. He sees the strat- egy. They do the same thing. Two tight ends on Lawrence, two wide receivers in the slot. Lawrence doesn't get a sack. We win again. But after the game everyone is asking me all over again: "what's the matter with Taylor?" I grab Lawrence in the locker room and say to him, "I'm going to change your first name from Lawrence to What's The Matter With?" At practice that next week he was What's The Matter With? "What you doin' over there What's The Matter With?" "Hey, What's The Matter With?, how come you aren't making plays?" By Thursday it's not funny to him. And I mean it is really *not* funny.

The next game we have is against the Vikings on Mon- day Night Football. Tommy Kramer is the quarterback. They don't employ the strategy. He knocks Kramer out of the game, causes two fumbles and recovers one of them. I'm leaving the field, walking down the tunnel towards the locker room for the press conference. And out of nowhere this . . . *thing* comes and jumps on my back. I didn't know he was coming. He basically knocks me over. He's still got his helmet on. Sweat's still pouring down his face. He comes right up into my face and hollers, "I tell you what Coachy, they aren't going to ask you What's The Matter With?!!"

Parcells believed Taylor's greatness was an act of will, a refusal to allow the world to understand him as anything less than great. "That's why I loved him so much," he said. "He responded to *anything* that threatened his status." When in the middle of his career Taylor became addicted to cocaine, Parcells interpreted the problem as a simple extension of the man's character. Lawrence Taylor trusted in one thing, the power of his own will. He assumed that his will could control NFL football games, and that it could also control his own chemical desires.

He was right about the NFL games. By November 18, 1985, when the Giants went into Robert F. Kennedy Stadium in Washington, DC, to play the Redskins, opposing teams have taken to lining up their players in new and creative ways simply to deal with him. The Redskins are a case in point. Early in the very first game in which his Redskins had faced this new force, back in 1981, Joe Gibbs had watched Taylor sprint past the blocker as if he wasn't there and clobber Joe Theismann from behind. "I was standing there," said Gibbs, "and I said, 'What? Did you see that? Oh Lord.'" Gibbs had flopped about looking for a solution to this new problem, and had come up with the "one back offense"—a formation, widely imitated in the NFL, that uses one running back instead of two. Until that moment, football offenses had typically used running backs to block linebackers who came charging after quarterbacks. But running backs were smaller, weaker, and, surprisingly often, given their job description, slower than Lawrence Taylor. Lynn Cain, a running back for the Atlanta Falcons, was the first to dramatize the problem. The first time Cain went to block Taylor he went in very low, got up underneath him, and sent Taylor flying head over heels. The next play Cain tried it again—and was carried off the field on a stretcher. "People figured out *very* quickly that they couldn't block Lawrence with a running back," Parcells said. "Then the question became: who do you block him with?" Hence Joe Gibbs's first solution: to remove the running back from the game and insert, across the line from Lawrence Taylor, a bigger, stronger tight end. The one back offense.

That will be the strategy tonight, but Joe Theismann knows too well its imperfections. Having that extra blocker to help the tackle addressed the problem, Theismann thought, without solving it. Too often Taylor came free. The week of practice leading up to the game had been a seminar on Lawrence Taylor. "If you looked at our overhead projector or our chalkboard," said Theismann, "all the other Giants players were X's or O's. Lawrence was the only one who had a number: fifty-six. He was a little red fifty-six and the number was always highlighted and circled. The goal was: let's identify where Lawrence is on every play." Taylor moved around a lot, to confuse the defense, but he and his coach were happiest when he came from his own right side and the quarterback's left. "The big reason I put him over there," said Bill Parcells, "is the right side is the quarterback's blind side, since most quarterbacks are right-handed. And no one wants to get his ass knocked off from the back side." Lawrence Taylor was more succinct: "Why the hell would I want to come from where he can see me?" But then he added: "It wasn't really called the blind side when I came into the league. It was called the right side. It *became* the blind side after I started knocking people's heads off."

Where Taylor is at the start of the play, of course, isn't the problem. It's where he ends up. "When I dropped back," says Theismann, "the first thing I still did was to glance over my shoulder to see if he was coming. If he was dropping back in coverage, a sense of calm came over me. If he was coming, I had a sense of urgency."

Four Mississippi: Taylor is coming. From the snap of the ball Theismann has lost sight of him. He doesn't see Taylor carving a wide circle behind his back; he doesn't see Taylor outrun his blocker upfield and then turn back down; and he doesn't see the blocker diving, frantically, at Taylor's ankles. He doesn't see Taylor leap, both arms over his head, and fill the sky behind him. Theismann prides himself on his ability to stand in the pocket and disregard his fear. He thinks this quality is a prerequisite in a successful NFL quarterback. "When a quarterback looks at the rush," he says, "his career is over." Theismann has played in 163 straight games, a record for the Washington Redskins. He's led his team to two Super Bowls, and won one. He's thirty-six years old. He's certain he still has a few good years left in him. He's wrong. He has less than half a second.

The game is on ABC's *Monday Night Football*, and 17.6 million people have tuned in. Frank Gifford is in the booth, flanked by O. J. Simpson and Joe Namath. "Theismann's in a lot of trouble," the audience hears Gifford say, just before Taylor's arms jackknife Theismann's head to his knees and Taylor's torso pins Theismann's right leg to the ground. Four other players, including, oddly, the Redskins' John Riggins, pile on. They're good for dramatic effect but practically irrelevant. The damage is done by Taylor alone. One hundred and ninety-six pounds of quarterback come to rest beneath a thousand or so pounds of other things. Then Lawrence Taylor pops to his feet and begins to scream and wave and clutch his helmet with both hands, as if in agony.

His reaction is a mystery until ABC Sports clarifies the event, by replaying it over and again, in slow motion. "Again, we'll look at it with the reverse angle one more time," says Frank Gifford. "And I suggest if your stomach is weak, you just don't watch." People watched; the replay was almost surely better attended than the original play. Doug Flutie was probably a representative viewer. Flutie had just finished a glorious college quarterbacking career at Boston College and started a professional one in the USFL. On the evening of November 18, 1985, he was at home with his mother.

She had the football game on; he had other things to do. "I heard my mother scream," he told a reporter. "And then I saw the replay. It puts fear in your heart and makes you wonder what the heck you're doing playing football."

THERE'S AN INSTANT before it collapses into some generally agreed-upon fact when a football play, like a traffic accident, is all conjecture and fragments and partial views. Everyone wants to know the whole truth but no one possesses it. Not the coach on the sidelines, not the coach in the press box, and certainly not the quarterback—no one can see the whole field and take in the movement of twenty-two bodies, each with his own job assignment. In baseball or basketball all the players see, more or less, the same events. Points of view vary, but slightly. In football many of the players on the field have no idea what happened—much less why it happened—until after the play is done. Even then, most of them will need to watch a videotape to be sure. The fans, naturally more interested in effect than cause, follow the ball, and come away thinking they know perfectly well what just happened. But what happened to the ball, and to the person holding the ball, was just the final link in a chain of events that began well before the ball was snapped. At the beginning of the chain that ended Joe Theismann's career was an obvious question: who was meant to block Lawrence Taylor?

Two players will be treated above all others as the authorities on the play: Joe Theismann and Lawrence Taylor. The victim didn't have a view of the action; the perpetrator was so intent on what he was doing that he didn't stop to look. "The play was a blur," said Taylor. "I had taken the outside. I was thinking: keep him in the pocket and squeeze him. Then I broke free." Why he broke free he couldn't say, as he didn't actually notice who was trying to block him. Theismann, when asked who was blocking Taylor on that play, will reply, "Joe Jacoby, our left tackle." He won't *blame* Jacoby, as the guy was one of the two or three finest left tackles of his era, and was obviously just doing his best. That's why it made no sense, in Joe Theismann's opinion, for an NFL team to blow big bucks on an offensive lineman: there was only so much a lineman could do. Even when his name was Joe Jacoby.

That was one point of view. Another was Jacoby's who, on that night, was standing on the sidelines, in street clothes. He'd strained ligaments in his knee and was forced to sit out. When Joe Jacoby played, he was indeed a splendid left tackle. Six seven and 315 pounds, he was shaped differently from most left tackles of his time, and more like the left tackle of the future. "A freak of nature ahead of his time," his position coach, Joe Bugel, called him, two decades later. Jacoby wasn't some lump of cement; he was an athlete. In high school he'd been a star basketball player. He could run, he could jump, he had big, quick hands. "We put him at left tackle for one reason," said Bugel, "to match up against Lawrence Taylor." The first time they'd met, Jacoby had given Lawrence Taylor fits— he was a 300-pounder before the era of 300-pounders, with hands so big they felt like hooks. Taylor had been forced to create a move just for Jacoby. "Geritol," Taylor called it, "because after the snap I tried to look like an old man running up to him." Unable to overwhelm him physically, Taylor sought to lull Jacoby into a tactical mistake. He'd come off the ball at a trot to lure Jacoby into putting his hands up before he reached him. The moment he did— *Wham!*—he'd try to knock away Jacoby's hands before he latched on. A burst of violence and he was off to the races.

Still, Jacoby was one of the linemen that always gave Taylor trouble, because he was so big and so quick and so long. "The hardest thing for me to deal with," said Taylor, "was that big, agile left tackle."

Offensive linemen were the stay-at-home mothers of the NFL: everyone paid lip service to the importance of their contribution yet hardly anyone could tell you exactly what that was. In 1985 the left tackle had no real distinction. He was still expected to believe himself more or less interchangeable with the other linemen. The Washington Redskins' offensive line was perhaps the most famous in NFL history. It had its own nickname: the Hogs. Fans dressed as pigs in their honor. And yet they weren't understood, even by their own teammates, in the way running backs or quarterbacks were understood, as individual players with particular skills. "Even people who said they were fans of the Hogs had no idea who we were," said Jacoby. "They couldn't even tell the black ones from the white ones. I had people see me and scream, 'Hey May!' " (Right tackle Mark May was black; Jacoby was not.)

That night, with Jacoby out, the Redskins moved Russ Grimm from his position at left guard to left tackle. Grimm was four inches shorter, 30 pounds lighter, and far less agile than Jacoby. "Little Porky Grimm," line coach Joe Bugel called him. As a result, he needed help, and got it, in the form of the extra tight end, a fellow named Don Warren. If Taylor made his move to the inside, Grimm was expected to deal with him; if Taylor went on a wide loop outside, Grimm was meant, at most, to punch him, to slow him down, and give Warren the time to stay with him. From his spot on the sidelines, Jacoby watched as Taylor went outside. Grimm couldn't lay a hand on him and so Warren was left alone with Taylor. "They weren't used to his speed," said Jacoby. He watched Taylor race upfield and leave Warren in the dust, then double back on the quarterback.

Jacoby then heard what sounded like a gunshot—the tibia and fibula in Joe Theismann's right leg snapping beneath Taylor. He watched as Grimm and Warren removed their helmets and walked quickly toward the sidelines, like men fleeing the scene of a crime. He listened as Grimm told him that Theismann's bone lay exposed, and his blood was spurting straight up in the air. "Russ was a hunter," said Jacoby. "He'd gutted deer. And he said, 'That's the most disgusting thing I've ever seen.'" And Jacoby thought: *It happened because I'm standing over here.* Years later he wouldn't be surprised that Theismann did not realize his great left tackle was standing on the sidelines. "But that's why his leg got broken," he said.

A few minutes later, six men bore Theismann on a stretcher to an ambulance. In ABC's booth, Joe Namath said, "I just hope it's not his last play in football." But it was. Nearly a year later Joe Theismann would be wandering around the Redskins locker room unable to feel his big toe, or to push off his right leg. He'd become a statistic: the *American Journal of Sports Medicine* article on the injuries to NFL quarterbacks between 1980 and 2001 would count Theismann's two broken bones as just one of a sample of 1,534— 77.4 percent of which occur, just as this one had, during games, on passing plays. The game continued and the Redskins, surprisingly, won, 28–23. And most people who did not earn their living in the NFL trying to figure out how to protect their increasingly expensive quarterbacks shoved the incident to the back of their minds. Not ten minutes after Theismann was hauled off the field, Lawrence Taylor himself pounced on a fumble and ran to the bench, jubilant. Frank Gifford sought to persuade his audience that Taylor was still obviously feeling upset about what he had done to Joe Theismann. But the truth is that he didn't look at all upset. He looked as if he'd already gotten over it.

What didn't make sense on that night was Taylor's initial reaction. He leapt out of the pile like a man on fire. Those who had watched Taylor's career closely might have expected a bit more sangfroid in the presence of an injured quarterback. The destruction of Joe Theismann may have been classified an accident, but it wasn't an aberration. It was an extension of what Lawrence Taylor had been doing to NFL quarterbacks for four and a half years. It wasn't even the first time Taylor had broken a quarterback's leg, or ended a quarterback's career. In college, in the Gator Bowl, he had taken out the University of Michigan's quarterback, John Wangler. Before Taylor hit him, Wangler had been a legitimate NFL prospect. ("I was invited to try out for the Lions and the Cowboys," Wangler said later. "But everyone was kind of afraid of the severity of my injury.")

As it turned out, there was a simple explanation: Taylor was claustrophobic. His claustrophobia revealed itself in the way he played the game: standing up looking for the best view, refusing to bend over and get down in the dirt with the other players, preferring the long and open outside route to the quarterback over the short, tight inside one. It revealed itself, also, in the specific fear of being trapped at the bottom of a pile and not being able to escape. "That's what made me so frantic," he said. "I've already dreamed it—if I get on the bottom of a pile and I'm really hurt. And I can't get out." Now he lay at, or near, the bottom of a pile, on top of a man whose leg he'd broken so violently that the sound was heard by Joe Jacoby on the sidelines. And he just had to get out. He leapt to his feet screaming, hands clutching the sides of his helmet, and—the TV cameras didn't pick this up—lifting one foot unconsciously and rubbing his leg with it. It was the only known instance of Lawrence Taylor imagining himself into the skin of a quarterback he had knocked from a game. "We all have fears," he said. "We all have fears."

▬

CHAPTER TWO

THE MARKET FOR
FOOTBALL PLAYERS

S OMEONE HAD SENT Tom Lemming a tape, but then Tom Lemming received thousands of tapes from thousands of football coaches and parents who wanted their kids to make the various high school All-American teams he selected. He at least glanced at all of them—usually quickly. This tape was different; this tape he watched in wonder. He knew right away that this boy was a special case. He lived and played in Memphis, Tennessee, and Memphis was always rich in raw high school football talent—so that wasn't it. "The tape was grainy and you couldn't see very well," said Lemming. "But when he came off the line, it looked like one whole wall was moving. And it was just one player! You had to look at it twice to believe it: he was that big. And yet he would get out and go chase down, and catch, these fast little linebackers. When I saw the tape I guess I didn't really believe it. I saw how he moved and I wondered how big he really was—because no one who is that big should be able to move that fast. It just wasn't possible."

As he drove into Memphis in March of 2004, Lemming

thought: everything about Michael Oher, including his surname, was odd. He played for a small private school, the Briarcrest Christian School, with no history of generating Division I college football talent. The Briarcrest Christian School team didn't typically have black players, either, and Michael Oher was black. But what made Michael Oher especially peculiar was that no one in Memphis had anything to say about him. Lemming had plenty of experience "discovering" great players. Each year he drove 50,000 to 60,000 miles and met, and grilled, between 1,500 and 2,000 high school juniors. He got inside their heads months before the college recruiters were allowed to shake their hands. It didn't happen as much as it used to, but he still found future NFL stars to whom the recruiters were oblivious. For instance, no one outside of Newport News, Virginia, had ever heard of Michael Vick—future number one pick in the entire NFL draft and quarterback of the Atlanta Falcons—before Lemming stumbled upon him and wrote him up in his newsletter. But even in the case of Michael Vick, the people closest to him knew he had talent. Michael Vick was no secret in Newport News, Virginia. Michael Oher was as good as invisible, even in Memphis, Tennessee. Lemming asked around, and the local high school coaches either didn't know who he was or didn't think he was any good. He hadn't made so much as the third string all-city team. He hadn't had his name or picture in any newspaper. An Internet search for "Oher" yielded nothing on him. The only proof of his existence was this grainy videotape.

From the tape alone, Lemming couldn't say how much Michael Oher had helped his team, just that he was big, fast, and fantastically explosive. "To make my lists they almost always have to have production," said Lemming. By "production" he meant honors and achievements—not mere potential. "He was different from just about every other kid I picked to be a high school All-American in that he didn't have any." But if Michael Oher in the flesh was anything like Michael Oher on the videotape, Lemming was afraid *not* to make an exception of him. He had his reputation to protect. Nothing was as embarrassing to him as leaving a kid off his lists who, four years later, was a first-round NFL draft pick. And the last time he had seen a player with this awesome array of physical gifts was back in 1993, when he went to the Sizzler Steakhouse in Sandusky, Ohio, and interviewed a high school junior working behind the counter named Orlando Pace.

"Michael Oher's athletic ability and his body—the only thing you could compare it to was Orlando Pace," said Lemming. "He kind of even looked like Orlando Pace. He wasn't as polished as Orlando. But Orlando wasn't Orlando in high school." Pace had gone from Lemming's All-American team to Ohio State, where he'd played left tackle and won the Outland Award given to the nation's finest college offensive lineman. In 1997, he'd signed the largest rookie contract in NFL history, to play left tackle for the St. Louis Rams, and he was about to sign an even bigger one (seven years, $52.8 million). Pace became, and would remain, the team's highest paid player—more highly paid than the star quarterback, Marc Bulger, the star running back, Marshall Faulk, and the star wide receiver, Isaac Bruce. He was an offensive lineman but not just any offensive lineman. He protected the quarterback's blind side.

When Tom Lemming walked into the football meeting room at the University of Memphis, looking for Michael Oher, the ghost of Lawrence Taylor was waiting. Taylor's legacy had led to a queasy tilting of the finances on the NFL's line of scrimmage. The players on the blind side of a right-handed quarterback—both offensive and defensive—became, on average, far more highly paid than the players on the visible side. This was strange. There was no financial distinction between left and right guards. Right-side linebackers who (unlike Taylor) routinely played off the line of scrimmage continued to be paid the same, on average, as left-side linebackers. Right-side cornerbacks, even further from the line of scrimmage, were paid the same as left-side cornerbacks. Only the two players engaged in the battle for control of the turf between the line of scrimmage and the right-handed quarterback's back were paid more than their counterparts on the side that the typical, right-handed quarterback faced. A lot more. By 2004, the five most highly paid NFL left tackles were earning nearly $3 million a year more than the five most highly paid right tackles, and more than the five most highly paid running backs and wide receivers.*

The fantastic general rise in overall NFL salaries since 1993, when players were granted the right of free agency, obscured a more striking shift in relative pay. The players all made so much more money each year than they had the year before that few paid much attention to the trends within the trend. But there were several, and this was the most revelatory. In the early 1980s, the notion that a single lineman should be paid much more than any other—and more than star running backs, wide receivers, and, in several cases, quarterbacks—would have been considered heretical had it not been so absurd. The offensive line never abandoned, at least in public, its old, vaguely socialistic ideology. All for one, one for all, as to do our jobs well we must work together, and thus no one of us is especially important. But by the mid-1990s the market dis-

---

* Most NFL teams line up in what is called a 4-3 defense. In the 4-3, the seven defenders closest to the line of scrimmage are arranged like this:

X X X

X' X X X

In this formation the right defensive end, X', becomes the leading blind side pass rusher. Bill Parcells—and a few other NFL coaches—prefer to line up their defense in a 3-4, which looks like this:

X' X X X

X X X

In the 3-4, the outside right-side linebacker (X') plays the role of lead blind side rusher.

agreed: it had declared this one member of the offensive line a superstar. Not some interchangeable homunculus, not low-skilled labor, but a rare talent. This judgment was not rendered overnight; it was the end of a long story, of football coaches and general managers sifting and judging and scrambling to determine the relative importance of the positions on a football field, and to find the people best suited to play them. And at the beginning of the story was Tom Lemming.

BACK IN 1978, at the age of twenty-three, Lemming had an idea: he'd travel America and meet the top high school football players in the country, and decide which ones were the best. There was no videotape, so he had to visit high schools and ask to see the 16mm film of their players. While there he'd interview the players, get a sense of their characters, and extract from them everything from their college preference to their grade point averages. Then he'd publish a book ranking them. "I had such excitement knowing I was doing something no one else was doing," he said later. "No one had ever gone to see everyone in the country." When he drove away from his home in Chicago he had to wonder who was going to pay for his bizarre enterprise. No one, at first: In the early days he spent every other night sleeping in his car at an Oasis truck stop. ("But then people started shooting people in Oasises, so I had to find different places to park.") The first year his budget allowed him to meet and interview every notable high school football player east of the Mississippi. The next year he crossed the Mississippi and went right to the base of the Rockies. "I would go as far as my cash would take me," he said. "I was sort of like Lewis and Clark, except instead of waiting for resupply I was waiting for enough radio shows to promote my books." In 1983 he crossed the Rockies and never looked back.

It took him seven years to turn a profit, but by then he had a frantic following in college football. What must have seemed at first a mad notion—why would anyone care what some twenty-three-year-old guy with no experience thought about high school football players? Why would any high school football star waste his time answering the questions of a stranger and filling out intrusive forms?—became a thriving business. Bear Bryant, Dan Devine, Bo Schembechler—all these big-time football coaches took an interest in Lemming's work. He was, in effect, the only national football scout in America. Baseball had hundreds of scouts—guys who spent 365 days a year traveling the country to evaluate teenagers. Strictly speaking, of course, a sixteen-year-old football player wasn't a commodity in the way a sixteen-year-old baseball player was. A high school baseball player could be drafted to play in the pros; a high school football player could not. Less strictly speaking, high school football players were far more highly prized, in part because colleges could usurp a great deal of their (skyrocketing) market value. Eight times a year Lemming published a newsletter to which all but seven of the 117 Division I college football programs subscribed. After they'd read it, all these college football coaches would call Lemming for the kids' addresses, phone numbers, and anything else he might know about them. High school football players across the country, with the help of their fathers and their coaches, inundated Lemming's little office in Chicago with tapes of their performances, press clippings, and letters of recommendation. All they wanted was for him to make them famous.

There simply was no one else doing what Lemming was doing. Overnight he became, by default, the leading independent authority on the subject of U.S. high school football players. It was a booming market with an obvious gap: colleges on one side of the country had no information about players on the other. Even in the lawless days of football recruiting—before the NCAA began seriously to crack down, in the late 1980s—recruiters from big-time football schools hunted for talent mostly in their own backyards. Coach Bear Bryant's machine at the University of Alabama spent its time and energies on southern players; Bo Schembechler's machine at the University of Michigan spent its time and energy on players in the Midwest. In the late 1980s, when the NCAA began to pass, and enforce, elaborate rules governing the interaction between college football coaches and high school football players, the hole in the market widened. College football coaches were forbidden to so much as wink at a prospect until he began his senior year. By then Lemming had studied the prospect's play, his character, and his grade point average. Plus he'd have a pretty good idea of where the kid might like to go to college.

The flow of information improved—videotape, cell phones, the Internet all made his life a lot easier—and Lemming's ability to make sense of it improved as well. When he started out, he felt, he had been too impressed by sheer physical talent and insufficiently respectful of actual on-field achievement. He'd thought future great NFL running back Barry Sanders was too small, for instance, even though he'd run for a zillion yards in high school. He still made mistakes, but fewer. By the 1990s he had a vast, informal network of informants whom he trusted—high school coaches and fans, mainly—who allowed him to shrink the pool of 3 million high school football players down to a few thousand. He watched tapes of those players and winnowed the pool to about 1,500, whom he interviewed in person. From those he selected 400 for his annual book of the nation's top prospects, and from the book he culled his list of the Top 100 players in the nation. And finally, he selected his most rarified group, the 25 or so high school players he pronounced "All-Americans." His hit rate was very high. Of the twenty-five players he picked in 1995, for instance, fourteen wound up becoming number one draft choices in the NFL. In the mid-1990s, ESPN began to publish an All-American team, selected by Lemming. *USA Today* published another one, also mainly selected by Lemming. In 2000, the U.S. Army High School All-American football game was born, and broadcast on national television. Lemming selected the eighty players for the game. Reggie Bush, Vince Young, Adrian Petersen, Dwayne Jarrett, Chris Leak, LenDale White, Brady Quinn: the game became a turnstile for future Heisman Trophy candidates and top NFL draft picks.

As the noise grew louder, and the money got bigger, the politics became worse: coaches and players pestered Lemming to be included in his books, and on his lists, and in the Game. At some point he basically ceased to believe what anyone told him about a high school football player. "There's a reason I'm on the road six months a year," he said. "I would never rely on what people tell me. I have to see 'em." By the spring of 2004, he found himself interviewing the sons of players he had interviewed twenty-five years earlier. His business, and his influence, grew, but Lemming kept on doing what he'd always done. He still drove 50,000 to 60,000 miles each year and interviewed, in the flesh, between 1,500 and 2,000 high school football players. He was a one-man sifting machine.

One of the perks of Lemming's role in the market was a worm's-eye view of its trends. When he opened for business, he assumed he was simply identifying future college football stars. He didn't give much thought to their professional futures. College football was mainly a running game, for instance, and the NFL, increasingly, was a passing game. College football had an appetite for all sorts of players the pros had no use for: option quarterbacks, slow fullbacks, midget linebackers. That changed as the big-time football programs came to function as training schools for the NFL. To attract the best high school players they had to persuade them that they offered the smoothest path to the NFL. It helped, then, if they ran NFL-style offenses and defenses. Because of this—

and because of the steady flow of NFL coaches into college football—college football became more homogenous, and less distinguishable from the game played in the NFL. In the late 1980s, Lemming began to notice the erosion in the differences between college and pro football. By the mid-1990s he saw that, in identifying the best future college football players, he was identifying the best future professional ones, too.

The other, related trend was a trickle-down of NFL prototypes into America's high schools. The NFL would discover a passion for athletic (read: black) quarterbacks, or speedy pass rushers, and first the colleges and then the high schools would begin to supply them. There was a lag, of course. If Lawrence Taylor created a new vogue in the NFL for exceptionally violent and speedy pass rushers with his dimensions in 1981, it might be 1986 before Lemming encountered a big new wave of similarly shaped violent and speedy high school pass rushers. But the wave always came. What the NFL prized, America's high schools supplied, and America's colleges processed. "It goes from Sunday to Saturday to Friday, five years later," said Lemming. The types came and went—one decade there would be a vogue for speedy little receivers, the next decade the demand would be for tall, lanky receivers. And there were antitypes; Lord help the white running back or wide receiver or, until the early 1990s, the black quarterback. The Lawrence Taylor type, however, came and never left. When Lemming hit the road in 2004, he knew he would find big linebackers, and small defensive ends, whose chief future use would be to wreak havoc with the minds and bodies of quarterbacks. He also knew that he'd find the type that had arisen across the line of scrimmage in response. The guy who could stop the Lawrence Taylor type. The left tackle type.

When Tom Lemming looked at left tackles, he thought in terms of others he had selected for his All-American teams who went on to be stars in the NFL: Jonathan Ogden, Orlando Pace, Walter

Jones, Willie Roaf. These people looked nothing like most human beings, or even the players Lemming interviewed in the late 1970s and 1980s. "Two hundred and fifty pounds used to be huge for a high school lineman," he said. "Now you've got to be three hundred pounds or no one will look at you." Even in this land of giants, the left tackle type stood out. *Freak of nature*: when he found one of these rare beasts, that's the phrase that popped into Lemming's mind to describe him. When Lemming put high school junior Jonathan Ogden on the cover of his *Annual Prep Report*, Ogden was six foot nine inches tall and weighed 320 pounds. (He'd fill out in college.) When he did the same with Orlando Pace, Pace stood six six and weighed 310 pounds. (And hadn't stopped growing.) The ideal left tackle was big, but a lot of people were big. What set him apart were his more subtle specifications. He was wide in the ass and massive in the thighs: the girth of his lower body lessened the likelihood that Lawrence Taylor, or his successors, would run right over him. He had long arms: pass rushers tried to get in tight to the blocker's body, then spin off of it, and long arms helped to keep them at bay. He had giant hands, so that when he grabbed ahold of you, it meant something.

But size alone couldn't cope with the threat to the quarterback's blind side, because that threat was also fast. The ideal left tackle also had great feet. Incredibly nimble and quick feet. Quick enough feet, ideally, that the idea of racing him in a five-yard dash made the team's running backs uneasy. He had the body control of a ballerina and the agility of a basketball player. The combination was just incredibly rare. And so, ultimately, very expensive.

The price of protecting quarterbacks was driven by the same forces that drove the price of other kinds of insurance: it rose with the value of the asset insured, with the risk posed to that asset. Quarterbacks had become wildly expensive. Even the rookie quarterback contracts now included huge guarantees. The San Francisco 49ers had agreed to pay Alex Smith $56 million over seven years; and if his career ended tomorrow, they'd still owe him $24 million. The New York Giants were paying their young quarterback, Eli Manning, $54 million for his first seven years of service; if an injury ended his career, they were still on the line for $20 million. The highest paid NFL quarterback, Eli's brother, Peyton Manning of the Indianapolis Colts, had a seven-year contract worth $99.2 million. Several others made nearly $10 million a year. The money wasn't all guaranteed, but a career-ending injury still cost an NFL franchise millions of dollars—if Peyton Manning suffered a career-ending injury, the Colts were out of pocket about half of their entire 2005 payroll. And those lost dollars would be but a fraction of the Colts' misery; there would also be the cost of playing without their star quarterback. When a star running back or wide receiver is injured, the coaches worry about their game plans. When a star quarterback gets hurt, the coaches worry about their jobs.

Their anxiety came to be reflected in the pay of left tackles. By the 2004 NFL season, the *average* NFL left tackle salary was $5.5 million a year, and the left tackle had become the second highest paid position on the field, after the quarterback. In Super Bowl XL, played on February 5, 2006, the highest paid player on the field was Seattle quarterback Matt Hasselbeck—who had just signed a new six-year deal worth $8.2 million a year. The second highest paid player on the field was the man who protected Hasselbeck's blind side, left tackle Walter Jones, who made $7.5 million a year. (The closest Steeler trailed by $1.9 million.)

The other force that drove the price of quarterback insurance was the supply of human beings who could plausibly provide it. There weren't many people on the planet, and only a few in the NFL, with Walter Jones's combination of size, speed, agility, hands, feet, and arms. Jonathan Ogden, Orlando Pace, maybe Chris Samuels of the Redskins. They were the prototypes. And it was these men—Walter Jones, and the few NFL left tackles of his caliber—that Tom Lemming had in mind when he arrived in Memphis in March of 2004 and went looking for Michael Oher.

EVEN MORE THAN USUAL, Lemming needed to see this kid. It just smelled fishy: there was no way an American high school player in 2004 with this kind of talent could be such a mystery. Film occasionally deceived: maybe he wasn't as big as he looked. Maybe there was something seriously defective about his character. Football was a team game; there was a limit to the pathological behavior it would tolerate, especially in a high school player. "Baseball can tolerate a Barry Bonds," said Lemming. "In football you never do anything alone. Even though you're Joe Montana you still need Jerry Rice, and the nine other guys on offense, if you're going to be any good. That's why [NFL receiver] Terrell Owens got himself in so much trouble. He thought he was bigger than the game. And no one player is bigger than the game."

Lemming had seen hundreds of NFL-caliber players with social problems come to inglorious ends. In 1995, Lemming picked as a first team high school All-American a sensational defensive end from Louisiana named Eric Jefferson. Jefferson signed to play football for the University of Illinois, and Lemming and a lot of other people couldn't see him as anything but a future NFL star. Before he played a down of college ball he pled guilty to armed robbery and is now serving a five-year sentence in California state prison. In 1996, a Chicago kid named Michael Burden had been easily the nation's most promising defensive back ("a future NFL star without a doubt") when he was charged with rape. Ohio State still took him, and he even played a year—then got into trouble at school and vanished without a trace. In 1997, a defensive lineman named Boo Boo Williams had been the most likely future NFL player in the nation. "He was the next Reggie White," said Lemming, referring to the Hall of Fame pass rusher for the Green Bay Packers. As a junior in high school, Boo Boo was six five, 265 pounds, ran a 4.7 40, and bench-pressed 375 pounds, despite never lifting weights. He'd not merely won the heavyweight state wrestling champion; he had picked up the runner-up, a 220-pound star running back, and lifted him straight over his head, then tossed him to the ground. Boo Boo Williams was the most promising player in a graduating class that included all kinds of future NFL stars. But Boo Boo's grades were so bad that he was required to sit out of college ball not just one but two years. And then Boo Boo, too, vanished: poof.

And so it went in football. The game attracted the very people most likely to get in trouble outside the game: aggressive people. Lemming was wary of kids with bad grades, criminal records, or anything else that suggested they'd never get to college, much less through it. To play in the NFL for money it was practically necessary to play three years in college for free. It was true, as Lemming put it, that "there are some colleges that would take Charles Manson if he could run a four-four forty and get his work release." Their existence didn't prevent the premature end of a shocking number of potentially lucrative careers.

After he'd seen Michael Oher's tape, Lemming tried to reach the kid by phone. He found out that his surname was pronounced "Oar," but that's about all he learned. He was accustomed to the social lives of high school football stars: the handlers, the harems, the informal advisers, the coaches. The kids Lemming sought to meet were not, typically, hard to find. This kid not only had no handlers, he didn't appear to exist outside of school. He had no home; he didn't even have a *phone number*. Or so said the Briarcrest Christian School when Lemming called looking for Michael Oher. They had been mystified by Lemming's interest in their student, but they were also polite, and finally agreed to have someone drive Michael Oher over to the University of Memphis football facility for a face-to-face interview. "I'll never forget when he walked into the room," says Lemming. "He looked like a house walking into a bigger house. He walked in the door and he barely fit through the door." He wasn't just huge, he was huge in exactly the right ways. "There's the big blob three-hundred-pounder, and there's the solid kind," said Lemming. "He was the solid kind. You also see big guys, tall guys who weigh a lot, but they have thin legs. They're fine in high school, but in college they'll get pushed around. He was just massive everywhere."

What happened next was the strangest encounter of Lemming's twenty-seven-year football scouting career. Michael Oher sat down at the table across from him . . . and refused to speak. "He shook my hand and then didn't say a word," said Lemming. ("His hands: they were huge!") Lemming asked him the usual questions.

"What colleges are you interested in?"

"What do you want to major in?"

"Where do you think you'll be in ten years?"

They were met with total silence. Not knowing what else to do, Lemming handed the kid his questionnaire. Michael Oher looked at it and put it to one side. Lemming then handed him the ultimate prize: the form to play in the U.S. Army high school all-star football game. Michael Oher looked at it and put it, too, to one side. ("I noticed his arms were really long.")

"You want to fill it out or not?" asked Lemming, finally.

Michael Oher just shrugged.

In hopes of generating some kind of response, Lemming asked what he assumed was a simple question: "So, you want to play in the Army game or not?" It was the equivalent of asking a four-year-old if he'd like a lifetime supply of ice cream. But Michael Oher didn't say yes or no. "He made some sound of total indifference," said Lemming. "First guy ever to say that. First and last."

Lemming decided further interaction was pointless. Michael Oher left, and left behind blank forms and unanswered questions. In the past twenty-six years Lemming had interviewed between forty and fifty *thousand* high school football players. Never—not once—had a player simply refused to talk to him, or declined to fill in his forms. They *begged* to answer his questions and fill in his forms. Once, a player had had the audacity to delegate the form-filling to a coach and it had left a bad taste in Lemming's mouth. That incident had occurred in this very room, in Memphis, Tennessee. The player was named Albert Means. Albert Means's sure-thing career had gone up in smoke after the NCAA discovered a University of Alabama booster had paid his high school coaches one hundred fifty grand to guide him to Alabama. (And the Crimson Tide spent the next two seasons on probation.)

Lemming didn't exactly write off Michael Oher, but he put him to one side with a mental asterisk beside his name. "I thought he was trouble," he said. "It's not only size and strength and speed and athletic ability in football. Football's an emotional game. It's about aggression, tenacity, and heart. I didn't have any idea what was in his heart. I got no sense of anything about him." If Lemming picked twenty high school All-Americans, he expected ten of them to fulfill their potential. The other ten would be lost to injury or crime or bad grades or drugs. The sponsors of the U.S. Army All-American game worried a great deal about their good name. Every year there was a player or two they declined to invite because they didn't want dope in their rooms, or criminal records on their rosters, or even boorish behavior. Michael Oher fell into that category, Lemming decided, a character risk. Still, he couldn't deny his talent. "I didn't hold a grudge," said Lemming. "He wasn't rude to me. And I try to go with the best players. I thought he could be the best offensive lineman to come out of the South in the last five years. He was an instant All-American. I saw him as a number one NFL draft choice. Playing left tackle." But there was no way he'd invite Michael Oher to play in the U.S. Army All-American game.

What never crossed Tom Lemming's mind was that the player

he would rank the number one offensive lineman in the nation, and perhaps the finest left tackle prospect since Orlando Pace, hadn't the faintest idea who Lemming was or why he was asking him all these questions. For that matter, he didn't even think of himself as a football player. And he'd never played left tackle in his life.

CHAPTER THREE

CROSSING THE LINE

W HEN BIG TONY put the two boys in his car on the west side of Memphis and drove them out, he was taking the longest journey he could imagine, and yet he only had to travel about fifteen miles. Driving east, he left the third poorest zip code in the United States and headed toward some of the richest people on earth. He left a neighborhood in which he could drive all day without laying eyes on a white person for one where a black person was a bit of a curiosity. Memphis could make you wonder why anyone ever bothered to create laws segregating the races. More than a million people making many millions of individual choices generated an outcome not so different from a law forbidding black people and white people from mingling.

As Big Tony puttered along in his ancient Ford Taurus, he passed what was left of Hurt Village, a barracks-style housing project built for white working-class families in the mid-1950s, reoccupied by blacks, and, in the end, controlled by gangs: Hurt Village was where Big Tony had grown up. He passed schools that had once been all white and were now all black. He passed people, like himself, in old clothes driving old cars. He passed Second Presbyterian Church, from which Martin Luther King Jr. staged his last march before he was shot and killed—now abandoned and boarded shut. Further east, he passed the relatively prosperous black church, Mississippi Boulevard, housed in a building abandoned by the white Baptists when they fled further east to a new church so huge and sprawling that it had been dubbed Six Flags Over Jesus. Even God, in the west end of Memphis, felt like a hand-me-down. As Big Tony drove east he left what was, in effect, a secondhand city occupied by black people and entered the place for which it had been exchanged: a brand-new city, created by Born Again white people. And now here came Big Tony, chugging along in his beat-to-hell Taurus, chasing after them.

Everyone called him Big Tony—his actual name was Tony Henderson—because he stood six three and weighed nearly 400 pounds. It was in Big Tony's nature to cross lines, if for no other reason than when he looked down he couldn't see them. But today he had a motive: his mother had died. And her dying wish had been for him to go east. Big Tony's mother's name was Betty, but she went by "Betty Boo." Right up until Big Tony reached the sixth grade, Betty Boo had been the party girl of Hurt Village. She smoked, she drank, she ran around; then suddenly, in 1973, she gave up alcohol, then her three-pack-a-day cigarette habit, then sin itself. She announced she had been saved, and accepted Jesus Christ as her Lord and Savior—and spent most of the next twenty-five years mailing pamphlets and pressing Christian literature and videos into people's hands. She wasn't tedious about it, though, and all the kids in Hurt Village called her "Grandma." Her first real grandson was Tony's son, Steven. As Betty Boo lay dying, in the early summer of 2002, she asked Tony for one thing: that he take Steven out of public school and get him a Christian education. She wanted her grandson to become a preacher.

Big Tony would have preferred Steven to become an NBA point guard. Still, he didn't consider Betty Boo's request unreasonable. Steven was one of the best students in his class, and always had been. There wasn't any difficulty in Memphis finding a school that offered a Christian education: the nation's largest private school system had sprung up in the mid-1970s, in East Memphis, to do just that. The problem was that Steven wasn't the only child living in Tony's small house. Occasionally, one of the boys from Hurt Village would crash on his floor; but a few months before, a boy came to stay the night and never left. His name was Michael Oher, but everyone just called him "Big Mike." Tony liked Big Mike, but he also could see that Big Mike was heading at warp speed toward a bad end. He'd just finished the ninth grade at a public school, but Tony very much doubted he'd be returning for the tenth. He seldom attended classes, and showed no talent or interest in school. "Big Mike was going to drop out," said Big Tony. "And if he dropped out, he'd be like all his friends who dropped out: dead, in jail, or on the street selling drugs, just waiting to be dead or in jail."

Tony decided that as long as he was taking Steven out on this search for a Christian education, he should take Big Mike, too. Just a few days after he buried his mother, he put Steven and Big Mike in his car, and drove east. White Memphis had use for a great variety of Christian schools: Harding Christian Academy, which had been around forever; Christian Brothers, which was Catholic and all male; and the Evangelical Christian School, known as ECS. ECS was as close to a church as a school could get. ECS wouldn't accept kids unless both parents gave testimony of their experience of being Born Again—and the stories better be good. Finally, and furthest east, was the Briarcrest Christian School. Briarcrest, also evangelical, was as far east as you could get and still be in Memphis. Briarcrest, more than the others, had been created to get away from Big Tony.

From the point of view of its creators, Briarcrest was a miracle. Its founder, Wayne Allen, had long been distressed by the absence of the Bible from public schools; the white outrage over busing was a chance to do something about it. In the year after the court decision—on January 24, 1973—that forced the city to deploy 1,000 buses to integrate the public schools, the parents of white children yanked more than 7,000 children out of those schools. From the ashes arose an entire, spanking new private school system. The Briarcrest Christian School—originally named the Briarcrest Baptist School—was by far the biggest. It was a system unto itself: fifteen different campuses, inside fifteen different Baptist churches. Its initial enrollment was just shy of 3,000 children, and every last one of them was white. By the summer of 2002 Briarcrest had a handful of black students, but these tended to be, like the black families in the fancy white neighborhoods, imports from elsewhere. The school had existed in East Memphis for nearly thirty years and yet no one who worked there could recall a poor black person from the west side of Memphis marching through its front door to enroll his child. Big Tony was the first.

All Tony knew about Briarcrest was that John Harrington was the basketball coach who had coached in the public schools, where Tony had met him. But any doubt that the Briarcrest Christian School served up the sort of education Betty Boo had in mind was allayed by the sight of the passage from the Book of Matthew inscribed on the outside of the main building: *With men this is impossible; with God all things are possible.* Two very lost-looking boys at his heels, Big Tony marched beneath it and inside the building and went hunting for the basketball coach.

JOHN HARRINGTON HAD SPENT two decades coaching in the public schools and was about to begin his first year at Briarcrest. When Big Tony walked into his office, unannounced, Harrington knew he couldn't do anything for him. The problem presented by Big Tony was too large for the new guy. They chatted for a few minutes and then Harrington sent him over to see the senior coach at Briarcrest, Hugh Freeze. Freeze was only thirty-three, and with his white-blond hair and unlined face might have passed for even younger than he was—if he weren't so shrewd. His shrewdness was right on the surface, so it had an innocent quality to it, but it was there just the same. Slow to speak and quick to notice, Hugh Freeze had the gifts of a machine politician. He was a man of God—if he hadn't been a football coach, he said, he'd have liked to have been a preacher—but he was also, very obviously, adept at getting his way on earth without any help from the Almighty. He'd coached at Briarcrest for eight years, taken the boys' football team to the Tennessee State Championship game five years in a row, and the girls' basketball team to the last seven state championship games, where they had won four of them. This year his girls were ranked ninth in the nation. Freeze was at his desk preparing for the first day of the new school year when his secretary alerted him to the presence of someone who insisted on calling himself "Big Tony."

In walks this 400-pound black man in a mechanic's shirt with a little white name tag that says: *Big Tony*. This huge man introduces himself as Big Tony—again, no last name—and proceeds to tell Hugh about Steven. "He told me about his son, and how he wanted more for him than the school he was at," said Freeze. "I told him how admirable that was but he had to understand that it cost a lot of money to go to Briarcrest, and not everyone got in. You had to have good grades. Big Tony said he knew about the cost and the grades; but Steven was an honor student and he was able to pay whatever the financial aid didn't cover." Freeze gave him the financial aid forms and thought: *Good luck*. That's when Tony said, "And Coach, I've also got one of Steven's friends." He told him about Big Mike, a basketball player who, in Big Tony's modest opinion, might also be of use to the Briarcrest football team.

"Where are his parents?" asked Freeze. He felt a twinge of interest. If a man who weighed 400 pounds was referring to someone else as "Big Mike," he'd like to see the size of that someone else.

"It's a bad deal, Coach," said Tony. "No Dad, Mom's in rehab. I'm pretty much all he has."

"Who is the guardian?" asked Freeze. "Who has legal authority over him?"

"The mom."

Big Tony said he could get Big Mike's mom to fill in the forms, then just sat there, a bit uneasily. Finally, he asked, "You want to meet them?"

"The boys are *here*?"

"Right outside."

"Sure," said Freeze, "bring 'em on in." Tony went out and came back with Steven. Hugh sized him up: almost six feet, and maybe as much as 180 pounds. Plenty big enough for the Briarcrest Christian School Saints football team. "But where's the other one?" he asked.

"Big Mike! Come on in here!"

Hugh Freeze will never forget the next few seconds. "He just peeks around the corner, with his head down." Hugh didn't get a good first look—it was just a sliver of him but it suggested an improbably large whole. Then Michael Oher stepped around the corner and into his office.

Good God! He's a monster!

The phrase shrieked inside Hugh's brain. He'd never seen anything remotely like this kid—and he'd coached against players who had gone to the NFL. When football coaches describe their bigger players, they can sound like ranchers discussing a steer. They use words like "girth" and "mass" and "trunk size." Hugh wasn't exactly sure of the exact dimensions of Big Mike—six five, 330 pounds? Maybe. Whatever the dimensions, they couldn't do justice to the effect they created. That mass! That . . . girth! The kid's shoulders and ass were as wide as his doorway. And he'd only just turned *sixteen*.

"How can I get their transcripts?" asked Hugh.

Big Tony said he'd go get them and bring them in person.

Then Hugh tried to make conversation with this man-child. "I couldn't get him to talk to me," he said. "Not a word. He was in a shell."

A few days later, Big Tony delivered the transcripts to Hugh Freeze. Steven, as advertised, was a model student and Briarcrest could see no reason not to supply him with a Christian education. Big Mike was another story. Hugh was a football coach and so he tended to take an indulgent view of bad grades, but he had no pleasant category in his mind for Big Mike's. "I knew it was too good to be true," he said. He sat on the transcript for two days, but he knew that eventually he'd have to hand it over to Mr. Simpson, the principal, to pass judgment. But his wheels already were spinning.

Steve Simpson, like John Harrington, was new to Briarcrest. He'd spent thirty of his fifty-six years working in the Memphis Public School system. When you first met him, you thought that whatever happened next it wasn't likely to be pleasant. His social manner was, like his salt-and-pepper hair, clipped short. He had the habit of frowning when another would have smiled, and of taking a joke seriously. But after about twenty minutes you realized that though the hard surface was both thin and brittle, beneath was a pudding of sentiment and emotion. He teared up easily, and was quick to empathize. When you mentioned his name to people who knew him well, they often said things like, "Steve Simpson has a heart that barely fits in this building." When teachers came to Briarcrest from the public schools, they often felt liberated, and took great pleasure in advertising their Christian faith. When Simpson arrived in this new place, he placed front and center on his desk a framed passage from the Bible that he never would have placed on his public school desk. But it was special to him:

And God is able to provide you with every blessing in abundance, so that by always having enough of everything, you may share abundantly in His good works.

—II CORINTHIANS 9:8

Still, when the file on Michael Oher from the Memphis City School system hit his desk, Simpson was frankly incredulous. The boy had a measured IQ of 80, which put him in mankind's 9th percentile. An aptitude test he had taken in the eighth grade had measured his "ability to learn" and ranked him in the 6th percentile. The numbers looked like misprints: in a rich white private school, under the column marked "percentile," you never saw single-digit numbers. Of course, logically, you knew such people must exist; for someone to be in the 99th percentile, someone else had to be in the 1st. But you didn't expect to meet them at the Briarcrest Christian School. Academically, Briarcrest might not be the most ambitious school. It spent more time and energy directing its students to Jesus Christ than to Harvard. But the students all went on to college. And they all had at least an average IQ.

In his first nine years of school Michael Oher had been enrolled in eleven different institutions, and that included a hole of eighteen months, around the age of ten, when he apparently did not attend school at all. Either that or the public schools were so indifferent to his presence that they had neglected to register it formally. But it was worse than that. There were schools Big Tony mentioned that did not even appear on the transcripts. Their absence might be explained by another shocking fact: the boy seldom showed up at the schools where he was enrolled. Even when he received credit for attending, he was sensationally absent: forty-six days of a single term of his first-grade year, for instance. His *first* first-grade year, that is—Michael Oher had repeated first grade. He'd repeated second grade, too. And yet Memphis City Schools described these early years as the most accomplished of his academic career. They claimed that right through the fourth grade he was performing at "grade level." How could they *know* when, according to these transcripts, he hadn't even attended the third grade?

Simpson knew what everyone who had even a brief brush with the Memphis public schools knew: they passed kids up to the next grade because they found it too much trouble to flunk them. They functioned as an assembly line churning out products never meant to be market-tested. At several schools Michael Oher had been given F's in reading his first term, and C's the second term, which allowed him to finish the school year with what was clearly an ignoramus's D. They were giving him grades just to get rid of him, to keep the assembly line moving. And get rid of him they did: seldom had the boy returned to the school that had passed him the year before. His previous year, in the ninth grade, he'd spent at a high school called Westwood. According to his transcripts, he'd missed fifty days of school. Fifty days! Briarcrest had a rule that if a student missed fifteen days of any class he had to repeat the class no matter what his grade. And yet Westwood had given Michael Oher just enough D's to move him along. Even when you threw in the B in world geography, clearly a gift from the Westwood basketball coach who taught the class, the grade point average the boy would bring with him to Briarcrest began with a zero: 0.6.

If there was a less promising academic record, Mr. Simpson hadn't seen it—not in three decades of working with public school students. Mr. Simpson guessed, rightly, that the Briarcrest Christian School hadn't seen anything like Michael Oher, either. And yet here he was, courtesy of the football coach, seated across the desk staring hard at the floor. The boy seemed as lost as a Martian stumbling out of a crash landing. Simpson had tried to shake his hand. "He didn't know how to do it," he said. "I had to show him how to shake hands." Every question Simpson asked elicited a barely audible mumble. "I don't know if 'docile' is the right word," Simpson said later. "He seemed completely intimidated by authority. Almost nonverbal." That, in itself, Simpson found curious. Even though Michael Oher had no business applying to Briarcrest, he showed courage just being here. "It was really unusual to see a kid with those kinds of deficits that wanted an education," he said. "To *want* to be in this environment. A lot of kids with his background wouldn't come within two hundred miles of this place."

The disposition of Michael Oher's application to Briarcrest was Steve Simpson's decision, and normally he would have had no trouble making it: an emphatic, gusty rejection. Beneath the crest of the Briarcrest Christian School was the motto: *Decidedly Academic, Distinctly Christian.* Michael Oher was, it seemed to Simpson, neither. But Mr. Simpson was new to the school, and this great football coach, Hugh Freeze, had phoned Simpson's boss, the school president, a football fan, and made his pitch: *This wasn't a thing you did for the Briarcrest football team*, Freeze had said, *this was a thing you did because it was right!* Briarcrest was this kid's last chance! The president in turn had phoned Simpson and told him that if he felt right with it, he could admit the boy.

Simpson thought it over and said: sorry. There was just no chance Michael Oher could cut it in the tenth grade; the fourth grade might be a stretch for him. But the pressure from the football coach, coupled with a little twinge inside his own heart, led Simpson to reject the applicant gently. "There was just something about the boy's desire to be here," he said. "I couldn't justify sending him away without any hope." He granted a single concession: if Michael Oher enrolled in a home study program based in Memphis called the Gateway Christian School, and performed at a high level for a semester, Briarcrest would admit him the following semester. Simpson knew there wasn't much chance Gateway would pass him, and suspected he'd never hear from the football coach, or Michael Oher, again.

He was wrong. Two months later—six weeks into the school year—his phone rang. It was Big Tony. It was a sad sight, said Big

Tony, watching Big Mike stare at these books sent to him by the Gateway Christian School, without any ability to make heads or tails of them. Big Tony didn't have the time or the energy to work with him. Big Mike was trying so hard but getting nowhere, and it was too late for him to enroll in a public school. What should they do now?

That's when Mr. Simpson realized he'd made a mistake. In effect, he had removed a boy from the public school system. He'd tried to handle this problem the easy way, for him, and it had backfired. "It was one of those things," Simpson said. "I should have said, 'You don't qualify and there's no chance you will ever qualify.' When Big Tony called back, I thought, 'Man, look what I've done to these people. I sent them out of here with false hope.'" He went to the Briarcrest president, Tim Hilen, and told him that he had made a big mess for these people. Then he called Michael Oher— who appeared still to be living with Big Tony—and said, "We're gonna take a chance on you but you're not going to play ball." The message was delivered simultaneously to Hugh Freeze: no football, no basketball—the kid couldn't even sing in the choir until he proved to the school that he could handle the schoolwork. Michael didn't say much at all in response, but that didn't matter to Mr. Simpson. "My conscience would be clear if we gave him a chance," he said. His thoughts turned to the teachers: how would he explain this mess to them?

JENNIFER GRAVES HAD RUN Briarcrest's program for students with special needs for nine years. "I decided early on in my life," she said, "that Christ was calling me to work with the kids who did not have it so easy." But her mission took on a different and less hopeful tone when, six weeks into the school year, this huge black kid was dumped in her lap. She, too, had seen the file on Big Mike that had come over from the Memphis City School system. After the transcript came the boy himself, accompanied by Mr. Simpson.

"He said this is Michael Oher and you'll be working with him," recalled Graves. "And Michael didn't say a thing. His head was always down. He kept his head down and his mouth shut." And she thought: *Oh Lord what have we gotten ourselves into?* She knew the coaches thought that he might help their sports teams, but even that surprised her. "He was *fat*," she said. "I didn't see how he could move it around. We weren't real sure what we're going to do with him, and I'll bet they weren't either." After Michael left her office, she went right back to Mr. Simpson to ask what good he imagined would come from letting this child into the Briarcrest Christian School. "He said, 'Jennifer, let's give him until Christmas.'"

She took him around and placed him in the middle of every classroom. "By sixth period of the first day everyone knew who he was," she said. "And he hadn't said a word." It was a matter of days before the reports poured in from the teachers, every last one of them asking the same question of her that she asked of Mr. Simpson: why had they let this kid in? "Big Mike had no conception of what real school was about," she said. "He'd never have his books with him, didn't speak in class, nothing. He had no academic background, no foundation at all. His transcript said he'd had algebra but he'd obviously never laid eyes on it." Another shocking discovery: "I don't know that he'd ever even held a Bible."

At length, in response to an especially loud complaint from the English teacher, Graves brought Big Mike into her office. She pulled out a remedial English test, and gave it to him. "The first thing he was supposed to do," she recalled, "was to identify parts of speech. He says, 'What do I do?' And I say, 'You mark all the parts of speech.' He says, 'I don't know 'em.' So I say, 'Let's start out with nouns.' He says, 'I don't know 'em.' I tell him that 'a noun names a person, place, or thing.' He says, 'It does?' For him English was almost like a second language."

She noticed things about him. She noticed, for instance, that he wore the same pair of cutoff jeans every day, and that he hadn't the first idea how to interact with other people. Everyone in the school knew who he was—he was the biggest human being anyone had ever seen—and they tried to engage him, but he refused to comply. One day while she was sitting with Michael, sorting out some mess or other, her own little girls, aged six and nine, came into her office. "And they just stood there with their mouths open. They'd never seen anyone who looked like that. But then Big Mike left and my six-year-old asked, 'Mama, who was *that*?' And I told her it was Big Mike." The next few days the little girl went out of her way to find Big Mike in the school halls, just to say, "Hi, Big Mike!" And Big Mike just stared at her. The little girl came back to her mother, obviously frightened, and said, "Mama, he doesn't speak to me!" Graves called Big Mike into her office and explained that if he wanted to stare at the ground mutely in her presence, that was fine. "But when a little child tells you hello and you don't respond, you scare that little child." A few days later Graves caught sight of Big Mike in the hallways, smiling and shaking hands with a crowd of small, awed children.

Still, Michael Oher was only a few weeks into his tenure at the Briarcrest Christian School before several teachers suggested he should be on his way out. He wasn't merely failing tests, he wasn't even starting them. The only honest grade to give him in his academic subjects was zero. And it wasn't just the academic subjects. Briarcrest offered a class in weightlifting, and Jennifer Graves had gotten him into it on the assumption it might offer him some relief from relentless failure. If there was one class Big Mike should have been able to ace, this was it. But the weightlifting teacher, Coach Mark Boggess, said that the boy was neglecting even to change into gym clothes. He just sat around, lifting not even his eyes. Boggess doubled as the Briarcrest track coach, and already had made vague plans for Big Mike to put the shot for his team, once he became academically eligible. The third time he watched Michael sit through class in street clothes—not even bothering to change into his sweats—he doubted that would ever happen, and he jumped on him. "Michael, there are a lot of people in this school waiting to see you fail," he said. "Every little step that you make, people are watching. This is the one class in this whole school that can help you with your grades. All you have to do is show up. And right now, you're flunking *weightlifting*."

The situation appeared hopeless, and humiliating for all concerned. Word of the new boy's various failures inevitably reached Mr. Simpson, who also began to sense the dimensions of the void in the boy's life experiences. Michael Oher didn't know what an ocean was, or a bird's nest, or the tooth fairy. He couldn't very well be taught tenth-grade biology if he had no clue what was meant by the word "cell," and he couldn't very well get through tenth-grade English if he'd never heard of a verb or a noun. It was as if he had materialized on the planet as an overgrown sixteen-year-old. Jennifer Graves had the same misgivings: the boy reminded her of a story she had read in a psychology journal, about a child who had been locked away inside a closet for years. "That child didn't even have tactile sense," she said, "but it felt like the same sort of thing. Big Mike was a blank slate." The obvious problem, that he suffered from some learning disability, had been ruled out. Graves had called the Memphis school system and been told that Michael Oher had been tested for learning disabilities, and he had none. In short, they said, he was just stupid. "By their standards," she said, "he was achieving what was expected."

It was then that the Briarcrest biology teacher, Marilyn Beasley, came to Graves in despair. She said that giving Michael yet another weekly biology test was pointless: nothing came back. "We've got to find out what he does and doesn't know," she said. She proposed that Graves replace her in the biology class, and proctor the exam while she, Beasley, took Michael into a separate room and gave him the test verbally. The next day, Ms. Beasley took him into a room and sat down beside him, test in hand. By now she, like the other teachers, knew about his academic record. She had taught at Briar-crest for twenty-one years—and had entire classrooms of children with learning disabilities—and had never experienced a student so seemingly hopeless. "I had never encountered anybody at Michael's reading and comprehension level," she said. His brain did not appear to contain any sort of intellect.

As they sat down together she noticed, once again, how enor-mous his hands seemed when set beside hers. She had a son who was six one, but compared to Big Mike, his hands were the hands of a child. She picked up the test and read aloud the first question from the multiple choice exam:

Protozoans are classified based on:
a.   How they get their food
b.   How they reproduce
c.   How they move
d.   Both a and c

She waited for his answer and received nothing but a blank look. She knew the problem: many of the words, words every tenth-grader should know, were foreign to him. "Classified" overwhelmed him. "Science has its own vocabulary," she said. "He didn't know it. He didn't know what a cell was, or an atom. He didn't have the foundation to figure out meanings through prefixes and suffixes. He didn't know what the prefixes and suffixes were—they might as well have been Greek." The vast quantity of things he didn't know paralyzed his mind. A word at a time, she talked him through the problem.

"Michael, do you remember what a protozoan is?"

Just down the hall Jennifer Graves waited for what she assumed would be bad news. She was already wondering about the best way to ease Big Mike out of the school. An hour later Marilyn Beasley emerged with wonder on her face and a simple observation:

"He knows it."

"What?"

"Jennifer, he knows the material!"

Or, at any rate, he knew something. As he had given no sign of picking up anything, Beasley was shocked at how much he had absorbed. His brain wasn't dead; he simply had no idea how to learn in a classroom. Even so, he knew enough biology to get himself a C on the test, and a high D for the semester instead of an F. He wasn't yet eligible to play any sports, but Graves could see that he longed to. He'd missed the football season, but it was basketball he was most eager to play. She hinted that if the biology test was any indication of the contents of his mind, he might well be eligible to play ball after Christmas, and catch the last part of the season. "The first thing he did," she said, "was start hanging around the basketball court."

WHEN SEAN TUOHY first spotted Michael Oher sitting in the stands in the Briarcrest gym, staring at basketball practice, he saw a boy with nowhere to go but up. The question was how to take him there.

Sean was an American success story: he had come from nothing and made himself rich. He was forty-three years old. His hairline had receded but not quite to the point where you could call him bald and his stomach had expanded but not quite to the point where you could call him fat. He was keenly interested in social status—his own, and other people's—but not in the Old Southern kind. Not long after he'd become a figure in Memphis—a rich businessman who had his own jet and was the radio voice of the Memphis Grizzlies—he'd had feelers from the Memphis Country Club. He didn't encourage them because, as he put it, "I don't hang with the blues. I'd rather go to a high school football game on Friday night than go to a country club and drink four scotches and complain about my wife." Sean Tuohy loved success. He delighted in the sight of people moving up in the world. Country clubs were all about staying in one place.

When he introduced himself to Big Mike, Sean was already knee-deep in the various problems and crises of the few black students at Briarcrest. Sean's daughter, Collins, a junior at Briarcrest and Tennessee State champion in the pole vault, had guaranteed him almost constant exposure to them. She ran track, they ran track. The first time Sean decided to play a role in their social education had been a couple of years earlier, when the track team traveled to Chattanooga for a meet. Coincidentally, also in Chattanooga, a Briarcrest tennis player was playing a tournament at the fancy local country club. Sean thought the black kids at Briarcrest might benefit from some exposure to tennis and golf and other white country club sports; and he thought the Briarcrest tennis player would enjoy a cheering section. Gathering up all two of the black kids on the track team—which amounted to two thirds of the blacks at Briarcrest—he drove them to the Chattanooga Country Club. Sure enough, it was, for them, an entirely new experience. Neither had ever seen a tennis match in person. And while they had no idea how to keep score, they quickly worked out that the Briarcrest kid was making mincemeat of his opponent. After each point they'd stand and holler and raise their fists:

Woo!
Woo!
Woo!

Rather than explain tennis club etiquette, of which he vaguely disapproved anyway, Sean let them have their fun. Between sets they ran over to the concession stand where a little old lady sniffed at them, "I just think y'all are in bad taste." To which one of the kids replied, "You must be rootin' for that other little white guy." The lady went off in a huff and the kids returned to the match, where the Briarcrest player kept on winning. The breaking point came when one of the kids stood up and screamed: "Keep on! You beatin' him like a two dollar whore!" Sean tried to drag the boy by his oversized jersey back into his seat, but before he could get him down, the boy spotted the little old lady in the stands, glaring at him, and screamed: "It's got to be killing ya, ma'am! It's got to be killing ya!"

Afterward, Sean realized that it had been awhile since he had had so much fun. And by the time he met Big Mike, he had a new unofficial title: Life Guidance Counselor to whatever black athlete stumbled into the Briarcrest Christian School. The black kids reminded him, in a funny way, of himself.

Sean knew what it meant to be the poor kid in a private school, because he'd been one himself. First off, none of the rich kids realized that one big difference between public schools and private schools is that, in the public schools, lunch was free. Every day for several years in high school Sean arrived without lunch, or money to buy it, and bummed what he could from friends. "When food is finite," he said, "you'd be surprised how much time you spend thinking about it."

He also knew what it was like to think of sports as a meal ticket. His sense that his future depended on his athletic ability was driven home during his freshman year in high school, when his father, a legendary but ill-paid basketball coach, suffered a stroke and ceased to function. Sean had adored his father. From the age of three, when he had grabbed a basketball and followed him to work in the morning, he had spent the better part of his life on his father's heels, soaking in everything he could about basketball and life. Twenty-five years later he would say, "Everything I do is still all about my daddy." And yet when he lost his father, he, and everyone around him, went on about their lives as if the earth had not just opened and swallowed the most important person in his life. The fancy New Orleans private school was still, for him, free; lunch was not.

He'd left New Orleans for the University of Mississippi on a basketball scholarship. When he set out for Ole Miss he was a six one, 147-pound exception; he wasn't even sure he could cut it as a college basketball player. When he walked off the court after his final game, he'd set the NCAA record for career assists; and, twenty-five years later, he still holds all meaningful SEC assist records. After he'd led Ole Miss to its first (and still only) SEC Championship, in 1981, a photograph of him, perched on top of the rim and bleeding from a cut on his chin as he cut down the nets, appeared in the *New York Times*. At a college still trying to figure out why their white boys were being whipped so routinely by the other team's black boys, he was an instant legend.

That was the joy; the misery was his essential powerlessness. He was at the mercy of a single man who specialized in tearing his players apart and leaving them in pieces. From the moment he had arrived at the Ole Miss gym, Sean realized that his coach had him trapped: he could only afford to stay in school so long as he played basketball, and he played at his coach's pleasure. His entire identity hung in the balance. "From the age of five I had been trained to do this one thing, play basketball. And if I couldn't do that, where did it leave me?" And this coach, who had him by the short hairs, loved nothing more than to give them a yank: threatening to bench him, pull his scholarship, humiliate him in front of his hometown crowd when the Ole Miss team played in New Orleans. Early in his freshman year, for instance, the team had traveled to Bloomington-Normal, Illinois, to play in a tournament. In the first game they beat Loyola Chicago; in the finals they got beaten badly by a nationally ranked Illinois State team. The game ended just before midnight, and they were supposed to drive the four hours to the St. Louis airport, then catch an early morning commercial flight back to Memphis. Sean had played every minute of both games with a torn cartilage in his knee, and afterwards had to be treated by trainers. When he emerged from the locker room, he found a fleet of cars and only one spot left in them, right beside his coach. No one else on the team wanted to sit next to the coach. "For the next four and a half hours," he said, "not one word was spoken. Not one word. I got a cramp in my leg and I remember holding back a scream because I was afraid of getting in trouble."

They caught their plane, and returned to Memphis, where a bus picked them up and carried them the rest of the way to Oxford, Mississippi. "We drove onto campus. There isn't anyone there. It's Christmas Day. It's now eleven in the morning and we still haven't slept. Coach gets up in the front of the bus and says, 'Dressed, stretched, and taped. Thirty minutes.' And I just remember going: 'I don't know about y'all but I haven't slept.' "

Still, the players all trudged to the locker room, donned practice uniforms, and set out for the film room. That's how practice always started: by watching films of their most recent performance and being humiliated by Coach. The players found their seats, the lights went down, and Coach entered the room. He always took a wide circle on his way to his lounge chair in the back: the players felt watched. "I had played forty minutes of both games," Sean said. "My knee was swelled up as big as Dallas. We hadn't slept. It's my first Christmas away from home. Coach walked around so he was right behind me and stopped. Never once in four years did he call me 'Sean.' It was either 'Buddy' or 'Twelve.' Now he comes right up behind me and says,

" *'Hey Twelve. Merry Fucking Christmas.'*

"The lights went out and I cried for the next forty-five minutes. The assistant coach literally sat there rubbing my back and patting me."

For four years he'd played what he called "survival ball." He had to play, or he couldn't afford school. The New Jersey Nets drafted him in a late round to play in the NBA, but the desire had gone out of him. He left Ole Miss with a fiancée and a new religion. But he left without a penny.

Now, by the fall of 2002, he'd become, by just about every way they measured it in Memphis, a success. He'd been Born Again, and helped to create one of the fastest growing evangelical churches in Memphis, the Grace Evangelical Church. He'd married the Ole Miss cheerleader who, twenty-five years later, could still pass for an Ole Miss cheerleader. He owned a chain of eighty-five Taco Bells, KFCs, and Long John Silver restaurants, along with a mountain of debt. His financial life remained risky. If everything broke right, he might soon be worth as much as $50 million. If everything did not break right, he could always call games for the Memphis Grizzlies. What Atlanta was to the American South, Sean Tuohy was to the white southern male. Prosperous. Forever upgrading the trappings of his existence. Happy to exchange his past at a deep discount for a piece of the future.

It wasn't enough. The restaurants ran themselves, the Grizzlies gig was a night job, church was on Sundays. He needed overt drama in his life. He was a person for whom the clock was always running out, the game was always tied, and the ball was always in his hands. He'd played the role for so long that he'd become the role. And he now had all the time in the world for what he still loved more than anything: hanging around school gyms and acting as a kind of consultant to the coaches at Briarcrest in their dealings with their players. Sean was interested in poor jocks in the same way that a former diva might be interested in opera singers or a Jesuit scholar in debaters. What he liked about them was that he knew how to help them. "What I learned playing basketball at Ole Miss," he said, "was what not to do: beat up a kid. It's easy to beat up a kid. The hard thing is to build him up."

Collins had mentioned Big Mike to him. When she tried to pass him on the stairwell, she said, she had to back up to the top, because she couldn't fit past him. Without uttering a peep, the kid had become the talk of the school. Everyone was frightened of him, she said, until they realized that he was far more terrified of them. Sean had seen Big Mike around the halls three or four times. He'd noticed that he wore the same clothes every day: cutoff blue jeans and an oversized T-shirt. Now he saw him in the stands and thought: *I'll bet he's hungry.* Sean walked over and said, "You don't know me, but we have more in common than you might think."

Michael Oher stared intently at his feet.

"What did you have to eat for lunch today?" Sean asked.

"In the cafeteria," said the kid.

"I didn't ask where you ate," said Sean. "I asked what you ate."

"Had a few things," said the kid.

Sure you did, thought Sean. He asked if he needed money for lunch, and Mike said, "I don't need any money."

The next day, Sean went to the Briarcrest accounting department and arranged for Michael Oher to have a standing charge card at the lunch checkout counter. He'd done the same for several of the poorer black kids who had come to Briarcrest. In a couple of cases he had, in effect, paid their tuition, by giving money to a school fund earmarked for scholarships for those who couldn't afford tuition. "That was my only connection with Michael," he said later. "Lunch."

Sean left it at lunch, and at lunch it might have ended. But a few weeks later, the Briarcrest Christian School took its Thanksgiving Break. One cold and blustery morning Sean and his wife, Leigh Anne, were driving down one of the main boulevards of East Memphis when, off a bus just ahead of them, steps this huge black kid. He was dressed in the same pair of cutoff jeans and T-shirt he always wore. Sean pointed him out to his wife and said, "That kid I was telling you about—that's him. Big Mike."

"But he's wearing shorts," she said.

"Uh-huh. He always wears those."

"Sean, it's snowing!"

And so it was. At Leigh Anne's insistence, they pulled over. Sean reintroduced himself to Michael, and then introduced Michael to Leigh Anne.

"Where are you going?" he asked.

"To basketball practice," says Big Mike.

"Michael, you don't have basketball practice," says Sean.

"I know," says the boy. "But they got heat there."

Sean didn't understand that one.

"It's nice and warm in that gym," said the boy.

As they drove off, Sean looked over and saw tears streaming down Leigh Anne's face. And he thought: *Uh-oh, my wife's about to take over.*

The next day afternoon, Leigh Anne left her business—she had her own interior decorating outfit—turned up at Briarcrest, picked up the kid, and took off with him. A few hours later, Sean's cell phone rang. He picked up and heard his wife's voice on the other end of the line:

"Do you know how big a fifty-eight long jacket is?" she asked.

"How big?"

"Not big enough."

Leigh Anne Tuohy had grown up with a firm set of beliefs about black people but had shed them for another—and could not tell you exactly how it happened, other than to say that "I married a man who doesn't know his own color." Her father, a United States Marshal based in Memphis, raised her to fear and loathe blacks as much as he did. (Friends who saw Tommy Lee Jones in the movie *U.S. Marshal* would say to her, "Oh my God, that's your father!") The moment the courts ordered the Memphis Public School system integrated, in 1973, he pulled her out of public school and put her into the newly founded Briarcrest Christian School, where she'd become a member of the first graduating class. "I was raised in a very racist household," she said. As her father walked her up the aisle so that she might wed Sean, he looked around the church, filled with Sean's black ex-teammates, and asked, "Why are all these niggers here?" Even as an adult, when she mentioned in passing that she was on her way into a black neighborhood on the west side of Memphis for some piece of business, he insisted on escorting her. "And when he comes to get me, he shows up with this magnum strapped to his chest."

Yet by the time Michael Oher arrived at Briarcest, Leigh Anne Tuohy didn't see anything odd or even awkward in taking him in hand. This boy was new; he had no clothes; he had no warm place to stay over Thanksgiving Break. For Lord's sake, he was walking to school in the snow *in shorts*, when school was *out of session*, on the off chance he could get into the gym and keep warm. Of course she took him out and bought him some clothes. It struck others as perhaps a bit aggressively philanthropic; for Leigh Anne, clothing a child was just what you did if you had the resources. She had done this sort of thing before, and would do it again. "God gives people money to see how you're going to handle it," she said. And she intended to prove she knew how to handle it.

For Leigh Anne, the mystery began once Michael climbed into her gray minivan. "He got in the car and didn't say anything," she said. "Not one word."

"Tell me everything I need to know about you," she said.

She noticed his sneakers—all beat-up and raggedy.

"Who takes care of you?"

He didn't answer.

"I've noticed in the African American community the grand-mother often helps to raise the kids. Do you have a grandmother?"

He didn't, but he didn't explain.

This wouldn't do. Leigh Anne Tuohy was an extreme, and seemingly combustible, mixture of tenderness and willfulness. She cried when a goldfish died. On her daily walks, when she spotted an earthworm sizzling on the sidewalk, she picked it up and put it back on the grass. On the other hand, when a large drunk man pushed and cut his way in front of her in a line outside a football game, she grabbed him by the arm and screamed, "You just get your fat ass right back where it belongs. *Now!*" When she did things like this, her husband would shrug and say, "You have to understand that my wife has a heart the size of a *pea*. If you cross her, she will step on your throat and take you out and she won't *feel a thing*." Sean had decided, no matter what the potential gains, it was never worth provoking his wife.

And this child's reluctance to answer her questions had provoked her. "We're gonna keep talking about this," she said. "We can do this the easy way. Or we can do it the hard way. Take your pick."

That worked, sort of. She learned that he'd not laid eyes on his father in many years. He never had much to do with his grandmother, who was now gone. He had a sister but didn't know where she was. His mother was, Leigh Anne surmised, an alcoholic. "But he never actually used the word 'alcoholic.' He let me say it and never corrected me. I didn't know then, but Michael will let you believe what you want to believe." After torturing him for a bit, she decided to leave him be. She'd had too much success getting what she wanted to pay much attention to temporary setbacks: it was only a matter of time before he'd tell her everything. "I knew that 103.5 FM was kind of a black station so I had that playing," she said. "I didn't want him thinking this was some charity thing and 'oh poor, pitiful me.' So I said that the Briarcrest basketball team needed its players looking spiffy and we were just going out to make sure that happened."

If it were up to her, she would have driven him straight to Brooks Brothers or Ralph Lauren, but she realized it might make him feel uncomfortable.

"No offense, but where do you go to buy clothes?" she asked.

He mentioned a place—it was in a less affluent section of

Memphis. Not the safest neighborhood. She set off in that direction, heading west.

"You okay going there?" he asked.

"I'm okay going there with you. You're going to take care of me, right?"

"Right," he said. She sensed a little shift in him. Sooner or later she'd break him. "I can talk to a wall," she liked to say.

For the next couple of hours that's just what she did. She was facing a new problem: trying to guess, from his body language, what a sixteen-year-old black child of the ghetto might wear to his new white Christian school. They arrived at the first of many Big and Tall shops and ran smack into another problem: nothing fit him! He wasn't big *or* tall. He was big *and* tall. The selection of clothing into which he could painlessly squeeze himself was limited, and he reduced it by refusing to wear anything that wasn't loose-fitting. For twenty minutes or so she pulled the biggest articles of clothing she could find off shelves and racks, without a comment from the boy.

"Michael!" she finally said. "You got to tell me if you like it or not. I cannot read your mind. Or we'll be here till Christmas, with me trying to guess what you like."

She pulled down the absolute biggest shirt she could find.

"I think that's okay," he said, at length. For him it counted as a soliloquy.

"No! Not okay! You need to love it! If you don't love it in the store, you'll never wear it once you get it home. The store is where you like it best."

She pulled down a gargantuan brown and yellow Rugby shirt.

"I like that one," he said.

She was five one, 115 pounds of blond hair, straight white teeth, and the most perfect pink dress. He was black, poor, and three times her size. Everyone—*everyone*—stared at them. And as they moved from shop to shop, the surroundings, and the attention, became more discomforting. At the final Big and Tall Shop on the border of what had just been pronounced, by the 2000 United States Census, the third poorest zip code in the country, Leigh Anne said, "I've lived here my whole life and I've never been to this neighborhood." And Big Mike finally spoke up. "Don't worry," he said. "I got your back."

Along the way she asked him more questions. "But of course they were the wrong questions," she said later. She noticed little things about him, however, and in these were tiny clues. "I could tell he wasn't used to being touched," she said. "The first time I tried to touch him—he just freezes up."

When they were finished shopping, he was heaped with packages and yet he insisted he wanted to take the bus home. ("I am *not* letting him ride the bus with all these bags!") She drove him back—into what she assumed must be the worst neighborhood in Memphis. They stopped in at McDonald's. He ordered for himself two quarter pounders with cheese. On a hunch she bought six extra burgers for him to take home with him. At length, they reached what he said was his mother's house. It was an ominous dark redbrick building behind a tall metal gate. Across the street was an abandoned house. The scrub grass, the dead plants in pots, the flaking paint on the houses: everything, including the small children in the streets, looked uncared for. She parked and stepped out of the car, to help him with all the bags. That's when he sprang into action:

"Don't get out!" he said.

"I'll just help you with the bags."

"You don't need to get out of the car," he said.

He was so insistent that she stepped back inside the car and promised to stay put, with the doors locked, while he went in and found someone to help him with his packages. A few minutes later a line of small children streamed out of the front gates of the depressing apartment building and, antlike, lifted the sacks and carried them inside. When the last child had moved the last package, the gate closed behind him.

He hadn't given her the first clue of what he thought of her, or of their strange afternoon together. "Probably," she figured, "that I'm some nice lady who wanted something from him." So when he thanked her, she made a point of saying, "Michael, it was my pleasure. You don't owe me anything." And that, she thought, was that.

It wasn't, of course. He was different from the other children that she and Sean had helped out. For a start, he was obviously more destitute. And she couldn't explain why just then, but she was drawn to him and felt the urge to do things for him. He was just this big ol' kid who could have been mean and scary and thuggy, but everything about him was soft and gentle and sweet-natured. With him she felt completely safe; even if he wasn't saying anything, she sensed he was watching out for her.

She went home and thought about the problem still at hand: how to clothe the biggest sixteen-year-old boy she had ever laid eyes on. She flipped through her Rolodex. Several of her interior decorating clients were professional athletes. All but one were basketball players, and all of them were tall and *thin*. The other was Patrick Ramsey, the Washington Redskins' new starting quarterback. "I know how these athletes are about their clothes," she said. "They're very particular and they're tossing them out and getting new ones all the time." What more fertile source of extra-large hand-me-downs than the NFL? She called Ramsey, who said he was more than happy to dun his teammates for their old clothing. She gave him Michael's measurements, and Patrick Ramsey took them down.

A few days later, he called back. "You've got these measurements wrong," he said, matter-of-factly. She explained that she had taken the measurements herself, and written them down on a piece of paper. It must be Patrick who had them wrong. He read them back to her—20-inch neck, 40-inch sleeve, 50-inch waist, 58-inch chest, etc.—nope, he had them right.

"There's no one on our team as big as he is," Ramsey said.

She thought he was kidding.

"Leigh Anne," said the Redskins quarterback, "we only have one player on this team who is even close, and he wears Wrangler blue jeans and flannel shirts and no black kid is going to be caught dead wearing that stuff." That would be Jon Jansen, the Redskins' starting right tackle.

There was a moment of silence on the other end of the line.

"Who *is* this kid?"

CHAPTER FOUR

THE BLANK SLATE

Every one of the coaches at Briarcrest can recall the moment they realized that Big Mike was not any ordinary giant. For Hugh Freeze the moment was a football practice at which this new boy, who had just been admitted on academic probation, had no business. He just wandered onto the field, picked up a huge tackling dummy—the thing weighed maybe fifty pounds—and took off with it, at high speed. *"Did you see that!!!? Did you see the way that kid moved?"* Hugh asked another coach. "He ran with that dummy like it weighed nothing." Hugh's next thought was that he had misjudged the boy's mass. No human being who moved that quickly could possibly weigh as much as 300 pounds. "That's when I had them weigh him," said Hugh. "One of the coaches took him into the gym and put him on the scale, but he overloaded the scale." The team doctor drove him away and put him on what the Briarcrest coaches were later informed was a cattle scale: 344 pounds, it read. On the light side, for a cow, delightfully beefy for a high school sophomore football player. Especially one who could *run.* "I didn't know whether he could play," said Freeze. "But I knew this: we didn't have anyone like him on campus."

The basketball coach, John Harrington, had a similarly incidental encounter with Big Mike in action, inside the Briarcrest gym. Whenever a new kid he thought might play on his team showed up, Harrington tossed him a ball, unexpectedly, just to test his reactions and instincts. The first time Big Mike walked onto the Briarcrest court he was wearing his cutoff blue jeans and grubby sneakers. Harrington tossed him a ball anyway, just to see. Instead of taking it to the rim, or kicking it into the stands, as you might expect a boy his size to do, he caught it and swirled. He dribbled three times between his legs, spun, and, from the dead corner of the floor, nailed a three-point shot. "Walking into the gym he sort of became a different person," said Harrington. "He was doing things a guard would do. Here's this kid—what, six five and three hundred-something pounds, and he's moving like he's a hundred sixty-five pounds. My head's spinning."

Coach Boggess, the track coach, who doubled as the weightlifting instructor and tripled as an assistant football coach, had his own shocking encounter with the boy's freakish physical gifts. It came on the Briarcrest football field. Big Mike wasn't allowed to play, but every now and then he came out onto the field and played, in effect, by himself. One afternoon he took a sack of footballs out to midfield. Standing on the fifty-yard line he threw them, one by one, through the goalposts at the back of the end zone. As a rule, a good college quarterback's range was 60 yards—from midfield to the line along the back of the end zone. Here was this kid, a sophomore in high school, shaped nothing like a quarterback, chucking the ball 70–75 yards. And making it look *easy.*

From the moment he'd laid eyes on Michael Oher, Coach Boggess thought he might invite him onto the track team as a shot putter. He was shaped like a shot putter, and also like the shot itself, round and heavy. It hadn't occurred to Boggess to ask Big Mike to throw anything else until he saw him chucking these footballs and realized he was not merely huge and strong, but flexible and long-armed. There was elegance about him. High school track didn't have the javelin. That was a pity, Boggess thought, as he watched the footballs rocket through the goalposts. Still, there was the discus. "I hadn't thought of him throwing the discus," said Boggess, "because with the discus it's not how big you are, it's the technique you use. The discus is not physiologically suited to the football lineman-type body, in the way the shot put is. Those bodies don't have the grace to do it."

Throwing a discus is more complicated than it appears. The discus thrower needs to separate his lower half from his upper half so that the lower half rotates faster than the upper and creates a torque effect. To achieve the proper spin on the discus requires the body control of an ice skater. None of the Briarcrest coaches was able to teach "spinning" by example, as none of them could do it themselves. When they had a kid who was ambitious enough to try it, they showed him instructional videos.

In Michael Oher's case, the coaches' ignorance hardly mattered. When the first track meet rolled around that first spring, he hadn't spent a minute with the coaches. He was earning straight D's in the classroom and spending five hours a day with tutors, in exchange for being allowed to finish up the basketball season on the Briarcrest team. When Coach Boggess led him out Briarcrest's back door and onto the old grass field for that first meet, he sensed, rightly, that Michael Oher was witnessing track and field for the first time in his life. "He didn't know what a discus was," said Boggess. "He'd never seen one." The track coach inserted Michael at the back of the queue of discus throwers from the other schools, and left him to give it a whirl. Michael, for his part, never said a word, or asked a question. "I just watched them a couple of times," he said, much later, "and then I threw it."

Across the field Collins Tuohy, daughter of Sean and Leigh

Anne, future Tennessee State champion in the pole vault, watched the discus competition as she waited herself to compete. When Big Mike's first throw landed, she picked up her cell phone and called her father. "Daddy," she said, "I think you better come over here and see Michael throw the discus. It looks like a *Frisbee*."

Boggess watched, too. "I think I just laughed," he said. "It wasn't spinning or doing anything fancy. But, man, it *flew*."

Michael's first throw won him first place in that meet. But it was a crude victory, the track and field equivalent of bludgeoning when a sword was at hand. Big Mike wasn't spinning, and neither was the discus. "That first time he did it he didn't really have anyone to watch, because the other kids at that meet weren't really able to spin either," said Boggess. Still, he was amazed, even then, how much the kid looked like he knew what he was doing. Even on the first throw, after watching the kids in front of him, he acquired the basic snap release. Boggess had had kids on his team who never even got that far. At the bigger meets, Boggess knew, some of the discus throwers had serious technique, and would offer Michael a more sophisticated model to imitate. To Boggess, the striking thing was how quickly Michael Oher learned. He wasn't just big and strong and agile; he had a kind of physical intelligence. "He basically taught himself," said Boggess. "Because we couldn't teach him. I remember going out on the field one day and saying: *Oh my God, he's spinning. He's figured it out.* Evidently he just figured it out by watching."

That was the point: Big Mike was able to learn with his body, when he could see other people in action. It wasn't long before Boggess was watching, with glee, as his professional-looking high school discus thrower hit 166 feet—the longest throw in Tennessee in six years. He never had time to practice, as he had to be tutored after school. He just wandered out to the meets and threw whatever needed to be thrown. By the time he finished his quixotic track career, Michael Oher would break the West Tennessee sectional record in the discus, and threaten it in the shot put. In his spare time! It came so easily to him, said Boggess, that if his talent for throwing the discus did not wind up seeming so trivial when set beside his other talents, "they'd have taken him away and trained him up and he'd have been big time."

For his first year and a quarter, until the spring of his junior year, there was some question as to the highest use of Michael Oher. Once the teachers figured out he needed to be tested orally, he proved to them that he deserved high D's instead of low F's. It wasn't clear he was going to acquire enough credits to graduate with his class, but Mr. Simpson and Ms. Graves stopped thinking they were going to send him back out on the streets, and they let him play sports. He joined the basketball team at the end of his sophomore year, and soon afterwards the track and field team. In his junior year he finally got onto the football field.

The problem there, at first, resembled his problems in the classroom. He was a blank slate. He had no foundation, no idea what he was meant to do as a member of a team. He said he had played football his freshman year, at Westwood, but there was no sign of it in his performance. When Coach Hugh Freeze saw how fast he could move, he pegged him as a defensive tackle. And so, for the first five games of the 2003 season, he played defense. He wasn't any worse than his replacement, but he wasn't much better either. One of his more talented teammates, Joseph Crone, thought Big Mike's main contribution came before the game, when the opposing team stumbled out of their locker room or their bus, and took the measure of the Briarcrest Christian School. "They'd see all of us," said Crone, "and then they'd see Mike and say, *oh crap*."

That, at first, was his highest use: to intimidate the opposition before the game. During the games he seemed confused. When he wasn't confused, he was reluctant. Passive, almost. This was the last thing Coach Hugh Freeze expected. Freeze didn't know much about Michael Oher's past but he knew enough to assume that he'd had some kind of miserable childhood in the worst part of Memphis. A miserable childhood in the worst part of Memphis was typically excellent emotional preparation for what was required on a football defense: it made you angry, it made you aggressive, it made you want to tear someone's head off. The NFL was loaded with players who had mined a loveless, dysfunctional childhood for sensational acts of violence.

The trouble with Michael Oher as a football player was the trouble with Ferdinand as a bull: he didn't exhibit the anger of his breed. He was just a sweet kid who didn't particularly care to hit anybody, or, as Hugh put it, "He just wasn't aggressive. His mentality was not a defensive player's mentality." The depth of the problem became clear during Briarcrest's fourth game, when the team took buses up into Kentucky to play a pretty tough Calloway County team. Early in the game Michael caught his hand on an opponent's face mask and gashed the webbing between his fingers. "You'd a thought he was going to die," said Hugh. "Screaming and moaning and carrying on. I thought we were going to have to go and get a stretcher." His defensive tackle ran to the bench, clenched his hand, and refused to allow anyone to look at it.

In the stands Leigh Anne Tuohy watched as two, then three, then four grown men tried to subdue Michael Oher, and then coax him into allowing them to examine his hand. "He was in a fetal position," she said. Men were next to useless in getting Michael to do things, because he didn't trust men: she knew this about him, and more. After their shopping trip, when she turned up at Briarcrest, Michael had sought her out. He had mentioned that he hated to be called "Big Mike" and so from then on he was, to her and her family, Michael. "I don't know what happened," Leigh Anne said. "Whether it was attrition of other people, or whatever. But I became the person Michael came to. At his basketball games he'd just walk over and start talking to me. When I was at school, he'd find me and talk to me. I think everyone kind of noticed that he'd gotten close to me. Maybe before I noticed."

She walked down from the stands, crossed the track, walked onto the football field, and went straight to the bench.

"Michael, you need to open your hand," she said, crossly.

"It hurts," he said.

"I realize it hurts. But your head is going to hurt a lot worse when I hit you upside it."

He unclenched his hand, one giant finger at a time. The gash went to the bottom of the webbing and down the finger, where the bone was visible. "I wanted to throw up," said Leigh Anne. "It was gross." She pretended it wasn't and told him he needed to be taken to the hospital.

"The hospital!!" he wailed. She thought he was going to faint.

They were a good two and a half hours from home, so Carly Powers, the Briarcrest athletic director, took him to a Kentucky emergency room. "The first question he asked when we got in the car," said Powers, "and he kept asking it, 'Is it going to hurt? Is it going to hurt?' He was a nervous wreck. You could see it in his eyes. When we walked into that hospital, he was scared to death." Powers sensed that Big Mike had perhaps never seen the inside of a hospital.

A nurse checked them in, told Powers to wait in the lobby, and escorted Big Mike to the back. A few minutes later, Powers heard "this blood-curdling scream. And you can tell it's Big Mike." The nurse comes running out and says, "Mr. Powers, I think we're going to need you back here. We need your help to hold him down." Powers followed her back to see what the problem was. A needle, as it turned out. The doctors were trying to give Big Mike a simple shot to numb his hand, and Big Mike had taken one look at the needle and leapt off the table. A staff of three had tried to put him back on it, without success. "He'd never seen a needle," said Powers.

Even a rich private school was ill-equipped to deal with a parentless child. Like all schools, it was hard-wired to call, at the first sign of conflict, a grown-up. In the eight months since she had taken him shopping for clothes, Leigh Anne Tuohy had become that grown-up. Briarcrest teachers knew that, increasingly, Big Mike was spending time with Sean and Leigh Anne. Sean was becoming something like a private basketball coach to him, and Leigh Anne was grappling with the rest of his life. The Tuohys were now covering not only his school lunches but also, indirectly, his tuition. For this reason and one other, when Carly Powers, as athletic director, asked himself which adult he might call to talk reason to Big Mike, he settled on Leigh Anne. The other reason was that he'd never seen Leigh Anne fail to get her way. "She is going to get it done," said Powers, "or she is going to drive you nuts."

He called Leigh Anne's cell phone. She was on the bus with the Briarcrest cheerleaders, riding back to the school. After she had sorted Michael out on the bench, Leigh Anne sensed she had glimpsed another little sliver of his childhood. "I just thought: this kid has never been injured before," she said. "Or if he has been injured, he said, 'I'm not gonna tell anyone about it.' " She suspected this might be the first time he had no choice but to allow someone else to do something for him. "When he was sitting on the bench refusing to let those men look at him," she said, "it was as if he thought: 'If I just keep my hand clenched tightly to my chest, it'll go away.' "

Now Carly Powers was in her ear, saying, "Leigh Anne, you got to talk to him because he's being completely irrational." Carly handed his cell phone to Mike.

"Michael, you have to let them take care of you," she said.

"But it really hurts," he said.

"Michael, you're being a baby! You're acting like Sean Junior!" Sean Junior was nine.

"They trying to stick me with a needle!"

"It's better than getting your *hand cut off* when *gangrene* sets in."

He didn't say anything to that.

"Michael," she said, "people lose *limbs* because of things like this. You want to lose your arm?"

No, he didn't want to lose his arm.

"Okay," she said. "And please don't make it hard on Coach Powers because he's just trying to help. And if I have to drive down there, it's going to be *bad news*."

"All right."

Powers came on and asked Leigh Anne if she thought Big Mike had medical insurance, and Leigh Anne said there was no chance he had medical insurance or any other kind, and he should just put Sean's name on all the forms.

To food, clothing, and tuition add medical care. It was an odd situation. A boy without a nickel in his pocket, no private mode of transportation, no change of clothes, no history of medical care, had stumbled into one of the more expensive private schools in Memphis. Lunch materialized, courtesy of Sean Tuohy, though Michael never asked, and so never learned, where it had come from. Clothes materialized, courtesy of Leigh Anne. He still exhibited an odd tendency to show up at school in the same clothes every day, but now they were different clothes: long pants and the brown and yellow Rugby shirt Leigh Anne had bought for him. That shirt became so worn that Leigh Anne, the fiftieth time she saw him in it, threatened to rip it off his back. She noticed all the details. One of these was that the Rugby shirt was fitting him more snugly. "I'm not sure he's stopped growing," she told Sean.

Michael's biggest need—a place to sleep at night—wasn't, at first, an issue. He spent most nights on Big Tony's floor. But because Big Tony lived such a long way from school, Michael had bivouacked some nights here and there in East Memphis, several of them on the Tuohys' sofa. There were also nights when he took the express bus back to the poorest neighborhoods on the west side of town. There he stayed, Leigh Anne assumed, with his mother.

Transportation was the big issue: Michael had no money and no reliable way to get around. He was totally dependent on whoever might give him a lift, and he had no idea, when he arrived at school in the morning, where he might spend the night. He sort of shopped around every day for the best deal he could find. If he had no place else to stay, he went home with Big Tony. But then his safety net vanished, suddenly. It happened the night the team returned from Myrtle Beach.

The Briarcrest basketball team had flown to Myrtle Beach, South Carolina, in the winter of 2003 to play two games. It had been Michael's first trip on an airplane, and also his first trip outside of Memphis. The first game had been traumatic, and both he and his coach, John Harrington, came to think of it as the moment Michael began to accept who he was, and fit himself into the team. The back end of his sophomore year and the front end of his junior year he had been an obviously physically gifted but disappointing basketball player. "He had no concept of his role," said Harrington. "Basketball's all about players accepting their roles. You want to know why the Lithuanians beat the Americans? It's because the Lithuanians know and accept their roles." Michael, now six five and a half and 350 pounds, was built to control the area under a high school basket. (To put his width into perspective, Shaquille O'Neal, the Miami Heat center who is seven one and seemingly wide as a truck, weighs 330 pounds.) But he insisted to everyone that he was a shooting guard, and if they put him at center, he stepped out, dribbled around, shot threes, and generally pissed off his coach, as well as the parents of his teammates. Plus, he didn't play defense. "He was a liability on the defensive end," said Harrington. "That's why he didn't play but about half of most games."

That changed at Myrtle Beach. At Myrtle Beach, something happened. "At Myrtle Beach," said Harrington, "Big Mike got angry." The minute he walked onto the court for their first game, the crowd was on him. They called him names. *Black Bear. Nigger.* They called him names that neither he nor his coach cared to repeat. Harrington wasn't shocked by more subtle forms of racism away from the basketball court, but it had been a long time since he'd seen the overt version on it. "I don't think there's a white coach with a black kid on his team, or a black coach with a white kid, who could have any racism in him," he said. Big Mike responded badly; Harrington hadn't seen this side of him. He began to throw elbows. Then he stopped on the court, turned on the fans, and gave them the finger.

One of the handicaps of coaching at an evangelical Christian school is that a technical foul isn't regarded by your own fans as a rallying cry but a spiritual transgression: you really didn't want Briarcrest people to think that you didn't have your passions well under control. "At Myrtle Beach," said Harrington, "that was the closest I've ever come in my career to a technical foul." He yelled at the refs for a bit and then called them, and the opposing coach, over. Pointing to the fans causing the trouble, he said, "You can take care of this problem or Big Mike can take care of this problem. And I think it'll be a lot better for them and for you if you take care of it. Because he's gonna clean house." Big Mike overheard this exchange and apparently liked the sound of it. He stayed in the paint for the rest of the game, grabbed 15 rebounds and scored 27 points, and helped his team thrash a team to whom they'd been expected to lose. "I think he realized then that this kind of thing didn't just happen in Memphis," said Harrington. "It happened everywhere. And we were on his side."

Then they flew home. It was when they landed at the Memphis airport that Big Mike's chronic housing problem became a crisis. The other players all had parents to meet them. Big Tony's girlfriend had come to pick up Steven—who was also on the team—but Mike refused to get in her car. "I'm not spending another night in that lady's house," he told his basketball coach. Pressed, he explained that he had overheard her talking about him on the telephone and that she had said many rude things: that he was a freeloader, that she didn't like him in their house, that he was stupid, that he was never going to amount to anything. When the players had all gone home, Michael Oher and his basketball coach were left together in the Memphis airport. Harrington asked Big Mike where he wanted to go, and Big Mike gave him an address, and Harrington drove his emerging star into the worst neighborhood in Memphis. "Every hundred yards he said, 'You can just let me off here, Coach. You can just let me off here.' It was the middle of the night and I said, 'Mike, I'm driving you to your front door.' "

After he had let Big Mike off in front of a dark and seemingly empty building, Harrington telephoned his volunteer assistant coach, Sean Tuohy. He told him the problem. "And Sean said, 'Maybe it's time I looked into this.' "

The next few months there was a lot to look into. Michael stayed nights in East Memphis with at least five different Briarcrest families: the Franklins, the Freezes, the Saunders, the Sparkses, the Tuohys. He somehow persuaded another black kid on the Briarcrest basketball team, Quinterio Franklin, to let him use his house as a kind of base camp. One night after a track meet, Michael was left without a ride home and Leigh Anne offered to take him wherever he wanted to go. "Terio's," he said, and off they went . . . thirty miles into Mississippi. "It was a *trailer*," she said. From the outside she couldn't believe there was room enough inside the place for him. She insisted on following him in, to see where he slept. There she found an old air mattress on the floor, flat as a leaf. "I blow it up every night," he said. "But it runs out of air around midnight."

"That's it," she said. "Get all your crap. You're moving in with me."

Crossing a new line, Michael picked up a single Glad trash bag and followed her back into the car. Right up until that moment

Leigh Anne had hoped that what they and other Briarcrest families had done for Michael added up to something like a decent life. Now that she knew it didn't, she took over the management of that life. Completely. "The first thing we did," she said, "was have a cleansing of the clothes."

Together they drove to every house in Memphis where Michael had stashed his clothing. *Seven* houses and four giant trash bags later she was staring at "this pile of crap. It was stuff people had given him. Most of it still had the tags on it. Stuff he would never wear. I mean there were polo shirts with little penguins on them." For the next couple of weeks Michael slept on the Tuohys' sofa, and no one in the family stated the obvious: this was Michael Oher's new home, and probably would be for a long time. He was, in effect, a third child. "When I first saw him, I was like, 'Who the heck is this big black guy?'" said Sean Junior, aged nine at the time. "But Dad just said this was a kid we were trying to help out and so I just said all right." Sean Junior had his own uses for Michael: the two would vanish for hours on end into his bedroom and play video games. Just a few months after his arrival, Leigh Anne would point to Michael and say, "That is Sean Junior's best friend." "He got comfortable quickly," said Collins Tuohy, then sixteen. "When he kept staying and staying, Mom asked him if he wanted to move in. He said, 'I don't think I want to leave.' That's when Mom went out and bought the dresser and the bed."

After she organized his clothing, Leigh Anne stewed on where to put this huge human being. The sofa clearly would not do—"it was *ruining* my ten-thousand-dollar couch"—but she was worried that no ordinary bed would hold him, or, if it did, it might collapse in the middle of the night and he and it would come hurtling through the ceiling. Sean had mentioned that he recalled some of the larger football players at Ole Miss sleeping on futons. That day Leigh Anne went out and bought a futon and a dresser. The day the futon arrived, she showed it to Michael and said, "That's your bed."

And he said, "That's *my* bed?" And she said, "That's your bed." And he just stared at it a bit and said, "This is the first time I ever had my own bed."

That was late February 2004. Leigh Anne sat Michael down and established some rules. She didn't care if she ever saw his mother, and didn't need to know her problems, but he would be required to visit her. "I'm not going to have you say that I took you away from your mother. I don't care if you don't want to go, you're going." She didn't know who his friends were from back on the west side of Memphis but they were welcome in the house and he should bring them home. Didn't he have anyone he grew up with who he might like to bring over? He didn't offer up any names. "Anything you wanted to know you had to pry out of him," she said. And so she pried. "He finally mentioned someone named Craig but this Craig never materialized."

Sean, for his part, had long since given up interest in probing into Michael's past, or anything else. The boy had a gift for telling people as little as possible, and also for telling them what they wanted to hear. "The right answer for Michael is the answer that puts an end to the questions," said Sean. He finally decided that Michael had not "the slightest interest in the future or the past. He's just trying to forget about yesterday and get to tomorrow. He's in survival mode: completely focused on the next two minutes." He persuaded his wife to take a more detached view of the question, who is Michael Oher? and Leigh Anne agreed, at least in principle. "What does it matter if he doesn't know the names of his brothers and sisters," she said, unconvincingly. "Or where he went to school. Or if he went to school."

They decided to move forward with Michael on a need-to-know basis: if they needed to know some detail about his past, she harassed Michael until he gave her an answer. If they didn't—and mostly they didn't—she'd leave him alone. "It is what it is," she said. "The past is the past." In her big talk with Michael she told him,

"We're just going to go forward. There is nothing I can do about whatever might have happened to you before now. If it's going to cause you problems, and you're not going to be able to go forward without dealing with it, maybe we need to get help from someone smarter than I am."

He just looked at her and asked, "What does that mean?"

She tried to explain about psychiatrists, but it was obvious he didn't know what therapy meant. So she said to herself: *Oh, what the hell. There's no way he's ever going to lie on some couch and talk about himself.*

And, she half thought, his past actually didn't matter all that much to him. "Like the way a woman blocks out childbirth," she said, "I think he just blocked out a lot of his childhood."

Sean had a different take: Michael's mind was finely calibrated to get from one day to the next. Whatever had happened to him in the past he couldn't afford to dwell on it. He couldn't afford to be angry, or bitter. "Michael's gift," Sean said, "is that the Good Lord gave him the ability to forget. He's mad at no one and doesn't really care what happened. His story might be sad, but *he's* not sad."

But even if they had decided not to interrogate him, there was nothing that said she couldn't *notice* the little tics and quirks about him. Information took many forms and both Leigh Anne and Sean had a talent for acquiring it. When they stopped in at the Taco Bell just around the corner, for instance, Michael would order more food than he wanted. The next morning Sean would open the refrigerator and find the coagulated, extra Mexican pizza. "He was in the habit of guaranteeing himself an extra meal," said Sean. "I had to explain that he didn't need to do that. That he could get it whenever he wanted. He said, 'Really?' I said, 'Michael, I *own* the restaurant. You can go over there any time you want and eat for free.'" But the habit was hard to break. Sean would see him come into the house, extra free Mexican pizza in hand, and "it was like he would catch himself. He'd come in with the extra pizza and see me and go, 'Oh, man, I forgot.' " Collins noticed, "He hoarded *everything*: food, clothes, money. He'd get stuff and he'd hide it away." It was as if he didn't actually believe that this free stuff would remain free.

There were tiny revelations that had Leigh Anne upset for days, for what they implied about his childhood. She took Michael with her and Sean Junior to a Barnes & Noble. As they walked through the store, Sean Junior spotted *Where the Wild Things Are* and said, "Look, Mom, you used to read that to me when I was little." To which Michael replied, in the most detached tone, "I've never had anyone read me a book."

There were also things about him that caused Leigh Anne and Sean to think of him as an even deeper mystery. He refused to wear clothes that, in his opinion, didn't match. He refused to wear clothes that had even a spot on them. He *ironed* his T-shirt; and if he wore the same T-shirt every day, he ironed it every morning. "That ain't a socioeconomic issue," said Sean. "That's a where-the-hell-did-that-come-from? issue." Sean had him out one day, buying basketball sneakers for himself. He asked Michael if he'd like a pair and Michael said, sniffily, he didn't like the colors on display. "I said, 'Michael you have *none*. How can you turn down shoes when you don't have shoes?' And he said, 'Well, I don't want those unless they have it with the blue stripe.' 'For someone who has no shoes you're pretty damn picky about what shoes you get.' " When they finally found the sneaker shoe color that Michael liked, they had another argument about his shoe size. Michael refused to wear the size 15 shoes that the salesman proved he needed. He insisted that he wore a size 14, and so it was size 14 shoes Sean bought for him, even though it meant a bit of pain when he walked.

Around the house he was a neat freak. Leigh Anne ran a tight ship and within weeks it was clear that Michael was the only member of the crew who passed muster. "You might drop your underwear on the floor," said Sean, "but one minute later they'd be gone.

They might have wound up in the silverware drawer but they were not on the floor." Michael's were the only underwear never dropped. Collins, who was the same age as Michael, had never made her bed in her life and, no matter how often her mother hollered at her, never would. Michael not only made his bed, he removed the sheets from the futon, folded them, and returned the thing to its couchlike state. Every day, without exception. "It was like God made a child just for us," said Sean. "Sports for me, neat for Leigh Anne."

From the moment Michael moved in with them, Sean began to stew on his future. ("Because I figured I was going to have to pay for it.") Michael was approaching the end of his junior year in high school, and while they hadn't seen his transcripts, they knew his grades were poor. Since Myrtle Beach he'd been good enough on the basketball team that Sean thought he might be able to play at a small college. "And I figured if he wasn't, I could *make* him good enough," said Sean. At six five he wasn't tall enough to be a post player in major college basketball but he might make it in Division II. Sean had contacts in college basketball all over the South. He began to write letters on Michael's behalf to coaches at small schools—Murray State, Austin Peay. He had Leigh Anne go out and sign up Michael for every summer basketball camp she could find.

Then Hugh Freeze called Michael and said that this guy who wrote scouting reports on high school football players was coming through town and had agreed, on Hugh's recommendation, to see him. Accustomed to just doing what he was told around Briarcrest, Michael jumped in the passenger seat of a teammate's car and allowed himself to be driven to the University of Memphis. He sat through fifteen long minutes of this strange little guy's questions without the faintest interest in the encounter. "I just wanted him to stop talking so I could leave," he said later. Under Michael's mute gaze, Tom Lemming finally stopped talking. Michael left the forms Lemming gave him, unfilled. And that, Michael thought, was that.

Only it wasn't. Lemming's private scouting report was sent to the head coach at more than one hundred Division I college football programs and so more than one hundred head college football coaches learned that this kid in Memphis, whom no one had ever heard of, was the most striking left tackle talent he'd seen since he first met Orlando Pace. And Orlando Pace was now being paid $10 million a year to play left tackle for the St. Louis Rams. It was only a week or so after Lemming's report went out that the Briarcrest Saints football team met for two weeks of spring practice. Hugh Freeze was there, of course, as he was the head coach and ran the practices. Tim Long was there, too, because he coached the offensive line. Like several of the coaches, Long was a Briarcrest parent, but was also a six five, 300-pound former left tackle at the University of Memphis, and a fifth-round draft pick of the Minnesota Vikings. At first sight, Long had been awed by Michael Oher's raw ability. "When I first saw him," he said, "I thought: this guy is going to make us all famous." But then he'd coached him in the final games of his junior year, after Michael was moved to right tackle on the offensive line, and Long wondered why he wasn't a better player. One game he had pulled Michael out and sat him on the bench because he thought the team was better off playing another guy.

The only other coach at Briarcrest Spring Practice with any experience of college or pro sports was Sean Tuohy. Hugh Freeze had asked Sean to help out as an assistant coach—which meant his usual role as coach to the coach and unofficial Life Counselor to the players. When Sean told Leigh Anne he planned to coach football, she had laughed at the idea of it: her husband didn't know a first down from a free throw. And it was true: the first thing Sean learned about coaching football was that you shouldn't do it in a BMW. He came home the first day and told Leigh Anne, "I need to buy a pickup truck; I'm the only one without a pickup truck." A few days later he bought one.

That first afternoon of spring practice, Sean rolled up in his new truck to find the players lined up and stretching. The other coaches were there already. But there was this other, highly unusual cluster of identically dressed men: college football coaches who had turned up to watch practice. They stood to one side, but you could tell them by their identical dark slacks and coaching shirts with their school's emblem emblazoned on the chest: University of Michigan, Clemson University, University of Southern Mississippi, University of Tennessee, Florida State University. They weren't head coaches, just assistants. But still. College coaches of any sort weren't in the habit of coming to watch Briarcrest players. The Briarcrest football field was in the middle of nowhere and Michigan was in the middle of another nowhere. The Clemson guy mentioned to one of the Briarcrest coaches that he had driven eight hours just to be there. Few of the players had any idea, at first, why they were there. The coaches knew why, because Hugh Freeze had just told them, but they were still as surprised as the players. Carly Powers, the athletic director, said, "Big Mike hadn't been very good. You could tell he hadn't played before. The only thing he had going for him was his size." Tim Long said, "I don't know why they were there. I guess his size just got him noticed."

The most complicated set of social rules on the planet—the rules that govern the interaction of college football coaches and high school prospects—forbade the coaches from speaking directly to a high school junior until August before his senior year. They were allowed to visit his school twice, and watch him from a distance. So the coaches made a point of not saying anything directly; they just sat off to the side and stared. "I'll never forget it," said Tim Long. "We did calisthenics and agility. Then board drill, right away. We're ten minutes into it. Michael's first up."

The board drill—so named for the thin ten-foot-long board laid on the ground before it begins—is among the most violent drills in football. The offensive lineman takes his stance in the middle of the board and faces the defensive lineman. At the sound of the whistle, they do whatever they must to drive the other fellow off the end of the board. Facing off against Michael Oher during a football game was one thing: he was often unsure where to go, you more than likely had help from teammates, and, if you didn't, there was plenty of room to run and hide. Getting onto the board across from him, for a fight to the death, was something else. No one on the team wanted to do it.

At length, out stepped the team's biggest and most powerful defensive lineman, Joseph Crone. He was six two, maybe 270 pounds, and a candidate to attend college on a football scholarship. To him this new mission, going hat-on-hat with Big Mike, had the flavor of heroism. "The reason I stepped up," said Crone, "is that I didn't think anyone else wanted to go up against him. Because he was such a big guy."

Crone still didn't think of Michael Oher as an exceptional football player. But if he hadn't been a force on the field, Crone thought, it was only because he had no idea what he was supposed to do there. And Crone noticed that he had improved the past season and, by the final game, looked very good indeed. "He was figuring it out," said Crone. "How to move his feet, where to put his hands. How to get onto people so they couldn't get away." But even if Big Mike had no idea what he was doing on a football field, Crone found him an awesome physical specimen. He had a picture in his mind of the few opposing players who had made the mistake of being fallen upon by Big Mike. "They looked like pressed pennies," he said. "They'd get up and their backs would be one giant grass stain. I couldn't imagine being on the other side of the ball going against Mike." Now, by default, he was.

The two players dropped into their stances, with the eyes of the SEC, the Big Ten, Conference USA, and the ACC upon them. Joseph Crone's mind was working overtime: "I'm sitting there thinking, *Man, this guy is* HUGE. *I got to get low on him. I got to drive my feet.*"

"Best on best!" shouted Hugh Freeze, and blew his whistle.

When it was over—and it was over in a flash—the five coaches broke formation and made what appeared to be urgent private phone calls. Briarcrest athletic director Carly Powers turned to his left and found that one of the coaches, in his bid to separate himself from the others, had wandered up beside him. "He was whispering into his phone, *'My God, you've got to see this!'* " said Powers. The Clemson coach, Brad Scott (he was the former head football coach at the University of South Carolina), actually ran out onto the field, handed his card to Hugh Freeze, and said, "I seen all I need to see." If Michael Oher wanted a full scholarship to Clemson, it was his. "Then," says Tim Long, "the Clemson guy got in his car and drove eight or nine hours back home."

Hugh Freeze was as impressed, and surprised, as anyone: it could have been a training film. Big Mike had picked up 270 pounds and dealt with them as he might have dealt with thin air. "Joseph was a *man*. And Michael treated him like he was a hundred-pound weakling. And Joseph fought him! Those first two steps—they were as quick as any running back's. And when that body hits you, it's just an amazing force. And once he's on you, you can't get off of him. He kept his ol' back flat and just rose up as he took Joseph down the field."

Sean, who had been standing off to one side, walked over to Joseph and patted him on the helmet: he felt sorry for the kid. ("He just smashed me," said Crone. "I was like, 'God, that wasn't a fun experience.' ") Sean knew one of the assistant coaches, Rip Scherer of Southern Miss—he'd once been the head football coach at the University of Memphis. Southern Miss was the poor cousin in this gathering of representatives from elite college football teams. Scherer, looking a little low, now walked over to Sean and said,

"Well, we're obviously not going to be able to sign him. Who else you got?" In a single play Michael Oher had established himself as too rich for the blood of Southern Miss. "It was strange that day," said Tim Long. "His moment came and he was on. It was like he'd always been that good."

After that, the coaches came in platoons. Arkansas, Notre Dame, Ole Miss, Miami, Nebraska, Oklahoma State, Ohio State, and on and on. First, they were merely assistant coaches, but the assistant coaches would get on their cell phones—"no, you have to come see this"—and the top brass would dutifully materialize. "It got so I couldn't wait to get to practice to see who was there that day," said Tim Long. "You get there late and someone would say, 'Oops, you just missed Bob Stoops.' " (Stoops is the head football coach of the University of Oklahoma.) One afternoon the Briarcrest players and coaches looked up and saw the strange sight of Tennessee's most famous coach, Phil Fulmer, from the University of Tennessee, not walking but *running* to their practice. If ever there was a body not designed to move at speed it was Fulmer's. "I'd seen Phil Fulmer on TV," said Joseph Crone, who knew the moment he saw Fulmer that he was in for yet another unpleasant board drill. "But I'd never seen him in person." Fulmer had been in Memphis for a speech, and was meant to be on a plane back to Knoxville. Before he'd boarded, his recruiter had called and told him about this once-in-a-lifetime sight, and Fulmer decided he'd rather miss his flight. Then he drove the twenty miles out to the Briarcrest field—and parked in the wrong lot. "It's a hundred and fifty degrees," recalls Tim Long. "And there's Phil Fulmer racing across the parking lot. He's running down this dirt road. He gets there huffing and puffing, and says, 'I was told I need to see this for myself.' "

Fulmer watched Michael Oher for half an hour and then turned to Long and said, "He's the best in the nation." Which is what *USA*

Today was about to say—thanks largely to Tom Lemming. In the middle of spring practice, Michael Oher became a pre-season First Team High School All-American. From that moment on, Hugh Freeze had to give up pretty much everything he was doing, and retire to his office to deal with the long line of college football coaches who wanted to spend quality time at the Briarcrest Christian School. "I feel there wasn't a coach in the country who did not call or come in person," he said. "Washington, Oregon, Oregon State. I mean, these people were calling from everywhere and asking, 'Coach, do we have a shot?' All spring practice I had one college head coach in my office, and another waiting outside." When the coaches weren't at practice, they were stalking the hallways of Briarcrest. "The best way I can describe it," said Joseph Crone, "is it was like a group of vultures trying to get their prey."

They were predatory by nature but they often came just to say they had seen *it*, in the spirit of tourists making their first trip to the Grand Canyon. The people at Briarcrest had trouble thinking of themselves as an athletic tourist attraction, and they had their own curiosities. Carly Powers asked one of the coaches: "What makes Michael so good?" And his answer was: "He's a freak of nature." Steve Simpson had one of the coaches in his office and took the occasion to ask, "What has you all so excited?" "He said you just don't see kids who are that big and that athletic." Two of the SEC head coaches told Tim Long that Michael Oher was the best offensive lineman they had ever seen. All but one of them would take away only memories, but even these, to some, were worth the trip. "The first time I saw Mike," said Stacey Searles, who coached the offensive line at LSU, "he was in a three-on-three Oklahoma Drill. He was just dominating people. I'd seen him from a distance and thought, 'Wow, that's a good-looking kid.' He has as much strength and size and agility and power as any lineman I'd ever seen. Then I got closer and said, *Oh my*. He was a freak of nature—for somebody to be that big, that powerful, that fast, and that talented. Every two or three years there is a kid who jumps out at you, and he was that kid."

Tim Long, who had been a star in high school, and in college, and had played in the NFL, had never seen anything like it. Sean Tuohy, who had been the most highly recruited basketball player in the state of Louisiana his senior year in high school, had never seen anything like it. Sean was mystified: "I was under the impression Michael sucked at football," he said. "I was trying to get him a basketball scholarship." Now he'd nip into Briarcrest for one reason or another and couldn't get to where he was going without hitting some big-time college football recruiter. One day he walks into Hugh Freeze's office just in time to hear Hugh tell the coach from the University of Missouri, "I don't want to be this way, but you got no shot at him. You're wasting your time here." Another time he'd squeezed a few minutes out of Hugh's schedule to meet to discuss some personal business—probably how to cover the tuition of one of the black players—when the football recruiter from the University of Florida barged in.

"I want to see Oher," he said. He pronounced it like the airport. "O-Hair."

"It's not O-Hair," said Sean. "It's Oher. Like a boat oar."

As it was against the rules for the recruiters to speak to Michael before the start of his senior year, the Florida guy was literally there just to see Michael. Hugh told the Florida guy that Michael was in class, but he could go down and see him when class let out. Just before the bell rang, the three men—Hugh, Sean, the Florida guy— set out down the hallways in the direction of the classroom. The Florida guy was scrolling through the messages on his BlackBerry when the bell rang, and the door opened in front of him—and so he didn't see Michael until he was right on top of him. When he looked up, Michael was two feet away: a wall of a human being.

The Florida guy actually gave this little jump and a horror-movie gasp: *Uuuuuu!*

He'd seen Michael Oher. "That's when he started dialing," said Sean. "He was dialing so fast." Like the others, he knew he couldn't say a word to Michael; but he had *seen* him. With Michael just looking on, patiently, the Florida guy turned to Hugh Freeze and said, "You tell Michael Oher that the University of Florida is very interested in offering him a football scholarship." Then he walked away but not so far that Sean couldn't hear him, as he hissed into his cell phone: "Coach, you have got to come see this guy. No, you have to come see this guy." Reduced by NCAA regulations to a single sense, the coaches fetishized that sense. "Once you saw him on the hoof," said Kurt Roper, who led the Ole Miss recruiting effort at first, "you said . . . '*Wow!* This guy passes the look test. This guy looks like a big-time SEC lineman. And he's a *junior in high school.*'" Ole Miss had just sent a pair of offensive linemen to the NFL: Chris Spencer, a first-round draft pick of the Seattle Seahawks, and Marcus Johnson, a second-round pick of the Minnesota Vikings. And yet Roper had never seen a lineman of Michael Oher's caliber. "He was *by far* the best guy I'd ever seen," he said.

The frenzy over the player who would become the most highly sought after offensive lineman in the nation had begun, and it had only just begun. And no one had a very clear idea of who he was, where he came from, who his parents were—or even, truth be told, if he was a very good football player. Within two weeks Michael was both as famous and as unknown as a high school football player can be. There wasn't an offensive line coach in the country who wasn't aware of him, and a lot of the head coaches of the bigger football schools had seen him in the flesh. And yet the most basic details of his life were a mystery. One day in spring practice he made this point, inadvertently. He finished yet another board drill, flattened poor Joseph Crone yet again, and went down on one knee, and just stayed there. He was usually the first up and around, jumping on the balls of his feet, like a man half his size. Sean walked over to him.

"You doin' all right?" he asked.

"Pops," said Michael, "my dad died."

Before practice Big Tony had called the Briarcrest office to say that he'd just learned Michael's daddy had been murdered—thrown off an overpass on the west side of Memphis. *Three months ago.* It had been on the evening news—"Man Thrown Off Bridge"—but the man hadn't been identified. When he finally was, no one knew or cared how it happened. "I didn't even know he had a dad," said Sean. "I thought: *I'm sure Leigh Anne knows all this.*" It followed from this that Leigh Anne would deal with whatever it meant inside of Michael Oher, as she was the only one who was allowed inside.

"How do you feel about that?" asked Sean. "Want to take practice off?"

"No."

"When did it happen?"

"Three months ago. But they just told me."

Sean thought that was strange. So did Michael.

"Why do you think they didn't want me to know?" he asked.

And that was all he said about it. He just took it inside him and filed it away in whatever place he kept for such data. Briarcrest had all these people—tutors, teachers, coaches—who thought of themselves as intimately involved with Big Mike's progress, and they were. The teachers who worked there thought that one of the ways a Christian school was superior to a public school was the depth of the spiritual connection between the teachers and the pupils. "It's hard to bond over calculus," said Dr. Pat Williams, a teacher who had been at Briarcrest since its founding. "But it's not hard to bond over 'Will you pray for my family?' " And yet Big Mike didn't think the fact that his father had been killed—or anything else about himself—worth mentioning to anyone but Sean.

He stayed on one knee a long time. Sean went over to Hugh and told him to keep Michael out of action for a spell. Sean called Leigh Anne—the Center for Emotional Involvement. When Michael walked in the door that evening, Leigh Anne took him aside and told him how sorry she was to hear about his dad. "And I hope this doesn't sound callous and cold to you," she said. "But you didn't know the man." Michael acknowledged that was true. Leigh Anne said, "You know, this might be better, because one way or another you are going to have money, and you know that he would have found you and made claims upon you."

That Michael's fortune might come to him from the game of football, rather than the last will and testament of Sean Tuohy, was suddenly thinkable. The first person, credible to Sean, to hint that Michael Oher might have a real future in football was Nick Saban, the head coach at LSU, fresh off a national championship. Michael was on the Briarcrest basketball court, playing a pickup game, when Saban walked into the school. Saban of course couldn't speak to the boy, but he didn't need to. He'd seen his tape. Now Saban watched him as he moved around on the basketball court. When Michael dribbled the ball between his legs, drove to the basket and rose up and dunked, Saban balked. There was no way, he said, that Michael Oher weighed more than 285 pounds. He demanded to see the boy on a scale. That was easy: Briarcrest had bought a new scale, just for him. When Saban saw that Michael tipped the scale at 345 pounds, he said, "If he isn't a top fifteen pick in the NFL draft three years from now, someone done him wrong."

In the frenzy, Hugh Freeze learned exactly what he had on his hands. Not just a big ol' lineman. Not some cement block, inter-changeable with other cement blocks of similar dimensions. A future NFL left tackle. "All of those college coaches," said Hugh, "and I mean every last one of them, said, 'He'll play on Sundays. At left tackle.'"

That is what had them all so excited: Michael Oher fit as perfectly as any high school player they had ever seen the job description of NFL left tackle. And left tackle, as guardian of the quarterback's blind side, had become one of the most highly compensated jobs in the game. Hugh had played Michael on defense at first, and then, when that didn't work, moved him to right tackle. And so Michael Oher had never actually played left tackle. That was understandable: the left tackle wasn't a big deal in high school because the passing game, and thus the pass rush, weren't quite so important. Hugh now understood that in big-time college football, and in the NFL, the left tackle was some kind of huge deal. You find the freak of nature who can play the position brilliantly and you have one of the most valuable commodities in professional sports.

After spring practice Hugh informed the boy who had been playing left tackle that he was being moved to right tackle. Michael Oher was taking over his position.

—

CHAPTER FIVE

DEATH OF A LINEMAN

A BOY HAD COLLIDED with an event. The boy was in many ways unlikely. He had never thought of himself as a football player, and didn't have the first idea what the fuss was all about. The event was a shift in football strategy that raised, dramatically, the value of the one role on the football field the boy was uniquely suited to play. Of course, any kid in America in 2004 thought to have a shot at a professional football career was going to get his share of attention. But if Michael Oher had been just any ordinary offensive lineman he wouldn't have been viewed as a future NFL player. It was the existence of the new prototype—or, more accurately, the stereotype—of the NFL left tackle that made him so interesting to football coaches. They took one look at him and knew exactly what he was born to do. The market for football players had reshaped the offensive line and, in effect, broken out this one position and treated it as almost a separate occupation: What caused *that*?

The answer lay buried in the history of football strategy. Football history, like personal history, is cleaner and more orderly in retrospect than it is at the time. It tends not to have crisp beginnings and endings. It progresses an accident at a time. As the left tackle position evolved, it experienced as many false starts and dead ends and random mutations and unnatural selections as the other little evolutions deep inside football. But the Oakland Coliseum, on December 28, 1975, was, in retrospect, a seminal moment.

The playoff game is in its final minutes, and the Cincinnati Bengals trail the Oakland Raiders 31–28. The Bengals have the ball on the Raiders' thirty-seven-yard line and are driving furiously. High up in the Coliseum, in the Bengals' wing of the press box, an assistant coach named Bill Walsh selects the next play. Walsh knows that whatever play he calls, he won't be able to change it. There won't be time. The Bengals' head coach, the legendary Paul Brown, wants to be seen to call the plays and has created a time-consuming "process" to preserve the illusion. Invisible and unacknowledged, Walsh relays the play over the phone to a fellow assistant coach on the sidelines, Bill Johnson. Johnson whispers the play to Brown. And then Brown, all eyes in the crowd on him, pulls aside a player, barks out his instructions, and pushes him out onto the field to tell the quarterback. Bill Walsh runs the Cincinnati offense; Paul Brown seems to. It doesn't bother Walsh, much. The press box offers what he calls "the clinical atmosphere" in which he thrives. Looking down from the press box one can more easily see what goes right, and what goes wrong. And he is about to see his play go very wrong.

It begins promisingly enough. Wide receiver Charley Joiner cuts across the middle and breaks free. Bengals quarterback Kenny Anderson is the league's most accurate passer and seldom misses an open target. Then a familiar shadow rises behind him. Oakland has a blind side pass rusher, named Ted Hendricks and known as "the Mad Stork." All day long Walsh has fretted about what might happen if the Bengals need to pass, and the Mad Stork knows they need to pass; all day long he's worried about just this moment. "We tried to have a running back pick Hendricks up," he says. "And he did. Most of the time." Now Joiner's open, and Kenny Anderson is about to release the ball when out of nowhere—*Bam!* The Mad Stork buries him. And just like that it's over. The moment the Mad Stork slips the running back's block, the Bengals' season is as good as done.

"I made up my mind right then," said Walsh, "there had to be a better way. And if I was ever in that situation again, I'd handle the blind side rush differently."

It took six years before he found himself in that situation again—calling plays in a playoff game that must account for a great blind side pass rusher. But when he did, the situation was far more alarming.

Now it's January 3, 1982. Walsh drives with a friend to Candlestick Park, before his first and possibly last playoff game as an NFL head coach. His team, the San Francisco 49ers, is about to face the New York Giants, with a newly energized defense coached by Bill Parcells. The Giants' rookie linebacker Lawrence Taylor presents the greatest systematic threat Walsh's offense has ever faced; how Walsh copes with it will inform the future of football strategy. Walsh's coaching career is still something of an iffy proposition— six months earlier Walsh decided to quit football altogether, then reversed himself. He's still in an odd place, professionally: the most innovative offensive mind of his generation and nobody understands what he's thought up. Lose this game and they might never know.

The week before, the Giants had won their first playoff game against the favored Philadelphia Eagles. The Eagles' head coach, Dick Vermeil, was a good friend of Walsh's. "I talked to Dick before their game," said Walsh, "and asked him how he was going to handle Lawrence Taylor. He said, 'Stan can take him. Stan can get out there.'" (Stan was the Eagles' left tackle, Stan Walters.) "Well, Stan didn't get out there." And Stan Walters was no chump. He'd been to the Pro Bowl twice and the year before, 1980, had not allowed a single quarterback sack. Taylor ate him alive, and seemed to take special pleasure in the havoc he created inside the mind of Eagles quarterback Ron Jaworski. In describing his signature hammer blow, Taylor said, "I hit Jaworski that way—with an over-the-head ax job. I thought his dick was going to drop in the dirt." Watching tape of Taylor, Walsh worked overtime to answer the question: how to keep this beast off the back of his new young quarterback? It wasn't Joe Montana's body parts that Walsh was worried about. It was his ability to run this intricate little passing game, Walsh's greatest creation.

Walsh took an unusual view of quarterbacks: he thought they were only as good as the system they played in. After they'd led their team to victory, people pointed to their air of confidence, their cool under pressure, and the other intangible virtues of the presumably born leader. If they led their teams to Super Bowls, these prima donnas became all but irreplaceable, in the public mind. The intangibles were nice, thought Walsh, but they weren't the reason quarterbacks succeeded or failed. "The performance of a quarterback must be manipulated," said Walsh. "To a degree coaching can make a quarterback, and it certainly is the most important factor for his success. The design of the team's offense is the key to a quarterback's performance. One has to be tuned to the other." His offense would make heroes of his quarterbacks. But that didn't mean he had to believe in them personally.

Walsh's career to that point had been as quixotic as his view of the football offense. He'd played minor college ball, at San Jose State. As a coach he had bounced back and forth between college and the pros without sticking in either place. One year he was an assistant with the Oakland Raiders, the next he was the head coach of something called the San Jose Apaches in a chaotic semi-pro league soon to implode. When he arrived in Cincinnati in 1968, at the age of thirty-seven, to run the passing game for Bengals head coach Paul Brown, he faced a new problem: comically inadequate football players. "We were an AFL expansion team," said Walsh, "and you just didn't get any quality players. We got the dregs, players who never should have been in pro football." The newfound Bengals clearly weren't going to frighten or push anyone off the line of scrimmage. If they were going to move the ball, they were going to need to pass the ball.

But the Bengals' small players were all, by NFL standards, as defective as the big ones. His new quarterback, Virgil Carter, was a case in point. Carter wasn't able to get the ball more than about 20 yards downfield in any form other than a slow desperate wobble. Walsh's job, as he saw it, was to create a system that suited Virgil Carter's talents: guile, nimbleness, and an ability to throw accurately, as long as he didn't have to throw far. "We couldn't dominate anyone with the run, so Virgil became our central performer," he said later. "And so that's how it all started. When I was forced to use Virgil."

Walsh's solution to Carter's weak arm was to teach him to use the field in a new way. He spread the field horizontally; that is, from sideline to sideline. He had the receivers run short routes timed precisely to the steps of the quarterback. If Carter took a three-step drop, they ran one sort of route; if Carter took a five-step drop, they ran another. Carter didn't wait for his receivers to come open but threw to where he expected them to be—usually just a few yards away. The process was further speeded up by reducing the number of decisions the quarterback was forced to make. His presumed precision means that he doesn't need to pay nearly so much attention to the defensive formation. His short, timed passes, if executed properly, can be completed against any defense. On any given play there might be as many as five Bengals receivers running pass patterns. But when Virgil Carter came to the line of scrimmage, he had already made up his mind to which side of the field he would throw, so he had reduced the five potential receivers to a short list of three: a primary, an alternate, and an outlet. He saw how the defense had lined up and made a pre-snap decision about the viability of his primary receiver. And so, as he dropped back to pass, he had at most one decision to make: alternate or outlet?

By its very nature the enterprise demanded tedious repetition: for ball and receiver to arrive on a patch of turf the size of a welcome mat at the same moment, their timing had to be precise, and to be precise it had to be second nature. At first Walsh had a problem finding the extraordinary amount of time he needed to practice with his quarterbacks and receivers. "Paul Brown didn't want us out on the field so long," he said, "so I'd sneak out with them during lunch." It was more like a handoff on the other side of the line of scrimmage than an aerial attack, and his players at first found it strange. "He'd show up every Monday with this high school play he'd thought up and we'd laugh at it all week," said Bengals receiver Chip Myers. "That Sunday, it'd work three times."

Walsh's father had been a talented auto mechanic and he had expected his son to join him in the family business. Walsh moved on, but something of his father lingered in him. His offense felt *engineered*. The virtues it exalted above all others were precision, consistency, and predictability. Walsh had created the contraption to compensate for the deficiencies of his quarterback, but an offense based on a lot of short, well-timed passes turned out to offer surprising inherent advantages. First, it delivered the ball into a runner's hands on the other side of the line of scrimmage, thus removing the biggest defensive beasts from the space between him and the goal line. The pass had always been viewed as a complement to the run, but it could apparently function as a substitute as well.

Next, by shortening—and timing—the passing game, Walsh reduced its two biggest risks: interceptions and incompletion. "Our argument was that the chance of a completion drops dramatically over twelve yards," said Walsh. "So, we would throw a ten-yard pass.

Our formula was that we should get at least half our passing yardage from the run *after* the catch."

Finally, the Walsh plan addressed the football coach's visceral fear of an offense based on the passing game. For such an offense to be viable, lots of people need to go out for a pass. Walsh did not usually feel that five receivers was necessary, but he needed, at a minimum, three. But the more people who go out for a pass, the fewer who remain to block for the quarterback. The defense, alert to the pass, already is more than usually intent on killing the quarterback. By reducing the amount of time the quarterback held the ball, Walsh had minimized the risk that they would succeed. He had infused the passing game with two new qualities: dullness and safety. "People made fun of it," Walsh said. "They thought if you weren't throwing the ball twenty yards downfield, you weren't throwing the ball. They called it a nickel-and-dime offense."

In 1971, Virgil Carter, who had never completed as many as half of his passes, somehow led the entire league in completion percentage (62.2) and bumped his yards per attempt from 5.9 to 7.3. The Bengals surprised everyone and won their division. The next year Carter gave way to Ken Anderson, a little known passer out of even less well known Augustana College, who hadn't completed even half his passes in college. In Walsh's offense, Kenny Anderson did even better than Virgil Carter. When he saw Anderson play, Walsh later said, he realized that the offense he had designed to compensate for a weak-armed quarterback had a more general effectiveness; this passing game of his could survive on very little talent, but it could also exploit better material. In 1974, Anderson led the league in completion percentage and total yards and yards per attempt (8.13). After the Mad Stork ended the 1975 season, and Paul Brown retired, Walsh expected to take over as head coach. Brown had several times refused other NFL teams permission to interview Walsh for their head coaching jobs, without bothering to mention their interest to Walsh. Instead, Brown had told Walsh that he didn't think he'd ever make a good NFL head coach. Now Brown did his part to make his prediction come true, by arranging for another coach to replace him. "The selection of head coaches in the NFL always has been a mystery to me," said Walsh not long afterwards. "I expect to be a head coach. I want to be a head coach. He really *is* the game. Everybody else are production people in his show."

Walsh left Cincinnati in anger, to run the offense for the San Diego Chargers. There he inherited a struggling quarterback named Dan Fouts. In Walsh's passing system, Fouts went on to lead the league in completion percentage. Walsh himself quickly moved on to become a head football coach at Stanford University. He coached the Cardinals for two seasons, 1977 and 1978. In 1977, Stanford quarterback Guy Benjamin led the nation in passing and won the Sammy Baugh Award given to the nation's top college passer. In 1978, his replacement, Steve Dils, did the same. In 1979, Walsh, now forty-nine years old, finally was named an NFL head coach, of the team with the league's lowest payroll and the league's worst record, the San Francisco 49ers.

The 49ers also had, by most statistical measures, one of the NFL's worst quarterbacks, Steve Deberg. The year before Walsh arrived, Deberg, a recent tenth-round draft choice, had engineered the lowest scoring offense in the entire NFL. In leading his team to a 2–14 record, Deberg threw 302 passes and completed 137 of them, or 45.4 percent, not counting the 22 he delivered into the hands of the opposing team. The next year, in Bill Walsh's system of well-timed passes, the seemingly inept Deberg threw more passes (578) than any quarterback in the history of the NFL. His completion rate rose to an astonishing 60 percent, and he also completed more passes than any quarterback in the history of the NFL. Deberg also cut his interception rate in half and threw for more than an extra yard on each passing attempt (5.2 to 6.32).

The transformation of Steve Deberg—and the 49er offense—amounted to a football miracle. But if anyone noticed, Walshdidn't hear about it.

In a pattern now familiar in Walsh's offenses, a quarterback who seemed to deserve a raise was instead handed a pink slip. Walsh replaced Deberg in 1980 with a quarterback drafted in the third round who everyone said was too small and had too weak an arm to play in the NFL: Joe Montana. The next two years, Montana led the NFL in completion percentage (64.5 and 63.7) and also in avoiding interceptions. He would become, by general consensus, the finest quarterback ever to play the game. How good was he really? That's hard to know, because his coach held a magic wand, and every quarterback over whose head that wand passed instantly looked better than he'd ever been. When Joe Montana's play became sloppy during the 1987 season, Walsh replaced him, temporarily, with Steve Young—whose sensational performance caused a lot of 49er fans to wonder, and to feel guilty for wondering, if maybe Steve Young was even better than Joe Montana.

The performance of Walsh's quarterbacks suggested a radical thought: that in the most effective passing attack in the NFL, and on one of the most successful teams in the history of pro football, the quarterbacks were fungible. The system was the star. Walsh had imported into pro football the spirit of a Japanese auto plant—Total Quality Management. A lot of people in and around pro football were uncomfortable with the idea, and the benching of Joe Montana, for them, was the final straw. "Walsh was wanting to bench him and play his other guy," hollered former star quarterback Terry Bradshaw, doing his best to speak for the man on the street, "because if Young can go in there and do it, then Walsh looks like another genius again. You know, he really believes that genius tag. But the genius really wears number sixteen [Montana's number]. That's the genius, and he [Walsh] was messing with him."

And yet when Young eventually took over the San Francisco 49er offense for good, he led the league in passing five out of his first six years, won a Super Bowl, and wound up with his face on a bust in the Hall of Fame. Perhaps because Young had played for other NFL teams, he appreciated better than most what Walsh had brought to the passing game. "When I was at Tampa," Young told sports writer Glenn Dickey, after he took over the 49ers quarterback job, "the coaches told me to hold the ball until the receiver came open. By that time everybody was on top of me. Now I have a progression of receivers, and I hit the first one who's open. It might be only a three yard gain, and maybe I could have waited and hit a receiver another ten yards down the field, but I've completed the pass, moved the ball, and added to the frustration of defensive linemen trying to stop me."

Young, like Montana, came to be viewed as a born star whose success in pro football was inevitable. But before Young arrived there were others, and no one in their right minds mistook them for first-tier NFL quarterbacks. In 1986, for instance, Jeff Kemp, Dartmouth College graduate and son of future vice-presidential candidate Jack, stepped in for the injured Montana for ten games. Kemp was five eleven and had trouble seeing over the heads of his blockers. To clear the view, Walsh had the linemen go out after the pass rushers rather than fall back, as they typically would do. The tactic was less effective in delaying the rush but it did, momentarily, create a window through which Kemp might glimpse the field. The bill for his view arrived milliseconds after he released the football, when some monster hammered him into the ground. In his career leading up to the moment he replaced Joe Montana—a career spent entirely with the Los Angeles Rams—Kemp had completed fewer than half his passes. That year in San Francisco he completed nearly 60 percent of his passes, for an impressive 7.77 yards per attempt, and posted one of the highest passer ratings in the NFL. Then Kemp, too, was injured. His replacement was a fellow named Mike Moroski, so obscure that any question concerning his NFL career would be considered out of bounds in a game of Trivial Pursuit. Moroski had been with the 49ers for exactly two weeks before he became, by default, their starting quarterback. He completed 57.5 percent of *his* passes.

Eventually people must have noticed. As Walsh performed miracle after miracle with his quarterbacks, a more general trend emerged in NFL strategy: away from the run and toward the pass.* In 1978, NFL teams passed 42 percent of the time and ran the ball 58 percent of the time. Each year, right through until the mid-1990s, they passed more and ran less until the ratios were almost exactly reversed: in 1995, NFL teams passed 59 percent of the time and ran 41 percent of the time. It's not hard to see why; the passing game was improving, and the running game was stagnant. Every year NFL teams ran the ball thousands of times, and every year the league averaged between 3.9 and 4.1 yards per carry. With just the tiniest, seemingly random variations from year to year, the

---

* I'm grateful to Ben Alamar for both his thoughts on this subject and for doing most of the actual work. Alamar, a professor of sports management at Menlo College, did his first football research as a graduate student. He sought to answer the question: which is more likely to lead to team success, a good running attack or a good passing attack? And he found that a team with a relatively strong passing attack was far more likely to make the NFL playoffs. He tried to get a statistics or economics journal to publish his study, but found no takers. Five years later, to fill the void in interest in his football research, Alamar founded the *Journal of Quantitative Analyses in Sports.* Today he is employed as a consultant to an actual NFL team.

But Alamar is a special case; there are only a handful of people engaged in the statistical analysis of football players, and football strategies, and they don't meet and argue and review each other's work, the way baseball people do. (The Society of American Baseball Research has thousands of members and a tradition of peer review and annual conferences, and has, in recent years, supplied Major League Baseball front offices with a great deal of brain power. Its founder, Bill James, has a World Series ring from his work with the 2004 Boston Red Sox.) No doubt there are plenty of reasons for the relative paucity of football research, but a big one is that inquiring minds have been discouraged by the messiness of the game. It's relatively easy to assign credit and blame on a baseball field. On a football field, there is no such thing as individual achievement. A quarterback throws an interception and it might be his own fault; but it might also be the fault of the receiver who ran the wrong route, or the blocker who allowed him to be hit as he threw. Twenty-two players are involved in every football play. To value precisely the activity of any one of them, it is first necessary to account for the actions of the other twenty-one.

yield from this mill was monotonously consistent going all the way back to 1960. Some teams did a bit better, of course, and some did a bit worse. The league as a whole, however, never figured out how to make the running game yield even a fraction of a yard more than it always had. It was possible that the running game awaited some innovative coach to figure out how to make it work more efficiently. And it could be that the steel industry is just awaiting the CEO who can find gold in its mills.

The passing game behaved like an altogether different and more promising business. In 1960, an NFL pass netted you, on average, 4.6 yards. That was better than running the ball, but then you had to consider that a pass was still twice as likely to cost you the ball. Quarterbacks threw interceptions a bit more than 6 percent of the time while running backs fumbled the ball only about 3 percent of the time. The trade-off must have seemed unappealing to NFL coaches, as passing attempts per game actually fell a bit through the 1960s. By 1975, teams were throwing the ball, on average, just 24 times each game. Then something happened: teams began to pass more each year than they had the year before until, by the early

---

Still, as Alamar points out, there are all sorts of questions about football waiting to be answered as soon as someone bothers to collect the data. One example relevant to this story: how much does the performance of quarterbacks vary with the amount of time they spend in the pocket? A critical part of any passing game—another reason for the extreme importance of left tackles—is the amount of time a quarterback has to throw the ball. The difference between a quick decision-making quarterback and a slow one is typically fractions of a second: a difference impossible to see with the naked eye. In 2004, for example, the New York Giants lost to the Arizona Cardinals, and Giants quarterback Kurt Warner was sacked six times. The New York sports press, with just a couple of interesting exceptions, vilified the Giants' offensive line. Giants coach Tom Coughlin suspected another culprit. He stayed up that night reviewing game tape, and finally took out a stopwatch and put it on Kurt Warner: 2.5 seconds is a generous amount of time for an NFL quarterback to enjoy before he gets rid of the ball. Anything longer than 3 seconds is an eternity. On thirty of the thirty-seven pass plays the Giants ran against the Cardinals, Warner had held the ball 3.8 seconds or more. Coughlin left his offensive line intact, but the next day he benched Warner and installed rookie Eli Manning in his place.

"Time in the pocket and the rate at which the quarterback is under pressure are the two most important aspects of a team's performance (both offensively and defensively)," says Alamar. And yet no record of it is kept.

1990s, NFL quarterbacks were throwing the ball, on average, 34 times per game. All else being equal, this should have been a disaster for those quarterbacks. In a business with normal returns, the more you produce of a good the less you can sell it for. The passing game didn't exhibit normal returns. From a yield of 4.6 yards each throw, the average gain climbed steadily from the late 1970s until the early 1990s, until it settled in at around 7 yards per passing attempt. Each attempt was significantly more likely to be caught by a receiver. Right through the 1960s, NFL quarterbacks hit on fewer than 50 percent of their passes. In the 1970s, quarterbacks not only began to throw more often but to complete a higher percentage of their passes. Again, the trend was gradual but relentless, until the early 2000s when, on average, NFL quarterbacks made good on 60 percent of their throws.

The more closely you examined the passing business, the stranger it appeared. You might think, for instance, that the more the quarterback threw the ball, the less picky he'd be about where he threw it, and the more easily a defense could anticipate the pass and intercept it. Apparently not: the more often pro quarterbacks put the ball up in the air, the less likely it was to be intercepted. From the late 1970s until the mid-1990s, the interception rate fell steadily—from 6 percent all the way down to 3 percent. By 1995, a quarterback was no more likely to be intercepted than a runner was to fumble the ball. The running game was a dull, barely profitable business that exhibited little potential for growth. The passing game looked like a booming software company: the more quarterbacks produced, the bigger their profit margins. Adding to the mystery, the passing boom occurred as the number of teams in the league, and the number of games each team played, expanded. There were twice as many pro quarterbacks in 1995 as there were in 1960, and more nearly always means worse. In this peculiar instance, more meant better. In 1960, NFL quarterbacks threw 7,583 passes and completed 49.6 percent of them, while throwing

470 interceptions (6.2 percent of all passes were intercepted). In 2005, NFL quarterbacks threw 16,430 passes, completed 59.5 percent of them, and had 507 of them intercepted (only 3.1 percent of all passes were intercepted).

An obvious reason for the boom in the passing game is the changes made to the rules of the NFL game. In 1978, NFL linemen were permitted, for the first time in history, to use their hands when they blocked. Overnight the image of the lineman with his elbows stuck out in imitation of a coat hanger became charmingly antiquated. That same year defensive backs were forbidden to make contact with receivers more than five yards beyond the line of scrimmage. Both rule changes helped the passing game along. But rule changes alone didn't begin to explain why a system of passing created before the changes had proven so effective: they don't explain Bill Walsh's success with quarterbacks. What seems to have happened is that NFL offenses began to pass the ball more effectively, the new passing attacks pleased the crowds and were good for business, and so NFL rulemakers made a point of encouraging them. As Indianapolis Colts general manager Bill Polian, who sat on the committee to change the rules, puts it, "Innovation drove the rule changes rather than the other way around."

And the 1970s and early 1980s were a golden era for innovation in the passing game. The football field is usually a tightly strung ecosystem, an efficient economy: there is seldom a free lunch on it. Of course there are the weaknesses and strengths of individual players. The other team might have an inept cornerback, for instance, and the smart coach will know how to exploit him. *Systematic* opportunity is rare. Yet Walsh had stumbled upon a systematic opportunity. The short, precisely timed passing game might not offer an entirely free lunch, but the discount to the retail price was steep. Bill Polian remembers when he first studied the 49ers' offense on tape, in early 1991. Then the general manager of the AFC Champion Buffalo Bills, he was waiting to see which team in the soon-to-be-played NFC Championship game he would face in the Super Bowl, the 49ers or Bill Parcells's New York Giants. What he saw on the tape persuaded him that Bill Walsh's passing game would change football. "That was the Eureka moment for me," he said.

The Bills subsequently borrowed liberally from Walsh, as did the Colts once Polian moved there. As did many other teams, covertly. An astonishing number of Walsh's assistants—Andy Reid, Mike Sherman, Steve Mariucci, George Seifert, John Gruden, Mike Shanahan, Denny Green, Gary Kubiak—left to become NFL head coaches. When, in the mid-1990s, Brett Favre of the Green Bay Packers stepped onto center stage and took over the role of God's gift to the quarterbacking position, a Walsh disciple (Packer head coach and former Walsh assistant Mike Holmgren) stood behind the curtain pulling the strings. The story wasn't quite as simple as Bill Walsh created this offense—which came to be called "the West Coast offense"*—and everyone else ripped it off. But it was close: by the late 1990s, every NFL team had a rhythm passing game. "In that sense," says Bill Polian of the Indianapolis Colts, "everyone in the NFL today runs Bill Walsh's offense. Because the rhythm passing game is all Walsh."

---

* There's an arcane dispute waiting for anyone who wants to have one about the meaning of the phrase "West Coast offense." According to Paul Zimmerman, the term came from a piece he wrote for *Sports Illustrated*; it referred to the passing game created by Sid Gilman, and adopted by Don Coryell, at the San Diego Chargers, and others, including Walsh, mistakenly applied it to Walsh's offense. The full intellectual history of the passing game is beyond the scope of this book, but Gilman was obviously central to it. "A football field is 53 and a 1/3 yards wide by 100," Gilman told the *Houston Post*, in what in the mid-1960s counted as a radical observation. "We felt we should take advantage of the fact that the football field was that wide and that long. So our formations reflected the fact that we were going to put our outside ends wide enough so that we could take advantage of the entire width of the field. And then we were going to throw the ball far enough so that we forced people to cover the width AND the length." Gilman was the first pro football coach to spread the field and treat the pass as the primary offensive weapon, and Walsh studied his work

This single strand of the history of the game—the strand that would become the rope tied around Michael Oher's waist and haul him up in the world—is clearer than most. Over time, the statistics of NFL quarterbacks, on average, came to resemble the statistics of Bill Walsh's quarterbacks—because other coaches borrowed heavily from Walsh. The passing game was transformed from a risky business with returns not all that much greater than the running game to a clearly superior way to move the football down the field. As a result, the players most important to the passing game became, relatively, a great deal more valuable. The force that pulled on the rope around Michael Oher's waist was the mind of Bill Walsh.

But on the afternoon of January 3, 1982, that mind had not been fully appreciated. It hadn't infected anything except a few quarterbacks. Football strategy has no inevitable path it must follow. Walsh still had no sense that his ideas were likely to be pilfered, or that they were even recognized as ideas. The drift of the game was in his favor—"The rule changes played right into our hands," he said—but hardly inexorable. The only proof of any concept in the NFL was a championship ring. Walsh knew he couldn't win with offense alone any more than a defensive-minded coach could

---

closely. "I think the difference between me and a lot of other people was that other people really weren't willing to pick up on what Sid was doing," Walsh told me. "Except for [Raider coach] Al Davis. Because it was complex."

Walsh and Coryell followed in Gilman's footsteps to a fork in the road, then set out in different directions: Coryell went deep and Walsh went wide. In Coryell's system, the first receiver the quarterback looked for was the receiver going long: the high-risk option. The quarterbacks who played for Coryell passed for many yards, but also threw a lot of interceptions, and took a lot of punishment. To enable the receivers to get downfield they held the ball longer and gave pass rushers more time to get to them. This was the big difference in Walsh's approach from previous innovators of the passing game: it stripped a lot of the risk out of passing. It was more reliable and less explosive, more mechanical and less obviously artistic. It was also more appealing to other coaches and general managers looking for a passing game to steal. If "West Coast offense" came to refer to Walsh's passing game, and not Coryell's, it may have been because the spread of Walsh's demanded a catch phrase.

People who wish to stress Coryell's importance point to the success of his Hall of Fame quarterback Dan Fouts. The trouble with this is that Walsh coached Fouts first. When

win with defense alone. And defense, to Walsh's mind, was not a strategic challenge but a matter of finding better players. That was something that he hadn't been able to do. Toward the end of the 1980 season, after yet another close loss, in which his team had scored a surprising number of points, Walsh had made up his mind to quit. "I spent the five hour flight home sitting by myself," he later wrote. "I looked out the window so no one could see me break down. It was too much for anyone. I was emotionally, mentally, and physically exhausted. I decided I would resign as soon as the season ended; I believed I had done as much as I could do and the job was just too much for me."

He had lasted into the 1981 season, just, but a successful regular season wasn't enough. He was still at risk of winding up a cliché of free market capitalism: the inventor whose brainchild would lead to profit for others and nothing for himself. For fifteen seasons he had performed miracles with quarterbacks. He had just done something truly extraordinary: take the worst offense in the NFL and, in two years, turn it into the seventh best. And still no one knew. "If I had stopped then," he said, "it [his passing game] would have been discarded. There wasn't anyone else. Everyone was just watching to see how we would do. If it worked, nobody

---

Walsh arrived in San Diego in 1976, says Fouts, "I was a mess. I was on my way to being cut or traded or whatever." A year under Walsh, and Fouts was on his way to stardom. After Walsh left in 1977, and Coryell took over, in 1978, Fouts indeed passed more frequently, and for more yards, and probably had a lot more fun than he had under Walsh—but he also threw a lot more interceptions. Fouts is reluctant to credit Walsh or Coryell alone for his success: both were instrumental. "I don't know who gets the credit," he says. "There's only one Moses, but I'm not sure there's a Moses here." But Howard Mudd, who coached the Chargers' offensive line at the time, and watched Fouts's transformation, has no such ambivalence. "Bill Walsh *made* Dan Fouts," Mudd says. "He stopped reading all over the field. He was looking for the player to be open rather than reading the defense. He rehearsed this *constantly*. Walsh created a new efficiency. And that efficiency turned Dan around totally."

Both Mudd and Fouts note that Coryell, after he came to San Diego, preserved an important element of Walsh's passing game: the emphasis on routes timed precisely to the quarterback's movements. "That was the beauty of that offense," says Fouts. "The rhythm and the timing follows from the steps the quarterback takes."

said anything. If it didn't work, everyone said, 'Look, that shows this stuff doesn't work.' "* He'd brought to the NFL passing game the precision and efficiency of a Japanese auto factory. And now, at the very moment he was ready to export to America, Godzilla had arrived to tear the factory apart.

Inside football, the argument between brains and brawn never has been settled, and probably never will be. The argument less and less found its way into words off the field, but on the field it reprised itself in action and strategy, over and over again. And on the chilly wet afternoon in Candlestick Park, it was about to play out in an extreme form, with Walsh as the brains and Bill Parcells as the brawn. Parcells was deeply suspicious of the overt use of intellect on a football sideline. He knew that Walsh claimed to script the first 25 plays of every game in advance, but later said "that scripting was a bunch of bullshit. They never got past number eight." And Parcells's influence in football, as measured by the number of his assistants who would go on to coach other teams, was nearly as great as Walsh's: Bill Belichick, Al Groh, Tom Coughlin, Sean Payton. (By 2006, two thirds of the teams in the NFL had

---

* The bias against the pass was deeply ingrained in football. It was illegal until 1906, and even then severely restricted. It wasn't until 1933 that a quarterback was allowed to throw a forward pass from anywhere behind the line of scrimmage. Once legalized it was disdained, in large part because it had been legalized to make the game safer, and a big point in the game's favor, to those who played it, was its unsafety. Right up until the mid-1940s, in a rearguard attempt to slow the spread of wussiness, roughing the passer was actually encouraged. A small-college coach named Elmer Berry who had used an innovative passing attack to sneak up and beat bigger schools got so worked up about the anti-pass sentiment that he penned a counterblast, called *The Forward Pass in Football.* "Apparently many regard the forward pass simply as a valuable threat, something for occasional use, something to take a chance with, something the possibility of which makes the real game still workable," Berry wrote in 1921. "To a large degree this has been the attitude of the larger colleges. In general they have frowned upon the forward pass; opposed it, sneered at it, called it basketball and done what they could to retard its adoption. It has taken away from them the advantage of numbers, weight and power, made the game one of brains, speed and strategy—even, if you please, of luck—and rendered the outcome of their 'practice' games with smaller colleges uncertain."

been run by a coaching descendant of Walsh or Parcells.) After Parcells later won his first Super Bowl, in 1986, he said his style of football "never had anything to prove. It's the fancy-pants stuff that needs to prove itself." Walsh was the latest embodiment of fancy-pants. In 1981, people were starting to take notice of his new and improved little passing game, but Parcells had something new and improved, too: a passing game destructomatic called Lawrence Taylor. Just as Walsh was lowering the risk of throwing the ball, Parcells was raising the risk to the men who threw it.

At the end of the 1981 season Taylor was for Parcells still a shiny new toy with a complicated control panel that he was figuring out how to use. No matter what Parcells told his rookie linebacker to do, Taylor's instinct was to find the quarterback and kill him. Later in his career Taylor enjoyed letting people think he had a gift for freelancing, but during his rookie year, at least, he often didn't know what he was meant to do—and so, unable to think up a better idea, he just went after the passer. The sixth game of that season, against the St. Louis Cardinals, was a case in point. "The deal was," said Parcells, "that whichever side the tight end lined up on, the linebacker facing him was supposed to drop back into pass coverage. Usually the tight end lined up on the right side, and Lawrence blitzed. But early in the game they moved the tight end over to the left, to deal with Lawrence. He rushes anyway, and sacks the quarterback. I went over and said, 'Lawrence, they got the tight end on your side, you need to be back in coverage.' He says, 'Oh yeah, Coach, oh yeah.' I said, 'Watch out, 'cause they gonna do that again.' 'Yeah, yeah, Coach, okay. I'm ready.' Third quarter they do it again, they put the tight end on his side . . . *and Lawrence blitzes again.* This time he hits the quarterback, knocks the ball out of his hands, and [defensive end] George Martin picks it up and runs for a touchdown. Everyone's jumping on top of each other in the end zone and I'm pissed. I went and found him on the bench and he sees me and says, 'I didn't do it again, did I?' I said, 'Lawrence, we don't even *have* what you're doing.' And he says, 'Well, we better put it in on Monday, Coach, 'cause it works!' "

And Parcells loved it! "I'm a little Neanderthal," Parcells said. "I think defense is the key to any sport. That was my intent when I started coaching. That's what I wanted to coach. Not football. Football *defense*. It's not glamorous to those who are into what's aesthetically pleasing. But it's glamorous to *me*. 'Cause I think defense is the key to the game." It went without saying that the key to defense was passion and violence.

Walsh's temperament—and his football interests—couldn't have been more different. He preferred offense because offense was strategic. "There's just so much to offense that a coach really does have control of," he said. "Defense is just a matter of having the personnel." As a rookie NFL head coach, Bill Walsh was able to stand on the sideline in the pose of a man before a fire with a glass of port in one hand and a volume of Matthew Arnold's essays in the other. He kept about him a degree of calm that led *Los Angeles Times* columnist Jim Murray to write of him, "you half expect his headset is playing Mozart." Parcells lived out his emotional life inside the game; Walsh aimed to cleanse himself of emotion before the game ever started. The effort was immense, as he had a great deal of emotion to dispose of, and after some games he could be seen brushing tears from his eyes. But once "The Star-Spangled Banner" began to play, he said, "I'd tell myself, 'Here you go. Start pulling away, start computerizing. You must think clearly and *remove yourself*.' . . . It was like watching a game through a window."

Lawrence Taylor was a problem new to Walsh. Lawrence Taylor smashed the window. Walsh's system enabled Joe Montana to get rid of the ball faster than anyone in football, and normally that was fast enough. Now it wasn't. "Taylor was so quick," said Walsh, "that no matter how quickly we executed, he could still get there." To leave some running back or tight end to deal with Taylor was out of the question: Walsh needed his tight ends out spreading the field, and Taylor ate running backs for breakfast. The next most obvious candidate to block Taylor was the left tackle, as he lined up closest to the point where Taylor crossed the line of scrimmage. But the 49ers' left tackle, Dan Audick, was six two, 250 pounds, and even less well designed to handle Taylor than the Eagles' Stan Walters. "It's when I started to play left tackle," Audick said, "that the coaches were just starting to discover that they needed their best lineman at left tackle. I think they just wanted me to play the position as a kind of final experiment to verify their hypothesis" (Audick might not have been big or fast, but he was charming).

Walsh had brought his left tackle problem on himself. When he'd arrived in San Francisco, he had a very promising young left tackle, Ron Singleton. But then, as Walsh later put it, "Ron decided that he should be a marquee player, and subsequently sounded off in the locker room about how he should have been receiving credit and publicity." Walsh could put up, just, with his quarterbacks prancing around like superstars, but he had no space in his brain for the idea of linemen as celebrities. Singleton took the outlandish step of hiring an agent, who demanded the outrageous sum of $90,000 a year. When Walsh refused to pay it, the agent told people that Walsh was unwilling to negotiate because Singleton was black. That's when Walsh flipped. He had a staffer go to Singleton's locker, toss his belongings in a cardboard box, drive over to Singleton's house, and leave them on the doorstep. "That's how he knew he was fired," said Walsh. "He opened his front door and found the cardboard box." The player, or the agent, had misjudged the coach. Walsh's problem with Singleton's exalted self-image had nothing to do with the color of his skin but with the position he played. The man was a *lineman*.

In the end, Walsh decided that the episode had been a turning point for his team. Parting so unsentimentally with his left tackle showed everyone that he was not to be trifled with. It set a certain tone. On the other hand . . . who was going to block Lawrence Taylor?

I hit Jaworski that way—with an over-the-head ax job. I thought his dick was going to drop in the dirt.

The system was all about rhythm, and rhythm was precisely what you didn't have when you heard Taylor's footsteps behind you. Walsh needed to stop Taylor in his tracks, take him out of the game. Searching his locker room for a solution, he settled on a man named John Ayers. Ayers played left guard. He was six five, 270 pounds, and quick-footed. He grew up in Canyon, a small ranching town in west Texas, and in the off season he still worked as a cowboy, branding and castrating bulls, which was probably good practice. "John was born fifty years too late," said his wife, Laurel. "He'd have been a cowboy on a ranch. For twenty dollars a day. And been just as happy." Ayers said almost nothing and did what he was told and everyone liked him and few really knew him. He didn't think more than twice about how little he was paid, and it didn't occur to him to promote himself. "He was always in the background," said his wife. "He preferred it that way. He preferred the anonymity." He was, in short, Bill Walsh's idea of an offensive lineman. When Walsh spoke of his linemen, he sounded like a sea captain describing ships. "He had a low center of gravity," he said of Ayers. "You couldn't get his feet up off the ground. He had great balance. He had *ballast*." On each passing play Ayers would first check to make sure that no other Giant was blitzing up the middle, then skip backwards and to his left and meet the onrushing Taylor. Walsh thought he was quick enough to get in front of Taylor; the ballast would do the rest.

Informed that he would be dealing, from his left guard position, with this linebacker coming off the edge, Ayers was at first puzzled. Then he watched tapes of Lawrence Taylor. "They said there's this rookie linebacker who's tearing up the league," he told the *New York Times*. "I said, 'Well, good, that's the fullback's problem.' Then I took a look at him and said, 'Well, maybe the fullback can't get it done.'" His wife looked at tape with him. "I was scared to death that he had that assignment," she said. "All we heard about the week before the game was this big bad Lawrence Taylor."

On January 3, 1982, Bill Walsh drove to Candlestick Park, changed into his coaching shirt, met with the trainers and his coaches, then said a few low-key words to the players. He didn't feel there was any point in trying to motivate them at that point; mainly he was trying to calm them down. ("Whenever I tried to give an inspirational talk before the game, the other team would score first, so I didn't see the numbers in it.") Then he lined up to listen to "The Star-Spangled Banner." The rain began to fall and the field became such a mess that, after the kickoff, teams of men in dark blue windbreakers ran around replacing the divots. When Joe Montana took his position under the center, the wedges of grass were still strewn around him like cheap toupees. Walsh has made no secret of his general game plan: the night before he had informed the television announcers, Pat Summerall and John Madden, that he intended to throw the ball on 17 of the first 22 plays. He knew that Parcells knew, and Parcells knew that he knew, just as Walsh knew that on most of those 17 passing plays Lawrence Taylor would be coming for Joe Montana. And if they somehow hadn't surmised as much, Taylor would remind them, well in advance. "When Lawrence is pass-rushing," Giants defensive back Beasley Reece said, "he telegraphs it. It's like a cop putting sirens on top of his car. Lawrence puts a light on his helmet. His hands are flopping and his arms are swinging. He looks at the blocker the minute he attacks and destroys the blocker. Then he goes after the quarterback."

John Ayers's job was to look over and see if Taylor's hands were flopping. If he saw Taylor preparing to charge, he stepped back to meet him. It was only a matter of how the carefully planned collision ended: John Ayers is the one surprise. How he turns out, Walsh thought, would determine the outcome of the game.

On the first play from scrimmage Montana drops back, and Taylor comes. For a moment the field in front of him is empty. Then, out of nowhere, a figure appears and . . . *Pow!*

It was as if Taylor had run into the side of a house. What he had run into was 270 pounds of cowboy, who trained each off season by harnessing himself to a six-foot-tall tractor tire and hauling it sideways behind him for miles around a freshly ploughed field. The training showed. On every passing play Taylor looked like a man who had gone to get his quart of vanilla ice cream only to yank on the freezer door and find it locked. "It was the first time I'd seen it," he said. "It was the first time they'd brought the guard back to meet me. There was nothing I could do but try to run him over." He didn't run him over: the first pass was thrown. And the next. And the next. Watching Walsh's offense attack Parcells's defense was like watching a giant icicle plunging into a volcano. Steam rose, and you couldn't tell at first whether the icicle had melted or the fire had been extinguished.

Then the air cleared. At halftime the 49ers led 24–10 and Montana had completed 15 of 22 passes for 276 yards and two touchdowns. He'd picked to pieces the NFL's most dangerous defense. Montana once observed of Walsh's passing attack that "if you missed perfect, you wound up with great." He missed perfect on this day, but not by much. He threw a careless interception, and once took off from the pocket when he didn't really need to—and was chased down from behind by Lawrence Taylor. Otherwise, he played like a kid who'd been given the answers to the test in advance. "I'd never seen us execute like that," he said after the game. "That's why it didn't look tough for us. But it was. Our line was stopping them, and when I got that time, things became easy." The threat from the blind side had, thanks to John Ayers, vanished. "I couldn't figure out what to do with him," said Taylor, much later.

When Bill Parcells looked up at the end of the game, the scoreboard read 38–24, but it hadn't been as close as that. His defense hadn't allowed 38 points in any game all season, and they were lucky to have allowed only 38 today. Parcells was appalled, at not only the outcome but the interpretation of the outcome—that the difference in the game had been Walsh's strategy. There was no chance that some *left guard* was shutting down LT. "That would never have worked on a fast track," he said. "The only reason it worked was that the field was so bad that nobody could rush the passer. It was a mud pile. It was a slow track. If that was AstroTurf that would have never worked." And in the future, he would make damn sure it wouldn't work even in a mud pile. Later, when he watched the tape of the game, Parcells saw the weakness of Walsh's strategy. When Ayers dropped back, he left a hole in the middle of the line. Had the Giants blitzed a middle linebacker, he'd have had a clear path to Joe Montana. They never did. "We learned to deal with that as we went on," said Parcells. "We blitzed [Harry] Carson and teams stopped doing that. What they eventually had to do is slide the line to Taylor. We knew that unless they were extremely gifted at the left tackle position, they would have to compensate for him." And if they had to compensate for their left tackle, they created weakness elsewhere, and the game was half-won.

After the game Bill Walsh smiled sheepishly and told the television audience that he had suspected the game was won the minute he saw that his offense could throw the ball. The next week, in an NFC Championship game far more famous than this one, his team will beat the Dallas Cowboys. Two weeks later, with the lowest payroll in the NFL, they will win the Super Bowl. People wanted proof that this offense worked: he'd taken a team that had been 2–14 two years before to a championship. Q.E.D. But it was here, after they beat the Giants, and dealt with Lawrence Taylor and all that he implied, that Walsh came to a pair of conclusions about his football team. The first was that he needed to find himself a player like Lawrence Taylor to terrorize opposing quarterbacks. The second was that he needed to use his first pick of the next amateur draft to find a left tackle because, as Bill Parcells observed, the only way to handle this monster coming off the edge without disrupting the rhythm of the new passing attack was to have a left tackle with the physical ability to deal with him. The old left tackle was coming to the end of his natural life. Dan Audick was crushed when he lost his job after winning a Super Bowl, but he understood: the left tackle was no longer going to be just another lineman. In some ways he wouldn't be a lineman at all but a highly skilled player who happened never to get his hands on the ball. Bill Walsh had made the quarterback a lot more valuable, and so the man who protected the quarterback was going to be a whole lot more valuable, too. Whoever he was, he was going to have to be special. The old idea was about to die.

But it lived for this one last day. On this final day there was no need to compensate for Lawrence Taylor. John Ayers acted as an impenetrable wall between Taylor and his quarterback right to the end of the game. "My husband loved Joe Montana," said Laurel Ayers. "He was not going to let Joe Montana get hit by Lawrence Taylor, or get hurt." It was Taylor who finally relented. "It was obvious," said the 49ers' line coach, Bob McKittrick, right after the game. "You could see how frustrated Taylor was getting out there as the game progressed. I don't want to put him down, but he was quitting out there." Ayers, on the other hand, was a profile in toughness and pass-blocking technique. He was, for that one moment, the critical component of Bill Walsh's passing attack, and hardly a soul in Candlestick Park noticed. He was a reminder that what sets football apart from other sports is that what you don't see is often the most important thing. What John Ayers was doing seemed routine. But to the few who knew, and watched, it was a thing of beauty.

The ball is snapped and John Ayers sees Taylor coming, and slides quickly back one step and to his left. And as he slides, he steps to meet his future. He's stepping into 1985, when the turf will be fast and he won't be able to deal with Lawrence Taylor. . . . Another quick step, back and left, and it's 1986, and he's injured and on the sidelines when the Giants send Joe Montana to the hospital and the 49ers home on the way to their own Super Bowl victory. . . . A third quick step and he crouches like one power forward denying another access to the hoop. But now it's 1987 and Coach Bill Walsh is advising John Ayers to retire. Ayers ignores the advice and then learns that Walsh won't invite him back to training camp. . . . He takes his final quick step back and left and times his blow, to stop dead in his tracks the most terrifying force ever launched at an NFL quarterback. "I don't think I've ever played against a football player who had more drive and intensity to get to the quarterback," John Ayers will say, after it's all over, and he's been given the game ball by his teammates. "It was almost like he was possessed." . . . But now it's 1995, and John Ayers has just died of cancer, at forty-two, and left behind a wife and two children. Joe Montana charters a plane to fly a dozen teammates to Amarillo, Texas, to serve as pallbearers. At the funeral of John Ayers the letter of tribute from Bill Walsh is read aloud.

—

CHAPTER SIX

INVENTING MICHAEL

By THE TIME the Briarcrest Christian School Saints opened their 2004 season, Michael Oher had spent four months growing accustomed to the idea that he was a football star. He'd been featured in the *Memphis Commercial Appeal*, attended summer camps for elite football prospects at LSU, Ole Miss, North Carolina State, and the University of Oklahoma, and turned down invitations to summer at another fifty or so Division I football programs. He'd received more than a thousand letters from college football programs, and many dozens of Federal Express packages—and so he had learned, among other things, that when the letter came by FedEx it contained the offer of a full scholarship. The only major football school that hadn't offered him a full scholarship was Penn State. He'd received, additionally, four months of frantic private tutoring from both his head coach Hugh Freeze and his offensive line coach Tim Long, who had been drafted in 1985 by the Minnesota Vikings to play left tackle. (Injuries cut short Long's NFL career. He played pre-season games with the Vikings, the San Francisco 49ers, and the Indianapolis Colts, and just three regular season games, in 1987, with the 49ers.) In practices before the first game, Sean Tuohy thought Michael looked like a different football player—which is to say he almost looked as if he knew what he was doing. "Tim doesn't take any credit for it," said Sean, "but something he said to him changed everything. He showed him how to use his hands."

The technique Long taught Michael was called "getting fit." A lineman the size and power of Michel Oher needed only to get his hands on his defender to ruin his day. He was so strong, and his hands so big, that there was no opponent—certainly not in high school, probably not even in college—who, once hooked, could wriggle free. It was of course illegal for an offensive lineman to grab a defender broadly, sumo-style; the lineman had to master the art of grabbing narrowly, of keeping his hands in close, and seizing his opponent near the breastplate of his shoulder pads. That's what Tim Long taught Michael Oher to do: get fit. "Fire to fit," became Hugh Freeze's mantra: fire off the line of scrimmage and get fit on the defender before he knows what's hit him.

The college football coaches of America had taken one look at Michael Oher and had seen a future NFL left tackle. Sean and Leigh Anne Tuohy had their doubts. Michael had wandered into their lives, moved into their home, and quickly become entirely dependent on them. He was meant to be a football player but, until everyone started telling him he was a star football player, he had shown hardly any interest in football. When he'd been thrown into games during his junior year, he had spent most of his time wandering around the field in search of someone to fall over. He'd looked completely lost, and passive. The left tackle might be the one guy on the field whose job was to reduce the level of violence. But even the left tackle, if he was to succeed, needed to play with aggression. And the few people who had paid attention on the few occasions when Michael played in football games hadn't seen even a hint of aggression.

Michael's first test was not an official game, but a pre-season scrimmage at home, against a team from Munford, twenty-five miles outside of Memphis. Leigh Anne took her usual seat in the stands, on the fifty-yard line, two rows from the top, right beneath the "N" in "SAINTS." She sat in a cluster of players' mothers, all of whom had definite views about the quality of Briarcrest's coaching and football strategy. They kept a cell phone handy just in case, as Leigh Anne put it, "we had any opinions or thoughts on the game that we felt Hugh or Sean needed to know." She was the coach in the skybox, and already she watched football games in a way few Americans did: focused on the offensive line. A play would end and she would have missed entirely what had happened to the ball. "I don't know about 'keeping his pad level down' and 'getting fit' and all these key little nichey phrases that the football coaches use to talk about what linemen do," she said. "All I can tell is if Michael's laying on top of somebody. And if he's spreadeagled on top of somebody, that's good."

Sean also took his place, a few yards down the sidelines from Hugh Freeze, where he could get a different view of the action than the head coach. Hugh, who fully grasped Sean's near-magical ability to boost the confidence of teen-aged boys, had taught him football just so that he might put him in charge of the Briarcrest quarterbacks. Sean still kept one eye on Michael, but tonight he missed the signs. From the first play of the game the Munford defensive end who lined up directly across from Michael targeted him for special ridicule. The Munford player was about six two and couldn't have weighed more than 220 pounds, and yet he wouldn't shut up. Every play, he had something nasty to say.

Hey fat ass, I'm a kill you!

Hey fat ass! Fat people can't play football! I'm a run your fat ass over!

It was the last game of Michael Oher's football career in which the opposing team wouldn't have the first clue who he was. He didn't yet have an impressive highlight reel of game film to precede him, and the folks up in Munford apparently didn't read either the Memphis newspapers or Tom Lemming's newsletter. Michael's body was indeed wide, but deceptively so. Leigh Anne had just remeasured him for a pair of slacks and found he had a 50-inch waist and a 32-inch inseam. He had some fat on him, but his width was mainly bone and muscle—he didn't need all 50 inches in the waist of his pants, but pants any smaller in the waist failed to accommodate his thighs. His teammates and coaches now understood that Michael Oher, even by national football standards, was a physical oddity. "He's the biggest player anyone's ever seen, and he may be the fastest player on our team in the ten-yard dash," said Terio Franklin, the Briarcrest linebacker and kick returner with whom Michael briefly lived. Too wide for anyone to imagine him solid and too big for anyone to imagine him fast, Michael Oher had, one last time, the element of surprise. "Force equals mass times acceleration," Coach Hugh Freeze liked to say. "And when Michael's mass hits you at Michael's speed, it's just an amazing and unexpected force."

The Munford scouting report hadn't picked up Michael's size and speed. The Munford defensive end who lined up across from Michael Oher obviously took one look at him and saw a high school football cliché: the fat kid they stuck on the offensive line because there was no place else to put him except the tuba section of the band.

Hey fat ass! I'm a put your fat ass in the dirt!

The more he went on, the angrier Michael became, and yet no one noticed, possibly because no one was prepared to imagine the rage inside Michael Oher. Hugh Freeze ordered up plays that called for Michael to block a linebacker, or to pull and sweep around the right end, and leave the defensive end across from him alone. The first quarter and a half of the scrimmage was uneventful—until Hugh Freeze called a different sort of play.

Leigh Anne could always tell when something angered Michael.

"I can tell by his body language," she said. "You piss Michael off and he looks more like a bull in his stance." Early in the scrimmage he had a bull-like demeanor, but he hadn't done anything out of anger. Leigh Anne rose from her seat to beat the crowd to the concessions stand, and so had her back to the action when the people in the stands around her began to laugh.

"Where's he taking him?" she heard someone say.

"He's not letting go of that kid!" shouted someone else.

She turned around in time to see twenty football players running down one side of the field, after the Briarcrest running back with the ball. On the other side of the field Briarcrest's No. 74 was racing at speed in the opposite direction, with a defensive end in his arms.

From his place on the sideline Sean watched in amazement. Hugh had called a running play, around the right end, away from Michael's side. Michael's job was simply to take the kid who had been jabbering at him and wall him off. Just keep him away from the ball carrier. Instead, he'd fired off the line of scrimmage and gotten fit. Once he had his hands inside the Munford player's shoulder pads, he lifted him off the ground. It was a perfectly legal block, with unusual consequences. He drove the Munford player straight down the field for 15 yards, then took a hard left, toward the Munford sidelines. "The Munford kid's feet were hitting the ground every four steps, like a cartoon character," said Sean. As the kid strained to get his feet back on the ground, Michael ran him the next 25 or so yards to the Munford bench. When he got there he didn't stop, but piled right through it, knocking over the bench, several more Munford players, and scattering the team. He didn't skip a beat. Encircling the football field was a cinder track. He blocked the kid across the 10-yard-wide track, and then across the grass on the other side of the cinder track.

That's where Sean lost sight of him. What appeared to be the entire Munford football team leaped on top of Michael, and the officials raced over to peel them off. All Sean could make out was a huge pile of bodies. "Then Michael gets up," says Sean. "And it's like watching Gulliver. Bodies flying everywhere. Flags flying everywhere. And then the referee comes over to scream at us."

All the officials knew Sean Tuohy, both as the former star point guard at Ole Miss and as the current radio color man for the Memphis Grizzlies. They read the Memphis sports pages, and so they also knew of Michael Oher, newly heralded as the hottest football recruit to come out of Memphis in some time who, for some strange reason, was now living with Sean Tuohy. Looking for a grown-up to complain to, an official sprinted back across the field. He made straight for Sean.

"Coach Tuohy!" he hollered.

Sean stepped out onto the field. "What's goin' on?"

"Coach Tuohy, he just can't do that."

"Did the whistle blow?" asked Sean, who could have made a good living as a tort lawyer.

The whistle had not blown. The Briarcrest running back had kept his feet for a conveniently long time.

"No," said the referee. "But he's got to let go of him when he gets him to the sidelines. He can't just keep on running with him."

"C'mon," said Sean. "The play wasn't over."

"Sean," said the ref. "He took that boy across the track."

"Okay," said Sean. "I'll talk to him."

Beyond the Munford bench, the cinder track, and the stretch of grass, was a chain-link fence.

"So what's the penalty?" someone else asked.

"Excessive blocking."

As the referee walked off the 15-yard penalty, Sean hollered at Michael to get his ass to the bench, and Michael trotted over, with an air of perfect detachment. He couldn't have seemed less interested in the ruckus. "Everyone's freaking out," said Sean, "the refs are screaming, their whole team is wanting to fight, and he's totally calm, like he's out for a Sunday stroll." Technically, it was Hugh's job to talk to Michael, as, since Michael's apotheosis, Hugh had taken a special interest in the offensive line. But in Hugh's view, Michael was merely doing what he'd taught him to do: block until the whistle blows. Upon reflection, thought Hugh, "You tell Michael, 'I want you to block until the whistle blows.' Well, he takes that real literal."

Sean and Tim Long took Michael off to one side. "You can't do that, Michael," said Long, struggling to keep a straight face. "These guys are after you, and now you've made a scene." Long had never heard of a lineman penalized for "excessive blocking," but then he'd never seen a block quite so dramatic as this one. For his first time as a volunteer football coach Tim was having difficulty swallowing his desire to giggle. ("I'd never seen that before—the lineman takes his man fifteen yards down the middle of the field, and then he decides to turn him left and take him all the way to his sidelines and through the bench.") Sean wasn't laughing; Sean had his stern face on. This incident fell into the ever-expanding category of Things Michael Oher Needed to Understand to Succeed. When Long was finished, Sean explained to Michael that he was now a famous football recruit, and bigger than anyone on just about any football field on earth. Even if he was an offensive lineman, he had to play as if everyone in the stadium was watching his every move. No matter how rude or dirty the opposing player might be, Michael had to swallow his desire for such obvious revenge. He could win, he could dominate, he could even humiliate. He just shouldn't attract the attention of the legal authorities.

Michael listened to Sean's little speech without responding except to grunt "okay." He was still eerily calm, as if this whole fuss didn't really concern him. Finishing his lecture, Sean looked over at the Munford bench: Michael had picked up a 220-pound defensive end and moved him at least 60 yards. In *seconds*.

"Michael," said Sean. "Where were you taking him, anyway?"

"I was gonna put him on the bus," said Michael.

Parked on the other side of the chain-link fence was, in fact, the Munford team bus.

"The *bus*?" asked Sean.

"I got tired of him talking," said Michael. "It was time for him to go home."

Sean thought he must be joking. He wasn't. Michael had thought it all through in advance; he'd been waiting nearly half a football game to do just exactly what he had very nearly done. To pick up this trash-talking defensive end and take him not *to* the chain-link fence but *through* the chain-link fence. To the bus. And then put him on the bus. Sean began to laugh.

"How far did you get?" asked Sean.

"I got him up against the fence," said Michael. Now Michael began to chuckle.

"What did that guy say while you were taking him to the bus?" asked Sean.

"Nothin'!" said Michael. "He was just hanging on for dear life."

As the laughter rose up in him, Sean thought: *there might be a fire in this belly after all.* He didn't worry much what might happen if that fire was misdirected, off the football field. He figured football could channel it, usefully.

THE QUESTION ASKED about Michael Oher by the Washington Redskins' quarterback still hadn't been answered to anyone's satisfaction: *Who was this kid?* Collins Tuohy, Michael's age and soon to be crowned Homecoming Queen of Michael's Briarcrest class, was now also functioning, in effect, as Michael's sister. And Collins thought Michael's identity was a work in progress. At school a year ago you couldn't get him to take his eyes off the floor. Now she'd catch him smiling and laughing and bantering with other kids in the halls and, in general, playing Big Man on Campus. He'd told the track coach he wanted to try the long jump, as the shot put and discus were too easy. He'd told the football coaches that he was tired of blocking the opposing team's extra points: he was going to try to catch one. The senior class was planning a skit. Three of the girls intended to perform a song-and-dance routine, and they were looking for a striking-looking male lead singer. They'd asked Michael to play the part and he'd shocked everyone by agreeing to do it. "After hearing, 'you're so good,' 'you're so good,' 'you're so good,'" said Collins, "he's started thinking, maybe I *am* good."

As Leigh Anne gradually took over the management of Michael's life, she noticed changes, too. He was a lot more talkative, and a bit more sure of himself, at least on the surface. His point of view began to intrude on the narrative. He now wanted things, and acknowledged that he wanted them, and the first thing he said he wanted was a driver's license. She handed him the driver's test prep books, and agreed to take him to the Memphis Department of Motor Vehicles, but immediately there was a problem: he couldn't prove who he was. To get a driver's license he needed two forms of identification. He didn't have so much as a YMCA membership card on him, and he swore that his mother, wherever she was, didn't have anything either. Leigh Anne thought that the hospital where he was born must have preserved some record of the event, but Michael didn't know where he'd been born. "We started with nothing," said Leigh Anne. "There wasn't a shred of evidence he even existed." She put the problem to Hugh Freeze, and Hugh told her that it was the easiest thing in the world to drive out to the Social Security Administration Office and get a Social Security card. He'd done it himself.

So that's how they began, with the two of them driving out to the Memphis suburbs, and asking a man behind a government computer for proof of Michael's existence. "To get a Social Security card," the man explained patiently, "you need to have a birth certificate." Leigh Anne tried to explain that they only needed the card so that they might obtain a driver's license, but the man remained firm: with so many terrorists on the loose he couldn't be handing out Social Security cards to people without other personal identification. Leigh Anne was born knowing how to play the damsel in distress; after she'd done it, the man agreed to help them, on the condition that Leigh Anne provide some evidence that Michael attended school in Memphis. Back they drove to Briarcrest, the only institution Leigh Anne could think of that recognized Michael's existence. Steve Simpson kindly printed Michael a school I.D. and wrote a letter identifying Michael Jerome Oher as a Briarcrest student. Then they went back to the Social Security office, where the man behind the desk looked at the dummied-up Briarcrest I.D. and got cold feet. He'd said any form of I.D. but he didn't mean *any* form of I.D. He meant something a bit more . . . official.

"Look at me," said Leigh Anne. "We have nothing. He's had seven addresses and he's gone to fifteen different schools. He doesn't know the names of his brothers and sisters. He's never committed a crime so we don't even have a criminal record. We . . . have . . . *nothing*." The man behind the desk either had a soft spot for a pretty woman in desperate circumstances or a hunch that he'd be much safer, long term, if he just gave this lady whatever she wanted. In any case, he began to punch the buttons on his computer. "You know why I'm going to do this," he said. "I'm going to do this because I want to know why a short white blond lady has got a big black kid in here trying to get him a driver's license." So Leigh Anne told him the story, and the man went looking in his computer for evidence of the existence of Michael Oher. She finished her story before he found the evidence. After a few minutes of searching, he looked up and said: "There's no such person as Michael Jerome Oher."

Michael just sat there in silence. Leigh Anne begged the man to keep looking: did he have anything even close? He tried spelling Oher in various ways; he tried spelling Michael in various ways.

Finally he said, "There's a Michael Jerome *Williams*."

"That's me," said Michael.

It is? thought Leigh Anne, but said nothing.

"You've been issued six Social Security cards in the last eighteen months," said the man from Social Security. He wasn't happy about it.

Leigh Anne had no idea what that was about—"someone was probably selling them on the Internet"—and neither did Michael. To the Social Security administrator she said, "I promise if you give us just one more, it'll be the last time we ask." Grudgingly, and a bit suspiciously, the man printed out a Social Security card. Only when they were outside did Leigh Anne stop to look at it: "Michael Jerome Williams Junior," it read.

"Who the hell is Michael Jerome Williams?" she asked.

"That's my dad," said Michael. He didn't find anything interesting about that fact, and so didn't elaborate.

She now had a Social Security card that said his name was Michael Jerome Williams and a student I.D. that said his name was Michael Jerome Oher. Leigh Anne explained to Michael: No matter how nice the people at the Memphis DMV are, they aren't going to accept these as two forms of legal identification for one boy. She told him that if he wanted a driver's license she was going to have to visit his mother, and see if she had a birth certificate. "She doesn't have any birth certificate," said Michael. "She doesn't have anything." Since Michael had moved in, Leigh Anne had pestered Michael to go and visit his mother. Occasionally, and grudgingly, Michael went, or said he did; but as he had never let any of the Tuohys near his old inner-city home, they couldn't be sure. The drawbridge might come down between white and black Memphis, but Michael insisted on crossing it alone. "Michael," Leigh Anne would say. "She is your mother. She will always be your mother. And you are never going to be able to look at me and say, 'You took me away from my mother.'" Now she said, "If you won't go, I will."

"No," he said. "I'll go."

He left and returned a few hours later. It was tattered and smeared, and he held it like a piece of trash, crumpled up in a tight ball in his hand, but he'd found a birth certificate. A boy named Michael Jerome Williams was indeed born in Memphis, on May 26, 1986.

"You told me your birthday was May 28," said Leigh Anne.

Michael looked at his birth certificate and frowned. "They must have got the date wrong," he said.

"They don't get the date wrong on birth certificates, Michael," said Leigh Anne.

"No, they got it wrong," he insisted.

She dropped the matter, and his birthday remained May 28. Armed with the Social Security card, the birth certificate, and the letter from Principal Simpson of the Briarcrest Christian School, they drove the next day to the Department of Motor Vehicles. This time they had Collins in tow. Collins had herself just turned seventeen and so was eligible to have the restrictions removed from her license. The DMV was for some reason miles east, outside the Memphis beltway, on a road lined with anemic maples, porn shops, and churches. They passed a porn shop and then a church and then another porn shop and another church; it was as if the people of Memphis had chosen this place to fight the war between animal nature and the instinct to subdue it. The DMV was a blue wooden shack in the woods, but there wasn't a trace of nature inside. It hummed with fluorescent lights and automated voices and the bells from the row of testing machines in the back. The walls were white cinder block, the floors speckled linoleum. At the front desk were four large black ladies. Leigh Anne handed all the documents over to one of them, who took one look at them and said in a slow drawl, "Uh-uh. This school letter is a *copy*. You got to have an *original*."

And so they left Collins to become a fully authorized grown-up driver, and raced the fifteen miles out to the Briarcrest Christian School, where Mr. Simpson met them in the parking lot, with the original of his letter embossed with the Briarcrest seal. They went back to the DMV, and the large black lady looked at the paperwork again. "Uh-uh," she said. "To apply for his license, he needs proof of residence, too." A phone or electric bill addressed to him, or someone whose name might plausibly be associated with his, that placed him more precisely in the world.

This was tricky. They had, right now, at home, boxes of letters addressed to Michael from college football coaches and boosters and just people who wanted to get to know the future star. They had a personal letter from Congressman Harold Ford Jr., who seemed to want to become Michael's friend, and a stack of letters from a football coach at the University of Alabama, who seemed prepared to offer his hand in marriage. Leigh Anne had long ago quit counting the letters: more than a thousand, fewer than ten thousand. The trouble was they were all addressed to "Michael Oher," who, legally, didn't exist. The only thing to do was to drive west across the city and find Michael's mother and, God willing, some piece of mail with an address and a more useful name on it. It was now 3:30 p.m. and the DMV didn't let anyone through the door after four-thirty.

"Let's just pick this up another day," said Leigh Anne.

"No," said Michael. "I want to get my driver's license *today.*"

She'd never seen him so definite and purposeful. For the first time, when Leigh Anne said that she would accompany him to his mother's house, Michael didn't protest. Leaving Collins to stall the DMV, she and Michael took off for inner-city Memphis, at 90 miles per hour. Along the way Michael said, "No one in my whole family has ever had a driver's license." That's why it was so important for him to get his driver's license. It would make him different from his family.

At length, they roared up in front of the same redbrick public housing project where Leigh Anne had dropped him off after their day of shopping for clothes. Michael had phoned his mother en route to let her know they were on the way, and to ask her to find an old bill or something. Now the woman herself opened the door: she was very large and very black. Six foot one at least, with big bones and, Leigh Anne thought, a pretty face. Denise was her name but everyone called her "Dee Dee."

"How y'all doin today?"

She was drunk, or high, and slurring her words. She wore a muu-muu and a garish wig that Leigh Anne assumed she had thrown on when they'd called to tell her they were on their way. She didn't invite them in and Leigh Anne sensed that she didn't want to, either. If she had, Leigh Anne would have found only a single trace of the childhood of Michael Oher: a sentimental photograph of a little boy hugging a big-eyed tabby cat that he had taped to the wall in the room where as a little boy he had, on occasion, slept. The sun was setting, and behind her the small apartment was dark. Michael just stood away from her, keeping his distance.

"You better come over here and hug your mama!" she shouted at Michael.

Michael just walked over and stood there. He offered no resistance when she threw her arms around him, but he didn't respond in kind or, for that matter, utter a word. She hadn't bothered to go looking for an envelope with an address on it, and they were in a mad rush, so they didn't have time to talk. At Leigh Anne's request, Dee Dee went and found the key to her mailbox. They walked down together to the row of surprisingly large metal boxes. Dee Dee found hers, but just before she opened it, she said, "Oh, there's no telling what's in here." Then she yanked open the box and down came the avalanche: water bills, light bills, gas bills, phone bills, eviction notices. It looked to be about three months' worth of stuff, and when it was done falling out, a moraine of future trouble rose from the pavement. Leigh Anne needed only a single bill; she was spoiled for choice. She reached down and grabbed the one on top, thanked Dee Dee for her trouble, and drove 90 miles per hour with Michael back to the DMV. On the way, neither she nor Michael said a thing about what they'd just seen.

By the time they arrived at the DMV the doors were shut, but Collins had persuaded the ladies to hold it open just a few minutes more. There wasn't a soul in the place; when Michael walked to the testing area, he had it all to himself. Leigh Anne was now sufficiently exasperated to remind Michael what she had been telling him for weeks: "You have one chance to pass this test. I gave Collins one chance, and I'll give you one chance. I'm not coming down here again." Michael vanished behind the partition where Leigh Anne couldn't see him. For a moment there was only the hum of the fluorescent lights. Then she heard Michael in conversation with the ladies. She couldn't make out what they were saying, but he was clearly chattering up a storm. Then he went silent.

Moments later, Leigh Anne heard the first ominous sound: *Bing!* That would be the bell on the testing terminal signaling that he'd made a mistake. He was allowed to miss four questions; five and he'd fail, and they'd have to return and do this all over again. Which, despite her threats, she knew she would have to do. She took a seat against the white cinder-block wall beside the large sign with red letters that said APPLICANTS ONLY BEYOND THIS POINT, and began to pray.

She was uncomfortable leaving Michael alone to solve a problem by himself. She already assumed that his problems were *her* problems, for if they weren't, no problem ever would be solved. He was already, in this sense, her son. Her own extended family hadn't liked the idea of them taking Michael in, at least initially. ("The only one who could never handle it was Daddy," Leigh Anne said. "I truly think God took Daddy because He knew he couldn't handle it.") But then the more they came to know Michael, the less they fought it. Her mother, Virginia, was already playing the role of dot-ing grandmother to Michael, and she and Michael clearly adored each other. Outside the family, the reaction was still mixed—"we knew people were going to have issues because we had a daughter exactly the same age," said Leigh Anne. She often found herself greeted in the shops and restaurants and schools of East Memphis with the same leading line: "How have you *handled* it?"

What the woman—it was nearly always a woman—who asked Leigh Anne the question meant was, *How have you handled having your gorgeous, nubile, seventeen-year-old daughter living under the same roof with a huge young black man the same age?*

Leigh Anne explained about fifty times that Michael's relationship to both Collins and Sean Junior was so much like that of a sibling that you'd never guess they hadn't grown up together. Michael and Sean Junior would shut the door to Michael's room for hours and compete: video games, miniature basketball, and whatever else they could find that leveled the playing field between a four-foot six-inch, 85-pound ten-year-old boy and a six-foot five-inch, 350-pound teenager. Michael and Collins would bicker and squabble just the way teen-aged brothers and sisters have since they were first created. As Leigh Anne's feelings for Michael developed, the questions people asked became offensive to her. She'd been taking care of his material needs for a good year and a half, and his emotional ones, to the extent he wanted them taken care of, for almost as long. "I love him as if I birthed him," she said. About the hundredth time someone asked her how she handled his sexual urges, Leigh Anne snapped. "You just need to mind your own business. You worry about your life and I'll worry about mine," she'd said. Word must have gotten around because after that no one asked.

Bing!

They now faced a problem far more difficult than mere social disapproval. At the end of Michael's junior year, Leigh Anne had ordered up his Briarcrest transcripts. No one at Briarcrest had said anything to her about his grades, and so she assumed they must be at least barely acceptable. They weren't. He had a cumulative GPA of 1.56 going into his senior year, and the NCAA required a 2.56. Out of a class of 161 students, he ranked 161st. The expensive private school was not much better than the worst sort of public one in filling the void: the empty space in the life of a child who had no one at home to take care of him. He was being described in the Memphis papers as the next great college football star, but to be the next great college football star you had to get to college, and there was little chance of that. Just to graduate from Briarcrest he needed eight more full credits—and there were only seven periods in the day! Most kids only took five classes, and had free periods for the other two. "The numbers don't add up," she said. "If he got an A in every class he still wouldn't qualify."

Bing!

When she saw Michael's grades, steam came out of her ears. She marched into Briarcrest and hollered at a bunch of people, starting with the principal. The Briarcrest Christian School was just shuffling him along without ever intending for him to graduate. "This going-on-faith thing isn't working," she said. "They just kind of hoped it would happen. That's bull. This isn't a faith thing; this is a tangible thing." She signed him up to take seven classes, plus before-school Bible Study—which counted toward graduation but not for the NCAA. She called every one of the teachers and told them that they were now to deal directly with her. He'd leave the house each morning at 6:00 a.m. and be in class straight through until 3:30 p.m. When she saw how many books he'd need, she realized he was going to need an industrial-strength backpack to carry them in. North Face, she thought, might do the trick ("It gets to the top of Everest," she thought) and so she went out and bought him a North Face backpack. Michael had taken one look at it and said, "I don't want to take that to school."

"Why not?" she'd asked.

"That's the one all the little rich kids carry," he'd said.

"Michael," she'd said. "You *are* a little rich kid."

And he'd taken the backpack to school.

Bing!

The first test of Michael's senior year was a quiz on the summer reading. Bunyan's *The Pilgrim's Progress* had been assigned. Michael was incapable of reading it himself. She and Sean had taken turns every night that summer reading it aloud to him. It took two months and nearly killed them both: Sean hadn't read a book cover to cover since—well, possibly ever. John Grisham had been at Ole Miss Law School when Sean was dazzling people on the Ole Miss basketball court. Grisham was a Sean Tuohy fan and sent Sean signed copies of his thrillers. They just piled up in Sean's clothes closet, unread. Now Sean was up half the night, every other night, reading *The Pilgrim's Progress* . . . *aloud.* They had gone over every passage of the book with Michael before the test. Leigh Anne thought he'd score a perfect 100. He got a 59. After that first day of school he brought the test score home with him, along with a long reading list, and an assignment to write a term paper. At that point Leigh Anne had turned to Sean, and Sean said, "Don't look at me. I majored in basketball."

She took over Michael's academic life. Every day, without fail, she went through his North Face backpack. He'd fail a quiz or get a D on a paper and never think it worth mentioning. He wouldn't throw away his papers and test grades but he wouldn't volunteer them, either. She'd find the paper balled up at the bottom of the backpack. That was their biggest problem at first: he wouldn't tell you when there was a problem. He had the most intense desire to please, without the ability to do the things that pleased. He had spent his whole life treating his mind as a problem to be covered up. He had grown so accustomed to not sharing a thing about himself, or perhaps never being asked about himself, that he didn't even know how to begin.

He now called her "Mama." (Except when he was pissed off at

her for making him do something he didn't want to do, in which case he called her "Ms. Tuohy.") When he felt vulnerable, he came to her. She was now, without a doubt, the person on earth in whom Michael was most likely to confide. And in the last thirty-six hours she had learned that she didn't know either his name or his birthday! Information about himself he viewed either as so totally without value, or so very precious, that it shouldn't be shared with others. In the Briarcrest locker room before and after his basketball games, he changed in a bathroom stall. He was the single most private person she had ever met. Every now and again when Michael suspected he might have revealed something about himself to her, or after Leigh Anne had made some observation about him, he'd smile and say, "You think you really know me, don't you?"

All of which raised a question: what was he hiding? The thought had crossed Leigh Anne's mind: *maybe he's gay*.

She didn't know a lot of gay people. White Evangelical Christian Memphis—which is to say most of East Memphis—wasn't really designed to make black people feel comfortable in it, but if you had a choice of being black in East Memphis, or being gay in East Memphis, you'd think at least twice about it. White Memphis life was organized around the churches, and the churches, at any rate most of them, viewed homosexuality as either a sin to be expiated or a disease to be treated. The vast and fast-growing Grace Evangelical Church that the Tuohys had been instrumental in creating was no softer on homosexuality than any other. Black people were perfectly welcome at Grace Evan—it's just that none but Michael Oher ever came. Gay people, unless they were looking to be cured, were not.

Bing!

When Leigh Anne heard the fifth and final mistake she stopped praying and started cursing. "Shit!" she said, and then she began to curse him: *Why couldn't he study? Why didn't he learn? What more could she possibly do?* Then she heard another sound—of the large black woman who'd stayed behind to administer the test.

"Congratulations, Michael!" said a cheery voice. "You've passed the test. You come on over here and have your picture made!"

A few minutes later Michael emerged with one of the ladies, climbed into Sean's BMW 745, and zipped off for a fifteen-minute test drive. When he returned, they handed him the first driver's license anyone in his family had ever owned. On the way out the door, one of the ladies shouted after him, "Don't you forget, I'm gonna have that NFL sideline pass off you!"

THERE WAS A new force in Michael Oher's life: a woman paying extremely close attention to him who had an eye for detail, a nose for trouble, the heart of a lion, and the will of a storm trooper. A mother. "When I moved in with Leigh Anne and Sean, I felt loved," said Michael, "like part of a family. In the other houses I didn't feel like part of the family. I didn't feel like they wanted me there." The feeling was good for Michael and it was also, oddly enough, good for the Briarcrest Christian School football team. The team came out for their first real game in early September 2004. The opponent was Melrose, a public school that would wind up in the state championship game in the division for Tennessee's biggest schools. The game was in the Liberty Bowl, and it was, from the point of view of the Michael Oher fan club, deflating. At the half, Melrose led 8–0 and went on to win 16–6. Afterwards, Hugh came up to the suite where Leigh Anne and a few of the other mothers and coaches' wives had watched the game. "So what'd you think?" he asked Leigh Anne, not actually expecting her to have a critical thought.

"I think you have the number one left tackle in America and you ran the ball right eighty percent of the time," said Leigh Anne, sharply. "I don't know a lot about football but that just doesn't make a lot of sense to me."

Hugh Freeze's authority on football matters was seldom questioned. Hugh had his own style, and it was, by high school and even some college standards, extremely complicated. He ran flea-flickers and fumblerooskis and double reverses and a seemingly endless variety of passing plays involving as many receivers as possible. He had one play where the quarterback hit the running back with a little screen in the middle of the field, the running back pitched it back to a wide receiver looping through the backfield, and the wide receiver chucked it 30 yards downfield to the quarterback. Of course every pro and college and even high school team has a trick play or three they can go to from time to time. The difference was that Hugh went to them routinely.

He had all these elaborate plays, in part, to compensate for what he saw as Briarcrest's systematic lack of brute force. From time to time he'd get a talented running back or quarterback, but he always found his team overmatched on the line of scrimmage. He couldn't power his way to victory, so he set out to trick his way to victory, and he had done it, often. He'd led the Briarcrest Christian School Saints to five of the previous six Tennessee State Championship games and, in the bargain, raised the money for a brand-new million-dollar football complex ten miles outside of town, a thirty-thousand-dollar boom on which to place his end zone cameras, and not one but two sets of uniforms (120 green helmets *and* 120 gold helmets). He had six paid assistant coaches and three volunteers: a former NFL offensive lineman, a former All-SEC defensive end, and a former All-SEC point guard. The only reason he didn't charter a jet to fly his team to their away games in Nashville is that Sean talked him out of it, on the grounds that it might upset some of the more academically inclined people at Briarcrest who wondered where the football program found all this money. Hugh had just turned thirty-five years old and Sean was willing to bet that by the time he was forty-five, he'd be the head football coach at a major college. Hugh would make that bet, too. "He's so absolutely cocky," said Sean, "that if you don't love him like a brother, you absolutely hate him."

Sean and Leigh Anne both loved Hugh like a brother; on the other hand, Leigh Anne had watched the game and thought: *Hugh doesn't know how to use his most precious football asset.* He had done all his fancy stuff and it hadn't worked. Only toward the end of that game did he pound the ball over Michael's side of the field where—lo and behold—huge holes opened up. After Leigh Anne said what she said, Hugh went silent, turned to Sean, and said, "Sean, I think it's time for me to leave." With that he walked out—and wouldn't answer his cell phone when Sean called him. They'd played that game on a Saturday and so the next morning, of course, everyone went to church. After church, Hugh met in his million-dollar football field house with his ten assistant coaches to review film of the game. The lights went down; the room was solemn. For the first hour or so, Hugh didn't say a word about the outrageous challenge to his authority. Then they came to a play where Michael missed a block. Hugh froze the film.

"Now look at that block Michael Oher just made," he said. "Call Leigh Anne Tuohy about *that* one."

"I can call her all you want, Hugh," said Sean. "But she's right."

Leigh Anne had just fired the first shot in a war that was waiting to happen. After the film, Hugh got up and showed the coaches the game plan for the following week: a chalkboard that was already a blizzard of new formations and new plays. Tim Long sat in the front row and could no longer contain himself. Long had played in the NFL, and yet he had the classic lineman personality: he laid low, said little, followed orders, and insisted on his own relative unimportance. He was six five, 300 pounds, and yet had spent the past two years feeling intimidated by five-foot ten-inch Hugh Freeze, who had maybe played in high school. "He's the sharpest football guy I've ever known, so I just got so I felt kinda inferior to him," said Long. The night before, depressed after the loss to Melrose, Long had flipped on the TV. The movie *Tin Cup* was on, and he sat and watched the whole thing until one in the morning. Why weren't they running the ball behind Michael Oher? He had never seen an offensive lineman who was such a force of nature that he might control an entire football game, if used properly. Now he had. In two years Long had never had the nerve to get up in front of the coaches and speak. Now he did.

"Coach Freeze, I got something to say," he said.

"All right," said Hugh.

Long rose. "I'm not a man of many words," he said. "But last night I watched *Tin Cup*. And I watched that boy par the entire back nine using nothing but a seven-iron."

He let that sink in.

"Well, that's nice, Tim," Sean said from the back of the room. "But what the hell are you talking about?"

"We can win football games running *one* play," Long replied.

"All right, Tim," said Hugh. "What play would that be?"

"Coach Freeze," said Tim. "I think we can run Gap."

The play was called Gap because each lineman was responsible for his own gap, defined as the space between his inside eye and the head of the defender inside of him (the eye and the defender closest to the center). The quarterback handed the ball to the running back. The running back ran at the right butt cheek of the left tackle, Michael's gap, and followed it as far as it would take him. Michael's job was simply to run straight down the field and destroy everything in front of him.

Michael had brought to Briarcrest an argument that ran right through football on every level—high school, college, the NFL. It was the argument Bill Walsh met when he first stressed the passing game as it had never before been stressed. It was the argument between the football fundamentalists and the football liberals. The fundamentalists reduce football to a game of brute force—and some of them do it so well that they appear to have found the secret to football success. The liberals minimize the importance of brute force and seek to overcome brute force with guile—and some of them do it so well that they, too, appear to have found the key to football success. That was Hugh: small, blond, looking nothing like a football coach but every ounce the crafty chess master, or the military strategist. Whatever his politics, Hugh was, by nature, a football liberal.

Sean Tuohy thought there was another reason, apart from his desire to win, why Hugh made everything so complicated: the pleasure of thinking up new things. "Hugh thinks football is supposed to be fun," said Sean. "We've got a quarterback who is average at best. No running back. No speed at receiver. And Hugh wants to run the triple reverse."

Hugh wanted to run a triple reverse because in his seven years as head coach of the Briarcrest Christian School Hugh had never had a player he could count on to physically overpower the bigger kids from the bigger schools. Now he had one of the most awesome forces ever to walk onto a Tennessee football field; and he didn't at first grasp the implications of that. He thought he could keep coaching the way he had always coached, and win a state championship. He was furious at Leigh Anne because, as he later put it, "she don't know what she's talking about, so she should keep her mouth shut. She was speaking out of ignorance. Fact being, the entire first half, whenever we went Michael's side, Michael was going the wrong way. He lost focus, or wasn't thinking." To which he added: "When you're on the sidelines you don't know what's happening. It took me until halftime to figure it out." Now he had this giant looking down at him telling him he should give the ball to the goddamn running back and let God's gift to head football coaches escort him to the end zone.

"All right," said Hugh.

But he didn't mean it. It took him a full two weeks to suppress his true nature and coach football in a way he'd never coached before. ("It had to be his idea," said Long.) Briarcrest won the next two games, but against weak opponents. The fourth game they faced another big public school, called Treadwell. Treadwell had just humiliated another white Christian school about the size and caliber of Briarcrest, the Harding Academy; and the Treadwell coach, and several Treadwell players, were quoted in the Memphis newspaper saying that they had taken care of one of the Christian schools and didn't think the other would be much of a problem. Hugh had a problem on his hands: Treadwell was better than Briarcrest, if he played the style of football he preferred to play. Every one of Treadwell's skill players would have started on the Briarcrest team. If they were going to win, he'd have to change; and all the coaches knew it. The day before that game, Tim Long came to practice with a 7-iron tucked in his belt.

On Friday night, the players donned their green helmets. There was a reason for this: the light uniforms made them look fast, the dark uniforms made them look big. In his dark green helmet and his dark green uniform, Michael Oher looked about nine feet tall and eight feet wide. Before the game, Hugh gathered together not just his players and coaches but also the offensive line coach from LSU, Stacey Searles, fresh off a national championship, who had come to see Michael play. Hugh loved to give pre-game speeches. "I feel that's the gift God gave me," he said. "I feel that is what I was really gifted at. I never would be emotional during the week. I'd save it all for right before the game." Now he began to speak.

"I don't *mind* that their coach said in the newspaper that they gonna beat us," he started out, then paused for effect. "What I *mind* is that they compared us to Harding." He let that sink in. (The fact that Harding Academy of Memphis was, from ten paces, indistinguishable from the Briarcrest Christian School of Memphis was what made the comparison so deeply, and unforgivably, insulting.) "So what we gonna do when we get the ball, on the first play, is we're gonna run Gap."

"The second play we're gonna run Gap," he said. Now his players were looking at each other. There wasn't a soul in that locker room who didn't know what he meant: the taboo weapon would finally be deployed. Michael Oher would be pointed at the opposition and fired. The Briarcrest Christian School was about to go nuclear.

"Then we're gonna run Gap again," said Hugh. He could feel the thrill in the air.

"The fourth play, we're gonna run Gap."

"The fifth play," he continued, then looked around the room. "What are we gonna run?"

"Gap!" they all screamed. They could be heard by the fans outside the field house, 50 yards away.

"And the sixth play?"

"GAP!!"

"And the seventh play?"

"GAP!!!!!"

Hugh then went quiet, and led them in the prayer that always concluded these pre-game locker-room talks. The players repeated after him:

"For we can . . ." *For we can . . .*

"Do all things . . ." *Do all things . . .*

"Through Jesus Christ . . ." *Through Jesus Christ . . .*

"Who strengthens us . . ." *Who strengthens us . . .*

"Each and every day . . ." *Each and every day . . .*

"And may God . . ." *And may God . . .*

"Bless the Saints!!!" they screamed together at the tops of their lungs. At which point the line coach from LSU could no longer contain himself, and shouted: "Somebody's got to find me a helmet! I got to play tonight."

With that, the team ran out onto the field. Seven plays into the game the score was 14–0 and they had done nothing but give the ball to their stumpy five three running back—"the Oompaloompah," Sean called him—and told him to follow Michael Oher's right butt cheek. The Treadwell defensive lineman across from

Michael weighed 365 pounds, but they were the wrong sort of pounds, and Michael blasted them away before moving on to destroy other targets. They ran that same play over and over again. By the time they were done, the Briarcrest offense would know that one play better than a football team ever knew a play. And because they knew it so well, they ran it with conviction and confidence; the entire team moved like a single well-thrown spear, knowing that the head of the spear was among the most terrifying sights on an American high school football field.

The LSU line coach, Stacey Searles, had never seen anything like it. Between plays, Michael was as impressive as during them. He skipped and fidgeted and jumped around like a 165-pound man. *He walked on the balls of his feet.* Running on and off the field he moved like a running back. There was nothing lumbering about him; it was as if when gravity was doling out its assignments, Michael wasn't paying attention. The LSU coach finally turned to Sean and asked, "How many three-hundred-forty-five-pound guys skip?"

By the end of the first half, Briarcrest had scored 40 points. When Sean looked down the sidelines, he saw Hugh shaking his head sadly. "This ain't any fun," he said. And, for Hugh, it wasn't. For the fans in the stands inclined to watch offensive line play, or the viewers of the game films, the sight of Michael Oher operating at full force, with a simple assignment and a definite purpose, was a unique experience. They saw things they had never before seen. They saw defenders, at the snap of the ball, turn and run in the opposite direction. They saw defensive ends assigned to rush the quarterback run to the sidelines to avoid having to make contact with this awesome force in charge of protecting the quarterback. They saw a single offensive lineman determine the outcome of a football game. Tim Long, the former NFL lineman long accustomed to the idea that offensive linemen were built to be ignored, experienced football nirvana. "What was so much fun," he said later, "was when he would take a guy and run him right off the field. He ran one guy right out of the back of the end zone. He just went completely out of the picture."

They beat Treadwell 59–20, with Michael sitting out the last quarter, and the chicken necks—which was what they'd dubbed the freshmen and sophomores—on the field. *God Bless!!!!* read the Briarcrest scoreboard. "That was the defining moment for us," said Hugh. "From that moment we decided that this is what we're going to do and teams are going to have to stop this. No matter what defenses they presented, no matter what blitzes. We were running Gap."

The next game they faced a bigger and tougher public school, Carver High, to whom they had lost badly the year before. Carver had a tough little 200-pound nose tackle who had lived in the Briarcrest backfield. He lined up between the guard and the center and raced through the gap before the Briarcrest lineman could get to him. He'd created total havoc; and this year he was back, bigger and better. Hugh wanted to discourage the kid before he caused trouble again.

Hugh now understood that Michael learned much more quickly from pictures than from words or charts. There was no point drawing up X's and O's on the chalkboard for him. Before the game he showed Michael tapes of the previous year's game, to illustrate the nature of the problem. On the first play of the game Michael moved down from left tackle to left guard, and positioned himself directly across from the kid—who wore No. 30. Hugh had called for a quarterback sneak. He'd told Michael, "I don't want you to block number thirty. I don't want him to go under you. I want him to go for a ride." At the snap of the ball the kid tried to do his usual trick, and jumped into the gap between the center and Michael, but Michael was too quick. He got up under No. 30 and for the next few seconds the nose tackle looked like a man riding a tsunami: arms flailing madly, legs kicking wildly. You could almost

hear him gasping for air. Ten yards downfield he was delivered, violently, back to the earth, where he vanished for several seconds
beneath Michael, until Michael, with the indolence of an heir to a
great fortune getting out of bed in the morning, lifted himself off
the flattened body. On the second play Michael lined up at guard
again and Hugh called another quarterback sneak. At the snap of
the ball No. 30 just threw himself flat on the ground. After that
Michael moved back to left tackle, and No. 30 did his best to
remain inconspicuous.

They beat Carver and then played Christian Brothers, a school
five times the size of Briarcrest and a perennial Tennessee football
powerhouse. Across the line from Michael were a defensive end
and a linebacker who were Division I college football prospects; the
linebacker, Chris Mosby, would later sign to play linebacker for
the University of Kentucky. Still they ran Gap, straight into the
strength of the defense. Nine plays into the game, Michael went
out after Mosby and pancaked him. Mosby left the game and never
returned. "The Christian Brothers' game finished my thought
process," said Hugh Freeze. "When I saw Michael doing what he
was doing to those guys, I thought, 'You know, we just might line
up behind him and win a state championship. And really not
have to do anything else.' Mosby was the best player we saw. And
he wanted no part of him. I've never seen a lineman have that
effect, and I tell you what, I coached against Chad Clifton and Will
Ofenheusle."*

The funny thing was how unappreciated Michael remained. He
was the driving factor in every game and the average fan would
have had to force himself to pay attention to him, because the average fan watched the ball. Oh, he might notice that small, slow-
running backs were waltzing over the left tackle for 15 yards each

---

* Clifton is now the left tackle for the Green Bay Packers, and Ofenheusle, a star left tackle
for the University of Tennessee, was drafted in 2003 by the New York Jets.

carry. He might notice, after the play, how many times Briarcrest's No. 74 was lifting himself off the ground to reveal a previously invisible opponent flat on the grass beneath him. But he wouldn't really understand. Even Michael's own teammates didn't understand his consequences until they watched game film. "In games you'd be too caught up," said Terio Franklin. "But you'd look at the tape and you'd see he'd be knocking down three, four people on every play."

It took even Hugh Freeze several games to understand that a single offensive lineman, all by himself, could change the ecosystem on the football field. In response to Michael, the other team simply abandoned any hope of getting to the quarterback. In response to Michael, the other team stacked their players in all sorts of strange ways to compensate—thus creating openings elsewhere. Only after the fact, on film, could one fully appreciate the effect of this kind of power. Even the officials were unprepared; Michael dominated the opposition so thoroughly that the officials assumed he must be cheating, and they hurled their yellow flags at that assumption. As Tim Long put it, "The referees would see him killing everyone and try to level the playing field." Midway through the season, Hugh began to take the officials aside before the game and say, "Let me tell you three things about my number seventy-four. My number seventy-four doesn't hold. My number seventy-four will block until the whistle blows. And my number seventy-four is the quickest player on either team. He's not offside; he's the first off the ball." He asked the officials to watch, rather than assume. And when they watched, they saw that Hugh was right.

It wasn't until near the end of the season that an opposing team came up with a strategy for dealing with this new force. Briarcrest's archrival was the Evangelical Christian School (ECS). The two schools met every year in what Sean had dubbed the "Jesus Bowl," and in the 2004 Jesus Bowl ECS sent players to simply tackle Michael Oher, so he couldn't escort a running back down the field.

They'd assign a player, or sometimes two, to the job, and the strategy worked; ECS won that game. Afterwards Hugh thought, *That's just got to be illegal, you can't just tackle an offensive lineman*. He called the Tennessee Secondary School Athletic Association and found a perplexed authority, who told him, "Well, we never really thought about it, 'cause why would a defensive player tackle an offensive lineman?" As they'd never heard of anyone doing it, they weren't going to do anything to prevent it. The tactic presented Hugh with about the only chance he had all season to outsmart the opposition. He told Michael, "If they come low, fall on them as heavily as you can, with your arms splayed wide, so they can't call you for holding. If they try to take you head-on, destroy them." Hugh then stacked the left side of the line with extra blockers; they would serve as the downfield escort for the running back, after he had scampered through the large hole where Michael, and the defenders who tackled him, had been.

They made it into the playoffs in early December and found themselves just three games away from the state championship. The first game was against Harding Academy. The Harding coach, Paul Simmons, had taken one look at Michael Oher and seen a player unlike any big man his teams had ever faced. There was simply no way they could win if they didn't do something a little strange. "Our whole goal was to keep Michael Oher from blocking more than one person," said Simmons. He told his six two, 230-pound defensive end to take Michael out below the knees; if he went for his knees, he should be able to bring him down all by himself. "For a defensive end to cut block an offensive lineman is unheard of," said Simmons. "But if Michael buried the defensive end and only the defensive end, that was a victory for us." Michael still opened a hole. ("Instead of having a freeway," said Simmons, "they just had a pretty good path.") And as the game went on, Micheal began to figure out how to use his hands to keep the defensive end away from his knees.

Briarcrest beat Harding, barely, and then faced a team from across the state, Notre Dame. Notre Dame had the ball first. Hugh sent Michael out on defense. He lined up at nose tackle; but the moment the Notre Dame offense broke huddle and came to the line, he backed up and became a middle linebacker, 350 pounds rocking back and forth preparing to charge. The Notre Dame quarterback called time-out and ran to the sidelines to ask his coach what to do about it; the coach didn't really know. The game was never close.

The state championship game was played six hours away in Nashville, in Vanderbilt Stadium. It was a rematch of the Jesus Bowl—the Briarcrest Christian School against the Evangelical Christian School—but it didn't take long to see that Jesus was keeping his distance. Before the first half was over, one of the ECS players had been penalized for calling the referee a motherfucker, and one of the Briarcrest players had been flagged for skipping around the field gleefully, hollering, "We're gonna beat their fucking ass! We're gonna beat their fucking ass!" The problem on both sides was a total lack of balance, caused by Michael Oher, which was odd in view of ECS's victory in their first meeting earlier in the season. But Hugh had succeeded in neutralizing the strategy of tackling Michael, and keeping him on the line of scrimmage. Michael still opened a big hole, but he was no longer available to escort the running back downfield, and so Hugh simply lined up a couple of extra blockers on Michael's side to deal with the downfield tacklers. ECS gave it up, and played him straight. As Briarcrest marched downfield to score the first touchdown, the ECS coach, Jim Heinz, grasped that he was up against an unstoppable force. "Whatever Michael Oher wanted to do," said Heinz, "he did."

At some point early in the game, Hugh Freeze decided he didn't fully enjoy the sight of his team simply rolling over the opposition to the state championship. The truth was, he'd grown weary of winning with brute force; when that force was Michael

Oher, it was too easy. In the middle of the second quarter, Briar-crest had the ball first and goal on the ECS ten-yard line. They were leading, 10–0, and if they punched this one into the end zone, the game would be as good as over. Hugh saw Sean walking up the sidelines, no doubt to tell him to just keep running Gap over Michael's right butt cheek until they scored. Hugh sent in the play before he could get there.

"What'd you call?" asked Sean.

"Coach Tuohy, you just don't want to know," said Hugh.

"Hugh, we can just run off tackle three times and score," Sean begged.

"Coach Tuohy, that's not near as much fun," said Hugh. He'd been holding back for two and a half months now and he couldn't hold back any longer. "It was my one season in my coaching career where I didn't feel like myself," Hugh said. When his gut told him that no one in Vanderbilt Stadium expected him to run a trick play—well, that's when you ran a trick play. And his gut now told him that there wasn't a soul in Vanderbilt Stadium who expected him to do anything but run right behind Michael Oher.

When they broke the huddle, the short little fullback hid behind the right guard—when Hugh taught his fullbacks how to run the fumblerooski, he told them, "You should be sniffing the right guard's butt." When they got to the line the fullback squatted down, nose to the guard's rear end, and remained hidden from the defense. Apart from the center, who was on the ball, the Briarcrest offensive linemen never even bothered to drop down into their stances. They stood tall, as if unready for the snap but in fact obscuring the defense's view of their backfield. The center snapped the ball to the quarterback, who walked a step to his right, handed the ball between the legs of the squatting fullback (who buried it in his stomach), and then sprinted out as if running an option play. (This handoff was a wrinkle Hugh had added; in a true fum-blerooski, the quarterback puts the ball on the ground, creating a "fumble" that the guard picks up and runs with.) The right guard, right tackle, and halfback all sprinted right with the quarterback. Believing that the quarterback still had the ball, the defense— already slow to react because the play was so bizarre—chased after him. The fullback waited until the coast cleared and then stood up and raced in the opposite direction, around the left end, where his left guard and left tackle waited to escort him downfield.

Everyone did what he was supposed to do, except for Michael Oher. For some reason known only to himself, Michael just stood there from the start of the play until the end. The Briarcrest fullback got as far as the one-yard line before he was pushed out of bounds, by the man Michael should have blocked. On the next play they scored, but Sean was waiting for Michael when he trotted off the field.

"Michael, all you had to do was give that guy a little push and we'd have scored," he said. "What were you thinking?"

"Man, I know," said Michael. "But it was such a great play. I just wanted to watch."

Hugh Freeze had Michael playing the entire game not only left tackle on offense but also at nose tackle on defense. This ensured, among other things, that ECS players spent even more time than usual beneath him. Trailing 17–0, ECS ran a sweep. The ECS fullback led the ECS halfback around the end, and looked for someone to block. The fullback was a five eight, 165-pound gamer named Clarke Norton. Clarke, as it happened, was the son of friends of Sean and Leigh Anne Tuohy, and spent a lot of time inside the Tuohys' home. Clarke's job was to pick up the first defender he saw as he came around the right end. Expecting to encounter an ordinary-sized human, he ran straight into No. 74. "Everything went black for a moment," said Clarke. "Then he goes to throw me on the ground and I think, 'Oh my God, he's gonna kill me.'" But then Michael peered through the face mask and saw the boy he'd dined beside not two weeks before. Their eyes met.

"Oh. Hey, Clarky," said Michael, and carefully picked Clarke up and moved him out of harm's way, before running down the ball carrier. "I was like, 'Thank God for the Tuohy family,' " Clarke later said, "because I was about to die."

The season had begun with an act of vengeance; it ended with that act of mercy. A few of the ECS players, frustrated and ungrateful, in effect quit playing the game and turned their energies directly on the player most responsible for their unhappiness. As Briarcrest ran out the clock, the ECS defenders lunged at Michael's knees and tried to take him out. It was dangerous, unsportsmanlike, and probably also un-Christian; and after a few plays of this Michael walked over to an official and asked him to make them stop. The official had no sympathy. "Son," he said. "You been whipping everybody out here all night long. Why don't you just go back to the huddle and let this game be over with." A few minutes later, the Briarcrest Christian School Saints were state champions. Michael Oher was, by general consensus, the best football player in the state of Tennessee. The easy part was over.

CHAPTER SEVEN

THE PASTA COACH

A SURPRISINGLY LONG TIME before the Briarcrest Christian School Saints bulldozed their way to a Tennessee State Championship, Leigh Anne mailed the Tuohy family Christmas card. At the end of December 2004, she and Sean would become Michael's legal guardians, but even without the imprimatur of law Michael felt so much a part of the family that she couldn't imagine him out of the Christmas picture. Leigh Anne did everything two months before it needed to be done, and her Christmas card was no exception. She snapped the portrait of her three perfect children in October, and sent it out to several hundred friends and distant relatives, without it ever occurring to her that most of the recipients would have no idea about the strange new addition to the family. A few weeks later, the phone rang late one night. It was a North Carolina cousin.

"All right," he blurted into the phone. "I've just had my fifth beer. Who *the hell* is this black kid in y'all's Christmas card?"

She sprang the relationship on the college football coaches of America in the same take-it-or-leave-it spirit, without comment or explanation. She virtually dared them to ask who she thought she was to harbor the nation's most highly prized lineman. They'd fly into Memphis from all over the country thinking they were coming to sell another poor black kid with raw talent, few strings attached, and the usual vulnerabilities. What they found waiting for them, in effect, was an extremely well connected rich kid who was nearly impossible to impress—and guarded by a warrior princess.

Michael Oher didn't want money or shoes or clothes or cars. Sean and Leigh Anne bought him pretty much whatever he asked for, and his share in the Tuohy estate came to millions. He didn't want to see the NBA games at the FedEx Forum; Sean, who announced the games, had a season pass, courtside. He didn't want free plane tickets, or a fifty-yard line seat for the national championship college football game between USC and Oklahoma. A private jet would fly him to the Orange Bowl or anywhere else for that matter, and Fred Smith's corporate suite would host him once inside. Smith, the founder and CEO of Federal Express, as well as the Orange Bowl's sponsor, was a good friend of the Tuohys. Collins Tuohy was dating his son.

As half the college football coaches in America gathered on his front lawn, Sean assumed the same pose that he had adopted at the end of basketball games when he had the ball in his hands with six seconds to go and his team was down by a point. He feigned indifference. To avoid the appearance of interest, he required all college coaches to approach Michael not through him but through Hugh Freeze. This provided him with an alibi without actually fooling anyone. Everywhere they looked, the college football coaches of America saw evidence of Sean Tuohy's devotion to his alma mater, the University of Mississippi. He and Leigh Anne were building a second home in Oxford, just off campus, on the assumption that Collins would follow her mother's footsteps and become an Ole Miss cheerleader and leading member of the ancient Kappa Delta sorority. When the coaches walked into the living room of the Tuohys' lovely Memphis home, the first thing they saw was the Rebel Christmas tree: red and blue branches festooned with nothing but Ole Miss ornaments. On their way out they passed, in the front yard, a little stone statue of what at first appeared a gnome but, upon closer inspection, proved to be the Ole Miss mascot, "Colonel Rebel." A statue of Santa Claus joined him at Christmas, a giant Easter Bunny came out for Easter, but Colonel Rebel was the statue for all seasons. Sean himself was so well known as an Ole Miss alumnus that a Memphis radio station, on the eve of the University of Memphis–Ole Miss football game, stole his Rebel gnome, hid it, and offered a prize to whichever listener found it first. Leigh Anne and Sean had both been the first members of their families to go to Ole Miss, but their lives were as intertwined with the place as if they'd founded it.

Hugh Freeze, for his part, quickly complicated the wooing of Michael Oher by entering into talks to join the coaching staff at the University of Tennessee. Hugh didn't even pretend not to care where Michael played college football; he let Michael know early and often his opinion that the University of Tennessee was the place for him. Further expanding the web of intrigue surrounding Michael was Justin Sparks, the Briarcrest placekicker. Justin's parents, Robert and Linda Sparks, had family ties to Oklahoma State and Mississippi State, and a lot more money than the Tuohys. The Sparkses' Hawker-800 dwarfed Sean's small plane—which Leigh Anne had dubbed *Air Taco*. The Hawker-800 flew Michael to all Sparks-affiliated schools. And because Justin Sparks could kick a football so well, the number of Sparks-affiliated schools quickly expanded. Justin flew to LSU's summer football camp, and Michael flew with him. North Carolina State was the first to offer Justin a football scholarship and, with direct private jet service established between Memphis and Raleigh, North Carolina State became, to Michael Oher, an appealing place to play football.

But the web around Michael was tightly strung. Inside it, every move triggered a countermove. Nanoseconds after North Carolina State made its offer to Justin, Leigh Anne called the Ole Miss football coach, David Cutcliffe, and told him that if he wanted Michael Oher, he had better offer a scholarship to Justin, too. Cutcliffe quickly did.

During the five months between the start of his senior year and the day—February 1, 2005—when prized college football recruits announced their decisions, Michael Oher was surrounded by people intensely interested in that decision. In what came to be, perhaps inadvertently, a kind of Ole Miss pincer movement, Leigh Anne had brought in Sue Mitchell to tutor Michael every night. Miss Sue, as she was known, had spent her career as a teacher in the Memphis public schools. Now in her mid-fifties, and retired, Miss Sue's only remaining school tie was with Ole Miss, from which she had graduated. Every night for five hours, six nights a week, Miss Sue and Michael worked together. They grew very close. And the closer they grew, the more Miss Sue felt she had to let Michael know what a mistake he'd be making if he didn't go to Ole Miss. On the night before he was making his official visit to Tennessee, for instance, Miss Sue told him that he had to be very careful in Knoxville, Tennessee, as she'd just learned from a good friend acquainted with the mystery novelist Patricia Cornwell that Knoxville, Tennessee, was used by the FBI to study the effects of the soil on decomposing human body parts.

"They bury a hand and let it sit for six weeks, then dig it up and see what it looks like," she explained. "These body parts are just below the surface of Knoxville, but the main thing is where they store them, when they aren't burying them. Right underneath the football field!" When the coaches took him out on the field before the game, she said, Michael should pay less attention to the 107,000 people dressed in orange and cheering him at the top of their lungs than to the hands and feet of dead people set to poke up through the turf. She ended her speech with a cheery, "But it's your decision where you play football. Don't let me 'influence' you!"

Michael, for his part, did an excellent imitation of a ditzy debutante unable to decide which of the fifteen eager young men in her parlor she wanted to escort her to the ball. He of course told Leigh Anne and Sean that he really liked Ole Miss—but only after Leigh Anne and Sean explained to him that, if he had any intention of going to Ole Miss, they really ought to go through the process of formally adopting him, so that the many gifts they had already bestowed on him might be construed not as boosters' graft but parental love. Then he flew off to a Fellowship of Christian Athletes camp at the University of Oklahoma.

A few weeks later, a Memphis news station rolled into a Briarcrest football practice to ask Michael where he might like to go to college. "I really can see myself going to Oklahoma," Michael said, provoking a frenzy on the Oklahoma football fan Web sites, and instigating a number of calls from Oklahoma coaches. He made further, unofficial visits to Mississippi State, Oklahoma State, North Carolina State, Tennessee, LSU, and Ole Miss. After he'd told the Memphis television audience that Oklahoma was now "at the top of my list," he told Hugh Freeze that it was his "lifetime dream" to go to Tennessee. After he'd shared with his coach his love of Tennessee, he told Robert Sparks how much he also liked Oklahoma State and Mississippi State. And after North Carolina State became the first school to offer Justin Sparks a football scholarship, Michael told the N.C. State coaches how much he liked the idea of playing football for them, too.

The head coaches weren't allowed to visit Michael in Memphis until the end of the Briarcrest football season, but they were allowed to call him whenever they wanted to—which turned out to be whenever Michael would pick up the phone. He had a lifetime of homework to finish, he had football to play, and no hours in the day to waste chitchatting with the head football coach from schools in states he couldn't find on a map.

Sean Tuohy and Hugh Freeze agreed that on Wednesday night each week Michael should go to Hugh's house and receive phone calls. The coaches soon learned that Wednesday night was the night to find Michael Oher, and Hugh soon learned that any coach who happened to get Michael on the phone wound up thinking that Michael might like to play for him. For instance, the recruiter from Alabama, Sparky Woods, called, and Michael, who had not shown the faintest interest in Alabama, jumped on the phone with him and said how much he liked the idea of paying Alabama an official visit. As Michael was allowed to make only five official visits, he was telling the Alabama coach that he was on his short list of five. "If the coaches *ever* got Michael on the phone," Hugh said, "he was going to lead 'em on. Every one of those coaches came away thinking Michael Oher wanted to play for him."

But Michael didn't want to play for them; he merely wanted to fly to see them. Flying on private planes, Michael developed the opinion that pretty much anyplace in America he wanted to go was a delightful day trip from Memphis. One Friday afternoon, Sean came home to find Michael walking out of the house, with the air of a man going for a stroll down the block.

"Where you going?" Sean asked.

"N.C. State," said Michael. He had accepted the school's invitation to make an "official visit." Michael was allowed to make as many unofficial visits to N.C. State as he wanted and to those he could fly in Mr. Sparks's jet. But North Carolina State picked up the tab for the official visit, and they flew their recruits commercial. Sean knew this, and wondered why Michael was leaving the house empty-handed. The boy didn't have so much as a toothbrush on him.

"Where your bags?" asked Sean.

"Not taking any," said Michael. "I'm coming back today."

Sean explained that when you took an official visit, you flew commercial, and when you flew commercial, the miles between the Tuohy home and the North Carolina State football stadium took a lot longer to travel. Michael might need to change planes, and he'd certainly need to accommodate the airlines' schedules. A boy leaving Memphis on Saturday morning for a football game that afternoon in Raleigh, North Carolina, had no choice but to spend the night somewhere other than Memphis.

When Sean had finished, Michael turned around, marched back into the house, and said, "Then I'm not going."

Sean couldn't let that happen. Not turning up for an official visit to N.C. State would give the impression the fix was in for Ole Miss. He hollered at Michael to pack his bag and get his ass to the airport, and Michael did.

The wooing of Michael Oher was pure southern ritual: everyone knew, or thought they knew, everyone else's darker motives, and what didn't get said was far more important than what did. The men seized formal control of the process. The women, acting behind the scenes, assumed they were actually in charge. Of all the people around there was really only one who spoke his mind directly, and advertised his own naked self-interest: eleven-year-old Sean Junior. The first coach through the Tuohy home, Ole Miss assistant coach Kurt Roper, noticed right away that his prized recruit had a special feeling for this little kid. When Roper arrived, he asked Michael to show him around, and they wound up in his room, with Roper reduced to onlooker while Michael and Sean Junior engaged in some endless contest involving miniature basketballs. "You could tell just watching them shoot around," said Roper. "Those two were like brothers." And just in case he didn't pick up on this little kid's importance, Michael muttered something about how Roper "really ought to talk to SJ, because he's gonna have a say in where I go."

When Roper took Michael back downstairs for the sales pitch, Sean Junior followed. At the end of the pitch, to which Michael listened wordlessly, Sean Junior stood up. He didn't raise his hand but he might as well have. "Can I ask my question?" he asked. His voice cracked. He now had this squeaky drawl, to go with his big slow smile and straight black hair falling down over his eyes. He was the sort of little kid grown women took one look at and said, "Oh, isn't he just the *sweetest* thing you ever saw!"

"Uh, sure."

With that, Sean Junior took off on a surprisingly insistent rap. He explained how important it was for him to be near Michael, and how concerned he was that once Michael committed himself to some big-time college football program, he'd become totally inaccessible. Then came the question: if Michael Oher agreed to play football for Ole Miss, what level of access would be granted to his little brother?

"How about we get you an all-access pass?" said the Ole Miss recruiter.

"That'd be good."

LEIGH ANNE'S FIRST impression of the college coaches of America was that none of them had the first idea what he was getting into. Michael Oher was so far from being qualified to go to college that there was hardly any point to the discussion. Added to that was the obvious question: even if he somehow qualified to attend college, without the elaborate support system she had created for him, how would he cope once he got there? She wasn't worried about the spirit but the letter of higher education. School she viewed mostly as something you did well in so you could (a) play sports and (b) get out of it and make something of yourself in the wider world. In the wider world Michael was lost, and would remain lost no matter how much Shakespeare they made him read.

Michael wasn't stupid. He was ignorant, but a lot of people mistook ignorance for stupidity, and knowingness for intelligence. He'd been denied the life experience that led to knowingness, which every other kid at Briarcrest took for granted. Leigh Anne was now making it her personal responsibility to introduce him to the most basic facts of life, the sort of things any normal person would have learned by osmosis. "Every day I try to make sure he knows something he doesn't know," she said. "If you ask him, 'Where should I shop for a girl to impress her?' he'll tell you, 'Tiffany's.' I'll go through the whole golf game. He can tell you what six under is, and what's a birdie and what's par. I want him to know the difference between Monet and Matisse."

Restaurant dining was a subject unto itself. "You don't know how complicated it all is until you go with someone who has no idea," she said. When she took him to an Italian restaurant, she didn't order for two. She ordered up the entire menu, "just to show him what they were." Michael thus learned to distinguish pesto from alfredo, and puttanesca from marinara.

The trouble was that there really was no end to the quotidian details of upper-class American life bafflingly new to Michael Oher. Every time he turned around, he bumped into a thing with which he should have been completely familiar and wasn't. One day they were leaving the house to go to a track meet. It would be a three-hour flight on *Air Taco* and Michael needed to bring his North Face backpack so he could study on the road. They were still in the driveway when Leigh Anne noticed he didn't have it with him.

"Michael," she said, "go and get your backpack."

"I don't know where it is," he said.

"It's in the foyer," she said. "Just go in and get it."

He left the car reluctantly and returned to the house. She waited several long minutes, then followed him inside to see what on earth had gone wrong. Coming through the front door she found the backpack where it had been, in the foyer. There was no sign of Michael, and she walked through the house until she came upon him near the back door, loitering uneasily. He looked up at her and asked, "What's a foyer?" It took a minute to explain, as her explanations amounted to little lectures on the general subject. ("It's an entry hall some places. A foy-er some places. A foy-yay other places, depending on where you are in the South.") When she was done, Michael just shook his head.

"But let me tell you something," Leigh Anne said. "He absorbed it. He absorbed *everything*." More and more, as Michael put it, "I feel smarter. 'Cause I know what things are."

Leigh Anne Tuohy was trying to do for one boy what economists had been trying to do, with little success, for less developed countries for the last fifty years. Kick him out of one growth path and onto another. Jump-start him. She had already satisfied his most basic needs: food, clothing, shelter, transportation, and health care. He had pouted for three days after she had taken him to get the vaccines he should have had as a child. It was amazing he hadn't already died some nineteenth-century death from, say, the mumps. (When she tried to get him a flu shot the second year in a row, he said, "You white people are obsessed with that flu shot. You don't need one every year.") Now she was moving on to what she interpreted as his cultural deficiencies. She had watched her own penniless husband turn his athletic triumphs into business success and, indeed, a happy life. But there was nothing inevitable about the process; you needed to know how to translate one narrow kind of success into another, much broader kind. To Sean, the skill came naturally. It would never come naturally to Michael, but it might come unnaturally, if she worked on him. She would make him completely at home in white Christian entrepreneurial Memphis, but in the way that a blind man became comfortable in a well-furnished room. He'd memorize the contents of the room so perfectly that his blindness became irrelevant.

To others it might seem silly, or beside the point, for Michael to know how to read a wine list, or score a golf game, or distinguish between Gucci and Chanel, but to Leigh Anne it didn't seem silly at all. He had to know all sorts of ridiculous little things if he was ever going to feel at ease in their world. The rich world. It was one thing when she first met Michael and took him out to buy clothes—she could see why she shouldn't impose her tastes on a stranger. It was another matter entirely now that Michael was, in effect, her child. "I'm trying to make him more preppy," she said. "He just looks so nice in a Ralph Lauren sports jacket."

He went through phases where he wore headbands and throwback jerseys and pants that drooped down the back of his ass, and Sean had tried to explain to her that "yes, it's a thug look, but it's an *organized* thug look, a *high-priced* thug look." She didn't buy it; she fought back; and she took it as one of many small victories in the great war when Michael's friend Terio Franklin from Briarcrest called her one day and said, "Mizz Tuohy, I need some of those shirts with alligators on them—can you get me some?"

In every city in America, rich white kids worked overtime to look and sound like black kids from the ghetto. In Leigh Anne's new world, black kids were crossing the line from the other direction.

She wasn't shy, either, about impressing upon Michael the important distinctions within the white world, and a sense of his new social class. One morning she and Collins and Michael set out on a little trip to Alabama. On their way they stopped at a McDonald's. As they waited for their food, a scruffy-looking man came through in a pickup truck with a gun rack and some dead animal in the bed of his truck. "Lord, he's such a redneck," said Collins. Ten minutes down the road, Michael asked, "What's a redneck?" Collins tried to explain but couldn't quite get it across until she said, "Thomas Trubride is a redneck."*

Trubride was a Briarcrest classmate of theirs. "Thomas Trubride is a good guy," Michael said.

"A redneck is just someone who drives a pickup truck with guns in it," said Leigh Anne.

"That doesn't sound too bad to me," said Michael.

"It's not bad," said Leigh Anne. "It's just not who we are."

Increasingly, it wasn't. In many ways Michael was coming to resemble a naturalized citizen of East Memphis. Every Sunday he attended Grace Evangelical Church, and he was always the first one dressed to go in the morning. His grades had improved, dramatically, thanks to Miss Sue. At the end of the first semester he'd come home from the Briarcrest Christian School with four A's, two B's, and a C. The school's report cards included the students' cumulative class ranking. Up until then Michael had always finished dead last. On the strength of the first semester of his senior year, in a class of 163 students, he placed 162nd. "He's started making his move!" shouted Sean, gleefully. "He's picking them off one at a time, like Sergeant York."

But it wasn't just his grades. He had a family that loved him, and would take care of him, and *he was coming to take their love for granted*. Leigh Anne got these little hints of Michael's security in the relationship. For instance, one afternoon she received a phone call from the store manager of one of Sean's Taco Bells on the other side of Memphis. "Mizz Tuohy," the man drawled, "there is a big ol' black kid here who says we need to serve him for free 'cause he's your son." She had treated Michael as she treated their other two children, which is to say she lavished upon him most of the material

* Not his real name.

comforts and spiritual guidance known to mankind. "A year ago he didn't have a bed to sleep in and wouldn't look you in the eye," said Sean. "Now he's got a car, money in his pocket, and everyone knows who he is." No wonder he got better at football his senior year, thought Leigh Anne. He was charging off the ball with confidence because he was arriving at the football field with confidence.

A year and a half into the reeducation of Michael Oher she felt, for the first time, almost relaxed. One night she realized that for the first time since she began to feel responsible for Michael, she was worried about nothing. "It was nine at night and Sean was traveling with the Grizzlies," she said. "I was sitting alone in bed with the remote in my lap. I could hear Miss Sue working away with Michael at the kitchen table. And I thought: I am so happy. I don't have to worry. I don't have to do *anything.*"

Not long after that, she went out for her afternoon walk. The sky couldn't decide whether to rain or snow; it was a winter day not so very different from the one on which she had first met Michael. She was motoring along at a fantastic clip when her cell phone rang: "Mom, you have to come home," Collins shouted into the phone. "There's been an accident."

All Collins knew was that Michael had been driving Sean Junior out to Briarcrest to play basketball when Michael's truck collided with another car. Collins and Leigh Anne drove out together, but the accident had created a traffic jam, and they couldn't get within a half-mile of it. When Leigh Anne saw they couldn't drive any closer, she left Collins with the car and took off at a sprint. The first thing she saw was Michael's truck, totaled. Then Michael, sitting on the side of the road, crying.

When she got to him, he was sobbing so violently that she could barely understand what he was saying. She grabbed his cheeks in her hands and said, "Michael, listen to me, this could happen to anybody." Then she understood what he was saying: "SJ needs you.

Go over to SJ." Then she saw Sean Junior stretched out on the ground on the other side of the mangled truck. She ran to him in a panic. His face was an unrecognizable mass of swollen, oozing flesh. She wasn't entirely sure it was him until he spoke. "Mom," he said, "will the blood come out of my shirt?"

She laughed; how badly hurt could he be if he was worried about his shirt? She sent Michael home and climbed in the ambulance with SJ. And Michael kept right on sobbing. "I just wished it was me going to the hospital instead of SJ," he said later.

At the hospital, the doctors said they were amazed that Sean Junior hadn't been more seriously injured. His face was bruised, and incredibly swollen—"I never knew a human face could do that," said Leigh Anne. "I never knew lips could swell like that." But his bones were perfectly intact. Michael's truck had skidded on the ice across the divide at 25 miles per hour and crashed head-on into the big van, also traveling at 25 miles per hour. The driver of the van was fine, and so was Michael, but no four and a half foot tall boy should have been sitting in the front seat: the airbag had exploded directly into Sean Junior's face. The doctors saw this kind of thing fairly often, and in every other case the airbag busted the little kid's nose or cheekbones, and usually took out a bunch of teeth in the bargain.

Leigh Anne listened to the doctors discuss how bizarrely lucky Sean Junior had been in his collision with the airbag. Then she went back home and relayed the conversation to Michael, who held out his arm. An ugly burn mark ran right down the fearsome length of it. "I stopped it," he said.

In Michael Oher's file at the Briarcrest Christian School were the results of a test he had been given, by the Memphis City School system, at some point during the eighth grade. The test was designed to measure his aptitude for a variety of careers. It showed that he had an aptitude for almost nothing. He scored in the 3rd percentile in spatial relations. In a category called "the ability to learn," he had scored in the 5th percentile. But there was one quality he possessed in an extreme form, and in whatever test the public school system had used to measure it, Michael Oher had scored in the 90th percentile. The quality was labeled "Protective Instincts."

AROUND THE TIME of the accident, the head coaches of the schools on Michael's short list came for their formal visits, or tried to. Urban Meyer was named the new head coach at the University of Florida and called Hugh Freeze every single day for the next two weeks, hoping to be invited into the Tuohy home. Leigh Anne picked up the home phone once a week to find Mark Richt, the head football coach from the University of Georgia. One week Richt finally said to her, "Look, if I have any shot at all, I'll be there in an hour and a half." "I have to be honest with you," said Leigh Anne. "I have no desire to go to Athens, Georgia, every Saturday to watch my son play football." Richt graciously thanked her for not wasting his time, and promised not to pester her further. Some of the coaches gave up; more of them slinked into Briarcrest and found Michael there. But they all knew they remained outside the circle of trust. Michael formally decided who to have into the house, but Leigh Anne was never far away from the decision. In the end, they chose three: Nick Saban of LSU; Phil Fulmer of Tennessee; and David Cutcliffe of Ole Miss.

The assistant coaches of all three universities had spent the previous six months loitering in the vicinity of the Tuohy home and Briarcrest. Trooper Taylor, the recruiter from the University of Tennessee, might as well have had season tickets to Michael Oher's Briarcrest basketball games. "I just love watching high school basketball," he leaned over and told Sean Junior during one of the games. And who could argue the point, when he traveled six hours from Knoxville to do it? Now the head coaches arrived to close the deal with Michael, with the ceremonial air of great chefs condescending to grill the beef, after their sous-chefs had done the marinating.

Sean made a show of not being present when the coaches turned up in his living room (*See? I don't care!*). It was left to Leigh Anne to receive the famous football coaches with a big smile that disguised her gritted teeth. Leigh Anne didn't have Sean's ability to fake it. Sean could pretend all he wanted, but Michael simply *could not function* without the elaborate support system she had built for him: private tutors, constant monitoring, and a steady drip-drip-drip Chinese cultural reeducation program, administered by her, to assimilate him into their world. ("The Chinese government would have shot her at some point," said Sean, "'cause after she finished telling everyone else what to do, she would have tried to tell them what to do, too.")

Leigh Anne reasoned that, if Michael was going to be part of the family, he had to know what the family knew and behave as the family behaved. Ole Miss was an hour away, and she had, on her fingertips, every pullable string inside the place. The chancellor was a friend, the athletic director called Sean for advice, the locals, who still remembered Sean as the Great White Point Guard, asked him for his autograph. Leigh Anne could be as sweet as the day is long, and seldom did she need to be anything but sweet. But if her friends at Ole Miss didn't take care of her little 350-pound baby she could, and would, have their asses in a sling. She liked knowing that.

The first to enter was Nick Saban, of LSU, fresh off winning the national championship. He was at a serious disadvantage with Michael, however, because Michael had already visited LSU and been entertained for a lurid evening by a few of LSU's star football players. Michael refused to go into the details of the night, but when he came home his eyes were big and round. To Leigh Anne he said simply, "Mom, that's a *bad* place down there." Leigh Anne didn't want to know what had happened—she could guess—but she did ask Michael what they fed him: raw seafood. "I don't think he ate anything the whole weekend," she said.

With Michael's official visit to Ole Miss coming up, she picked up the phone, called Ole Miss recruiter Kurt Roper, and said, "I am faxing you a list of what Michael likes and what he doesn't like and you use it like a frickin' road map." Leigh Anne's list was straightforward and exact: "Don't take him to some titty bar and give him shots of tequila. Don't put him with guys who want to show him how to have sex in eighty-five different positions. Don't feed him a steak: he *hates* steak. Take him to Ole Venice [a restaurant in Oxford] and feed him Fettuccine Alfredo with chicken. Take him to a movie—and not *The Texas Chainsaw Massacre* because he'll just hide his face in his hands the whole time. And then let him go to bed." And the people at Ole Miss had done exactly that. And Michael had come home and said what a fine time he had had—and how Ole Miss wasn't at all like LSU.

Then Nick Saban arrived. Waiting for him were the Tuohys minus Sean, plus Miss Sue, Coach Hugh Freeze, and Briarcrest principal Steve Simpson—who Sean thought would get a kick out of being included. Whatever damage LSU had done to its reputation with Michael on his visit to the place was immediately forgotten—at least by Leigh Anne. Saban came into the house in his Armani suit and Gucci dress shoes and made a point of being polite to every single person in the room. Then he looked around, as if soaking in every last detail of the Olde English and Country French furnishings, and said, "What a lovely home. I just love those window treatments." *I just love those window treatments.* He didn't say, "I just love the way you put together the Windsor valances with the draw drapes," but he might as well have. Right then Leigh Anne decided that if Nick Saban wasn't the most polished and charming football coach in America, she was ready to marry whoever was.

Saban sat down beside the Ole Miss Christmas tree and

explained to Michael how he, and LSU, planned to make him not merely a great NFL player but also a college graduate. Michael said not one word. "These coaches would come into the house to talk to him," said Collins, who watched the whole process with disguised but intense interest, "and he was like a stone. The coaches talked the *whole* time." Ten minutes into the soliloquy Hugh Freeze rose, offered a big yawn, and announced that he really had to leave to go spend some time with his family.

Leigh Anne seethed. This was nothing more than the University of Tennessee spitting on LSU. "It was so *rude*," she said. "And he did it because LSU hadn't offered him a coaching job." Saban's response—to not miss a beat, to not take obvious offense—caused Leigh Anne to think even more highly of him. Now *that* was good manners. He knew everything from the names of the people who would tutor Michael to the place on campus where Michael would do his laundry. And he addressed his remarks not only to Michael but also to Leigh Anne. Michael didn't have any questions for him but Leigh Anne did; and he answered them beautifully.

When he was done, Sean Junior stepped out into the living room. "Um, can I ask my question?" he said, then explained his concern about having access to his beloved older brother—and revealed that the recruiter from Ole Miss had offered to give him an all-access pass.

The LSU coach smiled his charming smile and said that Sean Junior could have a pass that said he was welcome in the LSU locker room, even if Michael didn't play football for LSU. And if Michael did play football for LSU, they'd make sure SJ had the adjoining locker.

"Hmm," said Sean Junior. "That'd be good."

On Saban's way out the door, Michael finally had a question, and it was a pointed one:

"You staying?" he asked, offhandedly.

There were rumors in the air that Saban was being offered NFL jobs. There was no point in going to LSU to play football for the incredibly charming Nick Saban if Nick Saban wasn't going to be there. "I've been offered several NFL head coaching jobs since I've been at LSU," replied Saban, "and haven't taken one yet." Then he left and Collins turned to Leigh Anne and said, "That was a *great* political answer." (Three weeks later, the Miami Dolphins announced Nick Saban as their new head coach.)

Michael's next visitor was meant to be Ole Miss's David Cutcliffe. He was due to arrive in the living room on a Sunday, but he was fired the Friday before. *Oops!* The news didn't travel fast, it traveled instantaneously. Moments after Cutcliffe's dismissal, the Tuohys' home phone began to ring. The first caller was LSU's director of athletics, Skip Bertman, to say that even though Nick Saban had just announced he was leaving to coach the Miami Dolphins, and LSU no longer had a football coach, LSU was of course still extremely interested in having Michael Oher play for LSU. The next call came from Phil Fulmer, head coach of the University of Tennessee Volunteers, who was scheduled to visit Michael in a couple of weeks. Now, Fulmer said, he'd be coming right over.

Since the spring football practice that doubled as Michael's coming-out party, Phil Fulmer had become perfectly obsessed with Michael Oher. When the University of Tennessee traveled to play Ole Miss, Fulmer took his entire team on a wide detour to the middle of nowhere, to practice at the Briarcrest Christian School. His plan had been to roll up to Briarcrest in the Volunteers' swanky team buses, and, offensive lineman leading the charge, have the entire team surround Michael Oher and give him a cheer. Even more shrewdly, Fulmer staged his tableau on the very Friday that Michael was meant to make his official visit to Ole Miss. Michael was to become, in effect, Ole Miss's property at 3:00 p.m. sharp. Fulmer planned to arrive just before that, and detain him.

It didn't work out that way. Just before 3:00, Fulmer called the Ole Miss recruiter, Kurt Roper, said his team bus was stuck in

Memphis traffic, and persuaded Roper to wait until 3:30 to take Michael away. (In the small world of big-time football, assistant coaches know better than to annoy head coaches; a year later, Fulmer hired Roper at Tennesee.) Roper informed Leigh Anne who, of course, was furious. She told Roper that if Fulmer's bus came even one minute past 3:30 he was to take off. Caught between a rock and a hard place, Roper succumbed to the rock: Fulmer's buses rolled into Briarcrest at 3:31, just in time to pass Roper driving in the other direction, with Michael in the car.

Now Fulmer was coming alone, more or less. He started his official visit to Michael Oher, accompanied by his offensive line coach and his recruiting coordinator, at Briarcrest. Hugh Freeze found Michael and pulled him out of class, and Michael was immediately struck by how happy the Tennessee coaches, and Hugh Freeze, seemed about the firing of the Ole Miss football coach. That afternoon Fulmer happened to be giving a talk at the Tennessee high school football awards ceremony, at which Michael Oher would be named Player of the Year. Michael needed to go home and don a jacket and tie, but Fulmer asked if he could pick him up there and give him a lift. Michael never said no to anyone, and he didn't say no to Fulmer.

A few hours later, Fulmer was greeted at the Tuohys' front door by Ole Miss alumna Miss Sue. Neglecting to mention the human remains buried under his football field, Miss Sue asked him into the house. Miss Sue offered the Tennessee coach a seat in the chair beside the Ole Miss Christmas tree, which he declined. "I'll just stand here and wait," he said. Miss Sue took one look at Fulmer. He didn't have the slightest interest in saying so much as hello to her. He just stood there, awkwardly, in the blue blazer and khaki pants combo familiar to every little boy whose mama dressed him up for church. She decided he was a hick. He might be the head coach of the University of Tennessee but he didn't have half the wit or charm of Nick Saban, not to mention his looks. ("I happen to think Nick Saban is a *very* good looking man.")

Seconds later Collins raced down the stairs, a giant pair of black slacks in hand, chased by Michael, in his underpants, hollering at the top of his lungs, "Give me my pants!" He caught her in the living room, tucked her under his arm as if she were a football, looked up, and saw the head coach of the University of Tennessee. If Fulmer was disturbed by the scene, he didn't show it.

"Michael wasn't impressed by anyone who walked through our door," said Collins. "He just thought: 'Oh, here comes someone else I don't want to talk to who's trying to tell me why I need to go to their school.' " Now, airborne, she looked up at the Tennessee head football coach, said hello, and explained, "Michael is trying to wear *black* pants with his blue blazer to the awards ceremony. Tell him that doesn't match."

Collins watched Fulmer stand there, uneasily. She assumed he was trying to decide if he should agree with Michael or tell the truth. He told the truth. It had no effect.

Fulmer took Michael, in his black pants and blue blazer, away to the banquet, during which Michael had many pictures of his oddly dressed self taken by many newspapers. Afterwards, Fulmer insisted on driving him back home. This time when he and his entourage of assistant coaches walked through the door, Leigh Anne was waiting for them.

Phil Fulmer may not have thought Miss Sue worthy of his attention but he quickly set about ingratiating himself with Leigh Anne. He didn't notice her Windsor valances and draw drapes. He noticed the swimming pool. ("Y'all gotta pond! Ooooo, look at that pool out there.") Then he started making promises, and there wasn't much, it seemed to Leigh Anne, that the coach wouldn't promise if it meant getting Michael Oher to play for the University of Tennessee. To allay her concerns that she knew absolutely no one in Knoxville, Tennessee, he offered the Fulmer guesthouse as a home away from home. To make her feel better about the fact that Michael might be too far away to get home for Thanksgiving, he suggested they all have Thanksgiving dinner together, at the Fulmers'. Every year!

He couldn't be nicer in his own hokey way, thought Leigh Anne, kind of like the Andy Griffith character in *Mayberry R.F.D.* He couldn't have been phonier, thought Collins, who walked away and said, "That was just a lot of good ol' country boy hoopla. He was blowing a lot of smoke up our butt." Leigh Anne didn't see the point of thinking ill of a football coach just trying his best to get what he most desperately wanted, but it did cross her mind that "the difference between Phil Fulmer and Nick Saban was the difference between dealing with the town mayor and dealing with the White House."

The town mayor, for a start, didn't know when to leave. These visits usually lasted a couple of hours. It was ten o clock at night and neither Fulmer nor his retinue showed any signs of tiring. Finally Leigh Anne realized that he was waiting to have a word with the man of the house—so she got on the phone and told Sean to quit hiding and come home, so she could go to bed.

While they waited, Sean Junior seized the moment to take the floor. "Can I ask my question?" he said.

Maybe it was Coach Fulmer's demotic southern manner, or maybe it was just that SJ was growing bolder with age and experience. But this time he put his question bluntly. "What I want to know," he said, after explaining the access he'd been promised to various SEC football locker rooms, "is what's in it for me?"

"Locker room, hell," boomed Fulmer. "You ever been to a UT football game, son?" He set the scene: *one hundred and seven thousand* people all dressed in orange and screaming at the top of their lungs. The band forming a capital T on the field before the game. The Tennessee football team bursting out of the locker room and running through the T, led by none other than Phil Fulmer. When he'd finished, he said: "First home game is on national television. It's me and you running through the T, arm-in-arm."

"And I'll have the other arm," said his recruiting director, Trooper Taylor.

"That'd be good," said Sean Junior.

And so it was that Sean Senior returned home to find in his living room a very self-satisfied Tennessee football coach. He knew that Fulmer knew that there were only three schools left standing: Ole Miss, LSU, and Tennessee. Ole Miss had just fired its coach, and LSU had just lost theirs to the Miami Dolphins. That left Fulmer as the last man standing. Fulmer gave Sean his pitch—"the minute Michael walks on campus he's my starting left tackle"—and then told him, in the spirit of Grant consoling Lee, that he understood completely that such a prominent Ole Miss Rebel might have trouble watching his son become a Tennessee Volunteer. "Phil," said Sean, "if Archie can sit in the Tennessee stands for four years, I can sit in the Tennessee stands for four years."

Archie was Archie Manning, the Ole Miss football legend whose son Peyton had just been named the MVP of the NFL. Before that he had spurned his father's alma mater, Ole Miss, to go to Tennessee, where he had one of the greatest careers in the history of college quarterbacking. After Peyton announced he was going to Tennessee, the Manning family had *death threats.* Ten years later, there were still large numbers of Ole Miss alums with whom Archie Manning was no longer on speaking terms. Leigh Anne heard the exchange and said, "That's fine. But I don't look good in orange so I'm not wearing it."

With that, Phil Fulmer, his assistant coaches, and Hugh Freeze walked out the front door. Fulmer asked Michael to walk him to the car, and Michael—who never said no—walked him to the car. A minute became two minutes became three minutes. Sean turned to Leigh Anne and asked, "You think he's telling Fulmer that he's going to UT right now?" Leigh Anne didn't even want to think about it. At length, Michael came back inside.

"Did you commit to Tennessee?" asked Sean.

Michael just looked at him, and walked upstairs and went to bed.

Sean didn't leave it at that, of course. He was perfectly happy to seem as if he had no control over the process; he wasn't at all happy actually to have no control. He picked up the phone and called his friend, and Phil Fulmer's agent, Jimmy Sexton. Fulmer had only been on the road five minutes and yet Sexton had already spoken to him. "I just hung up with Phil," he said, "and Phil thinks he has him."

At that moment Sean decided to drop his pose of indifference. "If he thinks he's going to Tennessee," he said, "he's not going to Tennessee. I'm going to get LSU back in here."

He couldn't make Michael go to Ole Miss without crossing some kind of line he didn't want to cross. But he had no official ties to LSU; there was nothing the slightest bit unethical about putting him on *Air Taco* to Baton Rouge. Sean was from Louisiana, knew people at LSU, and could control Michael's experience there, in a way he could not at Tennessee. Hugh Freeze must have sensed Sean's intent to upset his own best-laid plans. One night when it was just the two of them, Hugh finally broke and hollered at Sean: "Coach Tuohy, you got to let him go to Tennessee!"

But until Michael declared his intentions, Sean would do nothing at all. And, left alone, Michael didn't declare anything. "I know Michael better than anyone," said Sean. "And I would look at him and say: what is going on in that head?"

Michael flew off to San Antonio on *Air Taco* and played in Tom Lemming's U.S. Army All-American game. Lemming invited him after Hugh Freeze called and told him "it was Michael's lifelong dream to play in the Army all-star game," and that the reason he hadn't filled in the forms was that he was embarrassed by his penmanship. Sean thought Michael had fled his meeting with Lemming in haste because "he thought that to play he was going to have to join the Army." Lemming didn't actually believe any of this, but he had a last-minute need for someone to play center for the East squad. Michael had never played center in his life, but he did the job beautifully. After the game, Lemming forgot his dark suspicions of Michael's character and declared in print that Michael Oher was far and away the nation's finest offensive line prospect. At the all-star game, ESPN reporters poked microphones into the faces of the nation's top prospects and asked them to declare their plans for college. Michael declined to answer.

Two weeks later, Ole Miss found itself another head coach. With USC about to play for the national championship, the USC defensive line coach, Ed Orgeron, formally agreed to replace David Cutcliffe. He flew to Mississippi for the press conference, where he announced that his first order of business was to persuade Michael Oher to become an Ole Miss Rebel. The press conference began in Oxford at one in the afternoon; at five Coach O was marching through the Tuohys' front door in Memphis. Memphis had never before seen or heard anything like him. This new coach had a neck that ran like a drainage pipe from his chin to his chest, and a chest that seemed to extend all the way down to his ankles. The ankles were thin and strangely feminine, and so the effect of the whole was of a great wooden barrel teetering on toothpicks. From the depths of the barrel emerged sounds so clotted and guttural that, when you first heard them, you did not recognize them as English, or, for that matter, human speech.

"YAAAWWW BEEE BAAWWW!"

Huh?

"YAAAWWW BEEE BAAWWW!"

That's what he bellowed as he burst through the door and got his first look at Michael in the flesh: "YAAAWWW BEEE BAAWWW!" ("You a big boy!") Then he gave Michael a huge bear hug, followed by the sales pitch.

Michael listened to the hearty Cajun coach for a good thirty minutes, as he listened to the other coaches, only in Coach O's case there was a twist: Michael couldn't understand a word he said. He seemed to be saying something about being a really good recruiter, who planned to turn the Ole Miss football program around, but that he needed a star recruit like Michael Oher to kick-start the process. "It was scary," said Michael later. "I never heard anything like that." Leigh Anne, Collins, and Sean Junior were equally lost. Only Sean, who grew up in southeast Louisiana, could understand what Coach O was trying to say. "Coach O is pure one hundred percent coon-ass," he explained, "and I grew up surrounded by coon-asses."

Still, as Michael never said anything to the coaches, or even signaled nonverbally his interest in what had been said, he was, in his way, Coach O's ideal listener. He sat in silence and pretended to understand. When Coach O finally finished, Michael asked his first sincere, formal question of the entire five months' recruiting process.

"What," he asked, "are you going to do for the kids that already committed to Ole Miss?"

"My jaw about hit the floor," said Collins, who had been fixing something in the kitchen. "Michael spoke!"

Coach O sensed, shrewdly, that there was a right answer and a wrong answer to this. "*Lemsday!*" he bellowed. "Let them stay!"

"That's all I want to know," said Michael. With that Coach O, who apparently had been forewarned, turned on Sean Junior, and beat him to the punch.

"All right big boy what you got for me?" he boomed. "I know you got something."

Even SJ was startled: word traveled fast. Apparently Coach O had heard that if he wanted to dance with Michael Oher, he'd need to pay the little fiddler. SJ's speech grew longer with each passing coach. He now explained that Ole Miss had initially offered a locker-room pass, but then LSU had topped that offer with the offer of not merely a locker-room pass but a locker. But then Coach Fulmer came along and tossed in his wild card: running with the team through the T in front of 107,000 screaming fans. When he was done, Coach O was ready to join the bidding war.

"Son," he said, in a grave tone. "First game of the season, you and Coach O will be walking through the Grove together."

"The Grove" was Ole Miss's answer to the T. Before each home game, tens of thousands of Rebel fans did not so much gather as swarm. They ate and drank and prepared their bodies for the chemical jolt of an SEC football game. The pre-game ritual climaxed with the Ole Miss players marching along a narrow brick path through the Grove that led to the stadium, known, more than a little hopefully, as "The Walk of Champions." The whole shebang was conducted in the spirit of an ancient rite, when it was in fact the brainchild of an Ole Miss football coach in the early 1980s.

"That'd be good," said Sean Junior.

On the way out the door, Coach O, obviously anxious to know what sort of impression he had made on Michael, asked Sean, "Whataamoo baadaat kwestON?" ("What did he mean by that question?")

"He wanted to know what you are going to do about Justin," said Sean. Justin was Justin Sparks, the Briarcrest placekicker and provider of jet transport to Michael, who was now planning on kicking for Ole Miss. Coach O signaled his relief with a smile and said, "Shaaa! Cudda tow me baaaa fo ahwak-n-heee." ("Sean! You could have told me that before I walked in here.")

"Don't worry. You gave him the right answer."

Actually, Michael was after something more important than the fate of his Briarcrest teammate. "I wanted to see what type of person he was," he said later. "If he's pulling scholarships that they'd promised kids, would you want to play for that kind of person? Be around that kind of person?" Coach O wasn't that kind of person, he decided; more interestingly, Coach O was the only coach who didn't promise him he'd crack the starting lineup his freshman year. Michael decided Coach O was all right.

The whole recruiting process had been interesting to Michael, in its way. It told him a lot about the people who had taken an interest in his future. His high school coach had used him to get himself a college football coaching job, and by the end he had taken to calling Hugh Freeze "The Snake." After Hugh laughed about it— this was the way their world worked—the nickname stuck. Michael had put Sean in a position to pressure him if he wanted, and Sean hadn't, at least not overtly. Leigh Anne and Miss Sue had pressured him plenty but for what seemed to him to be legitimate reasons— if he went too far away they couldn't take care of him, and he needed a lot of taking care of. Sean Junior was the most nakedly ambitious, but Michael sort of enjoyed the boy's naked ambition. "SJ worked it," said Michael, laughing. "He had locker-room passes, trips through the T. If I'd a kept on, he'd a been playing on a team."

The Orange Bowl was the cherry on top of the process, at least for Sean Junior. The Tuohys went to the national championship game as a family, and Coach O had arranged for them to attend USC's pre-game practice. While it was against NCAA rules for Coach O to so much as wink at Michael Oher, there was nothing that said his players couldn't amuse Michael. At the end of the practice USC's two biggest stars, quarterback Matt Leinert and running back Reggie Bush, along with the entire USC offensive line, came over to Michael, surrounded him, and offered fulsome praise of Coach O. As he eavesdropped on their banter, Sean Senior noticed a pair of shocking facts: (1) Michael was bigger than *all* the USC linemen; and (2) Sean Junior had somehow wormed his way into the scrum, and was sidling up to Reggie Bush.

"Hey, Reggie," Sean Junior was saying. The future Heisman Trophy winner looked down, obviously a little surprised. *How did this little kid get in here?*

"Whazzup dawg?" said Reggie Bush.

"You know, that's my brother," said SJ, pointing to Michael.

"Oh really," said Reggie Bush, perhaps thinking two words would suffice to abort a weird conversation. They didn't.

"Can I have your sweatbands?" said Sean Junior.

On February 1, 2005, Michael Oher held a press conference to announce where he intended to go to college. He faced a bank of microphones and explained how he'd decided he'd go to Ole Miss, as that's where his family had gone. To hear him talk, you'd have thought he'd descended from generations of Ole Miss Rebels. He answered a few questions from reporters, without actually saying anything, and then went home and waited for all hell to break loose. Up in Indianapolis, the NCAA was about to hear a rumor that white families in the South were going into the ghetto, seizing poor black kids, and *adopting* them, so that they might play football for their SEC alma maters. But it was still weeks before the NCAA investigator would turn up in the Tuohy living room.

After his press conference, Michael had to attend to the important business of playing miniature basketball with Sean Junior. Up they went into SJ's room, whose walls were a shrine to his father's Ole Miss playing career: trophies, pictures, flags, newspaper articles. Over the bed was a beautifully framed basketball net, with bloodstains on its cords. This was the net Sean Senior had cut down on national television, right after he'd led Ole Miss to its first and only SEC Tournament Championship. The net said something that never would be put into words, about the relationship between Ole Miss and the Tuohys—that the school was less source of identity than foil. Sean was always the smallest man on the court, and he was forever taking cheap shots and rising bloodied from the floor. Blood dripped from his chin as he cut down the net, sullying and sanctifying his prize. The moment he'd come down from the rim, however, his coach had grabbed the net from him, and claimed it as the property of the University of Mississippi. Into the

Ole Miss trophy case the net went. The next night Sean had gone out to a playground, cut down another net, broken into the Ole Miss trophy case, and swapped the net he'd stolen for the one he'd earned. "That's my blood," he said simply. "And so that's my net."

Under the bloody net Sean Junior and Michael resumed their endless struggle for supremacy in miniature basketball. SJ was far less interested in old school ties than his private haul of booty. "I was hoping to go to LSU," he said. "I had a locker and a field pass for the whole season." Special access to the hallowed ground of SEC football, inside the T and the Grove, was nice, but it didn't beat having his own locker in the locker room of the national champions. About Michael's motives, or his thinking, SJ couldn't have cared less. He never prodded him with the questions that obsessed the grown-ups, because they never occurred to him. But now he was, faintly, curious.

"When d'you decide?" asked Sean Junior.

"Back in September," said Michael. As the wooing of Michael Oher had started, in earnest, in September and run all the way to February, a lot of other people's valuable time had been wasted: all along Michael had known he was going to Ole Miss. "It was running across my mind to go to Tennessee, because everyone was saying I shouldn't go to a place in transition," he said. "But deep down inside I wanted to go to Ole Miss. It just felt like home." It felt like home, of course, because home now felt a lot like Ole Miss.

"But," he now told the little boy he loved like a brother, "it was kind of cool having all those coaches around here."

"Uh-huh," said Sean Junior, and promptly lost what little interest he'd had.

(The Tuohy family)

ABOVE A photo of Michael Oher when he was around ten years old.

BELOW Michael (#50) going up for a basket during the Briarcrest versus U.S.J. game in 2003.

(The Tuohy family)

RIGHT Michael during a Briarcrest Christian School game.

BELOW Michael leaving a game with Leigh Anne.

(The Tuohy family)

ST. BENEDICT EAGLES

HOME 14 PERIOD 4 GUEST 28

1 DOWN TO GO 10

Coca-Cola

(The Tuohy family)

(The Tuohy family)

(The Tuohy family)

ABOVE The Tuohy Christmas card (Sean Jr., Michael, and Collins).

LEFT Family lunch at the country club.

(The Tuohy family)

BELOW Michael and Leigh Anne.

ABOVE High-school graduation, May 2005.

(The Tuohy family)

(Ole Miss Athletics Media Relations)

ABOVE Michael (#74) playing during the
Ole Miss–Kentucky game in 2005.

(Photograph by Tabitha Soren)

(Photograph by Neal Slavin)

(Photograph by Neal Slavin)

ABOVE Michael Oher and his lineup: (left to right) Big Tony Henderson; Collins Tuohy; Sean Tuohy Jr.; Hugh Freeze, Michael's football coach at Briarcrest and now assistant coach at Ole Miss; Sue Mitchell, Michael's tutor; Leigh Anne Tuohy; Sean Tuohy; and Steven Payne, one of Michael's friends and Big Tony's son.

(Photograph by Tabitha Soren)

BELOW The Tuohy family on the Ole Miss football field.

(The Tuohy family)

—

CHAPTER EIGHT

CHARACTER COURSES

"THIS IS JOYCE THOMPSON, assistant director of enforcement at the NCAA. Today's date is March 30, 2005. And I am currently talking to prospective student-athlete Michael Oher. There are other individuals in the room at this time and I would like for them to state their names for the record."

"Sean Tuohy," said Sean.

So began the investigation of Michael Oher. Leigh Anne refused to participate, on the grounds that the whole thing was offensive. Collins was busy. Sean Junior failed to see the upside. But then, the upside was hard to see. Some college football coach, and quite possibly more than one college football coach, had gone to the NCAA and accused the Tuohys of abducting Michael and showering him with possessions in exchange for becoming the future left tackle of the Ole Miss Rebels. The NCAA had sent this lady to investigate. The lady was young, black, intelligent, childless, private school–educated, and with a manner and an accent that made her impossible to place as anything other than generically American. She had an off-the-rack professional quality about her, too, and if she didn't make a good living shining a faint light on the shady dealings between high school football players and the college boosters who love them, she probably could have made a better one reading the news at any local television station in the country.

She settled into one of Leigh Anne's antique English chairs and took in her surroundings. On a cabinet behind her stood a framed copy of the page in *USA Today* on which Michael Oher had just been named a First Team High School All-American football player. Joyce Thompson politely explained that she had come to find out if Michael Oher had violated any NCAA regulations. If he had, and she could prove it, he could put aside his football career for a while.

Then she switched on her tape recorder, and asked Michael for his name, address, phone number, and the names of the people with whom he lived. These he effortlessly supplied. It was the next question that tripped him up: "And who are your siblings?"

"Collins Tuohy and Sean Junior," said Michael.

She was about to move on but Sean, unbidden, jumped in. "That's his siblings *here*," he said. "He's got other siblings."

"And so who are your other siblings?" she asked.

Michael looked at her. "Uh—name 'em *all*?" he said, as if she had asked him to recite the Kama Sutra in the original Sanskrit.

Miss Joyce Thompson laughed. Yes, she said, could he please name them all. Michael sat with his hands folded in his lap—and now his fingers were extended. He was trying to count, without seeming to. It was humiliating not to be able to come out quickly with the names of his brothers and sisters, especially before this well-dressed, privately educated black lady from the NCAA.

"Marcus Oher. Andre Oher, Deljuan Oher," he blurted out.

The lady scribbled as fast as she could to keep up. "Deljuan?" she asked. "Can you spell that?"

"D . . . E . . . L . . ." the letters came slowly at first, then charged out of him in a wildly uncertain bull rush. "J-U-A-N?"

"Okay," she said, with a big smile.

"Rico Oher," he continued.

"Okay," she said.

"Carlos," he said.

"Okay," she said.

"John," he said.

"Okay," she said.

He'd stopped. Still staring at his hands in his lap, he repeated: *Marcus, Andre, Deljuan, Rico, Carlos, John.* He sounded like a small child reciting the alphabet from the beginning in an attempt to propel his mind to whatever follows "G."

"All brothers?" asked the lady from the NCAA.

Michael nodded and relaxed, and it was clear to Sean that he was going to seize on the finality in her voice to leave it at that. Marcus, Andre, Deljuan, Rico, Carlos, John. Sean didn't know how many there were, but he knew there were more than those six.

"No," said Sean. "We're not finished."

Michael thought. "Denise," he said, finally.

"Okay," said the lady from the NCAA, uneasily, putting pen back to notepad.

"Tyra," said Michael. Or, perhaps, "Tara."

"Tyra?" asked the NCAA lady. "T-Y-R-A?"

"Uhhhh . . ." He was unsure. "Yes," he finally said.

"Okay," she said, then began to laugh. "Are these still Oher?"

"Uhhhh—" said Michael, thinking for a moment. "Yes."

"He dudn't know that," said Sean. "Some are."

"Depthia," added Michael.

Sean watched Michael. He might not know the length of Michael's bloodlines but he knew the depth of his anxiety. Confronted by alien authority figures, Michael froze. He was more likely to tell this woman what he thought she wanted to hear than the truth.

"Depthia?" said the lady. "Can you spell that for me?"

"D—" Michael starts, and then gave up. "No."

"Oher or Williams?" asked the lady—because she knew that Michael's legal name was Michael Jerome Williams.

"Oher."

"They can't all be Oher!" said Sean. He knew that there were at least five different fathers.

"It *is Oher*," Michael insisted. Then he thought some more.

"Marcus Young," he said.

"Okay," said the NCAA lady. She was now shaking her head in wonder.

"David Young," said Michael.

"Okay," she said, scribbling away.

"How many's that?" asked Sean, with genuine curiosity.

"Thirteen," said the NCAA lady.

"*Thirteen?*" asked Michael. It was as if he couldn't imagine how she'd arrived at such an absurdly big number. Sean Senior took the list and handed it to Michael to study. Michael stared at this list for a very long time. As he did, the NCAA lady giggled nervously. Michael announced, "You put John down twice."

"So there's two Marcuses?" she said, taking back her list. "Not two Johns?"

That was right. Or so he said. It had taken ten minutes just to sort out the names of Michael's brothers and sisters. And that would be the easiest piece of personal information for the NCAA investigator to extract from Michael Oher.

"How did it come to be that—uh—you began living with the Tuohys?" she now asked.

"Uh—" said Michael. "When I came to Briarcrest my tenth-grade year. Uh. Coach Tuohy was—uh—a volunteer coach. . . . And, uh, I met him there. I decided to live with him summer after my junior year. He talked to me all the time. He was in my situation."

"Okay," said the lady, dubiously.

"He didn't have much growing up and I didn't have much growing up," said Michael.

"Okay," said the lady, even more dubiously.

"It wasn't the summer," said Sean. "It was before your birthday. It was about March of 2004. . . . But he lived here off and on all the way to then."

"Describe your living situation at the time," said the lady. "Because when you say that, you know, that Mr. Tuohy was in your same situation, I don't necessarily know what that means. So can you describe a little more about your situation?"

"How he didn't have a lot coming up," said Michael. To which he added nothing.

Her boss back in Indianapolis was an NCAA lifer named Dave Didion. Didion oversaw the investigations of the nation's top football prospects, and said he very much enjoyed the work because "it's like a jigsaw puzzle that comes in a box with no pictures on it." This jigsaw puzzle was even more perplexing: the box came locked. When the NCAA investigator asked Michael when he had last seen his father, he said, "When I was about ten," and left it at that. When she asked him why he didn't live with his mother, he didn't say anything at all. When she asked him who had paid his tuition at Briarcrest, he said he had no idea. When she asked him what he had done for food and clothing, his answer suggested he didn't really need food or clothing. Exasperated, she asked Sean if perhaps he had bought clothes for Michael. To which Sean replied he'd bought him "maybe a T-shirt"—which might have been strictly true, as Leigh Anne did the shopping.

Sean didn't trust these people. They didn't think in terms of right and wrong. All they cared about was keeping up appearances.

The NCAA rules existed, in theory, to maintain the integrity of college athletics. These investigators were meant to act as a police department. In practice, they were more like the public relations wing of an inept fire department. They might not be the last people on earth to learn that some booster or coach had bribed some high school jock, but they weren't usually the first either. Some scandal would be exposed in a local newspaper and they would go chasing after it, in an attempt to minimize the embarrassment to the system. They didn't care how things were, only how they could be made to seem. A poor black football star inside the home of this rich white booster could be made to seem scandalous, and so here they were, bothering Michael. The lady said she was just trying to establish the facts of the case, but the facts didn't describe the case. If the Tuohys were Ole Miss boosters—and they most certainly were—they had violated the letter of every NCAA rule ever written. They'd given Michael more than food, clothing, and shelter. They'd given him a life.

It didn't help that his new market value had already led Michael to become more cynical of the people around him. The point the NCAA lady was driving toward was now never very far from his mind: maybe these rich white folks had been so helpful to him the past two and a half years only because they had identified him as this precious asset. Case in point: his own high school coach. The Snake, who had been in quiet negotiations with Tennessee for a coaching job, had tried to talk him into going to Tennessee. Then right after Michael announced he was going to Ole Miss—and not Tennessee—The Snake announced that he, too, was going to Ole Miss. Coach O had offered him a job.

Sean tried to explain to Michael that that was just how the world worked—that Hugh Freeze was born to coach football and Ole Miss was lucky to have him—but Michael reserved the right to dwell on the selfish motives of others. For his senior yearbook, he'd selected his quote, from a rap song, which he'd expurgated for

Briarcrest Christian School consumption: "People ask me if I ever reach the top will I forget about them? So I ask people if I don't reach the top will y'all forget about me?"* He didn't go so far as to treat Leigh Anne with suspicion but, as Leigh Anne put it, "with me and Sean I can see him thinking, 'If they found me lying in a gutter and I was going to be flipping burgers at McDonald's, would they really have had an interest in me?'"

The thing was, you never knew when these doubts would surface. When the NCAA lady finally quit bugging him about his clothes, she turned to the matter of his new pickup truck. (*Who had told her about the truck?*) She asked Michael if Sean had bought the truck for him as a reward for signing with Ole Miss. Sean had tried to cut her off at the pass, and treated the question as absurd. But Michael had just chuckled. "You mean, I'd a got a truck if I'd gone to Tennessee?" he asked Sean, right there in front of the NCAA investigator. He might have been joking. Then again, he might not have.

The woman let that one go, or seemed to. Putting food, clothing, and transportation to one side, she moved on to shelter. Where, she asked, had Michael slept at night, both immediately before he had come to the Briarcrest Christian School, and immediately after?

"At Tony Henderson's," said Michael. Big Tony. The man whose mother's dying wish had led him to cart his son, and Michael Oher, out of the hood. Now, when Michael thought at all about Tony, he wondered why he was working so hard to stay friends with him. Once a week, it seemed, Tony reminded him of all he had done for him.

"Did you live with Tony all the way from eighth-grade year to sophomore year—or were there stops in between?" she asked.

---

* From Playa Fly, "Crownin' Me": "Nigga's ask me . . . / If I ever reach the top will I / forget about them . . . / So I ask nigga's if I don't reach the top, will yall forget / about me. . . ."

"Stops in between," he said.

"And so tell me . . ." she began.

"You ain't got enough paper for this," said Sean.

"You tell me where you lived," said the NCAA lady to Michael, ignoring Sean. "'Cause that's what I'm going to ask you. Was it just different stops per night? Who would you be living with?"

Michael began, haltingly, to list families, black and white, who had sheltered him during just the first year and a half at the Briarcrest Christian School. The lady took down the names, as she had taken down the names of his brothers and sisters, with growing incredulity. *In how many different homes could one sixteen-year-old boy sleep?*

"This is a *huge* undertaking," said Sean. "This is like an eighty-five-page document. This is a *monstrous* undertaking. It was a nomad existence."

"Okay," she said, but to Michael, not Sean. "And that's because of your limited resources growing up."

Michael didn't say anything, just nodded.

"That and because his mom was in and out of rehab centers constantly," said Sean.

"Is it safe to assume that you didn't have a permanent address with your mom?" asked the NCAA lady. Michael nodded. The woman became even more curious: then where *on earth* had he lived before he stumbled so luckily into Big Tony's house? How had he survived? Had he been homeless as a child? That's when Michael mumbled something about "foster homes."

Sean was aware that Michael had had some contact with the foster home system but not because Michael had volunteered the information. Not long before, the Briarcrest football team had thrown a party for itself at the Chickasaw Country Club. The busboy had come by their table, spotted Michael, and nearly dropped his tray. Michael had jumped up and given the busboy a bear hug.

Then they both began to weep. When Michael sat back down he explained, in a very few words, that they had been in a foster home together for a year, when he was around eight years old. Further details he declined to offer.

The NCAA lady now wanted the answer to a question the Tuohys had never asked: how many foster homes had Michael been in? Michael sat there thinking to himself.

"How many?" asked Sean. "Two? Three?" He was beginning to wonder why the NCAA needed to know all this stuff.

"Um," said Michael, finally. "Two, I think."

"And that's here in Memphis?" asked the lady.

Michael nodded.

"I'm saying," said Sean. "It's a book."

Not a good one. Michael's answers were as nourishing as a bag of stale potato chips, and as vexing as a Rubik's Cube. The lady was now officially frustrated. She'd come all the way from Indianapolis to interrogate Michael Oher, but she was getting no answers from Michael Oher, and too many from this rich white Ole Miss booster whose roof, for some reason, Michael Oher lived under. She stared intently at Michael and said, "Michael, you *have* to talk to me." It had no obvious effect. The most basic facts of his own life he either didn't know or didn't recall. She must have decided that Sean was the problem because when Sean tried to answer yet another question she'd directed at Michael, she turned on him and said, "I'll interview you later." She might as well have said, "Shut the hell up."

"I'm just concerned," said Sean. "With Michael, you got to pull it out of him. And I'll help you pull it out of him."

If Michael disagreed with this assessment, he didn't let on.

"Okay," said the NCAA lady, wearily.

For the next five hours the two of them tried, each in their own way, to coax from Michael Oher his personal history. This investigation obviously turned on the Tuohys' motives, and his. To understand motives she needed to know, or thought she needed to know, the complete biography of Michael Oher. But the biography of Michael Oher was a slippery subject. Indeed, the more you questioned Michael, the more you understood that his answers depended on the way you'd phrased the question. Ask him how many foster homes he had lived in and he would say he wasn't sure. Ask him if he had lived in two or three different foster homes, he would treat it as a multiple choice test, with two options, and would answer "two" or "three." Ask him, instead, if he had lived in nine or ten different foster homes, and he would have said "nine" or "ten." He treated the NCAA investigator as he treated everyone who asked him about himself: as an intrusion. To his one-word answers he would add *nothing*—not a scintilla of color commentary or new information.

Five hours into the interrogation, at ten o'clock at night, Miss Sue arrived and announced that she and Michael needed to study for a test. At that moment, late in Michael's senior year, his grades fell so short of the NCAA's requirements that whatever crimes against college football recruiting this NCAA lady found him to have committed were irrelevant. He wouldn't be allowed to attend Ole Miss on academic grounds. "But I'm not finished," protested the NCAA lady. Sean asked how much more time she needed and she said, "At least five more hours." Five more hours, both Sean and Miss Sue said, was exactly what Michael didn't have, and wouldn't have for many weeks.

And with that, the NCAA investigator walked out the door and past the statue of Colonel Rebel in the Tuohys' front yard. She'd be running this information by her superiors at the NCAA, she said. If they shared her dissatisfaction, she'd be back for more. When she was gone, Michael shed his stone face for a quivering one and went and found Leigh Anne. "That lady upset me," he said, tears in his eyes. "I never want to talk to her again." Leigh Anne's head swiveled

CHARACTER COURSES | 207

angrily until her eyes found Sean. "Don't you let that lady back in this house," she said, as if he had any control over the NCAA. And Sean thought: *Chalk this down as another sleepless night.*

TO GET INTO THE NFL Michael Oher needed to first get into college, and to get into college he needed to meet the NCAA's academic standards. The NCAA had a sliding scale of ACT scores and grade point averages; the higher the ACT, the lower the required GPA. Given Michael's best ACT score (12), to play college football he would need a 2.65 overall GPA. He'd finished his sophomore year with a 0.9. A better performance the back end of his junior year, when he'd moved into the Tuohy home, had raised his cumulative average to 1.564. That's when Leigh Anne took over more completely. Before Michael's senior year, she called every teacher at Briarcrest and asked them to tell her exactly what Michael must do to earn at least a B in their class. She didn't expect them to just hand Michael a grade—though she wouldn't have complained if they did. But to her way of thinking a B was the fair minimum to give any normal person willing to take the simple steps. She would hound Michael until he took those steps. Just give me the list of things he needs to do, she told the teachers, and he will do them.

And he did. Two days into his senior year he had come home, dropped his massive North Face book bag onto the kitchen table, and said, "I can't do this." Leigh Anne thought he was about to cry. The next morning she told him to suck it up and pushed him right back out the door. But that's when Leigh Anne had brought in Sue Mitchell.

As a tool for overhauling the grade point average of Michael Oher, as well as for broadening his experience of white people, Sue Mitchell had a number of things to recommend her. In her thirty-five-year career she had taught at several of the toughest Memphis public schools. At Bartlett High School, her final stop, she had taken over the cheerleading squad and whipped them into five-time national champions. She had applied to work at the Briarcrest Christian School, but Briarcrest had rejected her out of hand because, though Miss Sue said she believed in God, she had trouble proving it. ("The application did not have *one* question about education," Miss Sue said. "It was all about religion, and what I thought about homosexuality and drinking and smoking.") She hadn't been Born Again, and she didn't often go to church. She also advertised herself as a liberal. When Sean heard that, he hooted at her, "We had a black son before we had a Democrat friend!"

Still, in spite of these presumed defects, Miss Sue was relentless and effusive—the sort of woman who wants everything to be just great between her and the rest of the world but, if it isn't, can adjust and go to war. And that's what she did. She worked five nights a week, four hours each night, for free, to help get Michael Oher into Ole Miss. The Tuohy family looked on with interest. "There were days when he was just overwhelmed," said Collins, who saw the academic drama unfold both at school and at home. "He'd just close his book and say, 'I'm done.' " When he did this, Miss Sue opened the book for him. She didn't care about football, but she cared about *Ole Miss* football, and it gave her pleasure to think she was contributing, in her way, to the Lost Cause. She also, fairly quickly, became attached to Michael. There was just something about him that made you want to help him. He tried so hard, and for so little return. "One night it wasn't going so well and I got frustrated," she said, "and he said to me, 'Miss Sue, you have to remember I've only been going to school for two years.' "

His senior year he made all A's and B's. It nearly killed him, but he did it. The Briarcrest academic marathon, in which Michael had started out a distant last and instantly fallen further behind, came to a surprising end: in a class of 157 students, he finished 154th. He'd caught up to and passed three of his classmates. When Sean saw the final report card, he turned to Michael with a straight face and said, "You didn't lose, you just ran out of time." Then they both fell about laughing.

He'd had a truly bizarre academic career: nothing but D's and F's until the end of his junior year, when all of a sudden he became a reliable member of Briarcrest's honor roll. He was going to finish with a grade point average of 2.05. Yet, amazing as that was, it wasn't enough to get him past the NCAA. He needed a 2.65. And with no more classes to take, he obviously would not get it.

Now it was Sean's turn to intervene. Watching him pore over the NCAA rule book searching for ways to raise Michael's grades after grades had ceased to be given out called to mind a rich man's accountants cracking the tax code. He approached American higher education with cold calculation and joyful cynicism. One of the lessons he had picked up from his own career as an NCAA student-athlete was that good enough grades were available to anyone who bothered to exploit the loopholes. When Sean first arrived at Ole Miss, he learned, just in time, that freshman English had flunked many a jock. He went looking for a loophole and quickly found one: Beginner's Spanish. For some reason he didn't care to know, Ole Miss allowed freshmen to substitute a foreign language for the serious English class. He'd had eight years of Spanish in school, so the returns were impressive: two A's in Spanish without lifting a finger instead of the two D's in English for which he'd have had actually to read books.

Now Sean had been out of school for twenty-two years and so his grade-rigging skills were a bit rusty, but the skill for avoiding books was among the last to abandon the aging athlete. Plus he had help. Coach O was on board. Having completed his move from USC to Ole Miss, Coach O was now giving speeches to auditoriums filled with Ole Miss boosters. They didn't understand a word he said, but he could still whip them up into a frenzy. At some point in every speech he'd say that every championship team had a rock on which it was built and the name of his rock was Michael Oher.

From Coach O, Sean learned about the Internet courses offered by Brigham Young University. The BYU courses had magical properties: a grade took a mere ten days to obtain and could be used to replace a grade *from an entire semester* on a high school transcript. Pick the courses shrewdly and work quickly and the most tawdry academic record could be renovated in a single summer. Sean scanned the BYU catalogue and his eyes lit upon a promising series. It was called "Character Education." All you had to do in one of these "Character Courses" was to read a few brief passages from famous works—a speech by Lou Gehrig here, a letter by Abraham Lincoln there—and then answer five questions about it. How hard could it be? The A's earned from Character Courses could be used to replace F's earned in high school English classes. And Michael never needed to leave the house!

There was a hitch, of course; there was always a hitch. But like every great prestidigitator Sean knew that a hitch was also an opportunity. The BYU courses might be used to replace F's on Michael Oher's transcripts with A's, but only if they were taken during the school year—and the school year was almost over. That's when Sean discovered, deep in the recesses of the NCAA rules, yet another loophole: the student-athlete was allowed to generate fresh new grades for himself right up until August 1, so long as that student-athlete was "Learning Disabled."

Whatever that meant, thought Sean. He had no idea if Michael was actually learning-disabled, but now that it was important for him to be learning-disabled, Sean couldn't imagine any decent human being trying to argue that he wasn't. But just in case some dark soul wanted to make that case, Sean began to compose the rebuttal in his head. "He's just got to be LD," he said, as he flipped through the yellow pages of his mind looking for someone to provide him with the necessary paperwork. "It's some brain disorder in most people, but in his case it's 'cause he didn't sleep in a bed for the first fifteen years of his life."

Of course he couldn't just declare Michael learning-disabled himself: he needed a document signed by some pointy-headed shrink. Sean had no idea where to find such a person, and so he called the Briarcrest academic counselor, Linda Toombs, who came up with the name of a bona fide licensed psychological examiner— a woman named Jakatae Jessup. A few days later Sean wrote a big check to cover the cost of a battery of tests, and dropped both it and Michael at the front door of Jakatae Jessup's office in East Memphis.

Jakatae Jessup was white. She and her colleague, Julia Huckabee, also white, had no interest in God, or in football, or in the vast majority of East Memphis defined by both. They were, by Memphis standards, charming oddballs. "Krogerites," they called themselves—and defined the term as people who shopped at the Krogers grocery store on Sunday mornings, while the rest of Memphis went to church. Most of the children they tested came referred by public or private school administrators. These kids would be dropped off right after school and stay for several hours, with a break for dinner, which, as a part of the deal, the psychologists supplied. When Michael came through their door to have his brain examined, they were shocked by the implications. "My first thought," said Huckabee, "was that we're not going to have enough money to feed him."

They gave him the Wechsler Intelligence Test, and then a series of achievement tests. They asked him what 1 plus 1 equaled. They showed him a picture of an apple and asked him what it was. They asked him to draw a picture of a house. (Michael later told Leigh Anne he thought they were testing him for insanity.) The holes in his mind were obvious enough. He was still working well below grade level. He would probably never read a book for pleasure.

He'd never been taught phonics or, if he had, he'd been taught so badly that he might as well have not been taught at all. When a child knows the sound that goes with the letter, depending on its position in the word, and knows the sense of the word, depending on its position in the sentence, he can instinctively decode the language. A child who had been taught phonics can be given a nonsense word—"deprotonation," for example, or "mibgus"—and still be able to pronounce it. Michael had no idea. "I don't think he knows how to read yet," said Jessup. "I think he's just memorized a tremendous number of words." When he sat down with a reading assignment, he was like a man with a partial combination trying to open a locked safe.

Still, it didn't take his testers long to see that the new subject was highly unusual. They saw lots of children with glitches in their hard wiring, but they'd never seen anyone like Michael. He was eighteen years old, and he obviously hadn't learned very much—yet he had both the ability and the desire to learn. "You can watch somebody taking an IQ test and see how they learn from experience," said Jessup. "They get a problem, then a slightly harder version of the problem, and they can apply what they learned from the first problem to the second. Michael learned something from every single thing I put in front of him."

Reptile eggs look a lot like bird eggs. Some are _____ while others are oblong.

Michael knew the answer—"round"—but he wanted them to confirm it for him. "You're not supposed to tell a kid whether he's right or not," said Jessup, "but it was life or death for Michael. And it was clear we weren't going to go on until I wrote it down. I've never seen kids this old still absorbing knowledge the way he is. You see it in seven-year-olds."

At the age of sixteen, when he arrived at Briarcrest, Michael could still have been taught phonics. He wasn't, the psychologists surmised, because he had worked very hard to disguise his grotesque deficiencies from his teachers. "He was not letting people at Briarcrest know what he could or couldn't do," said Jessup. "Only Michael knew that there was a big gap between where he was and where he was perceived to be." Fearing that he wouldn't be given the chance to catch up on the sly—that he'd be outed as stupid— he was faking it, and hoping no one noticed. But he wasn't stupid. Far from it. "He's great if there is any context at all," said Jessup. "He can figure it out. He just needs a basic literacy program to decode words."

But that's not what most interested his intelligence testers. Michael Oher had been tested, and more than once, as a child. Those tests had pegged his IQ at 80. Now the two psychological examiners established that his IQ was currently somewhere between 100 and 110—which is to say that he was no more or less innately intelligent than most of the kids in his class at Briarcrest. The mind described by the new IQ test was not recognizably the same mind that had been tested five years earlier. "I compare it to photographs," said Jessup. "If you put Michael then side by side with Michael now, you would not be able to recognize these two people as the same."

That wasn't supposed to happen: IQ was meant to be a given, like the size of one's feet. It wasn't as simple as that, of course, but Jessup had never seen such concrete evidence of the absurdity of treating intelligence as a fixed quantity. "We speak of fluid and crystallized intelligence," she said. "Fluid is your ability to respond on the spot to a situation. Crystallized is what you've picked up along the way. The two are obviously related—how can you respond if you have no experience? When they tested Michael in the Memphis City Schools he was probably already deficient— both of those things had become compromised. He had so little experience. Then he had this rich *drowning* in experience that fed both of those."

Neither she nor her partner had ever seen anything like it, and they'd both been administering these sorts of tests for twenty years. She knew the literature and so she knew that studies of the effects of environment and nurture on mental development tend to create two study groups, the haves and the have-nots. "The have-nots learn whatever words they happen to hear on TV, the haves hear a million different words by the age of three," said Jessup. "But you only get to compare the two groups. You almost never see a case where the subject moves from one group to the other." Those low IQ scores Michael generated as a child, they guessed, were caused by his encountering, inside the problems, a hole in his experience, and then simply giving up. Problems on the page, he'd come to assume, were problems beyond his ability to solve. "What they [Briarcrest] taught Michael was not just reading and writing and math," said Jessup. "They taught him how to solve problems and how to learn. He stopped giving up."

When she'd finished the testing, Jessup called Sean Tuohy. She wanted to see him in person; what she had to say was too interesting to relate over the phone. She drove to the Tuohy home and delivered a fairly long lecture to which Sean listened politely. ("I understood about two words she said," he noted later.) When Jakatae Jessup was done, he had only one question for her.

"Is this going to get me by the NCAA, or not?" he asked.

It was. If Michael's IQ really was as low as advertised, Jessup explained, he wouldn't have been classified as learning-disabled: he was just learning as well as his brain would allow. Now that he was established to have greater capacities, his problems could only be interpreted as a disability. Michael, to everyone's delight, was certifiably LD.

THUS BEGAN THE great Mormon grade-grab. Mainly it involved Miss Sue grinding through the Character Courses with

Michael. Every week or so they replaced a Memphis public school F with a BYU A. Every assignment needed to be read aloud, and decoded. Here he was, late in his senior year in high school, and he'd never heard of a right angle, or the Civil War, or *I Love Lucy*. But getting the grades was far easier than generating in Michael any sort of pleasure in learning. When Briarcrest had given him a list of choices of books to write a report on, Miss Sue, thinking it might spark Michael's interest, picked *Great Expectations*. "Because of the character of Pip," she said. "He was poor and an orphan. And someone sort of found him. I just thought Michael might be able to relate." He couldn't. *Pygmalion* came next. Again, he hadn't the faintest interest in the thing. They got through it by performing the work aloud, with Michael assigned to the role of Freddie. "He does wonderful memory work," said Miss Sue. "It's a survival technique. You can give him anything and he'll memorize it." But that's all he did. Engaging with the material in any deeper way seemed impossible. He was as isolated from the great works of Western literature as he was from other people. "If you asked him why we're doing all this," she said, "he'd say, 'I got to do it to get to the league.'"

It was always work, and so it was always tiring, and every now and again Miss Sue needed a break. One night the Detroit Pistons were playing the San Antonio Spurs in the NBA finals, and Michael insisted on watching the game out of one eye. With the other eye he watched Miss Sue, and some book. If he wasn't going to take any more interest than that, she thought, why should she?

That's when Sean came through the door. Miss Sue handed Sean the reading assignment—Character Education I, Lesson II—and went to stretch out on the Tuohys' sofa.

The text was "The Charge of the Light Brigade." That Sean Tuohy would know a poem was as likely as Sylvia Plath hitting a jump shot at the buzzer, but Sean knew "The Charge of the Light Brigade." He hadn't seen it in twenty years but he still could nearly recite it by heart. He grabbed the sheet, got between Michael and the NBA finals, and said, "You ready, Bubba?" Then he boomed:

> *Half a league, half a league,*
> *Half a league onward,*
> *All in the valley of Death*
>   *Rode the six hundred.*
> *"Forward the Light Brigade!"*
> *"Charge for the guns!" he said:*
> *Into the valley of Death*
>   *Rode the six hundred.*

Rather than stop to explain, he raced on to the next, his favorite verse:

> *"Forward, the Light Brigade!"*
> *Was there a man dismay'd?*
> *Not tho' the soldier knew*
>   *Someone had blunder'd:*
> *Their's not to make reply,*
> *Their's not to reason why,*
> *Their's but to do and die:*
> *Into the valley of Death*
>   *Rode the six hundred . . .*

Now he realized he should give Michael a bit of help. "You know Death Valley at LSU?" he asked.

"Death Valley" is what LSU football fans had nicknamed the LSU football stadium. Michael had visited Death Valley. Now he was planning to ride into it, on the opposing team's bus.

"Well, this is where it comes from," said Sean. "This guy," he said, waving the work of Alfred, Lord Tennyson, "is writing about Ole Miss–LSU."

"The Charge of the Light Brigade" was now a football story, and Sean read it all the way through. Performed it, really. Then he read it again, more slowly. In his crackly North Mississippi–West Tennessee baritone, its sounds couldn't have been much less stately than the sounds Tennyson heard as he wrote:

> *Cannon to right of them*
> *Cannon to left of them,*
> *Cannon in front of them*
>   *Volley'd and thunder'd . . .*

He stopped again and asked: "So where are they now?" He compelled Michael to imagine the valley, and the surrounding artillery. Prostrate in the adjoining room, Miss Sue saw Michael's body language change. He usually leaned away from the lesson; this time he was leaning toward it. "Michael holds back so many things," she said. "Even his interest." For the first time since she met him, she could sense that he was conceding an interest. In a poem! She knew that he absorbed only what he could visualize. She thought: *Sean is making him SEE the poem.*

Sean charged on. Toward the end, Michael tried to stop him. Twice he asked, "Did they all die?" "Did they all die?" But Sean kept booming on, right through to the final stanza:

> *When can their glory fade?*
> *O the wild charge they made!*
>   *All the world wondered.*
> *Honor the charge they made!*
> *Honor the Light Brigade,*
>   *Noble six hundred!*

"They're all going to die?" asked Michael, when it was over.
"They're all going to die," said Sean.

Michael leaned over and switched off the NBA finals. "What's a league?" he asked.

Sean actually didn't know. Obviously, though not to Michael, a league was a unit of distance. Fortunately, BYU kept a crib sheet on line and Sean went to the computer and pulled it up. They went through the poem and replaced several of what Sean conceded were "goofy words"—*league, blunder'd, battery, shatter'd and sunder'd*—with words Michael knew. "Saber" was the exception. Michael didn't know what a saber was but when Sean explained, "it's a big long-ass sword, bigger than the knives you used in the hood," they agreed to let Tennyson keep it. Then Sean read it again.

> *Half a mile, half a mile,*
> *Half a mile onward . . .*

After the second reading Michael said, "Why would anybody do that?"

"The point is that this is about courage," said Sean.

"But they're going to all get killed!" he said.

"And you honor that," said Sean, "because they used courage, even if it was dumb."

From the next room Miss Sue hollered, "Michael Oher, if there's a war broke out, you head straight to Canada! Do you hear me?"

If Michael heard her he didn't show it.

"And sometimes courage *is* dumb," said Sean. "What they are saying is not that it's right or wrong. What they are saying is that it's not for us to question the coach. If you're the left tackle and the coach tells you to block the whole other team, you do it first, and you ask questions later."

"Why didn't we read any great poems like that at Briarcrest?" asked Michael.

And Sean thought: *You did. But it didn't mean anything to you, because they took it for granted that you knew what a saber was.*

"Let's read it again," said Michael.

NEARLY A MONTH after her first visit, Miss Joyce Thompson from the NCAA returned. This time she arrived early and found Michael at home alone. They sat together uncomfortably. She started to explain all over again the purpose of her visit—there were these rules forbidding people affiliated with college football programs doing any favors for big-time high school football players, etc.—when Michael interjected.

"I *should* be paid," he said.

She laughed, but nervously.

"They're making all this money off football," he said. "Why shouldn't they pay the players?"

She treated it as a silly question. It wasn't. The reason the NCAA needed investigators roaming the country to ensure that college football teams, and their boosters, weren't giving money or food or clothing or shelter or succor of any sort to the nation's best high school football players is that the nation's best high school football players were worth a lot more to the colleges than the tuition, room, and board they were allowed to pay them. The NCAA rules had created a black market—and done for high school football players what the Soviet police had once done for Levi's blue jeans. A market doesn't simply shut down when its goods become contraband. It just becomes more profitable for the people willing to operate in it. There were a number of colleges—and Ole Miss was one of them—for which the expropriation of the market value of pre-professional football players was something very like a core business. Whether NCAA investigators impeded, or enabled, this state of affairs was an open question.

Michael, newly alert to his own market value, had wondered

about that: if he was allowed to auction his services in the 2004 market for college football players, how much, exactly, would they have paid him? The going black market rate for a Memphis high school superstar five years earlier appeared to have been around $150,000. One hundred fifty grand is what the University of Alabama booster Logan Young paid to the high school coaches of Albert Means, in exchange for persuading him to play for the Crimson Tide. Who knows what the University of Alabama might have paid if it could have cut a deal with Means directly?

At any rate, in 2004, one hundred fifty grand sounded almost quaint.

But the NCAA lady didn't want to engage Michael on the subject. If there wasn't a principle to prevent rich college boosters from feeding, clothing, and educating black inner-city football players, the NCAA investigative unit would be out of business. She went back to trying to determine which rich white person had given what to Michael Oher. Before she got very far, one of those rich white people came through the side door. He wasn't happy to see her.

The first time the NCAA lady had walked into his living room, Sean Tuohy had been all false bonhomie. He'd held out his pleasantness the way a trainer, faced with an ill-tempered horse, might hold out a carrot, with the clear implication that it could always be withdrawn. Now it was. As Joyce Thompson, NCAA investigator, switched on her tape recorder and asked the very same questions he had already spent five hours answering, Sean began to redden.

"Michael," she asked. "Who took care of your basic needs?"

She went over the same questions: food, clothing, shelter, the truck. What about spending money? She had no more luck getting satisfying answers out of Michael this time than she had the last. But this time she had a Plan B. If he wasn't going to talk to her about who gave him what, she was going to press him about his grades. She'd seen his transcripts: how did he intend to get himself academically qualified? Michael didn't know, but Sean told her that they had just started the BYU program of correspondence courses.

"Can you tell me how you're doing it?" she asked.

Sean offered a basic summary, and then disclaimed any more detailed knowledge. The great Mormon grade-grab was being managed by Michael's tutor, Miss Sue.

"Do you take the test on the computer?" the lady asked Michael. "In a book?"

Once again Michael didn't answer. Sean did. And what followed sounded like a courtroom exchange.

Sean: I have no idea. You'd have to ask her [Miss Sue]. She's doing it.

NCAA Lady: But Michael's taking the class!

Sean: I have no idea, and I know he doesn't either. She's conducting it, so you'd have to ask her.

NCAA Lady: That wasn't explained? Or you don't know how that's done? Whether or not you take a lesson, you grade it, you hand it in?

Sean: No! I mean I think I was clear: I'm not being flippant. I don't know. And neither does he. We'll find out for you. And you can keep asking.

NCAA Lady: It just surprises me.

Sean (hollering): Well, it can surprise you. But we don't know.

NCAA Lady: You don't know what core subjects they are going to be in?

Sean: There'll be an English and a math.

Michael: Depends on how the ACT turned out.

That was another loophole Sean had found. Now that Michael had been certified as learning-disabled, he was allowed to retake the ACT tests as many times as he wanted, with Miss Sue on hand to help him parse the questions. That'd be worth a few extra points, and a few extra points on the ACT meant fewer needed on the GPA.

"Okay," said the NCAA lady, obviously hoping to encourage Michael, and not Sean, to elaborate. He didn't.

"I figure when I get to the second course, I'll look for the third one," said Sean. "And when I get to the third one, I'll look for the fourth one."

NCAA Lady: Okay.

Sean: What's wrong with that answer? You rolled your eyes. Let me tell you now: that's really rude. To look at me and roll your eyes like I don't know what I'm talking about. Or that I'm trying to mislead you.

NCAA Lady: All right. Now may I answer you?

Sean: Absolutely.

NCAA Lady: It's not that—

Sean: And I won't roll my eyes and accuse you of anything!

NCAA Lady: First of all, I'm not accusing you of anything.

Sean: It's the body language I'm getting.

NCAA Lady: Can I finish my statement?

Sean: Sure!

She then explained how surprised she was that Sean didn't know the details of the BYU study program, given how he seemed to have calculated every other angle on the court. How could he not know, for example, even the subject matter of these courses?

"It could be one of *nine* different courses," shouted Sean, brandishing a copy of Michael's high school transcripts. "He's still got eight F's on here."

Which brought them to the nub of the NCAA lady's displeasure. She must have been feeling like a Keystone Kop. She didn't understand these BYU courses. She didn't know exactly what Michael was doing to get himself academically up to snuff. She remained unclear who had given what to Michael, and when, so she had no real idea exactly how many of their rules against booster graft had been violated. All that was bad enough. But what really bothered her was that *Michael wasn't talking.* "This is the interview for Michael," she said to Sean. "And like last time you're doing most of the talking. And I need to hear from Michael."

"Well," said Sean, as if she'd just made the world's most preposterous demand. "*He* doesn't know."

NCAA Lady: Well, if that's the case, say, "I don't know."
Sean: He said he didn't know.
NCAA Lady: But you're still answering all his questions!
Sean: He said he didn't know. And so I did my best to answer it for you and you just didn't like the answer.
NCAA Lady (now staring straight through Michael): Well . . . I'm just trying to make sure that *you* don't know.
Sean: What part of "I don't know" fooled you?
NCAA Lady: That you're his legal guardian and you don't know if he's supposed to take English or math or science. That's the part that still baffles me.
Sean: Ma'am, I hate that it baffles you. But all you asked me to be is truthful. You didn't ask me to be smart.

It was then that Michael's face broke into a smile. More than a smile. When he registered what Pops had just said, he let loose this wheezing laugh . . . *heh* . . . *heh* . . . *heh* . . . *heh*. He sounded just like Muttley, the cartoon character, sidekick to Dick Dastardly. Michael Oher might never be sure of Sean Tuohy's deeper motives. But he could be sure of this: Pops was funny!

Michael watched with something like amusement as Sean and the NCAA lady sparred for the next few hours. The NCAA lady did what she could to remain calm and polite and retain the high ground while Sean yelled at her and turned red in the face and hurled abuse from the ground below. (He kept calling the NCAA "The Evil Empire.") The NCAA lady asked some detailed question, and one of two things followed. Either Michael supplied an unsatisfying answer or Sean hollered at her. Finally, the NCAA lady gave up, and let Michael go off to get another A in some course he couldn't even describe.

Once Michael was gone, the blood drained out of Sean's face. Out came the carrot. He apologized for being so upset, but said she had to understand that Michael had found the first round of questioning very disturbing. He felt he had failed Michael, he said, by letting her grill him like that. As he spoke, the NCAA lady studied him.

"Nothing was promised to you or your family?" she asked.

"*Me?*" said Sean. "I don't need anything."

His arms were extended in a way that said—*Behold! Do you not see the million-dollar house gorgeously appointed with hundreds of thousands of dollars in furnishings? Did you somehow miss the five cars in the driveway? The BMW? Do I need to call my pilots and order* Air Taco *to buzz NCAA headquarters?* Sean made this one point— that both he and Michael were too rich to be bought—several times. Once, after the NCAA lady had asked Michael if any Ole Miss boosters had given him any money to go to Ole Miss, Sean had said, "Ma'am, he's *richer* than any Ole Miss boosters." Sean Tuohy was up from nothing and now he had done so well for himself and his family that no one could give him anything he couldn't buy. He'd lived his life to be able to say that.

"Well, I know *that*," the NCAA lady said. Then she laughed, and relaxed. "But I just have to ask the question."

For the first time, she seemed human. Girlish, even. She ceased to be an investigator from the NCAA and became a woman named Joyce Thompson. And Joyce Thompson was genuinely curious about this domestic situation. A poor black giant monosyllab of the Memphis ghetto comes to live with, and apparently be loved by, a rich white right-wing family on the other side of town: how did that happen? She offered to turn off her tape recorder—Sean told her he didn't care if she left it on—and then set about satisfying her honest curiosity.

> *Joyce:* Is he normally quiet like that?
> *Sean:* When I met him that was *talkative*.
> *Joyce:* How many times would you say he was here?
> *Sean:* Hundreds. It was an open door to him.
> *Joyce:* Did he just show up?
> *Sean:* A lot of times he'd just show up.

She took that in.

> *Joyce:* How did you two ever meet?
> *Sean:* I told him I was Collins's daddy. That's how I introduced myself to him.
> *Joyce:* Did he open up to you?
> *Sean:* No. Gosh no. I barely got his name out of him.
> *Joyce:* And so at some point he came over here and he spent the night. When's the first time he spent the night?
> *Sean:* I don't know. Sometime during that basketball season. . . . This sounds bad but he was probably left at school one day, and I happened to be there.

She asked about Michael's childhood, and he told her how little they still knew of it. They talked about the problems of parenting. She confessed that she didn't know them firsthand. But she wondered how any mother could let her child wander the world looking for a bed without caring to know where he wound up. She wondered why on earth a rich white happy family in East Memphis would go to all this trouble for some poor black kid. And, finally, she wondered how Sean now felt about the experience. That final piece of curiosity led Sean to think aloud about the implications for his family of Michael Oher. "It's ruined us," he said. "Because so far as I can see, there's no downside. We can't look at a kid who's in trouble now without asking, 'If we had him, could we turn him around?' So what do we do when he leaves? Do we do it again?"

It was then that Joyce Thompson vanished and out came the NCAA investigator, with barely disguised shock. "Have you thought about doing this *again*?" she asked.

THERE WAS ONE final piece of unfinished business in Michael Oher's Briarcrest career. The senior yearbook picture was due, and Michael didn't have one. It was a Briarcrest tradition for every senior to have his baby picture in the annual. Her lack of a baby picture for Michael drove Leigh Anne to distraction. "You don't want to be the only senior who doesn't have a baby picture in the annual!" she said. She had made Michael give her the name of the foster home he admitted to having lived in when he was eight years old. She called the foster mother, who sounded vague; at any rate, she had nothing on him. She went down to his biological mother's apartment and harassed her for pictures. Finally, she had come upon a single shot, taken by an employee of Memphis Children's Services, when Michael was about ten years old. She had come home with it and given it to Michael.

Michael had looked at it and exclaimed, "Mama, that's me!"

"That sure is you!" she said.

Then he'd taken it into the den and stared at it for fifteen minutes.

But the picture didn't solve the problem. It wasn't a *baby* picture. One night Leigh Anne had an idea. She flipped on her computer and went online and found, as she put it, "the cutest picture of a little black baby I could find." She downloaded the stranger's photo, and sent it in to Briarcrest.

Briarcrest held its graduation ceremony in a church. The Tuohys were all in the audience, of course, and they had brought Miss Sue with them. Steve Simpson was there and so was Jennifer Graves, who said she'd never seen anyone work so hard for a piece of paper as Big Mike had worked to get his Briarcrest diploma. Big Tony was on hand—even though his son, Steven, wouldn't graduate until the following year. In spite of Big Tony's efforts to coax her out of her apartment, Michael's mother didn't make it. Dee Dee had told Big Tony that she wanted to see her son graduate from high school, as no one in her entire family ever had gotten past the tenth grade. Big Tony had arranged to pick her up that morning. But when he got to Dee Dee's apartment he found the lights out and the door locked. He thought he heard someone inside, but whoever it was refused to answer.

The Briarcrest president gave a long speech filled with many words of warning to the graduating class. He explained that when they left Briarcrest and went out into the world, they would encounter "all kinds of groups that claim some kind of privilege based on their lifestyles or perversions." (There was no need to say "gay"; they knew all about sodomy.) He spoke sternly about the danger of "seeking false happiness in a variety of narcissistic pleasures." After that final jolt of fear from God, the graduates were called down from their tiered seats at the back of the stage to collect their reward. Steve Simpson called their names, one by one; one by one they filed down. Michael wasn't called down until nearly the end. He sat waiting on the top tier, upper lip tucked beneath lower, either choking back his emotion or settling his nerves.

"Michael Jerome Oher," said Steve Simpson, and smiled.

The crowd had been told not to cheer for individuals, but a few people just had to break the rules. Miss Sue cried. Leigh Anne hooted and laughed and clapped. Collins was graduating too, but there was never any doubt Collins would graduate. It was Michael that was the news on this day. "He's so fired up," she said, as she watched him amble down, trying to keep his little scholar's cap from falling off. Sean smiled too, but Sean was paying closer atten- tion to the small group of underclassmen in formal wear gathering on the side of the stage. The Briarcrest Choir. One of the kids, a whey-faced doughboy, was twice as large as the others.

"You see that big guy in the middle," said Sean. "That might be Michael's replacement at left tackle. That's not comforting, that he sings in the choir."

The NCAA needed its proof of Michael's new and improved grade point average by August 1. On July 29 Michael took his final BYU test—another Character Course. Sean sent the test to Utah by Federal Express, and the BYU people promised to have the grade ready by two o'clock the following afternoon. "The Mormons may be going to hell," said Sean. "But they really are nice people." With Michael's final A in hand, Sean rushed the full package to the NCAA's offices in Indianapolis. The NCAA promptly lost it. Sean threatened to fly up on his plane with another copy and sit in the lobby until they processed it—which led the NCAA to find Michael's file. On August 1, 2005, the NCAA informed Michael Oher that he was going to be allowed to go to college, and play football.

Now came the time to figure out what that meant for his foot- ball career. In big-time college football it was highly unusual for a freshman to walk onto campus and start playing. And, when the freshman was an offensive lineman, it was almost unheard of. The offensive line had the most intellectually demanding jobs on the field, apart from the quarterback. Even the best ones expected to spend a season practicing with the team, learning the plays, but not actually playing in the games. In return, they were granted by the NCAA an extra year of eligibility.

But Coach O wasn't having any of this. He called Sean and told him (a) that Michael was already his best lineman, and (b) that Michael was such a high-profile recruit he needed to become a kind of shop window for future high-profile recruits. Michael would have to start for the Ole Miss Rebels his freshman year.

Sean drove down to Ole Miss to have a word with Coach O. He didn't think he could talk him out of sticking Michael in the starting lineup, and he wasn't sure he wanted to anyway. He thought it would be good for Michael to see right away what he was up against—to learn that natural ability might not be enough to "get to the league." But he worried that Coach O might not fully understand what a challenge big-time football would be for Michael. Michael had just turned nineteen. He'd never lifted weights or trained for football in the way that serious football players usually do. He hadn't had the time. He had played fifteen games in high school on the offensive line. In less than a month, he'd be starting in the SEC, across the line of scrimmage from grown men of twenty-two who had spent the past four years majoring in football, and were just six months away from being drafted to play in the NFL. As these beasts came after him, he'd need to think on his feet.

Coach O wasn't one for sitting behind a desk. When he had people into his office at Ole Miss, he'd install them on his long black leather sofa while he marched back and forth, giving pep talks. The subject of Michael Oher brought out the student in him; when Sean came, he sat behind a desk. Coach O actually had a yellow pad to write on. He didn't get up. He didn't answer the phone. He took three pages of notes.

The two of them talked about many aspects of Michael Oher, but eventually Sean got around to his mental development. Michael's mind, Sean said, "is like a house built on sand. He doesn't know what 'agenda' means, but he knows eight thousand more complicated words." Sean didn't worry all that much about Michael's schoolwork, as he planned to ship Miss Sue down to Oxford with him; Miss Sue could take care of Michael's grades. What he was worried about was Michael's ability to understand football plays. "Michael can read," he said, "but it just doesn't register very well. If you give him a play book filled with X's and O's, he'll say, 'Yeah, I get it.' Then he'll run on the field and won't have any idea what he's supposed to do. If you think you can just put it on a chalkboard and he's going to know the play, it's not going to happen. But if you take him aside and explain it to him using mustard bottles and ketchup bottles—some visual aide that enables him to *see* it—not only will he remember it, he'll remember it for the rest of his life."

"This is very important," said Coach O, scribbling notes.

"Coach," said Sean. "My faith believes that the Lord sends down gifts for everyone and our job is to find those gifts. Michael's gift is the gift of memory. When he knows it, he knows it."

Coach O stopped scribbling and looked up. "I'm going to tell you one thing, Sean," he bellowed. "He's got some pretty good fucking feet, too. You seen them feet? Now them feet: *that's* a fucking gift!"

—

CHAPTER NINE

BIRTH OF A STAR

T HE REDBRICK MONSTROSITY rises from a hollow beside a quiet road in the Buckhead section of Atlanta. To call it a home would be to give the wrong impression. It's less a shelter than a statement: the long sweeping driveway, the lawn that could double as a putting green, the giant white columns, the smooth stone porch inscribed with greetings in Latin. Through the leaded glass windows can be glimpsed sleek marble floors leading to a grand staircase lit by chandeliers with enough wattage to illuminate an opera house. It's the sort of place where the door really should be answered by an English butler, but Steve Wallace answers his own door. He wears shorts, T-shirt, and sandals, and has the pleasantly surprised air of a man who has just woken up from a dream that he is rich only to discover that he's actually rich. The only thing that the home and its owner have in common is that they are both huge. He walks across his great stone porch and onto his lawn to adjust the sprinkler. He limps; but they all limp. One nasty scar runs down his right knee and another lines his left ankle. Former

NFL linemen age painfully and die young. No life insurance sales-man in his right mind sells them coverage at the usual rates.

Hard as it is to believe now—as he returns to his mansion and passes through its stone halls toward the magnificent den with its elaborate audiovisual system—there was a time when Steve Wallace worried about such financial trivia as life insurance. He worried about making a living. He wasn't born with money; all he knew how to do was block, and in 1986, when he started his NFL career, blockers didn't get paid much. His first contract guaranteed him $90,000 a year, which was pretty good, but he wasn't sure how long it would last. He sat on the bench, and waited, without knowing exactly what he was waiting for. It turned out he was waiting for Bubba Paris to eat himself out of a job.

After the 49ers won their first Super Bowl, in 1982, Bill Walsh had used his first draft choice to select Paris. Bubba was meant to be the final solution to Walsh's biggest problem, the need to protect Joe Montana's blind side. "At three hundred pounds or less," said Walsh, "Bubba would have been a Hall of Fame left tackle. He was quick, active, bright, and he had a mean streak." Bubba also had a history of putting on weight, but, as Walsh said, "we felt we could deal with that. And we did. Briefly." Walsh fined Bubba for being overweight. He inserted clauses in Bubba's contracts that paid him bonuses for showing up for work under 300 pounds. He sent Bubba to Santa Monica to live at the Pritikin Diet Center. He even hired a fitness instructor to drive over to Bubba's house every morning and feed him less than Bubba fed himself. Walsh did everything he could think of to keep Bubba from expanding. And then one day the fitness instructor showed up at Bubba's house and, as Walsh put it, "The car was in the driveway, the drapes were closed, and nobody answered the door."

In his first four seasons Bubba's weight jumped around, but the trend line pointed up. Offered many choices between carrots and sticks, Bubba reached every time for another jelly doughnut. The 49ers won the Super Bowl again, after the 1984 season. But the next three seasons they went into the playoffs with high hopes and were bounced in the first round. In 1985 and 1986, they were beaten badly by the New York Giants, and in both games Lawrence Taylor wreaked havoc. He'd been too quick for Bubba. The 49er offense, usually so reliable, had scored only three points in each of those games. Joe Montana had been knocked out of the 1986 game with a concussion. The hits didn't always come from the blind side but the blind side was the sore spot. As 49er center Randy Cross said, "Increasingly, we game-planned specifically for that rush guy on the right side." The right side of the defense, the left side of the offense, was the turf Bubba Paris was meant to secure. "There's that old Roberto Duran idea from boxing," said Cross. "Get the head and the body dies. More and more teams were coming for our head."

It was at the end of the 1987 season that Bill Walsh's frustrations with his promising left tackle peaked. That left side of the line was now, obviously, the pressure point that a very good pass rusher could use to shut down the 49er passing game. And Bubba Paris just kept getting fatter, and slower, and less able to keep up with the ever-faster pass rush. During the regular season Bubba's weight hadn't mattered very much. He was waddling onto the field at well over 300 pounds, and the 49ers still cruised through the season. They'd finished with a record of 14–2. Amazingly, they had the number one offense *and* the number one defense in the NFL. Going into the playoffs, they were viewed as such an unstoppable force that the bookies had them as 14-point favorites to win the Super Bowl, no matter who they played.

They appeared to be a team without a weakness; but then, the regular season is not as effective as the playoffs at exposing a team's weakness. The stakes are lower, the opponents generally less able, their knowledge of your team less complete. It's when a team hits the playoffs that its weaknesses are most highly magnified; and in the 1987 playoffs, Walsh discovered that his seemingly perfect team had a flaw.

The first game was against the Minnesota Vikings, and it was supposed to be a cakewalk. But the Vikings had a sensational six five, 270-pound young pass rusher named Chris Doleman, and he came off the blind side like a bat out of hell. He was fast, he was strong, he was crafty, he was mean. He wore Lawrence Taylor's number, 56, and when he was asked who in football he most admired, Doleman said, "The one guy who has the desire to be the best, and the tenacity, is Lawrence Taylor. I'm not saying I want to be exactly like Lawrence . . ." Every blind side rusher knew about the anxiety of influence. Doleman wasn't exactly Lawrence Taylor but he was exactly in the tradition of Lawrence Taylor. He'd been drafted as an outside linebacker, but in the 4-3 defense, which the Vikings played, the outside linebacker wasn't chiefly a pass rusher. Finally it occurred to the Vikings coaches to try him as a right defensive end—that is, to make him a pass rusher. To give him the role in the 4-3 that Taylor played in the 3-4. He was an instant success.

Fearing that Doleman might shut down his passing game, Bill Walsh considered his trick of pulling a guard to deal with him. John Ayers had moved on, and the 49ers had no one quite so well designed to the job. Anyway, the trick was old: the Vikings would see it for what it was and quickly move to exploit the hole left in the middle of the 49er line. They had a weapon to serve just this purpose: right tackle Keith Millard. He lined up beside Doleman, and was himself—oddly, for a tackle—a speedy pass rusher. Send the guard to help with Doleman and you left Millard to run free. Walsh couldn't do that.

Thus Bill Walsh received another lesson about the cost of not having a left tackle capable of protecting his quarterback's blind side. This time the lesson was far more painful than the last. This time he had *expected* to win the Super Bowl. He had built the niftiest little passing machine in the history of the NFL, manned with talented players, and this one guy on the other team had his finger on the switch that shut it down. Chris Doleman hit Joe Montana early and often, but even when he didn't hit Montana he came so close that Montana couldn't step into his throws. Backup left tackle Steve Wallace watched from the sidelines. "He never let Joe get his feet set," he said later. What Doleman did to Joe Montana's feet was minor compared to what he did to his mind. "Every time Joe went back, he was peeping out of the corner of his eye first," said Wallace, "then looking at his receivers." The pass rush rendered Joe Montana so inept that in the second half Walsh benched him and inserted his backup, Steve Young. Young was left-handed, which enabled him to see Doleman coming. Young was also fast enough to flee—which he did, often. Against a team they were meant to beat by three touchdowns on their way to an inevitable Super Bowl victory, the 49ers lost 36–24. Afterwards, Vikings coach Jerry Burns told reporters that "the way to stop [the 49ers] is to pressure the quarterback. Our whole approach was to pressure Montana."

A football game is too complicated to be reduced to a single encounter. Lots of other things happened that afternoon in Candlestick Park. But the inability of his left tackle to handle the Vikings' right end was, in Walsh's view, a difference maker: it created fantastically disproportionate distortions in the game. "Bubba got beat," he said. "Doleman and Millard just *dominated* the game." After the game, Walsh was so shattered he walked right out of Candlestick Park without pausing to speak to his players. Always a bit leery of the way Walsh viewed them—as cogs in his intricate machine—the players would later point to that playoff loss as the beginning of the end of their feeling for their ingenious coach. "Walsh couldn't talk to us the day after," defensive back Eric Wright later told the *San Francisco Chronicle*. "He lost a lot of respect with the players. When it was going well, he was there. When the ship was shaky, he couldn't face us."

Walsh coached football just one more season, and he decided to hang his fortunes on something more dependable than the Bubba Paris Diet. But Bubba had no obvious replacement. His backup was Steve Wallace, and Wallace hadn't been trained as a left tackle. He'd been drafted by the 49ers in the fourth round in 1986, and was known chiefly for having blocked for running back Bo Jackson at Auburn. The joke was that Auburn had only three plays: Bo left, Bo right, and Bo up the middle. Having spent most of his college career run blocking, Wallace had to teach himself how to pass-block; but Wallace was a student of the game, willing to pay a steep price to play it, and the recipient of Walsh's highest compliment: nasty. As in: "Steve Wallace was a *nasty* football player."

A year after their loss to the Vikings, the 49ers found themselves in exactly the same place: in the playoffs, facing the Minnesota Vikings. The 49ers weren't as good as they had been the year before, and the Vikings were better. They, not the 49ers, now had the NFL's number one defense. It was led by Chris Doleman who was, if anything, even better at sacking quarterbacks.

The night before the game, Steve Wallace didn't sleep. "I'd just try to go to bed early and hope somewhere along the way I fell asleep," he said. The inability to fall asleep on the night before the game had already become a pattern for him. Apparently, it came with the left tackle position. Will Wolford, who protected Jim Kelly's blind side for the Buffalo Bills, had exactly the same experience. He started out his career as a guard—and slept—then moved to left tackle—and didn't. Late in his career, he moved back to guard, and, presto, he could sleep again. The left tackle position, as it had been reconceived by the modern pass-oriented offense, presented a new psychological challenge for the offensive lineman. In the old days, no one could really see what you were doing, and you usually had help from the lineman on the other side of you. That was still true at the other line positions. A mistake at guard cost a running back a few yards; a mistake at left tackle usually cost a sack, occasionally cost the team the ball, and sometimes cost the team the quarterback.

And—here was the main thing—you only needed to make one mistake at left tackle to have a bad game. The left tackle was defined by his weakest moment. He wasn't measured by the body of his work but by the outliers. "You have this tremendous ability to be embarrassed," said Wallace. "You know you can't afford three bad games in a row. They gonna say, 'Nice knowing you.' And it only takes *one* play—if he has one sack, then he's interviewed after the game. And you're the guy who gave up the sack. I could be good on thirty-four out of thirty-five pass plays, and all anyone would remember was that one sack."

This point was driven home to him the Saturday before the Vikings game, when Bill Walsh called the team into the auditorium for the pleasurable viewing of its past highlights. Walsh did this before every game. He thought it helped his players to see themselves at their best before they went out to play. The players watched Jerry Rice dash into the end zone, Ronnie Lott intercept a pass, and Joe Montana thread the ball between defenders. They whooped and hollered and cheered for each other. It was all good fun, all positive. But at the very end of the highlight reel, Walsh, perversely, had inserted a single negative play: the Doleman sack.

The sack came during the regular season in a game the 49ers won, 24–21. Doleman had got by Wallace just that once, but he had crushed Joe Montana. Wallace didn't need to be reminded of the play. That one sack was all he had thought about for days. Doleman had beaten him to the outside. Wallace had reached out to punch him but he, not Doleman, had lost his footing. Doleman rose up off Montana, jumped around celebrating, and then found Wallace, to editorialize.

"You got this *all day*," he'd said.

Wallace responded as he had done thirteen other times that season, by starting a fight. "I remember thinking: if I don't do something, he may get *ten* sacks," he said. "So I decided to mix it up." The NFL hadn't yet begun to levy big fines for fights, and Wallace had taken full advantage of the freebies. He now had a reputation as one of the league's dirtiest linemen—because he started so many fights. "I thought that's how it had to be," he said. "I had to fight if I was going to make it. And I had some folks to feed. And when you have some folks to feed you have a whole different mentality."

That really was how Wallace thought about these beasts bent on killing Joe Montana: *you go by me and my family goes hungry*. And it wasn't all that far from the truth. His first paychecks would be so thoroughly consumed by the $1,426 monthly note on the new house his parents had bought for themselves that he'd finally summoned the nerve to tell them to sell the house. He was deeply insecure. People were saying that he wasn't a good pass blocker, and he wasn't all that sure they were wrong. Just that morning—the morning Walsh played the tape of the Doleman sack—Doleman was quoted in the paper saying "the reason Wallace fights so much is to cover up his lack of ability."

Now he had to face Doleman again. Doleman was about to go to the Pro Bowl for the second straight year. No one on the team had forgotten what Doleman and Millard had done to them in the playoffs the year before. And yet Bill Walsh felt the need to replay that one sack. Over and over again Wallace watched Doleman beat him and crunch Joe Montana. He didn't understand why Walsh needed to humiliate him. He said nothing, of course, but was at once livid and ashamed. He wasn't going to sleep tonight anyway; now he wasn't going to sleep with a vengeance. "All night long I'm laying there thinking: *why did he show that one play?* A lot of times you can't understand what Walsh was doing until he's done it." At some point that night he decided "the lesson for me was to concentrate one play longer. As hard as you can possibly work, you can do it for one more play."

The next day, after he'd suited up, Wallace received another explanation for Walsh's perverse behavior. John McVay, the team's director of football operations, pulled him aside in the hallway and said, "You are going to be the key to this game. The game is going to turn on your performance." This wasn't the front office peptalking. McVay was a former NFL head coach—and he was completely serious.

This was new. Until this season, his first as a starting NFL left tackle, Steve Wallace had never experienced line play as an individualistic event. But that is what the left tackle position had become: a one-on-one encounter, a boxing match. The passing game, increasingly, was built around the idea of getting as many receivers out into patterns as quickly as possible. More receivers meant fewer pass blockers. Fewer pass blockers meant the left tackle had to deal with whatever was coming at him all by himself. Every now and then a running back might nip at Doleman's heels on his way out to catch a pass. On very rare occasions a tight end might line up beside Wallace and lend a shoulder. But mostly it would be just him and Doleman, one on one. And the importance of the private battle was now clear to him. "No one had ever said anything like that to me before," said Wallace. "No one had ever said, 'The game depends on you.' I never thought a lineman could be that important. I started thinking, 'Oh my goodness . . .'"

NUMBER 74 TROTS to the edge of the tunnel leading from the locker room to the field. He loves this moment. This moment is the offensive lineman's one shot at positive recognition. Later in his career he'll milk it for drama. He'd sprint so fast from the tunnel that the other players wouldn't put a hand out to slap his "because they were afraid I'd break it off." When he'd started playing football as a kid, he wanted to play tight end; even then, he preferred basketball. He enjoyed attention. It's still not natural to him to play a game in front of millions of people and go completely unnoticed. It's like playing the cantaloupe in the school play.

"At left tackle, Number Seventy-four, Steve Wallace!"

His name is announced to the packed stadium and he runs out. He's still so nervous and new that he concentrates on not stumbling. The day is sunny and bright but the turf, he notices, is slick and muddy. That's a break. Opposing teams who came to Candlestick Park were deceived by the sunshine. They'd think: on such a nice day the ground just must be firm. The ground was seldom firm. By the second quarter they'd be slipping and sliding, yet they wouldn't think to change their cleats. A pass rusher like Doleman counted on traction to turn the corner. If he forced Doleman to carve especially tight turns, Wallace knew, the turf might do the rest.

When he reaches the 49ers' sideline he looks across the field, to find Doleman. "I'm looking to see if he's all cocky, like, 'I'm gonna kick your butt,' you know." Back when Bubba was starting, he'd engaged in this tribal chest-pounding ritual with certain opponents. Before the game he'd look across the field, find the guy he was going up against, and literally start howling and beating his chest. Wallace is too worried about the task at hand to pound his chest. In any case, he doesn't catch Doleman's eye; but as he looks around, he notices another piece of luck: Jerry Markbreit. Markbreit will referee the game. He's Wallace's favorite ref. Jerry let left tackles get away with a lot, like where they'd line up. On passing plays he'd want to line up a few inches further back from the line of scrimmage than was strictly legal. If it became a race to cut off Doleman on a wide loop, those few inches might make all the difference. A lot of other refs would just flag you for not being exactly on the line. Jerry at least warned you before he flagged you.

The Vikings got the ball first. Steve Wallace thinks: *just get to halftime. Worry about the rest of the game then.* He couldn't even think about an entire game. Before he mucked out the Augean stables, Hercules probably carved them in half in his mind, too. Wallace thinks in terms of getting through the half without humiliation. He thinks: *make it to halftime without a sack, you got a chance.*

He watches the 49er defense try to stop the Vikings offense and prays they don't leave the 49er offense with their backs to their own goal line. *If we get the ball in a bad place,* he thinks, *Doleman's gonna be even harder to handle.*

They give up a field goal: 3–0 Vikings. The offense takes over on its own twenty-yard line. That was fine.

Wallace had made up his mind before the game that he would take a different approach. He'd play within himself. Doleman's words in the paper had stung: *the reason Wallace fights so much is to cover up his lack of ability.* "I said to myself: no matter what happens, I'm not going to fight him today. And it helped me to become a true left tackle."

When he looks back over his career from the end of it, he will say that this was the day he embraced his position. He is focused on his technique—on where his feet are, where his hands are, the timing of his contact. He adjusts according to the tiny hints that Doleman gave him of what he plans to do next. Wallace keeps a mental list of the different moves of pass rushers. He has names for them: the spin, the swim, the power, the shoulder grab, the arm drag, the hand slap, the hip toss, the dead leg ("they fake as if they're stopping just to make you freeze your feet"). Each guy was a little different; each guy had his own moves. Doleman hasn't yet learned to spin. He'd develop a spin move later and it would make him so good at getting to quarterbacks that he'd break the NFL's single-season sack record. But he has a swim move, where he brings his arms crashing down on top of the left tackle's arms, to break his hold. He also has a speed move—which is what he'd used to beat Wallace during the regular season.

Wallace worries about Doleman's initial move. He worries even more about the move Doleman will make in response to whaever Wallace has done to defend himself against the initial move. "It's *all* feet and hands," said Wallace. "Once your body gets engaged with a guy, he can very easily use a counter—once you've stopped his initial move, he pushes off. That's why you can't stop moving your feet."

The first series is a bust in which he plays no role. Bill Walsh decided, uncharacteristically, to open the game running the ball. He achieved nothing but predictability. After two runs for losses, on third and very long, everyone in the stadium knows that Montana will pass. The Vikings blitz with what appears to be their entire team and sack Montana. Three plays, minus nine yards, and punt.

But the defense quickly gets back the ball. It's during this second series that the heavyweight bout between Chris Doleman and Steve Wallace really begins. On the first play, Montana takes a five-step drop and Doleman comes with the same speed rush that he used to beat Wallace the first time they met. Wallace now understands that he'd gotten beat that one time because he'd been too jumpy, too eager to make contact. He prides himself on playing offense with the aggression of a defensive player, but that aggression is now counterproductive. The left tackle position is all about control—of self, and of the man coming at you. "Control the number," Wallace tells himself. "Control that inside number. As long as I can control that inside number, I can push through him." He fixates on the "6" on Doleman's jersey, the way a basketball defender stares at the midsection of the dribbling opponent.

Doleman lines up far outside and, at the snap of the ball,

sprints straight upfield. He's quicker than Wallace, and has the distinct advantage of running straight ahead while Wallace backpeddles. Wallace can't get a purchase on him; his only hope is to give him a single hard push at exactly the right moment. If he hits Doleman the moment after the snap, he will achieve nothing. He'll throw himself off balance, just as he did before, and speed Doleman on his journey upfield, en route to Joe Montana's back.

What happens on this first serious encounter between these two huge men happens so fast it's nearly impossible to comprehend with the naked eye in real time. Doleman sprints upfield, probably expecting to collide with Wallace on his first or second step—but he doesn't. Wallace has taken a new angle. "I had to make sure that his body was completely by me . . . Wait . . . Wait . . . Wait . . . Then I hit him."

He'd met Doleman as deep in the backfield as he possibly could without missing him altogether. They collided, briefly, at the spot where Doleman wanted to be making a sharp left to get at Montana. The hit kept Doleman from turning, and drove him further upfield. Steve Wallace had traded the pleasure of violence for the comfort of real estate.

Nobody notices, of course. His contribution was the opposite of drama. He'd removed the antagonist from the play entirely. What the fans and the television cameras see is 49er wide receiver John Taylor come wide open in the middle of the field. Joe Montana hits him with a pass, and Taylor races for a gain of twenty yards.

Doleman must have thought that first play was a fluke, because on the next one he tries exactly the same move. Upfield he comes, at speed, and once again Wallace takes him right on past the action. What the fans see is Jerry Rice catching a touchdown pass. What Chris Doleman sees, from a distance, is Joe Montana throwing a touchdown pass. What the fans at home hear is the announcer, John Madden, saying, "The 49ers need production out of three key people. Two of them just produced." The three key people to whom

Madden refers are Montana, Rice, and running back Roger Craig. They are stars; they accumulated the important statistics: yards, touchdowns, receptions, completions. Wallace is not considered a producer. He has no statistics.

The next time the 49ers get the ball, Steve Wallace suspects that Doleman might adjust. Doleman now knows that Wallace is quick enough and agile enough and intelligent enough to deal with his speed rush. He'll come with his bull rush.

In the playoff game the year before—which Wallace had watched from the sidelines—Doleman had opened the game with a bull rush and knocked Bubba Paris flat on his back. ("When you knock a three-hundred-thirty-pound guy on his ass," Wallace observed, "that's a very serious thing.") He expected the bull rush early. If Doleman established his ability to knock Wallace flat on his back—to run right over him—he'd force Wallace to plant his feet early, to brace himself. Planted feet doom a left tackle. Planted feet are slow feet. If he plants his feet, Wallace knows, Doleman will see that his feet are planted—and then he'll go right back to his speed rush. When a left tackle plants his feet, he gives the pass rusher a half step head start in his race to the quarterback. That half step might be the difference between a productive Joe Montana and a Joe Montana being carried off the field on a stretcher.

As in sumo wrestling, the awesome crudeness on the surface of the battle disguised the finesse underneath. Keeping Doleman off Montana's back is less a matter of brute force than leverage, angles, and anticipation. The outcome of the struggle turns on half steps and milliseconds. "I know early there are maybe three plays where he is going to try to bull-rush me," says Wallace. "And you know that if you're not ready, he's going to beat you like a dog for the rest of the day, because then you are setting with slow, controlled feet rather than happy feet. The trick is to see that bull rush coming early, and go out and pop him. You deliver a quick karate blow—

Pow!—like a real quick punch, to stun him. But your feet never stop. If your feet ever stop, you're beat."

Here comes the payoff for all those hours he spent studying game tape. He's watched many hours of Chris Doleman rushing passers. He's learned that Doleman tips his bull rush—and how can he not?—by the set of his stance, the tilt of his body, his attitude. Now Doleman comes with the bull rush. And he's ready for it.

What the fan sees is . . . nothing. Doleman is 270 pounds of raw, explosive muscle. There is probably not a human being among the 62,457 present who could withstand the force of his furious charge. To the naked eye, however, it looks like he's not even trying. He's just stuck on the line of scrimmage, leaning against Steve Wallace. Why watch that? Watch, instead, the real action: Jerry Rice catches another touchdown pass!

The next time the 49ers have the ball (they now lead 14–3), Wallace looks up to find Doleman gone. Doleman has moved to the other side of the field, in search of a better venue to practice his black art. On the other side of the field, however, he's in Montana's line of vision. He also must deal with two blockers, the right tackle plus the tight end. Two plays into the experiment he returns to his natural point of attack. For him it's the blind side, or nothing.

Today, it's nothing. Not one sack. A single tackle, and that comes on a rare play when Wallace isn't assigned to block him. "When you're locked in," says Wallace, "you can't explain it. You just feel it." Today, he was locked in.

At halftime the score is 21–3. Joe Montana has thrown three touchdown passes. Just as Montana received more than his share of the credit when things went well, he received more than his share of the blame when things went badly. Before the game, a lot of people were saying and writing that Joe Montana was washed up. Finished. Over the hill. Montana was only thirty-two years old. But the 49ers had lost their previous three playoff games. In those three games Montana had thrown four interceptions, zero touchdown passes, and for a grand total of 529 yards. This one half he'd thrown three touchdown passes and had been, as John Madden put it, "about as efficient as a quarterback can be." All talk of Joe Montana being finished, said the announcers, was obviously silly. Joe Montana was going to keep on playing, and become maybe the greatest quarterback ever to play the game.

No one ever mentions Steve Wallace's name. The cameras never once find him. His work is evidently too boring to watch for long without being distracted by whatever's happening to the football. Worse, the better he does his job, the more boring to watch he becomes. His job is to eliminate what people pay to see—the sight of Chris Doleman crushing Joe Montana.

In *Instant Replay*, a diary of a year playing on the offensive line for Vince Lombardi's Green Bay Packers, Jerry Kramer points out that without instant replay technology no one would ever notice line play. As Steve Wallace arrives in his magnificent rec room, and begins to fiddle with the remote control to his VCR, he suggests that there are limits to what instant replay will do for a lineman. He finds the old tape of the 1988 Vikings–49ers playoff game. He fast-forwards through the first three quarters of the game, pausing the tape only three times, after each of Jerry Rice's touchdowns. Each time Rice arrives in the end zone and turns, he is lifted high in the air by . . . Steve Wallace. Wallace made a habit of sprinting at full tilt downfield after a touchdown. The main side effect of this behavior was for a picture of Steve Wallace to appear, briefly, in the middle of the television screen. The blocks that made the touchdowns possible, he assumed, weren't worth watching.

Midway through the fourth quarter, the former left tackle locates a final moment of interest. The 49ers lead 28–9, and have the ball. The game is all but over. Just then, Roger Craig takes a handoff and sprints through the left side of the line for an 80-yard touchdown, the longest in 49er playoff history. Craig has sprinter speed but he barely has time to turn and raise his arms over his head before he collides with . . . Steve Wallace. Craig ran a forty-yard dash in about 4.5 seconds, and Wallace ran it in about 5.5 seconds, so, in theory, it should have taken at least 2 seconds for Steve Wallace to reach Roger Craig. If so, they were the briefest 2 seconds in the history of time.

"Did you see who the first guy down there with him was?!" shouts John Madden, who alone among the announcers paid some attention to offensive linemen. "The first guy in the end zone with Roger Craig is Steve Wallace! Steve Wallace was the guy who made the first block to break him loose!"

Wallace smiles and rewinds the tape—the game ended with the 49ers on top 34–9. Doleman had more or less given up trying to get to Montana by the middle of the third quarter. None of it matters. Steve Wallace wants to see this one play again. This business of All-for-one-and-one-for-all-and-who-cares-if-I-get-any-attention-or-credit-for-myself-so-long-as-the-team-wins was nice as far as it went. But it didn't go down to the bottom of Steve Wallace. "As long as you'd play hard and get a little grimy and dirty, Madden would take care of you," said Wallace. But even Madden needed a little help: that's why you chased the running back 80 yards to the end zone.

"The first guy in the end zone with Roger Craig is Steve Wallace! Steve Wallace was the guy who made the first block to break him loose!"

Having reviewed his one moment of glory a second time, the former left tackle clicks off his big-screen television, settles back into his fine leather sofa, and smiles. "It's all part of it," he says.

THAT SEASON THE 49ERS won the Super Bowl. After the game, Bill Walsh retired, but his innovation continued to sweep the league in various forms. The passing game grew ever more important, the quarterbacks ever more valuable. Yet there was still little change in the value of the people who protected the quarterback. Steve Wallace had no sense that he would one day be rich, and neither did any other lineman. The purest case study was Anthony Muñoz. By the late 1980s, Muñoz was regarded as the finest left tackle ever to play the game. He was quick, huge, versatile, and athletic—in addition to playing football at USC, he'd played third base for the baseball team. He came into the league in 1980 and became a fixture at the Pro Bowl. Even he was constrained in his financial demands by the conceit that one good lineman was no different from any other. All for one and one for all. "They would actually say that linemen are interchangeable and can be replaced at any time," Muñoz recalled. "They'd actually say we can just take another guy and toss him in there. But you were aware that the left tackle was especially important. He just wasn't paid as if he was especially important."

In 1987, after he had been to six straight Pro Bowls, a lot of people were saying Anthony Muñoz might just be the greatest offensive lineman in the history of the game. With his contract about to expire, Muñoz and his agent walked into the Cincinnati Bengals' front office and asked for a raise. The best NFL quarterbacks were now making more than $2 million dollars a year and the best pass rushers were making $1 million. "We were asking for half a million a year," recalled Muñoz, "and we were told that there was no lineman alive who was worth that much."

The people who evaluated football players and football strategies understood that the parts were inextricable from the whole, of course. You didn't get Joe Montana and Jerry Rice's "production" without production of some sort from Steve Wallace. Bill Walsh and John McVay obviously understood that if Wallace didn't do his job, then Montana couldn't do his. Take a half second away from Joe Montana's pocket time, and all those people saying Montana was washed up might have been right. But there was a difference between saying that Steve Wallace was necessary and acknowledging that what Steve Wallace did was extremely difficult—that it wasn't a job for just any old lineman.

The market for football players was rooted in subjective judgments and ancient prejudices. "Before free agency, they just paid you whatever they felt like paying you, and your only recourse was to withhold services," said Tom Condon, an offensive lineman for the Kansas City Chiefs in the 1980s who went on to become a leading players' agent. But there were hints of how a free market in football players might differ from a shackled one. The amateur draft, for example, which had aspects of an open market. College players had no say in which NFL team they played for, but the NFL teams were free to choose among the college players, and the order of their choices revealed their preferences. And in 1988 the preferences of the Tampa Bay Buccaneers shocked a lot of football people. Ray Perkins was the Buccaneers' head coach at the time, and Perkins had been the head coach of the New York Giants when they'd drafted Lawrence Taylor. Perkins had the fourth pick of the first round and was expected to take one of the two available star wide receivers, Sterling Sharpe or Tim Brown. Instead, he took a left tackle named Paul Gruber. "We had Gruber rated the highest player on the board," Perkins told a *New York Times* reporter. "We would have taken him if we had the first pick of the draft. I've changed my mind about the left-tackle position. It's now a skill position because he lines up against more and more teams' best athlete, their right defensive end or linebacker, the Lawrence Taylor types. That's why I feel good about Gruber. He is one of the best athletes I've ever seen."

Whatever had caused Ray Perkins to change his mind about the left tackle was causing a lot of other people to change their minds, too. That became clear after the 1992 season when, to put an end to labor strife, NFL players and owners agreed to a new labor deal. The players accepted salary caps tied to leaguewide revenues, so that salaries would rise with revenues. In addition, players were granted the right of free agency. The new deal had a number of immediate effects. One was to make it possible for teams to go out and buy the players they thought they needed on the newly open market. Another was to focus NFL front office minds on how to allocate their dollars. Every team now had more or less the same number of dollars to spend on players—the number dictated by the cap—and so the team that spent the dollars most efficiently should win. What was the best way to spend those dollars? On a quarterback? On defense?

The new market officially opened on February 1, 1993, the day after the Super Bowl. Two months later, Peter King of *Sports Illustrated* reported its shocking early verdicts. More than any other football writer, King had earned the trust of NFL's front offices, and so was able to channel their thoughts. All the players lucky enough to be entering free agency were cutting sweet deals for themselves, he reported. But the real shock was the dollar value the new market assigned to offensive linemen. Just a few years earlier, the Bengals had told Anthony Muñoz that no offensive lineman on earth was worth half a million dollars a year. The Denver Broncos quickly signed a couple of free agent linemen, Brian Habib and Don Maggs, for three times that amount. A few days later, Vikings center Kirk Lowdermilk moved to the Indianapolis Colts for $2 million a year, then groped for the adjective to describe his feelings. "Stunned is not the word," he told King. "There is no word in the English language to describe it." A few days after Lowdermilk grappled with his new dollar value, the Green Bay Packers paid $1.52 million a year over three years to buy a guard named Harry Galbraith away from the Miami Dolphins.

The strange bidding frenzy for offensive linemen no one had ever heard of persisted. After the Los Angeles Rams offered $1 million a year to bid away a guard named Leo Goeas from the San Diego Chargers, the *San Diego Union-Tribune* ran an article under the headline: "Farewell, Leo Goeas, Whoever You Were." The newspaper sought comments from the Chargers' old left tackle Billy Shields, who had retired in 1983. "I played eleven years," said Shields, "and I didn't make a million dollars over my *entire career*."

That was the general drift of public commentary from NFL insiders: bafflement. The Bengals' offensive line coach Jim McNally called the explosion in pay for linemen "a fast rush to get players who probably aren't worth it." One AFC coach called the Habib deal "the worst contract I've ever seen in this league." Another skeptic pointed out that Don Maggs was a B-list left tackle and certainly not the guy to be guarding John Elway's blind side. Just the past season Maggs had been badly beaten by . . . Chris Doleman. Retired NFL linemen were the most disturbed; when Friedrich Engels coined the term "false consciousness" to describe the inability of the working class to understand the nature of its oppression, he might just as well have been writing about NFL linemen. The offensive linemen had swallowed hook, line, and sinker other people's opinion of their worth. They accepted as plain truth the widely held view that they were the team's most fungible members. You didn't see a lot of former quarterbacks wondering why current NFL quarterbacks were being paid millions of dollars; but these old linemen couldn't understand the new value placed on linemen. "There's a lot going on in football right now that makes no sense," said old Chicago Bears center Mike Pyle, who made fourteen grand a year back in the 1960s. "And this tops the list."

Of course the people shelling out the millions tried to explain themselves. They argued that the numbers spoke for themselves: just the previous season, nineteen out of the twenty-eight starting NFL quarterbacks had been knocked out of games with injuries *by mid-November*. The Broncos' director of football operations, Bob Ferguson, pointed out that his team's star quarterback John Elway had been sacked *fifty-two* times: Maggs and Habib were being paid to stop that kind of thing from happening. Ferguson actually went so far as to thank Broncos' owner Pat Bowlen for his willingness to spend football money in ways football money had never been spent. "You have to give credit here to Pat," he said, "because these were not famous guys. When I talked to him about Habib, he kept calling him 'Rashid.'"

In the midst of this upheaval, the only free agent A-list left tackle, Will Wolford of the Buffalo Bills, announced his new deal: he'd be leaving the Bills for the Indianapolis Colts, who had agreed to pay him $7.65 million over three years. That was more than any lineman had ever been paid, of course, but the money wasn't what was most astonishing. Wolford's agent, Ralph Cindrich, later said that at least four other teams had been willing to match the Colts' offer. What had set the Colts apart from the other bidders was a clause they agreed to insert into Wolford's new contract. It guaranteed that Will Wolford, left tackle, would remain the highest paid player on the Colts' offense for as long as he played on it. Better paid than the Colts' running backs, the Colts' wide receivers, or any of the other acknowledged stars. Even if the Colts went out and got themselves the NFL's most expensive quarterback, Wolford's salary would rise to eclipse his, too. "I thought linemen would get a little more money from free agency," said Wolford later. "But I didn't think *that* would happen. I was numb."

He wasn't the only one. The Bills were furious: how could any lineman demand a clause that guaranteed him he would be paid more than star quarterback Jim Kelly, or star running back Thurman Thomas? The NFL didn't like the idea of any player having a clause in his contract guaranteeing him more money than his teammates, and it made noises about voiding the deal. That's when Ralph Cindrich went on the warpath. He asked, pointedly, if the league would have the same reservations if the clause had been in some quarterback's contract. He accused the league, in the pages of the *New York Times*, of "discrimination against offensive linemen." And the NFL let the deal slide, but only after saying no such deal would be permitted in the future. "There's a mentality about linemen that goes back to high school," said Cindrich. "When you picked your football team, these were the last guys picked."

There wasn't a left tackle in the game who imagined himself to be as valuable as the star running back, much less the quarterback. How could this happen? How could the people paying these vast sums assign a value to a player that he wouldn't dare assign to himself? How could they justify it, when the left tackle had no statistics to measure his value—no "production"? Bill Polian was the general manager of the Bills in 1986, when the team used its first-round pick to take Will Wolford of Vanderbilt University. When Wolford jumped to the Colts, Polian was working in the league office and found himself embroiled in the discussions over the disturbing new contract. Then in 1997 he left—to become the GM of the Colts. "You want to know why this organization gave Will that contract?" he asked. "He got it for the simple reason that he shut down Lawrence Taylor in the Super Bowl."

Left tackles everywhere failed to sleep the night before they faced Lawrence Taylor. What they didn't appreciate was that there was gold in their anxiety. Their fear was a measure of their value. A year earlier, the Bills had lost to the New York Giants in Super Bowl XXV, 20–19. Yet Lawrence Taylor hadn't been a factor—and a lot of front office executives apparently noticed the relative tranquillity on the blind side of Bills quarterback Jim Kelly. In effect, they had asked themselves a question: if we were to play the Giants, how much would I pay to have Lawrence Taylor erased from the field of play? The number was higher than they ever imagined. Until the next year—because the number kept rising. And in 1995, Steve Wallace of the San Francisco 49ers became the first offensive lineman to sign a contract worth $10 million. The quarterback might still get all the glory. But the guy who watched his back would be moving into a bigger house.

That was the beginning of what became a massive revaluation

of the left tackle position. The NFL had a new designation: the "franchise player." A team could claim one player as its franchise player, and thus prevent him from becoming a free agent. In exchange, the team had to pay him the greater of 120 percent of his old salary or the average of the league's top five salaries at his position. Of the twenty-eight franchise players named in 1993, nine were left tackles, the most at any one position. (Steve Wallace was one of them.) These moves simply reflected the left tackle's rapidly rising cost. NFL teams saw, instantly, that a left tackle even after he'd been designated a franchise player was cheaper than a left tackle purchased on the open market.

All through the 1980s and into the 1990s, offensive linemen had competed with tight ends and kickers for the title of lowest paid players on the football field. In 1990, for instance, the average starting offensive lineman was paid $398,000 a year, while the average wide receiver made $504,000 a year, the average defensive end made $551,000 a year, the average running back made $620,000 a year, and the average quarterback made $1.25 million a year. The left tackle, Anthony Muñoz pointed out, made his living trying to prevent a guy making twice as much as he did from killing a guy who made three times more.* By the 2005 season, the left tackle would be paid more than anyone on the field except the quarterback, and the percentage difference between the two of them had shrunk dramatically. The average pay of the top five starting left tackles was $7.25 million a year, compared to $11.9 million for the quarterbacks.

The curious thing about this market revaluation is that nothing had changed in the game to make the left tackle position more valuable. Lawrence Taylor had been around since 1981. Bill Walsh's

---

* The data for defensive end pay, because it includes the salaries of both ends, underestimates what was paid to the ends, like Chris Doleman, coming off the blind side, who tended to be paid a lot more than their counterparts on the other side. For salary data, the author would like to thank the front office of the San Francisco 49ers and the NFLPA.

passing game had long since swept across the league. Passing attempts per game reached a new peak and remained there. There had been no meaningful change in strategy, or rules, or the threat posed by the defense to quarterbacks' health in ten years. There was no new data to enable NFL front offices to value left tackles—or any offensive linemen—more precisely. The only thing that happened is that the market was allowed to function. And the market assigned a radically higher value to the left tackle than had the old pre-market football culture.

And still no one really knew who he was. If he was never distinguished from his fellow linemen, it was because his contribution had always been indistinguishable from theirs. His exact value had always been a mystery, in part, because he never did anything by himself. To say that one lineman was more important than the others was as preposterous as arguing for the special value of a single synchronized swimmer. That was about to change: football strategy had broken up the collective. Or, rather, it had yanked this one member of the collective out into his own private business. Hardly anyone knew who he was—yet. But they knew the guy he was paid to stop! And two days after the game it would occur to them that Chris Doleman or Lawrence Taylor or Bruce Smith hadn't factored into the game. It was as if the star hadn't played.

That was the great left tackle's shot at recognition. He wasn't himself in the spotlight. No one was taking his picture. But he reflected the light of the star across from him. He was a kind of photographic negative.

UNTIL THEY STARTED paying left tackles huge sums of money, the NFL talent evaluators didn't really have a rigorous idea of what one looked like. There was no prototype. And for a brief period, right after the birth of free agency, all sorts of unlikely characters who would soon be dismissed as physically ill-equipped for the position made a fortune playing left tackle. Steve Wallace knew he could have used another 50 pounds. "I'd have given myself a big wide ass," he said. "I didn't have that girth in the butt." Will Wolford wasn't the prototype, either. In college he'd played right tackle; his first year with the Bills he'd played right guard. Like Wallace, he had been thrust into this strange new role on the offensive line— head to head with this wildly dangerous beast bent on killing the quarterback—and figured it out. He got by on guile rather than sheer physical ability. Like Wallace, he could have used a few more pounds. Plus his arms were too short. Judged physically not up to the task, he was moved back to guard in 1996 and retired after the 1998 season. As late as 2006 he said, "If I had long arms I'd still be playing."

Once the money started to fly, the talent evaluators became connoisseurs of left tackle flesh. The Wallaces and Wolfords were exposed as physically inadequate; the left tackle now had to meet a list of physical specifications rarely found in a human being. "I can sit in the draft room today and tell you the most likely things the scouts will say, when they talk about a college lineman," said Ernie Accorsi, the general manager of the New York Giants. "The first is, 'He's a tackle, but he'll have to be a guard in the pros.' The second is, 'He played left tackle in college, but he'll have to play right tackle in the pros.'" The left tackle was now meant to be the 300-plus-pound guy who was also among the best athletes on the field. Now that he was making rarefied sums of money, he was expected to be, by definition, rare. "It's tough to find three-hundred-fifty-pound guys who can move their feet," said Accorsi. "They are either six two, or their arms are too short or their hands are too small or their feet are too slow or they simply aren't athletic enough. You can coach a lot of things but you can't coach quick feet. You can't make a guy's arms longer, or his hands bigger. And you can't make them taller."

Accorsi inadvertently made an interesting point. It was probably true that the NFL couldn't lengthen the arms or stretch the torsos of fully grown men. On the other hand, they could wave millions of dollars in the air and let the American population know that the incentives had changed. Boys who thought they might make careers as power forwards, or shot putters, might now think twice before quitting the high school football team. Huge sums of money were there for the taking, so long as you met certain physical specifications.

Case in point: Jonathan Ogden. At the dawn of free agency, Ogden, the son of a Washington, DC, investment banker, had just graduated from the St. Albans School. He was six nine and weighed nearly 350 pounds, but his weren't the right sort of pounds, at least to begin with. When he arrived at UCLA, to play football and put the shot, Ogden's nickname was "Fat Albert." He liked football but he loved the shot put—and had a legitimate chance to make the U.S. Olympic team. At St. Albans he had played right tackle and enjoyed it, because teams typically ran the football behind the right tackle and run blocking was fun. At UCLA, his new coach told him he was moving to left tackle and becoming, chiefly, a pass blocker. Ogden bridled. "I called my father," he said, "and I told him, 'They're trying to make me play left tackle!' My dad told me just to do it—because if I was going to play football, left tackle was the position to play." For a few years after the birth of free agency it helped a young man suited to play left tackle to have an investment banker for a father. After that the finances became so obvious that no one needed an investment banker to interpret them.

Jonathan Ogden remained unsure of his future in football. His freshman year at UCLA wasn't especially encouraging. The leap from high school to college was giant, much bigger, in his view, than the leap from college to the pros. "My entire freshman year," he said, "was a blur." His high school team had about ten plays; his college team ran, more or less, a pro offense. Pass blocking—which struck him as an almost passive activity—was a lot less interesting to him than run blocking. But by his sophomore year he had figured out where he was meant to go, and what he was meant to do, and it came naturally to him. After that season—the 1994 season—*four* of the defensive ends he'd faced were taken in the first round of the NFL draft. He'd gone head to head with four extremely good blind side pass rushers—Willie McGinest, Shante Carver, Trev Alberts, Jamir Miller—and hadn't allowed a single sack. "It was then I thought, 'If they can be first-round picks, why can't I be a first-round pick?'"

Good question! Nobody called him Fat Albert anymore. Ogden had slimmed from 350 to 310 pounds and then built himself back up in the UCLA weight room to 345 pounds. Muscle had replaced fat. He was faster and quicker and stronger and altogether terrifying. Six foot nine inches and 345 very mobile pounds. "I had some weeks in college where I could have had a cup of coffee in one hand and blocked the guy with the other," said Ogden—and when this elicits a laugh, he raises his hand and says, "No. Seriously." There were games when they'd just give up, and he'd look around and say, "They're not rushing!" His junior year was when he first heard himself described with a term he'd hear ad nauseam for the rest of his football career: *freak of nature.* He heard scouts say, also, that he was a "finesse" player. He reckoned that scouts always had to have one critical reservation, and so they'd dreamed that one up for him, as he had no flaw. "Coming out of college I was the best pass blocker in the country," he said. "It wasn't even close. They had to have one 'but.'"

But . . . to accuse him of being a "finesse" player? "Who the hell were they looking at?" he asked. The *job* might not call for aggression. But the *player* was ferocious. At the end of Ogden's junior season, UCLA was getting creamed by Kansas in the Aloha Bowl. They were down by 31 points going into the fourth quarter, the game was clearly over, and yet the defensive end he'd been manhandling all day just kept coming hard. Ogden thought he could see what he was up to: he thought he might beat Jonathan Ogden and make a name for himself. Maybe the guy had been reading the stuff the NFL scouts were saying about him in the newspapers—that deep down Jonathan Ogden was soft. "He kept coming," said Ogden. "So I picked him up, slammed him to the ground, and drove him into the dirt. When I was on top of him, I said, 'Look, man, it can either be like this for the rest of the quarter or we can relax and finish the game.' And he actually slowed down!"

The Baltimore Ravens selected him with the fourth pick in the 1996 draft—and handed him the largest signing bonus of his year: $6.8 million. He celebrated with a trip to Las Vegas. He was sitting at the blackjack table when someone tapped him on the shoulder and said, "Hey, aren't you Jonathan Ogden?" He turned around: it was Charles Barkley, the basketball legend. Here he was, a supposedly obscure offensive lineman, and Charles Barkley knew who he was. And he hadn't played a down in the NFL. After that, Ogden put aside his ambition to put the shot for the U.S. Olympic team.

As a boy, Ogden had been terribly shy. When he'd been required to compete in a spelling bee he had turned his back on the audience, as he couldn't face them and spell at the same time. A few years into his sensational NFL career you couldn't find a soul who would describe Jonathan Ogden as shy. He was bright and chatty and funny—and about as sure of himself and his abilities as a human being can be. And why shouldn't he be? He did what he did alone, and he did it as well as anyone ever did it. He had the proof: his quarterbacks never got sacked. When they went back to pass, they knew that what was behind them didn't matter. Opposing players weren't pleased to see him. "It can be intimidating if you allow it to be," legendary pass rusher Bruce Smith told the *Washington Post* when the reporter asked him what it was like to go head to head with Jonathan Ogden. "I know when I walk up to the line of scrimmage and I have to look up, I only think to myself: 'What in the world did his parents feed him?' "

Before the 2000 season the Baltimore Ravens re-signed Ogden to a six-year deal worth $44 million. That was what one prominent agent referred to as "one of the great what-the-fuck moments in the history of pro football negotiations." At that moment Jonathan Ogden was being paid more money than any quarterback in the NFL—and eight times more than Trent Dilfer, the quarterback he'd be protecting.

Now the highest paid player on the field, Ogden was doing his job so well and so effortlessly that he had time to wonder how hard it would be for him to do some of the other less highly paid jobs. At the end of that 2000 season, en route to their Super Bowl victory, the Ravens played in the AFC Championship game. Ogden watched the Ravens' tight end, Shannon Sharpe, catch a pass and run 96 yards for a touchdown. Ravens center Jeff Mitchell told *The Sporting News* that as Sharpe raced into the end zone, Ogden had turned to him and said, "I could have made that play. If they had thrown that ball to me, I would have done the same thing."

Having sized up the star receivers, Ogden looked around and noticed that these quarterbacks he was protecting were . . . rather ordinary. Here he was, leaving them all the time in the world to throw the ball, and they still weren't doing it very well. They kept getting fired! Even after they'd won the Super Bowl, the Ravens got rid of their quarterback, Trent Dilfer, and went looking for a better one. What was wrong with these people? Ogden didn't go so far as to suggest that *he* should play quarterback, but he came as close as any lineman ever had to the heretical thought. "If you're going to throw the ball," he said, "just make it work. Nothing against all the quarterbacks we've had since I've been here—all twenty of them, it seems. But if we're going to complete ten of thirty passes, no TDs and two picks, then let's just run the ball. At least I can have some fun."

The left tackle had become a star, but of a curious kind. He knew he was a star, and his teammates and coaches knew it, too. But to the general fan he remained obscure. The TV cameras still weren't on Ogden, and their indifference to his work hadn't escaped him. "There's a little bit of satisfaction in playing well, but not that much," he said. "Nobody pays any attention to what I do as a lineman. All those offensive linemen in the Hall of Fame. I mean, they all deserve to be there. But who knows who they are? The first one you can think of is Anthony Muñoz. The only one you can think of is Anthony Muñoz." Generally overlooked, Ogden offered conspicuous displays of his athletic ability, just for the hell of it. It was as if he wanted the coaches who sat down and studied the game film to know how he measured up against the people getting all the attention.

That game against the Tampa Bay Buccaneers, for example. The Ravens quarterback throws an interception. The cornerback who has picked off the pass flies down the sideline—it's 60 yards to the end zone and there's nothing between him and it. Most of the Ravens just watch: there's no chance they'll catch the speedster, so why bother? A couple give it the old college try and lumber after him for twenty yards or so, with no real intention of catching him, like old dogs chasing after a new sports car. Jonathan Ogden, however, actually tries. He doesn't have an angle, and, really, how is a six nine, 350-pound man going to catch a five eleven, 185-pound man employed specifically for his foot speed? The angle is all wrong, and yet . . . he seems to be catching up. As Ogden runs, you can't see his facial expressions or read his mind, but his body language is eloquent: *you little supposedly fleet-footed sonofabitch. Me and you. One on one. Twenty-yard dash. I'll leave you in the dust.*

There's no way that Jonathan Ogden, NFL left tackle, can be faster than an NFL cornerback, but don't tell him that. He knows that he's special—one of a kind. Or, perhaps, first of a breed. "To be the next me, it's really not easy," he said. "'Cause you really can't

teach some of the things I've been able to do. You can't teach someone to be six nine. You can't teach someone how, when they are off
balance, to recover. To be good, you almost have to be born to play
left tackle." To be born to play left tackle you must be born to do a
great deal more than play left tackle. With the cornerback 15 yards
from the end zone, Ogden still trails him by 10 yards. Between the
monster and the midget is a single player, another Tampa Bay
defensive back serving, unnecessarily, as an escort. Realizing,
finally, that he won't catch the cornerback, Ogden decides to use
this poor unsuspecting fellow as a human missile. Still running at
full tilt, he grabs this 200-pound man and launches him at his
teammate—and just misses. The cornerback who picked off the
pass and ran it back for a touchdown has no idea what nearly hit
him. He races into the end zone and celebrates his wonderful self.
The crowd cooperates, and gives him all their attention. But they
shouldn't have.

—

CHAPTER TEN

THE EGG BOWL

Iɴ 1958, ᴡʜᴇɴ ᴀ ʙʟᴀᴄᴋ ᴛᴇᴀᴄʜᴇʀ from Gulfport, Mississippi, named Clennon King tried to enroll in Ole Miss, and was instead carted away by Mississippi state troopers to an insane asylum, the football coach couldn't have imagined it had anything to do with him. When, in 1962, James Meredith came and stayed, the campus was engulfed in riots, and the football coach watched as his practice field became a staging area for army helicopters—but his team still went 10–0 and ended the season as national champions. But not long after that Ole Miss coaches set out to recruit the black athlete and found that history interfered. "There just aren't that many white guys in Mississippi who can play," said one of the Ole Miss football coaches. "The game is so much about speed now. The defense is so much about speed now. We need the best black kids if we're going to have a chance." But they seldom attracted the best black players; and since the early 1970s the Ole Miss football team has had about it a delicious fatalism. The civil rights movement achieved many things, and one of them was to create a plausible analogy between Ole Miss football and the Confederate army.

In part because of the needs of their local football team, there wasn't a town in America more concerned than Oxford, Mississippi, with seeming to have dispensed with race as an issue. The effort the locals put into avoiding obvious racism rendered the near-total lack of interaction between black people and white people in Oxford, Mississippi, almost as invisible as it was in the rest of the country. The history of the place was inescapable, however, if for no other reason than all these extremely annoying outsiders kept dragging it into otherwise pleasant conversations. As late as the fall of 2004 coaches from other SEC schools—including the University of Alabama—were phoning up Michael Oher and telling him that he shouldn't go to Ole Miss because black people weren't welcome there. And if Michael Oher hadn't put down the phone and found himself staring at his very own white Ole Miss family, he might have taken an interest in the subject. Mississippi's past had created the climate for Mississippi's present, and it would continue to do so until the present was otherwise notified. Bobby Nix, a white Ole Miss graduate from the early 1980s who now tutored football players, made this point routinely. To help the black kids feel as if they belonged at Ole Miss, Nix often took them into the places frequented by the old white affluent Ole Miss crowd. The Grove, say, or the Square. Usually he would end up feeling awkward and self-conscious. "When you show up with them," he said, "you'll get this look. It's like you have the crying baby on the airplane."

That look could have meant any number of things. The color of their skin was just the beginning of what set the Ole Miss football players apart. They had gold caps on their teeth and blue tattoos on their skins. They wore different clothes: oversized ersatz sports apparel so loose fitting that every stiff breeze threatened to leave them naked in the streets. They drove different cars—these jalopies outfitted with hubcaps worth twice the market value of the entire vehicle. You'd see them driving around in these bizarre-looking rigs with the front seats tilted so far back that the driver appeared to be an astrologist hard at work in a fully reclined Barcalounger. Many of them didn't speak or write standard English; to all but the most attentive white Ole Miss football fan, the black football players were barely comprehensible. Many of them, according to their tutors, were *less* well prepared for college than Michael Oher. The typical incoming player in Michael's class had third-grade level reading skills. Several had never taken math. *Ever.*

But if they wanted to play college football—if they wanted a shot at "the league"—they had to go through the tedious charade of pretending to be ordinary college students. Of the seventy players who survived Coach O's first grueling spring practice, more than forty were classified as "academically at risk," which meant, among other things, that they spent a great deal of their time inside a redbrick building with dark windows on the fringes of the Ole Miss campus, being spoon-fed books by an army of tutors. "We tell them that they are employees of a corporation," said Nix, one of the more experienced of those tutors. "And that they might be dropped at any time for lack of performance." A big part of the tutor's job was to steer the players away from the professors and courses most likely to lead to lack of performance. The majority of the football team wound up majoring in "Criminal Justice." What Criminal Justice had going for it was that it didn't require any math or language skills. Criminal Justice classes were also almost always filled with other football players. Of course, football players weren't the only Ole Miss students majoring in Criminal Justice. But when the Criminal Justice program took the field trip to Parchman Farm— aka the Mississippi State Penitentiary—the football players were the only students with friends on the *inside.*

When people on the streets looked at the black football players, and made Bobby Nix feel as if he was holding the crying baby on the airplane, they might have had other things in mind but the color of their skin. And in other places, Nix might have discounted those looks. Here in Oxford he couldn't. Here every look was filtered by the past.

The perception that Ole Miss's treatment of black people might not be up to the high standards of, say, the University of Alabama was just one of the many problems Coach O faced when he set out to convince the region's top high school football players to come play for him—but he couldn't ignore it. Coach O had been hired by Ole Miss in large part because he had proven himself to be a gifted recruiter of black football players. He'd never been a head coach, or run a football offense. And while he had an obvious knack for firing up a football defense, his single most important career achievement was to have recruited a pair of national championship football teams for the University of Southern California. When Coach O had arrived in the late 1990s the USC football team was faring poorly, and losing the best Los Angeles inner-city athletes to other schools. Coach O decided that what he needed was an example. Talk just one great inner-city high school player into committing to USC, prove that he can have a great experience, and others would follow. His opinion leader had been a defensive lineman named Shuan Cody—a *USA Today* High School All-American who, after three years at USC, went on to become a second-round draft pick of the Detroit Lions. When Coach O looked at Michael Oher, he saw Shuan Cody. But he was more than that. Not only was Michael Oher black, famous, and the best offensive lineman anywhere near Oxford, Mississippi. Michael Oher had a white sister who was an Ole Miss cheerleader and belonged to one of the snootiest white sororities on campus. The possibilities were endless.

IT DIDN'T TAKE LONG for word to arrive back at Ole Miss that the new head coach was out there saying he planned to build his football team on the back of Michael Oher. Ole Miss's two starting tackles, Bobby Harris and Tre Stallings, dug out Michael Oher's high school recruiting tape just to have a look at this new guy everyone was talking about. Stallings and Harris both were entering their senior seasons with at least a shot at playing in the NFL— Stallings would be taken in the sixth round by the Kansas City Chiefs, and Harris would sign a free agent contract with the San Francisco 49ers. Stallings, especially, expected to be the center of attention when people paid attention to Ole Miss offensive linemen. Then he rolled the tape of Michael Oher playing left tackle for the Briarcrest Christian School. "We both just laughed," said Harris. "I'd have to say he was the best lineman I'd ever seen with my own eyes—Terrence Metcalf [of the Chicago Bears] would be second. He was just maulin' people. Tre and me just looked at each other and said, 'He a beast!' "

Coach O handed the same tape to George DeLeone. DeLeone, in his thirty-sixth year of coaching offensive linemen, in college and the pros, had just arrived at Ole Miss from Syracuse University. He popped in Michael's tape, and as he watched he thought, *Oh my God.* "The flexibility in those hips! The arch in that back! That mass! Those feet!" he exclaimed, as he rewatched. DeLeone had seen plenty of future star NFL linemen back as college prospects. "Orlando Pace," he said, "or Andre Gurode with the Cowboys. In my judgment Michael Oher looks just like those guys did at this stage. It's a kinesthetic sense. You can't teach it."

In modern times Ole Miss's football team had enjoyed only the briefest and most fleeting moments of glory but had always been good at sending offensive linemen to the NFL. In the most recent NFL draft—the draft of 2005—their center Chris Spencer was picked in the first round by the Seattle Seahawks, and one of their guards, Marcus Johnson, was taken in the second round by the Minnesota Vikings. Before that, Terrence Metcalf had gone to the Bears, Todd Wade to the Texans, Stacey Andrews to the Bengals, Ben Claxton to the Falcons, Tutan Reyes to the Panthers, and Keydrick Vincent to the Steelers. None of those players had been in the starting lineup his freshman year. George DeLeone assumed Michael Oher would be treated like any other great offensive line prospect. He'd be red-shirted, sit out a year, and learn the system. In his thirty-six years of college coaching DeLeone had inserted a freshman into his starting lineup just once. And that had been back in 1986, on a losing Syracuse team, in a far weaker college conference than the one Ole Miss played in. Even then, Blake Bednarz—that was the kid's name—had started several years in high school, weight trained seriously, and arrived at Syracuse with a good understanding of his position. And he'd stunk! "Blake ended up being a great player for us," said DeLeone, "but he wasn't one that year."

Now Coach O was insisting that Michael Oher start for Ole Miss . . . immediately! The kid had played a grand total of fifteen high school games on the offensive line. "He's a kid who has never really been in a weight program," said DeLeone. "And he'll be going up against grown men who have been in the weight room for five years. And he's doing it in the best league in the country for defensive linemen." To make matters worse, the college game had grown a lot more complicated in the past twenty years. The Ole Miss offense would be a combination of the Atlanta Falcons' running game and the Tampa Bay Buccaneers' passing game. DeLeone assumed that no matter how quickly the kid took to the game he'd need a full season to learn whom to block, and how to block him—and now he was being told by Coach O that Michael had some kind of learning disability, and that he'd have to teach him the plays using ketchup and mustard bottles. "A visual learner," Coach O had called him. Whatever that meant.

With the first game of the season less than two months away, DeLeone hopped in his car and drove the hour and a half from Oxford, Mississippi, to the Tuohy home in Memphis. Ditching the

Ole Miss playbook with its X's and O's, he gamely set out to teach Michael Oher what was essentially an NFL offense. The kitchen chairs stood in for linebackers. The fancy dining room chairs—the Tuohy lady had just enough of them, luckily—served as the defensive and offensive lines. Coach O had told him to get the kid out on the field as quickly as possible, so DeLeone turned him into a right guard. It wasn't the kid's natural position. His natural position was left tackle. But the right guard had physical help on either side of him, and verbal instructions, from both the center and the tackle. It was the easiest position to learn, but, even so, DeLeone did not believe any true freshman could learn it. "Michael Oher is without question one of the greatest athletes I have ever seen for a guy his size," said DeLeone. "But what we're asking him to do is impossible to do."

In the safety of the Tuohys' kitchen they made progress—the kid was driving the fancy dining room chairs off the line nicely—when Leigh Anne came through the door. When she saw Michael firing off the line and getting fit with her furniture she took control of the defense. "The linebackers can stay," she said, tensely. "But you put my two thousand dollar dining room chairs back! Right now!" She then proceeded to tell him that she had examined his playbook with its X's and its O's and that it was "never going to work."

Coach DeLeone had a better idea than changing the playbook: keep Michael on the bench. How could an offensive line coach in good conscience stick any freshman into an SEC football game, much less a lineman who didn't know the plays? The first few games he actually tried this ploy. Coach O had made him start Michael Oher; but in the middle of the second quarter, when Coach O's attention was diverted, he'd have an upperclassman tap Michael on the shoulder and quietly inform him he was being replaced. Michael would go sit on the bench until Coach O noticed he was there, and flip out.

Leigh Anne he assumed he could ignore; Coach O he assumed he could not. "Everyone who coaches college football is intense," said DeLeone. "But O's intensity is at another level."

ALRIGHTEERIGHTEERIGHTEE *righteeerighteeeee!! Hooo! . . . Hooo! . . . Hooo! . . . Hooo! LessgoooooLessgoooooLesssgooooo!"*

It was seven o'clock in the morning, and already Coach O was out roaming the halls of the practice facility, hollering at the top of his lungs.

The players filed past him, wearily. The linemen came as a group, a study in ectomorphism. Fourteen 300-pound men lumbering down a narrow hallway was a sight worth seeing. Their movements were regular, synchronized, and slow. Each step was a discrete event, requiring conscious effort. They transferred all their weight onto one leg, paused in preparation for the next three-foot-long journey, and then shoved off. They looked like a herd of circus elephants. All but one, the biggest of them all, who skipped along lightly on the balls of his feet.

Michael Oher now had a swagger about him. A lot of people he didn't know were talking about him. Before the season *Sports Illustrated* had named him one of the five freshman football players in the country to watch. At one of his first practices, newly installed at right guard, Michael could only shake his head as a defensive end bull rushed the left tackle and sacked the quarterback. But after the play he walked over to the defensive end and said, "If I was left tackle you wouldn't know what our backfield *looked like.* You'd need a road map." But he wasn't the left tackle; Bobby Harris was.

"Hoo! Hoo! Hoo! Bobbah Harris YouWAKEyet????!!!! C'mon Bobbah Bobbahbobbahbobbah! . . . WhatyouthinkBobbyHarris??"

"Aw-rye coach," said Bobby Harris.

"Mikka Oh! Mikka Oh! Howdooosaaaaaa!"

(Michael Oher! Michael Oher! How you doin' son?)

"*ReddostahCOMpeet'n?*"

(Ready to start competing?)

"*Lessturnbackdaclock. Two a days all over again! Hoo! Hoo! Hoo! Hoo!*" His voice broke and became a piercing, dog-whistle-like shriek, and then he vanished around a corner.

A human geyser of adrenaline and testosterone, he had maintained this pitch from the first day of spring practice until this morning, the day before the team was scheduled to play its final game of the season. He'd done it in spite of presiding over what had to be one of America's most dysfunctional football teams. He'd been handed a weak and dispirited group of players and instantly set about trying to determine who among them met his standards. After three grueling weeks of spring practice, seventeen of Ole Miss's eighty-five football players quit. Some decamped for other colleges; some just went home. Coach O immediately went looking for their replacements. Now, as the season entered its final week, his nose for available football carrion would be the envy of any vulture. He knew by heart the rosters of many junior college teams. He knew where to post ads on the Internet to solicit college football players. When Hurricane Katrina drove the Tulane University football team out of New Orleans, there, at the city limits, stood Coach O, hoping to lure away Tulane's finest—prompting the Tulane head coach to call him, publicly, "lower than dirt."

Coach O wasn't lower than dirt. He was a desperate man in a dire situation. Here he was in his first, and possibly only, shot at making it as a head coach in big-time college football. And he had no players! His defense was actually very good—and Coach O, who ran the defense, ran it well. But Coach O had no real experience with a football offense, and his offensive coaches weren't giving him a lot of help. Each week they trotted out plays that might be run with success only by physically superior football players. And each week the Ole Miss offense ran onto the field without the faintest hope of success. Going into the final game of the season the

Rebels were 3–7, but their record did not capture the flavor of their despair. In seven SEC games they were 1–6 and their lone win came against Kentucky, which was seldom a thing to be proud of. Their offense had scored the grand total of 77 points. Of the 117 Division I-A football teams Ole Miss ranked 115th in points scored. "We must have the worst offense in college football," said Michael, and he wasn't far wrong.

The coaching staff had passed through all the stages of grief— denial, shock, anger, sadness, resignation—and entered a stage overlooked by the psychology textbooks: the terror of total humiliation. They were about to travel to Starkville, Mississippi, to face the Mississippi State Bulldogs. The Ole Miss–Mississippi State game was called the Egg Bowl, in honor of the egg-shaped trophy passed back and forth for the previous twelve or thirteen centuries between the two schools. It had been several years since Ole Miss had lost the egg; no senior on the Ole Miss football team had suffered the indignity of surrendering the egg. It had been several years, for that matter, since Mississippi State had beaten any other team in the SEC. As Hugh Freeze, who was now Coach O's closest confidante and chief aide de camp, put it, "This is a game we don't need to be losing. You don't lose to Mississippi State."

A football game between Ole Miss and Mississippi State was more than just a football game—but then that was thought to be true of many Ole Miss football games. Before the previous game, against LSU, the second-to-last game of the season, Ole Miss's dean of students, Sparky Reardon, tried to explain the extreme emotions associated with the event. "It's kind of like the situation in the Middle East," he told the Ole Miss student newspaper. "Fans of one grow up hating the other and really don't know why." The twist to the Mississippi State rivalry was that the fans knew exactly why they hated each other. The game served as a proxy for the hoary Mississippi class struggle, between the white folks who wore shirts with collars on them and the white folks who did not. Mississippi

State was a land grant college, originally called Mississippi A&M. The desperate contempt Ole Miss football fans felt for Mississippi State was echoed in the feelings of fans of the University of Texas for Texas A&M and fans of the University of Oklahoma for Oklahoma State—formerly known as Oklahoma A&M. These schools were not rivals; they were subordinates. Theirs was not a football team to be beaten but an insurrection to be put down. This notion was most vivid in the Ole Miss imagination: that the state of Mississippi, with the sole exception of the town of Oxford, was once a Great Lake of Rednecks. In recent decades the earth had warmed, and the shores of Great Lake Redneck had receded, so that, strictly speaking, perhaps it should not be described as a lake. But still, the residue was a very large puddle. And the one place in the puddle deep enough to ruin a shiny new pair of tassel loafers was Starkville, Mississippi.

And now the only thing between the players and the game was this final morning of preparation. The players stumbled in and parsed themselves into small groups according to their positions. The running backs went off into a room with their fellow running backs, the linebackers disappeared with linebackers. The fourteen offensive linemen herded themselves into what instantly appeared to be an inadequate room, and settled behind desks that seemed designed for midgets. Michael took his usual seat, in the back of the room.

If Michael Oher felt any social anxiety leaving Memphis for Oxford he hadn't shown it. Once or twice he'd asked questions of Miss Sue about Ole Miss that suggested a certain vague apprehension. "Is it true they got fraternities that won't let in black guys?" (It was true.) "Will I be the only person at Ole Miss who doesn't drink?" (The small club of teetotalers was accepting all applicants.) But his wasn't the ordinary story of the boy going away to college. He'd left home, but home had come along for the ride. Miss Sue was still his private tutor. Hugh Freeze was still his football coach.

Sean and Leigh Anne were, on many nights, in the house they'd built a couple of hundred yards off the Ole Miss campus. Before the first home game of the season Sean Junior had walked just ahead of him through the Grove, hand in hand with Coach O. And when they'd gotten to the stadium Collins was right there on the sidelines, leading cheers.

He felt right at home, in his own way. He didn't run with a crowd but he had many friends. He floated back and forth between white Ole Miss and black Ole Miss. He enjoyed his own company and kept much of himself to himself. When the other linemen chattered he just sat and watched them.

"There was a *transvestite* in Chevron this morning," said one of the other linemen. "It was scary."

Several of them started, at the horror of it. The circus elephants had stumbled upon their mouse.

"And it wasn't buying anything either," said the 300-pound lineman. "It was just standing there. *Staring.*"

"Aw, man!" said another gargantuan fellow.

"Jesus," said a third.

Michael just shook his head and said nothing. When the digital clock turned from 7:29 to 7:30 Coach DeLeone came into the room, hunched and limping and deeply weary. T-shirt, sweat pants, reading glasses, gray hair cut in the style of a marine sergeant: if you had to guess what he did for a living you would guess George DeLeone was a retired military man, with a string of Purple Hearts. In fact he was a former undersized college lineman whose knee injuries still plagued him. He didn't look happy, but then he had no reason to be happy. The offense had been abysmal, and the Internet pundits and the newspaper columnists were pointing to his offensive line as the problem. His situation was grim: he was on the verge of losing his job. Now he hoped to persuade his linemen to join him in grimness and to see the gravity of their predicament.

"All right, men," he said, as he fiddled with the overhead projector. "I want to thank you for everything you've done for me this year."

No one said a word. Then one of them realized: "Coach, was that a joke?"

They all laughed, even Michael.

"We all set, ready to go, or we gonna laugh?" barked DeLeone, wrong-footing them utterly. "Guys! Can we just have one game where we come in on Sunday, look at the tape, and say, 'This is how we can play as an offensive line'? Let's play this game with some frickin' pride on the offensive line. That means something to me, and I hope it means something to you. We can laugh next week. Laugh Sunday night. Now . . ."

He calmed down, without any help from his players, and pulled out his plastic sheets—the sheets with the X's and O's on them. Then he switched on the overhead projector and assumed his usual position beside it.

Bobby Harris gave a huge yawn.

"Sit up please, Bobby," said Coach DeLeone.

Bobby sat up.

"Thank you."

The final lesson of their miserable season took the form of a pop quiz: Coach DeLeone called the name of a lineman and a play. The lineman was meant to respond with his assignment on that play. The air was soon thick with jargon and code. "Rip" and "Liz" and "Willie" and "Philly" and "Rum" and "Pookie" and "Trios" and "A-Gaps" and "3-Techniques." A gifted student of language would require a month to grasp it all. Throughout DeLeone kept one eye on his most troubling pupil, Michael Oher. Michael was now Ole Miss's starting right guard. A third of the time he had no idea where he was meant to go, or whom he was meant to block. The other two thirds, when he knew what he was supposed to do, and was sure of himself, he'd beaten up on much older opposing players. He'd pancaked a linebacker at Tennessee, and another at Alabama, both future NFL draft picks. After he'd crushed the Tennessee kid, and as he sat on top of him, he'd gotten into his face and said, "You lucky, if I'd come here to school, you'd be getting this every day." You had to like the kid's confidence—taking it that way to a senior all-conference linebacker. And, as confused as he was at times, he'd had games after which the film revealed him as the best performing lineman on the team. "He's getting by on his raw athletic ability," said Matt Luke, a former college lineman himself turned Ole Miss assistant coach. "It's the best I've ever seen. And my entire college line except me is in the NFL."

The games in which Michael had excelled also happened to be the games before which Sean Tuohy had sat down with him for six hours or so and reviewed the plays. Now he sat rubbing his knees, pushing down so hard on them with his hands he seemed to be trying to rip off a layer of his own skin. ("That's a nervous reaction he has," said Leigh Anne.)

He'd put fifty hours into this course for every hour he had put into math or English. But of all the courses he had taken, the course in playing offensive line had proved the most difficult. It *was* the most difficult. The plays were all new to him, and in a code foreign to him, and on each play there were a mind-numbing number of variations. On a football team, only the quarterback experienced the same level of complexity as the offensive line. As Michael struggled to organize inside his mind the blizzard of new material, this sixty-something-year-old coach with his funny East Coast accent kept hollering in his ear. Coach DeLeone prided himself on his rigor and the high expectations he had for his players. "One of my players misses a class I'm here at six in the morning running him," he said. "I know this: I don't see a lot of history professors out there running people around the building."

Today—the last day of preparation for the Mississippi State

Bulldogs—is in theory a review. In fact, the coaches, grasping at straws, have put in new plays, with new terminology. Michael Oher isn't the only lineman who has no clue what's going on.

"Michael Oher!"

Michael stirred, uneasily.

"Twenty-eight Gem," barked his coach. "Gem tells the right guard to do what?"

"Go get the Mac," Michael said. The Mac is the middle line-backer. Unless he's the Mike. The main thing is he's not the Willie or the Sam—the nicknames for the other linebackers.

"Go get the Mac," said DeLeone, approvingly.

Michael knew that much. But—he was thinking, as he sat there—the Mac moved around. So did every other player on a college defense. What if the Mac wasn't where he was supposed to be? "The problem is," he said later, "I got eight guys running in front of me two seconds before the ball's snapped." Back at Briarcrest they had three basic running plays, and Michael had been assigned to block the same man no matter what the defense. Ole Miss had dozens of running plays, with half a dozen different blocking assignments on each of them. Whom he blocked, and how he blocked them, depended on where the defenders stood at the snap of the ball. There was a good reason for the new complexity. In high school if some defender came free and went unblocked—well, the team would take that risk for the sake of keeping things simple. In college the coaches couldn't risk a defender going completely unblocked, because the defenders were so routinely dangerous. A defender who went completely unblocked in the SEC could end the quarterback's season.

"This is the last time to talk about these assignments," DeLeone shouted. "We got to nail this, men!"

It was as if Coach DeLeone had read his thoughts. Even though he'd given him the right answer, the coach seemed upset. He was getting himself all worked up again.

"You must step up!" shouted Coach DeLeone.

He'd changed gears. He meant this literally—that when the ball was snapped the linemen needed to step forward, not backward. "Both guards last week stepped on the quarterback," the line coach continued. "This *cannot* happen this week." Last week they'd played LSU and lost 40–7. Against LSU the Ole Miss quarterback had gone down several times, in the most embarrassing way possible, with his foot pinned to the ground by one of his own linemen. At least one of those feet had been Michael's.

"You must step up!!" He was screaming again. "You must step up!! We got that, Michael Oher??"

Coach DeLeone's face was red, but his toenail was still black and blue from having been stepped on during practice, two months before, by Michael Oher.

"Yes, sir," said Michael. He thought: *If this old guy doesn't calm down, he's gonna have a heart attack right here and die.* But, once again, the coach calmed himself. "What's the deal with Mississippi State?" he asked, innocently.

The linemen searched in each other's blank faces for the right answer, but failed to locate it. It was Bobby Harris who finally ventured a guess.

"That we hate them?" he said.

"Someone is saying that the Mississippi State coach is guaranteeing a win," said DeLeone, incredulously. "They think that much of us that they're *guaranteeing* a win?"

Ah—that was it. A faint stab at a motivational speech. But that wasn't Coach DeLeone's job. Which was just as well, as it was time to go listen to Coach O.

TEN MINUTES LATER Coach O had his football team arranged before him. One final pre-game speech to deliver before he could put this dreadful season behind him. He waited for them to quit horsing around, which they always seemed to need to do for at least ninety seconds, and then strolled with authority to the podium.

"Let me say this about Mississippi State," he began.

He paused for dramatic effect.

"They hate you, we hate them."

He paused again. No one could disagree.

"I purposefully have not had much for the other team. 'Cause I don't respect them much. I say I respect them in the paper. I don't respect 'em. I don't have *nuthin'* for them. The other guy has been putting up the scores of last year."

He hardly needed to explain himself because everyone in the room already understood. They might not have read the papers but they had at least heard the rumor that Sylvester Croom, Mississippi State's head coach, has been riling up his players by posting the scores from past defeats at the hands of Ole Miss. Croom also stood accused of trash-talking. He'd gone in front of a group of Mississippi State boosters, spoken about Ole Miss, and gotten himself quoted in the papers. All he'd actually said was "I don't ever think about Ole Miss. If our kids play as well as they can, we're going to beat their butt." But every right-thinking Ole Miss football fan and player must agree that Croom has violated football decorum— which is of course only what you'd expect from a Mississippi State football coach. "This is totally wrong," Coach O now says. "Let's put these guys *way* below our program. Think about class and Ole Miss. Think about how we are, think about how they are."

A Great Lake of Rednecks!

"Understand that their team is going to come out fired up," he continues. "He [Coach Croom] didn't even let 'em go home for Thanksgiving. Wanted 'em all living in a hotel in Starkville. *Dumpy ass* hotel in Starkville. I can just about imagine it."

Coach O actually didn't share the social pretensions of his employer. He was just a good ol' boy who didn't present himself as anything but a good ol' boy—he said his boyhood idea of going out to a fancy restaurant was driving thirty miles to Kentucky Fried Chicken. He'd have been perfectly content in a dumpy ass hotel in Starkville. He was just speaking from the Ole Miss script—and doing it well, in view of the circumstances.

The circumstances were that the Ole Miss football team, like the Mississippi State football team, consisted mostly of poor black kids from Mississippi. When the Ole Miss defense gathered in a single room, the only white people were coaches. On the football field the players became honorary white people, but off it they were still black, and unnatural combatants in Mississippi's white internecine war. Even as Coach O worked to fire them up for the game, many of the seniors had their bags packed and their cars running. After the game they'd vanish, en masse, from the Ole Miss campus. They'd just walk right out of the locker room and get in their cars and drive away. Several who might have stayed and picked up their degrees will decide it wasn't worth hanging around five months to do it. They'll have spent four years shuttling between their off-campus apartments, their Criminal Justice classes, and football practice on the off chance of making it to the NFL.

Coach O was finished imagining the dumpy ass hotel in Starkville. It clearly pained him to dwell on the negative qualities of their opponents; he was by nature a positive man. He wanted to end on a positive note. "You come to school here," he said, seriously. "You graduate. You go to the NFL. That's what I want our program to be." And then he began to ramble, sounding like a man talking in his sleep.

"Just gonna win tomorrow," he said. "Focus. Details. Let's focus."

THE NEXT MORNING the Ole Miss Rebels' buses rolled into Starkville. At Ole Miss there was money in the air; here there was just hostility, and the sights and sounds of resentment. Every State fan carried a cowbell, and rang it incessantly, as they hurled insults at the Ole Miss players. The players changed into their uniforms on cold concrete floors, and hung their street clothes in old wooden cubbyholes. Once dressed, they crowded into the foyer outside the locker room, like soldiers on a troop carrier about to storm a beach. That's when one spotted, beneath a pile of cardboard boxes, empty Gatorade bottles, and surgical tape, an oddly shaped trophy badly in need of polishing.

"*Dat* da egg?" he asked, incredulously.

Another player looked over, then another. The Ole Miss staff had brought the old trophy along with them, in case they lost and had to hand it over.

"Dat is da egg," said someone else.

With that, they raced out onto the field, to the clanging of cowbells and hoots of derision. Never mind the barnlike quality of the locker room; never mind the rickety old stadium itself: the football field was a work of art. There was no substance on earth more lush or thick or green or beautiful. Turfology, as it happened, was Mississippi State's great academic strength. At the mention of State's turf-tending skills, the Ole Miss snob would become serious and acknowledge that, whatever you might want to say about State, they knew how to grow golf courses. "Don't forget to look down and check out the grass!" had been one of two pieces of advice Sean had given Michael before he left for the game. The other was, "Never take your helmet off in Starkville."

And Michael didn't, but more out of shame than fear of being brained by a beer bottle. The game took the Ole Miss team through a speeded-up version of the emotions of their season. First came hope: five plays into the game the Ole Miss quarterback, Ethan Flatt, hit his fastest receiver, Taye Biddle, for a 41-yard touchdown pass. But Biddle, one of the seniors who would quit school immediately after the game, might as well have kept on running out the back of the end zone and into his car. Ole Miss never called that play again. Instead, their offensive brain trust decided to use their unbelievably slow, fifth-string running back to test the strong interior of the Mississippi State defense. In the press box before the game, the Ole Miss offensive coordinator, Noel Mazzone, happened to walk past a TV on which was playing a North Carolina State football game. Six months earlier, Mazzone had left his job running the North Carolina State offense to take the job of running the Ole Miss offense. Seeing his former team on TV he snorted and said, loudly enough for journalists to overhear, "Should have stayed there, at least they had some players."

Bill Walsh had shown how much an imaginative coach might achieve even with mediocre talent; Noel Mazzone was demonstrating how little could be achieved by a coach who did not admit any role for the imagination. The next five times Ole Miss had the ball Mazzone used the opportunity to prove that his slow, fifth-string running back couldn't run through a giant pile of bodies in the middle of the field. Once the Ole Miss offense faced third and long, as it invariably did, everyone in the stadium knew a pass was coming. There was nothing for the Ole Miss quarterback to do but drop back and wait to be buried under the Mississippi State blitz. Most of the time, just before he was crushed, he managed to throw an incomplete pass or an interception.

Three punts and two interceptions later Mississippi State led 21–7. Rather than try a different strategy—say, the surprising pass play that had worked the first time they had the ball—the Ole Miss coaches tried different players. First they switched their fifth-string running back out for their sixth-string running back. (Between them they ran the ball twenty-five times for 31 yards.) Then they switched their first-string quarterback out for their second-string quarterback—the fellow who had started the season as the first-string quarterback. (Between them they threw four interceptions.) The frantic search for the right combination of players reflected their more general football worldview: they believed in talent rather than strategy. They placed less emphasis on how players were used than who they were. Whoever had the best players won: it was as simple as that.

It was a bleak and deterministic worldview, implying, as it did, that there was little a strategist could do to raise the value of his players. More to the point, it was a false view, at least for running a football offense. The beauty of the football offense was that it allowed for a smart strategist to compensate for his players' limitations. He might find better ways to use players, to maximize their strengths and minimize their weaknesses. He might even change the players' sense of themselves. But Ole Miss not only lacked a smart strategist: it lacked a coach who understood the importance of strategy. The genius of Bill Walsh was missing; so, for that matter, was the genius of Leigh Anne Tuohy. There wasn't a soul on the Ole Miss sidelines thinking seriously how to make the most of what another person could do. They were all stuck dwelling on what other people couldn't do.

After each failed series the linemen trotted to the bench and plunked themselves down for a chalk talk delivered by assistant line coach Matt Luke. This served mainly to highlight their near-total confusion. After one series the right tackle, Tre Stallings, confessed he had gone the wrong way because he thought the center, Daryl Harris, had shouted "Philly," when he had in fact shouted "Willie." After another series there ensued a long argument—for them— about the difference between "G" and "Gem." After a third series three of the linemen got screamed at for firing out and blocking linebackers instead of blocking the linemen right in front of them. After a fourth series a coach thrust a headset at Michael Oher so that Michael could listen to Coach DeLeone, up in the press box, holler at him to try harder. After a fifth series the left guard, Andrew Wicker, hurled his helmet on the ground and shouted,

"We're getting our ass kicked by *State*." And they were—largely because none of them had any clear idea what he was meant to do on any given play.

By halftime hope was rapidly giving way to denial. At the start of the third quarter denial gave way to depression, with hardly a pause for the intermediate stages of bargaining and anger. The change came on a single play. With Ole Miss down 21–14, the team had the ball and began, slowly, to move it. It was, as always, third and long, and the Ole Miss quarterback, Michael Spurlock, called for a pass. That in itself posed a problem, as he was only about five nine, and unable to see over the linemen. To compensate for his stature, Spurlock had the habit of just taking off toward the sideline the minute he received the ball. The price he paid for his new view of the field was to render himself nearly useless as a passer— he was running too fast to throw the ball with accuracy—and to confuse the linemen assigned to protect him, as they had no idea where he was.

On this play it hardly mattered. Ole Miss had lined up with two tight ends: both ran the wrong way and missed their blocks. Ole Miss had a tailback: he, too, ran the wrong way and failed to block the defender he was meant to block. Three of the five Ole Miss linemen—Michael plus the center plus the left guard—all blocked a single Mississippi State defensive tackle. With most of Ole Miss's blockers ungainfully employed, a Bulldog linebacker shot through a gap and sacked the Rebel quarterback for a 20-yard loss, almost killing him in the bargain. After that Coach DeLeone, watching from the press box, yanked Michael Oher from the game. Michael ended his season on the bench, a simmering symbol of his coach's frustration.

From his seat beside his wife, high in the stands, Sean Tuohy watched the loss take shape with the calm of an asset manager who long ago banked his annual returns. In the grand scheme of Michael's career this one game—this entire season—didn't matter.

Just by taking the field as a freshman, Michael's stock remained high. Sean's main goal had been to make sure that Michael didn't have the same experience of college sports that he had had, and that Michael didn't wind up depending on the mercy or the intelligence of his coaches. Now Sean understood that the Ole Miss coaches needed Michael far more than he needed them. Their careers were at stake; Michael could always transfer—a fact Leigh Anne had brought to the attention of the Ole Miss coaches more than once. Leigh Anne had already told Coach O that if Noel Mazzone and George DeLeone returned to run the Ole Miss offense for one more year, Michael would not—and the two coaches were almost sure to be gone after this game. Michael didn't need to worry about the bigger picture; the bigger picture was arranging itself to maximize his value. "See how his face looks right now," said Sean, his binoculars trained on Michael. Michael's upper lip was tucked under his lower, and his eyes stared straight ahead at nothing. "That's how he looks when he's planning on not talking to anyone for a while." He could afford to pout.

THE DAY AFTER his team's embarrassing 35–14 loss to Mississippi State, Coach O fired his offensive coordinator and began to look for a new offensive line coach. Then he sat down and wrote out his depth chart for the 2006 football season. The first name he moved around was Michael Oher's. Michael became Ole Miss's starting left tackle. "If I could do it over," said the head coach, "I'd have just put him there to begin with and let him figure it out."

The plan started with Michael Oher but didn't end there. Coach O might not have Bill Walsh's gift for taking average talent and tricking it into being better, but he knew how to find and attract great talent. Over the next few months he set out to pluck the finest football talent from the junior colleges and high schools of America—and, to judge from the high marks he received from the recruiting services, he appeared to have succeeded. At the center of this effort, oddly enough, was Michael Oher. "In every conversation Michael's name came up," he said. "He was my tool. And when we had the top guys on campus, I had him show them around."

Michael walked away from his freshman season wondering what that had all been about. And then, strangely, the honors began to roll in. He was named a First Team Freshman All-American, and First Team Freshman All-SEC. He was named pre-season All-SEC by magazines and also by the SEC's coaches. *College Football Weekly* listed him the best player on the Ole Miss offense. His value, once perceived, was indestructible. He could play on one of the worst football offenses in the nation and nobody would hold it against him. The experience had been a blur. But all anyone seemed to care about was that (a) he was still the biggest guy on the field and a freakishly gifted athlete, (b) he'd picked up the college game faster than anyone had the right to expect, and (c) when he knew what he was supposed to do, he'd knocked some folks around. And while that wasn't as often as anyone would have liked, it had been often enough that players and coaches now knew he'd eventually figure it out.

So often given the benefit of doubts, Michael Oher now set out to confirm the wisdom of the people who showed such faith in him. After the season, for the first time in his life, he hit the weight room. Six months later he emerged a different shape; he went in a square and came out an inverted triangle. He went in being able to bench-press 225 pounds and came out bench-pressing nearly 400 pounds. He went in weighing 345 pounds and came out weighing 320—without, it seemed, an ounce of fat on him.

But there still lingered this ominous feeling about him. He might be injured at any time, of course, but that wasn't the source of the feeling. There was another, more disturbing risk, because it was harder to pin down. He could never shake entirely the place he had come from, and he could never change entirely who he was born. Every now and then, for instance, he'd go back to his old neighborhood and when he did bad things often happened. At Leigh Anne's urging he had gone to see his mother—and the next thing Leigh Anne knew she was getting a call from a clearly flustered Big Tony, and the only words she could understand were "truck" and "dead" and that Michael was in the custody of the Memphis police. When Michael had arrived at his mother's house he'd found the police there, arresting her. For some reason she'd been driving around in a truck that belonged to a man the police had just found, murdered. The police had asked Michael why he was there, he'd told them, and they'd put him in handcuffs and taken him to central lockup. Sean had sprung him, then given Michael a little speech about black people and the police and the unlikelihood of the former being treated graciously or even fairly by the latter. When a police officer told Michael to do something, no matter how rudely he put it, Michael was to say "yes, sir" and do it. And his first telephone call should be to Sean Tuohy.

In theory, when Michael went away to Ole Miss, he put some distance between himself and the hand reaching out from his past. But Michael had left behind inner-city social risks only to find that inner-city social risks had followed him to Oxford, Mississippi. One friend and teammate, having failed his Ole Miss classes, left school and went right back to his old neigborhood to peddle drugs—because it was the only way he knew how to make money. His three closest friends on the Ole Miss team all had children. One, Jamarca Stanford, had become a father at fifteen. Another friend was a tough defensive end named Peria (he pronounced it Pur-*Ray*) Jerry. Peria had so little knowledge of math or English he might as well never have been to school. Miss Sue not only tutored him, and got him reading and adding fractions, she mothered him incessantly. Michael didn't fully approve—he thought Miss Sue was *his*. One day he blurted out to Miss Sue, "You love Peria more than you love me." "I'll never love any of them more than I love you," said Miss Sue. "But he's catching up!" said Michael, outraged.

And he was: one day Peria looked at Miss Sue with tears in his eyes and said, "Nobody ever loved me till you," and it was all Miss Sue could do not to break down right there. Peria was so big that you forgot he was still, in most ways, just another needy child.

There were at least a dozen black football players from impoverished backgrounds auditioning for the role of Eliza Doolittle. ("I wish I could get me an adopted family," said Peria.) No one asked Leigh Anne for a shirt with a little alligator on it. But they all longed for some connection and the sense of being taken care of. Michael brought them home to Memphis, and so Leigh Anne got some idea of the risks to keeping Michael on the straight and narrow. To Thanksgiving dinner, for instance, Michael had invited a freshman linebacker named Quentin Taylor, who had no place else to go. At the start of the meal Michael leaned over and whispered, sternly, "Quentin, you're supposed to put your napkin in your lap." Right after that, Quentin let it drop that he had fathered three children by two different mothers. Leigh Anne pulled the carving knife from the turkey and said, "Quentin, you can do what you want and it's your own business. But if Michael Oher does that I'm cutting his penis off." From the look on Quentin's face Michael could see he didn't think she was joking. "She would, too," said Michael, without breaking a smile.

All these surprisingly good things were happening to Michael Oher. Still there was a sense that something surprisingly bad could happen at any time. And it did.

ONE AFTERNOON, long after their miserable season was over, Michael sat on the front steps of his dormitory with a couple of teammates. Up walked another teammate, a freshman linebacker named Antonio Turner. Antonio had visited the Tuohy home in

Memphis, and apparently he didn't like what he had seen. Now he made a number of unflattering remarks about white people generally and about Michael's "cracker family" specifically. When he called Michael a "cracker," Michael gave him a shove, and Antonio punched him in the face—then ran. Michael gave chase, and the two of them raced in circles around a parked car like a couple of cartoon characters. Finally, Antonio said something about Collins and Leigh Anne Tuohy. What exactly he said no one ever exactly learned—and Michael refused to repeat it. But it had something to do with Antonio's intention to have sex with Michael's white sister, but only after he'd had sex with Michael's white mother. Whereupon Michael said he was going to his dorm room to change his clothes, because he didn't want to get Antonio's blood on his nice shirt.

When Michael walked back into the dorm to find a shirt he didn't mind spoiling with Antonio's blood, Antonio took off at a sprint. He ran to the redbrick study hall with the darkened windows used by the football players and monitored by tutors. Surrounded by teammates and white tutors, he figured he'd be safe. He figured wrong.

Michael knew he didn't need to run. He knew where Antonio had gone—there was no place else to go where Antonio would think he was safe. Michael walked across campus, calmly stalking his prey. Finally, he came to the study hall. There, in a small room filled with half a dozen players and tutors, he found Antonio, and charged.

Force equals mass times acceleration, as Hugh Freeze said, and when Michael's mass comes at you at Michael's speed, it's just an incredible force. With that incredible force he drove Antonio into the ground. Then he picked him up with one hand by the throat and lifted him straight off the ground. Antonio weighed 230 pounds but in Michael's big hand he looked, as one player later put it, "like a rag doll." Michael beat Antonio around the face and threw him across the room as, around the room, huge football players took cover beneath small desks.

That's when a lot of people at once began to scream hysterically and Michael noticed the little white boy on the floor, in a pool of blood. He hadn't seen the little white boy—the three-year-old son of one of the tutors. Who had put the little white boy there? When he'd charged Antonio, the boy somehow had been hit and thrown up against the wall. His head was now bleeding badly. Seeing the body lying in his own blood, Michael ran.

Antonio, a sobbing wreck, was taken to the home of running back coach Frank Wilson, for his own protection. He was still alive, and the Ole Miss coaches planned to keep him that way. Back in the study hall Miss Sue sat listening to another football player, a linebacker named Robert Russell. She told him she didn't understand why these disputes must be resolved with violence. "Miss Sue," he said, "Michael and I weren't raised that way. No matter how much you try to wash us up behind the ears, we're going to go back to what we know."

Hugh Freeze called Leigh Anne, who was up in Memphis. Like a zoo director discussing a crazed rhinoceros with its trainer, he said, "You got to get down here and find him. You're the only one who can control him." Leigh Anne jumped in her car, took off for Oxford—and then stopped. Michael was gone, no one knew where he was, and she didn't actually believe she could find him. She pulled over to the side of the road and called Sean, who was somewhere on the West Coast with the Memphis Grizzlies. It was Sean who said, "He's running because that's all he knows how to do." He wasn't out looking for someone to kill. He was just trying to escape his predicament. Just a few months earlier Sean would have been shocked. But now he knew that when Michael got into trouble, he ran. He knew it because not long after Michael had left for Ole Miss he'd had an argument with Miss Sue and vanished for two days. He wouldn't return phone calls—nothing. Late one night, Sean and Leigh Anne had turned to each other in bed and considered the possibility that Michael Oher might never come back. That he'd just used them to get what he'd wanted and that he actually had no real feelings for them. "You think this is it?" Leigh Anne had asked. And the truth was, Sean didn't know. "Your mind does funny things when it's idle," said Sean. "But that's when I decided that the downside was that we'd helped some kid—so even if he'd been playing us all along there really was no downside."

But he knew something else, too. He knew that Michael had spent his life running. Not long before, he'd been in his Memphis office when a woman named Bobby Spivey, who worked for the Tennessee Department of Children's Services, finally returned his call. Spivey was the officer who had handled Michael's case. Sean had phoned her three times to see what he could learn about the missing years in Michael's life, and each time he found himself in conversation with Spivey's voice mail box.* Now, finally, Spivey herself was on his speaker phone, and embarrassed to say that most of the details of Michael's case were unavailable. The Department of Children's Services had lost his file. She remembered very clearly some things about Michael Oher, however. She recalled, for instance, the night that Children's Services had sent the police to remove seven-year-old Michael Oher from his mother's care.

"It was raining that night," said Bobby Spivey. "She was homeless. She was on drugs. Someone called the police and said she was walking around in the rain with her kids."

She recalled that Michael Oher had been taken away and put into a foster home—but that he hadn't stayed. "He was a runaway

---

* He called only after I'd found Bobby Spivey's name and pestered him to use his status as legal guardian to learn what he could about Michael's early childhood.

a majority of the time," she said, laconically. "He was real quiet. He wasn't disrespectful. He just ran." Eventually, the Memphis branch of the Tennessee Department of Children's Services had given up looking for Michael Oher. "He ran so much that we stopped trying to stop him," said this woman who had handled his case. The government had officially taken charge of Michael at the age of seven, she said, but lost track of him around his tenth birthday. She was curious to know what had become of him.

CHAPTER ELEVEN

FREAK OF NURTURE

NCAA Lady: Can I ask you this—

Sean: He has no hate. No animosity. His memories are all good.

NCAA Lady: To be quite honest with you—do you fully know his childhood?

Sean: Oh, absolutely not. First of all he doesn't have a great relationship with *me*. Because he never had a daddy. I'm more of just an older man. He'll talk to my daughter or my wife. But we don't ask questions like that. Because a lot of times we don't want the answers.

NCAA Lady: You don't care.

Sean: I only care about what he cares about.

NCAA Lady: You don't ask, I should say.

Sean: We're trying to take care of geometry class tomorrow. What happened when he was four years old—if he's okay by it, we're okay by it. The timeline to us, we figure it'll come one day. We're in no hurry. We got a long time.

———

DENISE OHER COULDN'T SAY who murdered her father—just that he had been shot several times in his bed when she was a little girl. She couldn't tell you exactly when she had been removed from her mother's custody. She knew her mother was an alcoholic and totally incapable of taking care of her and her half-brother, Robert Faulkner. Her mother never cooked her a meal, read her a book, or took her to school—at least, not that she could recall. One day the police came for them, and took her and Robert away to an orphanage. She still didn't feel especially cared for—she never felt loved or anything like that. She skipped plenty of school, and even more when, at the age of fifteen, her mother somehow sprung her from the institution. Once out she fell in with the wrong crowd. It led her to drugs and other things and, at twenty, she gave birth to a baby boy. Four more babies soon followed. Around the neighborhood people would say, "Dee Dee is a breeder." And she was: inside of six years she had five little boys. Their father, she felt sure, was a man named Odell Watkins, but he declined the offer from the Department of Children's Services to acknowledge his paternity. Instead he took a DNA test. The test proved, just as she'd said all along, that Odell Watkins was the father.

By the late summer of 1985 Dee Dee was twenty-seven years old, and finished with Odell Watkins. She wasn't even half-finished having babies, however, and the father of her next child had just arrived on her front porch. He came directly to her from Robert, her brother.

Since they'd left the orphanage Robert had gotten the nickname "Skillet." Oddly enough, it was a skillet, and then a horseshoe, that Robert later used to crush his wife's skull after she told him she wanted a divorce. His wife's brutal murder landed Robert on Death Row at River Bend over in Nashville; but that all came later. The first time Robert had been thrown in jail for murder he'd been sent away for just a few years. Denise couldn't tell you who Robert had killed, or why. She just knew that her brother had been convicted for murder and sent away to Fort Pillow prison, where he'd met a man named Michael Jerome Williams. Why Michael Jerome Williams had been in jail Dee Dee either didn't know or would soon forget. All she knew was that Robert had wanted to send word to her of his well-being and that Michael Jerome Williams, on his way out of jail, had been kind enough to serve as messenger. "When I met him I wasn't with nobody," said Dee Dee. "We got to talking and we wound up together. But he was a little bitty fellow. Five foot six, maybe."

Soon after Michael Williams visited her, Dee Dee discovered she was pregnant again. She had no money, no job, and was now flirting with a serious drug problem—but still she didn't worry about the welfare of this new baby. "God put it there," she said, "and He ain't going to put no mouth on this earth he can't feed." Unlike Odell Watkins, Michael Williams didn't dispute his paternity, and she named the baby after him: Michael Jerome Williams.

But right around the time the child was born, Michael Jerome Williams vanished. The Department of Children's Services went looking for him, and it was a full year before they found him—back in prison. By then Dee Dee had decided she didn't want her baby named for Michael Jerome Williams. Though she made no effort to change the baby's legal name, she began to call him "Michael Oher." Oher was her family name, which she had taken from her mother.

In the next four years Denise bore four more children, by several different fathers, none of whom stuck around. By the time Michael was five years old, and his memory kicked in to record events for posterity, Dee Dee was caring for seven boys and three girls, all under the age of fifteen. Only she wasn't really caring for anyone, as she'd become addicted to crack cocaine. "On the first of the month she'd get a check," recalled Marcus, Michael's eldest brother, "and she'd leave and we wouldn't see her until the tenth. . . . Them drugs tear everything up." As Dee Dee had no income except for whatever the government sent her on the first of each month, the children had no money for provisions. They had no food or clothing, except what they could scrounge from churches and the street. Surprisingly often, given the abundance of public housing in Memphis, they had no shelter. When asked what he recalls of his first six years, Michael said, "Going for days having to drink water to get full. Going to other people's houses and asking for something to eat. Sleeping outside. The mosquitoes." The winter was cold, but the summer was worse because the heat was so oppressive and the mosquitoes bit all night long.

Yet, by the time Michael turned seven his greatest fear was that some man in a uniform would come and take him away from his mother. His mother had her problems but she was never overtly cruel: she never hit them, for instance, and she often said she loved them. She just wasn't around that much and, when she was around, had nothing to give them. Marcus, now sixteen years old, knew that the police sometimes broke up families such as theirs. They'd heard snippets about foster homes, and the snippets hadn't been reassuring. The police just took you away and dumped you with people whose only interest in you was the cash they received for your presence. Michael's brothers spoke of the possibility that the police might take them away, and decided that, whatever happened, they would try to stick together.

On April 14, 1994, the Memphis courts, for the first time, registered Michael's existence. Listing Michael's name, as well as the names of his siblings, it rendered the following verdict: "It appears to this Court that said children are in need of immediate protection of this Court and that said children are subject to an immediate threat of said children's health to the extent that delay for a hearing would be likely to result in severe or irreparable harm."

A month before Michael's eighth birthday, the police cars rolled up in front of the shed behind the cottage that Denise had told the children belonged to a cousin of hers. The three little girls were out in front. Andre and Rico were someplace else. The four other boys—Marcus, Deljuan, Carlos, and Michael—were inside the shed. "We seen them pull up and we already knew what they were coming for," said Marcus. "We done seen it happen before with other people. We really thought they were going to scatter us up." Seeing the police, Marcus turned to his brothers and said, "Run!"

Michael prided himself on his foot speed. "I can fly," he liked to say. Speed was essential to the new plans he had for himself—plans he would cling to, with an amazing tenacity, for the next ten years. On June 20, 1993, he had been inside someone else's house and seen a basketball game on television. On that night Michael Jordan was using the Phoenix Suns as his foil for the public display of his greatness. The moment he saw Michael Jordan play basketball, Michael Oher knew who he was meant to be: the next Michael Jordan. Because he was seven, he thought it was an original idea. Because he was quiet, the idea went unexpressed, and so undisturbed.

But Michael Oher now had a secret ambition, and it would define much of what he did with himself for the next ten years. The ambition stood in defiance of a world that had assigned him no value. His father hadn't valued him enough to meet him. His mother hadn't valued him enough to feed him. He'd never been to a doctor, or been given medicine of any sort. He'd missed nearly as much school as he'd made. His older brothers cared for him and were good at finding food. But they had their own problems; they had no real ability to nurture. No one invested in Michael Oher, and so he yielded no visible returns. Michael did not consider himself without value, however. From the moment he laid eyes on Michael Jordan, he was, himself, destined to become the richest and most famous black athlete on earth.

When the police cars came and his brother screamed at him to run, Michael didn't really know what was going on. He just saw Marcus (sixteen), Deljuan (thirteen), and Carlos (eleven) sprinting out the back door. He flew after them. To be the next Michael Jordan, Michael Oher needed to be quick and agile—and he was. His older brothers were still faster than he was, but Michael pumped his little legs as fast as they'd go, and he finally caught up to them. When they'd finished running they stood on the second floor of an abandoned auto repair shop down the street, huffing and puffing. From a broken window they watched their mother scream as the police took away her three baby girls—Denise, Tara, and Depthia—and put them in the back of the squad car. Marcus told his brothers that they'd probably never see those little girls again, and he was right.

Dee Dee wasn't capable of caring for her children, and she knew it, but she didn't want anyone taking them away from her. The boys wanted to stay together; they felt safe together; together they at least had each other. They all knew that the police would be back for the boys, and so they left the shed. Dee Dee got her hands—she wouldn't say how—on an old beat-up Monte Carlo. For weeks she and the seven boys slept in the car. "Bodies on top of each other," is how Deljuan, who was now thirteen, recalled it. "We'd get up in the morning and go wash ourselves in the bathroom of a service station."

Unwilling to leave the small area on the west side of Memphis where she'd been born and raised, Dee Dee found herself at a disadvantage. A few weeks after the police nabbed her daughters, they caught up to Carlos and Michael on a day they attended school. The police took them from school to the home of a woman they'd never met, named Velma Jones. "Velma was a big lady," said Carlos, "about three hundred seventy-five pounds, and she got angry when you made her move." The children found her terrifying—and their fear was only heightened when she showed them what she did to children who misbehaved: sat on them. That was Michael's most vivid memory of the first few days, being sat on by Velma Jones. Carlos recalled being taken, with Michael, to the home of Velma's equally gargantuan twin sister, Thelma, who made them mop out the raw sewage that had spilled into her basement from a burst pipe. It was the first of a long series of unpleasant chores the boys were expected to perform for the fat twins.

BUT THAT WAS JUST the beginning of their misery. The house teemed with other foster children, older and bigger than Michael and Carlos, who picked on them. (When asked how many foster children the State of Tennessee had deposited with her, Velma later said, "I really don't know. I just got so much love and patience and energies. They just brought 'em to me.") Velma had a single biological child whom, in Carlos's view, she spoiled. She sent Carlos and Michael out to sell newspapers on Sundays, and when they returned she took away the money they'd made and gave it to her child. "Living with The Twins wudn't no happy thing," said Carlos. "They just treated us like we weren't people. Every night Mike cried hisself to sleep." The two boys slept in their first bunk bed, only Michael's lower bunk couldn't be called a bed, as it had no mattress. "I was sleeping on wood," he said. Carlos remembers Michael saying, almost every night, 'Carlos, I just want to go home.'"

Two nights into their stay Michael ran away, all by himself. ("I can fly.") He was just seven years old, but still he ran right across Memphis and found his mother. Dee Dee told him that she had to take him right back to the foster home or they would all get in trouble, and Michael cried all the way back. A few weeks later he ran again—with the same result. Once his mother came to visit him. "That was a happy day," he said. "Yes, that was my one happy day." He and Carlos stayed with Velma Jones for nearly two years. Then, one afternoon, Velma sat them down and told them they were going to be sent to Knoxville. She might as well have said they were being sent to the moon. Neither had ever left a tiny little area in western Memphis. She told them to go back to their room, pack their few things, and prepare to leave. They went back to their room, ignored their few things, and jumped out the window.

This time it took the police two days to track them down. The Department of Children's Services had noted by now that Michael was a runner, and they must have requested some sort of psychological evaluation. At any rate, instead of packing him straight back to foster care, they took him to St. Joseph's Hospital. There he was deposited on what he took to be "the floor for bad kids." They subjected him to tests that caused him to conclude later that they were seeing if he'd gone crazy. But it wasn't half-bad; and the living conditions were a vast improvement on the foster home. "We had good food," he said. "I had a bed with a mattress. They even had videos."

Michael had just turned ten years old. After two weeks in the hospital, he ached to go home. "It got old," he said. "You want to be free after a while." Incredible as it might seem to anyone who knew only the bare facts of his case rather than his emotional predisposition, he missed his mother. It was as if Dee Dee had been put on earth to answer a question: how little can a mother care for her children and still retain their affection? His mother hadn't cared for him, but still he loved her. "I guess you're just supposed to love your mom," he said later. "Just because she's your mom." That hard-to-shake feeling would explain why, much later, when he was asked for the first time about his mother and her problems with drugs, he would stare blankly and pretend the subject didn't bother him. But when asked a second time, his brown eyes filled with tears.

The doors on both ends of the floor were locked. The hospital was old—it would soon be torn down—and Michael noticed that the big metal doors at one end of the hall rattled. "I remember it like it was yesterday, actually," he said later. "We'd play up and down the floor. And at the end of the floor was an exit. One of those two-door exits that closed together with a lock between 'em. I got a sheet of paper and folded it together and stuck it down there. And it opened." At his moment of discovery there were too many people wandering around for him to escape cleanly. He kept his secret, and his piece of paper, to himself the rest of the day. "That night when I went to bed I kissed the paper and put it under my little pillow," he said. Between his room and the locked door a nurse's station intervened. The nurse at the window could monitor the entire hall. Early the next morning, when the halls were clear, he crawled on his belly directly beneath the window of the nurse's station. He reached the door without being seen, jimmied it open with his paper tool, and fled.

Now he found himself in a dark, concrete stairwell. Downward he plunged. "Door here, door there, and I was out," he said. "Like a thief in the night." ("We never did figure how he got out of there," said Bobby Spivey, of the Memphis Department of Children's Services.)

When he reached the street Michael still had no idea where he was. He wound up wandering for hours to cover what he later realized had been no more than half a mile between the hospital and a housing project called Dixie Homes. He arrived to find that his mother had moved again, from Dixie Homes into one of the most depressing public housing projects in Memphis: Hurt Village. Hurt Village had been built for white people back in the 1950s. The opening of its 450 units spread over 29 acres had been hailed by the mayor as "a great day in the history of Memphis." By the late 1980s it was occupied only by blacks, who were fleeing the place as fast as they could. Hurt Village had become an inferno of gangs and drugs and crime. The city had decided to rip it down, but didn't have the money to do the job. To spare themselves the expense of relocating the residents, the Memphis Public Housing Authority simply stopped maintaining their apartments. Without functioning air-conditioning, stoves, or refrigerators, the units became so unlivable that anyone who could leave, did. Once they'd left, the city came in and boarded up the abandoned apartment.

It was in Hurt Village that Michael found his mother. He checked in, then ran back to Dixie Homes and hid inside the place she'd vacated. Carlos soon materialized, and together they went on the lam. During the day they remained hidden; at night they came out and foraged. "Every day you were scared that the police might get you," said Michael. "You see the police, you just duck and dive." Two weeks later, feeling pretty sure they were in the clear, they left the vacant apartment at Dixie Homes and rejoined their mother at Hurt Village. The Hurt Village apartment had only two bedrooms, and Dee Dee had borne still more children. She kept one bedroom for herself; the seven children now in her charge shared a bed in the other. "Lots of feet, lots of hands, lots of heads—but we managed," said Michael.

This place in which Michael would grow up over the next five years was, by 1996, a portrait of social dysfunction. Hurt Village still had roughly a thousand residents. There were no two-parent families: zero. Only a tiny handful of the residents held jobs. They had a mean education level between fourth and fifth grade. Seventy-five percent of the adult residents suffered from some form of mental illness. (Drug addiction counted as a mental illness.) Knowing that Hurt Village was soon to be torn down, and replaced with some other social experiment, a group of social scientists from the University of Memphis, funded by the U.S. Department of Housing and Urban Development, began to collect data on the place. "It was its own little community," said Cynthia Sadler, an anthropologist who worked on the project. "They did not associate with people outside of Hurt Village, and people outside of Hurt Village did not associate with them." The zip code for Hurt Village, 38105, was social poison outside of Hurt Village. Several residents told the researchers that they'd ceased looking for work because potential employers would see their zip code and reject them out of hand. "In all our travels," said another researcher, TK Buchanan, "we never came across a single Cadillac welfare queen."

By the time Michael arrived, Hurt Village was largely controlled by gangs. The Vice Lords were the biggest gang in Memphis, but the Gangster Disciples were the fastest growing and they ran Hurt Village. Delvin Lane ran the GDs, and he had an army of fifty-eight gang members in Hurt Village alone. In the early 1990s Delvin had been a dynamic quarterback for Booker T. Washington High School. He'd been set to go off to the University of Wyoming on a football scholarship. That opportunity vanished when he was sent off instead to jail, on an aggravated assault charge. He remained a natural leader, a quarterback, and, when he got out of jail, he used his talent to administer a huge and growing drug business. The GDs sold several different drugs but crack was most profitable, Delvin said, because it was the most portable and the most easily hidden. The first of the month, when the welfare checks rolled in, he made sure he had plenty of crack cocaine. Dee Dee would be waiting, cash in hand.

For Michael's first three years in Hurt Village, Delvin was the closest thing to the man in charge. Delvin didn't actually live in Hurt Village but he held meetings there, and when he and his army rolled in for these they were an impressive sight: a caravan of twenty to thirty fancy cars from which emerged these expensively dressed guys *completely unarmed*. Everyone knew they had no guns on them, in case the police showed up; everyone also knew that within yards they had stashed an arsenal of Uzis and 380s and sawed-off shotguns, in case the Vice Lords showed up. A twelve-man security squad armed with 17-shot 9mm pistols—two clips apiece—controlled key positions. Flanking Delvin were his two biggest bodyguards. One was called "Tombstone." Tombstone was six four, 310 pounds, and the most frightening human being anyone had ever seen—until they caught sight of Delvin's second bodyguard, Rico Harris. Rico was known as "Big Brim," and he stood six seven and weighed 450 pounds. Big Brim's official title was "Chief of Security," and his job, literally, was to watch Delvin's back. His blind side. "Big Brim was extremely valuable to me," said Delvin. "Especially in a club environment. Big Brim could hit one person and knock five of them down. If I'm in a club and Brim is there, I got no worries. But if it's a smaller guy there, I got to find other guys to help."

For the first eighteen months after he'd fled St. Joseph's, Michael stayed away from school, for fear of being taken by the authorities. For that year and a half he played what he thought of as a game of hide and seek with the Department of Children's Services. In retrospect, it was never clear that the State of Tennessee knew the game was on. The amazing thing, thought Michael, was that no grown-up ever turned him in, or even questioned his status. Hundreds of adults saw him on the streets day and night—people from Hurt Village, people who knew his mother—and no one ever wondered what he was doing running around in the middle of a weekday. "No one ever said, 'What are you doing out of school?' he recalled. "No one made me do anything." He guessed that if he hid out for long enough, the bad people at the Department of Children's Services would give up looking and forget about him. And they did.

By the time he turned twelve years old Michael Oher was completely free of social obligations. He might as well have been alone on a raft floating down the Mississippi River—which flowed, unnoticed, less than a mile from Hurt Village. He stole a bike and rode it wherever he wanted to. He played games from morning until late at night. Every now and then the older guys started shooting their guns at each other—but that was just pure entertainment. "We'd sit on the hill and watch them shoot it out," Michael recalled. "It was like being in the Wild West." He didn't feel himself unsafe;

the older guys with the guns left him and the other little kids alone. He played basketball ten and twelve hours a day, and grew ever more certain that he was destined to be the next Michael Jordan. Hurt Village had long since come to epitomize the despair of inner-city life, but it didn't occur for a minute to Michael to leave. "It was fun," he said. "Everything was fun. Nobody stopped me from doing anything."

He still had the old problems: where to find food and clothing. But now that he was older he was more capable of caring for himself. He got better at foraging for food, from neighbors and churches and the street. "I knew that on the first of the month you were supposed to have money to eat," he said. "Everyone else got food and you got nothing." He was growing so fast in every direction. Often he'd fall, and sometimes when he'd fall he'd hurt himself. Once he went over the front of his bike and opened a great gash on his elbow. He never went to the hospital; he didn't even know what stitches were. Instead, he assumed that there was no injury, left untreated, that would not heal. The insight extended into his internal well-being. He must have calculated that emotional connections with other people were more trouble than they were worth, for, with one exception, he stopped making them. The exception came when his basketball got away from him and broke a neighbor's flower pot. The lady was nice about it; it turned out she was new to Hurt Village and had a son named Craig. Craig Vail was a shy, quiet, small boy, who also loved to play basketball. He and Craig soon became inseparable; and Michael would later say that Craig was the one person in the whole world he fully trusted.

He also now had a kind of shadow brother: Big Zach. Zachary Bright lived a few doors down from Michael in Hurt Village. Big Zach was ten years older than Michael, but their resemblance was a constant source of wonder to the neighbors. "Everybody used to say, 'Zach, you got a brother!' " recalled Zachary Bright. " 'Guy down the sidewalk looks just like you!' " Zach went and had a look at Michael Oher for himself and couldn't deny the family resemblance. Their skin color was an identical dark chocolate. Their features, in the context of their huge selves, seemed small and delicate. They both had ears designed for men half their size, and narrow eyes that closed almost shut when they laughed or became angry.

They shared a similar athletic ability, too. In 1994, two years before Michael turned up in Hurt Village, Zachary Bright had graduated from Kingsbury High School. After his junior year he'd been one of the most highly sought after college football prospects in Tennessee. He'd had scholarship offers from nearly every major football school in the country. In a high school all-star game Big Zach's *backup* was Cletidus Hunt—who eventually went on to play for the Green Bay Packers. And in that game Big Zach had played defensive tackle, which wasn't his natural position. His natural position was left tackle on offense. He was six six and, while he weighed only 265 pounds, he had a frame that would support a lot more, once he received proper nutrition. He had great long arms and the grace and agility of a star basketball player. "Zachary Bright has the potential to be a big-time offensive tackle," Tom Lemming had written in his annual review of high school football stars.

Coach Bobby Bowden of Florida State had the same thought. Bowden had flown Big Zach down to Tallahassee, where he'd spent two days and nights being wined and dined by Heisman Trophy winner and future NBA guard Charlie Ward and future NFL superstar Derrick Brooks. Florida State had his locker ready and a jersey (No. 71) with BRIGHT stenciled on the back. But Big Zach's girlfriend had already given birth to their first child. She didn't want to go to Florida State, and the truth was he didn't really feel like doing his schoolwork or making his grades. Surrounded by friends who told him that he'd be wasting his time to even try college, he quit. He never even finished high school. When the next school year started, and Big Zach didn't show up for it, Bobby Bowden himself came up from Florida State to Hurt Village, in search of his prized recruit. Big Zach hid out with his girlfriend and their new baby until Bowden was gone.

Big Zach would one day reflect upon that strange and wasteful period in his life. "Guys who were around said, 'Everyone can't make it to the NFL,' " he said. "Telling me I wasn't really gonna make it. Years passed by. I was still thinking I was at the top of my game. But my time was passing me on by. After a while I decided I was too old for it." He'd shake his head in wonder at all he had thrown away and say, "I feel like I could a did something, if I were to start over and do it again. I didn't know how close I was. All I had to do was knock on the NFL door."

But the wisdom, and the sadness, came much later; in 1996 he was just two years out of high school and still having fun. And suddenly all these people started coming up to him to ask if that kid now living a few doors down the block was his little brother. He grabbed the kid and took him out on the basketball court to see how he handled himself.

Well, as it turned out. ("But it was more like football than basketball," said Zach.) Michael Oher was no longer Michael Oher: he was "Big Mike." Michael loathed that nickname; it was the enemy of what he hoped to become. "I didn't want to be big," said Michael. He wanted to be lithe and fast; he wanted to be Michael Jordan. The wider he became the more preposterous was that ambition, but it proved easier to ignore his width than to abandon his dream. Everyone might be calling him "Big Mike," but no one ever took a picture of him. There weren't many mirrors around, either. He seldom was faced with his own reflection. He fiddled with optical illusions, and took to wearing his shoes too small and his clothes too big. He did push-ups and sit-ups, thinking they kept him thin. He developed the odd habit—for a boy his size—of always looking for something high over his head to jump up and hit, or tap, or jump up on. Every game they played he arranged it so that his role in it stressed, and trained, his quickness and his agility. Craig was his only real friend, and Craig reassured him that no matter what anybody called him he was still, like Jordan, a born outside threat. He just had to keep working on his quick first step and his crossover dribble.

Of course, Michael could sense his own swelling mass, but only by its effects. He was pleasantly shocked when one day, while wrestling, he just picked up a kid as if he weighed nothing and hurled him across the yard. On the other hand, he was no longer winning the foot races against the other kids—but at least he was still running them. They'd go out into the turning lane on Danny Thomas Boulevard like they always did, but now he'd be given a head start. He devoted so much time and energy to defying his own size that it couldn't help but yield results. Even as he became one of the biggest human beings in Hurt Village, he remained quick and agile. He willed himself to be graceful—to remain a little man, inside a big man's body. Later, college coaches who came to watch him would see a freak of nature. But where had nature left off, and nurture taken over? It was, as always, hard to say.

Between the ages of ten and fifteen Michael Oher was left alone with his fantasy. He learned nothing in school, confined himself to the incredibly narrow life available inside Hurt Village, and developed nothing in himself apart from his athletic ability. No one told him he should be doing anything other than what he was doing. If Hurt Village was an island in the Memphis economy, Michael's home was a hidden cave on that island. It probably helped that Delvin Lane's Gangster Disciples discouraged its members from messing with little kids. At any rate, Michael didn't have anything to do with the gangs or anyone else but Craig. He dipped in and out of school, and was moved along from one grade to the next, meaninglessly. He watched every one of his older brothers drop out. Marcus quit after the ninth grade, Andre and Deljuan and Rico after the eleventh, and Carlos after the tenth. Each had fathered at least one child, and among them they had fathered ten. But Michael remained happy and free, without the faintest premonition that anything would ever change, or needed to.

Then, just before his fifteenth birthday, he met Tony Henderson. Big Tony had grown up in Hurt Village, too. He came back often in search of kids to play for the football and basketball teams he coached. If you had the skills and the size, it was hard to hide from Big Tony. Big Zach had played for Big Tony; so had Tombstone and Big Brim.

Big Tony's first impression of Big Mike was that his family life was unusually troubled, even by the standards of Hurt Village. His second impression was that Big Mike had no friends. "I never saw him hanging around nobody," said Tony. "He was real quiet." He quickly figured out that Big Mike, like half the other kids he knew, was living to be the next Michael Jordan, and Tony did what he could to help him realize the dream. The summer before Michael's freshman year in high school Tony, through a friend, sneaked Michael into the basketball camp run by Carver High School. The first day Tony's friend called him to say that Big Mike had fled the camp. Big Tony hustled on over and found Big Mike walking the streets, a mile away, with tears streaming down his face. He was fifteen miles from Hurt Village and he didn't have a dime in his pockets. He was walking home, he said. The coaches had taken one look at him and told him he wasn't a perimeter player—that he wasn't Michael Jordan. And once he'd taken his newly assigned position in the low post, the bigger older kids alongside him had started shoving and hitting him. "Mike was a big ol' kid," said Tony, "but he didn't want to be touched. They got mad at him because he wouldn't knock the other kids down. The coach told him he'd never be nothing, and Mike started crying."

Big Tony was friends with Harold Johnson, the basketball coach at Westwood High. Westwood was a long way from Hurt Village, but Tony figured if he was driving his son Steven to Westwood he might as well drive Big Mike, too. At Westwood Big Mike played football, too, but his heart wasn't in it. The coach just threw out the balls and went and sat in the shade, and Big Mike coasted through the year as a defensive tackle on a bad team.

That was a shame, thought Big Tony, because Big Mike was getting seriously big. He reminded Tony of Big Zach: his size alone meant he'd attract the attention of college football coaches. For that to happen, however, he needed to get through high school, and that didn't seem even remotely possible. He was failing his freshman classes and, on many days, didn't even bother to show up for them. Other days Big Tony would drop Steven and Big Mike at school, and return that afternoon to find only Steven waiting. "He wasn't going back," said Big Tony. "Big Mike was going to drop out." The only reason Big Mike hadn't already gotten himself into a world of trouble, Big Tony thought, was that he was so loosely connected to the people around him. He wasn't at the same risk as Big Zach for the simple reason that he didn't have a crowd of friends tempting him with the fast life.

Still, there was only so much distance any young man who dropped out of high school could put between himself and the 'hood. "He didn't have nothing to turn to," said Big Tony. "What chance did he have to go straight? He had *no* chance." As Michael neared the end of his freshman year in high school, he had before him one obvious career path. Once he quit school he would have waiting for him a single, well-paying, high-status job: bodyguard to Delvin Lane. Or rather, since Delvin had moved on, to Delvin's successor. The job was to watch the back of the guy who ran the only real business in the neighborhood. Left tackle of the ghetto.

That's when Betty Boo died, and stated as her dying wish that her grandson receive a Christian education. And as odd as it felt to Big Tony to put Steven in his car and drive him into the heart of rich, white Memphis, it felt odder still to ignore his mother's dying wish. And Big Tony thought, *if I'm taking Steven I might as well take Big Mike, too.*

ONE OF THE TACTICAL disadvantages of being a six five, 350-pound black kid in a school built for white kids is that other people tend to recall their encounters with you in far more vivid detail than you do. The main thing Michael Oher would remember of his first few weeks at the Briarcrest Christian School was his own terror and confusion. All white kids looked alike; and they were all bizarrely enthusiastic and friendly. "Everyone was exactly the same," he said. "For three or four weeks, every time I turned the corner I'd see some white kid shouting hello to me and I'd think: *I just saw you!*" His senior year he'd figure out that, while he hated to read, he liked to write. Assigned to write a personal essay, he chose as his subject his first days at Briarcrest. "White Walls," he titled his piece. It began:

> I look and I see white everywhere: white walls, white floors, and a lot of white people.... The teachers are not aware that I have no idea of anything they are talking about. I do not want to listen to anyone, especially the teachers. They are giving homework and expecting me to do the problems on my own. I've never done homework in my life. I go to the bathroom, look in the mirror, and say, "This is not Mike Oher. I want to get out of this place."

The other thing he remembered about those first frightful days was his hunger. The free food had been the main reason he bothered to go to public school as often as he had. These Christians didn't give you lunch, and that shocked him.

Hunger and confusion did not prevent him from noting significant details about white people. He'd had no interaction with them before this. Now as he studied them he judged them ill-designed for survival. Astonishingly prone to exaggerating the severity of the most trivial illness or injury, they were forever racing off to doctors and hospitals, as if they were about to die. "They'd get a twisted ankle or something and they're walking around school with a *boot*!" Michael said. "I was like, 'What are y'all doing? You got to just walk it off!' "

In addition to their pathological friendliness, and their constant need for medical attention, they exhibited a bizarre tendency to leave their most valuable possessions unattended. Steven was in the grade below him, and so they didn't cross paths very often, but when they did they shared their incredulity: *these white kids left gold watches, hand TVs, name brand shoes, and wallets just lying around.* It was as if the doors to Ali Baba's cave had sprung open. The boys' locker room alone was a cornucopia; all you had to do was swoop your hand through once and you'd come away with fistfuls of cash. "A burglar's dream," Michael called it. One night they came home with money that wasn't theirs, and Big Tony found out and tried to explain to them a little bit about white people and how, lacking street smarts, they had established some rules to preserve their species and that, odd as those rules might seem, Steven and Michael needed to obey them. Rule number one was that a kid did not steal, or fight, or get into trouble of any sort; and what was a rule for white kids was an iron law for a black kid. Because a black kid who got into trouble in the white world was a black kid on his way out of that world.

—

CHAPTER TWELVE

AND MOSES STUTTERED

IN THE HOURS FOLLOWING Michael Oher's disappearance, hell broke loose. The Ole Miss study center for football players became a crime scene. The ambulance came for the little white boy, who continued to bleed from his head wound, and took him away. Campus police raced in, followed by the Oxford city police. Miss Sue screamed into the phone to Leigh Anne: "He's going to jail! They're going to put him in jail!" The teammate Michael had attacked, Antonio Turner, was hustled off, bruised and battered, to a coach's house, to be guarded like a witness in a protection program. The little boy's father—Bobby Nix, the tutor who had been at such pains to get the black players out into white Oxford—was understandably beside himself. He and his wife had already lost a child, and now he'd just seen his three-year-old son lying on the floor in a pool of blood, a victim of a black football player's rage. He said he was pressing charges.

Michael saw none of it: he was long gone. Ignoring the calls from Leigh Anne and the text messages from Sean, he drove around Oxford in a fog of anger and confusion. He was angry because Antonio had said what he'd said and then struck him; he was confused because he was newly vulnerable. He now had these people he loved, who loved him. Through them, other people could get to him. He was no longer just another poor black kid going nowhere. He understood that most people, white and black, treated him a lot differently than they would have if he wasn't a football star. But he couldn't bring himself to be cynical about the Tuohy family. He knew other people, white and black, were saying that these rich white Ole Miss boosters had identified him early on as a future NFL lineman and bought him the way you'd buy a cheap stock or a racehorse. That they might not need his money but they liked his status, and had envisioned how he might serve the Briarcrest and Ole Miss football teams. Michael didn't believe it. "I wasn't anything when I first got to them, and they loved me anyway," he said. "Nothing was in it for them."

A few hours after he'd fled the scene of the crime, he noticed that the tone of Sean's text messages had changed. They started out urgent. Now they were just funny.

Mike Tyson! U coming back into the ring for another round?

Michael began to compose himself. Three years ago he'd have just kept on running and never looked back. He wouldn't admit that he was different, but he couldn't deny that *things* were different. He was no longer a black object skipping along the surface of a white background; he'd been woven into the white fabric. So . . . why was he running? Who was he running from? For that matter—where was he running *to*?

He opened his cell phone.

At that moment Sean was sitting on the floor of a movie theater's lobby in Seattle, worrying that Michael might be looking for a bridge to throw himself from. He'd been traveling with the Memphis Grizzlies, and the team had an off day. Sean and his friend Brian Cardinal, the Grizzlies' forward, had gone to see a movie, *16*

Blocks with Bruce Willis. The first call about Michael had come as they walked into the theater. With his cell phone nearly out of juice, Sean found the plug in the lobby and set about trying to fix things. First he called Coach O, who, bless his heart, refused to be anything but calm. Then he called Hugh Freeze, and learned that (a) the little boy needed stitches in his head but was otherwise fine, and (b) the police, if and when they found Michael, intended to take him to jail. That wasn't good. Jail meant, at the very least, news stories. Jail meant the wrong kind of reputation.

Sean now considered how to play it. The poor white kid had been born with a talent for seeing the court, taking in every angle and every other player, and then attacking in the most efficient way possible. The talent translated beautifully from basketball into life. He knew that Leigh Anne had cheered for one of the senior officers of the Ole Miss campus police, Michael Harmon, back when he'd been a flanker on the Ole Miss football team, and considered him a friend. Bobby Nix, the father of the injured boy, had been Sean's fraternity brother at Ole Miss. Dr. Thomas Wallace, the vice chancellor of the university and an old friend of Sean's, was now serving as Michael's "mentor." Sean sat there on the theater floor, thinking how best to play this possession, while, every ten minutes, Brian Cardinal popped his head out of the theater door and said, "You haven't missed anything yet."

And he hadn't—the real action was right there on the lobby floor. After he'd left yet another text message for Michael—*make it funny*, he thought, *so he doesn't throw himself off a bridge*—Sean decided he needed a lawyer. The Ole Miss football team, and the school itself, he decided, should be allowed to handle matters as they saw fit. (Especially since he knew how they'd see fit.) And so he called his old friend Steve Farese.

Farese was the defense attorney then representing, among other clients, the nice lady in Selma, Tennessee, who had shot her Baptist preacher husband in the back and killed him. For Steve Farese, a single bullet fired into one's husband's back counted as a trivial offense: a human being could hardly think up a thing to do that Farese couldn't construe as innocent. The FedEx pilot accused of stuffing his wife in the trunk of his car and setting it on fire? Innocent! The rapper charged with rape? Innocent! The Ole Miss quarterback, Eli Manning, charged with peeing on the side of a campus building? Off and starting for the New York Giants! When Sean reached Farese, and explained that the police were about to take his son in and book him, Farese became excited. "Oh, no, no, no, no, they are not," he said. "Sean, this is just an *unfortunate accident*."

That's when Michael called.

"Pops," he said, "you're my first call. Just like I promised."

"Michael," said Sean, "this isn't exactly what I had in mind."

Sean sorted it out; of course he sorted it out. He told Michael to turn himself in to campus police who, he felt sure, would keep him from the clutches of the Oxford police. He called Bobby Nix and anyone else whose opinion might matter. He explained the situation in a way that they'd completely understand and offered to pay for whatever needed paying for. And, after a long round of fulsome apologies and ten hours of community service, Michael was restored to his former status of model citizen—and the incident never even hit the campus newspaper. It just went away, the way it would have gone away for some well-to-do white kid. Of course, lessons were learned and points of view exchanged. Coach O, for instance, pulled Michael into his office to discuss The Responsibilities of Being Michael Oher. Rather dramatically, Coach O extracted from his desk a thick folder stuffed with newspaper clippings, and dropped it with a thud. *"Dajus da crap dey wrote bout me last sittee days!"* he boomed. (That's just the crap they wrote about me in the last sixty days!) He went on to lecture Michael on the burdens of conspicuous success. "Let me tell you something, son," he concluded (in translation). "It is lonely at the top. I hate you had to learn about this at such a young age, but there are going to be many Antonio Turners. This is the first of many incidents."

MICHAEL OHER'S CAREER as a football player wasn't a sure thing—there was no such thing in football as a sure thing. But his odds in life had changed, dramatically. In just the past three years he had encountered countless threats to his future that might have put an end to it had he remained socially unconnected to white people: illiteracy, bad grades, car crashes, a night with the Memphis police, an NCAA investigation, men in the street who offered to become his agent. Any one of these might have sent him right back to the prison of his past. It was part of being hopelessly poor that events conspired to keep you poor; if it wasn't one thing, it was another. That cycle, in Michael's case, had been broken. He was like a quarterback who had gone from playing in an unimaginative offense, incapable of making him look good, to playing in an offense designed by Bill Walsh.

There's an instant before it collapses into some generally agreed-upon fact when a life, like a football play, is all conjecture and fragments and partial views. Everyone wants to know the whole truth but no one possesses it. But Michael Oher already had collapsed into a generally agreed-upon fact: he was a success. The world that had once taken no notice of Michael Oher was now so invested in him that it couldn't afford to see him fail. Of course, he wasn't the first black kid to rise from poverty and make it in the white world. But Michael was different, because the white world had so unusually aided and abetted his rise. The white world had watched Michael Oher happen, or thought they had, and so could imagine how he might be replicated. He haunted that world.

The Briarcrest Christian School, for starters, wrestled internally with the implications of Michael Oher. Applications to the school from black inner-city kids shot through the roof—"They all saw what happened to Michael and they now want to go to Briarcrest, too," said Sean. The school's new president, Bill McGee, did not like the idea of throwing open the doors to poor black athletes who couldn't read or write, but the school's staff could see the benefits. "Yeah, we helped Michael Oher," said Carly Powers, the Briarcrest athletic director. "But I tell you something else. Michael Oher helped our school. He gave a lot of people here some hope that if you help some of these kids, it is possible that they'll come around and make something of their lives." Jennifer Graves, who oversaw students with special needs, and so supervised Michael's academic life, saw an even higher purpose in Michael. "Michael got saved when he was at Briarcrest," said Graves. "What better way to spread the word of Jesus than for Michael Oher to stand up and say it? What kid in the Memphis City Schools wouldn't listen?" She knew that Michael was still intensely private—and that his gift for avoiding social entanglements had probably made a lot of what had happened to him possible. But when it was pointed out to her that Michael didn't seem like the most obvious spokesman for any cause, she just smiled and said, "And Moses stuttered."*

The coaches who had come to Briarcrest to woo Michael Oher also had trouble banishing him from their thoughts. Nick Saban was now coaching the Miami Dolphins, but he sent the Tuohys a Christmas card. ("If I was still at LSU Michael would be playing for me!") And, every now and again, Saban mentioned to scouts and sports agents that he was waiting for this phenomenal left tackle at Ole Miss to age, so that he could draft him.

If Nick Saban was still interested, Phil Fulmer was obsessed. Fulmer's University of Tennessee, widely considered before the 2005 season to have a shot at the national championship, had fin-

---

* Exodus 6:12: "But Moses said to the Lord, 'If the Israelites will not listen to me, why would Pharaoh listen to me, since I speak with faltering lips?' "

ished a disastrous 5–6. But at the start of the season they scored a huge victory at home against the highly ranked LSU Tigers. After the game the euphoric Fulmer spoke to the television cameras on the field, then rumbled into the Tennessee locker room. He found his agent, Jimmy Sexton, waiting for him. "He'd just beaten LSU," recalled Sexton, "and the first thing he says to me is 'See if you can get Michael Oher to transfer.'"

Fulmer returned to the Briarcrest Christian School. With the departure of Hugh Freeze—and Michael Oher—the Briarcrest football program fell on hard times. But the team still had one big-time prospect, a pass rushing defensive end named Greg Hardy. "The Freak," as he was known, because he was six six and 245 pounds with lightning reflexes and sprinter speed. The Freak was a quarterback's worst nightmare. The Freak was also black and, right up to the moment Briarcrest let him in, the recipient of a Memphis public school education. He wasn't a great student, but his grades were good enough to qualify him to play college football. And Phil Fulmer was seriously interested in him.

But, as Fulmer stood on the sidelines of the Briarcrest practice field and watched, he couldn't help but notice, just down the side-line, a familiar figure: Sean Tuohy. The Tennessee football coach edged a little closer until at length he caught Sean's eye.

"You gonna adopt this one, too?" he asked.

"I don't know," said Sean. "I'm waiting to see how good he is."*

He was only half-joking. His experience with Michael Oher had left Sean alive to the possibilities. If these poor black kids were good enough at sports that the wider world had a natural interest in them, all they'd need was a little push, in the form of love and attention from someone like Leigh Anne, and they'd be on their way. "The problem isn't intelligence," he said. "It's access to the sys-

---

* In the end, the Freak accepted a football scholarship to Ole Miss, in part, he said, because he wanted to play with Michael Oher.

tem." But Briarcrest had a new policy of shunning the inner-city black athlete, and it infuriated him. "They really aren't as obsessed as they should be with giving opportunities to academically challenged kids," he said. Sean was willing to provide the funds to pay for kids to go to Briarcrest, and yet Briarcrest was newly unwilling to take them.

SEAN JUNIOR MUST HAVE noticed his father's new interest in helping out, financially, every poor black boy who could hit a jump shot and every black girl who could pitch a softball. SJ was the only white player on his twelve-and-under AAU basketball team, and most of the black players were conspicuously poor. Just about every one of them had applied to Briarcrest, and if Briarcrest hadn't rejected them, his father was ready to bankroll them all. It got SJ to thinking about his own situation.

He now had a question he wanted to ask.

Three years earlier, Sean Junior, like his big sister Collins, had been more than happy to take Michael in. He didn't really view Michael as black or poor or a potential drain on the family's resources. He was more interested in Michael's capacity to serve as an entertaining big brother and wily co-conspirator. Still, now that Collins and Michael were off at Ole Miss, SJ couldn't help but feel left out. Collins was Miss Everything and dating Cannon Smith, the son of the billionaire founder of Federal Express. Michael was already being spoken of as a first-round NFL draft pick. Just the other day, a scout for the Chicago Bears had taken Michael aside and told him that he could be the best lineman ever to come out of Ole Miss. Even if he didn't actually have any money yet, SJ thought, Michael was sure to become really rich. And all he had gotten out of the deal was a single trip with Coach O through the Grove.

And so he had a question. He was in the back of a car one day, being chauffeured by his mother to one of his AAU basketball games, when he thought to ask it.

"Mom," he said, "can I ask you something about you and Dad's will?"

"Uh huh," she said, warily.

"Collins is going to marry Cannon and so she'll be a billionaire," he said.

"I wouldn't say that's a done deal."

"Michael is going to be a first-round draft choice in the NFL, so he'll be really rich."

"Uh huh," she said. "So?"

"So" asked Sean Junior, "why are they even *in* the will?"

"Because," said Leigh Anne. "That's just the way it's done."

THE TUOHY MOST directly responsible for the transformation of Michael Oher, Leigh Anne had the most trouble ignoring his implications. "Look at him," she would say, whenever Michael stood more than about ten feet away. "He has everything: integrity, ambition, and a future." Then she'd think a moment, with the critical detachment of a sculptor whose work was nearly, but not quite, finished. "The only thing he needs now is to learn to give."

Then she'd think again. Michael might be, very nearly, a finished product. He didn't need her time and attention—but that only raised an obvious question: who did? The inner city of Memphis alone teemed with kids whose athletic ability had market value. Very few ever reached their market. As Michael himself said, "If all the guys who could play got a chance to play, there would have to be two NFLs because one wouldn't be enough." Sports was the closest thing in America to pure meritocracy, the one avenue of ambition widely thought to be open to all. (Pity the kid inside Hurt Village who was born to play the piano, or manage people, or trade bonds.) And Michael Oher was in possession of what had to be among the more conspicuous athletic gifts. Apart from the seven foot tall basketball player, the six five, 350-pound kid who could fly had to be about the easiest future star to identify. And yet, without outside intervention even his talent would quite likely have been thrown away. Michael Oher would have become just another big fat man: Big Mike. If Michael Oher's talent could be missed—whose couldn't? Those poor black kids were like left tackles: people whose value was hidden in plain sight.

Leigh Anne thought about this, a lot. And one morning in early 2006 Sean was interrupted from lifting himself out of bed by his wife, who was brandishing the sports section of the morning paper. The Memphis *Commercial Appeal* had reported the story of a young man named Arthur Sallis. Sallis had been the star fullback on Memphis's East High team, which had been state champions in 1999 and runners-up in 2000. He'd averaged, incredibly, more than 10 yards a carry. "When I'm dreaming," he once told a reporter, "I'm suiting up and going on the field. It's like there's no stopping me. It's like I can't go down." Before Sallis's senior year, his high school coach Wayne Randall received phone calls from every head coach in the SEC. The Kentucky coach, Hal Mumme, told Randall that Sallis was one of the finest football players he had ever seen.

Sallis had been offered scholarships by the University of Kentucky and Ole Miss, but he never took them. High school proved to be the end of Arthur Sallis's football career. His grades were poor, and he was disqualified by NCAA rules. Prevented by the NCAA from going to college on a football scholarship Sallis had stayed home, in his old neighborhood, on the west side of Memphis.

In this Arthur Sallis was only typical. As it happened, East High—Sallis's public school—had been part of a study made of Memphis inner-city athletes. The study revealed that, for every six public school kids with the ability to play college sports, five failed to qualify academically. What was unusual about Arthur Sallis was the persistence of his desire to make something of his life, in spite of the odds against him. He never knew his father, and his mother was an alcoholic in and out of jail. "From the time he was a little boy Arthur lived by himself, out on the streets," said Coach Randall. In high school he'd gotten into all kinds of trouble, but most of it was driven by his need to get money to live. "I used to joke," said Randall, "that Arthur was the only football player I ever had who I had to keep a lawyer on retainer for."

But after high school, with his football coach's help, Arthur Sallis had gone straight. He eked out a living with his own carpet cleaning business. He'd fathered a baby girl, and was raising her by himself. "He was doing all the things a responsible person should be doing," said his former coach. Then, a few months after Arthur Sallis left high school, he caught two men stealing a car and tried to stop them. For his trouble he got himself shot, point-blank, once in the back and once in the chest. He very nearly died. When his old high school coach visited him in the hospital Sallis told him, "If God gets me out of this, Coach, I'm never going to be out on the street again."

He had been true to his word. The newspaper Leigh Anne dropped in Sean's lap told the story of what happened next. Arthur Sallis wasn't on the streets, but at home with his four-year-old daughter, when three men broke in. Sallis grabbed one, and another shot him three times in the head. Arthur Sallis could have been a teammate of Michael Oher's at Ole Miss. Instead, at the age of twenty-two, he was dead.

Sean was only just waking up, and yet his wife was pacing back and forth in front of him, angry and upset. She was crying but she was also pissed off, and that, in his experience, was a dangerous combination. "Do you realize that you could take this kid's name out and put Michael's name in and have the same story?" she said. "Why didn't *this* kid fall on our doorstep?"

Then and there Leigh Anne made a decision: she wasn't fin-

ished. "I want a *building*," she said. "We're going to open a foundation that's only going to help out kids with athletic ability who
don't have the academics to go to college. Screw the NCAA. I don't
care what people say. I don't care if they say we're only interested in
them because they're good at sports. Sports is all we know about.
And there are *hundreds* of kids in Memphis alone with this story."

Sean was now fully alert. *Hundreds* of kids. A *building*. His personal finances were always a bit more uncertain than he let on, even
to his wife. Sean's way of life depended on his ability to hide his
fears and anxieties. Everything was always good and if it wasn't, he
could fix it. He conveyed the impression so well that people naturally handed him things to fix; and people who were broken drifted
to him, in hopes of being fixed. His own success and well-being
were taken as given, but they weren't. Four years ago Taco Bell had
been in a down cycle, and he'd teetered on the brink of bankruptcy.
In the nick of time, Taco Bell made some changes in its menus and
its sales had boomed. ("The quesadilla saved my ass," he
explained.) But his fast-food stores were never a sure thing. "I'm
not financially secure where I can sit back and do nothing," he said.
"But I like my chances." On the other hand, if his wife was now
going to attack single-handedly America's most intractable social
problem, he liked his chances a bit less.

Leigh Anne must have seen him thinking because she left him
to get himself up and dressed, found her phone, and called Michael
Oher. "Michael, you better get off your ass and get to work," she
said. "Because we got things we got to do with your money."

It wasn't clear to Michael what, if anything, he owed the world.
He now received lots of phone calls from poor black friends and
family, and all of them wanted money. His mother called him a lot
more than she used to, and it bothered him enough that he often
didn't return her calls. "People don't understand that I made the
newspaper but nothing comes with that," he said. "I haven't made
a dollar yet." Not long after college coaches informed him that he

had a future in the NFL, Michael informed Leigh Anne that, if he indeed made it to the NFL, he intended to buy a house with thirteen bedrooms so that his mother and siblings would be guaranteed shelter. Now he wasn't so sure he wanted to do that. "They had the same chances I had," he said. "They need to get off their lazy asses and work. They need to start hearing 'no.'"

People are no better at seeing the various paths their lives might have taken than football fans are at seeing the many different things that might have happened on any single play. People note outcomes, and reason backward from them. Michael noted his outcome and concluded that his life was always going to work out. He refused to believe there was ever the faintest possibility that he was going to be anything other than a huge success. He had set out to become Michael Jordan and he was fulfilling that destiny, in his way. "I was always going to college," he said. "I guess I thought that if things didn't work out in the NBA, I'd have the NFL as my backup." If he didn't give a lot of credit to others for having changed his life—if he didn't feel that he owed much to many—it was, in part, because he didn't really believe he had changed. "I'm the same way I've always been," he said. "I'm exactly the same guy I was back in Hurt Village. The only thing that's changed for me is the environment."

The change in environment was no small thing, and it took the help of many people—Big Tony, the Briarcrest teachers, the families that had housed him—for him to function in the new environment. Still, when Michael thought about who he wanted to help, if he had the power to help, the only person he could think of was Craig.

In his first year and a half at the Briarcrest Christian School, Michael hadn't seen as much of Craig as he would have liked. Craig lived back on the west side of Memphis and that suddenly seemed a long way away. But the moment Michael had gotten his driver's license he knew what he wanted to do with it. When he and Leigh

Anne arrived home from the DMV, Michael asked Leigh Anne if he could drive back to western Memphis and bring back an old friend. For nearly a year Leigh Anne had been pressing him to bring home his old friends, but he'd never done it. Off he drove and soon returned with this shy, quiet, sweet-natured boy whom Michael introduced as "Craig." This was the one friend Michael had told them about—his one close friend in the world—in whose existence Leigh Anne had ceased to believe. She had come to think of Craig, like Harvey the rabbit, as an imaginary friend. Now Harvey stood uncomfortably in her foyer. "I never been this far from home," Craig said.

Michael claimed that Craig was the one person in the world he fully trusted, and so Craig became a regular visitor to the Tuohy home. For his part Craig was perplexed: his friend leaves the 'hood to go to a new school and the next thing he knows he's not merely shacked up with these rich white people on the other side of Memphis but claiming they are his *family*. "Big Mike call me one day and I ask him what he's doing," said Craig. "He say, 'I'm just driving to get something to eat with my brother.' I ask him, 'Which brother is that?' He say, 'My brother, Sean Junior.' I say, '*Who?*'"

Now Michael said, "If I ever make it to the NFL Craig *has* to come. We got so close 'cause he just like me. We the same people, just different size." Craig didn't have any more money than anyone else from his former life. And while Craig was his only real friend, Craig had never asked him for a thing. "I offer him something, he says, 'I'm good, I'm all right.'" That was one of the traits he admired most in Craig: he didn't go around acting like some victim. He had his pride.

At any rate he and Craig now spent more time together. One night Michael took him to see the Memphis Grizzlies play. They were making their way toward Sean's courtside seats when Craig noticed that a lot of people were staring at them and pointing. "They were all saying, 'That's Michael Oher! That's Michael Oher!'"

Craig already knew that people in poor black Memphis assumed that Michael Oher was going to the league. "They all talk about him," he said. "Nobody call him Big Mike anymore. They just call him Michael Oher." Now he saw that Michael's fame had spread beyond poor black Memphis, to courtside at the Memphis Grizzlies game, and realized: "Everyone in Memphis know who Michael Oher is!"

As they found their seats, Craig asked Michael if he noticed the many people pointing and staring at him. Michael smiled and Craig could tell that he not only noticed but loved it. "What if you don't make it to the NFL?" was the question Craig wanted to ask next, but he didn't. Instead he asked, "When you think you be ready for the league?" At that Michael laughed and said, "I'm ready *now.*"

Craig laughed. The world might have changed, but his friend had not. "He's the same guy," Craig said. "Everyone say Michael got cocky. What they don't know is that he was *always* cocky. He just didn't show it."

Still, Craig thought Michael must be joking. He wasn't.

"I could take Dwight Freeney right now," said Michael, seriously.

Dwight Freeney played for the Indianapolis Colts. He was the most feared pass rushing defensive end in the NFL, and maybe the fastest the NFL had ever seen. He'd arrived in the NFL in 2002 with his 4.3 forty-yard dash and his wild spin moves, and quickly figured out where he needed to be: the blind side. Two seasons later he rocked the order of the football universe when he went by Jonathan Ogden and sacked the Ravens' quarterback not once but twice. No one went by Jonathan Ogden—but Freeney had.

Freeney understood he was a man working in a tradition. When he was eight years old he'd seen a highlight film of Lawrence Taylor and right then and there knew who he was going to be when he grew up. "If you ask me to list my favorite players, I'd tell you LT and there'd be nobody second," he said. "There'd just be LT." Freeney took it for granted his job was to defeat the superstar of the offensive line. Best on best. That was his great strength: finding ways to win the most important one-on-one contest on the football field. And so when he heard that there was this kid down in Memphis who thought he was on his way to the league and said he "could take Dwight Freeney right now," he just laughed and said, "That's the way he's got to be." But he was curious enough to ask, "Who is this kid?"

Dwight Freeney stood outside the Colts' locker room, sweating in his pads, helmet in his hand, and listened patiently to a summary of the brief career of Michael Oher. How Michael had been one of thirteen children born to a mother who couldn't care for them, and so had more or less raised himself on the streets of Memphis. How he hadn't reported to serious football practice until his junior year in high school—but by then was six five, 350 pounds, and had been timed running the forty-yard dash in 4.9 seconds. How his forty-yard dash time didn't really capture his speed: to appreciate his quickness you needed to watch him in short bursts. How he'd been one of the best basketball players in the state of Tennessee, and held his own on the court with high school All-Americans, and still secretly believed his natural position was shooting guard. How, on the brink of adulthood, with a measured IQ of 80, no formal education and no experience of white people, he had so insinuated himself into rich white Memphis that white people no longer noticed the color of his skin. How he was now six six and 325 pounds and the starting left tackle at Ole Miss, and a fair bet to be named to the All-SEC team at the end of next season. How, fast and strong as he had been at 350 pounds, he was faster and stronger now. How every day he felt a little bit less a lost boy and a little bit more a man with a mission.

Dwight Freeney understood the rules of his game. In the NFL, on the quarterback's blind side, you came and you went. You had your moment when you played so perfectly in the sun that you were mistaken for the sun—and then you were eclipsed. The summer before the start of the 2006 season was still his moment, and would remain his moment—until it wasn't. Until he lost a step. Or got hurt. Or until the next Jonathan Ogden showed up and was maybe a step quicker, or fractionally more gifted, than the original. As he listened to the biography of Michael Oher, Dwight Freeney's expression changed. He was no longer smiling.

"What's his name again?" he asked.

"Michael Oher."

"You tell Michael Oher I'll be waiting for him," he said, and walked into the locker room.

AFTERWORD TO THE PAPERBACK EDITION

—

IN THE SEASON AFTER this book's publication Michael started every game as Ole Miss's left tackle. The Ole Miss football team was so consistently inept that it was hard to believe anyone on it could be any good, but Michael's play landed him on the All-SEC Second Team, while his grade point average (3.75) landed him, for a semester, on the University of Mississippi Dean's List. (He was honored at halftime during one Ole Miss basketball game for his *schoolwork.*) After what was otherwise a miserable season the Ole Miss offensive line coach, Art Kehoe, still said that never in his twenty-seven years coaching big-time college football linemen had he coached a player with more natural ability than Michael Oher. "He's still an inexperienced player," said Kehoe, "because he basically didn't play in high school. But he's getting better every day. He's got exceptionally low pad level; he's very, very quick off the ball; he's very good in pass protection and very aggressive with his hands, like a street fighter." When Kehoe was asked who of the hundreds of offensive linemen he has coached that Michael Oher reminded him of, he said, "He's a combination of Leon Searcy and Eric Winston." Searcy was picked in the first round of the 1992 draft by the Pittsburgh Steelers, played eleven seasons in the NFL, and made the Pro Bowl. Winston was a first-round talent drafted in the third round in 2006 by the Houston Texans, as he'd suffered a severe knee injury and it was unclear if he'd recover. He recovered and, as a rookie, became the Texans' starting right tackle. "Is he good enough to go to the NFL? There's no doubt in my mind," said Kehoe. Kehoe's main concern about Michael was "to keep him focused on being a good player for *Ole Miss*." (Rather than a good player, say, for the Green Bay Packers.)

For his part, Michael was still telling people what they wanted to hear: he planned to stay in school. But to close friends on the Ole Miss football team he admitted that if, after his junior year, the NFL planned to make him a first- or second-round pick, he was taking his business to the NFL. If his mind had begun to drift to thoughts of future professional glory, it was hard to blame him. One of his best friends on the team, linebacker Patrick Willis, was about to be drafted in the first round of the 2007 NFL draft and handed millions of dollars. (Willis, oddly enough, was also a poor black kid from Tennessee who'd been adopted by white parents.) If it could happen to Patrick, there was no reason it couldn't happen to him. "Patrick's a great player," said Hugh Freeze, "but he doesn't have what Michael has." In early 2007, at the suggestion of a sports agent, Michael drove to Nashville, to train with a handful of upperclassman who'd gathered there to prepare for the NFL Combine. The Combine is where NFL scouts put prospects through a series of sometimes bizarre drills, to determine their fitness for pro football. The agent thought it would serve Michael well to see what future NFLers looked like up close, and it did. "I did great," he said. "I didn't think anybody there had anything I didn't have." Most had less: he was already stronger, faster, and more athletically gifted than players expecting to go in the first three rounds of the upcoming draft. *And he was still developing.*

There is no sophomore playing on a college offensive line of whom NFL scouts are willing to say, "When he gets old enough to turn pro, we'll make him a first-round draft pick." In the first place, a college football player is not allowed to enter the NFL draft until after his junior year, and scouts tend to be overwhelmed by the players immediately at hand. In the second place, there is always the risk that a player will be injured, jailed, tossed out of school, or otherwise rendered useless to the game: so why bother with a football player until you need to? But Michael is proving a bit of an exception; when scouts came to Ole Miss in early 2007 to have a second look at Patrick Willis, several asked to see "the Oher kid." Just to see if what they'd heard was true. "If Michael wants to enter the draft after his junior year," says Jimmy Sexton, an agent who represents many NFL players and also, interestingly, many NFL coaches. "It's not a question of if he'll get drafted. It's just a question of how high."

Michael Oher has completed the swap: one life for another. He doesn't care to look back. He hardly ever talks to his mother these days; although when his brothers call, he usually calls them back. He seldom returns to the place he grew up. He spends most of his time with the football team, or in class, or with the Tuohys. A world once rigged to insure his failure now seems rigged to insure his success, and he claims to see nothing odd, or unsettling, about it.

But I do. If I had more patience with this story, I might have waited ten years to tell it. To see, for instance, what became of Michael as a professional football player, and a grown-up, before I wrote about him. But it seemed to me that the most important part of the Michael Oher story was over: his value was no longer neglected. He'd gone from among the least valued fifteen-year-olds on the planet to among the most highly prized eighteen-year-olds. In the market for him great forces were at work. Some of those forces arose from changes in football strategy: professional football now exalts the value of the task that Michael Oher's body is ideally suited to perform. But the greater forces arose from a series of social accidents—his wandering out of poor black Memphis into rich white Memphis, being taken in by a rich white family, and, above all, his willingness to endure an immense amount of trouble and discomfort to better his lot. Michael Oher might have been born to play left tackle in the NFL, but if he had remained in the environment into which he was born, no one would have ever known about his talent. I still find this remarkable. When we list all the problems afflicting the American inner city we don't usually include its inability to identify its star athletes, and export them. But even boys with talent to play in the NFL can be born into circumstances so low that their talents are never noticed.

Now that Michael Oher has been noticed, the discussions about him have a different tone. No longer do people ask, "What are we going to do with him?" Or "How are we going to save him?" They ask: "How do we maximize his incredible value?" As he enters his junior year at Ole Miss, Michael Oher remains on the fringes of the professional football mind. But if he were a corporate stock, Wall Street analysts would rate him a strong buy. With a bit better management, imagine how many more like him there might be.

—April 2007

AUTHOR'S NOTE

—

I'M STILL SLIGHTLY EMBARRASSED by how I came upon the story told by this book, and how slow I was to pick up on it. In the fall of 2003, while passing through Memphis, I called Sean Tuohy. Sean and I had been classmates for thirteen years at the Isidore Newman School in New Orleans, Louisiana. When very young we'd been good friends—there was a stretch between the first grade and the fourth during which I routinely followed him out of school to a dirt basketball court behind his house, to see how long it would take for him to score one hundred points against me. (Not long, usually.) But I hadn't seen or heard from him in twenty-five years when I called to tell him that I was writing a magazine article about our former high school baseball coach. That evening I heard about Michael Oher, who was quickly becoming a member of Sean's family—and paid almost no attention. I wrote the article about our coach for the *New York Times Magazine*, which became a book called *Coach* in which Sean appeared briefly, and moved on.

A few months later, kicking around the NFL for another magazine piece, I learned that the left tackle had become much more highly paid than other offensive linemen, and I wondered how that happened and what the left tackles themselves made of it. Then I learned from Sean that Michael was now being hounded by college football coaches who saw in him a future NFL left tackle. Now I was paying attention. Shortly thereafter Sean came to visit me. We went to dinner again, but this time my wife, Tabitha, came along. When we got around to the subject of Michael Oher it took Sean about ten minutes to get her laughing, twenty to get her crying, and thirty to ruin the meal. But it was worth it, because in the car on the way home she said, "I don't understand why you are writing about anything else." I had had the same thought but had dismissed it, as it seemed somehow unsporting, like hunting in a baited field, to turn to one's kindergarten classmate for literary material. It was one thing to include Sean as a foil in my memoir; it was another to ransack his life for a book. So now that it's time to slice up and distribute my gratitude, my wife deserves an extra big piece. If she hadn't pushed me to acknowledge my interest in Michael Oher, I'm not sure I'd have pursued it.

I must also thank Sean and Leigh Anne Tuohy. To them this book was a matter of some indifference. Actually, that's not quite right. Sean pretended to be indifferent but was actually a little bit amused; Leigh Anne pretended to be indifferent but was actually a tiny bit dubious. None of the Tuohys ever asked why I was spending so much time hanging around Memphis, or their living room. No one ever asked me what I planned to write; no one ever hinted at a desire to see the manuscript before it went to print. They gave me their time, and their points of view, and left it at that. I'll always be grateful for their openness and their generosity.

In learning about football I had a lot of help from people in college football and the NFL. Bill Walsh and Bill Parcells between them sat patiently through many sessions and countless hours of interrogation. Pat Hanlon and Ernie Accorsi of the New York Giants showed me the inside of an NFL front office several years ago, and both have continued to educate me. At the Indianapolis

Colts, Craig Kelley and Bill Polian were more helpful than they know; at the San Francisco 49ers, Paraag Marathe was a steady source of knowledge and insight. Kevin Byrne of the Baltimore Ravens and Patrick Wixted of the Washington Redskins made my life a lot more fun than it should have been in their locker rooms. The Tennessee Titans' defensive coordinator, Jim Schwartz, has been kind enough over the last few years to serve as an occasional sounding board.

I also had help from many current and former NFL players. When I first set out to interview professional football players I was struck by how much easier they were to talk to than professional baseball players, who tend to treat questions as insults. I'd like to thank a few of them here for making an extra effort with me: Lawrence Taylor, Steve Wallace, Jonathan Ogden, Harry Carson, Tariq Glenn, Dwight Freeney, Anthony Muñoz, Tim Long, Joe Jacoby, Lindsay Knapp, Joe Theismann, Dan Audick, Randy Cross, and Will Wolford. To understand the market for football players I had the help of several agents: Tom Condon, Gary O'Hagan, Ralph Cindrich, and Don Yee. Yee's client, D'Brickashaw Ferguson, the new left tackle of the New York Jets, wound up on the cutting-room floor; but he, too, was generous with his time. Laurel Ayers, widow of John Ayers, offered a moving and indispensable view of her husband. Langston Rogers made it possible for me to interview essentially the entire Ole Miss football team, and made me feel welcome from the moment I first set foot on the Ole Miss campus back in the fall of 2004. Hugh Freeze was a constant source of football insight; if I were the Ole Miss athletic director I'd just hand Hugh the offense and let him run it. There can't be many coaches who know more about offensive line play than George DeLeone, who has left Ole Miss and now runs the offense at Temple University. I appreciate the many hours he spent trying to explain what he knows to me.

Saleem Choudhry opened his archives at the Pro Football Hall of Fame in Canton, Ohio, and helped me to dig through them. The editors of *Total Football II: The Official Encyclopedia of the National Football League* have my enduring gratitude for compiling such a fantastic resource. Kevin Lamb's essay on the evolution of football strategy, especially, was an inspiration. Rick Figueiredo made it possible for me to watch old 49er games. Tony Horwitz, Jacob Weisberg, and Eddie Epstein read the first draft of this book and offered me good conceptual advice. Rob Neyer went through it line by line and repaired a shockingly large quantity of my prose.

Inside W. W. Norton, which has published all but one of my books, I stressed out the production line even more than I usually do. Nancy Palmquist and Amanda Morrison did a wonderful job making sure that the misery I caused them wasn't in turn inflicted on readers. Don Rifkin was kind enough to triple-check everything. Debra Morton Hoyt created a lovely package.

On the streets of Memphis I also needed a lot of help. Wyatt Aiken proved to be the perfect tour guide of local spiritual life. Big Tony Henderson is one of those people who makes a lot of improbable things happen, and he worked his magic often on my behalf. Delvin Lane would count as my highest-ranking friend in the Gangster Disciples, if he hadn't relinquished his title as gang leader. When Delvin was Born Again, and decided to dedicate his life to Christ, he assumed he might be killed in the bargain. (The penalty for a senior figure quitting the Gangster Disciples was, typically, death.) So I'm grateful, I suppose, to the other Gangster Disciples for making an exception of Delvin, and permitting him to live, and to educate me. Without the help of Phyllis Betts at the University of Memphis, who spearheads the social science investigation of Hurt Village, this book would have been even less well informed than it is about life in the Memphis inner city. Debra Kirkwood shared her knowledge of the Tennessee foster care system; Pat Williams related his experience helping to found the Briarcrest

Christian School; and Liz Marable offered insight into the Memphis public schools, and Michael's mind—acquired from the many hours she spent teaching basic math to him.

Michael was a funny subject because, at least at first, he had so little interest in talking about himself. He hoarded personal information the way he hoarded everything else. His memory might be a relative strength in his schoolwork, but it seemed to have neglected to record his own life experiences. When I asked Michael about his past, he claimed not to recall it and couldn't understand why I found it interesting. He wasn't happy to let people get to know him, and it didn't appear he was going to make an exception for me. After a year of pestering him, I felt doomed to learn about my main character exclusively from others. Then one day Michael phoned me out of the blue. "Are you the guy who keeps asking every other person in the world questions about me when you could just come and ask me?" he said. Our conversations soon became a lot more interesting. He remembered much about his past, often in vivid detail. One of the pleasures of working on this book has been those long conversations with Michael. I'll be cheering for him, I assume, for a long time to come.

MKTG
ONLINE

ACCESS TEXTBOOK CONTENT ONLINE— INCLUDING ON SMARTPHONES!

Includes Videos & Other Interactive Resources!

MANAGE MY COURSE ∨   STUDENT

MKTG10

CHAPTER
1

An Overview of Marketing

CHAPTER
2

Strategic Planning for Competitive Advantage

4LTR PRESS

Access MKTG **ONLINE** at www.cengagebrain.com

1 | An Overview of Marketing

LEARNING OUTCOMES
After studying this chapter, you will be able to…

1-1 Define the term *marketing*

1-2 Describe four marketing management philosophies

1-3 Discuss the differences between sales and market orientations

1-4 Describe several reasons for studying marketing

After you finish this chapter go to **PAGE 13** for **STUDY TOOLS.**

lofoto/Shutterstock.com

1-1 WHAT IS MARKETING?

What does the term *marketing* mean to you? Many people think *marketing* means personal selling. Others think it means advertising. Still others believe marketing has to do with making products available in stores, arranging displays, and maintaining inventories of products for future sales. Actually, marketing includes all of these activities and more.

Marketing has two facets. First, it is a philosophy, an attitude, a perspective, or a management orientation that stresses customer satisfaction. Second, marketing is an organization function and a set of processes used to implement this philosophy.

The American Marketing Association's definition of marketing focuses on the second facet. According to the AMA, **marketing** is the activity, set of institutions, and processes for creating, communicating, delivering, and exchanging offerings that

> "Marketing is too important to be left only to the marketing department."
>
> —DAVID PACKARD, COFOUNDER OF HEWLETT-PACKARD

have value for customers, clients, partners, and society at large.[1]

Marketing involves more than just activities performed by a group of people in a defined area or department. In the often-quoted words of David Packard, co-founder of Hewlett-Packard, "Marketing is too important to be left only to the marketing department." Marketing entails processes that focus on delivering value and benefits to customers, not just selling goods, services, and/or ideas. It uses communication, distribution, and pricing strategies to provide customers and other stakeholders with the goods, services, ideas, values, and benefits they desire when and where they want them. It involves

marketing the activity, set of institutions, and processes for creating, communicating, delivering, and exchanging offerings that have value for customers, clients, partners, and society at large building long-term, mutually rewarding relationships when these benefit all parties concerned. Marketing also entails an understanding that organizations have many connected stakeholder "partners," including employees, suppliers, stockholders, distributors, and others.

Research shows that companies that consistently reward employees with incentives and recognition are those that perform best, while disgruntled, disengaged workers cost the United States economy upward of $350 billion a year in lost productivity.[2] In 2014, Google captured the number one position in *Fortune*'s "100 Best Companies to Work For" for the third year in a row. The company pays 100 percent of employees' health care premiums, offers paid sabbaticals, and provides bocce courts, a bowling alley, and twenty-five cafés—all for free. Google has also never had a layoff. One so-called Googler reported that "employees are never more than 150 feet away from a well-stocked pantry."[3]

One desired outcome of marketing is an **exchange**—people giving up something in order to receive something else they would rather have. Normally,

Zuma Press, Inc./Alamy

Google offers many amenities to its employees, part of the reason *Fortune* ranked it as the best company to work for in 2012, 2013, and 2014.

we think of money as the medium of exchange. We "give up" money to "get" the goods and services we want. Exchange does

exchange people giving up something in order to receive something else they would rather have

not require money, however. Two (or more) people may barter or trade such items as baseball cards or oil paintings.

An exchange can take place only if the following five conditions exist:

1. There must be at least two parties.
2. Each party has something that might be of value to the other party.
3. Each party is capable of communication and delivery.
4. Each party is free to accept or reject the exchange offer.
5. Each party believes it is appropriate or desirable to deal with the other party.[4]

Exchange will not necessarily take place even if all these conditions exist, but they must exist for exchange to be possible. For example, suppose you place an advertisement in your local newspaper stating that your used automobile is for sale at a certain price. Several people may call you to ask about the car, some may test-drive it, and one or more may even make you an offer. All five conditions that are necessary for an exchange to occur exist in this scenario. But unless you reach an agreement with a buyer and actually sell the car, an exchange will not take place.

Notice that marketing can occur even if an exchange does not occur. In the example just discussed, you would have engaged in marketing by advertising in the local newspaper even if no one bought your used automobile.

 ## 1-2 MARKETING MANAGEMENT PHILOSOPHIES

Four competing philosophies strongly influence an organization's marketing processes. These philosophies are commonly referred to as production, sales, market, and societal marketing orientations.

1-2a Production Orientation

A **production orientation** is a philosophy that focuses on the internal capabilities of the firm rather than on the desires and needs of the marketplace. A production orientation means that management assesses its resources and asks these questions: "What can we do best?" "What can our engineers design?" "What is easy to produce, given our equipment?" In the case of a service organization, managers ask, "What services are most convenient for the firm to offer?" and "Where do our talents lie?" The furniture industry is infamous for its disregard of customers and for its slow cycle times. For example, most traditional furniture stores (think Ashley or Haverty's) carry the same styles and varieties of furniture that they have carried for many years. They always produce and stock sofas, coffee tables, arm chairs, and end tables for the living room. Master bedroom suites always include at least a queen- or king-sized bed, two dressers, and two side tables. Regardless of what customers may actually be looking for, this is what they will find at these stores—and they have been so long-lived because what they produce has matched up with customer expectations. This has always been a production-oriented industry.

There is nothing wrong with assessing a firm's capabilities; in fact, such assessments are major considerations in strategic marketing planning (see Chapter 2). A production orientation falls short because it does not consider whether the goods and services that the firm produces most efficiently also meet the needs of the marketplace. Sometimes what a firm can best produce is exactly what the market wants. Apple has a history of production orientation, creating computers, operating systems, and other gadgetry because it can and hoping to sell the result. Some items have found a waiting market (early computers, iPod, iPhone). Other products, like the Newton, one of the first versions of a PDA, were simply flops.

In some situations, as when competition is weak or demand exceeds supply, a production-oriented firm can survive and even prosper. More often, however, firms that succeed in competitive markets have a clear understanding that they must first determine what customers want and then produce it, rather than focus on what company management thinks should be produced and hope that the product is something customers want.

1-2b Sales Orientation

A **sales orientation** is based on the belief that people will buy more goods and services if aggressive sales techniques are used and that high sales result in high profits. Not only are sales to the final buyer emphasized, but intermediaries are also encouraged to push manufacturers' products more aggressively. To sales-oriented firms, marketing means selling things and collecting money.

production orientation
a philosophy that focuses on the internal capabilities of the firm rather than on the desires and needs of the marketplace

sales orientation the belief that people will buy more goods and services if aggressive sales techniques are used and that high sales result in high profits

LIGHTNING DOES NOT STRIKE TWICE

One of the dangers of a sales orientation is failing to understand what is important to the firm's customers. When that occurs, sales-oriented firms sometimes use aggressive incentives to drive sales. For example, after Apple received complaints about the $49 selling price of its Thunderbolt cable, the company reduced the cable's price to $39 and introduced a shorter $29 version. The company hoped to spark sales of the optical data transfer cable, compatible only with Apple's newest line of computers and laptops.[5]

JMiks/Shutterstock.com

"Josh Lowensohn, "Apple's Thunderbolt Cable Gets a Price Drop, Shorter Version," CNET, January 9, 2013, http://news.CNET.com/8301-13579_3-57563157-37/apples-thunderbolt-cable-gets-a-price-drop-shorter-version (Accessed January 10, 2015)."

The fundamental problem with a sales orientation, as with a production orientation, is a lack of understanding of the needs and wants of the marketplace. Sales-oriented companies often find that, despite the quality of their sales force, they cannot convince people to buy goods or services that are neither wanted nor needed.

1-2c Market Orientation

The **marketing concept** is a simple and intuitively appealing philosophy that articulates a market orientation. It states that the social and economic justification for an organization's existence is the satisfaction of customer wants and needs while meeting organizational objectives. What a business thinks it produces is not of primary importance to its success. Instead, what customers think they are buying—the perceived value—defines a business. The marketing concept includes the following:

- Focusing on customer wants and needs so that the organization can distinguish its product(s) from competitors' offerings
- Integrating all the organization's activities, including production, to satisfy customer wants
- Achieving long-term goals for the organization by satisfying customer wants and needs legally and responsibly

The recipe for success is to develop a thorough understanding of your customers and your competition, your distinctive capabilities that enable your company to execute plans on the basis of this customer understanding, and how to deliver the desired experience using and integrating all of the resources of the firm. For example, Kellogg's recently introduced Open for Breakfast, a forum the company uses to connect with consumers about what they are eating for breakfast. The program is also used to share stories about the foods the company makes and its pledge to care for the environment.[6]

Firms that adopt and implement the marketing concept are said to be **market oriented**, meaning they assume that a sale does not depend on an aggressive sales force but rather on a customer's decision to purchase a product. Achieving a market orientation involves obtaining information about customers, competitors, and markets; examining the information from a total business perspective; determining how to deliver superior customer value; and implementing actions to provide value to customers.

Some firms are known for delivering superior customer value and satisfaction. For example, in 2014, J.D. Power and Associates ranked Cadillac highest in customer satisfaction among luxury automotive brands, while Buick ranked

Oliver Hoffmann/Shutterstock.com

marketing concept the idea that the social and economic justification for an organization's existence is the satisfaction of customer wants and needs while meeting organizational objectives

market orientation a philosophy that assumes that a sale does not depend on an aggressive sales force but rather on a customer's decision to purchase a product; it is synonymous with the marketing concept

highest among mass-market brands.[7] Rankings such as these, as well as word-of-mouth from satisfied customers, drive additional sales for these automotive companies.

Understanding your competitive arena and competitors' strengths and weaknesses is a critical component of a market orientation. This includes assessing what existing or potential competitors intend to do tomorrow and what they are doing today. For example, BlackBerry (formerly Research in Motion) failed to realize it was competing against computer companies as well as telecom companies, and its wireless handsets were quickly eclipsed by offerings from Google, Samsung, and Apple. Had BlackBerry been a market-oriented company, its management might have better understood the changes taking place in the market, seen the competitive threat, and developed strategies to counter the threat. Instead, it reentered the market after a five-year slump with the wholly redesigned BlackBerry 10 operating system and sleek new flagship phones. These new products were fairly well received, but they failed to push BlackBerry back into the smartphone spotlight. By contrast, American Express's success has rested largely on the company's ability to focus on customers and adapt to their changing needs over the past 160 years.[8]

1-2d Societal Marketing Orientation

The **societal marketing orientation** extends the marketing concept by acknowledging that some products that customers want may not really be in their best interests or the best interests of society as a whole. This philosophy states that an organization exists not only to satisfy customer wants and needs and to meet organizational objectives but also to preserve or enhance individuals' and society's long-term best interests. Marketing products and containers that are less toxic than normal, are more durable, contain reusable materials, or are made of recyclable materials is consistent with a societal marketing orientation. The American Marketing Association's definition of marketing

Lunasee Studios/Shutterstock.com

recognizes the importance of a societal marketing orientation by including "society at large" as one of the constituencies for which marketing seeks to provide value.

Although the societal marketing concept has been discussed for more than thirty years, it did not receive widespread support until the early 2000s. Concerns such as climate change, the depleting of the ozone layer, fuel shortages, pollution, and health issues have caused consumers and legislators to become more aware of the need for companies and consumers to adopt measures that conserve resources and cause less damage to the environment.

Studies reporting consumers' attitudes toward, and intentions to buy, environmentally friendly products show widely varying results. A Nielsen study found that while eighty-three percent of consumers worldwide believe companies should have environmental programs, only twenty-two percent would pay more for an eco-friendly product. The key to consumer purchasing lies beyond labels proclaiming sustainability, natural ingredients, or "being green." Customers want sustainable products that perform better than their unsustainable counterparts.[9] Unilever, whose brands include Dove, Lipton, Hellmann's, and Ben & Jerry's, is one company that puts sustainability at the core of its business. It has promised both to cut its environmental footprint in half and to source all its agricultural products in ways that do not degrade the earth by 2020. The company also promotes the well-being of one billion people by producing foods with less salt and fat and has developed campaigns advocating hand washing and teeth brushing.[10]

1-2e Who Is in Charge?

The Internet and the widespread use of social media have accelerated the shift in power from manufacturers and retailers to consumers and business users. This shift began when customers began using books, electronics, and the Internet to access information, goods, and services. Customers use their widespread knowledge to shop smarter, leading executives such as former Procter & Gamble CEO A. G. Lafley to conclude that "the customer is boss."[11] Founder of Walmart and Sam's Club Sam Walton echoed this sentiment when he reportedly once said, "There is only one boss. The customer. And he can fire everybody in the company

societal marketing orientation the idea that an organization exists not only to satisfy customer wants and needs and to meet organizational objectives but also to preserve or enhance individuals' and society's long-term best interests

from the chairman on down, simply by spending his money somewhere else."[12] The following quotation, attributed to everyone from L.L.Bean founder Leon Leonwood Bean to Mahatma Gandhi, has been a guiding business principle for more than seventy years: "A customer is the most important visitor on our premises. He is not dependent on us. We are dependent on him. He is not an interruption in our work. He is the purpose of it. He is not an outsider in our business. He is part of it. We are not doing him a favor by serving him. He is doing us a favor by giving us an opportunity to do so."[13] And as Internet use and mobile devices become increasingly pervasive, that control will continue to grow. This means that companies must create strategy from the outside in by offering distinct and compelling customer value.[14] This can be accomplished only by carefully studying customers and using deep market insights to inform and guide companies' outside-in view.[15]

 ## 1-3 DIFFERENCES BETWEEN SALES AND MARKET ORIENTATIONS

The differences between sales and market orientations are substantial. The two orientations can be compared in terms of five characteristics: the organization's focus, the firm's business, those to whom the product is directed, the firm's primary goal, and the tools used to achieve the organization's goals.

1-3a The Organization's Focus

Personnel in sales-oriented firms tend to be inward looking, focusing on selling what the organization makes rather than making what the market wants. Many of the historic sources of competitive advantage—technology, innovation, economies of scale—allowed companies to focus their efforts internally and prosper. Today, many successful firms derive their competitive advantage from an external, market-oriented focus. A market orientation has helped companies such as Zappos.com and Bob's Red Mill Natural Foods outperform their competitors. These companies put customers at the center of their business in ways most companies do poorly or not at all.

CUSTOMER VALUE The relationship between benefits and the sacrifice necessary to obtain those benefits is known as **customer value**. Customer value is not simply a matter of high quality. A high-quality product that is available only at a high price will not be perceived as a good value, nor will bare-bones service or low-quality goods selling for a low price. Price is a component of value (a $4,000 handbag is perceived as being more luxurious and of higher quality than one selling for $100), but low price is not the same as good value. Instead, customers value goods and services that are of the quality they expect and that are sold at prices they are willing to pay.

Value can be used to sell a Mercedes-Benz as well as a Tyson frozen chicken dinner. In other words, value is something that shoppers of all markets and at all income levels look for. Lower-income consumers are price sensitive, but they will pay for products if they deliver a benefit that is worth the money.[16] Conversely, wealthy customers with money to spend may value the social message of their purchases above all else. These shoppers are being courted by a new breed of social shopping sites. The basic premise is that a well-known fashion name (be it a fashion editor, elite socialite, or celebrity) moderates sites by handpicking pieces from favorite retailers, such as Barneys New York or Saks Fifth Avenue. Shoppers then purchase the curated items, and the site receives commission for each purchase. There are many of these sites; Moda Operandi has highlighted (and sold out of) woven skirts for $4,000 each, Motilo focuses on French fashion (including couture pieces), and *Fino File* is an online, shopable magazine, with pieces ranging from $80 tops to $1,000 boots. With reports of growing subscribers and sold-out merchandise, it is clear that these sites are attracting customers who value curated style.[17]

CUSTOMER SATISFACTION The customers' evaluation of a good or service in terms of whether that good or service has met their needs and expectations is called **customer satisfaction**. Failure to meet needs and expectations results in dissatisfaction with the good or service. Some companies, in their passion to drive down costs, have damaged their relationships with customers. Bank of America, Comcast, Dish Network, and AT&T are examples of companies where executives lost track of the delicate balance between efficiency and service.[18] Firms that have a reputation for delivering high levels of customer satisfaction do things differently from their competitors. Top management is obsessed with customer satisfaction, and employees throughout the organization understand the link between their job and satisfied customers. The

> **customer value** the relationship between benefits and the sacrifice necessary to obtain those benefits
>
> **customer satisfaction** customers' evaluation of a good or service in terms of whether it has met their needs and expectations

▶ **Offer products that perform:** This is the bare minimum requirement. After grappling with the problems associated with its Vista operating system, Microsoft listened to its customers and made drastic changes for Windows 7, which received greatly improved reviews. Microsoft's subsequent release, Windows 8, performed even better than Windows 7, but consumers were much slower to embrace the operating system's incremental improvements.

▶ **Earn trust:** A stable base of loyal customers can help a firm grow and prosper. To attract customers, online eyewear company Coastal.com offers a First Pair Free program, whereby new customers receive their first pair of prescription eyeglass for free. Moreover, Coastal.com offers 366-day returns and encourages its staff members to do whatever it takes to ensure that customers are delighted by a smooth and stress-free experience. Coastal.com's dedication to earning customers' trust is evident—in 2013, the company received the STELLA Service elite seal for excellence in outstanding customer service.[19]

▶ **Avoid unrealistic pricing:** E-marketers are leveraging Internet technology to redefine how prices are set and negotiated. With lower costs, e-marketers can often offer lower prices than their brick-and-mortar counterparts. The enormous popularity of auction sites such as eBay and the customer-bid model used by Priceline and uBid.com illustrates that online customers are interested in bargain prices. In fact, as smartphone usage grows, brick-and-mortar stores are up against customers who compare prices using their smartphones and purchase items for less online while standing in the store.

▶ **Give the buyer facts:** Today's sophisticated consumer wants informative advertising and knowledgeable salespeople. It is becoming very difficult for business marketers to differentiate themselves from competitors. Rather than trying to sell products, salespeople need to find out what the customer needs, which is usually a combination of friendliness, understanding, fairness, control, options, and information.[20] In other words, salespeople need

Northfoto/Shutterstock.com

to start with the needs of the customer and work toward the solution.

▶ **Offer organization-wide commitment in service and after-sales support:** Upscale fashion retailer Nordstrom is widely known for its company-wide support system. If a customer finds that a competitor has reduced the price of an item also sold at Nordstrom, Nordstrom will match the other retailer's price and credit the customer's account—even long after the sale is made. Customer service agents at each of Nordstrom's 117 locations are knowledgeable and eager to assist customers before, during, or after a sale, and strive to make the return process as painless as possible. This attention to customer service is carried through to Nordstrom's online store as well: every order receives free shipping, as well as free return shipping. However and wherever they place their orders, customers know that Nordstrom will support them throughout—and long after—the checkout process.[21]

▶ **Co-create:** Some companies and products allow customers to help create their own experience. For example, Case-Mate, a firm that makes form-fitting cases for cell phones, laptops, and other personal devices, allows customers to design their own cases by uploading their own photos. Customers who do not have designs of their own can manipulate art from designers using the "design with" feature at case-mate.com. Either way, customers produce completely unique covers for their devices.

culture of the organization is to focus on delighting customers rather than on selling products.

Coming back from customer dissatisfaction can be tough, but there are some key ways that companies begin to improve customer satisfaction. Forrester Research discovered that when companies experience gains in the firm's Customer Experience Index (CxPi), they have implemented one of two major changes. Aetna, a major health insurance provider, executed the first type of change—changing its decentralized, part-time customer service group into a full-time, centralized customer service team. Aetna's CxPi score rose six points in one year. Office Depot executed the second type of change—addressing customer "pain points" and making sure that what customers need is always available to them. By streamlining its supply chain and adding more stylish office products,

Office Depot satisfied business customers and female shoppers, increasing its CxPi by nine points.[22]

BUILDING RELATIONSHIPS Attracting new customers to a business is only the beginning. The best companies view new-customer attraction as the launching point for developing and enhancing a long-term relationship. Companies can expand market share in three ways: attracting new customers, increasing business with existing customers, and retaining current customers. Building relationships with existing customers directly addresses two of the three possibilities and indirectly addresses the other.

Relationship marketing is a strategy that focuses on keeping and improving relationships with current customers. It assumes that many consumers and business customers prefer to have an ongoing relationship with one organization rather than switch continually among providers in their search for value. Chicago-based software company 37signals decided to focus its marketing budget on helping current customers get more out of the software they already have rather than targeting new customers. The company would rather expand current customers' awareness of what is possible with its products than focus on short term sales.[23] This long-term focus on customer needs is a hallmark of relationship marketing.

Most successful relationship marketing strategies depend on customer-oriented personnel, effective training programs, employees with the authority to make decisions and solve problems, and teamwork.

Customer-Oriented Personnel For an organization to be focused on building relationships with customers, employees' attitudes and actions must be customer oriented. An employee may be the only contact a particular customer has with the firm. In that customer's eyes, the employee *is* the firm. Any person, department, or division that is not customer oriented weakens the positive image of the entire organization. For example, a potential customer who is greeted discourteously may well assume that the employee's attitude represents the whole firm.

Customer-oriented personnel come from an organizational culture that supports its people. Marriott, a multibillion dollar worldwide hotel chain, believes that treating employees well contributes to good customer service. The company has been among Fortune's "100 Best Companies to Work For" every year since the magazine introduced the list in 1998. For example, during the recent recession, Marriott ensured that all of its employees kept their benefits despite shorter shifts. For its focus on customer satisfaction, Marriott received the number three ranking on MSN.com's 2014 Customer Service Hall of Fame.[24]

Some companies, such as Coca-Cola, Delta Air Lines, Hershey, Kellogg, Nautilus, and Sears, have appointed chief customer officers (CCOs). These customer advocates provide an executive voice for customers and report directly to the CEO. Their responsibilities include ensuring that the company maintains a customer-centric culture and that all company employees remain focused on delivering customer value.

Marriott's customer-oriented focus is evident in initiatives like the Fairfield Inn & Suites "Some Like It Hot" food truck, which serves hot, made-to-order breakfasts to customers for free.

The Role of Training Leading marketers recognize the role of employee training in customer service and relationship building. Sales staff at the Container Store receive more than 240 hours of training and generous benefits compared to an industry average of 8 hours of training and modest benefits.

Empowerment In addition to training, many market-oriented firms are giving employees more authority to solve customer problems on the spot. The term used to describe this delegation of authority is **empowerment**. Employees develop ownership attitudes when they are treated like part-owners of the business and are expected to act the part. These employees manage themselves, are more likely to work hard, account for their own performance and that of the company, and take prudent risks to build a stronger business and sustain the company's success.

> **relationship marketing** a strategy that focuses on keeping and improving relationships with current customers
>
> **empowerment** delegation of authority to solve customers' problems quickly—usually by the first person the customer notifies regarding a problem

An emphasis on cooperation over competition can help a company's performance improve. That is why many companies have moved to using teams to get jobs done.

Rawpixel/Shutterstock.com

In order to empower its workers, the Ritz-Carlton chain of luxury hotels developed a set of twelve "Service Values" guidelines. These brief, easy-to-understand guidelines include statements such as "I am empowered to create unique, memorable and personal experiences for our guests" and "I own and immediately resolve guest problems." The twelve Service Values are printed on cards distributed to employees, and each day a particular value is discussed at length in Ritz-Carlton team meetings. Employees talk about what the value means to them and offer examples of how the value can be put into practice that day.[25]

Teamwork Many organizations that are frequently noted for delivering superior customer value and providing high levels of customer satisfaction, such as Southwest Airlines and Walt Disney World, assign employees to teams and teach them team-building skills. **Teamwork** entails collaborative efforts of people to accomplish common objectives. Job performance, company performance, product value, and customer satisfaction all improve when people in the same department or work group begin supporting and assisting each other and emphasize cooperation instead of competition. Performance is also enhanced when cross-functional teams align their jobs with customer needs. For example, if a team of

teamwork collaborative efforts of people to accomplish common objectives

telecommunications service representatives is working to improve interaction with customers, back-office people such as computer technicians or training personnel can become part of the team, with the ultimate goal of delivering superior customer value and satisfaction.

1-3b The Firm's Business

A sales-oriented firm defines its business (or mission) in terms of goods and services. A market-oriented firm defines its business in terms of the benefits its customers seek. People who spend their money, time, and energy expect to receive benefits, not just goods and services. This distinction has enormous implications. As Michael Mosley, director of office operations at health care provider Amedisys Home Health, notes, "We're in the business of making people better."[26] Answering the question "What is this firm's business?" in terms of the benefits customers seek, instead of goods and services, offers at least three important advantages:

- It ensures that the firm keeps focusing on customers and avoids becoming preoccupied with goods, services, or the organization's internal needs.

- It encourages innovation and creativity by reminding people that there are many ways to satisfy customer wants.

- It stimulates an awareness of changes in customer desires and preferences so that product offerings are more likely to remain relevant.

Because of the limited way it defines its business, a sales-oriented firm often misses opportunities to serve customers whose wants can be met through a wide range of product offerings instead of through specific products. For example, in 1989, 220-year-old Britannica had estimated revenues of $650 million and a worldwide sales force of 7,500. Just five years later, after three consecutive years of losses, the sales force had collapsed to as few as 280 representatives. How did this respected company sink so low? Britannica managers saw that competitors were beginning to use CD-ROMs to store huge masses of information but chose to ignore the new computer technology as well as an offer to team up with Microsoft. In 2012, the company announced that it would stop printing its namesake books and instead focus on selling its reference works to subscribers through its Web site and apps for tablets and smartphones.[27]

Having a market orientation and a focus on customer wants does not mean offering customers everything they want. It is not possible, for example, to profitably manufacture and market automobile tires that will last for 100,000 miles for twenty-five dollars. Furthermore, customers' preferences must be mediated by sound professional judgment as to how to deliver the benefits they seek. As Henry Ford once said, "If I had asked people what they wanted, they would have said faster horses."[28] Consumers have a limited set of experiences. They are unlikely to request anything beyond those experiences because they are not aware of benefits they may gain from other potential offerings. For example, before the Internet, many people thought that shopping for some products was boring and time-consuming but could not express their need for electronic shopping.

1-3c Those to Whom the Product Is Directed

A sales-oriented organization targets its products at "everybody" or "the average customer." A market-oriented organization aims at specific groups of people. The fallacy of developing products directed at the average user is that relatively few average users actually exist. Typically, populations are characterized by diversity. An average is simply a midpoint in some set of characteristics. Because most potential customers are not "average," they are not likely to be attracted to an average product marketed to the average customer. Consider the market for shampoo as one simple example. There are shampoos for oily hair, dry hair, and dandruff. Some shampoos remove the gray or color hair. Special shampoos are marketed for infants and elderly people. There are even shampoos for people with average or normal hair (whatever that is), but this is a fairly small portion of the total market for shampoo.

A market-oriented organization recognizes that different customer groups want different features or benefits. It may therefore need to develop different goods, services, and promotional appeals. A market-oriented organization carefully analyzes the market and divides it into groups of people who are fairly similar in terms of selected characteristics. Then the organization develops marketing programs that will bring about mutually satisfying exchanges with one or more of those groups. For example, Toyota developed a series of tongue-in-cheek videos and interactive Web pages featuring comedian Michael Showalter to advertise the 2013 Yaris subcompact sedan. Toyota used absurdist humor and an ironic slogan ("It's a car!") to appeal to Internet-savvy teens and young adults—a prime market for inexpensive subcompact cars.[29]

CUSTOMER RELATIONSHIP MANAGEMENT Beyond knowing to whom they are directing their products or services, companies must also develop a deeper understanding of their customers. One way of doing this is through *customer relationship management*.

Customer relationship management (CRM) is a company-wide business strategy designed to optimize profitability, revenue, and customer satisfaction by focusing on highly defined and precise customer groups. This is accomplished by organizing the company around customer segments, establishing and tracking customer interactions with the company, fostering customer-satisfying behaviors, and linking all processes of the company from its customers through its suppliers. The difference between CRM and traditional mass marketing can be compared to shooting a rifle versus a shotgun. Instead of scattering messages far and wide across the spectrum of mass media (the shotgun approach), CRM marketers now are homing in on ways to effectively communicate with each customer (the rifle approach).

Companies that adopt CRM systems are almost always market oriented, customizing product and service offerings based on data generated through interactions between the customer and the company. This strategy transcends all functional areas of the business, producing an internal system where all of the company's decisions and actions are a direct result of customer information. We will examine specific applications of CRM in several chapters throughout this book.

The emergence of **on-demand marketing** is taking CRM to a new level. As technology evolves and becomes more sophisticated, consumer expectations of their decision- and buying-related experiences have risen. Consumers (1) want to interact anywhere, anytime; (2) want to do new things with varied kinds of information in ways that create value; (3) expect data stored about them to be targeted specifically to their needs or to personalize their experiences; and (4) expect all interactions with a company to be easy. In response to these expectations, companies are developing new ways to integrate and personalize each stage of a customer's decision journey, which in turn should increase relationship-related behaviors. On-demand marketing delivers relevant experiences throughout the consumer's decision and buying process that are integrated across both physical and virtual environments. Trends such as the growth of mobile connectivity, better-designed Web sites, inexpensive communication through technology, and advances in handling big data have allowed companies to start designing

> **customer relationship management (CRM)** a company-wide business strategy designed to optimize profitability, revenue, and customer satisfaction by focusing on highly defined and precise customer groups
>
> **on-demand marketing** delivering relevant experiences, integrated across both physical and virtual environments, throughout the consumer's decision and buying process

on-demand marketing programs that appeal to consumers. For on-demand marketing to be successful, companies must deliver high-quality experiences across all touch points with the customer, including sales, service, product use, and marketing.

An example of on-demand marketing is Commonwealth Bank of Australia's new smartphone app that integrates and personalizes the house hunting experience. A prospective homebuyer starts by taking a picture of a house he or she likes. Using special software and location-based technology, the app finds the house and provides the list price and other information, connects with the buyer's financial data, and determines whether the buyer can be preapproved for a mortgage. This fast series of interactions decreases the hassle of searching real-estate agents' sites for a house and then connecting with agents, banks, and/or mortgage brokers—a process that traditionally takes up to a week.[30]

Arena Creative/Shutterstock.com

Using the correct tools for the job will help an organization achieve its goals. Marketing tools for success are covered throughout this book.

1-3d **The Firm's Primary Goal**

A sales-oriented organization seeks to achieve profitability through sales volume and tries to convince potential customers to buy, even if the seller knows that the customer and product are mismatched. Sales-oriented organizations place a higher premium on making a sale than on developing a long-term relationship with a customer. In contrast, the ultimate goal of most market-oriented organizations is to make a profit by creating customer value, providing customer satisfaction, and building long-term relationships with customers. The exception is so-called nonprofit organizations that exist to achieve goals other than

profits. Nonprofit organizations can and should adopt a market orientation. Nonprofit organization marketing is explored further in Chapter 12.

1-3e **Tools the Organization Uses to Achieve Its Goals**

Sales-oriented organizations seek to generate sales volume through intensive promotional activities, mainly personal selling and advertising. In contrast, market-oriented organizations recognize that promotion decisions are only one of four basic marketing mix decisions that must be made: product decisions, place (or distribution) decisions, promotion decisions, and pricing decisions. A market-oriented organization recognizes that each of these four components is important. Furthermore, market-oriented organizations recognize that marketing is not just a responsibility of the marketing department. Interfunctional coordination means that skills and resources throughout the organization are needed to create, communicate, and deliver superior customer service and value.

1-3f **A Word of Caution**

This comparison of sales and market orientations is not meant to belittle the role of promotion, especially personal selling, in the marketing mix. Promotion is the means by which organizations communicate with present and prospective customers about the merits and characteristics of their organization and products. Effective promotion is an essential part of effective marketing. Salespeople who work for market-oriented organizations are generally perceived by their customers to be problem solvers and important links to supply sources and new products. Chapter 18 examines the nature of personal selling in more detail.

WHY STUDY MARKETING?

Now that you understand the meaning of the term *marketing*, why it is important to adopt a marketing orientation, and how organizations implement this philosophy, you may be asking, "What's in it for me?" or "Why should I study marketing?" These are important questions whether you are majoring in a business field other than marketing (such as accounting, finance, or management information systems) or a nonbusiness field (such as journalism, education, or agriculture). There are several important reasons to study marketing: Marketing plays an important role in society, marketing is important to businesses, marketing offers outstanding career opportunities, and marketing affects your life every day.

1-4a Marketing Plays an Important Role in Society

The total population of the United States exceeds 320 million people.[31] Think about how many transactions are needed each day to feed, clothe, and shelter a population of this size. The number is huge. And yet it all works quite well, partly because the well-developed U.S. economic system efficiently distributes the output of farms and factories. A typical U.S. family, for example, consumes two and a half tons of food a year.[32] Marketing makes food available when we want it, in desired quantities, at accessible locations, and in sanitary and convenient packages and forms (such as instant and frozen foods).

1-4b Marketing Is Important to Businesses

The fundamental objectives of most businesses are survival, profits, and growth. Marketing contributes directly to achieving these objectives. Marketing includes the following activities, which are vital to business organizations: assessing the wants and satisfactions of present and potential customers, designing and managing product offerings, determining prices and pricing policies, developing distribution strategies, and communicating with present and potential customers.

All businesspeople, regardless of specialization or area of responsibility, need to be familiar with the terminology and fundamentals of accounting, finance, management, and marketing. People in all business areas need to be able to communicate with specialists in other areas. Furthermore, marketing is not just a job done by people in a marketing department. Marketing is a part of the job of everyone in the organization. Therefore, a basic understanding of marketing is important to all businesspeople.

1-4c Marketing Offers Outstanding Career Opportunities

Between one-fourth and one-third of the entire civilian workforce in the United States performs marketing activities. Marketing offers great career opportunities in such areas as professional selling, marketing research, advertising, retail buying, distribution management, product management, product development, and wholesaling. Marketing career opportunities also exist in a variety of nonbusiness organizations, including hospitals, museums, universities, the armed forces, and various government and social service agencies.

1-4d Marketing in Everyday Life

Marketing plays a major role in your everyday life. You participate in the marketing process as a consumer of goods and services. About half of every dollar you spend pays for marketing costs, such as marketing research, product development, packaging, transportation, storage, advertising, and sales expenses. By developing a better understanding of marketing, you will become a better-informed consumer. You will better understand the buying process and be able to negotiate more effectively with sellers. Moreover, you will be better prepared to demand satisfaction when the goods and services you buy do not meet the standards promised by the manufacturer or the marketer.

STUDY TOOLS 1

LOCATED AT BACK OF THE TEXTBOOK

☐ Rip out Chapter Review Card

LOCATED AT WWW.CENGAGEBRAIN.COM

☐ Review Key Terms Flashcards and create your own

☐ Track your knowledge & understanding of key concepts in marketing

☐ Complete practice and graded quizzes to prepare for tests

☐ Complete interactive content within the MKTG Online experience

☐ View the chapter highlight boxes within the MKTG Online experience

2 | Strategic Planning for Competitive Advantage

LEARNING OUTCOMES

After studying this chapter, you will be able to...

2-1 Understand the importance of strategic planning

2-2 Define strategic business units (SBUs)

2-3 Identify strategic alternatives and know a basic outline for a marketing plan

2-4 Develop an appropriate business mission statement

2-5 Describe the components of a situation analysis

2-6 Identify sources of competitive advantage

2-7 Explain the criteria for stating good marketing objectives

2-8 Discuss target market strategies

2-9 Describe the elements of the marketing mix

2-10 Explain why implementation, evaluation, and control of the marketing plan are necessary

2-11 Identify several techniques that help make strategic planning effective

After you finish this chapter go to **PAGE 29** for **STUDY TOOLS.**

Phase4Studios/Shutterstock.com

2-1 THE NATURE OF STRATEGIC PLANNING

Strategic planning is the managerial process of creating and maintaining a fit between the organization's objectives and resources and the evolving market opportunities. The goal of strategic planning is long-run profitability and growth. Thus, strategic decisions require long-term commitments of resources.

A strategic error can threaten a firm's survival. On the other hand, a good strategic plan can help protect and grow the firm's resources. For instance, if the March of Dimes had decided to focus only on fighting polio, the organization would no longer exist because polio is widely viewed as a conquered disease. The March of Dimes survived by making the strategic decision to switch to fighting birth defects.

Strategic marketing management addresses two questions: (1) What is the organization's main activity at a particular time? (2) How will it reach its goals? Here are some examples of strategic decisions:

- In an effort to halt decreasing sales and compete with other fast food and fast causal chains, McDonald's has unveiled plans to allow customers to customize their orders for the first time. The new offering, called Create a Taste, lets customers use their tablet computers to choose toppings for their sandwiches.[1]

- Coach, the iconic leather goods company that became successful with wallets and handbags, is making an effort to reinvent itself as a lifestyle brand. The company has introduced a variety of products, including

strategic planning the managerial process of creating and maintaining a fit between the organization's objectives and resources and the evolving market opportunities

footwear, women's apparel, jewelry, sunglasses, and watches. It even designed a luxury baseball glove for men.[2]

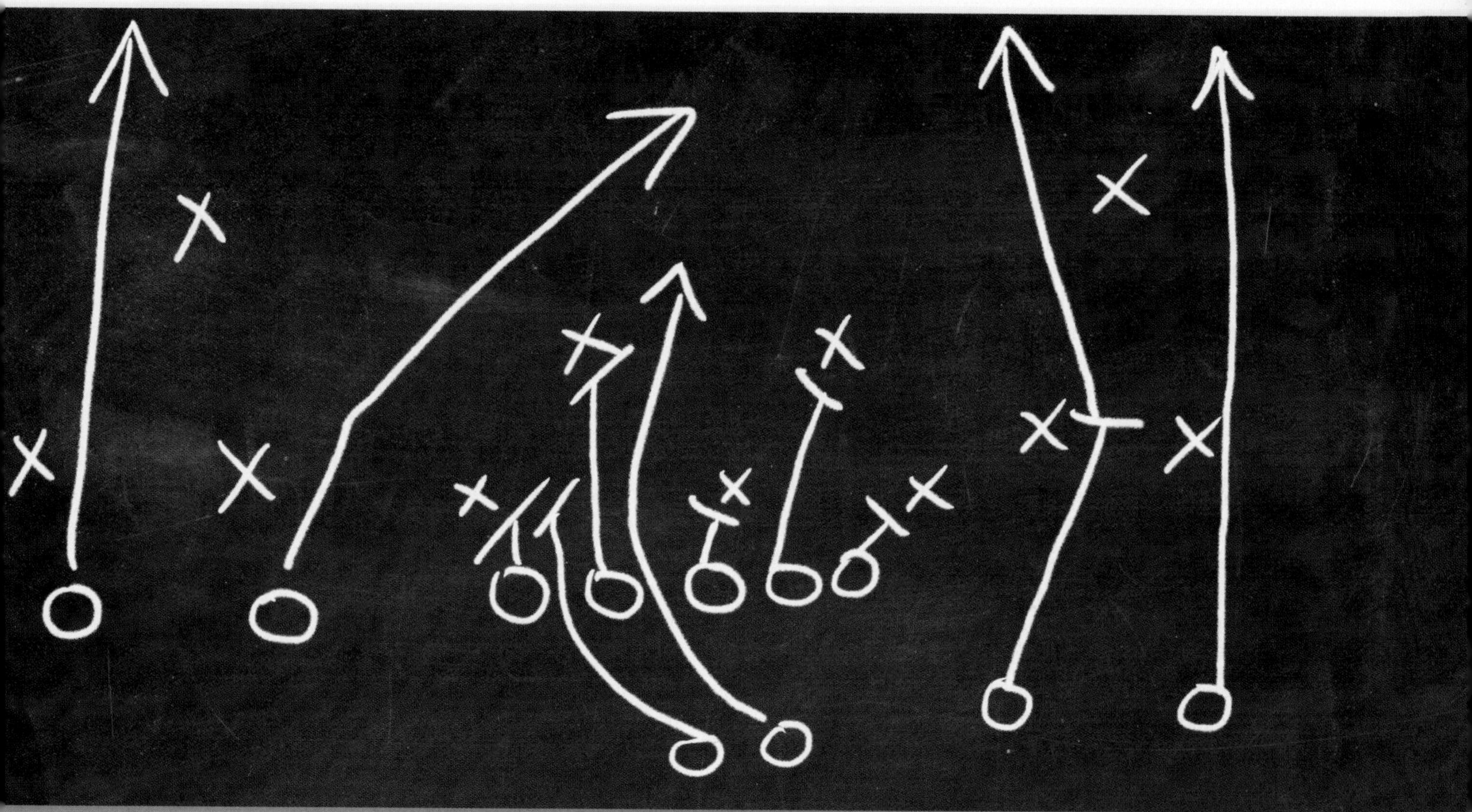

- Following founder Howard Schultz's vision of maintaining an entrepreneurial approach to strategy, Starbucks recently opened the Starbucks Reserve Roastery and Tasting Room in Seattle to appeal to upscale coffee lovers. The company also has plans to expand its food and beverage menu.[3]

All these decisions have affected or will affect each organization's long-run course, its allocation of resources, and ultimately its financial success. In contrast, an operating decision, such as changing the package design for Post Grape-Nuts cereal or altering the sweetness of a Kraft salad dressing, probably will not have a big impact on the long-run profitability of the company.

2-2 STRATEGIC BUSINESS UNITS

Large companies may manage a number of very different businesses, called strategic business units (SBUs). Each SBU has its own rate

> "There are a lot of great ideas that have come and gone in [the digital advertising] industry. Implementation many times is more important than the actual idea."
>
> —DAVID MOORE, CEO OF 24/7 REAL MEDIA

of return on investment, growth potential, and associated risks, and requires its own strategies and funding. When properly created, an SBU has the following characteristics:

- A distinct mission and a specific target market
- Control over its resources
- Its own competitors
- A single business or a collection of related businesses
- Plans independent of the other SBUs in the total organization.

In theory, an SBU should have its own resources for handling basic business functions: accounting, engineering, manufacturing, and marketing. In practice, however, because of company tradition, management philosophy, and production and distribution economies, SBUs sometimes share manufacturing facilities, distribution channels, and even top managers.

strategic business unit (SBU) a subgroup of a single business or collection of related businesses within the larger organization

STRATEGIC ALTERNATIVES

Source: Deckers Consumer Direct Corporation

EXHIBIT 2.1 ANSOFF'S OPPORTUNITY MATRIX

	Present Product	New Product
Present Market	*Market Penetration* Starbucks sells more coffee to customers who register their reloadable Starbucks cards.	*Product Development* Starbucks develops powdered instant coffee called Via.
New Market	*Market Development* Starbucks opens stores in Brazil and Chile.	*Diversification* Starbucks launches Hear Music and buys Ethos Water.

There are several tools available that a company, or SBU, can use to manage the strategic direction of its portfolio of businesses. Three of the most commonly used tools are Ansoff's strategic opportunity matrix, the Boston Consulting Group model, and the General Electric model. Selecting which strategic alternative to pursue depends on which of two philosophies a company maintains about when to expect profits—right away or after increasing market share. In the long run, market share and profitability are compatible goals. For example, Amazon lost hundreds of millions of dollars its first few years, and the company posted quarterly net losses as recently as 2013. Amazon's primary goal is market share—not profit. It sacrifices short-term profit for long-term market share, and thus larger long-term profits.[4]

2-3a Ansoff's Strategic Opportunity Matrix

One method for developing alternatives is Ansoff's strategic opportunity matrix (see Exhibit 2.1), which matches products with markets. Firms can explore these four options:

- **Market penetration:** A firm using the **market penetration** alternative would try to increase market share among existing customers. FTR Energy Services, a division of Frontier Communications, introduced a Green-e certified energy service into New York, Ohio, and Indiana markets served by Frontier's telephone and broadband services. Though these markets were already served by separate, well-established energy companies, FTR Energy hoped to penetrate the energy market by allowing customers to lock in competitive rates and offering five percent cash back on energy usage.[5] Customer databases, discussed in Chapter 9, would help managers implement this strategy.

- **Market development:** **Market development** means attracting new customers to existing products. Ideally, new uses for old products stimulate additional sales among existing customers while also bringing in new buyers. McDonald's, for example, has opened restaurants in Russia, China, and Italy and is eagerly expanding into Eastern European countries. In the nonprofit arena, the growing emphasis on continuing education and executive development by colleges and universities is a market development strategy.

- **Product development:** A **product development** strategy entails the creation of new products for present markets. In January 2014, Beats Electronics launched Beats Music, a subscription-based streaming music service that offers advanced personalization systems and forward-thinking family sharing plans. Beats hopes this service's novel features, sleek design, and celebrity endorsements will catapult it to the front of the music streaming pack, which is currently fronted by competitors such as Spotify and Rdio.[6]

- **Diversification: Diversification** is a strategy of increasing sales by introducing new products into new markets. For example, UGG, a popular footwear

UGG, a popular footwear brand, introduced an upscale men's footwear collection that was inspired by Jimi Hendrix and Jim Morrison.

market penetration
a marketing strategy that tries to increase market share among existing customers

market development
a marketing strategy that entails attracting new customers to existing products

product development
a marketing strategy that entails the creation of new products for present markets

diversification a strategy of increasing sales by introducing new products into new markets

brand known for its casual boots, has introduced an upscale men's footwear collection. The shoes are inspired by rock'n'roll legends such as Jimi Hendrix and Jim Morrison, and are meant to appeal to new customers. "There are some UGG customers that will be interested in the Collection product, but it will also bring in new customers for us," says Leah Larson, UGG's vice president and creative director.[7] A diversification strategy can be risky when a firm is entering unfamiliar markets. However, it can be very profitable when a firm is entering markets with little or no competition.

2-3b The Innovation Matrix

Critics of Ansoff's matrix mention that the matrix does not reflect the reality of how businesses grow—that modern businesses plan growth in a more fluid manner based on current capabilities rather than the clear-cut sectors outlined by the opportunity matrix. To reflect this, Bansi Nagji and Geoff Tuff, global innovation managers at Monitor Group, have recently developed a system that enables a company to see exactly what types of assets need to be developed and what types of markets are possible to grow into (or create) based on the company's core capabilities, as shown in Exhibit 2.2.

The layout of the innovation matrix demonstrates that as a company moves away from its core capabilities

(the lower left) it traverses a range of change and innovation rather than choosing one of the four sectors in Ansoff's matrix. These ranges are broken down into three levels:

1. **Core Innovation:** Represented by the yellow circle in Exhibit 2.2, these decisions implement changes that use existing assets to provide added convenience to existing customers and potentially entice customers from other brands. Packaging changes, such as Tide's laundry detergent pods, fall into this category.

2. **Adjacent Innovation:** Represented by the orange arc in Exhibit 2.2, these decisions are designed to take company strengths into new markets. This space uses existing abilities in new ways. For example, Botox, the popular cosmetic drug, was originally developed to treat intestinal problems and to treat crossed eyes. Leveraging the drug into cosmetic medicine has dramatically increased the market for Botox.

3. **Transformational Innovation:** Represented by the red arc in Exhibit 2.2, these decisions result in brand-new markets, products, and often new businesses. The company must rely on new, unfamiliar assets to develop the type of breakthrough decisions that fall in this category. The wearable, remote-controlled GoPro documentary video camera is a prime example of developing an immature market with a brand-new experience.[8]

2-3c The Boston Consulting Group Model

Management must find a balance among the SBUs that yields the overall organization's desired growth and profits with an acceptable level of risk. Some SBUs generate large amounts of cash, and others need cash to foster growth. The challenge is to balance the organization's portfolio of SBUs for the best long-term performance.

To determine the future cash contributions and cash requirements expected for each SBU, managers can use the Boston Consulting Group's portfolio matrix. The **portfolio matrix** classifies each SBU by its present or forecast growth and market share. The underlying assumption is that market share and profitability are strongly linked. The measure of market share used in the portfolio approach is *relative market share*, the ratio between the company's share and

> **portfolio matrix** a tool for allocating resources among products or strategic business units on the basis of relative market share and market growth rate

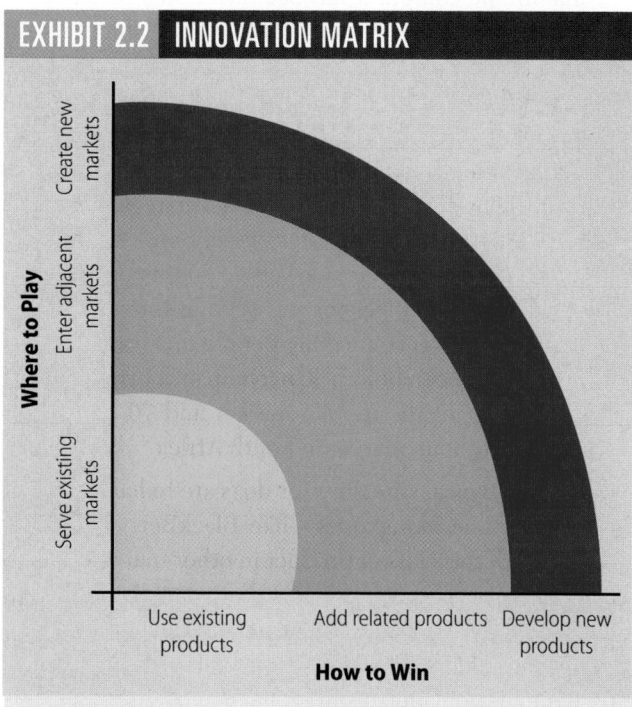

EXHIBIT 2.2 INNOVATION MATRIX

Where to Play:
- Create new markets
- Enter adjacent markets
- Serve existing markets

How to Win:
- Use existing products
- Add related products
- Develop new products

Based on Bansi Nagji and Geoff Tuff, "A Simple Tool You Need to Manage Innovation," *Harvard Business Review*, May 2012 http://hbr.org/2012/05/managing-your-innovation-portfolio/ar/1 (Accessed June 1, 2012).

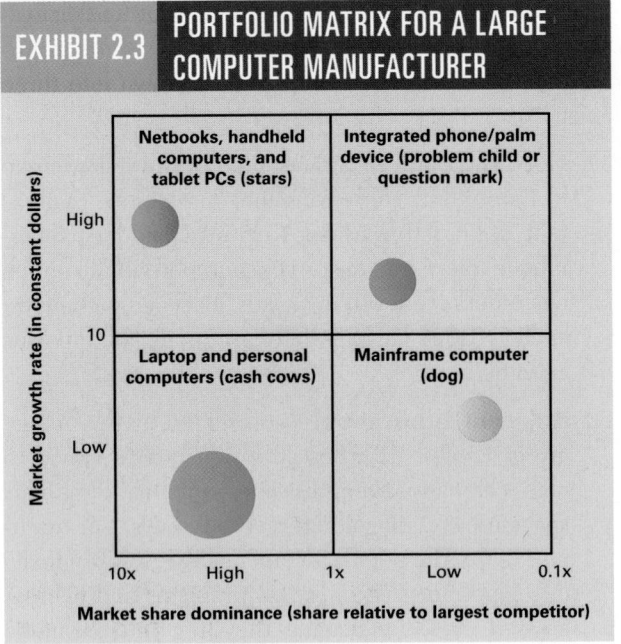

EXHIBIT 2.3 — PORTFOLIO MATRIX FOR A LARGE COMPUTER MANUFACTURER

Market growth rate (in constant dollars)

- Netbooks, handheld computers, and tablet PCs (stars)
- Integrated phone/palm device (problem child or question mark)
- Laptop and personal computers (cash cows)
- Mainframe computer (dog)

High — 10 — Low

10x — High — 1x — Low — 0.1x

Market share dominance (share relative to largest competitor)

the share of the largest competitor. For example, if a firm has a 50 percent share and the competitor has five percent, the ratio is 10 to 1. If a firm has a 10 percent market share and the largest competitor has 20 percent, the ratio is 0.5 to 1.

Exhibit 2.3 is a hypothetical portfolio matrix for a computer manufacturer. The size of the circle in each cell of the matrix represents dollar sales of the SBU relative to dollar sales of the company's other SBUs. The portfolio matrix breaks SBUs into four categories:

- **Stars:** A **star** is a fast-growing market leader. For example, the iPad is one of Apple's stars. Star SBUs usually have large profits but need lots of cash to finance rapid growth. The best marketing tactic is to protect existing market share by reinvesting earnings in product improvement, better distribution, more promotion, and production efficiency. Management must capture new users as they enter the market.

- **Cash cows:** A **cash cow** is an SBU that generates more cash than it needs to maintain its market share. It is in a low-growth market, but the product has a dominant market share. Personal computers and laptops are categorized as cash cows in Exhibit 2.3. The

star in the portfolio matrix, a business unit that is a fast-growing market leader

cash cow in the portfolio matrix, a business unit that generates more cash than it needs to maintain its market share

problem child (question mark) in the portfolio matrix, a business unit that shows rapid growth but poor profit margins

dog in the portfolio matrix, a business unit that has low growth potential and a small market share

basic strategy for a cash cow is to maintain market dominance by being the price leader and making technological improvements in the product. Managers should resist pressure to extend the basic line unless they can dramatically increase demand. Instead, they should allocate excess cash to the product categories where growth prospects are the greatest. For example, Heinz has two cash cows: ketchup and Weight Watchers frozen dinners.

- **Problem children:** A **problem child**, also called a **question mark**, shows rapid growth but poor profit margins. It has a low market share in a high-growth industry. Problem children need a great deal of cash. Without cash support, they eventually become dogs. The strategy options are to invest heavily to gain better market share, acquire competitors to get the necessary market share, or drop the SBU. Sometimes a firm can reposition the products of the SBU to move them into the star category. Elixir guitar strings, made by W. L. Gore & Associates, maker of Gore-Tex and Glide floss, were originally tested and marketed to Walt Disney theme parks to control puppets. After trial and failure, Gore repositioned and marketed heavily to musicians, who have loved the strings ever since.

- **Dogs:** A **dog** has low growth potential and a small market share. Most dogs eventually leave the marketplace. In the computer manufacturer example, the mainframe computer has become a dog. Another example is BlackBerry's smartphone line, which started out as a star for its manufacturer in the United States. Over time, the BlackBerry moved into the cash cow category, and then more recently, to a question mark, as the iPhone and Android-based phones captured market share. Even if it never regains its star status in the United States, BlackBerry has moved into other geographic markets to sell its devices. In parts of Africa, Blackberry is seen as a revolutionary company that is connecting people in a way that they have never been before. The company currently owns 48 percent of the mobile market and 70 percent of the smartphone market in South Africa.[9]

While typical strategies for dogs are to harvest or divest, sometimes companies—like BlackBerry—are successful with this class of product in other markets. Other companies may revive products that were abandoned as dogs. In early 2014, Church's Chicken brought its Purple Pepper dipping sauce back to the market using a "Back by Popular Demand" promotional campaign.[10]

After classifying the company's SBUs in the matrix, the next step is to allocate future resources for each. The four basic strategies are to:

- **Build:** If an organization has an SBU that it believes has the potential to be a star (probably a problem child at present), building would be an appropriate goal. The organization may decide to give up short-term profits and use its financial resources to achieve this goal. Apple postponed further work on the iPad to pursue the iPhone. The wait paid off when Apple was able to repurpose much of the iOS software and the iPhone's App Store for the iPad, making development less expensive and getting the product into the marketplace more quickly.[11]

- **Hold:** If an SBU is a very successful cash cow, a key goal would surely be to hold or preserve market share so that the organization can take advantage of the very positive cash flow. Fashion-based reality series *Project Runway* is a cash cow for the Lifetime cable television channel and parent companies Hearst and Disney. New seasons and spin-off editions such as *Project Runway: Under the Gunn* are expected for years to come.[12]

- **Harvest:** This strategy is appropriate for all SBUs except those classified as stars. The basic goal is to increase the short-term cash return without too much concern for the long-run impact. It is especially worthwhile when more cash is needed from a cash cow with long-run prospects that are unfavorable because of a low market growth rate. For instance, Lever Brothers has been harvesting Lifebuoy soap for a number of years with little promotional backing.

- **Divest:** Getting rid of SBUs with low shares of low-growth markets is often appropriate. Problem children and dogs are most suitable for this strategy. Nestle, for example, is in the process of selling its PowerBar SBU. Once the pioneering brand in the nutritional bar market, PowerBar has become an underperforming brand.[13]

2-3d The General Electric Model

The third model for selecting strategic alternatives was originally developed by General

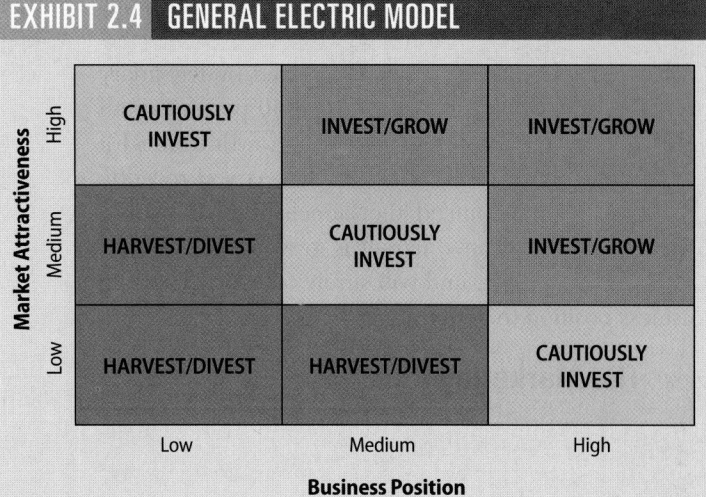

AP Images/Bernadette Tuazon

Electric. The dimensions used in this model—market attractiveness and company strength—are richer and more complex than those used in the Boston Consulting Group model, but are harder to quantify.

Exhibit 2.4 presents the GE model. The horizontal axis, Business Position, refers to how well positioned the organization is to take advantage of market opportunities. Business position answers questions such as: Does the firm have the technology it needs to effectively penetrate the market? Are its financial resources adequate? Can manufacturing costs be held down below those of the competition? Can the firm cope with change? The vertical axis measures the attractiveness of a market, which is expressed both quantitatively and qualitatively. Some attributes of an attractive market are high profitability, rapid growth, a lack of government regulation, consumer insensitivity to a price increase, a lack of competition, and availability of technology. The grid is divided into three overall attractiveness zones for each dimension: high, medium, and low.

Those SBUs (or markets) that have low overall attractiveness (indicated by the red cells in Exhibit 2.4) should be avoided if the organization is not already serving them. If the firm is in these markets, it should either harvest or divest those SBUs. The organization should selectively maintain markets with medium attractiveness (indicated by the yellow cells in Exhibit 2.4). If attractiveness begins to slip, then the organization should withdraw from the market.

Conditions that are highly attractive—a thriving market plus a strong business position (the green cells in Exhibit 2.4)—are the best candidates for investment. For example, when Beats Electronics launched a new line of over-the-ear headphones in 2008, the consumer headphone market

EXHIBIT 2.4 GENERAL ELECTRIC MODEL

		Low	Medium	High
Market Attractiveness	High	CAUTIOUSLY INVEST	INVEST/GROW	INVEST/GROW
	Medium	HARVEST/DIVEST	CAUTIOUSLY INVEST	INVEST/GROW
	Low	HARVEST/DIVEST	HARVEST/DIVEST	CAUTIOUSLY INVEST
		Low	Medium	High
		Business Position		

was strong but steady, led by inexpensive, inconspicuous earbuds. Four years later, the heavily branded and premium-priced Beats by Dr. Dre—helmed by legendary hip-hop producer Dr. Dre—captured 40 percent of all U.S. headphone sales, fueling market growth from $1.8 billion in 2011 to $2.4 billion in 2012. As you recently learned, Beats announced the launch of Beats Music in early 2014. This new market is growing quickly and is highly competitive, and will surely take Beats' strong business position to penetrate.[14]

2-3e The Marketing Plan

Based on the company's or SBU's overall strategy, marketing managers can create a marketing plan for individual products, brands, lines, or customer groups. **Planning** is the process of anticipating future events and determining strategies to achieve organizational objectives in the future. **Marketing planning** involves designing activities relating to marketing objectives and the changing marketing environment. Marketing planning is the basis for all marketing strategies and decisions. Issues such as product lines, distribution channels, marketing communications, and pricing are all delineated in the **marketing plan**. The marketing plan is a written document that acts as a guidebook of marketing activities for the marketing manager. In this chapter, you will learn the importance of writing a marketing plan and the types of information contained in a marketing plan.

2-3f Why Write a Marketing Plan?

By specifying objectives and defining the actions required to attain them, you can provide in a marketing plan the basis by which actual and expected performance can be compared. Marketing can be one of the most expensive and complicated business activities, but it is also one of the most important. The written marketing plan provides clearly stated activities that help employees and managers understand and work toward common goals.

Writing a marketing plan allows you to examine the marketing environment in conjunction with the inner workings of the business. Once the marketing plan is written, it serves as a reference point for the success of future

planning the process of anticipating future events and determining strategies to achieve organizational objectives in the future

marketing planning designing activities relating to marketing objectives and the changing marketing environment

marketing plan a written document that acts as a guidebook of marketing activities for the marketing manager

activities. Finally, the marketing plan allows the marketing manager to enter the marketplace with an awareness of possibilities and problems.

2-3g Marketing Plan Elements

Marketing plans can be presented in many different ways. Most businesses need a written marketing plan because a marketing plan is large and can be complex. Details about tasks and activity assignments may be lost if communicated orally. Regardless of the way a marketing plan is presented, some elements are common to all marketing plans. Exhibit 2.5 shows these elements, which include defining the business mission, performing a situation analysis, defining objectives, delineating a target market, and establishing components of the marketing mix. Other elements that may be included in a

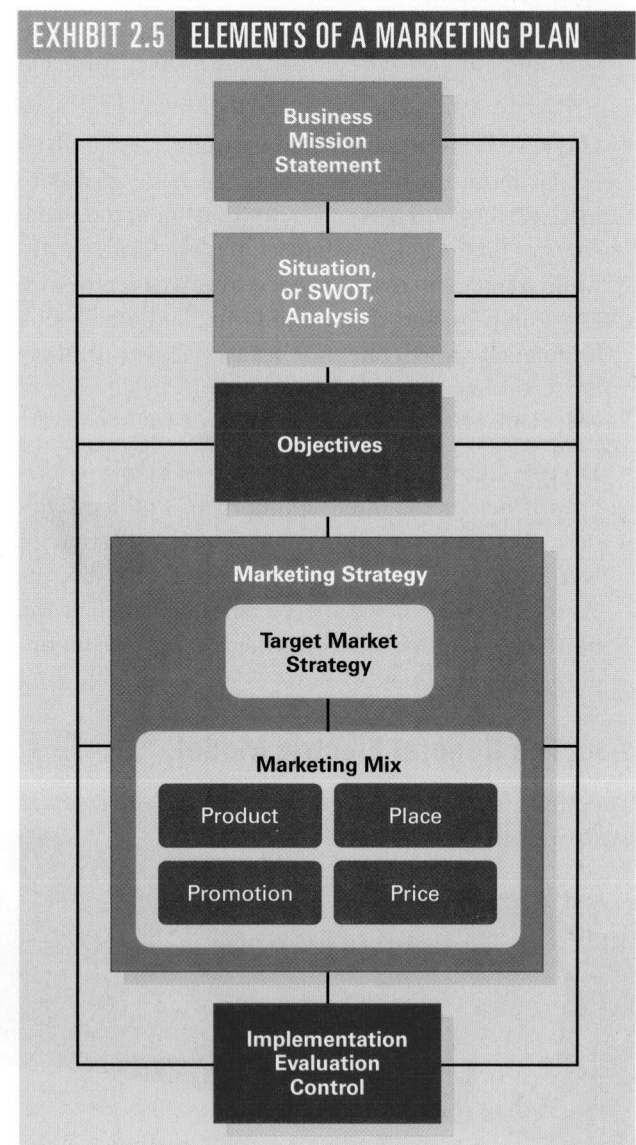

EXHIBIT 2.5 ELEMENTS OF A MARKETING PLAN

- Business Mission Statement
- Situation, or SWOT, Analysis
- Objectives
- Marketing Strategy
  - Target Market Strategy
  - Marketing Mix
    - Product
    - Place
    - Promotion
    - Price
- Implementation Evaluation Control

plan are budgets, implementation timetables, required marketing research efforts, or elements of advanced strategic planning.

2-3h Writing the Marketing Plan

The creation and implementation of a complete marketing plan will allow the organization to achieve marketing objectives and succeed. However, the marketing plan is only as good as the information it contains and the effort, creativity, and thought that went into its creation. Having a good marketing information system and a wealth of competitive intelligence (covered in Chapter 9) is critical to a thorough and accurate situation analysis. The role of managerial intuition is also important in the creation and selection of marketing strategies. Managers must weigh any information against its accuracy and their own judgment when making a marketing decision.

Note that the overall structure of the marketing plan (Exhibit 2.5) should not be viewed as a series of sequential planning steps. Many of the marketing plan elements are decided simultaneously and in conjunction with one another. Further, every marketing plan has different content, depending on the organization, its mission, objectives, targets, and marketing mix components. There is not one single correct format for a marketing plan. Many organizations have their own distinctive format or terminology for creating a marketing plan. Every marketing plan should be unique to the firm for which it was created. Remember, however, that although the format and order of presentation should be flexible, the same types of questions and topic areas should be covered in any marketing plan.

2-4 DEFINING THE BUSINESS MISSION

The foundation of any marketing plan is the firm's mission statement, which answers the question "What business are we in?" The way a firm defines its business mission profoundly affects the firm's long-run resource allocation, profitability, and survival. The mission statement is based on a careful analysis of benefits sought by present and potential customers and an analysis of existing and anticipated environmental conditions. The firm's mission statement establishes boundaries for all subsequent decisions, objectives, and strategies.

A mission statement should focus on the market or markets the organization is attempting to serve rather

Care must be taken when stating a business mission. Companies like Procter and Gamble have earned the right to be broad in their mission's wording.

Bryan Busovicki/Shutterstock.com

than on the good or service offered. Otherwise, a new technology may quickly make the good or service obsolete and the mission statement irrelevant to company functions. Business mission statements that are stated too narrowly suffer from **marketing myopia**—defining a business in terms of goods and services rather than in terms of the benefits customers seek. In this context, *myopia* means narrow, short-term thinking. For example, Frito-Lay defines its mission as being in the snack-food business rather than in the corn chip business. The mission of sports teams is not just to play games but also to serve the interests of the fans.

Alternatively, business missions may be stated too broadly. "To provide products of superior quality and value that improve the lives of the world's consumers" is probably too broad a mission statement for any firm except Procter & Gamble. Care must be taken when stating what business a firm is in. For example, the mission of Ben & Jerry's centers on three important aspects of its ice cream business: (1) Product: "To make, distribute and sell the finest quality all natural ice cream and euphoric concoctions with a continued commitment to incorporating wholesome, natural ingredients and promoting business practices that respect the Earth and the Environment"; (2) Economic: "To operate the Company on a sustainable financial basis of profitable growth, increasing

mission statement a statement of the firm's business based on a careful analysis of benefits sought by present and potential customers and an analysis of existing and anticipated environmental conditions

marketing myopia defining a business in terms of goods and services rather than in terms of the benefits customers seek

value for our stakeholders and expanding opportunities for development and career growth for our employees"; and (3) Social: "To operate the Company in a way that actively recognizes the central role that business plays in society by initiating innovative ways to improve the quality of life locally, nationally, and internationally."[15] By correctly stating the business mission in terms of the benefits that customers seek, the foundation for the marketing plan is set. Many companies are focusing on designing more appropriate mission statements because these statements are frequently displayed on the companies' Web sites.

2-5 CONDUCTING A SITUATION ANALYSIS

Marketers must understand the current and potential environment in which the product or service will be marketed. A situation analysis is sometimes referred to as a **SWOT analysis**—that is, the firm should identify its internal strengths (**S**) and weaknesses (**W**) and also examine external opportunities (**O**) and threats (**T**).

When examining internal strengths and weaknesses, the marketing manager should focus on organizational resources such as production costs, marketing skills, financial resources, company or brand image, employee capabilities, and available technology. For example, when Dell's stock fell sharply throughout the mid-2010s, management needed to examine strengths and weaknesses in the company and its competition. Dell had a $6 billion server business (strength), but the shrinking PC market accounted for a significant 24 percent of sales (weakness). Competitors like IBM and Hewlett-Packard (HP) were moving heavily into software and consulting, so to avoid them, Dell moved into the enterprise IT and services market. The shift was not enough to offset poor sales in other areas, however, and in 2013, the company entered buyout talks with private investors such as Blackstone and company founder Michael S. Dell. Dell ultimately went private and continues to sell computers, software, and related services.[16] Another issue to consider in this section of the marketing plan is the historical background of the firm—its sales and profit history.

When examining external opportunities and threats, marketing managers must analyze aspects of the marketing environment. This process is called **environmental scanning**—the collection and interpretation of information about forces, events, and relationships in the external environment that may affect the future of the organization or the implementation of the marketing plan. Environmental scanning helps identify market opportunities and threats and provides guidelines for the design of marketing strategy. Increasing competition from overseas firms and the fast growth of digital technology essentially ended Kodak's consumer film business. After emerging from bankruptcy, Kodak has repositioned the firm as a smaller, business-to-business company that offers commercial printing and digital imaging services.[17] The six most often studied macroenvironmental forces are social, demographic, economic, technological, political and legal, and competitive. These forces are examined in detail in Chapter 4.

2-6 COMPETITIVE ADVANTAGE

Performing a SWOT analysis allows firms to identify their competitive advantage. A competitive advantage is a set of unique features of a company and its products that are perceived by the target market as significant and superior to those of the competition. It is the factor or factors that cause customers to patronize a firm and not the competition. There are three types of competitive advantage: cost, product/service differentiation, and niche.

Yarygin/Shutterstock.com

Hydraulic fracturing is a competitive advantage for the United States in the global natural gas market.

SWOT analysis identifying internal strengths (S) and weaknesses (W) and also examining external opportunities (O) and threats (T)

environmental scanning collection and interpretation of information about forces, events, and relationships in the external environment that may affect the future of the organization or the implementation of the marketing plan

competitive advantage a set of unique features of a company and its products that are perceived by the target market as significant and superior to those of the competition

2-6a Cost Competitive Advantage

Cost leadership can result from obtaining inexpensive raw materials, creating an efficient scale of plant operations, designing products for ease of manufacture, controlling overhead costs, and avoiding marginal customers. Hydraulic fracturing (or fracking) is a controversial mining technique used to release petroleum, natural gas, and other valuable chemicals from layers of rock in the earth's crust. In the United States, fracking has revealed a vast supply of natural gas locked in shale rock, greatly reducing the cost of energy across the country and making the United States a primary player in the global natural gas market. According to George Blitz, vice president of energy and climate change at Dow Chemical Company, the shale gas boom has given the United States the biggest competitive advantage the industry has seen in several decades.[18] Having a **cost competitive advantage** means being the low-cost competitor in an industry while maintaining satisfactory profit margins. Costs can be reduced in a variety of ways:

- **Experience curves: Experience curves** tell us that costs decline at a predictable rate as experience with a product increases. The experience curve effect encompasses a broad range of manufacturing, marketing, and administrative costs. Experience curves reflect learning by doing, technological advances, and economies of scale. Firms like Boeing use historical experience curves as a basis for predicting and setting prices. Experience curves allow management to forecast costs and set prices based on anticipated costs as opposed to current costs.

- **Efficient labor:** Labor costs can be an important component of total costs in low-skill, labor-intensive industries such as product assembly and apparel manufacturing. Many U.S. publishers and software developers send data entry, design, and formatting tasks to India, where skilled engineers are available at lower overall cost.

- **No-frills goods and services:** Marketers can lower costs by removing frills and options from a product or service. Southwest Airlines, for example, offers low fares but no seat assignments or meals. Low costs give Southwest a higher load factor and greater economies of scale, which, in turn, mean lower prices.

- **Government subsidies:** Governments can provide grants and interest-free loans to target industries. Such government assistance enabled Japanese semiconductor manufacturers to become global leaders.

- **Product design:** Cutting-edge design technology can help offset high labor costs. BMW is a world leader in designing cars for ease of manufacture and assembly.

Reverse engineering—the process of disassembling a product piece by piece to learn its components and obtain clues as to the manufacturing process—can also mean savings. Reverse engineering a low-cost competitor's product can save research and design costs. The car industry often uses reverse engineering.

- **Reengineering:** Reengineering entails fundamental rethinking and redesign of business processes to achieve dramatic improvements in critical measures of performance. It often involves reorganizing functional departments such as sales, engineering, and production into cross-disciplinary teams.

- **Production innovations:** Production innovations such as new technology and simplified production techniques help lower the average cost of production. Technologies such as computer-aided design (CAD) and computer-aided manufacturing (CAM) and increasingly sophisticated robots help companies such as Boeing, Ford, and General Electric reduce their manufacturing costs.

- **New methods of service delivery:** Medical expenses have been substantially lowered by the use of outpatient surgery and walk-in clinics. Online-only magazines deliver great savings, and even some print magazines are exploring ways to go online to save material and shipping costs.

2-6b Product/Service Differentiation Competitive Advantage

Because cost competitive advantages are subject to continual erosion, product/service differentiation tends to provide a longer-lasting competitive advantage. The durability of this strategy tends to make it more attractive to many top managers. A **product/service differentiation competitive advantage** exists when a firm provides something that is unique and valuable to buyers beyond simply offering a lower price than that of the competition. Examples include brand names (Lexus), a strong dealer network (Caterpillar for construction work), product reliability (Maytag appliances), image (Neiman Marcus in retailing), or service

cost competitive advantage being the low-cost competitor in an industry while maintaining satisfactory profit margins

experience curves curves that show costs declining at a predictable rate as experience with a product increases

product/service differentiation competitive advantage the provision of something that is unique and valuable to buyers beyond simply offering a lower price than that of the competition

Customers have a loyalty to Caterpillar due to its strong network of dealerships.

Kevin Brine/Shutterstock.com

(Zappos). Uniqlo, a fast-fashion retailer with 840 stores in Japan and 1,170 stores outside Japan, is among the top five global clothing retailers. The company provides high-quality casual wear at reasonable prices. It differentiates itself from the competition in several ways. First, it develops and brands innovative fabrics like HeatTech, which turns moisture into heat and has air pockets in the fabric to retain that heat. HeatTech is thin and comfortable, and enables stylish designs different from the standard apparel made for warmth. Second, Uniqlo emphasizes the in-store experience, which involves carefully hiring, training, and managing all touchpoints with the customer. Every morning, for example, Uniqlo employees practice interacting with shoppers. Finally, the company has a recycling effort that moves millions of articles of discarded Uniqlo clothing to needy people around the world.[19]

2-6c Niche Competitive Advantage

A **niche competitive advantage** seeks to target and effectively serve a single segment of the market (see Chapter 8). For small companies with limited resources that potentially face giant competitors, niche targeting may be the only viable option. A market segment that has good growth potential but is not crucial to the success of major competitors is a good candidate for developing a niche strategy.

Many companies using a niche strategy serve only a limited geographic

niche competitive advantage the advantage achieved when a firm seeks to target and effectively serve a small segment of the market

sustainable competitive advantage an advantage that cannot be copied by the competition

market. Stew Leonard's is an extremely successful but small grocery store chain found only in Connecticut and New York. Blue Bell Ice cream is available in only about 26 percent of the nation's supermarkets, but it ranks as one of the top three best-selling ice creams in the country.[20]

The Chef's Garden, a 225-acre Ohio farm, specializes in growing and shipping rare artisan vegetables directly to its customers. Chefs from all over the world call to order or request a unique item, which is grown and shipped by the Chef's Garden. The farm provides personal services and specialized premium vegetables that aren't available anywhere else and relies on its customers to supply it with ideas for what they would like to be able to offer in their restaurants. The excellent service and feeling of contribution keep chefs coming back.[21]

2-6d Building Sustainable Competitive Advantage

The key to having a competitive advantage is the ability to sustain that advantage. A **sustainable competitive advantage** is one that cannot be copied by the competition. For example, Netflix, the online movie subscription service, has a steady hold over the movie rental market. No company has come close to the incomparable depth of titles available to be sent directly to homes or streamed online. Blockbuster tried to set up a similar online subscription service tied to new releases and Amazon.com offers free streaming to Prime members, but so far neither has been able to compete with the convenience and selection offered by Netflix. Netflix's 27.5 million subscribers have a twenty-eight-day delay on most of the latest movies, but Netflix says that only a couple hundred customers have complained about the delay. Redbox Instant, an up-and-coming streaming service from Verizon and Coinstar, builds on the popular Redbox kiosk-based rental service, allowing customers to stream movies *and* rent up to four physical DVDs for just $8 a month. Redbox Instant does not offer television shows, however—a key advantage of Netflix's service.[22] In contrast, when Datril was introduced into the pain-reliever market, it was touted as being exactly like Tylenol, only cheaper. Tylenol responded by lowering its price, thus destroying Datril's competitive advantage and ability to remain on the market. In this case, low price was not a sustainable competitive advantage. Without a competitive advantage, target customers do not perceive any reason to patronize an organization instead of its competitors.

The notion of competitive advantage means that a successful firm will stake out a position unique in some manner from its rivals. Imitation by competitors indicates

The ability to stream movies and rent up to four physical DVDs for just $8 a month is a compelling competitive advantage for Redbox Instant.

Courtesy of Chapel House Photography

a lack of competitive advantage and almost ensures mediocre performance. Moreover, competitors rarely stand still, so it is not surprising that imitation causes managers to feel trapped in a seemingly endless game of catch-up. They are regularly surprised by the new accomplishments of their rivals.

Rather than copy competitors, companies need to build their own competitive advantages. The sources of tomorrow's competitive advantages are the skills and assets of the organization. Assets include patents, copyrights, locations, equipment, and technology that are superior to those of the competition. Skills are functions such as customer service and promotion that the firm performs better than its competitors. Marketing managers should continually focus the firm's skills and assets on sustaining and creating competitive advantages.

Remember, a sustainable competitive advantage is a function of the speed with which competitors can imitate a leading company's strategy and plans. Imitation requires a competitor to identify the leader's competitive advantage, determine how it is achieved, and then learn how to duplicate it.

2-7 SETTING MARKETING PLAN OBJECTIVES

Before the details of a marketing plan can be developed, objectives for the plan must be stated. Without objectives, there is no basis for measuring the success of marketing plan activities.

A **marketing objective** is a statement of what is to be accomplished through marketing activities.

A strong marketing objective for Purina might be: "To increase sales of Purina brand cat food between January 1, 2016 and December 31, 2016 by 15 percent, compared to 2012 sales of $300 million."

Objectives must be consistent with and indicate the priorities of the organization. Specifically, objectives flow from the business mission statement to the rest of the marketing plan.

Carefully specified objectives serve several functions. First, they communicate marketing management philosophies and provide direction for lower-level marketing managers so that marketing efforts are integrated and pointed in a consistent direction. Objectives also serve as motivators by creating something for employees to strive for. When objectives are attainable

marketing objective a statement of what is to be accomplished through marketing activities

MARKETING OBJECTIVES SHOULD BE ...

▶ **Realistic:** Managers should develop objectives that have a chance of being met. For example, it may be unrealistic for start-up firms or new products to command dominant market share, given other competitors in the marketplace.

▶ **Measurable:** Managers need to be able to quantitatively measure whether or not an objective has been met. For example, it would be difficult to determine success for an objective that states, "To increase sales of cat food." If the company sells one percent more cat food, does that mean the objective was met? Instead, a specific number should be stated, "To increase sales of Purina brand cat food from $300 million to $345 million."

▶ **Time specific:** By what time should the objective be met? "To increase sales of Purina brand cat food between January 1, 2016, and December 31, 2016."

▶ **Compared to a benchmark:** If the objective is to increase sales by 15 percent, it is important to know the baseline against which the objective will be measured. Will it be current sales? Last year's sales? For example, "To increase sales of Purina brand cat food by 15 percent over 2012 sales of $300 million."

and challenging, they motivate those charged with achieving the objectives. Additionally, the process of writing specific objectives forces executives to clarify their thinking. Finally, objectives form a basis for control: the effectiveness of a plan can be gauged in light of the stated objectives.

 ## 2-8 DESCRIBING THE TARGET MARKET

Marketing strategy involves the activities of selecting and describing one or more target markets and developing and maintaining a marketing mix that will produce mutually satisfying exchanges with target markets.

2-8a Target Market Strategy

A market segment is a group of individuals or organizations who share one or more characteristics. They therefore may have relatively similar product needs. For example, parents of newborn babies need formula, diapers, and special foods.

The target market strategy identifies the market segment or segments on which to focus. This process begins with a **market opportunity analysis (MOA)**—the description and estimation of the size and sales potential of market segments that are of interest to the firm and the assessment of key competitors in these market segments. After the firm describes the market segments, it may target one or more of them. There are three general strategies for selecting target markets.

Target markets can be selected by appealing to the entire market with one marketing mix, concentrating on one segment, or appealing to multiple market segments using multiple marketing mixes. The

characteristics, advantages, and disadvantages of each strategic option are examined in Chapter 8. Target markets could be eighteen- to twenty-five-year-old females who are interested in fashion (*Vogue* magazine), people concerned about sugar and calories in their soft drinks (Diet Pepsi), or parents without the time to potty train their children (Booty Camp classes where kids are potty trained).

Any market segment that is targeted must be fully described. Demographics, psychographics, and buyer behavior should be assessed. Buyer behavior is covered in Chapters 6 and 7. If segments are differentiated by ethnicity, multicultural aspects of the marketing mix should be examined. If the target market is international, it is especially important to describe differences in culture, economic and technological development, and political structure that may affect the marketing plan. Global marketing is covered in more detail in Chapter 5.

2-9 THE MARKETING MIX

The term marketing mix refers to a unique blend of product, place (distribution), promotion, and pricing strategies (often referred to as the four Ps) designed to produce mutually satisfying exchanges with a target market. The marketing manager can control each component of the marketing mix, but the strategies for all four components must be blended to achieve optimal results. Any marketing mix is only as good as its weakest component. For example, the first pump toothpastes were distributed over cosmetics counters and failed. Not until pump toothpastes were distributed the same way as tube toothpastes did the products succeed. The best promotion and the lowest price cannot save a poor product. Similarly, excellent products with poor placing, pricing, or promotion will likely fail.

Successful marketing mixes have been carefully designed to satisfy target markets. At first glance, McDonald's and Wendy's may appear to have roughly identical marketing mixes because they are both in the fast-food hamburger business. However, McDonald's has been most successful at targeting parents with young children for lunchtime meals, whereas Wendy's targets the adult crowd for lunches and dinner. McDonald's has playgrounds, Ronald McDonald the clown, and children's Happy Meals. Wendy's has salad bars, carpeted restaurants, and no playgrounds.

Style-photography/Shutterstock.com

marketing strategy the activities of selecting and describing one or more target markets and developing and maintaining a marketing mix that will produce mutually satisfying exchanges with target markets

market opportunity analysis (MOA) the description and estimation of the size and sales potential of market segments that are of interest to the firm and the assessment of key competitors in these market segments

marketing mix (four Ps) a unique blend of product, place (distribution), promotion, and pricing strategies designed to produce mutually satisfying exchanges with a target market

Variations in marketing mixes do not occur by chance. Astute marketing managers devise marketing strategies to gain advantages over competitors and best serve the needs and wants of a particular target market segment. By manipulating elements of the marketing mix, marketing managers can fine-tune the customer offering and achieve competitive success.

2-9a Product Strategies

Of the four Ps, the marketing mix typically starts with the product. The heart of the marketing mix, the starting point, is the product offering and product strategy. It is hard to design a place strategy, decide on a promotion campaign, or set a price without knowing the product to be marketed.

The product includes not only the physical unit but also its package, warranty, after-sale service, brand name, company image, value, and many other factors. A Godiva chocolate has many product elements: the chocolate itself, a fancy gold wrapper, a customer satisfaction guarantee, and the prestige of the Godiva brand name. We buy things not only for what they do (benefits) but also for what they mean to us (status, quality, or reputation).

Products can be tangible goods such as computers, ideas like those offered by a consultant, or services such as medical care. Products should also offer customer value. Product decisions are covered in Chapters 10 and 11, and services marketing is detailed in Chapter 12.

2-9b Place (Distribution) Strategies

Place, or distribution, strategies are concerned with making products available when and where customers want them. Would you rather buy a kiwi fruit at the 24-hour grocery store within walking distance or fly to Australia to pick your own? A part of this P—place—is physical distribution, which involves all the business activities concerned with storing and transporting raw materials or finished products. The goal is to make sure products arrive in usable condition at designated places when needed. Place strategies are covered in Chapters 13 and 14.

2-9c Promotion Strategies

Promotion includes advertising, public relations, sales promotion, and personal selling. Promotion's role in the marketing mix is to bring about mutually satisfying exchanges with target markets by informing, educating, persuading, and reminding them of the benefits of an organization or a product. A good promotion strategy, like using a beloved cartoon character such as Sponge-Bob SquarePants to sell gummy snacks, can dramatically increase sales. Each element of this P—promotion—is coordinated and managed with the others to create a promotional blend or mix. These integrated marketing communications activities are described in Chapters 16, 17, and 18. Technology-driven and social media aspects of promotional marketing are covered in Chapter 19.

2-9d Pricing Strategies

Price is what a buyer must give up in order to obtain a product. It is often the most flexible of the four Ps—the quickest element to change. Marketers can raise or lower prices more frequently and easily than they can change other marketing mix variables. Price is an important competitive weapon and is very important to the organization because price multiplied by the number of units sold equals total revenue for the firm. Pricing decisions are covered in Chapters 20 and 21.

The Game of Organizing E-Mail

E-mail has become a necessity for students and business professionals, as well as an integral part of many personal lives. With so much riding on e-mail, inboxes can overflow and important e-mails can fall by the wayside. One company is out to change that. Baydin is a software developer that sells Boomerang, a product that allows users to "snooze" e-mails. The user sets the time for the e-mail to reappear in the inbox, and Boomerang moves it into a folder out of the inbox until the specified time. To promote their e-mail management products for Outlook, Baydin also developed *The Email Game*. The game sets a timer for each message and accrues points for decisions made in a timely manner. Baydin guarantees the game will get you through your e-mail 40 percent faster or your money back.[23]

"How to Play the Email Game," The Email Game, http://emailgame.baydin.com/index.html (Accessed February 12, 2015).

© olexius/Shutterstock 14973/013

2-10 FOLLOWING UP ON THE MARKETING PLAN

One of the keys to success overlooked by many businesses is to actively follow up on the marketing plan. The time spent researching, developing, and writing a useful and accurate marketing plan goes to waste if the plan is not used by the organization. One of the best ways to get the most out of a marketing plan is to correctly implement it. Once the first steps to implementation are taken, evaluation and control will help guide the organization to success as laid out by the marketing plan.

2-10a Implementation

Implementation is the process that turns a marketing plan into action assignments and ensures that these assignments are executed in a way that accomplishes the plan's objectives. Implementation activities may involve detailed job assignments, activity descriptions, time lines, budgets, and lots of communication. Implementation requires delegating authority and responsibility, determining a time frame for completing tasks, and allocating resources. Sometimes a strategic plan also requires task force management. A *task force* is a tightly organized unit under the direction of a manager who, usually, has broad authority. A task force is established to accomplish a single goal or mission and thus works against a deadline.

Implementing a plan has another dimension: gaining acceptance. New plans mean change, and change creates resistance. One reason people resist change is that they fear they will lose something. For example, when new-product research is taken away from marketing research and given to a new-product department, the director of marketing research will naturally resist this loss of part of his or her domain. Misunderstanding and lack of trust also create opposition to change, but effective communication through open discussion and teamwork can be one way of overcoming resistance to change.

Although implementation is essentially "doing what you said you were going to do," many organizations repeatedly experience failures in strategy implementation. Brilliant marketing plans are doomed to fail if they are not properly implemented. These detailed communications may or may not be part of the written marketing plan. If they are not part of the plan, they should be specified elsewhere as soon as the plan has been communicated. Strong, forward-thinking leadership can overcome resistance to change, even in large, highly integrated companies where change seems very unlikely.

2-10b Evaluation and Control

After a marketing plan is implemented, it should be evaluated. **Evaluation** entails gauging the extent to which marketing objectives have been achieved during the specified time period. Four common reasons for failing to achieve a marketing objective are unrealistic marketing objectives, inappropriate marketing strategies in the plan, poor implementation, and changes in the environment after the objective was specified and the strategy was implemented.

Once a plan is chosen and implemented, its effectiveness must be monitored. **Control** provides the mechanisms for evaluating marketing results in light of the plan's objectives and for correcting actions that do not help the organization reach those objectives within budget guidelines. Firms need to establish formal and informal control programs to make the entire operation more efficient.

Perhaps the broadest control device available to marketing managers is the **marketing audit**—a thorough, systematic, periodic evaluation of the objectives, strategies, structure, and performance of the marketing organization. A marketing audit helps management allocate marketing resources efficiently.

Although the main purpose of the marketing audit is to develop a full profile of the organization's marketing effort and to provide a basis for developing and revising the marketing plan, it is also an excellent way to improve communication and raise the level of marketing consciousness within the organization. It is a useful vehicle for selling the philosophy and techniques of strategic marketing to other members of the organization.

2-10c Post-audit Tasks

After the audit has been completed, three tasks remain. First, the audit should profile existing weaknesses and inhibiting factors, as well as the firm's strengths and the new opportunities available to it. Recommendations have to be judged and prioritized so that those with the potential to contribute most to improved marketing performance can be implemented first. The usefulness of the data also depends on the auditor's skill in interpreting and presenting the data so decision makers can quickly grasp the major points.

---

implementation the process that turns a marketing plan into action assignments and ensures that these assignments are executed in a way that accomplishes the plan's objectives

evaluation gauging the extent to which the marketing objectives have been achieved during the specified time period

control provides the mechanisms for evaluating marketing results in light of the plan's objectives and for correcting actions that do not help the organization reach those objectives within budget guidelines

marketing audit a thorough, systematic, periodic evaluation of the objectives, strategies, structure, and performance of the marketing organization

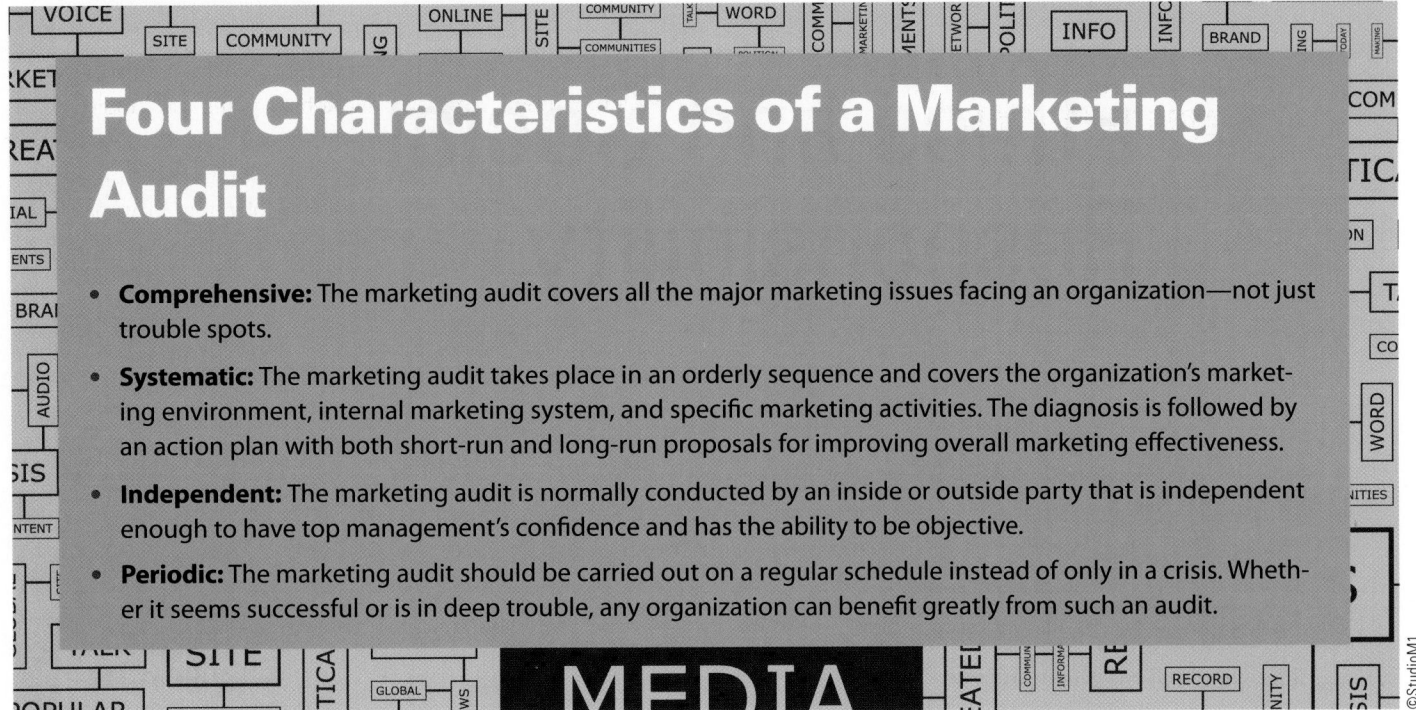

Four Characteristics of a Marketing Audit

- **Comprehensive:** The marketing audit covers all the major marketing issues facing an organization—not just trouble spots.

- **Systematic:** The marketing audit takes place in an orderly sequence and covers the organization's marketing environment, internal marketing system, and specific marketing activities. The diagnosis is followed by an action plan with both short-run and long-run proposals for improving overall marketing effectiveness.

- **Independent:** The marketing audit is normally conducted by an inside or outside party that is independent enough to have top management's confidence and has the ability to be objective.

- **Periodic:** The marketing audit should be carried out on a regular schedule instead of only in a crisis. Whether it seems successful or is in deep trouble, any organization can benefit greatly from such an audit.

©StudioM1

The second task is to ensure that the role of the audit has been clearly communicated. It is unlikely that the suggestions will require radical change in the way the firm operates. The audit's main role is to address the question "Where are we now?" and to suggest ways to improve what the firm already does.

The final post-audit task is to make someone accountable for implementing recommendations. All too often, reports are presented, applauded, and filed away to gather dust. The person made accountable should be someone who is committed to the project and who has the managerial power to make things happen.

 2-11 EFFECTIVE STRATEGIC PLANNING

Effective strategic planning requires continual attention, creativity, and management commitment. Strategic planning should not be an annual exercise in which managers go through the motions and forget about strategic planning until the next year. It should be an ongoing process because the environment is continually changing and the firm's resources and capabilities are continually evolving.

Sound strategic planning is based on creativity. Managers should challenge assumptions about the firm and the environment and establish new strategies. For example, major oil companies developed the concept of the gasoline service station in an age when cars needed frequent and rather elaborate servicing. These major companies held on to the full-service approach, but independents were quick to respond to new realities and moved to lower-cost self-service and convenience store operations. Major companies took several decades to catch up.

Perhaps the most critical element in successful strategic planning is top management's support and participation. At Google, for example, top managers support their employees' strategic plans and even assist in entry-level employees' development as strategic planners. This has created a top-to-bottom culture of strategic excellence at Google.[24]

STUDY TOOLS 2

LOCATED AT BACK OF THE TEXTBOOK

- ☐ Rip out Chapter Review Card

LOCATED AT WWW.CENGAGEBRAIN.COM

- ☐ Review Key Terms Flashcards and create your own
- ☐ Track your knowledge & understanding of key concepts in marketing
- ☐ Complete practice and graded quizzes to prepare for tests
- ☐ Complete interactive content within the MKTG Online experience
- ☐ View the chapter highlight boxes within the MKTG Online experience

3 Ethics and Social Responsibility

LEARNING OUTCOMES

After studying this chapter, you will be able to...

3-1 Explain the determinants of a civil society

3-2 Explain the concept of ethical behavior

3-3 Describe ethical behavior in business

3-4 Discuss corporate social responsibility

3-5 Describe the arguments for and against society responsibility

3-6 Explain cause-related marketing

After you finish this chapter go to **PAGE 44** for **STUDY TOOLS.**

3-1 DETERMINANTS OF A CIVIL SOCIETY

Have you ever stopped to think about the social glue that binds society together? That is, what factors keep people and organizations from running amok and doing harm, and what factors create order in a society like ours? The answer lies in **social control**, defined as any means used to maintain behavioral norms and regulate conflict.[1] **Behavioral norms** are standards of proper or acceptable behavior. Social control is part of your life at every level, from your family, to your local community, to the nation, to the global civilization. Several modes of social control are important to marketing:

1. **Ethics: Ethics** are the moral principles or values that generally govern the conduct of an individual or a group. Ethical rules and guidelines, along with customs and traditions, provide principles of right action.

2. **Laws:** Often, ethical rules and guidelines are codified into law. Laws created by governments are then enforced by governmental authority. This is how the dictum "Thou shall not steal" has become part of formal law throughout the land. Law, however, is not a perfect mechanism for ensuring good corporate and employee behavior. This is because laws often address the lowest common denominator of socially acceptable behavior. In other words, just because something is legal does not mean that it is ethical. For example, according to a recent study by Arizona State University, fast food restaurants disproportionally aim their child-focused marketing efforts at middle-income, rural, and predominately black communities.[2]

In a national study of more than 6,000 fast-food restaurants, researchers found that those situated in middle-income neighborhoods, rural communities, and predominately black neighborhoods were more likely to target children with ads featuring cartoon characters; displays on restaurant exteriors featuring movie, television, and sports stars; and indoor play areas and indoor displays of kids' meal toys. Overall, one-fifth of restaurants sampled in the study used one or more strategies targeting children. Fast-food companies in the U.S. spend nearly one-quarter of their marketing budgets to target kids age 2 to 17.[3] Is this ethical? What is your opinion?

3. **Formal and Informal Groups:** Businesses, professional organizations (such as the American Marketing Association and the American Medical Association), and clubs (such as Shriners and Ducks Unlimited) all have codes of conduct. These codes prescribe acceptable and desired behaviors of their members.

4. **Self-regulation:** Self-regulation involves the voluntary acceptance of standards established by nongovernmental entities, such as the American Association of Advertising Agencies (AAAA) or the National Association of Manufacturers. The AAAA has a self-regulation arm that deals with deceptive advertising. Other associations have regulations relating to child labor, environmental issues, conservation, and a host of other issues.

5. **The Media:** In an open, democratic society, the media play a key role in informing the public about the actions of individuals and organizations—both good and bad. The Children's Online Privacy Protection Act (COPPA) requires Web site operators to obtain verifiable consent from parents before collecting personal information about children under age thirteen. Recently, Yelp paid a $450,000 fine for collecting information on children under thirteen. Mobile app developer TinyCo was likewise fined $300,000.[4] Google has announced new versions of Chrome and YouTube tailored specifically for kids under the age of 13. To date, Google has not announced the safeguards it will use to meet COPPA standards. Since the vast majority of Google's revenue comes from advertising and the value of the company's ads is tied to its massive trove of user data,

social control any means used to maintain behavioral norms and regulate conflict

behavioral norms standards of proper or acceptable behavior. Several modes of social control are important to marketing

ethics the moral principles or values that generally govern the conduct of an individual or a group

COPPA compliance is very important to Google and advertisers alike.[5]

6. **An Active Civil Society:** An informed and engaged society can help mold individual and corporate behavior. The last state in the union to get a Walmart store was Vermont. Citizen campaigns against the big-box retailer were deciding factors in management's decision to avoid the state. The planned Keystone Pipeline has brought out environmentalists on one side of the debate and the petroleum industry on the other. Proponents argue that the oil pipeline snaking from Alberta, Canada, to Houston, Texas, will not only bring essential infrastructure to North American oil producers, but it will also provide jobs, long-term energy independence, and a boost to the economy.[6] TransCanada, proposed builder of the pipeline, says that it will be the safest and most advanced oil pipeline operation in North America. Opponents claim that the pipeline will create few post-construction jobs and will carry tar-sands oil (which is more hazardous than conventional oil). They argue that tar-sands refining has created toxic dust storms and that the pipeline would contribute little to U.S. energy independence.[7] The arguments on both sides are a product of an engaged and free society.

All six of the preceding factors—individually and in combination—are critical to achieving a socially coherent, vibrant, civilized society. These six factors (the social glue) are more important today than ever before due to the increasing complexity of the global economy and the melding of customs and traditions within societies.

3-2 THE CONCEPT OF ETHICAL BEHAVIOR

It has been said that ethics is something everyone likes to talk about but nobody can define. Others have suggested that defining ethics is like trying to nail Jell-O to a wall. You begin to think that you understand it, but that is when it starts squirting out between your fingers.

Simply put, ethics can be viewed as the standard of behavior by which conduct is judged. Standards that are legal may not always be ethical, and vice versa. Laws are the values and standards enforceable by the courts. Ethics, then, consists of personal moral principles. For example, there is no legal statute that makes it a crime for someone to "cut in line." Yet, if someone does not want to wait in line and cuts to the front, it often makes others very angry.

If you have ever resented a line-cutter, then you understand ethics and have applied ethical standards in life. Waiting your turn in line is a social expectation that exists because lines ensure order and allocate the space and time needed to complete transactions. Waiting your turn is an expected but unwritten behavior that plays a critical role in an orderly society.

So it is with ethics. Ethics consists of those unwritten rules we have developed for our interactions with one another. These unwritten rules govern us when we are sharing resources or honoring contracts. "Waiting your turn" is a higher standard than the laws that are passed to maintain order. Those laws apply when physical force or threats are used to push to the front of the line. Assault, battery, and threats are forms of criminal conduct for which the offender can be prosecuted. But the law does not apply to the stealthy line-cutter who simply sneaks to the front, perhaps using a friend and a conversation as a decoy. No laws are broken, but the notions of fairness and justice are offended by one individual putting himself or herself above others and taking advantage of others' time and position.

Ethical questions range from practical, narrowly defined issues, such as a businessperson's obligation to be honest with customers, to broader social and philosophical questions, such as whether a company is responsible for preserving the environment and protecting employee rights. Many ethical dilemmas develop from conflicts between the differing interests of company owners and their workers, customers, and surrounding community. Managers must balance the ideal against the practical—that is, the need to produce a reasonable profit for the company's shareholders against honesty in business practices and concern for environmental and social issues.

3-2a Ethical Theories

People usually base their individual choice of ethical theory on their life experiences. The following are some of the ethical theories that apply to marketing.[8]

DEONTOLOGY The **deontological theory** states that people should adhere to their obligations and duties when analyzing an ethical dilemma. This means that a

deontological theory ethical theory that states that people should adhere to their obligations and duties when analyzing an ethical dilemma

Sideways Design/Shutterstock.com

person will follow his or her obligations to another individual or society because upholding one's duty is what is considered ethically correct. For instance, a deontologist will always keep his promises to a friend and will follow the law. A person who follows this theory will produce very consistent decisions because they will be based on the individual's set duties.

Note that deontological theory is not necessarily concerned with the welfare of others. For example, suppose a salesperson has decided that it is her ethical duty (and very practical!) to always be on time to meetings with clients. Today she is running late. How is she supposed to drive? Is the deontologist supposed to speed, breaking the law to uphold her duty to society, or is the deontologist supposed to arrive at her meeting late, breaking her duty to be on time? This scenario of conflicting obligations does not lead us to a clear, ethically correct resolution, nor does it protect the welfare of others from the deontologist's decision.

UTILITARIANISM The **utilitarian ethical theory** is founded on the ability to predict the consequences of an action. To a utilitarian, the choice that yields the greatest benefit to the most people is the choice that is ethically correct. One benefit of this ethical theory is that the utilitarian can compare similar predicted solutions and use a point system to determine which choice is more beneficial for more people. This point system provides a logical and rational argument for each decision and allows a person to use it on a case-by-case context.

There are two types of utilitarianism: act utilitarianism and rule utilitarianism. *Act utilitarianism* adheres exactly to the definition of utilitarianism as just described. In act utilitarianism, a person performs the acts that benefit the most people, regardless of personal feelings or societal constraints such as laws. *Rule utilitarianism*, however, takes into account the law and is concerned with fairness. A rule utilitarian seeks to benefit the most people but through the fairest and most just means available. Therefore, added benefits of rule utilitarianism are that it values justice and doing good at the same time.

As is true of all ethical theories, however, both act and rule utilitarianism contain numerous flaws. Inherent in both are the flaws associated with predicting the future. Although people can use their life experiences to attempt to predict outcomes, no human being can be certain that his predictions will be true. This uncertainty can lead to unexpected results, making the utilitarian look unethical as time passes because his choice did not benefit the most people as he predicted.

Another assumption that a utilitarian must make is that he has the ability to compare the various types of consequences against each other on a similar scale. However, comparing material gains such as money against intangible gains such as happiness is impossible because their qualities differ so greatly.

CASUIST The **casuist ethical theory** compares a current ethical dilemma with examples of similar ethical dilemmas and their outcomes. This allows one to determine the severity of the situation and to create the best possible solution according to others' experiences. Usually, one will find examples that represent the extremes of the situation so that a compromise can be reached that will include the wisdom gained from the previous situations.

One drawback to this ethical theory is that there may not be a set of similar examples for a given ethical dilemma. Perhaps that which is controversial and ethically questionable is new and unexpected. Along the same line of thinking, this theory assumes that the results of the current ethical dilemma will be similar to results in the examples. This may not be necessarily true and would greatly hinder the effectiveness of applying this ethical theory.

MORAL RELATIVISM **Moral relativism** is a belief in time-and-place ethics, that is, the truth of a moral judgment is relative to the judging person or group.[9] According to a moral relativist, for example, arson is not always wrong—if you live in a neighborhood where drug dealers are operating a crystal meth lab or crack house, committing arson by burning down the meth lab may be ethically justified. If you are a parent and your child is starving, stealing a loaf of bread is ethically correct. The proper resolution to ethical dilemmas is based upon weighing the competing factors at the moment and then making a determination to take the lesser of the evils as the resolution. Moral relativists do not believe in absolute rules. Their beliefs center on the pressure of the moment and whether the pressure justifies the action taken.

VIRTUE ETHICS Aristotle and Plato taught that solving ethical dilemmas requires training—that individuals solve ethical dilemmas when they develop and nurture a set of virtues.[10]

utilitarian ethical theory
ethical theory that is founded on the ability to predict the consequences of an action

casuist ethical theory
ethical theory that compares a current ethical dilemma with examples of similar ethical dilemmas and their outcomes

moral relativism an ethical theory of time-and-place ethics; that is, the belief that ethical truths depend on the individuals and groups holding them

A **virtue** is a character trait valued as being good. Aristotle taught the importance of cultivating virtue in his students and then having them solve ethical dilemmas using those virtues once they had become an integral part of his students' being through their virtue training.

Some modern philosophers have embraced this notion of virtue and have developed lists of what constitutes a virtuous businessperson. Some common virtues for business people are self-discipline, friendliness, caring, courage, compassion, trust, responsibility, honesty, determination, enthusiasm, and humility. You may see other lists of virtues that are longer or shorter, but here is a good start for core business virtues.

3-3 ETHICAL BEHAVIOR IN BUSINESS

Depending upon which, if any, ethical theory a businessperson has accepted and uses in his or her daily conduct, the action taken may vary. For example, faced with bribing a foreign official to get a critically needed contract or shutting down a factory and laying off a thousand workers, a person following a deontology strategy would not pay the bribe. Why? A deontologist always follows the law. However, a moral relativist would probably pay the bribe.

While the boundaries of what is legal and what is not are often fairly clear (for example, do not run a red light, do not steal money from a bank, and do not kill anyone), the boundaries of ethical decision making are predicated on which ethical theory one is following. The law typically relies on juries to determine if an act is legal or illegal. Society determines whether an action is ethical or unethical. A number of women have accused comedian Bill Cosby of sexual molestation and rape. Society would view this as unethical behavior, but at the time of this writing, Mr. Cosby had not been indicted. If he is subjected to a trial, a jury will determine if an illegal act was committed. In a business-related case, a federal prosecutor in San Francisco recently indicted Federal Express for shipping illegal prescription drugs. If successful, the case would extend a shipping company's responsibility from its own conduct to the conduct of its customers. This case raises a lot of questions about what a company can and should know about its customers.

What makes the Federal Express case different is that the company has chosen to fight it out in court. Businesspeople

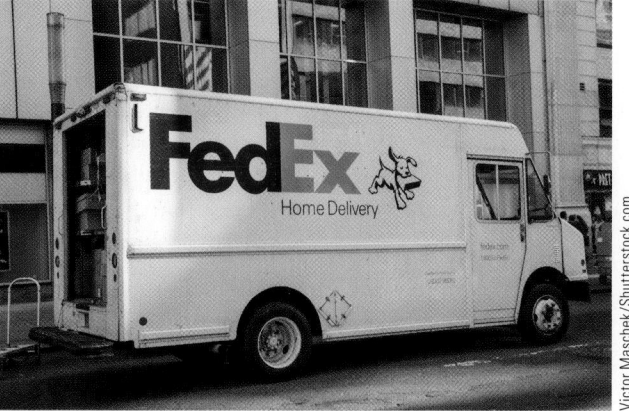

Shipping companies may ultimately be responsible for the conduct of its customers.

Victor Maschek/Shutterstock.com

generally argue that an indictment or a criminal charge can cause unacceptable damage, including the loss of operating licenses, government contracts, and customers. A company's only realistic choice may be to settle, even if it has a good chance of being acquitted. Some think this gives prosecutors too much power.[11] Consider the ethics of the FedEx case from a number of different perspectives.

Morals are the rules people develop as a result of cultural values and norms. Culture is a socializing force that dictates what is right and wrong. Moral standards may also reflect the laws and regulations that affect social and economic behavior. Thus, morals can be considered a foundation of ethical behavior.

Morals are usually characterized as good or bad. "Good" and "bad" have many different connotations. One such connotation is "effective" and "ineffective." A good salesperson makes or exceeds the assigned quota. If the salesperson sells a new computer system or HDTV to a disadvantaged consumer—knowing full well that the person cannot keep up the monthly payments—is that still a good salesperson? What if the sale enables the salesperson to exceed his or her quota?

"Good" and "bad" can also refer to "conforming" and "deviant" behaviors. A doctor who runs large ads offering discounts on open-heart surgery would be considered bad, or unprofessional, because he or she is not conforming to the norms of the medical profession. "Good" and "bad" also express the distinction between law-abiding and criminal behavior. And finally, different religions define "good" and "bad" in markedly different ways. A Muslim who eats pork would be considered bad by other Muslims, for example. Religion is just one of the many factors that affect a businessperson's ethics.

virtue a character trait valued as being good

morals the rules people develop as a result of cultural values and norms

3-3a Morality and Business Ethics

Today's business ethics actually consist of a subset of major life values learned since birth. The values businesspeople use to make decisions have been acquired through family, educational, and religious institutions.

Ethical values are situation specific and time oriented. Everyone must have an ethical base that applies to conduct in the business world and in personal life. One approach to developing a personal set of ethics is to examine the consequences of a particular act. Who is helped or hurt? How long do the consequences last? What actions produce the greatest good for the greatest number of people? A second approach stresses the importance of rules. Rules come in the form of customs, laws, professional standards, and common sense. "Always treat others as you would like to be treated" is an example of a rule.

A third approach to personal ethics emphasizes the development of moral character within individuals. In this approach, ethical development is thought to consist of three levels.[12]

- *Preconventional morality*, the most basic level, is childlike. It is calculating, self-centered, and even selfish, based on what will be immediately punished or rewarded. Fortunately, most businesspeople have progressed beyond the self-centered and manipulative actions of preconventional morality.

- *Conventional morality* moves from an egocentric viewpoint toward the expectations of society. Loyalty and obedience to the organization (or society) become paramount. A marketing decision maker operating at this level of moral development would be concerned only with whether a proposed action is legal and how it will be viewed by others.

- *Postconventional morality* represents the morality of the mature adult. At this level, people are less concerned about how others might see them and more concerned about how they see and judge themselves over the long run. A marketing decision maker who has attained a postconventional level of morality might ask, "Even though it is legal and will increase company profits, is it right in the long run? Might it do more harm than good in the end?"

3-3b Ethical Decision Making

Ethical questions rarely have cut-and-dried answers. Studies show that the following factors tend to influence ethical decision making and judgments:[13]

- **Extent of ethical problems within the organization:** Marketing professionals who perceive fewer ethical problems in their organizations tend to disapprove more strongly of "unethical" or questionable practices than those who perceive more ethical problems. Apparently, the healthier the ethical environment, the more likely it is that marketers will take a strong stand against questionable practices.

- **Top management's actions on ethics:** Top managers can influence the behavior of marketing professionals by encouraging ethical behavior and discouraging unethical behavior. Researchers found that when top managers develop a strong ethical culture, there is reduced pressure to perform unethical acts, fewer unethical acts are performed, and unethical behavior is reported more frequently.[14]

- **Potential magnitude of the consequences:** The greater the harm done to victims, the more likely that marketing professionals will recognize a problem as unethical.

- **Social consensus:** The greater the degree of agreement among managerial peers that an action is harmful, the more likely that marketers will recognize a problem as unethical. Research has found that a strong ethical culture among coworkers decreases observations of ethical misconduct. In companies with strong ethical cultures, 9 percent of employees observed misconduct, compared with 31 percent in companies with weaker cultures.[15]

- **Probability of a harmful outcome:** The greater the likelihood that an action will result in a harmful outcome, the more likely that marketers will recognize a problem as unethical.

- **Length of time between the decision and the onset of consequences:** The shorter the length of time between the action and the onset of negative consequences, the more likely that marketers will perceive a problem as unethical.

- **Number of people to be affected:** The greater the number of persons affected by a negative outcome, the more likely that marketers will recognize a problem as unethical.

As you can see, many factors determine the nature of an ethical decision. In October 2014, drugstore chain CVS ceased all sales of cigarettes and other tobacco products, becoming the first national pharmacy to do so.

CVS President and CEO Larry Merlo said that the decision better aligned the company with its purpose of improving customer health, and that it was simply the right thing to do.[16] Which of the above factors do you think contributed to CVS' decision?

AP Images/Sipa USA/Anthony Behar

In this February 2014 photo, cigarettes and other tobacco products can be seen on sale behind the counter at a New York City CVS location. As of October 1, 2014, CVS became the first chain of national pharmacies to remove cigarettes from its shelves.

3-3c Ethical Guidelines and Training

In recent years, many organizations have become more interested in ethical issues. One sign of this interest is the increase in the number of large companies that appoint ethics officers—from virtually none several years ago to over 40 percent of large corporations today.[17] In addition, many companies of various sizes have developed a **code of ethics** as a guideline to help marketing managers and other employees make better decisions. Creating ethics guidelines has several advantages:

- A code of ethics helps employees identify what their firm recognizes as acceptable business practices.
- A code of ethics can be an effective internal control of behavior, which is more desirable than external controls such as government regulation.
- A written code helps employees avoid confusion when determining whether their decisions are ethical.
- The process of formulating the code of ethics facilitates discussion among employees about what is right and wrong and ultimately leads to better decisions.

code of ethics a guideline to help marketing managers and other employees make better decisions

Ethics training is an effective way to help employees put good ethics into practice. The Ethics

GOOGLE'S CODE OF ETHICS

Google's now-famous guiding principle of personal conduct is simply "Don't be evil." This generally means providing Google users with unbiased access to information, focusing on user needs, and giving them the best products and services that the company can provide. Google's code of ethics is a means of putting "Don't be evil" into practice. A summary of the primary components of Google's code is as follows:

I. **Serve Our Users**
   Our users value Google not only because we deliver great products and services, but because we hold ourselves to a higher standard in how we treat users and operate in general. This requires integrity, useful products, preserving privacy, security, freedom of expression, and being responsive to users.

II. **Respect Each Other**
   We are committed to a supportive work environment where employees have the opportunity to reach their fullest potential. Each Googler is expected to do his or her utmost to create a respectful workplace culture that is free of harassment, intimidation, bias, and unlawful discrimination of any kind.

III. **Avoid Conflicts of Interest**
   While working at Google, we have an obligation to always do what's best for the company and our users. When you are in a situation in which competing loyalties could cause you to pursue a personal benefit for you, your friends, or your family at the expense of Google or its users, you may be faced with a conflict of interest. All of us should avoid conflicts of interest and circumstances that reasonably present the appearance of a conflict.

IV. **Preserve Confidentiality**

V. **Protect Google's Assets**

IV. **Ensure Financial Integrity and Responsibility**
   Financial integrity and fiscal responsibility are core aspects of corporate professionalism. This is more than accurate reporting of our financials, though that's certainly

> important. The money we spend on behalf of Google is not ours; it's the company's, and ultimately, our shareholders'. Each person at Google—not just those in finance—has a role in making sure that money is appropriately spent, our financial records are complete and accurate, and internal controls are honored.
>
> VII. **Obey the Law**
> Each of Google's seven tenants of its code is followed by several pages of detail that fully explain the guiding principle. Space requirements don't allow reprinting the code in full.[18]

Resource Center's National Business Ethics Survey (NBES) found that 81 percent of companies provide ethics training. Coincidentally, the survey found that a historically low 41 percent of workers reported that they had observed misconduct on the job.[19] Still, simply giving employees a long list of *dos* and *don'ts* does not really help employees navigate the gray areas or adapt to a changing world market. In Carson City, Nevada, all governmental lobbyists are required to attend a course on ethics and policy before they can meet with lawmakers. The training outlines exactly how and when lobbyists are allowed to interact with lawmakers and how to report any money they spend. A clear understanding of ethical expectations is essential to an industry like lobbying, where illicit—often illegal—actions are taken to promote individual causes.

Do ethics training programs work? According to the NBES, it seems that they do. The number of employees who said they had felt pressure to commit an ethics violation—to cut corners or worse—dropped from 13 percent in 2011 to 9 percent in 2013.[20]

THE MOST ETHICAL COMPANIES Each year, *Ethisphere* magazine (targeted toward top management and focused on ethical leadership) examines more than 5,000 companies in thirty separate industries, seeking the world's most ethical companies. It then lists the top 100. The magazine uses a rigorous format to identify true ethical leadership. A few of the selected winners are shown in Exhibit 3.1.

ETHICS AND SMALL BUSINESS Large firms like those listed in Exhibit 3.1 often have ethics officers and extensive ethics training for employees. Small companies, however, are often on their own when facing ethical issues. Simply managing the business often demands extensive amounts of time for entrepreneurs, so ethics training and awareness may not be a priority. One area in which small firms sometimes suffer ethical lapses is in promotion. The Internet has changed promotional strategy because small companies can create their own ads and get them out quickly to the marketplace. A recent study found that the number of false advertising lawsuits involving small firms is continually rising.[21] One lawyer who represents small advertisers says, "In order to keep up with the big players, they feel like they have to exaggerate and they can get in trouble."[22] For example, Hello Products sells toothpaste in flavors such as "pink grapefruit" and "mojito mint." When this line of toothpastes launched, it was touted as "99% natural"

University of Virginia professor, Bobby Parmar, demonstrates BizHero, an online game that teaches business ethics and decision making.

AP Images/The Daily Progress/Nate Delesline III

EXHIBIT 3.1 — SELECTED WINNERS OF THE WORLD'S MOST ETHICAL COMPANIES

Company	Industry
Rockwell Collins	Aerospace and Defense
Gap, Inc.	Apparel
Levi Strauss & Co.	Apparel
Cummins, Inc.	Automotive
Ford Motor Company	Autos
Accenture	Business Services
Dun & Bradstreet	Business Services
Manpower Group	Business Services
Dell Inc.	Computer Hardware
Intel Corporation	Computer Hardware
Google	Computer Services
Adobe Systems	Computer Software
Microsoft	Computer Software
Symantec	Computer Software
Colgate-Palmolive Company	Consumer Products
Kimberly-Clark Corporation	Consumer Products
Waste Management	Environmental Services
Kellogg Company	Food and Beverage
PepsiCo	Food and Beverage
L'OREAL	Health and Beauty
Cleveland Clinic	Healthcare Services
3M Company	Industrial Manufacturing
Deere & Company	Industrial Manufacturing
General Electric	Industrial Manufacturing
Time Warner	Media
Safeway	Retail Food Stores

Source: "2014 World's Most Ethical Companies," Ethisphere, http://ethisphere.com (Accessed January 20, 2015).

on the company's website and on the toothpaste packaging itself. After the firm delivered its first shipment, it received a letter from Procter & Gamble wanting Hello to retract its "99% natural" claim. Hello settled its dispute with P&G by agreeing to change the label to "Naturally Friendly." Hello ended up with 100,000 tubes that couldn't be sold. The firm ultimately gave them away on the streets of Manhattan hoping to get a little promotional mileage out of the old tubes.[23]

Foreign Corrupt Practices Act (FCPA) a law that prohibits U.S. corporations from making illegal payments to public officials of foreign governments to obtain business rights or to enhance their business dealings in those countries

corporate social responsibility (CSR) a business's concern for society's welfare

stakeholder theory ethical theory stating that social responsibility is paying attention to the interest of every affected stakeholder in every aspect of a firm's operation

---

3-3d Ethics in Other Countries

Studies suggest that ethical beliefs vary little from culture to culture. Certain practices, however, such as the use of illegal payments and bribes, are far more acceptable in some places than in others, though enforced laws are increasingly making the practice less accepted. One such law, the **Foreign Corrupt Practices Act (FCPA)**, was enacted because Congress was concerned about U.S. corporations' use of illegal payments and bribes in international business dealings. This act prohibits U.S. corporations from making illegal payments to public officials of foreign governments to obtain business rights or to enhance their business dealings in those countries. The act has been criticized for putting U.S. businesses at a competitive disadvantage. Many contend that bribery is an unpleasant but necessary part of international business, especially in countries such as China, where business gift giving is widely accepted and expected. But, as prosecutions under the FCPA have increased worldwide, some countries are implementing their own anti-bribery laws. For example, even though China is among the three countries with the most international corruption cases prosecuted under the FCPA, the country is working to develop its own anti-bribery laws.

3-4 CORPORATE SOCIAL RESPONSIBILITY

Corporate social responsibility (CSR) is a business's concern for society's welfare. This concern is demonstrated by managers who consider both the long-range best interests of the company and the company's relationship to the society within which it operates.

3-4a Stakeholders and Social Responsibility

An important aspect of social responsibility is **stakeholder theory**. Stakeholder theory says that social responsibility is paying attention to the interest of every affected stakeholder in every aspect of a firm's operation. The stakeholders in a typical corporation are shown in Exhibit 3.2.

- *Employees* have their jobs and incomes at stake. If the firm moves or closes, employees often face a severe hardship. In return for their labor, employees expect wages, benefits, and meaningful work. In return for their loyalty, workers expect the company to carry them through difficult times.

EXHIBIT 3.2 STAKEHOLDERS IN A TYPICAL CORPORATION

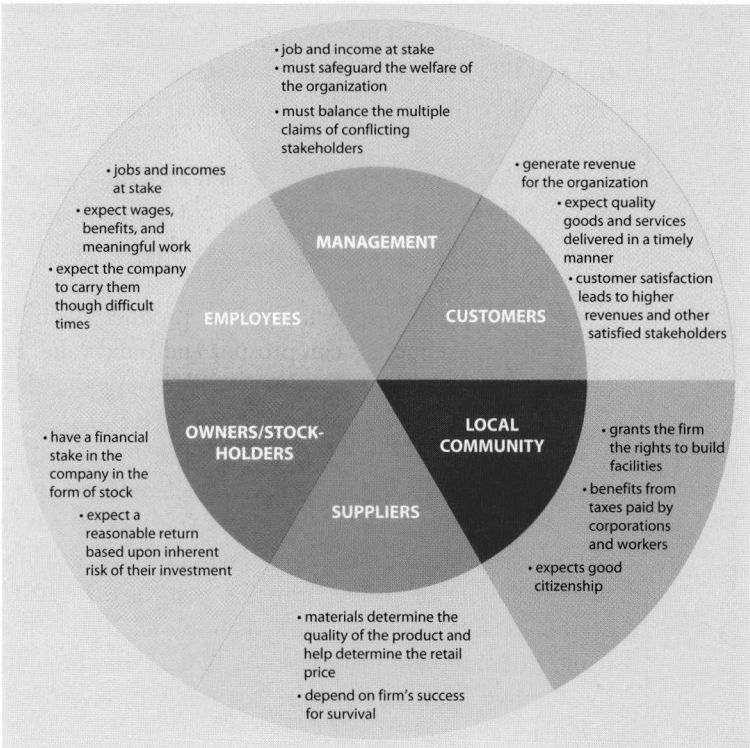

then production grinds to a halt. The materials supplied determine the quality of the product produced and create a cost floor, which helps determine the retail price. In turn, the firm is the customer of the supplier and is therefore vital to the success and survival of the supplier. A supplier that fails to deliver quality products can create numerous problems for a firm. For example, Burger King stopped buying beef from an Irish supplier whose patties were found to contain traces of horse meat in Britain and Ireland.[24]

- *Owners* have a financial stake in the form of stock in a corporation. They expect a reasonable return based upon the amount of inherent risk on their investment. Sometimes managers and employees receive a portion of their compensation in company stock. When Apple launched its initial public stock offering, 30 Apple employees became instant millionaires.[25] Similarly, more than 10,000 Microsoft employees have become millionaires from their stock holdings.[26]

3-4b Pyramid of Corporate Social Responsibility

One theorist suggests that total corporate social responsibility has four components: economic, legal, ethical, and philanthropic. The **pyramid of corporate social responsibility** portrays economic performance as the foundation for the other three responsibilities (see Exhibit 3.3). At the same time that it pursues profits (economic responsibility), however, a business is expected to obey the law (legal responsibility); to do what is right, just, and fair (ethical responsibilities); and to be a good corporate citizen (philanthropic responsibility). These four components are distinct but together constitute the whole. Still, if the company does not make a profit, then the other three responsibilities are moot.

 ## ARGUMENTS FOR AND AGAINST SOCIAL RESPONSIBILITY

CSR can be a divisive issue. Some analysts believe that a business should focus on making a profit and leave social and environmental problems to nonprofit organizations and government. Economist

> **pyramid of corporate social responsibility** a model that suggests corporate social responsibility is composed of economic, legal, ethical, and philanthropic responsibilities and that a firm's economic performance supports the entire structure

- *Management* plays a special role, as they also have a stake in the corporation. Like employees, managers have their jobs and incomes at stake. On the other hand, management must safeguard the welfare of the organization. Sometimes this means balancing the multiple claims of conflicting stakeholders. For example, stockholders want a higher return on investment and perhaps lower costs by moving factories overseas. This naturally conflicts with the interests of employees, the local community, and perhaps suppliers.

- *Customers* generate the revenue for the organization. In exchange, they expect high-quality goods and services delivered in a timely manner. Customer satisfaction leads to higher revenues and the ability to enhance the satisfaction of other stakeholders.

- *The local community*, through its government, grants the firm the right to build facilities. In turn, the community benefits directly from local taxes paid by the corporation and indirectly by property and sales taxes paid by the workers. The firm is expected to be a good citizen by paying a fair wage, not polluting the environment, and so forth.

- *Suppliers* are vital to the success of the firm. For example, if a critical part is not available for an assembly line,

EXHIBIT 3.3 THE PYRAMID OF CORPORATE SOCIAL RESPONSIBILITY

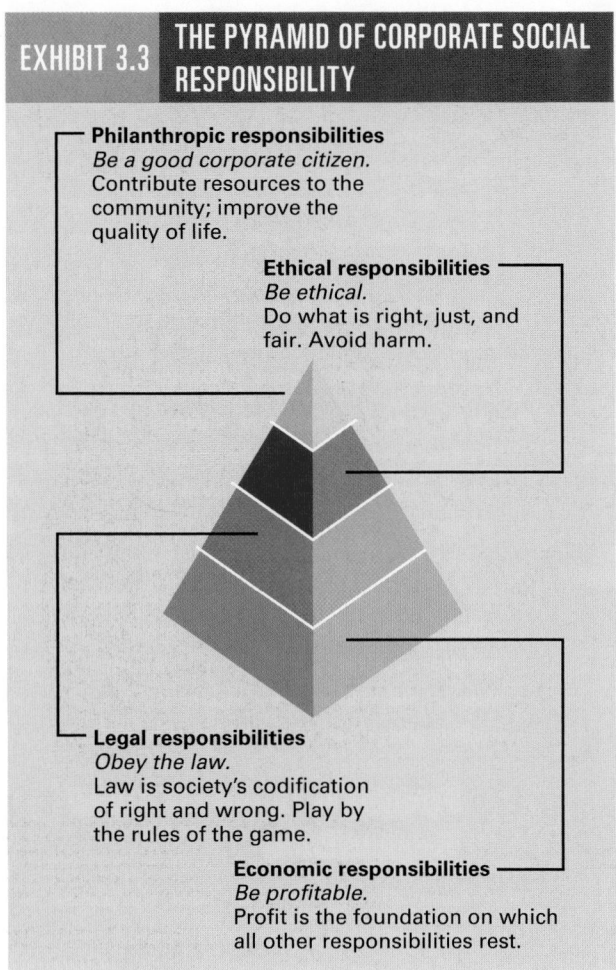

Philanthropic responsibilities
Be a good corporate citizen.
Contribute resources to the community; improve the quality of life.

Ethical responsibilities
Be ethical.
Do what is right, just, and fair. Avoid harm.

Legal responsibilities
Obey the law.
Law is society's codification of right and wrong. Play by the rules of the game.

Economic responsibilities
Be profitable.
Profit is the foundation on which all other responsibilities rest.

Milton Friedman believed that the free market, not companies, should decide what is best for the world.[27] Friedman argued that when business executives spend more money than necessary—to purchase delivery vehicles with hybrid engines, pay higher wages in developing countries, or even donate company funds to charity—they are spending shareholders' money to further their own agendas. It would be better to pay dividends and let the shareholders give the money away if they choose.

On the other hand, CSR has an increasing number of supporters based on several compelling factors. One is that it is simply the right thing to do. Some societal problems, such as pollution and poverty-level wages, have been brought about by corporations' actions; it is the responsibility of business to right these wrongs. Businesses also have the resources, so businesses should be given the chance to solve social problems. For example, businesses can provide a fair work environment, safe products, and informative advertising.

Recent research has found that being socially responsible and training front line employees about social responsibility can have a positive impact on the firm. In a business-to-business environment, researchers found that social responsibility activities can raise customer trust and identification with the firm. These factors, in turn, build customer loyalty, which often leads to higher profits.[28]

Another, more pragmatic, reason for being socially responsible is that if businesses do not act responsibly, then government will create new regulations and perhaps levy fines against them.

Finally, social responsibility can produce a direct profit. Smart companies can prosper and build value by tackling social problems. Starbucks rolled out a reusable plastic tumbler that customers could buy for $1 instead of using a disposable cardboard cup for each coffee they buy. Not only does the reusable tumbler reduce energy use, landfill waste, and litter, it saves Starbucks the cost of the disposable cups and encourages customers to buy their daily cup of coffee from the company. In 2015, Starbucks introduced a $30 double-walled tumbler made from recycled materials. Customers who brought the tumbler back to the store for refills received free coffee for a month.[29]

Richard B. Levine/Newscom

This reusable tumbler was purchased from a Starbucks location in the Chelsea neighborhood of New York City. Consumers have long criticized Starbucks' use of disposable containers, so the introduction of the reusable cup benefited both the company and its customers.

3-5a Sustainability

A popular theory in social responsibility is called **sustainability**. This refers to the idea that socially responsible companies will outperform their peers by focusing on the world's social and environmental problems and viewing them as opportunities to build profits and help the world at the same time.

Perhaps the company that most exemplifies the sustainability movement is Patagonia. The firm has recently launched a program called the Responsible Economy. Rick Ridgeway, Head of Sustainability for Patagonia, says, "Responsible Economy is about the role consumption plays in the continued decline of our planet's health."[30] Patagonia's goal is to get people to pay attention to environmental stress. Then, the company hopes, they will buy quality products that do not end up in a landfill after a few months.

Patagonia has placed ads on Black Friday—typically the busiest shopping day of the year—that read "don't buy our products." While this seems counterintuitive for a for-profit company, Patagonia has doubled in size and tripled its profits in recent years. CEO Rose Marcario says that the promotion has been very successful because what the ad *really* means is "don't buy more than you need" and "the more you consume, the more it strains the world's resources."[31] Marcario notes that Patagonia has released a film called "Worn Well" that stresses the durability of Patagonia's products and suggests that they can be handed down from generation to generation. Patagonia backs up this bold marketing strategy with a guarantee—if something happens, regardless of age, Patagonia will fix it for free.

Patagonia also funds various activities outside of the firm that support sustainability. Recently, the company paid for a documentary film called "Dam Nation," which advocates dam removal around the world. Marcario claims that there is a huge movement in China to dam virtually all natural rivers. This, she says, would mean less biodiversity.[32] Patagonia also announced a new $13 million project to put solar panels on homes in Hawaii because Marcario felt that solar infrastructure was not growing in Hawaii the way it should.[33]

Sustainability is not simply "green marketing," though environmental sustainability is an important component of the sustainability philosophy. An environmentally sustainable process contributes to keeping the environment healthy by using renewable resources and by avoiding actions that depreciate the environment.

3-5b Growth of Social Responsibility

The social responsibility of businesses is growing around the world. Companies around the globe are coming under increasing pressure from governments, advocacy groups,

DON'T BUY THIS JACKET

It's Black Friday, the day in the year retail turns from red to black and starts to make real money. But Black Friday, and the culture of consumption it reflects, puts the economy of natural systems that support all life firmly in the red. We're now using the resources of one-and-a-half planets on our one and only planet.

Because Patagonia wants to be in business for a good long time—and leave a world inhabitable for our kids—we want to do the opposite of every other business today. We ask you to buy less and to reflect before you spend a dime on this jacket or anything else.

Environmental bankruptcy, as with corporate bankruptcy, can happen very slowly, then all of a sudden. This is what we face unless we slow down, then reverse the damage. We're running short on fresh water, topsoil, fisheries, wetlands – all our planet's natural systems and resources that support business, and life, including our own.

The environmental cost of everything we make is astonishing. Consider the R2® Jacket shown, one of our best sellers. To make it required 135 liters of

COMMON THREADS INITIATIVE

REDUCE
WE make useful gear that lasts a long time
YOU don't buy what you don't need

REPAIR
WE help you repair your Patagonia gear
YOU pledge to fix what's broken

REUSE
WE help find a home for Patagonia gear you no longer need
YOU sell or pass it on*

RECYCLE
WE will take back your Patagonia gear that is worn out
YOU pledge to keep your stuff out of the landfill and incinerator

REIMAGINE
TOGETHER we reimagine a world where we take only what nature can replace

water, enough to meet the daily needs (three glasses a day) of 45 people. Its journey from its origin as 60% recycled polyester to our Reno warehouse generated nearly 20 pounds of carbon dioxide, 24 times the weight of the finished product. This jacket left behind, on its way to Reno, two-thirds its weight in waste.

And this is a 60% recycled polyester jacket, knit and sewn to a high standard; it is exceptionally durable, so you won't have to replace it as often. And when it comes to the end of its useful life we'll take it back to recycle into a product of equal value. But, as is true of all the things we can make and you can buy, this jacket comes with an environmental cost higher than its price.

There is much to be done and plenty for us all to do. Don't buy what you don't need. Think twice before you buy anything. Go to patagonia.com/CommonThreads or scan the QR code below. Take the Common Threads Initiative pledge, and join us in the fifth "R," to reimagine a world where we take only what nature can replace.

patagonia patagonia.com

* If you sell your used Patagonia product on eBay® and take the Common Threads Initiative pledge, we will co-list your product on patagonia.com for no additional charge.

TAKE THE PLEDGE

Source: Patagonia

Patagonia's decision to Responsible Economy is so strong that the company advises customers not to buy its products if they don't absolutely need to.

investors, prospective employees, current employees, and consumers to make their organizations more socially responsible. In turn, firms are seeing social responsibility as an opportunity. A recent global survey from the Nielsen Company, one of the world's largest marketing research firms, found that

sustainability the idea that socially responsible companies will outperform their peers by focusing on the world's social problems and viewing them as opportunities to build profits and help the world at the same time

55 percent of respondents around the world were willing to pay extra for products and services from companies providing positive social and environmental impact (see Exhibit 3.4).[34] More than half of the survey participants had bought at least one product or service in the past six months from a socially responsible company.[35]

UNITED NATIONS GLOBAL COMPACT

One way that U.S. firms can do more is by joining the United Nations Global Compact (UNGC). The UNGC, the world's largest global corporate citizenship initiative, has seen its ranks swell over the past few years. In 2001—the first full year after its launch—just sixty-seven companies joined, agreeing to abide by ten principles (see "The Ten Principles of the United Nation's Global Compact"). In 2015, there were more than 8000 business participants.[36]

Smaller companies that wish to join the social responsibility and sustainability movement are turning to the B Corp movement.[37] To become a B Corp Certified company, a firm must score at least 80 points on a 200-point assessment. Criteria include things like fair compensation

for workers, how much waste the company produces, and the company's work with local businesses. Firms such as Patagonia, Ben & Jerry's, online crafts marketplace Etsy, and cleaning products maker Method Products have qualified. New Seasons Market, a 13-store grocery chain in Oregon, stamps the B Corp logo on all of its grocery bags and gives employees B Corp badges to wear. The logo helps attract socially-minded shoppers and helps in recruiting new workers.

Fisherss/Shutterstock.com

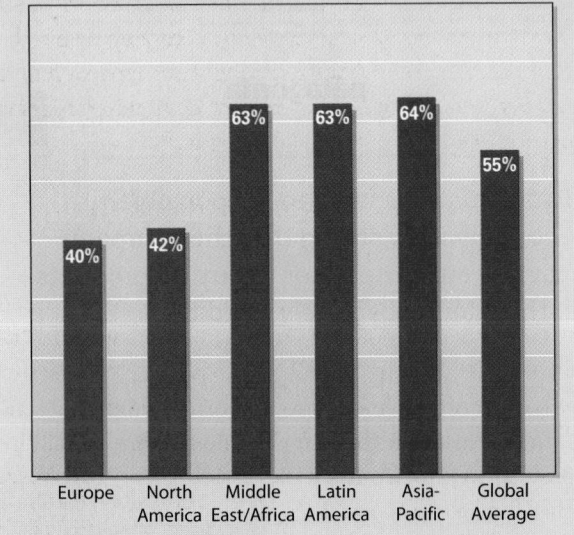

EXHIBIT 3.4 — PERCENT OF RESPONDENTS WILLING TO PAY EXTRA FOR PRODUCTS AND SERVICES FROM COMPANIES COMMITTED TO POSITIVE SOCIAL AND ENVIRONMENTAL IMPACT

Europe	North America	Middle East/Africa	Latin America	Asia-Pacific	Global Average
40%	42%	63%	63%	64%	55%

Source: "It Pays to Be Green: Corporate Social Responsibility Meets the Bottom Line," *Nielsen*, June 17, 2014, www.nielsen.com/us/en/insights/news/2014/it-pays-to-be-green-corporate-social-responsibility-meets-the-bottom-line.html (Accessed November 3, 2015).

THE TEN PRINCIPLES OF THE UNITED NATION'S GLOBAL COMPACT

Human Rights

▶ **Principle 1:** Businesses should support and respect the protection of internationally proclaimed human rights.

▶ **Principle 2:** Businesses should make sure that they are not complicit in human rights abuses.

Labor

▶ **Principle 3:** Businesses should uphold the freedom of association and the effective recognition of the right to collective bargaining.

▶ **Principle 4:** Businesses should uphold the elimination of all forms of forced and compulsory labor.

▶ **Principle 5:** Businesses should uphold the effective abolition of child labor.

▶ **Principle 6:** Businesses should uphold the elimination of discrimination in respect of employment and occupation.

Environment

▶ **Principle 7:** Businesses should support a precautionary approach to environmental challenges.

▶ **Principle 8:** Businesses should undertake initiatives to promote greater environmental responsibility.

▶ **Principle 9:** Businesses should encourage the development and diffusion of environmentally friendly technologies.

Anti-Corruption

▶ **Principle 10:** Businesses should work against corruption in all its forms, including extortion and bribery

Source: https://www.unglobalcompact.org/AboutThe GC/TheTenPrinciples/index.html

3-5c Green Marketing

An outgrowth of the social responsibility and sustainability movements is green marketing. **Green marketing** is the development and marketing of products designed to minimize negative effects on the physical environment or to improve the environment. One approach that firms use to indicate that they are part of the green movement is to use third-party eco-logos. Examples include the chasing-arrows recycling logo (the product is either recyclable or contains recycled materials); the Energy Star logo (the product is energy efficient); and Certified Organic (the U.S. Department of Agriculture created standards relative to soil quality, animal raising practices, pest and weed control, and the use of additives). These logos can enhance a product's sales and profitability.

Nearly four in 10 Americans (about 93 million people) say that they are dedicated to buying green products and services. Green purchasing is driven by young adults (age 18 to 34) and Hispanics; about half of the respondents in these groups report that they regularly seek out green products. Young adults are also more likely to be interested in a company's green practices and to avoid companies with poor environmental records.[38]

When a firm takes an action that is perceived as not environmentally friendly, it can create a significant amount of negative publicity. The *New Yorker* magazine recently ran a story about furniture and decorative accessories company Restoration Hardware. The article notes:

The first stirrings of dissent came from the UPS drivers. They began posting on Brown Café, an anonymous message board, about the thirty-three-hundred page catalogue bundles sent out by Restoration Hardware. "My building for the last few days is slammed with RF catalogues (17 pounds each) with another trailer full coming in next week," one wrote. One driver described orders to give the catalogues to passersby, if necessary, rather than return them to UPS distribution centers. "I see them all over my route in the recycle bins."

Then, customers rebelled. In Palo Alto, seven volunteers returned two thousand pounds of the catalogues to a Restoration Hardware store in one day, on hand trucks.

One page of the catalogue is devoted to Restoration Hardware's environmental impact. First, the company claims that sending out the catalogues all at once is more responsible than spreading them throughout the year. It does not acknowledge that, in 2003, when it mailed six catalogues annually, it used half as many total pages. Second, the company says that it purchases paper certified by the Programme for the Endorsement of Forest Certification. However, as *Business Week* explained, other retailers, such as Pottery Barn, buy paper from forests certified by the Forest Stewardship Council, which has stricter environmental standards. Third, Restoration Hardware points out that it purchases carbon offsets through UPS to fund conservation projects. Those offsets, while helpful, cover only the shipping, not the paper production, the most harmful of the process, because of the energy used to break down wood into pulp. The company responded to the *New Yorker's* questions about its environmental practices by emailing a press release containing information identical to what's in the catalogue.[39]

3-5d Leaders in Social Responsibility and Green Marketing

According to *Corporate Responsibility* magazine, the top four corporate citizens of 2014 were Bristol-Myers Squibb, Johnson & Johnson, Gap, and Microsoft.[40] Bristol-Myers Squibb currently funds more than 125 health care initiatives around the world. For example, it is a member of the Medicines Patent Pool in Geneva, Switzerland, which makes drugs available at low costs to people in the developing world with HIV/AIDS. The firm estimates that these projects are benefiting

Kevin Schafer/Moment Mobile/Getty Images

Restoration Hardware, a furniture and decorating company, recently caught grief for overproducing their catalogs, thus causing them to develop a reputation of not being environmentally friendly.

green marketing the development and marketing of products designed to minimize negative effects on the physical environment or to improve the environment

4 The Marketing Environment

LEARNING OUTCOMES

After studying this chapter, you will be able to…

4-1 Discuss the external environment of marketing and explain how it affects a firm

4-2 Describe the social factors that affect marketing

4-3 Explain the importance to marketing managers of current demographic trends

4-4 Explain the importance to marketing managers of growing ethnic markets

4-5 Identify consumer and marketer reactions to the state of the economy

4-6 Identify the impact of technology on a firm

4-7 Discuss the political and legal environment of marketing

4-8 Explain the basics of foreign and domestic competition

After you finish this chapter go to **PAGE 65** for **STUDY TOOLS**.

Dmitrijs Dmitrijevs/Shutterstock.com

4-1 THE EXTERNAL MARKETING ENVIRONMENT

Perhaps the most important decisions a marketing manager must make relate to the creation of the marketing mix. Recall from Chapters 1 and 2 that a marketing mix is the unique combination of product, place (distribution), promotion, and price strategies. The marketing mix is, of course, under the firm's control and is designed to appeal to a specific group of potential buyers, or target market. A **target market** is a group of people or organizations for which an organization designs, implements, and maintains a marketing mix intended to meet the needs of that group, resulting in mutually satisfying exchanges.

target market a group of people or organizations for which an organization designs, implements, and maintains a marketing mix intended to meet the need of that group, resulting in mutually satisfying exchanges

Managers must alter the marketing mix because of changes in the environment in which consumers live, work, and make purchasing decisions. Also, as markets mature, some new consumers become part of the target market; others drop out. Those who remain may have different tastes, needs, incomes, lifestyles, and buying habits than the original target consumers. Technology, and the resulting change in buying habits, meant that consumers no longer have those "Kodak Moments" when taking pictures

of a birthday party or an exceptional sunset. Digital photography has sent 35-millimeter film the way of the horse and buggy. Unfortunately, shifting technology ultimately led to the bankruptcy of Eastman Kodak.

Although managers can control the marketing mix, they cannot control elements in the external environment that continually mold and reshape the target market. Controllable and uncontrollable variables affect the target market, whether it consists of consumers or business purchasers. The uncontrollable elements in the center of the environment continually evolve and create changes in the target market. Think, for example, about how social media have changed your world. In contrast, managers can shape and reshape the marketing mix to influence the target market. That is, managers react to changes in the external environment and attempt to create a more effective marketing mix.

4-1a Understanding the External Environment

Unless marketing managers understand the external environment, the firm cannot intelligently plan for the future. Thus, many organizations assemble a team of specialists to continually collect and evaluate environmental information, a process called *environmental scanning*. The goal in gathering the environmental data is to identify future market opportunities and threats.

UNDERSTAND CURRENT CUSTOMERS You must first understand how customers buy, where they buy, what they buy, and when they buy. McDonald's had a rough year in 2014, suffering a net loss as customers moved on to different venues. While upcoming chains like Five Guys limit their offering to around a half dozen items, customers find the McDonald's menu confusing and too big. More upscale fast-casual restaurants like Chipotle Mexican Grill and Shake Shack are luring customers, particularly younger ones, by offering better quality food and the ability to customize their meals. For its part, McDonald's is in the process of changing its marketing mix to counter this trend and regain its lost market share around the globe.

In a brand-new McDonald's outlet near the company's headquarters in Oak Brook, Illinois, customers do not have to queue at the counter. They can go to a touch screen and build their own burger by choosing a bun, toppings, and sauces from a list of more than 20 ingredients including grilled mushrooms, guacamole, and caramelized onions. Customers then sit down and wait an average of seven minutes until a server brings their burgers to their table. The company is planning to roll out these "Create Your Taste" burgers in up to 2,000 restaurants by late 2015, and possibly more if they do well. McDonald's is also trying to engage with customers on social media and is working on a smartphone app as well as testing mobile-payment systems such as Apple Pay, Softcard, and Google Wallet.[1]

McDonald's is also changing its slogan of the past ten years from "I'm Lovin' It" to "Lovin' Beats Hatin'." The idea of the shift is to promote happiness over hate. So far, reaction to the new slogan has been underwhelming. The "It" in the old slogan can be tied back to McDonald's main product—food. Not so with the new slogan. The word "hatin'" is negative, and most advertisers try to avoid negative words in their slogans.[2] Clearly, McDonald's new slogan seems to have problems with both clarity (no ties to food) and likability.

Does McDonald's understand its current customers? By the time you read this text, you should be able to answer this question.

UNDERSTAND HOW CONSUMER DECISIONS ARE MADE Hotel chains like Hyatt, Holiday Inn, and Marriott must understand the decision process that consumers use when selecting a hotel. Boston research firm Chadwick Martin Bailey (CMB) found that mobile, social, and online factors influence leisure travelers very differently at different stages in the purchase process. Mobile devices play an important role in the initial research phase of hotel planning but are used sparingly to book hotel stays. More than 60 percent of travelers use a mobile device— 47 percent use a smartphone—during their hotel purchase journey, but only 6 percent book their hotel via a smartphone. Mobile applications are used infrequently throughout the hotel purchase journey. In total, only 6 percent of shoppers use a mobile app.

Consumer reviews trump social media in influence, research, evaluation, and final decision making. Only 13 percent of bookers use social media during the purchase process versus the 59 percent who consult consumer reviews.

Price-comparison sites play an important role—even when they are not the final purchase location. Nearly half of travelers (49 percent) used a price-comparison site such as Expedia, Priceline, or Kayak. Thirty-six percent of those who use one or more of these sites ultimately book their stay with them.[3] The challenge for hotels, then, is to decide how to align their marketing budgets to intercept potential travelers and deliver the right promotion on the appropriate device and through the right channel.

IDENTIFY THE MOST VALUABLE CUSTOMERS AND UNDERSTAND THEIR NEEDS Often, 20 percent of a firm's customers produce eighty percent of the firm's revenue. An organization must understand what drives that loyalty and then take steps to ensure that those drivers are maintained and enhanced. Airlines use loyalty programs to satisfy and retain their best customers. For example, persons who fly more than 100,000 miles a year on American Airlines are called Executive Platinum members. They are granted priority boarding and seating, free domestic upgrades, no fees for checked luggage, coupons for international upgrades, and other benefits.

UNDERSTAND THE COMPETITION Successful firms know their competitors and attempt to forecast those competitors' future moves. Competitors threaten both a firm's market share and its profitability. With 55 million wireless customers and growing, T-Mobile is projected to overtake Sprint as the nation's third largest mobile carrier. What is behind this

Tupungato/Shutterstock.com

This image of a T-Mobile store in Vienna, Switzerland, is a reminder that with 55 million wireless customers and growing, T-Mobile is projected to overtake Sprint as the third largest mobile carrier in the world-trailing Verizon and AT&T.

meteoric rise? After examining the competition, T-Mobile decided to be as different as possible from its rivals. As an innovation leader, T-Mobile is changing the way that carriers offer services. T-Mobile was first to eliminate monthly contracts and offer international data roaming at no extra cost. It was also the first to announce it would allow customers to roll over data capacity from month-to-month. The carrier still has a long way to go to overtake Verizon or AT&T, but its marketing strategy is fostering rapid growth.[4]

4-1b Environmental Management

No single business is large or powerful enough to create major change in the external environment. Thus, marketing managers are basically adapters rather than agents of change. For example, despite the huge size of firms like General Electric, Walmart, Apple, and Caterpillar, they do not control social change, demographics, or other factors in the external environment.

Just because a firm cannot fully control the external environment, however, does not mean that it is helpless. Sometimes a firm can influence external events. For example, extensive lobbying by FedEx has enabled it to acquire virtually all the Japanese routes it has sought. When a company implements strategies that attempt to shape the external environment within which it operates, it is engaging in **environmental management**. The factors within the external environment that are important to marketing managers can be classified as social, demographic, economic, technological, political and legal, and competitive.

 ## 4-2 SOCIAL FACTORS

Social change is perhaps the most difficult external variable for marketing managers to forecast, influence, or integrate into marketing plans. Social factors include our attitudes, values, and lifestyles. Social factors influence the products people buy; the prices paid for products; the effectiveness of specific promotions; and how, where, and when people expect to purchase products.

4-2a American Values

A *value* is a strongly held and enduring belief. During the United States' first 200 years, four basic values strongly influenced attitudes and lifestyles:

- **Self-sufficiency:** Every person should stand on his or her own two feet.

- **Upward mobility:** Success would come to anyone who got an education, worked hard, and played by the rules.

- **Work ethic:** Hard work, dedication to family, and frugality were moral and right.

- **Conformity:** No one should expect to be treated differently from anybody else.

These core values still hold for a majority of Americans today. A person's values are key determinants of what is important and not important, what actions to take or not to take, and how one behaves in social situations.

People typically form values through interaction with family, friends, and other influencers such as teachers, religious leaders, and politicians. The changing environment can also play a key role in shaping one's values.

Values influence our buying habits. Today's consumers are demanding, inquisitive, and discriminating. No longer willing to tolerate products that break down, they are insisting on high-quality goods that save time, energy, and often calories. U.S. consumers rank the characteristics of product quality as (1) reliability, (2) durability, (3) easy maintenance, (4) ease of use, (5) a trusted brand name, and (6) a low price. Shoppers are also concerned about nutrition and want to know what is in their food; many have environmental concerns as well.

4-2b The Growth of Component Lifestyles

People in the United States today are piecing together **component lifestyles**. A lifestyle is a mode of living; it is the way people decide to live their lives. With component lifestyles, people are choosing products and services that meet diverse needs and interests rather than conforming to traditional stereotypes.

In the past, a person's profession—for instance, banker—defined his or her lifestyle. Today, a person can be a banker and also a gourmet, fitness enthusiast, dedicated single parent, and Internet guru. Each of these lifestyles is associated with different goods and services and represents a target audience. Component lifestyles increase the complexity of consumers' buying habits. Each consumer's unique lifestyle can require a different marketing mix.

> **environmental management** when a company implements strategies that attempt to shape the external environment within which it operates

> **component lifestyles** the practice of choosing goods and services that meet one's diverse needs and interests rather than conforming to a single, traditional lifestyle

4-2c How Social Media Have Changed Our Behavior

In 2015, nearly half of the world's population—3 billion people—were on the Internet. Beyond accessing the Internet via computer, tablet, or smartphone, today there is much talk about the Internet of Things. In 2008, the number of "things" (clothing, thermostats, washing machines, fitness trackers, and lightbulbs, for example) connected to the Internet exceeded the number of people on earth. By 2020 there will be 50 billion connected tools, devices, and even cattle.[5] Yes, Dutch startup Sparked is developing a wireless sensor for cattle. When one is sick or pregnant, the sensor sends a message to the farmer. Similarly, Corventis makes a wireless cardiac monitor that doctors can use to monitor people for health risks in real time. And this is just the beginning—the Internet of Things has the potential to change life as we know it in nearly every area of life.

Social media are making profound changes in the way we obtain and consume information—consumers are interacting; sharing beliefs, values, ideas, and interests; and, of course, making purchases at a dizzying rate. These media have even played a major role in the beginnings of revolutions!

What exactly are social media? They are Web-based and mobile technologies that allow the creation and exchange of user-generated content. Social media encompasses a wide variety of content formats—you have most likely used sites such as Facebook, YouTube, Twitter, Tumblr, Instagram, and Pinterest, each of which serves a different function (see Chapter 18). These media have changed the way we communicate, keep track of others, browse for products and services, and make purchases. Social networking is part of regular life for people of all ages. Of the 3 billion Internet users, 2 billion use social media. From 2014 to 2015, 222 million people opened their first social media account.[6] Slightly more women than men use social media. At 89 percent, the heaviest users by age are 18- to 29-year-olds. Usage rates are lower among older age groups.[7]

More than one minute out of every five spent on the Internet worldwide is dedicated to social networking. Facebook, Instagram, Pinterest, LinkedIn, and Twitter are the most-used social networking sites worldwide. Facebook, by far, is the world's most popular, with more than 1.4 billion users. Sixty-six percent of Millennials around the world use Facebook.[8] A recent survey of persons using the Internet in America found:

- Multi-platform use is on the rise. Fifty-two percent of online adults now use two or more social media sites—a 10 percent increase since 2013.

- For the first time, more than half of all online adults 65 and older (56 percent) use Facebook. This represents 31 percent of all seniors.

- For the first time, roughly half of Internet-using young adults ages 18 through 29 (53 percent) use Instagram. Half of all Instagram users (49 percent) use the site daily.

- For the first time, the share of Internet users with college educations using LinkedIn reached 50 percent.

- Women dominate Pinterest. Forty-two percent of online women now use the platform, compared with 13 percent of online men.[9]

HOW FIRMS USE SOCIAL MEDIA Social networking has changed the game when it comes to opinion sharing. Now, consumers can reach many people at once with their views—and can respond to brands and events in real time. In turn, marketers can use social media to engage customers in their products and services. Marketers have learned that social media are not like network television, where a message is pushed out to a mass audience. Instead, social media enable firms to create conversations with customers and establish meaningful connections. In other words, social media marketing can humanize brands. Marketers for brands like Charmin tissues and Oreo cookies post custom videos about their products to Facebook and then invite feedback. Clearly it's a winning strategy—Facebook now attracts over a billion video views per day.[10]

A successful social media company requires creativity. For example, Airline WestJet recently asked travelers on one flight what they wanted for Christmas. While the passengers were airborne, WestJet shoppers raced to buy and wrap the requested items. These presents were then delivered to the recipients via the destination airport's baggage carousel. The campaign's YouTube video received more than 38 million views.[11] Most importantly, it created a positive image and goodwill for WestJet.

When fast-food chain Wendy's released the Pretzel Bacon Cheeseburger, it quickly became the chain's most successful product launch ever. Fans tweeted about their love for the new burger, and Wendy's turned the tweets (misspellings and all) into a series of silly love song music videos (including one staring Nick Lachey). In addition to being reported on all of the major news channels, the videos received 7.5 million Facebook views.[12]

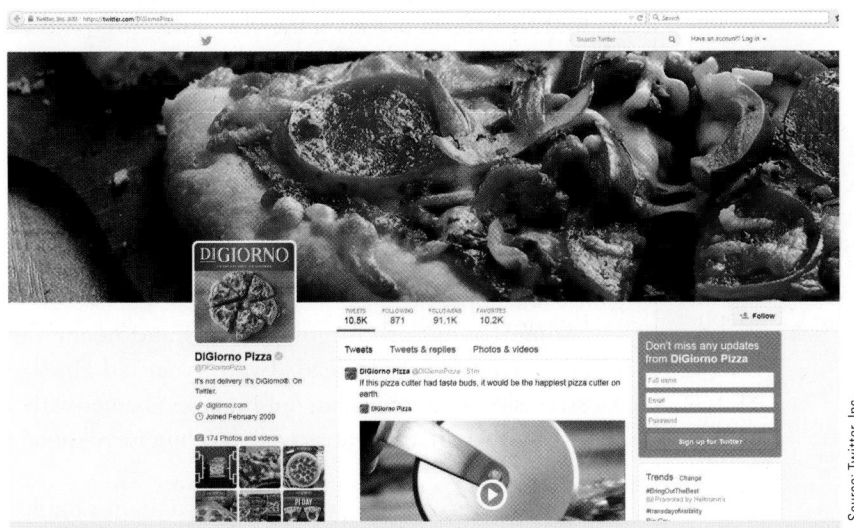

DiGiorno has done a great job of using social media to convey their message as a brand.

On average, about 6,000 tweets are posted on Twitter every second. That equates to 350,000 tweets per minute and 500 million tweets (by 248 million unique users) per day. [13] Frozen pizza manufacturer DiGiorno has proven to be a master at making its tweets stand out from the crowd. The company frequently employs humor, Internet memes, and casual language to endear itself to customers. Here are a few winners:

> *KNOCK KNOCK who's there DELIVERY PIZZA delivery pizza who HAHAHA JK DELIVERY PIZZA WON'T BE HERE FOR HOURS*
> —DiGiorno Pizza (@DiGiornoPizza)

> *"I've got too much on my plate," said no one ever with pizza on their plate.*
> —DiGiorno Pizza (@DiGiornoPizza)

> *Keep Calm and Pizza O-WAIT WHAT THERE'S PIZZA OMG I'M SO FREAKING OUT ABOUT THIS*
> —DiGiorno Pizza (@DiGiornoPizza)

> *March madness was named after a guy who didn't eat pizza once in the month of march one time. True story*
> —DiGiorno Pizza (@DiGiornoPizza)[14]

Even though the topics are random, the tweets all relate back to pizza, cheese, or delivery. These tweets are often retweeted, which spreads the word to larger audiences.

DiGiorno also tweets at other Twitter users, replies to celebrities, and makes comments about live events. DiGiorno noticed that #SoundofMusicLive was trending and capitalized on the 18 million people watching the event by sending out a tweet using the hashtag. This stunt is called "newsjacking" and it earned DiGiorno 2,000 new followers by the time the two hour special was over. The tweets included:

> DOUGH a crust an unbaked crust RAY, a guy that likes pizza ME a pizza liked by a guy named ray FAH no idea what fah is SO so LA a city T tee
> —DiGiorno Pizza (@DiGiornoPizza)

> #TheSoundOFMusicLive Can't believe pizza isn't one of her favorite things smh
> —DiGiorno Pizza (@DiGiornoPizza)

> THE KITCHEN IS ALIVE, WITH THE SMELL OF FRESH-BAKED PIZZA #TheSoundOFMusicLive
> —DiGiorno Pizza (@DiGiornoPizza)15

As its Twitter success continued, DiGiorno dropped the use of others' hashtags and created its own for college football. #DiGiorNOYOUDIDNT became an instant success as the company used it to make harmless, yet entertaining digs at teams. For example:

> IS YOUR DEFENSE A DELIVERY PIZZA? BECAUSE IT LOOKS LIKE THEY'RE NOT SHOWING UP TONIGHT
>
> #DiGiorNOYOUDIDNT

> YO, THIS GAME IS LIKE A DIGIORNO PIZZA BECAUSE IT WAS DONE AFTER TWENTY MINUTES
>
> #Super Bowl #SuperSmack #DiGiorNOYOUDIDNT
> —DiGiorno Pizza (@DiGiornoPizza)[16]

We will explore social media marketing in greater depth in Chapter 18.

4-3 DEMOGRAPHIC FACTORS

Another uncontrollable variable in the external environment—also extremely important to marketing managers—is demography, the study of people's vital statistics, such as age, race and ethnicity, and location. Demographics are significant because the basis for any market is people.

> **demography** the study of people's vital statistics, such as age, race and ethnicity, and location

Demographic characteristics are strongly related to consumer buying behavior in the marketplace.

4-3a Population

People are directly or indirectly the basis of all markets, making population the most basic statistic in marketing. There are more than seven billion people alive today. China has the largest population with 1.39 billion persons; India is second with 1.23 billion.[17] The U.S. population is slightly over 318 million. Older Americans have moved to retirement communities like the Villages in Central Florida. This area is the nation's fastest growing metropolitan area. Midland and Odessa, in western Texas, are the second and third fastest growing areas in the country. Both cities have seen an employment boom in recent years amid new techniques to extract oil and natural gas. This growth may slow or stop in coming years as global oil prices tumbled in 2015.[18]

Rural areas away from the oil fields, meanwhile, posted their first-ever net loss of population in 2012. The populations of the United States' rural regions—from the Great Plains to the Mississippi delta to rural New England—are aging. These populations are not receiving many young transplants to replace those who die or migrate to urban areas. In many parts of the country, multigenerational households are increasingly common. More than 57 million people live in households with at least two adult generations. About 24 percent of young adults age 25 to 34 live in multiple generation households.[19]

Population is a broad statistic that is most useful to marketers when broken into smaller, more specific increments. For example, age groups present opportunities to focus on a section of the population and offer opportunities for marketers. These groups are called tweens, teens, Millennials (or Generation Y), Generation X, and baby boomers. Each cohort has its own needs, values, and consumption patterns.

TWEENS America's tweens (ages 8 to 12) are a population of more than twenty million. With access to information, opinions, and sophistication well beyond their years (and purchasing power to match), these young consumers are directly or indirectly responsible for sales of over $180 billion annually. Tweens themselves spend about $43 billion per year, and the remainder is spent by parents and family members for them.[20]

With such spending power, this age group is very attractive to many markets. One of the fastest growing tween markets is mobile games and other advertising- and microtransaction-based smartphone apps. In the United States, nearly 78 percent of tweens own a mobile phone and almost half (47 percent) have smartphones.[21] That number jumps to 75 percent among tweens in the United Kingdom, and 83 percent among tweens in Poland. Both boys and girls are playing mobile games to pass time in between classes and at home, and many marketers have tapped into this growing market by catering to tweens' desire for fast-paced, highly stylized games and apps.[22]

Some tweens are forgoing games and becoming young entrepreneurs instead. Twelve-year-old Hartley Messer's sleepover travel kit, for example, "comes with a super cute bag that's great as well as a super cool pencil case for school."[23]

Messer's prospects—young girls—dab on samples of creams and sniff their wrists as their mothers look on. "The Skinny Mini lip gloss is made to slide into your jeans or Lululemon pockets," adds Messer, who sells moisturizers, lip gloss, acne cream, and other products made by Willagirl Inc.

Known as "Willagirls," teens and tweens like Messer host Tupperware-like get-togethers at home, school, or just about anywhere 8- to 12-year-olds hang out. Invites typically are extended via text message, since "nobody uses email anymore," Messner says.[24]

Willagirl's young sales reps receive 25 percent of total sales for a potential monthly income of $320 to $3,500 according to a pamphlet sellers distribute at their parties. Party hosts also receive 15 percent of retail sales from the party in free products, plus one half-priced item if party sales exceed $400.

Founder and CEO Christy Prunier says Willagirl's sales reps don't buy their own inventory in advance. Instead, they take orders from customers, which the company fulfills as orders come in. They're never sitting on products," she says. "It's not work. It's what these girls like to do and their moms are thrilled that they're saving money and developing important skills."[25] They do, however, earn money by recruiting other sellers.

A *Quirk's* study on "global kids" found that tweens in 12 developed countries are surprisingly worldly and share much in common because of the Internet and social media. Global kids are plugging in at younger ages, and the vast majority frequently use electronic entertainment or communication devices including digital cameras (93 percent), video game consoles (84 percent), digital music players (78 percent), and cell phones (77 percent). According to the study, these kids are engaging in a wide range of activities, from playing games (92 percent) to doing schoolwork (76 percent) on these devices.

Global kids are active and grounded. They are highly engaged, very busy, and they value learning. When shown a list of more than 30 activities such as reading, camping, sports, and crafts, global kids said on average that they participated in 25 activities. And, in a world seemingly obsessed with money and celebrity, global kids placed "being smart" and "getting a good education" near the top of socially desirable attributes. In the United States, these attributes topped even fame and fortune. Globally, "getting a good education" and "being rich" are in a dead heat among tweens.[26]

TEENS There are approximately 25 million teenagers in the United States, and they spend approximately 72 hours per week tuned in electronically to television, the Internet, music, video games, and cell phones. About 95 percent of U.S. teens use the Internet. Of those online, approximately 90 percent use social media. They still prefer face-to-face communication to communicating electronically, however. Twenty-five percent of teens claim that social networking makes them less shy. Teens also note that networking enables them to keep in touch with friends that they can't see on a regular basis (89 percent); helps them get to know other students better (69 percent); and enables them to connect with people who share common interests (55 percent). Teens commonly use the following websites:

Facebook	90 percent
Twitter	49 percent
Tumblr	33 percent (more popular with girls)
4chan	23 percent (more popular with boys)
Pinterest	20 percent
Foursquare	12 percent

Sixty-two percent also go online to get the news and current events.[27]

In many households, teens are now passing technology down to their parents, not the other way around. Researchers have found that teens are commonly the ones telling their parents to buy smartphones and tablets and are often the driving force behind their families' technology upgrades.[28]

Teens command an immense amount of buying power. Worldwide, they spend approximately

Approximately 90 percent of teenagers that use the internet, also use some form of social media.

Antonio Guillem/Shutterstock.com

$819 billion every year.[29] In the United States and Canada, teens have almost $118 billion to spend.[30] Although much of that money comes from parents, teens make many shopping decisions. Seventy-one percent do at least some of the family shopping and 4 percent do all of the family shopping. Yet, only 13 percent are told what brands to buy.[31]

Twice a year, Piper Jaffary takes a survey of teen lifestyles and attitudes. Over a 27-year period, the firm has found several factors that remain the same. First, teens continue to seek peer affirmation. Second, their spending is mostly discretionary (as illustrated above). Third, they are early adopters of change. Some key findings from the most recent survey are that:

- Teen males are spending more—up 4 percent from fall 2013.

- For the first time in the survey history, food exceeded clothing as a percentage of teen spending.

- Top clothing brands continue to include Nike, Action Sports, Forever 21, American Eagle, Polo Ralph Lauren, and Hollister.

- At home, cable subscriptions are becoming less essential for teens while online streaming is more critical. Outside the home, IMAX continues to grow share among teens.

- Music listenership has grown for Pandora and local radio, largely at the cost of MP3s and CDs.

- Eighty-five percent of teen gamers play mobile games.[32]

MILLENNIALS Millennials, or **Generation Y**, are people born between 1979 and 1994. Initially, Millennials were a smaller cohort than baby boomers. However, due to immigration and the aging of the boomer generation, the seventy-seven million Gen Yers in the United States passed the boomers in total population in 2010. Millennials are currently in two different stages of the life cycle.

The youngest members of Gen Y, born in 1994, are just entering young adulthood. In contrast, the oldest Gen Yers, born in 1979, turned 37 years old in 2016. They have started their careers, and many have become parents for the first time, leading to dramatic lifestyle changes. They care for their babies rather than go out, and they spend money on baby products. Gen Yers already spend more than $200 billion annually; over their lifetimes, they will likely spend about $10 trillion. Many older Millennials graduated from college during the Great Recession and had difficulty finding good jobs. Almost a third still live at home with their parents. They also own the bulk of America's $1 trillion in student debt.[33] Younger Millennials do have several things in their favor. First, the recession is over and America is slowly recovering. Second, the size of the Millennial group is massive. There are more people in their 20s (44.5 million) than in their 30s, 40s, or 50s.[34] The sheer size of the 20-old group will create a significant amount of economic growth. This, in turn, will mean more and better jobs.

Millennials may be the most tech-savvy generation yet, spending more time surfing the Web and on social media than they do watching television, listening to radio, or reading newspapers, but they still use and value traditional media. Gen Yers expect brands to be on social media. They also like to use social media to share photos of things they are doing and keep up with people in their network. Fifty-one percent of Millennials have an Instagram account and 42 percent use Snapchat, a photo-sharing app. When it comes to daily use, photo-focused social applications are slightly more popular than their text-focused competitors; 31 percent of Millennials post on Instagram on a daily basis, while 29 percent tweet every day.[35]

As to the subject matter of Millennials' photos, clues can be found in where they spend their time and money: travel, outdoor activities, and experiences like concerts.[36]

Millennials are very aware of the data that sites like Instagram and others collect on them. One survey found that 52 percent of Gen Yers in the United States have no issue with brands and Web sites using data to provide a better customer experience.[37] This is in stark contrast to European Millennials—only 37 percent of Millennials in the United Kingdom and just 13 percent of Millennials in the Netherlands agree.[38]

GENERATION X Generation X—people born between 1965 and 1978—consists of fifty million U.S. consumers. It was the first generation of latchkey children—products of dual-career households or, in roughly half of the cases, of divorced or separated parents. Gen Xers often spent more time without adult support and guidance than any other age cohort. This experience made them independent, resilient, adaptable, cautious, and skeptical.[39]

Gen Xers are in their primary earning years and have acquired a disproportionate amount of spending power relative to the size of their group. They have an estimated 31 percent of total income dollars.[40] Gen Xers have higher average incomes than their Millennial and baby boomer counterparts. Higher incomes have contributed to Gen Xers' optimistic outlook on the future. Two-thirds are either "satisfied" or "very satisfied" with their lives, yet they are also concerned about crime, climate change, and their health.[41]

Saving money is a major priority for Gen Xers. About half note that providing for their children's college expenses is a major goal. They also want to become financially independent, buy or upgrade a home, and provide an estate for their heirs.[42] When asked, "what makes your generation unique?" Gen Xers responded:

- Technology use (12 percent)
- Work ethic (11 percent)
- Conservative/Traditional (7 percent)
- Smarter (6 percent)
- Respectful (5 percent)[43]

Gen Xers tend to be frugal and seek value when making purchases. They place a high value on education and knowledge and tend to do a significant amount of research before making a major purchase. Marketers need to provide a lot of accurate information about their products—particularly why their goods or services are a great value—to reach Gen Xers.

BABY BOOMERS There are approximately 75 million **baby boomers** (persons born between 1946 and 1964) in the United States. With average life expectancy at an all-time high of 77.4 years, more and more Americans over fifty consider middle age a new start on life. The size of the baby boom cohort group has

Millennials people born between 1979 and 1994

Generation X people born between 1965 and 1978

baby boomers people born between 1946 and 1964

been decreasing in size since 2012. The pace of this decline will accelerate as the baby boomers grow older. When the first baby boomers turned 65 in 2011, there were 77 million of them. In 2030, when the baby boomers will be between 66 and 84 years old, that number is projected to drop to 60 million.[44]

While baby boomers' current incomes are relatively low because many have retired, they accumulated a substantial amount of wealth over their working years. It is estimated that boomers control 67 percent ($28 trillion) of the country's wealth.[45] Baby boomers outspend other generations by an estimated $400 billion a year on consumer goods and services. They even outspend younger adults by 2:1 on a per-capita basis when making online purchases.[46] Boomers outspend other cohorts in categories such as gifts, personal care products, medical care, food away from home, and entertainment. Many boomers want to age in place, that is, not move to a retirement community. As a result, they often remodel their existing homes to the tune of around $25 billion per year.[47]

Like other cohort groups, boomers believe that price and quality are very important when making purchase decisions. Baby boomers tend to be influenced more by traditional advertising, sales reps, and word-of-mouth recommendations than other groups. Yet they are also very active in seeking product information online. Boomers tend to use laptops and tablets more than smartphones when conducting product research. While boomers make fewer product purchases online than do some other cohorts, the same is not true for services. Boomers now make 90 percent of their travel purchases online.[48]

Marketers targeting baby boomers must avoid the perception that boomers are old. Words such as "senior," "elderly," and "aged" can quickly drive away potential customers. Boomers today are active and feel entitled to enjoy the good life. Adult diaper company Depends targets consumers age 60 and older, yet the actors in its advertising are in their 40s and 50s.[49] Marketers can also subtly change their products and packaging to appeal to boomers. Depends are today sold as underwear rather than diapers, for example. Simplifying instructions for product assembly and use makes life easier for boomers. Enlarging font size may enable boomers to avoid reaching for their reading glasses. Realizing that holding up

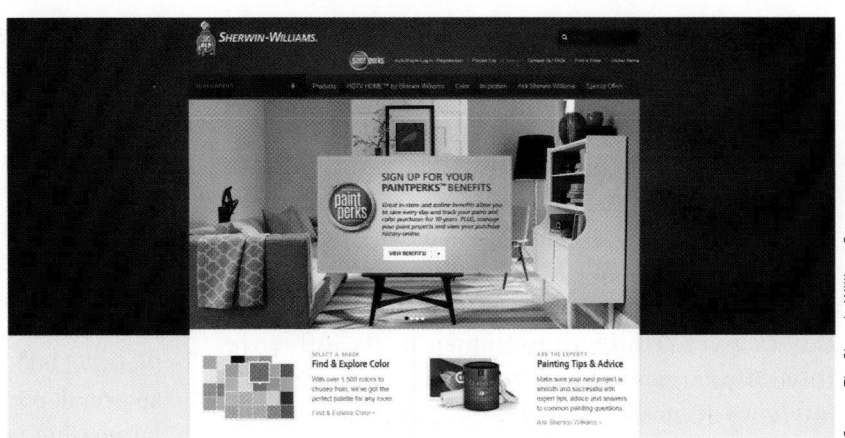

Source: The Sherwin-Williams Company

a heavy paint can and reaching for your glasses at the same time can be tough, Sherwin Williams completely redesigned its can with a clean, crisp look and large fonts.[50]

4-4 GROWING ETHNIC MARKETS

The American demographic profile is rapidly changing as racial and ethnic groups continue to grow. The minority population today is about 118 million. By 2050, around one in three U.S. residents will be Hispanic. The United States will flip completely to a majority-minority makeup in 2041, meaning that whites of European ancestry will make up less than 50 percent of the population. Already, minorities make up about half of all Americans under the age of five.[51] As the demographic environment of America evolves, so too must the marketing mix change to reach growing target markets.

4-4a Marketing to Hispanic Americans

The term *Hispanic* encompasses people of many different backgrounds. Nearly 60 percent of Hispanic Americans are of Mexican descent. Puerto Ricans, the next largest group, make up just under ten percent of Hispanics. Other groups, including Central Americans, Dominicans, South Americans, and Cubans, each account for less than five percent of all Hispanics.

According to surveys, Hispanics believe that the number one way they contribute to American society is through their commitment to family. Over three-fourths say that the traditional family is the main building block of a healthy community.[52] Research has found that many adults who have been in the United States for a number of years become acculturated, but not to the mainstream U.S. culture. That is, they do not use much English for their everyday activities. Instead, they acculturate to the locally dominant Spanish-speaking Hispanic community, referred to as the primal 45-Latino society.[53] The primal culture tends to be regional. It differs widely enough that Latinos from one region may be unaware of the food, slang, and even music from another region. A good example is the difference in primal cultures between Los Angeles (which draws much of its influence from Mexico) and Miami (which draws much of its influence from Cuba). The same is true for brands purchased. Hispanics are more likely to purchase Jerritos soda if they are integrated into the primal Los Angeles culture than if they live elsewhere in the United States.[54]

Hispanic Millennials now account for 25 percent of all Hispanics living in the United States.[55] Many Hispanic Millennials were born in the United Sates or came when they were very young, and unlike older generations, they have become more acculturated into mainstream America. Hispanic Millennials are less likely than their peers to live at home with their parents. Of those who do live at home, 86 percent contribute to the family's finances. Moreover, they often act as language translators and cultural advisors to their Spanish-dominant family members. Normally, purchase decisions revolve around the Millennial son or daughter who is helping to interpret and manage bills.

Bilingual Hispanic Millennials share common behaviors and beliefs with both older Hispanics and their Millennial peers. They are more optimistic about politics and economics than non-Hispanic Millennials, and they have a stronger faith in the American dream. Bilingual Millennials also place more value on higher education.[56]

Hispanic Millennials in the U.S. are particularly prone to taking a bilingual, bicultural approach to their media consumption. Forty percent of Hispanic Millennials consume an equal amount of Spanish and English media.[57] Spending on Hispanic media now tops $8.3 billion in the United States.[58] The leading advertisers targeting Hispanics are Procter & Gamble, AT&T, and L'Oreal. The 2014 World Cup was very popular in the Hispanic market, and Kraft Foods targeted Hispanics with its "Flavor of the Championship" campaign. Throughout this campaign, Kraft used social media to suggest appropriate recipes for World Cup viewing parties. Finally, Hispanics, particularly Millennials, have embraced technology. They are more likely to download apps, chat, stream video, listen to music, and play games than non-Hispanics.[59]

4-4b Marketing to African Americans

There are approximately 44 million African Americans (14 percent of the country's population). They are young—53 percent are under the age of 35—giving them a strong influence on the latest trends, especially in regards to music and pop culture. Higher academic achievement has translated into increases in household income; 44 percent of all African American households now earn $50,000 or more and 23 percent earn more than $75,000. Higher household incomes, coupled with an overall population growth, are driving the substantial purchasing power of the African American consumer upwards. Total purchasing power is expected to reach $1.3 trillion within a few years.[60]

Black Americans want companies to recognize their unique culture. A recent study found that 87 percent feel that ethnic recognition is important, compared to 59 percent of the general population. Seventy-three percent of African American adults age 18 to 54 state that cultural/ethnic heritage is a critical part of their identity. Among African Americans age 18 to 54 with a household income greater than $50,000, 77 percent indicate that their heritage is an important part of who they are, as compared to 58 percent of the general population.[61]

Also compared to the general population, African Americans are 30 percent more likely to believe that diversity in advertising is important and 38 percent are more likely to make a purchase when advertisements include African American people. Further, 44 percent of African Americans are more likely to support companies that are owned by African Americans or other minority groups and 43 percent are more likely to purchase products endorsed by African American celebrities or musicians.[62]

Black Americans tend to be loyal to both brands and stores; they spend 18 percent more than the general population on store brands. African Americans also are more likely to patronize convenience, drug stores, and dollar stores than other groups. Relative to other cohorts, they spend more on groceries and hair care products.[63] Featuring nonwhite Americans has become a cornerstone of Cheerios' promotional strategy. A recent Honey Nut Cheerios commercial features musician Usher and Buzz Bee dancing and discussing heart health while Usher's song "She Came to Give It to You" plays in the background. Usher was chosen for the spot because of his broad appeal—he has more than 50.5 million Facebook fans.[64]

4-4c Marketing to Asian Americans

The Asian American population reached 19 million in 2015. U.S. births have been the primary driving force behind the increase in the Hispanic and African American populations. By contrast, Asian American population growth has been fueled primarily by immigration. Seventy-four percent of Asian Americans were foreign-born.[65] California and Hawaii are home to the largest Asian American populations. Asian Americans, who still represent only 6 percent of the U.S. population, have the highest average family income of all groups. At $67,000, it exceeds the average U.S. household income by roughly $15,000.[66] About 53 percent of Asian Americans over age 25 have at least a bachelor's degree.[67] Because Asian Americans are younger (the average age is 34), better educated, and have higher incomes than average, they are sometimes called a "marketer's dream." Asian Americans are heavy users of technology. Moreover, they are early adopters of the latest digital gadgets. They visit computer and consumer electronics Web sites 36 percent more often and spend 72 percent more time at these sites than the total population.[68] Because of their high level of education, Asian Americans are thriving in America's technology sector.

Women shop for symbolic Chinese New Year flowers at a New York City Chinatown flower market.

Although Asian Americans embrace the values of the larger U.S. population, they also hold on to the cultural values of their particular subgroup. Consider language: many Asian Americans, particularly Koreans and Chinese, speak their native tongue at home (though Filipinos are far less likely to do so). Cultural values are also apparent in the ways different groups make big-ticket purchases. In Japanese American homes, husbands alone make large purchase decisions nearly half the time; wives decide only about six percent of the time. In Filipino families, however, wives make these decisions a little more often than their husbands do, although, by far, most decisions are made by husbands and wives jointly or with the input of other family members.

Asian Americans like to shop at stores owned and managed by other Asian Americans. Small businesses such as flower shops, grocery stores, and appliance stores are often best equipped to offer the products that Asian Americans want. For example, at first glance, the Hannam Chain supermarket in Los Angeles's Koreatown seems like any other grocery store. But next to the Kraft American singles and the State Fair corn dogs are jars of whole cabbage kimchi. A snack bar in another part of the store cooks up aromatic mung cakes, and an entire aisle is devoted to dried seafood.

Asian Americans are big adopters of technology. More than 70 percent use smartphones—the highest rate of any ethnic group.[69] Social media continues to be a primary way to reach Asian Americans. Mobile chat apps like Kakao, Viber, Tango, WeChat and WhatsApp are also starting to become very popular in the Asian American community. Many Asian Americans use these apps to communicate with family and friends back in their home countries.

ECONOMIC FACTORS

In addition to social and demographic factors, marketing managers must understand and react to the economic environment. The three economic areas of greatest concern to most marketers are consumers' incomes, inflation, and recession.

4-5a Consumers' Incomes

As disposable (or after-tax) incomes rise, more families and individuals can afford the "good life." In recent years, however, average U.S. incomes have actually fallen. The annual median household income in the United States in 2015 was approximately $52,000, though the median household income varies widely from state to state. This means half of all U.S. households earned less, and the other half earned more. Census data shows that average family incomes, when adjusted for inflation (discussed later in the chapter), fell around eight percent between 2007 and 2012. However, it rose slightly in 2013 and 2014.[70] The unemployment rate was 5.6 percent in early 2015, which is the lowest it had been in six years. Scars from the Great Recession continue to affect the United States as 2.8 million people continue to suffer from long-term unemployment (defined as not having a job for 27 weeks or longer).[71]

Education is the primary determinant of a person's earning potential. For example, just 1 percent of workers with only a high school education earn over $100,000 annually. By comparison, 13 percent of college-educated workers earn six figures or more. People with a bachelor's degree take home an average of 38 percent more than those with just a high school diploma. Over a lifetime, an individual with a bachelor's degree will earn more than twice as much total income as a nondegree holder.[72]

In recent years, stores that cater to lower-income consumers—like Family Dollar and Dollar General—have done well. P&G has found that its typical middle-class customers are increasingly unwilling to spend their money on household staples with extra features, such as Tide with bleach. Many customers have switched to cheaper brands, while P&G brands like Bounce fabric softener and Bounty paper towels suffered. To regain market share, P&G has launched its bargain-priced Gain dish soap. The firm has also reduced some package sizes of Tide in order to sell them at Walmart for less than ten dollars.

4-5b Purchasing Power

Even when incomes rise, a higher standard of living does not necessarily result. Increased standards of living are a function of purchasing power. **Purchasing power** is measured by comparing income to the relative cost of a standard set of goods and services in different geographic areas, usually referred to as the *cost of living*. Another way to think of purchasing power is income minus the cost of living (i.e., expenses). In general, a cost of living

purchasing power a comparison of income versus the relative cost of a standard set of goods and services in different geographic areas

inflation a measure of the decrease in the value of money, expressed as the percentage reduction in value since the previous year

index takes into account housing, food and groceries, transportation, utilities, health care, and miscellaneous expenses such as clothing, services, and entertainment. HomeFair.com's salary calculator uses these metrics when it determines that the cost of living in New York City is almost three times the cost of living in Youngstown, Ohio. This means that a worker living in New York City must earn nearly $279,500 to have the same standard of living as someone making $100,000 in Youngstown.

When income is high relative to the cost of living, people have more discretionary income. That means they have more money to spend on nonessential items (in other words, on wants rather than needs). This information is important to marketers for obvious reasons. Consumers with high purchasing power can afford to spend more money without jeopardizing their budget for necessities like food, housing, and utilities. They also have the ability to purchase higher-priced necessities—for example, a more expensive car, a home in a more expensive neighborhood, or a designer handbag versus a purse from a discount store.

4-5c Inflation

Inflation is a measure of the decrease in the value of money, generally expressed as the percentage reduction in value since the previous year, which is the rate of inflation. Thus, in simple terms, an inflation rate of five percent means you will need 5 percent more units of money than you would have needed last year to buy the same basket of products. If inflation is 5 percent, you can expect that, on average, prices have risen by about 5 percent since the previous year. Of course, if pay raises are matching the rate of inflation, then employees will be no worse off in terms of the immediate purchasing power of their salaries.

In times of low inflation, businesses seeking to increase their profit margins can do so only by increasing their efficiency. If they significantly increase prices, no one will purchase their goods or services. The Great Recession brought inflation rates to almost zero. In January 2015, the inflation rate was 0.8 percent.[73]

In creating marketing strategies to cope with inflation, managers must realize that, regardless of what happens to the seller's cost, the buyer is not going to pay more for a product than the subjective value he or she places on it. No matter how compelling the justification might be for a 10 percent price increase, marketers must always examine its impact on demand. Many marketers try to hold prices level for as long as is practical.

4-5d Recession

A **recession** is a period of economic activity characterized by negative growth. More precisely, a recession is defined as occurring when the gross domestic product falls for two consecutive quarters. Gross domestic product is the total market value of all final goods and services produced during a period of time. The official beginning of the Great Recession of 2008–2009 was December 2007. While the causes of the recession are very complex, this one began with the collapse of inflated housing prices. Those high prices led people to take out mortgages they could not afford from banks that should have known the money would not be repaid. By 2008, the recession had spread around the globe. A very slow economic recovery began in July 2009 and continues to this day.

iStockphoto.com/jjgroup

4-6 TECHNOLOGICAL FACTORS

Technological success is based upon innovation, and innovation requires imagination and risk taking. Bringing new technology to the marketplace requires a corporate structure and management actions that will lead to success. Great corporate leaders must embed innovation into the lifeblood of the company. Managers should hire employees with a tolerance for risk. Then, workers must be told not to fear innovation failure. Not everything works the first time. Some of the greatest innovations in recent years, such as 3-D printing, hydraulic fracturing, social media, and the iPhone, all had setbacks before a successful product was created.

Shell, one of the world's largest oil producers, has created the Idea Factory, a technology-forward development platform consisting of four pillars. These are:

- **Game Changer:** This program works at the early or "blue sky" stage of innovation. If a start-up proves its concept, and it aligns with Shell's goals and passes a rigorous approval process, it qualifies for funding and technological help from Shell's engineers.

- **Shell Technology Ventures:** Shell's venture capital arm funds start-ups and entrepreneurs.

- **Shell Tech Works:** This program looks for technology created in other industries but that addresses areas that also apply to Shell.

- **Universities:** Shell collaborates with universities from around the world to complement its internal research and development department.

Some of the innovations that have come from Shell's Idea Factory include visualization tools to print 3-D pictures of rock and oil formations, solar power technologies that assist oil recovery, space robots, and the world's largest floating structure—a floating liquefaction plant for natural gas.[74]

4-6a Research

The United States, historically, has excelled at both basic and applied research. **Basic research** (or *pure research*) attempts to expand the frontiers of knowledge but is not aimed at a specific, pragmatic problem. Basic research aims to confirm an existing theory or to learn more about a concept or phenomenon. For example, basic research might focus on high-energy physics. **Applied research**, in contrast, attempts to develop new or improved products. The United States has dramatically improved its track record in applied research. For example, the United States leads the world in applying basic research to aircraft design and propulsion systems.

4-6b Stimulating Innovation

Companies attempting to innovate often limit their searches to areas they are already familiar with. This can help lead to incremental progress but rarely leads to a dramatic breakthrough. Companies are now using several approaches such as Shell's Idea Factory to keep innovation strong. These include:

- **Building scenarios:** Some firms use teams of writers to imagine detailed opportunities and threats for their companies, partners, and collaborators in future markets. With more than 1 billion smartphones in use around the world, more and

> **recession** a period of economic activity characterized by negative growth, which reduces demand for goods and services
>
> **basic research** pure research that aims to confirm an existing theory or to learn more about a concept or phenomenon
>
> **applied research** research that attempts to develop new or improved products

more companies are creating mobile-friendly sites and mobile apps. However, Senior Vice President at Forrester Research John Bernoff advises that simply cramming a piece of a Web site into a mobile experience is a recipe for disaster that will result in complaints and lost customers. Instead, he says, firms must identify mobile moments and context. A mobile moment is the point in time at which a customer pulls out a mobile device to get immediate access to the information that he or she wants.[75] Rob Moore, chief technical officer at Hertz, figured out number of key mobile moments during which he could make customers happier. For example, he found that customers preferred searching the lot for the best available car right from the airport bus. Krispy Kreme figured out that one of its key moments was right when fresh doughnuts came off of the line. To take advantage of this moment, the company built an app that lets customers know when hot doughnuts are available near them. Half a million downloads later, Krispy Kreme's same-store sales are up by double digits—without advertising.[76]

- **Enlisting the Web:** A few companies have created Web sites that act as literal marketplaces of ideas where innovators can go to look for help with scientific and business challenges.

- **Talking to early adopters:** Early adopters tend to be innovators themselves. They are risk takers and look for new things or wish for something better to help in daily tasks at home and work.

- **Using marketing research:** Firms find out what customers like and dislike about their products and competitors' products.

- **Creating an innovative environment:** Companies let employees know that they have the "freedom to fail." They create intranets to encourage sharing ideas. Most importantly, top management must lead by example to create an atmosphere where innovation is encouraged and rewarded.

- **Catering to entrepreneurs:** Policies that reserve blocks of time for scientists or engineers to explore

leedsn/ShutterStock.com

their own ideas have worked well at some companies. At 3M, scientists can spend fifteen percent of their time on projects they dream up themselves—a freedom that led to the development of the yellow Post-It note. Google is well known in the tech industry for its "20% time" policy, which grants employees a day a week to follow their entrepreneurial passions.[77]

Although developing new technology internally is a key to creating and maintaining a long-term competitive advantage, external technology is also important to managers for two reasons. First, by acquiring the technology, the firm may be able to operate more efficiently or create a better product. Second, a new technology may render existing products obsolete.

Radio frequency identification (RFID) chips were supposed to be a game changer for inventory tracking. Walmart tried using them, but was less than satisfied. JC Penney found that the chips interfered with existing anti-theft sensors. The company removed the anti-theft sensors, and shoplifting surged. Zara, a fashion chain that operates in 88 countries, claims to have learned from others' mistakes and is using RFID chips in a new way. A Zara employee suggested putting the RFID chips inside items' security tags. The security tag's plastic case protects the chip, preventing interference and allowing for reuse.

Before the new tags, taking inventory took 40 employees about five hours to complete. Now, ten employees walking down store aisles while waving pistol-like scanners can finish in half the time.[78] Each time a garment is sold, data from its chip prompts the stockroom to send out an identical item. Previously, store employees using paper sales reports restocked shelves a few times a day. If a customer can't find an item, a salesperson can point an iPod camera at a similar item's bar code and, using data gathered by the chips, see whether the desired item is available in the store, at a nearby Zara store, or online.[79]

4-7 POLITICAL AND LEGAL FACTORS

Business needs government regulation to protect innovators of new technology, the interests of society in general, one business from another,

and consumers. In turn, government needs business because the marketplace generates taxes that support public efforts to educate our youth, pave our roads, protect our shores, and the like.

Every aspect of the marketing mix is subject to laws and restrictions. It is the duty of marketing managers or their legal assistants to understand these laws and conform to them, because failure to comply with regulations can have major consequences for a firm. Sometimes just sensing trends and taking corrective action before a government agency acts can help avoid regulation.

4-7a Federal Legislation

Federal laws that affect marketing fall into several categories of regulatory activity: competitive environment, pricing, advertising and promotion, and consumer privacy. The key pieces of legislation in these areas are summarized in Exhibit 4.1. The primary federal laws that protect consumers are shown in Exhibit 4.2. The Patient Protection and Affordable Care Act, commonly called Obamacare, has had a significant impact on marketing. A few key provisions of the Act are that:

- Large employers must offer coverage to full-time workers.
- Workers cannot be denied coverage.
- A person cannot be dropped when he or she is sick.
- A worker cannot be denied coverage for a preexisting condition.
- Young adults can stay on their parents' plans until age 26.[80]

In 2010, Congress passed the Restoring American Financial Stability Act, which brought sweeping changes to bank and financial market regulations. The legislation created the Consumer Financial Protection Bureau (CFPB) to oversee checking accounts, private student loans, mortgages, and other financial products. The agency deals with unfair, abusive, and deceptive practices. Some groups have expressed concerns that the CFPB is assembling massive databases on credit cards, credit monitoring, debt cancellation products, auto loans, and payday loans. CFPB officials claim that they need the information to make effective rules and enforce those policies. One way or another, the CFPB has certainly had a significant impact on several United States businesses—the agency has recovered more than $1.6 billion from financial services firms in the name of wronged consumers.[81]

4-7b State and Local Laws

Legislation that affects marketing varies state by state. Oregon, for example, limits utility advertising to 0.5 percent of the company's net income. California has forced industry to improve consumer products and has enacted legislation to lower the energy consumption

EXHIBIT 4.1 PRIMARY U.S. LAWS THAT AFFECT MARKETING

Legislation	Impact on Marketing
Sherman Act of 1890	Makes trusts and conspiracies in restraint of trade illegal; makes monopolies and attempts to monopolize misdemeanors.
Clayton Act of 1914	Outlaws discrimination in prices to different buyers; prohibits tying contracts (which require the buyer of one product to also buy another item in the line); makes illegal the combining of two or more competing corporations by pooling ownership of stock.
Federal Trade Commission Act of 1914	Created the Federal Trade Commission to deal with antitrust matters; outlaws unfair methods of competition.
Robinson-Patman Act of 1936	Prohibits charging different prices to different buyers of merchandise of like grade and quantity; requires sellers to make any supplementary services or allowances available to all purchasers on a proportionately equal basis.
Wheeler-Lea Amendments to FTC Act of 1938	Broadens the Federal Trade Commission's power to prohibit practices that might injure the public without affecting competition; outlaws false and deceptive advertising.
Lanham Act of 1946	Establishes protection for trademarks.
Celler-Kefauver Antimerger Act of 1950	Strengthens the Clayton Act to prevent corporate acquisitions that reduce competition.
Hart-Scott-Rodino Act of 1976	Requires large companies to notify the government of their intent to merge.
Foreign Corrupt Practices Act of 1977	Prohibits bribery of foreign officials to obtain business.

EXHIBIT 4.2 PRIMARY U.S. LAWS PROTECTING CONSUMERS

Legislation	Impact on Marketing
Federal Food and Drug Act of 1906	Prohibits adulteration and misbranding of foods and drugs involved in interstate commerce; strengthened by the Food, Drug, and Cosmetic Act (1938) and the Kefauver-Harris Drug Amendment (1962).
Federal Hazardous Substances Act of 1960	Requires warning labels on hazardous household chemicals.
Kefauver-Harris Drug Amendment of 1962	Requires that manufacturers conduct tests to prove drug effectiveness and safety.
Consumer Credit Protection Act of 1968	Requires that lenders fully disclose true interest rates and all other charges to credit customers for loans and installment purchases.
Child Protection and Toy Safety Act of 1969	Prevents marketing of products so dangerous that adequate safety warnings cannot be given.
Public Health Smoking Act of 1970	Prohibits cigarette advertising on television and radio and revises the health hazard warning on cigarette packages.
Poison Prevention Labeling Act of 1970	Requires safety packaging for products that may be harmful to children.
National Environmental Policy Act of 1970	Established the Environmental Protection Agency to deal with various types of pollution and organizations that create pollution.
Public Health Cigarette Smoking Act of 1971	Prohibits tobacco advertising on radio and television.
Consumer Product Safety Act of 1972	Created the Consumer Product Safety Commission, which has authority to specify safety standards for most products.
Child Protection Act of 1990	Regulates the number of minutes of advertising on children's television.
Children's Online Privacy Protection Act of 1998	Empowers the FTC to set rules regarding how and when marketers must obtain parental permission before asking children marketing research questions.
Aviation Security Act of 2001	Requires airlines to take extra security measures to protect passengers, including the installation of stronger cockpit doors, improved baggage screening, and increased security training for airport personnel.
Homeland Security Act of 2002	Protects consumers against terrorist acts; created the Department of Homeland Security.
Do Not Call Law of 2003	Protects consumers against unwanted telemarketing calls.
CAN-SPAM Act of 2003	Protects consumers against unwanted e-mail, or spam.
Credit Card Act of 2009	Provides many credit card protections.
Restoring American Financial Stability Act of 2010	Created the Consumer Financial Protection Bureau to protect consumers against unfair, abusive, and deceptive financial practices.
Patient Protection and Affordable Care Act	Overhauled the U.S. healthcare system; mandated and subsidized health insurance for individuals.

of refrigerators, freezers, and air conditioners. Several states, including California and North Carolina, are considering levying a tax on all in-state commercial advertising.

Many states and cities are attempting to fight obesity by regulating fast-food chains and other restaurants. For example, California and New York have passed a law banning trans fats in restaurants and bakeries, New York City chain restaurants must now display calorie counts on menus, and Boston has banned trans fats in restaurants. New York City enacted a law prohibiting restaurants from selling soft drinks larger than 16 ounces, but the ban was overturned a day before it was to go into effect.

> **Consumer Product Safety Commission (CPSC)** a federal agency established to protect the health and safety of consumers in and around their homes

4-7c Regulatory Agencies

Although some state regulatory bodies actively pursue violators of their marketing statutes, federal regulators generally have the greatest clout. The Consumer Product Safety Commission, the Federal Trade Commission, and the Food and Drug Administration are the three federal agencies most directly and actively involved in marketing affairs. These agencies, plus others, are discussed throughout the book, but a brief introduction is in order at this point.

CONSUMER PRODUCT SAFETY COMMISSION

The sole purpose of the **Consumer Product Safety Commission (CPSC)** is to protect the health and safety of consumers in and around their homes. The CPSC has the power to set mandatory safety standards for almost all products consumers use (about 15,000 items) and can fine offending firms up to $500,000 and sentence their officers to up to a year in prison. It can also ban dangerous products from the marketplace. The CPSC oversees about 400 recalls per year. In 2008, Congress passed the Consumer Product Safety Improvement Act. The law is aimed primarily at children's products, which are defined as those used by individuals 12 years old or younger. The law addresses items such as cribs, electronics and video games, school supplies, science kits, toys, and pacifiers. The law requires mandatory testing and labeling and increases fines and prison time for violators.

FOOD AND DRUG ADMINISTRATION The **Food and Drug Administration (FDA)**, another powerful agency, is charged with enforcing regulations against selling and distributing adulterated, misbranded, or hazardous food and drug products. In 2009, the Tobacco Control Act was passed. This act gave the FDA authority to regulate tobacco products, with a special emphasis on preventing their use by children and young people and reducing the impact of tobacco on public health. Another recent FDA action is the "Bad Ad" program. It is geared toward health care providers to help them recognize misleading prescription drug promotions and gives them an easy way to report the activity to the FDA.

FEDERAL TRADE COMMISSION The **Federal Trade Commission (FTC)** is empowered to prevent persons or corporations from using unfair methods of competition in commerce. The FTC consists of five members, each holding office for seven years. Over the years, Congress has greatly expanded the powers of the FTC. Its responsibilities have grown so large that the FTC has created several bureaus to better organize its operations. One of the most important is the Bureau of Competition, which promotes and protects competition. The Bureau of Competition:

- reviews mergers and acquisitions, and challenges those that would likely lead to higher prices, fewer choices, or less innovation;

- seeks out and challenges anti-competitive conduct in the marketplace, including monopolization and agreements between competitors;

- promotes competition in industries where consumer impact is high, such as health care, real estate, oil and gas, technology, and consumer goods; and

- provides information and holds conferences and workshops for consumers, businesses, and policy makers on competition issues for market analysis.

The FTC's Bureau of Consumer Protection works for the consumer to prevent fraud, deception, and unfair business practices in the marketplace. The Bureau of Consumer Protection claims that it:

- enhances consumer confidence by enforcing federal laws that protect consumers;

- empowers consumers with free information to help them exercise their rights and to spot and avoid fraud and deception; and

- wants to hear from consumers who want to get information or file a complaint about fraud or identity theft.[82]

Another important FTC bureau is the Bureau of Economics. It provides economic analysis and support to antitrust and consumer protection investigations. Many consumer protection issues today involve the Internet.

4-7d Consumer Privacy

The popularity of the Internet for direct marketing, for collecting consumer data, and as a repository for sensitive consumer data has alarmed privacy-minded consumers. In 2003, the U.S. Congress passed the CAN-SPAM Act in an attempt to regulate unsolicited e-mail advertising. The act prohibits commercial e-mailers from using false addresses and presenting false or misleading information, among other restrictions.

Internet users who once felt fairly anonymous when using the Web are now disturbed by the amount of information marketers collect about them and their children as they visit various sites in cyberspace. The FTC, with jurisdiction under the Children's Online Privacy Protection Act, requires Web site operators to post a privacy policy on their home page and a link to the policy on every page where personal information is collected. An area of growing concern to privacy advocates is called *behavioral targeting*, which is discussed in more detail in Chapters 9 and 16. Behavioral targeting is used by researchers to better target advertising to Web surfers and users of search engines and social media.

Despite federal efforts, online tracking has become widespread and pervasive. A vast amount of personal data is collected through application software, commonly called *apps*. For example, some widely used apps on Facebook gather volumes of

Food and Drug Administration (FDA) a federal agency charged with enforcing regulations against selling and distributing adulterated, misbranded, or hazardous food and drug products

Federal Trade Commission (FTC) a federal agency empowered to prevent persons or corporations from using unfair methods of competition in commerce

information when they are downloaded. A Wall Street Journal analysis of the 100 most popular Facebook apps found that some seek e-mail addresses, current locations, and even sexual preferences. Information is collected not only from app users but also from their Facebook friends.

Successful tracking has created a $137 billion online-advertising business that is growing rapidly. There are more than 300 companies collecting data about users.[93] More than half the time, data collectors piggyback on each other. When a user visits a Web site that has a code for one type of tracking technology, the data collection triggers other tracking technologies that are not embedded on the site. Piggybacking means that Web sites really do not know how much data are being gathered about their users.

Acxiom uses more than 23,000 computer servers to collect, collate, and analyze consumer data. The firm has created the world's largest consumer database—the servers process more than fifty trillion data transactions a year. The database contains information on over 500 million consumers worldwide, with about 1,500 data points per person.[84] Acxiom customers include firms like E*Trade, Ford, Wells Fargo, Macy's, and many other major firms seeking consumer insights. Acxiom integrates online, mobile, and offline data to create in-depth consumer behavior portraits. The firm's proprietary software, PersonicX, assigns consumers to one of 70 detailed socioeconomic clusters. For example, the "savvy single" cluster includes mobile, upper-middle-class singles who do their banking online, attend pro sports events, are sensitive to prices, and respond to free-shipping offers.[85]

Many consumers don't want to be part of huge databases—they want their privacy back. Half of Americans are concerned about the wealth of personal data on the Internet.[86] Approximately 25 percent of American Internet users have downloaded privacy protection software.[87]

AVG PrivacyFix is a free program from antivirus software company AVG Technologies. The program's dashboard gives users a snapshot of what information they're actually sharing when they use social networks and services such as Facebook, LinkedIn, and Google. It pings users with a small red exclamation point if their privacy settings are weak and sends an alert when a visited website makes relevant changes to its privacy policies.[88]

Other products let people keep track of their personal data in other ways. Privowny, a free privacy toolbar for Firefox and Chrome, shows users which companies have their credit card numbers, phone numbers, and e-mail addresses. It also highlights sites that share user data.[89]

DuckDuckGo is a search engine that doesn't collect any information on its users and blocks all ad trackers from the search page.[90] Ixquick, another privacy-forward search engine, attracts more than 4 million users a day.[91]

 ## 4-8 COMPETITIVE FACTORS

The competitive environment encompasses the number of competitors a firm must face, the relative size of the competitors, and the degree of interdependence within the industry. Management has little control over the competitive environment confronting a firm.

4-8a Competition for Market Share and Profits

As U.S. population growth slows, global competition increases, costs rise, and available resources tighten,

A vending machine is a perfect example of competition for market share. Several brands are competing for the business of the person who has the munchies.

Lissandra Melo/Shutterstock.com

firms find that they must work harder to maintain their profits and market share, regardless of the form of the competitive market. Sometimes technology advances can usher in a whole new set of competitors that can change a firm's business model. For example, one of the United States' most competitive companies is Amazon. The firm has more than 245 million customers that rely on Amazon for everything from flat screen televisions to dog food.[92] The Reputation Institute has found Amazon to have the best reputation in America.[93] Amazon's success, spurred by extremely competitive prices, hurt Sears, JCPenney, Borders, and Best Buy, and even contributed to Circuit City's going out of business. At first glance, Google and Amazon don't seem to be competitors. Google is a search engine that sells ads and Amazon is a retailer that sells and delivers goods. However, Google is slowly getting into the market for on-demand goods and has launched a same-day delivery service called Google Express in several major markets. Google doesn't own massive warehouses like Amazon, but works with local retailers like Walgreens and Walmart. Conversely, people don't tend to think of Amazon as search engine, but if someone is looking for something to buy, she is probably looking on Amazon. Almost a third of people looking for something to buy start on Amazon.[94] Both companies already compete fiercely in the media streaming industry. Is this the beginning of the clash of the titans? Only time will tell.

4-8b Global Competition

Boeing is a very savvy international business competitor. Now Airbus, Boeing's primary competitor, is going to start assembling planes in the United States.

Many foreign competitors also consider the United States to be a ripe target market. Thus, a U.S. marketing manager can no longer focus only on domestic competitors. In automobiles, textiles, watches, televisions, steel, and many other areas, foreign competition has been strong. In the past, foreign firms penetrated U.S. markets by concentrating on price, but the emphasis has switched to product quality. Nestlé, Sony, and Rolls-Royce are noted for quality, not cheap prices. Global competition is discussed in much more detail in Chapter 5.

STUDY TOOLS 4

LOCATED AT BACK OF THE TEXTBOOK

☐ Rip out Chapter Review Card

LOCATED AT WWW.CENGAGEBRAIN.COM

☐ Review Key Terms Flashcards and create your own

☐ Track your knowledge & understanding of key concepts in marketing

☐ Complete practice and graded quizzes to prepare for tests

☐ Complete interactive content within the MKTG Online experience

☐ View the chapter highlight boxes within the MKTG Online experience

5 Developing a Global Vision

Lightspring/Shutterstock.com

LEARNING OUTCOMES

After studying this chapter, you will be able to…

5-1 Discuss the importance of global marketing

5-2 Discuss the impact of multinational firms on the world economy

5-3 Describe the external environment facing global marketers

5-4 Identify the various ways of entering the global marketplace

5-5 List the basic elements involved in developing a global marketing mix

5-6 Discover how the Internet is affecting global marketing

After you finish this chapter go to **PAGE 87** for **STUDY TOOLS.**

5-1 REWARDS OF GLOBAL MARKETING AND THE SHIFTING GLOBAL BUSINESS LANDSCAPE

Today, global revolutions are underway in many areas of our lives: management, politics, communications, and technology. The word *global* has assumed a new meaning, referring to a boundless mobility and competition in social, business, and intellectual arenas. **Global marketing**—marketing that targets markets throughout the world—has become an imperative for business.

U.S. managers must develop a global vision not only to recognize and react to international marketing opportunities but also to remain competitive at home. Often a U.S. firm's toughest domestic competition comes from foreign companies. Consider the impact of Toyota and Honda on Ford and General Motors, for example. Moreover, a global vision enables a manager to understand that customer and distribution networks operate worldwide, blurring geographic and political barriers and making them increasingly irrelevant to business decisions. In summary, having a **global vision** means recognizing and reacting to international marketing opportunities, using effective global marketing strategies, and being aware of threats from foreign competitors in all markets.

World trade climbed from $200 billion in 1991 to more than $18 trillion in merchandise exports alone in 2015. Growth is not occurring evenly around the globe, however. In 2015, the United States was projected to

global marketing marketing that targets markets throughout the world

global vision recognizing and reacting to international marketing opportunities, using effective global marketing strategies, and being aware of threats from foreign competitors in all markets

grow by 3.2 percent. The European Union (discussed later in the chapter) was projected to grow 1.3 percent over the same span, while Japan was forecasted to grow just 0.8 percent due to struggles with economic policy. China's projected 2015 growth of 7.1 percent may seem gargantuan by comparison, but this actually represents the country's lowest growth rate in 15 years.[1] These low growth rates indicate that marketers are facing many challenges to their customary practices. Product development costs are rising, the life of products is getting shorter, and new technology is spreading around the world faster than ever. But marketing winners relish the pace of change instead of fear it.

Adopting a global vision can be very lucrative for a company. General Electric is involved in everything from private label credit cards to jet engines and health care equipment. There are now 24 countries outside of the United States where General Electric has annual sales of $1 billion or more. Today, the company has an order backlog of $244 billion.[2]

Despite the increasing availability of foreign customers, small businesses still account for only approximately 34 percent of U.S. exporting volume. Whether global business is daunting because of the various trade laws or tariffs, or because the markets are unfamiliar, small businesses are taking only slow, hesitant steps into the global market.

Of course, global marketing is not a one-way street whereby only U.S. companies sell their wares and services throughout the world. Foreign competition in the domestic market was once relatively rare but now is found in almost every industry. In fact, in many industries, U.S. businesses have lost significant market share to imported products. In electronics, cameras, automobiles, fine china, tractors, leather goods, and a host of other consumer and industrial products, U.S. companies have struggled at home to maintain their market shares against foreign competitors.

5-1a Importance of Global Marketing to the United States

Many countries depend more on international commerce than the United States does. For example, France, the United Kingdom, and Germany derive 28, 30, and 46 percent of their respective **gross domestic products (GDP)** from world trade—considerably more than the United States' 14 percent.[3] Gross domestic product is

> **gross domestic product (GDP)** the total market value of all final goods and services produced in a country for a given time period

The Impact of Exports

Although some countries depend more on international commerce than the United States does, the impact of international business on the U.S. economy is still impressive:

- The United States exports about thirteen percent of its industrial production.[4]
- More than 11 million Americans hold jobs that are supported by exports.[5]
- Every U.S. state has realized net employment gains directly attributed to foreign trade.
- The United States exports more than $2.3 trillion in goods and services each year.[6]
- Every $1 billion in additional exports creates about 5,000 new U.S. jobs.[7]

the total market value of all final goods and services produced in a country for a given time period (usually a year or a quarter of a year). *Final* in this sense refers to final products that are sold, not to intermediate products used in the assembly of a final product. For example, if the value of a brake (an intermediate product) and that of a car (the final product) were both counted, the brake would be counted twice. Therefore, GDP counts only final goods and services in its valuation of a country's production.

The main types of goods that the United States exports are automobiles, agricultural goods, machines, airplanes, computers, chemicals, and petroleum products. Services that the United States exports are primarily educational, financial, legal, licensing-, and travel-related. When a foreign tourist visits the United States, all the money she spends while stateside is counted as a travel-related export. Why is this? Because she is buying a service product (travel) and is simply coming to the United States to pick it up!

Traditionally, only very large multinational companies have seriously attempted to compete worldwide. However, more and more small and medium sized companies have begun pursuing international markets, and some are even beginning to play a critical role in driving export growth. Today, a record 287,000 small and medium size firms export goods from the United States. The U.S. government is working with these firms to expand small business trade. The Export–Import bank of the United States, for example, helps thousands of small businesses obtain financing to expand their export sales. In 2014, the Export-Import Bank authorized $20.5 billion to support 164,000 U.S. jobs.[8]

In addition, the Small Business Administration backed more than 2,400 loans to 3,500 small businesses, supporting $3.4 billion in small business export sales.

JOB OUTSOURCING AND INSHORING The notion of **outsourcing** (sending U.S. jobs abroad) has been highly controversial for several decades. Many executives have said that it leads to corporate growth, efficiency, productivity, and revenue growth. Most companies see cost savings as a key driver in outsourcing. But outsourcing also has its negative side. For instance, Detroit has suffered as many factories in the auto industry have been shut down and relocated around the world. Ford manufactures the Fiesta compact sedan in several countries

Ford manufactures the Fiesta in several countries, but no Fiestas are being built in the United States.

outsourcing sending U.S. jobs abroad

Imports Can Help Too

Many people view exports as generally good for the United States and view imports as generally harmful to the United States. Indeed, waves upon waves of U.S. factories have had to close over the years because they could not compete with low-cost imports. China is widely known as the largest supplier of imports to the United States. Some claim that Chinese goods are so cheap because Chinese manufacturers pay their employees inhumane wages. Although China's wages are still relatively low, they have doubled since 2008. Further, nearly half of the United States' non-oil imports come from developed, high-wage countries like France, Germany, Ireland, and Switzerland. These countries all have higher average wages than does the United States, so low wages (and low prices) are only one factor driving the popularity of imports.[9]

While some employers can't compete with lower-cost imports, many U.S. workers actually owe their jobs to imports. Transportation workers move goods around the country. Workers for manufacturers, wholesalers, and retailers research and place orders with foreign suppliers for products ranging from paper boxes to computer servers.

More than 60 percent of U.S. imports are raw materials, components, and machinery used to make goods or grow crops.[10] American manufacturers use these imported inputs when locally produced substitutes are either not available or too expensive. Imported inputs thus keep American manufacturing competitive—both locally and globally.

around the world—including Mexico—but no Fiestas are being built in the United States.

Recently, some companies have begun to suspect that outsourcing's negatives outweigh its positives. Improperly designed parts and products have caused production delays, and rising wages in the developing world have rendered American rates more competitive. Increased fuel and transportation costs associated with long-distance shipping, coupled with falling U.S. energy costs, have given impetus to **inshoring**, returning production jobs to the United States. Rapid consumer product innovation has led to the need to keep product designers, marketing researchers, logistics experts, and manufacturers in close proximity so that they can work quickly as a team. Thus, shrinking development and manufacturing timelines have further contributed to inshoring.

Walmart is also aiding the cause by promising to stock more "Made in the USA" goods. The firm plans to buy $50 billion of such goods as a start. This decision has already caused a ripple of effects. Redman & Associates, which manufactures battery-powered children's cars in China, recently announced a new factory in Rogers, Arkansas—not too far from Walmart's Bentonville, Arkansas headquarters.[11]

BENEFITS OF GLOBALIZATION Traditional economic theory says that globalization relies on

competition to drive down prices and increase product and service quality. Business goes to the countries that operate most efficiently and/or have the technology to produce what is needed. In summary, globalization expands economic freedom, spurs competition, and raises the productivity and living standards of people in countries that open themselves to the global marketplace. For less developed countries, globalization also offers access to foreign capital, global export markets, and advanced technology while breaking the monopoly of inefficient and protected domestic producers. Faster growth, in turn, reduces poverty, encourages democratization, and promotes higher labor and environmental standards. Though government officials in developing countries may face more difficult choices as a result of globalization, their citizens enjoy greater individual freedom. In this sense, globalization acts as a check on governmental power by making it more difficult for governments to abuse the freedom and property of their citizens.

Globalization deserves credit for helping lift many millions out of poverty and for improving standards of living of low-wage families. In developing countries around the world, globalization has created a vibrant middle class that has elevated the standard of living for hundreds of millions of people.

inshoring returning production jobs to the United States

MULTINATIONAL FIRMS

The United States has a number of large companies that are global marketers. Many of them have been very successful. A company that is heavily engaged in international trade, beyond exporting and importing, is called a **multinational corporation**. A multinational corporation moves resources, goods, services, and skills across national boundaries without regard to the country in which its headquarters is located.

Multinationals often develop their global business in stages. In the first stage, companies operate in one country and sell into others. Second-stage multinationals set up foreign subsidiaries to handle sales in one country. In the third stage, multinationals operate an entire line of business in another country. The fourth stage has evolved primarily due to the Internet and involves mostly high-tech companies. For these firms, the executive suite is virtual. Their top executives and core corporate functions are in different countries, wherever the firms can gain a competitive edge through the availability of talent or capital, low costs, or proximity to their most important customers.

A multinational company may have several worldwide headquarters, depending on where certain markets or technologies are located. Britain's APV, a maker of food-processing equipment, has a different headquarters for each of its worldwide businesses.

Many U.S.-based multinationals earn a large percentage of their total revenue abroad. Caterpillar, the construction-equipment company, receives 67 percent of its revenue from overseas markets, and General Electric earns 54 percent of its revenue abroad. Other large American exporters include General Motors, Ford, Hewlett-Packard, and IBM.

5-2a Are Multinationals Beneficial?

Although multinationals comprise far less than 1 percent of U.S. companies, they account for about nineteen percent of all private jobs, 25 percent of all private wages, 48 percent of total exports of goods, and a remarkable 74 percent of nonpublic research and development (R&D) spending.[12] For decades, U.S. multinationals have driven an outsized share of U.S. productivity growth, the foundation of rising standards of living for everyone.

multinational corporation a company that is heavily engaged in international trade, beyond exporting and importing

capital intensive using more capital than labor in the production process

The role of multinational corporations in developing nations is a subject of controversy. The ability of multinationals to tap financial, physical, and human resources from all over the world and combine them economically and profitably can benefit any country. They also often possess and can transfer the most up-to-date technology. Critics, however, claim that often the wrong kind of technology is transferred to developing nations. Usually, it is **capital intensive** (requiring a greater expenditure for equipment than for labor) and thus does not substantially increase employment. A "modern sector" then emerges in the nation, employing a small proportion of the labor force with relatively high productivity and income levels and with increasingly capital-intensive technologies. In addition, multinationals sometimes push for very quick production turn-around times, which has led to long hours and dangerous working conditions. In 2013, a Bangladesh garment factory collapsed and more than 1,100 people died as they rushed to meet production quotas for firms such as Benetton and Marks & Spencer.[13] Other critics say that the firms take more wealth out of developing nations than they bring in, thus widening the gap between rich and poor nations. The petroleum industry in particular has been heavily criticized in the past for its actions in some developing countries.

To counter such criticism, more and more multinationals are taking a proactive role in being good global citizens. Sometimes companies are spurred to action by government regulation; in other cases, multinationals are attempting to protect their good brand names. Some companies, such as Apple, Walmart, Calvin Klein, and Tommy Hilfiger, have begun conducting factory inspections to protect the health and safety of their workers. Coca-Cola has trained a half million women in 44 countries to

Coca-Cola has made an effort to provide opportunities for over half a million women in 44 countries.

become small-scale businesspeople. Coca-Cola has nurtured female owners of "sari-sari" convenience stores in the Philippines, farmers growing mangos in Kenya, and poor villagers building tiny recycling operations out of discarded bottles from trash heaps in Mexico.[14]

5-2b Global Marketing Standardization

Traditionally, marketing-oriented multinational corporations have operated somewhat differently in each country. They use a strategy of providing different product features, packaging, advertising, and so on. However, Ted Levitt, a former Harvard professor, has described a trend toward what he refers to as "global marketing," with a slightly different meaning.[15] He contends that communication and technology have made the world smaller so that almost all consumers everywhere want all the things they have heard about, seen, or experienced. Thus, he sees the emergence of global markets for standardized consumer products on a huge scale, as opposed to segmented foreign markets with different products. In this book, *global marketing* is defined as individuals and organizations using a global vision to effectively market goods and services across national boundaries. To make the distinction, we can refer to Levitt's notion as **global marketing standardization**.

Global marketing standardization presumes that the markets throughout the world are becoming more alike. Firms practicing global marketing standardization produce "globally standardized products" to be sold the same way all over the world. Most smartphones and tablets, for example, are standardized globally except for the languages displayed. These devices allow the user to switch easily from one language to another. Uniform production should enable companies to lower production and marketing costs and increase profits. Levitt has cited Coca-Cola, Colgate-Palmolive, and McDonald's as successful global marketers. His critics point out, however, that the success of these three companies is really based on variation, not on offering the same product everywhere. McDonald's, for example, changes its salad dressings and provides self-serve espresso for French tastes. It sells bulgogi burgers in South Korea and falafel burgers in Egypt. Further, the fact that Coca-Cola and Colgate-Palmolive sell some of their products in more than 160 countries does not signify that they have adopted a high degree of standardization for all their products globally. Only three Coca-Cola brands are standardized, and one of them, Sprite, has a different formulation in Japan.

Companies with separate subsidiaries in other countries can be said to operate using a multidomestic strategy. A **multidomestic strategy** occurs when multinational firms enable individual subsidiaries to compete independently in domestic markets. Simply put, multidomestic strategy is how multinational firms use strategic business units (see Chapter 2). Colgate-Palmolive uses both strategies: Axion paste dishwashing detergent, for example, was formulated for developing countries, and La Croix Plus detergent was custom made for the French market.

Nevertheless, some multinational corporations are moving beyond multidomestic strategies toward a degree of global marketing standardization. Colgate toothpaste and Nike shoes are marketed the same ways globally, using global marketing standardization.

5-3 EXTERNAL ENVIRONMENT FACED BY GLOBAL MARKETERS

A global marketer or a firm considering global marketing must consider the external environment. Many of the same environmental factors that operate in the domestic market also exist internationally. These factors include culture, economic development, the global economy, political structure and actions, demographic makeup, and natural resources.

5-3a Culture

Central to any society is the common set of values shared by its citizens that determines what is socially acceptable. Culture underlies the family, the educational system, religion, and the social class system. The network of social organizations generates overlapping roles and status positions. These values and roles have a tremendous effect on people's preferences and thus on marketers' options. A company that does not understand a country's culture is doomed to failure in that country. Cultural blunders lead to misunderstandings and often perceptions of rudeness or even incompetence. For example, when people in India shake hands, they sometimes do so rather limply. This is not a sign of weakness or disinterest; instead, a soft handshake conveys respect. Avoiding eye contact is also a sign of deference in India.

When eBay entered China in 2001, it did quite well because it had no competition. But when the Chinese

global marketing standardization
production of uniform products that can be sold the same way all over the world

multidomestic strategy
when multinational firms enable individual subsidiaries to compete independently in domestic markets

With a keen understanding of Chinese culture, Taobao proved to be stiff competition for eBay in China

Source: Taobao.com

competitor Taobao launched, eBay quickly lost ground. Its market share dropped from eighty percent to 7 percent in just five years. If you looked at eBay's site in China, you would recognize it—it looks very similar to eBay's United States site. This failure to adapt to Chinese culture led to eBay's decline: Americans do not want celebrity gossip or social interaction when they shop online, but the Chinese do.

Taobao is more than a one-stop shop for online shoppers—it is a social forum as well. The site features pictures and descriptions—very long descriptions—of products, but shoppers can also chat online about current trends, share shopping tips, and catch up on celebrity news at Taobao. Chinese shoppers are more inclined to follow fashion trends than American shoppers are, so Taobao lists trends in order of popularity, unlike eBay. Finally, when eBay entered China, it did not allow direct communication between buyers and sellers. As in the United States, all communication was handled by eBay's messaging system. This system was not well received in China because Chinese are much less likely than Americans to buy from strangers. Chinese Internet users expect Web sites to be much denser than many Western Internet users are used to. That is, Chinese Web sites tend to have more links, many more images, and longer page lengths than Western Web sites do. Eye-grabbing animations and floating images are common on Chinese sites. A page with less text, fewer embedded links, and nice imagery might be called "well-designed" by Western Internet users but "boring" by Chinese ones.

User experience issues also plague the digital divide between China and the West. In China, form fields like "first name," "middle name," and "last name" often confuse users. If you ask for name information this way in an online form, many Chinese users will be left scratching their heads. The simplest and most common approach to accommodate this cultural difference is to ask simply "name" instead of "first," "middle," and "last name." Similarly, addresses are not written in line with street names in Japan. For Japanese consumers, this small issue can make it incredibly hard to order products from Western Web sites.[16]

Language is another important aspect of culture that can create problems for marketers. Marketers must take care in translating product names, slogans, instructions, and promotional messages so as not to convey the wrong meaning. Free translation software, such as babelfish.com or Google Translate, allows users to input text in one language and output in another language. But marketers must take care using the software, as it can have unintended results—the best being unintelligible, the worst being insulting.

Each country has its own customs and traditions that determine business practices and influence negotiations with foreign customers. In many countries, personal relationships are more important than financial considerations. For instance, skipping social engagements in Mexico may lead to lost sales. Negotiations in Japan often include long evenings of dining, drinking, and entertaining, and only after a close personal relationship has been formed do business negotiations begin.

Making successful sales presentations abroad requires a thorough understanding of the country's culture. Germans, for example, do not like risk and need strong reassurance. A successful presentation to a German client will emphasize three points: the bottom-line benefits of the product or service, that there will be strong service support, and that the product is guaranteed. In southern Europe, it is an insult to show a price list. Without negotiating, you will not close the sale. The English want plenty of documentation for product claims and are less likely to simply accept the word of the sales representative. Scandinavian and Dutch companies are more likely to approach business transactions as Americans do than are companies in any other country.

5-3b Economic Factors

A second major factor in the external environment facing the global marketer is the level of economic development in the countries where it operates. In general, complex and sophisticated industries are found in developed countries, and more basic industries are found in less developed nations. Average family incomes are higher in the more developed countries compared to the less developed countries. Larger incomes mean greater purchasing power and demand, not only for consumer goods and services, but also for the machinery and workers required to produce consumer goods.

According to the World Bank, the average *gross national income (GNI)* per capita for the world is $10,679.[17] GNI is a country's GDP (defined earlier) together with its income received from other countries (mainly interest and dividends) less similar payments made to other countries. The United States' GNI per capita is $53,470, but it is not the world's highest. That honor goes to Bermuda at $104,610. Of course, there are many very poor countries: Rwanda, $630; Afghanistan, $690; Ethiopia, $470; Liberia, $410; and Democratic Republic of Congo, $430.[18] GNI per capita is one measure of the ability of a country's citizens to buy various goods and services. A marketer with a global vision can use these data to aid in measuring market potential in countries around the globe.

Not only is per capita income a consideration when going abroad, but so is the cost of doing business in a country. Although it is not the same as the cost of doing business, we can gain insights into expenses by examining the cost of living in various cities.[19]

5-3c The Global Economy

A global marketer today must be fully aware of the intertwined nature of the global economy. In the past, the size of the U.S. economy was so large that global markets tended to move up or down depending on its health. It was said, "If America sneezes, then the rest of the world catches a cold." This is still true today. Slow growth in America—and even slower growth in Europe and Japan—have hampered global economic progress. Even China's astronomical growth rate is much lower today than in recent years. Unfortunately, politics is playing an increasingly important role in how multinational firms serve their markets in countries like China and Russia. Despite politics, the BRIC (Brazil, Russia, India, and China) countries will play an increasingly important role in the global economy for years to come. By 2020, Brazil's market will top $1.6 trillion. The consumer markets in India and China are together projected to top $10 trillion in 2020.[20]

There are more consumers trading up to higher-priced, higher-quality products in emerging markets than there are in developed nations. This holds especially true for big-ticket items like housing, cars, and large appliances. Seventy percent of consumers in China and 67 percent of consumers in India cite "brand name and reputation" as key reasons for trading up to higher-priced goods and services.[21]

About half of all Indians have a mobile subscription. In fact, more people in India have mobile phones than have toilets. The Indian middle class spends three hours a day on mobile—more time than they spend on TV. Clearly, targeting consumers via mobile is critical in India.[22]

5-3d Political Structure and Actions

Political structure is a fourth important variable facing global marketers. Government policies run the gamut from no private ownership and minimal individual freedom to little central government and maximum personal freedom. As rights of private property increase, government-owned industries and centralized planning tend to decrease. But a political environment is rarely at one extreme or the other. India, for instance, is a republic with elements of socialism, monopoly capitalism, and competitive capitalism in its political ideology.

A recent World Bank study found that less regulation fosters the strongest economies. The least regulated and most efficient economies are concentrated among countries with well-established common-law traditions, including Australia, Canada, New Zealand, the United Kingdom, and the United States. On par with the best performers are Singapore and Hong Kong. Not far behind are Denmark, Norway, and Sweden—social democracies that recently streamlined their business regulation. In the United States, starting a new business—the future lifeblood of any economy—on average takes 7 procedures, 25 days, and costs the entrepreneur 32 percent of income per capita in fees. While it takes as little as one procedure, half a day, and almost nothing in fees in New Zealand, a businessperson must wait 208 days in Suriname and 144 in Venezuela.[23]

It is not uncommon for international politics to affect business laws. China recently started investigating dozens of America's largest multinationals—companies structured to compete with other corporations, not governments. Among the investigated companies, Google left China after enduring cyber-attacks and governmental pressure to release user information. Apple CEO Tim Cook expressed "sincere apologies" in the wake of Beijing's media campaign against the company. Adobe shut down both its China headquarters and ended its research and development in the country.[24] Not all of

China's oversight is excessive, however. Mead Johnson and Abbott Laboratories were fined $110 million by Chinese authorities for price fixing. Glaxo Smith Kline was fined $490 million for bribing doctors to prescribe its drugs.[25] Walmart was fined $9.8 million for misleading pricing, selling poor quality products, and selling donkey meat that turned out to be fox. But Walmart is also doing something rare for a Western company: telling the Chinese government that it needs to clean up its *own* act.

In the U.S. and most other countries, manufacturers rather than retailers are responsible for ensuring product quality. In China, however, retailers are accountable. In 2014, Walmart executives met with China's Food and Drug Administration and urged officials to step up their inspections of food purveyors. Walmart later reported that it ended relationships with 300 suppliers in 2014 because they didn't pass the retailer's testing and safety standards. Those 300 suppliers had paperwork proving that they passed muster with local food watchdogs, however. Clearly, international business can be a proxy for political jousting when governments enter the mix.[26]

Russia has also directly attacked American companies in the wake of political disagreement. In 2014, Russia seized the Crimean peninsula, leading to an onslaught of sanctions from the European Union, the United States, and others. Russia fought back, banning these countries from selling billions of dollars worth of fruits, vegetables, fish, and meat to Russians. Russia then went after McDonald's, closing down a number of restaurants for "sanitary conditions."[27]

LEGAL CONSIDERATIONS As you can see, legal considerations are often intertwined with the political environment. In France, nationalistic sentiments led to a law that requires pop music stations to play at least forty percent of their songs in French (even though French teenagers love American and English rock and roll).

Many legal structures are designed to either encourage or limit trade:

- **Tariff:** a tax levied on the goods entering a country. Because a tariff is a tax, it will either reduce the profits of the firms paying the tariff or raise prices to buyers, or both. Normally, a tariff raises prices of the imported goods and makes it easier for domestic firms to compete. In general, the U.S. economy is open to imports. America has tariffs on 1,000 product categories, but at a relatively low rate of 1.4 percent.[28] Exceptions to this are footwear and apparel, which carry a rate that is ten percent higher. In 2014, China and the U.S. slashed tariffs on a range of technology products. The agreement covered $1 trillion in trade and benefited companies like Apple, Intel, and Microsoft.[29] Nearly every piece of military gear that recruits get when they show up for training is made in the United States. The Pentagon recently conceded that even running shoes should be made domestically. New Balance will likely review the contract outlining production of up to 250,000 pairs of running shoes per year.[30]

- **Quota** a limit on the amount of a specific product that can enter a country. Several U.S. companies have sought quotas as a means of protection from foreign competition. The United States, for example, has a quota on raw cane sugar.

- **Boycott:** the exclusion of all products from certain countries or companies. Governments use boycotts to exclude companies from countries with which they have a political dispute. Several Arab nations have boycotted products made in Israel.

- **Exchange control:** a law compelling a company earning foreign exchange from its exports to sell it to a control agency, usually a central bank. A company wishing to buy goods abroad must first obtain a foreign currency exchange from the control agency. Some countries with foreign exchange controls are Argentina, Brazil, China, Iceland, India, North Korea, Russia, and Venezuela.

- **Market grouping (also known as a common trade alliance):** occurs when several countries agree to work together to form a common trade area that enhances trade opportunities. The best-known market grouping is the European Union (EU), which will be discussed later in this chapter.

- **Trade agreement:** an agreement to stimulate international trade. Not all government efforts are meant to stifle imports or investment by foreign corporations. The largest Latin American trade agreement is **Mercosur**, which includes Argentina, Bolivia, Brazil, Chile, Colombia, Ecuador, Paraguay, Peru, Uruguay,

Mercosur the largest Latin American trade agreement; includes Argentina, Bolivia, Brazil, Chile, Colombia, Ecuador, Paraguay, Peru, Uruguay, and Venezuela

Robinimages2013/Shutterstock.com

NEW BALANCE'S STATESIDE STRIDE

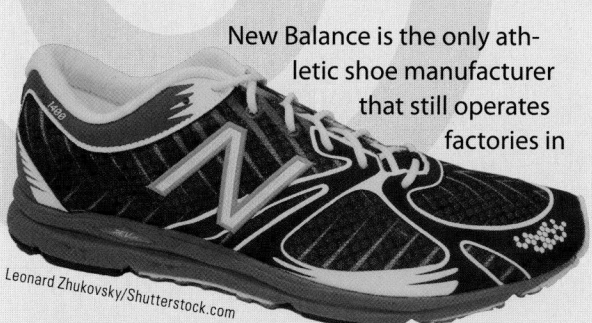

New Balance is the only athletic shoe manufacturer that still operates factories in

Leonard Zhukovsky/Shutterstock.com

the United States. These plants produce about a quarter of the shoes that New Balance sells domestically—the rest are imported.

The company has invested in new machines and cut out waste at its U.S. plants, which together employ 1,350 people. But even in its most streamlined form, shoe making remains relatively labor-intensive. New Balance reports that despite its investments, it still costs 25 to 35 percent more to produce shoes in the United States than it does in Asia.

Why does New Balance continue to produce shoes in the United States. even though that means settling for less profit? The U.S. factories' flexibility allows the company to count turn-around times in days rather than weeks, making up for some of the company's higher costs. However, a push by rivals to do away with tariffs on imported running shoes—part of a larger trade deal—could finally tip the scales against New Balance's American strategy.

and Venezuela. The elimination of most tariffs among the trading partners has resulted in trade revenues of more than $16 billion annually. The economic boom created by Mercosur will undoubtedly cause other nations to seek trade agreements on their own or to enter Mercosur.

THE URUGUAY ROUND, THE FAILED DOHA ROUND, AND BILATERAL AGREEMENTS The **Uruguay Round** is a trade agreement that has dramatically lowered trade barriers worldwide. Adopted in 1994, the agreement has been signed by 159 nations. It is the most ambitious global trade agreement ever negotiated. The agreement has reduced tariffs by one-third worldwide—a move that has raised global income by over $235 billion annually.[31] Perhaps most notable is the recognition of new global realities. For the first time, a trade agreement covers services, intellectual property rights, and trade-related investment measures such as exchange controls.

The Uruguay Round made several major changes in world trading practices:

- **Entertainment, pharmaceuticals, integrated circuits, and software:** The rules protect patents, copyrights, and trademarks for twenty years. Computer programs receive 50 years of protection, and semiconductor chips receive 10 years of protection. But many developing nations were given a decade to phase in patent protection for drugs. Also France, which limits the number of U.S. movies and television shows that can be shown, refused to liberalize market access for the U.S. entertainment industry.

- **Financial, legal, and accounting services:** Services came under international trading rules for the first time, creating a vast opportunity for these competitive U.S. industries. Now, it is easier for managers and key personnel to be admitted to a country. Licensing standards for professionals, such as doctors, cannot discriminate against foreign applicants. That is, foreign applicants cannot be held to higher standards than domestic practitioners.

- **Agriculture:** Europe is gradually reducing farm subsidies, opening new opportunities for such U.S. farm exports as wheat and corn. Japan and Korea are beginning to import rice. But U.S. growers of sugar and citrus fruit have had their subsidies trimmed.

- **Textiles and apparel:** Strict quotas limiting imports from developing countries are being phased out, causing further job losses in the U.S. clothing trade. But retailers are the big winners, because past quotas have added $15 billion a year to clothing prices.

- **A new trade organization:** The **World Trade Organization (WTO)** replaced the old **General Agreement on Tariffs and Trade (GATT)**, which was created in 1948. The WTO eliminated the extensive loopholes of which GATT members took advantage. Today, all WTO members must

Uruguay Round a trade agreement to dramatically lower trade barriers worldwide; created the World Trade Organization

World Trade Organization (WTO) a trade organization that replaced the old General Agreement on Tariffs and Trade (GATT)

General Agreement on Tariffs and Trade (GATT) a trade agreement that contained loopholes enabling countries to avoid trade-barrier reduction agreements

fully comply with all agreements under the Uruguay Round. The WTO also has an effective dispute settlement procedure with strict time limits to resolve disputes. Beijing recently lost a case on rare earth metals such as molybdenum and tungsten. The WTO charged that China's policies violated global trade rules and that Beijing was using export quotas to restrict trade. China claimed that the laws were for environmental protection. But the WTO said that this was an invalid reason for limiting exports.[32]

The latest round of WTO trade talks began in Doha, Qatar, in 2001. For the most part, the periodic meetings of WTO members under the Doha Round have been very contentious. One of the most contentious goals of the round was for the major developing countries, known collectively as BRIC (Brazil, Russia, India, and China), to lower tariffs on industrial goods in exchange for European and American tariff and subsidy cuts on farm products. Concerned that lowering tariffs would result in an economically damaging influx of foreign cotton, sugar, and rice, China and India demanded a safeguard clause that would allow them to raise tariffs on those crops if imports surged. A breakthrough came in 2014 when the United States and India reached an agreement over food security issues. Now India and the United States are looking forward to pushing the Doha Round to a conclusion.[33] Will it happen? Only time will tell.

Because many countries still view the Doha Round as virtually dead-in-the-water, several other coalitions have formed to negotiate alternative free-trade alliances. The Transatlantic Trade and Investment Partnership, which saw negotiations begin in 2013 and continue into 2015, is a proposed partnership between the United States and the European Union. The agreement would be a major benefit to Europe because of the continent's continued economic weakness.[34] A second set of negotiations are being conducted for the Trans-Pacific Partnership. The major goals of this partnership, formed by Australia, Brunei, Chile, Malaysia, New Zealand, Peru, Singapore,

The Doha Round suffers from fears of mass imports on agricultural goods that would economically stunt domestic producers.

Jim Barber/ShutterStock.com

Vietnam, and the United States, are to enhance trade and investment, promote innovation, and spur economic growth and development. The negotiations also center on control of data, intellectual property protection, and environmental and safety standards. The agreement, still being negotiated as of 2015, will cover about 40 percent of the world's gross domestic product and a third of all global trade.[35]

A third agreement, the Pacific Alliance, was signed in 2012 by Colombia, Chile, Peru, and Mexico to create a single region for the free movement of goods, services, investment, capital, and people. Full implementation of the Pacific Alliance, which created a market of 210 million people, began in 2014.[36] Costa Rica was recently accepted as a fifth member of the Alliance.

NORTH AMERICAN FREE TRADE AGREEMENT

At the time it was instituted, the **North American Free Trade Agreement (NAFTA)** created the world's largest free trade zone. Ratified by the U.S. Congress in 1993, the agreement includes Canada, the United States, and Mexico, with a combined population of 450 million. Since NAFTA's implementation in 1994, trade with Canada and Mexico has grown three and a half fold to $1.2 trillion. These countries now buy about one-third of U.S. merchandise exports.[37] The Act supports 14 million U.S. jobs.

The main impact of NAFTA was to open the Mexican market to U.S. companies. When the treaty went into effect, tariffs on about half the items traded

North American Free Trade Agreement (NAFTA) an agreement between Canada, the United States, and Mexico that created the world's then-largest free trade zone

across the Rio Grande disappeared. The pact removed a web of Mexican licensing requirements, quotas, and tariffs that limited transactions in U.S. goods and services. For instance, the pact allowed United States and Canadian financial-services companies to own subsidiaries in Mexico.

In August 2007, the three member countries met in Canada to tweak NAFTA but not make substantial changes. For example, the members agreed to further remove trade barriers on hogs, steel, consumer electronics, and chemicals. They also directed the North American Steel Trade Committee, which represents the three governments, to focus on subsidized steel from China.

DOMINICAN REPUBLIC–CENTRAL AMERICA FREE TRADE AGREEMENT The **Dominican Republic–Central America Free Trade Agreement (CAFTA-DR)** was instituted in 2005. Because it joined after the original agreement was signed, the Dominican Republic was amended to the original agreement title (Central America Free Trade Agreement, or CAFTA). Besides the United States and the Dominican Republic, the agreement includes Costa Rica, El Salvador, Guatemala, Honduras, and Nicaragua.

As of 2015, all consumer and industrial goods exported to CAFTA-DR countries are no longer subject to tariffs. Tariffs on agricultural goods will be phased out by 2020. The agreement also covers intellectual property rights, transparency, electronic commerce, and telecommunications. The CAFTA-DR countries comprise the 14th largest U.S. export market in the world. Today, the U.S. exports more than $30 billion in goods to the five Central American countries and Dominican Republic.[38]

EUROPEAN UNION The **European Union (EU)** is one of the world's most important free trade zones and now encompasses most of Europe. More than a free trade zone, it is also a political and economic community. As a free trade zone, it guarantees the freedom of movement of people, goods, services, and capital between member states. It also maintains a common trade policy with outside nations and a regional development policy. The EU represents member nations in the WTO. Recently, the EU also began venturing into foreign policy as well, getting involved in issues such as Iran's refining of uranium.

The European Union currently has twenty-eight member states: Austria, Belgium, Bulgaria, Croatia, Cyprus, the Czech Republic, Denmark, Estonia, Finland, France, Germany, Greece, Hungary, Ireland, Italy, Latvia, Lithuania, Luxembourg, Malta, Netherlands, Poland, Portugal, Romania, Slovakia,

Slovenia, Spain, Sweden, and the United Kingdom. There are currently six candidate countries: Albania, Iceland, the Republic of Macedonia, Montenegro, Serbia, and Turkey. In addition, the western Balkan countries of Bosnia and Herzegovina and Kosovo are recognized as potential candidates.[39]

In early 2010, Greece entered a financial crisis that highlighted the challenges of a large currency union where member nations maintain responsibility for their own fiscal policies. Unable to devalue its currency to boost sales of products without injuring other member nations, Greece turned to member states for a bailout. In 2015, the anti-austerity Syriza party was elected in Greece. The newly elected officials vowed to have Greek debt forgiven and to enact a program of stimulus spending. The only leverage Greece has is to threaten to stop using the euro currency, an act that would cause a banking crises and a severe recession at home.[40]

The EU is the largest economy in the world (with the United States very close behind). The EU is also a huge market, with a population of nearly 500 million and a GDP of $18.4 trillion.[41] The United States and the EU have the largest bilateral trade and investment relationship in world history. Together, they account for almost half of the entire world GDP and nearly one-third of world trade flows. United States and EU companies have invested trillions of dollars in each other's economies, contributing to significant job growth on both sides of the Atlantic. The relationship between these two economic superpowers has also shaped the global economy as a whole—the United States and the EU are primary trade partners for almost every other country in the world.[42]

The EU is a very attractive market for multinational firms. But the EU presents marketing challenges because, even with standardized regulations, marketers will not be able to produce a single European product for a generic European consumer. With more than 14 different languages and individual national customs, Europe will always be far more diverse than the United States. Thus, product differences will continue to be necessary. Atag Holdings NV, a diversified Dutch company whose main business is kitchen appliances, was confident it could cater to both the "potato" and "spaghetti" belts—marketers' terms for

Dominican Republic-Central America Free Trade Agreement (CAFTA-DR) a trade agreement instituted in 2005 that includes Costa Rica, the Dominican Republic, El Salvador, Guatemala, Honduras, Nicaragua, and the United States

European Union (EU) a free trade zone encompassing 28 European countries

consumer preferences in northern and southern Europe. But Atag quickly discovered that preferences vary much more than that. Ovens, burner shape and size, knob and clock placement, temperature range, and colors vary greatly from country to country. Although Atag's kitchenware unit has lifted foreign sales to 25 percent of its total from 4 percent in the mid-1990s, it now believes that its diversified products and speed in delivering them—rather than the magic bullet of a Europroduct—will keep it competitive.

An entirely different type of problem facing global marketers is the possibility of a protectionist movement by the EU against outsiders. For example, European automakers have proposed holding Japanese imports at roughly their current ten percent market share. The Irish, Danes, and Dutch do not make cars and have unrestricted home markets; they would be unhappy about limited imports of Toyotas and Nissans. But France has a strict quota on Japanese cars to protect Renault and Peugeot. These local carmakers could be hurt if the quota is raised at all.

THE WORLD BANK, THE INTERNATIONAL MONETARY FUND, AND THE G-20 Two international financial organizations are instrumental in fostering global trade. The **World Bank** offers low-interest loans to developing nations. Originally, the purpose of the loans was to help these nations build infrastructure such as roads, power plants, schools, drainage projects, and hospitals. Now the World Bank offers loans to help developing nations relieve their debt burdens. To receive the loans, countries must pledge to lower trade barriers and aid private enterprise. In addition to making loans, the World Bank is a major source of advice and information for developing nations. The **International Monetary Fund (IMF)** was founded in 1945, one year after the creation of the World Bank, to promote trade through financial cooperation and eliminate trade barriers in the process. The IMF makes short-term loans to member nations that are unable to meet their budgetary expenses. It operates as a lender of last resort for troubled nations, such as Greece. In exchange for these emergency loans, IMF lenders frequently extract significant commitments from the borrowing nations to address the problems that led to the crises. These steps may include curtailing imports or even devaluing the currency. Greece, working with both the IMF and the EU, has raised taxes to unprecedented levels, cut government spending (including pensions), and implemented labor reforms such as reducing minimum wage as part of its austerity measures to receive loans from the IMF and the European Union.

The **Group of Twenty (G-20)** finance ministers and central bank governors was established in 1999 to bring together industrialized and developing economies to discuss key issues in the global economy. The G-20 is a forum for international economic development that promotes discussion between industrial and emerging-market countries on key issues related to global economic stability. By contributing to the strengthening of the international financial system and providing opportunities for discussion on national policies, international cooperation, and international financial institutions, the G-20 helps to support growth and development across the globe. The members of the G-20 are shown in Exhibit 5.1.

Argentina Australia Brazil Canada
China France Germany India
Indonesia Italy Japan Mexico
Russia Saudi Arabia South Africa South Korea
Turkey United Kingdom United States European Union

Arteffficient/Shutterstock.com

World Bank an international bank that offers low-interest loans, advice, and information to developing nations

International Monetary Fund (IMF) an international organization that acts as a lender of last resort, providing loans to troubled nations, and also works to promote trade through financial cooperation

Group of Twenty (G-20) a forum for international economic development that promotes discussion between industrial and emerging-market countries on key issues related to global economic stability

EXHIBIT 5.1	MEMBERS OF THE G-20		
Argentina	European Union	Italy	South Africa
Australia	France	Japan	Republic of Korea
Brazil	Germany	Mexico	Turkey
Canada	India	Russia	United Kingdom
China	Indonesia	Saudi Arabia	United States

Members of the G-20 met in Brisbane, Australia in November 2014. The meeting focused on raising global growth to deliver better living standards and create high-quality jobs. In Brisbane, the G-20 set a goal to lift global GDP by two percent by 2018. This alone would add more than $2 trillion to the global economy and would create millions of new jobs.[43]

5-3e Demographic Makeup

The world's wealth is not evenly distributed. In fact, it is very highly concentrated. Only 0.7 percent of the world's population has assets valued at $1 million or more. This group owns an astounding 44 percent of all the world's wealth. The next 7.9 percent of the population owns an additional 41 percent of the world's wealth. That leaves 91.4 percent of the population controlling the remaining 14.7 percent of the wealth.[44] Two primary determinants of any consumer market are wealth and population.

China, India, and Indonesia are three of the most densely populated nations in the world. But that fact alone is not particularly useful to marketers. They also need to know whether the population is mostly urban or rural, because marketers may not have easy access to rural consumers. Belgium, for example, with about ninety percent of the population living in urban settings, is a more attractive market.

Another key demographic consideration is age. There is a wide gap between the older populations of the industrialized countries and the vast working-age populations of developing countries. This gap has enormous implications for economies, businesses, and the competitiveness of individual countries. It means that while Europe and Japan struggle with pension schemes and the rising cost of health care, countries like Brazil, China, and Mexico can reap the fruits of a *demographic dividend*. Caused by shifting birthrate trends, the demographic dividend results in a temporary bulge in the number of working-age people. This often leads to falling labor costs, a healthier and more educated population, and the entry of millions of women into the workforce. Population experts have estimated that one-third of East Asia's recent economic upswing can be attributed to a beneficial age structure. But the miracle occurred only because the governments had policies in place to educate their people, create jobs, and improve health.

5-3f Natural Resources

A final factor in the external environment that has become more evident in the past decade is the shortage of natural resources. For example, petroleum shortages have created huge amounts of wealth for oil-producing countries such as Norway, Saudi Arabia, and the United Arab Emirates. Both consumer and industrial markets have blossomed in these countries. Other countries—such as Indonesia, Mexico, and Venezuela—were able to borrow heavily against oil reserves in order to develop more rapidly. On the other hand, industrial countries such as Japan, the United States, and much of Western Europe experienced an enormous transfer of wealth to the petroleum-rich nations. The high price of oil has created inflationary pressures in petroleum-importing nations. Now, however, new technologies like fracking are facilitating the economic recovery of oil and gas from the tar sands of Canada and shale rock of America. This will significantly reduce U.S. demand for foreign oil.

Steep declines in the price of oil in 2014 and 2015 had a very negative impact on America's oil producers—particularly shale oil companies. Falling prices proved an economic boon to American consumers, however. Thanks to oil dropping to below $50 a barrel, the typical American household saved about $750 in 2015. People who depend upon home heating oil also saved around $750.[45]

Petroleum is not the only natural resource that affects international marketing. Warm climate and lack of water mean that many of Africa's countries will remain importers of foodstuffs. The United States, on the other hand, must rely on Africa for many precious metals. Vast differences in natural resources create international dependencies, huge shifts of wealth, inflation and recession, export opportunities for countries with abundant resources, and even a stimulus for military intervention.

Kokhanchikov/Shutterstock.com

The shortage of natural resources has become a major issue in the external environment in the last decade.

5-4 GLOBAL MARKETING BY THE INDIVIDUAL FIRM

A company should consider entering the global marketplace only after its management has a solid grasp of the global environment.

Companies decide to "go global" for a number of reasons. Perhaps the most important is to earn additional profits. Managers may believe that international sales will result in higher profit margins or more added-on profits. A second stimulus is that a firm may have a unique product or technological advantage not available to other international competitors. Such advantages should result in major business successes abroad. In other situations, management may have exclusive market information about foreign customers, marketplaces, or market situations not known to others. While exclusivity can provide an initial motivation for international marketing, managers must realize that competitors can be expected to catch up with the firm's information advantage. Finally, saturated domestic markets, excess capacity, and potential for economies of scale can also be motivators to go global. Economies of scale mean that average per-unit production costs fall as output is increased.

Many firms form multinational partnerships—called strategic alliances—to assist them in penetrating global markets; strategic alliances are examined in Chapter 7. Five other methods of entering the global marketplace are, in order of risk, exporting, licensing and franchising, contract manufacturing, joint venture, and direct investment (see Exhibit 5.2).

is currently the world's largest exporter, but the United States and Germany are not far behind.

Small companies comprise the majority of U.S. exporters. Businesses with fewer than 500 employees accounted for 294,589 of 301,238 U.S. exporters (about 98 percent) in 2012, the last year for which data is available.[46] Just over half were small manufacturers and wholesalers. Together they generated $460 billion in foreign trade—about 34 percent of total U.S. exports.

While paperwork is a headache for some small companies, it's not their biggest concern according to a survey of small businesses fielded by the National Small Business Association and the Small Business Exporters Association. Asked to identify the largest challenges to selling goods and services to foreign customers, 41 percent of respondents selected, "I worry about getting paid."[47]

"I think the biggest issue is getting a staff up overseas, as well as the cost of business travel, and of communication with far-flung clients," said Chris Coccio, chief executive of Sono-Tek Corp., which develops ultrasonic spray coating technology. Sono-Tek's primary overseas clients include contract manufacturers for electronic companies and medical firms. According to Coccio, about 60 percent of the company's roughly $10 million in annual revenue comes from sales to non-U.S. markets.[48]

Sono-Tek exports widely in Europe as well as to many parts of Asia (including China, Japan, and the Philippines). Its products can also be found in Mexico and Brazil. About 80 percent of the company's sales and marketing budget is spent on international sales, "so there clearly is extra cost per sales dollar," says Coccio.

5-4a Exporting

When a company decides to enter the global market, exporting is usually the least complicated and least risky alternative. **Exporting** is selling domestically produced products to buyers in other countries. A company can sell directly to foreign importers or buyers. China

exporting selling domestically produced products to buyers in other countries

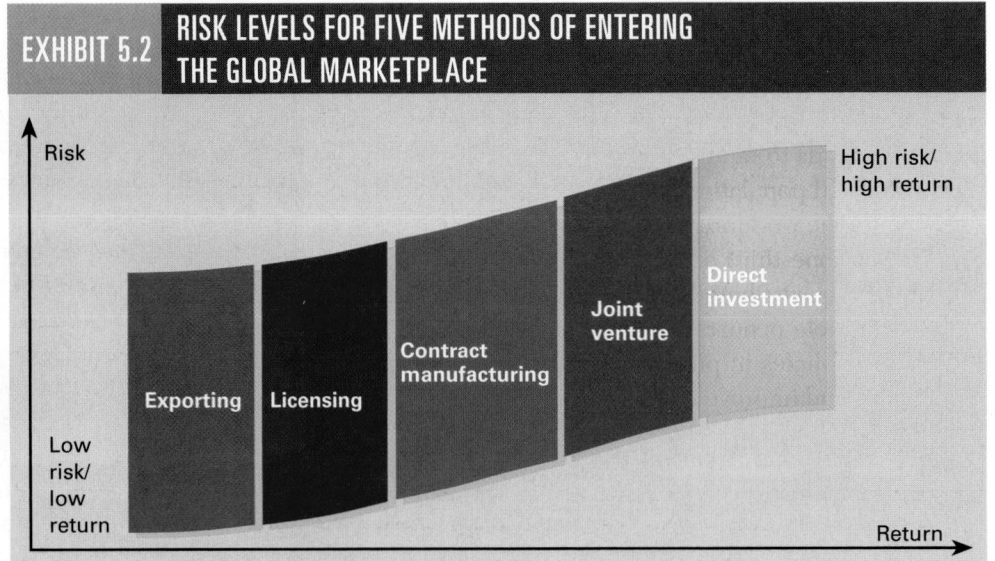

EXHIBIT 5.2 RISK LEVELS FOR FIVE METHODS OF ENTERING THE GLOBAL MARKETPLACE

On the whole, Coccio remains an advocate for exporting. "Without it, we would be one-third of our size," he says. Receiving payment is a regular concern when exporting goods, but "to deal with this our payment terms are front-end loaded with most of the payment prior to shipment."[49]

Instead of selling directly to foreign buyers, a company may decide to sell to intermediaries located in its domestic market. The most common intermediary is the export merchant, also known as a **buyer for export**, which is usually treated like a domestic customer by the domestic manufacturer. The buyer for export assumes all risks and sells internationally for its own account. The domestic firm is involved only to the extent that its products are bought in foreign markets.

A second type of intermediary is the **export broker**, who plays the traditional broker's role by bringing buyer and seller together. The manufacturer still retains title and assumes all the risks. Export brokers operate primarily in agricultural products and raw materials.

Export agents, a third type of intermediary, are foreign sales agents/distributors who live in the foreign country and perform the same functions as domestic manufacturers' agents, helping with international financing, shipping, and so on. The U.S. Department of Commerce has an agent/distributor service that helps about 5,000 U.S. companies each year find an agent or distributor in virtually any country of the world. A second category of agents resides in the manufacturer's country but represents foreign buyers. This type of agent acts as a hired purchasing agent for foreign customers operating in the exporter's home market.

5-4b Licensing and Franchising

Another effective way for a firm to move into the global arena with relatively little risk is to sell a license to manufacture its product to someone in a foreign country. **Licensing** is the legal process whereby a licensor allows another firm to use its manufacturing process, trademarks, patents, trade secrets, or other proprietary knowledge. The licensee, in turn, pays the licensor a royalty or fee agreed on by both parties.

A licensor must make sure it can exercise sufficient control over the licensee's activities to ensure proper quality, pricing, distribution, and so on. Licensing may also create a new competitor in the long run, if the licensee decides to void the license agreement. International law is often ineffective in stopping such actions. Two common ways of maintaining effective control over licensees are shipping one or more critical components from the United States and locally registering patents and trademarks to the U.S. firm, not to the licensee. Garment companies maintain control by delivering only so many labels per day; they also supply their own fabric, collect the scraps, and do accurate unit counts.

Franchising is a form of licensing that has grown rapidly in recent years. More than 400 U.S. franchisors operate more than 40,000 outlets in foreign countries, bringing in sales of more than $13 billion.[50] More than half of the international franchises are for fast-food restaurants and business services.

5-4c Contract Manufacturing

Firms that do not want to become involved in licensing or to become heavily involved in global marketing may engage in **contract manufacturing**, which is private label manufacturing by a foreign company. The foreign company produces a certain volume of products to specification, with the domestic firm's brand name on the goods. The domestic company usually handles the marketing. Thus, the domestic firm can broaden its global marketing base without investing in overseas plants and equipment. After establishing a solid base, the domestic firm may switch to a joint venture or direct investment.

5-4d Joint Venture

Joint ventures are somewhat similar to licensing agreements. In an international **joint venture**, the domestic firm buys part of a foreign company or joins with a foreign company to create a new entity. Thanks to a joint venture between General Electric and CFM International, workers assemble the best-selling aircraft engine in history in a huge factory just south of Paris. The engine's core, consisting of the

buyer for export an intermediary in the global market that assumes all ownership risks and sells globally for its own account

export broker an intermediary who plays the traditional broker's role by bringing buyer and seller together

export agent an intermediary who acts like a manufacturer's agent for the exporter; the export agent lives in the foreign market

licensing the legal process whereby a licensor allows another firm to use its manufacturing process, trademarks, patents, trade secrets, or other proprietary knowledge

contract manufacturing private label manufacturing by a foreign company

joint venture when a domestic firm buys part of a foreign company or joins with a foreign company to create a new entity

combustion chamber and related elements, is produced in a GE factory near Cincinnati, Ohio and shipped to France. Once the core arrives in France, engineers and technicians in blue overalls carefully marry the core to French-made turbo fans, turbines, and compressors. Combined, these parts form jet engines weighing two and a half tons each. Every month, about 65 of these engines are tested and shipped out. Like many successful joint ventures, one partner recently decided to acquire the other. General Electric made a $13.5 billion offer for CFM, and after much bickering with the French government, the deal was approved in November 2014.[51]

While this collaboration was successful, joint ventures can also be very risky. Many fail. Sometimes joint venture partners simply cannot agree on management strategies and policies. Often, joint ventures are the only way a government will allow a foreign company to enter its country. Joint ventures enable the local firm to acquire managerial skills and new technology.

5-4e Direct Investment

Active ownership of a foreign company or of overseas manufacturing or marketing facilities is called **direct foreign investment**. Direct foreign investment by U.S. firms is currently about $5.4 trillion.[52] Direct investors have either a controlling interest or a large minority interest in the firm. Thus, they have the greatest potential reward and the greatest potential risk. Because of problems with contract manufacturing and joint ventures in China, multinationals are going it alone. Today, nearly five times as much foreign direct investment comes into China in the form of stand-alone efforts as comes in for joint ventures.

A firm may make a direct foreign investment by acquiring an interest in an existing company or by building new facilities. It might do so because it has trouble transferring some resource to a foreign operation or getting that resource locally. One important resource is personnel, especially managers. If the local labor market is tight, the firm may buy an entire foreign firm and retain all its employees instead of paying higher salaries than competitors.

The United States is a popular place for direct investment by international companies. Foreign direct investment in the United States accounts for approximately $2.8 trillion.[53] The United States continues to receive more foreign investment flows than any country in the world. The United Kingdom is home

direct foreign investment active ownership of a foreign company or of overseas manufacturing or marketing facilities

to the largest investors in the United States, followed by Japan, the Netherlands, Canada, and France. U.S. affiliates of foreign firms employ more than 5.8 million people in the United States. These companies spend more than $50 billion on U.S. research and development and export over $345 billion worth of goods manufactured in the United States.[54]

5-5 THE GLOBAL MARKETING MIX

To succeed, firms seeking to enter into foreign trade must still adhere to the principles of the marketing mix. Information gathered on foreign markets through research is the basis for the four Ps of global marketing strategy: product, place (distribution), promotion, and price. Marketing managers who understand the advantages and disadvantages of different ways of entering the global market and the effect of the external environment on the firm's marketing mix have a better chance of reaching their goals.

The first step in creating a marketing mix is developing a thorough understanding of the global target market. Often this knowledge can be obtained through the same types of marketing research used in the domestic market (see Chapter 9). However, global marketing research is conducted in vastly different environments. Conducting a survey can be difficult in developing countries where telephone ownership is growing but is not always common and mail delivery is slow or sporadic. Drawing samples based on known population parameters is often difficult because of the lack of data. In some cities in Africa, Asia, Mexico, and South America, street maps are unavailable, streets are unidentified, and houses are unnumbered. Moreover, the questions a marketer can ask may differ in other cultures. In some cultures, people tend to be more private than in the United States and will not respond to personal questions on surveys. For instance, in France, questions about one's age and income are considered especially rude. In other situations, a question may simply not be relevant. A research company recently did an automobile-related study in Saudi Arabia. When asked for opinions about an advertisement that stressed fuel economy, a respondent was silent at first. Finally, he said, "Water is more expensive here than gas. We don't really think about fuel economy."[55]

5-5a Product Decisions

With the proper information, a good marketing mix can be developed. One important decision is whether to alter the product or the promotion for the global marketplace. Other options are to radically change the product or to adjust either the promotional message or the product to suit local conditions.

ONE PRODUCT, ONE MESSAGE The strategy of global marketing standardization, which was discussed earlier, means developing a single product for all markets and promoting it the same way all over the world. For instance, P&G uses the same product and promotional themes for Head & Shoulders in China as it does in the United States. The advertising draws attention to a person's dandruff problem, which stands out in a nation of black-haired people. Head & Shoulders is now the best-selling shampoo in China despite costing over 300 percent more than local brands. Procter & Gamble markets its rich portfolio of personal-care, beauty, grooming, health, and fabric products in more than 180 countries. The firm has 20 brands that sell more than $1 billion annually around the world. Some brands, such as Duracell batteries, are heavily standardized. P&G has moved away from standardization for other brands, however. Its Axe line of male grooming products uses a constantly running sociological study in order to keep its video ads up to date with the latest trends among young men. Axe's promotion, bottle size, and pricing also change according to which country is being targeted.[56]

Global marketing standardization can sometimes backfire. Unchanged products may fail simply because of cultural factors. Any type of war game tends to do very poorly in Germany, even though Germany is by far the world's biggest game-playing nation. A successful game in Germany is highly detailed and has a thick rulebook. In Russia, Campbell's Soups failed because housewives prefer to make soup from scratch.

Sometimes the desire for absolute standardization must give way to practical considerations and local market dynamics. For example, because of the negative connotations of the word *diet* among European females, the European version of Diet Coke is Coca-Cola Light. Even if the brand name differs by market—as with Lay's potato chips, which are called Sabritas in Mexico—a strong visual relationship may be created by uniform application of the brandmark and graphic elements on packaging.

PRODUCT INVENTION In the context of global marketing, product invention can be taken to mean either creating a new product for a market or drastically changing an existing product. For example, more than 100 unique Pringles potato chip flavors have

been invented for international markets. Prawn Cocktail (the United Kingdom), Seaweed (Japan), Blueberry (China), Cinnamon Sweet Potato (France), and Bangkok Grilled Chicken Wing (Thailand) are some of the many Pringles flavors available outside the United States.[57] Chinese consumers found Oreo cookies "too sweet," while Indian consumers said that they were "too bitter." In response, Kraft changed the recipe in each country and created a new Green Tea Oreo flavor for China.

PRODUCT ADAPTATION Another alternative for global marketers is to alter a basic product to meet local conditions. In India, Starbucks sells a tandoori paneer roll. KFC makes a "paneer zinger." Burger King sells its classic Whopper hamburger alongside a cheese-based Paneer King burger. This is largely how international food brands court India's 1.25 billion consumers—by playing to local tastes. But Domino's is doing more than simply creating new products in its attempt to woo Indian customers. It has reimagined everything about itself, from changing the flour it uses to maintaining a delicate balance between local tastes and Western influence. This dedication to adaptation has made Domino's India's largest international foreign-food chain; the company currently has 806 stores across 170 cities—more than twice as many as McDonald's.[58]

Pizza dough and toppings have much in common with Indian roti (flat bread) and subji (vegetables). Pizza also carries two important keystones of local Indian culture—shared plates and food that can be eaten with your hands. After eight months of research, Domino's introduced a small pizza called "Pizza Mania." It sells for 60 cents, is made in 2.5 minutes, and takes just six minutes to bake. The company also created a "cheese burst" (topped with chicken, salami, and classic Indian spices) and the "Taco Indiana" dish inspired by northern India's kebabs and parathas. In southern India, where pizza is less popular, research led to a spicy taw banana pizza.[59]

5-5b Promotion Adaptation

Another global marketing strategy is to maintain the same basic product but alter the promotional strategy. For example, bicycles are mainly pleasure vehicles in the United States, but in many parts of the world, they are a family's main mode of transportation. Thus, promotion in these countries should stress durability and efficiency. In contrast, U.S. advertising may emphasize escaping and having fun.

Language barriers, translation problems, and cultural differences have generated numerous headaches for international marketing managers. For example, a toothpaste claiming to give users white teeth was especially inappropriate in many areas of Southeast Asia, where the well-to-do chew betel nuts and black teeth are a sign of higher social status.

In many parts of the world, businesses market to customers via Web-connected smartphones by placing ads in everything from interactive games to graphics-laden productivity apps. Not so in rural India. To better reach the country's 833 million villagers, Unilever is delivering free Bollywood music and jokes to basic cell phones via old-fashioned phone calls. Users of Unilever's mobile phone music service listen to four product ads in between the popular tunes and cheesy jokes presented throughout each 15-minute program. Consumers like the offering; at least 2 million people subscribe to the free service.[60]

5-5c Place (Distribution)

Solving promotional and product problems does not guarantee global marketing success. The product must still get adequate distribution. For example, Europeans do not play sports as much as Americans do, so they do not visit sporting-goods stores as often. Realizing this, Reebok started selling its shoes in about 800 traditional shoe stores in France. In just one year, the company doubled its French sales.

Taiwanese convenience stores are quite different from what is found in the United States. Beyond the staple snacks, they provide an array of services including dry cleaning, train and concert ticket reservations, traffic fine and utility payment, hot sit-down meals, mail drop-off, and book pickup. They also deliver everything from refrigerators to multicourse banquets. As you might expect, heavy convenience store patronage is the norm in Taiwan.

Taiwan's major convenience store chains recently added seating areas to keep their customers around longer. This has resulted in convenience stores becoming popular hangouts for everyone from suited businesspeople conducting meetings to students using the stores' free wifi.[61]

Similarly, Starbucks targets white-collar consumers in China by providing larger eat-in areas with comfortable sofas, high-speed Internet access, and a business atmosphere. This allows Starbucks customers to sit in its coffee shops for casual business meetings.

In India's small cities, where eating out is often a family event, Domino's offers large dine-in spaces. Its locations are situated exactically throughout the country; the pizza chain studies each neighborhood, its streets, and traffic flow before deciding to launch a new store. Then, each store's surrounding area is meticulously mapped (down to every intersection and traffic light) to find the fastest delivery routes. In India, Domino's still offers its "30 minute or it's free" policy—a promotion the company ended in America in 1993.[62]

In many developing nations, channels of distribution and the physical infrastructure are inadequate. South Africa has perhaps the best infrastructure in all of Africa, but even there distributing products in a safe and cost-effective way is a monumental task. Though *spazas* (informal convenience stores) comprise approximately thirty percent of South Africa's national retail market, no formal distribution system exists—many shop owners cannot even afford delivery vans. To counter this distributional hurdle, Nestlé established eighteen distribution centers to deliver Nespray, a mineral-rich milk powder, directly to the spazas scattered across rural South Africa.[63]

American companies importing goods from overseas facilities to the United States are facing other problems. Logistics has been a growing challenge for U.S. companies seeking to cut costs by shifting more production to countries where manufacturing is cheaper. Now, however, the rising costs for shipping goods are adding to their profit pressures. The surge in global trade in recent years has added to strains and charges for all forms of transport. As a result, some manufacturers are developing costly buffer stocks—which can mean setting up days' or weeks' worth of extra components—to avoid shutting down production lines and failing to make timely deliveries. Others are shifting to more expensive but more reliable modes of transport, such as airfreight, which is faster and less prone to delays than ocean shipping. Still others are inshoring as discussed earlier in the chapter.

5-5d Pricing

Once marketing managers have determined a global product and promotion strategy, they can select the remainder of the marketing mix. Pricing presents some unique problems in the global sphere. Exporters must not only cover their production costs but also consider transportation costs, insurance, taxes, and tariffs. When deciding on a final price, marketers must also determine how much customers are willing to spend on a particular product. Marketers also need to ensure that their foreign buyers will pay the price. Because developing nations lack mass purchasing power, selling to them often poses special pricing problems. Sometimes a product can be simplified in order to lower the price. A firm must not assume low-income countries are willing to accept lower quality, however. L'Oréal was unsuccessful selling cheap shampoo in India, so the company targets the rising class. It now sells a $17 Paris face powder and a $25 Vichy sunscreen. Both products are very popular.

Walmart's low-price business model has been slow to catch on with Chinese shoppers, many of whom like to shop for bargains online and in mom-and-pop stores.[64] Chinese consumers expect foreign retailers to offer the highest quality shopping environments, not the warehouse-like design common to United States Walmart stores. The company recently decided to close 29 underperforming stores in China.[65]

EXCHANGE RATES The **exchange rate** is the price of one country's currency in terms of another country's currency. If a country's currency *appreciates*, less of that country's currency is needed to buy another country's currency. If a country's currency *depreciates*, more of that currency will be needed to buy another country's currency.

How do appreciation and depreciation affect the prices of a country's goods? If, say, the U.S. dollar depreciates relative to the Japanese yen, U.S. residents will need to pay more dollars to buy Japanese goods. To illustrate, suppose the dollar price of one yen is $0.012 and that a Toyota is priced at ¥2 million. At this exchange rate, a U.S. resident pays $24,000 for a Toyota ($0.012 × ¥2 million = $24,000). If the dollar depreciates to $0.018 to ¥1, then the U.S. resident will need to pay $36,000 for the same Toyota.

As the dollar depreciates, the prices of Japanese goods rise for U.S. residents, so they buy fewer Japanese goods—thus, U.S. imports may decline. At the same time, as the dollar depreciates relative to the yen, the yen appreciates relative to the dollar. This means prices of U.S. goods fall for the Japanese, so they buy more U.S. goods—and U.S. exports rise.

Currency markets operate under a system of **floating exchange rates**. Prices of different currencies "float" up and down based on the demand for and the supply of each currency. Global currency traders create the supply of and demand for a particular country's currency based on that country's investment, trade potential, and economic strength. Sanctions imposed because of Russia's annexation of Crimea and its engagement in the Ukrainian conflict in 2014 and 2015 have resulted in the Russian ruble plunging in value. On August 3, 2014, the exchange rate was 35.75 rubles to the U.S. dollar. By January 29, 2015, the rate was 68.75 rubles to the dollar.[66]

DUMPING **Dumping** is the sale of an exported product at a price lower than that charged for the same or a like product in the "home" market of the exporter. This practice is regarded as a form of price discrimination that can potentially harm the importing nation's competing industries. Dumping may occur as a result of exporter business strategies that include (1) trying to increase an overseas market share, (2) temporarily distributing products in overseas markets to offset slack demand in the home market, (3) lowering unit costs by exploiting large-scale production, and (4) attempting to maintain stable prices during periods of exchange rate fluctuations.

Historically, the dumping of goods has presented serious problems in international trade. As a result, dumping has led to significant disagreements among countries and diverse views about its harmfulness. Some trade economists view dumping as harmful only when it involves the use of "predatory"

> **exchange rate** the price of one country's currency in terms of another country's currency

> **floating exchange rates** a system in which prices of different currencies move up and down based on the demand for and the supply of each currency

> **dumping** the sale of an exported product at a price lower than that charged for the same or a like product in the "home" market of the exporter

> If a country's currency depreciates, more of that currency will be needed to buy another country's currency.

OtnaYdur/Shutterstock.com

practices that intentionally try to eliminate competition and gain monopoly power in a market. They believe that predatory dumping rarely occurs and that anti-dumping rules are a protectionist tool whose cost to consumers and import-using industries exceeds the benefits to the industries receiving protection.

In January 2015, the United States Commerce Department declared anti-dumping duties for passenger and light truck tires imported from China. More than 30 different manufacturers were involved in dumping at various prices. The duty rates ranged from 19 to 88 percent.[67]

COUNTERTRADE Global trade does not always involve cash. Countertrade is a fast-growing way to conduct global business. In **countertrade**, all or part of the payment for goods or services is in the form of other goods or services. Countertrade is thus a form of barter (swapping goods for goods), an age-old practice whose origins have been traced back to cave dwellers. The U.S. Department of Commerce says that roughly thirty percent of all global trade is countertrade.[68] In fact, both India and China have made billion-dollar government purchasing lists, with most of the goods to be paid for by countertrade.

One common type of countertrade is straight barter. The Malaysian government purchased 20 diesel-electric locomotives from General Electric in exchange for a supply of 200,000 metric tons of palm oil. Sometimes, countertrades involve both cash and goods. General Motors sold locomotive and diesel engines to Yugoslavia in exchange for $4 million and Yugoslavian cutting tools.[69] Another form of countertrade is the compensation agreement. Typically, a company provides technology and equipment for a plant in a developing nation and agrees to take full or partial payment in goods produced by that plant. For example, General Tire Company supplied equipment and know-how for a Romanian truck tire plant. In turn, General Tire sold the tires it received from the plant in the United States under the Victoria brand name. Both sides benefit even though they do not use cash.

5-6 THE IMPACT OF THE INTERNET

In many respects, going global is easier than it has ever been before. Opening an e-commerce site on the Internet immediately puts a company in the international marketplace. Sophisticated language translation software can make any site

countertrade a form of trade in which all or part of the payment for goods or services is in the form of other goods or services

accessible to people around the world. Global shippers such as UPS, FedEx, and DHL help solve international e-commerce distribution complexities. E4X Inc. offers software to ease currency conversions by allowing customers to pay in the currency of their choice. E4X collects the payment from the customer and then pays the site in U.S. dollars. Nevertheless, the promise of "borderless commerce" and the global "Internet economy" are still being restrained by the old brick-and-mortar rules, regulations, and habits. For example, Lands' End is not allowed to mention its unconditional refund policy on its e-commerce site in Germany because German retailers, which normally do not allow returns after 14 days, sued and won a court ruling blocking mention of it.

5-6a Social Media in Global Marketing

Because Facebook, YouTube, and other social media are popular around the world, firms both large and small have embraced social media marketing. Every passenger hopes for the opportunity to get a free upgrade to business class when flying. To help raise awareness of the launch of Air France's new business class cabins in Asia, Fred & Farid Shanghai created a social game in which travelers could compete to win a free upgrade to business class just prior to boarding. The agency transformed the boarding gates of Changi Airport in Singapore and Kansai Airport in Osaka, Japan into social gaming arenas where passengers could download a mobile game (similar to fruit ninja) and try to get a high score. Over 400 passengers were invited to compete against one another and monitor all the competitors on a large scoreboard during their wait.[70]

Fashion label H&M promoted its summer products on Twitter and Facebook using the hashtag #DivideOpinion. For each #DivideOpinion post, H&M captured a fashion item in two distinctive scenes (for example, a sheer lace top styled for both a romantic-inspired outfit and a street-style outfit) and asked its followers to reply with which look was better and why. The best responses received a trip to Los Angeles for each winner and a friend. With this campaign, H&M reinvented a popular idea often seen in fashion magazines for the mobile market. By comparing two products (rather than three or four) against one another, H&M was able to target mobile users who want quick snippets of information and whose screens do not allow for more than a couple of images at a time. This campaign was successful in its effort to drive excitement around H&M's summer fashions.[71]

Managers of global social media campaigns must always be aware of the cultures of the countries in

Source: Twitter

Source: Twitter

which they operate. Global energy drink giant Red Bull sparked a major spat with Kenyans after it posted a video that seemed to imply that Kenyans were backwards to Facebook. The video clip featured South African motorcycle rider Brian Capper, who started the video off by expressing his shock at how many people spoke English in Nairobi. "I've been blown away with the amount of people that speak English. I had absolutely no idea what to expect from that point of view; just about everybody I spoke to spoke English, which was really surprising for me," said the rider. "They are unbelievably knowledgeable … they know what's going on with the rest of the world."[72] Capper's comments did not go down well with many, as Red Bull's Facebook page quickly filled with angry comments such as:

"Seems like a nice guy and cool video, but seriously, what era is he and the Red Bull crew living in! Surprised about the English and saying 3rd world country, eyes need to be open to 2015 Kenya! And the dude is from SA as well, so should really know better."

"Don't you just love the ignorance of these people! Surprised that Kenyans speak English? We speak better English than you dude. All in all, great biking skills! Now go back to school."[73]

These reactions are reminiscent of a similar outcry after Korean Air termed Kenyans "primitive" in an online advertising campaign about the company's direct flights to Nairobi. The advertisement read in part: "Fly to Nairobi with Korean Air and enjoy the grand African savanna, the safari tour, and the indigenous people full of primitive energy." The words 'primitive energy' annoyed many Kenyans, who forced the airline to retract the ad and issue an apology on social media.[74]

STUDY TOOLS 5

LOCATED AT BACK OF THE TEXTBOOK

☐ Rip out Chapter Review Card

LOCATED AT WWW.CENGAGEBRAIN.COM

☐ Review Key Terms Flashcards and create your own

☐ Track your knowledge & understanding of key concepts in marketing

☐ Complete practice and graded quizzes to prepare for tests

☐ Complete interactive content within the MKTG Online experience

☐ View the chapter highlight boxes within the MKTG Online experience

Consumer Decision Making

leaada/Shutterstock.come

LEARNING OUTCOMES

After studying this chapter, you will be able to…

6-1 Explain why marketing managers should understand consumer behavior

6-2 Analyze the components of the consumer decision-making process

6-3 Explain the consumer's postpurchase evaluation process

6-4 Identify the types of consumer buying decisions and discuss the significance of consumer involvement

6-5 Identify and understand the cultural factors that affect consumer buying decisions

6-6 Identify and understand the social factors that affect consumer buying decisions

6-7 Identify and understand the individual factors that affect consumer buying decisions

6-8 Identify and understand the psychological factors that affect consumer buying decisions

After you finish this chapter go to **PAGE 113** for **STUDY TOOLS.**

6-1 THE IMPORTANCE OF UNDERSTANDING CONSUMER BEHAVIOR

Consumers' product and service preferences are constantly changing. Marketing managers must understand these desires in order to create a proper marketing mix for a well-defined market. So it is critical that marketing managers have a thorough knowledge of consumer behavior. **Consumer behavior** describes how consumers make purchase decisions and how they use and dispose of the purchased goods or services. The study of consumer behavior also includes factors that influence purchase decisions and product use.

consumer behavior
processes a consumer uses to make purchase decisions, as well as to use and dispose of purchased goods or services; also includes factors that influence purchase decisions and product use

Understanding how consumers make purchase decisions can help marketing managers in several ways. For example, if the product development manager for Trek bicycles learns through research that a more comfortable seat is a key attribute for purchasers of mountain bikes, Trek can redesign the seat to meet that criterion. If the firm cannot change the design in the short run, it can use promotion in an effort to change consumers' decision-making criteria. Trek, for example, could promote the ultra-light weight, durability, and performance of its current mountain bikes.

Buying a mountain bike, or anything else, is all about value. **Value** is a personal assessment of the net worth one obtains from making a purchase. To put it another way, value is what you get minus what you give up. When you buy something, you hope to get benefits like relief from hunger, durability, convenience, prestige, affection, happiness, a sense of belonging...the list goes on. In order to receive these benefits, you must give something up. You may sacrifice money, self-image, time, convenience, effort, opportunity, or a combination thereof. Value can also mean an enduring belief shared by a society that a specific mode of conduct is personally or socially preferable to another mode of conduct. This definition of "value" will be discussed later in the chapter.

Purchases are made based upon **perceived value**, which is what you *expect* to get. The actual value may be more or less than you expected. Recently, one of your authors bought a well-known brand of coffee maker with a thermal carafe. He likes to drink coffee all morning, but found that traditional coffee makers' heating elements tended to turn the coffee bitter and thick-tasting after a few hours. The thermal carafe has no such heating element, so the coffee stays fresh. That is, if the coffee actually makes it into the carafe. The carafe lid has a valve that lets the coffee drip into the carafe basin.

However, the valve tends to stick, and after about a week of use, the valve stuck during a fill-up and coffee went all over the kitchen counter. No value there! (For the curious, the author has moved on to a new traditional-style coffee maker.)

The value received from a purchase can be broken down into two categories. **Utilitarian value** is derived from a product or service that helps the consumer solve problems and accomplish tasks. Buying a washing machine and dryer gives you a convenient means of cleaning your clothes. Buying a new pair of eyeglasses lets you better view the computer screen. Utilitarian value, then, is a means to an end. Value is provided because the purchase allows something good to happen.

The second form of value is **hedonic value**. Hedonic value is an end in itself rather than as a means to an end. The purchase tends to give us good feelings, happiness, and satisfaction. The value is

value a personal assessment of the net worth one obtains from making a purchase, or the enduring belief that a specific mode of conduct is personally or socially preferable to another mode of conduct

perceived value the value a consumer *expects* to obtain from a purchase

utilitarian value a value derived from a product or service that helps the consumer solve problems and accomplish tasks

hedonic value a value that acts as an end in itself rather than as a means to an end

provided entirely through the experience and emotions associated with consumption, not because another end is accomplished. Taking a ski vacation or a trip to the beach gives us hedonic value. Spending a day in a spa is a source of hedonic value. A coffee maker provides utilitarian value, but the coffee itself provides hedonic value.

Utilitarian and hedonic values are not mutually exclusive. In some cases, the purchase experience can give you both hedonic and utilitarian value. Morton's The Steakhouse is considered to be one of the top steak restaurant chains in America. Going to a Morton's and enjoying the atmosphere and a fine steak will give you hedonic value. At the same time, it satisfies your hunger pangs and thus provides utilitarian value. Some of the best consumer experiences are high in both utilitarian and hedonic value.[1]

Acquiring value comes from making a purchase. How does one go about making the decision to buy? We will explore this topic next.

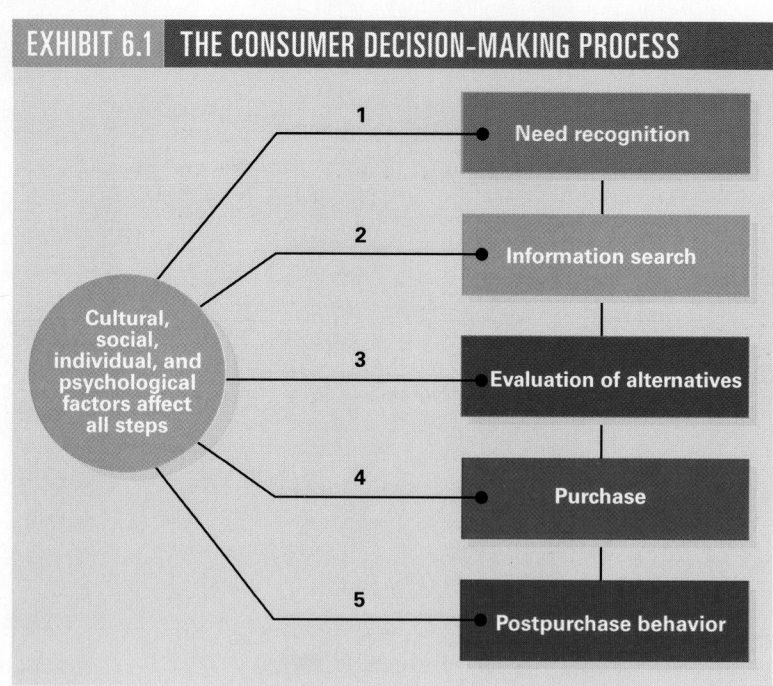

EXHIBIT 6.1 THE CONSUMER DECISION-MAKING PROCESS

Cultural, social, individual, and psychological factors affect all steps

1 Need recognition
2 Information search
3 Evaluation of alternatives
4 Purchase
5 Postpurchase behavior

6-2 THE CONSUMER DECISION-MAKING PROCESS

When buying products, particularly new or expensive items, consumers generally follow the consumer decision-making process shown in Exhibit 6.1: (1) need recognition, (2) information search, (3) evaluation of alternatives, (4) purchase, and (5) postpurchase behavior. These five steps represent a general process that can be used as a guide for studying how consumers make decisions. It is important to note, though, that consumers' decisions do not always proceed in order through all of these steps. In fact, the consumer may end the process at any time or may not even make a purchase. The section on the types of consumer buying decisions later in the chapter discusses why a consumer's progression through these steps may vary. We begin, however, by examining the basic purchase process in greater detail.

6-2a Need Recognition

The first stage in the consumer decision-making process is need recognition. **Need recognition** is the result of an imbalance between actual and desired states. The imbalance arouses and activates the consumer decision-making process. A **want** is the recognition of an unfulfilled need and a product that will satisfy it. For example, have you ever gotten blisters from an old running shoe and realized you needed new shoes? Or maybe you have seen a new sports car drive down the street and wanted to buy it. Need recognition is triggered when a consumer is exposed to either an internal or an external **stimulus**, which is any unit of input affecting one or more of the five senses: sight, smell, taste, touch, and hearing. *Internal stimuli* are occurrences you experience, such as hunger or thirst. For example, you may hear your stomach growl and then realize you are hungry. *External stimuli* are influences from an outside source. In today's digital age, stimuli can come from a multitude of sources. Perhaps it was a YouTube video that created a purchase desire. Perhaps it was a Google search on a smartphone or an interactive advertisement playing on a large touch-enabled screen. Or perhaps it was a friend's video posted on Facebook using a new GoPro camera.

The imbalance between actual and desired states is sometimes referred to as the *want–got gap*. That is,

consumer decision-making process a five-step process used by consumers when buying goods or services

need recognition result of an imbalance between actual and desired states

want recognition of an unfulfilled need and a product that will satisfy it

stimulus any unit of input affecting one or more of the five senses: sight, smell, taste, touch, hearing

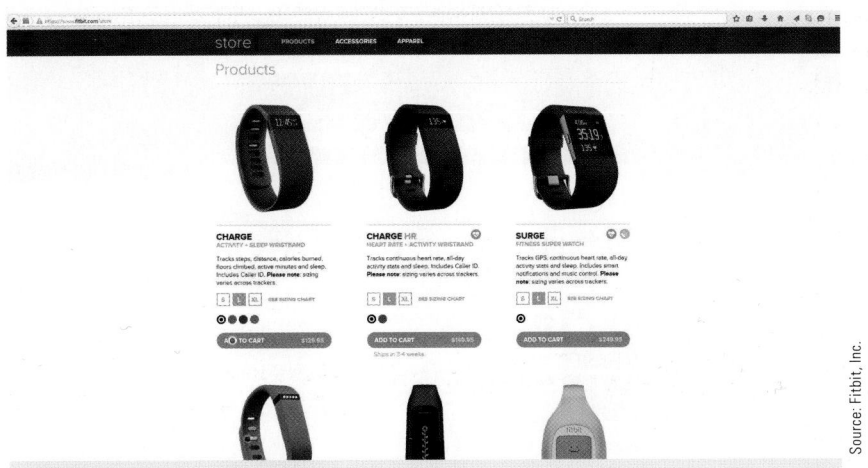

Source: Fitbit, Inc.

> A want can be for a specific product, or it can be for a certain attribute or feature of a product.

there is a difference between what a customer has and what he or she would like to have. This gap does not always trigger consumer action. The gap must be large enough to drive the consumer to do something. Just because your stomach growls once does not mean that you necessarily will stop what you are doing and go eat.

A marketing manager's objective is to get consumers to recognize this want–got gap. Advertising, sales promotion, and social media often provide this stimulus. Surveying buyer preferences provides marketers with information about consumer needs and wants that can be used to tailor products and services. Marketing managers can create wants on the part of the consumer. An ad promoting a healthy, active lifestyle and the fun of fitness tracking may inspire you to purchase a wearable fitness tracker like a Fitbit Charge HR or a Runtastic Orbit. A want can be for a specific product, or it can be for a certain attribute or feature of a product. A runner may purchase the Orbit, for example, because the band pairs with the Runtastic app to display information about recent runs right on the wearer's wrist.

6-2b Information Search

After recognizing a need or want, consumers search for information about the various alternatives available to satisfy it. For example, you know you are interested in seeing a movie, but you are not sure what to see. So you visit the Rotten Tomatoes Web site to see what is getting great reviews by both critics and your peers on Facebook. This is a type of information search, which can occur internally, externally, or both. In an **internal information search**, the person recalls information stored in the memory. This stored information stems largely from previous experience with a product. For example, while traveling with your family, you may choose to stay at a hotel you have stayed in before because you remember that the hotel had clean rooms and friendly service.

In contrast, an **external information search** seeks information in the outside environment. There are two basic types of external information sources: nonmarketing-controlled and marketing-controlled. A **nonmarketing-controlled information source** is a product information source that is not associated with marketers promoting a product. These information sources include personal experiences (trying or observing a new product), personal sources (family, friends, acquaintances, and coworkers who may recommend a product or service), and public sources (such as Rotten Tomatoes, *Consumer Reports*, and other rating organizations that comment on products and services). Once you have read reviews on Rotten Tomatoes to decide which movie to see (public source), you may search your memory for positive theater experiences to determine where you will go (personal experience). Or you might rely on a friend's recommendation to try out a new theater (personal source). Marketers gather information on how these information sources work and use it to attract customers. For example, car manufacturers know that younger customers are likely to get information from friends and family, so they try to develop enthusiasm for their products via word of mouth and social media.

Living in the digital age has changed the way consumers get nonmarketing-controlled information. It can be from blogs, Amazon, social media, Web forums, or consumer opinion sites such as www.consumerreview.com, www.tripadvisor.com, or www.epinions.com. Eighty percent of U.S. consumers research electronics, computers, and media online before making an in-store purchase, and a quarter of shoppers utilize at least four sources for product information. To give you an idea of the number of searches this

internal information search the process of recalling past information stored in the memory

external information search the process of seeking information in the outside environment

nonmarketing-controlled information source a product information source that is not associated with advertising or promotion

implies, Google averages more than 12 billion searches a month.[2] This number is only going to expand.

The Internet has changed the quality of information available to make purchase decisions. In the past, consumers used quality proxies to help determine what to buy. A proxy could be a brand name ("it is made by Sony so it must be good"), price ("higher price meant higher quality"), or origin ("made in the USA is better"). Today, consumers can appraise a product based upon how it is evaluated by others. If you are looking for a hotel in New York City, for example, you can easily view a ranking of all New York hotels based upon thousands of reviews on Web sites like TripAdvisor. This provides much better information than simply relying on a brand name (such as Hilton) because you have the direct experience of others to guide you.[3] A word of caution, however: researchers using data from a large private label retailer's Web site found that approximately 5 percent of product reviews were submitted by people with no record of ever having purchased the products they were reviewing.[4] Expedia avoids this problem by only allowing customers who have purchased a service (such as a flight, car, or hotel room) to write a review. Similarly, Amazon identifies whether a review matches a confirmed transaction.

Social media are playing an ever-increasing role in consumer information search. Thirty percent of shoppers made a purchase via social media in 2014. Forty-four percent will discover new products via social networks, and 49 percent will make purchases based upon referrals from social media, recommendations from friends in their social networks, or promotions from brands that they follow on Facebook or Twitter.[5]

Although the use of a mobile device to make purchases is rising, consumers primarily use their smartphones and tablets to research products before buying. One survey found that 70 percent of respondents planned to research products on their mobile devices and then purchased them in-store.[6] In-store research and price comparisons conducted on mobile devices while shopping have become standard practice for many consumers.

Source: TripAdvisor

The internet has changed the quality of information available to make purchase decisions.

Not every information search is about comparing Product or Service Firm A with Product or Service Firm B. Yet, the online search can still influence purchase patterns. For example, a shopper may browse recipe Web sites or watch cooking demonstration videos before deciding on a dinner party menu. This research helps the shopper decide which ingredients to purchase at the supermarket.

A **marketing-controlled information source** is biased toward a specific product because it originates with marketers promoting that product. Marketing-controlled information sources include mass media advertising (radio, newspaper, television, and magazine advertising), sales promotion (contests, displays, premiums, and so forth), salespeople, product labels and packaging, and digital media. In 2016, the web influenced more than half of all retail transactions, representing sales of almost $2 trillion.[7]

The extent to which an individual conducts an external search depends on his or her perceived risk, knowledge, prior experience, and level of interest in the good or service. Generally, as the perceived risk of the purchase increases, the consumer enlarges the search and considers more alternative brands. For example, suppose that you want to purchase a surround-sound system for your home entertainment system. The decision is relatively risky because of the expense and technical nature of the surround-sound system, so you are motivated to search for information about models, prices, options, compatibility with existing entertainment products, and capabilities. You may decide to compare attributes of many speaker systems because the value of the time expended finding the

marketing-controlled information source a product information source that originates with marketers promoting the product

"right" stereo will be less than the cost of buying the wrong system.

A consumer's knowledge about the product or service will also affect the extent of an external information search. A consumer who is knowledgeable and well informed about a potential purchase is less likely to search for additional information. In addition, the more knowledgeable consumers are, the more efficiently they will conduct the search process, thereby requiring less time to search. For example, many consumers know that Spirit Airlines and other discount airlines have much lower fares, so they generally use the discounters and do not even check fares at other carriers.

The extent of a consumer's external search is also affected by confidence in one's decision-making ability. A confident consumer not only has sufficient stored information about the product but also feels self-assured about making the right decision. People lacking this confidence will continue an information search even when they know a great deal about the product. Consumers with prior experience in buying a certain product will have less perceived risk than inexperienced consumers. Therefore, they will spend less time searching and limit the number of products they consider.

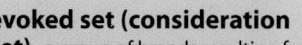
Radu Bercan/Shutterstock.com

A third factor influencing the external information search is product experience. Consumers who have had a positive experience with a product are more likely to limit their search to items related to the positive experience. For example, when flying, consumers are likely to choose airlines with which they have had positive experiences, such as consistent on-time arrivals, and avoid airlines with which they have had a negative experience, such as lost luggage.

Finally, the extent of the search is positively related to the amount of interest a consumer has in a product. A consumer who is more interested in a product will spend more time searching for information and alternatives. For example, suppose you are a dedicated runner who reads jogging and fitness magazines and catalogs. In searching for a new pair of running shoes, you may enjoy reading about the new brands available and spend more time and effort than other buyers in deciding on the right shoe.

The consumer's information search should yield a group of brands, sometimes called the buyer's **evoked set** (or **consideration set**), which are the consumer's most preferred alternatives. From this set, the buyer will further evaluate the alternatives and make a choice. Consumers do not consider all brands available in a product category, but they do seriously consider a much smaller set. For example, from the many brands of pizza available, consumers are likely to consider only the alternatives that fit their price range, location, take-out/delivery needs, and taste preferences. Having too many choices can, in fact, confuse consumers and cause them to delay the decision to buy, or in some instances, cause them not to buy at all.

6-2c Evaluation of Alternatives and Purchase

After getting information and constructing an evoked set of alternative products, the consumer is ready to make a decision. A consumer will use the information stored in memory and obtained from outside sources to develop a set of criteria. Recent research has shown that exposure to certain cues in your everyday environment can affect decision criteria and purchase. For example, when NASA landed the *Pathfinder* spacecraft on Mars, it captured media attention worldwide. The candy maker Mars also noted a rather unusual increase in sales. Although the Mars bar takes its name from the company's founder and not the planet, consumers apparently responded to news about the planet Mars by purchasing more Mars bars.

The environment, internal information, and external information help consumers evaluate and compare alternatives. One way to begin narrowing the number of choices in the evoked set is to pick a product attribute and then exclude all products in the set that do not have that attribute. For example, assume Jane and Jill, both college sophomores, are looking for their first apartment. They need a two-bedroom apartment, reasonably priced and located near campus. They want the apartment to have a swimming pool, washer and dryer, and

> **evoked set (consideration set)** a group of brands resulting from an information search from which a buyer can choose

covered parking. Jane and Jill begin their search with all fifty apartments in the area and systematically eliminate complexes that lack the features they need. Hence, they may reduce their list to ten apartments that possess all of the desired attributes. Now, they can use cutoffs to further narrow their choices. Cutoffs are either minimum or maximum levels of an attribute that an alternative must pass to be considered. Suppose Jane and Jill set a maximum of $1,000 per month for rent. Then all apartments with rent higher than $1,000 will be eliminated, further reducing the list of apartments from ten to eight. A final way to narrow the choices is to rank the attributes under consideration in order of importance and evaluate the products based on how well each performs on the most important attributes. To reach a final decision on one of the remaining eight apartments, Jane and Jill may decide proximity to campus is the most important attribute. As a result, they will choose to rent the apartment closest to campus.

If new brands are added to an evoked set, the consumer's evaluation of the existing brands in that set changes. As a result, certain brands in the original set may become more desirable. Suppose Jane and Jill find two apartments located an equal distance from campus, one priced at $800 and the other at $750. Faced with this choice, they may decide that the $800 apartment is too expensive given that a comparable apartment is cheaper. If they add a $900 apartment to the list, however, then they may perceive the $800 apartment as more reasonable and decide to rent it.

The purchase decision process described above is a piecemeal process. That is, the evaluation is made by examining alternative advantages and disadvantages along important product attributes. A different way consumers can evaluate a product is according to a categorization process. The evaluation of an alternative depends upon the particular category to which it is assigned. Categories can be very general (motorized forms of transportation), or they can be very specific (Harley-Davidson motorcycles). Typically, these categories are associated with some degree of liking or disliking. To the extent that the product can be assigned membership in a particular category, it will receive an evaluation similar to that attached to the category. If you go to the grocery store and see a new organic food on the shelf, you may evaluate it on your liking and opinions of organic food.

So, when consumers rely on a categorization process, a product's evaluation depends on the particular category to which it is perceived as belonging. Given this, companies need to understand whether consumers are using categories that evoke the desired evaluations. Indeed, how a product is categorized can strongly influence consumer demand. For example, what products come to mind when you think about the "morning beverages" category? To the soft drink industry's dismay, far too few consumers include sodas in this category. Several attempts have been made at getting soft drinks on the breakfast table, but with little success.

Brand extensions, in which a well-known and respected brand name from one product category is extended into other product categories, is one way companies employ categorization to their advantage. Brand extensions are a common business practice. For example, mixed martial arts promotional organization Ultimate Fighting Championship (UFC) has built its brand on pay-per-view events, cable and network television broadcasts, and merchandising. The UFC launched a 24-hour full-service gym in Long Island, New York. In addition to martial arts–themed activities, the UFC Gym features standard fitness equipment, a café, and signature classes like Hot Hula and Hi-Octane Conditioning.

TO BUY OR NOT TO BUY Ultimately, the consumer has to decide whether to buy or not buy. Specifically, consumers must decide:

1. Whether to buy
2. When to buy
3. What to buy (product type and brand)

Source: UFC Gym

The UFC Gym extends the Ultimate Fighting Championship's combative nature and gritty aesthetic into a new product category.

4. Where to buy (type of retailer, specific retailer, on-line or in store)

5. How to pay

As mentioned previously, technology has forever changed the way we make our purchase decisions. Imagine that Mike and Linda have just bought their first home and are now looking to purchase a washer and dryer. They start their journey by visiting several big-box retailers' Web sites. They identify three models they are interested in at one store's site and save them to a wish list. Because space in their starter home is limited—and because is the washer and dryer constitute a relatively big purchase in their eyes—they decide to see the items in person before deciding on which to buy.

The couple finds the nearest physical outlet on the retailer's Web site, gets directions using Google Maps, and then drives over to view the desired products. Even before they walk through the doors, a transmitter mounted at the retailer's entrance identifies Mike and Linda and sends a text message to their smartphones welcoming them and providing personalized offers and recommendations based on their unique histories with the store. In this case, they receive links to the wish list they created as well as updated specs and prices for the washers and dryers they had shown interest in (captured in their click trails on the store's Web site). Additionally, they receive notification of a sale ("15 percent off selected brand appliances—today only!") that applies to two of the items they had added to their wish list.

When Mike and Linda tap on their wish list in the store's app, they are provided with a store map directing them to the appliances section and a "call button" to speak with an expert. They meet with the salesperson, ask some questions, take some measurements, and close in on a particular brand and model of washer and dryer. Because the store employs sophisticated tagging technologies, information about the washer and dryer are automatically synced with other apps on the couple's smartphones. They scan reviews using the *Consumer Reports* app, share the appliance specs to their messaging apps and send them to their parents for advice, ask Facebook friends to weigh in on the purchase, and compare the retailer's prices against others. Mike and Linda also take advantage of a virtual designer feature in the retailer's mobile app that, with the entry of just a few key pieces of information, allows them to preview how the washer and dryer might look in their home.

All of the input is favorable, so the couple decides to take advantage of the 15 percent offer and buy the appliances. They use Mike's smartwatch to authenticate

payment and walk out of the store with a date and time for delivery. A week later, on the designated day, they receive confirmation that a truck is in their area and that they will be texted within a half hour of arrival time ("No need to cancel other plans just to wait for your order to arrive!"). Three weeks after the appliances are delivered, the couple receives a message from the retailer with offers for other appliances and home-improvement services tailored toward first-year home owners…and the cycle begins again.[8]

PLANNED VERSUS IMPULSE PURCHASE The previous example represents a *fully planned purchase* based upon a lot of information. People rarely buy a new washer and dryer simply on impulse. Often, consumers will make a *partially planned purchase* when they know the product category they want to buy (shirts, pants, reading lamp, car floor mats) but wait until they get to the store or go online to choose a specific style or brand. Finally, there is the *unplanned purchase*, which people buy on impulse. Research has found that 75 percent of adults in the United States have made an impulse purchase. We often think of impulse purchasing as buying inexpensive items at the grocery store checkout. This, however, is not always the case. In the survey above, 16 percent said that they spent $500 to $1,000 on impulse purchases while 10 percent spent more than $1,000.[9] The purchase may be in a planned category (for example, soup), but decisions regarding the brand (Campbell's), package (can), and type (tomato) are all made on impulse. Researchers using in-store video cameras observed that when shoppers make impulse buys, they tend to touch and examine the item more, stand further from the shelf, and are less likely to refer to their shopping lists, coupons, or in-store circulars.[10]

 ## 6-3 POSTPURCHASE BEHAVIOR

When buying products, consumers expect certain outcomes from the purchase. How well these expectations are met determines whether the consumer is satisfied or dissatisfied with the purchase. For example, if a person bids on a used KitchenAid mixer from eBay and wins, she may have fairly low expectations regarding performance. If the mixer's performance turns out to be of superior quality, then the person's satisfaction will be high because her expectations were exceeded. Conversely, if the person bids on a new Kitchen Aid mixer expecting superior quality and performance, but the mixer breaks within one month, she will be very dissatisfied because her expectations were not met. Price often influences the level of expectations for a product or service.

For the marketer, an important element of any postpurchase evaluation is reducing any lingering doubts that the decision was sound. When people recognize inconsistency between their values or opinions and their behavior, they tend to feel an inner tension called **cognitive dissonance**. For example, suppose Angelika is looking to purchase an e-reader. After evaluating her options, she has decided to purchase an iPad, even though it is much more expensive than other dedicated e-readers. Prior to choosing the iPad, Angelika may experience inner tension or anxiety because she is worried that the current top-of-the-line technology, which costs much more than the middle-of-the-line technology, will be obsolete in a couple months. That feeling of dissonance arises as her worries over obsolescence battle her practical nature, which is focused on the lower cost of a Kindle Paperwhite and its adequate—but less fancy—technology.

Consumers try to reduce dissonance by justifying their decision. They may seek new information that reinforces positive ideas about the purchase, avoid information that contradicts their decision, or revoke the original decision by returning the product. In some instances, people deliberately seek contrary information in order to refute it and reduce dissonance. Dissatisfied customers sometimes rely on word of mouth to reduce cognitive dissonance by letting friends and family know they are displeased.

Marketing managers can help reduce dissonance through effective communication with purchasers. For example, a customer service manager may slip a note inside the package congratulating the buyer on making a wise decision. Postpurchase letters sent by manufacturers and dissonance-reducing statements in instruction booklets may help customers feel at ease with their purchase. Advertising that displays the product's superiority over competing brands or guarantees can also help relieve the possible dissonance of someone who has already bought the product. Apple's Genius Bar and customer service will ease cognitive dissonance for purchasers of an iPad because they know that the company is there to support them.

An excellent opportunity for a company to reduce (or if handled poorly,

increase) cognitive dissonance is when a customer has a question or complaint and tries to contact the company. Too many firms view their contact centers as cost centers and every contact as a problem to be minimized by making it as hard as possible to speak to a customer representative. Have you ever gone through four or five automated sequences, pushing a series of buttons, only to be told, "We are experiencing a higher than normal call volume and you can expect a lengthy delay." Not only does this raise cognitive dissonance, it can also destroy brand loyalty. Marketing-oriented companies perceive the contact center as an opportunity to engage customers and reinforce the brand promise. At these companies, there is no long menu of buttons to push. Instead, a service rep answers on the first or second ring and is empowered to solve customer problems. A recent study found that positive contact experiences resulted in consumers being 15 times more likely to say that they would definitely buy again than those with negative contact experiences. Of four different channels for a company to interact with its customers, telephone was most effective. Eighty-six percent of respondents said that speaking on the phone with a service rep enabled them to resolve their issues. Chat earned a 70 percent success rate, e-mail 44 percent, and Facebook 27 percent.[11]

TYPES OF CONSUMER BUYING DECISIONS AND CONSUMER INVOLVEMENT

All consumer buying decisions generally fall along a continuum of three broad categories: routine response behavior, limited decision making, and extensive decision making (see Exhibit 6.2). Goods and services in these three categories can best be described in terms of five factors:

- Level of consumer involvement
- Length of time to make a decision
- Cost of the good or service
- Degree of information search
- Number of alternatives considered

The level of consumer involvement is perhaps the most significant determinant in classifying buying decisions. **Involvement** is the amount of time and effort a buyer invests in the search, evaluation, and decision processes of consumer behavior.

cognitive dissonance inner tension that a consumer experiences after recognizing an inconsistency between behavior and values or opinions

involvement the amount of time and effort a buyer invests in the search, evaluation, and decision processes of consumer behavior

EXHIBIT 6.2 CONTINUUM OF CONSUMER BUYING DECISIONS

	Routine	Limited	Extensive
Involvement	Low	Low to moderate	High
Time	Short	Short to moderate	Long
Cost	Low	Low to moderate	High
Information Search	Internal only	Mostly internal	Internal and external
Number of Alternatives	One	Few	Many

Frequently purchased, low-cost goods and services are generally associated with **routine response behavior**. These goods and services can also be called *low-involvement products* because consumers spend little time on search and decision before making the purchase. Usually, buyers are familiar with several different brands in the product category but stick with one brand. For example, a person may routinely buy Tropicana orange juice. Consumers engaged in routine response behavior normally do not experience need recognition until they are exposed to advertising or see the product displayed on a store shelf. Consumers buy first and evaluate later, whereas the reverse is true for extensive decision making. A consumer who has previously purchased whitening toothpaste and was satisfied with it will probably walk to the toothpaste aisle and select that same brand without spending twenty minutes examining all other alternatives.

iStockphoto.com/Kickstand

Limited decision making typically occurs when a consumer has previous product experience but is unfamiliar with the current brands available. Limited decision making is also associated with lower levels of involvement (although higher than routine decisions) because consumers expend only moderate effort in searching for information or in considering various alternatives. For example, what happens if the consumer's usual brand of whitening toothpaste is sold out? Assuming that toothpaste is needed, the consumer will be forced to choose another brand. Before making a final decision, the consumer will likely evaluate several other brands based on their active ingredients, their promotional claims, and the consumer's prior experiences.

Consumers practice **extensive decision making** when buying an unfamiliar, expensive product or an infrequently bought item. This process is the most complex type of consumer buying decision and is associated with high involvement on the part of the consumer. This process resembles the model outlined in Exhibit 6.1. These consumers want to make the right decision, so they want to know as much as they can about the product category and available brands. People usually experience the most cognitive dissonance when buying high-involvement products. Buyers use several criteria for evaluating their options and spend much time seeking information. Buying a home or a car, for example, requires extensive decision making.

The type of decision making that consumers use to purchase a product does not necessarily remain constant. For instance, if a routinely purchased product no longer satisfies, consumers may practice limited or extensive decision making to switch to another brand. And people who first use extensive decision making may then use limited or routine decision making for future purchases. For example, when a family gets a new puppy, they will spend a lot of time and energy trying out different toys to determine which one the dog prefers. Once the new owners learn

routine response behavior
the type of decision making exhibited by consumers buying frequently purchased, low-cost goods and services; requires little search and decision time

limited decision making the type of decision making that requires a moderate amount of time for gathering information and deliberating about an unfamiliar brand in a familiar product category

extensive decision making
the most complex type of consumer decision making, used when buying an unfamiliar, expensive product or an infrequently bought item; requires use of several criteria for evaluating options and much time for seeking information

that the dog prefers a bone to a ball, however, the purchase no longer requires extensive evaluation and will become routine.

6-4a Factors Determining the Level of Consumer Involvement

The level of involvement in the purchase depends on the following factors:

- **Previous experience:** When consumers have had previous experience with a good or service, the level of involvement typically decreases. After repeated product trials, consumers learn to make quick choices. Because consumers are familiar with the product and know whether it will satisfy their needs, they become less involved in the purchase. For example, a consumer purchasing cereal has many brands to choose from—just think of any grocery store cereal aisle. If the consumer always buys the same brand because it satisfies his hunger, then he has a low level of involvement. When a consumer purchases a new category of cereal for the first time, however, it likely will be a much more involved purchase.

- **Interest:** Involvement is directly related to consumer interests, as in cars, music, movies, bicycling, or on-line games. Naturally, these areas of interest vary from one individual to another. A person highly involved in bike racing will be more interested in the type of bike she owns and will spend quite a bit of time evaluating different bikes. If a person wants a bike only for recreation, however, he may be fairly uninvolved in the purchase. He may just choose a bike from the most convenient location and in a reasonable price range.

- **Perceived risk of negative consequences:** As the perceived risk in purchasing a product increases, so does a consumer's level of involvement. The types of risks that concern consumers include financial risk, social risk, and psychological risk.

  - Financial risk is exposure to loss of wealth or purchasing power. Because high risk is associated with high-priced purchases, consumers tend to

become extremely involved. Therefore, price and involvement are usually directly related: As price increases, so does the level of involvement. For example, someone who is purchasing a new car for the first time (higher perceived risk) will spend a lot of time and effort making this purchase.

- Social risks occur when consumers buy products that can affect people's social opinions of them (for example, driving an old, beat-up car or wearing unstylish clothes).

- Psychological risks occur if consumers believe that making the wrong decision might cause some concern or anxiety. For example, some consumers feel guilty about eating foods that are not healthy, such as regular ice cream rather than fat-free frozen yogurt.

- **Social visibility:** Involvement also increases as the social visibility of a product increases. Products often on social display include clothing (especially designer labels), jewelry, cars, and furniture. All these items make a statement about the purchaser and, therefore, carry a social risk.

High involvement means that the consumer cares about a product category or a specific good or service. The product or service is relevant and important, and means something to the buyer. High involvement can

yellowdog/Cultura RM/Alamy

Purchase involvement depends on level of interest. If this shopper is looking to use a bike as her main mode of transportation, then she is highly involved in this purchase decision.

take a number of different forms. The most important types are discussed below:

- *Product involvement* means that a product category has high personal relevance. Product enthusiasts are consumers with high involvement in a product category. The fashion industry has a large segment of product enthusiasts. These people are seeking the latest fashion trends and want to wear the latest clothes.

- *Situational involvement* means that the circumstances of a purchase may temporarily transform a low-involvement decision into a high-involvement one. High involvement comes into play when the consumer perceives risk in a specific situation. For example, an individual might routinely buy low-priced brands of liquor and wine. When the boss visits, however, the consumer might make a high-involvement decision and buy more prestigious brands.

- *Shopping involvement* represents the personal relevance of the process of shopping. Some people enjoy the process of shopping even if they do not plan to buy anything. For others, shopping is an enjoyable social activity. Many consumers also engage in **showrooming**—examining merchandise in a physical retail location without purchasing it, and then shopping online for a better deal on the same item.

- *Enduring involvement* represents an ongoing interest in some product, such as kitchen gadgets, or activity, such as fishing. The consumer is always searching for opportunities to consume the product or participate in the activity. Enduring involvement typically gives personal gratification to consumers as they continue to learn about, shop for, and consume these goods and services. Therefore, there is often linkage between enduring involvement, shopping, and product involvement.

- *Emotional involvement* represents how emotional a consumer gets during some specific consumption activity. Emotional involvement is closely related to enduring involvement because the things that consumers care most about will eventually create high emotional involvement. Sports fans typify consumers with high emotional involvement.

6-4b Marketing Implications of Involvement

Marketing strategy varies according to the level of involvement associated with the product. For high-involvement product purchases, marketing managers

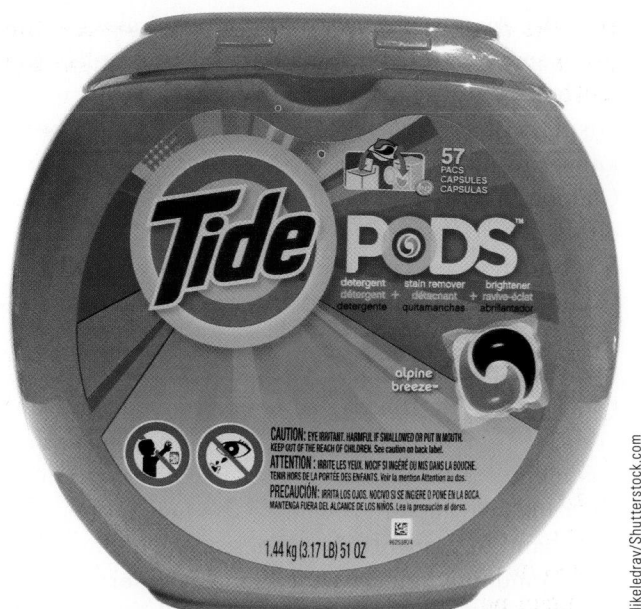

Mikeledray/Shutterstock.com

Tide uses bright, eye-catching packaging to draw customers to what is otherwise a low-involvement product.

have several objectives. First, promotion to the target market should be extensive and informative. A good ad gives consumers the information they need for making the purchase decision and specifies the benefits and unique advantages of owning the product. For example, Ford has a vehicle with many custom options that is marketed to small business owners. One example of a recent print ad shows how one entrepreneur customized his Ford Transit to help improve the efficiency of his home theater and electronics installation business. Ford highlights the fact that unique businesses need unique and customizable transportation. The Transit comes in three body lengths, each offering a unique volume and payload capacity. There are also three different roof heights to choose from, and of course, several different engines.

For low-involvement product purchases, consumers may not recognize their wants until they are in the store. Therefore, in-store promotion is an important tool when promoting low-involvement products. Marketing managers focus on package design so the product will be eye-catching and easily recognized on the shelf. Examples of products that take this approach are Campbell's soups, Tide detergent, Velveeta cheese, and Heinz

showrooming the practice of examining merchandise in a physical retail location without purchasing it, and then shopping online for a better deal on the same item

ketchup. In-store displays also stimulate sales of low-involvement products. A good display can explain the product's purpose and prompt recognition of a want. Displays of snack foods in supermarkets have been known to increase sales many times above normal. Coupons, cents-off deals, and two-for-one offers also effectively promote low-involvement items.

Linking a product to a higher-involvement issue is another tactic that marketing managers can use to increase the sales or positive publicity of a relatively low-involvement product. In 2015, McDonald's tweaked its long-running advertising campaign from "I'm Lovin' It," which focused on McDonald's various menu items, to "Choose Lovin'." The notion of choosing love and offering love is a much more emotional and high-involvement message. The fast food chain randomly selected a million customers and let them pay for their meals with acts of love. Participants could do things like hug family members or call their moms and tell them that they loved them to "choose lovin'."[12]

Researchers have found that another way to increase involvement is to offer products on a "limited availability" basis. McDonald's, for example, has regularly cycled its McRib sandwich on and off its menu for more than 30 years. Marketers can use several ways to trigger limited availability, including daily specials (for example special soup *du jour*), day of the week (for example, Sunday brunch), promotional periods

(for example, item availability for a limited time only), harvest time (for example, corn in the summer), and small production runs (for example, limited edition items). Limited availability creates a "get it now or never" mentality. Researchers have found that consuming such products leads to more consumer enjoyment than if the items were always available.[13]

It is important to understand that the consumer decision-making process does not occur in a vacuum. On the contrary, underlying cultural, social, individual, and psychological factors strongly influence the decision process. These factors have an effect from the time a consumer perceives a stimulus through postpurchase behavior. Cultural factors, which include culture and values, subculture, and social class, exert a broad influence over consumer decision making. Social factors sum up the social interactions between a consumer and influential groups of people, such as reference groups, opinion leaders, and family members. Individual factors, which include gender, age, family life cycle stage, personality, self-concept, and lifestyle, are unique to each individual and play a major role in the type of products and services consumers want. Psychological factors determine how consumers perceive and interact with their environments and influence the ultimate decisions consumers make. They include perception, motivation, and learning. Exhibit 6.3 summarizes these influences, and the following sections cover each in more detail.

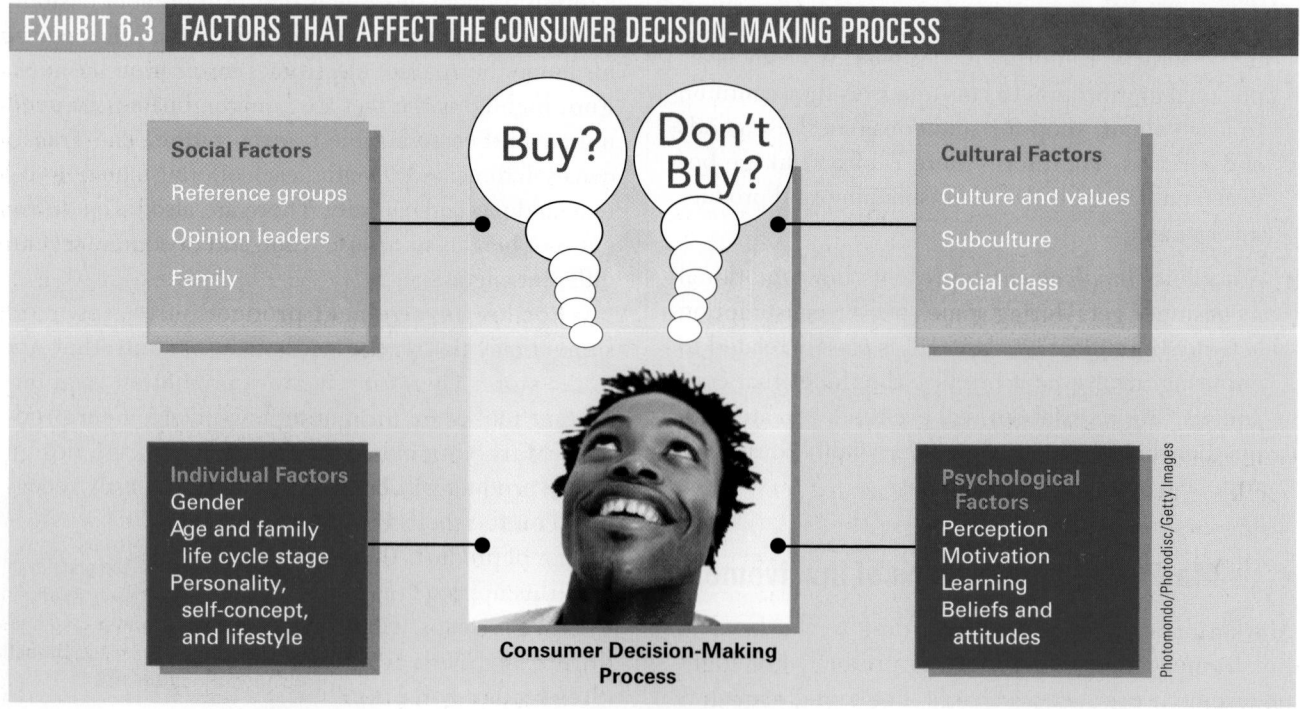

EXHIBIT 6.3 FACTORS THAT AFFECT THE CONSUMER DECISION-MAKING PROCESS

Social Factors
Reference groups
Opinion leaders
Family

Cultural Factors
Culture and values
Subculture
Social class

Buy? Don't Buy?

Individual Factors
Gender
Age and family life cycle stage
Personality, self-concept, and lifestyle

Psychological Factors
Perception
Motivation
Learning
Beliefs and attitudes

Consumer Decision-Making Process

Photomondo/Photodisc/Getty Images

6-5 CULTURAL INFLUENCES ON CONSUMER BUYING DECISIONS

Of all the factors that affect consumer decision making, cultural factors exert the broadest and deepest influence. Marketers must understand the way people's culture and its accompanying values, as well as their subculture and social class, influence their buying behavior.

6-5a Culture and Values

Culture is the set of values, norms, attitudes, and other meaningful symbols that shape human behavior and the artifacts, or products, of that behavior as they are transmitted from one generation to the next. It is the essential character of a society that distinguishes it from other cultural groups. The underlying elements of every culture are the values, language, myths, customs, rituals, and laws that guide the behavior of the people.

Culture is pervasive. Cultural values and influences are the ocean in which individuals swim, and yet most are completely unaware that it is there. What people eat, how they dress, what they think and feel, and what language they speak are all dimensions of culture. Culture encompasses all the things consumers do without conscious choice because their culture's values, customs, and rituals are ingrained in their daily habits.

Culture is functional. Human interaction creates values and prescribes acceptable behavior for each culture. By establishing common expectations, culture gives order to society. Sometimes these expectations are enacted into laws. For example, drivers in our culture must stop at a red light. Other times these expectations are taken for granted: grocery stores and hospitals are open 24 hours, whereas banks are open only during "bankers' hours," typically nine in the morning until five in the afternoon.

Culture is learned. Consumers are not born knowing the values and norms of their society. Instead, they must learn what is acceptable from family and friends. Children learn the values that will govern their behavior from parents, teachers, and peers. As members of our society, they learn to shake hands when they greet someone, to drive on the right-hand side of the road, and to eat pizza and drink Coca-Cola.

Culture is dynamic. It adapts to changing needs and an evolving environment. The rapid growth of technology in today's world has accelerated the rate of cultural change. Our culture is beginning to tell us when it is okay to send a text message and when it is considered impolite. Assume that you are on a first date with someone in a nice, romantic restaurant and your date is talking to you about his or her favorite things to do. Pulling out your smartphone to check a text will probably lead to a very short date. Cultural norms will continue to evolve because of our need for social patterns that solve problems.

The most defining element of a culture is its values. Recall that "value" can refer to an enduring belief shared by a society that a specific mode of conduct is personally or socially preferable to another mode of conduct. People's value systems have a great effect on their consumer behavior. Consumers with similar value systems tend to react alike to prices and other marketing-related inducements. Values also correspond to consumption patterns. For example, Americans place a high value on convenience. This value has created lucrative markets for products such as breakfast bars, energy bars, and nutrition bars that allow consumers to eat on the go. Values can also influence consumers' television viewing habits or the magazines they read. For instance, people who strongly object to violence avoid crime shows and vegetarians avoid cooking magazines that feature numerous meat-based recipes.

6-5b Subculture

A culture can be divided into subcultures on the basis of demographic characteristics, geographic regions, national and ethnic background, political beliefs, and religious beliefs. A **subculture** is a homogeneous group of people who share elements of the overall culture as well as cultural elements unique to their own group. Within subcultures, people's attitudes, values, and purchase decisions are even more similar than they are within the broader culture. Subcultural differences may result in considerable variation within a culture in what, how, when, and where people buy goods and services.

Once marketers identify subcultures, they can design special marketing to serve their needs. The United States' growing Hispanic

> **culture** the set of values, norms, attitudes, and other meaningful symbols that shape human behavior and the artifacts, or products, of that behavior as they are transmitted from one generation to the next
>
> **subculture** a homogeneous group of people who share elements of the overall culture as well as unique elements of their own group

Bloody/Shutterstock.com

The popularity of biker events has created an opportunity for fans of Harley-Davidson to get together and create their own subculture.

SandiMako/Shutterstock.com

population has made South and Central American subcultures a prime focus for many companies, for example. Recall that marketing to Hispanics was discussed in Chapter 4.

In the United States alone, countless subcultures can be identified. Many are concentrated geographically. People who belong to the Church of Jesus Christ of Latter-Day Saints, for example, are clustered mainly in Utah; Cajuns are located in the bayou regions of southern Louisiana. Many Hispanics live in states bordering Mexico, whereas the majority of Chinese, Japanese, and Korean Americans are found on the West Coast. Other subcultures are geographically dispersed. Computer hackers, people who are hearing or visually impaired, Harley-Davidson bikers, military families, and university professors may be found throughout the country. Yet they have identifiable attitudes, values, and needs that distinguish them from the larger culture.

Today, America has a rapidly growing number of binational households. In such households, one spouse was born and raised in the United States while the other was originally from another country. This often creates cultural complexity in family purchase decision making. Researchers have found that the partner with the greatest cultural competence (knowledge of the customs of the country of residence) plays the family role of cultural bridge,

social class a group of people in a society who are considered nearly equal in status or community esteem, who regularly socialize among themselves both formally and informally, and who share behavioral norms

arbitrator, and translator. This spouse compensates for her relative advantage in purchase decision making by giving up control in other decisions. Therefore, the immigrant spouse may gain greater influence in decisions relating to vacations, education, and food.[14]

6-5c Social Class

The United States, like other societies, has a social class system. A **social class** is a group of people who are considered nearly equal in status or community esteem, who regularly socialize among themselves both formally and informally, and who share behavioral norms.

A number of techniques have been used to measure social class, and a number of criteria have been used to define it. One view of contemporary U.S. status structure is shown in Exhibit 6.4.

As you can see from Exhibit 6.4, the upper and upper middle classes comprise the small segment of affluent and wealthy Americans. In terms of consumer buying patterns, the affluent are more likely to own their own homes and purchase new cars and trucks and are less likely to smoke. The very rich flex their financial muscles by spending more on vacation homes, jewelry, vacations and cruises, and housekeeping and gardening services. The most affluent consumers are more likely to attend art auctions and galleries, dance performances, operas, the theater, museums, concerts, and sporting events. What types of things do the wealthiest of the wealthy buy? The most expensive new car in the world is the Lamborghini Veneno. It goes from 0 to 60 miles per hour in 2.8 seconds and has a top speed of 221 mph. Only three of these cars are made a year at a price of $4,500,000 each.[15] Unfortunately, if you want one, you must get on a waiting list.

The majority of Americans today define themselves as middle class, regardless of their actual income or educational attainment. This phenomenon most likely occurs because working-class Americans tend to aspire to the middle-class lifestyle, while some of those who do achieve some affluence call themselves middle-class as a matter of principle.

The working class is a distinct subset of the middle class. Interest in organized labor is one of the most common attributes among the working class.

EXHIBIT 6.4 U.S. SOCIAL CLASSES

Upper Classes		
Capitalist class	1%	People whose investment decisions shape the national economy; income mostly from assets, earned or inherited; university connections
Upper middle class	14%	Upper-level managers, professionals, owners of medium-sized businesses; well-to-do, stay-at-home homemakers who decline occupational work by choice; college educated; family income well above national average
Middle Classes		
Middle class	33%	Middle-level white-collar, top-level blue-collar; education past high school typical; income somewhat above national average; loss of manufacturing jobs has reduced the population of this class
Working class	32%	Middle-level blue-collar, lower-level white-collar; income below national average; largely working in skilled or semi-skilled service jobs
Lower Classes		
Working poor	11–12%	Low-paid service workers and operatives; some high school education; below mainstream in living standard; crime and hunger are daily threats
Underclass	8–9%	People who are not regularly employed and who depend primarily on the welfare system for sustenance; little schooling; living standard below poverty line

This group often rates job security as the most important reason for taking a job. The working-class person depends heavily on relatives and the community for economic and emotional support.

Lifestyle distinctions between the social classes are greater than the distinctions within a given class. The most significant difference between the classes occurs between the middle and lower classes, where there is a major shift in lifestyles. Members of the lower class have annual incomes at or below the poverty level—$11,770 for individuals and $24,250 for families of four (as defined by the federal government).[16]

Social class is typically measured as a combination of occupation, income, education, wealth, and other variables. For instance, affluent upper-class consumers are more likely to be salaried executives or self-employed professionals with at least an undergraduate degree. Working-class or middle-class consumers are more likely to be hourly service workers or blue-collar employees with only a high school education. Educational attainment, however, seems to be the most reliable indicator of a person's social and economic status. Those with college degrees or graduate degrees are more likely to fall into the upper classes, while those with some college experience fall closest to traditional concepts of the middle class.

Marketers are interested in social class for two main reasons. First, social class often indicates which medium to use for promotion. Suppose an insurance company seeks to sell its policies to middle-class families. It might advertise during the local evening news because middle-class families tend to watch more television than other classes do. If the company wanted to sell more policies to upscale individuals, it might place an ad in a business publication like the *Wall Street Journal*. The Internet,

Greta Gabaglio/Shutterstock.com

Knowing what products appeal to which social classes can help mareters determine where to best distribute their products.

long the domain of more educated and affluent families, has become an increasingly important advertising outlet for advertisers hoping to reach blue-collar workers and homemakers.

Second, knowing what products appeal to which social classes can help marketers determine where to best distribute their products. Affluent Americans, one-fifth of the U.S. population, have changed their buying habits since the Great Recession ended. They are now willing to spend more of their discretionary income on one-of-a-kind items. Full-priced and upscale retailers such as Neiman Marcus have experienced greater sales gains than have discount chains. Because many lower-income consumers are still struggling to recover from job loss, retailers such as Walmart are selling smaller packages of items because customers do not have enough cash to buy more standard-size products.

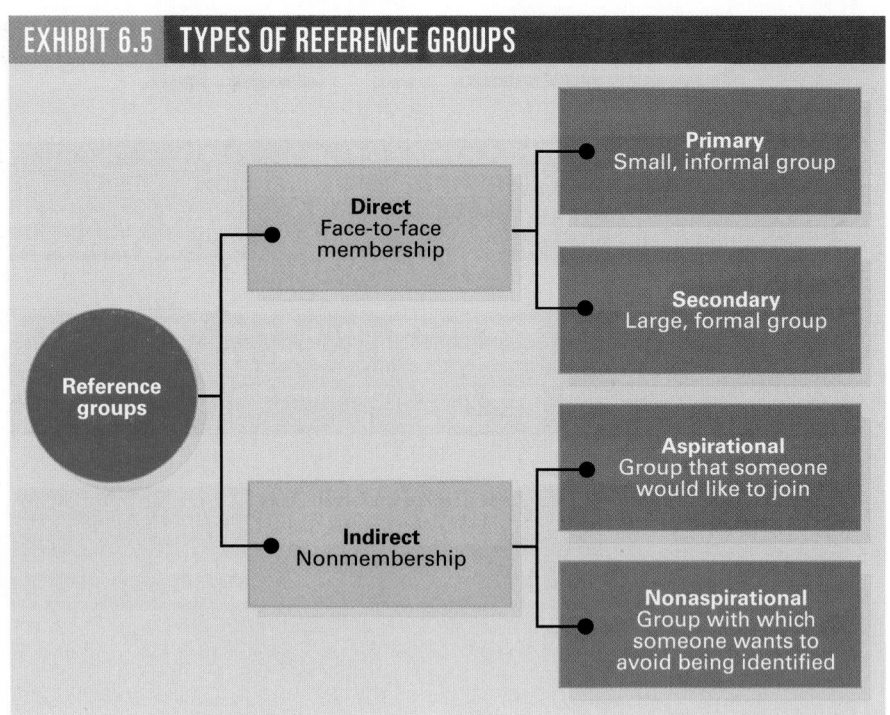

EXHIBIT 6.5 TYPES OF REFERENCE GROUPS

6-6 SOCIAL INFLUENCES ON CONSUMER BUYING DECISIONS

Many consumers seek out the opinions of others to reduce their search and evaluation effort or uncertainty, especially as the perceived risk of the decision increases. Consumers may also seek out others' opinions for guidance on new products or services, products with image-related attributes, or products for which attribute information is lacking or uninformative. Specifically, consumers interact socially with reference groups, opinion leaders, and family members to obtain product information and decision approval.

reference group all of the formal and informal groups in society that influence an individual's purchasing behavior

primary membership group a reference group with which people interact regularly in an informal, face-to-face manner, such as family, friends, and coworkers

secondary membership group a reference group with which people associate less consistently and more formally than a primary membership group, such as a club, professional group, or religious group

aspirational reference group a group that someone would like to join

norm a value or attitude deemed acceptable by a group

6-6a Reference Groups

People interact with many reference groups. A **reference group** consists of all the formal and informal groups that influence the buying behavior of an individual. Consumers may use products or brands to identify with or become a member of a group. They learn from observing how members of their reference groups consume, and they use the same criteria to make their own consumer decisions.

Reference groups can be categorized very broadly as either direct or indirect (see Exhibit 6.5). Direct reference groups are membership groups that touch people's lives directly. They can be either primary or secondary. A **primary membership group** includes all groups with which people interact regularly in an informal manner, such as family, friends, members of social media, and coworkers. Today, they may also communicate by e-mail, text messages, Facebook, Skype, or other social media as well as face-to-face. In contrast, people associate with a **secondary membership group** less consistently and more formally. These groups might include clubs, professional groups, and religious groups.

Consumers also are influenced by many indirect, nonmembership reference groups to which they do not belong. An **aspirational reference group** is a group a person would like to join. To join an aspirational group, a person must at least conform to the norms of that group. (A **norm** consists of the values and attitudes deemed acceptable by the group.) Thus, a person who

Members of the Hell's Angels biker gang protest in Oslo, Norway, against police bias towards motorcycle gangs.

Uncleru/Shutterstock.com

wants to be elected to public office may begin to dress more conservatively, as other politicians do. He or she may go to many of the restaurants and social engagements that city and business leaders attend and try to play a role that is acceptable to voters and other influential people.

Nonaspirational reference groups, or dissociative groups, influence our behavior when we try to maintain distance from them. A consumer may avoid buying some types of clothing or cars, going to certain restaurants or stores, or even buying a home in a certain neighborhood to avoid being associated with a particular group. For middle- and upper-middle-class

Professional athletes serve as opinion leaders when they choose a specific shoe they feel helps them perform at a high level.

Thearon W. Henderson/Getty Images

professionals who take an interest in Harley-Davidson motorcycles, biker gangs serve as both an aspirational and a nonaspirational reference group. Though the professionals (derisively called RUBS—rich urban bikers—by hardcore Harley enthusiasts) aspire to the freedom, community, and tough posturing of biker gangs, they do not aspire to the perpetual life on the road, crime, or violence of gangs. Thus, a professional may buy a Harley because of the gangs, but he may intentionally buy a specific model not typically associated with those gangs.

Reference groups are particularly powerful in influencing the clothes people wear, the cars they drive, the electronics they use, the activities they participate in, the foods they eat, and the luxury goods they purchase. In short, the activities, values, and goals of reference groups directly influence consumer behavior. For marketers, reference groups have three important implications: (1) They serve as information sources and influence perceptions; (2) they affect an individual's aspiration levels; and (3) their norms either constrain or stimulate consumer behavior.

6-6b Opinion Leaders

Reference groups and social media groups (for example, your friends on Facebook) frequently include individuals known as group leaders, or **opinion leaders**—persons who influence others. Obviously, it is important for marketing managers to persuade such people to purchase their goods or services. They are often the most influential, informed, plugged-in, and vocal members of society. Technology companies have found that teenagers, because of their willingness to experiment, are key opinion leaders for the success of new technologies.

Opinion leadership is a casual phenomenon and is usually inconspicuous, so locating opinion leaders offline can be a challenge. An opinion leader in one field, such as cooking, may not be an opinion leader in another, such as sports. In fact, it is rare to find an opinion leader who spans multiple diverse domains. Thus, marketers often try to create opinion leaders. They may use high school cheerleaders to

nonaspirational reference group a group with which an individual does not want to associate

opinion leader an individual who influences the opinions of others

model new fall fashions or civic leaders to promote insurance, new cars, and other merchandise. On a national level, companies sometimes use movie stars, sports figures, and other celebrities to promote products, hoping they are appropriate opinion leaders. The effectiveness of celebrity endorsements varies, though, depending largely on how credible and attractive the spokesperson is and how familiar people are with him or her. Endorsements are most likely to succeed if a reasonable association between the spokesperson and the product can be established.

Increasingly, marketers are looking to social media to find opinion leaders, but the sheer volume of posts and platforms makes determining true opinion leaders challenging. So, marketers are focusing their attention on platforms such as Facebook, Pinterest, and Tumblr because those sites better identify the social trends that are shaping consumer behavior. With their unprecedented ability to network and communicate with each other, people often rely on each other's opinions more than marketing messages when making purchase decisions. And social media are becoming a key way that people communicate their opinions.

Social media have made identification of opinion leaders easier than ever before. Klout, for example, collects data from 13 social networks and search data from Bing and Google to measure a person's influence. The firm also looks at offline data such as how often the individual is mentioned in traditional media like magazines and newspapers. Klout then tabulates a score for each person ranging from 1 to 100.

Klout's Perks program has expanded from offering certain opinion leaders coupons and product samples to helping brands send out invitations for product launches, promotional events, and concerts. The company recently launched VIP Perks, a program that tracks opinion leaders' mobile devices to tell when they enter a store or restaurant. Marketers have used the program to offer social influencers with high Klout scores seat upgrades at Cirque Du Soleil shows and access to VIP airport lounges.[17] Research has found that when social media influencers purchase a new product, they tend to share this information right away with their social networks.[18]

6-6c Family

The family is the most important social institution for many consumers, strongly influencing values, attitudes, self-concept, and buying behavior. For example, a family that strongly values good health will have a

socialization process how cultural values and norms are passed down to children

grocery list distinctly different from that of a family that views every dinner as a gourmet event. Moreover, the family is responsible for the **socialization process**, the passing down of cultural values and norms to children. Children learn by observing their parents' consumption patterns, so they tend to shop in similar patterns.

Decision-making roles among family members tend to vary significantly, depending on the type of item purchased. Family members assume a variety of roles in the purchase process. *Initiators* suggest, initiate, or plant the seed for the purchase process. The initiator can be any member of the family. For example, Sister might initiate the product search by asking for a new bicycle as a birthday present. *Influencers* are members of the family whose opinions are valued. In our example, Mom might function as a price-range watchdog, an influencer whose main role is to veto or approve price ranges. Brother may give his opinion on certain makes of bicycles. The *decision maker* is the family member who actually makes the decision to buy or not to buy. For example, Dad or Mom is likely to choose the final brand and model of bicycle to

Image Courtesy of The Advertising Archives

By working with children to develop a drink they like, Innocent Smoothies for kids can advertise kid-friendly flavors with healthy benefits, satisfying moms and kids.

buy after seeking further information from Sister about cosmetic features such as color and then imposing additional criteria of his or her own, such as durability and safety. The *purchaser* (probably Dad or Mom) is the one who actually exchanges money for the product. Finally, the *consumer* is the actual user—in this case, Sister.

Marketers should consider family purchase situations along with the distribution of consumer and decision-maker roles among family members. Ordinary marketing views the individual as both decision maker and consumer. Family marketing adds several other possibilities: sometimes more than one family member or all family members are involved in the decision, sometimes only children are involved in the decision, sometimes more than one consumer is involved, and sometimes the decision maker and the consumer are different people. In most households, when parental joint decisions are being made, spouses consider their partner's needs and perceptions to maintain decision fairness and harmony. This tends to minimize family conflict. When couples agree to narrow down their options before making a purchase, they are more likely to be satisfied with the eventual outcome and less likely to feel regret.

6-6d Individual Differences in Susceptibility to Social Influences

Social influence plays an important role in consumer behavior, but not all persons are equally influenced in their purchase decisions. Some have a strong need to build the images others have of them by buying products used by other members of their reference groups. Seeking approval of others through the "correct" product ownership is very important to these consumers. This is particularly true for conspicuous items (those that others can easily see) such as clothes, jewelry, cars, and even mobile devices. These individuals have a strong desire to avoid negative impressions in public settings. For example, wearing the wrong bather suit at the university swimming pool would be very distressing to this type of consumer.

Consumers differ in their feelings of connectedness to other consumers. A consumer with a **separated self-schema** perceives himself as distinct and separate from others. A person with a **connected self-schema** sees himself as an integral part of a group. Research has found that individuals who feel connected respond more favorably to advertisements that promote group belonging and cohesion.

The influence of other people on how a consumer behaves is strongest when that consumer knows or feels

that she is being watched. Researchers have found this to be especially true when individuals are consuming or buying personal products. Some people will not buy memberships to athletic clubs because they don't want to work out with (or even around) a group of people. They fear how they may appear to others.[19]

 ## 6-7 INDIVIDUAL INFLUENCES ON CONSUMER BUYING DECISIONS

While individuality impacts a person's susceptibility to social influences, factors such as gender, age, life cycle stage, personality, self-concept, and lifestyle also play important roles in consumer decision making. Individual characteristics are generally stable over the course of one's life. For instance, most people do not change their gender, and the act of changing personality or lifestyle requires a complete reorientation of one's life. In the case of age and life cycle stage, these changes occur gradually over time.

6-7a Gender

Physiological differences between men and women result in many different needs, such as with health and beauty products. Just as important are the distinct cultural, social, and economic roles played by men and women and the effects that these have on their decision-making processes. A recent survey found that 52 percent of women have purchased a product based upon a marketer's portrayal of women.[20] Messages and videos for companies such as Nike, Always, and Under Armour were perceived as very positive. The Dove "Real Beauty" campaign was named the number one ad of the 21st century by *Advertising Age*. Under Armour's "I Will What I Want" ad also fared well for its portrayal of women pushing back against the idea of perfection and simply embracing themselves (see an example at www .youtube.com/watch?v=ZY0cdXr_1MA).

Trends in gender marketing are influenced by the changing roles of men and women in society. For example, men used to rely on the women in their lives to shop for them. Today, however, more men are shopping for themselves. More than seventy percent of men shop online and about 48 percent shop

> **separated self-schema** a perspective whereby a consumer sees himself or herself as distinct and separate from others
>
> **connected self-schema** a perspective whereby a consumer sees himself or herself as an integral part of a group

from mobile devices. When doing so, men use smartphones twice as often as they use tablets. Men are price-conscious, often scanning QR codes rather than typing in URLs to retrieve promotional materials, coupons, and product information. In fact, a Harris Interactive poll found that, "men have become the chief coupon-cutters of the mobile era."[21]

6-7b Age and Family Life Cycle Stage

A consumer's age and family life cycle stage can have a significant impact on his or her behavior. How old a consumer is generally indicates what products he or she may be interested in purchasing. Consumer tastes in food, clothing, cars, furniture, and recreation are often age related.

Related to a person's age is his or her place in the family life cycle. As Chapter 8 explains in more detail, the *family life cycle* is an orderly series of stages through which consumers' attitudes and behavioral tendencies evolve through maturity, experience, and changing income and status. Marketers often define their target markets in terms of family life cycle, such as "young singles," "young married couples with children," and "middle-aged married couples without children." For instance, young singles spend more than average on alcoholic beverages, education, and entertainment. New parents typically increase their spending on health care, clothing, housing, and food and decrease their spending on alcohol, education, and transportation. Households with older children spend more on food, entertainment, personal care products, and education, as well as cars and gasoline. After their children leave home, spending by older couples on vehicles, women's clothing, and health care typically increases. For instance, the presence of children in the home is the most significant determinant of the type of vehicle that's driven off the new car lot. Parents are the ultimate need-driven car consumers, requiring larger cars and trucks to haul their children and all their belongings. It comes as no surprise, then, that for all households with children, SUVs rank either first or second among new-vehicle purchases, followed by minivans.

NONTRADITIONAL LIFE CYCLES Marketers should also be aware of the many nontraditional life cycle paths that are common today and provide insights into the needs and wants of such consumers as

divorced parents, lifelong singles, and childless couples. Three decades ago, married couples with children under the age of 18 accounted for about half of U.S. households. Today, such families make up only 23 percent of all households, while people living alone or with nonfamily members represent more than thirty percent. Furthermore, according to the U.S. Census Bureau, the number of single-mother households grew by 25 percent over the last decade. The shift toward more single-parent households is part of a broader societal change that has put more women on the career track.

SINGLE PARENTS Careers often create a *poverty of time* for single parents. To cope with the dual demands of a career and raising children, single parents are always on the lookout for time saving products like quick-preparation foods and no-iron clothing. Rightly so, more and more marketers are catering to the single parent market. eTargetMedia maintains a list of over 9,500,000 active single parents that it rents out for both e-mail and postal advertising campaigns. The firm says that the list is ideal for offers pertaining to education, childcare, insurance, photo sharing, parenting magazines and books, camps, and children's recreation.[22]

LIFE EVENTS Another way to look at the life cycle is to look at major events in one's life over time. Life-changing events can occur at any time. A few examples are death of a spouse, moving, birth or adoption of a child, retirement, job loss, divorce, and marriage. Typically, such events are quite stressful, and consumers will often take steps to minimize that stress. Many times, life-changing events will mean new consumption patterns. For example, a recently divorced person may try to improve his or her appearance by joining a health club and dieting. Someone moving to a different city will need a new dentist, grocery store, auto service center, and doctor, among other things. Marketers realize that life events often mean a chance to gain a new customer. The Welcome Wagon offers free gifts and services for area newcomers. Lowe's sends out a discount coupon to those moving to a new community. And when you put your home on the market, you will quickly start receiving flyers from moving companies promising a great price on moving your household goods.

Gelpi JM/Shutterstock.com

6-7c Personality, Self-Concept, and Lifestyle

Each consumer has a unique personality. **Personality** is a broad concept that can be thought of as a way of organizing and grouping how an individual typically reacts to situations. Thus, personality combines psychological makeup and environmental forces. It includes people's underlying dispositions, especially their most dominant characteristics. Although personality is one of the least useful concepts in the study of consumer behavior, some marketers believe personality influences the types and brands of products purchased. For instance, the type of car, clothes, or jewelry a consumer buys may reflect one or more personality traits.

Eurobanks/iStock/Thinkstock

Self-concept, or self-perception, is how consumers perceive themselves. Self-concept includes attitudes, perceptions, beliefs, and self-evaluations. Although self-concept may change, the change is often gradual. Through self-concept, people define their identity, which in turn provides for consistent and coherent behavior.

Self-concept combines the **ideal self-image** (the way an individual would like to be perceived) and the **real self-image** (how an individual actually perceives himself or herself). Generally, we try to raise our real self-image toward our ideal (or at least narrow the gap). Consumers seldom buy products that jeopardize their self-image. For example, someone who sees herself as a trendsetter would not buy clothing that does not project a contemporary image.

Human behavior depends largely on self-concept. Because consumers want to protect their identity as individuals, the products they buy, the stores they patronize, and the credit cards they carry support their self-image. No other product quite reflects a person's self-image as much as the car he or she drives. For example, many young consumers do not like family sedans like the Honda Accord or Toyota Camry and say they would buy one for their mom but not for themselves. Likewise, younger parents may avoid purchasing minivans because they do not want to sacrifice the youthful image they have of themselves just because they have new responsibilities. To combat decreasing sales, marketers of the Nissan Quest minivan decided to reposition it as something other than a "mom mobile" or "soccer mom car." They chose the ad copy "Passion built it. Passion will fill it up," followed by "What if we made a minivan that changed the way people think of minivans?"

By influencing the degree to which consumers perceive a good or service to be self-relevant, marketers can affect consumers' motivation to learn about, shop for, and buy a certain brand. Marketers also consider self-concept important because it helps explain the relationship between individuals' perceptions of themselves and their consumer behavior.

Many companies now use psychographics to better understand their market segments. For many years, marketers selling products to mothers conveniently assumed that all moms were fairly homogeneous and concerned about the same things—the health and well-being of their children—and that they could all be reached with a similar message. But recent lifestyle research has shown that there are traditional, blended, and nontraditional moms, and companies like Procter & Gamble and Pillsbury are using strategies to reach these different types of mothers. Psychographics is also effective with other market segments. Psychographics and lifestyle segmentation are discussed in more detail in Chapter 8.

6-8 PSYCHOLOGICAL INFLUENCES ON CONSUMER BUYING DECISIONS

An individual's buying decisions are further influenced by psychological factors: perception, motivation, and learning. These factors are what consumers use to interact with their world. They are the tools consumers use to recognize their feelings, gather and analyze information, formulate thoughts and opinions, and take action. Unlike the other three influences on consumer behavior, psychological influences can be affected by a person's environment because they are

> **personality** a way of organizing and grouping the consistencies of an individual's reactions to situations
>
> **self-concept** how consumers perceive themselves in terms of attitudes, perceptions, beliefs, and self-evaluations
>
> **ideal self-image** the way an individual would like to be perceived
>
> **real self-image** the way an individual actually perceives himself or herself

applied on specific occasions. For example, you will perceive different stimuli and process these stimuli in different ways depending on whether you are sitting in class concentrating on the instructor, sitting outside of class talking to friends, or sitting in your dorm room streaming a video.

6-8a Perception

The world is full of stimuli. A stimulus is any unit of input affecting one or more of the five senses: sight, smell, taste, touch, and hearing. The process by which we select, organize, and interpret these stimuli into a meaningful and coherent picture is called **perception**. In essence, perception is how we see the world around us. We act based upon perceptions that may or may not reflect reality. Suppose you are driving to the grocery and you see a house with smoke pouring from the roof. Your perception is that the house is on fire, so you quickly stop to warn any occupants and to call 911. As you approach the house, you hear laughter coming from the back yard. As you peek around the corner, you see a family burning a big pile of leaves and the wind carrying the smoke over the roof. There is no house fire. When you get to the grocery, you see a big, beautiful ripe pineapple and immediately put it in your cart. When you get home, you cut into the pineapple—only to find that it has a rotten core and is inedible. In both cases, you acted based upon perceptions that did not reflect reality.

People cannot perceive every stimulus in their environment. Therefore, they use **selective exposure** to decide which stimuli to notice and which to ignore. A typical consumer is exposed to nearly 3,000 advertising messages a day but notices only between 11 and 20.

The familiarity of an object, contrast, movement, intensity (such as increased volume), and smell are cues that influence perception. Consumers use these cues to identify and define products and brands. Double Tree hotels always have fresh chocolate chip cookies at the reception desk and the entire area smells like just-baked cookies. For most travelers, this cues feelings of warmth and comfort. Cutting-edge consumer research has found that a cluttered, chaotic environment results in consumers spending more. Why does this occur? The perception of a cluttered environment impairs self-control. Disorganized surroundings threaten one's sense of personal control, which in turn taxes one's self-regulatory abilities.[23]

The shape of a product's packaging, such as Coca-Cola's signature contour bottle, can influence perception. Color is another cue, and it plays a key role in consumers' perceptions. Packaged foods manufacturers use color to trigger unconscious associations for grocery shoppers who typically make their shopping decisions in the blink of an eye. Think of the red and white Campbell's soup can and the green and white Green Giant frozen vegetable box, for example.

Two other concepts closely related to selective exposure are selective distortion and selective retention. **Selective distortion** occurs when consumers change or distort information that conflicts with their feelings or beliefs. For example, suppose a college student buys a Dell tablet. After the purchase, if the student gets new information about an alternative brand, such as an Asus Transformer, he or she may distort the information to make it more consistent with the prior view that the Dell is just as good as the Transformer, if not better. Business travelers who are Executive Platinum frequent flyers on American Airlines may distort or discount information about the quality of United Airlines' business class service. The frequent flyer may think to herself, "Yes, the service is OK but the seats are uncomfortable and the planes are always late."

Selective retention is remembering only information that supports personal feelings or beliefs. The consumer forgets all information that may be inconsistent. After reading a pamphlet that contradicts one's political beliefs, for instance, a person may forget many of the points outlined in it. Similarly, consumers may see a news report on suspected illegal practices by their favorite retail store but soon forget the reason the store was featured on the news.

Which stimuli will be perceived often depends on the individual. People can be exposed to the same stimuli under identical conditions but perceive them very differently. For example, two people viewing a television commercial may have different interpretations of the advertising message. One person may be thoroughly engrossed by the message and become highly motivated to buy the product. Thirty seconds after the ad ends, the second person may not be able to recall the content of the message or even the product advertised.

perception the process by which people select, organize, and interpret stimuli into a meaningful and coherent picture

selective exposure a process whereby a consumer notices certain stimuli and ignores others

selective distortion a process whereby a consumer changes or distorts information that conflicts with his or her feelings or beliefs

selective retention a process whereby a consumer remembers only that information that supports his or her personal beliefs

MARKETING IMPLICATIONS OF PERCEPTION

Marketers must recognize the importance of cues, or signals, in consumers' perception of products. Marketing managers first identify the important attributes, such as price or quality, that the targeted consumers want in a product and then design signals to communicate these attributes. For example, consumers will pay more for candy in expensive-looking foil packages. But shiny labels on wine bottles signify less expensive wines; dull labels indicate more expensive wines. Marketers also often use price as a signal to consumers that the product is of higher quality than competing products. Of course, brand names send signals to consumers. The brand names of Close-Up toothpaste, DieHard batteries, and Caress moisturizing soap, for example, identify important product qualities. Names chosen for search engines and sites on the Internet, such as Yahoo!, Amazon, and Bing, are intended to convey excitement and intensity and vastness.

Consumers also associate quality and reliability with certain brand names. Companies watch their brand identity closely, in large part because a strong link has been established between perceived brand value and customer loyalty. Brand names that consistently enjoy high perceived value from consumers include Google, Disney, National Geographic, Mercedes-Benz, and Fisher-Price. Naming a product after a place can also add perceived value by association. Brand names using the words Santa Fe, Dakota, or Texas convey a sense of openness, freedom, and youth, but products named after other locations might conjure up images of pollution and crime. Marketing managers are also interested in the *threshold level of perception*, the minimum difference in a stimulus that the consumer will notice. This concept is sometimes referred to as the "just-noticeable difference." For example, how much would Apple have to drop the price of its 15-inch MacBook Pro with Retina display before consumers perceived it as a bargain—$100? $300? $500? Alternatively, how much could Hershey shrink its milk chocolate bar before consumers noticed that it was smaller, but selling for the same price?

Besides changing such stimuli as price, package size, and volume, marketers can change the product or attempt to reposition its image. But marketers must be careful when adding features. How many new services will discounter Target need to add before consumers perceive it as a full-service department store? How many sporty features will General Motors have to add to

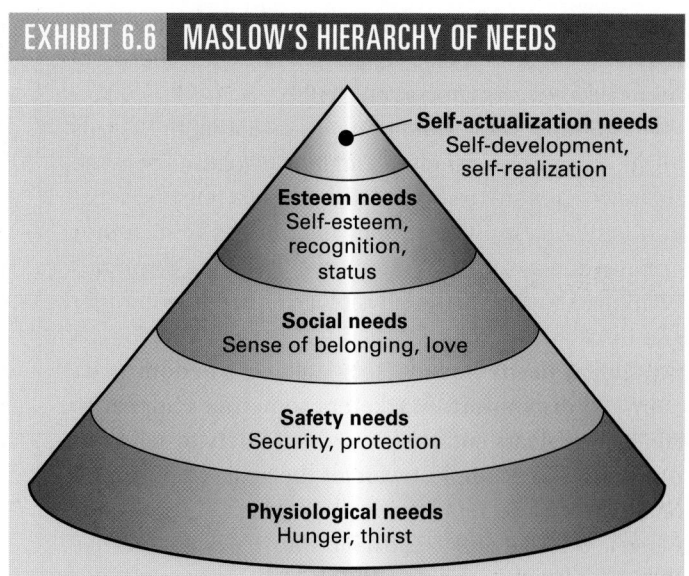

EXHIBIT 6.6 | MASLOW'S HIERARCHY OF NEEDS

- **Self-actualization needs** — Self-development, self-realization
- **Esteem needs** — Self-esteem, recognition, status
- **Social needs** — Sense of belonging, love
- **Safety needs** — Security, protection
- **Physiological needs** — Hunger, thirst

a basic two-door sedan before consumers start perceiving it as a sports car?

Marketing managers who intend to do business in global markets should be aware of how foreign consumers perceive their products. For instance, in Japan, product labels are often written in English or French, even though they may not translate into anything meaningful. Many Japanese associate foreign words on product labels with the exotic, the expensive, and high quality.

6-8b Motivation

By studying motivation, marketers can analyze the major forces influencing consumers to buy or not buy products. When you buy a product, you usually do so to fulfill some kind of need. These needs become motives when they are aroused sufficiently. For instance, suppose this morning you were so hungry before class that you needed to eat something. In response to that need, you stopped at Subway for a breakfast sandwich. In other words, you were motivated by hunger to stop at Subway. A **motive** is the driving force that causes a person to take action to satisfy specific needs.

Why are people driven by particular needs at particular times? One popular theory is **Maslow's hierarchy of needs**, illustrated in Exhibit 6.6, which arranges needs in ascending order of

motive a driving force that causes a person to take action to satisfy specific needs

Maslow's hierarchy of needs a method of classifying human needs and motivations into five categories in ascending order of importance: physiological, safety, social, esteem, and self-actualization

importance: physiological, safety, social, esteem, and self-actualization. As a person fulfills one need, a higher-level need becomes more important.

The most basic human needs—that is, the needs for food, water, and shelter—are *physiological*. Because they are essential to survival, these needs must be satisfied first. Ads showing a juicy hamburger or a runner gulping down Gatorade after a marathon are examples of appeals to satisfy the physiological needs of hunger and thirst.

Safety needs include security and freedom from pain and discomfort. Marketers sometimes appeal to consumers' fears and anxieties about safety to sell their products. For example, aware of the aging population's health fears, the retail medical imaging centers Heart Check America and HealthScreen America advertise that they offer consumers a full body scan for early detection of health problems such as coronary disease and cancer. Some companies or industries advertise to allay consumer fears. For example, in the wake of the September 11, 2001, terrorist attacks, the airline industry found itself having to conduct an image campaign to reassure consumers about the safety of air travel.

After physiological and safety needs have been fulfilled, *social needs*—especially love and a sense of belonging—become the focus. Love includes acceptance by one's peers, as well as sex and romantic love. Marketing managers probably appeal more to this need than to any other. Ads for clothes, cosmetics, and vacation packages suggest that buying the product can bring love.

Love is acceptance without regard to one's contribution. Esteem is acceptance based on one's contribution to the group. *Self-esteem needs* include self-respect and a sense of accomplishment. Esteem needs also include prestige, fame, and recognition of one's accomplishments. Montblanc pens, Mercedes-Benz automobiles, and Neiman Marcus stores all appeal to esteem needs.

The highest human need is *self-actualization*. It refers to finding self-fulfillment and self-expression, reaching the point in life at which "people are what they feel they should be." Maslow believed that very few people ever attain this level. Even so, advertisements may focus on this type of need. For example, American Express ads convey the message that acquiring an AmEx card is one of the highest attainments in life. The Centurion card, often called simply "the black card," requires a $5,000 initiation fee and carries an annual fee of $2,500.

6-8c Learning

Almost all consumer behavior results from **learning**, which is the process that creates changes in behavior through experience and practice. It is not possible to observe learning directly, but we can infer when it has occurred by a person's actions. For example, suppose you see an advertisement for a new and improved cold medicine. If you go to the store that day and buy that remedy, we infer that you have learned something about the cold medicine.

There are two types of learning: experiential and conceptual. *Experiential learning* occurs when an experience changes your behavior. For example, if the new cold medicine does not relieve your symptoms, you may not buy that brand again. *Conceptual learning*, which is not acquired through direct experience but based upon reasoning, is the second type of learning. Assume, for example, that you are standing at a soft drink machine and notice a new diet flavor with an artificial sweetener. Because someone has told you that diet beverages leave an aftertaste, you choose a different drink. You have learned that you would not like this new diet drink without ever trying it.

Reinforcement and repetition boost learning. Reinforcement can be positive or negative. If you see a vendor selling frozen yogurt (stimulus), buy it (response), and find the yogurt to be quite refreshing (reward), your behavior has been positively reinforced. On the other hand, if you buy a new flavor of yogurt and it does not taste good (negative reinforcement), you will not buy that flavor of yogurt again (response). Without positive or negative reinforcement, a person will not be motivated to repeat the behavior pattern or to avoid it. Thus, if a new brand evokes neutral feelings, some marketing activity, such as a price change or an increase in promotion, may be required to induce further consumption. Learning theory is helpful in reminding marketers that concrete and timely strategies are what reinforce desired consumer behavior.

Repetition is a key strategy in promotional campaigns because it can lead to increased learning. Most marketers use repetitive advertising so that consumers will learn what their unique advantage is over the competition. Generally, to heighten learning, advertising messages should be spread out over time rather than clustered together.

A related learning concept useful to marketing managers is **stimulus generalization**. In theory,

learning a process that creates changes in behavior, immediate or expected, through experience and practice

stimulus generalization a form of learning that occurs when one response is extended to a second stimulus similar to the first

stimulus generalization occurs when one response is extended to a second stimulus similar to the first. Marketers often use a successful, well-known brand name for a family of products because it gives consumers familiarity with and knowledge about each product in the family. Such brand name families spur the introduction of new products and facilitate the sale of existing items. OXO relies on consumers' familiarity with its popular kitchen and household products to sell office and medical supplies; Sony's film division relies on name recognition from its home technology, such as the PlayStation. Clorox bathroom cleaner relies on familiarity with Clorox bleach, and Dove shampoo relies on familiarity with Dove soap. Branding is examined in more detail in Chapter 10.

Another form of stimulus generalization occurs when retailers or wholesalers design their packages to resemble well-known manufacturers' brands. Such

Dcwcreations/Shutterstock.com

imitation conveys the notion that the store brand is as good as the national manufacturer's brand.

The opposite of stimulus generalization is **stimulus discrimination**, which means learning to differentiate among similar products. Consumers may perceive one product as more rewarding or stimulating, even if it is virtually indistinguishable from competitors. For example, some consumers prefer Miller Lite and others prefer Bud Light.

With some types of products—such as aspirin, gasoline, bleach, and paper towels—marketers rely on promotion to point out brand differences that consumers would otherwise not recognize. This process, called *product differentiation*, is discussed in more detail in Chapter 8. Usually, product differentiation is based on superficial differences. For example, Bayer tells consumers that it is the aspirin "doctors recommend most."

stimulus discrimination a learned ability to differentiate among similar products

STUDY TOOLS 6

LOCATED AT BACK OF THE TEXTBOOK

☐ Rip out Chapter Review Card

LOCATED AT WWW.CENGAGEBRAIN.COM

☐ Review Key Terms Flashcards and create your own

☐ Track your knowledge & understanding of key concepts in marketing

☐ Complete practice and graded quizzes to prepare for tests

☐ Complete interactive content within the MKTG Online experience

☐ View the chapter highlight boxes within the MKTG Online experience

7 | Business Marketing

Dusit/Shutterstock.com

LEARNING OUTCOMES

After studying this chapter, you will be able to...

7-1 Describe business marketing

7-2 Describe trends in B-to-B Internet marketing

7-3 Discuss the role of relationship marketing and strategic alliances in business marketing

7-4 Identify the four major categories of business market customers

7-5 Explain the North American Industry Classification System

7-6 Explain the major differences between business and consumer markets

7-7 Describe the seven types of business goods and services

7-8 Discuss the unique aspects of business buying behavior

After you finish this chapter go to **PAGE 130** for **STUDY TOOLS.**

7-1 WHAT IS BUSINESS MARKETING?

Business marketing (also called industrial, business-to-business, B-to-B, or B2B marketing) is the marketing of goods and services to individuals and organizations for purposes other than personal consumption. The sale of a personal computer (PC) to your college or university is an example of business marketing. A **business product**, or **industrial product**, is used to manufacture other goods or services, to facilitate an organization's operations, or to resell to other customers. A **consumer product** is bought to satisfy an individual's personal wants or needs. The key characteristic distinguishing business products from consumer products is intended use, not physical form.

business marketing (industrial, business-to-business, B-to-B, or B2B marketing) the marketing of goods and services to individuals and organizations for purposes other than personal consumption

business product (industrial product) a product used to manufacture other goods or services, to facilitate an organization's operations, or to resell to other customers

consumer product a product bought to satisfy an individual's personal wants or needs

How do you distinguish between a consumer product and a business product? A product that is purchased for personal or family consumption or as a gift is a consumer good. If that same product, such as a PC or a cell phone, is bought for use

in a business, it is a business product. Some common items that are sold as both consumer goods and business products are office supplies (e.g., pens, paper, and staple removers). Some items, such as forklifts, are more commonly sold as business products than as consumer goods.

The size of the business market in the United States and most other countries substantially exceeds that of the consumer market. In the business market, a single customer can account for a huge volume of purchases. For example, IBM's purchasing department spends more than $40 billion annually on business products. Procter & Gamble, Apple, Merck, Dell, and Kimberly-Clark each spend more than half of their annual revenue on business products.[1]

Some large firms that produce goods such as steel, computer memory chips, or production equipment market exclusively to business customers. Other firms market to both businesses and to consumers. Hewlett-Packard marketed exclusively to business customers in the past but now markets laser printers and personal computers to consumers. Sony, traditionally a consumer marketer, now sells office automation products to businesses. Kodak used to sell its cameras exclusively to consumers, but has opted to sell its commercial printing services to businesses

> The key characteristic distinguishing business products from consumer products is intended use, not physical form.

since emerging from bankruptcy in 2013. All of these companies have had to make organizational and marketing changes to expand into the new market categories.

7-2 TRENDS IN B-TO-B INTERNET MARKETING

Over the past decade, marketers have become more and more sophisticated in their use of the Internet. Companies have had to transition from "We have a Web site because our customer does" to having a site that attracts, interests, satisfies, informs, and retains customers. B-to-B companies are increasingly leveraging the Internet as an effective sales and promotion platform (much like B-to-C companies have done for decades). B-to-B companies use the Internet in three major ways. First, they use their Web sites to facilitate communication and orders. Second, they use digital marketing to increase brand awareness. Third, they use digital marketing—primarily in the form of content marketing—to position their businesses as thought leaders and therefore generate sales leads. Companies selling to business buyers face the same challenges as all marketers, including determining the target market and deciding how best to reach it.

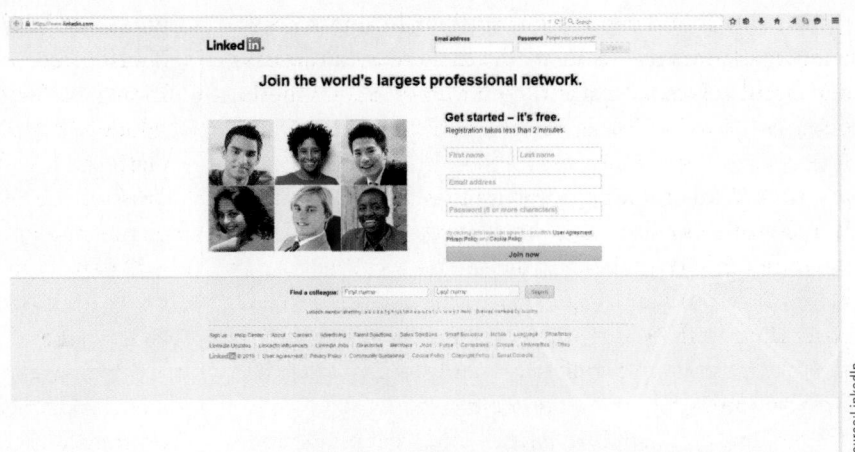

Source: LinkedIn

Most B-to-B companies see LinkedIn as the most beneficial platform through which to distribute content.

Every year, new applications that provide additional information about customers are developed. These applications often also lower costs, increase supply chain efficiency, or enhance customer retention, loyalty, and trust. Increasingly, business customers expect suppliers to know them personally, monitor people's movement within their company, and offer personal interaction through social media, e-mail, and personal mailers. As such, we have seen B-to-B marketers use technology like smartphones and tablets to facilitate orders and enhance customer experiences.

A few years ago, many people thought the Internet would eliminate the need for distributors. Why would customers pay a distributor's markup when they could buy directly from the manufacturer with a few mouse clicks? This has occurred less frequently than many expected because distributors often perform important functions such as providing credit, aggregating supplies from multiple sources, making deliveries, and processing returns. Many business customers, especially small firms, depend on knowledgeable distributors for information and advice that is not available to them online.

Social media usage has been the most pervasive B-to-B and B-to-C marketing trend of the past five years. Most companies use e-mail marketing, search engine optimization, paid search, and display advertising to pull customers to their Web sites. This field of marketing requires vigilant adjustment to keep track of new applications and platforms, as well as constant evaluation to determine whether these new avenues are beneficial to (or used by) customers. Generally, B-to-C marketers were faster to adopt social media as part of the promotional mix. B-to-B marketers did not initially see the value in these tools. However, that has changed as social media has become more popular.

Content marketing is a strategic marketing approach focused on creating and distributing valuable, relevant, and consistent content. The goal of this content is to attract and retain a clearly defined audience, and ultimately, drive profitable customer action. This strategy has played an important role for B-to-B marketers. Content marketing includes media such as videos, podcasts, webinars, blog posts, white papers, e-books, slide decks, and more. Sharing valuable insights and interesting content can position a company as a though leader in an area. A 2014 study by the Content Marketing Institute and MarketingProfs found that 86 percent of respondents use content marketing, but many struggle with developing effective content. More than 55 percent of respondents stated plans to increase their content marketing usage in 2015.[2] Most companies use content marketing to increase brand awareness and generate leads. Increasing engagement comes in at a close third. Interestingly, while most B-to-C companies favor Facebook as their primary social media platform, most B-to-B companies see LinkedIn as the most beneficial platform through which to distribute content. Regardless of the platform used, the key to social media-based content marketing for B-to-B marketers is to create compelling and useful content for customers. For example, HubSpot and Marketo develop white papers and e-books on topics such as generating leads through social media for customers and potential customers.

Content marketing a strategic marketing approach that focuses on creating and distributing content that is valuable, relevant and consistent.

As they build reputations in their business areas, many marketers use social media to increase awareness and build relationships and community. Social media platforms like YouTube, LinkedIn, Twitter, and Facebook provide great conversational platforms for doing just that. While building community is important, B-to-B marketers are also using social media to gather leads (as you may have gathered from the HubSpot and Marketo white paper example). Other goals include product promotion, traffic building, search engine optimization (SEO), competitive intelligence and listening, customer feedback and support, and product development.

As platforms such as mobile and streaming video grow, marketers must develop new ways to measure campaign effectiveness. For example, after using social analytics to determine the most effective hashtag from its "Internet of Everything" campaign, Cisco was able to increase usage of one particularly effective hashtag by 440 percent. Global information and measurement company Nielsen recently launched Nielsen Online Campaign Ratings, a "much-anticipated advertising measurement solution."[3] According to data collected through this new platform, less than half of all online advertisement impressions reach their intended audiences. Depending on the medium used, customer targeting varies between a 30 percent and 50 percent coverage rate.[4] Some metrics that are particularly useful for increasing the success of a social media campaign are awareness, engagement, and conversion. *Awareness* is the attention that social media attracts, such as the number of followers or fans. Awareness is generally used as the first step in the marketing funnel, and social media is often paired with paid digital media like display advertising and text-based ads to increase its effectiveness. *Engagement* refers to the interactions between the brand and the audience, such as comments, retweets, shares, and searches. The

The Top Social Media Tools for B-to-B Marketers

BtoB Marketing Magazine surveyed hundreds of B-to-B marketers regarding their social media usage, and while LinkedIn, Facebook, and Twitter were used by the majority of respondents, LinkedIn was the most used social media tool overall (chosen by 94 percent of respondents). Runners up were Twitter (89 percent), Facebook (77 percent), YouTube (77 percent), and Google+ (61 percent). LinkedIn is so popular because it drives more traffic and leads than other platforms for B-to-B marketers. The company has only increased its favor among B-to-B marketers by adding new B-to-B-friendly features like sponsored company updates, groups connected to topics, products and services pages, and a thought leader blogging program.[5]

B-to-B marketers have begun making use of social advertising platforms such as advertisement exchanges on LinkedIn and promoted tweets on Twitter. Video, used for everything from product demonstrations to customer testimonials, is also proving to be an extremely compelling platform for many B-to-B marketers. After finding that attorney profiles were the most viewed parts of its Web site, for example, law firm Levenfeld Pearlstein decided to create a series of videos featuring attorney interviews. In these videos, attorneys answered questions about themselves and the firm, thereby telling a richer story about the company.[6]

© plexius/Shutterstock 149737013

Twin Design/Shutterstock.com

purpose of engagement is to get customers to respond to brand-led posts and to start conversations themselves. *Conversions* occur when action is taken and include everything from downloading a piece of content (like a white paper) to actually making a purchase.[7] Each of these metrics affects the return on investment.

mnoa357/Shutterstock.com

H&R Block partnered with Arizona's private, Catholic school system in a marketing campaign highlighting the Private Education Tax Credit.

7-3 RELATIONSHIP MARKETING AND STRATEGIC ALLIANCES

As explained in Chapter 1, relationship marketing is a strategy that entails seeking and establishing ongoing partnerships with customers. Relationship marketing has become an important business marketing strategy as customers have become more demanding and competition has become more intense. Loyal customers are also more profitable than those who are price sensitive and perceive little or no difference among brands or suppliers.

Relationship marketing is increasingly important as business suppliers use platforms like Facebook, Twitter, and other social networking sites to advertise themselves to businesses. Social networking sites encourage businesses to shop around and research options for all their needs. This means that, for many suppliers, retaining their current customers has become a primary focus, whereas acquiring new customers was the focus in the past. Maintaining a steady dialogue between the supplier and the customer is a proven way to gain repeat business.[8]

7-3a Strategic Alliances

A **strategic alliance**, sometimes called a **strategic partnership**, is a cooperative agreement between business firms. Strategic alliances can take the form of licensing or distribution agreements, joint ventures, research and development consortia, and partnerships. They may be between manufacturers, manufacturers and customers, manufacturers and suppliers, and manufacturers and channel intermediaries.

Business marketers form strategic alliances to strengthen operations and better compete. In 2013,

strategic alliance (strategic partnership) a cooperative agreement between business firms

news conglomerate Time formed a strategic alliance with wireless carrier Sprint. Under the partnership, Time's content would automatically be delivered to Sprint's SprintZone app, which comes preloaded on all Sprint devices. According to Cyrus Beagley, general manager of Time's Advertising Sales & Marketing Group, the purpose of the partnership was to "create a really compelling daily content snacking experience that leverages the breadth of our brands."[9]

Sometimes alliance partners are fierce competitors. Take, for example, the partnership between Amazon and Netflix. In 2014, Amazon introduced the Fire TV and the Fire TV Stick, both of which allow users to stream digital media to their home televisions. This product supports several media services, including Netflix, despite that Netflix offers competing services. Instead of trying to compete with Netflix, Amazon included its services in order to offer its customers a satisfactory product.[10]

Other alliances are formed between companies that operate in completely different industries. For example, tax preparation company H&R Block partnered with Arizona's private Catholic school system in a marketing campaign highlighting the Private Education Tax Credit, which allows low-income students to attend the state's high-performing Catholic schools. The partnership generated good publicity for H&R Block while effectively serving the schools' customers (the students' parents). In the first year of the partnership, H&R Block clients generated $167,000 in tax credit

EXHIBIT 7.1 STRATEGIC ALLIANCE: STARBUCKS AND GREEN MOUNTAIN

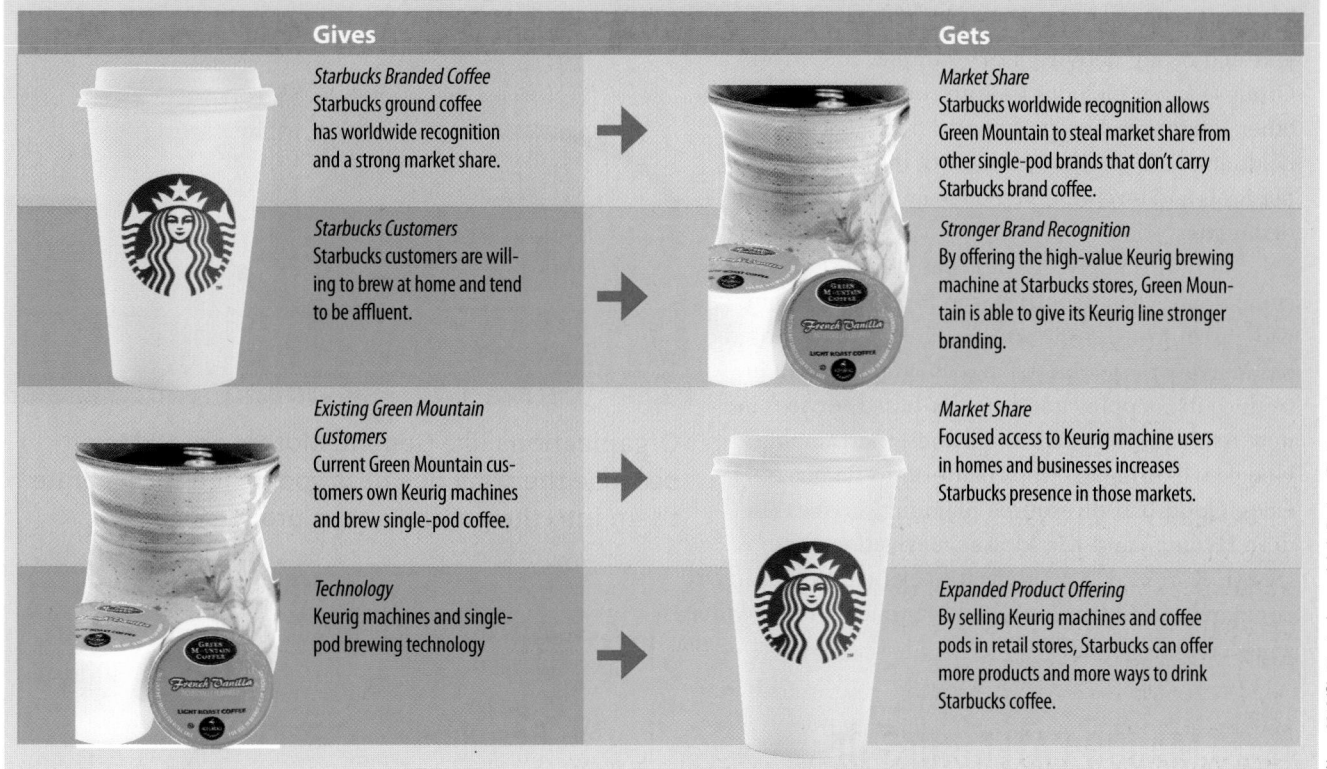

Gives		Gets	
Starbucks Branded Coffee Starbucks ground coffee has worldwide recognition and a strong market share.	→	**Market Share** Starbucks worldwide recognition allows Green Mountain to steal market share from other single-pod brands that don't carry Starbucks brand coffee.	
Starbucks Customers Starbucks customers are willing to brew at home and tend to be affluent.	→	**Stronger Brand Recognition** By offering the high-value Keurig brewing machine at Starbucks stores, Green Mountain is able to give its Keurig line stronger branding.	
Existing Green Mountain Customers Current Green Mountain customers own Keurig machines and brew single-pod coffee.	→	**Market Share** Focused access to Keurig machine users in homes and businesses increases Starbucks presence in those markets.	
Technology Keurig machines and single-pod brewing technology	→	**Expanded Product Offering** By selling Keurig machines and coffee pods in retail stores, Starbucks can offer more products and more ways to drink Starbucks coffee.	

gifts, sending ninety-two students to private Catholic schools.[11] Exhibit 7.1 demonstrates the benefits Starbucks and Green Mountain Coffee receive from each other through their strategic alliance.

For an alliance to succeed in the long term, it must be built on commitment and trust. **Relationship commitment** means that a firm believes an ongoing relationship with some other firm is so important that it warrants maximum efforts at maintaining it indefinitely.[12] A perceived breakdown in commitment by one of the parties often leads to a breakdown in the relationship.

Trust exists when one party has confidence in an exchange partner's reliability and integrity.[13] Some alliances fail when participants lack trust in their trading partners. Consider, for example, the failed partnership between Phones 4U, an independent phone retailer based in the United Kingdom, and Vodaphone, a British telecommunications company. While the two companies could have created a successful partnership, Vodaphone made the decision to cut ties with Phones 4U in 2014.[14] Vodaphone claimed that Phones 4U refused to improve upon the terms of their agreement when the contract came up for renewal, but Phones 4U believed that it was misled during negotiations and that cutting ties was an unfair decision. This decision forced Phones 4U to lay off thousands of employees and left the company struggling to restructure its business.

7-3b Relationships in Other Cultures

Although the terms *relationship marketing* and *strategic alliances* are fairly new and popularized mostly by American business executives and educators, the concepts have long been familiar in other cultures. Businesses in China, Japan, Korea, Mexico, and much of Europe rely heavily on personal relationships.

In Japan, for example, exchange between firms is based on personal relationships that are developed through what is called *amae*, or indulgent dependency. *Amae* is the feeling of nurturing concern for, and dependence upon, another. Reciprocity and personal relationships contribute to *amae*. Relationships between companies can develop into a **keiretsu**—a network of interlocking corporate affiliates. Within a *keiretsu*, executives may sit on the boards of

relationship commitment a firm's belief that an ongoing relationship with another firm is so important that the relationship warrants maximum efforts at maintaining it indefinitely

trust the condition that exists when one party has confidence in an exchange partner's reliability and integrity

keiretsu a network of interlocking corporate affiliates

Wayne0216/Shutterstock.com; Jaimie Duplass/Shutterstock.com

their customers or their suppliers. Members of a *keiretsu* trade with each other whenever possible and often engage in joint product development, finance, and marketing activity. For example, the Toyota Group *keiretsu* includes 14 core companies and another 170 that receive preferential treatment. Toyota holds an equity position in many of these 170 member firms and is represented on many of their boards of directors.

Many firms have found that the best way to compete in Asian countries is to form relationships with Asian firms. For example, Google Enterprise has allied with several Asian tech companies to introduce its mapping and location-based services in new Asian markets. Through these partnerships, Google will bring its Maps platform to Ramco Services' cloud-based resource planning services (India), Hyundai and Kia Motors' navigation systems (South Korea), HSR International Realtors' property comparisons (Singapore), and Nintendo's Wii U video game console (Japan).[15]

Organizations like General Motors are OEMs because they buy business goods and incorporate them into the products they produce.

Linda Parton/Shutterstock.com

7-4 MAJOR CATEGORIES OF BUSINESS CUSTOMERS

The business market consists of four major categories of customers: producers, resellers, governments, and institutions.

7-4a Producers

The producer segment of the business market includes profit-oriented individuals and organizations that use purchased goods and services to produce other products, to incorporate into other products, or to facilitate the daily operations of the organization. Examples of producers include construction, manufacturing, transportation, finance, real estate, and food service firms. In the United States, there are more than thirteen million firms in the producer segment of the business market. Some of these firms are small, and others are among the world's largest businesses.

Producers are often called **original equipment manufacturers**, or **OEMs**. This term includes all in-

original equipment manufacturers (OEMs)
individuals and organizations that buy business goods and incorporate them into the products they produce for eventual sale to other producers or to consumers

dividuals and organizations that buy business goods and incorporate them into the products they produce for eventual sale to other producers or to consumers. Companies such as

General Motors that buy steel, paint, tires, and batteries are said to be OEMs.

7-4b Resellers

The reseller market includes retail and wholesale businesses that buy finished goods and resell them for a profit. A retailer sells mainly to final consumers; wholesalers sell mostly to retailers and other organizational customers. There are approximately 1.5 million retailers and 500,000 wholesalers operating in the United States. Consumer product firms like Procter & Gamble, Kraft Foods, and Coca-Cola sell directly to large retailers and retail chains and through wholesalers to smaller retail units. Retailing is explored in detail in Chapter 14.

Business product distributors are wholesalers that buy business products and resell them to business customers. They often carry thousands of items in stock and employ sales forces to call on business customers. Businesses that wish to buy a gross of pencils or a hundred pounds of fertilizer typically purchase these items from local distributors rather than directly from manufacturers such as Empire Pencil or Dow Chemical.

7-4c Governments

A third major segment of the business market is government. Government organizations include thousands of federal, state, and local buying units. Collectively, these government units account for the greatest volume of purchases of any customer category in the United States.[16]

Companies like Kroger are resellers of products offered by P&G and Coca-Cola.

AP Images/Al Behrman

Marketing to government agencies can be an overwhelming undertaking, but companies that learn how the system works can position themselves to win lucrative contracts and build lasting, rewarding relationships.[17] Marketing to government agencies traditionally has not been an activity for companies seeking quick returns. The aphorism "hurry up and wait" is often cited as a characteristic of marketing to government agencies. Contracts for government purchases are often put out for bid. Interested vendors submit bids (usually sealed) to provide specified products during a particular time. Sometimes the lowest bidder is awarded the contract. When the lowest bidder is not awarded the contract, strong evidence must be presented to justify the decision. Grounds for rejecting the lowest bid include lack of experience, inadequate financing, or poor past performance. Bidding allows all potential suppliers a fair chance at winning government contracts and helps ensure that public funds are spent wisely.

FEDERAL GOVERNMENT Name just about any good or service and chances are that someone in the federal government uses it. The U.S. federal government buys goods and services valued at more than $875 billion per year, making it the world's largest customer.[18]

Although much of the federal government's buying is centralized, no single federal agency contracts for all the government's requirements, and no single buyer in any agency purchases all that the agency needs. We can view the federal government as a combination of several large companies with overlapping responsibilities and thousands of small independent units. One popular source of information about government procurement is *FedBizOpps*. Until recently, businesses hoping to sell to the federal government found the document (previously called *Commerce Business Daily*) unorganized, and it often arrived too late to be useful. The online version (www.cbd-net.com) is timelier and allows contractors to find leads using key word searches. Other examples of publications designed to explain how to do business with the federal government include *Doing Business with the General Services Administration*, *Selling to the Military*, and *Selling to the U.S. Air Force*.

STATE, COUNTY, AND CITY GOVERNMENT Selling to states, counties, and cities can be less frustrating for both small and large vendors than selling to the federal government. Paperwork is typically simpler and more manageable than it is at the federal level. But vendors must decide which of the more than 89,000 government units are likely to buy their wares. State and local buying agencies include school districts, highway departments, government-operated hospitals, housing agencies, and many other departments and divisions.

7-4d Institutions

The fourth major segment of the business market consists of institutions that seek to achieve goals other than the standard business goals of profit, market share, and return on investment. This segment includes schools, hospitals, colleges and universities, churches, labor unions, fraternal organizations, civic clubs, foundations, and other so-called nonbusiness organizations. Some institutional purchasers operate similar to governments in that the purchasing process is influenced, determined, or administered by government units. Other institutional purchasers are organized more like corporations.[19]

 7-5 ## THE NORTH AMERICAN INDUSTRY CLASSIFICATION SYSTEM

The **North American Industry Classification System (NAICS) is an industry classification system introduced in 1997 to replace the standard industrial classification system (SIC).** NAICS (pronounced *nakes*) is a system for classifying North American business establishments. The system, developed jointly by the United States, Canada, and Mexico, provides

> **North American Industry Classification System (NAICS)**
> a detailed numbering system developed by the United States, Canada, and Mexico to classify North American business establishments by their main production processes

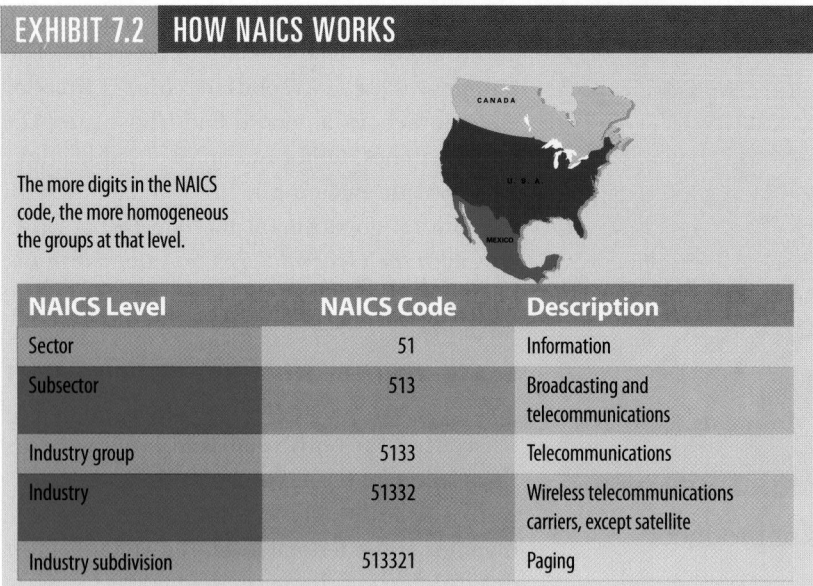

EXHIBIT 7.2 HOW NAICS WORKS

The more digits in the NAICS code, the more homogeneous the groups at that level.

NAICS Level	NAICS Code	Description
Sector	51	Information
Subsector	513	Broadcasting and telecommunications
Industry group	5133	Telecommunications
Industry	51332	Wireless telecommunications carriers, except satellite
Industry subdivision	513321	Paging

a common industry classification system for the North American Free Trade Agreement (NAFTA) partners. Goods- or service-producing firms that use identical or similar production processes are grouped together.

NAICS is an extremely valuable tool for business marketers engaged in analyzing, segmenting, and targeting markets. Each classification group is relatively homogeneous in terms of raw materials required, components used, manufacturing processes employed, and problems faced. Therefore, if a supplier understands the needs and requirements of a few firms within a classification, requirements can be projected for all firms in that category. The number, size, and geographic dispersion of firms can also be identified. This information can be converted to market potential estimates, market share estimates, and sales forecasts. It can also be used for identifying potential new customers. NAICS codes can help identify firms that may be prospective users of a supplier's goods and services. The more digits in a code, the more homogeneous the group. A sample of how NAICS codes function is listed in Exhibit 7.2. For a complete listing of all NAICS codes, see www.naics.com/search.htm.

7-6 BUSINESS VERSUS CONSUMER MARKETS

The basic philosophy and practice of marketing are the same whether the customer is a business organization or a consumer. Business markets do, however, have characteristics different from consumer markets.

derived demand the demand for business products

7-6a Demand

Consumer demand for products is quite different from demand in the business market. Unlike consumer demand, business demand is derived, inelastic, joint, and fluctuating.

DERIVED DEMAND The demand for business products is called **derived demand** because organizations buy products to be used in producing their customers' products. For instance, the number of drills or lathes that a manufacturing firm needs is derived from, or based upon, the demand for products that are produced using these machines. Following the Great Recession, California timber harvests fell by over 50 percent due to dramatic reductions in building construction. Since hitting a record low in 2009, the industry has rebounded each year, due in part to increased exports of whole logs to China and a slowly recovering construction industry in the United States.[20] Because demand is derived, business marketers must carefully monitor demand patterns and changing preferences in final consumer markets, even though their customers are not in those markets. Moreover, business marketers must carefully monitor their customers' forecasts because derived demand is based on expectations of future demand for those customers' products.

Some business marketers not only monitor final consumer demand and customer forecasts, but also try to influence final consumer demand. Aluminum producers use television and magazine advertisements to point out the convenience and recycling opportunities that aluminum offers to consumers who can choose to purchase soft drinks in either aluminum or plastic containers.

INELASTIC DEMAND The demand for many business products is inelastic with regard to price. *Inelastic demand* means that an increase or decrease in the price of the product will not significantly affect demand for the product. This will be discussed further in Chapter 19.

The price of a product used in the production of, or as part of, a final product is often a minor portion of the final product's total price. Therefore, demand for the final consumer product is not affected. If the price of automobile paint or spark plugs rises significantly, say, 200 percent in one year, do you think the number of new automobiles sold that year will be affected? Probably not.

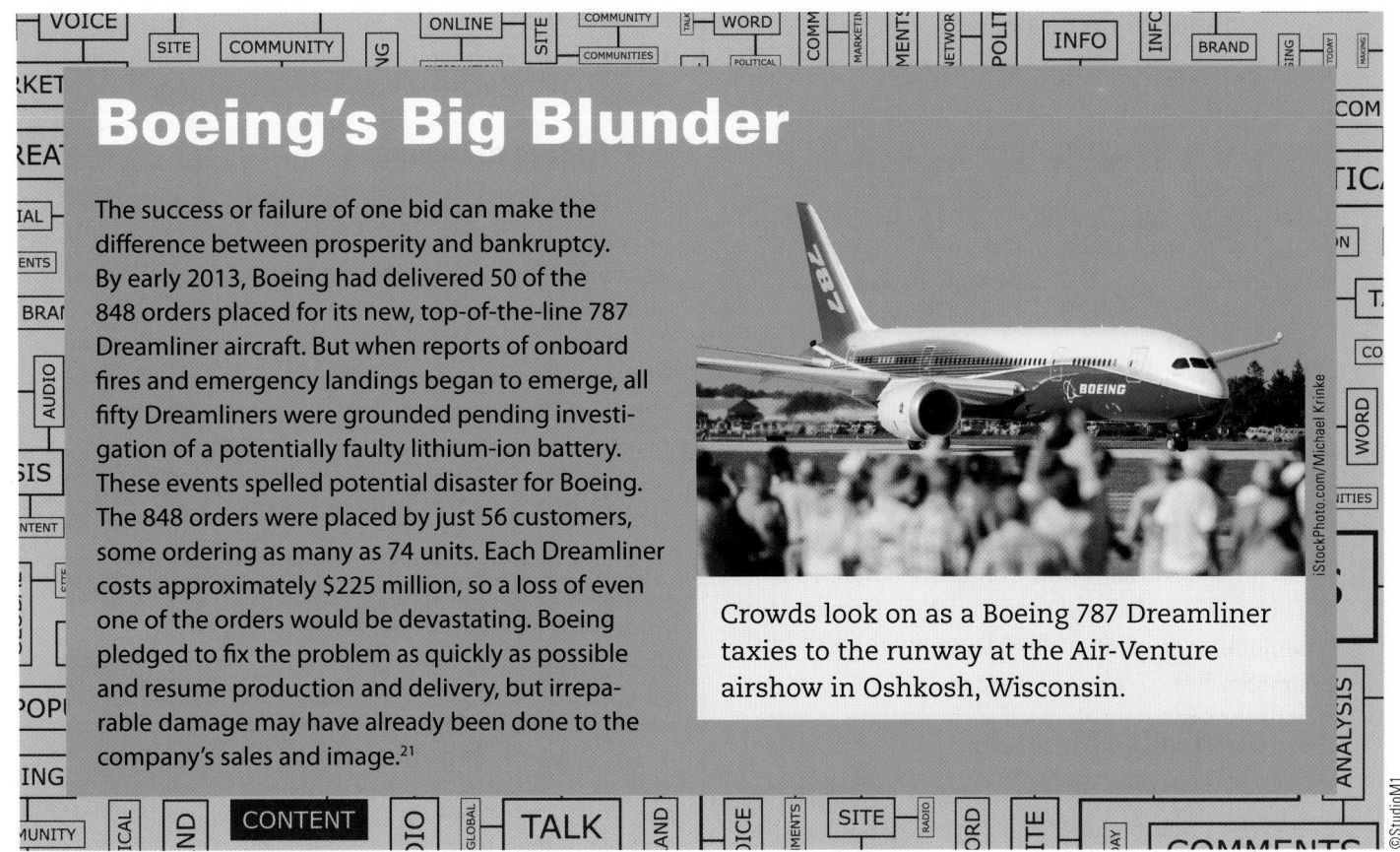

Boeing's Big Blunder

The success or failure of one bid can make the difference between prosperity and bankruptcy. By early 2013, Boeing had delivered 50 of the 848 orders placed for its new, top-of-the-line 787 Dreamliner aircraft. But when reports of onboard fires and emergency landings began to emerge, all fifty Dreamliners were grounded pending investigation of a potentially faulty lithium-ion battery. These events spelled potential disaster for Boeing. The 848 orders were placed by just 56 customers, some ordering as many as 74 units. Each Dreamliner costs approximately $225 million, so a loss of even one of the orders would be devastating. Boeing pledged to fix the problem as quickly as possible and resume production and delivery, but irreparable damage may have already been done to the company's sales and image.[21]

Crowds look on as a Boeing 787 Dreamliner taxies to the runway at the Air-Venture airshow in Oshkosh, Wisconsin.

JOINT DEMAND **Joint demand** occurs when two or more items are used together in a final product. For example, a decline in the availability of memory chips will slow production of microcomputers, which will in turn reduce the demand for disk drives. Likewise, the demand for Apple operating systems exists as long as there is demand for Apple computers. Sales of the two products are directly linked.

FLUCTUATING DEMAND The demand for business products—particularly new plants and equipment—tends to be less stable than the demand for consumer products. A small increase or decrease in consumer demand can produce a much larger change in demand for the facilities and equipment needed to make the consumer product. Economists refer to this phenomenon as the **multiplier effect** (or **accelerator principle**).

Cummins Inc., a producer of heavy-duty diesel engines, uses sophisticated surface grinders to make parts. Suppose Cummins is using 20 surface grinders. Each machine lasts about 10 years. Purchases have been timed so two machines will wear out and be replaced annually. If the demand for engine parts does not change, two grinders will be bought this year. If the demand for parts declines slightly, only eighteen

grinders may be needed, and Cummins will not replace the worn ones. However, suppose that next year demand returns to previous levels plus a little more. To meet the new level of demand, Cummins will need to replace the two machines that wore out in the previous year, the two that wore out in the current year, plus one or more additional machines. The multiplier effect works this way in many industries, producing highly fluctuating demand for business products.

7-6b Purchase Volume

Business customers tend to buy in large quantities. Just imagine the size of Kellogg's typical order for the wheat bran and raisins used to manufacture Raisin Bran. Or consider that in 2013, the Chicago Transit Authority (CTA) began accepting bids to fulfill a purchase order of 846 new rail cars to replace its aging fleet. The purchase budget was estimated at $2 billion—quite a bit larger than the CTA's $2.25 ride fare.[22]

> **joint demand** the demand for two or more items used together in a final product
>
> **multiplier effect (accelerator principle)** phenomenon in which a small increase or decrease in consumer demand can produce a much larger change in demand for the facilities and equipment needed to make the consumer product

7-6c Number of Customers

Business marketers usually have far fewer customers than consumer marketers. The advantage is that it is a lot easier to identify prospective buyers, monitor current customers' needs and levels of satisfaction, and personally attend to existing customers. The main disadvantage is that each customer becomes crucial—especially for those manufacturers that have only one customer. In many cases, this customer is the U.S. government.

7-6d Concentration of Customers

Manufacturing operations in the United States tend to be more geographically concentrated than consumer markets. More than half of all U.S. manufacturers concentrate the majority of their operations in the following eight states: California, New York, Ohio, Illinois, Michigan, Texas, Pennsylvania, and New Jersey.[23] Most large metropolitan areas host large numbers of business customers.

7-6e Distribution Structure

Many consumer products pass through a distribution system that includes the producer, one or more wholesalers, and a retailer. In business marketing, however, because of many of the characteristics already mentioned, channels of distribution for business marketing are typically shorter. Direct channels, where manufacturers market directly to users, are much more common. The use of direct channels has increased dramatically in the past decade with the introduction of various Internet buying and selling schemes. One such technique is called a **business-to-business online exchange**, which is an electronic trading floor that provides companies with integrated links to their customers and suppliers. The goal of B-to-B exchanges is to simplify business purchasing and to make it more efficient. Alibaba.com is a B-to-B e-commerce portal based in China that allows companies from all over the world to purchase goods and services from Chinese suppliers. Recently, the Web site has begun expanding to include suppliers from countries outside of China, including the United States. Alibaba.com serves buyers in more than 190 countries worldwide and has suppliers representing more than 40 major product categories. The mission of Alibaba.com is to allow suppliers to reach a global audience and to help buyers quickly find the products and services they need.[24]

> **business-to-business online exchange** an electronic trading floor that provides companies with integrated links to their customers and suppliers
>
> **reciprocity** a practice whereby business purchasers choose to buy from their own customers

7-6f Nature of Buying

Unlike consumers, business buyers usually approach purchasing rather formally. Businesses use professionally trained purchasing agents or buyers who spend their entire career purchasing a limited number of items. They get to know the items and the sellers well. Some professional purchasers earn the designation of Certified Purchasing Manager (CPM) after participating in a rigorous certification program.

7-6g Nature of Buying Influence

Typically, more people are involved in a single business purchase decision than in a consumer purchase. Experts from fields as varied as quality control, marketing, and finance, as well as professional buyers and users, may be grouped in a buying center (discussed later in this chapter).

7-6h Type of Negotiations

Consumers are used to negotiating price on automobiles and real estate. In most cases, however, American consumers expect sellers to set the price and other conditions of sale, such as time of delivery and credit terms. In contrast, negotiating is common in business marketing. Buyers and sellers negotiate product specifications, delivery dates, payment terms, and other pricing matters. Sometimes these negotiations occur during many meetings over several months. Final contracts are often very long and detailed.

7-6i Use of Reciprocity

Business purchasers often choose to buy from their own customers, a practice known as **reciprocity**. For example, General Motors buys engines for use in its automobiles and trucks from BorgWarner, which in turn buys many of the automobiles and trucks it needs from General Motors. This practice is neither unethical nor illegal unless one party coerces the other and the result is unfair competition. Reciprocity is generally considered a reasonable business practice. If all possible suppliers sell a similar product for about the same price, does it not make sense to buy from those firms that buy from you?

7-6j Use of Leasing

Consumers normally buy products rather than lease them. But businesses commonly lease expensive equipment such as computers, construction equipment and vehicles, and automobiles. Leasing allows firms to reduce capital outflow, acquire a seller's latest products, receive better services, and gain tax advantages.

The leaser, the firm providing the product, may be either the manufacturer or an independent firm. The benefits to the leaser include greater total revenue from leasing compared to selling and an opportunity to do business with customers who cannot afford to buy.

7-6k Primary Promotional Method

Business marketers tend to emphasize personal selling in their promotion efforts, especially for expensive items, custom-designed products, large-volume purchases, and situations requiring negotiations. The sale of many business products requires a great deal of personal contact. Personal selling is discussed in more detail in Chapter 17.

7-7 TYPES OF BUSINESS PRODUCTS

Business products generally fall into one of the following seven categories, depending on their use: major equipment, accessory equipment, raw materials, component parts, processed materials, supplies, and business services.

7-7a Major Equipment

Major equipment includes capital goods such as large or expensive machines, mainframe computers, blast furnaces, generators, airplanes, and buildings. (These items are also commonly called **installations**.) Major equipment is depreciated over time rather than charged as an expense in the year it is purchased. In addition, major equipment is often custom designed for each customer. Personal selling is an important part of the marketing strategy for major equipment because distribution channels are almost always direct from the producer to the business user.

7-7b Accessory Equipment

Accessory equipment is generally less expensive and shorter-lived than major equipment. Examples include portable drills, power tools, microcomputers, and computer software. Accessory equipment is often charged as an expense in the year it is bought rather than depreciated over its useful life. In contrast to major equipment,

The market tends to set the price of raw materials, and individual producers have little pricing flexibility.

accessories are more often standardized and are usually bought by more customers. These customers tend to be widely dispersed. For example, all types of businesses buy microcomputers.

Local industrial distributors (wholesalers) play an important role in the marketing of accessory equipment because business buyers often purchase accessories from them. Regardless of where accessories are bought, advertising is a more vital promotional tool for accessory equipment than for major equipment.

7-7c Raw Materials

Raw materials are unprocessed extractive or agricultural products—for example, mineral ore, timber, wheat, corn, fruits, vegetables, and fish. Raw materials become part of finished products. Extensive users, such as steel or lumber mills and food canners, generally buy huge quantities of raw materials. Because there is often a large number of relatively small sellers of raw materials, none can greatly influence price or supply. Thus, the market tends to set the price of raw materials, and individual producers have little pricing flexibility. Promotion is almost always via personal selling, and distribution channels are usually direct from producer to business user.

major equipment (installations) capital goods such as large or expensive machines, mainframe computers, blast furnaces, generators, airplanes, and buildings

accessory equipment goods, such as portable tools and office equipment, that are less expensive and shorter-lived than major equipment

raw materials unprocessed extractive or agricultural products, such as mineral ore, lumber, wheat, corn, fruits, vegetables, and fish

7-7d Component Parts

Component parts are either finished items ready for assembly or products that need very little processing before becoming part of some other product. Caterpillar diesel engines are component parts used in heavy-duty trucks. Other examples include spark plugs, tires, and electric motors for automobiles. A special feature of component parts is that they can retain their identity after becoming part of the final product. For example, automobile tires are clearly recognizable as part of a car. Moreover, because component parts often wear out, they may need to be replaced several times during the life of the final product. Thus, there are two important markets for many component parts: the OEM market and the replacement market.

The availability of component parts is often a key factor in OEMs meeting their production deadlines. In September 2013, a massive fire at an SK Hynix factory in Wuxi, China halted the manufacture of much of the world's OEM-grade computer memory. This greatly reduced the availability of memory and sent the price of the remaining inventory through the roof. The price of a single stick of memory jumped nearly 42 percent overnight, forcing many OEMs to halt production while an alternate source could be found.[25]

The replacement market is composed of organizations and individuals buying component parts to replace worn-out parts. Because components often retain their identity in final products, users may choose to replace a component part with the same brand used by the manufacturer—for example, the same brand of automobile tires or battery. The replacement market operates differently from the OEM market, however. Whether replacement buyers are organizations or individuals, they tend to demonstrate the characteristics of consumer markets that were discussed in the previous section. Consider, for example, a replacement part for a piece of construction equipment such as a bulldozer or a crane. When a piece of equipment breaks down, it is usually important to acquire a replacement part and have it installed as soon as possible. Purchasers typically buy from local or regional dealers. Negotiations do not occur, and neither reciprocity nor leasing is usually an issue.

component parts either finished items ready for assembly or products that need very little processing before becoming part of some other product

processed materials products used directly in manufacturing other products

supplies consumable items that do not become part of the final product

business services expense items that do not become part of a final product

7-7e Processed Materials

Processed materials are products used directly in manufacturing other products. Unlike raw materials, they have had some processing. Examples include sheet metal, chemicals, specialty steel, treated lumber, corn syrup, and plastics. Unlike component parts, processed materials do not retain their identity in final products.

Timber, harvested from forests, is a raw material. Fluff pulp, a soft, white absorbent, is produced from loblolly pine timber by mills such as International Paper Co. The fluff pulp then becomes part of disposable diapers, bandages, and other sanitary products.[26]

Most processed materials are marketed to OEMs or to distributors servicing the OEM market. Processed materials are generally bought according to customer specifications or to some industry standard, as is the case with steel and plywood. Price and service are important factors in choosing a vendor.

7-7f Supplies

Supplies are consumable items that do not become part of the final product—for example, lubricants, detergents, paper towels, pencils, and paper. Supplies are normally standardized items that purchasing agents routinely buy. Supplies typically have relatively short lives and are inexpensive compared to other business goods. Because supplies generally fall into one of three categories—maintenance, repair, or operating supplies—this category is often referred to as MRO items. Competition in the MRO market is intense. Bic and Paper Mate, for example, battle for business purchases of inexpensive ballpoint pens.

7-7g Business Services

Business services are expense items that do not become part of a final product. Businesses often retain outside providers to perform janitorial, advertising, legal, management consulting, marketing research, maintenance, and other services. Contracting an outside provider makes sense when it costs less than hiring or assigning an employee to perform the task, when an outside provider is needed for particular expertise, or when the need is infrequent.

BUSINESS BUYING BEHAVIOR

As you probably have already concluded, business buyers behave differently from consumers. Understanding how purchase decisions are made in organizations is a first step in developing a business selling strategy. Business buying behavior has five important aspects: buying centers, evaluative criteria, buying situations, business ethics, and customer service.

7-8a Buying Centers

In many cases, more than one person is involved in a purchase decision. A salesperson must determine the buying situation and the information required from the buying organization's perspective to anticipate the size and composition of the buying center.[27]

A **buying center** includes all those people in an organization who become involved in the purchase decision. Membership and influence vary from company to company. For instance, in engineering-dominated firms like Bell Helicopter, the buying center may consist almost entirely of engineers. In marketing-oriented firms like Toyota and IBM, marketing and engineering have almost equal authority. In consumer goods firms like Clorox Corporation, product managers and other marketing decision makers may dominate the buying center. In a small manufacturing company, almost everyone may be a member.

The number of people involved in a buying center varies with the complexity and importance of a purchase decision. The average buying center includes more than one person and up to four per purchase.[28] The composition of the buying group will usually change from one purchase to another and sometimes even during various stages of the buying process. To make matters more complicated, buying centers do not appear on formal organization charts.

For example, even though a formal committee may have been set up to choose a new plant site, it is only part of the buying center. Other people, like the company president, often play informal yet powerful roles. In a lengthy decision-making process, such as finding a new plant location, some members may drop out of the buying center when they can no longer play a useful role. Others whose talents are needed then become part of the center. No formal announcement of "who is in" and "who is out" is ever made.

ROLES IN THE BUYING CENTER As in family purchasing decisions, several people may each play a role in the business purchase process:

- The *initiator* is the person who first suggests making a purchase.

- *Influencers/evaluators* are people who influence the buying decision. They often help define specifications and provide information for evaluating options.

Technical personnel are especially important as influencers.

- *Gatekeepers* are group members who regulate the flow of information. Frequently, the purchasing agent views the gatekeeping role as a source of his or her power. A secretary may also act as a gatekeeper by determining which vendors get an appointment with a buyer.

- The *decider* is the person who has the formal or informal power to choose or approve the selection of the supplier or brand. In complex situations, it is often difficult to determine who makes the final decision.

- The *purchaser* is the person who actually negotiates the purchase. It could be anyone from the president of the company to the purchasing agent, depending on the importance of the decision.

- *Users* are members of the organization who will actually use the product. Users often initiate the buying process and help define product specifications.

IMPLICATIONS OF BUYING CENTERS FOR THE MARKETING MANAGER Successful vendors realize the importance of identifying who is in the decision-making unit, each member's relative influence in the buying decision, and each member's evaluative criteria. Key influencers are frequently located outside of the purchasing department. Successful selling strategies often focus on determining the most important buying influences and tailoring sales presentations to the evaluative criteria most important to these buying center members. An example illustrating the basic buying center roles is shown in Exhibit 7.3.

Marketers are often frustrated by their inability to reach c-level (chief) executives who play important roles in many buying centers. Marketers who want to build executive-level contacts must become involved in the buying process early on. This is when eighty percent of executives get involved—when major purchase decisions are being made. Executives often ensconce themselves in the buying process because they want to understand current business issues, establish project objectives, and set the overall project strategy.[29] Senior executives are typically not involved in the middle phases of the buying process but often get involved again later in the process to monitor the deal's closing. Executives look for four characteristics in sales representatives:

- The ability to marshal resources

- An understanding of the buyer's business goals

> **buying center** all those people in an organization who become involved in the purchase decision

EXHIBIT 7.3 BUYING CENTER ROLES FOR COMPUTER PURCHASES

Role	Illustration
Initiator	Division general manager proposes to replace company's computer network.
Influencers/evaluators	Corporate controller's office and vice president of information services have an important say in which system and vendor the company will deal with.
Gatekeepers	Corporate departments for purchasing and information services analyze company's needs and recommend likely matches with potential vendors.
Decider	Vice president of administration, with advice from others, selects vendor the company will deal with and system it will buy.
Purchaser	Purchasing agent negotiates terms of sale.
Users	All division employees use the computers.

- Responsiveness to requests
- Willingness to be held accountable

Some firms have developed strategies to reach executives throughout the buying process and during non-buying phases of the relationship. For example, FedEx Corp. has initiated a marketing effort called "access" aimed at c-level executives. It includes direct mail, e-mail, and a custom magazine prepared exclusively for c-level executives. It also hosts exclusive leadership events for these senior executives. Other firms have developed programs utilizing a combination of print, online, and events to reach the elusive c-level audience.[30]

View Apart/Shutterstock.com

Some firms have developed strategies to reach "c-level" executives, with FedEx leading the way.

7-8b Evaluative Criteria

Business buyers evaluate products and suppliers against three important criteria: quality, service, and price.

QUALITY In this case, *quality* refers to technical suitability. A superior tool can do a better job in the production process and superior packaging can increase dealer and consumer acceptance of a brand. Evaluation of quality also applies to the salesperson and the salesperson's firm. Business buyers want to deal with reputable salespeople and companies that are financially responsible. Quality improvement should be part of every organization's marketing strategy.

SERVICE Almost as much as they want satisfactory products, business buyers want satisfactory service. A purchase offers several opportunities for service. Suppose a vendor is selling heavy equipment. Prepurchase service could include a survey of the buyer's needs. After thorough analysis of the survey findings, the vendor could prepare a report and recommendations in the form of a purchasing proposal. If a purchase results, postpurchase service might consist of installing the equipment and training those who will be using it. Postsale services may also include maintenance and repairs.

Another service that business buyers seek is dependability of supply. They must be able to count on delivery of what was ordered when it is scheduled to be delivered. Buyers also welcome services that help them sell their finished products. Services of this sort are especially appropriate when the seller's product is an identifiable part of the buyer's end product.

PRICE Business buyers want to buy at low prices—at the lowest prices, under most circumstances. However, a buyer who pressures a supplier to cut prices to a point at which the supplier loses money on the sale almost forces shortcuts on quality. The buyer also may, in effect, force the supplier to quit selling to him or her. Then a new source of supply will have to be found.

7-8c Buying Situations

Often, business firms, especially manufacturers, must decide whether to make something or buy it from an outside supplier. The decision is essentially one of economics. Can an item of similar quality be bought at a lower price elsewhere? If not, is manufacturing it in-house the best use of limited company resources? For example, Briggs & Stratton Corporation, a major manufacturer of four-cycle engines, might be able to save $150,000 annually on outside purchases by spending $500,000 on the equipment needed to produce gas throttles internally. Yet Briggs & Stratton could also use that $500,000 to upgrade its carburetor assembly line, which would save $225,000 annually. If a firm does decide to buy a product instead of making it, the purchase will be a new buy, a modified rebuy, or a straight rebuy.

NEW BUY A **new buy** is a situation requiring the purchase of a product for the first time. For example, suppose a manufacturing company needs a better way to page its managers while they are working on the shop floor. Currently, each of the several managers has a distinct ring—for example, two short and one long—that sounds over the plant intercom whenever he or she is being paged by anyone in the factory. The company decides to replace its buzzer system of paging with handheld wireless radio technology that will allow managers to communicate immediately with the department initiating the page. This situation represents the greatest opportunity for new vendors. No long-term relationship has been established for this product, specifications may be somewhat fluid, and buyers are generally more open to new vendors.

If the new item is a raw material or a critical component part, the buyer cannot afford to run out of supply. The seller must be able to convince the buyer that the seller's firm can consistently deliver a high-quality product on time.

MODIFIED REBUY A **modified rebuy** is normally less critical and less time-consuming than a new buy. In a modified rebuy situation, the purchaser wants some change in the original good or service. It may be a new color, greater tensile strength in a component part, more respondents in a marketing research study, or additional services in a janitorial contract.

Because the two parties are familiar with each other and credibility has been established, the buyer and seller can concentrate on the specifics of the modification. But in some cases, modified rebuys are open to outside bidders. The purchaser uses this strategy to ensure that the new terms are competitive. An example would be the manufacturing company buying radios with a vibrating feature for managers who have trouble hearing the ring over the factory noise. The firm may open the bidding to examine the price, quality, and service offerings of several suppliers.

STRAIGHT REBUY A **straight rebuy** is a situation vendors prefer. The purchaser is not looking for new information or other suppliers. An order is placed and the product is provided as in previous orders. Usually, a straight rebuy is routine because the terms of the purchase have been agreed to in earlier negotiations. An example would be the previously cited manufacturing company purchasing additional radios for new managers from the same supplier on a regular basis.

One common instrument used in straight rebuy situations is the purchasing contract. Purchasing contracts are used with products that are bought often and in high volume. In essence, the purchasing contract makes the buyer's decision making routine and promises the salesperson a sure sale. The advantage to the buyer is a quick, confident decision, and to the salesperson, reduced or eliminated competition. Nevertheless, suppliers must remember not to take straight rebuy relationships for granted. Retaining existing customers is much easier than attracting new ones.

7-8d Business Ethics

As we noted in Chapter 3, *ethics* refers to the moral principles or values that generally govern the conduct of an individual or a group. Ethics can also be viewed as the standard of behavior by which conduct is judged.

Although we have heard a lot about corporate misbehavior in recent years, most people, and most companies, follow ethical practices. To help achieve this, over half of all major corporations offer ethics training to employees. Many companies also have codes of ethics that help guide buyers and sellers. For example, Home Depot has a clearly written code of ethics available on its corporate Web site that acts as an ethical guide for all its employees.

7-8e Customer Service

Business marketers are increasingly recognizing the benefits of developing a formal system to monitor customer opinions and perceptions of the quality of customer service. Companies such as FedEx, IBM, and Oracle build their strategies not only around products but also around highly developed service skills.[31] These companies understand that keeping current customers satisfied is just as important as attracting new ones, if not

new buy a situation requiring the purchase of a product for the first time

modified rebuy a situation in which the purchaser wants some change in the original good or service

straight rebuy a situation in which the purchaser reorders the same goods or services without looking for new information or investigating other suppliers

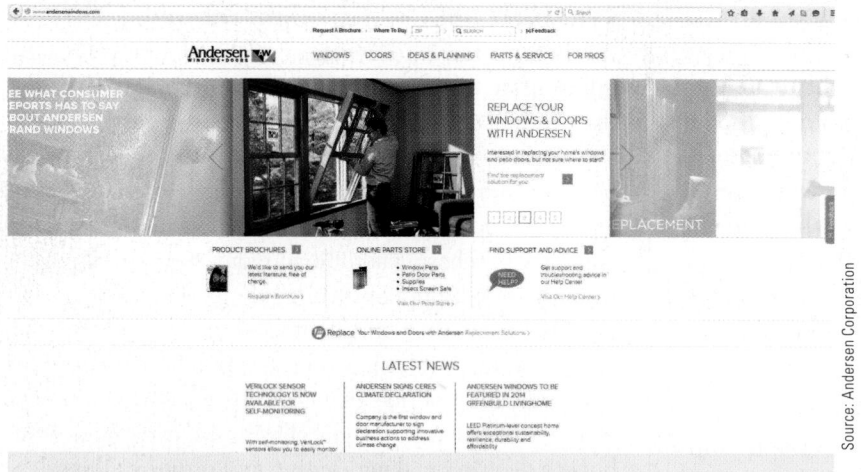

Source: Andersen Corporation

Andersen Windows and Doors assesses the loyalty of its trade customers by their willingness to carry its windows and doors.

more so. Leading-edge firms are obsessed not only with delivering high-quality customer service but also with measuring satisfaction, loyalty, relationship quality, and other indicators of nonfinancial performance. Delivering consistent, high-quality customer service is an important basis for establishing competitive advantage and differentiating one's company from competitors. Cisco Systems uses a Web-based survey to determine the pre-sale and postsale satisfaction of customers.[32]

Most firms find it necessary to develop measures unique to their own strategies, value propositions, and target markets. For example, Andersen Corporation assesses the loyalty of its trade customers by their willingness to continue carrying its windows and doors, recommend its products to colleagues and customers, increase their volume with the company, and put its products in their own homes. Basically, each firm's measures should not only ask "What are your expectations?" and "How are we doing?" but should also reflect what the firm wants its customers to do.

Some customers are more valuable than others. They may have greater value because they spend more, buy higher-margin products, have a well-known name, or have the potential of becoming a bigger customer in the future. Some companies selectively provide different levels of service to customers based on their value to the business. By giving the most valuable customers

superior service, a firm is more likely to keep them happy, hopefully increasing retention of these high-value customers and maximizing the total business value they generate over time.

To achieve this goal, the firm must be able to divide customers into two or more groups based on their value. It must also create and apply policies that govern how service will be allocated among groups. Policies might establish which customers' phone calls get "fast tracked" and which customers are directed to use the Web and/or voice self-service, how specific e-mail questions are routed, and who is given access to online chat and who is not.

Providing different customers with different levels of service is a very sensitive matter. It must be handled very carefully and very discreetly to avoid offending lesser-value, but still important, customers.

STUDY TOOLS 7

LOCATED AT BACK OF THE TEXTBOOK

☐ Rip out Chapter Review Card

LOCATED AT WWW.CENGAGEBRAIN.COM

☐ Review Key Terms Flashcards and create your own

☐ Track your knowledge and understanding of key concepts in marketing

☐ Complete practice and graded quizzes to prepare for tests

☐ Complete interactive content within the MKTG Online experience

☐ View the chapter highlight boxes within the MKTG Online experience

MKTG ONLINE

PREPARE FOR TESTS ON THE STUDYBOARD!

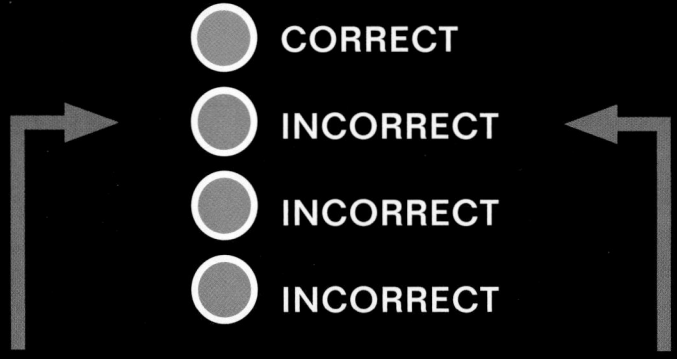

CORRECT

INCORRECT

INCORRECT

INCORRECT

Personalize Quizzes from Your StudyBits

Take Practice Quizzes by Chapter

CHAPTER QUIZZES

Chapter 1

Chapter 2

Chapter 3

Chapter 4

4LTR PRESS

Access MKTG ONLINE at www.cengagebrain.com

8 Segmenting and Targeting Markets

LEARNING OUTCOMES

After studying this chapter, you will be able to…

8-1 Describe the characteristics of markets and market segments

8-2 Explain the importance of market segmentation

8-3 Discuss the criteria for successful market segmentation

8-4 Describe the bases commonly used to segment consumer markets

8-5 Describe the bases for segmenting business markets

8-6 List the steps involved in segmenting markets

8-7 Discuss alternative strategies for selecting target markets

8-8 Explain how CRM can be used as a targeting tool

8-9 Explain how and why firms implement positioning strategies and how product differentiation plays a role

After you finish this chapter go to **PAGE 148** for **STUDY TOOLS.**

8-1 MARKETS AND MARKET SEGMENTS

The term *market* means different things to different people. We are all familiar with the supermarket, stock market, labor market, fish market, and flea market. All these types of markets share several characteristics. First, they are composed of people (consumer markets) or organizations (business markets). Second, these people or organizations have wants and needs that can be satisfied by particular product categories. Third, they have the ability to buy the products they seek. Fourth, they are willing to exchange their resources, usually money or credit, for desired products. In sum, a **market** is (1) people or organizations with (2) needs or wants and with (3) the ability and (4) the willingness to buy. A group of people or an organization that lacks any one of these characteristics is not a market.

market
people or organizations with needs or wants and the ability and willingness to buy

Within a market, a **market segment** is a subgroup of people or organizations sharing one or more characteristics that cause them to have similar product needs. At one extreme, we can define every person and every organization in the world as a market segment because each is unique. At the other extreme, we can define the entire consumer market as one large market segment and the business market as another large segment. All people have some similar characteristics and needs, as do all organizations.

From a marketing perspective, market segments can be described as somewhere between the two extremes. The process of dividing a market into meaningful, relatively similar, and identifiable segments, or groups, is called **market segmentation**. The purpose of market segmentation is to enable the marketer to tailor marketing mixes to meet the needs of one or more specific segments.

8-2 THE IMPORTANCE OF MARKET SEGMENTATION

Until the 1960s, few firms practiced market segmentation. When they did, it was more likely a haphazard effort than a formal marketing strategy. Before 1960, for example, the Coca-Cola Company produced only one beverage and aimed it at the entire soft drink market. Today, Coca-Cola offers more than a dozen different products to market segments based on diverse consumer preferences for flavors, calorie, and caffeine content. Coca-Cola offers traditional soft drinks, energy drinks (including POWERade), flavored teas, fruit drinks (Minute Maid), and water (Dasani).

Market segmentation plays a key role in the marketing strategy of almost all successful organizations and is a powerful marketing tool for several reasons. Most important, nearly all markets include groups of people or organizations with different product needs and preferences. Market segmentation helps marketers define customer needs and wants more precisely. Because market segments differ in size and potential, segmentation helps decision makers to more accurately define marketing objectives and better allocate resources. In turn, performance can be better evaluated when objectives are more precise.

Jax & Bones has successfully appealed to affluent customers with high-end pet products. For example, the company produces a $200 dog bed that

market segment
a subgroup of people or organizations sharing one or more characteristics that cause them to have similar product needs

market segmentation
the process of dividing a market into meaningful, relatively similar, and identifiable segments or groups

it sells in upscale retailers such as Bloomingdale's, Pottery Barn, and Barneys New York. The company's owner creates pet beds that reflect the latest colors, fabrics, textures, and styles. When memory foam became popular in human beds, Jax & Bones added memory foam to its beds. Last year, when gray, silver, and blue were popular in home design, these colors were incorporated into Jax & Bones' beds.[1]

8-3 CRITERIA FOR SUCCESSFUL SEGMENTATION

Marketers segment markets for three important reasons. First, segmentation enables marketers to identify groups of customers with similar needs and to analyze the characteristics and buying behavior of these groups. Second, segmentation provides marketers with information to help them design marketing mixes specifically matched with the characteristics and desires of one or more segments. Third, segmentation is consistent with the marketing concept of satisfying customer wants and needs while meeting the organization's objectives.

To be useful, a segmentation scheme must produce segments that meet four basic criteria:

1. **Substantiality:** A segment must be large enough to warrant developing and maintaining a special marketing mix. This criterion does not necessarily mean that a segment must have many potential customers. For example, marketers of custom-designed homes and business buildings, commercial airplanes, and large computer systems typically develop marketing programs tailored to each potential customer's needs. In most cases, however, a market segment needs many potential customers to make commercial sense. In the 1980s, home banking failed because not enough people owned personal computers. Today, a larger number of people own computers, and home banking is a thriving industry.

2. **Identifiability and measurability:** Segments must be identifiable and their size measurable. Data about the population within geographic boundaries, the number of people in various age categories, and other social and demographic characteristics are often easy to get, and they provide fairly concrete measures of segment size. Suppose that a social service agency wants to identify segments by their readiness to participate in a drug and alcohol program or in prenatal care. Unless the agency can measure how many people are willing, indifferent, or unwilling to participate, it will have trouble gauging whether there are enough people to justify setting up the service.

3. **Accessibility:** The firm must be able to reach members of targeted segments with customized marketing mixes. Some market segments are hard to reach—for example, senior citizens (especially those with reading or hearing disabilities), individuals who do not speak English, and the illiterate.

4. **Responsiveness:** Markets can be segmented using any criteria that seem logical. Unless one market segment responds to a marketing mix differently than other segments, however, that segment need not be treated separately. For instance, if all customers are equally price conscious about a product, there is no need to offer high-, medium-, and low-priced versions to different segments.

8-4 BASES FOR SEGMENTING CONSUMER MARKETS

Marketers use segmentation bases, or variables, which are characteristics of individuals, groups, or organizations, to divide a total market into segments. The choice of segmentation bases is crucial because an inappropriate segmentation strategy may lead to lost sales and missed profit opportunities. The key is to identify bases that will produce substantial, measurable, and accessible segments that exhibit different response patterns to marketing mixes.

Markets can be segmented using a single variable, such as age group, or several variables, such as age group, gender, and education. Although it is less precise, single-variable segmentation has the advantage of being simpler and easier to use than multiple-variable segmentation. The disadvantages of multiple-variable segmentation are that it is often harder to use than single-variable segmentation; usable secondary data are less likely to be available; and as the number of segmentation bases increases, the size of individual segments decreases. Nevertheless, the current trend is toward using more rather than fewer variables to segment most markets. Multiple-variable segmentation is clearly more precise than single-variable segmentation.

Consumer goods marketers commonly use one or more of the following characteristics to segment markets: geography, demographics, psychographics, benefits sought, and usage rate.

segmentation bases (variables) characteristics of individuals, groups, or organizations

8-4a Geographic Segmentation

Geographic segmentation refers to segmenting markets by region of a country or the world, market size, market density, or climate. Market density means the number of people within a unit of land, such as a census tract. Climate is commonly used for geographic segmentation because of its dramatic impact on residents' needs and purchasing behavior. Snowblowers, water and snow skis, clothing, and air-conditioning and heating systems are products with varying appeal, depending on climate.

Consumer goods companies take a regional approach to marketing for four reasons. First, many firms need to find new ways to generate sales because of sluggish and intensely competitive markets. Second, computerized checkout stations with scanners give retailers an accurate assessment of which brands sell best in their region. Third, many packaged-goods manufacturers are introducing new regional brands intended to appeal to local preferences.

Fourth, a more regional approach allows consumer goods companies to react more quickly to competition. Macy's localizes the merchandising and shopping experience for every U.S. geographic region in which it operates. For example, Macy's stocks its downtown Chicago location to meet a high demand for women's shoes in larger sizes, while it stocks its Long Island location to meet high demand for electric coffee percolators. Men in some, but not all, of Macy's districts shop primarily for cuffed pants, so the company adjusts its product offerings accordingly.[2]

8-4b Demographic Segmentation

Marketers often segment markets on the basis of demographic information because it is widely available and often related to consumers' buying and consuming behavior. Some common bases of **demographic segmentation** are age, gender, income, ethnic background, and family life cycle.

AGE SEGMENTATION Marketers use a variety of terms to refer to different age groups. Examples include newborns, infants, young children, tweens, Millennials, Generation X, baby boomers, and seniors. Age segmentation can be an important tool, as a brief exploration of the market potential of several age segments illustrates.

Many companies have long targeted parents of babies and young children with products such as disposable diapers, baby food, and toys. Recently, other companies that have not traditionally marketed to young children are developing products and services to attract this group. For example, high-intensity fitness company CrossFit recently developed a program for kids in an attempt to tackle childhood obesity. The coaches for these group fitness classes create special workouts and games like "Hungry, Hungry Hippos" and "Farmers and Lumberjacks" to make classes fun and kid-friendly.[3]

The tween and teenage cohort following the Millennials is sometimes called Generation Z. This group accounts for 25.9 percent of the U.S. population and contributes $44 billion to the U.S. economy.[4] Born after 1995, Gen Zers are incredibly tech savvy, have short attention spans, and do not distinguish between their online and offline friends. To reach this cohort, marketers must make sure that their brands are communicated consistently across different channels.[5] To attract Generation Z, Google is considering offering user accounts to children under the age of 13. These accounts will include a way for parents to control account usage. Similarly, Facebook allows teens age 13 to 17 to post publicly on its site.[6] In another effort to reach tween shoppers, Macy's joined with the ABC Family television network to offer apparel seen on the popular series *Pretty Little Liars*. While they shopped on the store's Web site for clothing, teens and tweens had the opportunity to chat live with one of the show's stars.[7]

The Millennial market makes up 25 percent of the adult population in the United States.[8] This group is the most educated, diverse, and technology-proficient generation ever. Most of their media consumption is online, including reading news and watching television shows. Millennials have formidable purchasing power, but they distrust advertising and are more likely to listen to their peers regarding product decisions.[9] The top brand attributes important to Millennials include trustworthiness, creativity, intelligence, authenticity, and confidence. Millennials are more likely than other generations to take a company's social responsibility into account before making a purchase decision.[10] Brands like TOMS Shoes and Warby Parker appeal to this group because they offer social value and align their brands with a higher purpose. These brands also invite participation and co-creation, both of which appeal to Millennials.[11]

Szefei/istock/Thinkstock

geographic segmentation
segmenting markets by region of a country or the world, market size, market density, or climate

demographic segmentation
segmenting markets by age, gender, income, ethnic background, and family life cycle

Generation X is smaller than both the Millennials and the baby boomers, making up only sixteen percent of the total population. Members of Generation X are at a life stage where they are often stuck between supporting their aging parents and young children (earning Gen X the nickname "the sandwich generation"). They grew up as *latchkey kids*, meaning that they spent time alone at home while their (often divorced) parents worked long into the night. They are the best-educated generation—29 percent have earned a bachelor's degree or better. They tend to be disloyal to brands and skeptical of big business. Many of them are parents, and they make purchasing decisions with thought for and input from their families.[12] Gen Xers desire an experience, not just a product. This desire has led to an increase in offbeat events such as Vancouver, Canada's Dine Out Vancouver food festival. More than a series of tastings and tours, the 17-day festival features experiences such as a drag queen cabaret and dinner show inspired by the film *The Birdcage*, a brunch crawl, the Grape Debate (where top wine experts debate contemporary topics), and prix fixe menus at more than 230 restaurants throughout the city.[13]

Recall from Chapter 4 that people born between 1946 and 1964 are often called baby boomers. Boomers make up 24.7 percent of the total population and they constitute almost one-third of the adult population. According to the U.S. Consumer Expenditure Survey, baby boomers outspend other generations by approximately $400 billion a year.[14] They are living longer, healthier, more active and connected lives, and will spend time and money doing whatever is necessary to maintain vitality as they age. This group spends more than other age brackets on dining out, housing, alcohol, and healthcare. Moreover, boomers' spending on vehicles is growing faster than any other demographic. Marketers should target boomers based on their core values, such as healthy eating and aging well. General Mills' Cheerios ads have long focused on heart health to reach boomers, for example.[15]

Consumers age seventy and older are part of the war generation and the Great Depression generation. Together, this group is often called the silent generation for its ability to quietly persevere through great hardships. The smallest generation of the last 100 years, members of this group tend to live modestly, save their money, and be civic minded. Many in this group view retirement not as a passive time, but as an active time they use to explore new knowledge, travel, volunteer, and spend time with family and friends.[16] However, as consumers age, they do require some modifications in the way they live and the products they purchase. According to gerontologist Stephen Golant, for example, aging individuals may need to install "well-placed handrails or grab bars, ramps, easy-access bathrooms, easy-access kitchens, stair lifts, widened doors or hallways, and modified sink faucets or cabinets" in their homes.[17]

GENDER SEGMENTATION In the United States, women make 85 percent of purchases of consumer goods each year.[18] They are an experienced purchasing group with the responsibility of purchasing the majority of household items. They also are increasingly part of what were once considered all-male markets, such as financial markets. Women tend to view money and wealth differently than men do. They do not seek to accumulate money for the sake of accumulation, but rather associate it with security, independence, and quality of life for themselves and their families. They also tend to research investments in-depth more than men do. Thus, financial advisors need to use different strategies to appeal to women.[19] Freshness Burger, Japan's biggest hamburger chain, recently unveiled a burger wrapper with the bottom half of a woman's face printed on it. As a woman eats a burger, she can cover the bottom half of her face with the wrapper, making it appear that she is not chowing down, but is instead smiling serenely. After Freshness Burger launched the wrapper, sales to women jumped more than 200 percent.[20] Marketers of products such as clothing, cosmetics, food, personal-care items, magazines, jewelry, and gifts still commonly segment markets by gender, and many of these marketers are going after the less-traditional male market. For example, Kraft used to target its Velveeta Shells and Cheese exclusively at busy moms. While conducting market research, Kraft "found a segment of men already making and cooking Shells and Cheese that we frankly weren't talking to," said Tiphanie Maronta, senior brand manager for Velveeta meals. To reach this new market, Kraft developed a series of humorous Eat Like That Guy You Know television ads that featured slacker heroes such as limo drivers and ham radio operators.[21] Similarly, Procter & Gamble sponsored "man-aisles" in some Walmart, Target, and Walgreen's stores in the U.S. and Canada.

Mayakova/Shutterstock.com

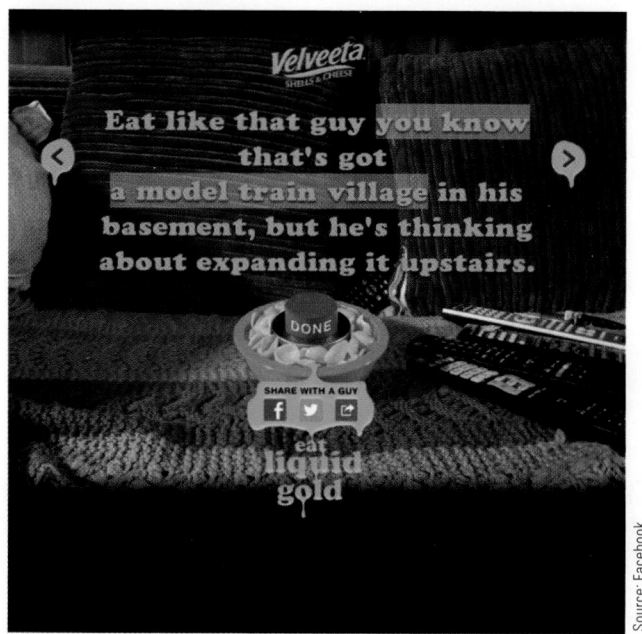

Source: Facebook

These aisles group all men's products in one place and use shelf displays and small TV screens to guide men to skin-care items.[22]

INCOME SEGMENTATION Income is a popular demographic variable for segmenting markets because income level influences consumers' wants and determines their buying power. Many markets are segmented by income, including the markets for housing, clothing, automobiles, and food. Dollar stores, traditionally targeted at lower-income consumers, surged in growth as they began to target middle-income consumers during the Great Recession. In 2012, Dollar General announced that its fastest-growing customer segment was shoppers who earned more than $70,000 a year.[23] Wholesale clubs Costco and Sam's Club appeal to many income segments. High-income customers looking for luxury want outstanding customer service. Because they spend large amounts of money, luxury consumers expect to be treated extraordinarily well and to feel a personal connection to a product or brand. Luxury product showrooms and retail locations must constantly evolve to accommodate these customers' needs and to provide an exceptional, high-tech in-store experience.[24] On the other hand, some companies have found success in marketing to the very poor. People living in developing nations are emerging as reliable customers for multinational companies like Coca-Cola and McDonald's.[25]

ETHNIC SEGMENTATION In the past, ethnic groups in the United States were expected to conform to a homogenized, Anglo-centric ideal. This was evident both in how mass-produced products were marketed as well as in the selective way that films, television, advertisements, and popular music portrayed America's diverse population. Until the 1970s, ethnic foods were rarely sold except in specialty stores. Increasing numbers of ethnic minorities and increased buying power have changed this. Hispanic Americans, African Americans, and Asian Americans are the three largest ethnic groups in the United States. In the American Southwest, Caucasian populations comprise less than half the population and have become the minority to other ethnic groups combined. To meet the needs and wants of expanding ethnic populations, some companies, such as McDonald's and Kmart, make products geared toward specific ethnic groups. For example, Kmart has teamed up with Selena Gomez and Sofia Vergara, both popular Hispanic actors, to develop clothing lines that appeal to Latina consumers.[26] Many department stores carry Fashion Fair Cosmetics, a line of beauty products created specifically for (and marketed toward) African American women.[27]

FAMILY LIFE CYCLE SEGMENTATION The demographic factors of gender, age, and income often do not sufficiently explain why consumer buying behavior

Bennett Raglin/WireImage/Getty Images

Kmart has teamed up with Hispanic actress, Sofia Vergara, in order to appeal their clothing to Latina consumers.

varies. Frequently, consumption patterns among people of the same age and gender differ because they are in different stages of the family life cycle. The **family life cycle (FLC)** is a series of stages determined by a combination of age, marital status, and the presence or absence of children.

family life cycle (FLC)

a series of stages determined by a combination of age, marital status, and the presence or absence of children

The life cycle stage consisting of the married-couple household used to be considered the traditional family in the United States. Today, however, married couples make up less than half of households, down from nearly eighty percent in the 1950s. Single adults are increasingly in the majority. Already, unmarried Americans make up 42 percent of the workforce, 40 percent of home buyers, and one of the most potent consumer groups on record. Exhibit 8.1 illustrates numerous FLC

EXHIBIT 8.1 FAMILY LIFE CYCLE

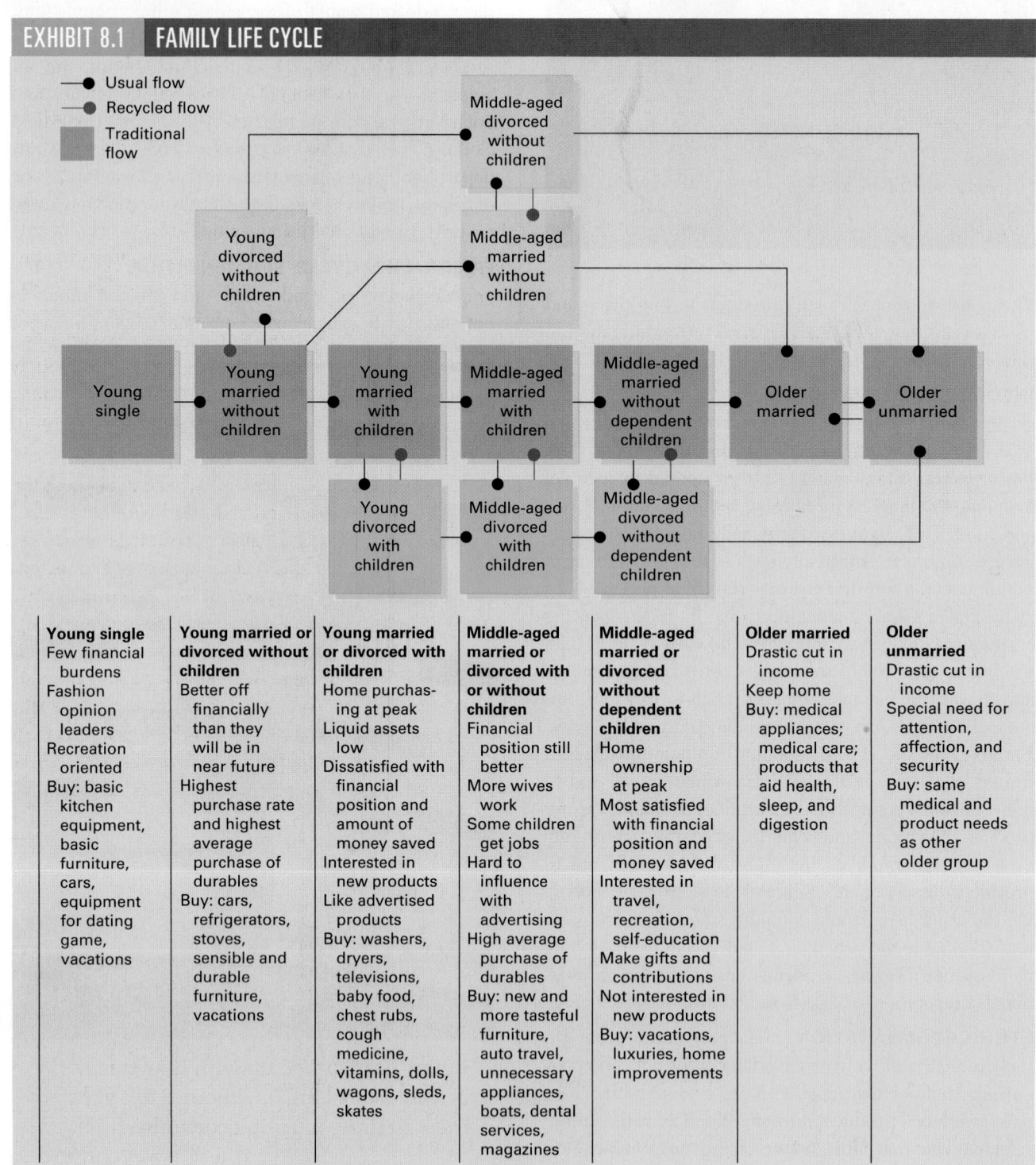

patterns and shows how families' needs, incomes, resources, and expenditures differ at each stage. The horizontal flow shows the traditional FLC. The lower part of the exhibit gives some of the characteristics and purchase patterns of families in each stage of the traditional life cycle. The exhibit also acknowledges that about half of all first marriages end in divorce. If young marrieds move into the young divorced stage, their consumption patterns often revert to those of the young single stage of the cycle.

About four out of five divorced persons remarry by middle age and reenter the traditional life cycle, as indicated by the "recycled flow" in the exhibit. Consumers are especially receptive to marketing efforts at certain points in the life cycle. For example, baby boomers have increased needs for health care services, while families with babies need diapers, toys, and baby clothes.

8-4c Psychographic Segmentation

Age, gender, income, ethnicity, FLC stage, and other demographic variables are usually helpful in developing segmentation strategies, but often, they do not paint the entire picture. Demographics provide the skeleton, but psychographics add meat to the bones. **Psychographic segmentation** is market segmentation on the basis of the following psychographic segmentation variables:

- **Personality:** Personality reflects a person's traits, attitudes, and habits. Clothing is the ultimate personality descriptor. Fashionistas wear high-end, trendy clothes, and hipsters enjoy jeans and T-shirts with tennis shoes. People buy clothes that they feel represent their personalities and give others an idea of who they are.

- **Motives:** Marketers of baby products and life insurance appeal to consumers' emotional motives—namely, to care for their loved ones. Using appeals to economy, reliability, and dependability, carmakers like Subaru and Suzuki target customers with rational motives. Carmakers like Mercedes-Benz, Jaguar, and Cadillac appeal to customers with status-related motives.

- **Lifestyles:** Lifestyle segmentation divides people into groups according to the way they spend their time, the importance of the things around them, their beliefs, and socioeconomic characteristics such as income and education. For example, record stores specializing in vinyl are targeting young people who are listening to independent labels and often pride themselves on being independent of big business.

LEED-certified appliances appeal to environmentally conscious "green" consumers. PepsiCo is promoting its no-calorie, sugar-free flavored water, Aquafina FlavorSplash, to consumers who are health conscious.

- **Geodemographics: Geodemographic segmentation** clusters potential customers into neighborhood lifestyle categories. It combines geographic, demographic, and lifestyle segmentations. Geodemographic segmentation helps marketers develop marketing programs tailored to prospective buyers who live in small geographic regions, such as neighborhoods, or who have very specific lifestyle and demographic characteristics. College students, for example, often share similar demographics and lifestyles and tend to cluster around campus. Knowing this, marketing teams for startups and tech companies like Google often launch ambassador programs at insular college campuses. Student brand ambassadors for the Google Pizza Program bought pizza for their computer science peers during tough times and around deadlines. This helped the company create buzz and form ties with talented programmers. Through these programs, students are transformed into word-of-mouth marketers to their geodemographic peers.[28]

Psychographic variables can be used individually to segment markets or can be combined with other variables to provide more detailed descriptions of market segments. One approach is for marketers and advertisers to purchase information from a collector, such as eXelate Media, in order to reach the audience they want. eXelate, part of consumer research firm Nielsen, gathers information about Web-browsing habits through cookies placed on Web sites. Nielsen, using eXelate, organizes groups according to this information. One group, the "young digerati," includes 25- to 45-year-olds who:

- Are tech savvy
- Are affluent
- Live in trendy condos
- Read the *Economist*
- Have an annual income of $88,000

An automaker can purchase that list and the list of people who visit car blogs and then target ads to the young digerati interested in cars.[29]

> **psychographic segmentation** segmenting markets on the basis of personality, motives, lifestyles, and geodemographics
>
> **geodemographic segmentation** segmenting potential customers into neighborhood lifestyle categories

8-4d Benefit Segmentation

Benefit segmentation is the process of grouping customers into market segments according to the benefits they seek from the product. Most types of market segmentation are based on the assumption that this variable and customers' needs are related. Benefit segmentation is different because it groups potential customers on the basis of their needs or wants rather than on some other characteristic, such as age or gender. The snack-food market, for example, can be divided into six benefit segments: nutritional snackers, weight watchers, guilty snackers, party snackers, indiscriminate snackers, and economical snackers.

Customer profiles can be developed by examining demographic information associated with people seeking certain benefits. This information can be used to match marketing strategies with selected markets. Dish Network developed Sling TV, a streaming live television service that is available on devices such as gaming consoles and mobile devices, to appeal to people who want to get away from traditional TV sets and cable boxes. The service costs $20 a month for a basic package (additional channels can be purchased), and there are no set-up fees or commitments. Sling TV emphasizes family-friendly programming, which is especially attractive to families with young children.[30]

8-4e Usage-Rate Segmentation

Usage-rate segmentation divides a market by the amount of product bought or consumed. Categories vary with the product, but they are likely to include some combination of the following: former users, potential users, first-time users, light or irregular users, medium users, and heavy users. Segmenting by usage rate enables marketers to focus their efforts on heavy users or to develop multiple marketing mixes aimed at different segments. Because heavy users often account for a sizable portion of all product sales, some marketers focus on the heavy-user segment.

The **80/20 principle** holds that 20 percent of all customers generate 80 percent of the demand. Although the percentages usually are not exact, the general idea often holds true. Multinational corporations require vast amounts of computer storage, but these giant enterprises make up just a small percentage of the data storage market. When storage manufacturer Actifio found that eighty percent of its customers were midsize enterprises that bought computer storage in relatively modest batches of 100 terabytes (about 100,000 gigabytes), it developed the Actifio 100T, a storage appliance that allowed midsize enterprises to scale up to two petabytes (about two million gigabytes) of capacity. In this way, Actifio's 80 percent of low-demand customers could transition over time toward its 20 percent of high-demand customers.[31]

Developing customers into heavy users is the goal behind many frequency/loyalty programs like the airlines' frequent flyer programs. Most supermarkets and other retailers have also designed loyalty programs that reward the heavy-user segment with deals available only to them, such as in-store coupon dispensing systems, loyalty card programs, and special price deals on selected merchandise.

 8-5

BASES FOR SEGMENTING BUSINESS MARKETS

The business market consists of four broad segments: producers, resellers, government, and institutions. (For a detailed discussion of the characteristics of these segments, see Chapter 7.) Whether marketers focus on only one or on all four of these segments, they are likely to find diversity among potential customers. Thus, further market segmentation offers just as many benefits to business marketers as it does to consumer product marketers.

8-5a Company Characteristics

Company characteristics, such as geographic location, type of company, company size, and product use, can be important segmentation variables. Some markets tend to be regional because buyers prefer to purchase from local suppliers, and distant suppliers may have difficulty competing in terms of price and service. Therefore, firms that sell to geographically concentrated industries benefit by locating close to their markets.

Segmenting by customer type allows business marketers to tailor their marketing mixes to the unique needs of particular types of organizations or industries. For example, the Amazon Webstore platform allows businesses

---

benefit segmentation the process of grouping customers into market segments according to the benefits they seek from the product

usage-rate segmentation dividing a market by the amount of product bought or consumed

80/20 principle a principle holding that 20 percent of all customers generate 80 percent of the demand

from single-person operations to multinational corporations to operate Amazon-hosted online shops. Entrepreneurs can easily set up templatized shops featuring products that are warehoused and fulfilled by Amazon, while enterprise-level corporations like Fruit of the Loom, Spalding, and Bacardi can use the platform to manage large-scale, customized Web stores. Amazon Webstore's Web site, http://webstore.amazon.com, caters to companies' diverse needs with an array of hosting packages and information pages segmented by both business size and business type.[32]

Volume of purchase (heavy, moderate, light) is a commonly used basis for business segmentation. Another is the buying organization's size, which may affect its purchasing procedures, the types and quantities of products it needs, and its responses to different marketing mixes. Banks frequently offer different services, lines of credit, and overall attention to commercial customers based on their size. Many products, especially raw materials like steel, wood, and petroleum, have diverse applications. How customers use a product may influence the amount they buy, their buying criteria, and their selection of vendors. For example, a producer of springs may have customers who use the product in applications as diverse as making machine tools, bicycles, surgical devices, office equipment, telephones, and missile systems.

8-5b Buying Processes

Many business marketers find it helpful to segment customers and prospective customers on the basis of how they buy. For example, companies can segment some business markets by ranking key purchasing criteria, such as price, quality, technical support, and service. Atlas Overhead Door has developed a commanding position in the industrial door market by providing customized products in just 4 weeks, which is much faster than the industry average of 12 to 15 weeks. Atlas's primary market is companies with an immediate need for customized doors.

The purchasing strategies of buyers may provide useful segments. Two purchasing profiles that have been identified are satisficers and optimizers. **Satisficers** contact familiar suppliers and place the order with the first one to satisfy product and delivery requirements. **Optimizers** consider numerous suppliers (both familiar and unfamiliar), solicit bids, and study all proposals carefully before selecting one.

The personal characteristics of the buyers themselves (their demographic characteristics, decision style, tolerance for risk, confidence level, job responsibilities, and so on) influence their buying behavior and thus offer a viable basis for segmenting some business markets.

 ## 8-6 STEPS IN SEGMENTING A MARKET

The purpose of market segmentation, in both consumer and business markets, is to identify marketing opportunities.

1. **Select a market or product category for study:** Define the overall market or product category to be studied. It may be a market in which the firm already competes, a new but related market or product category, or a totally new market.

2. **Choose a basis or bases for segmenting the market:** This step requires managerial insight, creativity, and market knowledge. There are no scientific procedures for selecting segmentation variables. However, a successful segmentation scheme must produce segments that meet the four basic criteria discussed earlier in this chapter.

3. **Select segmentation descriptors:** After choosing one or more bases, the marketer must select the segmentation descriptors. Descriptors identify the specific segmentation variables to use. For example, if a company selects demographics as a basis of segmentation, it may use age, occupation, and income as descriptors. A company that selects usage-rate segmentation needs to decide whether to go after heavy users, nonusers, or light users.

4. **Profile and analyze segments:** The profile should include the segments' size, expected growth, purchase frequency, current brand usage, brand loyalty, and long-term sales and profit potential. This information can then be used to rank potential market segments by profit opportunity, risk, consistency with organizational mission and objectives, and other factors important to the firm.

5. **Select markets:** Selecting markets is not a part of but a natural outcome of the

> **satisficers** business customers who place an order with the first familiar supplier to satisfy product and delivery requirements
>
> **optimizers** business customers who consider numerous suppliers (both familiar and unfamiliar), solicit bids, and study all proposals carefully before selecting one

TOO MANY COOKS

Campbell Soup Co. has classified home cooks into six distinct profile types: the passionate kitchen master, the familiar taste pleaser, the familiar taste pleaser (Mexican), the constrained wishful eater, the disciplined health manager, and the uninvolved quick fixer. The company uses these types as a foundation to develop and market new products and create recipes. For example, the passionate kitchen master loves to cook, usually has the time to do so, and knows how to make many dishes without a recipe. On the other end of the spectrum is the uninvolved quick fixer, who doesn't enjoy cooking and would be happy to snack all day. Campbell's develops unique approaches for each, as members of one market will not likely be persuaded to buy by a marketing mix targeted at the other. [33]

segmentation process. It is a major decision that influences and often directly determines the firm's marketing mix. This topic is examined in greater detail later in this chapter.

6. **Design, implement, and maintain appropriate marketing mixes:** The marketing mix has been described as product, place (distribution), promotion, and pricing strategies intended to bring about a mutually satisfying exchange relationship with a market. These topics are explored in detail in Chapters 10 through 20.

Markets are dynamic, so it is important that companies proactively monitor their segmentation strategies over time. Often, once customers or prospects have been assigned to a segment, marketers think their task is done. Once customers are assigned to an age segment, for example, they stay there until they reach the next age bracket or category, which could be ten years in the future. Thus, the segmentation classifications are static, but the customers and prospects are changing. Dynamic segmentation approaches adjust to fit the changes that occur in customers' lives. For example, American Eagle mainly targets 10-year-old boys and girls

target market a group of people or organizations for which an organization designs, implements, and maintains a marketing mix intended to meet the needs of that group, resulting in mutually satisfying exchanges

with its 77 kids stores. However, some segments are targeted by too many players, and choosing to enter those kinds of segments can be particularly challenging. For example, there are so many online fashion stores using flash sales to attract bargain hunters that *DailyWorth* put together a list of nine that it thinks are *actually* worth visiting. [34]

 ## 8-7 STRATEGIES FOR SELECTING TARGET MARKETS

So far, this chapter has focused on the market segmentation process, which is only the first step in deciding whom to approach about buying a product. The next task is to choose one or more target markets. A **target market** is a group of people or organizations for which an organization designs, implements, and maintains a marketing mix intended to meet the needs of that group, resulting in mutually satisfying exchanges.

Because most markets will include customers with different characteristics, lifestyles, backgrounds, and income levels, it is unlikely that a single marketing mix will attract all segments of the market. Thus, if a marketer wishes to appeal to more than one segment of the market, it must develop different marketing mixes. The three general strategies for selecting target markets—undifferentiated, concentrated, and multisegment targeting—are illustrated in Exhibit 8.2, which also illustrates the advantages and disadvantages of each targeting strategy.

8-7a Undifferentiated Targeting

A firm using an **undifferentiated targeting strategy** essentially adopts a mass-market philosophy, viewing the market as one big market with no individual segments. The firm uses one marketing mix for the entire market. A firm that adopts an undifferentiated targeting strategy assumes that individual customers have similar needs that can be met with a common marketing mix.

The first firm in an industry sometimes uses an undifferentiated targeting strategy. With no competition, the firm may not need to tailor marketing mixes to the preferences of market segments. Henry Ford's famous comment about the Model T is a classic example of an undifferentiated targeting strategy: "They can have their car in any color they want, as long as it's black." At one time, Coca-Cola used this strategy with a single

EXHIBIT 8.2 ADVANTAGES AND DISADVANTAGES OF TARGET MARKETING STRATEGIES

Targeting Strategy	Advantages	Disadvantages
Undifferentiated Targeting	• Potential savings on production/marketing costs	• Unimaginative product offerings • Company more susceptible to competition
Concentrated Targeting	• Concentration of resources • Can better meet the needs of a narrowly defined segment • Allows some small firms to better compete with larger firms • Strong positioning	• Segments too small or changing • Large competitors may more effectively market to niche segment
Multisegment Targeting	• Greater financial success • Economies of scale in producing/marketing	• High costs • Cannibalization

product and a single size of its familiar green bottle. Marketers of commodity products, such as flour and sugar, are also likely to use an undifferentiated targeting strategy.

One advantage of undifferentiated marketing is the potential for saving on production and marketing. Because only one item is produced, the firm should be able to achieve economies of mass production. Also, marketing costs may be lower when there is only one product to promote and a single channel of distribution. Too often, however, an undifferentiated strategy emerges by default rather than by design, reflecting a failure to consider the advantages of a segmented approach. The result is often sterile, unimaginative product offerings that have little appeal to anyone.

Another problem associated with undifferentiated targeting is that it makes the company more susceptible to competitive inroads. Hershey lost a big share of the candy market to Mars and other candy companies before it changed to a multisegment targeting strategy. Coca-Cola forfeited its position as the leading seller of cola drinks in supermarkets to PepsiCo in the late 1950s, when Pepsi began offering several sizes of containers.

You might think a firm producing a standard product such as toilet tissue would adopt an undifferentiated strategy. However, this market has industrial segments and consumer segments. Industrial buyers want an economical, single-ply product sold in boxes of a hundred rolls (or jumbo rolls a foot in diameter to use in public restrooms). The consumer market demands a more versatile product in smaller quantities. Within the consumer market, the product is differentiated with designer print or no print, as cushioned or noncushioned, and as economy priced or luxury priced. Undifferentiated marketing can succeed in certain situations, though. A small grocery store in a small, isolated town may define all of the people who live in the town as its target market. It may offer one marketing mix and generally satisfy everyone in town. This strategy is not likely to be as effective if there are three or four grocery stores in town.

8-7b Concentrated Targeting

With a **concentrated targeting strategy**, a firm selects a market **niche** (one segment of a market) for targeting its marketing efforts. Because the firm is appealing to a single segment, it can concentrate on understanding the needs, motives, and satisfactions of that segment's members and on developing and maintaining a highly specialized marketing mix. Some firms find that concentrating resources and meeting the needs of a narrowly defined market segment is more profitable than spreading resources over several different segments.

Intelligentsia Coffee & Tea, a Chicago-based coffee roaster/retailer, targets serious coffee drinkers with hand-roasted, ground, and poured super-gourmet

undifferentiated targeting strategy a marketing approach that views the market as one big market with no individual segments and thus uses a single marketing mix

concentrated targeting strategy a strategy used to select one segment of a market for targeting marketing efforts

niche one segment of a market

A bag of Intelligentsia coffee sits on a shelf before being shipped from the company's Chicago, Illinois headquarters

Daniel Acker/Bloomberg /Getty Images

coffee or tea served by seriously educated baristas. The company also offers training classes for the at-home or out-of-town coffee aficionado. Starting price—$200 per class.

Small firms often adopt a concentrated targeting strategy to compete effectively with much larger firms. For example, Enterprise Rent-A-Car, number one in the car rental industry, started as a small company catering to people with cars in the shop. Some other firms use a concentrated strategy to establish a strong position in a desirable market segment. Porsche, for instance, targets an upscale automobile market through "class appeal, not mass appeal."

Concentrated targeting violates the old adage "Don't put all your eggs in one basket." If the chosen segment is too small or if it shrinks because of environmental changes, the firm may suffer negative consequences.

For instance, OshKosh B'gosh was highly successful selling children's wear in the 1980s. It was so successful, however, that the children's line came to define OshKosh's image to the extent that the company could not sell clothes to anyone else. Attempts at marketing older children's clothing, women's casual clothes, and maternity wear were all abandoned. Recognizing it was in the children's wear business, the company expanded into products such as kids' shoes, children's eyewear, and plush toys.

A concentrated strategy can also be disastrous for a firm that is not successful in its narrowly defined target market. Before Procter & Gamble (P&G) introduced Head & Shoulders shampoo, several small firms were already selling antidandruff shampoos. Head & Shoulders was introduced with a large promotional campaign, and the new brand captured over half the market immediately. Within a year, several of the firms that had been concentrating on this market segment went out of business.

8-7c Multisegment Targeting

A firm that chooses to serve two or more well-defined market segments and develops a distinct marketing mix for each has a **multisegment targeting strategy**. P&G offers 18 different laundry detergents, each targeting a different segment of the market. For example, Tide is a tough, powerful cleaner, and Era is good for stain treatment and removal. Zipcar, a membership-based car sharing company that provides car rentals to its members billable by the hour or day, shifted its targeting strategy from urban centers, adding services for business and universities like the University of Minnesota, which has five Zipcar stations located around its campus. On campuses across the nation, Zipcar targeting is further subdivided into faculty/staff and student markets.[35]

Multisegment targeting offers many potential benefits to firms, including greater sales volume, higher profits, larger market share, and economies of scale in manufacturing and marketing. Yet it may also involve greater product design, production, promotion, inventory, marketing research, and management costs. Before deciding to use this strategy, firms should compare the benefits and costs of multisegment targeting to those of undifferentiated and concentrated targeting.

Another potential cost of multisegment targeting is **cannibalization**, which occurs when sales of a new product cut into sales of a firm's existing products. For example, as sales of Apple's iPad mini have risen, sales of the 9.7-inch iPad have fallen—so much so that Sharp

multisegment targeting strategy a strategy that chooses two or more well-defined market segments and develops a distinct marketing mix for each

cannibalization a situation that occurs when sales of a new product cut into sales of a firm's existing products

Zipcar representative Travis Reik explains the car sharing process to University of Mississippi junior, Abby Oliver, shortly after Ole Miss accounced a partnership with the company.

Stan Carroll/The Commercial Appeal/ZUMA Press, Inc/Alamy

Corp had to significantly cut back its production of the larger iPad's screens. Given that the tablet market continues to grow rapidly, this trend suggests that buyers may be choosing the less-expensive mini over the larger option—not opting for both, as Apple might have hoped.[36]

8-8 CRM AS A TARGETING TOOL

Recall from Chapter 1 that CRM entails tracking interactions with customers to optimize customer satisfaction and long-term company profits. Companies that successfully implement CRM tend to customize the goods and services offered to their customers based on data generated through interactions between carefully defined groups of customers and the company. CRM can also allow marketers to target customers with extremely relevant offerings. Birchbox, a company that creates custom boxes of beauty, grooming, and lifestyle product samples, uses CRM to personalize the customer experience. Birchbox reps get to know each customer via profile information, carefully monitoring product reviews, and general activity on the company's Web site. They then put together customized samples and editorial content that feels personal to customers. If a customer likes a sample, he can use Birchbox to buy the full product.[37]

As many firms have discovered, a detailed and segmented understanding of customers can be advantageous. There are at least four trends that will lead to the continuing growth of CRM: personalization, time savings, loyalty, and technology.

- **Personalization:** One-size-fits-all marketing is no longer relevant. Consumers want to be treated as the individuals they are, with their own unique sets of needs and wants. By its personalized nature, CRM can fulfill this desire.

- **Time savings:** Direct and personal marketing efforts will continue to grow to meet the needs of consumers who no longer have the time to spend shopping and making purchase decisions. With the personal and targeted nature of CRM, consumers can spend less time making purchase decisions and more time doing the things that are important to them.

- **Loyalty:** Consumers will be loyal only to those companies and brands that have earned their loyalty and reinforced it at every purchase occasion. CRM techniques focus on finding a firm's best customers, rewarding them for their loyalty, and thanking them for their business.

- **Technology:** Mass-media approaches will decline in importance as advances in market research and database technology allow marketers to collect detailed information on their customers. New technology offers marketers a more cost-effective way to reach customers and enables businesses to personalize their messages. For example, My.Yahoo.com greets each user by name and offers information in which the user has expressed interest. Similarly, RedEnvelope.com helps customers keep track of special occasions and offers personalized gift recommendations. With the help of database technology, CRM can track a business's customers as individuals, even if they number in the millions.

CRM is a huge commitment and often requires a 180-degree turnaround for marketers who spent the last half of the twentieth century developing and implementing mass-marketing efforts. Although mass marketing will probably continue to be used, especially to create brand awareness or to remind consumers of a product, the advantages of CRM cannot be ignored.

8-9 # POSITIONING

Marketers segment their markets and then choose which segment, or segments, to target with their marketing mix. Then, based on the target market(s), they can develop the product's **positioning**, a process that influences potential customers' overall perception of a brand, product line, or organization in general. **Position** is the place a product, brand, or group of products occupies in consumers' minds relative to competing offerings. Consumer goods marketers are particularly concerned with positioning. Coca-Cola has multiple cola brands, each positioned to target a different market. For example, Coca-Cola Zero is positioned on its bold taste and zero calories, Caffeine Free Coca-Cola is positioned as a no-caffeine alternative, and Tab is positioned as a cola drink for dieters.[38]

Positioning assumes that consumers compare products on the basis of important features. Marketing efforts that emphasize irrelevant features are therefore likely to misfire. For example, Crystal Pepsi and a clear version of Coca-Cola's Tab failed because consumers perceived the "clear" positioning as more of a marketing gimmick than a benefit.

Effective positioning requires assessing the positions occupied by competing products, determining the important dimensions underlying these positions, and choosing a position in the market where the organization's marketing efforts will have the greatest impact. In 2013, NBC Universal partnered with *Esquire* magazine to rebrand and reposition ailing cable television channel G4 as the Esquire Network. Transitioning away from a focus on nerd culture, video games, and immature humor, the channel was repositioned to target men age 18 to 49 who are upwardly mobile and highly educated—a demographic NBC Universal believes is underserved by current television offerings. While certain G4 programs like *American Ninja Warrior* were carried over to the new network, new programs focusing on cooking and travel were added to appeal to an older, more sophisticated demographic.[39] One positioning strategy that many firms use to distinguish their products from competitors is based on **product differentiation**. The distinctions between products can be either real or perceived. For example, Kentucky Fried Chicken differentiates itself from other fast-food fried chicken restaurants with its secret blend of eleven herbs and spices (perceived), as well as unique offerings like the Double Down, Famous Bowl, and Bucket & Bites Meal (real).[40] However, many everyday products, such as bleaches, aspirin, unleaded regular gasoline, and some soaps, are differentiated by such trivial means as brand names, packaging, color, smell, or "secret" additives. The marketer attempts to convince consumers that a particular brand is distinctive and that they should demand it.

Some firms, instead of using product differentiation, position their products as being similar to competing products or brands. Two examples of this positioning are

Unique menu items help Kentucky Fried Chicken differentiate itself from other fast-food fried chicken restaurants.

AP Images/Wilfredo Lee

positioning developing a specific marketing mix to influence potential customers' overall perception of a brand, product line, or organization in general

position the place a product, brand, or group of products occupies in consumers' minds relative to competing offerings

product differentiation a positioning strategy that some firms use to distinguish their products from those of competitors

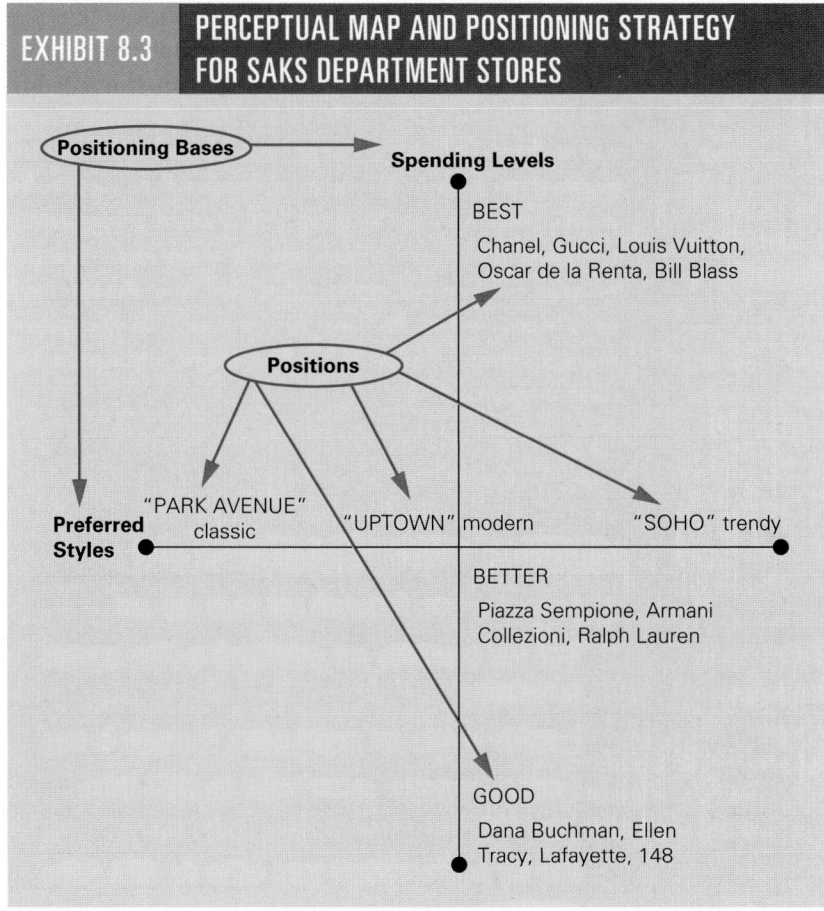

artificial sweeteners advertised as tasting like sugar and margarine as tasting like butter.

8-9a Perceptual Mapping

Perceptual mapping is a means of displaying or graphing, in two or more dimensions, the location of products, brands, or groups of products in customers' minds. For example, Saks Incorporated, the department store chain, stumbled in sales when it tried to attract a younger core customer. To recover, Saks invested in research to determine its core customers in its fifty-four stores across the country. The perceptual map in Exhibit 8.3 shows how Saks uses customer demographics such as spending levels and preferred styles to build a matrix that charts the best mix of clothes and accessories to stock in each store.

8-9b Positioning Bases

Firms use a variety of bases for positioning, including the following:

- **Attribute:** A product is associated with an attribute, product feature, or customer benefit. In engineering its products, Seventh Generation focuses on removing common toxins and chemicals from household products to make them safe for everyone in the household.

- **Price and quality:** This positioning base may stress high price as a signal of quality or emphasize low price as an indication of value. Neiman Marcus uses the high-price strategy; Walmart has successfully followed the low-price and value strategy. The mass merchandiser Target has developed an interesting position based on price and quality. It is an "upscale discounter," sticking to low prices but offering higher quality and design than most discount chains.

- **Use or application:** Stressing uses or applications can be an effective means of positioning a product with buyers. Danone introduced its Kahlúa liqueur using advertising to point out 228 ways to consume the product.

- **Product user:** This positioning base focuses on a personality or type of user. Gap Inc. has several different brands: Gap stores offer basic casual pieces, such as jeans and T-shirts, to middle-of-the-road consumers at mid-level prices; Old Navy offers low-priced, trendy casual wear geared to youth and college-age groups; and Banana Republic is a luxury brand offering fashionable, luxurious business and casual wear to twenty-five- to thirty-five-year-olds.[41]

- **Product class:** The objective here is to position the product as being associated with a particular category of products—for example, positioning a margarine brand with butter. Alternatively, products can be disassociated with a category.

- **Competitor:** Positioning against competitors is part of any positioning strategy. Apple positions the iPhone as cooler and more up-to-date than Windows-based smartphones, and Samsung positions the Galaxy series as cooler and more up-to-date than the iPhone.

- **Emotion:** Positioning using emotion focuses on how the product makes customers feel. A number of companies use this approach.

> **perceptual mapping** a means of displaying or graphing, in two or more dimensions, the location of products, brands, or groups of products in customers' minds

For example, Nike's "Just Do It" campaign did not tell consumers what "it" is, but most got the emotional message of achievement and courage. Luxury smartphone manufacturer Vertu shifted from a high-price message to an emotional one, positioning the $10,880 Ti model as the phone that will make "nothing else ever feel the same."[42]

8-9c Repositioning

repositioning changing consumers' perceptions of a brand in relation to competing brands

Sometimes products or companies are repositioned in order to sustain growth in slow markets or to correct positioning mistakes. **Repositioning** is changing consumers' perceptions of a brand in relation to competing brands. For example, in its early years, the Hyundai brand was synonymous with cheap, low-quality cars. To reposition its brand, Hyundai redesigned its cars to be more contemporary-looking and started a supportive warranty program. Consumer perceptions changed because customers appreciated the new designs and were reassured of the cars' performance by the generous warranties. Today, Hyundai's brand reputation has vastly improved.[43]

STUDY TOOLS 8

LOCATED AT BACK OF THE TEXTBOOK
☐ Rip Out Chapter Review Card

LOCATED AT WWW.CENGAGEBRAIN.COM
☐ Review Key Terms Flashcards and create your own
☐ Track your knowledge and understanding of key concepts in marketing
☐ Complete practice and graded quizzes to prepare for tests
☐ Complete interactive content within the MKTG Online experience
☐ View the chapter highlight boxes within the MKTG Online experience

MKTG ONLINE
REVIEW FLASHCARDS ANYTIME, ANYWHERE

Flashcards
our StudyBits

Review Key
Flashcards
Loaded o
StudyB

4LTR PRESS

ess MKTG ONLINE at www.cengage

Marketing Research

...ES

...you will be able to...

...earch and explain its importance to ...aking

9-4 Describe the growing importance of mobile resea...

...volved in conducting a marketing

9-5 Discuss the growing importance of scanner-base...

9-6 Explain when marketing research should be con...

...impact of the Internet on marketing

9-7 Explain the concept of competitive intelligence

After you finish this chapter go to **PAGE 171** for **STUDY TOOLS.**

...LE OF MARKETING RESEARCH

...esearch is the process of planning, collecting, and ...data relevant to a marketing decision. The results of ...e then communicated to management. Thus, market... ...the function that links the consumer, customer, and ...keter through information. Marketing research plays ...marketing system. It provides decision makers with ... ...ctiveness of the current marketing mix and insights ... ...changes. Furthermore, marketing research is a main ... ...management information systems. In other words, th... ...a marketing research project become data for mana... ...aking.

...he ...g, ...o a

Marketing research has three roles: descriptive, di- agnostic, and predictive. Its *descriptive* role includes

gathering and presenting factual statements. ... what is the historic sales trend in the indust... consumers' attitudes toward a product and ... ing? Its *diagnostic* role includes explaining

determining the impact on sales of a change in the design of the package. Its *predictive* function is to address "what if" questions. For example, how can the researcher use the descriptive and diagnostic research to predict the results of a planned marketing decision?

9-1a Management Uses of Marketing Research

Marketing research can help managers in several ways. First, it improves the quality of decision making, allowing marketers to explore the desirability of various alternatives before arriving at a path forward. Second, it helps managers trace problems. Was the initial decision incorrect? Did an unforeseen change in the external environment cause the plan to fail? How can the same mistake be avoided in the future? Questions like these can be answered through marketing research. Third, marketing research can help managers understand very detailed and complicated relationships. Most importantly, sound marketing research can help managers serve their customers accurately and efficiently. In order to be successful, manufacturers of fitness wearables like Activité Pop need to understand consumers' attitudes about their products. Marketing research has found that 80 percent of consumers have serious concerns about wearable Internet-connected technology. However, half of these same consumers would be willing to share personal data collected through such devices if offered compensation such as a coupon or discount. Consumers also report that they would like information about better workouts to reach their goals (22 percent); the best foods to eat (22 percent); and coupons for fitness gear (19 percent).[1] This marketing research is critical for companies developing new fitness tracking devices.

Marketing research also helps managers gauge the perceived value of their goods and services, as well as the level of customer satisfaction. Such *satisfaction research* can be carried out at the individual product, product line, company, or industry level. Research has determined, for example, that the auto repair business needs an overhaul. According to a new consumer survey from AutoMD.com, most consumers (83 percent) feel overcharged in the auto repair process and rank the experience of going to the repair shop/dealership on par with going to the dentist—and women respondents actually *preferred* the dentist.[2] While women have a more negative view of the repair shop/service center experience than men do, consumers across the board report that a more transparent process would improve the experience. They also report that not knowing what a repair should cost is the biggest challenge in the process and that they want real apples-to-apples repair job quotes.

9-1b Understanding the Ever-Changing Marketplace

Marketing research helps managers understand what is going on in the marketplace and take advantage of opportunities. Now, with big data analytics (discussed later), we can understand the marketing environment like never before. Historically speaking, marketing research has been practiced for as long as marketing has existed. The early Phoenicians carried out market demand studies as they traded in the various ports of the Mediterranean Sea. Marco Polo's diary indicates he performed marketing research as he traveled to China. There is even evidence that the Spanish systematically conducted "market surveys" as they explored the New World, and there are examples of marketing research conducted during the Renaissance.

Returning to the present, assume that you are the North American manager of promotion for Audi. You are considering a significant increase in your social media budget and wonder both what role word of mouth (WOM) advertising plays in the promotion process and how Audi compares with other brands. The Foresight Research Word of Mouth Immersion Report provides insights into these questions. The report shows that among auto owners, MINI, Subaru, and Volvo owners stand out as the most likely to recommend their brands (all are 96 percent likely to do so). According to Nancy Walter, vice president of business development at Foresight, "Word of mouth is a prominent influencer in new auto purchases. Almost one-third of new auto buyers say they were moderately or completely influenced by it, and that can go as high as 45 percent for a highly-influenced brand like Audi."[3]

Foresight calls the consumers most likely to give advice *TalkersPlus*. These highly influential buyers comprise 15 percent of the buyer population but generate 59 percent of the WOM. They are most likely to be brand-loyal males who comment about their new vehicle purchases online. They spend $246 more on accessories and are more likely to be influenced by social media, use a mobile device, and attend motorsports events.

To put the giving and getting sides of WOM into perspective, Foresight developed the Amplifier Index, a measure that shows the strength of WOM for a brand, segment, or buyer characteristic. Audi's Amplifier Index score of 2.51, for example, reflects high levels of creating and nurturing brand advocacy. Audi beats out second-place Mercedes-Benz (at 2.14) and is more than double the industry average of 1.22. Although this material represents just a small section of the report, you can see how it can help Audi's promotion manager begin to understand WOM's role in auto purchases.

 ## 9-2 STEPS IN A MARKETING RESEARCH PROJECT

Virtually all firms that have adopted the marketing concept engage in some marketing research because it offers decision makers many benefits. Some companies spend millions on marketing research; others, particularly smaller firms, conduct informal, limited-scale research studies.

Whether a research project costs $200 or $2 million, the same general process should be followed. The marketing research process is a scientific approach to decision making that maximizes the chance of getting accurate and meaningful results. Exhibit 9.1 traces the seven steps in the research process, which begins with the recognition of a marketing problem or opportunity. As changes occur in the firm's external environment, marketing managers are faced with the questions "Should we change the existing marketing mix?" and, if so, "How?" Marketing research may be used to evaluate product, promotion, distribution, or pricing alternatives.

Biotechnology company Genentech gave its sales force iPads loaded with iDetail, an app that facilitates sales calls to the company's clients. Genentech quickly discovered, however, that many sales representatives chose not to use the tablets in their presentations. To find the root of the problem, the company turned to marketing research. This research found that the iDetail app was difficult to navigate and use, the font size was too small, and the prescription and safety information was difficult to find. The sales force also needed better information on how to effectively engage clients when using iDetail. Based on the findings of this market research, Genentech implemented additional training for sales reps using the iDetail app.[4]

The iDetail story illustrates an important point about problem/opportunity definition. The **marketing research problem** is information oriented. It involves determining what information is needed and how that information can be obtained efficiently and

marketing research problem determining what information is needed and how that information can be obtained efficiently and effectively

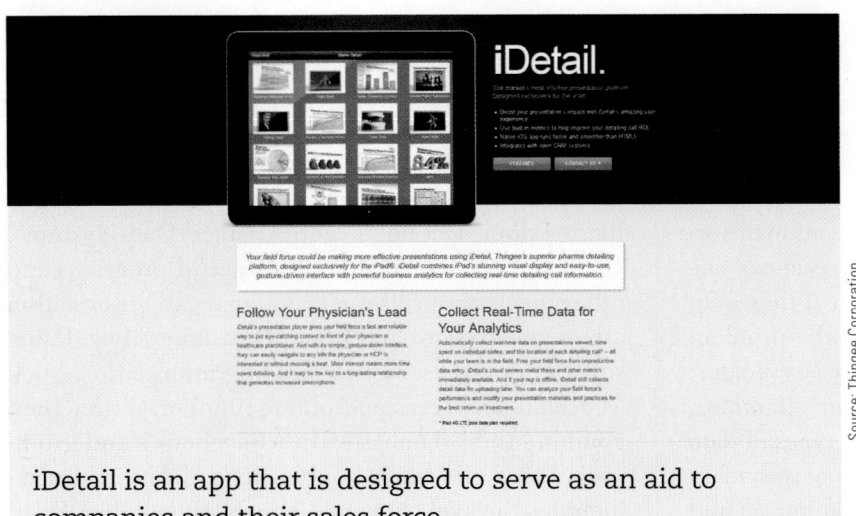

Source: Thingee Corporation

iDetail is an app that is designed to serve as an aid to companies and their sales force.

effectively. The **marketing research objective**, then, is the goal statement. The marketing research objective defines the specific information needed to solve the marketing problem and provides insightful

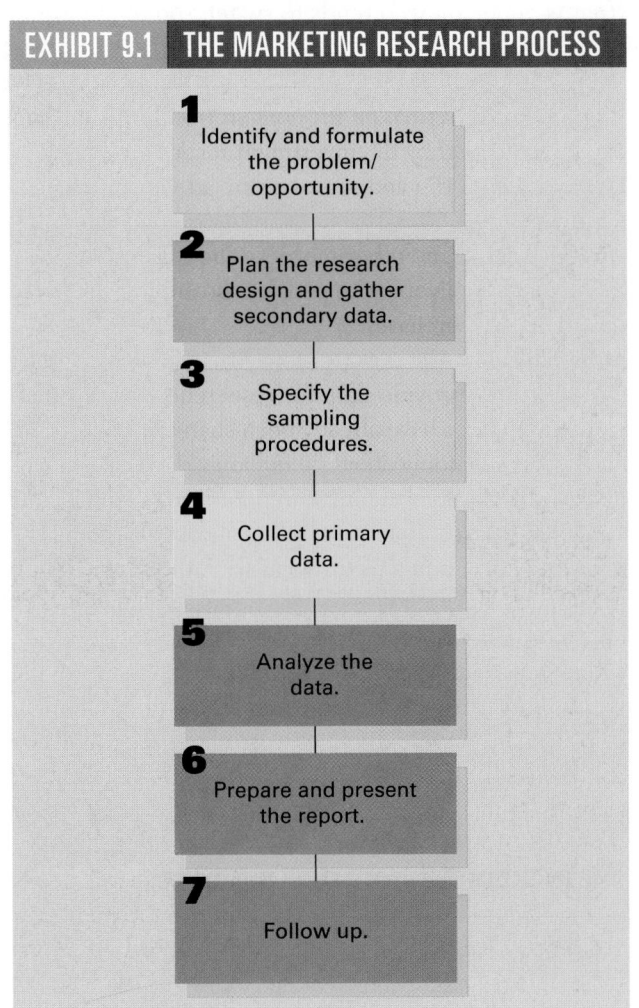

EXHIBIT 9.1 THE MARKETING RESEARCH PROCESS

1 Identify and formulate the problem/opportunity.

2 Plan the research design and gather secondary data.

3 Specify the sampling procedures.

4 Collect primary data.

5 Analyze the data.

6 Prepare and present the report.

7 Follow up.

decision-making information. This requires specific pieces of information needed to solve the marketing research problem. Managers must combine this information with their own experience and other information to make proper decisions. Genentech's marketing research problem was to gather specific information about why a number of sales reps weren't using iDetail. The marketing research objective was to determine exactly what the company should do to solve the problem.

In contrast, the **management decision problem** is action oriented. Management problems tend to be much broader in scope and far more general than marketing research problems, which must be narrowly defined and specific if the research effort is to be successful. Sometimes several research studies must be conducted to solve a broad management problem. For Genentech, the management decision problem was determining how to make the sales force more effective.

9-2a Secondary Data

A valuable tool throughout the research process, particularly in the problem/opportunity identification stage, is **secondary data**—data previously collected for any purpose other than the one at hand. Secondary information originating within the company includes the company's Web sites, annual reports, reports to stockholders, blogs, product testing results perhaps made available to the news media, YouTube videos, social media posts, and house periodicals composed by the company's personnel for communication to employees, customers, or others. Often, this information is incorporated into a company's internal database.

Innumerable outside sources of secondary information also exist, some in the forms of government departments and agencies (federal, state, and local) that compile and post summaries of business data. Trade and industry associations also publish secondary data.

marketing research objective the specific information needed to solve a marketing research problem; the objective should be to provide insightful decision-making information

management decision problem a broad-based problem that uses marketing research in order for managers to take proper actions

secondary data data previously collected for any purpose other than the one at hand

Still more data are available in business periodicals and other news media that regularly publish studies and articles on the economy, specific industries, and even individual companies. The unpublished summarized secondary information from these sources corresponds to internal reports, memos, or special-purpose analyses with limited circulation. Competitive considerations in the organization may preclude publication of these summaries.

Secondary data save time and money if they help solve the researcher's problem. Even if the problem is not solved, secondary data have other advantages. They can aid in formulating the problem statement and suggest research methods and other types of data needed for solving the problem. In addition, secondary data can pinpoint the kinds of people to approach and their locations and serve as a basis of comparison for other data. The disadvantages of secondary data stem mainly from a mismatch between the researcher's unique problem and the purpose for which the secondary data were originally gathered, which are typically different. For example, a company wanted to determine the market potential for a fireplace log made of coal rather than compressed wood by-products. The researcher found plenty of secondary data about total wood consumed as fuel, quantities consumed in each state, and types of wood burned. Secondary data were also available about consumer attitudes and purchase patterns of wood by-product fireplace logs. The wealth of secondary data provided the researcher with many insights into the artificial log market. Yet nowhere was there any information that would tell the firm whether consumers would buy artificial logs made of coal.

The quality of secondary data may also pose a problem. Often, secondary data sources do not give detailed information that would enable a researcher to assess their quality or relevance. Whenever possible, a researcher needs to address these important questions: Who gathered the data? Why were the data obtained? What methodology was used? How were classifications (such as heavy users versus light users) developed and defined? When was the information gathered?

THE GROWING IMPORTANCE OF SOCIAL MEDIA DATA

Facebook owns and controls data collected from 890 million daily users and 1.4 billion monthly active users.[5] There are more than 284 million active Twitter users monthly, 80 percent of whom use mobile devices to tweet.[6] Instagram has over 300 million

big data the exponential growth in the volume, variety, and velocity of information and the development of complex, new tools to analyze and create meaning from such data

users. These Web sites' databases tell their marketers a lot about who you are and what you are like, though often on an anonymous basis.

In an effort to expand its information databases even further, Facebook now combines its social data with third-party information from data brokerages like Acxiom, Datalogix, and Alliance Data Systems. Using data collected from loyalty card programs and other mechanisms, these firms aggregate information about which items and brands consumers buy. Using software that obscures identifying information (such as e-mail addresses and phone numbers), they then combine their databases with Facebook's and group users based on certain combinations of data. This data includes the Web sites that Facebook members visit, e-mail lists they may have signed up for, and the ways they spend money, both online and offline—among many, many other metrics.[7] General Motors uses this new type of data synthesis to target younger buyers who might be interested in its Chevrolet Sonic. Pepsi uses it to show different ads based on whether a user regularly buys Pepsi, Diet Pepsi, or is a Pepsi switcher (that is, a person who tends to switch soda brands and is more price sensitive).

Another new Facebook tool allows advertisers to calculate their *return on investment* (total profit minus expenses divided by the investment made) on Facebook ads by tallying the actions taken by ad viewers. These actions include click-throughs, registrations, shopping cart checkouts, and other metrics. The tool also enables marketers to deliver ads to people who are most likely to make further purchases.[8]

Even photos shared on sites such as Flickr, Instagram, and Pinterest provide data for researchers. More than 20 billion photos have already been shared in Instagram, and users are adding about 60 million a day.[9] Companies like Ditto Labs and Piqora scan photos to glean insights about consumers. If a logo appears above a face, such as Smith ski goggles in a picture of a skier, the software logs the brand of apparel. Visual analysis can also show correlations between products, such as which beverages people drink while eating Kraft Macaroni and Cheese. Digital Labs' software can detect more than 3,000 different brand logos in pictures. Photos that were shot at a university, a bar, the beach, or a snowy mountain give clues about where and how customers use those brands.

THE INCREDIBLE WORLD OF BIG DATA

Big data is the exponential growth in the volume, variety, and velocity of information and the development of complex new tools to analyze and create meaning from such data.

In the past, the flow of data was slow, steady, and predictable. All data was quantitative (countable)—many firms collected sales numbers by store, by product line, and at most, perhaps by a few other measures. Today, data is constantly streaming in from social media, as well as other sources. Advanced big data databases allow the analysis of unstructured data such as e-mails, audio files, and YouTube videos.

In 2016, real-time advertising auctions are expected to account for a third of the $25 billion spent on digital display advertising in the United States.[10] Big data enables these auctions to take place in mere seconds. For example, suppose a bored woman sits waiting in an airline lounge. She scrolls through her iPhone and taps on a brightly colored icon to launch a free mobile game. In the instant before the app loads, predictive analytics firm Flurry collects data about the woman: here we have a new mother, business traveler, fashion follower, in her late 20s, and somewhere near JFK airport. Flurry then holds an automated auction among potential advertisers to fill an ad space that displays while the app is loading. In a fraction of a second, the mobile ad exchange picks the highest bidder with the best-fitting parameters, and the woman's screen flashes to an ad for Maui Jim sunglasses.[11]

Flurry provides an analytic tool that tells app developers how many people are using their apps. More than 540,000 apps now use the tool, which in turn funnels much of the user data back to Flurry. Flurry has a data pipe into more than 1.2 million mobile devices globally and pulls data from seven to ten apps per device. Flurry's analytic tool encrypts and combines identifying pieces of data to create anonymous IDs for each mobile device.[12] Mobile device users are then grouped into one of more than one hundred profiles such as "business traveler" or "sports fanatic."

Along with advanced data analysis tools came a software program called Hadoop, developed by Apache and named for a child's toy elephant. Traditionally, complex computer programs had to run on huge, expensive mainframe computers. Hadoop allows queries to be split up and run much more efficiently. Using Hadoop, different analytic tasks are distributed among numerous inexpensive computer servers, each of which solves part of the problem before reassembling the queries when the work is finished. Thus, with the aid of modern databases, software, and hardware, big data can be analyzed faster and cheaper than ever before.[13]

The ability to crunch numbers means nothing, however, if humans cannot use or even access that information. Most people cannot remember a string of numbers longer than their phone numbers. Modern databases sometimes contain billions of pieces of data, so the question quickly arose as to how big data could be presented in a meaningful way. The answer to this question is data visualization. An example of data visualization is shown in Exhibit 9.2. Visualization acts as an engine for bringing patterns to light—even the subtlest of patterns woven into the largest of data sets

Specialty women's apparel retailer Chicos uses big data analytics to find key brand influencers online and to determine how brand-related conversations impact sales. Sprint's Virgin Mobile uses analytics to tailor specific phone offers to particular customer types. For example, one effort promoted higher-end contract-free smartphones to individuals who could afford the monthly contractual plan but were likely to prefer the company's prepaid option. This offer resulted in increased customer retention and higher profits for Virgin Mobile. Online automotive market Edmunds.com uses big data analytics to help auto dealers predict how long a given car will remain on their lots. This helps dealers minimize the number of days a car remains unsold. Macy's adjusts pricing in near-real time for 73 million items based on demand and inventory. Walmart uses big data, including semantic search and synonym mining, to produce relevant search results for online shoppers. Semantic search improves purchase completion by 10 to 15 percent—a figure that is worth billions to Walmart.

One fast food chain is using cameras to determine what to display on its digital drive-through menu boards. When drive-through lines are longer, the menu board features products that can be served up quickly. When lines are shorter, the menu board features higher margin items that take longer to prepare. Similarly, the Los Angeles and Santa Cruz police departments are using big data to predict where crime will occur down to 500 square feet. Los Angeles has seen a 33 percent reduction in burglary and a 21 percent reduction in violent crime in areas where the software is being used.[14]

Big data analytics focuses very much on *what*. That is, its primary purpose is to uncover what patterns and relationships exist in this database. Often, the insights gained from *what* are all a marketer needs to create a strategy. Suppose that Amazon's analytic software uncovers that hundreds of online customers who bought *War and Peace* also bought *The Idiot*. Amazon can use this data to send promotional e-mails to customers who bought one book but not the other. *Why* never comes into play when sending out these promotional e-mails. Still, marketers often do need to understand why, and that is where traditional marketing research comes into play. If Mars launches a new type of chocolate bar and

EXHIBIT 9.2 **DATA VISUALIZATION (CONTAINS IMAGE OF SEARCHES IN CHINA)**

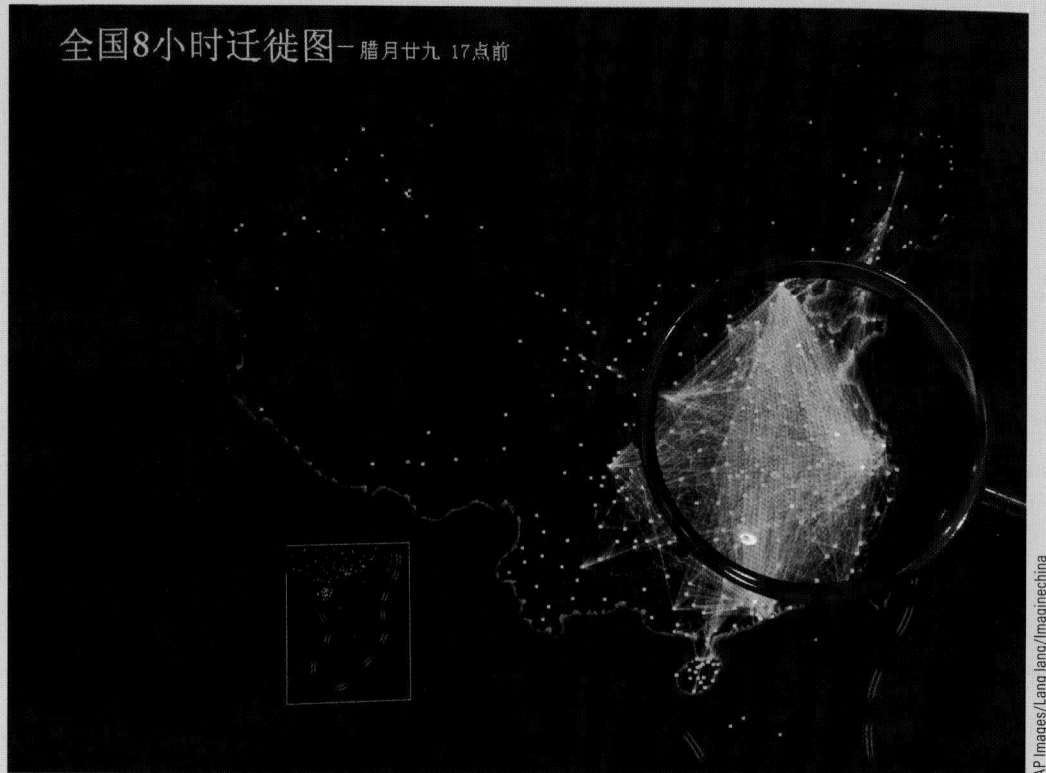

全国8小时迁徙图－腊月廿九 17点前

AP Images/Lang lang/Imaginechina

Baidu Migrate, an interactive heat map developed by China's largest search engine, uses smartphone data to visualize migration during the company's 40-day spring festival travel rush.

there are many initial purchases, but few repeat purchasers, then the driving question becomes "why?" In the following sections, we will return to the marketing research process to explain how such a question can be answered.

9-2b Planning the Research Design and Gathering Primary Data

Good secondary data and big data can help researchers conduct a thorough situation analysis. With that information, researchers can list their unanswered questions and rank them. Researchers must then decide the exact information required to answer the questions. The **research design** specifies which research questions must be answered,

research design specifies which research questions must be answered, how and when the data will be gathered, and how the data will be analyzed

primary data information that is collected for the first time; used for solving the particular problem under investigation

how and when the data will be gathered, and how the data will be analyzed. Typically, the project budget is finalized after the research design has been approved.

Sometimes research questions can be answered by gathering more secondary data; otherwise, primary data may be needed. **Primary data**, or information collected for the first time, are used for solving the particular problem under investigation. The main advantage of primary data is that they can answer specific research questions that secondary data cannot answer. Suppose that Olive Garden is considering discontinuing about a third of its menu and adding an equal number of new items. All of the new dishes have done very well in taste tests. The research question is whether or not to make such a major change in the menu. Primary data from a recent research project found that almost 70 percent of restaurant patrons won't try a new menu item (actual data). Of the 30 percent willing to try a new menu item, only 17 percent will order a completely new dish. Consumers tend to replace their preplanned menu items ("I'm going to have lasagna") with a new menu item only if the new

EXHIBIT 9.3 CHARACTERISTICS OF TRADITIONAL FORMS OF SURVEY RESEARCH

Characteristic	In-Home Personal Interviews	Mall Intercept Interviews	Central-Location Telephone Interviews	Self-Administered and One-Time Mail Surveys	Mail Panel Surveys	Executive Interviews	Focus Groups
Cost	High	Moderate	Moderate	Low	Moderate	High	Low
Time span	Moderate	Moderate	Fast	Slow	Relatively slow	Moderate	Fast
Use of interviewer probes	Yes	Yes	Yes	No	Yes	Yes	Yes
Ability to show concepts to respondent	Yes (also taste tests)	Yes (also taste tests)	No	Yes	Yes	Yes	Yes
Management control over interviewer	Low	Moderate	High	N/A	N/A	Moderate	High
General data quality	High	Moderate	High to moderate	Moderate to low	Moderate	High	Moderate
Ability to collect large amounts of data	High	Moderate	Moderate to low	Low to moderate	Moderate	Moderate	Moderate
Ability to handle complex questionnaires	High	Moderate	High, if computer aided	Low	Low	High	N/A

dish is the same type of food as the product they had originally planned to order.[15] Thus, Olive Garden replacing a third of its menu is not a good idea. Primary data are current, and researchers know the source. Sometimes researchers gather the data themselves rather than assign projects to outside companies. Researchers also specify the methodology of the research. Secrecy can be maintained because the information is proprietary. In contrast, much secondary data is available to all interested parties for relatively small fees or free.

Gathering primary data can be expensive; costs can range from a few thousand dollars for a limited survey to several million for a nationwide study. For instance, a nationwide, 15-minute telephone interview with 1,000 adult males can cost $50,000 or more for everything, including a data analysis and report. Because primary data gathering is so expensive, many firms do not bother to conduct in-person interviews. Instead, they use the Internet. Larger companies that conduct many research projects use another cost-saving technique. They *piggyback studies*, or gather data on two different projects using one questionnaire. Nevertheless, the disadvantages of primary data gathering are usually offset by the advantages. It is often the only way of solving a research problem. And with a variety of techniques available for research—including surveys, observations, and experiments—primary research can address almost any marketing question.

SURVEY RESEARCH The most popular technique for gathering primary data is **survey research**, in which a researcher either interacts with people or posts a questionnaire online to obtain facts, opinions, and attitudes. Exhibit 9.3 summarizes the characteristics of traditional forms of survey research.

In-Home Personal Interviews Although in-home personal interviews often provide high-quality information, they tend to be very expensive because of the interviewers' travel time and mileage costs. Therefore, they are rapidly disappearing from the American and European researchers' survey toolbox. They are, however, still popular in many less developed countries around the globe.

Mall Intercept Interviews The **mall intercept interview** is conducted in the common area of a shopping mall or in a market research office within the mall. To conduct this type of interview, the research firm rents office space in the mall or pays a significant daily fee. One drawback is that it is hard to get a representative sample of the population. One advantage is the ability of the

> **survey research** the most popular technique for gathering primary data, in which a researcher interacts with people to obtain facts, opinions, and attitudes
>
> **mall intercept interview** a survey research method that involves interviewing people in the common areas of shopping malls

interviewer to probe when necessary—a technique used to clarify a person's response and ask for more detailed information.

Mall intercept interviews must be brief. Only the shortest ones are conducted while respondents are standing. Often, researchers invite respondents into the office for interviews, which are still generally less than fifteen minutes long. The overall quality of mall intercept interviews is about the same as telephone interviews.

Marketing researchers use computer technology to speed the mall interview process. One technique is **computer-assisted personal interviewing**. The researcher conducts in-person interviews, reads questions to the respondent off a computer screen, and directly keys the respondent's answers into the computer. A second approach is **computer-assisted self-interviewing**. A mall interviewer intercepts and directs willing respondents to nearby computers. Each respondent reads questions off a computer screen and directly keys his or her answers into the computer. A third use of computer technology is fully automated self-interviewing. Respondents are guided by interviewers or independently approach a centrally located computer station or kiosk, read questions off a screen, and directly key their answers into the station's computer.

Telephone Interviews

Telephone interviews cost less than personal interviews, but cost is rapidly increasing due to respondent refusals to participate. Most telephone interviewing is conducted from a specially designed phone room called a **central-location telephone (CLT) facility**.

A CLT facility has many phone lines, individual interviewing stations,

Tupungato/Shutterstock.com

headsets, and sometimes monitoring equipment. The research firm typically will interview people nationwide from a single location. The federal "Do Not Call" law does not apply to survey research.

Most CLT facilities offer computer-assisted interviewing. The interviewer reads the questions from a computer screen and enters the respondent's data directly into the computer, saving time. Hallmark Cards found that an interviewer administered a printed questionnaire for its Shoebox greeting cards in 28 minutes. The same questionnaire administered with computer assistance took only 18 minutes. The researcher can stop the survey at any point and immediately print out the survey results, allowing the research design to be refined as necessary.

MAIL SURVEYS Mail surveys have several benefits: relatively low cost, elimination of interviewers and field supervisors, centralized control, and actual or promised anonymity for respondents (which may draw more candid responses). A disadvantage is that mail questionnaires usually produce low response rates. The resulting sample may therefore not represent the surveyed population. Another serious problem with mail surveys is that no one probes respondents to clarify or elaborate on their answers. If a respondent uses the word "convenience," there is no way to clarify exactly what he means. Convenience could refer to location, store hours, or a host of other factors.

Mail panels offer an alternative to the one-shot mail survey. A mail panel consists of a sample of households recruited to participate by mail for a given period. Panel members often receive gifts in return for their participation. Essentially, the panel is a sample used several times. In contrast to one-time mail surveys, the response rates from mail panels are high. Rates of 70 percent (of those who agree to participate) are not uncommon.

Executive Interviews
An **executive interview** involves interviewing businesspeople at their offices concerning industrial products or services, a process that is very expensive. First, individuals involved in the purchase decision for the product in question must be identified and located, which can itself be expensive and time-consuming. Once a qualified person is located, the next step is to get that person to agree to be interviewed

computer-assisted personal interviewing an interviewing method in which the interviewer reads questions from a computer screen and enters the respondent's data directly into the computer

computer-assisted self-interviewing an interviewing method in which a mall interviewer intercepts and directs willing respondents to nearby computers where each respondent reads questions off a computer screen and directly keys his or her answers into the computer

central-location telephone (CLT) facility a specially designed phone room used to conduct telephone interviewing

executive interview a type of survey that involves interviewing businesspeople at their offices concerning industrial products or services

and to set a time for the interview. Finally, an interviewer must go to the particular place at the appointed time. Long waits are frequently encountered; cancellations are not uncommon. This type of survey requires the very best interviewers because they are frequently interviewing on topics that they know very little about.

Focus Groups A **focus group** is a type of personal interviewing. Often recruited by random telephone screening, seven to ten people with certain desired characteristics form a focus group. These qualified consumers are usually offered an incentive (typically $30 to $50) to participate in a group discussion. The meeting place (sometimes resembling a living room, sometimes featuring a conference table) has audiotaping and perhaps videotaping equipment. It also likely has a viewing room with a one-way mirror so that clients (manufacturers or retailers) can watch the session. During the session, a moderator, hired by the research company, leads the group discussion. Focus groups can be used to gauge consumer response to a product or promotion and are occasionally used to brainstorm new-product ideas or to screen concepts for new products. Focus groups also represent an efficient way of learning how products are actually used in the home. Lewis Stone, former manager of Colgate-Palmolive's research and development division, says the following about focus groups:

> If it weren't for focus groups, Colgate-Palmolive Co. might never know that some women squeeze their bottles of dishwashing soap, others squeeeeeze them, and still others squeeeeeeeeeze out the desired amount. Then there are the ones who use the soap 'neat.' That is, they put the product directly on a sponge or washcloth and wash the dishes under running water until the suds run out. Then they apply more detergent.

Stone was explaining how body language, exhibited during focus groups, provides insights into a product that are not apparent from reading questionnaires on habits and practices. Panelists' descriptions of how they perform tasks highlight need gaps, which can improve an existing product or demonstrate how a new product might be received.

QUESTIONNAIRE DESIGN All forms of survey research require a questionnaire. Questionnaires ensure that all respondents will be asked the same series of questions. Questionnaires include three basic types of questions: open-ended, closed-ended, and scaled-response (see Exhibit 9.4). An **open-ended question** encourages an answer phrased in the respondent's

own words. Researchers get a rich array of information based on the respondent's frame of reference (What do you think about the new flavor?). In contrast, a **closed-ended question** asks the respondent to make a selection from a limited list of responses. Closed-ended questions can either be what marketing researchers call dichotomous (Do you like the new flavor? Yes or No.) or multiple choice. A **scaled-response question** is a closed-ended question designed to measure the intensity of a respondent's answer.

Closed-ended and scaled-response questions are easier to tabulate than open-ended questions because response choices are fixed. On the other hand, unless the researcher designs the closed-ended question very carefully, an important choice may be omitted. For example, suppose a food study asked this question: "Besides meat, which of the following items do you normally add to tacos that you prepare at home?"

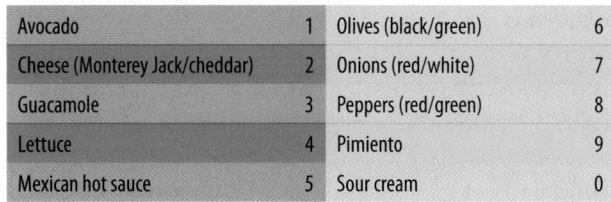

Avocado	1	Olives (black/green)	6
Cheese (Monterey Jack/cheddar)	2	Onions (red/white)	7
Guacamole	3	Peppers (red/green)	8
Lettuce	4	Pimiento	9
Mexican hot sauce	5	Sour cream	0

The list seems complete, doesn't it? However, consider the following responses: "I usually add a green, avocado-tasting hot sauce," "I cut up a mixture of lettuce and spinach," "I'm a vegetarian—I don't use meat at all," and "My taco is filled only with guacamole." How would you code these replies? As you can see, the question needs an "other" category.

A good question must be clear and concise and avoid ambiguous language. The answer to the question "Do you live within ten minutes of here?" depends on the mode of transportation (maybe the person walks), driving speed, perceived time, and other factors. Language should also be clear. As such, jargon should be avoided, and wording should be geared to the target audience. A question such as "What is the level of efficacy of your preponderant dishwasher powder?" would probably

focus group seven to ten people who participate in a group discussion led by a moderator

open-ended question an interview question that encourages an answer phrased in the respondent's own words

closed-ended question an interview question that asks the respondent to make a selection from a limited list of responses

scaled-response question a closed-ended question designed to measure the intensity of a respondent's answer

Open-Ended Questions	Closed-Ended Questions	Scaled-Response Question
1. What advantages, if any, do you think ordering from a mail-order catalog offers compared to shopping at a local retail outlet? (*Probe*: What else?)	**Dichotomous** 1. Did you heat the Danish product before serving It? Yes . . . . 1 No . . . . 2 2. The federal government doesn't care what people like me think. Agree . . . . 1 Disagree 2	Now that you have used the rug cleaner, would you say that you . . . (*Circle one.*) Would definitely buy it . . . . 1 Would probably buy it . . . . 2 Might or might not buy it . . . . 3 Probably would not buy it . . . . 4 Definitely would not buy it 5
2. Why do you have one or more of your rugs or carpets professionally cleaned rather than cleaning them yourself or having someone else in the household clean them?	**Multiple Choice** 1. I'd like you to think back to the last footwear of any kind that you bought. I'll read you a list of descriptions and would like for you to tell me which category they fall into. (*Read list and circle proper category*.) Dress and/or formal . . . . 1 Casual . . . . 2 Canvas/trainer /gym shoes . . . . 3 Specialized athletic shoes . . . . 4 Boots 5	
3. What is it about the color of the eye shadow that makes you like it the best?	2. In the last three months, have you used Noxzema skin cream . . . . (*Circle all that apply.*) As a facial wash . . . . 1 For moisturizing the skin . . . . 2 For treating blemishes . . . . 3 For cleansing the skin . . . . 4 For treating dry skin . . . . 5 For softening skin . . . . 6 For sunburn . . . . 7 For making the facial skin smooth 8	

be greeted by a lot of blank stares. It would be much simpler to say "Are you (1) very satisfied, (2) somewhat satisfied, or (3) not satisfied with your current brand of dishwasher powder?"

Stating the survey's purpose at the beginning of the interview may improve clarity, but it may also increase the chances of receiving biased responses. Many times, respondents will try to provide answers that they believe are "correct" or that the interviewer wants to hear. To avoid bias at the question level, researchers should avoid leading questions and adjectives that cause respondents to think of the topic in a certain way.

Finally, to ensure clarity, the interviewer should avoid asking two questions in one—for example, "How did you like the taste and texture of the Pepperidge Farm coffee cake?" This should be divided into two questions, one concerning taste and the other texture.

observation research a research method that relies on four types of observation: people watching people, people watching an activity, machines watching people, and machines watching an activity

mystery shoppers researchers posing as customers who gather observational data about a store

OBSERVATION RESEARCH In contrast to survey research, **observation research** entails watching what people do or using machines to watch what people do. Specifically, it can be defined as the systematic process of recording the behavioral patterns of people, objects, and occurrences without questioning them. A market researcher using the observation technique witnesses and records information as events occur or compiles evidence from records of past events. Carried a step further, observation may involve watching people or phenomena and may be conducted by human observers or machines. Examples of these various observational situations are shown in Exhibit 9.5.

Some common forms of people-watching-people research are one-way mirror observations, mystery shoppers, and behavioral targeting. A one-way mirror allows the researchers to see the participants, but the participants cannot see the researchers.

Mystery Shoppers **Mystery shoppers** are researchers posing as customers who gather observational data about a store (for example, are the shelves neatly stocked?) and collect data about customer/employee

EXHIBIT 9.5 OBSERVATIONAL SITUATIONS

Situation	Example
People watching people	Observers stationed in supermarkets watch consumers select frozen Mexican dinners; the purpose is to see how much comparison shopping people do at the point of purchase.
People watching an activity	An observer stationed at an intersection counts traffic moving in various directions.
Machines watching people	Movie or videotape cameras record behavior as in the people-watching-people example above.
Machines watching an activity	Traffic-counting machines monitor traffic flow.

interactions. The interaction is not an interview, and communication occurs only so that the mystery shopper can observe the actions and comments of the employee. Mystery shopping is, therefore, classified as an observational marketing research method even though communication is often involved. Restaurant chains like Subway use mystery shoppers to evaluate store cleanliness and quality of service.

Behavioral Targeting **Behavioral targeting (BT)**, sometimes simply called tracking, began as a simple process by placing cookies in users' browsers or mobile apps to track which Web sites they visited, how long they lingered, what they searched for, and what they bought. All of this information can be tracked anonymously—a "fly on the wall" perspective. While survey research is a great way to find out the "why" and the "how," behavioral targeting lets the researcher find out the "how much," the "how often," and the "where." Also, through **social media monitoring**, using automated tools to monitor online buzz, chatter, and conversations, a researcher can learn what is being said about the brand and the competition. Tracking is the basis for input into online databases. Companies like Tapad track customers across multiple devices—personal desktop computers, laptops, smartphones, and tablets, for example. If a customer is using multiple devices at the same time, Tapad knows, and knows what she is doing on each.

ETHNOGRAPHIC RESEARCH Ethnographic research comes to marketing from the field of anthropology. The technique is becoming increasingly popular in marketing research. **Ethnographic research**, or the study of human behavior in its natural context, involves observation of behavior and physical setting. Ethnographers directly observe the population they are studying. As

"participant observers," ethnographers can use their intimacy with the people they are studying to gain richer, deeper insights into culture and behavior—in short, what makes people do what they do?

Managers at Cambridge SoundWorks recently faced a perplexing problem. Male customers stood wide-eyed and wallets-ready when sales reps showed off the company's hi-fi "blow-your-hair-back" stereo speakers in retail outlets across the country, but sales were slumping. Why didn't such unabashed enthusiasm for the product translate into more—and bigger ticket—sales?

To find out, the Andover, Massachusetts-based stereo equipment manufacturer and retailer hired research firm Design Continuum to follow a dozen prospective customers over the course of two weeks. After the two weeks were up, the researchers concluded that the high-end speaker market suffered from something they referred to as "the spouse acceptance factor." While men adored the big black boxes, women hated their unsightly appearance. Concerned about how speakers might look in the living room, women frequently talked their husbands out of buying the cool (but hideous) stereo equipment. Even those who purchased the products had trouble showing them off. Men would attempt to display the loudspeakers as trophies in their living rooms while women would hide them behind plants, vases, and chairs. "Women would come into the store, look at the speakers, and say, 'that thing is ugly,'" said principal at Design Continuum Ellen Di Resta. "The men would lose the argument and leave the store without a stereo. The solution was to give the target market what men and women *both* wanted: a great sound system that looks like furniture so you don't have to hide it."

Armed with this knowledge, Cambridge SoundWorks unveiled a new line of spouse-friendly speakers. The furniture-like Newton Series of speakers and home theater systems comes in an array of colors and finishes. The result? The Newton Series is the fastest-growing and best-selling product line in Cambridge SoundWorks' history.[16]

VIRTUAL SHOPPING

Advances in computer technology have enabled researchers to simulate an actual retail store environment on a computer screen. Depending on the type of simulation, a shopper can "pick up" a package by touching

behavioral targeting (BT) a form of observation marketing research that combines a consumer's online activity with psychographic and demographic profiles compiled in databases

social media monitoring the use of automated tools to monitor online buzz, chatter, and conversations

ethnographic research the study of human behavior in its natural context; involves observation of behavior and physical setting

Advances in computer technology have enabled researchers to simulate an actual retail store environment.

its image on the monitor and rotate it to examine all sides. Like buying on most online retailers, the shopper touches the shopping cart to add an item to the basket. During the shopping process, the computer unobtrusively records the amount of time the consumer spends shopping in each product category, the time the consumer spends examining each side of a product, the quantity of the product the consumer purchases, and the order in which items are purchased.

A major apparel retailer using a computer simulated environment recently found that men have trouble putting outfits together. Men also hesitate to pick up clothing items because they can't fold them back the same way. With this knowledge, the apparel chain made two major changes: it began selling items together as complete outfit solutions and folded shirts and other clothes more simply. Sales of men's clothes increased by 40 percent.[17]

Virtual shopping research is growing rapidly. According to the United States Department of Agriculture, approximately 50,000 new consumer packaged goods are introduced each year.[18] All are vying for very limited retail shelf space. Any process, such as virtual shopping, that can speed product development time and lower costs is always welcomed by manufacturers. Some companies outside of retail have even begun experimenting with virtual shopping and other simulated environment

experiment a method of gathering primary data in which the researcher alters one or more variables while observing the effects of those alterations on another variable

sample a subset from a larger population

universe the population from which a sample will be drawn

tools—many telecom, financial, automotive, aviation, and fast-food companies are using such tools to better serve their customers.

EXPERIMENTS An **experiment** is a method a researcher can use to gather primary data. The researcher alters one or more variables—price, package design, shelf space, advertising theme, advertising expenditures—while observing the effects of those alterations on another variable (usually sales). The best experiments are those in which all factors except one are held constant. The researcher can then observe what changes in sales, for example, result from changes in the amount of money spent on advertising.

Holding all other factors constant in the external environment is a monumental and costly, if not impossible, task. Such factors as competitors' actions, weather, and economic conditions are beyond the researcher's control. Yet market researchers have ways to account for the ever-changing external environment. Mars, the candy company, was losing sales to other candy companies. Traditional surveys showed that the shrinking candy bar was not perceived as a good value. Mars wondered whether a bigger bar sold at the same price would increase sales enough to offset the higher ingredient costs. The company designed an experiment in which the marketing mix stayed the same in different markets but the size of the candy bar varied. The substantial increase in sales of the bigger bar quickly proved that the additional costs would be more than covered by the additional revenue. Mars increased the bar size—along with its market share and profits.

9-2c Specifying the Sampling Procedures

Once the researchers decide how they will collect primary data, their next step is to select the sampling procedures they will use. A firm can seldom take a census of all possible users of a new product, nor can they all be interviewed. Therefore, a firm must select a sample of the group to be interviewed. A **sample** is a subset from a larger population.

Several questions must be answered before a sampling plan is chosen. First, the population, or **universe**, of interest must be defined. This is the group from which the sample will be drawn. It should include all the people whose opinions, behavior, preferences, attitudes, and so on, are of interest to the marketer. For example, in a study whose purpose is to determine the market for a new canned dog food, the universe might be defined to include all current buyers of canned dog food.

SAMPLE

Pashabo/Shutterstock.com

UNIVERSE

Guy Shapira/Shutterstock.com

After the universe has been defined, the next question is whether the sample must be representative of the population. If the answer is yes, a probability sample is needed. Otherwise, a nonprobability sample might be considered.

PROBABILITY SAMPLES A **probability sample** is a sample in which every element in the population has a known statistical likelihood of being selected. Its most desirable feature is that scientific rules can be used to ensure that the sample represents the population.

One type of probability sample is a **random sample**—a sample arranged in such a way that every element of the population has an equal chance of being selected as part of the sample. For example, suppose a university is interested in getting a cross section of student opinions on a proposed sports complex to be built using student activity fees. If the university can acquire an up-to-date list of all the enrolled students, it can draw a random sample by using random numbers from a table (found in most statistics books) to select students from the list. Common forms of probability and nonprobability samples are shown in Exhibit 9.6.

NONPROBABILITY SAMPLES Any sample in which little or no attempt is made to get a representative cross section of the population can be considered a **nonprobability sample**. Therefore, the probability of selection of each sampling unit is not known. A common form of a nonprobability sample is the **convenience sample**, which uses respondents who are convenient or readily accessible to the researcher—for instance, employees, friends, or relatives.

Nonprobability samples are acceptable as long as the researcher understands their nonrepresentative nature. Because of their lower cost, nonprobability samples are sometimes used in marketing research.

TYPES OF ERRORS Whenever a sample is used in marketing research, two major types of errors may occur: measurement error and sampling error. **Measurement error** occurs when there is a difference between the information desired by the researcher and the information provided by the measurement process. For example, people may tell an interviewer that they purchase Crest toothpaste when they do not. Measurement error generally tends to be larger than sampling error.

Sampling error occurs when a sample somehow does not represent the target population. Sampling error can be one of several types. Nonresponse error occurs when the sample actually interviewed differs from the sample drawn. This error happens because the original people selected to be interviewed either refused to cooperate or were inaccessible.

Frame error, another type of sampling error, arises if the sample drawn from a population differs from the target population. For instance, suppose a telephone survey is conducted to find out Chicago beer drinkers' attitudes toward Coors. If a Chicago telephone directory is used as

probability sample a sample in which every element in the population has a known statistical likelihood of being selected

random sample a sample arranged in such a way that every element of the population has an equal chance of being selected as part of the sample

nonprobability sample any sample in which little or no attempt is made to get a representative cross section of the population

convenience sample a form of nonprobability sample using respondents who are convenient or readily accessible to the researcher—for example, employees, friends, or relatives

measurement error an error that occurs when there is a difference between the information desired by the researcher and the information provided by the measurement process

sampling error an error that occurs when a sample somehow does not represent the target population

frame error an error that occurs when a sample drawn from a population differs from the target population

EXHIBIT 9.6 TYPES OF SAMPLES

Probability Samples	
Simple Random Sample	Every member of the population has a known and equal chance of selection.
Stratified Sample	The population is divided into mutually exclusive groups (such as gender or age); then random samples are drawn from each group.
Cluster Sample	The population is divided into mutually exclusive groups (such as geographic areas); then a random sample of clusters is selected. The researcher then collects data from all the elements in the selected clusters or from a probability sample of elements within each selected cluster.
Systematic Sample	A list of the population is obtained—e.g., all persons with a checking account at XYZ Bank—and a skip interval is obtained by dividing the sample size by the population size. If the sample size is 100 and the bank has 1,000 customers, then the skip interval is 10. The beginning number is randomly chosen within the skip interval. If the beginning number is 8, then the skip pattern would be 8, 18, 28, ...
Nonprobability Samples	
Convenience Sample	The researcher selects the easiest population members from which to obtain information.
Judgment Sample	The researcher's selection criteria are based on personal judgment that the elements (persons) chosen will likely give accurate information.
Quota Sample	The researcher finds a prescribed number of people in several categories—e.g., owners of large dogs versus owners of small dogs. Respondents are not selected on probability sampling criteria.
Snowball Sample	Additional respondents are selected on the basis of referrals from the initial respondents. This method is used when a desired type of respondent is hard to find—e.g., persons who have taken round-the-world cruises in the last three years. This technique employs the old adage "Birds of a feather flock together."

the *frame* (the device or list from which the respondents are selected), the survey will contain a frame error. Not all Chicago beer drinkers have landline phones, and many phone numbers are unlisted. An ideal sample (in other words, a sample with no frame error) matches all important characteristics of the target population to be surveyed. Could you find a perfect frame for Chicago beer drinkers?

Random error occurs when the selected sample is an imperfect representation of the overall population. Random error represents how accurately the chosen sample's true average (mean) value reflects the population's true average (mean) value. For example, we might take a random sample of beer drinkers in Chicago and find that 16 percent regularly drink Coors beer. The next day, we might repeat the same sampling procedure and discover that 14 percent regularly drink Coors beer. The difference is due to random error. Error is common to all surveys, yet it is often not reported or is underreported. Typically, the only error mentioned in a written report is sampling error.

random error an error that occurs when the selected sample is an imperfect representation of the overall population

field service firm a firm that specializes in interviewing respondents on a subcontracted basis

9-2d Collecting the Data

Marketing research field service firms are used to collect some primary data. A **field service firm** specializes in interviewing respondents on a subcontracted basis. Many have offices, often in malls, throughout the country. A typical marketing research study involves data collection in several cities, which may require the marketer to work with a comparable number of field service firms. Besides conducting interviews, field service firms provide focus group facilities, mall intercept locations, test product storage, and kitchen facilities to prepare test food products.

9-2e Analyzing the Data

After collecting the data, the marketing researcher proceeds to the next step in the research process: data analysis. The purpose of this analysis is to interpret and draw conclusions from the mass of collected data. The marketing researcher tries to organize and analyze those data by using one or more techniques common to marketing research: one-way frequency counts, cross-tabulations, and more sophisticated statistical analysis. Of these three techniques, one-way frequency counts are the simplest. One-way frequency tables simply record the responses to a question. For example, the

EXHIBIT 9.7 POPCORN CROSS-TABULATION

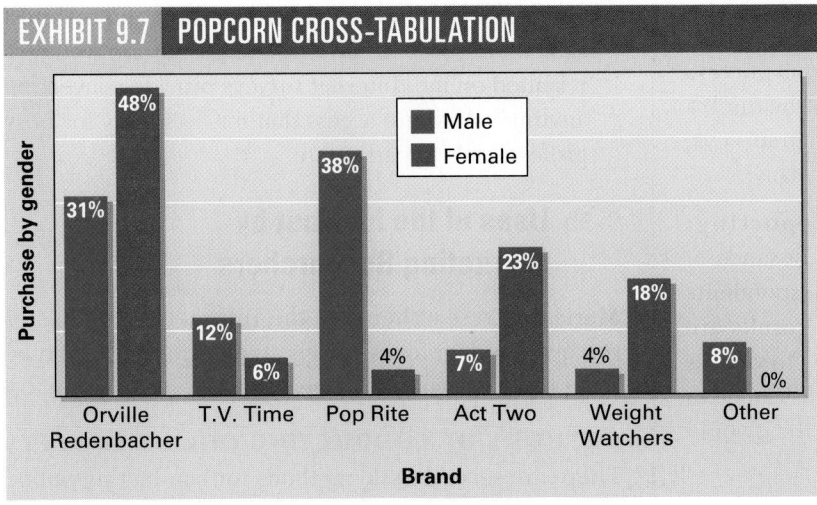

EXHIBIT 9.7 POPCORN CROSS-TABULATION

Purchase by gender / Brand

- Male
- Female

Orville Redenbacher: 31% / 48%
T.V. Time: 12% / 6%
Pop Rite: 38% / 4%
Act Two: 7% / 23%
Weight Watchers: 4% / 18%
Other: 8% / 0%

answers to the question "What brand of microwave popcorn do you buy most often?" would provide a one-way frequency distribution. One-way frequency tables are always done in data analysis, at least as a first step, because they provide the researcher with a general picture of the study's results. A **cross-tabulation** lets the analyst look at the responses to one question in relation to the responses to one or more other questions. For example, in Exhibit 9.7, what is the association between gender and the brand of microwave popcorn bought most frequently?

Researchers can use many other more powerful and sophisticated statistical techniques, such as hypothesis testing, measures of association, and regression analysis. A description of these techniques goes beyond the scope of this book but can be found in any good marketing research textbook. The use of sophisticated statistical techniques depends on the researchers' objectives and the nature of the data gathered.

9-2f Preparing and Presenting the Report

After data analysis has been completed, the researcher must prepare the report and communicate the conclusions and recommendations to management. This is a key step in the process. If the marketing researcher wants managers to carry out the recommendations, he or she must convince them that the results are credible and justified by the data collected.

Researchers are usually required to present both written and oral reports on the project. Today, the written report is often no more than a copy of the PowerPoint slides used in the oral presentation. Both reports should be tailored to the audience. They should begin with a clear, concise statement of the research objectives, followed by a complete but brief and simple explanation of the research design or methodology employed. A summary of major findings should come next. The conclusion of the report should also present recommendations to management.

Most people who enter marketing will become research users rather than research suppliers. Thus, they must know what to notice in a report. As with many other items we purchase, quality is not always readily apparent. Nor does a high price guarantee superior quality. The basis for measuring the quality of a marketing research report is the research proposal. Did the report meet the objectives established in the proposal? Was the methodology outlined in the proposal followed? Are the conclusions based on logical deductions from the data analysis? Do the recommendations seem prudent, given the conclusions?

9-2g Following Up

The final step in the marketing research process is to follow up. The researcher should determine why management did or did not carry out the recommendations in the report. Was sufficient decision-making information included? What could have been done to make the report more useful to management? A good rapport between the product manager, or whoever authorized the project, and the market researcher is essential. Often, they must work together on many studies throughout the year.

 ### 9-3 THE PROFOUND IMPACT OF THE INTERNET ON MARKETING RESEARCH

More than 90 percent of U.S. marketing research companies conduct some form of online research. Paper questionnaires are going the way of the horse and buggy in marketing research Online survey research has replaced computer-assisted telephone interviewing as the most popular mode of data collection. The majority of online research is done through incentivized panels (discussed later in the chapter).

> **cross-tabulation** a method of analyzing data that lets the analyst look at the responses to one question in relation to the responses to one or more other questions

9-3a Advantages of Internet Surveys

The huge growth in the popularity of Internet surveys is the result of the many advantages offered by the Internet. The specific advantages of Internet surveys, which are often sent to mobile devices, are many:

- **Rapid development, real-time reporting:** Internet surveys can be broadcast to thousands of potential respondents simultaneously. Respondents complete surveys simultaneously; then results are tabulated and posted for corporate clients to view as the returns arrive. The effect: survey results can be in a client's hands in significantly less time than would be required for traditional paper surveys.

- **Dramatically reduced costs:** The Internet can cut costs by 25 to 40 percent and provide results in half the time it takes to do traditional telephone surveys. Traditional survey methods are labor-intensive efforts incurring training, telecommunications, and management costs. Electronic methods eliminate these completely. While costs for traditional survey techniques rise proportionally with the number of interviews desired, electronic solicitations can grow in volume with little increase in project costs.

- **Personalized questions and data:** Internet surveys can be highly personalized for greater relevance to each respondent's own situation, thus speeding the response process.

- **Improved respondent participation:** Internet surveys take half as much time to complete as phone interviews, can be accomplished at the respondent's convenience (for example, after work hours), and are much more stimulating and engaging. As a result, Internet surveys enjoy much higher response rates.

- **Contact with the hard-to-reach:** Certain groups—doctors, high-income professionals, top management in Global 2000 firms—are among the most surveyed on the planet and the most difficult to reach. Many of these groups are well represented online. Internet surveys provide convenient anytime/anywhere access that makes it easy for busy professionals to participate.

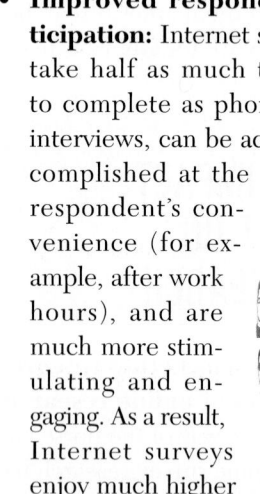

iStockphoto.com/bgblue

9-3b Uses of the Internet by Marketing Researchers

Marketing researchers use the Internet to administer surveys, conduct focus groups, and perform a variety of other types of marketing research.

METHODS OF CONDUCTING ONLINE SURVEYS

There are several basic methods for conducting online surveys: Web survey systems, survey design and Web hosting sites, and online panel providers.

Web Survey Systems Web survey systems are software systems specifically designed for Web questionnaire construction and delivery. They consist of an integrated questionnaire designer, Web server, database, and data delivery program designed for use by nonprogrammers.

The Web server distributes the questionnaire and files responses in a database. The user can query the server at any time via the Web for completion statistics, descriptive statistics on responses, and graphical displays of data. Some popular online survey research software packages are Sawtooth CiW, Infopoll, SurveyMonkey, and SurveyPro.

Google Consumer Surveys Google, with more than a billion unique visitors worldwide, has entered the do-it-yourself Web survey arena. It does this in a rather unique manner; see www.google.com/insights/consumersurveys/home. Certain Web sites host premium content that usually requires a subscription or access fee. With Google Consumer Surveys, however, a visitor can gain access to the premium content by answering a couple of questions instead of paying the fee. Surveys are limited to two questions. The first is typically a screening question such as, "Have you purchased anything online in the past ninety days?" The second question is more substantive, such as "Which promotion would you be most interested in—free shipping, 15% off, free returns, or saving $25 on your next purchase of $150?" Basic demographic and location information are inferred from Google's big data database. Google Consumer Surveys are fast and cheap, but some researchers have questioned the sampling methodology while others have suggested that the two-question format is too restrictive.[19]

Online Panel Providers Often, researchers use online panel providers for a ready-made sample population. Online panel providers such as Survey Sampling International and e-Rewards pre-recruit people who agree to participate in online market research surveys.

Some online panels are created for specific industries and may have a few thousand panel members, while the large commercial online panels have millions of people waiting to be surveyed. When people join online panels, they answer an extensive profiling questionnaire that enables the panel provider to target research efforts to panel members who meet specific criteria.

Some critics of online panels suggest that they are not representative of the target population. Others claim that offering incentives to join a panel leads to bias and misleading results. One such critic called online panels "a club of people who signed up to take point-and-click surveys for points redeemable for cash and gifts."[20] Online panel researchers contend that they use a number of interventions to detect poor quality online surveys. These include speed detection, straight-line response detection, challenge questions, IP address location checking, digital fingerprinting to identify multiple registrations, and analysis of aggregate responses.

ONLINE FOCUS GROUPS A number of research firms are currently conducting focus groups online. The process is fairly simple. The research firm builds a database of respondents via a screening questionnaire on its Web site. When a client comes to a firm with a need for a particular focus group, the firm goes to its database and identifies individuals who appear to qualify. It sends an e-mail to these individuals, asking them to log on to a particular site at a particular time scheduled for the group. Many times, these groups are joined by respondents on mobile devices. The firm pays them an incentive for their participation.

The firm develops a discussion guide similar to the one used for a conventional focus group, and a moderator runs the group by typing in questions online for all to see. The group operates in an environment similar to that of a chat room so that all participants see all questions and all responses. The firm captures the complete text of the focus group and makes it available for review after the group has finished.

Online focus groups also allow respondents to view things such as a concept statement, a mockup of a print ad, or a short product demonstration video. The moderator simply provides a URL for the respondents to go to in another browser window.

© olexius/Shutterstock 149737013

Benefits of Web Community Research

The popularity and marketing power of Web communities stems from several key benefits:

- Provide cost-effective, flexible research.
- Help companies create customer-focused organizations by putting employees into direct contact with consumers.
- Achieve customer-derived innovation.
- Establish brand advocates who are emotionally invested in a company's success.
- Engage customers in a space where they are comfortable, allowing clients to interact with them on a deeper level.
- Offer real-time results, enabling clients to explore ideas that normal time constraints prohibit.

More advanced virtual focus group software reserves a frame (section) of the screen for stimuli to be shown. Here, the moderator has control over what is shown in the stimulus area. Many online groups are now conducted with audio and video feeds as well. One advantage of this approach is that the respondent does not have to do any work to see the stimuli. There are many other advantages of online groups:

- **Better participation rates:** Typically, online focus groups can be conducted over the course of days; once participants are recruited, they are less likely to pull out due to time conflicts.

- **Cost-effectiveness:** Face-to-face focus groups incur costs for facility rental, airfare, hotel, and food. None of these costs is incurred with online focus groups.

- **Broad geographic scope:** Time is flexible online; respondents can be gathered from all over the world.

- **Accessibility:** Online focus groups allow access to individuals who otherwise might be difficult to recruit (for example, business travelers, senior executives, mothers with infants).

WEB COMMUNITY RESEARCH A Web community is a carefully selected group of consumers who agree to participate in an ongoing dialogue with a particular corporation. All community interaction takes place on a custom-designed Web site. During the life of the community—which may last anywhere from six months to a year or more—community members respond to questions posed by the corporation on a regular basis. In addition to responding to the corporation's questions, community members talk to one another about topics that are of interest to them. When Procter & Gamble was developing scents for a new product line, it asked members of its online community to record the scents that they encountered over the course of a day that made them feel good. By week's end, Procter & Gamble had received images, videos, and simple text tributes to cut grass, fresh paint, Play Dough, and other aromas that revealed volumes about how scent triggers not just nostalgia, but also feelings of competence, adventurousness, comfort, and other powerful emotions.[21]

9-4 THE GROWING IMPORTANCE OF MOBILE RESEARCH

Although desktop and laptop computers are the primary devices used for completing online research, the picture is changing rapidly. Mobile survey traffic now accounts

Nearly one in four mobile surveys are taken outside of the home—often at work.

Nopporn/Shutterstock.com

for approximately 30 percent of interview responses. Nearly one in four mobile surveys are taken outside of the home—often at work.[22]

Mobile surveys are designed to fit into the brief cracks of time that open up when a person waits for a plane, is early for an appointment, commutes to work on a train, or stands in a line. Marketers strive to engage respondents "in the moment" because mobile research provides immediate feedback when a consumer makes a decision to purchase, consumes a product, or experiences some form of promotion. As new and better apps make the survey experience easier and more intuitive, the use of mobile surveys will continue to rise. As screen size decreases, so do survey completion rates. Seventy-six percent of surveys are completed on desktop; 70 percent on tablet; and 59 percent on mobile phone.[23] New responsive design technology automatically adjusts the content and navigation of a Web site to fit the dimensions and resolution of any screen it is viewed on.[24]

One advertiser wanted to conduct a survey on the televised advertisements that ran during the Super Bowl. The client wanted to measure real-time reactions, but most people do not sit in front of their desktop computers during the big game. They do, however, multitask using their smartphones. Respondents were recruited in advance of game day, and then during the game, surveys were pushed out in real time to collect feedback on commercials as they aired.[25]

An *ethnography shop-along* used to mean accompanying a participant on a shopping trip, but with today's mobile qualitative research tools, shop-alongs can be completely self-guided. Mondelez Canada recently set out to launch Potato Thins, a low-calorie snack food, in the United States. Potato Thins are packaged in a resealable pouch, differentiating the product and allowing customers to consume small portions of the bag at a time. Before the launch, Mondelez Canada set up a research experiment to determine which grocery store shelf location would give Potato Thins the biggest boost. The key concern for Mondelez was to learn about shoppers' logic and motivations when it comes to in-store navigation and healthy snacking. Survey participants were sent on a "snacking safari" whereby they recorded their shopping and purchase habits by taking photos on their mobile devices. Researchers found that consumers demonstrated one of two distinct behaviors when shopping for snacks—hunting or browsing.

When hunting, consumers tended to ignore signage, as they knew which aisles to head for. When browsing, participants went up and down the aisles of the store, gathering the items they needed and keeping an eye out for new items.[26]

After the shopping safari, respondents were introduced to Potato Thins. Researchers asked whether they should be placed in the chip or cracker aisle, and the majority of participants picked the cracker aisle. One participant said, "I could see them in the snack food area, close to the chips. However, I would likely miss purchasing them, as I tend to avoid going down that aisle as it's too tempting and not healthy. So I suppose that it would be better to merchandise them close to the crackers." Researchers also concluded that the bag may look out of place on the chip aisle due to its size. One participant said, "The size of the package is quite small, so if you wanted to serve these rather than regular chips you would have to purchase quite a number of packages."[27]

 ## 9-5 SCANNER-BASED RESEARCH

Scanner-based research is a system for gathering information from respondents by continuously monitoring the advertising, promotion, and pricing they are exposed to and the things they buy. Scanner-based research also entails the aggregation of scanner data from retailers, analysis, and identification of sales trends by industry, company, product line, and individual brand. The variables measured are advertising campaigns, coupons, displays, and product prices. The result is a huge database of marketing efforts and consumer behavior.

The two major scanner-based suppliers are SymphonyIRI Group Inc. and the Nielsen Company. Each has about half of the market. However, SymphonyIRI is the founder of scanner-based research. SymphonyIRI's first product is called **BehaviorScan**. It delivers different TV advertisements to selected homes within the same market and then uses scanner purchase data to analyze the impact of the advertising on consumers' actual buying behavior.[28]

Another SymphonyIRI's product is **InfoScan**, a scanner-based sales-tracking service for the consumer packaged-goods industry. Retail sales, detailed consumer purchasing information (including measurement of store loyalty and total grocery basket expenditures), and promotional activity by manufacturers and retailers are monitored and evaluated for all bar-coded products. Data are collected weekly from supermarkets, drugstores, and mass merchandisers.

Some companies have begun using neuromarketing to study microscopic changes in skin moisture, heart rate, brain waves, and other biometrics to see how consumers react to things such as package designs and ads. **Neuromarketing** is the process of researching brain patterns and measuring certain physiological responses to marketing stimuli. It is a fresh attempt to better understand consumers' responses to promotion and purchase motivations.

 ## 9-6 WHEN SHOULD MARKETING RESEARCH BE CONDUCTED?

When managers have several possible solutions to a problem, they should not instinctively call for marketing research. In fact, the first decision to make is whether to conduct marketing research at all.

Some companies have been conducting research in certain markets for many years. Such firms understand the characteristics of target customers and their likes and dislikes about existing products. Under these circumstances, further research would be repetitive and waste money. P&G, for example, has extensive knowledge of the coffee market. After it conducted initial taste tests with Folgers Instant Coffee, P&G went into national distribution without further research. Sara Lee followed the same strategy with its frozen croissants, as did Quaker Oats with Chewy Granola Bars. This tactic, however, can backfire. Marketers may think they understand a particular

scanner-based research a system for gathering information from a single group of respondents by continuously monitoring the advertising, promotion, and pricing they are exposed to and the things they buy

BehaviorScan a scanner-based research program that tracks the purchases of 3,000 households through store scanners in each research market

InfoScan a scanner-based sales-tracking service for the consumer packaged-goods industry

neuromarketing a field of marketing that studies the body's responses to marketing stimuli

market thoroughly and so bypass market research for a product, only to have the product fail and be withdrawn from the market.

If information were available and free, managers would rarely refuse more, but because marketing information can require a great deal of time and expense to accumulate, they might decide to forgo additional information. Ultimately, the willingness to acquire additional decision-making information depends on managers' perceptions of its quality, price, and timing. Research should be undertaken only when the expected value of the information is greater than the cost of obtaining it.

9-6a Customer Relationship Management

Recall from the beginning of the chapter that databases and big data play a key role in marketing decision making. A key subset of data management systems is a customer relationship management (CRM) system. CRM was introduced in Chapters 1 and 8. The key to managing relationships with customers is the CRM cycle (Exhibit 9.8).

To initiate the CRM cycle, a company must *identify customer relationships with the organization*. This may simply entail learning who the customers are or where they are located, or it may require more detailed information about the products and services they are using. Next, the company must *understand the interactions with current customers*. Companies accomplish this by collecting data on all types of communications a customer has with the company.

Using this knowledge of its customers and their interactions, the company then *captures relevant customer data on interactions*. Big data analytics are used not only to enhance the collection of customer data but also to *store and integrate customer data* throughout the company, and ultimately, to "get to know" customers on a more personal level. Customer data are the firsthand responses that are obtained from customers through investigation or by asking direct questions.

Every customer wants to be a company's main priority. Yet not all customers are equally important in the eyes of a business. Consequently, the company must *identify its profitable*

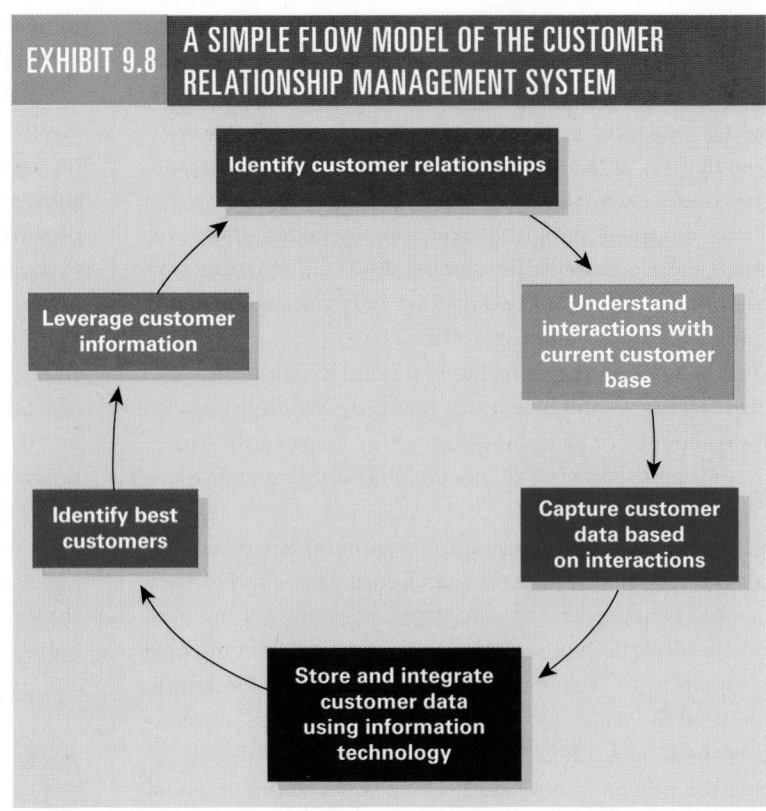

EXHIBIT 9.8 A SIMPLE FLOW MODEL OF THE CUSTOMER RELATIONSHIP MANAGEMENT SYSTEM

- Identify customer relationships
- Understand interactions with current customer base
- Capture customer data based on interactions
- Store and integrate customer data using information technology
- Identify best customers
- Leverage customer information

and unprofitable customers. Big data analytics compile actionable data about the purchase habits of a firm's current and potential customers. Essentially, analytics transform customer data into customer information a company can use to make managerial decisions. Big data analytics are examined in more detail in Chapter 14.

Once customer data are analyzed and transformed into usable information, the information must be *leveraged*. The CRM system sends the customer information to all areas of a business because the customer interacts with all aspects of the business. Essentially, the company is trying to enhance customer relationships by getting the right information to the right person in the right place at the right time.

9-7 COMPETITIVE INTELLIGENCE

Derived from military intelligence, competitive intelligence is an important tool for helping a firm overcome a competitor's advantage. Specifically, competitive intelligence can help identify the advantage and play a major role in determining how it was achieved. It also helps a firm identify areas where it can achieve its own competitive advantages.

Competitive intelligence (CI) helps managers assess their competitors and their vendors in order to

competitive intelligence (CI) an intelligence system that helps managers assess their competition and vendors in order to become more efficient and effective competitors

become more efficient and effective competitors. Intelligence is analyzed information. It becomes decision-making intelligence when it has implications for the organization. For example, a primary competitor may have plans to introduce a product with performance standards equal to those of the company gathering the information but with a 15 percent cost advantage. The new product will reach the market in eight months. This intelligence has important decision-making and policy consequences for management. CI and environmental scanning (see Chapter 2) combine to create marketing intelligence.

The Internet is an important resource for gathering CI, but noncomputer sources can be equally valuable. Some examples include company salespeople, industry experts, CI consultants, government agencies, Uniform Commercial Code filings, suppliers, periodicals, the Yellow Pages, and industry trade shows.

STUDY TOOLS 9

LOCATED AT BACK OF THE TEXTBOOK
☐ Rip out Chapter Review Card

LOCATED AT WWW.CENGAGEBRAIN.COM
☐ Review Key Terms Flashcards and create your own

☐ Track your knowledge and understanding of key concepts in marketing

☐ Complete practice and graded quizzes to prepare for tests

☐ Complete interactive content within the MKTG Online experience

☐ View the chapter highlight boxes within the MKTG Online experience

10 | Product Concepts

Paket/Shutterstock.com

LEARNING OUTCOMES

After studying this chapter, you will be able to…

10-1 Define the term *product*

10-2 Classify consumer products

10-3 Define the terms *product item*, *product line*, and *product mix*

10-4 Describe marketing uses of branding

10-5 Describe marketing uses of packaging and labeling

10-6 Discuss global issues in branding and packaging

10-7 Describe how and why product warranties are important marketing tools

After you finish this chapter go to **PAGE 186** for **STUDY TOOLS.**

10-1 WHAT IS A PRODUCT?

The product offering, the heart of an organization's marketing program, is usually the starting point in creating a marketing mix. A marketing manager cannot determine a price, design a promotion strategy, or create a distribution channel until the firm has a product to sell. Moreover, an excellent distribution channel, a persuasive promotion campaign, and a fair price have no value when the product offering is poor or inadequate.

A **product** may be defined as everything, both favorable and unfavorable, that a person receives in an exchange. A product may be a tangible good like a pair of shoes, a service like a haircut, an idea like "don't litter," or any combination of these three. Packaging, style, color, options, and size are some typical product features. Just as important are intangibles such as service, the seller's image, the manufacturer's reputation, and the way consumers believe others will view the product.

To most people, the term *product* means a tangible good. However, services and ideas are also products. (Chapter 12 focuses specifically on the unique aspects of marketing services.) The marketing process identified in Chapter 1 is the same whether the product marketed is a good, a service, an idea, or some combination of these.

> **product** everything, both favorable and unfavorable, that a person receives in an exchange

10-2 TYPES OF CONSUMER PRODUCTS

Products can be classified as either business (industrial) or consumer, depending on the buyer's intentions. The key distinction between the two types of products is their intended use. If the intended use is a business purpose, the product is classified as a business or industrial product. As explained in Chapter 7, a business product is used to manufacture other goods or services, to facilitate an organization's operations, or to resell to other customers. A consumer product is bought to satisfy an individual's personal wants or needs. Sometimes the same item can be classified as either a business or a consumer product, depending on its intended use. Examples include lightbulbs, pencils and paper, and computers.

We need to know about product classifications because business and consumer products are marketed differently. They are marketed to different target markets and tend to use different distribution, promotion, and pricing strategies.

Chapter 7 examined seven categories of business products: major equipment, accessory equipment, component parts, processed materials, raw materials, supplies, and services. This chapter examines an effective way of categorizing consumer products. Although there are several ways to classify them, the most popular approach

> A marketing manager cannot determine a price, design a promotion strategy, or create a distribution channel until the firm has a product to sell.

includes these four types: convenience products, shopping products, specialty products, and unsought products. This approach classifies products according to how much effort is normally used to shop for them.

10-2a Convenience Products

A **convenience product** is a relatively inexpensive item that merits little shopping effort—that is, a consumer is unwilling to shop extensively for such an item. Candy, soft drinks, aspirin, small hardware items, dry cleaning, and car washes fall into the convenience product category.

Consumers buy convenience products regularly, usually without much planning. Nevertheless,

> **convenience product**
> a relatively inexpensive item that merits little shopping effort

consumers do know the brand names of popular convenience products, such as Coca-Cola, Bayer aspirin, and Old Spice deodorant. Convenience products normally require wide distribution in order to sell sufficient quantities to meet profit goals. For example, the gum brand Extra is available everywhere, including Walmart, Walgreens, gas stations, newsstands, and vending machines.

10-2b Shopping Products

A **shopping product** is usually more expensive than a convenience product and is found in fewer stores. Consumers usually buy a shopping product only after comparing several brands or stores on style, practicality, price, and lifestyle compatibility. They are willing to invest some effort into this process to get the desired benefits.

There are two types of shopping products: homogeneous and heterogeneous. Consumers perceive *homogeneous* shopping products as basically similar—for example, washers, dryers, refrigerators, and televisions. With homogeneous shopping products, consumers typically look for the lowest-priced brand that has the desired features. For example, they might compare Kenmore, Whirlpool, and General Electric refrigerators.

In contrast, consumers perceive *heterogeneous* shopping products as essentially different—for example, furniture, clothing, housing, and universities. Consumers often have trouble comparing heterogeneous shopping products because the prices, quality, and features vary so much. The benefit of comparing heterogeneous shopping products is "finding the best product or brand for me"; this decision is often highly individual. For example, it would be difficult to compare a small, private college with a large, public university, or IKEA with La-Z-Boy.

10-2c Specialty Products

When consumers search extensively for a particular item and are very reluctant to accept substitutes, that item is a **specialty product**. Omega watches, Rolls-Royce automobiles, Bose speakers, Ruth's Chris Steak House, and highly specialized forms of medical care are generally considered specialty products.

Consumers perceive houses as heterogeneous because of variety and differences.

Marketers of specialty products often use selective, status-conscious advertising to maintain a product's exclusive image. Distribution is often limited to one or a very few outlets in a geographic area. Brand names and quality of service are often very important.

10-2d Unsought Products

A product unknown to the potential buyer or a known product that the buyer does not actively seek is referred to as an **unsought product**. New products fall into this category until advertising and distribution increase consumer awareness of them.

Some goods are always marketed as unsought items, especially needed products we do not like to think about or care to spend money on. Insurance, burial plots, and similar items require aggressive personal selling and highly persuasive advertising. Salespeople actively seek leads to potential buyers. Because consumers usually do not seek out this type of product, the company must go directly to them through a salesperson, direct mail, or direct response advertising.

10-3 PRODUCT ITEMS, LINES, AND MIXES

Rarely does a company sell a single product. More often, it sells a variety of things. A product item is a specific version of a product that can be designated as a distinct offering among an organization's products. Campbell's Cream of Chicken soup is an example of a product item (see Exhibit 10.1).

A group of closely related product items is called a **product line**. For example, the column in Exhibit 10.1

karamysh/Shutterstock.com

shopping product a product that requires comparison shopping because it is usually more expensive than a convenience product and is found in fewer stores

specialty product a particular item for which consumers search extensively and are very reluctant to accept substitutes

unsought product a product unknown to the potential buyer or a known product that the buyer does not actively seek

product item a specific version of a product that can be designated as a distinct offering among an organization's products

product line a group of closely related product items

titled "Soups" represents one of Campbell's product lines. Different container sizes and shapes also distinguish items in a product line. Diet Coke, for example, is available in cans and various plastic containers. Each size and each container are separate product items.

An organization's **product mix** includes all the products it sells. All Campbell's products—soups, sauces, frozen entrées, beverages, and biscuits—constitute its

Dcwcreations/Shutterstock.com

product mix. Each product item in the product mix may require a separate marketing strategy.

In some cases, however, product lines and even entire product mixes share some marketing strategy components. UPS promotes its various services by demonstrating its commitment to its line of work with the tagline "We [heart] Logistics." Organizations derive several benefits from organizing related items into product lines:

- **Advertising economies:** Product lines provide economies of scale in advertising. Several products can be advertised under the umbrella of the line. Campbell's can talk about its soups being "M'm, M'm, Good!" and promote the entire line.

- **Package uniformity:** A product line can benefit from package uniformity. All packages in the line may have a common look and still keep their individual identities. Again, Campbell's soup is a good example.

- **Standardized components:** Product lines allow firms to standardize components, thus reducing manufacturing and inventory costs. For example, General Motors uses the same parts on many automobile makes and models.

- **Efficient sales and distribution:** A product line enables sales personnel for companies like Procter & Gamble to provide a full range of choices to customers. Distributors and retailers are often more inclined to stock the company's products if it offers a full line. Transportation and warehousing costs are likely to be lower for a product line than for a collection of individual items.

- **Equivalent quality:** Purchasers usually expect and believe

> **product mix** all products that an organization sells

EXHIBIT 10.1   CAMPBELL'S PRODUCT LINES AND PRODUCT MIX

	Width of the Product Mix				
Depth of the Product Lines — DEPTH	**Soups**	**Sauces**	**Frozen Entrées**	**Beverages**	**Biscuits**
	Cream of Chicken	Cheddar Cheese	Macaroni and Cheese	Tomato Juice	Arnott's:
	Cream of Mushroom	Alfredo	Golden Chicken	V-Fusion Juices	Water Cracker
	Vegetable Beef	Italian Tomato	Fricassee	V8 Splash	Butternut Snap
	Chicken Noodle	Hollandaise	Traditional Lasagna		Chocolate Ripple
	Tomato				Spicy Fruit Roll
	Bean with Bacon				Chocolate Wheaten
	Minestrone				
	Clam Chowder				
	French Onion				
	and more				

Karkas/ShutterStock.com

Women's swimming suits are known for coming in wide varieties of styles from functional to poolside lounging.

that all products in a line are about equal in quality. Consumers expect that all Campbell's soups and all Gillette razors will be of similar quality.

Product mix width (or breadth) refers to the number of product lines an organization offers. In Exhibit 10.1, for example, the width of Campbell's product mix is five product lines. **Product line depth** is the number of product items in a product line. As shown in Exhibit 10.1, the sauces product line consists of four product items; the frozen entrée product line includes three product items.

Firms increase the *width* of their product mix to diversify risk. To generate sales and boost profits, firms spread risk across many product lines rather than depend on only one or two. Firms also widen their product mix to capitalize on established reputations. For example, in order to expand its portfolio of beverage-related businesses, Starbucks purchased specialty upscale tea retailer Teavana, which sells loose-leaf teas, tea accessories, and food items. With this purchase, Starbucks wants to position tea as it does coffee—as a luxury beverage rather than a commodity. [1]

Firms increase the *depth* of their product lines to attract buyers with different preferences, to increase sales and profits by further segmenting the market, to capitalize on economies of scale in production and marketing, and to even out seasonal sales patterns.

product mix width the number of product lines an organization offers

product line depth the number of product items in a product line

product modification changing one or more of a product's characteristics

planned obsolescence the practice of modifying products so those that have already been sold become obsolete before they actually need replacement

10-3a Adjustments to Product Items, Lines, and Mixes

Over time, firms change product items, lines, and mixes to take advantage of new technical or product developments or to respond to changes in the environment. They may adjust by modifying products, repositioning products, or extending or contracting product lines.

PRODUCT MODIFICATION Marketing managers must decide if and when to modify existing products. **Product modification** is a change in one or more of a product's characteristics:

- **Quality modification:** a change in a product's dependability or durability. Reducing a product's quality may let the manufacturer lower the price and appeal to target markets unable to afford the original product. Conversely, increasing quality can help the firm compete with rival firms. For example, Barnes & Noble offers a color version of its Nook that runs Android apps, allowing it to compete with tablet and netbook makers, such as Dell and Asus. Increasing quality can also result in increased brand loyalty, greater ability to raise prices, or new opportunities for market segmentation.

- **Functional modification:** a change in a product's versatility, effectiveness, convenience, or safety. In 2015, Cat's Pride introduced a new litter, Fresh & Light Ultimate Care, that has a unique ultra-lightweight formula that is good for both cats and their owners. It weighs half as much as traditional scoopable clay cat litters, has premium clumping ability, and features a dust-free formula.[2]

- **Style modification:** an aesthetic (how the product looks) product change rather than a quality or functional change. Clothing and auto manufacturers commonly use style modifications to motivate customers to replace products before they are worn out.

Planned obsolescence is a term commonly used to describe the practice of modifying products so that those that have already been sold become obsolete before they actually need replacement. For example, products such as printers and cell phones become obsolete because technology changes so quickly.

Some argue that planned obsolescence is wasteful; some claim it is unethical. Marketers respond that consumers favor style modifications because they like changes in the appearance of goods such as clothing and cars. Marketers also contend that consumers, not manufacturers and marketers, decide when styles are obsolete.

REPOSITIONING Repositioning, as Chapter 8 explained, involves changing consumers' perceptions of a brand. Known primarily for its fat-, sugar-, and salt-laden product offerings, McDonald has long fought to reposition itself as a healthy fast food alternative. The company recently announced that it would no longer market some of its less nutritional options to children, and would instead incorporate fruits and vegetables into combo meals for children and adults alike. Further, McDonald's announced that it would utilize menu boards and national television advertising to help consumers understand the nutritional choices available to them.[3] Changing demographics, declining sales, and changes in the social environment often motivate a firm to reposition an established brand. Retailer Target, for example, plans to reposition its brand toward Hispanic shoppers. The company's research showed that while only 38 percent of its shoppers said that the store was their favorite, 54 percent of Hispanic Millennials said that Target was their favorite store. Several departments, including the baby department, will be renovated to focus on marketing to Hispanic moms. Target also plans to be the first brand to launch a Spanish-language ad campaign on an English-language network.[4]

PRODUCT LINE EXTENSIONS A **product line extension** occurs when a company's management decides to add products to an existing product line in order to compete more broadly in the industry. Krispy Kreme recently developed a new series of ready-to-drink iced coffees that it plans to sell in Walmart stores that carry Krispy Kreme products. The drinks are relatively inexpensive, convenient, and are offered in the signature Krispy Kreme donut flavors. The company hopes to attract more coffee drinkers, as well as Walmart customers, to their products. In addition, Krispy Kreme will attempt to attract a bigger share of the home-brew consumer market by selling packages of its coffee blends at some Sam's Clubs locations in the Southeast.[5]

Krispy Kreme developed a line of beverages that it made available to sell in Walmart stores.

A company can add too many products, or demand can change for the type of products that were introduced over time. When this happens, a product line is overextended. Product lines can be overextended when:

- Some products in the line do not contribute to profits because of low sales or they cannibalize sales of other items in the line.

- Manufacturing or marketing resources are disproportionately allocated to slow-moving products.

- Some items in the line are obsolete because of new-product entries in the line or new products offered by competitors.

PRODUCT LINE CONTRACTION Sometimes marketers can get carried away with product extensions. (Does the world really need 31 varieties of Head & Shoulders shampoo?) Contracting product lines is a strategic way to deal with overextension. In March 2013, Internet pioneer Yahoo announced that it would be cutting seven products—the Yahoo BlackBerry app, Sports IQ, Yahoo Message Boards, Yahoo Avatars, Yahoo Clues, Yahoo App Search, and Yahoo Updates. "Ultimately, we're making these changes in an effort to sharpen our focus," said Jay Rossiter, Yahoo's executive vice president for platforms. "By continuing to hone in on our core products and experiences, we'll be able to make our existing products the very best they can be."[6]

Indeed, three major benefits are likely when a firm contracts an overextended product line. First, resources become

> **product line extension**
> adding additional products to an existing product line in order to compete more broadly in the industry

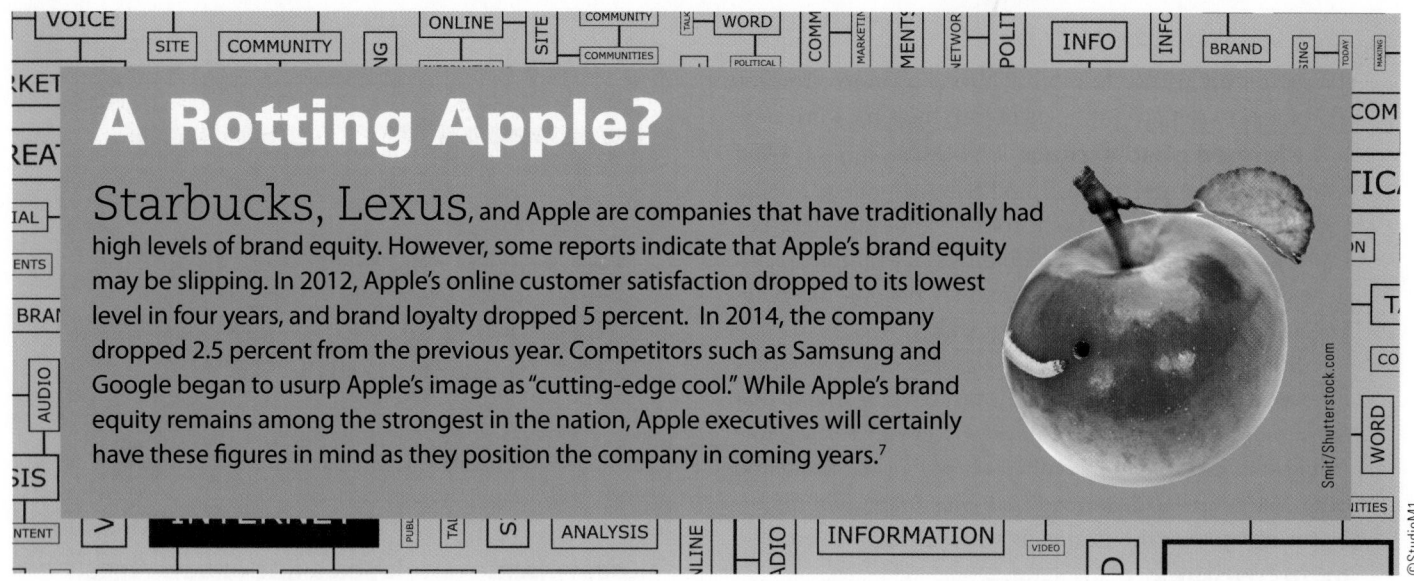

A Rotting Apple?

Starbucks, Lexus, and Apple are companies that have traditionally had high levels of brand equity. However, some reports indicate that Apple's brand equity may be slipping. In 2012, Apple's online customer satisfaction dropped to its lowest level in four years, and brand loyalty dropped 5 percent. In 2014, the company dropped 2.5 percent from the previous year. Competitors such as Samsung and Google began to usurp Apple's image as "cutting-edge cool." While Apple's brand equity remains among the strongest in the nation, Apple executives will certainly have these figures in mind as they position the company in coming years.[7]

Smit/Shutterstock.com

©StudioM1

concentrated on the most important products. Second, managers no longer waste resources trying to improve the sales and profits of poorly performing products. Third, new-product items have a greater chance of being successful because more financial and human resources are available to manage them.

10-4 BRANDING

The success of any business or consumer product depends in part on the target market's ability to distinguish one product from another. Branding is the main tool marketers use to distinguish their products from those of the competition.

A **brand** is a name, term, symbol, design, or combination thereof that identifies a seller's products and differentiates them from competitors' products. A **brand name** is that part of a brand that can be spoken, including letters (GM, YMCA), words (Chevrolet), and numbers (WD-40, 7-Eleven). The elements of a brand that cannot be spoken are called the **brand mark**—for example, the well-known Mercedes-Benz and Delta Air Lines symbols.

brand a name, term, symbol, design, or combination thereof that identifies a seller's products and differentiates them from competitors' products

brand name that part of a brand that can be spoken, including letters, words, and numbers

brand mark the elements of a brand that cannot be spoken

brand equity the value of a company or brand name

global brand a brand that obtains at least a one-third of its earnings from outside its home country, is recognizable outside its home base of customers, and has publicly available marketing and financial data

brand loyalty consistent preference for one brand over all others

10-4a Benefits of Branding

Branding has three main purposes: product identification, repeat sales, and new-product sales. The most important purpose is *product identification*. Branding allows marketers to distinguish their products from all others. Many brand names are familiar to consumers and indicate quality.

The term **brand equity** refers to the value of a company or brand name. A brand that has high awareness, perceived quality, and brand loyalty among customers has high brand equity—a valuable asset indeed. See Exhibit 10.2 for some classic examples of companies that leverage their brand equity to the fullest.

The term **global brand** refers to a brand that obtains at least one-third of its earnings from outside its home country, is recognizable outside its home base of customers, and has publicly available marketing and financial data. Yum! Brands, which owns Pizza Hut, KFC, and Taco Bell, is a good example of a company that has developed strong global brands. Yum! believes that it must adapt its restaurants to local tastes and different cultural and political climates. In Japan, for instance, KFC sells tempura crispy strips. In northern England, KFC focuses on gravy and potatoes, and in Thailand, it offers rice with soy or sweet chili sauce.

The best generator of *repeat sales* is satisfied customers. Branding helps consumers identify products they wish to buy again and avoid those they do not. **Brand loyalty**, a consistent preference for one brand over all others, is quite high in some product categories. More than half the consumers in product categories such as cigarettes, mayonnaise, toothpaste, coffee, headache remedies, bath soap, and ketchup are loyal to one brand. Many students go to college and purchase the same brands they used at home rather than

YUM! believes that it must adapt its restaurants to local tastes and different cultural and political climates.

Tupungato/Shutterstock.com

EXHIBIT 10.2 THE POWER OF BRAND EQUITY

Product Category	Dominant Brand Name
Children's Entertainment	Disney
Laundry Detergent	Tide
Tablet Computer	Apple
Toothpaste	Crest
Microprocessor	Intel
Soup	Campbell's
Bologna	Oscar Meyer
Ketchup	Heinz
Bleach	Clorox
Greeting Cards	Hallmark
Overnight Mail	FedEx
Copiers	Xerox
Gelatin	Jell-O
Hamburgers	McDonald's
Baby Lotion	Johnson & Johnson
Tissues	Kleenex
Acetaminophen	Tylenol
Coffee	Starbucks
Information Search	Google

Source: Data from Chris Moorman.

choosing by price. Brand identity is essential to developing brand loyalty.

The third main purpose of branding is to *facilitate new-product sales*. Having a well-known and respected company and brand name is extremely useful when introducing new products.

10-4b Branding Strategies

Firms face complex branding decisions. Firms may choose to follow a policy of using manufacturers' brands, private (distributor) brands, or both. In either case, they must then decide among a policy of individual branding (different brands for different products), family branding (common names for different products), or a combination of individual branding and family branding.

MANUFACTURERS' BRANDS VERSUS PRIVATE BRANDS The brand name of a manufacturer—such as Kodak, La-Z-Boy, and Fruit of the Loom—is called a **manufacturer's brand**. Sometimes "national brand" is used as a synonym for "manufacturer's brand." This term is not always accurate, however, because many manufacturers serve only regional markets. Using "manufacturer's brand" precisely defines the brand's owner.

A **private brand**, also known as a private label or store brand, is a brand name owned by a wholesaler or a retailer. Target's Archer Farms brand is a popular private label, for example. Private labels are increasing in popularity and price as customers develop loyalties to store brands such as Archer Farms. According to research conducted in the United Kingdom, 44 percent of shoppers believe that private label brands are simply repackaged national brands. Fifty-nine percent believe that national brands are more expensive only because more money is spent advertising them. Seventy percent believe that private label foods are just as good or better than national brands.[8] Today, private label products have a 23 percent unit share and

manufacturer's brand the brand name of a manufacturer

private brand a brand name owned by a wholesaler or a retailer

Key Advantages of Carrying Manufacturers' Brands	Key Advantages of Carrying Private Brands
• Heavy advertising to the consumer by manufacturers such as Procter & Gamble helps develop strong consumer loyalties.	• A wholesaler or retailer can usually earn higher profits on its own brand. In addition, because the private brand is exclusive, there is less pressure to mark down the price to meet competition.
• Well-known manufacturers' brands, such as Kodak and Fisher-Price, can attract new customers and enhance the dealer's (wholesaler's or retailer's) prestige.	• A manufacturer can decide to drop a brand or a reseller at any time or even become a direct competitor to its dealers.
• Many manufacturers offer rapid delivery, enabling the dealer to carry less inventory.	• A private brand ties the customer to the wholesaler or retailer. A person who wants a DieHard battery must go to Sears.
• If a dealer happens to sell a manufacturer's brand of poor quality, the customer may simply switch brands and remain loyal to the dealer.	• Wholesalers and retailers have no control over the intensity of distribution of manufacturers' brands. Walmart store managers don't have to worry about competing with other sellers of Sam's American Choice products or Ol' Roy dog food. They know that these brands are sold only in Walmart and Sam's Club stores.

a nineteen percent dollar share of the food and beverage market.[9]

Retailers love consumers' greater acceptance of private brands. Because overhead is low and there are no marketing costs, private label products bring 10 percent higher profit margins, on average, than manufacturers' brands. More than that, a trusted store brand can differentiate a chain from its competitors. Exhibit 10.3 illustrates key issues that wholesalers and retailers should consider in deciding whether to sell manufacturers' brands or private brands. Many firms offer a combination of both.

Instead of marketing private brands as cheaper and inferior to manufacturers' brands, many retailers are creating and promoting their own **captive brands**. These brands carry no evidence of the store's affiliation, are manufactured by a third party, and are sold exclusively at the chains. This strategy allows the retailer to ask a price similar or equal to manufacturers' brands, and the captive brands are typically displayed alongside mainstream products. A recent study showed that 88 percent of consumers prefer store brands over name brands. These consumers believe that many store brands are just as good as, or better than, their favorite name brands.[10] For example, Simple Truth and Simple Truth Organic are Kroger's lines of natural and organic products designed to meet consumer desire for upscale brands. in 2014, these private brands accounted for $1.2 billion in sales for Kroger.[11]

captive brand a brand manufactured by a third party for an exclusive retailer, without evidence of that retailer's affiliation

individual branding using different brand names for different products

family branding marketing several different products under the same brand name

co-branding placing two or more brand names on a product or its package

INDIVIDUAL BRANDS VERSUS FAMILY BRANDS

Many companies use different brand names for different products, a practice referred to as **individual branding**. Companies use individual brands when their products vary greatly in use or performance. For instance, it would not make sense to use the same brand name for a pair of dress socks and a baseball bat. Procter & Gamble targets different segments of the laundry detergent market with Bold, Cheer, Dash, Dreft, Era, Gain, and Tide.

In contrast, a company that markets several different products under the same brand name is practicing **family branding**. Jack Daniel's family brand includes whiskey, coffee, barbeque sauce, heat-and-serve meat products like brisket and pulled pork, mustard, playing cards, and clothing lines.

CO-BRANDING Co-branding entails placing two or more brand names on a product or its package. Three common types of co-branding are ingredient branding, cooperative branding, and complementary branding. *Ingredient branding* identifies the brand of a part that makes up the product. For example, Church & Dwight co-branded an entire line of Arm & Hammer laundry detergents with OxiClean, a popular household cleaner and stain remover. OxiClean is also co-branded with Kaboom shower cleaner and Xtra detergent.[12] *Cooperative branding* occurs when two brands receiving equal treatment (in the context of an advertisement) borrow from each other's brand equity. A promotional contest jointly sponsored by Ramada Inn, American Express, and United Airlines used cooperative branding. Guests at Ramada who paid with an American Express card were automatically entered in a contest and were eligible to win more than 100 getaways for two at any Ramada in the continental United States

Source: Sears Brand LLC

Craftsman and Harley-Davidson have partnered together to offer tool storage units.

- Shapes, such as the Jeep front grille and the Coca-Cola bottle.

- Ornamental colors or designs, such as the decoration on Nike tennis shoes, the black-and-copper color combination of a Duracell battery, Levi's small tag on the left side of the rear pocket of its jeans, or the cutoff black cone on the top of Cross pens.

- Catchy phrases, such as Prudential's "Own a Piece of the Rock," Mountain Dew's "This Is How We Dew," and Nike's "Just Do It!"

- Abbreviations, such as Bud, Coke, or the Met.

and round-trip airfare from United. In 2014, Bruegger's Bagels and Jamba Juice announced that five co-branded and co-operated locations would be opened across Florida. "Pairing Bruegger's Bagels with [Jamba Juice parent company] Great Service Restaurants is a fantastic match," said Paul Carolan, chief development officer for Le Duff America, which owns Bruegger's Bagels. "Great Service Restaurants shares our passion for community, quality, and providing exceptional guest experiences."[13] Finally, with complementary branding, products are advertised or marketed together to suggest usage, such as a spirits brand (Seagram's) and a compatible mixer (7Up).

Co-branding is a useful strategy when a combination of brand names enhances the prestige or perceived value of a product or when it benefits brand owners and users. Co-branding may also be used to increase a company's presence in markets where it has little room to differentiate itself or has limited market share. For example, Doc Popcorn and Dippin' Dots plan to join together to open their first co-branded store. The companies will sell sweet and savory flavors of popcorn as well as ice cream products under the same roof. This move will allow both brands to continue to grow domestically and internationally over the coming years. [14]

10-4c Trademarks

A **trademark** is the exclusive right to use a brand or part of a brand. Others are prohibited from using the brand without permission. A **service mark** performs the same function for services, such as H&R Block and Weight Watchers. Parts of a brand or other product identification may qualify for trademark protection. Some examples are:

- Sounds, such as the MGM lion's roar.

It is important to understand that trademark rights come from use rather than registration. An intent-to-use application is filed with the U.S. Patent and Trademark Office, and a company must have a genuine intention to use the mark when it files and must actually use it within three years of the granting of the application. Trademark protection typically lasts for ten years.[15] To renew the trademark, the company must prove it is using the mark. Rights to a trademark last as long as the mark is used. Normally, if the firm does not use it for two years, the trademark is considered abandoned, and a new user can claim exclusive ownership of the mark.

The Digital Millennium Copyright Act (DMCA) explicitly applies trademark law to the digital world. This law includes financial penalties for those who violate trademarks or register an otherwise trademarked term as a domain name. The DMCA has come under some criticism for its more restrictive provisions. In 2013, controversy erupted over the reinstitution of a section prohibiting individuals from unlocking their smartphones—a consumer who disables her phone's restriction to a specific carrier may be subject to a prison term of up to five years and a $500,000 fine.[16]

Companies that fail to protect their trademarks face the possibility that their product names will become generic. A **generic product name** identifies a product by class or type and cannot be trademarked. Former brand names that were not sufficiently protected by their owners and were subsequently declared to be generic product names

trademark the exclusive right to use a brand or part of a brand

service mark a trademark for a service

generic product name identifies a product by class or type and cannot be trademarked

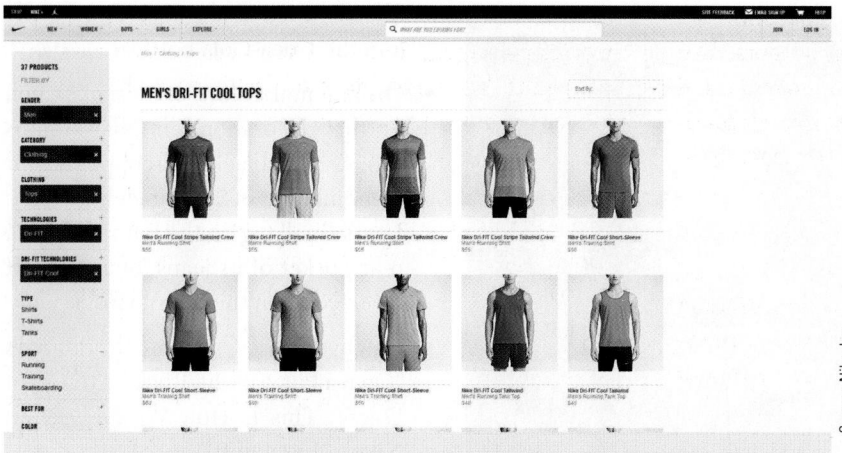

Nike and Under Armour have file lawsuits against one another in the recent past for trademark infringement; one instance being the use of the term "DRI-FIT".

Source: Nike, Inc.

by U.S. courts include aspirin, cellophane, linoleum, thermos, kerosene, monopoly, cola, and shredded wheat.

Companies such as Rolls-Royce, Cross, Xerox, Levi Strauss, Frigidaire, and McDonald's aggressively enforce their trademarks. Rolls-Royce, Coca-Cola, and Xerox even run newspaper and magazine ads stating that their names are trademarks and should not be used as descriptive or generic terms. In 2013, athletic apparel company Under Armour filed a trademark infringement lawsuit against Nike over the company's use of advertising phrases "I Will" and "Protect this house." According to Under Armour, Nike's use of phrases such as "I will protect my home court" in online and social media outlets infringed upon an Under Armour marketing campaign that used similar phrases. Ten years earlier, Nike filed a suit against Under Armour over the use of the term "DRI-FIT."[17]

To try to stem the number of trademark infringements, violations carry steep penalties. But despite the risk of incurring a penalty, infringement lawsuits are still common. Serious conflict can occur when brand names resemble one another too closely. Fashion brand Gucci has accused Guess of trademark violations for years. In 2015, a French court ruled in Guess's favor, finding that no trademark infringement, counterfeiting, or unfair competition between the two brands occurred. The court found that Guess had diluted Gucci's logos, not copied them. An American court ruled, however, that Guess was guilty of copying four of Gucci's five trademarked logos. This example also illustrates that there is no such thing as a global trademark.[18]

Companies must also contend with fake or unauthorized brands. Knockoffs of trademarked clothing lines are easy to find in cheap shops all over the world,

and loose imitations are found in some reputable department stores as well. Today, whole stores are faked in China. Stores selling real iPhones and iPads in stores with sparse décor and bright lighting may seem like authentic Apple stores but are frequently imitating the real deal. Numerous fast-food restaurants have become victims of knockoff stores throughout China: Pizza Huh (Pizza Hut), Mak Dak (McDonald's), and Taco Bell Grande (Taco Bell) mimic the American chains' layouts and products. FBC, KFG, KLG, MFC, and OFC all lift Kentucky Fried Chicken's iconic logo, color scheme, and menu.[19]

In Europe, you can sue counterfeiters only if your brand, logo, or trademark is formally registered. Formal registration used to be required in each country in which a company sought protection. However, today a company can register its trademark in all European Union member countries with one application.

10-5 PACKAGING

Packages have always served a practical function— that is, they hold contents together and protect goods as they move through the distribution channel. Today, however, packaging is also a container for promoting the product and making it easier and safer to use.

10-5a Packaging Functions

The three most important functions of packaging are to contain and protect products; promote products; and facilitate the storage, use, and convenience of products. A fourth function of packaging that is becoming increasingly important is to facilitate recycling and reduce environmental damage.

CONTAINING AND PROTECTING PRODUCTS The most obvious function of packaging is to contain products that are liquid, granular, or otherwise divisible. Packaging also enables manufacturers, wholesalers, and retailers to market products in specific quantities, such as ounces.

Physical protection is another obvious function of packaging. Most products are handled several times between the time they are manufactured, harvested, or otherwise produced and the time they are consumed or used. Many products are also shipped, stored, and inspected several times between production and consumption. Some, like milk, need to be refrigerated. Others, like beer, are sensitive to light. Still others, like medicines and bandages, need to be kept sterile. Packages protect products from breakage, evaporation, spillage, spoilage, light, heat, cold, infestation, and many other conditions.

PROMOTING PRODUCTS Packaging does more than identify the brand, list the ingredients, specify features, and give directions. A package differentiates a product from competing products and may associate a new product with a family of other products from the same manufacturer. However, some products' packaging lacks useful information. The FDA is looking to remedy inconsistent and incomplete food packaging information by adding more facts to nutrition labels. These changes include listing the number of servings in each container and printing the calorie count for each serving in larger, bolder type. The FDA hopes that these changes will catch consumers' eyes and help them better manage their health.[20]

Mahathir Mohd Yasin/Shutterstock.com

Packages use designs, colors, shapes, and materials to try to influence consumers' perceptions and buying behavior. For example, marketing research shows that health-conscious consumers are likely to think that any food is probably good for them as long as it comes in green packaging. Packaging can also influence consumer perceptions of quality and/or prestige. England's Brothers Cider recently revamped its label and can designs in a move to reposition Toffee Apple Cider, Festival Pear Cider, and other cider flavors as premium adult beverages. The company replaced bright green bottles with tinted brown ones, and swapped colorful graphic labels for designs that employ a mix of classic and modern typefaces. To bolster its new prestigious image, Brothers rolled out its package redesign alongside a $7.6 million countrywide marketing push.[21]

FACILITATING STORAGE, USE, AND CONVENIENCE Wholesalers and retailers prefer packages that are easy to ship, store, and stock on shelves. They also like packages that protect products, prevent spoilage or breakage, and extend the product's shelf life.

Consumers' requirements for storage, use, and convenience cover many dimensions. Consumers are constantly seeking items that are easy to handle, open, and reclose, although some consumers want packages that are tamperproof or childproof. Research indicates that hard-to-open packages are among consumers' top

complaints—especially when it comes to clamshell electronics packaging. Indeed, Quora users voted clamshell packaging "the worst piece of design ever done." There is even a Wikipedia page devoted to "wrap rage," the anger associated with trying to open clamshells and other poorly designed packages.[22] As oil prices force the cost of plastics used in packaging skyward, companies such as Amazon, Target, and Walmart are pushing suppliers to do away with excessive and infuriating packaging. Such packaging innovations as zipper tear strips, hinged lids, tab slots, screw-on tops, simple cardboard boxes, and pour spouts were introduced to solve these and other problems. Easy openings are especially important for kids and aging baby boomers.

Some firms use packaging to segment markets. For example, a C&H sugar carton with an easy-to-pour, reclosable top is targeted to consumers who do not do a lot of baking and are willing to pay at least 20 cents more for the package. Different-sized packages appeal to heavy, moderate, and light users. Campbell's soup is packaged in single-serving cans aimed at the elderly and singles market segments. Packaging convenience can increase a product's utility and, therefore, its market share and profits.

FACILITATING RECYCLING AND REDUCING ENVIRONMENTAL DAMAGE One of the most important packaging issues today is eco-consciousness, a trend that has recently been in and out of consumer and media attention. Studies conflict as to whether consumers will pay more for eco-friendly packaging, though consumers repeatedly iterate the desire to purchase such products. A 2013 Harris Interactive study found that 78 percent of customers buy green products and services, up from sixty-nine percent in 2012. Twenty percent of respondents said that they purchased eco-friendly products to improve their health, while 47 percent reported that they did so to improve the environment.[23]

10-5b Labeling

An integral part of any package is its label. Labeling generally takes one of two forms: persuasive or informational. **Persuasive labeling** focuses on a promotional theme or logo, and consumer information is secondary. Note that the standard promotional claims—such as "new," "improved," and

> **persuasive labeling** a type of package labeling that focuses on a promotional theme or logo, and consumer information is secondary

THE DISAPPEARING PACKAGE

Some firms use innovative packaging to target environmentally concerned market segments. Package designer Aaron Mickelson's the Disappearing Package project showcased several inventive ways to make packaging more sustainable. Mickelson's designs include bar soap packaging that dissolves under shower water, trash bag packaging that doubles as a container and can be used as a trash bag itself, perforated tea bag booklets (eliminating the need for a box), and a rolled up tear-away detergent pod package with product information printed across the outside of the conjoined pods.[25]

Brand & product info are printed directly on the surface with soap-soluble ink.

Courtesy of Chapel House Photography

Aaron Mickelson's innovative packaging project included concepts such as this one—a reusable container with a soap-soluble label that rinsed off—allowing the container to be repurposed for other foods or household items.

informational labeling a type of package labeling designed to help consumers make proper product selections and lower their cognitive dissonance after the purchase

universal product codes (UPCs) a series of thick and thin vertical lines (bar codes) readable by computerized optical scanners that represent numbers used to track products

the purchase. Most major furniture manufacturers affix labels to their wares that explain the products' construction features, such as type of frame, number of coils, and fabric characteristics. The Nutritional Labeling and Education Act of 1990 mandated detailed nutritional information on most food packages and standards for health claims on food packaging. An important outcome of this legislation has been guidelines from the Food and Drug Administration for using terms such as *low fat*, *light*, *reduced cholesterol*, *low sodium*, *low calorie*, *low carb*, and *fresh*. Getting the right information is very important to consumers, so some universities and corporations are working on new technologies to help consumers shop smart. For example, researchers at the Eindhoven University of Technology, the Universitá di Catania, CEA-Liten, and STMicroelectronics have developed a low-cost plastic converter that tests whether packaged foods are safe to eat. The converter then displays information about the food's freshness directly on its packaging, eliminating the need for "best before" dates that serve as cautious estimates at best. This not only reassures customers that they are buying fresh food; it prevents still-edible food from being thrown away once it is bought.[24]

GREENWASHING There are numerous products in every product category that use *greenwashing* to try and sell products. Greenwashing is when a product or company attempts to give the impression of environmental friendliness whether or not it is environmentally friendly.

As consumer demand for green products appeared to escalate, green certifications proliferated. Companies could create their own certifications and logos, resulting in more than 300 possible certification labels, ranging in price from free to thousands of dollars. Consumer distrust and confusion caused the Federal Trade Commission to issue new rules. Starting in late 2011, new regulations apply to labeling products with green-certification logos. If the same company that produced the product performed the certification, that relationship must be clearly marked. This benefits organizations such as Green Seal, which uses unbiased, third-party scientists and experts to verify claims about emissions or biodegradability, and hopes to increase consumer confidence in green products.[26]

10-5c Universal Product Codes

The **universal product codes (UPCs)** that appear on most items in supermarkets and other high-volume outlets were first introduced in 1974. Because the numerical codes appear as a series of thick and thin vertical lines, they are often called *bar codes*. The lines are read by computerized optical scanners that match codes with brand names, package sizes, and prices. They also

"super"—are no longer very persuasive. Consumers have been saturated with "newness" and thus discount these claims.

Informational labeling, by contrast, is designed to help consumers make proper product selections and lower their cognitive dissonance after

print information on cash register tapes and help retailers rapidly and accurately prepare records of customer purchases, control inventories, and track sales. The UPC system and scanners are also used in scanner-based research (see Chapter 9).

10-6 GLOBAL ISSUES IN BRANDING AND PACKAGING

When planning to enter a foreign market with an existing product, a firm has three options for handling the brand name:

- **One brand name everywhere:** This strategy is useful when the company markets mainly one product and the brand name does not have negative connotations in any local market. The Coca-Cola Company uses a one-brand-name strategy in more than 195 countries around the world. The advantages of a one-brand-name strategy are greater identification of the product from market to market and ease of coordinating promotion from market to market.

- **Adaptations and modifications:** A one-brand-name strategy is not possible when the name cannot be pronounced in the local language, when the brand name is owned by someone else, or when the brand name has a negative or vulgar connotation in the local language. The Iranian detergent Barf, for example, might encounter some problems in the U.S. market.

- **Different brand names in different markets:** Local brand names are often used when translation or pronunciation problems occur, when the marketer wants the brand to appear to be a local brand, or when regulations require localization. Unilever's Axe line of male grooming products is called Lynx in England, Ireland, Australia, and New Zealand. PepsiCo changed the name of its eponymous cola to Pecsi in Argentina to reflect the way the word is pronounced with an Argentinian accent.

In addition to global branding decisions, companies must consider global packaging needs. Three aspects of packaging that are especially important in international marketing are labeling, aesthetics, and climate considerations. The major *labeling* concern is properly translating ingredient, promotional, and instructional information on labels. Care must also be employed in meeting all local labeling requirements. Several years ago, an Italian judge ordered that all bottles of Coca-Cola be removed from retail shelves because the ingredients were not properly labeled. Labeling is also harder in countries like Belgium and Finland, which require packaging to be bilingual.

Package *aesthetics* may also require some attention. Even though simple visual elements of the brand, such as a symbol or logo, can be a standardizing element across products and countries, marketers must stay attuned to cultural traits in host countries. For example, colors may have different connotations. Red is associated with witchcraft in some countries, green may be a sign of danger, and white may be symbolic of death. Such cultural differences could necessitate a packaging change if colors are chosen for another country's interpretation. In the United States, green typically symbolizes an eco-friendly product, but that packaging could keep customers away in a country where green indicates danger. Aesthetics also influence package size. Soft drinks are not sold in six-packs in countries that lack refrigeration. In some countries, products such as detergent may be bought only in small quantities because of a lack of storage space. Other products, such as cigarettes, may be bought in small quantities, and even single units, because of the low purchasing power of buyers.

Extreme climates and long-distance shipping necessitate sturdier and more durable packages for goods sold overseas. Spillage, spoilage, and breakage are all more important concerns when products are shipped long distances or frequently handled during shipping and storage. Packages may also need to ensure a longer product life if the time between production and consumption lengthens significantly.

10-7 PRODUCT WARRANTIES

Just as a package is designed to protect the product, a warranty protects the buyer and gives essential information about the product. A warranty confirms the quality or performance of a good or service. An **express warranty** is a written guarantee. Express warranties range from simple statements—such as "100-percent cotton" (a guarantee of quality) and "complete satisfaction guaranteed" (a statement of performance)—to extensive documents written in technical language. In contrast, an **implied warranty** is an unwritten guarantee that the good or service is fit for the purpose for which it was sold. All sales have an implied warranty under the Uniform Commercial Code.

> **warranty** a confirmation of the quality or performance of a good or service
>
> **express warranty** a written guarantee
>
> **implied warranty** an unwritten guarantee that the good or service is fit for the purpose for which it was sold

Congress passed the Magnuson-Moss Warranty–Federal Trade Commission Improvement Act in 1975 to help consumers understand warranties and get action from manufacturers and dealers. A manufacturer that promises a full warranty must meet certain minimum standards, including repair "within a reasonable time and without charge" of any defects and replacement of the merchandise or a full refund if the product does not work "after a reasonable number of attempts" at repair. Any warranty that does not live up to this tough prescription must be "conspicuously" promoted as a limited warranty.

STUDY TOOLS 10

LOCATED AT BACK OF THE TEXTBOOK

☐ Rip out Chapter Review Card

LOCATED AT WWW.CENGAGEBRAIN.COM

☐ Review Key Terms Flashcards and create your own

☐ Track your knowledge and understanding of key concepts in marketing

☐ Complete practice and graded quizzes to prepare for tests

☐ Complete interactive content within the MKTG Online experience

☐ View the chapter highlight boxes within the MKTG Online experience

TEACH³
INTRODUCTION TO EDUCATION
NOW WITH TEACH ONLINE

HIST⁴
U.S. HISTORY
NOW WITH HIST ONLINE

BCOM⁸
BUSINESS COMMUNICATION
NOW WITH BCOM ONLINE

SPEAK³
PUBLIC SPEAKING
NOW WITH SPEAK ONLINE

ORGB⁵
ORGANIZATIONAL BEHAVIOR
NOW WITH ORGB ONLINE

GLOBAL³
GLOBAL BUSINESS
NOW WITH GLOBAL ONLINE

IPC³
INTERPERSONAL COMMUNICATION
NOW WITH IPC ONLINE

COMM⁴
SPEECH COMMUNICATION
NOW WITH COMM ONLINE

GOVT⁸
PRINCIPLES OF AMERICAN GOVERNMENT
NOW WITH GOVT ONLINE

MKTG¹⁰
PRINCIPLES OF MARKETING
NOW WITH MKTG ONLINE

MIS⁶
MANAGEMENT INFORMATION SYSTEMS
NOW WITH MIS ONLINE

WORLD RELG³
INTRODUCTION TO WORLD RELIGIONS
NOW WITH RELG ONLINE

CFIN⁵
CORPORATE FINANCE
NOW WITH CFIN ONLINE

BUSN⁹
INTRODUCTION TO BUSINESS
NOW WITH BUSN ONLINE

SELL⁵
NOW WITH SELL ONLINE

MGMT⁹
PRINCIPLES OF MANAGEMENT
NOW WITH MGMT ONLINE

LEARNING **YOUR** WAY

www.cengage.com/4ltrpress

11 Developing and Managing Products

Luminaimages./Shutterstock.com

LEARNING OUTCOMES

After studying this chapter, you will be able to…

11-1 Explain the importance of developing new products and describe the six categories of new products

11-2 Explain the steps in the new-product development process

11-3 Understand why some products succeed and others fail

11-4 Discuss global issues in new-product development

11-5 Explain the diffusion process through which new products are adopted

11-6 Explain the concept of product life cycles

After you finish this chapter go to **PAGE 203** for **STUDY TOOLS.**

11-1 THE IMPORTANCE OF NEW PRODUCTS

New products are important to sustain growth, increase revenues and profits, and replace obsolete items. Each year *Fast Company* rates and ranks its most innovative companies, based on the ability to buck tradition in the interest of reaching more people, building a better business, and spurring mass-market appeal for unusual or highly technical products or services. In 2015, the top five companies were Warby Parker, Apple, Alibaba, Google, and Instagram.[1] All of these firms have reputations for relying heavily on technology.

11-1a Introduction of New Products

Some companies spend a considerable amount of money each year developing new products. At Pfizer, the world's largest research-based pharmaceutical company, approximately $1.2 billion is spent on research and development for every new product released.[2] Other companies with large R&D spending include Toyota ($9.9 billion per year), IBM ($6.3 billion per year), and Procter & Gamble ($2 billion per year).[3]

Sometimes it is difficult to decide when to replace a successful product. Gillette Co. has a history of introducing new shaving systems (razors and accompanying blades) before the previous generation of products begins experiencing a sales decline. In fact, Gillette *expects* to cannibalize the sales of older models with its newer introductions. In early 2015, Apple reintroduced the MacBook line of laptops, effectively replacing the popular MacBook Air line. Apple executives agreed that the MacBook Air needed to be replaced to keep customers

satisfied, but the design of the new MacBook required complex decisions, tradeoffs, and risks. The new version features a retina display, thinner design, and a longer-lasting battery.[4] Clearly, the introduction of a new product is a monumental undertaking with a lot of open-ended questions—even for an established, multi-billion dollar company like Apple.

11-1b Categories of New Products

The term **new product** is somewhat confusing because its meaning varies widely. Actually, the term has several "correct" definitions. A product can be new to the world, to the market, to the producer or seller, or some combination of these. There are six categories of new products:

- **New-to-the-world products (also called *discontinuous innovations*):** These products create an entirely new market. For example, in early 2013, Taiwanese electronics company Polytron Technologies unveiled a completely transparent smartphone prototype. The device's new-to-the-world "Switchable Glass" technology employs liquid crystal molecules that display images only when electric current is run through them. Without power, the smartphone is completely see-through.[5] New-to-the-world products represent the smallest category of new products.

> ## The average fast-moving consumer goods company introduces seventy to eighty new products per year.

- **New product lines:** These products, which the firm has not previously offered, allow it to enter an established market. For example, Moleskine's first products were simple black-covered journals. Since then, the company has expanded into pens, travel bags, and even digital creative tools available on the iPhone and iPad.[6]

- Additions to existing product lines: This category includes new products that supplement a firm's established line. Fast-food restaurant chain Taco Bell and snack food manufacturer Frito-Lay have a longstanding partnership that has resulted in several product line additions. After the nacho cheese-flavored Doritos Locos taco proved to be the biggest launch in Taco Bell history, CEO Greg Creed announced that Cool Ranch– and

new product a product new to the world, the market, the producer, the seller, or some combination of these

New 2015 Ford F-150s feature high-strength, military-grade, aluminum-alloy bodies and beds.

Flamas-flavored versions of the Doritos Locos taco would soon be added to Taco Bell's product line. Indeed, in March 2013, the Cool Ranch Doritos Locos taco was added to Taco Bell menus across America.[7]

- **Improvements or revisions of existing products:** The "new and improved" product may be significantly or only slightly changed. In May 2013, MillerCoors announced a new Miller Lite bottle that would only be available in bars and restaurants. According to the company, the new bottle shape featured "broad shoulders and a contoured grip." While the beer inside did not change, the revision was significant enough that the bottle could be called a new product.[8]

- **Repositioned products:** These are existing products targeted at new markets or market segments, or ones repositioned to change the current market's perception of the product or company, which may be done to boost declining sales. Mercedes is repositioning its ultra-luxurious Maybach line as a sub-brand to appeal to its most status-conscious customers. Although Mercedes is already known for luxurious vehicles, the Maybach line is intended to "set a new benchmark for exclusivity." The Mercedes-Maybach line will feature exceptionally comfortable and spacious seating and lavishly designed interiors.[9]

- **Lower-priced products:** This category refers to products that provide performance similar to competing brands at a lower price. The HP LaserJet Color MFP is a scanner, copier, printer, and fax machine combined. This new product is priced lower than many conventional color copiers and much lower than the combined price of the four items purchased separately.

11-2 THE NEW-PRODUCT DEVELOPMENT PROCESS

The management consulting firm Booz Allen Hamilton has studied the new-product development process for more than 30 years. Analyzing five major studies undertaken during this period, the firm has concluded that the companies most likely to succeed in developing and introducing new products are those that take the following actions:

- Make the long-term commitment needed to support innovation and new-product development.
- Use a company-specific approach, driven by corporate objectives and strategies, with a well-defined new-product strategy at its core.
- Capitalize on experience to achieve and maintain competitive advantage.
- Establish an environment—a management style, organizational structure, and degree of top management support—conducive to achieving company-specific new-product and corporate objectives.

Most companies follow a formal new-product development process, usually starting with a new-product strategy. Exhibit 11.1 traces the seven-step process, which is discussed in detail in this section. The exhibit is funnel-shaped to highlight the fact that each stage acts as a screen to filter out unworkable ideas.

11-2a New-Product Strategy

A **new-product strategy** links the new-product development process with the objectives of the marketing department, the business unit, and the corporation. A new-product strategy must be compatible with these objectives, and in turn, all three of the objectives must be consistent with one another.

A new-product strategy is part of the organization's overall marketing strategy. It sharpens the focus and provides general guidelines for generating, screening, and evaluating new-product ideas. The new-product strategy specifies the roles that new products must play in the organization's overall plan and describes the characteristics of products the organization wants to offer and the markets it wants to serve.

new-product strategy a plan that links the new-product development process with the objectives of the marketing department, the business unit, and the corporation

Bill Pugliano/Getty Images

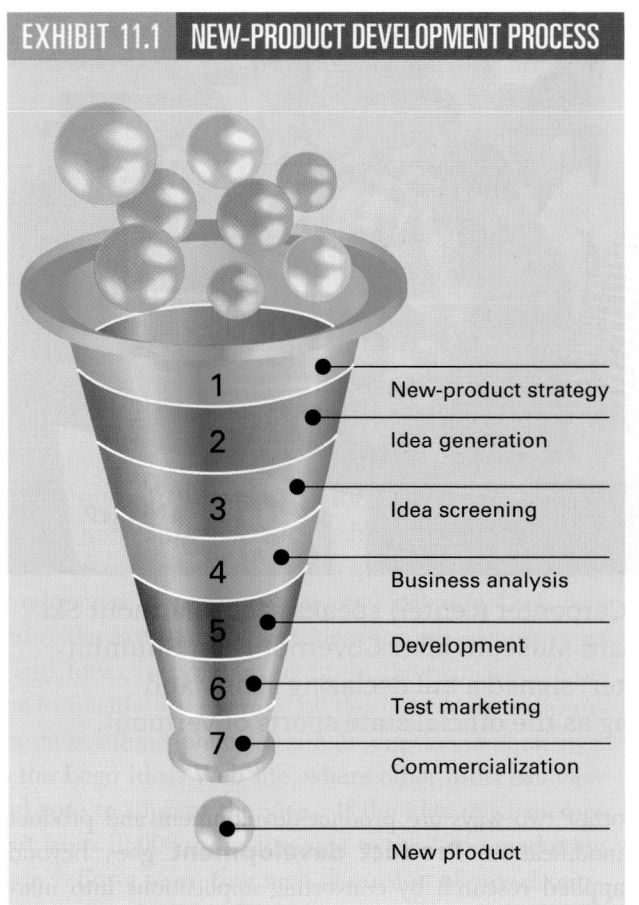

EXHIBIT 11.1 NEW-PRODUCT DEVELOPMENT PROCESS

1. New-product strategy
2. Idea generation
3. Idea screening
4. Business analysis
5. Development
6. Test marketing
7. Commercialization

New product

11-2b Idea Generation

New-product ideas come from many sources, including customers, employees, distributors, competitors, research and development (R&D), consultants, and other experts.

CUSTOMERS The marketing concept suggests that customers' wants and needs should be the springboard for developing new products. Companies can derive insight from listening to Internet chatter or reading blogs, which often indicate early trends or areas consumers are interested in seeing develop or change. Another approach for generating new-product ideas is using what some companies are calling "customer innovation centers." The idea is to provide a forum for meeting with customers and directly involving them in the innovation process.

EMPLOYEES Sometimes employees know a company's products and processes better than anyone else. Many firms have formal and informal processes in place for employees to propose new product ideas. To encourage participation, some companies run contests, hold votes, and set up idea kiosks.[10]

PricewaterhouseCoopers uses a system called iPlace to encourage employee innovation. The system is so successful that 60 percent of employees participate in the idea-generation process; 140 of the 3,300 ideas have already been implemented.[11]

For Havianas Customers, Customization is Key

In the saturated summer sandals market, flip-flop manufacturer Havianas utilizes customization as a way to stand out. Havianas' online customization tool allows customers to combine different patterns and colors to create their own unique pairs of flip flops.[12]

Source: Havaianas

© olexius/Shutterstock 149731013

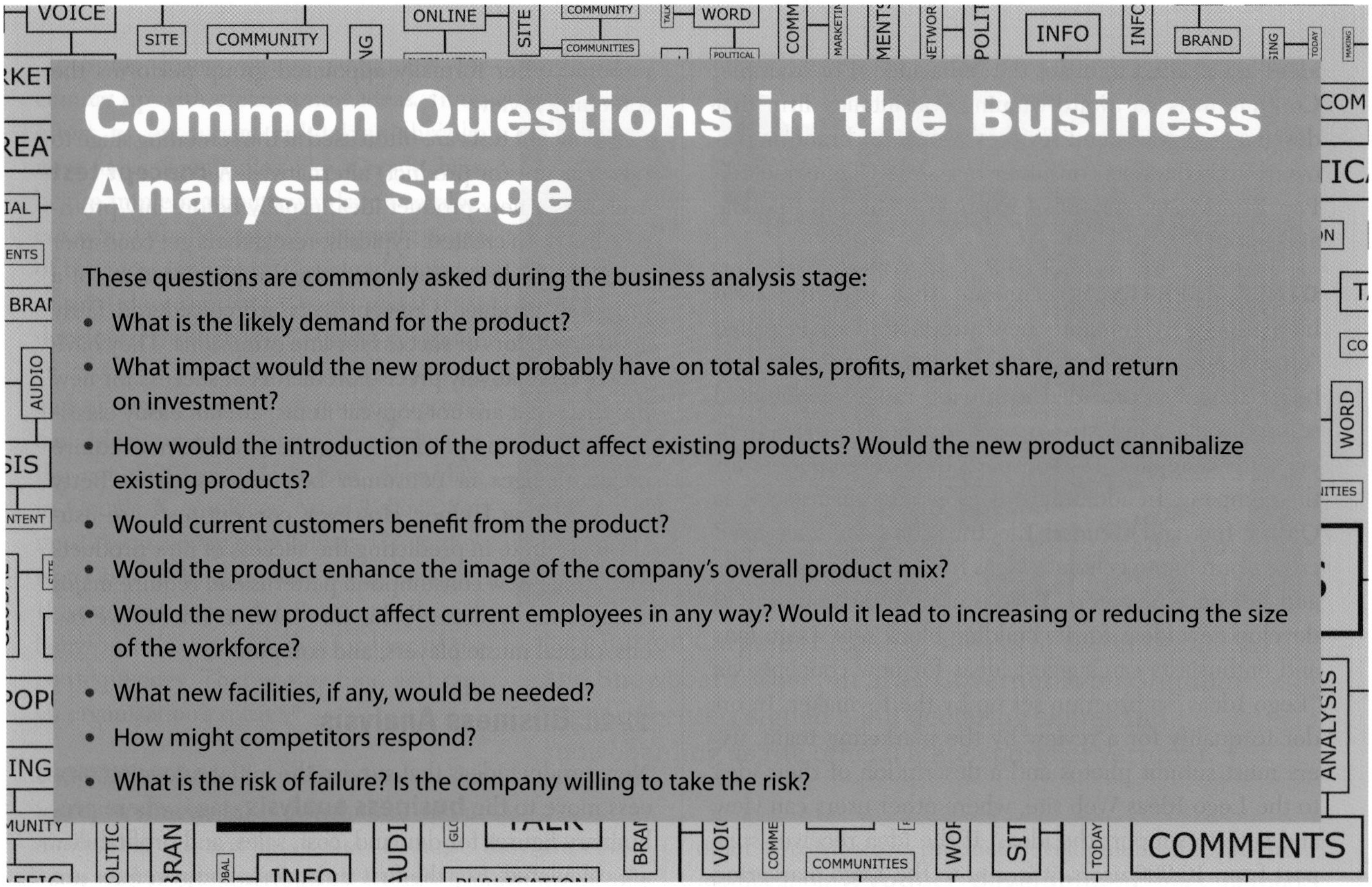

©StudioM1

Common Questions in the Business Analysis Stage

These questions are commonly asked during the business analysis stage:

- What is the likely demand for the product?
- What impact would the new product probably have on total sales, profits, market share, and return on investment?
- How would the introduction of the product affect existing products? Would the new product cannibalize existing products?
- Would current customers benefit from the product?
- Would the product enhance the image of the company's overall product mix?
- Would the new product affect current employees in any way? Would it lead to increasing or reducing the size of the workforce?
- What new facilities, if any, would be needed?
- How might competitors respond?
- What is the risk of failure? Is the company willing to take the risk?

Understanding the market potential is important because costs increase dramatically once a product idea enters the development stage.

11-2e Development

In the early stage of **development**, the R&D or engineering department may develop a prototype of the product. A process called 3D printing, or additive manufacturing, is sometimes used to create three-dimensional prototypes quickly and at a relatively low cost. During this stage, the firm should start sketching a marketing strategy. The marketing department should decide on the product's packaging, branding, labeling, and so forth. In addition, it should map out preliminary promotion, price, and distribution strategies. The feasibility of manufacturing the product at an acceptable cost should be thoroughly examined. The development stage can last a long time and thus be very expensive. It took ten years to develop Crest toothpaste, fifteen years to develop the Polaroid Colorpack camera and the Xerox copy machine, 18 years to develop Minute Rice, and 51 years to develop the television. Video game developer Ubisoft took more than five years to develop open-world action game Watch Dogs and more than six years to develop racing game The Crew. The time invested in

development the stage in the product development process in which a prototype is developed and a marketing strategy is outlined

3D Printing (or additive manufacturing) is sometimes used to create three-dimensional prototypes quickly and at a relatively low cost.

Stefano Tinti/Shutterstock.com

development, however, can often have a tremendous payoff. Watch Dogs broke launch day sales for Ubisoft, selling more than 4 million units during its first week.[19]

The development process works best when all the involved areas (R&D, marketing, engineering, production, and even suppliers) work together rather than sequentially, a process called **simultaneous product development**. This approach allows firms to shorten the development process and reduce costs. With simultaneous product development, all relevant functional areas and outside suppliers participate in all stages of the development process. Rather than proceeding through highly structured stages, the cross-functional team operates in unison. Involving key suppliers early in the process capitalizes on their knowledge and enables them to develop critical component parts.

The Internet is a useful tool for implementing simultaneous product development. On the Web, multiple partners from a variety of locations can meet regularly to assess new-product ideas, analyze markets and demographics, and review cost information. Ideas judged to be feasible can quickly be converted into new products. The best-managed global firms leverage their global networks by sharing best practices, knowledge, and technology.[20] Without the Internet, it would be impossible to conduct simultaneous product development from different parts of the world. Some firms use online brain trusts to solve technical problems. InnoCentive Inc. is a network of 80,000 self-selected science problem solvers in 173 countries. Its clients include NASA, *Popular Science*, and *The Economist*. When one of InnoCentive's partners selects an idea for development, it no longer tries to develop the idea from the ground up with its own resources and time. Instead, it issues a brief to its network of thinkers, researchers, technology entrepreneurs, and inventors around the world, hoping to generate dialogue, suggestions, and solutions.

Innovative firms are also gathering a variety of R&D input from customers online. Wheaties NEXT Challenge allowed customers to vote for which elite athlete would be featured on the next Wheaties cereal box by logging workouts through the MapMyFitness program. For each workout that was logged, a vote was cast for the participant's favorite Wheaties athlete. More than 71,000 people participated in the challenge.[21]

Laboratory tests are often conducted on prototype models during the development stage. User safety is an important aspect of laboratory testing, which actually subjects products to much more severe treatment than is expected by end users. The Consumer Product Safety Act of 1972 requires manufacturers to conduct a "reasonable testing program" to ensure that their products conform to established safety standards.

Many products that test well in the laboratory are also tried out in homes or businesses. Examples of product categories well suited for such use tests include human and pet food products, household cleaning products, and industrial chemicals and supplies. These products are all relatively inexpensive, and their performance characteristics are apparent to users. For example, P&G tests a variety of personal and home-care products in the community around its Cincinnati, Ohio, headquarters.

11-2f Test Marketing

After products and marketing programs have been developed, they are usually tested in the marketplace. **Test marketing** is the limited introduction of a product and a marketing program to determine the reactions of potential customers in a market situation. Test marketing allows management to evaluate alternative strategies and to assess how well the various aspects of the marketing mix fit together. Even established products are test marketed to assess new marketing strategies.

The cities chosen as test sites should reflect market conditions in the new product's projected market area. Yet no "magic city" exists that can universally represent market conditions, and a product's success in one city does not guarantee that it will be a nationwide hit. When selecting test market cities, researchers should therefore find locations where the demographics and purchasing habits mirror the overall market. The company should also have good distribution in test cities. Wendy's uses Columbus, Ohio as a test market for new burgers. Because the city has a nearly perfect cross-section of America's demographic breakdown, it is the perfect testing ground for new products. Most recently, Wendy's tested the reception of its Ciabatta Bacon Cheeseburger.[22] Moreover, test locations should be isolated from the media. If the television stations in a particular market reach a very large area outside that market, the advertising used for the test product may pull in many consumers from outside the market. The product may then appear more successful than it really is.

simultaneous product development a team-oriented approach to new-product development

test marketing the limited introduction of a product and a marketing program to determine the reactions of potential customers in a market situation

Wendy's uses Columbus, Ohio, as a test market for new burgers and menu items.

THE HIGH COSTS OF TEST MARKETING Test marketing frequently takes one year or longer, and costs can exceed $1 million. Some products remain in test markets even longer. In an effort to expand its product offerings, Starbucks launched the Dark Barrel Latte in select Ohio and Florida locations in September 2014. Some describe this new latte as having a taste similar to Guinness beer. As of this printing, the drink is yet to become more widely available.[23]

Despite the cost, many firms believe it is better to fail in a test market than in a national introduction. Because test marketing is so expensive, some companies do not test line extensions of well-known brands.

simulated (laboratory) market testing the presentation of advertising and other promotional materials for several products, including a test product, to members of the product's target market

commercialization the decision to market a product

The high cost of test marketing is not just financial. One unavoidable problem is that test marketing exposes the new product and its marketing mix to competitors before its introduction. Thus, the element of surprise is lost. Competitors can also sabotage or "jam" a testing program by introducing their own sales promotion, pricing, or advertising campaign. The purpose is to hide or distort the normal conditions that the testing firm might expect in the market.

ALTERNATIVES TO TEST MARKETING Many firms are looking for cheaper, faster, safer alternatives to traditional test marketing. In the early 1980s, Information Resources Inc. pioneered one alternative: scanner-based research (discussed in Chapter 9). A typical supermarket scanner test costs about $300,000. Another alternative to traditional test marketing is **simulated (laboratory) market testing**. Advertising and other promotional materials for several products, including the test product, are shown to members of the product's target market. These people are then taken to shop at a mock or real store, where their purchases are recorded. Shopper behavior, including repeat purchasing, is monitored to assess the product's likely performance under true market conditions. Research firms offer simulated market tests for $25,000 to $100,000, compared to $1 million or more for full-scale test marketing.

The Internet offers a fast, cost-effective way to conduct test marketing. P&G uses the Internet to assess customer demand for potential new products. Many products that are not available in grocery stores or drugstores can be sampled from P&G's Web site devoted to samples and coupons, www.pgeveryday.com.[24]

Despite these alternatives, most firms still consider test marketing essential for most new products. The high price of failure simply prohibits the widespread introduction of most new products without testing.

11-2g Commercialization

The final stage in the new-product development process is **commercialization**, the decision to market a product. The decision to commercialize the product sets several tasks in motion: ordering production materials and equipment, starting production, building inventories, shipping the product to field distribution points, training the sales force, announcing the new product to the trade, and advertising to potential customers.

The time from the initial commercialization decision to the product's actual introduction varies. It can range from a few weeks for simple products that use existing equipment to several years for technical products that require custom manufacturing equipment. And the total cost of development and initial introduction can be staggering.

WHY SOME PRODUCTS SUCCEED AND OTHERS FAIL

Despite the amount of time and money spent on developing and testing new products, a large proportion of new product introductions fail. Products fail for a number of reasons. One common reason is that they simply do not offer any discernible benefit compared to existing products. Another commonly cited factor in new-product failures is a poor match between product features and customer desires. For example, there are telephone systems on the market with more than 700 different functions, although the average user is happy with just ten functions. Other reasons for failure include overestimation of market size, incorrect targeting or positioning, a price too high or too low, inadequate distribution, poor promotion, or simply an inferior product.

Estimates of the percentages of new products that fail vary. Many estimates range as high as 80 to 90 percent.[25] Failure can be a matter of degree, however. Absolute failure occurs when a company cannot recoup its development, marketing, and production costs—the product actually loses money for the company. A relative product failure results when the product returns a profit

SEVEN CHARACTERISTICS OF SUCCESSFUL PRODUCT INTRODUCTIONS

Firms that routinely experience success in new-product introductions tend to share the following seven characteristics:

- A history of listening carefully to customers
- An obsession with producing the best product possible
- A vision of what the market will be like in the future
- Strong leadership
- A commitment to new-product development
- A project-based team approach to new-product development
- Getting every aspect of the product development process right

but fails to achieve sales, profit, or market share goals. Examples of product failures in 2014 include the Amazon Fire Phone, detergent-free laundry systems, the Nike FuelBand, and Burger King's Satisfries, a healthier alternative to regular fries.[26]

High costs and other risks of developing and testing new products do not stop many companies, such as Newell Rubbermaid, Colgate-Palmolive, Campbell Soup Company, and 3M, from aggressively developing and introducing new products. These companies depend on new products to increase revenues and profits. The most important factor in successful new-product introduction is a good match between the product and market needs—as the marketing concept would predict. Successful new products deliver a meaningful and perceivable benefit to a sizable number of people or organizations and are different in some meaningful way from their intended substitutes.

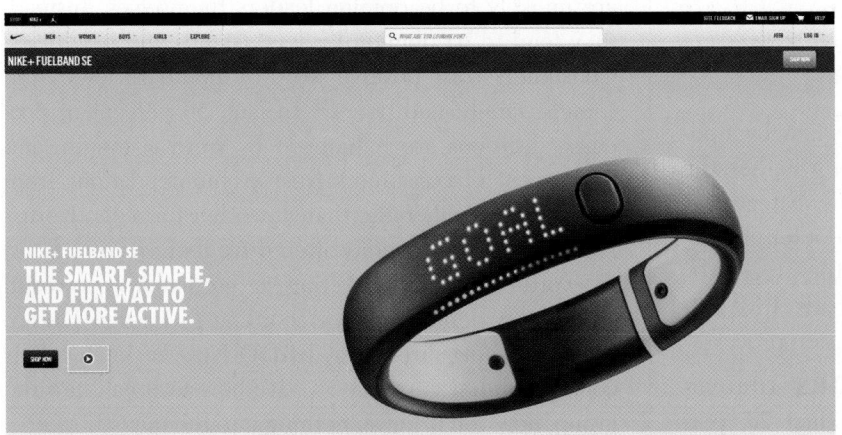

High costs of new products do not stop large companies from aggressively developing them, even if they fail.

Source: Nike, Inc.

GLOBAL ISSUES IN NEW-PRODUCT DEVELOPMENT

Increasing globalization of markets and competition provides a reason for multinational firms to consider new-product development from a worldwide perspective. A firm that starts with a global strategy is better able to develop products that are marketable worldwide. In many multinational corporations, every product is developed for potential worldwide distribution, and unique market requirements are satisfied during development whenever possible.

Some global marketers design their products to meet regulations in their major markets and then, if necessary, meet smaller markets' requirements country by country. Nissan develops lead-country car models that, with minor changes, can be sold in most markets. With this approach, Nissan has been able to reduce the number of its basic models from 48 to 18. Some products, however, have little potential for global market penetration without modification. Succeeding in some countries (such as China) often requires companies to develop products that meet the unique needs of these populations.[27] In other cases, companies cannot sell their products at affordable prices and still make a profit in many countries.

11-5 THE SPREAD OF NEW PRODUCTS

Managers have a better chance of successfully marketing products if they understand how consumers learn about and adopt products.

11-5a Diffusion of Innovation

An **innovation** is a product perceived as new by a potential adopter. It really does not matter whether the product is "new to the world" or some other category of new product. If it is new to a potential adopter, it is an innovation in this context. **Diffusion** is the process by which the adoption of an innovation spreads. Five categories of adopters participate in the diffusion process.

INNOVATORS Innovators are the first 2.5 percent of all those who adopt the product. Innovators are eager to try new ideas and products, almost as an

innovation a product perceived as new by a potential adopter

diffusion the process by which the adoption of an innovation spreads

obsession. In addition to having higher incomes, they are more worldly and more active outside their community than noninnovators. They rely less on group norms and are more self-confident. Because they are well educated, they are more likely to get their information from scientific sources and experts. Innovators are characterized as being venturesome.

EARLY ADOPTERS Early adopters are the next 13.5 percent to adopt the product. Although early adopters are not the very first, they do adopt early in the product's life cycle. Compared to innovators, they rely much more on group norms and values. They are also more oriented to the local community, in contrast to the innovators' worldly outlook. Early adopters are more likely than innovators to be opinion leaders because of their closer affiliation with groups. Early adopters are a new product's best friends. Because viral, buzz, and word-of-mouth advertising is on the rise, marketers focus a lot of attention identifying the group that begins the viral marketing chain—the influencers. Part of the challenge is that this group of customers is distinguished not by demographics but by behavior. Influencers come from all age, gender, and income groups, and they do not use media any differently than other users who are considered followers. The characteristic influencers share is their desire to talk to others about their experiences with goods and services. A desire to earn the respect of others is a dominant characteristic among early adopters.

EARLY MAJORITY The next 34 percent to adopt are called the early majority. The early majority weighs the pros and cons before adopting a new product. They are likely to collect more information and evaluate more brands than early adopters, thereby extending the adoption process. They rely on the group for information but are unlikely to be opinion leaders themselves. Instead, they tend to be opinion leaders' friends and neighbors. Consumers trust positive word-of-mouth reviews from friends, family, and peers.[28] In fact, 50 percent of purchase decisions are influenced by word-of-mouth, and 92 percent of consumers trust recommendations from friends and family more than any other form of advertising.[29] Product discussions often drive teen conversations, so word-of-mouth marketing is particularly powerful among this demographic. According to Lauren Hutter, group planning director at BBDO New York, "It's their countercultural currency . . . It's how to break into the group, how you bring something into the mix."[30]

While word-of-mouth marketing is important to teens, actually getting them to discuss products concretely can be difficult. According to Eric Pakurar, executive director and head of strategy at G2 USA, "They kind of ping-pong back and forth. They do a little research, then talk to their friends, and then do a little more research and check back with their friends and family."[31] Other groups, such as Millennials, also report word-of-mouth as the most important source of product information.[32] Many feel a responsibility to help friends and family make wise purchase decisions.

All word of mouth is not positive. Four out of five U.S. consumers report telling people around them about negative customer service experiences. Forty-two percent of consumers share customer service experiences on social media, roughly half of which is negative.[33] The early majority is an important link in the process of diffusing new ideas because they are positioned between earlier and later adopters. A dominant characteristic of the early majority is deliberateness.

LATE MAJORITY The late majority is the next 34 percent to adopt. The late majority adopts a new product because most of their friends have already adopted it. Because they also rely on group norms, their adoption stems from pressure to conform. This group tends to be older and below average in income and education. They depend mainly on word-of-mouth communication rather than on the mass media. The dominant characteristic of the late majority is skepticism.

LAGGARDS The final 16 percent to adopt are called laggards. Like innovators, laggards do not rely on group norms. Their independence is rooted in their ties to tradition. Thus, the past heavily influences their decisions. By the time laggards adopt an innovation, it has probably been outmoded and replaced by something else. For example, they may have bought their first color television set after flat screen televisions were already widely diffused. Laggards have the longest adoption time and the lowest socioeconomic status. They tend to be suspicious of new products and alienated from a rapidly advancing society. The dominant value of laggards is tradition. Marketers typically ignore laggards, who do not seem to be motivated by advertising or personal selling and are virtually impossible to reach online.

Note that some product categories may never be adopted by 100 percent of the population. The adopter categories refer to all of those who will eventually adopt a product, not the entire population.

11-5b Product Characteristics and the Rate of Adoption

Five product characteristics can be used to predict and explain the rate of acceptance and diffusion of a new product:

- **Complexity:** the degree of difficulty involved in understanding and using a new product. The more complex the product, the slower is its diffusion.

- **Compatibility:** the degree to which the new product is consistent with existing values and product knowledge, past experiences, and current needs. Incompatible products diffuse more slowly than compatible products.

- **Relative advantage:** the degree to which a product is perceived as superior to existing substitutes. Because it can store and play back thousands of songs, the iPod and its many variants have a clear relative advantage over the portable CD player.

- **Observability:** the degree to which the benefits or other results of using the product can be observed by others and communicated to target customers. For instance, fashion items and automobiles are highly visible and more observable than personal-care items.

- **"Trialability":** the degree to which a product can be tried on a limited basis. It is much easier to try a new toothpaste or breakfast cereal, for example, than a new personal computer.

11-5c Marketing Implications of the Adoption Process

Two types of communication aid the diffusion process: *word-of-mouth communication* among consumers and communication from marketers to consumers. Word-of-mouth communication within and across groups, including social media and viral communication, speeds diffusion. Opinion leaders discuss new products with their followers and with other opinion leaders. Marketers must therefore ensure that opinion leaders have the types of information desired in the media that they use. Suppliers of some products, such as professional and health care services, rely almost solely on word-of-mouth communication for new business.

Many large-scale companies like Procter & Gamble, Cisco Systems, and Salesforce.com seek out opinion leaders among their employees. Some companies conduct surveys to identify opinion leaders while others use technology to map connections between individuals and postings. Once identified, these influential employees are provided with specially tailored communication training and are invited to attend senior management briefings. The hope is that these opinion leaders will field co-workers' questions and build positive buzz. Influencers are frequently rewarded for their skills with promotions and other forms of recognition.[34]

The second type of communication aiding the diffusion process is *communication directly from the marketer to potential adopters*. Messages directed toward early adopters should normally use different appeals than messages directed toward the early majority, the late majority, or the laggards. Early adopters are more important than innovators because they make up a larger group, are more socially active, and are usually opinion leaders.

As the focus of a promotional campaign shifts from early adopters to the early majority and the late majority, marketers should study the dominant characteristics, buying behavior, and media characteristics of these target markets. Then they should revise messages and media strategy to fit. The diffusion model helps guide marketers in developing and implementing promotion strategy.

11-6 PRODUCT LIFE CYCLES

The product life cycle (PLC) is one of the most familiar concepts in marketing. Few other general concepts have been so widely discussed. Although some researchers and consultants have challenged the theoretical basis and managerial value of the PLC, many believe it is a useful marketing management diagnostic tool and a general guide for marketing planning in various life cycle stages.

The PLC is a biological metaphor that traces the stages of a product's acceptance, from its introduction (birth) to its decline (death). As Exhibit 11.2 shows, a product progresses through four major stages: introduction, growth, maturity, and decline.

The PLC concept can be used to analyze a brand, a product form, or a product category. The PLC for a product form is usually longer than the PLC for any one brand. The exception would be a

brand that was the first and last competitor in a product form market. In that situation, the brand and product form life cycles would be equal in length. Product categories have the longest life cycles. A **product category** includes all brands that satisfy a particular type of need, such as shaving products, passenger automobiles, or soft drinks.

The time a product spends in any one stage of the life cycle may vary dramatically. Some products, such as fad items, move through the entire cycle in weeks. Fads are typically characterized by a sudden and unpredictable spike in sales followed by a rather abrupt decline. Examples of fad items are Silly Bandz, Beanie Babies, and Crocs. Other products, such as electric clothes washers and dryers, stay in the maturity stage for decades. Exhibit 11.2 illustrates the typical life cycle for a consumer durable good, such as a washer or dryer. In contrast, Exhibit 11.3 illustrates typical life cycles for styles (such as formal, business, or casual clothing), fashions (such as miniskirts or baggy jeans), and fads (such as leopard-print clothing). Changes in a product, its uses, its image, or its positioning can extend that product's life cycle.

The PLC concept does not tell managers the length of a product's life cycle or its duration in any stage. It does not dictate marketing strategy. It is simply a tool to help marketers forecast future events and suggest appropriate strategies.

11-6a Introductory Stage

The **introductory stage** of the PLC represents the full-scale launch of a new product into the marketplace. Computer databases for personal use, room-deodorizing

---

product life cycle (PLC) a concept that provides a way to trace the stages of a product's acceptance, from its introduction (birth) to its decline (death)

product category all brands that satisfy a particular type of need

introductory stage the full-scale launch of a new product into the marketplace

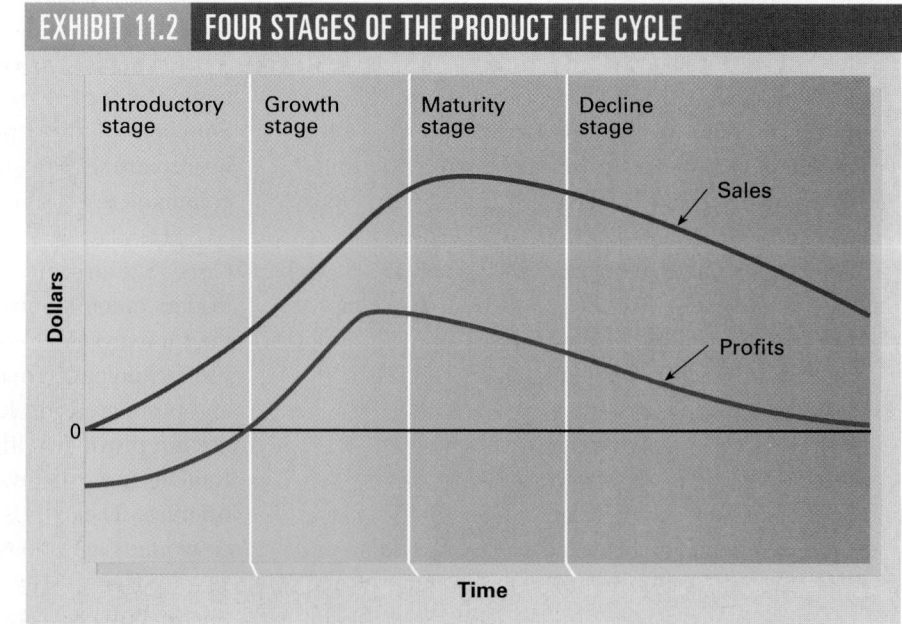

EXHIBIT 11.2 FOUR STAGES OF THE PRODUCT LIFE CYCLE

Introductory stage | Growth stage | Maturity stage | Decline stage

Sales

Profits

Dollars

0

Time

EXHIBIT 11.3 PRODUCT LIFE CYCLES FOR STYLES, FASHIONS, AND FADS

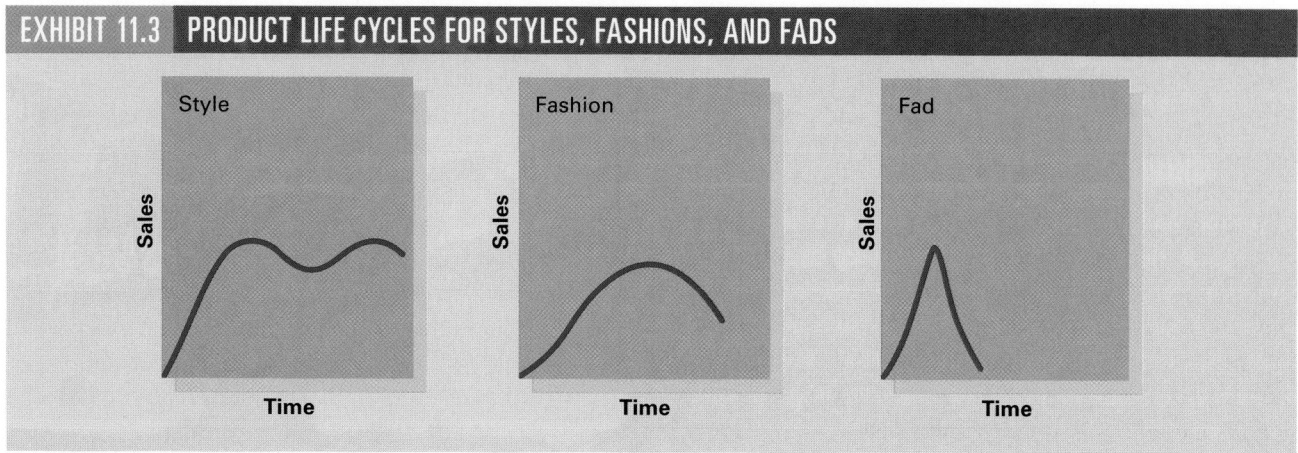

air-conditioning filters, and wind-powered home electric generators are all product categories that have recently entered the PLC. A high failure rate, little competition, frequent product modification, and limited distribution typify the introductory stage of the PLC.

Marketing costs in the introductory stage are normally high for several reasons. High dealer margins are often needed to obtain adequate distribution, and incentives are needed to get consumers to try the new product. Advertising expenses are high because of the need to educate consumers about the new product's benefits. Production costs are also often high in this stage, as product and manufacturing flaws are identified and corrected and efforts are undertaken to develop mass production economies.

Sales normally increase slowly during the introductory stage. Moreover, profits are usually negative because of R&D costs, factory tooling, and high introduction costs. The length of the introductory phase is largely determined by product characteristics, such as the product's advantages over substitute products, the educational effort required to make the product known, and management's commitment of resources to the new item. A short introductory period is usually preferred to help reduce the impact of negative earnings and cash flows. As soon as the product gets off the ground, the financial burden should begin to diminish. Also, a short introduction helps dispel some of the uncertainty as to whether the new product will be successful.

Promotion strategy in the introductory stage focuses on developing product awareness and informing consumers about the product category's potential benefits. At this stage, the communication challenge is to stimulate primary demand—demand for the product in general rather than for a specific brand. Intensive personal selling is often required to gain acceptance for the product among wholesalers and retailers. Promotion of convenience products often requires heavy consumer sampling and couponing. Shopping and specialty products demand educational advertising and personal selling to the final consumer.

11-6b Growth Stage

If a product category survives the introductory stage, it then advances to the **growth stage** of the life cycle. In this stage, sales typically grow at an increasing rate, many competitors enter the market, and large companies may start to acquire small pioneering firms. Profits rise rapidly in the growth stage, reach their peak, and begin declining as competition intensifies. Emphasis switches from primary demand promotion (e.g., promoting e-readers) to aggressive brand advertising and communication of the differences between brands (e.g., promoting Kindle versus Nook).

Distribution becomes a major key to success during the growth stage, as well as in later stages. Manufacturers scramble to sign up dealers and distributors and to build long-term relationships. Others are able to market direct to consumers using electronic media. Without adequate distribution, it is impossible to establish a strong market position.

As the economy recovers, more companies are entering the growth stage, and more workers are being hired. Because of this employment boom, staffing agencies are seeing a huge increase in revenues. On Assignment, a company that places temporary and permanent workers in several different industries, ranked third on *Fortune's* list of the fastest growing companies for 2014. In 2012, On Assignment acquired IT staffing agency ApexSystems,

growth stage the second stage of the product life cycle when sales typically grow at an increasing rate, many competitors enter the market, large companies may start to acquire small pioneering firms, and profits are healthy

becoming the second largest infotech staffing agency in the U.S. The company's stock rose 26.6 percent the day after the acquisition[35]

11-6c Maturity Stage

A period during which sales increase at a decreasing rate signals the beginning of the **maturity stage** of the life cycle. New users cannot be added indefinitely, and sooner or later the market approaches saturation. Normally, this is the longest stage of the PLC. Many major household appliances are in the maturity stage of their life cycles.

For shopping products such as durable goods and electronics, and many specialty products, annual models begin to appear during the maturity stage. Product lines are lengthened to appeal to additional market segments. Service and repair assume more important roles as manufacturers strive to distinguish their products from others. Product design changes tend to become stylistic (How can the product be made different?) rather than functional (How can the product be made better?).

As prices and profits continue to fall, marginal competitors start dropping out of the market. Dealer margins also shrink, resulting in less shelf space for mature items, lower dealer inventories, and a general reluctance to promote the product. Thus, promotion to dealers often intensifies during this stage in order to retain loyalty.

Heavy consumer promotion by the manufacturer is also required to maintain market share. Cutthroat competition during this stage can lead to price wars. Another characteristic of the maturity stage is the emergence of "niche marketers" that target narrow, well-defined, underserved segments of a market. Starbucks Coffee targets its gourmet line at new, young, affluent coffee drinkers, the only segment of the coffee market that is growing.

11-6d Decline Stage

A long-run drop in sales signals the beginning of the **decline stage**. The rate of decline is governed by how rapidly consumer tastes change or substitute products are adopted. Many convenience products and fad items lose their market overnight, leaving large inventories of unsold items, such as designer jeans. Others die more slowly. Landline telephone service

maturity stage a period during which sales increase at a decreasing rate

decline stage a long-run drop in sales

Startbucks targets its gourmet line at new, young drinkers;—the only segment that is growing.

is an example of a product in the decline stage of the product life cycle. Nearly 40 percent of American homes do not have a landline, which represents a continued steady increase since 2010—and a steady drop in the use of landlines.[36] People abandoning landlines to go wireless and households replacing landlines with Internet phones have both contributed to this long-term decline.

Some firms have developed successful strategies for marketing products in the decline stage of the PLC. They eliminate all nonessential marketing expenses and let sales decline as more and more customers discontinue purchasing the products. Eventually, the product is withdrawn from the market.

11-6e Implications for Marketing Management

The new-product development process, the diffusion process, and the PLC concept all have implications for marketing managers. The funnel shape of Exhibit 11.1 indicates that many new product ideas are necessary to produce one successful new product. The new-product development process is sometimes illustrated as a decay curve with roughly half of the ideas approved at one stage rejected at the next stage. While the actual numbers vary widely among firms and industries, the relationship between the stages can be generalized. This reinforces the notion that an organized effort to generate many ideas from various sources is important for any firm that wishes to produce a continuing flow of new products.

The major implication of the diffusion process to marketing managers is that the message may need to

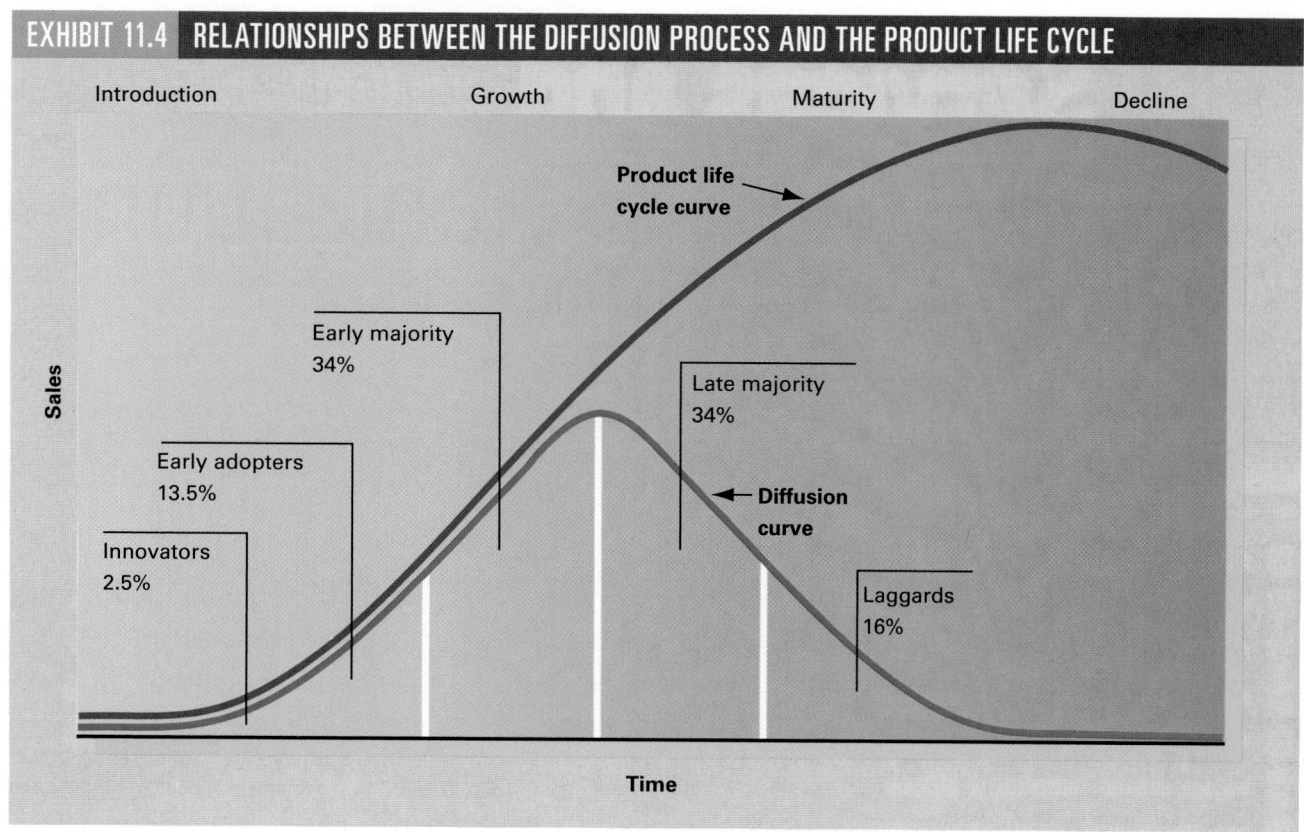

EXHIBIT 11.4 RELATIONSHIPS BETWEEN THE DIFFUSION PROCESS AND THE PRODUCT LIFE CYCLE

change over time. The targeted adopter and media may need to shift based on how various categories of adopters gather product information. A message developed for and targeted toward early adopters will not be perceived similarly by late majority adopters.

Exhibit 11.4 shows the relationship between the adopter categories and stages of the PLC. Note that the various categories of adopters buy products in different stages of the life cycle. Almost all sales in the maturity and decline stages represent repeat purchases.

STUDY TOOLS 11

LOCATED AT BACK OF THE TEXTBOOK

☐ Rip Out Chapter Review Card

LOCATED AT WWW.CENGAGEBRAIN.COM

☐ Review Key Terms Flashcards and create your own

☐ Track your knowledge and understanding of key concepts in marketing

☐ Complete practice and graded quizzes to prepare for tests

☐ Complete interactive content within the MKTG Online experience

☐ View the chapter highlight boxes within the MKTG Online experience

12 Services and Nonprofit Organization Marketing

LEARNING OUTCOMES

After studying this chapter, you will be able to...

12-1 Discuss the importance of services to the economy

12-2 Discuss the differences between services and goods

12-3 Describe the components of service quality and the gap model of service quality

12-4 Develop marketing mixes for services

12-5 Discuss relationship marketing in services

12-6 Explain internal marketing in services

12-7 Describe nonprofit organization marketing

12-8 Discuss global issues in services marketing

After you finish this chapter go to **PAGE 216** for **STUDY TOOLS.**

12-1 THE IMPORTANCE OF SERVICES

A service is the result of applying human or mechanical efforts to people or objects. Services involve a deed, a performance, or an effort that cannot be physically possessed. Today, the service sector substantially influences the U.S. economy. According to the Office of the United States Trade Representative, service industries accounted for 68 percent of U.S. gross domestic product (GDP) in 2014. These industries are responsible for four out of five U.S. jobs. Recent Census data shows that most service sectors reported revenue growth in 2014. The largest gains came in the real estate, administrative and support, and information services sectors.[1]

The marketing process described in Chapter 1 is the same for all types of products, whether they are goods or services. In addition, although a comparison of goods and services marketing can be beneficial, in reality it is hard to distinguish clearly between manufacturing and service firms. Indeed, many manufacturing firms can point to service as a major factor in their success. For example, maintenance and repair services offered by the manufacturer are important to buyers of copy machines. Nevertheless, services have some unique characteristics that distinguish them from goods, and marketing strategies need to be adjusted for these characteristics.

service the result of applying human or mechanical efforts to people or objects

12-2 HOW SERVICES DIFFER FROM GOODS

Services have four unique characteristics that distinguish them from goods. Services are intangible, inseparable, heterogeneous, and perishable.

12-2a Intangibility

The basic difference between services and goods is that services are intangible performances. Because of their **intangibility**, they cannot be touched, seen, tasted, heard, or felt in the same manner that goods can be sensed.

Evaluating the quality of services before or even after making a purchase is harder than evaluating the quality of goods because, compared to goods, services tend to exhibit fewer search qualities. A **search quality** is a characteristic that can be easily assessed before purchase—for instance, the color of an appliance or automobile. At the same time, services tend to exhibit more experience and credence qualities. An **experience quality** is a characteristic that can be assessed only after use, such as the quality of a meal in a restaurant. A **credence quality** is a characteristic that consumers may have difficulty assessing even after purchase because they do not have the necessary knowledge or experience. Medical and

consulting services are examples of services that exhibit credence qualities.

These characteristics also make it harder for marketers to communicate the benefits of an intangible service than to communicate the benefits of tangible goods. Thus, marketers often rely on tangible cues to communicate a service's nature and quality. For example, Travelers Insurance Company uses an umbrella symbol as a tangible reminder of the protection that insurance provides.

The facilities that customers visit, or from which services are delivered, are a critical tangible part of the total service offering. Messages about the organization are communicated to customers through such elements as the décor, the clutter or neatness of service areas, and the staff's manners and dress. Hotels know that guests form opinions quickly and are more willing than ever before to tweet them within the first fifteen minutes of

intangibility the inability of services to be touched, seen, tasted, heard, or felt in the same manner that goods can be sensed

search quality a characteristic that can be easily assessed before purchase

experience quality a characteristic that can be assessed only after use

credence quality a characteristic that consumers may have difficulty assessing even after purchase because they do not have the necessary knowledge or experience

their stay. Some hotels go to great lengths to make their guests feel at home right away. For example, employees at Ritz-Carlton hotels are trained to greet guests, bid them goodbye, and always address them by name. If a guest asks for directions to another part of the hotel, employees are required to escort them rather than pointing or giving complicated verbal directions.[2]

12-2b Inseparability

Goods are produced, sold, and then consumed. In contrast, services are often sold, produced, and consumed at the same time. In other words, their production and consumption are inseparable activities. This **inseparability** means that, because consumers must be present during the production of services like haircuts or surgery, they are actually involved in the production of the services they buy. That type of consumer involvement is rare in goods manufacturing.

Simultaneous production and consumption also means that services normally cannot be produced in a centralized location and consumed in decentralized locations, as goods typically are. Services are also inseparable from the perspective of the service provider. Thus, the quality of service that firms are able to deliver depends on the quality of their employees.

12-2c Heterogeneity

One great strength of McDonald's is consistency. Whether customers order a Big Mac in Chicago or Seattle, they know exactly what they are going to get. This is not the case with many service providers. Because services have greater **heterogeneity**, or variability of inputs and outputs, they tend to be less standardized and uniform than goods. For example, physicians in a group practice or barbers in a barbershop differ within each group in their technical and interpersonal skills. Because services tend to be labor intensive and production and consumption are inseparable, consistency and quality control can be hard to achieve.

Standardization and training help increase consistency and reliability. In the information technology sector, a number of certification programs are available to ensure that technicians are capable of working on (and within) complex enterprise software systems. Certifications such as the Cisco Certified Network Associate, CompTIA Security+, and Microsoft Certified Professional ensure a consistency of knowledge and ability among those who can pass these programs' rigorous exams.[3]

12-2d Perishability

Perishability is the fourth characteristic of services. **Perishability** refers to the inability of services to be stored, warehoused, or inventoried. An empty hotel room or airplane seat produces no revenue that day. The revenue is lost. Yet service organizations are often forced to turn away full-price customers during peak periods.

One of the most important challenges in many service industries is finding ways to synchronize supply and demand. The philosophy that some revenue is better than none has prompted many hotels to offer deep discounts on weekends and during the off-season.

12-3 SERVICE QUALITY

Because of the four unique characteristics of services, service quality is more difficult to define and measure than is the quality of tangible goods. Business executives rank the improvement of service quality as one of the most critical challenges facing them today.

12-3a Evaluating Service Quality

Research has shown that customers evaluate service quality by the following five components:

- **Reliability:** the ability to perform the service dependably, accurately, and consistently. Reliability is performing the service right the first time. This

Quality service is a must if a company wants to keep the customers coming back.

---

inseparability the inability of the production and consumption of a service to be separated; consumers must be present during the production

heterogeneity the variability of the inputs and outputs of services, which causes services to tend to be less standardized and uniform than goods

perishability the inability of services to be stored, warehoused, or inventoried

reliability the ability to perform a service dependably, accurately, and consistently

component has been found to be the one most important to consumers.

- **Responsiveness:** the ability to provide prompt service. Examples of responsiveness include calling the customer back quickly, serving lunch fast to someone who is in a hurry, or mailing a transaction slip immediately. The ultimate in responsiveness is offering service twenty-four hours a day, seven days a week.

- **Assurance:** the knowledge and courtesy of employees and their ability to convey trust. Skilled employees, who treat customers with respect and make customers feel that they can trust the firm, exemplify assurance.

- **Empathy:** caring, individualized attention to customers. Firms whose employees recognize customers and learn their specific requirements are providing empathy.

- **Tangibles:** the physical evidence of the service. The tangible parts of a service include the physical facilities, tools, and equipment used to provide the service, as well as the appearance of personnel.[4]

Overall service quality is measured by combining customers' evaluations for all five components.

12-3b The Gap Model of Service Quality

A model of service quality called the **gap model** identifies five gaps that can cause problems in service delivery and influence customer evaluations of service quality.[5] These gaps are illustrated in Exhibit 12.1.

- **Gap 1:** the gap between what customers want and what management thinks customers want. This gap results from a lack of understanding or a misinterpretation of the customers' needs, wants, or desires. A firm that does little or no customer satisfaction research is likely to experience this gap. To close gap 1, firms must stay attuned to customer wishes by researching customer needs and satisfaction.

- **Gap 2:** the gap between what management thinks customers want and the quality specifications that management develops to provide the service. Essentially, this gap is the result of management's inability to translate customers' needs into delivery systems within the firm. For example, KFC used to rate its managers according to "chicken efficiency," or how much chicken they threw away at closing; customers who came in late would either have to wait for chicken to be cooked or settle for chicken several hours old.

> **responsiveness** the ability to provide prompt service
>
> **assurance** the knowledge and courtesy of employees and their ability to convey trust
>
> **empathy** caring, individualized attention to customers
>
> **tangibles** the physical evidence of a service, including the physical facilities, tools, and equipment used to provide the service
>
> **gap model** a model identifying five gaps that can cause problems in service delivery and influence customer evaluations of service quality

Has starbucks fallen into gap 3?

Starbucks used to stress the importance of "legendary service" during the company's extensive training program for new hires. However, a rash of labor cuts in recent years has both diminished the quality of Starbucks's barista training and forced employees to work longer hours with less help and resources—often resulting in a single stressed-out barista frantically working to serve a growing line of customers. The creeping incompetence, inaccuracy, and inattentiveness of Starbucks baristas was satirized in a Saturday Night Live skit in which even the automated Verismo espresso machine was neglectful and derisive toward its customers.[6]

© olexus/Shutterstock 149737013

ChameleonsEye/Shutterstock.com

EXHIBIT 12.1 GAP MODEL OF SERVICE QUALITY

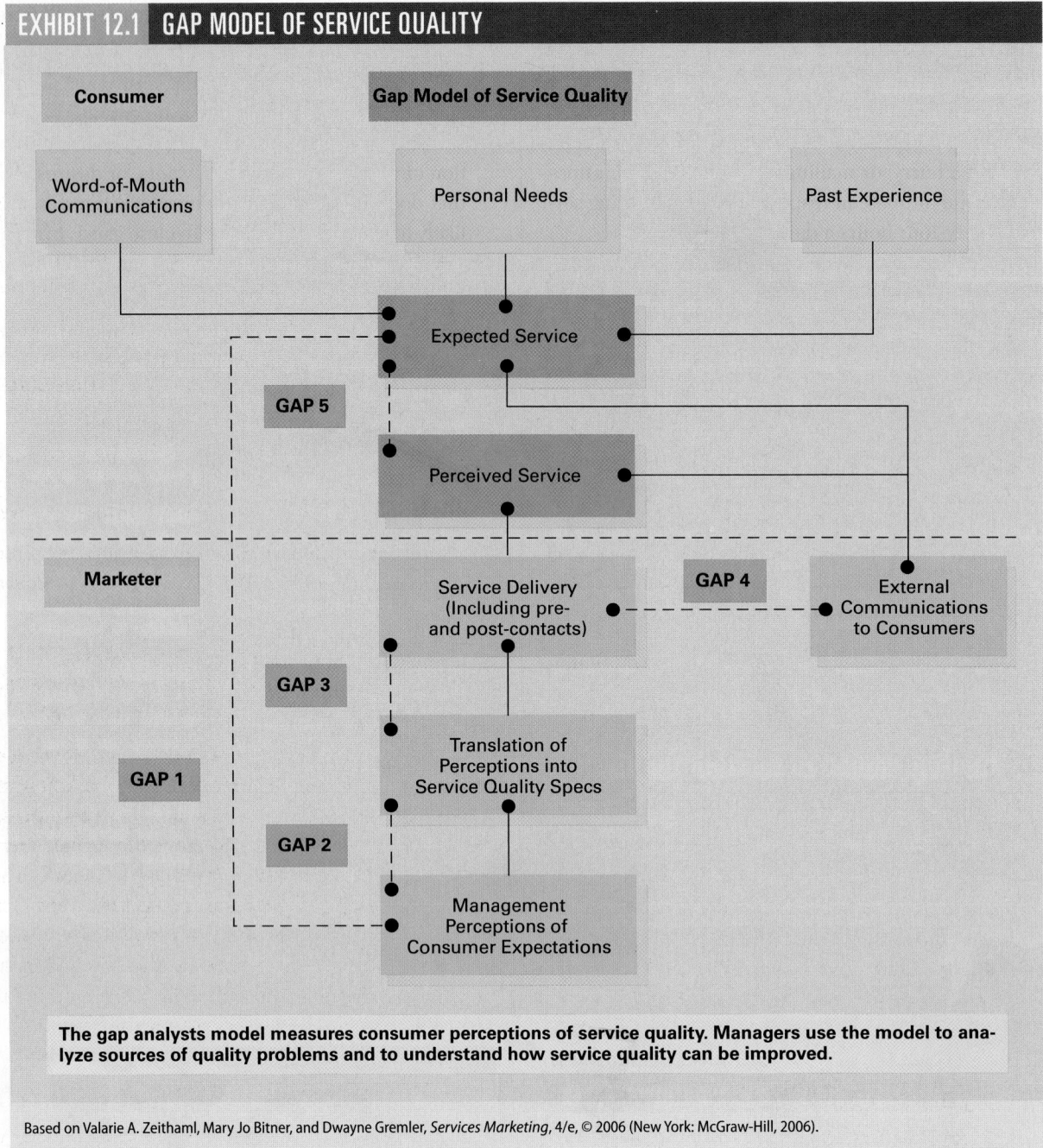

The gap analysts model measures consumer perceptions of service quality. Managers use the model to analyze sources of quality problems and to understand how service quality can be improved.

Based on Valarie A. Zeithaml, Mary Jo Bitner, and Dwayne Gremler, *Services Marketing*, 4/e, © 2006 (New York: McGraw-Hill, 2006).

- **Gap 3:** the gap between the service quality specifications and the service that is actually provided. If both gaps 1 and 2 have been closed, then gap 3 is due to the inability of management and employees to do what should be done. Management needs to ensure that employees have the skills and the proper tools to perform their jobs. Other techniques that help to close gap 3 are training employees so they know what management expects and encouraging teamwork.

- **Gap 4:** the gap between what the company provides and what the customer is told it provides. This is clearly a communication gap. It may include misleading or deceptive advertising campaigns promising more than the firm can deliver or doing "whatever it takes" to get the business. To close this gap, companies need to create realistic customer expectations through honest, accurate communication about what the firms can provide.

- **Gap 5:** the gap between the service that customers receive and the service they want. This gap can be positive or negative. For example, if a patient expects to wait twenty minutes in the physician's office before seeing the physician but actually waits only ten minutes, the patient's evaluation of service quality will be high. However, a 40-minute wait would result in a lower evaluation.

When one or more of these gaps is large, service quality is perceived as low. As the gaps shrink, service quality perception improves. In early 2013, Fifth Third Bank joined a growing number of financial institutions working quickly to close a persistent, gaping gap 1—customers' desire for full-featured mobile banking. To meet the needs of highly mobile, technologically tuned-in customers, Fifth Third launched a powerful mobile app whereby customers can view transactions, pay bills, transfer funds, or deposit checks simply by taking pictures of them with their smartphones. "The ways in which consumers interact with their bank are constantly evolving," said Larry McClanahan, vice president and director of Digital Delivery for Fifth Third Bank. "The enhancements we've made . . . reflect this shift in consumer preference and expectations."[7]

Several other companies consistently get their service quality right. According to MSN, the top five companies in terms of great customer service are:

1. Amazon
2. Hilton Worldwide
3. Marriott International
4. Chick-fil-A
5. American Express[8]

These companies have three core beliefs in common: good service starts at the top, service is seen as a continual challenge, and companies work best when people want to work for them.

12-4 MARKETING MIXES FOR SERVICES

Services' unique characteristics—-intangibility, inseparability of production and consumption, heterogeneity, and perishability—make marketing more challenging. Elements of the marketing mix (product, place, promotion, and pricing) need to be adjusted to meet the special needs created by these characteristics.

12-4a Product (Service) Strategy

A product, as defined in Chapter 10, is everything a person receives in an exchange. In the case of a service organization, the product offering is intangible and consists

in large part of a process or a series of processes. Product strategies for service offerings include decisions on the type of process involved, core and supplementary services, standardization or customization of the service product, and the service mix.

SERVICE AS A PROCESS Two broad categories of things get processed in service organizations: people and objects. In some cases, the process is physical, or tangible, while in others the process is intangible. Based on these characteristics, service processes can be placed into one of four categories:

- *People processing* takes place when the service is directed at a customer. Examples are transportation services and health care.

- *Possession processing* occurs when the service is directed at customers' physical possessions. Examples are lawn care, dry cleaning, and veterinary services.

- *Mental stimulus processing* refers to services directed at people's minds. Examples are theater performances and education.

- *Information processing* describes services that use technology or brainpower directed at a customer's assets. Examples are insurance and consulting.[9]

Because customers' experiences and involvement differ for each of these types of services, marketing strategies may also differ. For example, people-processing services require customers to enter the *service factory*, which is a physical location, such as an aircraft, a physician's office, or a hair salon. In contrast, possession-processing services typically do not require the presence of the customer in the service factory. Marketing strategies for the former would therefore focus more on an attractive, comfortable physical environment and employee training on employee–customer interaction issues than would strategies for the latter.

CORE AND SUPPLEMENTARY SERVICE PRODUCTS The service offering can be viewed as a bundle of activities that includes the **core service**, which is the most basic benefit the customer is buying, and a group of **supplementary services** that support or enhance the core service. Exhibit 12.2 illustrates these concepts for a luxury hotel. The core service is providing bedrooms for rent which involves people processing. The supplementary services, some of which involve information processing, include food services, reservations, parking, phone, and television services.

core service the most basic benefit the consumer is buying

supplementary services a group of services that support or enhance the core service

Nike/Getty Images.com

EXHIBIT 12.2 — CORE AND SUPPLEMENTARY SERVICES FOR A LUXURY HOTEL

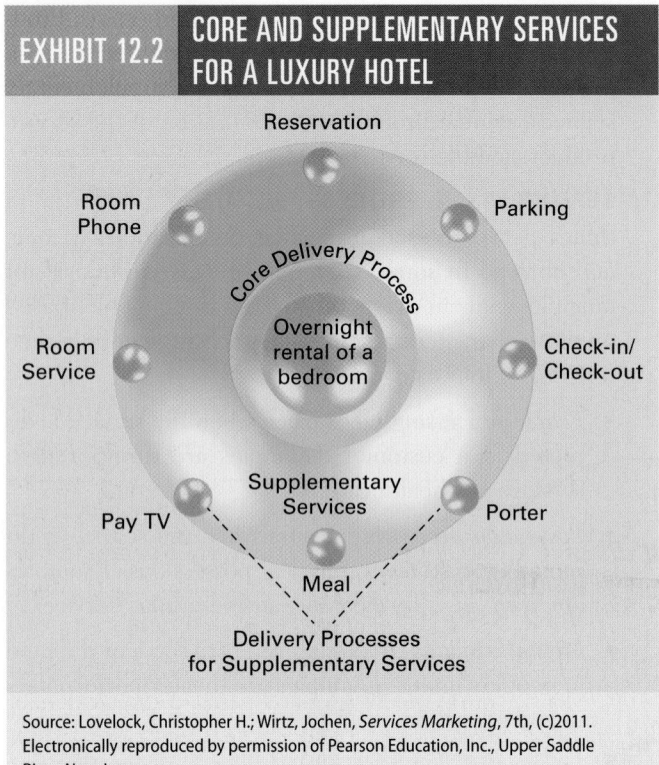

Source: Lovelock, Christopher H.; Wirtz, Jochen, *Services Marketing*, 7th, (c)2011. Electronically reproduced by permission of Pearson Education, Inc., Upper Saddle River, New Jersey.

In many service industries, the core service becomes a commodity as competition increases. Thus, firms usually emphasize supplementary services to create a competitive advantage. On the other hand, some firms are positioning themselves in the marketplace by greatly reducing supplementary services.

mass customization a strategy that uses technology to deliver customized services on a mass basis

CUSTOMIZATION/STANDARDIZATION An important issue in developing the service offering is whether to customize or standardize it. Customized services are more flexible and respond to individual customers' needs. They also usually command a higher price. Standardized services are more efficient and cost less.

Instead of choosing to either standardize or customize a service, a firm may incorporate elements of both by adopting an emerging strategy called **mass customization**. Mass customization uses technology to deliver customized services on a mass basis, which results in giving each customer whatever she or he asks for. Application Programming Interface (API) banking represents a new way to think about banking services and how to deliver these services to different customer groups. For example, API banking could allow a bank to offer Millennials a mobile banking app with tools to pay down student debt while offering Baby Boomers a similar app but with special services focused on retirement planning.[10]

THE SERVICE MIX Most service organizations market more than one service. For example, TruGreen offers lawn care, shrub care, carpet cleaning, and industrial lawn services. Each organization's service mix represents a set of opportunities, risks, and challenges. Each part of the service mix should make a different contribution to achieving the firm's goals. To succeed, each service may also need a different level of financial support. Designing a service strategy, therefore, means

Joleon Lescott and James Vaughn design customized Nike trainers in Liverpool, England's NikeTown iD Studio. Nike iD is an example of mass customization, employing technology to deliver customized shoes, apparel and bags on a mass basis.

deciding what new services to introduce to which target market, what existing services to maintain, and what services to eliminate.

12-4b Place (Distribution) Strategy

Distribution strategies for service organizations must focus on such issues as convenience, number of outlets, direct versus indirect distribution, location, and scheduling. A key factor influencing the selection of a service provider is *convenience*. An interesting example of this is Mac & Mia, a premium trunk club for children's clothing. This service targets parents of small children who have little or no time to shop. After a parent completes a style profile for his or her child at Mac & Mia's Web site, a company representative fills a box with a selection of hand-picked clothing and accessories and ships it out. Parents keep what they want and return what they don't within five days using an included prepaid envelope. The company provides busy parents an easy, fun, and convenient way to buy needed items for their kids.[11]

An important distribution objective for many service firms is the number of outlets to use or the number of outlets to open during a certain time. Generally, the intensity of distribution should meet, but not exceed, the target market's needs and preferences. Having too few outlets may inconvenience customers; having too many outlets may boost costs unnecessarily. Intensity of distribution may also depend on the image desired. Having only a few outlets may make the service seem more exclusive or selective.

The next service distribution decision is whether to distribute services to end users *directly* or *indirectly* through other firms. Because of the intangible nature of services, many service firms have to use direct distribution or franchising. Examples include legal, medical, accounting, and personal-care services. The newest form of direct distribution is the Internet. Most major airlines are now using online services to sell tickets directly to consumers, which results in lower distribution costs for the airlines. Other firms with standardized service packages have developed indirect channels using independent intermediaries. For example, Bank of America offers teller and loan services to customers in small satellite facilities at Albertsons grocery stores in Texas.

The *location* of a service most clearly reveals the relationship between its target market strategy and distribution strategy. For time-dependent service providers such as airlines, physicians, and dentists, *scheduling* is often a more important factor.

12-4c Promotion Strategy

Consumers and business users have more trouble evaluating services than goods because services are less tangible. In turn, marketers have more trouble promoting intangible services than tangible goods. Here are four promotion strategies they can try:

- **Stressing tangible cues:** A tangible cue is a concrete symbol of the service offering. To make their intangible services more tangible, hotels turn down the bedcovers and put mints on the pillows.

- **Using personal information sources:** A personal information source is someone consumers are familiar with (such as a celebrity) or someone they admire or can relate to personally. Service firms may seek to simulate positive word-of-mouth communication among present and prospective customers by using real customers in their ads.

- **Creating a strong organizational image:** One way to create an image is to manage the evidence, including the physical environment of the service facility, the appearance of the service employees, and the tangible items associated with a service (such as stationery, bills, and business cards). For example, McDonald's golden arches are instantly recognizable. Another way to create an image is through branding.

- **Engaging in postpurchase communication:** Postpurchase communication refers to the follow-up

Celebrity is a powerful promotional tool for services and nonprofits alike. Here, actor and Eastern Congo Initiative founder, Ben Affleck, testifies before a Senate Foreign Relations Committee hearing on the Congo.

activities that a service firm might engage in after a customer transaction. Postcard surveys, telephone calls, and other types of follow-up show customers that their feedback matters.

12-4d Price Strategy

Considerations in pricing a service are similar to the pricing considerations to be discussed in Chapter 19. However, the unique characteristics of services present two special pricing challenges.

First, in order to price a service, it is important to define the unit of service consumption. For example, should pricing be based on completing a specific service task (cutting a customer's hair), or should it be time based (how long it takes to cut a customer's hair)? Some services include the consumption of goods, such as food and beverages. Restaurants charge customers for food and drink rather than the use of a table and chairs.

Second, for services that are composed of multiple elements, the issue is whether pricing should be based on a "bundle" of elements or whether each element should be priced separately. A bundled price may be preferable when consumers dislike having to pay "extra" for every part of the service (e.g., paying extra for baggage or food on an airplane), and it is simpler for the firm to administer. Alternatively, customers may not want to pay for service elements they do not use. Many furniture stores now have "unbundled" delivery charges from the price of the furniture. Customers who wish to can pick up the furniture at the store, saving on the delivery fee.

Marketers should set performance objectives when pricing each service. Three categories of pricing objectives have been suggested:

- Revenue-oriented pricing focuses on maximizing the surplus of income over costs. This is the same approach that many manufacturing companies use. A limitation of this approach is that determining costs can be difficult for many services.

- Operations-oriented pricing seeks to match supply and demand by varying prices. For example, matching hotel demand to the number of available rooms can be achieved by raising prices at peak times and decreasing them during slow times.

- Patronage-oriented pricing tries to maximize the number of customers using the service. Thus, prices vary with different market segments' ability to pay, and methods of payment (such as credit) are offered that increase the likelihood of a purchase. Senior citizen and student discounts at movie theaters and restaurants are examples of patronage-oriented pricing.[12]

A firm may need to use more than one type of pricing objective. In fact, all three objectives probably need to be included to some degree in a pricing strategy, although the importance of each type may vary depending on the type of service provided, the prices that competitors are charging, the differing ability of various customer segments to pay, or the opportunity to negotiate price. For customized services (such as construction services), customers may also have the ability to negotiate a price.

12-5 RELATIONSHIP MARKETING IN SERVICES

Many services involve ongoing interaction between the service organization and the customer. Thus, they can benefit from relationship marketing, the strategy described in Chapter 1, as a means of attracting, developing, and retaining customer relationships. The idea is to develop strong loyalty by creating satisfied customers who will buy additional services from the firm and are unlikely to switch to a competitor. Satisfied customers are also likely to engage in positive word-of-mouth communication, thereby helping to bring in new customers.

Many businesses have found that it is more cost-effective to hang on to the customers they have than to focus only on attracting new ones. A bank executive, for example, found that increasing customer retention by two percent can have the same effect on profits as reducing costs by 10 percent.

Services that purchasers receive on a continuing basis (e.g., cable television, banking, insurance) can be considered membership services. This type of service naturally lends itself to relationship marketing. When services involve discrete transactions (e.g., in a movie theater, at a restaurant, or on public transportation), it may be more difficult to build membership-type relationships with customers. Nevertheless, services involving discrete transactions may be transformed into membership relationships using marketing tools. For example, the service could be sold in bulk (e.g., a theater series subscription or a commuter pass on public transportation). Or a service firm could offer special benefits to customers who choose to register with the firm (e.g., loyalty programs for hotels and airlines). The service firm that has a more formalized relationship with its customers has an advantage because it knows who its customers are and how and when they use the services offered.[13]

Relationship marketing can be practiced at four levels:

- **Level 1: Financial.** The firm uses pricing incentives to encourage customers to continue doing business with it. Frequent-flyer programs are an example of level 1 relationship marketing. This level of relationship marketing is the least effective in the long term because its price-based advantage is easily imitated by other firms.

- **Level 2: Social.** This level of relationship marketing also uses pricing incentives but seeks to build social bonds with customers. The firm stays in touch with customers, learns about their needs, and designs services to meet those needs. Level 2 relationship marketing is often more effective than level 1 relationship marketing.

- **Level 3: Customization**. A customization approach encourages customer loyalty through intimate knowledge of individual customers (often referred to as *customer intimacy*) and the development of one-to-one solutions to fit customers' needs.

- **Level 4: Structural.** At this level, the firm again uses financial and social bonds but adds structural bonds to the formula. Structural bonds are developed by offering value-added services that are not readily available from other firms.[14] The MGM Grand hotel in Las Vegas offers an entire floor of Stay Well suites that feature air purification systems to reduce allergens and toxins in the air; healthy energizing lighting developed to reduce jet lag and regulate circadian rhythms; and vitamin C-infused water in showers to neutralize chlorine and soften skin and hair.[15]

12-6 INTERNAL MARKETING IN SERVICE FIRMS

Services are performances, so the quality of a firm's employees is an important part of building long-term relationships with customers. Employees who like their jobs and are satisfied with the firm they work for are more likely to deliver superior service to customers. In other words, a firm that makes its employees happy has a better chance of retaining customers. Thus, it is critical that service firms practice **internal marketing**, which means treating employees as customers and developing systems and benefits that satisfy their needs. While this strategy may also apply to goods manufacturers, it is even more critical in service firms. This is because in service industries, employees deliver the brand promise—their performance as a brand representative—directly to customers. To satisfy employees, companies have designed and instituted a wide variety of programs such as flextime, on-site day care, and concierge services. Google offers its employees benefits such as free chef-prepared

Companies like Google have designed and instituted a wide variety of programs such as flextime, on-site daycare and concierge service for their employees.

organic foods, free health and dental insurance, subsidized massages, nap pods, and on-site phycians.[16]

12-7 NONPROFIT ORGANIZATION MARKETING

A nonprofit organization is an organization that exists to achieve some goal other than the usual business goals of profit, market share, or return on investment. Both nonprofit organizations and private-sector service firms market intangible products, and both often require the customer to be present during the production process. Both for-profit and nonprofit services vary greatly from producer to producer and from day to day, even from the same producer.

Few people realize that nonprofit organizations account for more than twenty percent of the economic activity in the United States. The cost of government (i.e., taxes), the predominant form of nonprofit organization, has become the biggest single item in the American family budget—more than housing, food, or health care. Together, federal, state, and local governments collect tax revenues that amount to more than one-third of the U.S. GDP. In addition to government entities, nonprofit organizations include hundreds of thousands of private museums, theaters, schools, and churches.

internal marketing treating employees as customers and developing systems and benefits that satisfy their needs

nonprofit organization an organization that exists to achieve some goal other than the usual business goals of profit, market share, or return on investment

12-7a What Is Nonprofit Organization Marketing?

Nonprofit organization marketing is the effort by nonprofit organizations to bring about mutually satisfying exchanges with target markets. Although these organizations vary substantially in size and purpose and operate in different environments, most perform the following marketing activities:

- Identify the customers they wish to serve or attract (although they usually use other terms, such as clients, patients, members, or sponsors)

- Explicitly or implicitly specify objectives

- Develop, manage, and eliminate programs and services

- Decide on prices to charge (although they use other terms, such as fees, donations, tuition, fares, fines, or rates)

- Schedule events or programs, and determine where they will be held or where services will be offered

- Communicate their availability through brochures, signs, public service announcements, or advertisements

Often, the nonprofit organizations that carry out these functions do not realize they are engaged in marketing.

12-7b Unique Aspects of Nonprofit Organization Marketing Strategies

Like their counterparts in business organizations, nonprofit managers develop marketing strategies to bring about mutually satisfying exchanges with target markets. However, marketing in nonprofit organizations is unique in many ways—including the setting of marketing objectives, the selection of target markets, and the development of appropriate marketing mixes.

OBJECTIVES In the private sector, the profit motive is both an objective for guiding decisions and a criterion for evaluating results. Nonprofit organizations do not seek to make a profit for redistribution to owners or shareholders. Rather, their focus is often on generating enough funds to cover expenses.

Most nonprofit organizations are expected to provide equitable, effective, and efficient services that respond to the wants and preferences of multiple constituencies. These include users, payers, donors, politicians, appointed officials, the media, and the general public. Nonprofit organizations cannot measure their success or failure in strictly financial terms.

nonprofit organization marketing the effort by nonprofit organizations to bring about mutually satisfying exchanges with target markets

Singer, Nick Lachey, volunteered his time at the Freestore Foodbank in Cincinnati, as he promoted the kick-off of The Everybody Wins Tour. Having a celebrity as a spokesperson is something that organizations regularly do to draw attention to their cause.

Joe Robbins/WireImage/Getty Images

The lack of a financial "bottom line" and the existence of multiple, diverse, intangible, and sometimes vague or conflicting objectives make prioritizing objectives, making decisions, and evaluating performance hard for nonprofit managers. They must often use approaches different from the ones commonly used in the private sector.

TARGET MARKETS Three issues relating to target markets are unique to nonprofit organizations:

- **Apathetic or strongly opposed targets:** Private-sector organizations usually give priority to developing those market segments that are most likely to respond to particular offerings. In contrast, nonprofit organizations must often target those who are apathetic about or strongly opposed to receiving their services, such as vaccinations and psychological counseling.

- **Pressure to adopt undifferentiated segmentation strategies:** Nonprofit organizations often adopt undifferentiated strategies (see Chapter 8) by default. Sometimes they fail to recognize the advantages of targeting, or an undifferentiated approach may appear to offer economies of scale and low per-capita costs. In other instances, nonprofit organizations are pressured or required to serve the maximum number of people by targeting the average user.

- **Complementary positioning:** The main role of many nonprofit organizations is to provide services, with available resources, to those who are not adequately served by private-sector organizations. As a result, the nonprofit organization must often complement, rather than compete with, the efforts of others. The positioning task is to identify underserved market segments and to develop marketing programs that match their needs rather than target the niches that may be most profitable. For example, a university library may see itself as complementing the services of the public library rather than as competing with it.

PRODUCT DECISIONS There are three product-related distinctions between business and nonprofit organizations:

- **Benefit complexity:** Nonprofit organizations often market complex behaviors or ideas. Examples include the need to exercise or eat right and the need to quit smoking. The benefits that a person receives are complex, long term, and intangible, and therefore are more difficult to communicate to consumers.

- **Benefit strength:** The benefit strength of many nonprofit offerings is quite weak or indirect. What are the direct, personal benefits to you of driving 55 miles per hour or donating blood? In contrast, most private-sector service organizations can offer customers direct, personal benefits in an exchange relationship.

- **Involvement:** Many nonprofit organizations market products that elicit very low involvement ("Prevent forest fires") or very high involvement ("Stop smoking"). The typical range for private-sector goods is much narrower. Traditional promotional tools may be inadequate to motivate adoption of either low- or high-involvement products.

PLACE (DISTRIBUTION) DECISIONS A nonprofit organization's capacity for distributing its service offerings to potential customer groups when and where they want them is typically a key variable in determining the success of those service offerings. For example, many large universities have one or more satellite campus locations to provide easier access for students in other areas. Some educational institutions also offer classes to students at off-campus locations through the use of interactive video technology or at home via the Internet.

The extent to which a service depends on fixed facilities has important implications for distribution decisions. Services like rail transit and lake fishing can be delivered only at specific points. Many nonprofit services, however, do not depend on special facilities.

PROMOTION DECISIONS Many nonprofit organizations are explicitly or implicitly prohibited from advertising, thus limiting their promotion options. Most federal agencies fall into this category. Other nonprofit organizations simply do not have the resources to retain advertising agencies, promotion consultants, or marketing staff.

Nonprofit organizations have a few special promotion resources to call on, however:

- **Professional volunteers:** Nonprofit organizations often seek out marketing, sales, and advertising professionals to help them develop and implement promotion strategies. In some instances, an advertising agency donates its services in exchange for potential long-term benefits. Donated services create goodwill; personal contacts; and general awareness of the donor's organization, reputation, and competency.

- **Sales promotion activities:** Sales promotion activities that use existing services or other resources are increasingly being used to draw attention to the offerings of nonprofit organizations. Sometimes nonprofit charities even team up with other companies for promotional activities.

- **Public service advertising:** A **public service advertisement (PSA)** is an announcement that promotes a program of a federal, state, or local government or of a nonprofit organization. Unlike a commercial advertiser, the sponsor of the PSA does not pay for the time or space. Instead, it is donated by the medium. PSAs are used, for example, to help educate students about the dangers of misusing and abusing prescription drugs, as well as where to seek treatment for substance abuse problems.

PRICING DECISIONS Five key characteristics distinguish the pricing decisions of nonprofit organizations from those of the profit sector:

- **Pricing objectives:** The main pricing objective in the profit sector is revenue or, more specifically, profit maximization, sales maximization, or target return on sales or investment. Many nonprofit organizations must also be concerned about revenue. Often, however, nonprofit organizations seek to either partially or fully defray costs rather than to achieve a profit for distribution to stockholders. Nonprofit organizations also seek to redistribute income—for instance, through taxation and sliding-scale fees. Moreover, they strive to allocate resources fairly among individuals or households or across geographic or political boundaries.

- **Nonfinancial prices:** In many nonprofit situations, consumers are not charged a monetary price but instead must absorb nonmonetary costs. The importance of those costs is illustrated by the large number of eligible citizens who do not take

public service advertisement (PSA) an announcement that promotes a program of a federal, state, or local government or of a nonprofit organization

Glynnis Jones/Shutterstock.com

First Lady, Chirlane McCray announces a $78 million budget proposed by her husband, Mayor Bill de Blasio, for mental health services at a press conference at the Empire State Building.

MarcelClemens/Shutterstock.com

advantage of so-called "free" services for the poor. In many public assistance programs, about half the people who are eligible do not participate. Nonmonetary costs include time, embarrassment, and effort.

- **Indirect payment:** Indirect payment through taxes is common to marketers of "free" services, such as libraries, fire protection, and police protection. Indirect payment is not a common practice in the profit sector.

- **Separation between payers and users:** By design, the services of many charitable organizations are provided for those who are relatively poor and are largely paid for by those who are better off financially. Although examples of separation between payers and users can be found in the profit sector (such as insurance claims), the practice is much less prevalent.

- **Below-cost pricing:** An example of below-cost pricing is university tuition. Virtually all private and public colleges and universities price their services below full cost.

12-8 GLOBAL ISSUES IN SERVICES MARKETING

The international marketing of services is a major part of global business, and the United States has become the world's largest exporter of services. Competition in international services

is increasing rapidly, but many U.S. service industries have been able to enter the global marketplace because of their competitive advantages. U.S. banks, for example, have advantages in customer service and collections management.

For both for-profit and nonprofit service firms, the first step toward success in the global marketplace is determining the nature of the company's core products. Then, the marketing mix elements (additional services, place, promotion, pricing, and distribution) should be designed to take into account each country's cultural, technological, and political environment.

STUDY TOOLS 12

LOCATED AT BACK OF THE TEXTBOOK

☐ Rip out Chapter Review Card

LOCATED AT WWW.CENGAGEBRAIN.COM

☐ Review Key Terms Flashcards and create your own

☐ Track your knowledge and understanding of key concepts in marketing

☐ Complete practice and graded quizzes to prepare for tests

☐ Complete interactive content within the MKTG Online experience

☐ View the chapter highlight boxes within the MKTG Online experience

Supply Chain Management and Marketing Channels

LEARNING OUTCOMES

After studying this chapter, you will be able to…

13-1 Define the terms *supply chain* and *supply chain management* and discuss the benefits of supply chain management

13-2 Discuss the concepts of internal and external supply chain integration and explain why each of these types of integration is important

13-3 Identify the eight key processes of excellent supply chain management and discuss how each of these processes affects the end customer

13-4 Understand the importance of sustainable supply chain management to modern business operations

13-5 Discuss how new technology and emerging trends are impacting the practice of supply chain management

13-6 Explain what marketing channels and channel intermediaries are and describe their functions and activities

13-7 Describe common channel structures and strategies and the factors that influence their choice

13-8 Discuss omnichannel and multichannel marketing in both B-to-B and B-to-C structures and explain why these concepts are important

After you finish this chapter go to **PAGE 242** for **STUDY TOOLS.**

Bill Pugliano/Getty Images News/Getty Images

13-1 SUPPLY CHAINS AND SUPPLY CHAIN MANAGEMENT

Many modern companies are turning to supply chain management for competitive advantage. A company's **supply chain** includes all of the companies involved in the upstream and downstream flow of products, services, finances, and information, extending from initial suppliers (the point of origin) to the ultimate customer (the point of consumption). The goal of **supply chain management** is to coordinate and integrate all of the activities performed by supply chain members into a seamless process, from the source to the point of consumption, ultimately giving supply chain managers "total visibility and control" of the materials, processes, money, and finished products both inside and outside the company they work for. The philosophy behind

supply chain the connected chain of all of the business entities, both internal and external to the company, that perform or support the logistics function

supply chain management a management system that coordinates and integrates all of the activities performed by supply chain members into a seamless process, from the source to the point of consumption, resulting in enhanced customer and economic value

supply chain management is that by visualizing and exerting control over the entire supply chain, supply chain managers can balance supply and demand needs, maximize strengths, and increase efficiencies at each level of the chain. Understanding and integrating supply and demand-related information at every level enables supply chain managers to optimize their decisions, reduce waste, and respond quickly to sudden changes in supply or demand.

> In today's marketplace, products are being driven by customer demand, and businesses' need to balance demand with supply in order to ensure economic profits.

Supply chain management, when performed well, reflects a completely customer-driven management philosophy. In the mass production era, manufacturers produced standardized products that were "pushed" down through marketing channels to consumers, who were convinced by salespeople to buy whatever was produced. In today's marketplace, however, customers who expect to receive product configurations and services matched to their unique needs are driving demand. The focus of businesses has shifted to determining how products and services are being "pulled" into the marketplace by customers, and on partnering with members of the supply chain to enhance customer value. For example, when Rolls-Royce launched its Ad Personam customer value program, the company used a build-to-order system that allowed every customer to design his or her car with more than a million combinations of leather, fabric, wood, and paint.[1] This differed from the mass-manufacturing approach companies used historically, whereby a company's focus on efficiency determined a far narrower range of cars and custom options.

This reversal of the flow of demand from "push" to "pull" has resulted in a radical reformulation of traditional marketing, production, and distribution functions toward a philosophy of **supply chain agility**. Agile companies synchronize their activities through the sharing of supply and demand market information, spend more time than their competitors focusing on activities that create direct customer benefits, partner closely with suppliers and service providers to reduce customer wait times for products, and constantly seek to reduce supply chain complexity through the evaluation and reduction (or elimination) of stock-keeping units (SKUs) that customers aren't buying, among other strategies. By managing the product pipeline in this way, companies are able to reduce supply chain costs while at the same time offering better service levels, and in doing so, deliver more desirable products at better prices to customers.

13-1a Benefits of Effective Supply Chain Management

Supply chain management is a key means of differentiation for a firm, and therefore represents a critical component in marketing and corporate strategy. Companies that focus on supply chain management commonly report lower inventory, transportation, warehousing, and packaging costs; greater logistical flexibility; improved customer service; and higher revenues. Research has shown a clear relationship between supply chain performance

supply chain agility an operational strategy focused on creating inventory velocity and operational flexibility simultaneously in the supply chain

supply chain orientation a system of management practices that are consistent with a "systems thinking" approach

In a supply chain, agility which involves being flexible, like star athletes, allows companies to adapt to customer needs.

and both profitability and company value. Additionally, because well-managed supply chains are able to provide better value to customers with only marginal incremental expenditure on company assets, best-in-class supply chain companies such as Kimberly-Clark are becoming significantly more valuable investments for investors. Kimberly-Clark re-organized its supply chains by reducing distribution centers, increasing flexibility, and making its supply chain more "demand-driven." As a result, the company decreased forecasting errors by up to 35 percent each week, reduced fuel consumption by 2.4 million gallons per year, and reduced overall supply chain costs by millions of dollars per year[2]—all of which positively impact the company's bottom line.

13-2 SUPPLY CHAIN INTEGRATION

A key principle of supply chain management is that multiple entities (firms and/or their functional areas) should work together to perform tasks as a single, unified system, rather than as multiple individual units acting in isolation. Companies in a world-class supply chain combine their resources, capabilities, and innovations across multiple business boundaries so they are used for the best interest of the entire supply chain as a whole. The goal is that the overall performance of the supply chain will be greater than the sum of its parts.

As companies become increasingly focused on supply chain management, they come to possess a **supply chain orientation**. This means that they develop management practices that are consistent with a "systems thinking" approach. Supply chain oriented firms possess five characteristics that, in combination, set them apart from their partners:

1. *They are credible.* They have the capability to deliver on the promises they make.

2. *They are benevolent.* They are willing to accept short-term risks on behalf of others; are committed to others, and invest in others' success.

Gregory Shamus/Getty Images Sport/Getty Images

3. *They are cooperative.* They work with rather than against their partners when seeking to achieve goals.

4. *They have the support of top managers.* These managers possess the vision required to do things that benefit the entire supply chain in the short run so that they can enjoy greater company successes in the long run.

5. *They are effective at conducting and directing supply chain activity.* Thereby, they are better off in the long run financially than those who are not.

Management practices that reflect a highly coordinated effort between supply chain firms or across business functions within the same or different firms are "integrated." In other words, **supply chain integration** occurs when multiple firms or their functional areas in a supply chain coordinate business processes so they are seamlessly linked to one another. In a world-class supply chain, the customer may not know where the business activities of one company or business unit end and where those of another begin—each actor keeps their own interests in mind, but all appear to be reading from the same script, and from time to time, each makes sacrifices that benefit the performance of the system as a whole.

In the modern supply chain, integration can be either internal or external to a specific company or, ideally, both. From an internal perspective, the very best companies develop a managerial orientation toward **demand-supply integration (DSI).** Under the DSI philosophy, those functional areas in a company charged with creating customer demand (such as marketing, sales, or research/development) communicate frequently and are synchronized with the parts of the business charged with fulfilling the created demand (purchasing, manufacturing, and logistics). This type of alignment enhances customer satisfaction by ensuring that, for example, salespeople make promises to customers that can actually be delivered on by the company's logistics arm, or that raw materials being purchased actually meet customer specifications before they are placed into production. Simultaneously, the company gains efficiencies from ordering and using only those materials that lead directly to sales. In short, companies operating under a DSI philosophy are better at their business because all of the different divisions within the company "play from the same sheet of music."[3]

Additionally, the practice of world-class supply chain management requires that different companies act as if a single mission and leadership connect them. To accomplish this task across companies that have different ownership and interests, five types of external integration are sought by firms interested in providing top-level service to customers:[4]

- *Relationship integration* is the ability of two or more companies to develop social connections that serve to guide their interactions when working together. More specifically, relationship integration is the capability to develop and maintain a shared mental framework across companies that describes how they will depend on one another when working together. This includes the ways in which they will collaborate on activities or projects so that the customer gains the maximum amount of total value possible from the supply chain.

- *Measurement integration* reflects the idea that performance assessments should be transparent and measurable across the borders of different firms, and should also assess the performance of the supply chain as a whole while holding each individual firm or business unit accountable for meeting its own goals.

- *Technology and planning integration* refers to the creation and maintenance of information technology systems that connect managers across the firms in the supply chain. It requires information hardware and software systems that can exchange information when needed between customers, suppliers, and internal operational areas of each of the supply chain partners.

- *Material and service supplier integration* requires firms to link seamlessly to those outsiders that provide goods and services to them so that they can streamline work processes and thereby provide smooth, high-quality customer experiences. Both sides need to have a common vision of the total value creation process and be willing to share the responsibility for satisfying customer requirements to make supplier integration successful.

- *Customer integration* is a competency that enables firms to offer long-lasting, distinctive, value-added offerings to those customers who represent the greatest value to the firm or supply chain. Highly customer-integrated firms assess their own capabilities and then match them to customers whose

supply chain integration when multiple firms or business functions in a supply chain coordinate their activities and processes so that they are seamlessly linked to one another in an effort to satisfy the customer

demand-supply integration (DSI) a supply chain operational philosophy focused on integrating the supply-management and demand-generating functions of an organization

Max blain/ShutterStock.com

Relationally integrated supply chains have sets of rules, policies, and/or procedures that dictate how firms will work together and specify how conflicts among supply chain partners will be resolved.

desires they can meet and who offer large enough sales potential for the linkage to be profitable over the long term.

Success in achieving both the internal and external types of integration is very important. Highly integrated supply chains (those that are successful in achieving many or all of these types of integration) have been shown to be better at satisfying customers, managing costs, delivering high-quality products, enhancing productivity, and utilizing company or business unit assets, all of which translate into greater profitability for the firms and their partners working together in the supply chain.

Integration involves a balance between barriers and enablers. Companies that work closely with their suppliers encounter problems such as corporate culture, information hoarding, and trust issues. For example, Häagen-Dazs and General Mills share information with their vanilla suppliers to increase yields and improve sustainability practices, but at the same time, there is a danger. Giving supply chain partners this information enables those partners to share it with competitors. On the other hand, integration can be improved through long-term agreements, cross-organizational integrated product teams, and improved communication between partners. These factors all aid in integrating supply chain operations.[5]

13-3 THE KEY PROCESSES OF SUPPLY CHAIN MANAGEMENT

When firms practice good supply chain management, their functional departments or areas, such as marketing, research and development, and/or production, are integrated both within and across the linked firms. Integration, then, is "how" excellent supply chain management works. The business processes on which the linked firms work together represent the "what" of supply chain management—they are the objects of focus on which firms, departments, areas, and people work together when seeking to reduce supply chain costs or to generate additional revenues. **Business processes** are composed of bundles of interconnected activities that stretch across firms in the supply chain; they represent key areas that some or all of the involved firms are constantly working on to reduce costs and/or generate revenues for everyone throughout supply chain management. There are eight critical business processes on which supply chain managers must focus:

1. Customer relationship management
2. Customer service management
3. Demand management
4. Order fulfillment
5. Manufacturing flow management
6. Supplier relationship management
7. Product development and commercialization
8. Returns management[6]

13-3a Customer Relationship Management

The **customer relationship management (CRM) process** enables companies to prioritize their marketing focus on different customer groups according to each group's long-term value to the company or supply chain. Once higher-value customers are identified, firms should

---

business processes bundles of interconnected activities that stretch across firms in the supply chain

customer relationship management (CRM) process allows companies to prioritize their marketing focus on different customer groups according to each group's long-term value to the company or supply chain

focus more on providing customized products and better service to this group than to others. The CRM process includes customer segmentation by value and subsequent generation of customer loyalty for the most attractive segments. This process provides a set of comprehensive principles for the initiation and maintenance of customer relationships and is often carried out with the assistance of specialized CRM computer software. For example, C. H. Briggs, a specialty building materials distributor, integrated CRM software as part of an effort to serve its customers better. With this software, each company sales representative has access to every customer's purchasing history. With this information, representatives can shape the sales process for its most valuable customers and uncover opportunities to improve service for them, thereby optimizing decision-making throughout the company.[7]

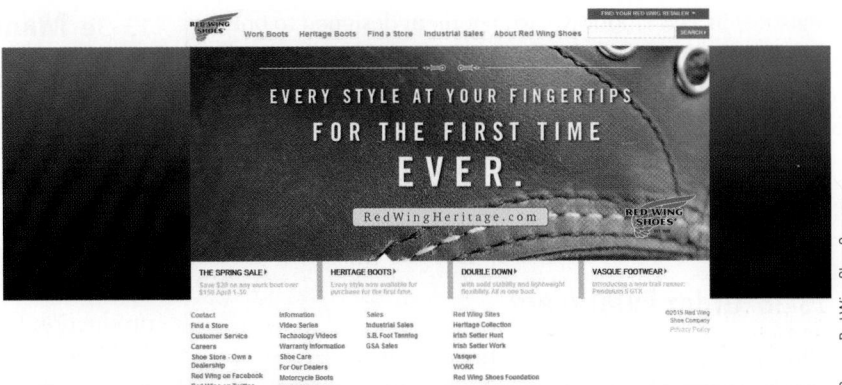

Source: Red Wing Shoe Company

Sales and Operations Planning quickly became a valuable asset to shoemaker, Red Wing Shoes—known for their rugged work boots.

13-3b Customer Service Management

Whereas the CRM process is designed to identify and build relationships with good customers, the customer service management process is designed to ensure that those customer relationships remain strong. The **customer service management process** presents a multi-company, unified response system to the customer whenever complaints, concerns, questions, or comments are voiced. When the process is well executed, it can have a strong positive impact on revenues, often as a result of quick positive response to negative customer feedback, and sometimes even in the form of additional sales gained through the additional customer contact. Customers expect service from the moment a product is purchased until it is disposed of, and the customer service management process allows for touch points between the buyer and seller throughout this life cycle. The use of customer care software enables companies to enhance their customer service management process. Dell's customer support software, Clear View, enables staff members at the tech company's customer service command centers to view information from Dell's internal systems (as well as that of its partners) in real-time. This information is combined with a geographical system that allows Dell to match each customer's complaint with the proper service dispatch center, making its response both rapid and effective.[8]

13-3c Demand Management

The **demand management process** seeks to align supply and demand throughout the supply chain by anticipating customer requirements at each level and creating customer-focused plans of action prior to actual purchases being made. At the same time, demand management seeks to minimize the costs of serving multiple types of customers who have variable wants and needs. In other words, the demand management process allows companies in the supply chain to satisfy customers in the most efficient and effective ways possible. Activities such as collecting customer data, forecasting future demand, and developing activities that smooth out demand help bring available inventory into alignment with customer desires.

Though it is very difficult to predict exactly what items and quantities customers will buy prior to purchase, demand management can ease pressure on the production process and allow companies to satisfy most of their customers through greater flexibility in manufacturing, marketing, and sales programs. One key way this occurs is through the sharing of customer demand forecasts and data during sales and operations planning (S&OP) meetings. During these meetings, the demand-generating functions of the business (marketing and sales) work together with the production side of the business (procurement, production, and

customer service management process presents a multi-company, unified response system to the customer whenever complaints, concerns, questions, or comments are voiced

demand management process seeks to align supply and demand throughout the supply chain by anticipating customer requirements at each level and creating demand-related plans of action prior to actual customer purchasing behavior

logistics) in a collaborative arrangement designed to both satisfy customers and minimize waste. When work boot manufacturer Red Wing Shoes implemented S&OP in 2013, it was able to reduce inventory by 27 percent while simultaneously increasing customer service rates by 8 to 10 percent, leading to significant costs savings that were passed along to customers.[9]

13-3d Order Fulfillment

One of the most fundamental processes in supply chain management is the order fulfillment process, which involves generating, filling, delivering, and providing on-the-spot service for customer orders. The **order fulfillment process** is a highly integrated process, often requiring persons from multiple companies and multiple functions to come together and coordinate to create customer satisfaction at a given place and time. The best order fulfillment processes reduce **order cycle time**—the time between order and customer receipt—as much as possible, while ensuring that the customer receives exactly what he or she wants. The shorter lead times are beneficial in that they allow firms to carry reduced inventory levels and free up cash that can be used on other projects. Overall, the order fulfillment process involves understanding and integrating the company's internal capabilities with customer needs, and matching these together so that the supply chain maximizes profits while minimizing costs and waste. Amazon now uses Kiva robots to help workers pack three to four times more orders per hour than before. These robots bring shelves of products to the human packers based on what is in each customer's order. The packers then pick out the correct items, pack them, and send the complete box off to another robot to be shipped. This process has greatly increased the speed of Amazon's order fulfillment process: recent research found that the work robots do at Amazon shaves more than an hour off the time needed to pick and pack the average order.[10]

order fulfillment process a highly integrated process, often requiring persons from multiple companies and multiple functions to come together and coordinate to create customer satisfaction at a given place and time

order cycle time the time delay between the placement of a customer's order and the customer's receipt of that order

manufacturing flow management process concerned with ensuring that firms in the supply chain have the needed resources to manufacture with flexibility and to move products through a multi-stage production process

supplier relationship management process supports manufacturing flow by identifying and maintaining relationships with highly valued suppliers

13-3e Manufacturing Flow Management

The **manufacturing flow management process** is concerned with ensuring that firms in the supply chain have the needed resources to manufacture with flexibility and to move products through a multi-stage production process. Firms with flexible manufacturing have the ability to create a wide variety of goods and/or services with minimized costs associated with changing production techniques. The manufacturing flow process includes much more than simple production of goods and services—it means creating flexible agreements with suppliers and shippers so that unexpected demand bursts can be accommodated, without disruptions to customer service or satisfaction.

The goals of the manufacturing flow management process are centered on leveraging the capabilities held by multiple members of the supply chain to improve overall manufacturing output in terms of quality, delivery speed, and flexibility, all of which tie directly to profitability. Depending on the product, supply chain managers may choose between a lean or agile supply chain strategy. In a lean supply chain, products are built before demand occurs, but managers attempt to reduce as much waste as possible. Lean supply chains first appeared within the Toyota Production System (TPS) as early as the 1950s. Agile strategies lie on the other end of the continuum—they prioritize customer responsiveness more so than waste reduction. Instead of trying to forecast demand and reduce waste, agile supply chains wait for demand to occur and use communication and flexibility to fill that demand quickly.[11]

13-3f Supplier Relationship Management

The **supplier relationship management process** is closely related to the manufacturing flow management process and contains several characteristics that parallel the customer relationship management process. The manufacturing flow management process is highly dependent on supplier relationships for flexibility. Furthermore, in a way similar to that found in the customer relationship management process, supplier relationship management provides structural support for developing and maintaining relationships with suppliers. Thus, by integrating these two ideas, supplier relationship management supports manufacturing flow by identifying and maintaining relationships with highly valued suppliers.

Just as firms benefit from developing close-knit, integrated relationships with customers, close-knit, integrated relationships with suppliers provide a means through which performance advantages can be gained. For example, careful management of supplier relationships is a key step toward ensuring that firms' manufacturing resources are utilized to their maximum potential. It is clear, then, that the supplier relationship management process has a direct impact on each supply chain member's bottom-line financial performance. In certain instances, it can be advantageous for the supply chain to integrate via a formal merger. American pharmaceutical company Bayer Health-Care recently purchased German-based Steigerwald Arzneimittelwerk, a partnering pharmacy supplier that specializes in herbal medicines. Purchasing a supplier gave Bayer HealthCare access to new medications. At the same time, purchasing a supplier based in Germany gave Bayer HealthCare enhanced access to European markets. Managing supplier relationships not only gave Bayer Health-Care better access to supplies, it also offered a chance to increase its customer base. The acquisition of one by the other simply sealed the deal by making the partnership permanent.[12]

Titus Green assembles a recycled iPhone at a Green Citizen recycling facility in Burlingame, California. Green Citizen collects and disposes old electronics in the San Francisco Bay area, tracking each device to ensure that it is recycled back into raw material or refurbished and resold.

13-3g Product Development and Commercialization

The **product development and commercialization process** (discussed in detail in Chapter 11) includes the group of activities that facilitate the joint development and marketing of new offerings among a group of supply chain partner firms. In many cases, more than one supply chain entity is responsible for ensuring new product success. Commonly, a multi-company collaboration is used to execute new-product development, testing, and launch, among other activities. The capability for developing and introducing new offerings quickly is key for competitive success versus rival firms, so it is often advantageous to involve many supply chain partners in the effort. The process requires the close cooperation of suppliers and customers, who provide input throughout the process and serve as advisers and co-producers for the new offering(s).

Designing a new product with the help of suppliers and customers can enable a company to introduce features and cost-cutting measures into final products. Customers provide information about what they want from the product, while suppliers can help to design for quality and manufacturability. Research has shown that when each supply chain partner shares responsibility for the design and manufacture of a new product, more obstacles can be identified early and opportunities for cost reduction are made possible. For example, Boeing involved a team of suppliers early in the development phase of its 787 Dreamliner aircraft, leading to a shift to a lighter composite material for the fuselage's outer shell. The lighter material is expected to make the aircraft substantially cheaper to operate on long haul flights.[13]

13-3h Returns Management

The final supply chain management process deals with situations in which customers choose to return a product to the retailer or supplier, thereby creating a reversed flow of goods within the supply chain. The **returns management process** enables firms to manage volumes of returned product efficiently while minimizing returns-related costs and maximizing the value of the returned assets to the firms

product development and commercialization process includes the group of activities that facilitates the joint development and marketing of new offerings among a group of supply chain partner firms

returns management process enables firms to manage volumes of returned product efficiently while minimizing returns-related costs and maximizing the value of the returned assets to the firms in the supply chain

in the supply chain. Returns have the potential to affect a firm's financial position in a major and negative way if mishandled. In certain industries, such as apparel e-retailing, returns can amount to as much as 40 percent of sales volume.

In addition to the value of managing returns from a pure asset-recovery perspective, many firms are discovering that returns management also creates additional marketing and customer service touch points that can be leveraged for added customer value above and beyond normal sales and promotion-driven encounters. Handling returns quickly creates a positive image, and gives the company an additional opportunity to please the customer, and customers who have positive experiences with the returns management process can become very confident buyers who are willing to reorder, since they know any problems they encounter with purchases will be quickly and fairly rectified. In addition, the returns management process allows the firm to recognize weaknesses in product design and/or areas for potential improvement through the direct customer feedback that initiates the process.

The mobile phone industry has been able to use returns management to its advantage. In a typical year, almost 100 million mobile phones are returned to manufacturers. With a return of between 35 and 75 percent of their original value in the secondary market, reselling 250,000 out of the 100 million returned phones would result in more than $20 million in additional revenue. Returns management also allows mobile phone companies to reclaim rare materials, such as gold, silver, and palladium. For example, reclaimed metals from one million mobile phones returned to one company brought in more than $2.8 million.[14]

 ## 13-4 SUSTAINABLE SUPPLY CHAIN MANAGEMENT

In response to the need for firms to both reduce costs and act as leaders in protecting the natural environment, many are adopting sustainable supply chain management principles as a key part of their supply chain strategy. **Sustainable supply chain management** involves the integration and balancing of environmental, social, and economic thinking into all phases of the supply chain management process. In doing so,

sustainable supply chain management a supply chain management philosophy that embraces the need for optimizing social and environmental costs in addition to financial costs

the organization both better addresses current business needs and develops long-term initiatives that allow it to mitigate risks and avail itself of future opportunities in ways that preserve resources for future generations and ensure long-term viability. Such activities include environmentally friendly materials sourcing; the design of products with consideration given to their social and environmental impact; and end-of-life product management that includes easy recycling and/or clean disposal. By enacting sustainable supply chain management principles, companies can simultaneously generate cost savings, protect the Earth's natural resources, and ensure that socially responsible business practices are enacted.

UPS works continuously to develop a more sustainable supply chain. By integrating new transportation technology into its fulfillment networks, UPS mechanics and employees are able to facilitate package delivery in ways that are more fuel- and emissions-efficient—the proof lies in the more than 3 percent reduction in fuel use per package per year. UPS has logged more than 200 million miles on alternative fuel vehicles and offers carbon-neutral delivery in 36 countries.[15]

In addition to environmental sustainability, modern businesses are also balancing economic success with social sustainability practices like human rights, labor rights, employee diversity initiatives, and quality of life concerns. A common misconception surrounding both environmental and social sustainability is that their practice increases supply chain costs disproportionately, and therefore should be enacted only when business leaders are willing to act altruistically or for the purposes of good public relations. However, recent research on these subjects has demonstrated a strong business case for supporting many sustainability initiatives. As examples, the recycling of used pallets is both an environmentally sustainable practice and cheaper than purchasing new ones, and the employment of disabled workers in distribution operations ensures both social sustainability (via opportunities for economically disadvantaged people) and better overall performance for the employer. The benefits of social sustainability efforts have been demonstrated by retailers such as Lowe's Home Improvement and Walgreen Stores, where the hiring and training of disabled workers has increased productivity in the host facilities by up to 20 percent. These companies have found that disabled workers are far less likely to miss work and are often as effective at performing job tasks as their abled counterparts—while frequently exceeding them in terms of process execution and safety standards.[16]

13-5 TRENDS IN SUPPLY CHAIN MANAGEMENT

Ken James/Bloomberg/Getty Images

Several technological advances and business trends are affecting the job of the supply chain manager today. Some of the business trends that are affecting supply chain management include outsourcing logistics, maintaining a secure supply chain and minimizing supply chain risk, and maintaining a sustainable supply chain. While these trends exert pressure on managers to change the way their supply chains function, electronic distribution is being used and changed frequently to help make supply chain management more integrated and easier to track.

More than 100 new all-electric UPS delivery vehicles were deployed in February 2013, eliminating the use of 126,000 gallons of fuel per year.

13-5a Outsourcing Logistics Functions

Partnering organizations are becoming increasingly efficient at dividing responsibility for supply chain management. **Outsourcing**, or **contract logistics**, is a rapidly growing initiative in which a manufacturer or supplier turns over an entire logistical function (often buying and managing transportation, warehousing, and/or light postponed manufacturing) to an independent **third-party logistics company (3PL)**. These service providers sell logistics solutions instead of physical products. Common 3PL products include warehouse space, transportation solutions, information sharing, manufacturing postponement, and enhanced technological innovations. When a firm's order fulfillment process is managed diligently, the amount of time between order placement and receipt of the customer's payment following order shipment (known as the *order-to-cash cycle*) is minimized as much as possible. Since many firms do not view order fulfillment as a core competency (versus, for example, product development or marketing), they often outsource this function to a 3PL that specializes in the order fulfillment process. The 3PL becomes a semi-permanent part of the firm's supply chain and is assigned to manage one or more specialized functions.[17] Other, more comprehensive partners, often known as **fourth-party logistics companies (4PLs) or logistics integrators**, create and manage entire solutions for getting products where they need to be, when they need to be there. Many times 3PLs and 4PLs provide a firm's only interaction with the customer,

so they need to represent the needs and interests of the entire firm and supply chain. Developing and training these firms' employees to be empowered and to respond to the customer's needs in the best interest of the supply chain is becoming increasingly important.

Outsourcing enables companies to cut inventories, locate stock at fewer plants and distribution centers, and still provide the same level of service or even better. The companies then can refocus investment on their core business. In the hospitality industry, Avendra negotiates with suppliers to obtain virtually everything a hotel might need, from food and beverages to golf course maintenance. For example, by relying on Avendra to manage many aspects of the supply chain, companies like Fairmont Hotels & Resorts and Inter-Continental Hotels Group can concentrate on their core function—providing hospitality. The most progressive companies are engaging in vested outsourcing relationships, whereby both parties collaborate deeply to find mutually beneficial arrangements that allow both parties to "win" by reducing overall costs while achieving better performance.[18]

outsourcing (contract logistics) a manufacturer's or supplier's use of an independent third party to manage an entire function of the logistics system, such as transportation, warehousing, or order processing

third-party logistics company (3PL) a firm that provides functional logistics services to others

fourth-party logistics company (4PL or logistics integrator) a consulting-based organization that assesses another's entire logistical service needs and provides integrated solutions, often drawing on multiple 3PLs for actual service

North American companies have been outsourcing logistics and shipping to companies overseas.

Because a logistics service provider is focused on logistical functions only, clients receive better service in a timely, efficient manner, thereby increasing their customers' satisfaction and boosting the perception of added value to a company's offerings. In many recent instances, North American companies have been **offshoring**, or outsourcing logistics to service providers located in countries with lower labor costs, such as Vietnam and Bangladesh. However, as fuel costs have risen and security issues become more prominent, many companies have begun to relocate outsourced operations closer to home. **Nearshoring** to locations such as Mexico or the Caribbean nations ensures low costs while reducing supply chain risk. Nearshoring not only allows a company to manufacture its

products more closely to major demand centers, it also gives the supplier a chance to make its presence known at a local level. Mexican-based IT firm Rural Sourcing Inc. has long worked with customers in Mexico, but an influx of American partners has led the company to grow an average of 150 percent annually over the last four years.[19]

13-5b Public-Private Partnerships

Sometimes, the magnitude of a supply chain dilemma is too great for a company and its suppliers or outsourcing partners to handle alone. Increasingly, this is leading firms to work together with government agencies in the form of **public-private partnerships (PPPs)**. PPPs are critical to the satisfaction of both company and societal interests and provide a mechanism by which very-large scale problems or opportunities can be addressed.

Though it is often assumed that industries and governments work poorly together (or in fact work against one another) when problems common to both emerge, a number of successful PPPs have formed over the past decade to diminish the negative impacts of potentially hazardous supply chain situations. For

> **offshoring** the outsourcing of a business process from one country to another for the purpose of gaining economic advantage
>
> **nearshoring** the transfer of an offshored activity from a distant to a nearby country
>
> **public-private partnerships (PPPs)** Critical to the satisfaction of both company and societal interests and provide a mechanism by which very-large scale problems or opportunities can be addressed

Efforts involving PPPs, like the Red Cross, will likely factor into the solution of future national and global supply chain.

example, immediately following the September 11, 2001, terror attacks on the United States, representatives from both industry and government collaborated to develop the Customs-Trade Partnership Against Terrorism (C-TPAT) in an effort to protect U.S.-based supply chains from terrorist disruption. The program currently has more than 10,000 company participants and has, in general terms, been successful at protecting cargo inbound for the United States while only minimally impacting the performance of its members' supply chains. Similarly, governmental agencies like the Federal Emergency Management Agency (FEMA) and non-government organizations like the Red Cross have benefitted from the inclusion of commercial logistics expertise in their disaster response systems.[20] Efforts involving.

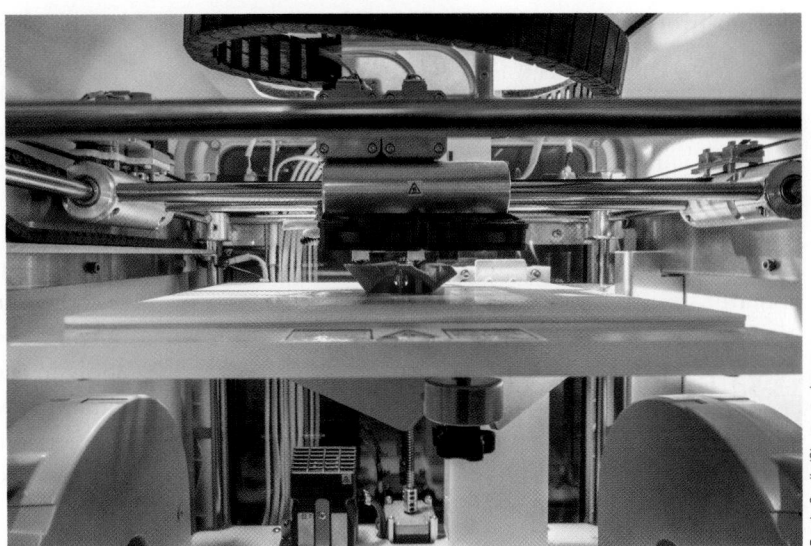

Using 3DP technology, objects are built to precise specifications using raw materials at or near the location where they will be consumed.

RomboStudio/Shutterstock.com

PPPs will likely factor into the solution of future national and global supply chain problems as well. For example, the dangerous combination of population growth and overuse of aging infrastructure has led to a situation whereby congestion and deterioration of roads imperils the timely shipment of goods. The U.S. Federal Highway Administration is openly soliciting proposals that would take some of the stress off of the U.S. highway network, including collaborating on building new toll roads and extending railways dedicated to cargo. These sorts of PPP-led advancements will play a critical role in the price of retail goods in upcoming years due to the costs associated with product and material delays.[21]

13-5c Electronic Distribution

Electronic distribution is the most recent development in the logistics arena. Broadly defined, **electronic distribution** includes any kind of product or service that can be distributed electronically, whether over traditional forms such as fiber-optic cable or through satellite transmission of electronic signals. Companies like E*TRADE, Apple (iTunes), and Movies.com have built their business models around electronic distribution.

In the near future, however, electronic distribution will not be limited only to products and services that are mostly composed of information that can therefore be easily digitized. Experiments with **three-dimensional printing (3DP)** have been successful in industries such as auto parts, biomedical, and even fast food. Using 3DP technology, objects are built to precise specifications using raw materials at or near the location where they will be consumed. Charge Bikes prints customized titanium bicycle parts based on customer specifications, thus reducing the need to transport complete frames around the world before they can be assembled and sold.[22] Shipping raw materials such as powdered titanium is cheaper than shipping finished bicycles because it can be packaged in a perfectly cubic container, making transportation much more efficient and cost effective. Powdered titanium is used only when it is needed, so virtually no waste is produced during printing. Web sites like 3DLT.com offer consumers templates for toys, dishes, and furniture that can be printed using the 3DP technology that is becoming increasingly available.[23]

Many industry experts project that 3DP (sometimes referred to as *additive manufacturing*) will radically transform the ways global supply chains work by changing the basic platforms of business. With 3DP, smaller, localized supply chains will become the norm and small manufacturers will produce many more

electronic distribution
a distribution technique that includes any kind of product or service that can be distributed electronically, whether over traditional forms such as fiber-optic cable or through satellite transmission of electronic signals

three-dimensional printing (3DP) the creation of three-dimensional objects via an additive manufacturing (printing) technology that layers raw material into desired shapes

custom products than ever before over very short lead times. And because such platforms will remove much of the need for transportation of finished goods to distribution centers and retailers, 3DP is expected to have a very positive impact on businesses' carbon footprints and the environment at large. At the same time, these platforms should make it possible to deliver unique goods more quickly, creating perceptions of better service.[24]

13-5d Global Supply Chain Management

Global markets present their own sets of challenges for supply chain managers. Strategically, there are many reasons why a company might wish to globalize its supply chain. The allure of foreign markets is strong, due to increasing demand for imported products worldwide. Cheap labor advantages and trade barriers/tariffs have encouraged firms to expand their global manufacturing operations. At the same time, globalization has brought about great uncertainty for modern companies, and specifically, their supply chains. Moving operations offshore exposes companies to risks associated with geopolitical conflict, foreign nationalization of assets and knowledge diffusion, and highly variable quality standards. Foreign suppliers are often less reliable, and due to the lengthening of the supply chain, variability in transportation service can lead to service failures. It is important to consider how sourcing and logistics will be impacted by supply chain globalization.

From a supply management standpoint, it often makes sense to procure goods and services from offshore suppliers. From an economic perspective, lower labor rates, government subsidies, and low materials costs are attractive, but are sometimes outweighed by the costs of quality variation and loss of intellectual property. Still, moving offshore also exposes the company to new technologies, introduces competition to domestic suppliers who have

become lackadaisical, and build brand equity. Companies moving offshore must carefully consider the pros and cons, and build supply management systems that can manage very diverse tasks. Logistically, it is critical for importers of all sizes to understand and cope with the legalities of trade in other countries. Shippers and distributors must be aware of the permits, licenses, and registrations they may need to acquire, and depending on the types of product they are importing, the tariffs, quotas, and other regulations that apply in each country. Sometimes, the complexities of handling overseas logistics are too great to overcome. As companies lengthen their global supply chains in search of cost advantages, other less obvious risks emanating from outside the immediate supply chain are also starting to come into play. Longer shipping lanes can expose shipments to natural disasters and extreme weather; political instability and trade restrictions can abruptly halt or slow shipments; fluctuations in currency values and border delays can diminish the value of products while they are on the path to the customer; and theft and piracy can present a greater threat due to increased time of exposure. For these reasons, many companies are now creating contingency plans so they can react quickly when something goes wrong.[25]

Indeed, as the world continues to globalize, supply chain management will undoubtedly continue to take on a globalized flavor. Worldwide, the resources needed to manufacture and sell increasingly demanded goods are becoming scarcer, and market boundaries are melting together. Free trade is expanding, and consumers in nations where demand has been traditionally low are viewing goods and placing orders via the Internet. Efforts to achieve world-class global supply chain management mean that the balancing of supply and demand—and the satisfaction of more and more customers worldwide—are becoming a reality for many companies.

egd/Shutterstock.com

Shippers and distributors must be aware of the permits, licenses, and registrations they may need to acquire, and depending on the types of product they are importing, the tariffs, quotas, and other regulations that apply in each country.

13-5e Supply Chain Analytics and Technology

In addition to outsourcing, globalization, PPPs, and 3D printing, other advancements in data and technology are beginning to exert an impact on the effectiveness and efficiency of the supply chain. First, a rapidly increasing prevalence of powerful computers and methods for capturing customer, supplier, and company information over the past two decades has resulted in the appearance of **big data**, a colloquial term for the explosive availability of data that has traditionally been hard to capture, store, manage, and analyze. The emergence of big data has presented both great opportunities and significant problems for supply chain managers. There is indeed more information available about supply chain operations than ever before, but the challenge of extracting usable date from this information is also very great. In order to harvest more useful information, many companies are using **cloud computing** to collaborate on big data projects and analyze findings in a quick and cost-effective manner.

As a result, many organizations are seeking to develop capabilities for **supply chain analytics**. Supply chain analytics programs that can interpret

Makeitdouble/Shutterstock.com

big data have great potential for improving supply chain operations. For example, the use of bigger and better data should allow supply chain forecasting to become more accurate; shipments to be re-routed in the event of traffic or bad weather; and warehouses to be stocked with exactly the products customers want (and none they don't want). Each of these ambitions, if realized, would offer lower prices for customers and lead to greater customer satisfaction.

Advanced technology enabled by big data is also improving supply chain operations. Fundamentally, the acquisition and analysis of big data allows a company to replace human reasoning with faster and more efficient decision making that is based on information rather than intuition. As a result, and combined with supply chain analytics, a company can automate many of its supply chain processes rather than using human labor. Many tasks that are done repetitively and require significant precision can be accomplished more cheaply and accurately by robots. For example, scientists at the University of California have developed robots—powered by cloud-based data about surgical patients—that are capable of performing basic hip and knee replacement surgery.[26] Cloud-based robots are already being used for large-scale production tasks like automobile and airplane manufacturing.

A final consideration related to technological advancement: sensory equipment that connects physical objects to decision-making analytics via the Internet is beginning to emerge. Recall the Internet of Things (IoT), which allows physical objects to relay specific information over the Internet without overt human interaction. The potential impact of the Internet of Things is tantalizing, but the technology is

Mr Aesthetics/Shutterstock.com

big data the rapidly collected and difficult-to-process large-scale datasets that have recently emerged, and which push the limits of current analytical capability

cloud computing the practice of using remote network servers to store, manage, and process data

supply chain analytics data analyses that support the improved design and management of the supply chain

currently in its infant stage. Connections between cargo vessels or trucks and transportation networks may eventually lead to the development of smart transportation modes that re-route in real time based on local traffic patterns, weather events, and accidents. Alternatively, the traffic grid could react to a need for emergency supplies by enabling a sequence of green stoplights along a critical emergency route. The possibilities are essentially endless for the IoT to positively impact the supply chain. Many companies have already launched projects related to the development of IoT-enabled supply chain management strategies.

13-6 MARKETING CHANNELS AND CHANNEL INTERMEDIARIES

A marketing channel can be viewed as a canal or pipeline through which products, their ownership, communication, financing and payment, and accompanying risk flow to the consumer. A **marketing channel** (also called a **channel of distribution**) is a business structure of interdependent organizations that reaches from the point of production to the consumer and facilitates the downstream physical movement of goods through the supply chain. Channels represent the "place" or "distribution" element of the marketing mix (product, price, promotion, and place), in that they provide a route for company products and services to flow to the customer. In essence, the marketing channel is the "downstream" portion of the supply chain that connects a producer with the customer. Whereas "upstream" supply chain members are charged with moving component parts or raw materials to the producer, members of the marketing channel propel finished goods toward the customer, and/or provide services that facilitate additional customer value.

Many different types of organizations participate in marketing channels. **Channel members** (also called *intermediaries*, *resellers*, and *middlemen*) negotiate with one another, buy and sell products, and facilitate the change of ownership between buyer and seller in the course of moving finished goods from the manufacturer into the hands of the final consumer. As products move toward the final consumer, channel members facilitate the distribution process by providing specialization and division of labor, overcoming discrepancies, and providing contact efficiency.

13-6a How Marketing Channels Work

According to the concepts of *specialization and division of labor*, breaking down a complex task into smaller, simpler ones and assigning these to specialists creates greater efficiency and lower average production costs via economies of scale. Marketing channels attain economies of scale through specialization and division of labor by aiding upstream producers (who often lack the motivation, financing, or expertise) in marketing to end users or consumers. In most cases, such as for consumer goods like soft drinks, the cost of marketing directly to millions of consumers—taking and shipping individual orders—is prohibitive. For this reason, producers engage other channel members such as wholesalers and retailers to do what the producers are not well suited to do. Some channel members can accomplish certain tasks more efficiently than others because they have built strategic relationships with key suppliers or customers or have unique capabilities. Their specialized expertise enhances the overall performance of the channel.

Because customers, like businesses, are specialized, they also rely on other entities for the fulfillment of most of their needs. Imagine what your life would be like if you had to grow your own food, make your own clothes, produce your own television shows, and assemble your own automobile! Luckily, members of marketing channels are available to undertake these tasks for us. However, not all goods and services produced by channel members exist in the form we'd most prefer, at least at first. Marketing channels are valuable because they aid producers in creating time, place, and exchange utility for customers, such that products become aligned with their needs. Producers, who sit at the top of the supply chain, provide **form utility** when they transform oats grown on a distant farm into the Cheerios that we like to eat for breakfast. **Time** and **place utility** are created by channel members, when, for example, a transport company hired by the producer physically moves boxes of cereal to a store near our homes in time for our next

marketing channel (channel of distribution) a set of interdependent organizations that eases the transfer of ownership as products move from producer to business user or consumer

channel members all parties in the marketing channel who negotiate with one another, buy and sell products, and facilitate the change of ownership between buyer and seller in the course of moving the product from the manufacturer into the hands of the final consumer

form utility the elements of the composition and appearance of a product that make it desirable

time utility the increase in customer satisfaction gained by making a good or service available at the appropriate time

place utility the usefulness of a good or service as a function of the location at which it is made available

Igor Strukov/Shutterstock.com Sheila Fitzgerald/Shutterstock.com MNStudio/Shutterstock.com

scheduled shopping trip. And the retailer, who is often the closest channel member to the customer, provides a desired product for some amount of money we are reasonably willing to give, creates **exchange utility** in doing so.

13-6b Functions and Activities of Channel Intermediaries

Intermediaries in a channel negotiate with one another, facilitate transfer of ownership for finished goods between buyers and sellers, and physically move products from the producer toward the final consumer. The most prominent difference separating intermediaries is whether they take title to the product. *Taking title* means they actually own the merchandise and control the terms of the sale—for example, price and delivery date. Retailers and merchant wholesalers are examples of intermediaries that take title to products in the marketing channel and resell them. **Merchant wholesalers** are organizations that facilitate the movement of products and services from the manufacturer to producers, resellers, governments, institutions, and retailers. All merchant wholesalers take title to the goods they sell, and most of them operate one or more warehouses where they receive finished goods, store them, and later reship them to retailers, manufacturers, and institutional clients. Since wholesalers do not dramatically alter the form of a good nor sell it directly to the consumer, their value hinges on their providing time and place utility and contact efficiency to retailers.

Other intermediaries do not take title to goods and services they market but do facilitate exchanges of ownership between sellers and buyers. **Agents and brokers** facilitate the sales of products downstream by representing the interests of retailers, wholesalers, and manufacturers to potential customers. Unlike merchant wholesalers, agents or brokers only facilitate sales and generally have little input into the terms of the sale. They do, however, get a fee or commission based on sales volume. For example, grocery chains often employ the services of food brokers, who provide expertise for a range of products within a category. The broker facilitates the sale of many different manufacturers' products to the grocery chain by marketing the producers' stocks, but the broker never actually takes ownership of any food products.

Many different variations in channel structures are possible, with choices made based in large part on the numbers and types of wholesaling intermediaries that are most desirable. Generally, product characteristics, buyer considerations, and market conditions determine the types and number of intermediaries the producer should use, as follows:

- Customized or highly complex products such as computers, specialty foods, or custom uniforms are usually sold through an agent or broker, who may represent one or multiple companies. In contrast, standardized product such as soda or toothpaste are often sold through a merchant wholesaler and retailer channel.

- Buyer considerations such as purchase frequency or customer wait time influence channel choice. When there is no time pressure, customers may save money on books by ordering online and taking direct distribution from a wholesaler. However,

exchange utility the increased value of a product that is created as its ownership is transferred

merchant wholesaler an institution that buys goods from manufacturers and resells them to businesses, government agencies, and other wholesalers or retailers and that receives and takes title to goods, stores them in its own warehouses, and later ships them

agents and brokers wholesaling intermediaries who do not take title to a product but facilitate its sale from producer to end user by representing retailers, wholesalers, or manufacturers

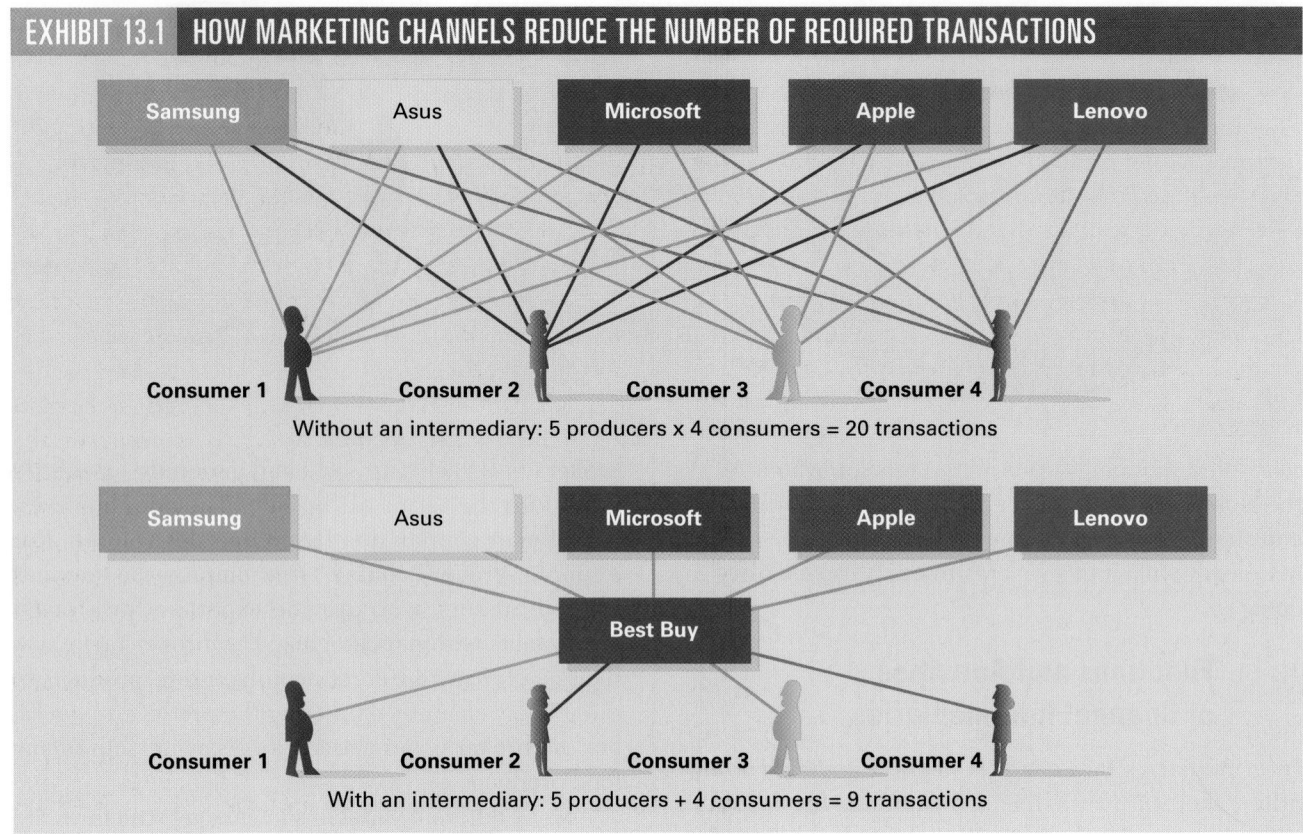

Without an intermediary: 5 producers x 4 consumers = 20 transactions

With an intermediary: 5 producers + 4 consumers = 9 transactions

if a book is needed immediately, it will have to be purchased at retail—at the school bookstore—and will include a markup.

- Market characteristics such as how many buyers are in the market and whether they are concentrated in a general location also influence channel design. In a home sale, the buyer and seller are localized in one area, which facilitates the use of a simple agent/broker relationship, whereas mass-manufactured goods such as automobiles may require parts from all over the world and therefore many intermediaries.

Retailers are those firms in the channel that sell directly to consumers as their primary function. A critical role fulfilled by retailers within the marketing channel is that they provide contact efficiency for consumers. Suppose you had to buy your milk at a dairy, your meat at a stockyard, and so forth. You would spend a great deal of time, money, and energy just shopping for just a few groceries. Retailers simplify distribution by reducing the number of transactions required by consumers, and by making an assortment of goods available in one location. Consider the example illustrated in Exhibit 13.1. Four consumers each want to buy a tablet computer. Without

retailer a channel intermediary that sells mainly to consumers

a retail intermediary like Best Buy, tablet manufacturers Samsung, Asus, Microsoft, Apple, and Lenovo would each have to make four contacts to reach the four consumers who are in the target market, for a total of twenty transactions. But when Best Buy acts as an intermediary between the producer and consumers, each producer needs to make only one contact, reducing the number to nine transactions. This benefit to customers accrues whether the retailer operates in a physical store location or online format.

13-6c Channel Functions Performed by Intermediaries

Intermediaries in marketing channels perform three essential functions that enable goods to flow between producer and consumer. *Transactional* functions involve contacting and communicating with prospective buyers to make them aware of existing products and to explain their features, advantages, and benefits. Intermediaries in the channel also provide *logistical* functions. Logistical functions typically include transportation and storage of assets, as well as their sorting, accumulation, consolidation, and/or allocation for the purpose of conforming to customer requirements. The third basic channel function, *facilitating*, includes research and financing.

Research provides information about channel members and consumers by getting answers to key questions: Who are the buyers? Where are they located? Why do they buy? Financing ensures that channel members have the money to keep products moving through the channel to the ultimate consumer. Although individual members can be added to or deleted from a channel, someone in the channel must perform these essential functions. Producers, wholesalers, retailers, or consumers can perform them, and sometimes nonmember channel participants such as service providers elect to perform them for a fee.

 13-7 CHANNEL STRUCTURES

A product can take any of several possible routes to reach the final consumer. Marketers and consumers each search for the most efficient channel from many available alternatives. Constructing channels for a consumer convenience good such as candy differs from doing the same for a specialty good like a Prada handbag. Exhibit 13.2 illustrates four ways manufacturers can route products to consumers. When possible, producers use a **direct channel** to sell directly to consumers in order to keep purchase prices low. Direct marketing activities—including telemarketing, mail order and catalog shopping, and forms of electronic retailing such as online shopping and shop-at-home television networks—are good examples of this type of channel structure. There are no intermediaries. Producer-owned stores and factory outlet stores—like Sherwin-Williams, Polo Ralph Lauren, Oneida, and WestPoint Home—are also examples of direct channels.

By contrast, when one or more channel members are small companies lacking in marketing power, an *agent/broker channel* may be the best solution. Agents or brokers bring manufacturers and wholesalers together for negotiations, but they do not take title to merchandise. Ownership passes directly from the producer to one or more wholesalers and/or retailers, who sell to the ultimate consumer.

Most consumer products are sold through distribution channels similar to the other two alternatives: the retailer channel and the wholesaler channel. A *retailer channel* is most common when the retailer is large and can buy in large quantities directly from the manufacturer. Walmart, Sears, and car dealers are examples of retailers that often bypass a wholesaler. *A wholesaler channel* is commonly used for low-cost items that are frequently purchased, such as candy, cigarettes, and magazines.

13-7a Channels for Business and Industrial Products

As Exhibit 13.3 illustrates, five channel structures are common in business and industrial markets. First, *direct channels* are typical in business and industrial markets. For example, manufacturers buy large quantities of raw materials, major equipment,

direct channel a distribution channel in which producers sell directly to consumers

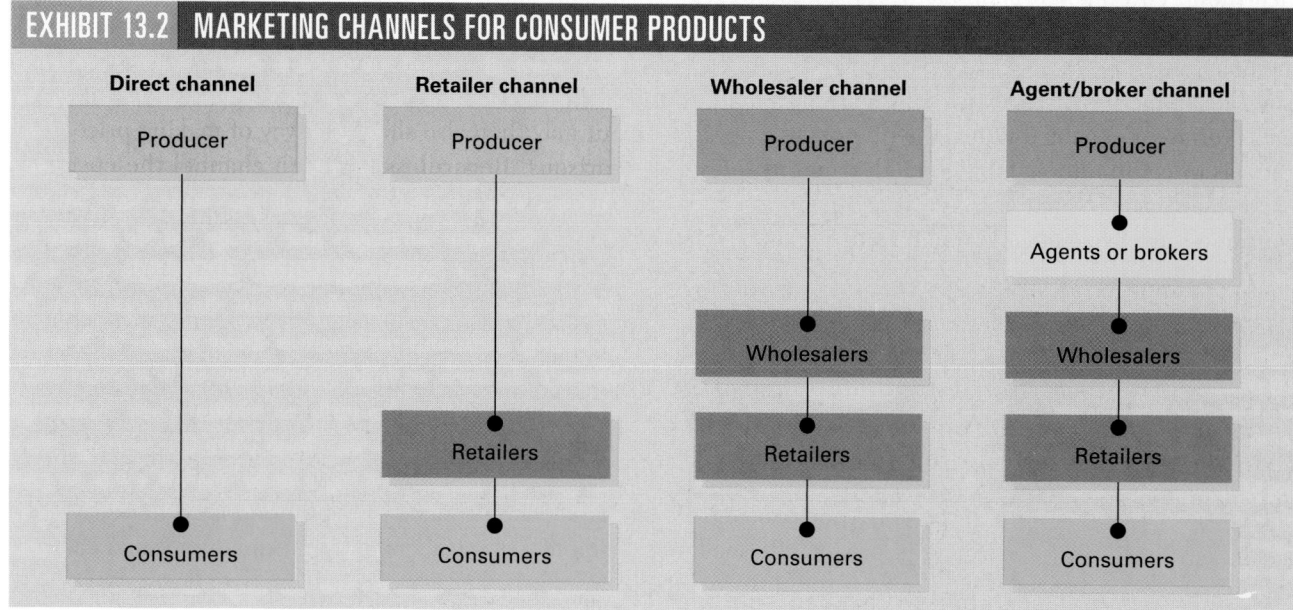

EXHIBIT 13.2 MARKETING CHANNELS FOR CONSUMER PRODUCTS

Direct channel	Retailer channel	Wholesaler channel	Agent/broker channel
Producer	Producer	Producer	Producer
			Agents or brokers
		Wholesalers	Wholesalers
	Retailers	Retailers	Retailers
Consumers	Consumers	Consumers	Consumers

EXHIBIT 13.3 CHANNELS FOR BUSINESS AND INDUSTRIAL PRODUCTS

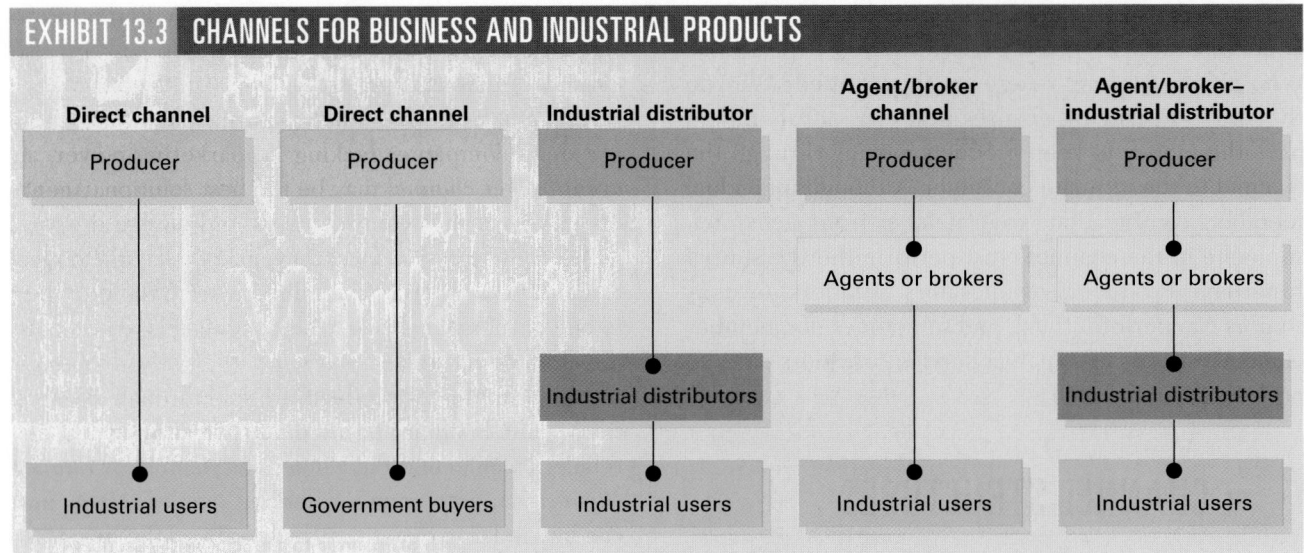

processed materials, and supplies directly from other producers. Manufacturers that require suppliers to meet detailed technical specifications often prefer direct channels. For instance, Apple uses a direct channel to purchase high-resolution retina displays for its innovative iPad tablet line. To ensure sufficient supply for iPad manufacturing, Apple takes direct shipments of screens from Sharp, LG, and Samsung.[27]

Alternatively, companies selling standardized items of moderate or low value often rely on *industrial distributors*. In many ways, an industrial distributor is like a supermarket for organizations. Industrial distributors are wholesalers and channel members that buy and take title to products. Moreover, they usually keep inventories of their products and sell and service them. Often small manufacturers cannot afford to employ their own sales force. Instead, they rely on manufacturers' representatives or selling agents to sell to either industrial distributors or users. Additionally, the Internet has enabled virtual distributors to emerge and has forced traditional industrial distributors to expand their business models. Many manufacturers and consumers are bypassing distributors and going direct, often via the Internet.

13-7b Alternative Channel Arrangements

Rarely does a producer use just one type of channel to move its product. It usually employs several different strategies, which include the use of multiple distribution, nontraditional channels, and strategic channel alliances. When a producer selects two or more channels to distribute the same product to target markets, this arrangement is called **dual or multiple distribution**. Dual or multiple distribution systems differ from single channel systems, and managers should recognize the differences. Multiple distribution channels must be organized and managed as a group, and managers must orchestrate their use in synchronization if whole system is to work well. As consumers increasingly embrace online shopping, more retailers are employing a multiple distribution strategy. This arrangement allows retailers to reach a wider customer base, but may also lead to competition between distribution channels through cannibalization (whereby one channel takes sales away from another). When multiple separate channels are used, they must all complement each other. Some customers use "showrooming" as a way of learning about products, but may then also shop as a way of making price comparisons. Regardless of which channel the customer chooses when making the final purchase, they should receive the same messages and "image" of the products.

The use of **nontraditional channels** may help differentiate a firm's product from the competition by providing additional information about products. Nontraditional channels include approaches such as mail-order television or video channels, or infomercials. Although nontraditional channels may limit a brand's coverage, they can give a producer serving a niche market a way to gain market access and customer attention without having to establish physical channel intermediaries and can also provide another sales avenue for larger firms.

dual distribution (multiple distribution) the use of two or more channels to distribute the same product to target markets

nontraditional channels non-physical channels that facilitate the unique market access of products and services

VERA BRADLEY

Vera Bradley signed a deal with Mitsubishi Corporation and its partner, Look, Inc., to distribute its handbags, luggage and accessories.

AP Photos/Michael Conroy

Furthermore, companies often form **strategic channel alliances** that enable them to use another manufacturer's already-established channel. Alliances are used most often when the creation of marketing channel relationships may be too expensive and time consuming. For example, U.S.-based Vera Bradley, Inc. signed a deal with Mitsubishi Corporation and its partner Look, Inc. to distribute the former's handbags, luggage, and accessories in the Japanese department stores and boutiques in their respective networks. This alliance helps Vera Bradley reach new markets in foreign cities and diversifies its revenue base, while minimizing its risks of going abroad.[28]

In addition to using primary traditional and nontraditional channels to flow products toward customer markets, many businesses also employ secondary channels, using either an active or passive approach. For example, though most automobile manufacturers sell their finished products to end users through networks of owned or franchised dealers, they also sell cars to rental agencies such as Enterprise or Hertz, who then rent them to potential customers. Similarly, fashion apparel companies might distribute their premium products, such as silk ties or branded watches, through primary channels such as department stores or specialty stores, while using an off-brand or discount outlet for distribution of low-end products. In each case, the goal of the company is the same: to engage a segment of customers who might otherwise never experience the product by offering it at a more easily affordable price or under trial conditions.

Marketers must also be aware, however, that some unintended secondary channels also exist. In some countries, **gray marketing channels** may be used to sell stolen or counterfeited products, which could detract from the profitability of the primary and secondary channels controlled by the business. Counterfeit products such as North Face outerwear, Rolex watches, and Prada handbags can be very difficult to distinguish from the real thing, and their presence provides unintended competition for the producer when such products are distributed through unauthorized intermediaries.

Along with marketing channels that move products downstream to end customers, retailers and manufacturers also manage channels that move products upstream, in the direction of the producer. These **reverse channels** enable consumers to return products to the retailer or manufacturer in the event of a product defect, or at the end of the product's useful life to the consumer. The retailers or manufacturers can then recycle the product and use components to manufacture new products, or refurbish and resell the same product in a secondary market. Several large companies, including Apple, Best Buy, and Walmart, offer opportunities to recycle items ranging from plastic bags and batteries to televisions and Christmas trees. Consumers and companies alike view reverse channels as not just a way to reduce the firm's environmental impact, but also as a means to gain some financial benefits as well.[29] For example, Apple will pay consumers for their old Apple products if they qualify for resale, or if their component parts are valuable for manufacturing new products.[30] **Drop and shop** programs use convenience to get consumers to recycle products, like batteries or cell phones, during a regular trip to the store.

13-7c Digital Channels

With technology changing rapidly, many companies are turning to digital channels to facilitate product

strategic channel alliance a cooperative agreement between business firms to use the other's already established distribution channel

gray marketing channels secondary channels that are unintended to be used by the producer, and which often flow illegally obtained or counterfeit product toward customers

reverse channels channels that enable customers to return products or components for reuse or remanufacturing

drop and shop a system used by several retailers that allow customers to bring used products for return or donation at the entrance of the store

A key advantage of Uber and similar apps is their frictionless payment interface.

Source: Uber Technologies, Inc.

distribution. **Digital channels** are pathways for moving product and information toward customers such that they can be sent and/or received with electronic devices, such as computers, smartphones, tablets, or video game consoles. Digital channels allow for either push- or pull-based information and product flows to occur, and sometimes simultaneously. For example, a downloaded video game or music file purchased by a customer can also include a digital ad for more games or a new music player.

In response to the growth of digital channels, customers are turning in droves to **M-commerce**, whereby a mobile device is used to assess, compare, and/or buy products. For example, suppose you need a ride from one point in Chicago to another. Instead of having to hail a cab or walk to the nearest elevated train station, you can use Uber's smartphone app to contact a local driver who will take you directly to your destination. A key advantage of Uber and similar apps is their frictionless payment interface. When you are done with your ride, you just get out of the car and walk away while the app charges your credit or debit card and pays the driver.[31] M-commerce is currently experiencing the largest growth in both retail and channel decision-making, in part because of its more than $20 billion annual revenue.

M-commerce also enables consumers using wireless mobile devices to connect to the Internet and shop. Essentially, M-commerce goes beyond text message advertisements to allow consumers to purchase goods and services using wireless mobile devices. M-commerce users adopt the new technology because it saves time and offers more convenience in a greater number of locations. The use of M-commerce has become increasingly important as users grow in both number and purchasing power. Consumers have become more reliant on digital technologies, as shown in the world's first fully digital generation, the Millennials, and firms that fail to react to this trend risk losing a rapidly growing group of M-commerce customers[32].

Many major companies, ranging from Polo Ralph Lauren to Sears, already offer shopping on mobile phones, and the growth potential is huge. Along with smartphone use, consumers are shopping with tablets just as much, if not more, than with company Web sites. One study even found that tablets accounted for twice as much in Web-based sales as smartphone purchases[33]. M-commerce in the United States will exceed $41 billion by 2017 and sales made on mobile devices on a global scale will exceed $110 billion in the same time frame.[34] In the United States, 87 percent of adults own a cellphone, 45 percent own a smartphone, 31 percent own a tablet, and 26 percent own an e-reader.[35] Fifty-five percent of adults use the Internet on their mobile devices, and 31 percent report that they go online with their mobile device more than they do with a desktop or laptop computer.[36] The gap between the number of smartphones owned and smartphones used for purchases is closing rapidly. During the holiday season, about 30 percent of smartphone owners check prices using some kind of price comparison app or read reviews online while inside a store, and almost 50 percent use their smartphones to call a friend or family member for purchase advice.[37] Overall, more than two-thirds of Americans use their mobile devices to obtain shopping information.[38]

Along with smartphone technology, companies are starting to look into other digital channels with which to connect with their customers. Social shopping allows multiple retailers to sell products to customers through social media sites. Aaramshop brings hundreds of neighborhood grocery stores to customers through Facebook. Customers makes their purchases online and their specific neighborhood stores take care of delivering the items directly to customers' homes.[39] Home delivery extends beyond groceries in many heavily populated

digital channels
electronic pathways that allow products and related information to flow from producer to consumer

M-commerce the ability to conduct commerce using a mobile device for the purpose of buying or selling goods or services

areas. In China and India, McDonald's has started delivering directly to its customers instead of making consumers come to them.

Firms are also using social media Web sites as digital channels—even in some cases without offering a purchasing opportunity. Companies create profiles on Web sites like Pinterest or Facebook and use them not only to give customers information about their products, but also to collect customer information. According to one recent study, 38 percent of all online customers follow at least one retailer on a social networking site. Many customers use these Web sites to find product information or get information on special deals, and those who follow a company's blog or profile on a social media site often end up clicking through to the firm's Web site.[40]

While some services group retailers together in order to bring products to customers, others allow consumers to combine and order larger amounts. Web sites like Groupon and Livingsocial give customers the opportunity to fulfill their individual needs at group prices. Many of these sites are organized and managed by intermediaries between manufacturers and customers, but others may be customer initiated or even created by firms to better promote their own products and manage demand.[41]

13-7d Factors Affecting Channel Choice

Marketing managers must answer many questions before choosing a marketing channel. A book manufacturer must decide, for example, what roles physical and electronic distribution will play in the overall marketing strategy and how these two paths will fare against each other. In addition, managers must decide what level of distribution intensity is appropriate and must ensure that the channel strategy they choose is consistent with product, promotion, and pricing strategies. The choice of channels depends on a holistic analysis of market factors, product factors, and producer factors.

MARKET FACTORS Among the most important market factors affecting distribution channel choices are market considerations. Specifically, managers should answer the following questions: Who are the potential customers? What do they buy? Where do they buy? When do they buy? How do they buy? Additionally, the choice of channel depends on whether the producer is selling to consumers directly, or through other industrial buyers, due to differences in the buying routines of these groups. The geographic location and size of the market are also important factors guiding channel selection. As a rule, if the target market is concentrated in one or more specific areas, then direct selling through a sales force is appropriate, whereas intermediaries would be less expensive in broader markets.

PRODUCT FACTORS Complex, customized, and expensive products tend to benefit from shorter and more direct marketing channels. These types of products sell better through a direct sales force. Examples include pharmaceuticals, scientific instruments, airplanes, and mainframe computer systems. On the other hand, the more standardized a product is, the longer its distribution channel can be and the greater the number of intermediaries that can be involved without driving up costs. For example, with the exception of flavor and shape, the formula for chewing gum is fairly standard from producer to producer. As a result, the distribution channel for gum tends to involve many wholesalers and retailers.

The product stage in the life cycle is also an important factor in choosing a marketing channel. In fact, the choice of channel may change over the life of the product. As products become more common and less intimidating to potential users, producers tend to look for alternative channels. Similarly, perishable products such as vegetables and milk have a relatively short life span, and fragile products like china and crystal require a minimum amount of handling. Therefore, both require

Levi Strauss launched Signature, a line of low cost jeans available exclusively at Wal-Mart. According to the company, the Signature line offers superior fit, comfort, and style for less than $20.

fairly short marketing channels. Online retailers such as eBay facilitate the sale of unusual or difficult-to-find products that benefit from a direct channel.

PRODUCER FACTORS

Several factors pertaining to the producer itself are important to the selection of a marketing channel. In general, producers with large financial, managerial, and marketing resources are better able to perform their own marketing, and thus will use more direct channels. These producers have the ability to hire and train their own sales forces, warehouse their own goods, and extend credit to their customers. Smaller or weaker firms, on the other hand, must rely on intermediaries to provide these services for them. Compared to producers with only one or two product lines, producers that sell several products in a related area are able to choose channels that are more direct. Sales expenses then can be spread over more products.

A producer's desire to control pricing, positioning, brand image, and customer support also tends to influence channel selection. For instance, firms that sell products with exclusive brand images, such as designer perfumes and clothing, usually avoid channels in which discount retailers are present. Manufacturers of upscale products, such as Gucci (handbags) and Godiva (chocolates), may sell their wares only in expensive stores in order to maintain an image of exclusivity. Many producers have opted to risk their image, however, and test sales in discount channels. For example, Levi Strauss expanded its distribution network to include JCPenney, Sears, and Walmart.

Source: Spotify AB, Source: Gilt Groupe, Inc., Source: JackThreads, Source: Netflix, Inc.

intensive distribution a form of distribution aimed at having a product available in every outlet where target customers might want to buy it

selective distribution a form of distribution achieved by screening dealers to eliminate all but a few in any single area

exclusive distribution a form of distribution that establishes one or a few dealers within a given area

13-7e Levels of Distribution Intensity

Organizations have three options for intensity of distribution: intensive distribution, selective distribution, or exclusive distribution. **Intensive distribution** is a form of distribution aimed at maximum market coverage. Here, the manufacturer tries to have the product available in every outlet where potential customers might want to buy it. If buyers are unwilling to search for a product, it must be made very accessible to buyers. The next level of distribution, **selective distribution**, is achieved by screening dealers and retailers to eliminate all but a few in any single area. Because only a few are chosen, the consumer must seek out the product. For example, HBO selectively distributes its popular television shows through a series of its own subscription-based channels (HBO, HBO on Demand, and HBO Go for mobile devices) and sells subscriptions or single episodes through Apple, Amazon.com, and Sony's online stores but does not stream them through Netflix or Hulu Plus. The most restrictive form of market coverage is **exclusive distribution**, which entails only one or a few dealers within a given area. Because buyers may have to search or travel extensively to buy the product, exclusive distribution is usually confined to consumer specialty goods, a few shopping goods, and major industrial equipment. Products such as Rolls-Royce automobiles, Chris-Craft powerboats, and Pettibone tower cranes are distributed under exclusive arrangements.

EMERGING DISTRIBUTION STRUCTURES

In recent years, rapid changes in technology and communication have led to the emergence of new, experimental distribution methods and channel structures. For example, fashion flash sale sites like Gilt, JackThreads, and Ruelala have recently boomed in popularity. On these sites, new designer clothing items are made available every day—often at a discount from 15 to 80 percent, and always for an extremely limited time. The average fashion flash sale shopper is between 25 and 40 years of age and makes $100,000 a year—an ideal demographic for many marketers.

Another emerging channel structure involves renting items that are usually only sold to end consumers. For example, some Web sites allow customers to rent and return high fashion products (renttherunway.com and fashionrenting.com), handbags and accessories (lovemeandleaveme.com), and even furniture (fashionfurniture.com). Rental versus retail channels open up an entirely new customer base for certain products that were once reserved for a much smaller group.

For many years, subscription services such as book-of-the-month clubs have provided customers products periodically over time. More recently, subscription services have expanded far beyond books and magazines to include clothing (bombfell.com), shoes (shoedazzle.com), crafting kits (craftaholicsanonymous.net), and wine (www.clubw.com). Many Web sites require subscriptions to view premium content, and streaming media services like Spotify, Netflix, and OnLive offer a wholly new type of subscription service.

Digital marketplaces like Steam and the Google Play Store constitute another recent trend in marketing channels. Digital licensing adds an interesting facet to customer sales; instead of selling a tangible product, digital marketplaces sell the rights to songs, movies, and television shows through their Web sites and applications. Instead of leaving home to purchase a physical album, game, or movie, consumers can select specific media and download them directly to their computers or mobile devices.

13-8 OMNICHANNEL VERSUS MULTICHANNEL MARKETING

Marketing channels are valuable because they provide a route for products and services to reach the customer. Customers have different preferences, however, as to which channels to use when browsing, seeking information, comparing products to one another, and making a purchase. A single customer may use different channels for each of these activities, including both traditional and digital channels! For example, a customer might first learn about a new smartwatch when browsing a catalog, then conduct research about it on the company's Web site. She might later go to a physical retail location to try out the product, before finally purchasing the device using a mobile app. Because of these varying preferences through different stages of the shopping cycle, many companies have begun to employ a multichannel marketing strategy, whereby customers are offered information, goods, services, and/or support through one or more synchronized channels. Recent studies have demonstrated that customers who use multiple channels when shopping become more engaged during the purchase process, and tend to spend more than customers who shop one channel only. The exception is when customers are buying simple, utilitarian products that are well known and intended for frequent use. Since customers are already familiar with these product types, single-channel designs are just as effective.[42]

Because consumers use multiple channels during the shopping experience, it has become important for channel members to create a seamless shopping

AND-ONE/iStock/Thinkstock

experience across all physical and digital channels. Facilitating such customer activities as checking a store's inventory online, purchasing an item through an app for in-store pickup, allowing online purchases to be returned in-store, and enabling mobile payment while shopping in-store are only a few strategies that producers and retailers are using to give customers the appearance that multiple channels are behaving as one.[43]

However, it is important to understand that the multichannel design does create redundancy and complexity in the firm's distribution system. Selling through multiple channels is typically accompanied by the construction of multiple, parallel supply chains, each with its own inventory, processes, and performance metrics. Multichannel systems typically have meant that each channel would operate different transportation and distribution systems, hold and account for its own inventory, and otherwise act as independent sales and profit centers, with little knowledge of the operations of the other. This proved problematic for one retailer who was selling its products both in physical stores and on its Web site. The company had a distribution center in Kentucky for its Internet retailing business, and another near Chicago for its physical stores located there. When a customer in Chicago visited the local store looking for a certain product, the shelves were empty, and he was directed to order products from the company's Web site if he wanted one in time for the holidays. He did so, and the product was shipped to his home—at significant expense—from the Kentucky distribution center, while unused product sat only miles from his home in the Chicago distribution center, waiting to be stocked on local store shelves.

Because of situations like these, many companies are transitioning to an omnichannel distribution operation that supports their multichannel retail operations and unifies their retail interfaces so that all customers receive equal and efficient service. For example, retailers such as The Gap and Burberry allow customers to reserve items online for pickup in nearby stores, have employed a find-in-store feature on their Web sites that displays real-time stock information so customers can avoid unnecessary trips to the mall, and are beginning to provide in-store computer terminals or iPads for customers to search their Web sites for offerings the customer's local store may not carry. By making their inventory data available to customers in real-time, these retailers have effectively merged their multiple distribution channels in such a way that creates greater customer control over the shopping experience, leading to greater satisfaction and loyalty. We discuss further implications of this strategy in Chapter 15.

STUDY TOOLS 13

LOCATED AT BACK OF THE TEXTBOOK

☐ Rip out Chapter Review Card

LOCATED AT WWW.CENGAGEBRAIN.COM

☐ Review Key Terms Flashcards and create your own

☐ Track your knowledge and understanding of key concepts in marketing

☐ Complete practice and graded quizzes to prepare for tests

☐ Complete interactive content within the MKTG Online experience

☐ View the chapter highlight boxes within the MKTG Online experience

MKTG
ONLINE

ACCESS TEXTBOOK CONTENT ONLINE—INCLUDING ON SMARTPHONES!

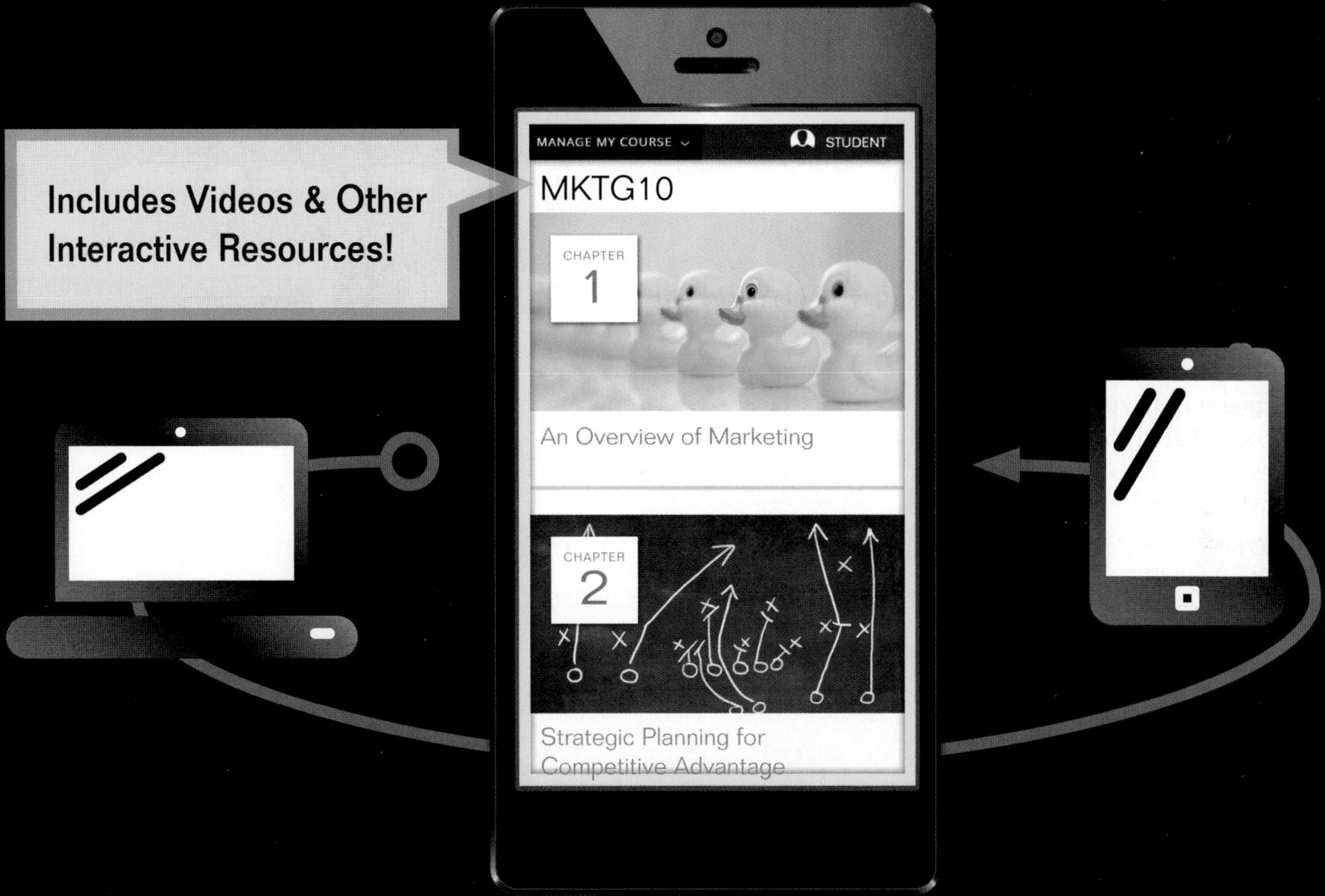

Includes Videos & Other Interactive Resources!

MANAGE MY COURSE · STUDENT

MKTG10

CHAPTER 1

An Overview of Marketing

CHAPTER 2

Strategic Planning for Competitive Advantage

4LTR PRESS

Access MKTG ONLINE at www.cengagebrain.com

14 | Retailing

iStockphoto.com/kevinjeon00

LEARNING OUTCOMES

After studying this chapter, you will be able to…

14-1 Explain the importance of the retailer within the channel and the U.S. economy

14-2 List and understand the different types of retailers

14-3 Explain why nonstore retailing is on the rise and list the advantages of its different forms

14-4 Discuss the different retail operations models and understand why they vary in strategy and format

14-5 Explain how retail marketing strategies are developed and executed

14-6 Discuss how services retailing differs from goods retailing

14-7 Understand how retailers address product/service failures and discuss the opportunities that service failures provide

14-8 Summarize current trends related to customer data, analytics, and technology

After you finish this chapter go to **PAGE 260** for **STUDY TOOLS.**

14-1 THE IMPORTANCE OF RETAILING

Retailing represents all the activities directly related to the sale of goods and services to the ultimate consumer for personal, nonbusiness use. Retailing has enhanced the quality of our daily lives in countless ways. When we shop for groceries, hair care, clothes, books, or other products and services, we are doing business with **retailers**. The millions of goods and services provided by retailers mirror the diverse needs, wants, and trends of modern society. The U.S. economy depends heavily on the retail sector. Approximately two-thirds of the U.S. gross domestic product comes from retail activity, and retail sales account for nearly 30 percent of all consumer spending.[1]

retailing all the activities directly related to the sale of goods and services to the ultimate consumer for personal, nonbusiness use

retailer a channel intermediary that sells mainly to consumers

Retailing affects everyone, both directly and indirectly. The retailing industry is one of the largest employers in the United States, with almost 3.8 million U.S. retailers employing more than 29 million people—about one in five American workers. And the industry is expected to grow to more than 16 million by 2018.[2] In addition, almost 10 percent of all businesses are classified as retailers.[3] Yet, retailing is still largely a mom-and-pop industry. Almost nine out of ten retail companies employ fewer than twenty employees, and according to the National Retail Federation, over 95 percent of all retailers operate just one store.[4] Most retailers are quite small, but a few giant organizations such as Walmart dominate the industry. Walmart's annual U.S. sales are greater than the combined sales of the four next largest U.S. retailers. As the retail environment changes, so too do retailers. Trends and innovations relating to customer data, social media, and alternative forms of shopping are constantly developing, and retailers have no choice but to react. The *best* retailers actually lead the way by anticipating change and developing new and exciting ways to interact with customers. We discuss each of these issues and more in this chapter.

14-2 TYPES OF RETAILERS AND RETAIL OPERATIONS

Retail establishments can be classified in several ways, such as type of ownership, level of service, product assortment, and price. These variables can be combined in several ways to create numerous unique retail operating models. Exhibit 14.1 depicts the major types of retailers and classifies them by their key differentiating characteristics.

14-2a Ownership Arrangement

Depending on its ownership arrangement, a retailer can gain advantages from having a broad brand identity, or from having the freedom to take risks and innovate. Retail ownership takes one of three forms—they can be independently owned, part of a chain, or a franchise outlet.

- An **independent retailer** is owned by a person or group and is not operated as part of a larger network. Around the world, most retailers are independent, with each owner operating a singular store within a local community.

- A **chain store** is a group of retailers (of one or more brand names) owned and operated by a single organization. Under this form of ownership, a home office for the entire chain handles

> **independent retailer** a retailer owned by a single person or partnership and not operated as part of a larger retail institution
>
> **chain store** a store that is part of a group of the same stores owned and operated by a single organization

EXHIBIT 14.1 TYPES OF STORES AND THEIR CHARACTERISTICS

Type of Retailer	Level of Service	Product Assortment	Price	Gross Margin
Department store	Moderately high to high	Broad	Moderate to high	Moderately high
Specialty store	High	Narrow	Moderate to high	High
Supermarket	Low	Broad	Moderate	Low
Drugstore	Low to moderate	Medium	Moderate	Low
Convenience store	Low	Medium to narrow	Moderately high	Moderately high
Full-line discount store	Moderate to low	Medium to broad	Moderately low	Moderately low
Specialty discount store	Moderate to low	Medium to broad	Moderately low to low	Moderately low
Warehouse club	Low	Broad	Low to very low	Low
Off-price retailer	Low	Medium to narrow	Low	Low
Restaurant	Low to high	Narrow	Low to high	Low to high

retail buying; creates unified operating, marketing, and other administrative policies; and works to ensure consistency across different locations. The Gap and Starbucks are retail chains.

- A **franchise** is a retail business where the operator is granted a license to operate and sell a product under the brand name of a larger supporting organizational structure, such as Subway or Supercuts. Under this arrangement, a **franchisor** originates the trade name, product, methods of operation, and so on. A **franchisee**, in return, pays the franchisor for the right to use its name, product, and business methods, and takes advantage of the franchisor's brand equity and operational expertise. The most successful franchises are increasingly services retailers. Three of the top five franchises recognized by Entrepreneur Magazine are primarily service rather than goods providers.[5]

---

franchise a relationship in which the business rights to operate and sell a product are granted by the franchisor to the franchisee

franchisor the originator of a trade name, product, methods of operation, and the like that grants operating rights to another party to sell its product

franchisee an individual or business that is granted the right to sell another party's product

---

14-2b Level of Service

The service levels that retailers provide range from full-service to self-service. Some retailers, such as exclusive clothing stores, offer very high or even customized service levels. They provide alterations, credit, delivery, consulting, liberal return policies, layaway, gift-wrapping, and personal shopping. By contrast, retailers such as factory outlets and warehouse clubs offer virtually no service. After stock is set out for sale, the customer is responsible for any information gathering, acquisition, handling, use, and product assembly. At the extreme low end of the service continuum, a retailer may take the form of a product kiosk or vending machine.

14-2c Product Assortment

Retailers can also be categorized by the *width* and depth of their product lines. Width refers to the assortment of products offered; *depth* refers to the number of different brands offered within each assortment. Specialty stores such as Best Buy, Staples, and GameStop have the thinnest product assortments, usually carrying single or narrow product lines that are considerably deep. For example, a specialty pet store like PetSmart is limited to pet-related products, but may carry as many as twenty brands of dog food in a large variety of flavors, shapes, and sizes. On the other end of the spectrum, full-line discounters typically carry very wide assortments of merchandise that are fairly shallow.

Stores often modify their product assortments in order to accommodate factors in the external environment. Petitions started by concerned patrons in Australia and the United States caused major retailers to remove the Grand Theft Auto 5 video game and action figures from the popular television show Breaking Bad from store shelves. These patrons believed that the products' violent nature and association with the illegal drug culture were harmful to society.[6] Similarly, food products ranging from milk to vitamins to dog treats have been excluded from retail product lines in order to better ensure customer safety.

14-2d Price

Price is the fourth way to position retail stores. Traditional department stores and specialty stores typically charge the full "suggested retail price." In contrast, discounters, factory outlets, and off-price retailers use low prices and discounts to lure shoppers. The last column in Exhibit 14.1 shows the typical **gross margin**—how much the retailer makes as a percentage of sales after the cost of the goods sold is subtracted. (Margins will be covered in more detail in Chapter 19.) Today, prices in any store format might vary not just from day to day, but from minute to minute! Online retailers and traditional brick-and-mortar stores that have invested in electronic tagging systems are increasingly adopting dynamic pricing strategies that allow them to adjust to an item's surging popularity or slow movement in real time.[7]

14-2e Types of In-Store Retailers

Traditionally, retailers fall into one of several distinct types of retail stores, each of which features a product assortment, types of services, and price levels that align with the intended customers' shopping preferences. Recently, however, retailers began experimenting with alternative formats that blend the features and benefits of the traditional types. For instance, supermarkets are expanding their nonfood items and services, discounters are adding groceries, drugstores are becoming more like convenience stores, and department stores are experimenting with smaller stores. Nevertheless, many stores still fall into the traditional archetypes:

- **Department stores** such as JCPenney and Macy's carry a wide range of products and specialty goods, including apparel, cosmetics, housewares, electronics, and sometimes furniture. Each department acts as a separate profit center, but central management sets policies about pricing and the types of merchandise carried.

AP Images/Casper Star-Tribune/Alan Rogers

This December 2012 photo shows a wall that typically displays about 25 military-style rifles. Like many gun stores across American, Casper, Wyoming's Rocky Mountain Discount Sports sold out of firearms after the Sandy Hook shootings in Newtown, Connecticut.

- **Specialty stores** typically carry a deeper but narrower assortment of merchandise within a single category of interest. The specialized knowledge of their salesclerks allows for more attentive customer service. The Children's Place, Williams-Sonoma, and Foot Locker are well-known specialty retailers.

- **Supermarkets** are large, departmentalized, self-service retailers that specialize in food and some nonfood items. Some conventional supermarkets are being replaced by much larger *superstores*. Superstores offer one-stop shopping for food and nonfood needs, as well as services such as pharmacists, florists, salad bars, photo processing kiosks, and banking centers.

- **Drugstores** primarily provide pharmacy-related products and services, but many also carry an extensive selection of cosmetics, health and beauty aids, seasonal merchandise, greeting cards, toys, and some non-refrigerated

gross margin the amount of money the retailer makes as a percentage of sales after the cost of goods sold is subtracted

department store a store housing several departments under one roof

specialty store a retail store specializing in a given type of merchandise

supermarket a large, departmentalized, self-service retailer that specializes in food and some nonfood items

drugstore a retail store that stocks pharmacy-related products and services as its main draw

convenience foods. As other retailer types have begun to add pharmacies and direct mail prescription services have become more popular, drugstores have competed by adding more services such as 24-hour drive-through windows and low-cost health clinics staffed by nurse practitioners.

- A **convenience store** resembles a miniature supermarket but carries a much more limited line of high-turnover convenience goods. These self-service stores are typically located near residential areas and offer exactly what their name implies: convenient locations, long hours, and fast service in exchange for premium prices. In exchange for higher prices, however, customers are beginning to demand more from convenience store management, such as higher quality food and lower prices on staple items such as gasoline and milk.

- **Discount stores** compete on the basis of low prices, high turnover, and high volume. Discounters can be classified into several major categories:

  - **Full-line discount stores** such as Walmart offer consumers very limited service and carry a vast assortment of well-known, nationally branded goods such as housewares, toys, automotive parts, hardware, sporting goods, garden items, and clothing.

  - **Supercenters** extend the full-line concept to include groceries and a variety of services, such as pharmacies, dry cleaning, portrait studios, photo finishing, hair salons, optical shops, and restaurants. For supercenter operators such as Target,

convenience store a miniature supermarket, carrying only a limited line of high-turnover convenience goods

discount store a retailer that competes on the basis of low prices, high turnover, and high volume

full-line discount store a discount store that carries a vast depth and breadth of product within a single product category

supercenter a large retailer that stocks and sells a wide variety of merchandise including groceries, clothing, household goods, and other general merchandise

specialty discount store a retail store that offers a nearly complete selection of single-line merchandise and uses self-service, discount prices, high volume, and high turnover

category killer a large discount store that specializes in a single line of merchandise and becomes the dominant retailer in its category

warehouse club a large, no-frills retailer that sells bulk quantities of merchandise to customers at volume discount prices in exchange for a periodic membership fee

off-price retailer a retailer that sells at prices 25 percent or more below traditional department store prices because it pays cash for its stock and usually doesn't ask for return privileges

Ken Wolter/Shutterstock.com

Sam's Club is an American chain of membership-only retail warehouse clubs owned and operated by Walmart.

customers are drawn in by food but end up purchasing other items from the full-line discount stock.

- Single-line **specialty discount stores** such as Foot Locker offer a nearly complete selection of merchandise within a single category and use self-service, discount prices, high volume, and high turnover to their advantage. A **category killer** such as Best Buy is a specialty discount store that heavily dominates its narrow merchandise segment.

- A **warehouse club** sells a limited selection of brand name appliances, household items, and groceries. These are sold in bulk from warehouse outlets on a cash-and-carry basis to members only. Currently, the leading stores in this category are Sam's Club, Costco, and BJ's Wholesale Club.

- **Off-price retailers** such as TJ Maxx, Ross, and Marshall's sell at prices 25 percent or more below traditional department store prices because they buy inventory with cash and they don't require return privileges. These stores often sell manufacturers' overruns, irregular merchandise, and/

or overstocks that they purchase at or below cost. A **factory outlet** is an off-price retailer that is owned and operated by a single manufacturer and carries one line of merchandise—its own. Manufacturers can realize higher profit margins using factory outlets than they would by disposing of the goods through independent wholesalers and retailers. **Used goods retailers** turn customers into suppliers: pre-owned items bought back from customers are resold to different customers. Used goods retailers can be either brick-and-mortar locations (such as Goodwill stores) or electronic marketplaces (such as eBay).

- **Restaurants** provide both tangible products—food and drink—and valuable services—food preparation and presentation. Most restaurants are also specialty retailers in that they concentrate their menu offerings on a distinctive type of cuisine—for example, Olive Garden Italian restaurants and Starbucks coffeehouses.

Laura Riquelme/Shutterstock.com

Tupperware, like the companies mentioned in the Direct Retailing section, directly markets itself to potential customers by offering a chance to purchase products inside the consumer's home.

 14-3 THE RISE OF NONSTORE RETAILING

The retailing formats discussed so far entail physical stores where merchandise is displayed and to which customers must travel in order to shop. In contrast, **nonstore retailing** enables customers to shop without visiting a physical store location. Nonstore retailing adds a level of convenience for customers who wish to shop from their current locations. Due to broader changes in culture and society, nonstore retailing is currently growing faster than in-store retailing. The major forms of nonstore retailing are automatic vending, direct retailing, direct marketing, and Internet retailing (or *e-tailing*). In response to the recent successes seen by nonstore retailers, traditional brick-and-mortar retailers have begun seeking a presence in limited nonstore formats. For example, Target has begun to heighten its Internet presence by offering movies via streaming video. The new Target Ticket platform allows customers to purchase movies and popular television shows cheaply and without subscription fees, which allows Target to compete with services such as Apple's iTunes and Netflix.[8]

- **Automatic vending** entails the use of machines to offer goods for sale—for example, the soft drink, candy, or snack vending machines commonly found in public places and office buildings. Retailers are continually seeking new opportunities to sell via vending. As a result, modern vending machines today sell merchandise such as DVDs, digital cameras, perfumes, and even ice cream. A key aspect of their continuing success is the proliferation of cashless payment systems in response to consumers' diminishing preference for carrying cash.

- **Self-service technologies (SST)** comprise a form of automatic vending where services are the primary focus. Automatic teller machines, pay-at-the-pump gas stations, and movie ticket kiosks allow customers to make purchases that once required assistance from a company employee. However, as with any sort of self-service technology, automatic vending comes with failure risks due to human or technological error.

factory outlet an off-price retailer that is owned and operated by a manufacturer

used goods retailer a retailer whereby items purchased from one of the other types of retailers are resold to different customers

restaurant a retailer that provides both tangible products—food and drink—and valuable services—food preparation and presentation

nonstore retailing shopping without visiting a store

automatic vending the use of machines to offer goods for sale

self-service technologies (SST) technological interfaces that allow customers to provide themselves with products and/or services without the intervention of a service employee

Unless customers expect that they can easily recover from such errors, they may end up shopping elsewhere.

- **Direct retailing** representatives sell products door-to-door, in offices, or at in-home sales parties. Companies like Avon, Mary Kay, and The Pampered Chef have used this approach for years. Man Cave, a new home sales party developed for men, has been described as "like Mary Kay on steroids." Man Cave representatives invite male friends and family over for testosterone-fueled parties at which Man Cave products are used and Man Cave foods are eaten. Affiliates earn commissions for the sale of beer mugs, grilling tools, frozen steaks, and other Man Cave products.[9]

- **Direct marketing (DM)** includes techniques used to elicit purchases from consumers' homes, offices, and other convenient locations. Common DM techniques include telemarketing, direct mail, and mail-order catalogs. Shoppers using these methods are less bound by traditional shopping situations. Time-strapped consumers and those who live in rural or suburban areas are most likely to be DM shoppers because they value the convenience and flexibility it provides. DM occurs in several forms:

  - **Telemarketing** is a form of DM that employs outbound and inbound telephone contacts to sell directly to consumers. Telemarketing is a highly effective marketing technique; recent estimates indicate that 5,000 U.S. companies will spend over $15 billion on inbound and outbound calls by 2015.[10]

  - Alternatively, **direct mail** can be a highly efficient or highly inefficient retailing method, depending on the quality of the mailing list and the effectiveness of the mailing piece. With direct mail, marketers can precisely target their customers according to demographic,

geographic, and/or psychographic characteristics. Direct mailers are becoming more sophisticated in targeting the right customers. **Microtargeting** based on data analytics of census data, lifestyle patterns, financial information, and past purchase and credit history allows direct mailers to pick out those most likely to buy their products.[11] U.S. companies spend more than $45 billion annually on direct marketing—a larger share of advertising expenditures than any other media except television. More than $11.5 billion of that is spent on data and software solutions intended to heighten customer responsiveness.[12]

- **Shop-at-home television networks** such as HSN and QVC produce television shows that display merchandise to home viewers. Viewers can phone in their orders directly on toll-free lines and shop with their credit cards. The shop-at-home industry has quickly grown into a multi-billion-dollar business with a loyal customer following and high customer penetration.

- **Online retailing**, or **e-tailing**, enables a customer to shop over the Internet and have items delivered directly to her door. Global online shopping accounts for more than $1.3 trillion in sales today and is expected to reach $2.5 trillion by 2018.[13] Interactive shopping tools and live chats substitute for the in-store interactions with salespeople and product trials that customers traditionally use to make purchase decisions. Shoppers can look at a much wider variety of products online because physical space restrictions do not exist. While shopping, customers can take their time deciding what to buy.

In addition to retailer Web sites, consumers are increasingly using social media applications as shopping platforms. Social networking sites such as Facebook, Instagram, and Twitter enable users to immediately purchase items recommended by their social connections, a phenomenon known as *social shopping*. Companies are eager to establish direct linkages between social networking platforms and their own Web sites due to the belief that a product or service recommended by a friend will receive higher consideration from the potential customer.

RETAIL OPERATIONS MODELS

The retail formats covered so far are co-aligned with unique operating models that guide the decisions made by their managers. Each operating

---

direct retailing the selling of products by representatives who work door-to-door, office-to-office, or at home sales parties

direct marketing (DM) techniques used to get consumers to make a purchase from their home, office, or other nonretail setting

telemarketing the use of the telephone to sell directly to consumers

direct mail the delivery of advertising or marketing material to recipients of postal or electronic mail

microtargeting the use of direct marketing techniques that employ highly detailed data analytics in order to isolate potential customers with great precision

shop-at-home television network a specialized form of direct response marketing whereby television shows display merchandise, with the retail price, to home viewers

online retailing (e-tailing) a type of shopping available to consumers with personal computers and access to the Internet

Back Stock

Floor Stock

model can be summarized as a set of guiding principles. For example, off-price retailers de-emphasize customer service and product selection in favor of lower prices, which are achieved through a greater focus on lean inventory management.

Alternatively, specialty shops generally adopt a high-service approach that is supported by an agile approach to inventory. By keeping a greater amount of **floor stock** (inventory displayed for sale to customers) and **back stock** (inventory held in reserve for potential future sale in a retailer's storeroom or stockroom) on hand, a broader range of customer demands can be accommodated. This operating model also implies higher prices for customers, however, so retail managers must make sure that they deliver on the promises their firms make to customers in order to secure their loyalty. At the same time, these retail managers must control demand via promotions and other sales events in order to sell off slow moving and perishable items, thereby making more room for items that are more popular.

These sorts of tradeoffs have been partially responsible for the recent emergence of hybrid retail operating models. As an example of a hybrid strategy, the Spanish women's fashion retailer Zara employs a specialty retail format with a twist: It uses a mass merchandising inventory strategy. Zara offers high quality products and excellent customer service to draw customers into its stores but never replenishes specific inventory items that are sold. Rather, its designers and buyers are continually introducing new products in small or medium quantities. Once a product sells out, a new one replaces it, allowing for a very lean operation. This strategy not only lowers inventory costs (and thereby increases profitability) but also creates an aura of exclusivity around each piece that the retailer sells: Each skirt, blouse, and accessory is effectively a limited edition item. This strategy also

has the ancillary benefit of driving customers back to the store in order to see what new products have arrived, and thus has the potential to increase repurchases.[14]

The tradeoffs inherent to retail operating models have both spurred the recent success of online-only retailers and led to a surge in online storefront development among retailers who have traditionally operated in physical formats only. A key advantage of online retail is that no physical retail store space is needed for displaying and selling merchandise. Lower cost remote distribution centers can be used since all of the showcasing occurs on the company's Web site. By moving online, a specialty store can gain the operational benefits of a mass merchandiser. It can showcase exclusive or trendy items in an almost-free space to potential customers located around the world, and can then fulfill demand from one of several localized distribution centers in a very short time. Fulfillment times are specified by the customer (according to their willingness to pay for greater shipping and delivery speed), and even this tradeoff is becoming less of a sticking point every year. Amazon's Prime subscription program, for example, includes free two-day shipping. The company recently revealed that it is experimenting with same day delivery via unmanned drones, and is already offering same-day delivery by traditional means within several limited geographic areas.[15] Startup company Deliv positioned itself in 2015 as a cutting-edge crowdsourced courier service. Deliv provides its more than 250 national and regional U.S. retail partners (such as Macy's and Footlocker) a means of competing with Amazon by offering same-day home delivery.[16] It will be very exciting to see

> **floor stock** inventory displayed for sale to customers
>
> **back stock** inventory held in reserve for potential future sale in a retailer's storeroom or stockroom

how these advances continue to change retail strategies and operations in the years to come.

Today, most retail stores remain operationally and tactically similar to those that have been in business for hundreds of years; with one or more physical locations that the customer must visit in order to purchase a stocked product, and with strategies in place to attract customers to visit. The sorts of differences we have described among retail operating models imply that managing one type of store instead of another can involve very different experiences. But most of the decisions that retail managers make can be distilled down to six categories of activity, referred to as the retailing mix. These categories, described in the next section, are relatively universal to all forms of retailing, but are applied in different ways based on the retail format.

14-5 EXECUTING A RETAIL MARKETING STRATEGY

Retail managers develop marketing strategies based on the goals established by stakeholders and the overall strategic plans developed by company leadership. Strategic retailing goals typically focus on increasing total sales, reducing costs of goods sold, and improving financial ratios such as return on assets or equity. At the store level, more tactical retailing goals include increased store traffic, higher sales of a specific item, developing a more upscale image, and creating heightened public awareness of the retail operation and its products or services. The tactical strategies that retailers use to obtain their goals include having a sale, updating décor, and launching a new advertising campaign. The key strategic tasks that precede these tactical decisions are defining and selecting a target market and developing the retailing mix to successfully meet the needs of the chosen target market.

14-5a Defining a Target Market

The first and foremost task in developing a retail strategy is to define the target market. This process begins with market segmentation, the topic of Chapter 8. Successful retailing has always been based on knowing the customer. Sometimes retailing chains flounder when management loses sight of the customers the stores should be serving. Customers' desires and preferences change over their personal and professional

retailing mix a combination of the six Ps—product, promotion, place, price, presentation, and personnel—to sell goods and services to the ultimate consumer

lifespans, and it is important for retailers to be sensitive to these changes by migrating them to new and different products as their buying patterns evolve.

Target markets in retailing are often defined by demographics, geographic boundaries, and psychographics. For example, Blaze Pizza targets Millennial shoppers by providing a "build your own" pizza experience that mirrors the personal food design processes of Subway and Chipotle. This technique appeals to the Millennial psychographic characteristics of achievement and creativity.[17] Determining a target market is a prerequisite to creating the retailing mix. For example, Target's merchandising approach for sporting goods is to match its product assortment to the demographics of the local store and region.

14-5b Choosing the Retailing Mix

As previously noted, defining a retail operation entails combining the elements of the retailing mix to come up with a single retailing method to attract the target market. The **retailing mix** consists of six Ps: the four Ps of the marketing mix (*product*, *promotion*, *place*, and *price*) plus *presentation* and *personnel* (see Exhibit 14.2). The combination of the six Ps projects a store's (or Web site's) image and influences customers' perceptions. Using these impressions, shoppers position one store or Web site against another. Managers must make sure that the positioning is aligned with target customers' expectations.

PRODUCT The first element in the retailing mix is the product offering, also called the product assortment or merchandise mix. Developing a product offering is essentially a question of the width and depth of the product assortment. Price, store/Web site design, displays, and service are important to customers in determining where to shop, but the most critical factor is merchandise selection. This reasoning also holds true for online retailers. Amazon.com, for instance, offers enormous width in its product assortment with millions of different items, including books, music, toys, videos, tools and hardware, health and beauty aids, electronics, and software. Conversely, online specialty retailers such as Lemon and Mint and Bridge 55 focus on a single category of merchandise, hoping to attract loyal customers with a larger depth of products at lower prices and excellent customer service. Many online retailers purposely focus on single product line niches that could never attract enough foot traffic to support a traditional brick-and-mortar store. For instance, Web sites such as bugbitingplants.com and petflytrap.com sell and ship live carnivorous plants in the United States. After

EXHIBIT 14.2 THE RETAILING MIX

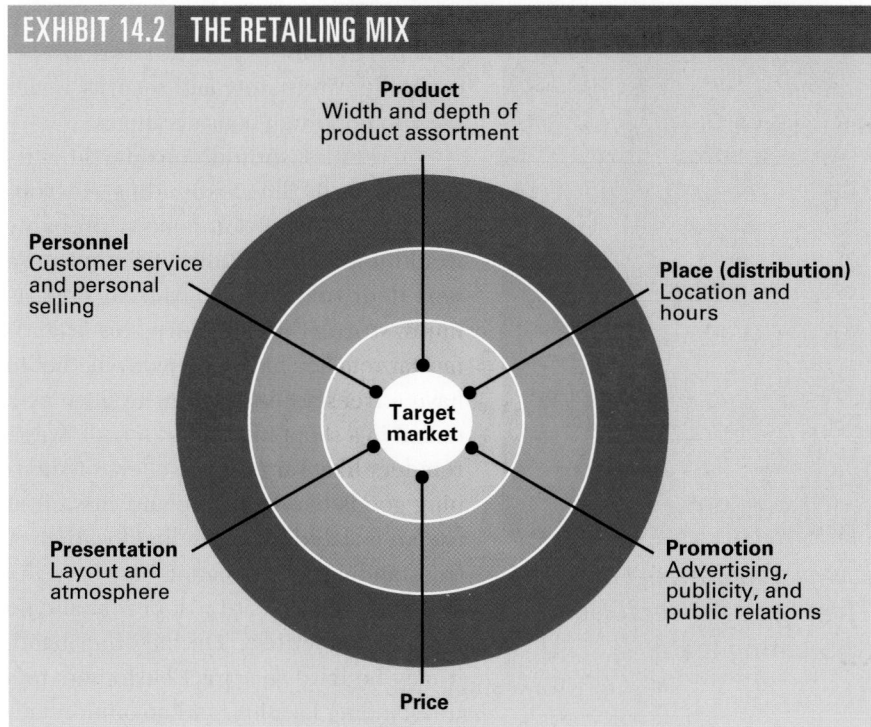

Product
Width and depth of product assortment

Place (distribution)
Location and hours

Personnel
Customer service and personal selling

Target market

Promotion
Advertising, publicity, and public relations

Presentation
Layout and atmosphere

Price

determining what products will satisfy target customers' desires, retailers must find sources of supply and evaluate the products. When the right products are found, the retail buyer negotiates a purchase contract.

PROMOTION Retail promotion strategy includes advertising, public relations and publicity, and sales promotion. The goal is to help position the store or Web site in customers' minds. Retailers design intriguing ads, stage special events, and develop promotions aimed at their target markets. Today's grand-openings are a carefully orchestrated blend of advertising, merchandising, goodwill, and glitter. All the elements of an opening—press coverage, special events, media advertising, and store displays—are carefully planned. Other promotions that are often used successfully include sales events, coupons, and discounts for certain products or customer groups. One risk associated with store promotions, however, is **brand cannibalization**: a situation whereby the promotion intended to draw in new customers simply shifts current customers from buying one brand to another brand. For example, when TGI Fridays began offering $10 appetizers to boost unit sales, sales of some main course items decreased.[18] Brand cannibalization is dangerous to the retailer for two reasons. First, the retailer incurs significant expense in executing the promotion itself. Second, the promotion creates inaccurate sales forecasts for both the promoted and cannibalized products, leading to stockouts of the promoted brand and financial losses from discounting surplus inventory of the cannibalized brand. The latter types of losses can sometimes be significantly greater than the cost of the promotion itself. Therefore, retail managers should design their promotional activities carefully, with gaining new customers being the primary objective.

Much retail advertising is focused on the local level. Local advertising by retailers usually provides specific information about their stores, such as location, merchandise, hours, prices, and special sales. In contrast, national retail advertising generally focuses on image. For example, Target uses advertisements similar to designer fashion advertisements to depict high-quality goods. Paired with the ubiquitous red target and tag line "Expect more. Pay less," Target is demonstrating that it sells products that consumers normally aspire to own at prices they can afford.

Target's advertising campaigns also take advantage of cooperative advertising, another popular retail advertising practice. Traditionally, marketers would pay retailers to feature their products in store mailers, or a marketer would develop a television campaign for the product and simply tack on several retailers' names at the end. But Target's advertising uses a more collaborative trend by integrating products such as Tide laundry detergent or Coca-Cola into the actual campaign. Another common form of cooperative advertising involves promotion of exclusive products. For example, Target hires famous trendy designers for temporary partnerships, during which they develop reasonably priced product lines available exclusively at Target stores. Recently, Target teamed up with Neiman Marcus to offer a collection of holiday luxury items. These items were sold both at Target and Neiman Marcus stores, as well as on both stores' outlet Web stores.

PLACE The retailing axiom "location, location, location" has long emphasized the importance of place to the retail mix. The physical *location* decision is

brand cannibalization the reduction of sales for one brand as the result of the introduction of a new product or promotion of a current product by another brand

The Victoria's Secret Fashion Show is a major part of the company's marketing strategy. Their "Angels" serve as key members of the company's marketing team.

important first because the retailer is making a large, semi-permanent commitment of resources that can reduce its future flexibility. Second, the physical location will almost inevitably affect the store's future growth and profitability. Many retailers work with consultants and/or city planners to determine the best sites for current sales as well as potential growth in the future.

Physical site location begins by choosing a community. Important factors to consider are the area's economic growth potential, the amount of competition, and geography. For instance, retailers like TJ Maxx and Walmart often build stores in new communities that are still under development. Fast-food restaurants tend to place a priority on locations with other fast-food restaurants because being located in clusters helps to draw customers for each restaurant. Even after careful research, however, the perfect location can be elusive in the face of changing markets. Mobile food trucks circumvent this problem by being able to relocate at will. By moving from spot to spot over the course of a day and parking outside events and heavily trafficked areas, mobile food trucks can maximize their exposure and adapt to changing markets.

After identifying a geographic region or community, retailers must choose a specific site. In addition to growth potential, the important factors to consider are neighborhood socioeconomic characteristics, traffic flows, land costs, zoning regulations, and public

destination store a store that consumers purposely plan to visit prior to shopping

transportation. A particular site's visibility, parking, entrance and exit locations, accessibility, and safety and security issues are also important considerations.

A retailer should consider how its store fits into the surrounding environment. Retail decision makers probably would not locate a Dollar General store next door to a Neiman Marcus department store. Furthermore, brick-and-mortar retailers have to decide whether to have a freestanding unit or to become a tenant in a shopping center or mall. Large retailers like Target and sellers of shopping goods like furniture and cars often use an isolated, freestanding location. A freestanding store location may have the advantages of low site cost or rent and no nearby competitors. On the other hand, it may be hard to attract customers to a freestanding location, and no other retailers are around to share costs. To be successful, stores in isolated locations must become "destination stores." A **destination store** is a store consumers seek out and purposely plan to visit. Web sites can also be destinations for shoppers. Amazon is a destination Web site for a wide variety of products, and Google is a destination Web site for search information.

Freestanding units are increasing in popularity as brick-and-mortar retailers strive to make their stores more convenient to access, more enticing to shop, and more profitable. Freestanding sites now account for more than half of all retail store construction starts in the United States as more and more retailers are deciding not to locate in pedestrian malls. Perhaps the greatest reason for developing a freestanding site is greater visibility. Retailers often feel they get lost in huge shopping centers and malls, but freestanding units can help stores develop an identity with shoppers. Also, an aggressive expansion plan may not allow time to wait for shopping centers to be built. Drugstore chains like Walgreens have been purposefully relocating their existing shopping center stores to freestanding sites, especially street corner sites for drive-through accessibility.

Shopping centers first appeared in the 1950s when the U.S. population started migrating to the suburbs. The first shopping centers were *strip centers*, typically located along busy streets. They usually included a supermarket, a variety store, and perhaps a few specialty stores. Then *community shopping centers* emerged, with one or two small department stores, more specialty stores, a couple of restaurants, and several apparel stores. These community shopping centers provided off-street parking and a broader variety of merchandise. *Regional malls* offering a much wider variety of merchandise started appearing in the mid-1970s. Regional malls are either entirely enclosed or roofed to allow shopping in any weather. Most are landscaped with trees, fountains, sculptures, and the like to enhance the shopping environment. They have acres of free parking. The *anchor stores* or *generator stores* (often major department stores) are usually located at opposite ends of the mall to create heavy foot traffic.

According to shopping center developers, *lifestyle centers* are emerging as the newest generation of shopping centers. Lifestyle centers typically combine outdoor shopping areas composed of upscale retailers and restaurants, with plazas, fountains, and pedestrian streets. They appeal to retail developers looking for an alternative to the traditional shopping mall, a concept rapidly losing favor among shoppers. Though shopping malls bring multiple retail locations together, location is often not the most important motivator for a customer to choose a specific store. Instead, most shoppers look for stores that guarantee product availability, more service employees, and time saving opportunities.

Many smaller specialty lines are opening shops inside larger stores to expand their retail opportunities without risking investment in a separate store. Toys"R"Us worked with Macy's to open stores-within-a-store at numerous Macy's locations. The 1,500-square-foot toy sections offered dolls, puzzles, and other potential stocking stuffers.[19] The Toys"R"Us modules reflect a popular trend of pop-up shops—tiny, temporary stores that stay in one location for only a few months. Pop-up shops help retailers reach a wide market while avoiding high rent at retail locations. They have become the marketing tool du jour for large companies.

PRICE Another important element in the retailing mix is price. Retailing's ultimate goal is to sell products to consumers, and the right price is critical to ensure sales. Because retail prices are usually based on the cost of the merchandise, an essential part of pricing is efficient and timely buying. Another pricing strategy is "value-based pricing," which focuses on the value of the product to the customer more than the cost of the product to the supplier. Price is also a key element in a retail store's positioning strategy. Higher prices often indicate a level of quality and help reinforce the prestigious image of retailers, as they do for Lord & Taylor and Neiman

Marcus. On the other hand, discounters and off-price retailers, such as Target and TJ Maxx, offer a good value for the money.

PRESENTATION The presentation of a retail store helps determine the store's image and positions the retail store in consumers' minds. For instance, a retailer that wants to position itself as an upscale store would use a lavish or sophisticated presentation. The main element of a store's presentation is its **atmosphere**, the overall impression conveyed by a store's physical layout, décor, and surroundings. The atmosphere might create a relaxed or busy feeling, a sense of luxury or efficiency, a friendly or cold attitude, a sense of organization or clutter, or a fun or serious mood. Urban Outfitters stores, targeted to Generation Y consumers, use raw concrete, original brick, rusted steel, and unfinished wood to convey an urban feel. These are the most influential factors in creating a store's atmosphere:

- *Employee type and density:* Employee type refers to an employee's general characteristics—for instance, neat, friendly, knowledgeable, or service oriented. Density is the number of employees per thousand square feet of selling space. Whereas low employee density creates a do-it-yourself, casual atmosphere, high employee density denotes readiness to serve the customer's every whim.

- *Merchandise type and density:* A prestigious retailer like Nordstrom or Neiman Marcus carries the best brand names and displays them in a neat, uncluttered arrangement. Discounters and off-price retailers often carry seconds or out-of-season goods crowded into small spaces and hung on long racks by category—tops, pants, skirts, and so on—creating the impression that "We've got so much stuff, we're practically giving it away."

- *Fixture type and density:* Fixtures can be elegant (rich woods) or trendy (chrome and smoked glass); they can even consist of old, beat-up tables, as in an antiques store. The fixtures should be consistent with the general atmosphere the store is trying to create.

- *Sound:* Sound can be pleasant or unpleasant for a customer. Music can entice some customers to stay in the store longer and buy more or to eat quickly and leave a table for others. It can also control the pace of the store traffic, create an image, and attract or direct the shopper's attention.

- *Odors:* Smell can either stimulate or

atmosphere the overall impression conveyed by a store's physical layout, décor, and surroundings

detract from sales. Research suggests that people evaluate merchandise more positively, spend more time shopping, and are generally in a better mood when an agreeable odor is present. Retailers use fragrances as an extension of their retail strategy.

- *Visual factors:* Colors can create a mood or focus attention and therefore are an important factor in atmosphere. Red, yellow, and orange are considered warm colors and are used when a feeling of warmth and closeness is desired. Cool colors like blue, green, and violet are used to open up closed-in places and create an air of elegance and cleanliness. Many retailers have found that natural lighting, either from windows or skylights, can lead to increased sales. Outdoor lighting can also affect a customer's choice of retailer.

The **layout** of retail stores is also a key factor in their success. The goal is to use all of the store's space effectively, including aisles, fixtures, merchandise displays, and non-selling areas. In addition to making shopping easy and convenient for the customer, an effective layout has a powerful influence on traffic patterns and purchasing behavior. Layout also includes where products are placed in the store. Many technologically advanced retailers are using a technique called *market-basket analysis* to sift through the data collected by their point-of-purchase scanning equipment. The analysis looks for products that are commonly purchased together to help retailers find ideal locations for each product. Walmart uses market-basket analysis to determine where in the store to stock products for customer convenience. Kleenex tissues, for example, are in the paper-goods aisle and also beside the cold medicines.

Retailers can better acquire and use assets when they customize store layouts and merchandise mixes to the tastes of local consumer bases. For example, O'Reilly Auto Parts designs each of its retail outlets with the wants and needs of local auto drivers in mind, creating a neighborhood-specific strategy for each location. By customizing layout and product mix to the vehicles owned and operated in a particular area, the company can simultaneously provide greater levels of availability and reduce inventory, creating savings that the company passes along to customers.[20]

PERSONNEL People are a unique aspect of retailing. Most retail sales involve a customer–salesperson relationship, if only briefly. Sales personnel provide their customers with the amount of service prescribed by the retail strategy of the store.

layout the internal design and configuration of a store's fixtures and products

Retail salespeople serve another important selling function: They persuade shoppers to buy. They must therefore be able to persuade customers that what they are selling is what the customer needs. Salespeople are trained in two common selling techniques: trading up and suggestion selling. *Trading* up means persuading customers to buy a higher-priced item than they originally intended to purchase. To avoid selling customers something they do not need or want, however, salespeople should take care when practicing trading-up techniques. *Suggestion selling*, a common practice among most retailers, seeks to broaden customers' original purchases with related items. For example, if you buy a new printer at Office Depot, the sales representative will ask if you would like to purchase paper, a USB cable, and/or extra ink cartridges. Suggestion selling by sales or service associates should always help shoppers recognize true needs rather than sell them unwanted merchandise.

Providing great customer service is one of the most challenging elements in the retail mix because customer expectations for service vary greatly. What customers expect in a department store is very different from what they expect in a discount store. Customer expectations also change. Ten years ago, shoppers wanted personal, one-on-one attention. Today, many customers are happy to help themselves as long as they can easily find what they need.

 14-6 RETAILING DECISIONS FOR SERVICES

The fastest-growing part of our economy is the service sector. Although distribution in the service sector is difficult to visualize, the same skills, techniques, and strategies used to manage inventory can also be used to manage service inventory, such as hospital beds, bank accounts, or airline seats. The quality of the planning and execution of distribution can have a major impact on costs and customer satisfaction.

Because service industries are so customer oriented, service quality is a priority. To manage customer relationships, many service providers, such as insurance carriers, physicians, hair salons, and financial services, use technology to schedule appointments, manage accounts, and disburse information. Service distribution focuses on four main areas:

- *Minimizing wait times:* Minimizing the amount of time customers wait in line is a key factor in maintaining the quality of service.

Quality of service is directly tied to how long people have to wait in line.

Andrey_Popov/Shutterstock.com

- *Managing service capacity:* If service firms don't have the capacity to meet demand, they must either turn down some prospective customers, let service levels slip, or expand capacity.

- *Improving service delivery:* Service firms are now experimenting with different distribution channels for their services. Choosing the right distribution channel can increase the times that services are available or add to customer convenience.

- *Establishing channel-wide network coherence:* Because services are to some degree intangible, service firms also find it necessary to standardize their service quality across different geographic regions to maintain their brand image.

14-7 ADDRESSING RETAIL PRODUCT/ SERVICE FAILURES

In spite of retailers' best intentions and efforts to satisfy each and every customer, all retailers inevitably disappoint a subset of their customers. In some cases, customer disappointment occurs by design. No retailer can be everything to every customer, and by making strategic decisions related to targeting, segmentation, and the retailing mix, retailers implicitly decide which customers will be delighted and which will probably leave the store unsatisfied. In other cases, service failures are unintentional. A product may be located where customers cannot easily find it (or it may remain in the stockroom, entirely out of customer view), or an employee may provide mistaken information about a product's features or benefits. Customers are generally indifferent to the reasons for retailer errors, and their

reactions to mistakes such as product stockouts and unexpectedly poor quality products can range widely. Some may simply leave the store, while others will respond with anger or even revenge behaviors intended to prevent other customers from visiting the store.[21]

The best retailers have plans in place not only to recover from inevitable lapses in service but perhaps even to benefit from them. For these top-performing stores, service recovery is handled proactively as part of an overarching plan to maximize the customer experience. Actions that might be taken include:

- Notifying customers in advance of stockouts and explaining the reasons why certain products are not available

- Implementing liberal return policies designed to ensure that the customer can bring back any item for any reason (if the product fails to work as planned, or even if the customer simply doesn't like it)

- Issuing product recalls in conjunction with promotional offers that provide future incentives to repurchase

In short, the best retailers treat customer disappointments as opportunities to interact with and improve relations with their customers. Evidence indicates that successful handling of such failures can sometimes yield even higher levels of customer loyalty than if the failure had never occurred at all.

14-8 RETAILER AND RETAIL CUSTOMER TRENDS AND ADVANCEMENTS

Though retailing has been around for thousands of years, it continues to change every day. Retailers are constantly innovating. They are always looking for new products and services (or ways to offer them) that will attract new customers or inspire current ones to buy in greater quantities or more frequently. Many of the most interesting and effective retail innovations that have recently taken hold are related to the use of purchase and shopping data to better understand customer wants and needs. Finding new and better ways to entice customers into a store—and then to spend more money once there—is another hotbed of innovation. This chapter concludes with an examination into emerging trends and recent advancements in retailing.

It is important to recognize that, fundamentally, retailers decide what to sell on the basis of what their target market wants to buy. They base these decisions on market research, past sales, fashion trends, customer requests, and other sources. Recently, the need for more and better information has led many retailers to use **big data analytics**, a process whereby retailers use complex mathematical models to make better product mix decisions. Dillard's, Target, and Walmart use big data analytics to determine which products to stock and at what prices, how to manage markdowns, and how to advertise to draw target customers. The data these and other companies collect at the point of sale and throughout their stores enable retailers and suppliers alike to gain better customer insights. For example, instead of simply unloading products into the distribution channel and leaving marketing, sales and relationship building to local dealers, auto manufacturers use Web sites to keep in touch with customers and prospects. They inquire about lifestyles, hobbies, and vehicle needs in an effort to develop long-lasting relationships in the hopes that these consumers will reward them with brand loyalty in the future.

Retailers are increasingly using **beacons**—devices that send out connecting signals to customers' smartphones and tablets. These devices recognize when a customer is in or near the store and indicate to an automated system that the customer is ripe to receive a marketing message via e-mail or text. Beacons can also notify sales associates to offer (or not offer) a coupon at the point of sale. Some retailers are using an app called Swarm to map customer foot traffic data, which they use to make better decisions about product placement within the floor grid. Carefully

Big retailers like Target use big data analytics to determine which products to stock and at what price.

Sergey Yechikov/Shutterstock.com

designed beacons can even have an aesthetic appeal. At some retailers, cameras and beacons are built into mannequins located inside the store and in window displays. These beacons not only act as data collection devices, but also as primary displays for the clothing and jewelry that appeal to customers' eyes. [22]

14-8a Shopper Marketing and Analytics

Shopper marketing is an emerging retailing trend that employs market data to best serve customers as they prepare to make a purchase. Shopper marketing focuses first on understanding how a brand's target consumers behave as shoppers in different channels and formats, and then using this information in business-based strategies and initiatives that are carefully designed to deliver balanced benefits to all stakeholders— brands, channel members, and customers. It may sound simple, but it is anything but. Whereas brand manufacturers used to advertise widely and tried to ensure that their products were available wherever consumers shopped, now they are placing far more emphasis on partnering with specific retailers or Web sites. Brand manufacturers work with retailers on everything from in-store initiatives to customized retailer-specific products. Shopper marketing brings brand managers and account managers together to connect with consumers along the entire path-to-purchase,

big data analytics the process of discovering patterns in large data sets for the purposes of extracting knowledge and understanding human behavior

beacon a device that sends out connecting signals to customers' smartphones and tablets in order to bring them into a retail store or improve their shopping experience

shopper marketing understanding how one's target consumers behave as shoppers, in different channels and formats, and leveraging this intelligence to generate sales or other positive outcomes whether it be at home, on the go via mobile marketing, or in the store. Both manufacturers and retailers now think about consumers specifically while they are in shopping mode. They use **shopper analytics** to dig deeply into customers' shopping attitudes, perceptions, emotions, and behaviors—and are thereby able to learn how the shopping experience shapes these differences. More and more companies are conducting or participating in large-scale data analytics projects to better understand how shoppers think when they shop at a store or on a Web site and what factors influence their thought processes.

Shopper marketing is becoming increasingly popular as businesses see the implications of this new method of customer research. One implication is the strategic alignment of customer segments. Brands' core target consumers are compared to retailers' most loyal shoppers in an effort to find intersecting areas where brands and retailers can pool their resources. The ideal outcome is a more focused marketing effort and a three-way win for brands, channel members, *and* customers.

Shopper marketing also has significant implications for retailers' supply chains. As in-store initiatives become more unique and short-term and products become more customized, supply chains must react more quickly to customer demand changes. Thus, shopper marketing has increased the need for sophisticated analytics and metrics. As with many modern business efforts, shopper marketing forces managers to coordinate better, measure more, think more creatively, and move faster.

14-8b Future Developments in Retail Management

A retailing trend with great growth potential is the leveraging of technology to increase touchpoints with customers and thereby generate greater profitability. The use of mobile devices and social media while browsing, comparison shopping, and actually making a purchase is becoming extremely pervasive, leading retailers to rethink how they should appeal to shoppers in the decision-making mode. Recall that customers who "showroom" visit a physical retail store to examine product features or quality firsthand, but then eventually make the purchase online. This practice has motivated a showrooming response from retailers themselves, who reduce the amount of stock kept on hand, rent or lease smaller spaces, and ramp up their fulfillment capabilities at distribution centers. Showrooming and data analytics have even led to the development of virtual reality apps that enable customers to see themselves wearing articles of desired clothing without physically putting them on! These

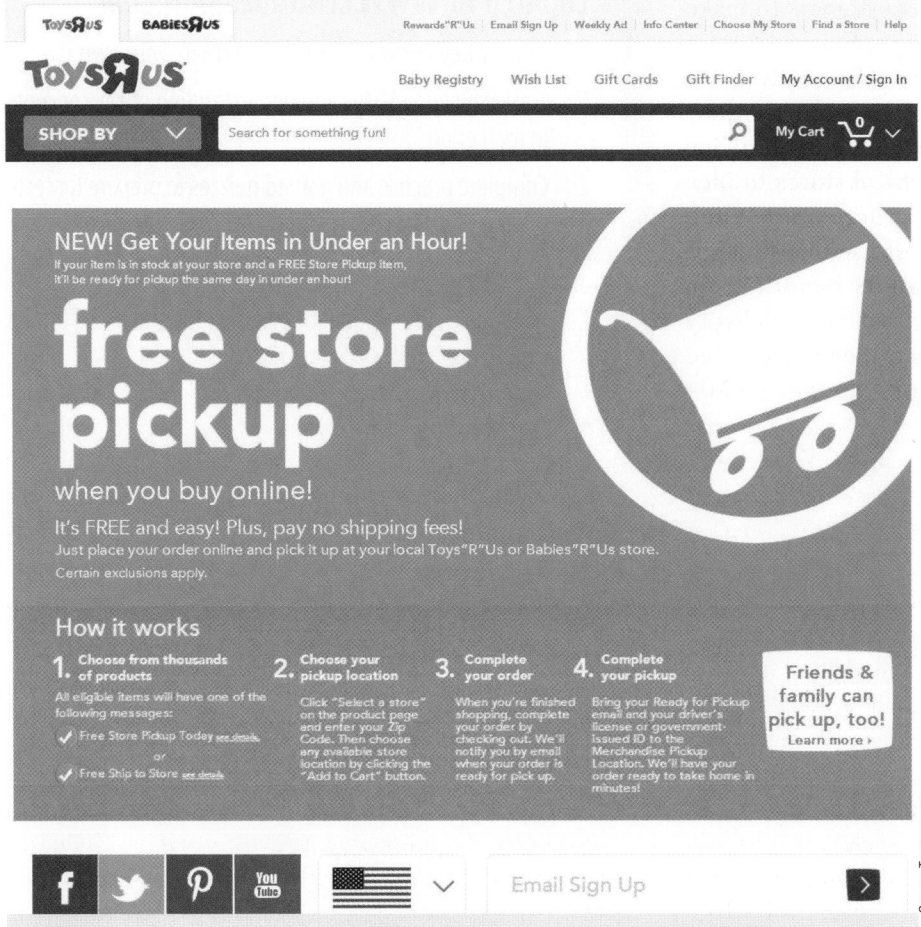

Source: Toysrus.com

National toy store chain Toys'R'Us offers a click-and-collect service whereby customers can make purchases online and then pick their items up in-store.

shopper analytics searching for and discovering meaningful patterns in shopper data for the purpose of fine-tuning, developing, or changing market offerings approaches have led some retailers to pursue a strategy of **retail channel omnification** (recall Chapter 13's discussion of omnichannel distribution operations). Retailers like Nordstrom used to treat their physical stores as entirely different businesses from their online stores, with each channel having a unique distribution system and a dedicated inventory. Now, retailers are combining these ventures into a single system that is responsible for delivering on customer demand regardless of whether it originated in a physical store or in cyberspace.[23] This single system avoids redundancies in inventory and transportation, saving costs and enabling retailers to offer competitive prices across their various outlets. Customers of Nordstrom, Nordstrom Rack, Nordstrom.com, hautelook.com, and nordstromrack.com can seamlessly transition between each of these channels when shopping, returning purchased goods or scheduling services such as alterations.

However, not all retailers are embracing omnification as the way of the future. The alternative strategy, **click-and-collect**, also enables customers to make their purchases online. Rather than waiting for orders to arrive at their homes, customers drive to physical stores to pick their orders up.[24] When retailers use this strategy, customers benefit from greater speed of delivery (in fact, they become the delivery vehicle), while retailers themselves benefit from the fact that customers must enter their stores in order to claim their purchases. Once inside, customers can be marketed to, increasing the likelihood that they will purchase add-on items or otherwise engage in impulse buying. It remains to be seen whether one or both of these strategies will stand the test of time, but it is certain that retailers are preparing for the inevitability of the Internet as an important shopping and purchasing medium for the foreseeable future.

retail channel omnification the reduction of multiple retail channel systems into a single, unified system for the purpose of creating efficiencies or saving costs

click-and-collect the practice of buying something online and then traveling to a physical store location to take delivery of the merchandise

STUDY TOOLS 14

LOCATED AT BACK OF THE TEXTBOOK

- ☐ Rip out Chapter Review Card

LOCATED AT WWW.CENGAGEBRAIN.COM

- ☐ Review Key Terms Flashcards and create your own
- ☐ Track your knowledge and understanding of key concepts in marketing
- ☐ Complete practice and graded quizzes to prepare for tests
- ☐ Complete interactive content within the MKTG Online experience
- ☐ View the chapter highlight boxes within the MKTG Online experience

MKTG ONLINE

STUDY YOUR WAY WITH STUDYBITS!

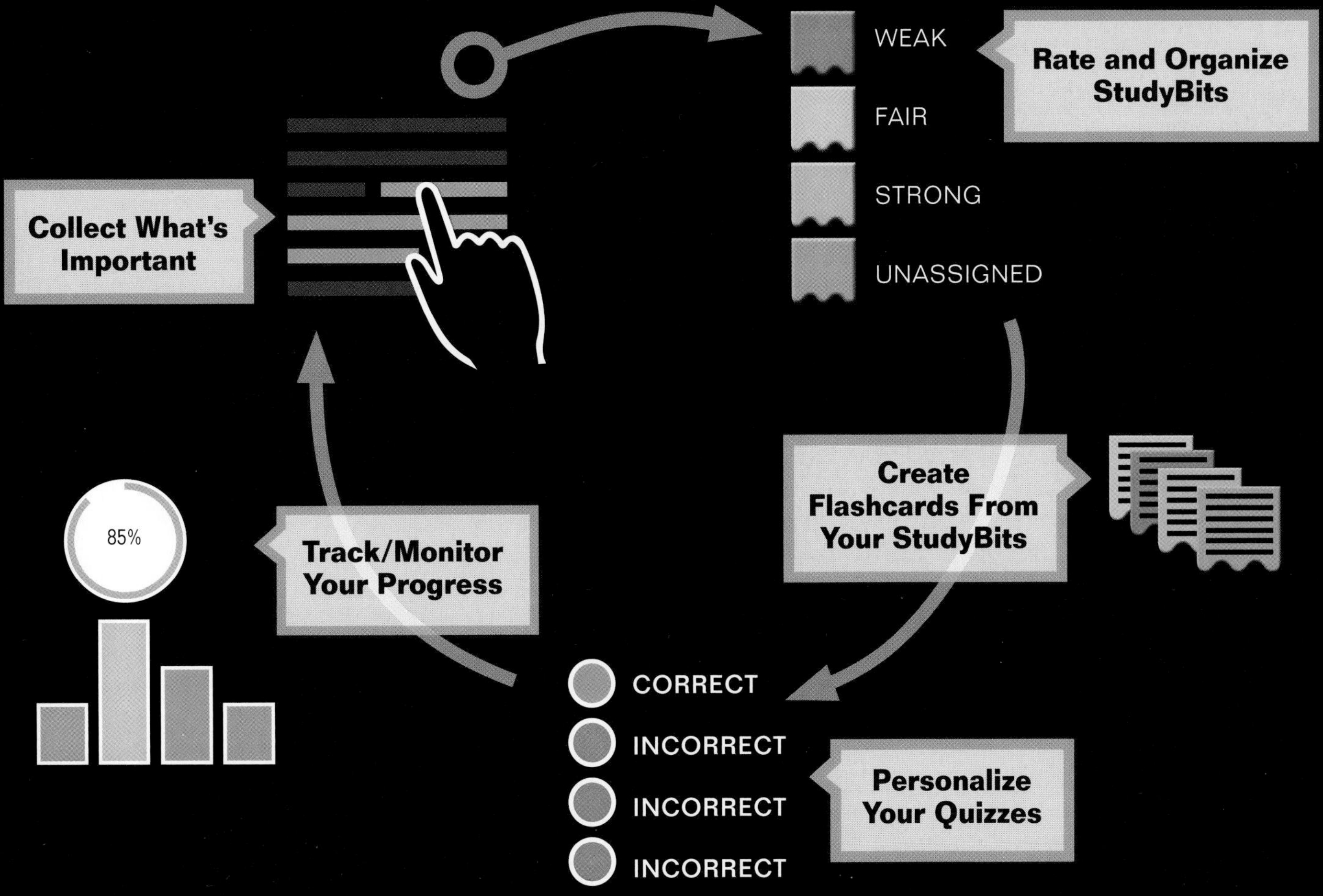

WEAK
FAIR
STRONG
UNASSIGNED

Rate and Organize StudyBits

Collect What's Important

Create Flashcards From Your StudyBits

85%

Track/Monitor Your Progress

CORRECT
INCORRECT
INCORRECT
INCORRECT

Personalize Your Quizzes

4LTR PRESS

Access MKTG ONLINE at www.cengagebrain.com

15 Marketing Communications

LEARNING OUTCOMES

After studying this chapter, you will be able to...

15-1 Discuss the role of promotion in the marketing mix

15-2 Describe the communication process

15-3 Explain the goals and tasks of promotion

15-4 Discuss the elements of the promotional mix

15-5 Discuss the AIDA concept and its relationship to the promotional mix

15-6 Discuss the concept of integrated marketing communications

15-7 Describe the factors that affect the promotional mix

After you finish this chapter go to **PAGE 279** for **STUDY TOOLS.**

iStockphoto.com/Uschools

15-1 THE ROLE OF PROMOTION IN THE MARKETING MIX

Few goods or services, no matter how well developed, priced, or distributed, can survive in the marketplace without effective **promotion**—communication by marketers that informs, persuades, and reminds potential buyers of a product in order to influence an opinion or elicit a response.

promotion communication by marketers that informs, persuades, and reminds potential buyers of a product in order to influence an opinion or elicit a response

promotional strategy a plan for the optimal use of the elements of promotion: advertising, public relations, personal selling, sales promotion, and social media

competitive advantage one or more unique aspects of an organization that cause target consumers to patronize that firm rather than competitors

Promotional strategy is a plan for the optimal use of the elements of promotion: advertising, public relations, personal selling, sales promotion, and social media. Promotion is a vital part of the marketing mix, informing consumers of a product's benefits and thereby positioning the product in the marketplace. As Exhibit 15.1 shows, the marketing manager determines the goals of the company's promotional strategy in light of the firm's overall goals for the marketing mix—product, place (distribution), promotion, and price. Using these overall goals, marketers combine the elements of the promotional strategy (the promotional mix) into a coordinated plan. The promotion plan then becomes an integral part of the marketing strategy for reaching the target market.

The main function of a marketer's promotional strategy is to convince target customers that the goods and services offered provide a competitive advantage over the competition. A **competitive advantage** is the set of unique features of a company and its products that are perceived by the target market as significant

and superior to those of the competition. Such features can include high product quality, rapid delivery, low prices, excellent service, or a feature not offered by the competition. Promotional strategies have changed a great deal over the years as many targeted customer segments have become more difficult to reach. Informative

| EXHIBIT 15.1 | ROLE OF PROMOTION IN THE MARKETING MIX |

Overall marketing objectives

Marketing mix
- Product
- Place (distribution)
- Promotion
- Price

Target market

Promotional mix
- Advertising
- Public relations
- Sales promotion
- Personal selling
- Social media

Promotion plan

television advertisements are no longer enough, forcing marketers to think more creatively. Most modern campaigns utilize a variety of newer tactics—such as digital paid media, social media, and influencer marketing—in addition to more traditional media like television and print. Dodge, for example, chose fictitious *Anchorman* character Ron Burgundy (played by Will Ferrell) as its pitchman for the Durango SUV. The promotional strategy, which involved more than 80 Web and television ads, drove a 59 percent sales boost in the first month and an 80 percent increase in Web traffic for Dodge. Lower-level Web activities such as selecting automobile options and searching for a dealer rose more than 100 percent. Dodge's YouTube video views topped 15 million within two months, prompting guest appearances on several CNN programs and dozens of local newscasts in selected states. This campaign led some to feel that the Ron Burgundy character was overexposed, but the strategy proved extremely successful for Dodge.[1]

 15-2 **MARKETING COMMUNICATION**

Promotional strategy is closely related to the process of communication. As humans, we assign meaning to feelings, ideas, facts, attitudes, and emotions.

Communication is the process by which meanings are exchanged or shared through a common set of symbols. When a company develops a new product, changes an old one, or simply tries to increase sales of an existing good or service, it must communicate its selling message to potential customers. Marketers communicate information about the firm and its products to the target market and various publics through their promotional programs.

15-2a Interpersonal Communication

Communication can be divided into two major categories: interpersonal communication and mass communication. **Interpersonal communication** is direct, face-to-face communication between two or more people. When communicating face-to-face, people see the other person's reaction and can respond almost immediately. Salespeople for French cosmetics store chain Sephora are trained on the company's most popular products, enabling them to assist customers and answer questions directly. A salesperson speaking directly with a customer is an example of an interpersonal marketing communication.

15-2b Mass Communication

Mass communication involves communicating a concept or message to large audiences. A great number of marketing communications are directed to consumers as a whole, usually through a mass medium such as television or newspapers. When a company advertises, it generally does not personally know the people with whom it is trying to communicate. Furthermore, the company often cannot respond immediately to consumers' reactions to its messages (unless they are using social media or other Internet-based marketing tools). Any clutter from competitors' messages or other distractions in the environment can reduce the effectiveness of the mass-communication effort. Continuing the previous example, Sephora uses many different mass media vehicles (including magazines, the Internet, and television) to reach its target audience.

Salespeople for Sephora are trained on the company's most popular products, this enables them to be more helpful to customers.

Radu Bercan/Shutterstock.com

15-2c The Communication Process

Marketers are both senders and receivers of messages. As *senders*, marketers attempt to inform, persuade, and remind the target market to take actions compatible with the need to promote the purchase of goods and services. As *receivers*, marketers listen to the target market in order to develop the appropriate messages, adapt existing messages, and spot new communication opportunities. In this way, most marketing communication is a two-way, rather than one-way, process. The two-way nature of the communication process is shown in Exhibit 15.2.

THE SENDER AND ENCODING The **sender** is the originator of the message in the communication process. In an interpersonal conversation, the sender may be a parent, a friend, or a salesperson. For an advertisement, press release, or social media campaign, the sender is the company or organization itself. It can sometimes be difficult to tell who the sender of a promotional message is, especially in the case of bold, avant-garde advertisements. Sometimes, senders intentionally cover up their identities in order to build buzz around an advertisement. For example, a video titled "Elevator Murder

communication the process by which we exchange or share meaning through a common set of symbols

interpersonal communication direct, face-to-face communication between two or more people

mass communication the communication of a concept or message to large audiences

sender the originator of the message in the communication process

EXHIBIT 15.2 COMMUNICATION PROCESS

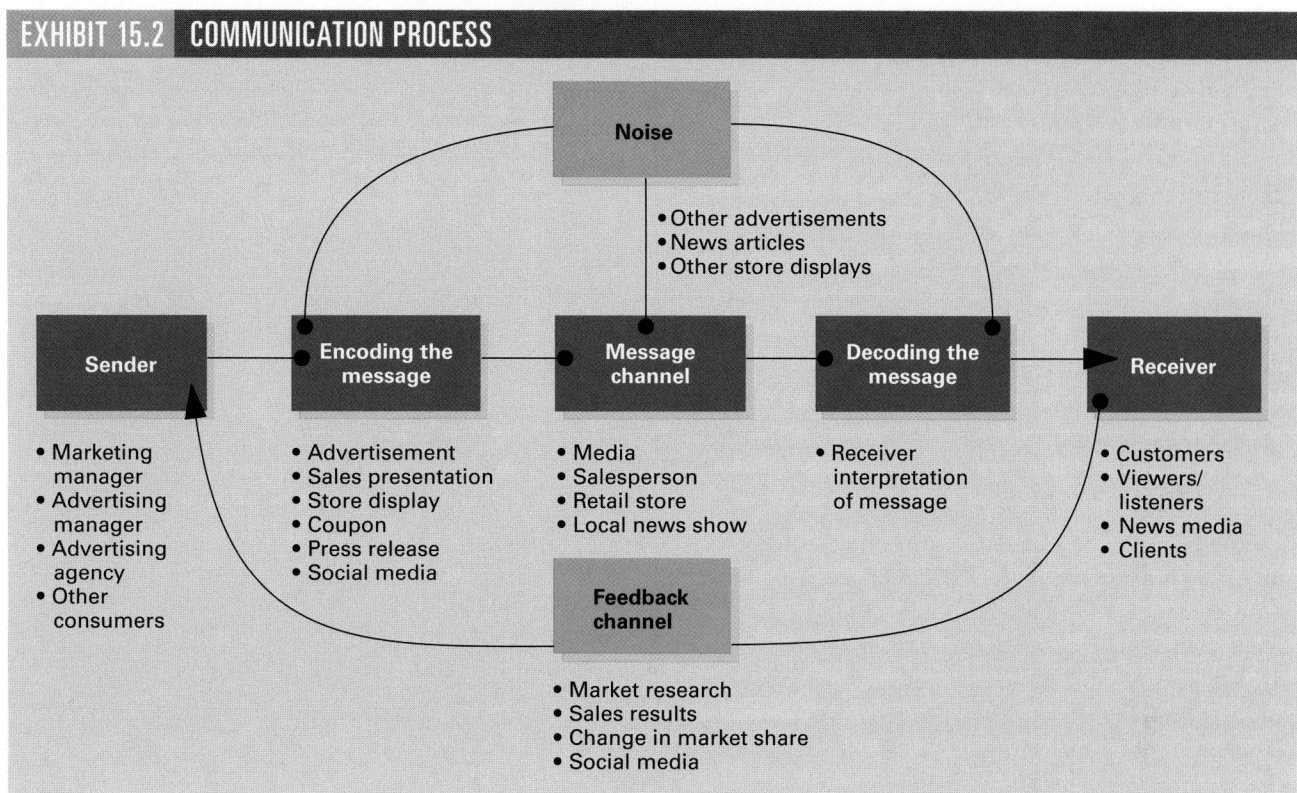

Experiment" recently went vital after mysteriously being uploaded to YouTube. In the video, the reactions of unsuspecting bystanders are secretly filmed as they witness a staged strangulation in a public New York City elevator. After the video went viral, it was revealed to be an advertisement for the Colin Farrell film *Dead Man Down*. The film's grim themes, extreme violence, and gritty settings were incorporated into the elevator prank video, which even used one of the film's plot points—murder in an elevator.

Encoding is the conversion of the sender's ideas and thoughts into a message, usually in the form of words or signs. A basic principle of encoding is that what the source says is not what matters, but what the receiver hears. In the case of "Elevator Murder Experiment," the video encoded sentiments such as "you won't know what to expect" and "difficult ethical choices will need to be made"—provocative selling points for a gruesome action thriller.[2] One way of conveying a message the receiver will hear properly is to use concrete words and pictures.

MESSAGE TRANSMISSION Transmission of a message requires a **channel**—a voice, radio, newspaper, computer, smartphone, or other communication medium. A facial expression or gesture can also serve as a channel. The *Dead Man Down's* marketing team used

social media as the primary channel on which it distributed the advertisement. After marketers posted the video to YouTube, individuals fascinated by the social experiment ran with it. They shared the video with their friends in person, posted it to Facebook and Twitter, and shared it through several other unorthodox channels. Eventually, local and national media outlets published print articles and ran television segments about the video, creating new channels for the campaign as they did so.[3] The response to these viral activities clearly created a lot of free publicity.

Reception occurs when the message is detected by the receiver and enters his or her frame of reference. In a two-way conversation such as a sales pitch given by a sales representative to a potential client, reception is normally high. Similarly, when the message is a recommendation from a friend, the reception is high as well. By contrast, the desired receivers may or may not detect the message when it is mass communicated because most media are cluttered by **noise**—anything that interferes

encoding the conversion of a sender's ideas and thoughts into a message, usually in the form of words or signs

channel a medium of communication—such as a voice, radio, or newspaper—for transmitting a message

noise anything that interferes with, distorts, or slows down the transmission of information

with, distorts, or slows down the transmission of information. In some media overcrowded with advertisers, such as newspapers and television, the noise level is high and the reception level is low.

THE RECEIVER AND DECODING Marketers communicate their message through a channel to customers, or **receivers**, who will decode the message. It is important to note that there can be multiple receivers as consumers share their experiences and their recommendations online through social networks and other types of social media, as happened when the "Elevator Murder Experiment" video went viral. Online conversations are becoming an increasingly influential way to promote products and services. Indeed, this new empowerment of the receiver has transformed marketing and advertising. Receivers can easily share new information with their friends and followers on social media, and those new receivers can then share that information as well. This leads to a more diverse interrelationship between senders and receivers of social media messages. **Decoding** is the interpretation of the language and symbols sent by the source through a channel. Common understanding between two communicators, or a common frame of reference, is required for effective communication. Therefore, marketing managers must ensure a proper match between the message to be conveyed and the target market's attitudes and ideas.

Even though a message has been received, it may not necessarily be properly decoded because of selective exposure, distortion, and retention. When people receive a message, they tend to manipulate it to reflect their own biases, needs, experiences, and knowledge. Therefore, differences in age, social class, education, culture, and ethnicity can lead to miscommunication. Further, because people do not always listen or read carefully, they can easily misinterpret what is said or written. In fact, researchers have found that consumers misunderstand a large proportion of both printed and televised communications. YouTubers who watched the "Elevator Murder Experiment" and simply clicked away without absorbing that it was an advertisement for *Dead Man Down* received the message but could not decode it because they did not have adequate information. Bright colors and bold graphics have been shown to increase consumers' comprehension of marketing communication. Even these techniques are not foolproof, however.

receiver the person who decodes a message

decoding interpretation of the language and symbols sent by the source through a channel

feedback the receiver's response to a message

Marketers targeting consumers in foreign countries must also worry about the translation and possible miscommunication of their promotional messages by other cultures. Global marketers must decide whether to standardize or customize the message for each global market in which they sell.

FEEDBACK In interpersonal communication, the receiver's response to a message is direct **feedback** to the source. Feedback may be verbal, as in saying "I agree," or nonverbal, as in nodding, smiling, frowning, or gesturing. Feedback can also occur digitally, as in a Facebook like. Mass communicators are often cut off from direct feedback, so they must rely on market research, social media, or analysis of viewer responses for indirect feedback. They might use such measurements as the percentage of television viewers who recognized, recalled, or stated that they were exposed to the company's messages. Indirect feedback enables mass communicators to decide whether to continue, modify, or drop a message.

Some people who observed the video (receivers) found the "Elevator Murder Experiment" advertising stunt tasteless and macabre, while others praised it as an ingenious use of social media. YouTube users provided direct feedback by commenting on the video's page and clicking either the "Like" or "Dislike" button (the video garnered nearly 10,000 likes, versus approximately 700 dislikes). Regardless of receivers' responses and feedback, the video was effective, garnering more than 2.6 million views in just three days.[4]

With the increase in online advertising, marketers are able to get more feedback than before the Internet became such a driving social force. Using Web analytics, marketers can see how long customers stay on a Web site and which pages they view. Moreover, social media enable companies such as Dell and Comcast to provide instant feedback by responding to consumers' posts on Facebook and to complaints posted on Twitter.

The Internet and social media have had an impact on the communication model in two major ways. First, consumers are now able to become senders (as opposed to only brands being senders). A consumer who makes a recommendation on Facebook or Yelp is essentially a sender, meaning that the communication model is much more complicated today than it was just a few years ago. Second, the communication model shows the feedback channel as primarily impersonal and numbers driven. In the traditional communication process, marketers can see the results of customer behavior (for example, a drop or rise in sales) but are able to explain those

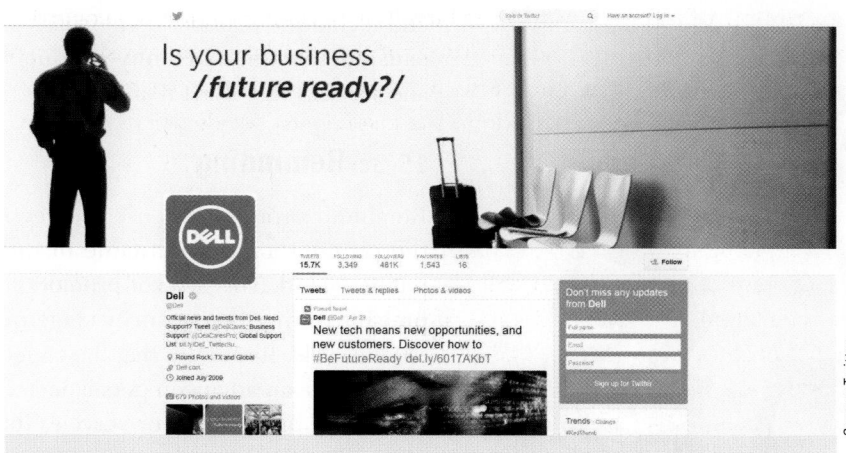

Social media enable companies to provide instant feedback by responding to consumers' posts on Twitter.

Source: Twitter

changes only by using their judgment. Today, customers use social media platforms like Facebook and Twitter to comment publically on marketing efforts. These platforms enable marketers to personalize the feedback channel by opening the door for direct conversations with customers. However, because social media conversations occur in real time and are public, any negative posts or complaints are highly visible. Thus, many companies have crisis communication strategies to deal with negative information and promote good brand reputations.

15-3 THE GOALS OF PROMOTION

People communicate with one another for many reasons. They seek amusement, ask for help, give assistance or instructions, provide information, and express ideas and thoughts. Promotion, on the other hand, seeks to modify behavior and thoughts in some way. For example, promoters may try to persuade consumers to eat at Burger King rather than at McDonald's. Promotion also strives to reinforce existing behavior—for instance, getting consumers to continue dining at Burger King once they have switched. The source (the seller) hopes to project a favorable image or to motivate purchase of the company's goods and services.

Promotion can perform one or more of four tasks: *inform* the target audience, *persuade* the target audience, *remind* the target audience, or *connect* with the audience. The ability to *connect* to consumers is one task that can be facilitated through social media. Often a marketer will try to accomplish two or more of these tasks at the same time.

15-3a **Informing**

Informative promotion seeks to convert an existing need into a want or to stimulate interest in a new product. It is generally more prevalent during the early stages of the product life cycle. People typically will not buy a product or service or support a nonprofit organization until they know its purpose and its benefits to them. Informative messages are important for promoting complex and technical products such as automobiles, computers, and investment services. For example, shortly after Google unveiled the Google Glass wearable computer and display, it released a series of commercials showing various practical uses for the device. A commercial titled "How It Feels" demonstrated point-of-view video and photo capture, messaging, video chatting, search, weather, mapping, and more. Even though it did not overtly explain the device's functions, the ad informed viewers how the device could record once-in-a-lifetime moments and provide the perfect solutions for life's little problems.[5] Informative promotion is also important for a "new" brand being introduced into an "old" product class. When the upstart video game console Ouya began its Kickstarter campaign, it used a video to inform backers about its unique benefits (such as its low cost, open development, free-to-play games, and Web-based game market).[6] When it launched, Ouya again used informative promotion to distinguish itself from seasoned competitors. New products cannot establish themselves against more mature products unless potential buyers are aware of them, value their benefits, and understand their positioning in the marketplace.

15-3b **Persuading**

Persuasive promotion is designed to stimulate a purchase or an action. Persuasion typically becomes the main promotion goal when the product enters the growth stage of its life cycle. By this time, the target market should have general product awareness and some knowledge of how the product can fulfill its wants. Therefore, the promotional task switches from informing consumers about the product category to persuading them to buy the company's brand rather than that of the competitor. At this time, the promotional message emphasizes the product's real and perceived competitive advantages, often appealing to emotional needs such as

#ALSICEBUCKETCHALLENGE

Crystal Eye Studio/Shutterstock.com

The ALS Association received a boost to awareness thanks to pro golfer Chris Kennedy kicking off the campaign.

and techniques can be too persuasive, causing consumers to buy products and services they don't really need.

15-3c Reminding

Reminder promotion is used to keep the product and brand name in the public's mind. This type of promotion prevails during the maturity stage of the life cycle. It assumes that the target market has already been persuaded of the merits of the good or service. Its purpose is simply to trigger a memory. Colgate toothpaste and other consumer products often use reminder promotion. Companies that produce products like automobiles and appliances advertise throughout the year in order to remind people about the brands when they are looking to purchase.

love, belonging, self-esteem, and ego satisfaction. For example, advertisers of Android-based smartphones try to persuade users to purchase their companies' devices instead of an iPhone (or even instead of another brand of Android phone). Advertising messages, therefore, highlight the unique technological benefits of Android phones such as a faster processors and larger screens.

Persuasion is important when the goal is to inspire direct action. In 2014, the ALS Association experienced a huge influx of donations through its "Ice Bucket Challenge" campaign. Pro Golfer Chris Kennedy kicked the vital hit off on his social network by pouring ice water over his head and then challenging others to do the same. The campaign spread all over Facebook and Twitter, was reported on cable television news shows, and eventually became part of popular culture. The effort raised $115 million, more than 20 times the usual donations received for that period of time. The "Ice Bucket Challenge" currently ranks as the largest social media fundraiser ever.[7] Persuasion can also be an important goal for very competitive mature product categories such as household items and soft drinks. In a marketplace characterized by many competitors, the promotional message often encourages brand switching and aims to convert some buyers into loyal users. Critics believe that some promotional messages

promotional mix the combination of promotional tools—including advertising, public relations, personal selling, sales promotion, and social media—used to reach the target market and fulfill the organization's overall goals

15-3d Connecting

The idea behind social media is to form relationships with customers and potential customers through technological ties such as Facebook, Twitter, YouTube, or other social media platforms. Indeed, some companies, such as Starbucks, have their own social networks that allow customers to share ideas, information, and feedback. By facilitating this exchange of information through a transparent process, brands are increasingly connecting with their customers in hopes they become brand advocates that promote the brand through their own social networks. Tools for connection include social networks, social games, social publishing tools, as well as social commerce. The ALS Association's "Ice Bucket Challenge" can also be considered an example of connecting since many people used videos posted to Facebook and Twitter to issue their challenges.

THE PROMOTIONAL MIX

Most promotional strategies use several ingredients—which may include advertising, public relations, sales promotion, personal selling, and social media—to reach a target market. That combination is called the **promotional mix**. The proper promotional mix is the one that management believes will meet the needs of the target market and fulfill the organization's overall goals. Data plays a very important role in how marketers distribute funding among their promotional mix tactics. The more funds allocated to each promotional ingredient and the more managerial emphasis placed on each technique, the more important that element is thought to be in the overall mix.

15-4a Advertising

Almost all companies selling a good or a service use advertising, whether in the form of a multi-million-dollar campaign or a simple classified ad in a newspaper. **Advertising** is any form of impersonal paid communication in which the sponsor or company is identified. Traditional media—such as television, radio, newspapers, magazines, pay-per-click online advertising, display advertising, direct mail, billboards, and transit advertising (such as on buses and taxis and at bus stops)—are most commonly used to transmit advertisements to consumers. Other options include Web sites, e-mail, blogs, videos, and interactive games. Marketers' budgets are shifting more and more toward these digital options (including

Adverising can show up in any way, shape or form. Here, a movie premier backdrop is used to promote products and sponsors (pictured are Kimberly Williams-Paisley and Brad Paisley).

social media). However, as the Internet becomes a more vital component of many companies' promotion and marketing mixes, consumers and lawmakers are increasingly concerned about possible violations of consumers' privacy. Social networking sites like Facebook and Google+ are having to re-examine their privacy policies.

One of the primary benefits of advertising is its ability to communicate to a large number of people at one time. Cost per contact, therefore, is typically very low. Advertising has the advantage of being able to reach the masses (for example, through national television networks), but it can also be microtargeted to small groups of potential customers, such as television ads on a targeted cable network. Although the *cost per contact* in advertising is very low, the *total cost* to advertise is typically very high. This hurdle tends to restrict advertising on a national basis. Chapter 16 examines advertising in greater detail.

15-4b Public Relations

Concerned about how they are perceived by their target markets, organizations often spend large sums to build a positive public image. **Public relations** is the marketing function that evaluates public attitudes, identifies areas within the organization the public may be interested in, and executes a program of action to earn public understanding and acceptance. Public relations helps an organization communicate with its customers, suppliers, stockholders, government officials, employees, and the community in which it operates. Marketers use public relations not only to maintain a positive image but also to educate the public about the company's goals and objectives, introduce new products, and help support the sales effort.

A public relations program can generate favorable **publicity**—public information about a company, product, service, or issue appearing in the mass media as a news item. Social media sites like Twitter can provide large amounts of publicity quickly. Organizations generally do not pay for the publicity and are not identified as the source of the information, but they can benefit tremendously from it. However, although organizations do not directly pay for publicity,

advertising impersonal, one-way mass communication about a product or organization that is paid for by a marketer

public relations the marketing function that evaluates public attitudes, identifies areas within the organization the public may be interested in, and executes a program of action to earn public understanding and acceptance

publicity public information about a company, product, service, or issue appearing in the mass media as a news item

it should not be viewed as free. Preparing news releases, staging special events, and persuading media personnel to broadcast or print publicity messages costs money. Public relations and publicity are examined further in Chapter 16.

15-4c Sales Promotion

Sales promotion consists of all marketing activities—other than personal selling, advertising, and public relations—that stimulate consumer purchasing and dealer effectiveness. Sales promotion is generally a short-run tool used to stimulate immediate increases in demand. Sales promotion can be aimed at end consumers, trade customers, or a company's employees. Sales promotions include free samples, contests, premiums, trade shows, vacation giveaways, and coupons. It also includes experiential marketing whereby marketers create events that enable customers to connect with brands. Increasingly, companies such as LivingSocial and Groupon have combined social networks and sales promotions. Facebook is a growing platform through which companies run sweepstakes. For example, JPMorgan Chase ran a sweepstakes where Facebook users entered a drawing for a $1,000 grocery store gift card by "liking" the Chase Freedom Facebook page. In the past, Chase Freedom has run other Facebook sweepstakes where players could "like" the page to win $1 million. In addition to being entered into the large drawing, players were entered for a chance to win $500 every hour. The company runs this type of sweepstakes to educate potential customers about its cash-back rewards program available through the Chase Freedom credit card.[8]

Marketers often use sales promotion to improve the effectiveness of other ingredients in the promotional mix, especially advertising and personal selling. Research shows that sales promotion complements advertising by yielding faster sales responses. In many instances, more marketing money is spent on sales promotion than on advertising.

Many companies are using Facebook as a platform to run contests and promote their products and services.

Source: Facebook

sales promotion marketing activities—other than personal selling, advertising, and public relations—that stimulate consumer buying and dealer effectiveness

personal selling a purchase situation involving a personal, paid-for communication between two people in an attempt to influence each other

15-4d Personal Selling

Personal selling is a purchase situation involving a personal, paid-for communication between two people in an attempt to influence each other. In this dyad, both the buyer and the seller have specific objectives they wish to accomplish. The buyer may need to minimize cost or assure a quality product, for instance, while the salesperson may need to maximize revenue and profits.

Traditional methods of personal selling include a planned presentation to one or more prospective buyers for the purpose of making a sale. Whether it takes place face-to-face or over the phone, personal selling attempts to persuade the buyer to accept a point of view. For example, a car salesperson may try to persuade a car buyer that a particular model is superior to a competing model in certain features, such as gas mileage. Once the buyer is somewhat convinced, the salesperson may attempt to elicit some action from the buyer, such as a test drive or a purchase. Frequently, in this traditional view of personal selling, the objectives of the salesperson are at the expense of the buyer, creating a win-lose outcome.

More current notions on personal selling emphasize the relationship that develops between a salesperson and a buyer. Initially, this concept was more typical in business-to-business selling situations, involving the sale of products like heavy machinery or computer systems. More recently, both business-to-business and business-to-consumer selling focus on building long-term relationships rather than on making a one-time sale.

Relationship selling emphasizes a win-win outcome and the accomplishment of mutual objectives that benefit both buyer and salesperson in the long term. Rather than focusing on a quick sale, relationship selling attempts to create a long-term, committed relationship based on trust, increased customer loyalty, and a continuation of the relationship between the salesperson and the customer. Personal selling, like other promotional mix elements, is increasingly dependent on the Internet. Most companies use their Web sites to attract potential buyers seeking information on products and services and to drive customers to their physical locations where personal selling can close the sale. Personal selling is discussed further in Chapter 17.

15-4e Content Marketing and Social Media

As promotional strategies change, and given brands' newfound ability to become publishers, content marketing has become a crucial part of promotion. Recall from Chapter 7 that content marketing entails developing valuable content for interested audience members and then using e-mail marketing, search engine optimization, paid search, and display advertising to pull customers to the company's Web site or social media channel so that they can learn about the brand or to make a purchase. Content created by brands is typically distributed through social media.

Recall that social media are promotion tools used to facilitate conversations and other interactions among people online. When used by marketers, these tools facilitate consumer empowerment. For the first time, consumers are able to speak directly to other consumers, the company, and Web communities. Social media include blogs, microblogs (such as Twitter), video platforms (such as You Tube, Twitch, and Vine), podcasting (online audio and video broadcasts), and social networks (such as Tumblr, Pinterest, Yik Yak, and Snapchat).

Initially, these tools were used primarily by individuals for self-expression. For example, a lawyer might develop a blog to talk about politics because that is her hobby. Or a college freshman might develop a profile on Facebook to stay in touch with his high school friends. But soon, businesses saw that these tools could be used to engage with consumers as well. Indeed, social media have become a "layer" in promotional strategy. Social media are ubiquitous—it just depends on how deep that layer goes for each brand. The rise of streaming video, for example, has created a completely new way for marketers to manage their image, connect with consumers, and generate interest in and desire for their companies' products. Now marketers are using social media as integral aspects of their campaigns and as a way to extend the benefits of their traditional media. Social media are discussed in more detail in Chapter 18.

15-4f The Communication Process and the Promotional Mix

The Internet has changed how businesses promote their brands. Traditionally, marketing managers have been in charge of defining the essence of the brand. This included complete brand control and mostly one-way communication between the brand and customers. All of the content and messages were focused on defining and communicating the brand value. The focus for many campaigns was pure entertainment, and the brand created all of the content for campaigns—from the Web site to television spots to print ads.

That approach has now changed. The consumer has much more control (which makes some brands quite nervous!). The communication space is increasingly controlled by the consumer, as is the brand message. Perception is reality as consumers have more control to adapt the brand message to fit their ideas. Instead of repetition, social media rely on the idea of customization and adaption of the message. Information is positioned as more valuable as opposed to being strictly entertaining. Probably the most important aspect is the idea of consumer-generated content, whereby consumers are able to both take existing content and modify it or to create completely new content for a brand. For example, Doritos has the "Crash the Super Bowl" promotion, where ordinary people are invited to create television commercials for Doritos that are then uploaded to www.crashthesuperbowl.com and voted on by millions of Doritos fans. The winning spots then run during the Super Bowl.

As a result of the impact of social media as well as the proliferation of new platforms, tools, and ideas, promotional tactics can also be categorized according to media type—paid, earned, or owned, as shown in Exhibit 15.3. **Paid media** is based on the traditional advertising model, whereby a brand pays for media space. Traditionally, paid media has included television, magazine, outdoor, radio, or newspaper advertising. Paid media also includes display advertising on Web sites, pay-per-click advertising on search engines, and even promoted tweets on Twitter. Paid media is quite important, especially as it migrates to the Web. Paid media is used with other media types to develop an integrated message strategy. **Earned media** is based on a public

> **paid media** a category of promotional tactic based on the traditional advertising model, whereby a brand pays for media space

> **earned media** a category of promotional tactic based on a public relations or publicity model that gets customers talking about products or services

EXHIBIT 15.3   DIGITAL MEDIA TYPES

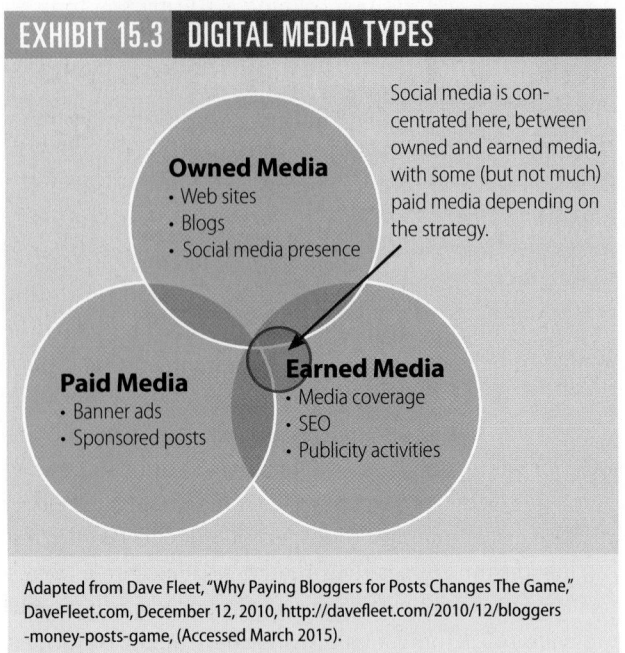

Owned Media
• Web sites
• Blogs
• Social media presence

Social media is concentrated here, between owned and earned media, with some (but not much) paid media depending on the strategy.

Paid Media
• Banner ads
• Sponsored posts

Earned Media
• Media coverage
• SEO
• Publicity activities

Adapted from Dave Fleet, "Why Paying Bloggers for Posts Changes The Game," DaveFleet.com, December 12, 2010, http://davefleet.com/2010/12/bloggers-money-posts-game, (Accessed March 2015).

for example, sharing a movie review on a social media site, is growing rapidly. Earned media is often created when people talk and share content on social media. Additionally, search engine optimization (SEO), whereby companies embed key words into content to increase their positioning on search engine results pages (SERPs), can also be considered earned media. **Owned media** is a new form of promotional tactic where brands are becoming publishers of their own content in order to maximize the brand's value to customers as well as increase their search rank in Google. Owned media includes the company's Web sites as well as its official presence on Facebook, Twitter, YouTube channels, blogs, and other platforms. This media is controlled by the brand but continuously keeps the customer and his or her needs in mind as it creates videos, blog posts, contests, photos, and other pieces of content. Owned media is often used as another term for content marketing, which is important to both B-to-B and B-to-C companies.

The elements of the promotional mix differ in their ability to affect the target audience. For instance, promotional mix elements may communicate with the consumer directly or indirectly. The message may flow one way or two ways. Feedback may be fast or slow, a little or a lot. Likewise, the communicator may have varying degrees of control over message delivery, content, and flexibility. Exhibit 15.4 outlines characteristics among the promotional mix elements with respect to mode of

relations or publicity model. The idea is to get people talking about the brand—whether through media coverage (as in traditional public relations) or through word of mouth (WOM). Word of mouth traditionally occurs face-to-face. Electronic word of mouth (EWOM),

owned media a new category of promotional tactic based on brands becoming publishers of their own content in order to maximize the brands' value to customers

	Advertising	Public Relations	Sales Promotion	Personal Selling	Social Media
Mode of Communication	Indirect and impersonal	Usually indirect and impersonal	Usually indirect and impersonal	Direct and face-to-face	Indirect but instant
Communicator Control over Situation	Low	Moderate to low	Moderate to low	High	Moderate
Amount of Feedback	Little	Little	Little to moderate	Much	Much
Speed of Feedback	Delayed	Delayed	Varies	Immediate	Intermediate
Direction of Message	One-way	One-way	Mostly one-way	Two-way	Two-way, multiple ways
Control over Message Content	Yes	No	Yes	Yes	Varies, generally no
Identification of Sponsor	Yes	No	Yes	Yes	Yes
Speed in Reaching Large Audience	Fast	Usually fast	Fast	Slow	Fast
Message Flexibility	Same message to all audiences	Usually no direct control over message audiences	Same message to varied targets	Tailored to prospective buyer	Some of the most targeted opportunities

communication, marketer's control over the communication process, amount and speed of feedback, direction of message flow, marketer's control over the message, identification of the sender, speed in reaching large audiences, and message flexibility.

From Exhibit 15.4, you can see that most elements of the promotional mix are indirect and impersonal when used to communicate with a target market, providing only one direction of message flow. For example, advertising, public relations, and sales promotion are generally impersonal, one-way means of mass communication. Because they provide no opportunity for direct feedback, it is more difficult to adapt these promotional elements to changing consumer preferences, individual differences, and personal goals.

Personal selling, on the other hand, entails direct two-way communication. The salesperson receives immediate feedback from the consumer and can adjust the message in response. Unlike other promotional tools, personal selling is very slow in dispersing the marketer's message to large audiences. Because a salesperson can communicate to only one person or a small group of persons at one time, it is a poor choice if the marketer wants to send a message to many potential buyers. Social media are also considered two-way communication, though not quite as immediate as personal selling. Social media can disperse messages to a wide audience and allow for engagement and feedback from customers through Twitter, Facebook, and blog posts.

15-5 PROMOTIONAL GOALS AND THE AIDA CONCEPT

The ultimate goal of any promotion is to get someone to buy a good or service or, in the case of nonprofit organizations, to take some action (for example, donate to a cause organization like Susan G. Komen). A classic model for reaching promotional goals is called the **AIDA concept**.[9] The acronym AIDA stands for *attention, interest, desire,* and *action*—the stages of consumer involvement with a promotional message. It mimics many "funnel-like" models that require audiences to move through a set of steps or stages.

15-5a The AIDA Model

This model proposes that consumers respond to marketing messages in a cognitive (thinking), affective (feeling), and conative (doing) sequence. First, a promotion manager may focus on attracting

a consumer's *attention* by training a salesperson to use a friendly greeting and approach or by using loud volume, bold headlines, movement, bright colors, and the like in an advertisement. Next, a good sales presentation, demonstration, or advertisement creates *interest* in the product and then, by illustrating how the product's features will satisfy the consumer's needs, arouses *desire*. Finally, a special offer or a strong closing sales pitch may be used to obtain purchase *action*.

The AIDA concept assumes that promotion propels consumers along the following four steps in the purchase-decision process:

1. **Attention:** The advertiser must first gain the attention of the target market. A firm cannot sell something if the market does not know that the good or service exists. When Apple introduced the iPad, it quickly became one of the largest electronics product launches in history. To create awareness and gain attention for its revolutionary tablet computer, Apple not only used traditional media advertising but also contacted influential bloggers and journalists so that they would write about the product in blogs, newspapers, and magazines. Because the iPad was a brand extension of the Apple computer, it required less effort than an entirely new brand would have. At the same time, because the iPad was an innovative new product

> **AIDA concept** a model that outlines the process for achieving promotional goals in terms of stages of consumer involvement with the message; the acronym stands for attention, interest, desire, and action

iStockphotos.com/Hocus-focus

The four steps of the AIDA process describe how consumers make purchases. These steps are:

1. **ATTENTION:** First, Apple uses a number of media outlets to gain the attention of the target market.

2. **INTEREST:** Next, it arranges iPad demonstrations and develops target messages to create interest among innovators and early adopters.

3. **DESIRE:** Then, Apple creates brand preference and convinces potential customers that they want the new iPad.

4. **ACTION:** Finally, having been attracted to the new iPad and convinced that they need it, customers purchase the iPad.

line, the promotion had to get customers' attention and create awareness of a new idea from an established company.

2. **Interest:** Simple awareness of a brand seldom leads to a sale. The next step is to create interest in the product. A print ad cannot tell potential customers all the features of the iPad. Therefore, Apple had to arrange iPad demonstrations and target messages to innovators and early adopters to create interest in the new tablet computer. To do this, Apple used both online videos on YouTube and personal demonstrations in Apple Stores. The iPad also received extensive media coverage from both online and traditional media outlets.

3. **Desire:** Potential customers for the Apple iPad may like the concept of a portable tablet computer, but they may not necessarily think that it is better than a laptop or smartphone. Therefore, Apple had to create brand preference with the iTunes Music Store, specialty apps, multiple functionality, and features such as better power management and a lighter weight unit. Specifically, Apple had to convince potential customers that the iPad was the best solution to their desire for a combination tablet computer and smartphone.

4. **Action:** Some potential target market customers may have been persuaded to buy an iPad but had yet to make the actual purchase. To motivate them to take action, Apple continued advertising to communicate the features and benefits more effectively. And the strategy worked—more than 250 million people own an iPad.[10]

Most buyers involved in high-involvement purchase situations pass through the four stages of the AIDA model on the way to making a purchase. The promoter's task is to determine where on the purchase ladder most of the target consumers are located and design a promotion plan to meet their needs. For example, if Apple learned from its market research that many potential customers were in the desire stage but had not yet bought an iPad for some reason, it could place advertising on Facebook and Google, and perhaps in video games, to target younger individuals and professionals with messages motivating them to buy an iPad.

The AIDA concept does not explain how all promotions influence purchase decisions. The model suggests that promotional effectiveness can be measured in terms of consumers progressing from one stage to the next. However, the order of stages in the model, as well as whether consumers go through all steps, has been much debated. A purchase can occur without interest or desire, perhaps when a low-involvement product is bought on impulse. Regardless of the order of the stages or consumers' progression through these stages, the AIDA concept helps marketers by suggesting which promotional strategy will be most effective.[11]

15-5b AIDA and the Promotional Mix

Exhibit 15.5 depicts the relationship between the promotional mix and the AIDA model. It shows that although advertising does have an impact in the later stages, it is most useful in gaining attention for goods or services. By contrast, personal selling reaches fewer people at first. Salespeople are more effective at creating customer interest for merchandise or a service and at creating desire. For example, advertising may help a potential computer purchaser gain knowledge about competing brands, but the salesperson may be the one who actually encourages the buyer to decide a particular brand is the best choice. The salesperson also has the advantage of having the computer physically there to demonstrate its capabilities to the buyer.

Public relations' greatest impact is as a method of gaining attention for a company, good, or service. Many companies can attract attention and build goodwill by sponsoring community events that benefit worthy causes such as an anti-bullying campaign or a global poverty program. Such sponsorships project a positive image of the firm and its products into the minds of consumers and potential consumers. Book publishers push to get their titles on the best-seller lists of major publications, such as *Publishers Weekly* or the *New York Times*. Book authors make appearances on talk shows and at bookstores to personally sign books and speak to fans. They also frequently engage with fans on social media like Facebook and Twitter.

Sales promotion's greatest strength is in creating strong desire and purchase intent. Coupons and other price-off promotions are techniques used to persuade

EXHIBIT 15.5 THE PROMOTIONAL MIX AND AIDA

	Attention	Interest	Desire	Action
Advertising	●	●	○	●
Public Relations	●	●	○	●
Sales Promotion	○	○	●	●
Personal Selling	○	●	●	●
Social Media	●	●	○	○

● Very effective ○ Somewhat effective ● Not effective

customers to buy new products. Frequent-buyer sales promotion programs, popular among retailers, allow consumers to accumulate points or dollars that can be redeemed for goods. Frequent buyer programs tend to increase purchase intent and loyalty and encourage repeat purchases.

Social media are a strong way to gain attention and interest in a brand, particularly if content goes viral. It can then reach a massive audience. Social media are also effective at engaging with customers and enabling companies to maintain interest in the brand if properly managed.

15-6 INTEGRATED MARKETING COMMUNICATIONS

Ideally, marketing communications from each promotional mix element (personal selling, advertising, sales promotion, social media, and public relations) should be integrated. That is, the message reaching the consumer should be the same regardless of whether it is from an advertisement, a salesperson in the field, a magazine article, a Facebook fan page, or a coupon in a newspaper insert.

From the consumer's standpoint, a company's communications are already integrated. Consumers do not think in terms of the five elements of promotion: personal selling, advertising, sales promotion, public relations, and social media. Instead, everything is an "ad." The only people who recognize the distinctions among these communications elements are the marketers themselves. Unfortunately, many marketers neglect this fact when planning promotional messages and fail to integrate their communication efforts from one element to the next. The most common rift typically occurs between personal selling and the other elements of the promotional mix.

This unintegrated, disjointed approach to promotion has propelled many companies to adopt the concept of **integrated marketing communications (IMC)**. IMC is the careful coordination of all promotional messages—traditional advertising, direct marketing, social media, interactive, public relations, sales promotion, personal selling, event marketing, and other communications—for a product or service to assure the consistency of messages at every contact point where a company meets the consumer. Following the concept of IMC, marketing managers carefully work out the roles that various promotional elements will play in the marketing mix. Timing of promotional activities is coordinated, and the results of each campaign are carefully monitored to improve future use of the promotional mix tools. Typically, a marketing communications director is appointed who has overall responsibility for integrating the company's marketing communications.

The IMC concept has been growing in popularity for several reasons. First, the proliferation of thousands of media choices beyond traditional television has made promotion a more complicated task. Instead of promoting a product just through mass-media options, like television and magazines, promotional messages today can appear in many varied sources.

Further, the mass market has also fragmented—more selectively segmented markets and an increase in niche marketing have replaced the traditional broad market groups that marketers promoted to in years past. Finally, marketers have slashed their advertising spending in favor of promotional techniques that generate immediate sales responses and those that are more easily measured, such as direct marketing. Online advertising has earned a bigger share of the budget as well due to its measurability. Thus, the interest in IMC is largely a reaction to the scrutiny that marketing communications has come under and, particularly, to suggestions that uncoordinated promotional activity leads to a strategy that is wasteful and inefficient.

15-7 FACTORS AFFECTING THE PROMOTIONAL MIX

Promotional mixes vary a great deal from one product and one industry to the next. Normally, advertising and personal selling are used to promote goods and services. These primary tools are often supported and supplemented by sales promotion. Public relations help develop a positive image for the organization and the product line. Social media have been used more for consumer goods, but business-to-business marketers are increasingly using these media. A firm may choose not to use all five promotional elements in its promotional mix, or it may choose to use them in varying degrees. The particular promotional mix chosen by a firm for a product or service depends on several factors: the nature of the product, the stage in the product life cycle, target market characteristics, the type of buying decision, funds available for promotion, and whether a push or a pull strategy will be used.

> **integrated marketing communications (IMC)** the careful coordination of all promotional messages for a product or a service to ensure the consistency of messages at every contact point at which a company meets the consumer

15-7a Nature of the Product

Characteristics of the product itself can influence the promotional mix. For instance, a product can be classified as either a business product or a consumer product. (Refer to Chapters 7 and 10.) As business products are often custom-tailored to the buyer's exact specifications, they are often not well suited to mass promotion. Therefore, producers of most business goods rely more heavily on personal selling than on advertising, but advertising still serves a purpose in the promotional mix. Advertising in trade media can also help locate potential customers for the sales force. For example, print media advertising often includes coupons soliciting the potential customer to "fill this out for more detailed information."

By contrast, because consumer products generally are not custom-made, they do not require the selling efforts of a company representative who can tailor them to the user's needs. Thus, consumer goods are promoted mainly through advertising or social media to create brand familiarity. Television and radio advertising, consumer-oriented magazines, and increasingly the Internet and other highly targeted media are used to promote consumer goods, especially nondurables. Sales promotion, the brand name, and the product's packaging are about twice as important for consumer goods as for business products. Persuasive personal selling is important at the retail level for goods such as automobiles and appliances.

The costs and risks associated with a product also influence the promotional mix. As a general rule, when the costs or risks of buying and using a product or service increase, personal selling becomes more important. Inexpensive items cannot support the cost of a salesperson's time and effort unless the potential volume is high. On the other hand, expensive and complex machinery, cars, and new homes represent a considerable investment. A salesperson must assure buyers that they are spending their money wisely and not taking an undue financial risk.

Social risk is an issue as well. Many consumer goods are not products of great social importance because they do not reflect social position. People do not experience much social risk in buying a loaf of bread. However, buying many specialty products such as jewelry and clothing involves a social risk. Many consumers depend on sales personnel for guidance in making the "proper" choice.

15-7b Stages in the Product Life Cycle

The product's stage in its life cycle is a big factor in designing a promotional mix (see Exhibit 15.6). During the *introduction stage*, the basic goal of promotion is to inform the target audience that the product is available. Initially, the emphasis is on the general product class—for example, smartphones. This emphasis gradually changes to gaining attention for a particular brand, such as Apple, Nokia, Samsung, Sony Ericsson, or Motorola. Typically, both extensive advertising and public relations inform the target audience of the product class or brand and heighten awareness levels. Sales promotion encourages early trial of the product, and personal selling gets retailers to carry the product.

When the product reaches the *growth stage* of the life cycle, the promotion blend may shift. Often a change is necessary because different types of potential buyers are targeted. Although advertising and public relations continue to be major elements of the promotional mix, sales promotion can be reduced because consumers need fewer incentives to purchase. The promotional strategy is to emphasize the product's differential advantage over the competition. Persuasive promotion is used to build and maintain brand loyalty during the growth stage. By this stage, personal selling has usually succeeded in getting adequate distribution for the product.

As the product reaches the *maturity stage* of its life cycle, competition becomes fiercer, and thus persuasive and reminder advertising are emphasized more strongly. Sales promotion comes back into focus as product sellers try to increase their market share.

All promotion, especially advertising, is reduced as the product enters the *decline stage*. Nevertheless, personal selling and sales promotion efforts may be maintained, particularly at the retail level.

Print media advertising often includes coupons soliciting the potential customer.

EXHIBIT 15.6 PRODUCT LIFE CYCLE AND THE PROMOTIONAL MIX

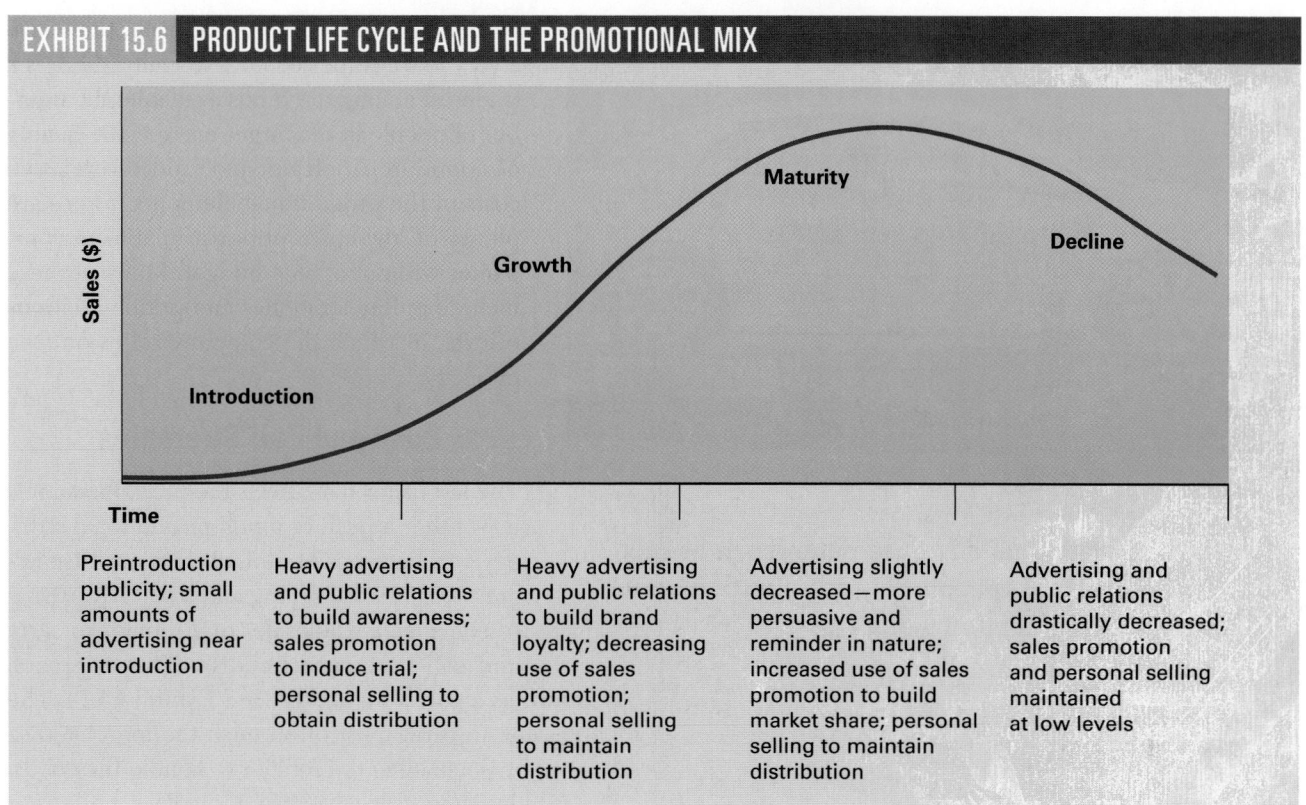

Introduction	Growth	Maturity	Decline
Preintroduction publicity; small amounts of advertising near introduction	Heavy advertising and public relations to build awareness; sales promotion to induce trial; personal selling to obtain distribution	Heavy advertising and public relations to build brand loyalty; decreasing use of sales promotion; personal selling to maintain distribution	Advertising slightly decreased—more persuasive and reminder in nature; increased use of sales promotion to build market share; personal selling to maintain distribution	Advertising and public relations drastically decreased; sales promotion and personal selling maintained at low levels

15-7c Target Market Characteristics

A target market characterized by widely scattered potential customers, highly informed buyers, and brand loyal repeat purchasers generally requires a promotional mix with more advertising and sales promotion and less personal selling. Sometimes, however, personal selling is required even when buyers are well informed and geographically dispersed. Although industrial installations may be sold to well-educated people with extensive work experience, salespeople must be present to explain the product and work out the details of the purchase agreement.

Often firms sell goods and services in markets where potential customers are hard to locate. Print advertising can be used to find them. The reader is invited to go online, call, or mail in a reply card for more information. As the online queries, calls, or cards are received, salespeople are sent to visit the potential customers.

15-7d Type of Buying Decision

The promotional mix also depends on the type of buying decision—for example, a routine decision or a complex decision. For routine consumer decisions like buying toothpaste, the most effective promotion calls attention to the brand or reminds the consumer about the brand. Advertising, and especially sales promotion, are the most productive promotion tools to use for routine decisions.

If the decision is neither routine nor complex, advertising and public relations help establish awareness for the good or service. Suppose a man is looking for a bottle of wine to serve to his dinner guests. As a beer drinker, he is not familiar with wines, yet he has read an article in a popular magazine about Silver Oak Cabernet and has seen an advertisement for the wine. He may be more likely to buy this brand because he is already aware of it. Online reviews are often important in this type of buying decision as well because the consumer has any number of other consumers' reviews easily accessible.

By contrast, consumers making complex buying decisions are more extensively involved. They rely on large amounts of information to help them reach a purchase decision. Personal selling is most effective in helping these consumers decide. For example, consumers thinking about buying a car typically research the car online using corporate and third party Web sites like Kelley Blue Book. However, few people buy a car without visiting the dealership. They depend on a salesperson to provide the information they need to reach a decision. In addition to online resources, print advertising may also be used for high-involvement purchase decisions because it can often provide a large amount of information to the consumer.

Despite a myriad of car advertisements, such as this one for Infiniti, most people rely on sales personnel for guideance when purchasing a car.

15-7e **Available Funds**

Money, or the lack of it, may easily be the most important factor in determining the promotional mix. A small, undercapitalized manufacturer may rely heavily on free publicity if its product is unique. If the situation warrants a sales force, a financially strained firm may turn to manufacturers' agents, who work on a commission basis with no advances or expense accounts. Even well capitalized organizations may not be able to afford the advertising rates of publications like *Time, Sports Illustrated,* and the *Wall Street Journal,* or the cost of running television commercials during *Modern Family, The Voice,* or the Super Bowl. The price of a high-profile advertisement in these media could support several salespeople for an entire year.

When funds are available to permit a mix of promotional elements, a firm will generally try to optimize its return on promotion dollars while minimizing the *cost per contact,* or the cost of reaching one member of the target market. In general, the cost per contact is very high for personal selling, public relations, and sales promotions like sampling and demonstrations. On the other hand, given the number of people national

push strategy a marketing strategy that uses aggressive personal selling and trade advertising to convince a wholesaler or a retailer to carry and sell particular merchandise

advertising and social media reach, they have a very low cost per contact. Usually, there is a trade-off among the funds available, the number of people in the target market, the quality of communication needed, and the relative costs of the promotional elements. There are plenty of low-cost options available to companies without a huge budget. Many of these include online strategies and public relations efforts, in which the company relies on free publicity.

15-7f **Push and Pull Strategies**

The last factor that affects the promotional mix is whether a push or a pull promotional strategy will be used. Manufacturers may use aggressive personal selling and trade advertising to convince a wholesaler or a retailer to carry and sell their merchandise. This approach is known as a **push strategy** (see Exhibit 15.7). The wholesaler, in turn, must often push the merchandise forward by persuading the retailer to handle the goods. The retailer then uses advertising, displays, and other forms of promotion to convince the consumer to buy the "pushed" products. Walmart uses aggressive discounts to push products out of its stores. For example, First Lady Michelle Obama praised the retailer for using drastically reduced prices to push fresh meat, produce, and other healthy options to consumers in low-income areas. The move proved to be a win-win strategy. Fresh foods generated 70 percent of Walmart's sales growth in recent

Lay's calls attention to its commitment to natural ingredients as a distinguishing attribute in order to help customers make a routine buying decision—purchasing Lay's snack food.

EXHIBIT 15.7 PUSH STRATEGY VERSUS PULL STRATEGY

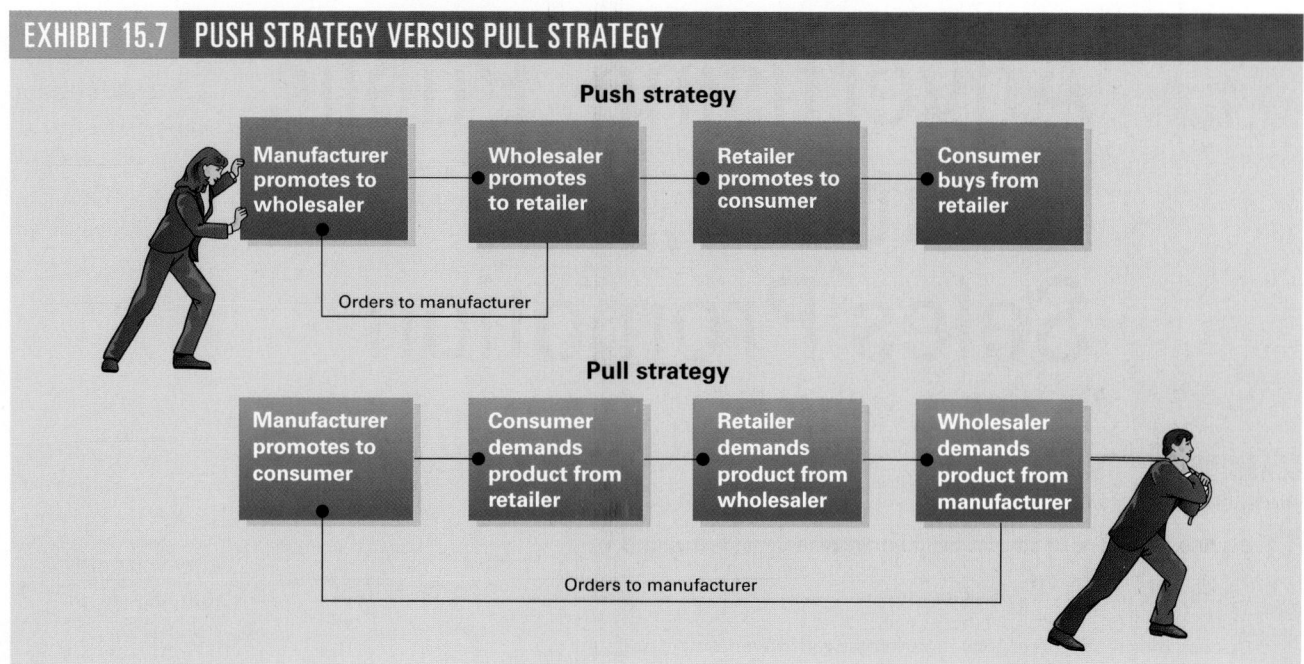

Push strategy

Manufacturer promotes to wholesaler → Wholesaler promotes to retailer → Retailer promotes to consumer → Consumer buys from retailer

Orders to manufacturer

Pull strategy

Manufacturer promotes to consumer → Consumer demands product from retailer → Retailer demands product from wholesaler → Wholesaler demands product from manufacturer

Orders to manufacturer

years, and customers have saved more than $2.3 billion on fresh fruits and vegetables by shopping at Walmart.[12] This concept also applies to services.

At the other extreme is a **pull strategy**, which stimulates consumer demand to obtain product distribution. Rather than trying to sell to the wholesaler, the manufacturer using a pull strategy focuses its promotional efforts on end consumers or opinion leaders. Social media and content marketing are the most recent (and best) example of pull strategy. The idea is that social media content does not interrupt a consumer's experience with media (like a commercial interrupts your favorite television program). Instead, the content invites customers to experience it on social media or a Web site. Consumer demand pulls the product through the channel of distribution (see Exhibit 15.7). Heavy sampling, introductory consumer advertising, cents-off campaigns, and couponing are part of a pull strategy.

Rarely does a company use a pull or a push strategy exclusively. Instead, the mix will emphasize one of these strategies. For example, pharmaceutical companies generally use a push strategy (personal selling and trade advertising) to promote their drugs and therapies to physicians. Sales presentations and advertisements in medical journals give physicians the detailed information they need to prescribe medication to their patients. Most pharmaceutical companies supplement this push promotional strategy with a pull strategy targeted directly to potential patients through advertisements in consumer magazines and on television.

> **pull strategy** a marketing strategy that stimulates consumer demand to obtain product distribution

STUDY TOOLS 15

LOCATED AT BACK OF THE TEXTBOOK
☐ Rip out Chapter Review Card

LOCATED AT WWW.CENGAGEBRAIN.COM
☐ Review Key Terms Flashcards and create your own

☐ Track your knowledge and understanding of key concepts in marketing

☐ Complete practice and graded quizzes to prepare for tests

☐ Complete interactive content within the MKTG Online experience

☐ View the chapter highlight boxes within the MKTG Online experience

16 | Advertising, Public Relations, and Sales Promotion

LEARNING OUTCOMES

After studying this chapter, you will be able to...

16-1 Discuss the effects of advertising on market share and consumers

16-2 Identify the major types of advertising

16-3 Discuss the creative decisions in developing an advertising campaign

16-4 Describe media evaluation and selection techniques

16-5 Discuss the role of public relations in the promotional mix

16-6 Define and state the objectives of sales promotion and the tools used to achieve them

After you finish this chapter go to **PAGE 301** for **STUDY TOOLS.**

16-1 THE EFFECTS OF ADVERTISING

Advertising was defined in Chapter 15 as impersonal, one-way mass communication about a product or organization that is paid for by a marketer. It is a popular form of promotion, especially for consumer packaged goods and services. Increasingly, as more and more marketers consolidate their operations, advertising is seen as an international endeavor. Promotion makes up a large part of most brands' budgets. Typically, promotional spending is divided into *measured* and *unmeasured media*. Measured media ad spending includes network and cable TV, newspapers, magazines, radio, outdoor, and Internet (though paid search and social media are not included). Spending must be estimated for unmeasured media, which includes direct marketing, promotions, co-op, coupons, catalogs, product placement, and event marketing. Global advertising expenditures increase by almost 5 percent per year. In 2015, they reached almost $550 billion. The United States is, by far,

the largest spender ($182 billion, representing a full third of spending globally). China, Japan, Germany, and the United Kingdom round out the top five countries in terms of advertising spending. Latin America is the fastest growing market, recently increasing by almost 10 percent annually.[1]

The top 25 largest U.S. advertisers spend more than $50 billion each year. Procter & Gamble is by far the largest advertiser, spending almost $5 billion annually on its wide variety of brands. Telecommunications companies like AT&T ($3.3 billion) and Verizon ($2.4 billion) are other top spenders. Automotive companies also spend a great deal of money on advertising in the U.S.—GM alone spends $3.1 billion a year.[2]

Advertising and marketing services, agencies, and other firms that provide marketing and communications services employ millions of people across America. Just as the producers of goods and services need marketers to build awareness of their products, media outlets such as magazines and Web sites need marketing teams to coordinate with producers and transmit those messages to customers. The longer one thinks about the business of marketing, the more unique positions within the industry become apparent. One particular area that has continued to see rapid growth is the data side of marketing. Companies are collecting huge amounts of information and need skilled, creative, Web-savvy people to interpret the data coming in from Web, mobile, and other digital ad campaigns. One Microsoft study estimates that ninety percent of enterprise companies have a dedicated budget for addressing data analytics. Forty-nine percent of the demand for data analytics is driven by sales and marketing departments. According to IDC program vice president Dan Vesset, "A lot of the ultimate potential is in the ability to discover potential connections, and to predict potential outcomes in a way that wasn't really possible before. Before, you only looked at these things in hindsight."[3]

16-1a Advertising and Market Share

The five most valuable U.S. brands are Apple ($124 billion), Microsoft ($63 billion), Google ($57 billion), Coca-Cola ($56 billion), and IBM ($48 billion). These were all top brands the year before and all gained value, but Google jumped from fifth to third place. Most of these brands were built over many years by heavy advertising and marketing investments long ago. Google is the only exception—its brand value was built using digital platforms.[4] Today's advertising dollars for successful consumer brands are spent on maintaining brand awareness and market share.

New brands with a small market share tend to spend proportionately more for advertising and sales promotion than those with a large market share, typically for two reasons. First, beyond a certain level of spending for advertising and sales promotion, diminishing returns set in. That is, sales and market share improvements slow down and eventually decrease no matter how much is spent on advertising and sales promotion. This phenomenon is called the **advertising response function**. Understanding the advertising response function helps marketers use budgets wisely. A market leader like Johnson & Johnson's Neutrogena typically spends proportionately less on advertising than a newer line such as Unilever's Vaseline Spray & Go brand. Neutrogena has already captured the attention of the majority of its target market. It only needs to remind customers of its product.

The second reason new brands tend to require higher spending for advertising and sales promotion is that a certain minimum level of exposure is needed to measurably affect purchase habits. If Vaseline advertised its Spray & Go moisturizers in only one or two publications and bought only one or two television spots, it would not achieve the exposure needed to penetrate consumers' perceptual defenses and affect purchase intentions.

advertising response function a phenomenon in which spending for advertising and sales promotion increases sales or market share up to a certain level but then produces diminishing returns

Eric Milos/Shutterstock.com

16-1b The Effects of Advertising on Consumers

Advertising affects peoples' daily lives, informing them about products and services and influencing their attitudes, beliefs, and ultimately, their purchases. Advertising affects the television programs people watch, the content of the newspapers they read, the politicians they elect, the medicines they take, and the toys their children play with. Consequently, the influence of advertising on the U.S. socioeconomic system has been the subject of extensive debate in nearly all corners of society.

Interestingly, despite a proliferation of new technology options, consumers still spend a lot of time consuming traditional media (where much of advertising exists). The average person, for example, spends about 273 minutes a day watching television.[5] Americans report an average of 5.3 leisure hours a day, and most of it is spent watching TV. As a result, American consumers are exposed to thousands of advertising messages each year.[6]

Though advertising cannot change consumers' deeply rooted values and attitudes, advertising may succeed in transforming a person's negative attitude toward a product into a positive one. For instance, serious or dramatic advertisements are more effective at changing consumers' negative attitudes. Humorous ads, on the other hand, have been shown to be more effective at shaping attitudes when consumers already have a positive image of an advertised brand.

Advertising also reinforces positive attitudes toward brands. A brand with a distinct personality is more likely to have a larger base of loyal customers and market share. The more consistent a brand's personality, the more likely a customer will build a relationship with that brand over his or her lifetime. Consider Apple, for example. Sixty percent of iPhone users report they would switch to Apple's latest iPhone without considering any other options, admitting to "blind loyalty."[7] This is why market leaders spend billions of dollars annually to reinforce and remind their loyal customers about the benefits of their products.

Advertising can also affect the way consumers rank a brand's attributes. In years past, car ads emphasized such brand attributes as roominess, speed, and low maintenance. Today, however, car marketers have added technology, safety, versatility, customization, and fuel efficiency to the list.

 ## 16-2 MAJOR TYPES OF ADVERTISING

A firm's promotional objectives determine the type of advertising it uses. If the goal of the promotion plan is to improve the image of the company or the industry, **institutional advertising** may be used. In contrast, if the advertiser wants to enhance the sales of a specific good or service, **product advertising** should be used.

16-2a Institutional Advertising

Historically, advertising in the United States has been product and service oriented. Today, however, companies market multiple products and need a different type of advertising. Institutional advertising, or corporate advertising, is designed to establish, change, or promote the corporation's identity as a whole. It usually does not ask the audience to do anything but maintain a favorable attitude toward the advertiser and its goods or services. A beer company running a series of television spots advocating designated driving is an example of institutional advertising.

A form of institutional advertising called **advocacy advertising** is typically used to safeguard against negative consumer attitudes and to enhance the company's credibility among consumers who already favor its position. Corporations often use advocacy advertising to express their views on controversial issues. For example, in celebration of the one-year anniversary of New York's Marriage Equality Act, Nabisco's Oreo posted a gay pride-themed image (an Oreo cookie with six rainbow-colored layers of cream filling) on its Facebook page. Accompanying the image were the phrases "Pride" and "Proudly support love!" Responses to the images were mixed: "I'm never eating Oreos again. This is just disgusting," wrote one commenter, while another replied, "I didn't think it was possible for me to love Oreo's more than I already did!!" Though controversial, the post drew a considerable amount of support from fans, generating approximately 15,000 shares and 87,000 "likes."[9] Alternatively, a firm's advocacy campaign might react to criticism or blame, or to ward off increases in regulation, damaging legislation, or the unfavorable outcome of a lawsuit.

16-2b Product Advertising

Unlike institutional advertising, product advertising promotes the benefits of a specific good or service. The product's stage in its life cycle often determines which type of product advertising is used: pioneering advertising, competitive advertising, or comparative advertising.

PIONEERING ADVERTISING Pioneering **advertising** is intended to stimulate primary demand for a new product or product category. Heavily used during the introductory

> **institutional advertising** a form of advertising designed to enhance a company's image rather than promote a particular product
>
> **product advertising** a form of advertising that touts the benefits of a specific good or service
>
> **advocacy advertising** a form of advertising in which an organization expresses its views on controversial issues or responds to media attacks
>
> **pioneering advertising** a form of advertising designed to stimulate primary demand for a new product or product category

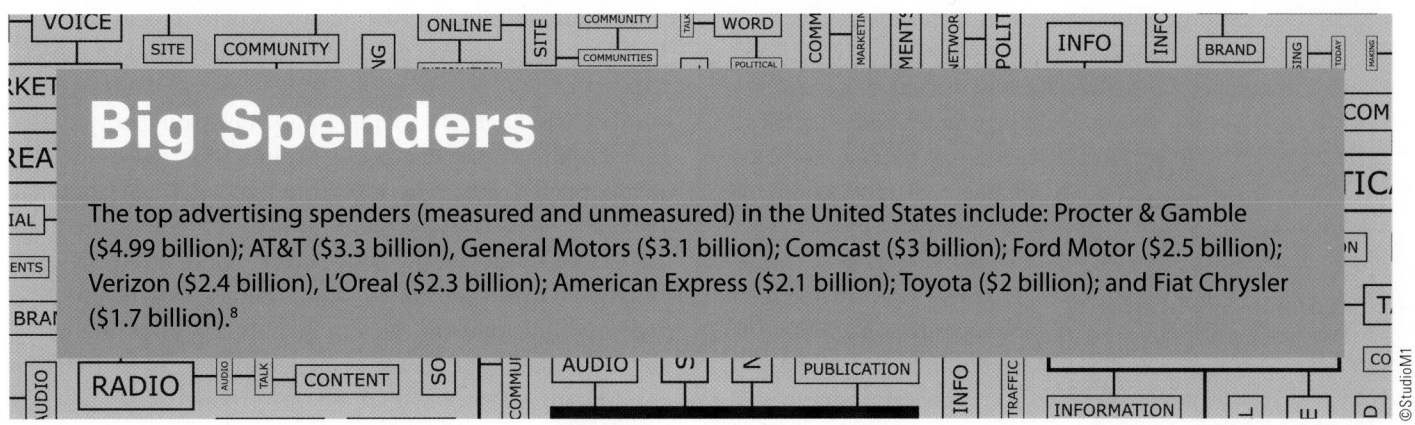

Big Spenders

The top advertising spenders (measured and unmeasured) in the United States include: Procter & Gamble ($4.99 billion); AT&T ($3.3 billion), General Motors ($3.1 billion); Comcast ($3 billion); Ford Motor ($2.5 billion); Verizon ($2.4 billion), L'Oreal ($2.3 billion); American Express ($2.1 billion); Toyota ($2 billion); and Fiat Chrysler ($1.7 billion).[8]

©StudioM1

stage of the product life cycle, pioneering advertising offers consumers in-depth information about the benefits of the product class. Pioneering advertising also seeks to create interest and, as such, can be quite innovative in its own right. For example, Motorola placed an ad for its new flagship smartphone, the Moto X, in *Wired*. The Moto X is highly customizable, featuring more than twenty different back plate and accent colors. Built in Austin, Texas, the Moto X is the first smartphone of its kind to be so customizable. Using an embedded LED array, microchip, and battery, the print ad allows the reader to push eleven different colored buttons, changing the color of the Moto X Smartphone pictured in the ad. A demonstration of the ad can be seen at www.youtube .com/watch?v=iMrZmSPpIRw.[10]

COMPETITIVE ADVERTISING Firms use competitive or brand advertising when a product enters the growth phase of the product life cycle and other companies begin to enter the marketplace. Instead of building demand for the product category, the goal of **competitive advertising** is to influence demand for a specific brand. Often, promotion becomes less informative and appeals more to emotions during this phase. Generally, this is where an emphasis on branding begins. Advertisements focus on showing subtle differences between brands, building recall of a brand name, and creating a favorable attitude toward the brand. GEICO uses competitive advertising that discusses the attributes of the brand, how little time it takes to get a quote, how much customers can save, and the ease of submitting a claim. All of its campaigns use humor to promote the brand above others in the industry but without actively comparing GEICO with other insurance companies.

COMPARATIVE ADVERTISING **Comparative advertising** directly or indirectly compares two or more competing brands on one or more specific attributes. Some advertisers even use comparative advertising against their own brands. Products experiencing slow growth or those entering the marketplace against strong competitors are more likely to employ comparative claims in their advertising. In contrast to GEICO's "Fifteen minutes can save you 15 percent or more on car insurance" tagline that

Miro Vrlik Photography/Shutterstock.com

GEICO uses competitive advertising that discusses attributes of the brand.

does not explicitly mention any other insurance company, 21st Century Insurance takes on its major competitors directly in its "Shopping Carts" television ad campaign. The ad features two cars, one labeled GEICO, the other 21st Century. As shopping carts pour down on the cars like rain, a voiceover explains that since both cars are covered, both get the same repairs.[11] Then the commercial goes on to explain that 21st Century Insurance customers who switch from GEICO save an average of $508 a year.[12] 21st Century is explicitly comparing its insurance rates with those of its main competitors and capitalizing on customers' desire for great coverage at the lowest prices.

Before the 1970s, comparative advertising was allowed only if the competing brand was veiled and unidentified. In 1971, however, the Federal Trade Commission (FTC) fostered the growth of comparative advertising by saying that the advertising provided information to the customer and that advertisers were more skillful than the government in communicating this information. Federal rulings prohibit advertisers from falsely describing competitors' products and allow competitors to sue if ads show their products or mention

competitive advertising
a form of advertising designed to influence demand for a specific brand

comparative advertising
a form of advertising that compares two or more specifically named or shown competing brands on one or more specific attributes

®, TM, © 2010 KELLOGG NA CO. PILLSBURY®, TOASTER STRUDEL® and the Doughboy are trademarks of the Pillsbury Company, LLC.

What form of advertising is the Kellogg Company using in this Pop-Tarts advertisement? What does that say about the Pop-Tarts brand?

their brand names in an incorrect or false manner. FTC rules also apply to advertisers making false claims about their own products.

16-3 CREATIVE DECISIONS IN ADVERTISING

Advertising strategies are typically organized around an advertising campaign. An advertising campaign is a series of related advertisements focusing on a common theme, slogan, and set of advertising appeals. It is a specific advertising effort for a particular product that extends for a defined period of time.

Before any creative work can begin on an advertising campaign, it is important to determine what goals or objectives the advertising should achieve. An **advertising objective** identifies the specific communication task that a campaign should accomplish for a specified target audience during a specified period. The objectives of a specific advertising campaign often depend on the overall corporate objectives and the product being advertised.

The DAGMAR approach (Defining Advertising Goals for Measured Advertising Results) is one method of setting objectives. According to this method, all advertising objectives should precisely define the target audience, the desired percentage change in some specified measure of effectiveness, and the time frame in which that change is to occur.

Once objectives are defined, creative work can begin on the advertising campaign. Advertising campaigns often follow the AIDA model, which was discussed in Chapter 15. Depending on where consumers are in the AIDA process, the creative development of an advertising campaign might focus on creating attention, arousing interest, stimulating desire, or ultimately leading to the action of buying the product. Specifically, creative decisions include identifying product benefits, developing and evaluating advertising appeals, executing the message, and evaluating the effectiveness of the campaign.

16-3a Identifying Product Benefits

A well-known rule of thumb in the advertising industry is "Sell the sizzle, not the steak"—that is, in advertising, the goal is to sell the benefits of the product, not its attributes. Customers do not buy attributes, they buy benefits. An attribute is simply a feature of the product such as its easy-open package, special formulation, or new lower price. A benefit is what consumers will receive or achieve by using the product, such as convenience or ease of use. A benefit should answer the consumer's question "What's in it for me?" Benefits might be such things as pleasure, improved health, savings, or relief. A quick test to determine whether you are offering attributes or benefits in your advertising is to ask "So?" Consider this example:

- **Attribute:** "DogsBestFriend is an all-natural skin care lotion for dogs that combines traditional medicines and Nigella sativa seed oils with the newest extraction technology." "So . . . ?"

- **Benefit:** "So . . . DogsBestFriend acts as a natural replacement for hydrocortisone, antihistamines, and topical antibiotics that is powerful enough to combat inflammation, itching, and pain, yet safe enough to use on dogs of all ages."[13]

advertising campaign a series of related advertisements focusing on a common theme, slogan, and set of advertising appeals

advertising objective a specific communication task that a campaign should accomplish for a specified target audience during a specified period

16-3b Developing and Evaluating Advertising Appeals

An **advertising appeal** identifies a reason for a person to buy a product. Developing advertising appeals, a challenging task, is typically the responsibility of the creative team (e.g., art directors and copywriters) in the advertising agency. Advertising appeals typically play off consumers' emotions or address some need or want consumers have.

Advertising campaigns can focus on one or more advertising appeals. Often the appeals are quite general, thus allowing the firm to develop a number of subthemes or mini campaigns using both advertising and sales promotion. Several possible advertising appeals are listed in Exhibit 16.1.

Choosing the best appeal from those developed usually requires market research. Criteria for evaluation include desirability, exclusiveness, and believability. The appeal first must make a positive impression on and be desirable to the target market. It must also be exclusive or unique. Consumers must be able to distinguish the advertiser's message from competitors' messages. Most importantly, the appeal should be believable. An appeal that makes extravagant claims not only wastes promotional dollars but also creates ill will for the advertiser.

The advertising appeal selected for the campaign becomes what advertisers call its **unique selling proposition**. The unique selling proposition often becomes all or part of the campaign's slogan. High-end leather goods manufacturer Saddleback Leather uses its Web site to build brand personality and convey the company's unique selling proposition: its products are extremely tough and rugged—just like the consumers who buy them. First-person narratives recount trips to Mexican bullfighting rings, shark diving in Bora Bora, backpacking along the red sand dunes of Texas, and other adventures in exotic, often perilous locations. Of course, Saddleback Leather's messenger bags and luggage are up to the task, accompanying their sojourning owner everywhere he goes— even into the ocean. Saddleback Leather's slogan drives home its products' unique selling proposition: "They'll fight over it when you're dead."[14]

advertising appeal a reason for a person to buy a product

unique selling proposition a desirable, exclusive, and believable advertising appeal selected as the theme for a campaign

EXHIBIT 16.1 COMMON ADVERTISING APPEALS

Appeal	Goal
Profit	Lets consumers know whether the product will save them money, make them money, or keep them from losing money.
Health	Appeals to those who are body conscious or who want to be healthy; love or romance is used often in selling cosmetics and perfumes.
Fear	Can center around social embarrassment, growing old, or losing one's health; because of its power, requires advertiser to exercise care in execution.
Admiration	Frequently highlights celebrity spokespeople.
Convenience	Is often used for fast-food restaurants and microwave foods.
Fun and Pleasure	Are the keys to advertising vacations, beer, amusement parks, and more.
Vanity and Egotism	Are used most often for expensive or conspicuous items such as cars and clothing.
Environmental Consciousness	Centers around protecting the environment and being considerate of others in the community.

16-3c Executing the Message

Message execution is the way an advertisement portrays its information. In general, the AIDA plan (see Chapter 15) is a good blueprint for executing an advertising message. Any ad should immediately draw the reader's, viewer's, or listener's attention. The advertiser must then use the message to hold interest, create desire for the good or service, and ultimately motivate a purchase.

The style in which the message is executed is one of the most creative elements of an advertisement. Exhibit 16.2 lists some examples of executional styles used by advertisers. Executional styles often dictate what type of media is to be employed to convey the message. For example, scientific executional styles lend themselves well to print advertising, where more information can be conveyed. Testimonials by athletes are one of the more popular executional styles.

Injecting humor into an advertisement is a popular and effective executional style. Humorous executional styles are more often used in radio and television advertising than in print or magazine advertising, where humor is less easily communicated. Recall that humorous ads are typically used for lower-risk, low-involvement, routine purchases such as candy, cigarettes, and casual jeans than for higher-risk purchases or for products that are expensive, durable, or flamboyant.[15]

Sometimes an executional style must be modified to make a marketing campaign more effective. Nowhere

EXHIBIT 16.2 **ELEVEN COMMON EXECUTIONAL STYLES FOR ADVERTISING**

Executional Style	Description
Slice-of-Life	Depicts people in normal settings, such as at the dinner table or in their car. McDonald's often uses slice-of-life styles showing youngsters munching on french fries from Happy Meals on family outings.
Lifestyle	Shows how well the product will fit in with the consumer's lifestyle. As his Volkswagen Jetta moves through the streets of the French Quarter, a Gen X driver inserts a techno music CD and marvels at how the rhythms of the world mimic the ambient vibe inside his vehicle.
Spokesperson/ Testimonial	Can feature a celebrity, company official, or typical consumer making a testimonial or endorsing a product. Sheryl Crow represented Revlon's Colorist hair coloring, while Beyoncé Knowles was named the new face of American Express. Dell Inc. founder Michael Dell touts his vision of the customer experience via Dell in television ads.
Fantasy	Creates a fantasy for the viewer built around use of the product. Carmakers often use this style to let viewers fantasize about how they would feel speeding around tight corners or down long country roads in their cars.
Humorous	Advertisers often use humor in their ads, such as Snickers' "Not Going Anywhere for a While" campaign featuring hundreds of souls waiting, sometimes impatiently, to get into heaven.
Real/Animated Product Symbols	Creates a character that represents the product in advertisements, such as the Energizer Bunny or Starkist's Charlie the Tuna. GEICO's suave gecko and disgruntled cavemen became cult classics for the insurance company.
Mood or Image	Builds a mood or image around the product, such as peace, love, or beauty. De Beers ads depicting shadowy silhouettes wearing diamond engagement rings and diamond necklaces portrayed passion and intimacy while extolling that "a diamond is forever."
Demonstration	Shows consumers the expected benefit. Many consumer products use this technique. Laundry detergent spots are famous for demonstrating how their product will clean clothes whiter and brighter. Fort James Corporation demonstrated in television commercials how its Dixie Rinse & ReUse disposable stoneware product line can stand up to the heat of a blowtorch and survive a cycle in a clothes washer.
Musical	Conveys the message of the advertisement through song. For example, Nike's ads depicted a marathoner's tortured feet and a surfer's thigh scarred by a shark attack while strains of Joe Cocker's "You Are So Beautiful" could be heard in the background.
Scientific	Uses research or scientific evidence to give a brand superiority over competitors. Pain relievers like Advil, Bayer, and Excedrin use scientific evidence in their ads.

is this more evident than in the political realm, where advertisements for issues and candidates must account for ever-changing poll numbers and public sentiments. In Barack Obama's second presidential election, campaign advertisements taking aim at the president shifted in tone from sharply combative and accusatory to concerned—even mournful—about the state of the economy. According to Republican pollster Frank Luntz, focus group research revealed that ads that attacked Obama too personally turned people off in ways that kept them turned off. The Republican campaign shifted its executional style, opting for advertisements that appealed to citizens' worries and frustrations. In one ad, a forlorn-looking woman declares, "I supported President Obama because he spoke so beautifully. But since then, things have gone from bad to much worse."[16]

16-3d Post-Campaign Evaluation

Evaluating an advertising campaign can be the most demanding task facing advertisers. How can an advertiser assess if the campaign led to an increase in sales or market share or elevated awareness of the product? Many advertising campaigns aim to create an image for the good or service instead of asking for action, so their real effect is unknown. So many variables shape the effectiveness of an ad that advertisers often must guess whether their money has been well spent. Nonetheless, marketers spend considerable time studying advertising effectiveness and its probable impact on sales, market share, or awareness.

Testing ad effectiveness can be done before and/or after the campaign. Before a campaign is released, marketing managers use pretests to determine the best advertising appeal, layout, and media vehicle. After advertisers implement a campaign, they use several monitoring techniques to determine whether the campaign has met its original goals. Even if a campaign has been highly successful, advertisers still typically do a post-campaign analysis to identify how the campaign might have been more efficient and what factors contributed to its success.

16-4 MEDIA DECISIONS IN ADVERTISING

A major decision for advertisers is the choice of medium—the channel used to convey a message to a target market. Media planning, therefore, is the series of decisions advertisers make regarding the selection and use of media, enabling the marketer to optimally and cost-effectively communicate the message to the target audience. Specifically, advertisers must determine which types of media will best communicate the benefits of their product or service to the target audience and when and for how long the advertisement will run.

Promotional objectives and the appeal and executional style of the advertising strongly affect the selection of media. Both creative and media decisions are made at the same time: creative work cannot be completed without knowing which medium will be used to convey the message to the target market. In many cases, the advertising objectives dictate the medium and the creative approach to be used. For example, if the objective is to demonstrate how fast a product operates, a television commercial that shows this action may be the best choice.

In 2015, U.S. advertisers spent about $180 billion on paid media monitored by national reporting services—newspapers, magazines, radio, television, the Internet, and outdoor/

medium the channel used to convey a message to a target market

media planning the series of decisions advertisers make regarding the selection and use of media, allowing the marketer to optimally and cost-effectively communicate the message to the target audience

BEST OF THE BEST

According to *Advertising Age,* these are the best advertising campaigns in recent years:

1. Newcastle's "If We Made It"
2. Save the Children's "Most Shocking Second a Day"
3. Coca Cola Life's "Parents"
4. Wren's "First Kiss"
5. John Lewis' "Monty the Penguin"[17]

cinema.[18] The remainder was spent on unmonitored media such as direct mail, trade exhibits, cooperative advertising, brochures, coupons, catalogs, and special events. More than 38 percent of every media dollar goes toward television ads (cable, syndicated, spot, and network); almost 25 percent toward Internet ads; 12 percent toward newspaper ads; 10 percent toward magazine ads; 9 percent toward radio ads; and 5 percent toward outdoor/cinema ads.[19] But these traditional mass-market media are declining in usage as more targeted media are emerging. Future growth lies primarily in the digital realm, both in paid media (display ads, video ads, and search ads) and earned media (social media).

16-4a Media Types

Advertising media are channels that advertisers use in mass communication. The six major advertising media are newspapers, magazines, radio, television, the Internet, and outdoor media. Exhibit 16.3 summarizes the advantages and disadvantages of some of these major channels. In recent years, however, alternative media channels have emerged that give advertisers innovative ways to reach their target audience and avoid advertising clutter.

NEWSPAPERS Newspapers are one of the oldest forms of media. The advantages of newspaper advertising include geographic flexibility and timeliness. Although there has been a decline in circulation as well as in the number of newspapers, nationally, there are still several major newspapers including the *Wall Street Journal, USA Today,* the *New York Times,* the *Los Angeles Times,* and the *Washington Post.* But most newspapers are local. Because newspapers are generally a

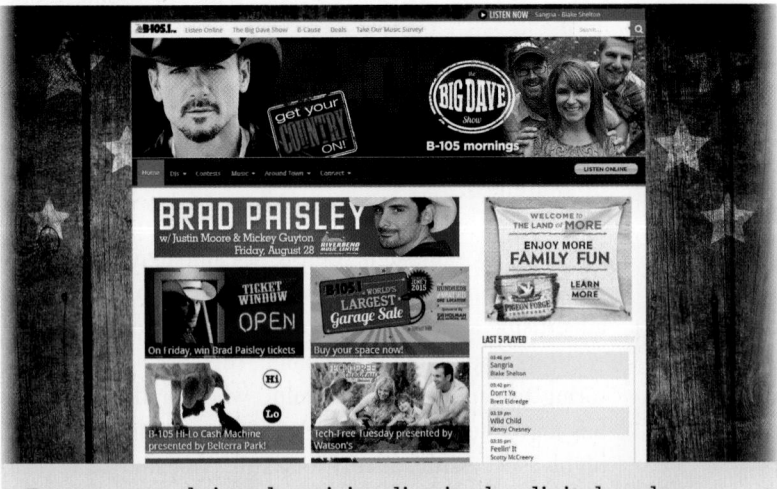

Source: Hubbard Radio, LLC

Future growth in advertising lies in the digital realm; this includes display ads, video ads, search ads and banner ads.

EXHIBIT 16.3 ADVANTAGES AND DISADVANTAGES OF MAJOR ADVERTISING MEDIA

Medium	Advantages	Disadvantages
Newspapers	Geographic selectivity and flexibility; short-term advertiser commitments; news value and immediacy; year-round readership; high individual market coverage; co-op and local tie-in availability; short lead time	Little demographic selectivity; limited color capabilities; low pass-along rate; may be expensive
Magazines	Good reproduction, especially for color; demographic selectivity; regional selectivity; local market selectivity; relatively long advertising life; high pass-along rate	Long-term advertiser commitments; slow audience buildup; limited demonstration capabilities; lack of urgency; long lead time
Radio	Low cost; immediacy of message; can be scheduled on short notice; relatively no seasonal change in audience; highly portable; short-term advertiser commitments; entertainment carryover	No visual treatment; short advertising life of message; high frequency required to generate comprehension and retention; distractions from background sound; commercial clutter
Television	Ability to reach a wide, diverse audience; low cost per thousand; creative opportunities for demonstration; immediacy of messages; entertainment carryover; demographic selectivity with cable stations	Short life of message; some consumer skepticism about claims; high campaign cost; little demographic selectivity with network stations; long-term advertiser commitments; long lead times required for production; commercial clutter
Internet	Fastest-growing medium; ability to reach a narrow target audience; relatively short lead time required for creating Web-based advertising; moderate cost; ability to measure ad effectiveness; ability to engage consumers through search engine marketing, social media, display advertising, and mobile marketing	Most ad exposure relies on "click-through" from display ads; measurement for social media needs much improvement; not all consumers have access to the Internet, and many consumers are not using social media
Outdoor Media	Repetition; moderate cost; flexibility; geographic selectivity	Short message; lack of demographic selectivity; high "noise" level distracting audience

mass-market medium, however, they may not be the best vehicle for marketers trying to reach a very narrow market. Newspaper advertising also encounters distractions from competing ads and news stories. Therefore, one company's ad may not be particularly visible.

The main sources of newspaper ad revenue are local retailers, classified ads, and cooperative advertising. In **cooperative advertising**, the manufacturer and the retailer split the costs of advertising the manufacturer's brand. For example, Estée Lauder may split the cost of an advertisement with Macy's department store provided that the ad focuses on Estée Lauder's products. One reason manufacturers use cooperative advertising is the impracticality of listing all their dealers in national advertising. Also, cooperative advertising encourages retailers to devote more effort to the manufacturer's lines.

MAGAZINES Magazines are another traditional medium that has been successful. Some of the top magazines according to circulation include *AARP*, *Better Homes and Gardens*, *Reader's Digest*, *National Geographic*, and *Good Housekeeping*. However, compared to the cost of other media, the cost per contact in magazine advertising is usually high. The cost per potential customer may be much lower, however, because magazines are often targeted to specialized audiences and thus reach more potential customers.

RADIO Radio has several strengths as an advertising medium: selectivity and audience segmentation, a large out-of-home audience, low unit and production costs, timeliness,

Brian A Jackson/Shutterstock.com

cooperative advertising
an arrangement in which the manufacturer and the retailer split the costs of advertising the manufacturer's brand

and geographic flexibility. Local advertisers are the most frequent users of radio advertising, contributing over 75 percent of all radio ad revenue. Like newspapers, radio also lends itself well to cooperative advertising.

TELEVISION Television broadcasters include network television, independent stations, cable television, and direct broadcast satellite television. Network television reaches a wide and diverse market, and cable television and direct broadcast satellite systems, such as DIRECTV and DISH Network, broadcast a multitude of channels devoted to highly segmented markets. Because of its targeted channels, cable television is often characterized as "narrowcasting" by media buyers. DIRECTV is testing the ability to serve ads based on household data (as opposed to demographic and geographic data). To stay relevant amidst new technologies, DIRECTV and other television-focused companies are beginning to recognize the need for better audience targeting.[20]

Advertising time on television can be very expensive, especially for network and popular cable channels. Special events and first-run prime-time shows for top-ranked television programs command the highest rates for a typical commercial. For example, running a thirty-second spot during the sitcom *How to Get Away with Murder* on *ABC* costs $146,113, while running one during NFL Sunday Football costs $627,300. Cable programs like ESPN's *Monday Night Football* command similarly hefty price tags.[20] A thirty-second spot during the Super Bowl costs approximately $4.5 million.[21] Despite its high cost, many brands feel that a Super Bowl ad is a good investment given the earned media leading up to the game, during the game, and after the game.[22] An alternative to a commercial spot is the **infomercial**, a 30-minute or longer advertisement, which is relatively inexpensive to produce and air. Advertisers say the infomercial is an ideal way to present complicated information to potential customers, which other advertising vehicles typically do not allow time to do. Beachbody's P90X and Insanity exercise DVDs are advertised through infomercials.

Probably the most significant trend of concern to television advertising is the rise in popularity of digital video recorders (DVRs) and on-demand viewing. For every hour of television programming, an average of 20 minutes is dedicated to nonprogram material (ads, public service announcements, and network promotions), so the popularity of DVRs among ad-weary viewers is hardly surprising. Like marketers and advertisers, networks are also highly concerned about ad skipping. If consumers are not watching advertisements, then marketers will spend a greater proportion of their advertising budgets on alternative media, and a critical revenue stream for networks will disappear.

THE INTERNET Online advertising has become a versatile medium to target specific groups. U.S. digital ad revenues exceed $50 billion annually and are expected to increase to $82 billion annually by 2018. This figure is projected to grow to more than $163 billion by 2016, at which point it will represent 26 percent of all advertising expenditures.[23] Online advertising includes search engine marketing (e.g., pay-per-click ads like Google AdWords), display advertising (e.g., banner ads, video ads), social media advertising (e.g., Facebook ads), e-mail marketing, and mobile marketing (including mobile advertising and SMS). Some online channels like Google offer the ability to *audience buy* (whereby advertisers can purchase ad space targeted to a highly specific group), but others, such as Turner Digital's FunnyOrDie.com, believe the complex cookie-based strategy poses too many risks.[24]

Popular Internet sites and search engines generally sell advertising space to marketers to promote their goods and services. Internet surfers click on these ads to be linked to more information about the advertised product or service. Both leading advertisers and companies whose ad budgets are not as large have become big Internet advertisers. Because of the relative low cost and high targetability, search engines generate nearly half of all Internet ad revenue. Display and banner ads are the next largest source of Internet revenue, followed by classifieds, mobile, and digital video.[25]

Another popular Internet advertising format is **advergaming**, whereby companies put ad messages in Web-based, mobile, console, or handheld video games to advertise or promote a product, service, organization, or issue. *Gamification*, the process of using game mechanics and a gaming mindset to engage an audience, is increasingly important for marketers to know about and utilize. Challenges, rewards, incentives, and competition are all important aspects in social media games like *Candy Crush Saga and Candy Crush Soda Saga*.[26] Some games amount to virtual commercials; others encourage players to buy in-game items and power-ups to advance; and still others allow advertisers to sponsor games or buy ad space for

infomercial a 30-minute or longer advertisement that looks more like a television talk show than a sales pitch

advergaming placing advertising messages in Web-based, mobile, console, or handheld video games to advertise or promote a product, service, organization, or issue

product placements. Many of these are social games, played on Facebook or mobile networks, where players can interact with one another. Social gaming has a huge audience—according to Facebook CEO Mark Zuckerberg, 235 million people play social games on Facebook every month. The Facebook gaming market is projected to more than double in the next three years, attracting 554 million people and generating $5.6 billion.[27]

More than three-fourths of Americans have mobile phones, and over one-third of those are smartphones. Fifty-five percent of mobile phone owners access the Web on their phones, making mobile Web sites and apps more important.[28] Mobile advertising has substantial upside potential given that there are more than six billion cell phone users in the world, and an increasing number of those users have smartphones or tablets with Internet access. Mobile advertising is finally reaching its tipping point, reaching almost $24 billion annually. This accounts for nearly all growth in digital advertising. The primary reason is that people are spending more of their time (19.4 percent) on mobile devices rather than on desktops and laptops.[29] As devices such as the iPad continue to grow in popularity, mobile advertising spending will continue to grow worldwide.

OUTDOOR MEDIA Outdoor or out-of-home advertising is a flexible, low-cost medium that may take a variety of forms. Examples include billboards, skywriting, giant inflatables, mini billboards in malls and on bus stop shelters, signs in sports arenas, and lighted moving signs in bus terminals and airports, as well as ads painted on cars, trucks, buses, water towers, manhole covers, drinking glass coasters, and even people, called "living advertising." The plywood scaffolding surrounding downtown construction sites often holds ads, which in places like Manhattan's Times Square, can reach over a million viewers a day.

Outdoor advertising reaches a broad and diverse market and is therefore ideal for promoting convenience products and services as well as directing consumers to local businesses. One of outdoor advertising's main advantages over other media is that its exposure frequency is very high, yet the amount of clutter from competing ads is very low. Outdoor advertising also can be customized to local marketing needs, which is why local businesses are the leading outdoor advertisers in any given region.

ALTERNATIVE MEDIA To cut through the clutter of traditional advertising media, advertisers are developing new media vehicles, like shopping carts in grocery stores, computer screen savers, interactive kiosks in department stores, advertisements run before movies at the cinema, posters on bathroom stalls, and *advertainments*—mini movies that promote a product and are shown online.

Marketers are looking for more innovative ways to reach captive and often bored commuters. For instance, subway systems are now showing ads via lighted boxes installed along tunnel walls. Other advertisers seek consumers at home. Some marketers have begun replacing hold music on customer service lines with advertisements and movie trailers. This strategy generates revenue for the company being called and catches undistracted consumers for advertisers. The trick is to amuse and interest this captive audience without annoying them during their ten- to fifteen-minute wait. After Yahoo! CEO Marissa Mayer called her company's on-hold message "garbage," audio production startup Jingle Punks hired Canadian rapper Snow (known for his 1992 hit "Informer") to write a humorous on-hold jingle for Yahoo! (you can hear the jingle at www.youtube.com /watch?v=vRmVDADlnOU). Yahoo! has yet to implement the jingle, however.[30]

There are a number of factors to consider before committing to any sort of advertising medium; this includes flexibility of the medium, noise level, and the life span of the medium.

16-4b Media Selection Considerations

An important element in any advertising campaign is the **media mix**, the combination of media to be used. Media mix decisions are typically based on several factors: cost per contact, cost per click, reach, frequency, target audience considerations, flexibility of the medium, noise level, and the life span of the medium.

Cost per contact, also referred to as **cost per thousand (CPM)**, is the cost of reaching one member of the target market. Naturally, as the size of the audience increases, so does the total cost. Cost per contact enables an advertiser to compare the relative costs of specific media vehicles (such as television versus radio or magazine versus newspaper), or more specifically, within a media category (such as *People* versus *US Weekly*). Thus, an advertiser debating whether to spend local advertising dollars for television spots or radio spots could consider the cost per contact of each. Alternatively, if the question is which magazine to advertise in, she might choose the one with the greater reach. In either case, the advertiser can pick the vehicle with the lowest cost per contact to maximize advertising punch for the money spent. **Cost per click** is the cost associated with a consumer clicking on a display or banner ad. Although there are several variations, this option enables the marketer to pay only for "engaged" consumers—those who opted to click on an ad.

Reach is the number of target customers who are exposed to a commercial at least once during a specific period, usually four weeks. Media plans for product introductions and attempts at increasing brand awareness usually emphasize reach. For example, an advertiser might try to reach seventy percent of the target audience during the first three months of the campaign. Reach is related to a medium's ratings, generally referred to in the industry as *gross ratings points*, or *GRP*. A television program with a higher GRP means that more people are tuning in to the show and the reach is higher. Accordingly, as GRP increases for a particular medium, so does cost per contact.

Because the typical ad is short-lived, and often only a small portion of an ad may be perceived at one time, advertisers repeat their ads so that potential customers will remember the message. **Frequency** is the number of times an individual is exposed to a given message during a specific period. Advertisers use average frequency to measure the intensity of a specific medium's coverage. For example, Coca-Cola might want an average exposure frequency of five for its Powerade television ads. That means that each of the television viewers who saw the ad saw it an average of five times.

Media selection is also a matter of matching the advertising medium with the product's target market. If marketers are trying to reach teenage females, they might select *Teen Vogue* magazine. A medium's ability to reach a precisely defined market is its **audience selectivity**. Some media vehicles, like general newspapers and network television, appeal to a wide cross section of the population. Others—such as *Brides*, *Popular Mechanics*, *Architectural Digest*, *Lucky*, MTV, ESPN, and Christian radio stations—appeal to very specific groups.

The *flexibility* of a medium can be extremely important to an advertiser. For example, because of layouts and design, the lead time for magazine advertising is considerably longer than for other media types and so is less flexible. By contrast, radio and Internet advertising provide maximum flexibility. If necessary, an advertiser can change a radio ad on the day it is aired.

Noise level is the level of distraction experienced by the target audience in a medium. Noise can be created by competing ads, as when a street is lined with billboards or when a television program is cluttered with competing

media mix the combination of media to be used for a promotional campaign

cost per contact (cost per thousand or CPM) the cost of reaching one member of the target market

cost per click the cost associated with a consumer clicking on a display or banner ad

reach the number of target consumers exposed to a commercial at least once during a specific period, usually four weeks

frequency the number of times an individual is exposed to a given message during a specific period

audience selectivity the ability of an advertising medium to reach a precisely defined market

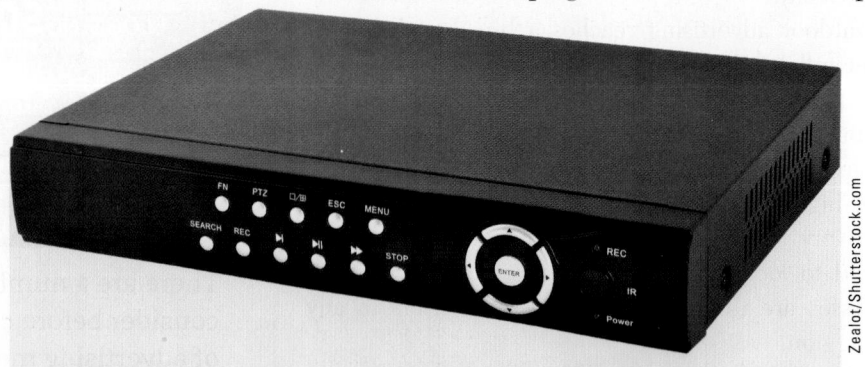

There are many ways for viewers to avoid watching commercials; this includes the use of a DVR.

Zealot/Shutterstock.com

ads. Whereas newspapers and magazines have a high noise level, direct mail is a private medium with a low noise level. Typically, no other advertising media or news stories compete for direct mail readers' attention.

Media have either a short or a long *life span*, which means that messages can either quickly fade or persist as tangible copy to be carefully studied. A radio commercial may last less than a minute, but advertisers can overcome this short life span by repeating radio ads often. In contrast, a magazine has a relatively long life span, which is further increased by a high pass-along rate.

Media planners have traditionally relied on the above factors in selecting an effective media mix, with reach, frequency, and cost often the overriding criteria. Well-established brands with familiar messages, however, probably need fewer exposures to be effective, while newer or unfamiliar brands likely need more exposures to become familiar. In addition, today's media planners have more media options than ever before. (Today, there are over 1,600 television networks across the country, whereas forty years ago there were only three.)

The proliferation of media channels is causing *media fragmentation* and forcing media planners to pay as much attention to where they place their advertising as to how often the advertisement is repeated. That is, marketers should evaluate reach *and* frequency in assessing the effectiveness of advertising. In certain situations, it may be important to reach potential consumers through as many media vehicles as possible. When this approach is considered, however, the budget must be large enough to achieve sufficient levels of frequency to have an impact. In evaluating reach versus frequency, therefore, the media planner ultimately must select an approach that is most likely to result in the ad being understood and remembered when a purchase decision is being made.

Advertisers also evaluate the qualitative factors involved in media selection. These include such things as attention to the commercial and the program, involvement, program liking, lack of distractions, and other audience behaviors that affect the likelihood that a commercial message is being seen and, hopefully, absorbed. While advertisers can advertise their product in as many media as possible and repeat the ad as many times as they like, the ad still may not be effective if the audience is not paying attention. Additional research highlights the benefits of cross-media advertising campaigns. According to Rick Mandler, VP of Digital Ad Sales at television network ABC, running an ad both on television and online delivers a lower median age, but delivers greater frequency and reach in the 18 to 24 age range, as well as greater overall reach for adults ages 18 to 49. ABC

Unified, a pioneering approach to cross-media advertising, is quickly gaining popularity among ABC's more than 200 advertisers.[31]

16-4c Media Scheduling

After choosing the media for the advertising campaign, advertisers must schedule the ads. A **media schedule** designates the medium or media to be used (such as magazines, television, or radio), the specific vehicles (such as *People* magazine, the show *Scandal* on television, or Rush Limbaugh's national radio program), and the insertion dates of the advertising.

There are four basic types of media schedules:

- A **continuous media schedule** allows the advertising to run steadily throughout the advertising period. Examples include Ivory soap and Charmin toilet tissue, which may have an ad in the newspaper every Sunday and a television commercial on NBC every Wednesday at 7:30 p.m. over a three-month time period. Products in the later stages of the product life cycle, which are advertised on a reminder basis, often use a continuous media schedule.

- With a **flighted media schedule**, the advertiser may schedule the ads heavily every other month or every two weeks to achieve a greater impact with an increased frequency and reach at those times. Movie studios might schedule television advertising on Wednesday and Thursday nights, when moviegoers are deciding which films to see that weekend.

- A **pulsing media schedule** combines continuous scheduling with flighted scheduling. It is continuous advertising that is simply heavier during the best sale periods. A retail department store may advertise on a year-round basis but place more advertising during certain sale periods such as Thanksgiving, Christmas, and back-to-school. Or beer may be advertised more heavily during the summer months and football

media schedule designation of the media, the specific publications or programs, and the insertion dates of advertising

continuous media schedule a media scheduling strategy in which advertising is run steadily throughout the advertising period; used for products in the later stages of the product life cycle

flighted media schedule a media scheduling strategy in which ads are heavily every other month or every two weeks to achieve a greater impact with an increased frequency and reach at those times

pulsing media schedule a media scheduling strategy that uses continuous scheduling throughout the year coupled with a flighted schedule during the best sales periods

season given the higher consumption levels at those times.

- Certain times of the year call for a **seasonal media schedule**. Products like Sudafed cold tablets and Coppertone sunscreen, which are used more during certain times of the year, tend to follow a seasonal strategy.

Research comparing continuous media schedules and flighted ones suggests that continuous schedules are more effective than are flighted ones at driving sales through television advertisements. This research suggests that it may be important to reach a potential customer as close as possible to the time at which he makes a purchase. Therefore, the advertiser should maintain a continuous schedule over as long a period of time as possible. Often called *recency planning*, this theory of scheduling is now commonly used for scheduling television advertising for frequently purchased products such as Coca-Cola and Tide detergent. Recency planning's main premise is that advertising works by influencing the brand choice of people who are ready to buy. Mobile advertising may be one of the most promising tactics for contacting consumers when they are thinking about a specific product. For example, a GPS-enabled mobile phone can get text messages for area restaurants around lunchtime to advertise specials to professionals working in a big city.

AP Images/John Shearer/Invision

Big Mama's and Papa's Pizzeria received more than $10 million in free publicity after Ellen DeGeneres placed an order with the restaurant during the 2014 Academy Awards broadcast.

 16-5 PUBLIC RELATIONS

Public relations is the element in the promotional mix that evaluates public attitudes, identifies issues that may elicit public concern, and executes programs to gain public understanding and acceptance. Public relations is a vital link in a forward-thinking company's marketing communication mix. Marketing managers plan solid public relations campaigns that fit into overall marketing plans and focus on targeted audiences. These campaigns strive to maintain a positive image of the corporation in the eyes of the public. As such, they should capitalize on the factors that enhance the firm's image and minimize the factors that could generate a negative image. The concept of earned media is based on public relations and publicity.

Publicity is the effort to capture media attention—for example, through articles or editorials in publications or through human-interest stories on radio or television programs. Corporations usually initiate publicity through press releases that further their public relations plans. A company about to introduce a new product or open a new store may send press releases to the media in the hope that the story will be published or broadcast. Savvy publicity can often create overnight sensations or build up a reserve of goodwill with consumers. Corporate donations and sponsorships can also create favorable publicity.

16-5a Major Public Relations Tools

Public relations professionals commonly use several tools, many of which require an active role on the part of the public relations professional, such as writing press releases and engaging in proactive media relations. Sometimes, however, these techniques create their own publicity.

NEW-PRODUCT PUBLICITY Publicity is instrumental in introducing new products and services. Publicity can help advertisers explain what's different about their new product by prompting free news stories or positive

seasonal media schedule a media scheduling strategy that runs advertising only during times of the year when the product is most likely to be used

public relations the element in the promotional mix that evaluates public attitudes, identifies issues that may elicit public concern, and executes programs to gain public understanding and acceptance

publicity an effort to capture media attention, often initiated through press releases that further a corporation's public relations plans

word of mouth about it. During the introductory period, an especially innovative new product often needs more exposure than conventional, paid advertising affords. Public relations professionals write press releases or develop videos in an effort to generate news about their new product. They also jockey for exposure of their product or service at major events, on popular television and news shows, or in the hands of influential people. Consider the publicity Apple generated for the release of the iPad Air, which included press coverage in traditional media as well as online blogs and forums. That was a small part of the entire marketing campaign.

PRODUCT PLACEMENT Marketers are increasingly using product placement to reinforce brand awareness and create favorable attitudes. **Product placement** is a strategy that involves getting one's product, service, or name to appear in a movie, television show, radio program, magazine, newspaper, video game, video or audio clip, book, or commercial for another product; on the Internet; or at special events. Including an actual product, such as a can of Pepsi, adds a sense of realism to a movie, television show, video game, book, or similar vehicle that cannot be created by a can simply marked "soda." Product placements are arranged through barter (trade of product for placement), through paid placements, or at no charge when the product is viewed as enhancing the vehicle it is placed in.

Global product placement expenditures total about $8 billion annually ($4.3 billion in the United States alone).[32] More than two-thirds of product placements are in movies and television shows, but placements in other alternative media are growing, particularly on the Internet and in video games. Digital technology now enables companies to "virtually" place their products in any audio or video production. Virtual placement not only reduces the cost of product placement for new productions but also enables companies to place their products in previously produced programs, such as reruns of television shows. Overall, companies obtain valuable product exposure, brand reinforcement, and increased sales through product placement.

CONSUMER EDUCATION Some major firms believe that educated consumers are more loyal customers. Financial planning firms often sponsor free educational seminars on money management, retirement planning, and investing in the hope that the seminar participants will choose the sponsoring organization for their future financial needs.

> **product placement** a public relations strategy that involves getting a product, service, or company name to appear in a movie, television show, radio program, magazine, newspaper, video game, video or audio clip, book, or commercial for another product; on the Internet; or at special events

The Many Duties of Public Relations Departments

Public relations departments may perform any or all of the following functions:

- **Press relations:** Placing positive, newsworthy information in the news media or in the hands of influential bloggers to attract attention to a product, a service, or a person associated with the firm or institution

- **Product publicity:** Publicizing specific products or services through a variety of traditional and online channels

- **Corporate communication:** Creating internal and external messages to promote a positive image of the firm or institution

- **Public affairs:** Building and maintaining local, national, or global community relations

- **Lobbying:** Influencing legislators and government officials to promote or defeat legislation and regulation

- **Employee and investor relations:** Maintaining positive relationships with employees, shareholders, and others in the financial community

- **Crisis management:** Responding to unfavorable publicity or a negative event placement, often at a much lower cost than in mass media like television ads

© plexus/Shutterstock 149737013

SPONSORSHIP Sponsorships are increasing both in number and as a proportion of companies' marketing budgets. Currently sitting at about $32 billion annually, U.S. sponsorship spending is likewise increasing.[33] Probably the biggest reason for the increasing use of sponsorships is the difficulty of reaching audiences and differentiating a product from competing brands through the mass media.

With **sponsorship**, a company spends money to support an issue, cause, or event that is consistent with corporate objectives, such as improving brand awareness or enhancing corporate image. The biggest category of sponsorships is sports, which accounts for almost 70 percent of spending in sponsorships and has seen steady growth in recent years.[34] Nonsports categories include entertainment tours and attractions, causes, arts, festivals, fairs and annual events, and association and membership organizations.

Corporations sponsor events in an attempt to market their product. The yearly Rose Bowl game has been sponsored by companies like Citi and Northwestern Mutual.

Although the most popular sponsorship events are still those involving sports, music, or the arts, companies have recently been turning to more specialized events such as tie-ins with schools, charities, and other community service organizations. Marketers sometimes even create their own events tied around their products. For example, energy drink manufacturer Red Bull hosted Stratos, a multimillion-dollar event where Austrian Felix Baumgartner skydived from the edge of space—nearly twenty-four miles above Earth's surface. Baumgartner became the first human to break the sound barrier in free fall, reaching 834 miles per hour before touching down safely in New Mexico. A major marketing victory for Red Bull, Stratos set its own record as the most-watched YouTube live stream of all time—more than eight million viewers tuned in to the event.[35]

Corporations sponsor issues as well as events. Sponsorship issues are quite diverse, but the three most popular are education, health care, and social programs. Firms often donate a percentage of sales or profits to a worthy cause favored by their target market.

EXPERIENTIAL MARKETING While the Internet enables consumers to connect with their favorite brands in a virtual environment, there is often nothing like experiencing the real thing live and in person. Experiential marketing involves engaging with consumers in a way that enables them to feel the brand—not just read about it. Experiential and event marketing have increased in recent years, with most of the growth coming from the world's largest brands. Examples of experiential marketing include American Express's Small Business Saturday, which promotes shopping at local businesses, and Clear Channel's effort to run a carnival-style dunk tank in New York City's Times Square.[36]

COMPANY WEB SITES Companies are increasingly using the Internet in their public relations strategies. Company Web sites are used to introduce new products; provide information to the media, including social media news releases; promote existing products; obtain consumer feedback; communicate legislative and regulatory information; showcase upcoming events; provide links to related sites (including corporate and non-corporate blogs, Facebook, and Twitter); release financial information; interact with customers and potential customers; and perform many more marketing activities. In addition, social media are playing a larger role in how companies interact with customers online, particularly through sites like Facebook, Yelp, or Twitter. Indeed, online reviews (good and bad) from opinion leaders and other consumers help marketers sway purchasing decisions in their favor.

16-5b Managing Unfavorable Publicity

Although marketers try to avoid unpleasant situations, crises do happen. In our free-press environment, publicity is not easily controlled, especially in a crisis.

sponsorship a public relations strategy in which a company spends money to support an issue, cause, or event that is consistent with corporate objectives, such as improving brand awareness or enhancing corporate image

Crisis management is the coordinated effort to handle the effects of unfavorable publicity, ensuring fast and accurate communication in times of emergency.

When the Villa Fresh Italian Kitchen ran "Dub the Dew," an online contest to name a green apple–flavored variety of Mountain Dew exclusive to the restaurant, it was not long before Internet trolls descended. These digital pranksters submitted absurd and offensive names (such as "diabeetus," "gushing granny," and "Hitler did nothing wrong"), and then voted their submissions to the top of the contest leaderboard en masse. The contest's Web site was quickly taken offline, and Mountain Dew tweeted that the contest "lost to the internet." In an attempt to manage the crisis, the Villa Fresh Italian Kitchen issued an apologetic statement: "'Dub the Dew,' a local market promotional campaign that was created by one of our customers—not Mountain Dew—was compromised. We are working diligently with our customer's team to remove all offensive content that was posted and putting measures in place to ensure this doesn't happen again."[37]

 16-6 ## SALES PROMOTION

In addition to using advertising and public relations, marketing managers can use sales promotion to increase the effectiveness of their promotional efforts. Sales promotion consists of marketing communication activities other than advertising, personal selling, and public relations, in which a short-term incentive motivates consumers or members of the distribution channel to purchase a good or service immediately, either by lowering the price or by adding value.

Sales promotion is usually cheaper than advertising and easier to measure. A major national television advertising campaign often costs $10 million or more to create, produce, and place. In contrast, promotional campaigns using the Internet or direct marketing methods can cost less than half that amount. It is also very difficult to determine how many people buy a product or service as a result of radio or television ads. With sales promotion, marketers know the precise number of coupons redeemed or the number of contest entries received.

Sales promotion usually has more effect on behavior than on attitudes. Giving the consumer an incentive to make an immediate purchase is the goal of sales promotion, regardless of the form it takes. Sales promotion is usually targeted toward either of two distinctly different markets. **Trade sales promotion** is directed to members of the marketing channel, such as wholesalers and retailers. **Consumer sales promotion** is targeted to the ultimate consumer market. The objectives of a promotion depend on the general behavior of targeted customers Exhibit 16.4.

> **crisis management** a coordinated effort to handle all the effects of unfavorable publicity or another unexpected unfavorable event
>
> **sales promotion** marketing communication activities other than advertising, personal selling, and public relations, in which a short-term incentive motivates consumers or members of the distribution channel to purchase a good or service immediately, either by lowering the price or by adding value
>
> **trade sales promotion** promotion activities directed to members of the marketing channel, such as wholesalers and retailers
>
> **consumer sales promotion** promotion activities targeted to the ultimate consumer market

EXHIBIT 16.4 TYPES OF CONSUMERS AND SALES PROMOTION GOALS

Type of Buyer	Desired Results	Sales Promotion Examples
Loyal customers People who buy your product most or all of the time	Reinforce behavior, increase consumption, change purchase timing	• Loyalty marketing programs, such as frequent buyer cards or frequent shopper clubs • Bonus packs that give loyal consumers an incentive to stock up or premiums offered in return for proofs of purchase
Competitor's customers People who buy a competitor's product most or all of the time	Break loyalty, persuade to switch to your brand	• Sampling to introduce your product's superior qualities compared to their brand • Sweepstakes, contests, or premiums that create interest in the product
Brand switchers People who buy a variety of products in the category	Persuade to buy your brand more often	• Any promotion that lowers the price of the product, such as coupons, price-off packages, and bonus packs • Trade deals that help make the product more readily available than competing products
Price buyers People who consistently buy the least expensive brand	Appeal with low prices or supply added value that makes price less important	• Coupons, price-off packages, refunds, or trade deals that reduce the price of the brand to match that of the brand that would have been purchased

From *Sales Promotion Essentials*, 2nd ed., by Don E. Schultz, William A. Robinson, and Lisa A. Petrison, published by McGraw-Hill Education.

For example, marketers who are targeting loyal users of their product need to reinforce existing behavior or increase product usage. An effective tool for strengthening brand loyalty is the *frequent buyer program*, which rewards consumers for repeat purchases. Other types of promotions are more effective with customers who are prone to brand switching or with those who are loyal to a competitor's product. A cents-off coupon, free sample, or eye-catching display in a store will often entice shoppers to try a different brand.

Once marketers understand the dynamics occurring within their product category and determine the particular customers and behaviors they want to influence, they can then go about selecting promotional tools to achieve these goals.

16-6a Tools for Trade Sales Promotion

As we'll discuss in section 16-6b, consumer promotions pull a product through the channel by creating demand. However, trade promotions *push* a product through the distribution channel (see Chapter 13). When selling to members of the distribution channel, manufacturers use many of the same sales promotion tools used in consumer promotions, such as sales contests premiums and point-of-purchase displays. Several tools, however, are unique to manufacturers and intermediaries:

- **Trade allowances:** A **trade allowance** is a price reduction offered by manufacturers to intermediaries such as wholesalers and retailers. The price reduction or rebate is given in exchange for doing something specific, such as allocating space for a new product or buying something during special periods. For example, a local Best Buy outlet could receive a special discount for running its own promotion on Sony surround sound systems.

- **Push money:** Intermediaries receive **push money** as a bonus for pushing the manufacturer's brand through the distribution channel. Often the push money is directed toward a retailer's salespeople. LinoColor, the leading high-end scanner company, produces a Picture Perfect Rewards catalog filled with merchandise retailers can purchase with points accrued for every LinoColor scanner they sell.

- **Training:** Sometimes a manufacturer will train an intermediary's

personnel if the product is rather complex—as frequently occurs in the computer and telecommunications industries. For example, representatives of major pharmaceutical companies receive extensive training because they need to provide accurate information to doctors and nurses.

- **Free merchandise:** Often a manufacturer offers retailers free merchandise in lieu of quantity discounts. Occasionally, free merchandise is used as payment for trade allowances normally provided through other sales promotions. Instead of giving a retailer a price reduction for buying a certain quantity of merchandise, the manufacturer may throw in extra merchandise "free" (i.e., at a cost that would equal the price reduction).

- **Store demonstrations:** Manufacturers can also arrange with retailers to perform an in-store demonstration. Food manufacturers often send representatives to grocery stores and supermarkets to let customers sample a product while shopping.

- **Business meetings, conventions, and trade shows:** Trade association meetings, conferences, and conventions are an important aspect of sales promotion and a growing, multi-billion-dollar market. At these shows, manufacturers, distributors, and other vendors have the chance to display their goods or describe their services to potential customers. Companies participate in trade shows to attract and identify new prospects, serve current customers, introduce new products, enhance corporate image, test the market response to new products, enhance corporate morale, and gather competitive product information.

Trade promotions are popular among manufacturers for many reasons. Trade sales promotion tools help manufacturers gain new distributors for their products, obtain wholesaler and retailer support for consumer sales promotions, build or reduce dealer inventories, and improve trade relations. Car manufacturers annually sponsor dozens of auto shows for consumers. The shows attract millions of consumers, providing dealers with increased store traffic as well as good leads.

16-6b Tools for Consumer Sales Promotion

Marketing managers must decide which consumer sales promotion devices to use in a specific campaign. The methods chosen must suit the objectives to ensure success of the overall promotion plan. The popular tools for consumer sales promotion, discussed in the following

trade allowance a price reduction offered by manufacturers to intermediaries such as wholesalers and retailers

push money money offered to channel intermediaries to encourage them to "push" products—that is, to encourage other members of the channel to sell the products

pages, have also been easily transferred to online versions to entice Internet users to visit sites, purchase products, or use services on the Web.

COUPONS AND REBATES A **coupon** is a certificate that entitles consumers to an immediate price reduction when the product is purchased. Coupons are a particularly good way to encourage product trial and repurchase. They are also likely to increase the amount of a product bought. Coupons can be distributed in stores as instant coupons on packaging, on shelf displays with pull-off coupon dispensers, and at cash registers, printed based on what the customer purchased; through freestanding inserts (FSIs); and through various Internet daily deal sites.

American Express is experimenting with Twitter to offer cardholders great deals at participating businesses.

iStockphoto.com/Magnez2

FSIs, the promotional coupons inserts found in newspapers, are the traditional way of circulating printed coupons. FSIs are used to distribute approximately 80 percent of coupons. Such traditional types of coupon distribution, which also include direct mail and magazines, have been declining for several years, as consumers use fewer coupons. About 3 billion coupons are redeemed annually. Mobile coupons have a much higher redemption rate than paper coupons.[38]

The Internet is changing the face of coupons. In addition to Internet coupon sites such as Valpak.com and Coolsavings.com, and social coupon sites such as Groupon and LivingSocial, there are also deal sites like DealSurf.com that aggregate offers from different sites for convenience. While daily deal sites have been quite popular with consumers, sites like Groupon and LivingSocial are coming under some fire as many small businesses claim they lose money or drown under the flood of coupon redemptions. American Express is using Twitter to drive card use. After syncing their credit cards to their Twitter accounts, American Express customers can send tweets using an approved hashtag (or "cashtag") to pay for items purchased through third-party retailers. Cardholders can also receive automatic discounts from partner businesses on Twitter when they make purchases with their American Express cards.[39]

A **rebate** is similar to a coupon in that a rebate offers the purchaser a price reduction; however, because the purchaser must mail in a rebate form and usually some proof of purchase, the reward is not as immediate. Manufacturers prefer rebates for several reasons. Rebates allow manufacturers to offer price cuts to consumers directly. Manufacturers have more control over rebate promotions because they can be rolled out and shut off quickly. Further, because buyers must fill out forms with their names, addresses, and other data, manufacturers use rebate programs to build customer databases. Perhaps the best reason of all to offer rebates is that although rebates are particularly good at enticing purchase, most consumers never bother to redeem them—only about 40 percent of consumers eligible for rebates collect them.[40]

PREMIUMS A **premium** is an extra item offered to the consumer, usually in exchange for some proof that the promoted product has been purchased. Premiums reinforce the consumer's purchase decision, increase consumption, and persuade nonusers to switch brands. A longstanding example of the use of premiums is the McDonald's Happy Meal, which rewards children with a small toy. Premiums can also include more product for the regular price, such as two-for-the-price-of-one bonus packs or packages that include more of the product. Some companies attach a premium to the product's package, such as a small sample of a complementary hair product attached to a shampoo bottle.

LOYALTY MARKETING PROGRAMS A **loyalty marketing program** builds long-term, mutually beneficial relationships between a company and its key customers. One of the most popular types of loyalty programs, the **frequent buyer program**, rewards loyal consumers for making multiple purchases. The objective of loyalty marketing programs is to build long-term, mutually beneficial relationships between a company and its key customers.

coupon a certificate that entitles consumers to an immediate price reduction when the product is purchased.

rebate a cash refund given for the purchase of a product during a specific period

premium an extra item offered to the consumer, usually in exchange for some proof of purchase of the promoted product

loyalty marketing program a promotional program designed to build long-term, mutually beneficial relationships between a company and its key customers

frequent buyer program a loyalty program in which loyal consumers are rewarded for making multiple purchases of a particular good or service

There are almost three billion loyalty program memberships in the United States; the average household has signed up for 18 programs.[41] Popularized by the airline industry through frequent-flyer programs, loyalty marketing enables companies to strategically invest sales promotion dollars in activities designed to capture greater profits from customers already loyal to the product or company. Co-branded credit cards are an increasingly popular loyalty marketing tool. Most department stores only offer loyalty programs if a customer opens their branded credit card. However, high-end chain Bloomingdales recently changed its rewards program to include anyone who will sign up. Members of the new Loyalist program receive one point for each dollar they spend and receive a $25 gift card after earning 5,000 points. While Bloomingdale's credit card holders receive more points per dollar spent, the company is hoping to monitor a greater number of its shoppers' spending habits by enabling non-cardholders to join Loyalist.[42]

Through loyalty programs, shoppers receive discounts, alerts on new products, and other types of enticing offers. In exchange, retailers are able to build customer databases that help them better understand customer preferences.

CONTESTS AND SWEEPSTAKES Contests and sweepstakes are generally designed to create interest in a good or service, often to encourage brand switching. *Contests* are promotions in which participants use some skill or ability to compete for prizes. A consumer contest usually requires entrants to answer questions, complete sentences, or write a paragraph about the product and submit proof of purchase. Winning a *sweepstakes*, on the other hand, depends on chance, and participation is free. Sweepstakes usually draw about ten times more entries than contests do.

While contests and sweepstakes may draw considerable interest and publicity, generally they are not effective tools for generating long-term sales. To increase their effectiveness, sales promotion managers must make certain the award will appeal to the target market. Offering several smaller prizes to many winners

Source: Mead Johnson & Company

Baby formula companies like Enfamil, will send samples to expectant mothers or homes where baby's were recently born.

instead of one huge prize to just one person often will increase the effectiveness of the promotion, but there is no denying the attractiveness of a jackpot-type prize.

SAMPLING **Sampling** allows the customer to try a product risk-free. In a recent study, in-store sampling proved to be the most successful promotional tactic when researchers introduced a new dairy product to grocery stores. In-store sampling events increased sales 116 percent, outperforming aisle displays (70 percent), ad circulars (63 percent), and temporary price reductions (48 percent).[43]

Samples can be directly mailed to the customer, delivered door-to-door, packaged with another product, or demonstrated or distributed at a retail store or service outlet. Sampling at special events is a popular, effective, and high profile distribution method that permits marketers to piggyback onto fun-based consumer activities—including sporting events, college fests, fairs and festivals, beach events, and chili cook-offs. Distributing samples to specific location types, such as health clubs, churches, or doctors' offices, is also one of the most efficient methods of sampling. Online sampling is catching up in popularity, however, with the growth of social media. Branded products not only run contests through Facebook, but also connect with fans, show

sampling a promotional program that allows the consumer the opportunity to try a product or service for free

commercials, and offer samples of new products in exchange for "liking" the brand.

POINT-OF-PURCHASE PROMOTION A **point-of-purchase (P-O-P) display** includes any promotional display set up at the retailer's location to build traffic, advertise the product, or induce impulse buying. P-O-P displays include shelf "talkers" (signs attached to store shelves), shelf extenders (attachments that extend shelves so products stand out), ads on grocery carts and bags, end-aisle and floor-stand displays, television monitors at supermarket checkout counters, in-store audio messages, and audiovisual displays. One big advantage of the P-O-P display is that it offers manufacturers a captive audience in retail stores. According to POPAI's Shopper Engagement Study, approximately 76 percent of all retail purchase decisions are made in-store. Fifty-seven percent of shoppers buy more than they anticipated once in the store, so P-O-P displays can be very effective.[44] Other strategies to increase sales include adding cards to the tops of displays, changing messages on signs on the sides or bottoms of displays, adding inflatable or mobile displays, and using signs that advertise the brand's sports, movie, or charity tie-in.

16-6c Trends in Sales Promotion

The biggest trend in sales promotion on both the trade and consumer side has been the increased use of the Internet. Social media-, e-mail-, and Web site–based promotions have expanded dramatically in recent years. Marketers are now spending billions of dollars annually on such promotions. Sales promotions online have proved both effective and cost-efficient—generating response rates three to five times higher than off-line promotions. The most effective types of online sales promotions are free merchandise, sweepstakes, free shipping with purchases, and coupons. One major goal of retailers is to add potential customers to their databases and expand marketing touch points.

Marketers have discovered that online coupon distribution provides another vehicle for promoting their products. The redemption rate of online coupons has been growing substantially while total coupon redemption has remained steady.[45] Online coupons can help marketers lure new customers, and with the speed of online feedback, marketers can track the success of a coupon in real time and adjust it based on changing market conditions.[46]

Online versions of loyalty programs are also popping up, and although many types of companies have these programs, the most successful are those run by hotel and airline companies. A final major trend in sales promotion is the utilization of sales promotions on social media and at the point of purchase. Google's Zero Moment of Truth (ZMOT) insights illustrate how important consumer feedback is to consumer purchases, highlighting the importance of behavioral data when serving up a targeted sales promotion.[47]

point of purchase (P-O-P) display a promotional display set up at the retailer's location to build traffic, advertise the product, or induce impulse buying

STUDY TOOLS 16

LOCATED AT BACK OF THE TEXTBOOK

☐ Rip out Chapter Review Card

LOCATED AT WWW.CENGAGEBRAIN.COM

☐ Review Key Terms Flashcards and create your own

☐ Track your knowledge and understanding of key concepts in marketing

☐ Complete practice and graded quizzes to prepare for tests

☐ Complete interactive content within the MKTG Online experience

☐ View the chapter highlight boxes within the MKTG Online experience

17 | Personal Selling and Sales Management

LEARNING OUTCOMES

After studying this chapter, you will be able to…

17-1 Understand the sales environment

17-2 Describe personal selling

17-3 Discuss the key differences between relationship selling and traditional selling

17-4 List and explain the steps in the selling process

17-5 Understand the functions of sales management

17-6 Describe the use of customer relationship management in the selling process

After you finish this chapter go to **PAGE 320** for **STUDY TOOLS.**

17-1 THE SALES ENVIRONMENT

Many people around the world work in some form of selling. Traditionally, salespeople engage in direct face-to-face contact with customers. This can take place either at the salesperson's place of business or at a secondary location (such as when a salesperson travels door-to-door or meets a customer at her office or home). Salespeople can be consumer-focused (as in the case of retail) or business-focused.

In many cases, consumer-focused salespeople require customers to come directly to a retail store, shortening the sales process time. Even though many retailers use multiple customer relationship management processes (including information kiosks, Web sites, and self-check outs), one-to-one interactions are often key to retail success. Most major retailers use trained salespeople—not just order takers—to enhance the customer experience. Nordstrom's, for example, offers a retail management internship that provides both hands-on selling experience and classroom learning for students looking for careers in retail management and sales.[1] By having knowledgeable salespeople, retailers can help their customers select the products or services that are best for them.

As previously discussed, some consumer-focused salespeople travel to their customers' locations. For example, many home improvement and maintenance salespeople meet potential customers at their homes. Certain cosmetics, small appliances, and magazine subscriptions are sold directly to customers at their homes. These salespeople are considered direct salespeople. Companies such as CUTCO Cutlery, AVON, and Mary Kay Cosmetics have been very successful in direct selling.

Business-focused salespeople call on other companies to sell their products. These business-to-business salespeople often spend a good deal of time traveling to customer locations to make sales calls, and the sales process generally takes a longer period of time. Often, business-to-business salespeople have more extensive sales training, are required to travel more, and receive a higher level of compensation.

The sales environment changes constantly as new competitors enter the market and old competitors leave. The ways that customers interact with salespeople and learn about products and suppliers are changing due to the rapid increase in new sales technologies. In order for companies to successfully sell products or services using a sales force, they must be very effective at personal selling, sales management, customer relationship management, and technology—all of which play critical roles in building strong long-term relationships with customers.

17-2 PERSONAL SELLING

As mentioned in Chapter 15, *personal selling* is a purchase situation involving a personal, paid-for communication between two people in an attempt to influence each other. In a sense, all businesspeople are salespeople. An individual may become a plant manager, a chemist, an engineer, or a member of any profession and yet still have to sell. During a job search,

applicants must "sell" themselves to prospective employers in an interview. Personal selling offers several advantages over other forms of promotion:

- Personal selling provides a detailed explanation or demonstration of the product. This capability is especially needed for complex or new goods and services.

- The sales message can be varied according to the motivations and interests of each prospective customer. Moreover, when the prospect has questions or raises objections, the salesperson is there to provide explanations and guidance. By contrast, advertising and sales promotion can respond only to the questions and objections that the copywriter *thinks* are important to customers.

- Personal selling should only be directed toward qualified prospects. Other forms of promotion include some unavoidable waste because many people in the audience are not prospective customers.

- Costs can be controlled by adjusting the size of the sales force (and resulting expenses) in one-person increments. On the other hand, advertising and sales promotion must often be purchased in fairly large amounts.

- Perhaps the most important advantage is that personal selling is considerably more effective than other forms of promotion in obtaining a sale and gaining a satisfied customer.

- Personal selling also has several limitations compared to other forms of promotion:

  - Cost per contact is much greater than for mass forms of communication, leading companies to be highly selective about where and when they use salespeople.

  - If the sales force is not properly trained, the message provided can be inconsistent and inaccurate. Continual sales force management and training are necessary.

  - Salespeople can convince customers to buy unneeded products or services. This can lead to increased levels of cognitive dissonance among buyers if a salesperson is being pushed to meet certain quotas.

Personal selling often works better than other forms of promotion given certain customer and product characteristics. Generally speaking, personal selling becomes more important as the number of potential customers decreases, as the complexity of the product increases, and as the value of the product grows (see Exhibit 17.1). For highly complex goods such as business jets and private communication systems, a salesperson is needed to determine the prospective customer's needs and wants, explain the product's benefits and advantages, and propose the exact features and accessories that will best meet the client's needs. Many upscale clothing retailers offer free personal shopping, whereby consultants select and suggest designer clothing they believe will fit the customer's style and specified need. Bloomingdales' personal shoppers help customers select gifts for others, provide guidance tailored to the individual's personal tastes, coordinate gift wrapping and alterations, help navigate the entire store from clothing to home goods, and even schedule reminders for special occasions.[2]

Technology plays an increasingly important role in personal selling. Instead of being handed traditional sales pamphlets and brochures, consumers are now able to easily learn about products and services by searching the Internet before entering a store. Many consumers compare product features, prices, and quality online before even deciding which store to visit. Even after entering a store, consumers use their smartphones to browse competitors' Web sites while evaluating products. In addition to their own research, consumers are being bombarded with in-store messages, coupons, and sale information using beacon technology like Apple's iBeacon. Suffice to say, consumers are more educated about products and services today than they've ever been before.

This shift in technology has changed the dynamic of how information is obtained. If salespeople do not stay well informed about the products they're selling, consumers may enter the store knowing even more than they do. This reduces the ability of the salesperson to build trust and confidence. Salespeople are increasingly turning to social media like LinkedIn, Facebook, blogs, and Twitter to help establish their expertise within a field. With more than 300 million members, LinkedIn positions itself as the world's largest professional network.[3] In addition to its networking function, LinkedIn offers sales solutions to help salespeople find prospects, qualify leads, and make product recommendations to decision makers.[4] LinkedIn also provides free advice on how to effectively sell using social media, including a six-step guide to aid salespeople in successful social selling.[5] LinkedIn also provides actionable social selling tips, making it a great resource for salespeople looking to harness the power of technology themselves.[6]

17-3 RELATIONSHIP SELLING

Historically, marketing theory and practice concerning personal selling have focused almost entirely on planned presentations to prospective customers for the sole purpose of making sales. Marketers were mostly concerned with making one-time sales and then moving on to the next prospect. Traditional personal selling methods attempted to persuade the buyer to accept a point of view or convince the buyer to take some action. Frequently, the objectives of the

EXHIBIT 17.1	COMPARISON OF PERSONAL SELLING AND ADVERTISING/SALES PROMOTION
Personal selling is more important if . . .	**Advertising and sales promotion are more important if . . .**
The product has a high value.	The product has a low value.
It is a custom-made product.	It is a standardized product.
There are few customers.	There are many customers.
The product is technically complex.	The product is easy to understand.
Customers are concentrated.	Customers are geographically dispersed.
Examples: Insurance policies, custom windows, airplane engines	**Examples:** Soap, magazine subscriptions, cotton T-shirts

Technology is leading the way in selling in all forms of business.

Jack Frog/Shutterstock.com

consultative selling, is a multistage process that emphasizes personalization, win-win outcomes, and empathy as key ingredients in identifying prospects and developing them as long-term, satisfied customers. The focus, therefore, is on building mutual trust between the buyer and seller through the delivery of long-term, value-added benefits that are anticipated by the buyer.

Relationship or consultative salespeople, therefore, become consultants, partners, and problem solvers for their customers. They strive to build long-term relationships with key accounts by developing trust over time. The emphasis shifts from a one-time sale to a long-term relationship in which the salesperson works with the customer to develop solutions for enhancing the customer's bottom line. The end result of relationship selling tends to be loyal customers who purchase from the company time after time, often with an increased share-of-purchase. A relationship selling strategy focused on retaining customers is often less expensive to a company than having to constantly prospect for and sell to new customers. Relationship selling provides many advantages over traditional selling in the consumer goods market. Still, relationship selling is more often used in selling situations for industrial-type goods, such as heavy machinery and computer systems, and services, such as airlines and insurance, than in selling situations for consumer goods. Exhibit 17.2 lists the key differences between traditional personal selling and relationship or consultative selling.

salesperson were at the expense of the buyer, creating a win–lose outcome. Although this type of sales approach has not disappeared entirely, it is being used less and less often by professional salespeople.

By contrast, modern views of personal selling emphasize the relationship that develops between a salesperson and a buyer. **Relationship selling**, or

> **relationship selling (consultative selling)** a sales practice that involves building, maintaining, and enhancing interactions with customers in order to develop long-term satisfaction through mutually beneficial partnerships

EXHIBIT 17.2 KEY DIFFERENCES BETWEEN TRADITIONAL SELLING AND RELATIONSHIP SELLING

Traditional Personal Selling	Relationship or Consultative Selling
Sell products (goods and services)	Sell advice, assistance, and counsel
Focus on closing sales	Focus on improving the customer's bottom line
Limited sales planning	Consider sales planning as top priority
Spend most contact time telling customers about product	Spend most contact time attempting to build a problem-solving environment with the customer
Conduct "product-specific" needs assessment	Conduct discovery in the full scope of the customer's operations
"Lone wolf" approach to the account	Team approach to the account
Proposals and presentations based on pricing and product features	Proposals and presentations based on profit impact and strategic benefits to the customer
Sales follow-up is short term, focused on product delivery	Sales follow-up is long term, focused on long-term relationship enhancement

Source: Robert M. Peterson, Patrick, L. Schul, and George H. Lucas Jr., "Consultative Selling: Walking the Walk in the New Selling Environment, "*National Conference on Sales Management Proceedings,* March 1996; and Ari Walker, *7 Ways to Stop "Selling" and Start Building Relationships,* http://marketing.about.com/od/salestraining/a/stopselling .htm (Accessed March 2015).

17-4 STEPS IN THE SELLING PROCESS

Completing a sale requires multiple steps. The **sales process**, or **sales cycle**, is simply the set of steps a salesperson goes through to sell a particular product or service. The sales process can be unique for each product or service offered. The actual sales process depends on the features of the product or service, characteristics of customer segments, and internal processes in place within the firm (such as how leads are gathered).

Some sales take only a few minutes to complete, but others may take much longer. Sales of technical products like a Boeing or Airbus airplane and customized goods and services typically take many months, perhaps even years, to complete. On the other end of the spectrum, sales of less technical products like stationery are generally more routine and often take less than a day to complete. Whether a salesperson spends a few minutes or a few years on a sale, there are seven basic steps in the personal selling process:

1. Generating leads
2. Qualifying leads
3. Approaching the customer and probing needs
4. Developing and proposing solutions
5. Handling objections
6. Closing the sale
7. Following up

Like other forms of promotion, the steps of selling follow the AIDA concept discussed in Chapter 16. Once a salesperson has located and qualified a prospect with the authority to buy, he or she tries to get the prospect's attention. A thorough needs assessment turned into an effective sales proposal and presentation should generate interest. After developing the customer's initial desire (preferably during the presentation of the sales proposal), the salesperson seeks action in the close by trying to get an agreement to buy. Follow-up after the sale, the final step in the selling process, not only lowers cognitive dissonance (refer to Chapter 6) but also may open up opportunities for repeat business, cross-sales of related products and services, and new customer referrals.

Traditional selling and relationship selling follow the same basic steps. They differ in the relative importance placed on key steps in the process. Traditional selling efforts are transaction oriented, focusing on generating as many leads as possible, making as many presentations as possible, and closing as many sales as possible. Minimal effort is placed on asking questions to identify customer needs and wants or matching these needs and wants to the benefits of the product or service. Often, traditional selling efforts allow little time for following up and ensuring that customers are satisfied with the products or services they received. Again, these types of sales generally generate lower levels of customer satisfaction and can result in more win-lose transactions for salespeople.

By contrast, salespeople practicing relationship selling emphasize a long-term investment in the time and effort needed to uncover each customer's specific needs and wants and meet them with the product or service offering. By doing their homework up front, salespeople often create the conditions necessary for a relatively straightforward close. In general, customers are more satisfied, engage in more repeat business, and provide higher shares-of-purchase over longer periods of time with relationship salespeople. In the following sections, we will examine each step of the personal selling process.

17-4a Step 1: Generating Leads

Initial groundwork must precede communication between the potential buyer and the salesperson. **Lead generation**, or **prospecting**, is the

> **sales process (sales cycle)** the set of steps a salesperson goes through in a particular organization to sell a particular product or service
>
> **lead generation (prospecting)** identification of those firms and people most likely to buy the seller's offerings

Julia Tim/Shutterstock.com

identification of those firms and people most likely to buy the seller's offerings. These firms or people become "sales leads" or "prospects."

Sales leads can be obtained in many different ways, most notably through advertising, trade shows and conventions, social media, webinars, or direct mail and telemarketing programs. Favorable publicity also helps to create leads. Company records of past client purchases are another excellent source of leads. Many sales professionals are also securing valuable leads from their firm's Web site.

A basic unsophisticated method of lead generation is done through **cold calling**—a form of lead generation in which the salesperson approaches potential buyers without any prior knowledge of the prospects' needs or financial status. Although cold calling is still used in generating leads, many sales managers have realized the inefficiencies of having their top salespeople use their valuable selling time searching for the proverbial "needle in a haystack." Passing the job of cold calling to a lower-cost employee, typically an internal sales support person, allows salespeople to spend more time and use their relationship-building skills on prospects who have already been identified.

Another way to gather a lead is through a **referral**—a recommendation from a customer or business associate. The advantages of referrals over other forms of prospecting are highly qualified leads, higher closing rates, larger initial transactions, and shorter sales cycles. Referrals are often as much as ten times more productive in generating sales than are cold calls. Unfortunately, although many clients are willing to give referrals, most salespeople do not ask for them. Effective sales training can help to overcome this reluctance to ask for referrals. To increase the number of referrals, some companies even pay or send small gifts to customers or suppliers that provide referrals. Generating referrals is one area that social media and technology can usually make much more efficient.

Salespeople should build strong networks to help generate leads. **Networking** is using friends, business contacts, coworkers, acquaintances, and fellow members in professional and civic organizations to identify potential clients. Indeed, a number of national networking clubs have been started for the sole purpose of generating leads and providing valuable business advice. Increasingly, sales professionals are also using online networking sites like LinkedIn to connect with targeted leads and clients around the world, 24 hours a day.

17-4b Step 2: Qualifying Leads

When a prospect shows interest in learning more about a product, the salesperson has the opportunity to follow up, or qualify, the lead. Typically, unqualified prospects give vague or incomplete answers to a salesperson's specific questions, try to evade questions on budgets, and request changes in standard procedures like prices and terms of sale. In contrast, qualified leads are real prospects who answer questions, value the salesperson's time, and are realistic about money and when they are prepared to buy.

Lead qualification involves determining whether the prospect has three things:

1. **A recognized need:** The most basic criterion for determining whether someone is a prospect for a product is a need that is not being satisfied. The salesperson should first consider prospects who are aware of a need but should not disregard prospects who have not yet recognized that they have one. With a little more information about the product, they may decide they do have a need for it. Preliminary questioning can often provide the salesperson with enough information to determine whether there is a need.

2. **Buying power:** Buying power involves both authority to make the purchase decision and access to funds to pay for it. To avoid wasting time and money, the salesperson needs to identify the purchasing authority and his or her ability to pay before making a presentation. Organizational charts and information about a firm's credit standing can provide valuable clues.

3. **Receptivity and accessibility:** The prospect must be willing to see the salesperson and be accessible to the salesperson. Some prospects simply refuse to see salespeople. Others, because of their stature in their organization, will see only a salesperson or sales manager with similar stature.

Often the task of lead qualification is handled by

cold calling a form of lead generation in which the salesperson approaches potential buyers without any prior knowledge of the prospects' needs or financial status

referral a recommendation to a salesperson from a customer or business associate

networking a process of finding out about potential clients from friends, business contacts, coworkers, acquaintances, and fellow members in professional and civic organizations

lead qualification determination of a sales prospect's (1) recognized need, (2) buying power, and (3) receptivity and accessibility

a telemarketing group or a sales support person who prequalifies the lead for the salesperson. Prequalification systems free sales representatives from the time-consuming task of following up on leads to determine need, buying power and receptiveness. Prequalification systems may even set up initial appointments with the prospect for the salesperson. The result is more time for the sales force to spend in front of interested customers.

Companies are increasingly using their Web sites and other software to qualify leads. When qualifying leads online, companies want visitors to register, indicate the products and services they are interested in, and provide information on their time frames and resources. Leads from the Internet can then be prioritized (those indicating short time frames, for instance, are given a higher priority) and then transferred to salespeople. Enticing visitors to register also enables companies to customize future electronic interactions.

Personally visiting unqualified prospects wastes valuable salesperson time and company resources. Many leads often go unanswered because salespeople are given no indication as to how qualified the leads are in terms of interest and ability to purchase. Inside salespeople and sales support staff assess leads to maximize successful meetings, while CRM systems provide resources to increase lead follow-up rates. Still, according to Salisify, salespeople only follow up on 10 percent of leads.[7]

17-4c Step 3: Approaching the Customer and Probing Needs

Before approaching customers, the salesperson should learn as much as possible about the prospect's organization and its buyers. This process, called the **preapproach**, describes the "homework" that must be done by the salesperson before contacting the prospect. This may include visiting company Web sites, consulting standard reference sources such as Moody's, Standard & Poor's, or Dun & Bradstreet, or contacting acquaintances or others who may have information about the prospect. Reading the prospect's social media sites (following the company's Twitter feed and reading its Facebook page, for example) is a great way to get to know the company culture, become acquainted with customer needs, and learn more about daily activities.[8] Another preapproach task is to determine whether the actual approach should be

preapproach a process that describes the "homework" that must be done by a salesperson before he or she contacts a prospect

needs assessment a determination of the customer's specific needs and wants and the range of options the customer has for satisfying them

a personal visit, a phone call, a letter, or some other form of communication. Note that the preapproach applies to most business-to-business sales and outside consumer sales, but it is usually not possible when consumers approach salespeople in the retail store environment.

During the sales approach, the salesperson either talks to the prospect or secures an appointment to probe the prospect further about his or her needs. Relationship selling theorists suggest that salespeople should begin developing mutual trust with their prospect during the approach. Salespeople must sell themselves before they can sell the product. Small talk that projects sincerity and some suggestion of friendship is encouraged to build rapport with the prospect, but remarks that could be construed as insincere should be avoided.

The salesperson's ultimate goal during the approach is to conduct a **needs assessment** to find out as much as possible about the prospect's situation. The salesperson should be determining how to maximize the fit between what he or she can offer and what the prospective customer wants. As part of the needs assessment, the consultative salesperson must know everything there is to know about the following:

- **The product or service:** Product knowledge is the cornerstone for conducting a successful needs analysis. The consultative salesperson must be an expert on his or her product or service, including technical specifications, features and benefits, pricing and billing procedures, warranty and service support, performance comparisons with the competition, other customers' experiences with the product, and current advertising and promotional campaign messages. For example, a salesperson who is attempting to sell a Canon copier to a doctor's office should be very knowledgeable about Canon's selection of copiers, their attributes, capabilities, technological specifications, and postpurchase servicing.

- **Customers and their needs:** The salesperson should know more about customers than he knows about himself. That's the secret to relationship and consultative selling, where the salesperson acts not only as a supplier of products and services but also as a trusted consultant and adviser. The professional salesperson brings each client business-building ideas and solutions to problems. For example, if the Canon salesperson is asking the "right" questions, then he or she should be able to identify copy-related areas where the doctor's office is losing or wasting money. Rather than just selling a copier, the Canon salesperson can act as a consultant on how the doctor's office can save money and time.

- **The competition:** The salesperson must know as much about the competitor's company and products as he or she knows about his or her own company. Competitive intelligence includes many factors: who the competitors are and what is known about them, how their products and services compare, advantages and disadvantages, and strengths and weaknesses. For example, if the competitor's Xerox copy machine is less expensive than the Canon copier, the doctor's office may be leaning toward purchasing the Xerox. But if the Canon salesperson can point out that the cost of long-term maintenance and toner cartridges is lower for the Canon copier, offsetting its higher initial cost, the salesperson may be able to persuade the doctor's office to purchase the Canon copier.

- **The industry:** Knowing the industry requires active research by the salesperson. This means attending industry and trade association meetings, reading articles published in industry and trade journals, keeping track of legislation and regulation that affect the industry, being aware of product alternatives and innovations from domestic and foreign competition, and having a feel for economic and financial conditions that may affect the industry. It is also important to be aware of economic downturns, as businesses may be looking for less expensive financing options.

Creating a *customer profile* during the approach helps salespeople optimize their time and resources. This profile is then used to help develop an intelligent analysis of the prospect's needs in preparation for the next step,

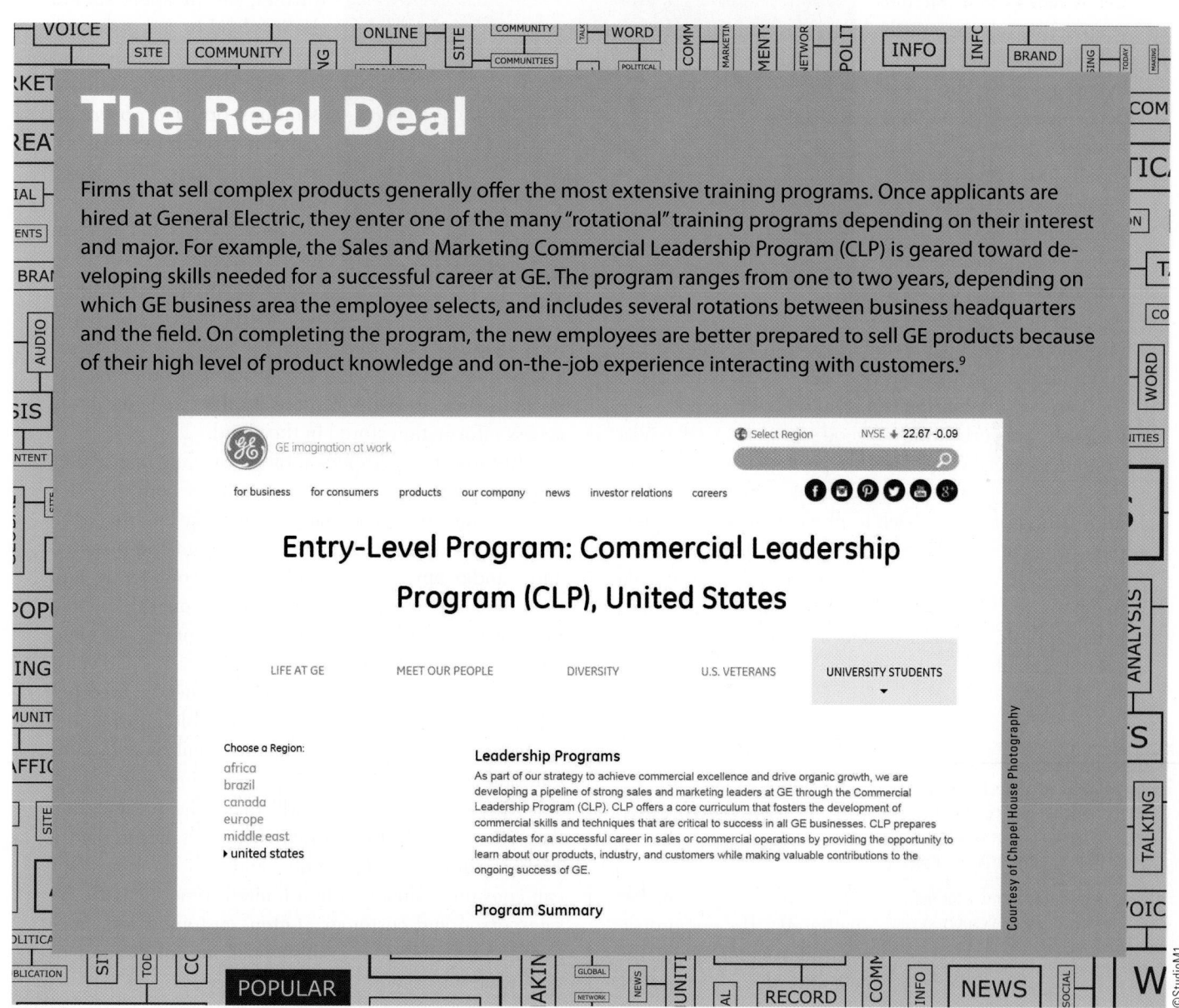

The Real Deal

Firms that sell complex products generally offer the most extensive training programs. Once applicants are hired at General Electric, they enter one of the many "rotational" training programs depending on their interest and major. For example, the Sales and Marketing Commercial Leadership Program (CLP) is geared toward developing skills needed for a successful career at GE. The program ranges from one to two years, depending on which GE business area the employee selects, and includes several rotations between business headquarters and the field. On completing the program, the new employees are better prepared to sell GE products because of their high level of product knowledge and on-the-job experience interacting with customers.[9]

Courtesy of Chapel House Photography

©StudioM1

developing and proposing solutions. Customer profile information is typically stored and manipulated using sales force automation software packages designed for use on laptop computers, smartphones, or tablets. Sales force automation software provides sales reps with a computerized and efficient method of collecting customer information for use during the entire sales process. Further, customer and sales data stored in a computer database can be easily shared among sales team members. The information can also be appended with industry statistics, sales or meeting notes, billing data, and other information that may be pertinent to the prospect or the prospect's company. The more salespeople know about their prospects, the better they can meet their needs.

A salesperson should wrap up the sales approach and need-probing mission by summarizing the prospect's need, problem, and interest. The salesperson should also get a commitment from the customer to some kind of action, whether it is reading promotional material or agreeing to a demonstration. This commitment helps to qualify the prospect further and justify additional time invested by the salesperson. When doing so, however, the salesperson should take care not to be too pushy or overbearing—a good salesperson will read a customer's social cues. The salesperson should reiterate the action he or she promises to take, such as sending information or calling back to provide answers to questions. The date and time of the next call should be set at the conclusion of the sales approach as well as an agenda for the next call in terms of what the salesperson hopes to accomplish, such as providing a demonstration or presenting a solution.

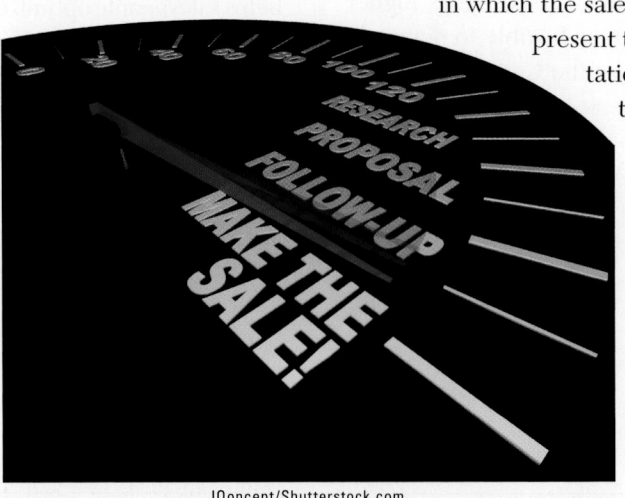

IQoncept/Shutterstock.com

sales proposal a formal written document or professional presentation that outlines how the salesperson's product or service will meet or exceed the prospect's needs

sales presentation a formal meeting in which the salesperson presents a sales proposal to a prospective buyer

17-4d Step 4: Developing and Proposing Solutions

Once the salesperson has gathered the appropriate information about the client's needs and wants,

the next step is to determine whether her company's products or services match the needs of the prospective customer. The salesperson then develops a solution, or possibly several solutions, in which the salesperson's product or service solves the client's problems or meets a specific need.

These solutions are typically presented to the client in the form of a sales proposal presented at a sales presentation. A **sales proposal** is a written document or professional presentation that outlines how the company's product or service will meet or exceed the client's needs. The **sales presentation** is the formal meeting in which the salesperson has the opportunity to present the sales proposal. The presentation should be explicitly tied to the prospect's expressed needs. Further, the prospect should be involved in the presentation by being encouraged to participate in demonstrations or by exposure to computer exercises, slides, video or audio, flip charts, photographs, and the like. Technology has become an important part of presenting solutions for many salespeople. In the past, salespeople took desktop PCs with them to make presentations. Today, they increasingly carry iPads and other tablets because they are lighter, more flexible, and can easily access information stored in the cloud.

Because the salesperson often has only one opportunity to present solutions, the quality of both the sales proposal and the presentation can make or break the sale. Salespeople must be able to present the proposal and handle any customer objections confidently and professionally. For a powerful presentation, salespeople must be well prepared, use direct eye contact, ask open-ended questions, be poised, use hand gestures and voice inflection, and focus on the customer's needs. Incorporating visual elements that impart valuable information, knowing how to operate the audio/visual or computer equipment being used for the presentation, and making sure the equipment works will make the presentation flow smoother. Nothing loses customers faster than a boring or ill-prepared presenter, and equipment mishaps can consume valuable (often limited) time for both the salesperson and customer. Often, customers are more likely to remember how salespeople present themselves than what they say.

17-5 SALES MANAGEMENT

There is an old adage in business that nothing happens until a sale is made. Without sales, there is no need for accountants, production workers, or even a company president. Sales provide the fuel that keeps the corporate engines humming. Companies such as Cisco Systems, International Paper, Johnson Controls, and thousands of other manufacturers would cease to exist without successful salespeople. Even companies such as Procter & Gamble and Kraft Foods, which mainly sell consumer goods and use extensive advertising campaigns, still rely on salespeople to move products through the channel of distribution. Thus, sales management must be one of every firm's most critical specialties. Effective sales management stems from a success-oriented sales force that accomplishes its mission economically and efficiently. Poor sales management can lead to unmet sales and profit objectives or even to the downfall of the corporation.

Just as selling is a personal relationship, so is sales management. Although the sales manager's basic job is to maximize sales at a reasonable cost while also maximizing profits, he or she also has many other important responsibilities and decisions:

1. Defining sales goals and the sales process
2. Determining the sales force structure
3. Recruiting and training the sales force
4. Compensating and motivating the sales force
5. Evaluating the sales force

17-5a Defining Sales Goals and the Sales Process

Effective sales management begins with a determination of sales goals. Without goals to achieve, salesperson performance would be mediocre at best, and the company would likely fail. Like any marketing objective, sales goals should be stated in clear, precise, and measurable terms and should always specify a time frame for their completion. Overall sales force goals are usually stated in terms of desired dollar sales volume, market share, and/or profit level. For example, a life insurance company may have a goal to sell $50 million in life insurance policies annually, to attain a twelve percent market share, and/or to achieve $1 million in profits.

Individual salespeople are also assigned goals in the form of quotas. A **quota** is a statement of the salesperson's sales goals, usually based on sales volume alone, but sometimes including other focuses such as key accounts (those with greatest potential), new account generation, volume of repeat sales, profit margin, and specific product mixes sold.

17-5b Determining the Sales Force Structure

Because personal selling is so costly, no sales department can afford to be disorganized. Proper design helps the sales manager organize and delegate sales duties and provide direction for salespeople. Sales departments are most often organized by geographic regions, product lines, marketing functions performed (such as account development or account maintenance), markets, industries, individual clients, or accounts. For example, the sales force for Hewlett-Packard (HP) could be organized into sales territories covering New England, the Midwest, the South, and the West Coast or into distinct groups selling different product lines. HP salespeople might also be assigned to specific industries or markets (such as the telecommunications industry), or to key clients (such as AT&T, Virgin Mobile, and Verizon).

Market or industry-based structures and key account structures are gaining popularity in today's competitive selling environment, especially with the emphasis on relationship selling. Being familiar with one industry or market allows sales reps to become experts in their

> **quota** a statement of the salesperson's sales goals, usually based on sales volume

Part of sales management is defining sales goals for the sales force.

iStockphoto.com/Hocus-focus

fields and thereby offer better solutions and service. Further, by organizing the sales force around specific customers, many companies hope to improve customer service, encourage collaboration with other arms of the company, and unite salespeople in customer-focused sales teams.

17-5c Recruiting and Training the Sales Force

Sales force recruitment should be based on an accurate, detailed description of the sales task as defined by the sales manager. For example, General Electric (GE) uses its Web site to provide prospective salespeople with explanations of different career entry paths and video accounts of what it is like to have a career at GE. Aside from the usual characteristics such as level of experience or education, what traits should sales managers look for in applicants?

- **Ego strength:** Great salespeople should have a strong, healthy self-esteem and the ability to bounce back from rejection.

- **Sense of urgency and competitiveness:** These traits push their sales to completion, as well as help them persuade people.

- **Assertiveness:** Effective salespeople have the ability to be firm in one-to-one negotiations, to lead the sales process, and to get their point across confidently without being overbearing or aggressive.

- **Sociable:** Wanting to interact with others is a necessary trait for great salespeople.

- **Risk takers:** Great salespeople are willing to put themselves in less-than-assured situations, and in doing so, often are able to close unlikely sales.

- **Capable of understanding complex concepts and ideas:** Quick thinking and comprehension allow salespeople to quickly grasp and sell new products or enter new sales areas.

- **Creativity:** Great salespeople develop client solutions in creative ways.

- **Empathetic:** Empathy—the ability to place oneself in someone else's shoes—enables salespeople to understand the client.

In addition to these traits, almost all successful salespeople say their sales style is relationship oriented rather than transaction oriented.[11]

After the sales recruit has been hired and given a brief orientation, initial training begins. A new salesperson generally receives instruction in company policies and practices, selling techniques, product knowledge, industry and customer characteristics, and nonselling duties such as filling out sales and market information reports and using a sales automation computer program. Continuous training then keeps salespeople up-to-date on changes in products and services, technology, the competitive landscape, and sales techniques, among other issues. Continuous training can occur during sales meetings, annual meetings, or during the course of everyday business.

Training can take place in a classroom environment, in the field, or using online modules. When conducting job training in the field via a live sales call, the trainer should be a more experienced salesperson or sales manager. This type of training provides real world experience for the trainee, but may reduce the effectiveness of the call because it often entails a reduced selling time. Another form of training involves the trainee working in inside sales, primarily phone-based sales, for an extended period of time before being given an outside territory to cover. This enables the trainee to develop selling skills with less-important and/or less-established accounts before facing the challenges of outside sales.

17-5d Compensating and Motivating the Sales Force

Compensation planning is one of the sales manager's toughest jobs. Only good planning will ensure that compensation attracts, motivates, and retains good salespeople. Generally, companies and industries with lower levels of compensation suffer higher turnover rates. This increases costs (including training and recruiting costs), decreases sales effectiveness, and harms relationship management. Therefore, compensation needs to be competitive enough to attract and motivate the best salespeople. Firms sometimes take profit into account when developing their compensation plans. Instead of paying salespeople on overall volume, they pay according to the profitability achieved from selling each product.

Still other companies tie a part of the salesperson's total compensation to customer satisfaction. As the emphasis on relationship selling increases, many sales managers believe that a portion of a salesperson's compensation should be tied to a client's satisfaction. To determine this, sales managers can survey clients on a salesperson's ability to create realistic expectations and his or her responsiveness to customer needs. At PeopleSoft, a division of Oracle, structure, culture, and strategies are all built around customer satisfaction. Sales force compensation is tied to both sales quotas and a satisfaction metric that enables clients to voice their opinions on the services provided.[12]

Although a compensation-based plan motivates a salesperson to sell, sometimes it is not enough to produce the volume of sales or the profit margin required by sales management. Sales managers therefore often offer rewards or incentives, such as recognition at ceremonies, plaques, and/or monetary-based rewards such as vacations, merchandise, pay raises, and cash bonuses. Cash awards are the most popular sales incentive and are used by virtually all companies. Mary Kay Cosmetics offers a unique type of incentive whereby salespeople can earn the use of different types of vehicles—from a lowly Ford Fiesta all the way up to the coveted pink Mary Kay Cadillac. To qualify for these vehicles, salespeople must reach certain sales quotas.[13]

Recognition and rewards may help increase overall sales volume, add new accounts, improve morale and goodwill, move slow items, and bolster slow sales. They can also be used to achieve short- and long-term objectives such as reducing overstocked inventory and meeting a monthly or quarterly sales goal. In motivating their sales force, however, sales managers must be careful not to encourage unethical behavior.

17-5e Evaluating the Sales Force

The final task of sales managers is evaluating the effectiveness and performance of the sales force. To evaluate the sales force, the sales manager needs feedback—that is, regular information from salespeople. Typical performance measures include sales volume, contribution-to-profit, calls per order, sales or profits per call, or percentage of calls achieving specific goals such as sales of products that the firm is heavily promoting.

Performance information helps the sales manager monitor a salesperson's progress through the sales cycle and pinpoint where breakdowns might be occurring. For example, by learning the number of prospects an individual salesperson has in each step of the sales cycle process and determining where prospects are falling out of the sales cycle, a manager can determine how effective a salesperson might be at lead generation, needs assessment, proposal generation, presenting, closing, and follow-up stages. This information can then tell a manager which sales skills might need to be reassessed or retrained. For example, if a sales manager notices that a sales rep seems to be letting too many prospects slip away after presenting proposals, it might mean he or she needs help with developing proposals, handling objections, or closing sales.

17-6 CUSTOMER RELATIONSHIP MANAGEMENT AND THE SALES PROCESS

As we have discussed throughout the text, customer relationship management (CRM) is the ultimate goal of a new trend in marketing that focuses on understanding customers as individuals instead of as part of a group. To do so, marketers are making their communications more customer specific using the CRM cycle, covered in Chapter 8, and by developing relationships with their customers through touch points and data mining. CRM was initially popularized as one-to-one marketing. But CRM is a much broader approach to understanding and serving customer needs than is one-to-one marketing.

Throughout the text, our discussion of a CRM system has assumed two key points. First, customers take center stage in any organization. Second, the business must manage the customer relationship across all points of customer contact throughout the entire organization. By identifying customer relationships, understanding the customer base, and capturing customer data, marketers and salespeople can leverage the information not only to develop deeper relationships but also to close more sales with loyal customers in a more efficient manner.

17-6a Identify Customer Relationships

Companies that have CRM systems follow a customer-centric focus or model. **Customer-centric** is an internal management philosophy similar to the marketing concept discussed in Chapter 1. Under this philosophy, the company customizes its product and service offering based on data generated through interactions between the customer and the company. This philosophy transcends all functional areas of the business, producing an internal system where all of the company's decisions and actions are a direct result of customer information.

Each unit of a business typically has its own way of recording what it learns, and perhaps even has its own customer information system. The departments' different interests make it difficult to pull all of the customer information together in one place using a common format. To overcome this problem, companies using CRM rely on knowledge

> **customer-centric** a philosophy under which the company customizes its product and service offerings based on data generated through interactions between the customer and the company

management. **Knowledge management** is a process by which customer information is centralized and shared in order to enhance the relationship between customers and the organization. Information collected includes experiential observations, comments, customer actions, and qualitative facts about the customer.

As Chapter 1 explained, *empowerment* involves delegating authority to solve customers' problems. Usually, organizational representatives, salespeople for example, are able to make changes during interactions with customers through phone, fax, e-mail, social media, or face-to-face.

An **interaction** occurs when a customer and a company representative exchange information and develop learning relationships. With CRM, the customer—not the organization—defines the terms of the interaction, often by stating his or her preferences. The organization responds by designing products and services around customers' desired experiences. Social media have created numerous new ways for companies to interact with customers—see Chapter 18 for more on this topic.

The success of CRM—building lasting and profitable relationships—can be directly measured by the effectiveness of the interaction between the customer and the organization. In fact, what further differentiates CRM from other strategic initiatives is the organization's ability to establish and manage interactions with its current customer base. The more latitude (empowerment) a company gives its representatives, the more likely the interaction will conclude in a way that satisfies the customer.

EXHIBIT 17.4   CUSTOMER-CENTRIC APPROACH FOR MANAGING CUSTOMER INTERACTIONS

interaction the point at which a customer and a company representative exchange information and develop learning relationships

touch points areas of a business where customers have contact with the company and data might be gathered

knowledge management the process by which customer information is centralized and shared in order to enhance the relationship between customers and the organization

17-6b Understand Interactions of the Current Customer Base

The interaction between the customer and the organization is the foundation on which a CRM system is built. Only through effective interactions can organizations learn about the expectations of their customers, generate and manage knowledge about them, negotiate mutually satisfying commitments, and build long-term relationships.

Exhibit 17.4 illustrates the customer-centric approach for managing customer interactions. Following a customer-centric approach, an interaction can occur through different communication channels, such as a phone, the Internet, or a salesperson. Any activity or touch point a customer has with an organization, either directly or indirectly, constitutes an interaction.

Companies that effectively manage customer interactions recognize that data provided by customers affect a wide variety of **touch points**. In a CRM system, touch points are all areas of a business where customers have contact with the company and data might be gathered. Touch points might include: a customer registering for a particular service; a customer communicating with customer service for product information; a customer completing and returning the warranty information card for a product; or a customer talking with salespeople, delivery personnel, and product installers. Data gathered at these touch points, once interpreted, provide information that affects touch points inside the company. Interpreted information may be redirected to marketing research to develop profiles of extended warranty purchasers, to production to analyze recurring problems and repair components, to accounting to establish cost-control models for repair service calls, and to sales for better customer profiling and segmentation.

WEB-BASED INTERACTIONS Web-based interactions are an increasingly popular touch point for customers to communicate with companies on their own terms. Web users can evaluate and purchase products, make reservations, input preferential data, and provide customer feedback on services and products. Data from these Web-based interactions are then captured, compiled, and used to segment customers, refine marketing efforts, develop new products, and deliver a degree of individual customization to improve customer relationships.

SOCIAL CRM As social media have become more popular, many companies have begun to use these media for "social CRM." ZDNet journalist Paul Greenberg recently named Salesforce, Microsoft, Blackbaud, Xactly, Infusionsoft, Accenture, and EY as companies to watch in the field of social CRM.[14] Essentially, social CRM takes the most successful aspects of traditional CRM, such as behavioral targeting, and expands them to include ways to engage customers through social media. This new paradigm includes a new customer recommendation value called the *net promoter score*. The net promoter score measures how much a customer influences the behavior of other customers through recommendations on social media. Its ultimate purpose is to gather all consumer interactions into a single database so that they can be analyzed and used to improve communication. Social CRM also enables marketers to focus more on the relationship aspect of CRM. For example, REI empowers customers to "carve your own adventure" through its YouTube channel. JetBlue uses Facebook and Twitter to provide advice and updates to travelers. To use social CRM effectively, companies must understand which sites customers use, whether they post opinions, and who the major influencers in the category are. They can then marry this information with behavioral data like purchases and purchase frequency.

POINT-OF-SALE INTERACTIONS Another touch point is through **point-of-sale interactions** in stores or at information kiosks. Many point-of-sale software programs enable customers to easily provide information about themselves without feeling violated. The information is then used for marketing and merchandising activities and to accurately identify the store's best customers and the types of products they buy. Data collected at point-of-sale interactions are also used to increase customer satisfaction through the development of in-store services and customer recognition promotions.

17-6c Capture Customer Data

Vast amounts of data can be obtained from the interactions between an organization and its customers. Therefore, in a CRM system, the issue is not how much data can be obtained, but rather what types of data should be acquired and how the data can effectively be used for relationship enhancement.

The traditional approach for acquiring data from customers is through channel interactions. Channel interactions include store visits, conversations with salespeople, interactions via the Web, traditional phone conversations, and wireless communications. In a CRM system, channel interactions are viewed as prime information sources based on the channel selected to initiate the interaction rather than on the data acquired. In some cases, companies use online chat to answer questions customers have about products they are looking for. For example, 24 Hour Fitness has an online chat window that opens when a

GET UNDER THE SKIN OF YOUR MAN.
TAKE OUR VALENTINE QUIZ.

MR. ACTION MR. SENSITIVE
MR. SMOOTH MR. EXTREME

FIND HIS PERFECT VALENTINE GIFT
Take our quiz to find the perfect products for your man and for your chance to WIN A ROMANTIC BREAK!

Go to facebook.com/LorealParisUK

L'ORÉAL
MEN EXPERT

EXPERT AT BEING A MAN

L'Oreal Paris/Advertising Archive

This advertisement for L'Oreal directs a highly segmented group of customers to its Facebook page, where the company will continue to engage them through social CRM.

point-of-sale interactions
a touch point in stores or information kiosks that uses software to enable customers to easily provide information about themselves without feeling violated

potential customer begins to review the Web site. If the visitor remains on the site, the online chat window asks if he or she needs help finding something specific.

Interactions between the company and the customer facilitate the collection of large amounts of data. Companies can obtain not only simple contact information (name, address, phone number) but also data pertaining to the customer's current relationship with the organization—past purchase history, quantity and frequency of purchases, average amount spent on purchases, sensitivity to promotional activities, and so forth.

In this manner, a large amount of information can be captured from one individual customer across several touch points. Multiply this by the thousands of customers across all of the touch points within an organization, and the volume of data can rapidly become unmanageable for company personnel. The large volume of data resulting from a CRM initiative can be managed effectively only through technology. Once customer data are collected, the question of who owns those data becomes extremely salient. In its privacy statement, Toysmart. com declared that it would never sell information registered at its Web site—including children's names and birth dates—to a third party. When the company filed for bankruptcy protection, it said that the information it collected constituted a company asset that needed to be sold off to pay creditors. Despite the outrage at this announcement, many dot-coms closing their doors found they had little in the way of assets and followed Toysmart's lead.

17-6d **Leverage Customer Information**

Data mining identifies the most profitable customers and prospects. Managers can then design tailored marketing strategies to best appeal to the identified segments. In CRM, this is commonly referred to as leveraging customer information to facilitate enhanced relationships with customers. Exhibit 17.5 shows some common CRM marketing database applications.

CAMPAIGN MANAGEMENT Through campaign management, all areas of the company participate in the development of programs targeted to customers. **Campaign management** involves monitoring and leveraging customer interactions to sell a company's products and to increase customer service. Campaigns are based directly on data obtained from customers through various

campaign management
developing product or service offerings customized for the appropriate customer segment and then pricing and communicating these offerings for the purpose of enhancing customer relationships

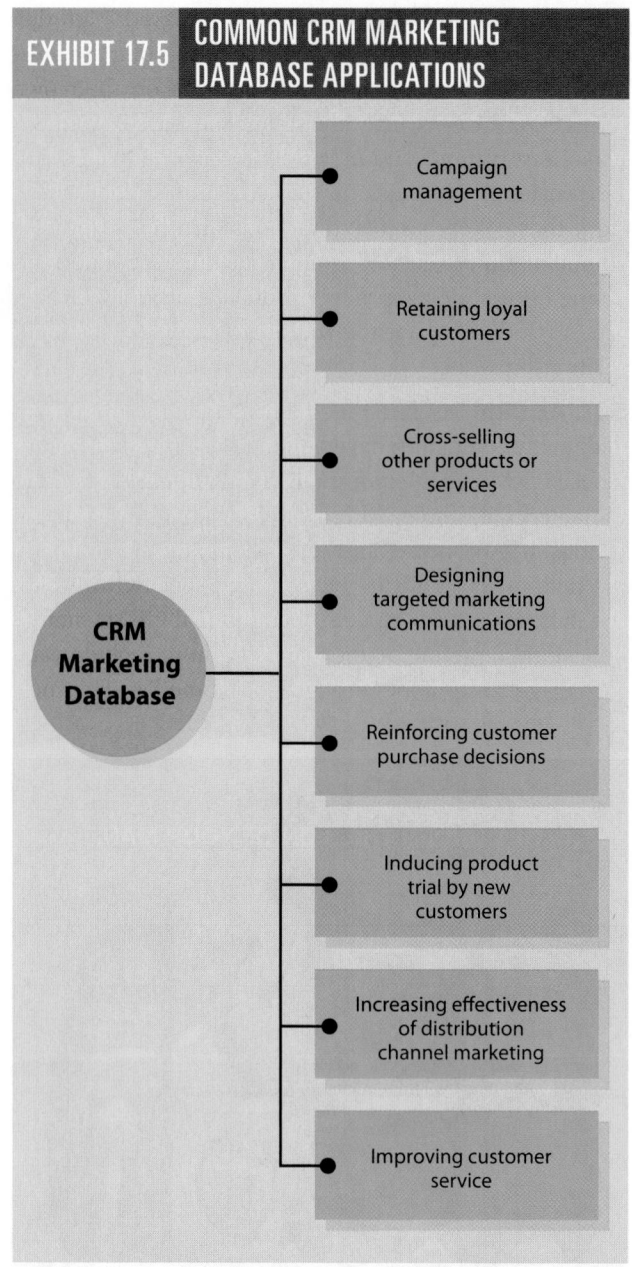

EXHIBIT 17.5 **COMMON CRM MARKETING DATABASE APPLICATIONS**

- Campaign management
- Retaining loyal customers
- Cross-selling other products or services
- Designing targeted marketing communications
- Reinforcing customer purchase decisions
- Inducing product trial by new customers
- Increasing effectiveness of distribution channel marketing
- Improving customer service

CRM Marketing Database

interactions. Campaign management includes monitoring the success of the communications based on customer reactions through sales, orders, callbacks to the company, and so on. If a campaign appears unsuccessful, it is evaluated and changed to better achieve the company's desired objective.

Campaign management involves developing customized product and service offerings for the appropriate customer segment, pricing these offerings attractively, and communicating these offers in a manner that enhances customer relationships. Customizing product and service offerings requires managing multiple interactions with customers, as well as giving priority to those products and services that are viewed as most desirable for a specifically designated customer. Even within a highly defined market segment, individual customer differences will emerge. Therefore, interactions among customers must focus on individual experiences, expectations, and desires.

RETAINING LOYAL CUSTOMERS If a company has identified its best customers, then it should make every effort to maintain and increase their loyalty. When a company retains an additional five percent of its customers each year, profits will increase by as much as 125 percent. What's more, improving customer retention by a mere two percent can decrease costs by as much as ten percent.[15]

Loyalty programs reward loyal customers for making multiple purchases. The objective is to build long-term, mutually beneficial relationships between a company and its key customers. More than 4,000 small- and medium-sized businesses across thirty-five states have teamed up with reward management firm Belly to develop unique rewards programs, such as getting to throw eggs at a food truck after a specified number of purchases or having the owner of your favorite bagel store sing to you after buying 100 bagels. The individualized rewards reflect each business's personality and (ideally) those of its customers, making the rewards programs highly motivating.[16] In addition to rewarding good customers, loyalty programs provide businesses with a wealth of information about their customers and shopping trends, which can be used to make future business decisions.

CROSS-SELLING OTHER PRODUCTS AND SERVICES CRM provides many opportunities to cross-sell related products. Marketers can use the database to match product profiles and consumer profiles so that they can cross-sell customers products that match their demographic, lifestyle, or behavioral characteristics. The financial services industry uses cross-selling better than most other industries do. Cross selling is a key part of Wells Fargo's strategy, for example, and is a large contributor to the company's success in the industry. After engaging with customers to determine their financial needs and aspirations, Wells Fargo reps work to determine how the company's wide range of products can synergize to meet or exceed those financial goals.[17]

Internet companies use product and customer profiling to reveal cross-selling opportunities while customers surf their sites. Past purchases, tracking programs, and the site a surfer is referred from give online marketers clues about the surfer's interests and what items to cross-sell. Amazon, for example, has used profiling to better meet customer needs for years. The company systematically compares individuals' shopping habits and online activities to other Amazon customers to make better tailored recommendations. Customers are also able to proactively rate products, review products, add products to wishlists, recommend products, and save products for a later purchase—all of which make for a more customized customer experience.[18]

A small company, such as this Gorilla Cheese food truck, may use the services of Belly to reward customers for their loyalty.

iStockphoto.com/Wdstock

DESIGNING TARGETED MARKETING COMMUNICATIONS Using transaction and purchase data, a database allows marketers to track customers' relationships to the company's products and services and modify the marketing message accordingly.

Customers can also be segmented into infrequent users, moderate users, and heavy users. A segmented communications strategy can then be developed based on which group the customer falls into. Communications to infrequent users might encourage repeat purchases through a direct incentive such as a limited-time price discount for ordering again. Online marketers for retailers like GNC and Newegg send out periodic e-mails with discounts to customers who made previous purchases. Communications to moderate users may use fewer incentives and more reinforcement of past purchase decisions. Communications to heavy users would be designed around loyalty and reinforcement of the purchase rather than around price promotions.

Source: General Nutrition Center

Online marketers for retailers like GNC will use email as a way to reach out to previous customers.

STUDY TOOLS 17

LOCATED AT BACK OF THE TEXTBOOK
☐ Rip Out Chapter Review Card

LOCATED AT WWW.CENGAGEBRAIN.COM
☐ Review Key Terms Flashcards and create your own
☐ Track your knowledge and understanding of key concepts in marketing
☐ Complete practice and graded quizzes to prepare for tests
☐ Complete interactive content within the MKTG Online experience
☐ View the chapter highlight boxes within the MKTG Online experience

MKTG ONLINE

PREPARE FOR TESTS ON THE STUDYBOARD!

- ○ CORRECT
- ○ INCORRECT
- ○ INCORRECT
- ○ INCORRECT

Personalize Quizzes from Your StudyBits

Take Practice Quizzes by Chapter

CHAPTER QUIZZES
- ▶ Chapter 1
- Chapter 2
- Chapter 3
- Chapter 4

4LTR PRESS

Access MKTG ONLINE at www.cengagebrain.com

18 Social Media and Marketing

LEARNING OUTCOMES

After studying this chapter, you will be able to...

18-1 Describe social media, how they are used, and their relation to integrated marketing communications

18-2 Explain how to create a social media campaign

18-3 Evaluate the various methods of measurement for social media

18-4 Explain consumer behavior on social media

18-5 Describe the social media tools in a marketer's toolbox and how they are useful

18-6 Describe the impact of mobile technology on social media

18-7 Understand the aspects of developing a social media plan

Source: Twitter, Inc.

After you finish this chapter go to **PAGE 339** for **STUDY TOOLS.**

18-1 WHAT ARE SOCIAL MEDIA?

The most exciting thing to happen to marketing and promotion in recent years is the increasing use of online technology to promote brands, particularly using social media. Social media have changed the way that marketers can communicate with their brands—from mass messages to intimate conversations. As marketing moves into social media, marketers must remember that for most people, social media are meant to be a social experience, not a marketing experience. In fact, the term *social media* means different things to different people, though most people think it refers to digital technology. The American Bar Association uses a definition developed by social media expert Brian Solis. According to Solis, **social media** is "any tool or service that uses the Internet to facilitate conversations."[1] However, social media can also be defined relative to traditional advertising like

social media any tool or service that uses the Internet to facilitate conversations

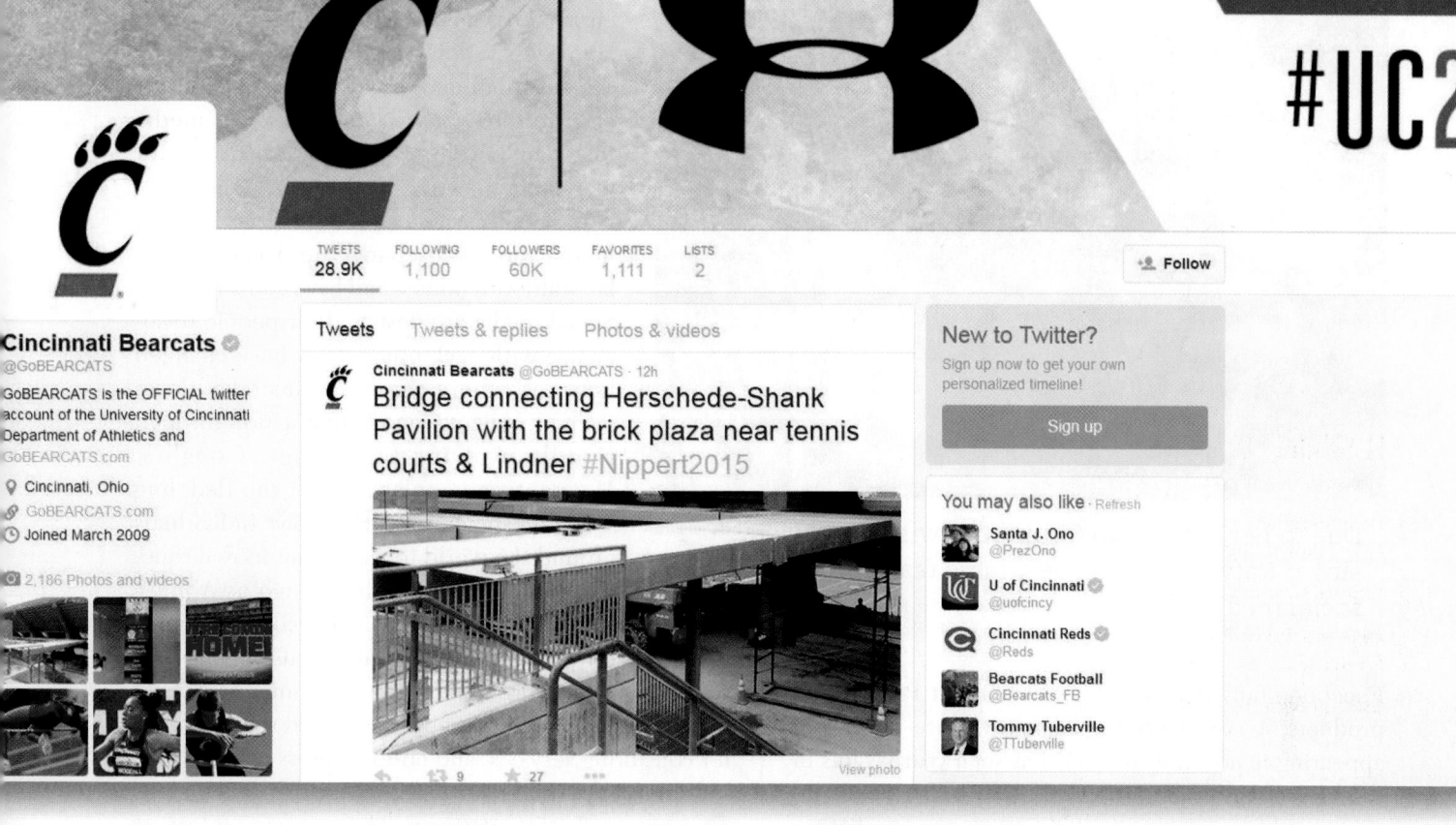

television and magazines: whereas traditional marketing media offer a mass media method of interacting with consumers, social media offer more one-to-one ways to meet consumers.

Social media have several implications for marketers and the ways that they interact with their customers. First, marketers must realize that they often do not control the content on social media sites. Consumers are sharing their thoughts, wishes, and experiences about brands with the world through social media. Because of this level of visibility and discussion, marketers must realize that having a great ad campaign is not enough—the product or service must be great, too.

Second, the ability to share experiences quickly and with such large numbers of people amplifies the impact of word of mouth in ways that can affect a company's bottom line. Singer Katy Perry has more than 66 million Twitter followers, and as such, has a very large reach.[2] YouTube is the company with the largest Twitter presence (more than 50 million followers), and

> "Interaction and engagement [on social media] is something that you don't necessarily see in traditional media. That's why we [at Ford] continue to accelerate our digital advertising investment to more than 25% of our media dollars."[3]
>
> —JIM FARLEY, FORD GLOBAL SALES AND MARKETING VICE PRESIDENT

Coca-Cola is the most liked brand on Facebook with almost 90 million fans.[4] The total reach of these brands is difficult to quantify, but it is unquestionably massive. Many companies use mascots to drive their marketing messages on social media. For example, Progressive auto insurance's perky saleswoman Flo has almost 5.5 million

Due to her more than 65 million Twitter followers, singer Katy Perry has a very large reach on social media.

Facebook fans that read her posts about Progressive products. According to the company, since Flo began appearing in ads, the company has seen yearly gains in the number of policies taken out.[5]

Third, social media allow marketers to listen. Domino's Pizza listened to what was being posted about its products (much of which was not nice) and decided to use that information to change its product. Social media, along with traditional marketing research, allowed Domino's to gain the insight needed to completely reinvent its pizza. Dell and Gatorade have taken social media monitoring to a whole new level as they literally put social media at the center of their marketing efforts. Premium sportswear company Lululemon was forced to acknowledge manufacturing problems after comments critical of the company's product quality were posted across its social media sites.[6]

Fourth, social media provide more sophisticated methods of measuring how marketers meet and interact with consumers than traditional advertising does. Currently, social media include tools and platforms like social networks, blogs, microblogs, and media sharing sites, which can be accessed through a growing number of devices including smartphones, e-readers, televisions, tablets, video game consoles, and netbooks. This technology changes daily, offering consumers new ways to experience social media platforms. As such, social media must constantly innovate to keep up with consumer demands.

Finally, social media allow marketers to have much more direct and meaningful conversations with customers. Social media offer a form of relationship building that will ultimately bring the customer and brand closer. Indeed, the culture of *participation* that social media foster may well prove to be a fifth "P" for marketing.

At the basic level, consumers of social media want to exchange information, collaborate with others, and have conversations. Social media are designed for people to socialize with each other. They have changed how and where conversations take place, even globalizing human interaction through rapidly evolving technology. Google + Hangouts, a popular facet of the fledgling Google + social network, allows individuals around the world to video chat in real time. Competing with products such as Apple's FaceTime and Microsoft's Skype, Hangouts offers unique innovations such as live streaming and recording. Various companies have used Hangouts to conduct team meetings and webinars, offer consulting services, and host live press conferences. Bakespace.com has successfully utilized Hangouts as a potent marketing platform. The company interacts with customers, shares recipes, and hosts chats with celebrity chefs using Hangouts. And as a chef might say, the proof is in the pudding—Bakespace.com has more than 450,000 people in its Hangouts circle, compared to just 14,000 fans on Facebook.[7] Clearly, conversations are happening online; it is up to the marketer to decide if engaging in those conversations will be profitable and to find the most effective method of entering the conversation.

Companies are beginning to understand the implications of their employees' activities on social media. In fact, there have been several examples of employees getting fired for airing their personal feelings on social media platforms. To combat this, many companies have begun developing social media policies as to what can be posted and what is inappropriate. Some companies have rules concerning corporate blogs, Facebook, Twitter, LinkedIn, comments, and even passwords. Adidas has adopted an "encouraging but strict" approach whereby employees may state their affiliation with Adidas but must also state that any personal views are just that— personal. Obviously, employees are still prohibited from sharing sensitive information. Similarly, Best Buy has a clear set of social media guidelines stating that any negative posts regarding religion, race, or ethnicity will not be tolerated.[8] Having a social media policy can certainly help mitigate risk, but it is not a guarantee that employees won't occasionally slip up.

Marketers are interested in online communication because it is wildly popular: brands, companies, individuals, and celebrities all promote their messages online. In fact, some social media are becoming so important that celebrities, sports stars, and even hotels are hiring coaches to help them strike the correct tone. Britney Spears, Carly Rae Jepsen, and Will.I.Am all have coaches that help them navigate the perilous landscape of Twitter. Coaches instruct clients on best practices and advise them how to leverage their personal brands in online spaces. They also monitor clients' Twitter feeds in real time, acting as editor, security guard, and advisor all at once. Some celebrities have social media advisors accompany them to galas and award shows, but coaches are often underutilized by the entertainment elite. As one celebrity coach noted, "It can get really busy if you're doing interviews on the red carpet, and it's just nice to have someone with you who can say, 'Hey, you should take a picture with your other-famous-person friend right now. Here you go, now you should tweet it.'"[9]

Some companies go so far as to require Facebook and Twitter training for high-profile employees. Approximately thirty percent of Adobe's employees have gone through some form of social media training. According to Cory Edwards, head of Adobe's Social Business Center of Excellence, Adobe's social media training "helps employees understand key principles such as disclosure and who to contact with questions. Guided by a set of core Adobe principles, the program aims to build employee social media fluency through awareness, empowerment, and excellence."[10]

18-1a How Consumers Use Social Media

Before beginning to understand how to leverage social media for brand building, it is important to understand which social media consumers are using and how they are using them. It is safe to assume that many of your customers are active on Facebook. Targeting can be accomplished by using less ubiquitous platforms. Qzone and Sina Weibo are two of the largest social media platforms in China, for example. Match.com, OkCupid, and Tinder are great platforms to reach young adult singles. Y8 and Big Fish Games offer a wide variety of social games. Teens tend to use platforms like Snapchat, Instagram, Twitch, Yik Yak, and Tumblr. While Facebook is used widely by older teens and adults, its popularity among younger consumers is decreasing.[11]

Videos are another of the most popular tools by which marketers reach consumers, and YouTube is by far the largest online video repository—it has more content than any major television network. Twitter's Vine, which limits videos to six seconds in length, is also widely popular. Flickr, Twitter, and blogs—all of which will be discussed in more detail later on—are some of the other most popular social media destinations among consumers. In 2015:

- Instagram grew by 50 percent to more than 300 million users; it is larger than Twitter and has one of the highest engagement levels of any social platform.
- Millennials spent more than two hours per day on their smartphones and used an average of six apps during that time.
- Facebook had more video views (12.3 billion) than YouTube (11.3 billion).
- Snapchat grew by 56 percent.[12]
- Tumblr added 120,000 new users per day.[13]

The bottom line, according to Universal McCann's Comparative Study on Social Media Trends, is that "if you are online, you are using social media."[14]

Increased usage of alternative platforms like smartphones and tablet computers has further contributed to the proliferation of social media usage. In the United States, ninety percent of American adults own a cell phone, while forty-five percent own a smartphone. These numbers jump to ninety-three percent and sixty-three percent for adults age eighteen to twenty-nine. Among all adults, 55 percent access the Internet on a mobile phone, and forty percent have accessed a social media Web site.[15] Tablet usage has hit critical mass among mobile surfers—one in four smartphone users owns a tablet as well. According to Mark Donovan, senior vice president of mobile at ComScore, "Tablets are one of the most rapidly adopted consumer technologies in history and are poised to fundamentally disrupt the way people engage with the digital world both on-the-go and perhaps most notably, in the home."[16] The overall impact of tablet computing on social media (and thus the discipline of marketing) is yet to be seen, but given the incredible impact that the smartphone has had in its short life span, tablets could indeed prove to be game changing.

SOCIAL COMMERCE A new area of growth in social media is **social commerce**, which combines social media with the

> **social commerce** a subset of e-commerce that involves the interaction and user contribution aspects of social online media to assist online buying and selling of products and services

basics of e-commerce. Social commerce is a subset of e-commerce that involves the interaction and user contribution aspects of social online media to assist online buying and selling of products and services.[17] Basically, social commerce relies on user-generated content on Web sites to assist consumers with purchases. Pinterest lets users collect ideas and products from all over the Web and "pin" favorite items to individually curated pinboards. Other users browse boards by theme, keyword, or product; click on what they like; and either visit the originating sites or re-pin the items on their own pinboards. Social commerce sites often include ratings and recommendations (as Amazon.com does) and social shopping tools (as Groupon does). In general, social commerce sites are designed to help consumers make more informed decisions on purchases and services.

Social commerce generated almost $24 billion in sales in 2014, with nearly half of all online sales coming through social media sites.[18] There are seven types of social commerce:

- Peer-to-peer sales platforms (like eBay and Etsy)
- Social networking Web sites driven by sales (like Pinterest and Twitter)

- Group buying platforms (like Groupon and Social Living)
- Peer recommendation sites (like Yelp and JustBoughtIt)
- User-curated shopping sites (like The Fancy and Lyst)
- Participatory commerce platforms (like Kickstarter and Threadless)
- Social shopping sites (like Motilo and GoTryItOn).[19]

As companies migrate to social commerce sites such as Pinterest, consumer interactions across the sites may change. One way that companies are leveraging Pinterest's user base is by running promotions. For example, Favorite Family Recipes offered two iPads as prizes for users who followed and pinned the logos of thirteen associated Pinterest boards.[20] This type of promotion can undermine the authenticity that many consumers rely on when using social commerce sites. However, some companies hope to cultivate authentic relationships by staying away from promotions. Whole Foods pins items that relate to the company's values but are not promotional or linked back to the Whole Foods site. Customers have built a relationship with Whole Foods based on upcycled products and recipes, rather than free products.[21]

18-1b Social Media and Integrated Marketing Communications

While marketers typically employ a social media strategy alongside traditional channels like print and broadcast, many budget pendulums are swinging toward social media. Forrester Research predicts that mobile marketing, social media, e-mail marketing, display advertising, and search marketing will grow to more than thirty-five percent of spending in the next few years, equaling spending on television today. The bulk of this budget will still go to search marketing and display advertising, but substantial investments will also be made in mobile marketing and social media.[22]

A unique consequence of social media is the widespread shift from one-to-many communication to many-to-many communication. Instead of simply putting a brand advertisement on television with

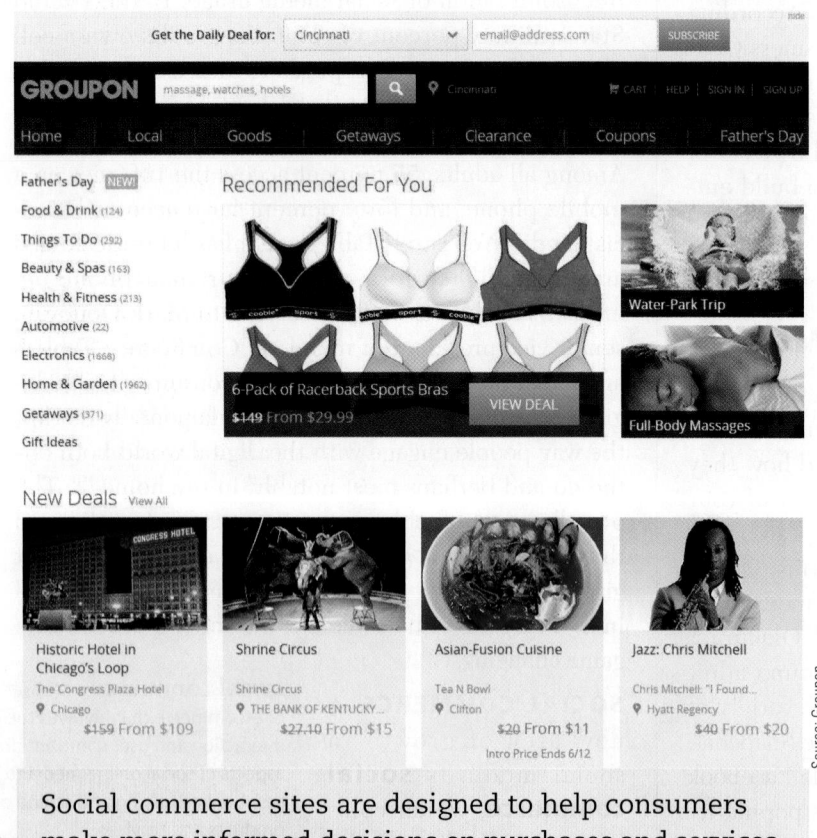

Social commerce sites are designed to help consumers make more informed decisions on purchases and services.

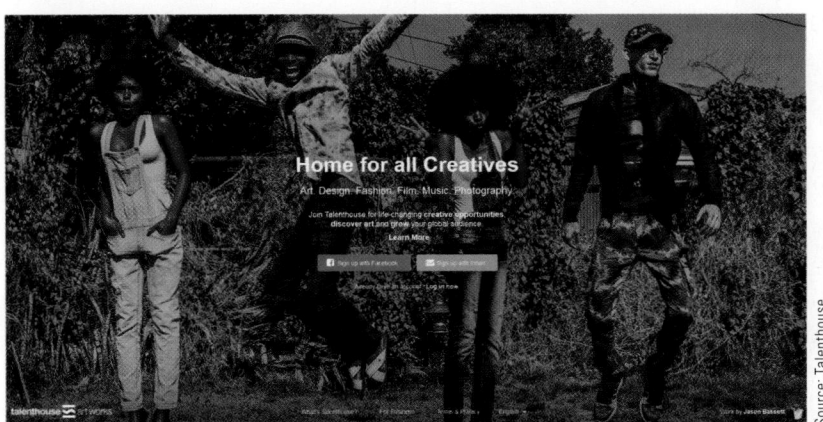

Source: Talenthouse

Talenthouse asks customers for their input when it comes to album art, performer wardrobes, etc. A winner is selected through social media voting.

no means for feedback, marketers can use social media to have conversations with consumers, forge deeper relationships, and build brand loyalty. Social media also allow consumers to connect with each other, share opinions, and collaborate on new ideas according to their interests.

With social media, the audience is often in control of the message, the medium, the response, or all three. This distribution of control is often difficult for companies to adjust to, but the focus of social marketing is unavoidably on the audience, and the brand must adapt to succeed. The interaction between producer and consumer becomes less about entertaining and more about listening, influencing, and engaging.

Using consumers to develop and market products is called **crowdsourcing**. Crowdsourcing describes how the input of many people can be leveraged to make decisions that used to be based on the input of only a few people.[23] Companies get feedback on marketing campaigns, new product ideas, and other marketing decisions by asking customers to weigh in. One company called Talenthouse is offering up the crowd to help musicians fulfill all sorts of needs—for example, someone to design album art or sew a dress for a lead singer. Talenthouse has users submit work to be voted on by Facebook and Twitter peers. The winner gets the job (though the musician has the final say in who wins). Some musicians see Talenthouse as a way to gain publicity or to help aspiring artists. English singer-songwriter Ellie Goulding set up a contest for Talenthouse competitors to submit a photograph that showed people connecting with music at a concert or festival. The winner received £1,000 (about $1,500), a new laptop, special promotion, and a job as the official photographer for an Ellie Goulding concert.[24] Crowdsourcing offers a way for companies to engage

heavy users of a brand and receive input, which in turn increases those users' brand advocacy and lessens the likelihood that a change will be disliked enough to drive away loyal customers.

18-2 CREATING AND LEVERAGING A SOCIAL MEDIA CAMPAIGN

Social media is an exciting new field, and its potential for expanding a brand's impact is enormous. Because the costs are often minimal and the learning curve is relatively low, some organizations are tempted to dive headfirst into social media. As with any marketing campaign, however, it is always important to start with a strategy. For most organizations, this means starting with a marketing or communications plan. Important evaluative areas such as situation analysis, objectives, and evaluation are still essential. It is important to link communication objectives (for example, improving customer service) to the most effective social media tools (for example, Twitter) and to be able to measure the results to determine if the objectives were met. It is also important to understand the various types of media involved.

The new communication paradigm created by a shift to social media marketing raises questions about categorization. In light of the convergence of traditional and digital media, researchers have explored different ways that interactive marketers can categorize media types, namely owned, earned, and paid media (recall these concepts from Chapter 15). The purpose of owned media is to develop deeper relationships with customers. A brand's Facebook presence, YouTube channel, Twitter presence, Pinterest presence, and presence on other social platforms constitute owned media. Additional content such as videos, webinars, recommendations, ratings, and blog posts are also considered owned media since they are sharable on social media platforms. In an interactive space, media are *earned* through word of mouth or online buzz about something the brand is doing. Earned media include viral videos, retweets, comments on blogs, and other forms of customer feedback resulting from a social media

crowdsourcing using consumers to develop and market products

Companies with an established brand recognition have deeper layers of social media—customers know and recognize instantly.

presence. When consumers pass along brand information in the form of retweets, blog comments, or ratings and recommendations, this is an example of earned media. In other words, the word of mouth is spread online rather than face-to-face. Paid media are similar to marketing efforts that utilize traditional media, like newspaper, magazine, and television advertisements. In an interactive space, paid media include display advertising, paid search words, and other types of direct online advertising.[25] Ads purchased on Facebook, for example, are considered paid media since the brand is paying for the text-based or visual ad that shows up on the right-hand side of Facebook profiles.

As a result, social media can really be thought of as an additional "layer" that many brands decide to develop. Some layers are quite deep—Doritos, Old Spice, and Nike can be said to have deeper layers of social media since these are brands that people talk about. Other brands, for example, many B-to-B brands, may have a more shallow social media layer and provide access on only one or two social media platforms. At the end of the day, it really depends on the type

social media monitoring
the process of identifying and assessing what is being said about a company, individual, product, or brand

of product being sold and the customer's propensity to participate in social media.

To leverage all three types of media, marketers must follow a few key guidelines. First, they must maximize owned media by reaching out beyond their existing Web sites to create portfolios of digital touch points. This is especially true for brands with tight budgets, as the organization may not be able to afford much paid media. Second, marketers must recognize that public and media relations no longer translates into earned media. Instead, marketers must learn how to listen and respond to stakeholders. This will stimulate word of mouth. Finally, marketers must understand that paid media must serve as a catalyst to drive customer engagement and expand into emerging channels.[26] If balanced correctly, all three types of media can be powerful tools for interactive marketers.

18-2a The Listening System

The first action a marketing team should take when initiating a social media campaign is simple—it should just listen. Customers are on social media and assume that the brand is there as well. They expect a new level of engagement with brands. Developing an effective listening system is necessary to both understanding and engaging an online audience. Marketers must not only hear what is being said about the brand, the industry, the competition, and the customer, but they must also pay attention to who is saying what and act upon that information. The specific ways that customers and noncustomers rate, rank, critique, praise, deride, recommend, snub, and generally discuss brands are all important. Thus, social media have created a new method of market research: customers telling marketers what they want and need (and do not want and do not need).

Once a company has started listening, it typically wants to develop a more formalized approach. **Social media monitoring** is the process of identifying and assessing what is being said about a company, individual, product, or brand. It can involve sentiment analysis and *text mining* specific key words on social networking Web sites, blogs, discussion forums, and other social media. Negative comments and complaints are of particular importance, both because they can illuminate unknown brand flaws and because they are the comments that tend to go viral. Listening is important because consumers believe that if negative comments about a brand go unanswered, that brand is insincere, and consumers will take their business elsewhere. Failure to respond to criticism typically leads to a larger crisis. Online tools such as Google Alerts, Google Blog Search, Twitter Search, Social Mention, Social Bakers and Socialcast are extremely helpful in monitoring social media. Larger companies typically use an enterprise system such as Salesforce.com's Radian6 CRM software to monitor social media.

18-2b Social Media Objectives

After establishing a listening platform, the organization should develop a list of objectives for its social media team to accomplish. These objectives must be developed with a clear understanding of how social media change the communication dynamic with and for customers. Remember, attempting to reach a mass audience with a static message will never be as successful as influencing people through conversation. Marketing managers must set objectives that reflect this reality. Here are some practical ideas that marketing managers should consider when setting social media objectives:

- **Listen and learn:** Monitor what is being said about the brand and competitors, and glean insights about audiences. Use online tools and do research to implement the best social media practices. If you have established a listening strategy, this objective should already be accomplished.

- **Build relationships and awareness:** Open dialogues with stakeholders by giving them compelling content across a variety of media. Engage in conversations, and answer customers' questions candidly. This will both increase Web traffic and boost your search engine ranking. This is where crowdsourcing can be useful for product development and communication campaign feedback.

- **Promote products and services:** The clearest path to increasing the bottom line using social media is to get customers talking about products and services, which ultimately translates into sales.

- **Manage your reputation:** Develop and improve the brand's reputation by responding to comments and criticism that appear on blogs and forums. Additionally, organizations can position themselves as helpful and benevolent by participating in other forums and discussions. Social media make it much easier to establish and communicate expertise.

- **Improve customer service:** Customer comments about products and services will not always be

positive. Use social media to search out displeased customers and engage them directly in order to solve their service issues.

 ## 18-3 EVALUATION AND MEASUREMENT OF SOCIAL MEDIA

Social media have the potential to revolutionize the way organizations communicate with stakeholders. Given the relative ease and efficiency with which organizations can use social media, a positive return on investment (ROI) is likely for many—if not most—organizations. A Forrester Research report found that ninety-five percent of marketers planned to increase or maintain their investments in social media. However, though they understand that it is a worthwhile investment, most marketers have not been able to figure out how to measure the benefits of social media.

As with traditional advertising, marketers lack hard evidence as to the relative effectiveness of these tools. Some marketers accept this unknown variable and focus on the fact that social media are less about ROI than about deepening relationships with customers; others work tirelessly to better understand the measurement of social media's effectiveness. A recent Ragan/NASDAQ OMX Corporate Solutions survey found that forty percent of marketers are unsure of what evaluative tools to use, and about seventy percent are only "somewhat satisfied" or "not satisfied at all" with how their companies measure social media. "I'm not sure what to measure or how," said one survey participant. "I know it's important, but I can't show my boss how many retweets a post received and expect him to care."[27]

While literally hundreds of metrics have been developed to measure social media's value, these metrics are meaningless unless they are tied to key performance indicators.[28] For example, a local coffee shop manager may measure the success of her social media presence by the raw number of friends on Facebook and followers on Twitter she has accumulated. But these numbers depend entirely on context. The rate of accumulation, investment per fan and follower, and comparison to similarly sized coffee shops are all important metrics to consider. Without context, measurements are meaningless. This is a hot topic, and several marketing blogs cover the areas of social media measurement. Jim Sterne's book *Social Media Metrics* is one of the best sources information on monitoring and using social media metrics.

18-4 SOCIAL BEHAVIOR OF CONSUMERS

Social media have changed the way that people interact in their everyday lives. Some say that social media have made people smarter by giving people (especially children) access to so much information and interactivity. Social media allow people to stay in touch in ways never before experienced. Social media have also reinvented civic engagement (recall that the ALS Association's "Ice Bucket Challenge" grew worldwide through social media like Facebook and Twitter). Social media have drastically changed the advertising business from an industry based on mass-media models (for example, television) to an industry based on relationships and conversations. This all has implications for how consumers use social media and the purposes for which they use those media.[29]

Once objectives have been determined and measurement tools have been implemented, it is important to identify the consumer the marketer is trying to reach. Who is using social media? What types of

Social media has reinvented civic engagement—see the ALS Ice Bucket Challenge as a prime example.

Marcos Mesa Sam Wordley/Shutterstock.com

WHICH METRICS ARE MOST EFFECTIVE?

Many social media marketers will simply need to start with good measurable objectives, determine what needs to be measured, and figure it out. Still, some social media metrics to consider include:

- **Buzz:** volume of consumer-created buzz for a brand based on posts and impressions, by social channel, by stage in the purchase channel, by season, and by time of day.

- **Interest:** number of "likes," fans, followers, and friends; growth rates; rate of virality or pass along; and change in pass along over time.

- **Participation:** number of comments, ratings, social bookmarks, subscriptions, page views, uploads, downloads, embeds, retweets, Facebook posts, pins, and time spent with social media platform.

- **Search engine ranks and results:** increases and decreases on searches and changes in key words.

- **Influence:** media mentions, influences of bloggers reached, influences of customers reached, and second-degree reach based on social graphs.

- **Sentiment analysis:** positive, neutral, and negative sentiment; trends of sentiment; and volume of sentiment.

- **Web site metrics:** clicks, click-through rates, and percentage of traffic.

social media do they use? How do they use social media? Are they just reading content, or do they actually create it? Does Facebook attract younger users? Do Twitter users retweet viral videos? These types of questions must be considered because they determine not only which tools will be most effective but also, more importantly, whether launching a social media campaign even makes sense for a particular organization.

Understanding an audience necessitates understanding how that audience uses social media. In *Groundswell*, Charlene Li and Josh Bernoff of

Forrester Research identify six categories of social media users:

1. **Creators:** Those who produce and share online content like blogs, Web sites, articles, and videos

2. **Critics:** Those who post comments, ratings, and reviews of products and services on blogs and forums

3. **Collectors:** Those who use RSS feeds to collect information and vote for Web sites online

4. **Joiners:** Those who maintain a social networking profile and visit other sites

5. **Spectators:** Those who read blogs, listen to podcasts, watch videos, and generally consume media

6. **Inactives:** Those who do none of these things[30]

A Forrester Research study determined that twenty-four percent of social media users function as creators, 36 percent function as critics, 23 percent function as collectors, 68 percent function as joiners, 73 percent function as spectators, and 14 percent function—or rather, do not function—as inactives.[31] Participation in most categories has slowed slightly, prompting analysts to recommend that marketers re-examine how they are engaging with their customers online.

Despite the apparent slowdown, research also shows that more social networking "rookies" are classified as joiners. Another bright spot is a new category, "conversationalists," or people who post status updates on social networking sites and microblogging services such as Twitter. Conversationalists represent 36 percent of users.[32] This type of classification gives marketers a general idea of who is using social media and how to engage them. It is similar to any type of market segmentation—especially the 80/20 rule. Those who are creating content and active on social media could be those consumers most likely to actively engage with a brand as well as actively post negative comments on social media. The critics and collectors make up most of this group. However, it is important not to miss the joiners and spectators, because they are eager to follow and act on the comments of their fellow customers.

18-5 SOCIAL MEDIA TOOLS: CONSUMER- AND CORPORATE-GENERATED CONTENT

Given that it is important for marketers to engage with customers on social media for the reasons mentioned earlier, there are a number of tools and platforms that can be employed as part of an organization's social media strategy. Blogs, microblogs, social networks, media creation and sharing sites, social news sites, location-based social networking sites, review sites, and virtual worlds and online gaming all have their place in a company's social marketing plan. These are all tools in a marketing manager's toolbox, available when applicable to the marketing plan but not necessarily to be used all at once. Because of the breakneck pace at which technology changes, this list of resources will surely look markedly different five years from now. More tools emerge every day, and branding strategies must keep up with the ever-changing world of technology. For now, the resources highlighted in this section remain a marketer's strongest set of platforms for conversing and strengthening relationships with customers.

18-5a Blogs

Blogs have become staples in many social media strategies and are often a brand's social media centerpiece. A **blog** is a publicly accessible Web page that functions as an interactive journal, whereby readers can post comments on the author's entries. Some experts believe that every company should have a blog that speaks to current and potential customers, not as consumers, but as people.[33] Blogs allow marketers to create content in the form of posts, which ideally build trust and a sense of authenticity in customers. Once posts are made, audience members can provide feedback through comments. Because it opens a dialogue and gives customers a voice, the comments section of a blog post is one of the most important avenues of conversation between brands and consumers.

Blogs can be divided into two broad categories: corporate and professional blogs, and noncorporate blogs such as personal blogs. **Corporate blogs** are sponsored by a company or one of its brands and are maintained by one or more of the company's employees. They disseminate marketing-controlled information and are effective platforms for developing thought leadership, fostering better relationships with stakeholders, maximizing search engine optimization, attracting new customers, endearing the organization with anecdotes and stories about brands, and providing an active forum for testing new ideas. Many companies, however, have moved

> **blog** a publicly accessible Web page that functions as an interactive journal, whereby readers can post comments on the author's entries
>
> **corporate blogs** blogs that are sponsored by a company or one of its brands and maintained by one or more of the company's employees

away from corporate blogs, replacing the in-depth writing and comment monitoring that come with blog maintenance with the quick, easy, and more social Facebook, Twitter, or Tumblr. Coca Cola, Walmart, and AllState operate some of the best big company corporate blogs. All are known for their creative and engaging content and the authenticity of their tone.[34]

On the other hand, **noncorporate blogs** are independent and not associated with the marketing efforts of any particular company or brand. Because these blogs contain information not controlled by marketers, they are perceived to be more authentic than corporate blogs. Mommy bloggers, women who review children's products and discuss family-related topics on their personal blogs, use noncorporate blogs. The goal of mommy blogs is to share parenting tips and experiences and become part of a community. Food blogs are especially popular, particularly those posting restaurant reviews, diet and exercise tips, and recipes.

Because of the popularity of these and other types of blogs, many bloggers receive products and/or money from companies in exchange for a review. Many bloggers disclose where they received the product or if they were paid, but an affiliation is not always clear. Because of this, bloggers must disclose any financial relationship with a company per Federal Trade Commission rules. Marketing managers need to understand the rules behind offering complimentary products to bloggers before using them as a way to capitalize on the high potential for social buzz; four out of five noncorporate bloggers post brand or product reviews. Even if a company does not have a formal social media strategy, chances are the brand is still out in the blogosphere, whether or not a marketing manager approached a blogger.

18-5b Microblogs

Microblogs are blogs that entail shorter posts than traditional blogs. Twitter, the most popular microblogging platform, requires that posts be no more than 140 characters in length. However, there are several other platforms, including Tumblr, Plurk, and, of course, Facebook's status updates. Unlike Twitter,

Source: Tumblr

Some social media platforms allow users to post longer pieces of text, videos, images and links.

these platforms allow users to post longer pieces of text, videos, images, and links. While some microblogs (such as Tumblr) do not have text length limits, their multimedia-based cultures discourage traditional blog-length text posts. The content posted on microblogs ranges from five-paragraph news stories to photos of sandwiches with the ingredients as captions (scanwiches.com). While Tumblr is growing rapidly, Twitter, originally designed as a short messaging system used for internal communication, is wildly popular and is used as a communication and research tool by individuals and brands around the world. Twitter is effective for disseminating breaking news, promoting longer blog posts and campaigns, sharing links, announcing events, and promoting sales. By following, retweeting, responding to potential customers' tweets, and tweeting content that inspires customers to engage the brand, corporate Twitter users can lay a foundation for meaningful two-way conversation quickly and effectively. Celebrities also flock to Twitter to interact with fans, discuss tour dates, and efficiently promote themselves directly to fans. Research has found that when operated correctly, corporate Twitter accounts are well respected and well received. Twitter can be used to build communities, aid in customer service, gain prospects, increase awareness, and, in the case of nonprofits, raise funds.

The ways a business can use microblogs to successfully engage with customers are almost limitless. A wide variety of companies find Tumblr's easy and customizable format a great way to promote an individual brand. Mashable uses its Tumblr to give a glimpse inside the offices and share the company's sense of humor. Ace Hotel, located in New York, Portland, Seattle, and Palm

noncorporate blogs
independent blogs that are not associated with the marketing efforts of any particular company or brand

microblogs blogs with strict post length limits

Springs, shows off its properties and local art exhibits on a spare, gallery-like Tumblr. Lure Fishbar shows off its delectable food on its Tumblr.[35]

18-5c Social Networks

Social networking sites allow individuals to connect—or network—with friends, peers, and business associates. Connections may be made around shared interests, shared environments, or personal relationships. Depending on the site, connected individuals may be able to send each other messages, track each other's activity, see each other's personal information, share multimedia, comment on each other's blog and microblog posts—or do all of these things. Depending on a marketing team's goals, several social networks might be engaged as part of a social media strategy: Facebook is the largest social network; Instagram and Snapchat are popular among younger audiences; LinkedIn is geared toward professionals and businesses who use it to recruit employees; and niche networks like Twitch, SoundCloud, Grindr, BlackPlanet, and ChristianMingle.com cater to specialized markets. There is a niche social network for just about every demographic and interest. Beyond those already established, an organization may decide to develop a brand-specific social network or community. Although each social networking site is different, some marketing goals can be accomplished on any such site. Given the right strategy, increasing awareness, targeting audiences, promoting products, forging relationships, highlighting expertise and leadership, attracting event participants, performing research, and generating new business are attainable marketing goals on any social network.

There is a niche social network for just about every demographic and interest.

EXHIBIT 18.1 FACEBOOK LINGO

Non-Individual (Usually Corporate)	Individual
Page	Profile
Fan of a page, tells fan's friends that the user is a fan, creates mini viral campaign	Friend a person, send private messages, write on the Wall, see friend-only content
Public, searchable	Privacy options, not searchable unless user enabled

FACEBOOK Facebook originated as a community for college students that opened to the general public as its popularity grew. It now has almost 1.5 billion monthly active users, making it the largest social networking site by far. Growth in new profiles is highest among baby boomers using Facebook as a way to connect with old friends and keep up with family. Facebook is popular not only with individuals, but also with groups and companies. How an individual uses Facebook differs from the way a group or company uses Facebook, as you can see in Exhibit 18.1. Individual Facebook users create profiles, while brands, organizations, and nonprofit causes operate as pages. As opposed to individual profiles, all pages are public and are thus subject to search engine indexing.

By maintaining a popular Facebook page, a brand not only increases its social media presence, it also helps to optimize search engine results. Pages often include photo and video albums, brand information, and links to external sites. One of the most useful page features is the Timeline. The Timeline allows a brand to communicate directly with fans via status updates, which enables marketers to build databases of interested stakeholders. When an individual becomes a fan of your organization or posts on your Timeline, that information is shared with the individual's friends, creating a mini viral marketing campaign. Other Facebook marketing tools include groups, applications, and ads. Facebook is an extremely important platform for social marketers.

Facebook has proved to be fertile ground for new marketing ideas and campaigns. Many companies use Facebook as a way to share photos of the business they are doing, whether that is images of the

social networking sites
Web sites that allow individuals to connect—or network—with friends, peers, and business associates

plant where the product is made or finished construction on a new project. Offering guides relevant to a company's product or service as a way to educate interested customers has worked well for Kitchen Cabinet Kings, which found that educated customers make more purchases. Threadless' Voting Hub Facebook page allows fans to share, promote, and vote on new t-shirt designs.[36]

LINKEDIN LinkedIn is used primarily by professionals who wish to build their personal brands online and businesses that are recruiting employees and freelancers. LinkedIn features many of the same services as Facebook (profiles, status updates, private messages, company pages, and groups) but is oriented around business and professional connections—it is designed to be information-rich rather than multimedia-rich. LinkedIn serves as a virtual rolodex, providing recruiters and job seekers alike a network to connect and conduct business. LinkedIn's question-and-answer forum, endorsement system, job classifieds platform, and acquisition of presentation-hosting Web site SlideShare set it apart from Facebook as a truly business-oriented space.[37] LinkedIn is the most effective social media platform for B-to-B marketing, as many use it for lead generation. Some companies use LinkedIn for recruiting, and others use it for thought leadership. Indeed, company pages on LinkedIn can serve as an effective hub for products and services, promotional videos, and company news.

Video creation and distribution have gained popularity among marketers because of video's rich ability to tell stories.

Rvlsoft/Shutterstock.com

18-5d Media Sharing Sites

Media sharing sites allow users to upload and distribute multimedia content like videos and photos. YouTube, Flickr, Pinterest, Instagram, Vine, and Snapchat are particularly useful to brands' social marketing strategies because they add a vibrant interactive channel on which to disseminate content. Suffice to say, the distribution of user-generated content has changed markedly over the past few years. Today, organizations can tell compelling brand stories through videos, photos, and audio.

Photo sharing sites allow users to archive and share photos. Flickr, Picasa, Twitpic, Photobucket, Facebook, and Imgur all offer free photo hosting services that can be utilized by individuals and businesses alike. Instagram is often used by brands to engage younger audience members. Snapchat is also useful, but since photos and videos are only visible for a few seconds, complex marketing messages cannot easily be conveyed.

Video creation and distribution have also gained popularity among marketers because of video's rich ability to tell stories. YouTube, the highest-trafficked video-based Web site and the third-highest-trafficked site overall, allows users to upload and stream their videos to an enthusiastic and active community.[38] YouTube is not only large (in terms of visitors), but it also attracts a diverse base of users: age and gender demographics are remarkably balanced.

Many entertainment companies and movie marketers have used YouTube as a showcase for new products, specials, and movie trailers. User-generated content can

media sharing sites Web sites that allow users to upload and distribute multimedia content like videos and photos

Ask Me Anything

Politicians, celebrities, and business leaders from all walks of life have used Reddit's Ask Me Anything (AMA) series to promote their issues, projects, and products. After an AMA is posted, Reddit users ask questions—sometimes complex or controversial questions—and the poster answers them as he or she chooses. Some of the site's most popular AMAs have included Bill Gates, Molly Ringwald, Snoop Lion, Neil deGrasse Tyson, Louis C.K., and President Barack Obama.[39]

© olexius/Shutterstock 149737013

also be a powerful tool for brands that can use it effectively. While YouTube is still the champ, Vine is quickly becoming another popular platform for corporate promotion.

A podcast, another type of user-generated media, is a digital audio or video file that is distributed serially for other people to listen to or watch. Podcasts can be streamed online, played on a computer, uploaded to a portable media player, or downloaded onto a smartphone. Podcasts are like radio shows that are distributed through various means and not linked to a scheduled time slot. While they have not experienced the exponential growth rates of other digital platforms, podcasts have amassed a steadily growing number of loyal devotees. For example, Etsy, an online marketplace for handmade and vintage wares, offers a podcast series introducing favorite craftspeople to the world—driving business for those individuals.

Since location site technology is relatively new, many brands are still figuring out how to best utilize Foursquare.

18-5e Social News Sites

Social news sites allow users to decide which content is promoted on a given Web site by voting that content up or down. Users post news stories and multimedia on crowdsourced sites such as Reddit for the community to vote on. The more interest from readers, the higher the story or video is ranked. Marketers have found that these sites are useful for promoting campaigns, creating conversations around related issues, and building Web site traffic.

If marketing content posted to a crowdsourced site is voted up, discussed, and shared enough to be listed among the most popular topics of the day, it can go viral across other sites, and eventually, the entire Web. Social bookmarking sites such as Delicious and StumbleUpon are similar to social news sites but the objective of their users is to collect, save, and share interesting and valuable links. On these sites, users categorize links with short, descriptive tags. Users can search the site's database of links by specific tags or can add their own tags to others' links. In this way, tags serve as the foundation for information gathering and sharing on social bookmarking sites.[40]

18-5f Location-Based Social Networking Sites

Considered by many to be the next big thing in social marketing, location sites like Foursquare and Loopt should be on every marketer's radar. Essentially, **location-based social networking sites** combine the fun of social networking with the utility of location-based GPS technology. Foursquare, one of the most popular location sites, treats location-based micronetworking as a game: Users earn badges and special statuses based on their number of visits to particular locations. Users can write and read short reviews and tips about businesses, organize meet-ups, and see which Foursquare-using friends are nearby. Foursquare updates can also be posted to linked Twitter and Facebook accounts for followers and friends to see. Location sites such as Foursquare are particularly useful social marketing tools for local businesses, especially when combined with sales promotions like coupons, special offers, contests, and events. Location sites can be harnessed to forge lasting relationships with and deeply ingrained loyalty from customers.[41] For example, a local restaurant can allow consumers to check in on Foursquare using their smartphones and receive coupons for that day's purchases. Since the location site technology is relatively new, many brands are still figuring out how best to utilize Foursquare. Facebook added Places to capitalize on this location-based technology, which allows people to "check in" and share their location with their online friends. It will be interesting to see how use of this technology grows over time.

18-5g Review Sites

Individuals tend to trust other people's opinions when it comes to purchasing.

social news sites Web sites that allow users to decide which content is promoted on a given Web site by voting that content up or down

location-based social networking sites Web sites that combine the fun of social networking with the utility of location-based GPS technology

Giving marketers the opportunity to respond their customers directly and put their business in a positive light, is why review sites like Yelp have thrived.

According to Nielsen Media Research, more than seventy percent of consumers said that they trusted online consumer opinions. This percentage is much higher than that of consumers who trust traditional advertising. Based on the early work of Amazon.com and eBay to integrate user opinions into product and seller pages, countless Web sites allowing users to voice their opinions have sprung up across every segment of the Internet market. **Review sites** allow consumers to post, read, rate, and comment on opinions regarding all kinds of products and services. For example, Yelp, the most active local review directory on the Web, combines customer critiques of local businesses with business information and elements of social networking to create an engaging, informative experience. On Yelp, users scrutinize local restaurants, fitness centers, tattoo parlors, and other businesses, each of which has a detailed profile page. Business owners and representatives can edit their organizations' pages and respond to Yelp reviews both privately and publicly. Yelp even rewards its most popular (and prolific) reviewers with Elite status. Businesses like Worthington, Ohio's Pies & Pints will throw Elite-only parties to allow these esteemed Yelpers to try out their restaurant, hoping to receive a favorable review. A Tiki Beach Party for Yelp Elites at Montreal, Canada's Le Lab garnered thirteen reviews averaging five stars out of five.[42] By giving marketers the opportunity to respond to their customers directly and put their businesses in a positive light, review

review sites Web sites that allow consumers to post, read, rate, and comment on opinions regarding all kinds of products and services

sites certainly serve as useful tools for local and national businesses.

18-5h Virtual Worlds and Online Gaming

Virtual worlds and online gaming present additional opportunities for marketers to engage with consumers. These include massive multiplayer online games (MMOGs) such as *League of Legends*, *Destiny*, and *The Elder Scrolls Online* as well as online communities (or virtual worlds) such as *Second- Life*, *Poptropica*, and *Habbo Hotel*. Although virtual worlds are unfamiliar to and even intimidating for many traditional marketers, the field is an important, viable, and growing consideration for social media marketing. Consultancy firm KZero Worldwide reported that almost 800 million people participate in some sort of virtual world experience, and the sector's annual revenue approaches $1 billion. Some of the most popular and profitable games, including *Diamond Dash* and *FarmVille 2*, are built on the Facebook platform. Much of these games' revenue comes from in-game advertising—virtual world environments are often fertile grounds for branded content. Organizations such as IBM and the American Cancer Society have developed profitable trade presences in *Second Life*, but others have abandoned the persistent online community as its user base has declined—the average number of users logged into *Second Life* has dropped almost 25 percent in the last four years.[43]

One area of growth is social gaming. Nearly twenty-five percent of people play games like *Words with Friends* and *Trivia Crack*, either within social networking sites like Facebook or on mobile devices. Interestingly, the typical player is a forty-five-year-old woman with a full-time job and college education (while users who play on mobile devices tend to be younger). Women are most likely to play with real-world friends or relatives as opposed to strangers. Most play multiple times per week, and more than thirty percent play daily. Facebook is by far the largest social network for gaming, though hi5 is hoping to win over more users with its large variety of games. The top five games on Facebook are *Candy Crush Saga*, *FarmVille 2*, *Texas HoldEm Poker*, *Pet Rescue Saga*, and *Dragon City*.[44] King's *Candy Crush Saga* entices more than ninety-three million users a day. These games are attractive because they can be played in just five minutes, perhaps while waiting for the train.[45] Many mobile games use mobile ads to generate revenue for the game-makers. As long as the ads are not overly intrusive, most users opt to play the free game with ads over the paid version that does not have ads.

Another popular strategy is to give an ad-free game away for free and then charge small sums of money for in-game items and power-ups. These *microtransactions* account for 21 percent of all mobile profits.[46] Though *Kim Kardashian: Hollywood* is free to download and play, for example, the game has earned more than $200 million from in-game microtransactions.[47]

Another popular type of online gaming targets a different group—MMOGs tend to draw eighteen to thirty-four-year-old males. In MMOG environments, thousands of people play simultaneously, and the games have revenues of more than $400 billion annually. Regardless of the type of experience, brands must be creative in how they integrate into games. Social and real-world-like titles are the most appropriate for marketing and advertising (as opposed to fantasy games), and promotions typically include special events, competitions, and sweepstakes. In some games (like *The Sims*), having ads increases the authenticity. For example, Nike offers shoes in *The Sims Online* that allow the player to run faster.

 ## 18-6 SOCIAL MEDIA AND MOBILE TECHNOLOGY

While much of the excitement in social media has been based on Web sites and new technology uses, much of the growth lies in new platforms. These platforms include the multitude of smartphones as well as iPads and other tablets. The major implication of this development is that consumers now can access popular Web sites like Facebook, Mashable, Twitter, and Foursquare from all their various platforms.

18-6a Mobile and Smartphone Technology

Worldwide, there are more than six billion mobile phones in use, seventeen percent of which are smartphones.[48] It is no surprise, then, that the mobile platform is such an effective marketing tool—especially when targeting a younger audience. Smartphones up the ante by allowing individuals to do nearly everything they can do with a computer—from anywhere. With a smartphone in hand, reading a blog, writing an e-mail, scheduling a meeting, posting to Facebook, playing a multiplayer game, watching a video, taking a picture, using GPS, and surfing the Internet might all occur during one ten-minute bus ride. Smartphone technology, often considered the crowning achievement in digital convergence and social media integration, has opened the door to modern mobile advertising as a viable marketing strategy.

Mobile advertising has grown as much as 80 percent per year in the U.S., but that rate is expected to slow to about 50 percent per year over the next few years. Digital advertising accounted for almost 34 percent of all U.S. ad spending in 2015, and mobile advertising alone made up about a third of that.[49] There are several reasons for the recent popularity of mobile marketing. First, an effort to standardize mobile platforms has resulted in a low barrier to entry. Second, especially given mobile marketing's younger audiences, there are more consumers than ever acclimating to once-worrisome privacy and pricing policies. Third, because most people carry their smartphones with them at all times, mobile marketing is uniquely effective at garnering customer attention in real time. Fourth, mobile marketing is measurable: metrics and usage statistics make it an effective tool for gaining insight into consumer behavior. Fifth, in-store notification technology such as Apple's iBeacon can send promotional messages based on real-time interactions with customers. Finally, mobile marketing's response rate is higher than that of traditional media types like print and broadcast advertisement. Some common mobile marketing tools include:

- **SMS (short message service):** 160-character text messages sent to and from cell phones. SMS is typically integrated with other tools.

- **MMS (multimedia messaging service):** Similar to SMS but allows the attachment of images, videos, ringtones, and other multimedia to text messages.

- **Mobile Web sites (MOBI and WAP Web sites):** Web sites designed specifically for viewing and navigation on mobile devices.

- **Mobile ads:** Visual advertisements integrated into text messages, applications, and mobile Web sites. Mobile ads are often sold on a cost-per-click basis.

- **Bluetooth marketing:** A signal is sent to Bluetooth-enabled devices, allowing marketers to send targeted messages to users based on their geographic locations.

- **Smartphone applications (apps):** Software designed specifically for mobile and tablet devices.

A popular use for barcode scanning apps is the reading and processing of Quick Response (QR) codes. When scanned by a smartphone's QR reader app, a QR code takes the user to a specific site with content about or a discount for products or services. Uses range from donating to a charity by scanning the code to simply checking out the company's Web site for more information. For example, Modify Watches offers a watch face with no hands. Instead it has a QR code that, when scanned, shows the correct time.[50]

Another smartphone trend is called "near field communication" (NFC), which uses small chips hidden in or behind products that, when touched by compatible devices, will transfer the information on the chip to the device. Barnes & Noble is hoping to work with publishers to ship hardcover books containing NFC chips to Barnes & Noble stores. The chips will be embedded with editorial reviews about that book from Barnes & Noble's Web site. When a NOOK user touches the hardcover with her NOOK, the book reviews will display on her tablet, helping her make a purchase decision.[51] The Samsung Galaxy S6 smartphone can track users' eye movements and shift screen content depending on where they are looking. While a relatively new technology, eye tracking has interesting implications for mobile marketing in the near future.[52]

Finally, mobile marketing is particularly powerful when combined with geo-location platforms such as Foursquare, whereby people can "check in" to places and receive benefits and special offers. These platforms allow retailers and other businesses to incentivize multiple visits, visits at certain times of the day, and positive customer reviews.

18-6b Apps and Widgets

Given the widespread adoption of Apple's iPhone, Android-based phones, and other smartphones, it is no surprise that millions of apps have been developed for the mobile market. Dozens of new and unique apps that harness mobile technology are added to mobile marketplaces every day. While many apps perform platform-specific tasks, others convert existing content into a mobile-ready format. Whether offering new or existing content, when an app is well branded and integrated into a company's overall marketing strategy, it can create buzz and generate customer engagement.

Web widgets, also known as gadgets and badges, are software applications that run entirely within existing online platforms. Essentially, a Web widget allows a developer to embed a simple application such as a weather forecast, horoscope, or stock market ticker into a Web site, even if the developer did not write (or does not understand) the application's source code. From a marketing perspective, widgets

allow customers to display company information (such as current promotions, coupons, or news) on their own Web sites or smartphone home screens. Widgets are often cheaper than apps to develop, can extend an organization's reach beyond existing platforms, will broaden the listening system, and can make an organization easier to find.[53]

18-7 THE SOCIAL MEDIA PLAN

To effectively use the tools in the social media toolbox, it is important to have a clearly outlined social media plan. The social media plan is linked to larger plans such as a promotional plan or marketing plan and should fit appropriately into the objectives and steps in those plans (for more information, review Chapters 2 and 16). It is important to research throughout the development of the social media plan to keep abreast of the rapidly changing social media world. There are six stages involved in creating an effective social media plan:

1. **Listen to customers:** This is covered in more detail in section 18-2a.

2. **Set social media objectives:** Set objectives that can be specifically accomplished through social media, with special attention to how to measure the results. Numerous metrics are available, some of which are mentioned throughout the chapter.

3. **Define strategies:** This includes examining trends and best practices in the industry.

4. **Identify the target audience:** This should line up with the target market defined in the marketing plan, but in the social media plan, pay special attention to how that audience participates and behaves online.

5. **Select the tools and platforms:** Based on the result of Step 4, choose the social media tools and platforms that will be most relevant. These choices are based on the knowledge of where the target audience participates on social media.

6. **Implement and monitor the strategy:** Social media campaigns can be fluid, so it is important to keep a close eye on what is successful and what is not. Then, based on the observations, make changes as needed. It also becomes important,

Twin Design/Shutterstock.com

EXHIBIT 18.2 SOCIAL MEDIA TRENDS

Trend	Change	Where Is It Now?
Yik Yak	Anonymous geolocated messaging	
Microsoft Office 365, Google Drive	Integration with file hosting	
Ello	Challengers to Facebook's dominance	
Bing	Rewards program offers prizes for using Bing Search	
The Internet of Things	Integration into wearables, appliances, apparel, and more	
Apple Pay, Google Wallet, Bitcoin, and NFC- enabled payment options	Replace credit cards with various forms of digital payment	
Loot Crate, Trunk Club, and NatureBox	Online and subscription-based personal shopping	
Twitch, Meerkat, and Periscope	Live video streaming for everybody	
Tinder and Grindr	The mainstreaming of geolocated dating apps	

therefore, to go back to the listening stage to interpret how consumers are perceiving the social media campaign.

Listening to customers and industry trends, as well as continually revising the social media plan to meet the needs of the changing social media market, are keys to successful social media marketing. There are numerous industry leaders sharing some of their best practices, and sources such as *Fast Company* and the *Wall Street Journal* report regularly on how large and small companies are successfully using social media to gain market share and sales. A good example of using social media strategies is HubSpot, a company that practices what it preaches. HubSpot advocates the benefits of building valuable content online and then using social media to pull customers to its Web site. Social engine profiles have increased HubSpot's Web site traffic, which has made its lead generation program much more effective.

18-7a The Changing World of Social Media

As you read through the chapter, some of the trends that are noted may already seem ancient to you. The rate of change in social media is astounding—usage statistics change daily for sites like Facebook and Twitter. Some things that are in the rumor mill as we write this may have exploded in popularity; others may have fizzled out without even appearing on your radar. In Exhibit 18.2, we have listed some of the items that seem to be on the brink of exploding on to the social media scene. Take a moment to fill in the current state of each in the third column. Have you heard of it? Has it come and gone? Maybe it is still rumored, or maybe it has petered out. This exercise highlights not only the speed with which social media change but also the importance of keeping tabs on rumors. Doing so may give you a competitive advantage by being able to understand and invest in the next big social media site.

STUDY TOOLS 18

LOCATED AT BACK OF THE TEXTBOOK

☐ Rip out Chapter Review Card

LOCATED AT WWW.CENGAGEBRAIN.COM

☐ Review Key Terms Flashcards and create your own

☐ Track your knowledge and understanding of key concepts in marketing

☐ Complete practice and graded quizzes to prepare for tests

☐ Complete interactive content within the MKTG Online experience

☐ View the chapter highlight boxes within the MKTG Online experience

19 | Pricing Concepts

LEARNING OUTCOMES

After studying this chapter, you will be able to…

19-1 Discuss the importance of pricing decisions to the economy and to the individual firm

19-2 List and explain a variety of pricing objectives

19-3 Explain the role of demand in price determination

19-4 Understand the concepts of dynamic pricing and yield management systems

19-5 Describe cost-oriented pricing strategies

19-6 Demonstrate how the product life cycle, competition, distribution and promotion strategies, customer demands, the Internet and extranets, and perceptions of quality can affect price

19-7 Describe the procedure for setting the right price

19-8 Identify the legal constraints on pricing decisions

19-9 Explain how discounts, geographic pricing, and other pricing tactics can be used to fine-tune a base price

After you finish this chapter go to **PAGE 361** for **STUDY TOOLS.**

19-1 THE IMPORTANCE OF PRICE

Price means one thing to the consumer and something else to the seller. To the consumer, it is the cost of something. To the seller, price is revenue—the primary source of profits. In the broadest sense, price allocates resources in a free-market economy. Marketing managers are frequently challenged by the task of price setting, but they know that meeting the challenge of setting the right price can have a significant impact on the firm's bottom line. Organizations that successfully manage prices do so by creating a pricing infrastructure within the company. This means defining pricing goals, searching for ways to create greater customer value, assigning authority and responsibility for pricing decisions, and creating tools and systems to continually improve pricing decisions.

19-1a What Is Price?

Price is that which is given up in an exchange to acquire a good or service. Price also plays two roles in the evaluation of product alternatives: as a measure of sacrifice and as an information cue. To some degree, these are two opposing effects.

THE SACRIFICE EFFECT OF PRICE Price is, again, "that which is given up," which means what is sacrificed to get a good or service. In the United States, the sacrifice is usually money, but it can be other things as well. It may also be time lost while waiting to acquire the good or service. Price might also include lost dignity for individuals who lose their jobs and must rely on charity.

THE INFORMATION EFFECT OF PRICE Consumers do not always choose the lowest-priced product in a category, such as shoes, cars, or wine, even when the products are otherwise similar. One explanation of this behavior, based upon research, is that we infer quality information from price. That is, higher quality equals higher price. The information effect of price may also extend to favorable price perceptions by others because higher prices can convey the prominence and status of the purchaser to other people. Thus, both a Swatch and a Rolex can tell time accurately, but they convey different meanings. The price–quality relationship will be discussed later in the chapter.

> "Trying to set the right price is one of the most stressful and pressure-filled tasks of the marketing manager."

VALUE IS BASED UPON PERCEIVED SATISFACTION Consumers are interested in obtaining a "reasonable price." "Reasonable price" really means "perceived reasonable value" at the time of the transaction. When high-end housewares retailer Williams-Sonoma launched a $279 bread maker, the company garnered only mediocre returns. Undeterred, Williams-Sonoma released a second, slightly larger bread maker with similar features for $429. The more expensive model flopped, but when it was released, sales of the smaller, less expensive model skyrocketed. Though nothing changed about the smaller model's features or marketing mix, the $429 model affected people's perceptions, making the $279 model look like a much better value.

price that which is given up in an exchange to acquire a good or service

19-1b The Importance of Price to Marketing Managers

As noted in the chapter introduction, prices are the key to revenues, which in turn are the key to profits for an organization. **Revenue** is the price charged to customers multiplied by the number of units sold. Revenue is what pays for every activity of the company: production, finance, sales, distribution, and so on. What is left over (if anything) is **profit**. Managers usually strive to charge a price that will earn a fair profit.

$$\text{Price} \times \text{Units} = \text{Revenue}$$

To earn a profit, managers must choose a price that is not too high or too low—a price that equals the perceived value to target consumers. If, in consumers' minds, a price is set too high, the perceived value will be less than the cost, and sale opportunities will be lost.

360b/Shutterstock.com

product's perceived value. Sometimes managers say that their company is trying to maximize profits—in other words, trying to make as much money as possible. Although this goal may sound impressive to stockholders, it is not good enough for planning.

In attempting to maximize profits, managers can try to expand revenue by increasing customer satisfaction, or they can attempt to reduce costs by operating more efficiently. A third possibility is to attempt to do both. Some companies may focus too much on cost reduction at the expense of the customer. Lowe's lost market share when it cut costs by reducing the number of associates on the floor. Customer service declined—and so did revenue. When firms rely too heavily on customer service, however, costs tend to rise to unacceptable levels. United States' airlines used to serve full meals on two-hour flights and offered pillows and blankets to tired customers. This proved to be unsustainable. A company can maintain or slightly cut costs while increasing customer loyalty through customer service initiatives, loyalty programs, customer relationship management programs, and allocating resources to programs that are designed to improve efficiency and reduce costs.

19-2 PRICING OBJECTIVES

To survive in today's highly competitive marketplace, companies need pricing objectives that are specific, attainable, and measurable. Realistic pricing goals then require periodic monitoring to determine the effectiveness of the company's strategy. For convenience, pricing objectives can be divided into three categories: profit oriented, sales oriented, and status quo.

19-2a Profit-Oriented Pricing Objectives

Profit-oriented pricing objectives include profit maximization, satisfactory profits, and target return on investment.

PROFIT MAXIMIZATION *Profit maximization* means setting prices so that total revenue is as large as possible relative to total costs. Profit maximization does not always signify unreasonably high prices, however. Both price and profits depend on the type of competitive environment a firm faces, such as whether it is in a monopoly position (being the only seller) or in a much more competitive situation. Also, remember that a firm cannot charge a price higher than the

Chinaview/Shutterstock.com

Airlines use to offer full meals on flights of two hours or more. Now, you are lucky to get a drink and peanuts.

revenue the price charged to customers multiplied by the number of units sold

profit revenue minus expenses

SATISFACTORY PROFITS Satisfactory profits are a reasonable level of profits. Rather than maximizing profits, many organizations strive for profits that are satisfactory to the stockholders and management—in other words, a level of profits consistent with the level of risk an organization faces. In a risky industry, a satisfactory profit may be thirty-five percent. In a low-risk industry, it might be seven percent.

TARGET RETURN ON INVESTMENT The most common profit objective is a target **return on investment (ROI)**, sometimes called the firm's return on total assets. ROI measures management's overall effectiveness in generating profits with the available assets. The higher the firm's ROI, the better off the firm is. Many companies use a target ROI as their main pricing goal. In summary, ROI is a percentage that puts a firm's profits into perspective by showing profits relative to investment.

Return on investment is calculated as follows:

$$\text{Return on investment} = \frac{\text{Net profits after taxes}}{\text{Total assets}}$$

Assume that in 2017 Johnson Controls had assets of $4.5 million, net profits of $550,000, and a target ROI of ten percent. This was the actual ROI:

$$\text{ROI} = \frac{\$550,000}{\$4,500,000} = 12.2 \text{ percent}$$

As you can see, the ROI for Johnson Controls exceeded its target, which indicates that the company prospered in 2017.

Comparing the 12.2 percent ROI with the industry average provides a more meaningful picture, however. Any ROI needs to be evaluated in terms of the competitive environment, risks in the industry, and economic conditions. Generally speaking, firms seek ROIs in the ten to thirty percent range. In some industries, such as the grocery industry, however, a return of under five percent is common and acceptable.

A company with a target ROI can predetermine its desired level of profitability. The marketing manager can use the standard, such as ten percent ROI, to determine whether a particular price and marketing mix are feasible.

In addition, however, the manager must weigh the risk of a given strategy even if the return is in the acceptable range.

19-2b Sales-Oriented Pricing Objectives

Sales-oriented pricing objectives are based on market share as reported in dollar or unit sales. Firms strive for either market share or to maximize sales.

EXHIBIT 19.1	TWO WAYS TO MEASURE MARKET SHARE (UNITS AND REVENUE)				
Company	Units Sold	Unit Price	Total Revenue	Unit Market Share	Revenue Market Share
A	1,000	$1.00	$1,000	50	25
B	200	4.00	800	10	20
C	500	2.00	1,000	25	25
D	300	4.00	1,200	15	30
Total	2,000		$4,000		

MARKET SHARE Market share is a company's product sales as a percentage of total sales for that industry. Sales can be reported in dollars or in units of product. It is very important to know whether market share is expressed in revenue or units because the results may be different. Consider four companies competing in an industry with 2,000 total unit sales and total industry revenue of $4,000 (see Exhibit 19.1). Company A has the largest unit market share at fifty percent, but it has only twenty-five percent of the revenue market share. In contrast, Company D has only a fifteen percent unit share but the largest revenue share: thirty percent. Usually, market share is expressed in terms of revenue and not units.

Many companies believe that maintaining or increasing market share is an indicator of the effectiveness of their marketing mix. Larger market shares have indeed often meant higher profits, thanks to greater economies of scale, market power, and ability to compensate top-quality management. Conventional wisdom also says that market share and ROI are strongly related. For the most part they are; however, many companies with low market share survive and even prosper. To succeed with a low market share, companies often need to compete in industries with slow growth and few product changes—for instance, industrial supplies. Otherwise, they must vie in an industry that makes frequently bought items, such as consumer convenience goods.

The conventional wisdom about market share and profitability is not always reliable, however. Because of extreme competition in some industries, many market share leaders either do not reach their target ROI or actually lose money. Procter & Gamble switched from market share

return on investment (ROI) net profit after taxes divided by total assets

market share a company's product sales as a percentage of total sales for that industry

Photomaker.kiev.ua/Shutterstock.com

The 5.7 inch Galaxy Round, released in October 2013, iterates on Samsung's Galaxy Note line of phablets by introducing a curved display.

status quo pricing a pricing objective that maintains existing prices or meets the competition's prices

demand the quantity of a product that will be sold in the market at various prices for a specified period

supply the quantity of a product that will be offered to the market by a supplier at various prices for a specified period

elasticity of demand consumers' responsiveness or sensitivity to changes in price

elastic demand a situation in which consumer demand is sensitive to changes in price

to ROI objectives after realizing that profits do not automatically follow from a large market share.

SALES MAXIMIZATION Rather than strive for market share, sometimes companies try to maximize sales. A firm with the objective of maximizing sales ignores profits, competition, and the marketing environment as long as sales are rising.

If a company is strapped for funds or faces an uncertain future, it may try to generate a maximum amount of cash in the short run. Management's task when using this objective is to calculate which price–quantity relationship generates the greatest cash revenue. Sales maximization can also be effectively used on a temporary basis to sell off excess inventory. It is not uncommon to find Christmas cards, ornaments, and other seasonal items discounted at 50 to 70 percent off retail prices after the holiday season has ended.

Maximization of cash should never be a long-run objective because cash maximization may mean little or no profitability.

19-2c Status Quo Pricing Objectives

Status quo pricing seeks to maintain existing prices or to meet the competition's prices. This third category of pricing objectives has the major advantage of requiring little planning. It is essentially a passive policy.

Often, firms competing in an industry with an established price leader simply meet the competition's prices. These industries typically have fewer price wars than those with direct price competition. In other cases, managers regularly shop competitors' stores to ensure that their prices are comparable.

Status quo pricing often leads to suboptimal pricing. This occurs because the strategy ignores customers' perceived value of both the firm's goods or services and those offered by its competitors. Status quo pricing also ignores demand and costs. Although the policy is simple to implement, it can lead to a pricing disaster.

19-3 THE DEMAND DETERMINANT OF PRICE

After marketing managers establish pricing goals, they must set specific prices to reach those goals. The price they set for each product depends mostly on two factors: the demand for the good or service and the cost to the seller for that good or service. When pricing goals are mainly sales oriented, demand considerations usually dominate. Other factors, such as distribution and promotion strategies, perceived quality, needs of large customers, the Internet, and the stage of the product life cycle, can also influence price.

19-3a The Nature of Demand

Demand is the quantity of a product that will be sold in the market at various prices for a specified period. The quantity of a product that people will buy depends on its price. The higher the price, the fewer goods or services consumers will demand. Conversely, the lower the price, the more goods or services they will demand.

Supply is the quantity of a product that will be offered to the market by a supplier or suppliers at various prices for a specified period. At higher prices, manufacturers earn more capital and can produce more products.

19-3b Elasticity of Demand

To appreciate the concept of demand , you should understand elasticity. **Elasticity of demand** refers to consumers' responsiveness or sensitivity to changes in price. **Elastic demand** is a situation in which consumer demand is sensitive to price changes. Conversely, **inelastic demand** means that an increase or a decrease in price will not significantly affect demand for the product.

FACTORS THAT AFFECT ELASTICITY
Several factors affect elasticity of demand, including the following:

- **Availability of substitutes:** When many substitute products are available, the consumer can easily switch from one product to another, making demand more elastic. The same is true in reverse: A person with complete renal failure will pay whatever is charged for a kidney transplant because there is no substitute.

- **Price relative to purchasing power:** If a price is so low that it is an inconsequential part of an individual's budget, demand will be inelastic. If the price of pepper doubles, for example, people won't stop putting pepper on their eggs or buying more when they run out.

- **Product durability:** Consumers often have the option of repairing durable products (like cars and washing machines) rather than replacing them, thus prolonging their useful life. In other words, people are sensitive to the price increase, and demand is more elastic.

- **A product's other uses:** The greater the number of different uses for a product, the more elastic demand tends to be. If a product has only one use, as may be true of a new medicine, the quantity purchased probably will not vary as price varies. A person will consume only the prescribed quantity, regardless of price. On the other hand, a product like steel has many possible applications. As its price falls, steel becomes more economically feasible in a wider variety of applications, thereby making demand relatively elastic.

Examples of both elastic and inelastic demand abound in everyday life. The slow recovery of the housing market following the Great Recession was in part a function of elasticity of demand. Housing prices dropped forty percent or more in cities like Phoenix, Las Vegas, and Miami. Ultimately, these low prices began bringing buyers back into the marketplace. On the other hand, demand for tickets to certain sporting and

Everett Collection/Shutterstock.com

The Rolling Stones are still selling out concerts with tickets priced at up to $400.

concert events is highly inelastic. The Rolling Stones are still selling out concerts with tickets priced at up to $400. Hershey, maker of Kisses, Milk Chocolate bars, and other classic candies, recently raised a majority of its products' prices by 8 percent. Chocolate consumption has historically been very inelastic; people tend to indulge even when prices spike.[1]

 19-4 THE POWER OF DYNAMIC PRICING AND YIELD MANAGEMENT SYSTEMS

When competitive pressures are high, a company must know when it can raise prices to maximize its revenues. More and more companies are turning to **dynamic pricing** to help adjust prices. Dynamic pricing is most useful when two product or service characteristics co-exist. First, the product/service expires at a given point in time. Airline flights and vacant hotel rooms eventually lose their ability to make money, as do products with "sell before" dates such as meat and dairy items. Second, capacity is fixed well in advance and can only be increased at a high cost. For example, Delta has eight flights a day to Chicago. To increase

inelastic demand a situation in which an increase or a decrease in price will not significantly affect demand for the product

dynamic pricing a strategy whereby prices are adjusted over time to maximize a company's revenues

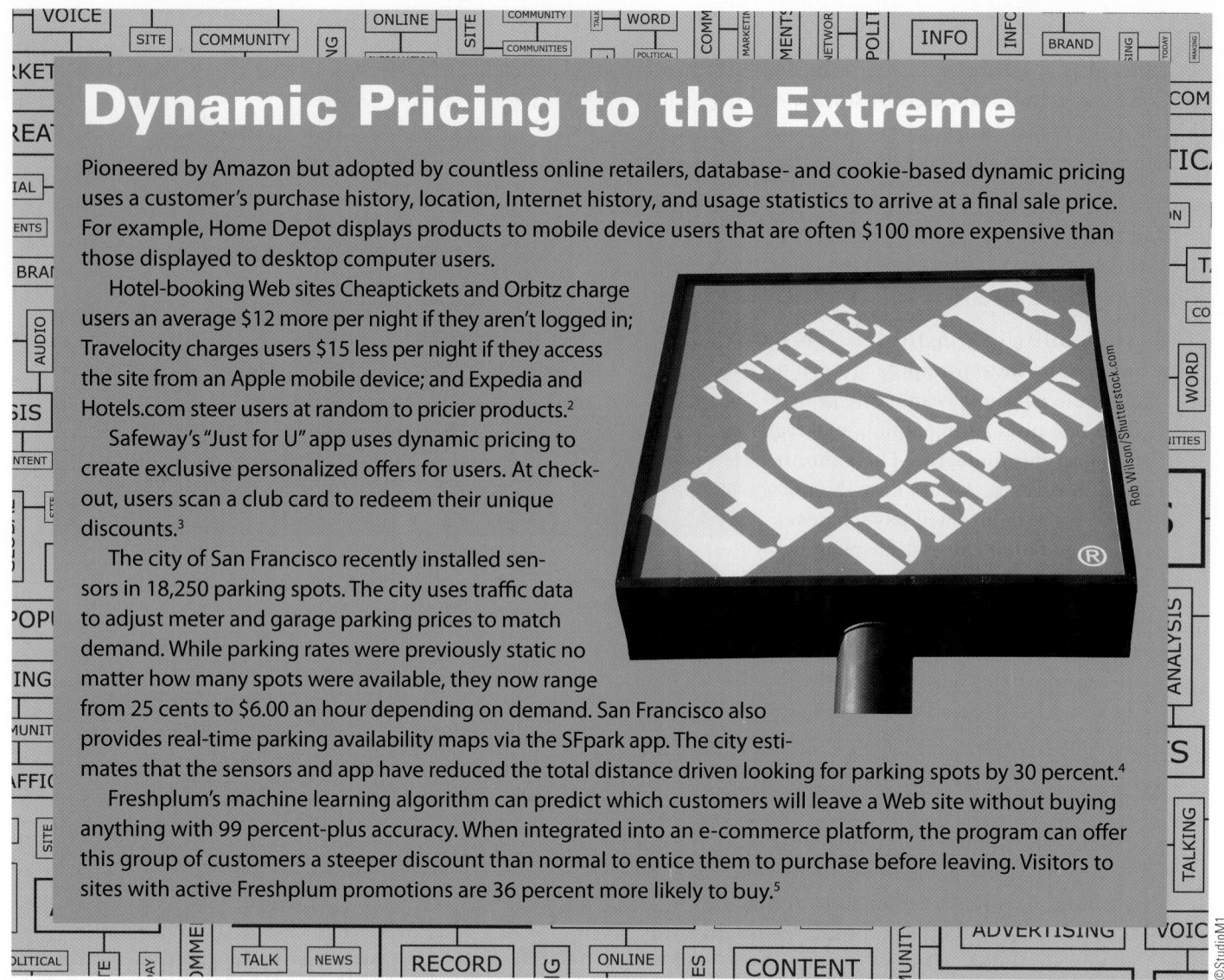

Dynamic Pricing to the Extreme

Pioneered by Amazon but adopted by countless online retailers, database- and cookie-based dynamic pricing uses a customer's purchase history, location, Internet history, and usage statistics to arrive at a final sale price. For example, Home Depot displays products to mobile device users that are often $100 more expensive than those displayed to desktop computer users.

Hotel-booking Web sites Cheaptickets and Orbitz charge users an average $12 more per night if they aren't logged in; Travelocity charges users $15 less per night if they access the site from an Apple mobile device; and Expedia and Hotels.com steer users at random to pricier products.[2]

Safeway's "Just for U" app uses dynamic pricing to create exclusive personalized offers for users. At checkout, users scan a club card to redeem their unique discounts.[3]

The city of San Francisco recently installed sensors in 18,250 parking spots. The city uses traffic data to adjust meter and garage parking prices to match demand. While parking rates were previously static no matter how many spots were available, they now range from 25 cents to $6.00 an hour depending on demand. San Francisco also provides real-time parking availability maps via the SFpark app. The city estimates that the sensors and app have reduced the total distance driven looking for parking spots by 30 percent.[4]

Freshplum's machine learning algorithm can predict which customers will leave a Web site without buying anything with 99 percent-plus accuracy. When integrated into an e-commerce platform, the program can offer this group of customers a steeper discount than normal to entice them to purchase before leaving. Visitors to sites with active Freshplum promotions are 36 percent more likely to buy.[5]

Rob Wilson/Shutterstock.com

©StudioM1

that number to twelve flights would probably be very expensive. A Hyatt hotel in Denver has 120 rooms available for February twenty-sixth. To increase the number to 160 would involve huge construction costs.

Developed in the airline industry, **yield management systems (YMS)** use complex mathematical software to profitably fill unused capacity. The software employs techniques such as discounting early purchases, limiting early sales at these discounted prices, and overbooking capacity. One of the key inputs in airlines' yield management systems is what has been the historical pattern of demand for a specific flight.

Now dynamic pricing and YMS are spreading beyond service industries as their popularity increases. The lessons of airlines and hotels are not entirely applicable to other industries, however, because plane seats and hotel beds are perishable—if they go empty, the revenue opportunity is lost forever. So it makes sense to slash prices to move toward capacity if it's possible to do so without reducing the prices that other customers pay. Cars and steel are not so perishable, but the capacity to make them is. An underused factory is a lost revenue opportunity. So it makes sense to cut prices to use up capacity if it is possible to do so while getting other customers to pay full price.

19-5 THE COST DETERMINANT OF PRICE

Sometimes companies minimize or ignore the importance of demand and decide to price their products largely or solely on the basis of costs.

yield management systems (YMS) a technique for adjusting prices that uses complex mathematical software to profitably fill unused capacity by discounting early purchases, limiting early sales at these discounted prices, and overbooking capacity

Prices determined strictly on the basis of costs may be too high for the target market, thereby reducing or eliminating sales. On the other hand, cost-based prices may be too low, causing the firm to earn a lower return than it should. Nevertheless, costs should generally be part of any price determination, if only as a floor below which a good or service must not be priced in the long run.

The idea of cost may seem simple, but it is actually a multifaceted concept, especially for producers of goods and services. A **variable cost** is a cost that varies with changes in the level of output; an example of a variable cost is the cost of materials. In contrast, a **fixed cost** does not change as output is increased or decreased. Examples include rent and executives' salaries. Costs can be used to set prices in a variety of ways. While markup pricing is relatively simple, break-even pricing uses more complicated concepts of cost.

19-5a Markup Pricing

Markup pricing, the most popular method used by wholesalers and retailers to establish a selling price, does not directly analyze the costs of production. Instead, **markup pricing** uses the cost of buying the product from the producer, plus amounts for profit and for expenses not otherwise accounted for. The total determines the selling price.

A retailer, for example, adds a certain percentage to the cost of the merchandise received to arrive at the retail price. An item that costs the retailer $1.80 and is sold for $2.20 carries a markup of forty cents, which is a markup of twenty-two percent of the cost ($0.40 ÷ $1.80). Retailers tend to discuss markup in terms of its percentage of the retail price—in this example, eighteen percent ($0.40 ÷ $2.20). The difference between the retailer's cost and the selling price (forty cents) is the gross margin.

The formula for calculating the retail price given a certain desired markup is as follows:

$$\text{Retail price} = \frac{\text{Cost}}{1 - \text{Desired return on Sales}}$$

$$= \frac{\$1.80}{1.00 - 0.18}$$

$$= \$2.20$$

If the retailer wants a 30 percent return, then:

$$\text{Retail price} = \frac{\$1.80}{1.00 - 0.30}$$

$$= \$2.57$$

The reason that retailers and others speak of markups on selling price is that many important figures in financial reports, such as gross sales and revenues, are sales figures, not cost figures.

To use markup based on cost or selling price effectively, the marketing manager must calculate an adequate gross margin—the amount added to cost to determine price. The margin must ultimately provide adequate funds to cover selling expenses and profit. Once an appropriate margin has been determined, the markup technique has the major advantage of being easy to employ.

Markups are often based on experience. For example, many small retailers markup merchandise 100 percent over cost. (In other words, they double the cost.) This tactic is called **keystoning**. Some other factors that influence markups are the merchandise's appeal to customers, past response to the markup (an implicit demand consideration), the item's promotional value, the seasonality of the good, its fashion appeal, the product's traditional selling price, and competition. Most retailers avoid any set markup because of such considerations as promotional value and seasonality.

19-5b Break-Even Pricing

Now, let's take a closer look at the relationship between sales and cost. **Break-even analysis** determines what sales volume must be reached before the company breaks even (its total costs equal total revenue) and no profits are earned.

The typical break-even model assumes a given fixed cost and a constant average variable cost (total cost divided by quantity of output). Suppose that Universal Sportswear, a hypothetical firm, has fixed costs of $2,000 and that the cost of labor and materials for each unit produced is fifty cents. Assume that it can sell up to 6,000 units of its product at $1 without having to lower its price.

Exhibit 19-2a illustrates Universal Sportswear's break-even point. As Exhibit 19.2b indicates, Universal Sportswear's total variable costs increase by fifty cents every time a new unit is produced, and total fixed costs remain constant at $2,000 regardless of the level of output. Therefore, for 4,000 units of output, Universal Sportswear has $2,000 in fixed costs and

variable cost a cost that varies with changes in the level of output

fixed cost a cost that does not change as output is increased or decreased

markup pricing the cost of buying the product from the producer, plus amounts for profit and for expenses not otherwise accounted for

keystoning the practice of marking up prices by 100 percent, or doubling the cost

break-even analysis a method of determining what sales volume must be reached before total revenue equals total costs

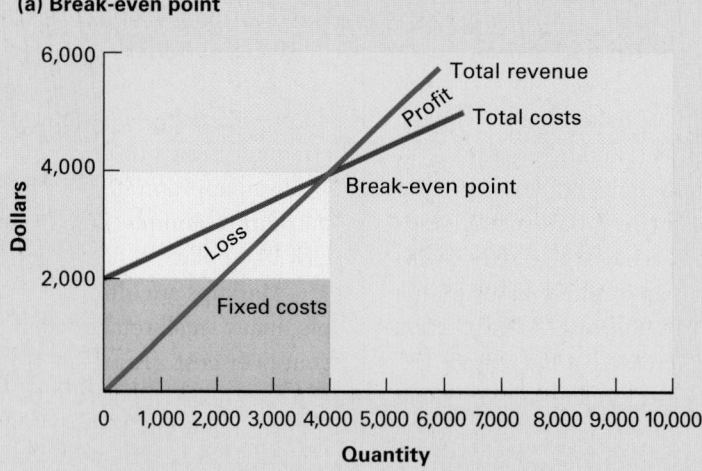

(a) Break-even point

(b) Costs and revenues

Output	Total fixed costs	Average variable costs	Total variable costs	Average total costs	Average revenue (price)	Total revenue	Total costs	Profit or loss
500	$2,000	$0.50	$ 250	$4.50	$1.00	$ 500	$2,250	($1,750)
1,000	2,000	0.50	500	2.50	1.00	1,000	2,500	(1,500)
1,500	2,000	0.50	750	1.83	1.00	1,500	2,750	(1,250)
2,000	2,000	0.50	1,000	1.50	1.00	2,000	3,000	(1,000)
2,500	2,000	0.50	1,250	1.30	1.00	2,500	3,250	(750)
3,000	2,000	0.50	1,500	1.17	1.00	3,000	3,500	(500)
3,500	2,000	0.50	1,750	1.07	1.00	3,500	3,750	(250)
*4,000	2,000	0.50	2,000	1.00	1.00	4,000	4,000	0
4,500	2,000	0.50	2,250	0.94	1.00	4,500	4,250	250
5,000	2,000	0.50	2,500	0.90	1.00	5,000	4,500	500
5,500	2,000	0.50	2,750	0.86	1.00	5,500	4,750	750
6,000	2,000	0.50	3,000	0.83	1.00	6,000	5,000	1,000

*Break-even point

$2,000 in total variable costs (4,000 units × $0.50), or $4,000 in total costs.

The advantage of break-even analysis is that it provides a quick estimate of how much the firm must sell to break even and how much profit can be earned if a higher sales volume is obtained. If a firm is operating close to the break-even point, it may want to see what can be done to reduce costs or increase sales.

Break-even analysis is not without several important limitations. Sometimes it is hard to know whether a cost is fixed or variable. If labor wins a tough guaranteed-employment contract, are the resulting expenses a fixed cost? More important than cost determination is the fact that simple break-even analysis ignores demand. How does Universal Sportswear know it can sell 4,000 units at $1? Could it sell the same 4,000 units at $2 or even $5?

19-6 OTHER DETERMINANTS OF PRICE

Other factors besides demand and costs can influence price. For example, the stages in the product life cycle, the competition, the product distribution strategy, the promotion strategy, guaranteed price matching, demands of large customers, and the perceived quality can all affect pricing.

19-6a Stages in the Product Life Cycle

As a product moves through its life cycle (see Chapter 11), the demand for the product and the competitive conditions tend to change:

- **Introductory stage:** Management usually sets prices high during the introductory stage. One reason is that it hopes to recover its development costs quickly. In addition, demand originates in the core of the market (the customers whose needs ideally match the product's attributes) and thus is relatively inelastic. On the other hand, if the target market is highly price sensitive, management often finds it better to price the product at the market level or lower. When companies introduce highly innovative products such as consumer electronics, medical devices, and pharmaceuticals, they must properly estimate the elasticity or demand for those products. This is particularly true today, when some life cycles are measured in months, not years.

- **Growth stage:** As the product enters the growth stage, prices generally begin to stabilize for several reasons. First, competitors have entered the market, increasing the available supply. Second, the product has begun to appeal to a broader market. Finally, economies of scale are lowering costs, and the savings can be passed on to the consumer in the form of lower prices.

- **Maturity stage:** Maturity usually brings further price decreases as competition increases and inefficient, high-cost firms are eliminated. Distribution channels become a significant cost factor, however, because of the need to offer wide product lines for highly segmented markets, extensive service requirements, and the sheer number of dealers necessary to absorb high-volume production. The manufacturers that remain in the market toward the end of the maturity stage typically offer similar prices. At this stage, price increases are usually cost initiated, not demand initiated. Nor do price reductions in the late phase of maturity stimulate much demand. Because demand is limited and producers have similar cost structures, the remaining competitors will probably match price reductions.

- **Decline stage:** The final stage of the life cycle may see further price decreases as the few remaining competitors try to salvage the last vestiges of demand. When only one firm is left in the market, prices begin to stabilize. In fact, prices may eventually rise dramatically if the product survives and moves into the specialty goods category, as horse-drawn carriages and vinyl records have.

19-6b The Competition

Competition varies during the product life cycle, of course, and so at times it may strongly affect pricing decisions. Although a firm may not have any competition at first, the high prices it charges may eventually induce another firm to enter the market.

One way to counter a competitor's prices is through price matching. Recall that showrooming is inspecting a product in a retail store and then buying it online. Seventy-two percent of male buyers and 56 percent of female buyers engage in showrooming when buying electronics. Forty-seven percent of female buyers engage in showrooming when buying apparel, clothing, and accessories. Four out of ten showrooming consumers plan to buy online from the outset but want to check the product out in person before ordering.[6] Fed up with losing sales, Best Buy announced in late 2013 that it would match the prices of all local competitors as well as online retailers such as Amazon, Apple, and Walmart.com. By 2015, Best Buy's sales had increased significantly.

Another way that Best Buy gets around price matching problems is to carry exclusive versions of products that have similar specifications to ones carried in other stores but have different model or serial numbers. Best

Sergey Yechikov/Shutterstock.com

In late 2013, Best Buy announced it would match the prices of its major competitors, Amazon, Apple, and Walmart.com.

Buy's premium collection of laptops, which includes approximately thirty popular models from brands such as Dell and Samsung, are carried exclusively and therefore cannot be price matched.

19-6c Distribution Strategy

An effective distribution network can sometimes overcome other minor flaws in the marketing mix. For example, although consumers may perceive a price as being slightly higher than normal, they may buy the product anyway if it is being sold at a convenient retail outlet.

Adequate distribution for a new product can often be attained by offering a larger-than-usual profit margin to distributors. A variation on this strategy is to give dealers a large trade allowance to help offset the costs of promotion and further stimulate demand at the retail level.

19-6d The Impact of the Internet and Extranets

The Internet, **extranets** (private electronic networks), and wireless setups are linking people, machines, and companies around the globe—and connecting sellers and buyers as never before. These links are enabling buyers to quickly and easily compare products and prices, putting them in a better bargaining position. At the same time, the technology allows sellers to collect detailed data about customers' buying habits, preferences, and even spending limits so that sellers can tailor their products and prices.

USING SHOPPING BOTS A shopping bot is a program that searches the Web for the best price for a particular item that you wish to purchase. Bot is short for robot. Shopping bots theoretically give pricing power to the consumer. The more information that the shopper has, the more efficient his or her purchase decision will be.

There are two general types of shopping bots. The first is the broad-based type that searches (trawls) a wide range of product categories such as Google Shopping, Nextag, and PriceGrabber. These sites operate using a Yellow Pages type of model in that they list every retailer they can find. The second is the niche-oriented type that searches for prices for only one type of product such as consumer electronics (CNET), event tickets (SeatGeek), or travel-related services (Kayak).

Shopping bots have been around for quite some time, and security protocols have been developed by some Internet

extranet a private electronic network that links a company with its suppliers and customers

retailers to limit bot trawls. Still, shopping bots remain a powerful and impactful marketing tool to this day.

INTERNET AUCTIONS The Internet auction business is huge. Among the most popular consumer auction sites are the following:

- **www.ubid.com:** Offers a large range of product categories. "My page" consolidates all of the user's activity in one place.

- **www.ebay.com:** The most popular auction site.

- **www.bidz.com:** Buys closeout deals in very large lots and offers them online in its no-reserve auctions.

Even though consumers are spending billions on Internet auctions, business-to-business auctions are likely to be the dominant form in the future. Recently, Whirlpool began holding online auctions. Participants bid on the price of the items that they would supply to Whirlpool but with a twist: they had to include the date when Whirlpool would have to pay for the items. The company wanted to see which suppliers would offer the longest grace period before requiring payment. Five auctions held over five months helped Whirlpool uncover savings of close to $2 million and more than doubled the grace period.

Whirlpool's success is a sign that the business-to-business auction world is shifting from haggling over prices to niggling over parameters of the deal. Warranties, delivery dates, transportation methods, customer support, financing options, and quality have all become bargaining chips.

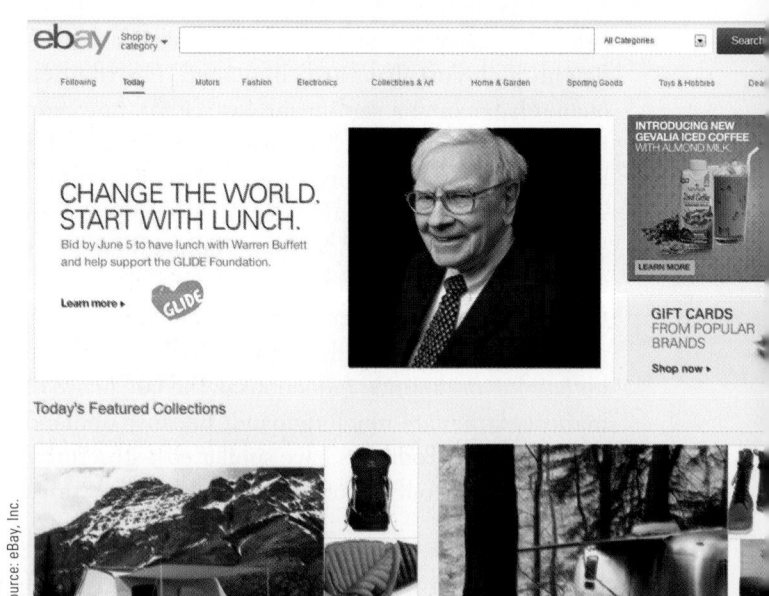

Ebay is the most popular internet auction site.

19-6e Promotion Strategy

Price is often used as a promotional tool to increase consumer interest. In many cases, consumer perceptions of a store's prices are more impactful than the actual prices themselves. Walmart, for example, has always promoted low prices. Many consumers view Target as a higher priced store than Walmart even though a recent study tracking prices on 55 items, both food and nonfood, revealed that Target's prices are consistently as low as or lower than Walmart's.[7] At the other end of the spectrum, Whole Foods is perceived as significantly more expensive than other grocery stores despite having prices that are largely in line with competitors. Whole Foods has made a concerted effort to change its pricing image by promoting lower prices and adding new lower-priced options. Similarly, Nordstrom is perceived as a pricier alternative to Macy's even though it has similar prices in many categories and lower prices in other categories. Clearly, price promotion alone does not always create a low price image. Upscale ambiance, expensive specialty offerings, premier locations, a high level of service, and a lack of price matching contribute to a high price image as well.[8]

Often, the amount saved is the most important information when promoting a discount. For example, starting with a retail price of $80, a 40 percent discount creates a savings of $32 for a net sale price of $58. Of these four numbers—80, 40, 32, and 58—the most effective one to promote is the absolute savings of $32.[9]

19-6f Demands of Large Customers

Manufacturers find that their large customers such as department stores often make specific pricing demands that the suppliers must agree to. Department stores are making greater-than-ever demands on their suppliers to cover the heavy discounts and markdowns on their own selling floors. They want suppliers to guarantee their stores' profit margins, and they insist on cash rebates if the guarantee is not met. They are also exacting fines for violations of ticketing, packing, and shipping rules. Cumulatively, the demands are nearly wiping out profits for all but the very biggest suppliers, according to fashion designers and garment makers.

Walmart is the largest retailer in the world, and the company uses that size to encourage companies to meet its needs. When Walmart decided that its grocery department needed to have everyday low prices instead of periodic rollbacks, it talked to its major suppliers, such as ConAgra, General Mills, and McCormick & Co., to discuss the possibility of offering a consistently lower price to drive business. Some companies, like ConAgra, are struggling to lower costs while grain and other ingredients are steadily increasing in price. Other companies, like Kraft, have been steadily lowering costs and are having an easier time meeting Walmart's demands. Walmart's demands are not all about keeping prices low, however. The company recently instituted a policy requiring suppliers to evaluate and disclose the full environmental costs of their products.[10] The risk of not working with Walmart? Either your product is important enough to drive traffic that Walmart keeps the item, or you lose the world's biggest sales outlet.

19-6g The Relationship of Price to Quality

As mentioned at the beginning of the chapter, when a purchase decision involves uncertainty, consumers tend to rely on a high price as a predictor of good quality. Reliance on price as an indicator of quality seems to occur for all products, but it reveals itself more strongly for some items than for others. Among the products that benefit from this phenomenon are coffee, aspirin, shampoo, clothing, furniture, whiskey, education, and many services. In the absence of other information, people typically assume that prices are higher because the products contain better materials, because they are made more carefully, or, in the case of professional services, because the provider has more expertise. A 2014 MIT study found that passengers of premier airlines like Delta and United Airlines complain about service failures ten times more often than do customers of low-cost airlines like Frontier and Southwest. Customers expect more from higher-cost airlines, so they are more likely to become upset when their expectations are not met.[11]

Markus Mainka/Shutterstock.com

Customers expect more from higher-cost airlines.

Researchers have found that price promotions of higher priced, higher quality brands tend to attract more business than do similar promotions of lower priced and lower quality brands. Higher prices increase expectation and set a reference point against which people can evaluate their consumption experiences (as was demonstrated in the recent airliner example). A bad experience with a higher priced product tends to increase the level of disappointment.[12] Finally, products that generate strong emotions, such as perfumes and fine watches, tend to get more "bang for the buck" in price promotions.[13]

19-7 HOW TO SET A PRICE ON A PRODUCT

Setting the right price on a product is a four-step process, as illustrated in Exhibit 19.3 and discussed throughout this chapter:

1. Establish pricing goals.
2. Estimate demand, costs, and profits.
3. Choose a price strategy to help determine a base price.
4. Fine-tune the base price with pricing tactics.

19-7a Establish Pricing Goals

The first step in setting the right price is to establish pricing goals. Recall that pricing objectives fall into three categories: profit oriented, sales oriented, and status quo. These goals are derived from the firm's overall objectives. A good understanding of the marketplace and of the consumer can sometimes tell a manager very quickly whether a goal is realistic.

All pricing objectives have trade-offs that managers must weigh. A profit maximization objective may require a bigger initial investment than the firm can commit to or wants to commit to. Reaching the desired market share often means sacrificing short-term profit because without careful management, long-term profit goals may not be met. Meeting the competition is the easiest pricing goal to implement. But can managers really afford to ignore demand

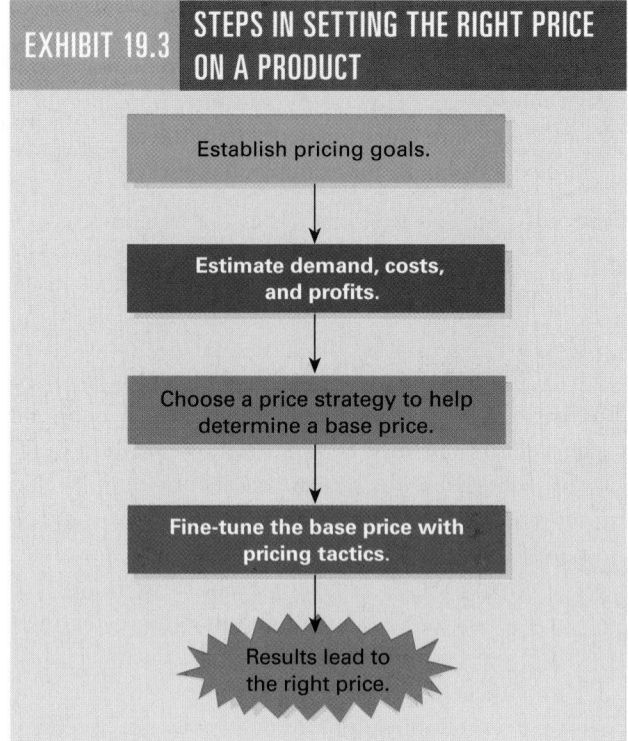

EXHIBIT 19.3 STEPS IN SETTING THE RIGHT PRICE ON A PRODUCT

Establish pricing goals.

↓

Estimate demand, costs, and profits.

↓

Choose a price strategy to help determine a base price.

↓

Fine-tune the base price with pricing tactics.

↓

Results lead to the right price.

Maksim Kabakou/Shutterstock.com

and costs, the life cycle stage, and other considerations? When creating pricing objectives, managers must consider these trade-offs in light of the target customer, the environment, and the company's overall objectives.

19-7b Estimate Demand, Costs, and Profits

Recall that total revenue is a function of price and quantity demanded and that quantity demanded depends on elasticity. Elasticity is a function of the perceived value to the buyer relative to the price. The types of questions managers consider when conducting marketing research on demand and elasticity are key. Some questions for market research on demand and elasticity are:

- What price is so low that consumers would question the product's quality?
- What is the highest price at which the product would still be perceived as a bargain?
- What is the price at which the product is starting to be perceived as expensive?
- What is the price at which the product becomes too expensive for the target market?

After establishing pricing goals, managers should estimate total revenue at a variety of prices. This usually requires marketing research. Next, they should determine corresponding costs for each price. They are then ready to estimate how much profit, if any, and how much market share can be earned at each possible price. Managers can study the options in light of revenues, costs, and profits. In turn, this information can help determine which price can best meet the firm's pricing goals.

19-7c Choose a Price Strategy

The basic, long-term pricing framework for a good or service should be a logical extension of the pricing objectives. The marketing manager's chosen **price strategy** defines the initial price and gives direction for price movements over the product life cycle.

The price strategy sets a competitive price in a specific market segment based on a well-defined positioning strategy. Changing a price level from premium to super premium may require a change in the product itself, the target customers served, the promotional strategy, or the distribution channels.

A company's freedom in pricing a new product and devising a price strategy depends on the market conditions and the other elements of the marketing mix. If a firm launches a new item resembling several others already on the market, its pricing freedom will be restricted. To succeed, the company will probably have to charge a price close to the average market price. In contrast, a firm that introduces a totally new product with no close substitutes will have considerable pricing freedom.

The conventional wisdom is that store brands such as Target's Archer Farms and Kroger's Simple Truth should be priced lower than manufacturer's national brands. In fact, private label products are priced an average of twenty-nine percent less than their national brand counterparts.[14] However, savvy retailers doing pricing strategy research have found that store brands do not necessarily have to be cheap. When store brands are positioned as gourmet or specialty items, consumers will even pay more for them than for gourmet national brands.

Companies that do serious planning when creating a price strategy usually select from three basic approaches: price skimming, penetration pricing, and status quo pricing.

PRICE SKIMMING **Price skimming** is sometimes called a "market-plus" approach to pricing because it denotes a high price relative to the prices of competing products. The term *price skimming* is derived from the phrase "skimming the cream off the top." Companies often use this strategy for new products when the product is perceived by the target market as having unique advantages. Often companies will use skimming and then lower prices over time. This is called "sliding down the demand curve." Manufacturers sometimes maintain skimming prices throughout a product's life cycle. A manager of the factory that produces Chanel purses (retailing for over $2,000 each) told one of your authors that it takes back unsold inventory and destroys it rather than selling it at a discount.

Price skimming works best when there is strong demand for a good or service. Apple, for example, uses skimming when it brings out a new iPhone or iPad. As new models are unveiled, prices on older versions are normally lowered. Firms can also effectively use price skimming when a product is well protected legally, when it represents a technological breakthrough, or when it has in some other way blocked the entry of competitors. Managers may follow a skimming strategy when production cannot be expanded rapidly because of technological difficulties, shortages, or constraints imposed by the skill and time required to produce a product (such as fine china, for example).

A successful skimming strategy enables management to recover its product development costs quickly. Even if the market perceives an introductory price as too high, managers can lower the price. Firms often believe it is better to test the market at a high price and then lower the price if sales are too slow. Successful skimming strategies are not limited to products. Well-known athletes, lawyers, and celebrity hairstylists are experts at price skimming. Naturally, a skimming strategy will encourage competitors to enter the market.

PENETRATION PRICING **Penetration pricing** is at the opposite end of the spectrum from skimming. Penetration pricing means

Sheila Fitzgerald/Shutterstock.com

price strategy a basic, long-term pricing framework that establishes the initial price for a product and the intended direction for price movements over the product life cycle

price skimming a pricing policy whereby a firm charges a high introductory price, often coupled with heavy promotion

penetration pricing a pricing policy whereby a firm charges a relatively low price for a product when it is first rolled out as a way to reach the mass market

charging a relatively low price for a product when it is first rolled out as a way to reach the mass market. The low price is designed to capture a large share of a substantial market, resulting in lower production costs. If a marketing manager has made obtaining a large market share the firm's pricing objective, penetration pricing is a logical choice.

Penetration pricing does mean lower profit per unit, however. Therefore, to reach the break-even point, it requires a higher volume of sales than would a skimming policy. The recovery of product development costs may be slow. As you might expect, penetration pricing tends to discourage competition.

A penetration strategy tends to be effective in a price-sensitive market. Price should decline more rapidly when demand is elastic because the market can be expanded through a lower price. The ultra-low-cost airline Spirit is now the most profitable U.S. airline. Its cut-rate fares include little more than a seat—nearly everything else is sold à la carte (adding an average $54.00 to the ticket price). The only complimentary item in the cabin is ice. If you want water with your ice, it costs $3.00. Yet this airline maintains the highest load numbers in the industry and it continues its rapid growth. Clearly, price matters.[15]

If a firm has a low fixed cost structure and each sale provides a large contribution to those fixed costs, penetration pricing can boost sales and provide large increases in profits—but only if the market size grows or if competitors choose not to respond. Low prices can attract additional buyers to the market. The increased sales can justify production expansion or the adoption of new technologies, both of which can reduce costs. And, if firms have excess capacity, even low-priced business can provide incremental dollars toward fixed costs.

Penetration pricing can also be effective if an experience curve will cause costs per unit to drop significantly. The experience curve proposes that per-unit costs will go down as a firm's production experience increases. Manufacturers that fail to take advantage of these effects will find themselves at a competitive cost disadvantage relative to others that are further along the curve.

The big advantage of penetration pricing is that it typically discourages or blocks competition from entering a market. The disadvantage is that penetration means gearing up for mass production to sell a large volume at a low price. If the volume fails to materialize, the company will face huge losses from building or converting a factory to produce the failed product.

Carlos Yudica/Shutterstock.com

STATUS QUO PRICING The third basic price strategy a firm may choose is status quo pricing. Recall that this pricing strategy means charging a price identical to or very close to the competition's price. Although status quo pricing has the advantage of simplicity, its disadvantage is that the strategy may ignore demand or cost or both. If the firm is comparatively small, however, meeting the competition may be the safest route to long-term survival.

19-8 THE LEGALITY OF PRICE STRATEGY

As mentioned in Chapter 4, some pricing decisions are subject to government regulation. Among the issues that fall into this category are unfair trade practices, price fixing, price discrimination, and predatory pricing.

19-8a Unfair Trade Practices

In more than half of the United States, **unfair trade practice acts** put a floor under wholesale and retail prices. Selling below cost in these states is illegal. Wholesalers and retailers must usually take a certain minimum percentage markup on their combined merchandise cost and transportation cost. The most common markup figures are 6 percent at the retail level and 2 percent at the wholesale level. If a specific wholesaler or retailer can provide conclusive proof that operating costs are lower than the minimum required figure, lower prices may be allowed.

The intent of unfair trade practice acts is to protect small local firms from giants like Walmart, which operates very efficiently on razor-thin profit margins. State enforcement of unfair trade practice laws has generally been lax, however, partly because low prices benefit local consumers.

19-8b Price Fixing

Price fixing is an agreement between two or more firms on the price they will charge for a product. Suppose two or more executives from competing firms meet to decide how much to charge for a product or to decide

unfair trade practice acts
laws that prohibit wholesalers and retailers from selling below cost

price fixing an agreement between two or more firms on the price they will charge for a product

which of them will submit the lowest bid on a certain contract. Such practices are illegal under the Sherman Act and the Federal Trade Commission Act. Offenders have received fines and sometimes prison terms. Price fixing is one area where the law is quite clear, and the U.S. Justice Department's enforcement is vigorous.

19-8c Price Discrimination

The Robinson-Patman Act of 1936 prohibits any firm from selling to two or more different buyers, within a reasonably short time, commodities (not services) of like grade and quality at different prices where the result would be to substantially lessen competition. The act also makes it illegal for a seller to offer two buyers different supplementary services and for buyers to use their purchasing power to force sellers into granting discriminatory prices or services.

The Robinson-Patman Act provides three defenses for a seller charged with price discrimination (in each case the burden is on the seller to prove the defense):

- **Cost:** A firm can charge different prices to different customers if the prices represent manufacturing or quantity discount savings.

- **Market conditions:** Price variations are justified if designed to meet fluid product or market conditions. Examples include the deterioration of perishable goods, the obsolescence of seasonal products, a distress sale under court order, and a legitimate going-out-of-business sale.

- **Competition:** A reduction in price may be necessary to stay even with the competition. Specifically, if a competitor undercuts the price quoted by a seller to a buyer, the law authorizes the seller to lower the price charged to the buyer for the product in question.

19-8d Predatory Pricing

Predatory pricing is the practice of charging a very low price for a product with the intent of driving competitors out of business or out of a market. Once competitors have been driven out, the firm raises its prices. This practice is illegal under the Sherman Act and the Federal Trade Commission Act. To prove predatory pricing, the Justice Department must show that the predator—the destructive company—explicitly tried to ruin a competitor and that the predatory price was below the predator's average variable cost.

Prosecutions for predatory pricing suffered a major setback when a federal judge threw out a predatory pricing suit filed by the Department of Justice against

Markus Mainka/Shutterstock.com

American Airlines went after low-cost competitors in the Dallas area by using predatory pricing.

American Airlines. The Department of Justice argued that the definition should be updated and that the test should be whether there was any business justification, other than driving away competitors, for American's aggressive pricing. Under that definition, the Department of Justice attorneys thought they had a great case. Whenever a fledgling airline tried to get a toehold in the Dallas market, American would meet its fares and add flights. As soon as the rival retreated, American would jack its fares back up.

Under the average variable cost definition, however, the case would have been almost impossible to win. The reason is that, like a high-tech industry, the airline industry has high fixed costs and low marginal costs. Once a flight is scheduled, the marginal cost of providing a seat for an additional passenger is almost zero. Thus, it is very difficult to prove that an airline is pricing below its average variable cost. The judge was not impressed by the Department of Justice's argument, however, and kept the average variable cost definition of predatory pricing.

19-9 TACTICS FOR FINE-TUNING THE BASE PRICE

After managers understand both the legal and the marketing consequences of price strategies, they should set a **base price**—the general price level at which the company expects

> **predatory pricing** the practice of charging a very low price for a product with the intent of driving competitors out of business or out of a market

> **base price** the general price level at which the company expects to sell the good or service

to sell the good or service. The general price level is correlated with the pricing policy: above the market (price skimming), at the market (status quo pricing), or below the market (penetration pricing). The final step, then, is to fine-tune the base price.

Fine-tuning techniques are approaches that do not change the general price level. They do, however, result in changes within a general price level. These pricing tactics allow the firm to adjust for competition in certain markets, meet ever-changing government regulations, take advantage of unique demand situations, and meet promotional and positioning goals. Fine-tuning pricing tactics include various sorts of discounts, geographic pricing, and other pricing strategies.

19-9a Discounts, Allowances, Rebates, and Value-Based Pricing

A base price can be lowered through the use of discounts and the related tactics of allowances, rebates, low or zero percent financing, and value-based pricing. Managers use the various forms of discounts to encourage customers to do what they would not ordinarily do, such as paying cash rather than using credit, taking delivery out of season, or performing certain functions within a distribution channel. The following are the most common tactics:

- **Quantity discounts:** When buyers get a lower price for buying in multiple units or above a specified dollar amount, they are receiving a **quantity discount**. A **cumulative quantity discount** is a deduction from list price that applies to the buyer's total purchases made during a specific period; it is intended to encourage customer loyalty. In contrast, a **noncumulative quantity discount** is a deduction from list price that applies to a single order rather than to the total volume of orders placed during a certain period. It is intended to encourage orders in large quantities.

- **Cash discounts:** A **cash discount** is a price reduction offered to a consumer, an industrial user, or a marketing intermediary in return for prompt payment of a bill. Prompt payment saves the seller carrying charges and billing expenses and allows the seller to avoid bad debt.

- **Functional discounts:** When distribution channel intermediaries, such as wholesalers or retailers, perform a service or function for the manufacturer, they must be compensated. This compensation, typically a percentage discount from the base price, is called a **functional discount** (or **trade discount**). Functional discounts vary greatly from channel to channel, depending on the tasks performed by the intermediary.

- **Seasonal discounts:** A **seasonal discount** is a price reduction for buying merchandise out of season. It shifts the storage function to the purchaser. Seasonal discounts also enable manufacturers to maintain a steady production schedule year-round.

- **Promotional allowances:** A **promotional allowance** (also known as a **trade allowance**) is a payment to a dealer for promoting the manufacturer's products. It is both a pricing tool and a promotional device. As a pricing tool, a promotional allowance is like a functional discount. If, for example, a retailer runs an ad for a manufacturer's product, the manufacturer may pay half the cost.

- **Rebates:** A **rebate** is a cash refund given for the purchase of a product during a specific period. The advantage of a rebate over a simple price reduction for stimulating demand is that a rebate is a temporary inducement that can be taken away without altering the basic price structure. A manufacturer that uses a simple price reduction for a short time may meet resistance when trying to restore the price to its original, higher level.

- **Zero percent financing:** To get consumers into automobile showrooms, manufacturers sometimes offer zero percent financing, which enable purchasers to borrow money to pay for new cars with no interest charge. This tactic creates a huge increase in sales, but is not without its costs. A five-year interest-free car loan typically represents a loss of more than $3,000 for the car's manufacturer.

---

quantity discount a price reduction offered to buyers buying in multiple units or above a specified dollar amount

cumulative quantity discount a deduction from list price that applies to the buyer's total purchases made during a specific period

noncumulative quantity discount a deduction from list price that applies to a single order rather than to the total volume of orders placed during a certain period

cash discount a price reduction offered to a consumer, an industrial user, or a marketing intermediary in return for prompt payment of a bill

functional discount (trade discount) a discount to wholesalers and retailers for performing channel functions

seasonal discount a price reduction for buying merchandise out of season

promotional allowance (trade allowance) a payment to a dealer for promoting the manufacturer's products

rebate a cash refund given for the purchase of a product during a specific period

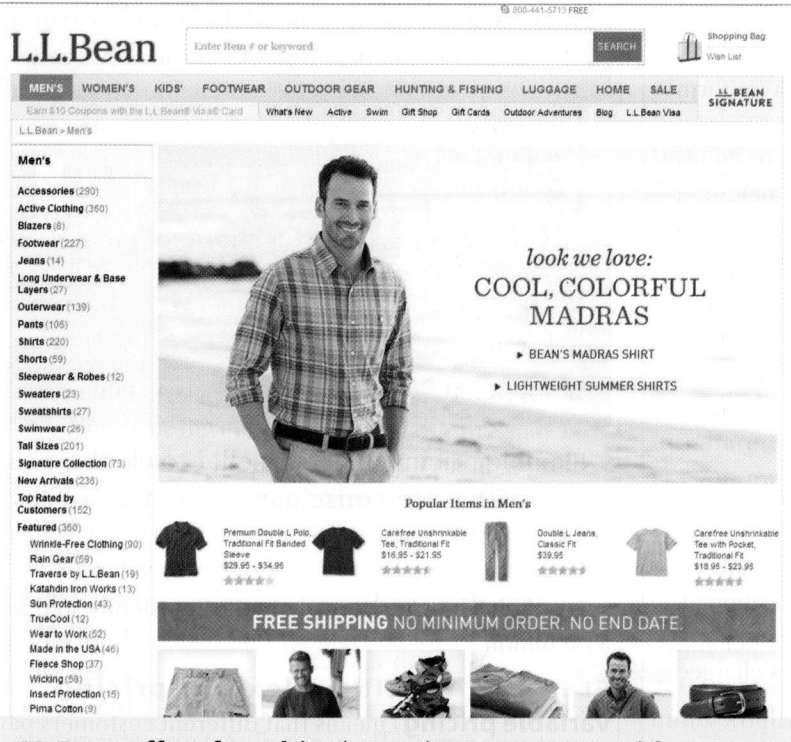

LL Bean offers free shipping to its customers, with no minimum amount.

the value of alternatives. In value-based pricing, therefore, the price of the product is set at a level that seems to the customer to be a good price compared with the prices of other options.

Research has found that loyal customers become even more loyal when they receive discounts. Also, customers who are loyal because of superior service and quality are less likely to bargain over price.[18]

19-9b Geographic Pricing

Because many sellers ship their wares to a nationwide or even a worldwide market, the cost of freight can greatly affect the total cost of a product. Sellers may use several different geographic pricing tactics to moderate the impact of freight costs on distant customers. The following methods of geographic pricing are the most common:

- **FOB origin pricing: FOB origin pricing**, also called FOB factory or FOB shipping point, is a price tactic that requires the buyer to absorb the freight costs from the shipping point ("free on board"). The farther buyers are from sellers, the more they pay, because transportation costs generally increase with the distance merchandise is shipped.

- **Uniform delivered pricing:** If the marketing manager wants total costs, including freight, to be equal for all purchasers of identical products, the firm will adopt uniform delivered pricing, or "postage stamp" pricing. With **uniform delivered pricing**, the seller pays the actual freight charges and bills every purchaser an identical, flat freight charge. This is sometimes called *postage stamp pricing* because a person can send a letter across the street or across the country for the same price.

- **Zone pricing:** A marketing manager who wants to equalize total costs among buyers within large geographic areas—but not necessarily all of the seller's

- **Free shipping:** Free shipping is another method of lowering the price for purchasers. Zappos, Nordstrom, and L.L. Bean offer free shipping with no minimum order amount. However, since shipping is an expense to the seller, it must be built into the cost of the product. Amazon spends about $6.6 billion on shipping but brings in only about $3.1 billion in payments for shipping.[16] Amazon, Best Buy, and Gap recently raised their minimum order requirements to receive free shipping. Based on a study of 113 major retailers, a customer must spend an average of $82 on merchandise to qualify for free shipping.[17]

VALUE-BASED PRICING Value-based pricing, also called *value pricing*, is a pricing strategy that has grown out of the quality movement. Value-based pricing starts with the customer, considers the competition and associated costs, and then determines the appropriate price. The basic assumption is that the firm is customer driven, seeking to understand the attributes customers want in the goods and services they buy and the value of that bundle of attributes to customers. Because very few firms operate in a pure monopoly, however, a marketer using value-based pricing must also determine the value of competitive offerings to customers. Customers determine the value of a product (not just its price) relative to

value-based pricing setting the price at a level that seems to the customer to be a good price compared to the prices of other options

FOB origin pricing a price tactic that requires the buyer to absorb the freight costs from the shipping point ("free on board")

uniform delivered pricing a price tactic in which the seller pays the actual freight charges and bills every purchaser an identical, flat freight charge

Companies offer local service, long distance, DSL Internet service, wireless, and even cable television in various bundled configurations. Telecom companies use bundling as a way to protect their market share and fight off competition by locking customers into a group of services. For consumers, comparison shopping may be difficult since they may not be able to determine how much they are really paying for each component of the bundle.

You inevitably encounter bundling when you go to a fast food restaurant. McDonald's Happy Meals and Value Meals are bundles, and customers can trade up these bundles by super sizing them. Super sizing provides a greater value to the customer and creates more profits for the fast food chain.

TWO-PART PRICING **Two-part pricing** means establishing two separate charges to consume a single good or service. Consumers sometimes prefer two-part pricing because they are uncertain about the number and the types of activities they might use at places like an amusement park. Also, the people who use a service most often pay a higher total price. Two-part pricing can increase a seller's revenue by attracting consumers who would not pay a high fee even for unlimited use. For example, a health club might be able to sell only 100 memberships at $700 annually with unlimited use of facilities, for a total revenue of $70,000. However, it could sell 900 memberships at $200 with a guarantee of using the racquetball courts ten times a month. Every use over ten would require the member to pay a $5 fee. Thus, membership revenue would provide a base of $180,000, with some additional usage fees throughout the year.

PAY WHAT YOU WANT To many people, paying what you want or what you think something is worth is a very risky tactic. Obviously, it would not work for expensive durables like automobiles. Imagine someone paying $1 for a new BMW! Yet this model has worked in varying degrees in digital media marketplaces, restaurants, and other service businesses. One of your authors has patronized a restaurant close to campus that asks diners to pay what they think their meals are worth. After several years, the restaurant is still in business. The owner says that the average lunch donation is around $8 for lunch. Social pressures can come into play in a "pay what you want" environment because an individual does not want to appear poor or cheap to his or her peers.

19-9d Consumer Penalties

More and more businesses are adopting **consumer penalties**—extra fees paid by consumers for violating the terms of a purchase agreement. Airlines often charge a fee for changing a return date on a ticket. Businesses impose consumer penalties for two reasons: they will allegedly (1) suffer an irrevocable revenue loss and/or (2) incur significant additional transaction costs should customers be unable or unwilling to complete their purchase obligations. For the company, these customer payments are part of doing business in a highly competitive marketplace. With profit margins in many companies increasingly coming under pressure, organizations are looking to stem losses resulting from customers not meeting their obligations. Some medical professionals charge a penalty fee if you don't show up for an appointment. However, the perceived unfairness of a penalty may affect some consumers' willingness to patronize a business in the future.

two-part pricing a price tactic that charges two separate amounts to consume a single good or service

consumer penalty an extra fee paid by the consumer for violating the terms of the purchase agreement

HamsterMan/Shutterstock.com

STUDY TOOLS 19

LOCATED AT BACK OF THE TEXTBOOK

☐ Rip out Chapter Review Card

LOCATED AT WWW.CENGAGEBRAIN.COM

☐ Review Key Terms Flashcards and create your own

☐ Track your knowledge & understanding of key concepts in marketing

☐ Complete practice and graded quizzes to prepare for tests

☐ Complete interactive content within the MKTG Online experience

☐ View the chapter highlight boxes within the MKTG Online experience

ENDNOTES

1

1. "Definition of Marketing," *American Marketing Association*, www.marketingpower.com/AboutAMA/Pages/DefinitionofMarketing.aspx (Accessed January 26 , 2015).

2. Lydia Dishman, "Secrets of America's Happiest Companies," *Fast Company*, January 10, 2013, www.fastcompany.com/3004595/secrets-americas-happiest-companies (Accessed January 26, 2015).

3. "Fortune 100 Best Companies to Work For," *CNN*, http://money.cnn.com/magazines/fortune/best-companies/ (Accessed January 25, 2015).

4. Philip Kotler and Kevin Lane Keller, *A Framework for Marketing Management*, 5th ed. (Upper Saddle River, NJ: Prentice Hall, 2011), 4–5.

5. Josh Lowensohn, "Apple's Thunderbolt Cable Gets a Price Drop, Shorter Version," *CNET*, January 9, 2013, http://news.CNET.com/8301-13579_3-57563157-37/apples-thunderbolt-cable-gets-a-price-drop-shorter-version (Accessed January 10, 2015).

6. Mark J. Miller, "Kellogg's is Open for Breakfast – and Your Opinion on its Brands," *Brand Channel*, January 20, 2015, www.brandchannel.com/home/post/2015/01/20/150120-Kellogg-Open-for-Breakfast (Accessed February 20, 2015).

7. "2014 U.S. Customer Service Index (CSI) Study," *J.D. Power and Associates*, January 26, 2015, http://www.jdpower.com/press-releases/2014-us-customer-service-index-csi (Accessed February 20, 2015).

8. Ian Paul, "RIM at CES: 5 Things to Know about BlackBerry 10," *PC World*, January 10, 2013, www.pcworld.com/article/2024740/rim-at-ces-5-things-to-know-about-blackberry-10.html (Accessed January 26, 2015).

9. "The 'Green' Gap between Environmental Concerns and the Cash Register," *Nielsen Wire*, August 31, 2011, http://blog.nielsen.com/nielsenwire/global/the-green-gap-between-environmental-concerns-and-the-cash-register (Accessed January 25, 2015).

10. Marc Gunther, "Unilever's CEO has a green thumb," *Fortune*, June 10, 2013, 125–130, http://connection.ebscohost.com/c/articles/89584471/unilevers-ceo-has-green-thumb (Accessed January 28, 2015).

11. A.G. Laffey and Ron Charon, cited in George S. Day and Christine Moorman, *Strategy from the Outside In: Profiting from Customer Value*, (New York City, NY: McGraw-Hill, 2010), 235.

12. Day and Moorman, 261–262.

13. "The Customer Is Not an Interruption in Our Work; He Is the Purpose of It," *Quote Investigator*, August 2, 2012, http://quoteinvestigator.com/2012/08/02/gandhi-customer (Accessed January 28, 2015).

14. Day and Moorman, 4.

15. *Ibid*.

16. "Using Advertising to Engage the Price Sensitive Consumer," *Dunnhumby*, http://info.dunnhumby.com/pricesensitivity2013 (Accessed January 29, 2015).

17. Eric Wilson, "Social Shopping: Everybody Wants In," *New York Times*, March 25, 2012, www.nytimes.com/imagepages/2012/03/25/fashion/25SOCIALSHOP_GRAPHIC.html?scp=1&sq=social%20shopping&st=cse (Accessed January 28, 2015).

18. Douglas A. McIntyre, Alexander Kent, Alexander E.M. Hess, Thomas C. Frolich and Ashley C. Allen, "Customer Service Hall of Shame," http://finance.yahoo.com/news/customer-hall-shame-161938050.html (Accessed January 29, 2015).

19. "Coastal.com Receives STELLAService Elite Seal for Outstanding Customer Service," *Fort Mill Times*, January 2, 2013, http://www.businesswire.com/news/home/20130102005748/en/Coastal.com-Receives-STELLAService-Elite-Seal-Outstanding-Customer (Accessed January 28, 2015).

20. Rosa Say, "The Six Basic Needs of Customers," *Lifehack*, April 27, 2013, www.lifehack.org/articles/work/the-six-basic-needs-of-customers.html (Accessed February 11, 2015).

21. Matt Granite, "Who Has the Best Customer Service," *WTSP*, January 11, 2013, www.wtsp.com/news/article/291523/397/Who-has-the-best-customer-service (Accessed January 28, 2015).

22. Harley Manning, "How The 'Most Improved' Companies Raised Their Customer Experience Game Last Year," *Harley Manning's Blog*, April 25, 2011, http://blogs.forrester.com/harley_manning/11-04-25-how_the_most_improved_companies_raised_their_customer_experience_game_last_year (Accessed January 29, 2015).

23. Jason Fried, "Marketing Without Marketing," *INC.*, December 2013/January 2014, 116.

24. Douglas A. McIntyre, Alexander Kent, Alexander E.M. Hess, Thomas C. Frolich and Ashley C. Allen, "Customer Service Hall of Shame."

25. David Kirkaday, "12 Service Values Ritz Carlton Uses (And You Can Too)," http://www.davidkirkaldy.com/12-service-values-ritz-carlton-uses-and-you-can-too/ (Accessed January 28, 2015).

26. Nicole Singleton, "'We're in the Business of Making People Better,'" *The Blount Countian*, January 2, 2013, http://www.blountcountian.com/news/2013-01-02/News/Were_in_the_business_of_making_people_better.html (Accessed January 30, 2015).

27. Shalini Ramachandran and Jeffrey A. Trachtenberg, "End of Era for Britannica," *Wall Street Journal*, March 14, 2013, http://online.wsj.com/news/articles/SB10001424052702304450004577280143864147250 (Accessed January 30, 2015).

28. Ekaterina Walter, "The Simple Secret of Business Innovation and Personal Growth," *Forbes*, November 26, 2013, http://www.forbes.com/sites/ekaterinawalter/2013/11/26/the-simple-secret-of-business-innovation-and-personal-growth/ (Accessed February 1, 2015).

29. "Yaris—It's a Car!" *Toyota*, www.toyota.com/itsacar (Accessed January 31, 2015).

30. Peter Dahlstrom and David Edelman, "The Coming Era of 'On-Demand' Marketing," *McKinsey*, April 2013, www.mckinsey.com/insights/marketing_sales/the_coming_era_of_on-demand_marketing (Accessed January 31, 2015).

31. U.S. Census Bureau, "U.S. & World Population Clocks," January 31, 2015, www.census.gov/main/www/popclock.html (Accessed February 20, 2015).

32. Nina Golgowski, "Average American Consumes One Ton of Food a Year While Equating a Gallon of Soda a Week," *Daily Mail*, January 1, 2012, www.dailymail.co.uk/news/article-2080940/Average-American-consumes-ton-food-year-equating-gallon-soda-week.html (Accessed January 14, 2014).

2

1. Dale Buss, "McDonald's Trims Menu, Expands Customization to Turn Around Brand," *Brand Channel*, December 11, 2014, www.brandchannel.com/home/post/2014/12/11/141211-McDonalds-DIY-Burgers.aspx?utm_campaign=141211-McDonalds-DIY-Burgers&utm_source=newsletter&utm_medium=email (Accessed February 8, 2015)

2. Barry Silverstein, "Coach Stretches Itself Thin with Brand Extensions as Sales Continue to Fall," *Brand Channel*, October 23, 2013, www.brandchannel.com/home/post/Coach-Brand-Struggles-102313.aspx (Accessed February 8, 2015).

3. Dale Buss, "Starbucks Goes Back to the Bean in 'Big Bet' on Upscale Coffee Lovers," *Brand Channel*, December 5, 2014, www.brandchannel.com/home/post/141205-Starbucks-Roastery.aspx (Accessed February 8, 2015).

4. Dan Caplinger, "Why Amazon.com, Zynga, and Deckers Outdoor Soared Today," *The Motley Fool*, October 25, 2013, http://www.fool.com/investing/general/2013/10/25/why-amazoncom-zynga-and-deckers-outdoor-soared-tod.aspx (Accessed February 11, 2015).

5. Troy L. Smith, "Frontier Inks Partnership to Provide Green Electricity," *Rochester Business Journal*, December 18, 2012, www.rbj.net/article.asp?aID=193463 (Accessed February 10, 2015).

6. Casey Newton, "Image Is Everything: Beats Music Bets on Style and Celebrity to Take On iTunes," *The Verge*, January 21, 2014, www.theverge.com/2014/1/21/5327594/image-is-everything-beats-music-bets-style-and-celebrity-take-on-itunes (Accessed February 11, 2015).

7. David Lipke, "Ugg Goes Upscale with Men's Collection Line," *Women's Wear Daily*, March 28, 2012, www.wwd.com/menswear-news/clothing-furnishings/ugg-goes-upscale-with-mens-collection-line-5833195 (Accessed February 10, 2015).

8. "GoPro Hero 3 HD Camera Picked as Top Device in 2013 according to iTrustNews," *PRWeb*, January 5, 2013, www.prweb.com/releases/prwebgopro-hero-3/gopro-hero-hd/prweb10293699.htmp (Accessed February 10, 2015).

9. Douglas Imaralu, "Can Africa Save Blackberry?" *Ventures*, May 30, 2014, www.ventures-africa.com/2014/05/can-africa-save-blackberry/ (Accessed February 8, 2015).

10. "Church's Chicken Purple Pepper Sauce Back by Popular Demand and Brand New Honey Buffalo BBQ Sauce to Complement Church's Fan Favorite Chicken Strips," *Restaurant News Release*, January 13, 2014, www.restaurantnewsrelease.com/churchs-chicken-purple-pepper-sauce-back-by-popular-demand-and-brand-new-honey-buffalo-bbq-sauce-to-complement-churchs-fan-favorite-tender-strips/8534625/ (Accessed February 12, 2015).

11. Peter Burrows and Jim Aley, "Why the iPad's Success May Spell the End of the Computer Industry as We Know It," *Bloomberg Businessweek*, March 26–April 1, 2012, 4–5. http://magsreview.com/bloomberg-businessweek/bloomberg-businessweek-march-26-2012/3264-nice-try.html (Accessed February 10, 2015).

12. Dave Walker, "'Under the Gunn,' Starring 'Project Runway's' Tim Gunn, Debuts on Lifetime," *NOLA*, January 16, 2014, http://www.nola.com/tv/index.ssf/2014/01/under_the_gunn_starring_projec.html (Accessed February 12, 2015).

13. Dale Buss, "To Stay Fit and Nimble in Slow Market, Nestle Plans to Shed Underperforming Brands," *Brand Channel*, October 4, 2013, www.brandchannel.com/home/post/2013/10/04/Nestle-Underperforming-Brands-100413.aspx (Accessed February 10, 2015).

14. Matthew Garrahan, "Dr Dre Beats New Paths in Music," *Financial Times*, January 11, 2013, www.ft.com/intl/cms/s/2/70a003d4-5bd7-11e2-bf31-00144feab49a.html (Accessed February 15, 2015); Todd Martens, "Beats Aligns with TopSpin, Picks Daisy Subscription Service Chief," January 10, 2013, www.latimes.com/entertainment/envelope/cotown/la-et-ct-beats-partners-with-topspin-daisy-subscription-service-20130110,0,305852.story (Accessed January 10, 2014).

15. "Ben & Jerry's Ice Cream - Ben & Jerry's Mission Statement," Ben & Jerry's, www.benjerry.com/activism/mission-statement (Accessed February 10, 2015).

16. Damon Poeter, "Report: Dell 'In Talks' to Go Private," *PC Magazine*, January 14, 2013, www.pcmag.com/article2/0,2817,2414282,00.asp (Accessed February 11, 2015); Donna Guglielmo, "Dell Officially Goes Private: Inside the Nastiest Tech Buyout Ever," *Forbes.com*, October 30, 2013, www.forbes.com/sites/connieguglielmo/2013/10/30/you-wont-have-michael-dell-to-kick-around-anymore/ (Accessed February 12, 2015).

17. Sheila Shayon, "Kodak Emerges from Bankruptcy with Focus on Digital Imaging, Commercial Printing," *Brand Channel*, April 9, 2013, www.brandchannel.com/home/post/2013/09/04/Kodak-Emerges-From-Bankruptcy (Accessed February 12, 2015).

18. Meg Handley, "Should the U.S. Export Natural Gas?," *U.S. News & World Report*, January 10, 2013, www.usnews.com/news/articles/2013/01/10/should-the-us-export-natural-gas (Accessed February 12, 2015).

19. David Aaker, "Why Uniqlo is Winning," *Marketing News*, January 2015, p. 24.

20. "Blue Bell History," www.bluebell.com/the_little_creamery/our_history.html (Accessed February 12, 2015).

21. "Our Story," *The Chef's Garden*, www.chefs-garden.com/our-story (Accessed January 5, 2014); "Research and Development," *The Chef's Garden*, www.chefs-garden.com/research-and-development (Accessed February 12, 2015).

22. Claire Atlinson, "Redbox Instant to Allow Subscribers to Stream Movies Straight to TVs," *New York Post*, January 10, 2013, www.nypost.com/p/news/business/up_stream_swim_SbrwwvfABL6e2EDfPJ7n2H (Accessed February 12, 2015).

23. "How to Play the Email Game," *The Email Game*, http://emailgame.baydin.com/index.html (Accessed February 12, 2015).

24. "Does Google's Lean Management Structure Make Them Even More Competitive?" *Collaboration*, February 23, 2014, www.collaboration-llc.com/blog/2014/02/23/does-googles-lean-management-structure-make-them-even-more-competitive/ (Accessed February 13, 2015).

3

1. "Social Control: From Hunter Gatherer Bands to the United Nations." *Anthropology Now*, April 17, 2014, http://anthropologynow.wordpress.com/tag/social-control (Accessed January 16, 2015).

2. "Fast-Food Marketers Target Kids in Certain Socioeconomic Groups More Than Others Study Shows." *Marketing News*, January 2015, 4.

3. *Ibid.*

4. Kimberlee Morrison, "Yelp Pays $450,000 FTC fine for COPPA Violation," *Social Times*, September 22, 2014, www.adweek.com/socialtimes/yelp-pays-450000-ftc-fine-coppa-violation/204977 (Accessed January, 14, 2015).

5. "Google to Launch Kid-Friendly Versions of Chrome, YouTube, Others in 2015," *Ars Technica*, December 3, 2014, http://arstechnica.com/gadgets/2014/12/google-to-launch-kid-friendly-versions-of-chrome-youtube-others-in-2015/ (Accessed January 13, 2015).

6. "Keystone XL Pipeline Project," *TransCanada*, http://keystone-xl.com/?gclid=CI-bwr3_mMMCFUok7A.od.xQAJw (Accessed January 13, 2015).

7. Rose Ann DeMoro, "10 Reasons to Oppose the Keystone XL Pipeline," *Huffington Post*, April 20, 2014, www.huffingtonpost.com/rose-ann-demoro/10-reasons-to-oppose-the-_1_b_4791713.html (Accessed January 13, 2015).

8. Catherine Rainbow, "Descriptions of Ethical Theories and Principles," *Davidson College*, www.bio.davidson.edu/people/kabernd/indep/carainbow/Theories.htm (Accessed January 10, 2015). Reprinted with permission.

9. "Relativism," *Vocabulary.com*, www.vocabulary.com/dictionary/relativism (Accessed January 20, 2014).

10. "Virtue Ethics," *Ethics*, http://ethicsmorals.com/ethicsvirtue.html (Accessed January 10, 2015).

11. "A Mammoth Guilt Trip," *The Economist*, August 20, 2014, 21-24.

12. "Moral Development: Lawrence Kohlberg and Carol Gilligan," *Academia.edu*, www.academia.edu/7829090/Moral_Development_Lawrence_Kohlberg_and_Carol_Gilligan (Accessed January 11, 2015).

13. Anusorn Singhapakdi, Scott Vitell, and Kenneth Kraft, "Moral Intensity and Ethical Decision Making of Marketing Professionals," *Journal of Business Research*, 36, no. 3, (1996): 245–255; Ishmael Akaah and Edward Riordan, "Judgments of Marketing Professionals about Ethical Issues in Marketing Research: A Replication and Extension," *Journal of Marketing Research*, 26, no. 1, (1989): 112–120; see also Shelby Hunt, Lawrence Chonko, and James Wilcox, "Ethical Problems of Marketing Researchers," *Journal of Marketing Research*, 21, no. 3, (1984): 309–324; Kenneth Andrews, "Ethics in Practice," *Harvard Business Review*, September 1989, 99–104; Thomas Dunfee, Craig Smith, and William T. Ross, Jr., "Social Contracts and Marketing Ethics," *Journal of Marketing*, 63, no. 3, (1999): 14–32; Jay Handelman and Stephen Arnold, "The Role of Marketing Actions with a Social Dimension: Appeals to the Institutional Environment," *Journal of Marketing*, 63, no. 3 (1999): 33–48; David Turnipseed, "Are Good Soldiers Good? Exploring the Link between Organizational Citizenship Behavior and Personal Ethics," *Journal of Business Research*, 55, no. 1, (2002): 1–15; and O.C. Ferrell, John Fraedrich, and Linda Ferrell, *Business Ethics: Ethical Decision Making and Cases*. 10th ed. (Stamford, CT: Cengage Learning) 2015, 128-137.

14. "A Strong Ethical Culture Is Key to Cutting Misconduct on the Job," *Ethics Resource Center*, June 23, 2010, http://ethics.org/news/strong-ethical-culture-key-cutting-misconduct-job (Accessed January 12, 2015); "Workplace Ethics in Transition," *Ethics.org*, www.ethics.org/resource/webcasts (Accessed January 12, 2015).

15. *Ibid.*

16. Brittany Umar, "CVS Says Not Selling Cigarettes Is the Right Thing to Do," *The Street*, February 5, 2014, www.thestreet.com/video/12310460/cvs-says-quitting-selling-cigarettes-is-the-right-thing-to-do.html (Accessed February 13, 2014).

17. Author's estimate.

18. "Code of Conduct," *Google*, http://investor.google.com/corporate/code-of-conduct.html (Accessed January 21, 2015).

19. Joe Mont, "Ethics Survey Finds Historically Low Rate of Workplace Misdeeds," *Compliance Week*, February 4, 2014, www.complianceweek.com/ethics-survey-finds-historically-low-rate-of-workplace-misdeeds/article/332690/ (Accessed January 19, 2015).

20. Joe Mont, "Ethics Survey Finds Historically Low Rate of Workplace Misdeeds."

21. "For Small Firms, New Perils in Ad Claims," *Wall Street Journal*, May 15, 2014, B5.

22. *Ibid.*

23. *Ibid.*

24. "Burger King Drops Supplier Linked to Horsemeat," *Times Union*, www.timesunion.com/news/ (accessed January 19, 2015).

25. "Apple IPO Makes Instant Millionaires," *EDN*, December 12, 2014, www.edn.com/electronics-blogs/edn-moments/44032761/ (Accessed January 16, 2015).

26. "Here's What You Don't Know About Microsoft, Today's Best Dow Stock," *The Motley Fool*, March 18, 2014, www.fool.com/investing/general/2014/03/18 (Accessed January 16, 2015).

27. "The Benefits and Costs of Socially Responsible Investing," *Morningstar*, January 7, 2015, http://news.morningstar.com/articlenet/article.aspx?id=679225.

28. Christian Homburg, Marcel Stierl, and Torsten Bornemann, "Corporate Social Responsibility in Business-to-Business Markets: How Organizational Customers Account for Supplier Corporate Social Responsibility Engagement," *Journal of Marketing*, November 2013, 53-72; Daniel Korschun, C.B. Bhattacharya, and Scott Swain, "Corporate Social Responsibility, Customer Orientation, and the Job Performance of Frontline Employees," *Journal of Marketing*, May 2014, 20-37.

29. "Made Greener Coffee Refill Tumbler, 16 fl. oz." *Starbucks*, http://store.starbucks.com/made-greener-coffee-refill-tumbler/011039302, default.pd.html (Accessed January 18, 2015).

30. "Questions for Rick Ridgeway," *Fortune*, September 16, 2013, 25.

31. Danielle Sacks, "Any Fight Worth Fighting – That's the Attitude We Take," *Fast Company*, February 2015, 34-36.

32. *Ibid.*

33. *Ibid.*

34. "It Pays to be Green: Corporate Social Responsibility Meets the Bottom Line," *Nielsen*, June 17, 2014, www.nielsen.com/us/en/insights/news/2014 (Accessed January 19, 2015).

35. *Ibid.*

36. "UN Global Compact Participants," *United Nations*, www.unglobalcompact.org/Participant-sandStakeholders/index.html (Accessed January 19, 2015).

37. "Certified B Corporations," *B Corporation*, www.bcorporation.net (Accessed January 18, 2015).

38. "Marketing to the Green Consumer," *Mintel*, www.mintel.com/marketing-to-the-green-consumers-us-March-2014 (Accessed January 18, 2015). To better understand the notion of "greenness" see: Andrew Gershoff and Judy Frels, "What Makes It Green? The Role of Centrality of Green Attributes in Evaluations of the Greenness of Products," *Journal of Marketing*, January 2015, 97-110.

39. Amy Merrick, "Restoration Hardware's Mail-Order Extravagance," August 7, 2014, *New Yorker*, www.newyorker.com/business/currency/restoration-hardwares-mail-order-extravagance (Accessed January 17, 2015); Barbara Wood, "Residents Return Stacks of Catalogs to Palo Alto Restoration Hardware," June 18, 2014, *Palo Alto Online*, www.paloaltoonline.com/news/2014/06/18/drowning-in-restoration-hardware-catalogs (Accessed January 17, 2015); Ben Elgin, "Cataloging Restoration Hardware's Cleanup of Its 17-Pound Delivery," June 20, 2014, *Bloomberg Business*, www.bloomberg.com/bw/articles/2014-06-20/inside-restoration-hardwares-messy-cleanup-of-its-17-pound-catalog-delivery (Accessed January 17, 2015); "Weaker Certification Schemes," March 3, 2014, *Greenpeace*, www.greenpeace.org/international/en/campaigns/forests/solutions/alternatives-to-forest-destruc/Weaker-Certification-Schemes/ (Accessed January 17, 2015).

40. "CR's 100 Best Corporate Citizens 2014," *CR Magazine*, www.thecro.com/files/100bestlist.pdf (Accessed January 18, 2015).

41. "Bristol-Myers Squibb Corporate Responsibility Report," *Bristol-Myers Squibb*, www.bms.com/Documents/foundation/BMS-Corporate-Responsibility-Report.pdf (Accessed January 18, 2015).

42. "Sustainability Report," *Johnson & Johnson*, www.jnj.com/sites/default/files/JNJ-Citizenship-Sustainability-Highlights-Report.pdf (Accessed January 18, 2015).

43. "2014 Citizenship Report," *Microsoft*, www.microsoft.com/About/corporatecitizenship/en-us/reporting (Accessed January 19, 2015).

44. Andrew Czaplewski, Eric Olson, and Peggy McNulty, "Going Green Puts Chipotle in the Black," *Marketing News*, March 2014, 31-37; "Good Business," *Marketing News*, July 2014, 27-29.

45. Michelle Andrews, Xueming Luo, Zheng Fang, and Jaakko Aspara, "Cause Marketing Effectiveness and the Moderating Role of Price Discounts," *Journal of Marketing*, November 2014, 120-142.

46. "Cause Related Marketing on Facebook: 3 Companies Doing Back to School Right," *Social Media Today*, September 3, 2014, www.socialmediatoday.comcontent/ (Accessed January 14, 2015).

47. "The Right to R&R," *Marketing News*, November 2014, 12-14.

48. *Ibid*.

4

1. "When the Chips Are Down," Economist, January 10, 2015, www.economist.com/node/21638115/print (Accessed January 29, 2015).

2. "Why Consumers are Hatin' McDonald's New Slogan," *CBS*, October 29, 2014, www.cbsnews.com/news (Accessed January 20, 2015).

3. "Travelers Research Hotels With Smartphones But Don't Book With Them," *Quirk's Marketing Research Review*, October 2014, 8.

4. "T-Mobile Continues to Steal Customers from Rivals," *CNET*, January 7, 2015, www.cnet.com/news/t-mobile-continues-to-steal-customers-from-rivals (Accessed January 20, 2015).

5. "Internet of Things (IoT)," *Cisco*, www.cisco.com/web/solutions/trends/iot/overview.html (Accessed February 23, 2015).

6. "Digital Social & Mobile Worldwide in 2015," *Wearesocial.net*, January 21, 2015, http://wearesocial.net/blog/2015/01 (Aaccessed January 21, 2015).

7. "Social Networking Fact Sheet," *Pew*, www.pewinternet.org/fact-sheets/ (Accessed January 21, 2015).

8. "Digital Social & Mobile Worldwide in 2015."

9. "Social Media Update 2014," *Pew*, January 9, 2015, www.pewinternet.org/2015/01/09/social-media-update-2014/ (Accessed January 21, 2015).

10. Heidi Cohen, "Video Becomes the Content of Choice," *Video Media Examiner*, www.videomediaexaminer.com/social-media-marketing-predictions-for-2015 (Accessed January 21, 2015).

11. "Social Media Campaign on the Year: WestJet Christmas Miracle," *CIO*, www.cio.com/article/2369784/social-media/155992-14-Must-See-Social-Media-Marketing-success-stories.html (Accessed January 21, 2015).

12. "Wendy's Pretzel Bacon Cheeseburger Love Songs," *CIO*, www.cio.com/article/2369784/social-media/155992-14-Must-See-Social-Media-Marketing-success-stories.html (Accessed January 21, 2015).

13. Lindsey Havansek, "It's Not Social Media Marketing, It's DiGiorno," *Social Media Today*, January 21, 2015, www.socialmediatoday.com/content/its-not-social-media-marketing-its-digiorno (Accessed January 21, 2015).

14. *Ibid*.

15. *Ibid*.

16. *Ibid*.

17. "Top Population by Country," *Photius*, www.photius.com/rankings/world2050_rank.html (Accessed January 21, 2015).

18. "Fracking and Retirees Drive U.S. Population Growth," *Businessweek*, March 27, 2014, www.businessweek.com/articles/2014-03-27 (Accessed January 21, 2015).

19. "Proof Young Americans Are Still Hurting From the Recession," *Huffington Post*, September 16, 2004, www.huffingtonpost.com/2014/09/16/multigenerational-homes-pew_N_5594440.html (Accessed January 21, 2015).

20. "Tweens By the Numbers: A Rundown of Recent Stats," *Chicago Now*, February 20, 2014, www.chicagonow.com/tween-us/2014/12 (Accessed January 22, 2015).

21. *Ibid*.

22. Jon Louis, "Tweens and Pre-Tweens Fastest Growing Users of Mobile Games & Facebook App," *Avant*, May 7, 2013, http://blog.avantexperience.com/tweens-and-pre-tweens-fastest-growing-users-of-mobile-games-facebook-app/ (Accessed January 22, 2015).

23. "Move Over Avon Lady, the Tweens Are Here," *Wall Street Journal*, June 17, 2014, B1-B2.

24. "Children Around the World Are Connected, Informed, and Concerned," *Quirk's Marketing Research Review*, November 2013, 16.

25. "The Digital World of Teens," *Pinterest*, www.pinterest.com/pin/16466354861535005 (Accessed January 22, 2015).

26. *Ibid*.

27. *Ibid*.

28. "Why Teens Are the Most Elusive and Valuable Customers in Tech," *Inc.*, www.inc.com/issie-lapowsky/inside-massive-tech-land-grab-teenabers.html (Accessed January 22, 2015).

29. Ian Johnston, "Consumer Buying Behavior of Teenagers & How to Market to Them," *AZCentral*, http://yourbusiness.azcentral.com/consumer-buying-behavior-teenagers-market-27398.html (Accessed September 22, 2014).

30. *Ibid*.

31. http://www.posttrib.chicagotribune.com/lifestyles/29705481-423 (Accessed January 22, 2015).

32. "Piper Jaffray Completes 27th Semi-Annual Taking Stock With Teens Marketing Research Project," *Piper Jaffray*, April 9, 2014, www.piperjaffray.com/2col.aspx?id=287&releaseid=1917315&title=Piper+Jaffray+completes+27th+semi-annual+Taking+stock+with+teens+Market+Research+Project (Accessed January 22, 2015).

33. "The 23-Year-Olds Will Save America," *Businessweek*, June 30 – July 6, 2014, 14–16.

34. *Ibid*.

35. "A Life Well Photographed," *Marketing News*, May 2014, 12-13; "Millennials-Best Friends, Gurus and One-Night Stands," *Quirk's Marketing Research Review*, February 2014, 28–31.

36. *Ibid*.

37. "With Millennials, Trust Opens Doors," *Quirk's Marketing Research Review*, October 2014, 12–14.

38. *Ibid*.

39. Dune Lawrence and Nora Zimmett, "Generation X Stymied by Boomers," *Bloomberg*, September 15, 2013, www.bloomberg.com/news/2011/09/15/generation-x-stymied-by-baby-boomers-refusing-to-give-up-jobs.html (Accessed January 22, 2015).

40. Rieva Lesonsky, "Gen X: How to Market to the Forgotten Generation," *American Express*, September 15, 2014, www.AmericanExpress.com/us/small-business/openforum/articles/gen-x-how-to-market-to-the-forgotten-generation (Accessed January 22, 2015).

41. *Ibid*.

42. *Ibid*.

43. "Generation X: America's Neglected Middle Child," *Pew*, June 5, 2014, www.pewresearch.org/fact-tank/2014/06/05/generation-x-america's-neglected-middle-child/ (Accessed January 22, 2015).

44. "The Baby Boom Cohort in the United States: 2012 to 2060," *United States Census Bureau*, May 2014, www.census.gov/prod/2014pubs/p25-1141.pdf (Accessed January 22, 2015).

45. "Resources: 50+Facts & Fiction," *Immersion Active*, November 12, 2014, www.immersionactive.com/resources/50-plus-facts-and-fiction/ (Accessed January 22, 2015).

46. *Ibid*.

47. *Ibid*.

48. "Are They Really Different?" *Quirk's Marketing Research Review*, February 2014, 32-36.

49. "4 Tips for Marketing to Baby Boomers in the Digital Age," *Contently*, July 16, 2014, www.contently.com/strategist/2014/07/16/4-tips-for-marketing-to-baby-boomers-in-the-digital-age/ (Accessed January 23, 2015).

50. *Ibid*.

51. "Are You Ready For the 'Majority-Minority Demographic?" *Media Post*, April 10, 2014, www.mediapost.com/publications/article/223044/are-you-ready-for-the-majority-minority-demographis.html (Accessed January 23, 2015).

52. "Focus on Faith and Family," *Quirk's Marketing Research Review,* February 2013, 16.

53. "Looking From a Different Perspective," *Quirk's Marketing Research Review,* August 2014, 46, 64–66.

54. *Ibid.*

55. "A One-Two Punch," *Marketing News,* December 2014, 12–13

56. *Ibid.*

57. *Ibid.*

58. "Ad Ages' 2014 Hispanic Fact Pack Is Out Now," *Advertising Age,* July 29, 2014, http://adage.com/article/hispanic-marketing/ad-age-s-2014-hispanic-fact-pack/294335/ (Accessed January 23, 2015).

59. *Ibid.*

60. "Connecting Through Culture: African Americans Favor Diverse Advertising," *Nielsen,* October 20, 2014, www.nielsen.com/us/en/insights/news/2014/connecting-through-culture-african-americans-favor-diverse-advertising.html (Accessed January 23, 2015).

61. *Ibid.*

62. *Ibid.*

63. "How Blacks Are Influencing Media, Marketing and Advertising," *BET,* www.bet.com/news/national/photos/Nielsen-company/ (Accessed January 23, 2015).

64. "Usher's Honey Nut Commercial Knows Its Audience," *Businessweek,* August 21, 2014, www.businessweek.com/articles/2014-08-21/ushers-honey-nut-cheerios-commercial-knows-its-audience (Accessed January 23, 2015).

65. "U.S. Hispanic and Asian Populations Growing, But For Different Reasons," *Pew,* June 26, 2014, www.pewresearch.org/fact-tank/2014/06/26 (Accessed September 23, 2014).

66. "Median Household Income in the United States in 2013, by Race or Ethnic Group (in U.S. Dollars)," *The Statistics Portal,* www.statista.com/statistics/233324/median-household-income-in-the-united-states-by-race (Accessed January 23, 2015).

67. Author's projection; "14 Important Statistics About Asian Americans," *Asian Nation,* www.asian-nation.org/14-statistics.shtml (Accessed January 23, 2015).

68. "State of the Asian American Consumer: Growing Market, Growing Impact Report," *Nielsen,* www.nielsen.com/asians (Accessed January 23, 2015).

69. "What's Next in Advertising to Asian Americans?" *Asian Fortune News,* April 30, 2014, http://asianfortunenews.com/2014/04/what's-next-in-advertising-to-asian-americans (Accessed January 23, 2015).

70. "Incomes End a 6-Year Decline, Just Barely," *Wall Street Journal,* September 17, 2014, A2.

71. "Labor Force Statistics From the Current Population Survey," *Bureau of Labor Statistics,* www.bls.gov/cps (Accessed January 23, 2015).

72. "Fast Facts: Income of Young Adults," *Institute of Education Sciences,* http://nces.ed.gov/fastfacts/display.asp?id=77 (Accessed January 23, 2015).

73. "Current US Inflation Rates: 2014-2015," *U.S. Inflation Calculator,* www.usinflationcalculator.com/inflation/current-inflation-rates/ (Accessed January 24, 2015).

74. "Innovation: A Look Inside the Idea Factory," *Wired,* www.wired.co.uk/promotions/shell-lets-go/innovation/the-idea-factory (Accessed January 24, 2015).

75. Josh Bernoff, "Strategic Thinking for the Mobile Mind Shift," *Marketing News,* July 2014, 24–25.

76. *Ibid.*

77. "20 Tips on Google's 20 Percent Time in Your Classroom," *Learning Personalized,* www.learningpersonalized.com/2015/01/06/20-tips-on-googles-20-percent-time-in-your-classroom/ (Accessed January 24, 2015).

78. "Zara Builds Its Business Around RFID," *Wall Street Journal,* September 19, 2014, B1-B2.

79. *Ibid.*

80. "Benefits of ObamaCare: Advantage of ObamaCare," *Obamacare Facts,* http://obamacarefacts.com/benefitsofobamacare/ (Accessed January 24, 2015.

81. "CFPB-2014 in Review–And What's Ahead for 2015," *Paul Hastings,* January 20, 2015, www.paulhastings.com/publications (Accessed January 24, 2015).

82. "Bureau of Consumer Protection," *Federal Trade Commission,* www.ftc.gov/about-ftc/bureaus-offices/bureau-consumer-protection (Accessed January 24, 2015).

83. "US Total Media Ad Spend Inches Up, Pushed by Digital," *eMarketor,* www.emarketor.com/Article/10101 (Accessed January 24, 2015).

84. Natasha Singer, "Mapping, and Sharing, the Consumer Genome," *New York Times,* June 16, 2012, www.nytimes.com/2012/06/17/technology/acxiom-the-quiet-giant-of-consumer-database-marketing.html; "Acxiom InfoBase Consumer List Mailing List," *NextMark,* http://Lists.nextmark.com/market?page=order/online/datacard&id=131838 (Accessed January 24, 2015).

85. "Personic X Lifestage Analysis," *Lab 3 Marketing,* http://Lab3marketing.com/direct-marketing/data-analytics/personicX-lifestage-analysis (Accessed January 24, 2015).

86. "Give Me Back My Privacy," *Wall Street Journal,* March 24, R1-R2.

87. *Ibid.*

88. "AVG PrivacyFix," *AVG,* www.avg.com/ww-en/privacyfix (Accessed January 24, 2015).

89. "Privowny," *Privowny,* http://privowny.com (Accessed January 24, 2015).

90. "DuckDuckGo," *DuckDuckGo,* https://duckduckgo.com (Accessed January 24, 2015).

91. http://2015newyear.org/tag/startpage-ixquick-passed-4-million-daily-searches-on-monday (Accessed January 24, 2015).

92. Daniel Kline, "How Many Customers Does Amazon Have?" *The Motley Fool,* May 24, 2014, www.fool.com/investing/general/2014/05/24/how-many-customers-does-amazon-have.aspx (Accessed January 25, 2015).

93. Susan Adams, "America's Most Reputable Companies, 2014," *Forbes,* May 13, 2014, www.forbes.com/sites/susanadams/2014/05/13/americas-most-reputable-companies-2014/ (Accessed January 25, 2015).

94. "Google Thinks Amazon Is Its Biggest Competitor," *Slate,* www.slate.com/articles/business/moneybox/2014/10/google_amazon_competition_how_amazon_prime_delivery_hurts_google_s_ad_business.html (Accessed January 25, 2015).

5

1. "2015 Global Economic Outlook: Better Than 2014 – But Not By Much," *Bloomberg Businessweek,* November 6, 2014, wwwbusinessweek.com/articles/2014-11-06/2015-global-economic-outlook-better-than-2014-but-not-by-much (Accessed January 25, 2015).

2. "GE Works," *GE,* February 27, 2014, www.ge.com/ar2013/pdf/GE_AR13.pdf (Accessed January 25, 2015).

3. "Exports of Goods and Services (% of GDP)," *The World Bank,* www.data.worldbank.org/indicator/NE.EXP.GNFS.2S (Accessed January 25, 2015).

4. "U.S. Exports 1950-2015," *Trading Economics,* www.tradingeconomics.com/united-states/exports (Accessed January 25, 2015).

5. "Export-Related Jobs," *International Trade Administration,* September 2014, www.trade.gov/MAS/IAN/employment (Accessed January 25, 2015).

6. "Exports of Goods and Services," *International Trade Administration,* www.trade.gov/MAS/IAN/employment (Accessed January 25, 2015).

7. "U.S. Exports Reach $2.37 Trillion, Set New Record for Fourth Straight Year," *United States Department of Commerce,* February 6, 2014, www.commerce.gov/news/press-releases/2014/02/06/us-exports-reach-23-trillion-2013-set-record-fourth-straight-year (Accessed January 25, 2015).

8. "Ex-ImBank Finishes Fiscal Year Strong, Providing Over 20.5 Billion to Finance US Small Business Exports and Supporting Over 160,000 American Jobs," *Export-Import Bank of the United States,* November 5, 2014, www.exim.gov/newsandevents/releases/2014/Fiscal/Year/Strong.cfm (Accessed January 25, 2015).

9. "Five Myths about Imports," *Wall Street Journal,* May 20, 2014, A11.

10. *Ibid.*

11. "Pitching to Walmart: Made in U.S.," *Wall Street Journal,* October 7, 2013, B1, B2.

12. Aaron Flaaen, "Multinational Firms in Context," *Federal Reserve Bank of Atlanta,* August 30, 2013, www.frbatlanta.org/documents/news/conferences/13rdc/s1_p1_intl_topics_Flaaen.pdf (Accessed January 26, 2015).

13. "Bangladesh Factory Collapse," *Huffington Post,* January 11, 2015, www.huffingtonpost.com/news/bangladesh-factory-collapse (Accessed January 26, 2015).

14. "As Foreign Aid Dries Up, Companies Take the Lead in Global Development," *Fortune,* July 24, 2014, 46.

15. Theodore Levitt, "The Globalization of Markets," *Harvard Business Review,* May 1983, 92–100.

16. "The Gentle Art of Crossing Borders," *Marketing Insights,* July/August 2014, 10-11.

17. "Gross National Income Per Capita," *The World Bank,* December 16, 2014, http://data.world.bank.org/data-catalog/GNI-per-capita-Atlas-and-PPR-table (Accessed March 19, 2015).

18. *Ibid.*

19. "The 10 Most Expensive Cities in the World," *Business Insider,* March 3, 2015, www.businessinsider.com/most-expensive-cities-2014 (Accessed January 26, 2015).

20. "In Search of the Middle," *Marketing News,* August 2014, 24.

21. *Ibid.*

22. *Ibid.*

23. "Doing Business 2014: Understanding Regulations for Small and Medium-Size Enterprises," *The World Bank,* http://openknowledge.worldbank.org/bitstream/handle/10986/16204/19984.pdf?sequence=1 (Accessed January 17m 2015).

24. "The New Cold War on Business," *Fortune,* October 8, 2014, 77-80.

25. "Beijing Pulls Back the Welcome Mat," *Fortune,* October 8, 2014, 88-92.

26. "Wal-Mart Fights Back in China," *Wall Street Journal,* April 14, 2014, A1-A14.

27. "The Putin Paradox," *Fortune,* October 8, 2014, 82-86.

28. "Five Myths about Imports," A11.

29. "Tariff Deal Is Big Step for Trade, Tech Firms," *Wall Street Journal,* November 12, 2014, B1, B4.

30. "New Balance, Saucony Vying for Soles of Military Recruits," *Boston Globe,* www.bostonglobe .com/business101/06/2015/new-balance-saucony -two-way-race-build-all-american-shoe/cqH1DMoy FKbninQ7Y9E5N/story.html (Accessed January 29, 2015).

31. "Uruguay Found Final Act Should Produce Overall U.S. Gains," *U.S. Government Account-ability Office,* www.gao.gov/products/GAO/GGD-94 -836 (Accessed January 29, 2015).

32. "Beijing Faces Setback in Rare-Earth Spat," *Wall Street Journal,* March 27, 2014, A12.

33. "After U.S. Deal, India to Push for Doha Agenda at WTO in 2015," *India Times,* December 18, 2014, http://articles.economictimes.indiatimes .com/2014-12-18/news/57196109_1_doha-round -trade-facilitation-agreement-doha-agenda (Accessed January 29, 2015).

34. "For a Fair, Transparent and Effective ISDS in TTIP," *EurActive,* January 16, 2015, http://euractiv .com/sections/trade-society/fair-transparent-and -effective-isds-ttip-311339 (Accessed January 29, 2015).

35. "Trades Big Breakout," *Politico,* January 2, 2015, www.politico.com/story/2015/01/trade-outlook -2015-113793.html (Accessed January 29, 2015).

36. "Most Dynamic Latin Countries Forge New Trade Accord," *Wall Street Journal,* February 11, 2014, A10.

37. "NAFTA Triumphant: Assessing Two Decades of Gains in Trade, Growth, and Jobs," *U.S. Chamber of Commerce,* www.uschamber.com /sites/default/files/legacy/reports/1112_INTL _NAFTA_20years.pdf (Accessed January 20, 2015).

38. "Dominican Republic-Central America-United States Free Trade Agreement (CAFTA-DR)," *Export.gov,* http://export.gov/FTA/cafta-dr /index.asp (Accessed March 19, 2015).

39. "Countries," *European Union,* http://europa .eu/about-eu/countries/index_en.htm (Accessed January 28, 2015).

40. "Why the Greek Elections Might be the Begin-ning of the End for the Euro," *Fortune,* January 26, 2015, http://fortune.com/2015/01/26/greek-elections -euro-end/ (Accessed January 28, 2015).

41. "2014 Autumn Economic Forecast: Slow Recovery with Very Low Inflation," *Europea,* November 4, 2014, http://europea.eu/rapid/press -release_IP_14_1362_en.htm (Accessed January 29, 2015).

42. "Countries and Regions: United States," *European Commission,* January 9, 2013, http:// ec.europa.eu/trade/creating-opportunities/bilateral -relations/countries/united-states/ (Accessed January 29, 2015).

43. "G20 Leaders' Communique Brisbane Summit, 15-16 November 2014," *G-20,* https://g20.org /wp-content/uploads/2014/12/brisbane_g20_leaders _summit_communique1.pdf (Accessed January 29, 2015).

44. "Global Wealth," *Economist,* October 18, 2014, 93.

45. "Lower Oil Prices Provide Benefits to US Workers," *New York Times,* January 17, 2015, www .nytimes.com/2015/01/18/business/economy/lower -oil-prices-offer-a-bonanza-to-us-workers.html? _r=o (Accessed January 29, 2015).

46. "The Costs of Expanding Overseas," *Wall Street Journal,* February 27, 2014, B6.

47. *Ibid.*

48. *Ibid.*

49. *Ibid.*

50. Author's estimate.

51. "Exhibit A in GE's Case for Alston Deal," *New York Times,* May 23, 2014, www.nytimes.com /2014/05/26/business/international/generalelectric _joint_venture_in_France.html (Accessed January 29, 2015).

52. "Direct Investment Positions: Country and Industry Detail, July 2014, *Bureau of Economic Analysis,* www.bea.gov/scb/pdf/2014/07%20 July/0714_direct_investment_positions.pdf (Accessed January 30, 2015).

53. "2015 Select USA Investment Summit is Now Open for Business," *United States Department of Commerce,* January 8, 2015, www.commerce.gov /blog/category/138 (Accessed January 30, 2015).

54. *Ibid.*

55. "The Gentle Art of Crossing Borders," *American Marketing Association,* July/August 2014, www.ama.org/publications/MarketingInsights/Pages /gentle-art-crossing-borders.aspx (Accessed January 30, 2015).

56. "How Procter & Gamble is Conquering Emerging Markets," *The Motley Fool,* www.fool .com/investing/general/2013/10/27/how-procter -gamble-is-conquering-emerging-markets.aspx (Accessed January 30, 2015).

57. "What is Selling Where? Pringles Chips," *Wall Street Journal,* April 24, 2013, D3

58. "How Domino's Won India," *Fast Company,* February 2015, 54.

59. *Ibid.*

60. "Pick Up. Your Ad Is Calling," *Business Week,* April 21-27, 2014, 19.

61. "How Convenient: In Taiwan, the 24/7 Store Does It All," *Wall Street Journal,* May 17-18, 2014, A1, A9.

62. "How Domino's Won…," 56.

63. "A Continent Goes Shopping," *The Economist,* August 18, 2013, www.economist.com/node /21560582 (Accessed January 30, 2015).

64. "Why Wal-Mart Hasn't Conquered Brazil," *Business Week,* May 8, 2014, 25.

65. *Ibid.*

66. "Russian Rubles to 1 US Dollar," *Exchange-rates.org,* January 29, 2015, www.exchange-rates.org /history/RUB/USD/T (Accessed January 30, 2015).

67. "Commerce Department Declares Anti -dumping Duties," *TireReview.com,* January 21, 2015, www.tirereview.com/commerce-department -declares-anti-dumping-duties/ (Accessed January 30, 2015).

68. "Suggested Reading about Countertrade," *Exporter-Sources.com,* http://exporters-sources.com /suggested-reading-about-countertrade (Accessed January 30, 2015).

69. "Countertrade," *All About Countertrade,* http://allaboutcountertrade.blogspot.com (Accessed January 30, 2015).

70. "Air France Launches the Upgrade Challenge Social Game," *Creative Guerrilla Marketing,* January 28, 2015, www .creativeguerrillamarketing.com/guerrilla-marketing /air-france-launches-the-upgrade-challenge-social -game/ (Accessed January 30, 2015).

71. "H&M Pushes Sales With Versatility Campaign on Twitter, Facebook," *Mobile Commerce Daily,* July 8, 2014, www.mobilecommercedaily.com/hm -pushes-sales-with-versatility-campaign-on-twitter -facebook/ (Accessed January 31, 2015).

72. "Red Bull Ad Sparks Social Media Outburst From Kenyans," *Jambonewspot,* January 15, 2015, www.jambonewspot.com/video-redbull-ad-sparks -social-media-outburst-kenyans/ (Accessed January 31, 2015).

73. *Ibid.*

74. *Ibid.*

6

1. The material on hedonic and utilitarian value was partially adapted from Barry Babin and Eric Harris, *CB* 6th ed., Cengage Learning, 2015, 28–29.

2. Craig Smith, "By the Numbers: 60 Amazing Google Search Statistics and Facts," *Expanded Ram-blings,* January 22, 2015, http://expandedramblings .com/index.php/by-the-number-a-gigantic-list-of -google-stats-and-facts/ (Accessed February 17, 2015).

3. "Dethroning the Brand," *Marketing News,* December 2014, 14.

4. Eric Anderson and Duncan Simester, "Reviews Without a Purchase: Low Ratings, Loyal Cus-tomers, and Deception," *Journal of Marketing Research,* June 2014, 249–269.

5. "Good Tidings For Retail," *Marketing News,* December 2014, 14.

6. *Ibid.*

7. Edwin von Bommel, David Edelman, and Kelly Ungerman, "Digitizing the Consumer Decision Journey," *McKinsey,* June 2014, www.mckinsey .com/insights/marketing_sales/digitizing_the _consumer_decision_journey/ (Accessed February 17, 2015).

8. von Bommel, et al, "Digitizing the Consumer Decision…"

9. "Survey: 3 in 4 Americans Make Impulse Purchases," *CreditCards.com,* November 23, 2014, www.creditcards.com/credit-card-news/impulse -purchase-survey.php (Accessed February 17, 2015).

10. Sam Hui, Yanliu Huang, Jacob Suher, and Jeff Inman, "Deconstructing the First Moment of Truth: Understanding Unplanned Consideration and Purchase Conversion Using In-Store Video Tracking," *Journal of Marketing Research,* August 2013, 445–462.

11. Crystal Collier and Gavin Sinter, "Meet Them Where They Want To Be," *Quirk's Marketing Research Review,* October 2014, 58–62.

12. "McDonald's Ad Campaign Banks On A New Payment Method: Love," *Christian Science Monitor,* February 2, 2015, www.csmonitor.com /Business/The-Bite/2015/0202/McDonald-s-ad -campaign-banks-on-a-new-payment-method-love (Accessed February 18, 2015).

13. Julio Sevilla and Joseph Redden, "Limited Availability Reduces the Rate of Satiation," *Journal of Marketing Research,* April 2014, 205–217.

14. Samantha Cross and Mary Gilly, "Cultural Competence and Cultural Compensatory Mechanisms in Binational Households," *Journal of Marketing,* May 2014, 121–139.

15. "Most Expensive Cars in the World: Top 10 List 2014-2015," *The Supercars,* www.thesupercars .org/top-cars/most-expensive-cars-in-the-world-top -10-list/ (Accessed February 18, 2015).

16. "2015 Poverty Guidelines," January 22, 2015, *United States Department of Health and Human*

Services, http://aspe.hhs.gov/poverty/15poverty.cfm (Accessed February 18, 2015).

17. "Sphere of Influence," *Marketing News*, November 2014, 16–17.

18. Hans Risselada, Peter Verdoef, and Tammo Bijmolt, "Dynamic Effects of Social Influence and Direct Marketing on the Adoption of High-Technology Products," *Journal of Marketing*, March 2014, 52–68.

19. This section was partially adapted from Babin and Harris, 156–157.

20. "Is Women's Empowerment Marketing the New 'Pink It and Shrink It'?" *Entrepreneur*, February 9, 2015, www.entrepreneur.com/article /242677 (Accessed February 20, 2015).

21. "Industry Statistics Shows Growth in Men Engaging in Online Shopping," *Mobile Commerce Insider*, June 18, 2013, www.mobilecommerceinsider .com/topics/mobileecommerceinsider/articles /342484-industry-statistics-show-growth-men -engaging-online-shopping.html (Accessed January 29, 2014).

22. "Reach Over 45 Million American Families," *eTarget Media*, www.etargetmedia.com/family -lists.html (Accessed February 20, 2015).

23. "Messes and Wrong Guesses," *Wall Street Journal*, February 15-16, 2014, C4.

7

1. Michael D. Hutt and Thomas W. Speh, *Business Marketing Management*, 12th ed. (Boston: Cengage, 2017).

2. Jeffrey Cohen "20 Most Important Stats from the 2015 B2B Content Marketing Report," *Social Media B2B*, October 6, 2014, www.socialmediab2b .com/2014/10/b2b-content-marketing-report -statistics-2015.com (Accessed February 20, 2015).

3. Autumn Truong, "5 B2B Social Media Lessons Cisco Learned in 2014," *Social Media B2B*, January 20, 2015 www.socialmediab2b.com (Accessed February 20, 2015).

4. "Online Measurement," *Nielsen*, www.nielsen. com/us/en/nielsen-solutions/nielsen-measurement /nielsen-online-measurement.html (Accessed March 22, 2015).

5. "2014 Social Media Benchmarking Report," *B2B Marketing Magazine*, www.b2bmarketing.net /magazine (Accessed February 27, 2015).

6. Jeffrey Cohen, "7 Examples of B2B Content Marketing," *Social Media B2B*, September 18, 2013, www.socialmediab2b.com/category/social -media-101/ (Accessed February 19, 2015).

7. Chris Lee, "Why Online Marketing Is as Simple as Five-a-side Football," *Econsultancy*, February 1, 2013, http://econsultancy.com/us/blog/62018-why -online-marketing-is-as-simple-as-five-a-side-football (Accessed March 22, 2015).

8. "The Best Repeat Business Practices," *eLocal. com*, March 8, 2012, www.elocal.com/content /home-expert-network/repeat-business-practices -2547 (Accessed March 22, 2015).

9. TJ Raphael, "Time Inc. Forms Strategic Alliance with Sprint Nextel Corp.," *Folio*, May 7, 2013, www.foliomag.com/2013/time-inc-forms-strategic -alliance-sprint-nextel-corp (Accessed March 22, 2015).

10. Eric Griffin, "12 Amazon Fire TV Tips for Streaming Fans," *PC Mag*, February 19, 2015, www.pcmag.com/slideshow/story/332129/12 -amazon-fire-tv-tips-for-streaming-fans (Accessed March 22, 2015).

11. "H&R Block Saluted for Partnership with Arizona Catholic Schools," *Ahwatukee Foothills News*, February 6, 2013, www.ahwatukee.com /money/article_bb3dc05e-6f26-11e2-b270 -001a4bcf887a.html (Accessed March 22, 2015).

12. Robert M. Morgan and Shelby D. Hunt, "The Commitment-Trust Theory of Relationship Marketing," *Journal of Marketing*, 58, no. 3, 1994, 23.

13. *Ibid*.

14. Nils Pratley, "Phones 4U Has Only Itself to Blame," *The Guardian*, September 15, 2014, www.theguardian.com/business/nils-pratley-on -finance/2014/sep/15/phones-4u-administrators (Accessed March 22, 2015).

15. Jamie Yap, "Maps, LBS Bolster Google Enterprise's Asia Roadmap," *ZDNet*, February 1, 2013, www.zdnet.com/maps-lbs-bolster-google -enterprises-asia-roadmap-7000010671/ (Accessed March 22, 2015).

16. "Doing Business with the US Government," *iSquare*, September 19, 2013, www.isquare.com /fhome18.cfm (Accessed March 22, 2015).

17. Hutt and Speh, 7.

18. *Ibid*.

19. *Ibid*.

20. "California Timber Industry Bussing Post-Recession," *Lake Tahoe News*, March 22, 2013, www.laketahoenews.net/2013/03/california-timber -industry-buzzing-post-recession/ (Accessed March 22, 2015).

21. Alan Levin and Susanna Ray, "Boeing 878 Dreamlines Is Grounded Worldwide by Regulators," *Bloomberg*, January 17, 2013, www.bloomberg .com/news/2013-01-16/boeing-787-dreamliner-fleet -grounded-by-u-s-after-emergency.html (Accessed March 22, 2015).

22. Jon Hilkevitch, "CTA to Spend $2 Billion for 846 New Rail Cars," *Chicago Tribune*, February 6, 2013, www.chicagotribune.com/news/local/breaking /chi-cta-to-spend-2-billion-for-846-new-rail-cars -20130206,0,1482382.story (Accessed March 22, 2015).

23. Hutt and Speh, 6.

24. Paul Demery, "Alibaba.com Looks for Growth Among U.S. Suppliers," *Internet Retailer*, February 4, 2015, www.internetretailer.com/2015/02/04 /alibabacom-looks-growth-among-us-suppliers (Accessed March 22, 2015).

25. Cyril Kowaliski, "SK Hynix Fire Sends Memory Prices Soaring," *The Tech Report*, Septermber 24, 2013, http://techreport.com/news/25416/sk-hynix -fire-sends-memory-prices-soaring (Accessed March 22, 2015).

26. Cameron McWhirter, "Chinese Diapers Save U.S. Paper Mill," *The Wall Street Journal*, August 13, 2012, B1.

27. Hutt and Speh, 52.

28. *Ibid*.

29. Stuart Leung, "Selling to Executives: Bringing Your Sales "A" Game to the C-Level," *SalesForce Blog*, February 24, 2014, http://blogs.salesforce.com /company/2014/02/selling-to-c-level-executives .html (Accessed March 22, 2015).

30. *Ibid*.

31. Hutt and Speh, 231.

32. *Ibid*.

8

1. "Biting Off the High End of the Market," *Inc.*, February 2015, 25.

2. Halah Touryalai, "How Macy's Is Winning the Retail Battle," *Forbes*, December 24, 2013, www.forbes.com/sites/halahtouryalai/2013/12/24 /how-macys-is-winning-the-retail-battle-hint-it -knows-which-u-s-cities-love-cuffed-pants (Accessed February 2, 2015).

3. Rebecca Spera, "CrossFit for Kids Focuses on Fun," *ABC*, January 21, 2015, http://abc13.com /health/crossfit-for-kids-focuses-on-fun/482997/ (Accessed February 26, 2015).

4. Sheila Shayton, "Never Mind Millennials – Gen Z May be the Hardest Marketing Nut to Crack," *Brand Channel*, August 20, 2014, www.brandchannel .com/home/post/2014/08/20/140820-Gen-Z -Marketing (Accessed February 21, 2015).

5. Christine Birkner, "Z Marks the Spot," *Marketing News*, December 2013, 14, www.ama.org /publications/MarketingNews/Pages/generation -z-digital-channels-innovation.aspx (Accessed February 21, 2015).

6. Sheila Shayton, "Never Mind Millennials–Gen Z May be the Hardest Marketing Nut to Crack."

7. Christine Birkner, "Attention, Shoppers," *Marketing News*, December 2013, 26–33, www .ama.org/publications/MarketingNews/Pages /tweens-consumer-research-brand-management .aspx (Accessed February 21, 2015).

8. "Who are Millennials?" *Millennial Marketing*, http://www.millennialmarketing.com/who-are -millennials/ (Accessed February 23, 2015).

9. Tom Ryan, "Are Retailers Ready for the Millennial Takeover?" *RetailWire*, November 4, 2013, www.retailwire.com/discussion/17128 /are-retailers-ready-for-the-millennial-takeover (Accessed February 22, 2015).

10. "Which Brand Attributes Matter Most to Millennials?" *RetailWire*, September29, 2014, www .retailwire.com/discussion/17807/which-brand -attributes-matter-most-to-millennials (Accessed February 21, 2015).

11. Jeff Fromm, "'Idea brands' Will Win Big with Millennials: Here's How to Attract Them," *Retail Customer Experience*, September 5, 2013, www.retailcustomerexperience.com/blog _print/11101 (Accessed February 21, 2015).

12. William F. Schroer, "Generations X, Y, Z and the Others," *The Social Librarian*, www.socialmarketing .org/newsletter/features/generation3.htm (Accessed February 22, 2015).

13. "Save the Date: Vancouver Turns Into Culinary Central During Dine Out Vancouver Festival 2015," *Tourism Vancouver*, www.tourismvancouver.com /articles/view/SAVE-THE-DATE-VANCOUVER -TURNS-INTO-CULINARY-CENTRAL-DURING -DINE-OUT-VANCOUVER-FESTIVAL-2015/652 /541/ (Accessed February 22, 2015).

14. Janet Eveleth, "Baby Boomers Are Shopping and Spending," *Examiner*, July 11, 2013, www .examiner.com/article/baby-boomers-are-shopping -and-spending (Accessed February 22, 2015).

15. Christine Birkner, "Senior Moment," *Marketing News*, September 2014, 12-13.

16. S. E. Smith, "What Is the Silent Generation?" *wiseGEEK*, January 23, 2013, www.wisegeek.com /what-is-the-silent-generation.htm (Accessed February 1, 2014).

17. Stephen M. Golant, "Aging in the American Suburbs: A Changing Population," *Aging Well*, www.agingwellmag.com/news/ex_06309_01.shtml (Accessed February 22, 2015).

18. Lauren Stiller Rikleen, "Not Buying Offensive Super Bowl Ads," *Boston Globe*, February 4, 2013, http://bostonglobe.com/opinion/2013/02/04 /not-buying-offensive-super-bowl-ads /1eNEMBDxLyLWFnHS7jKI2I/story.html (Accessed February 22, 2015).

19. "Men, Women and Money: How We View Finances Differently," *TransAmerica*, www.transamerica.com/yourlife/retirement/education/men-women-money-how-we-view-finances-differently (Accessed February 23, 2015).

20. Renee Montagne, "Japanese Burger Chain Finds Way to Appeal to Women," *NPR*, November 5, 2013, www.npr.org/2013/11/05/243185594/japanese-burger-chain-finds-way-to-appeal-to-women (Accessed February 22, 2015).

21. Annie Marie Cheker, "Groceries Become a Guy Thing," *Wall Street Journal*, October 16, 2013, http://online.wsj.com/news/articles/SB100014240527023036804045791394229728913 30 (Accessed February 23, 2015).

22. Ana Swanson, "What Super Bowl Manvertising Says About Men's New Role in America," *The Washington Post*, February 2, 2015, www.washingtonpost.com/blogs/wonkblog/wp/2015/02/02/what-super-bowl-manvertising-says-about-mens-new-role-in-america (Accessed February 26, 2015).

23. Marylouise Smith, "Dollar Stores Making a Buck in the Lebanon Valley," *Lebanon Daily News*, March 9, 2013, www.ldnews.com/ci_22749059/dollar-stores-making-buck-lebanon-valley (Accessed February 23, 2015).

24. Erin Shea, "How Luxury Retailers Can Take On Showrooming Threat," *Luxury Daily*, January 29, 2013, www.luxurydaily.com/how-luxury-retailers-can-take-on-threat-of-showrooming (Accessed February 22, 2015).

25. Judy Bankman, "Junk Food Marketing Makes Big Moves in Developing Countries," *Civil Eats*, October 2, 2013, http://civileats.com/2013/10/02/junk-food-marketing-makes-big-moves-in-developing-countries/ (Accessed February 23, 2015).

26. Breanne L. Heldman, "Adam Levine and Nicki Minaj Designing Clothes for Kmart," *Yahoo*, January 15, 2013, http://omg.yahoo.com/blogs/celeb-news/adam-levine-nicki-minaj-designing-clothes-kmart-194136723.html (Accessed February 23, 2015).

27. "Find a Store Near You," *Fashion Fair*, www.fashionfair.com/wtb2.php (Accessed February 23, 2015)

28. "Why You Need a Brand Ambassador Program (And 4 Companies that Are Doing it Right)," April 3, 2014, http://thenextweb.com/entrepreneur/2014/04/03/need-brand-ambassador-program-4-companies-right (Accessed February 23, 2015).

29. Laurie Sullivan, "Nielsen Taps eXelate's Data Pipeline," *MediaPost*, August 27, 2013, www.mediapost.com/publications/article/207917/nielsen-taps-exelates-data-pipeline.html (Accessed February 23, 2015); "The Start-Up Hunter," *Nielsen*, June 27, 2013, www.nielseninnovate.com/start-hunter (Accessed February 23, 2015).

30. Will Greenwald, "Sling TV," *PC Magazine*, February 17, 2015, www.pcmag.com/article2/0,2817,2475619,00.asp (Accessed February 26, 2015).

31. Joseph F. Kovar, "Actfio Looks to Simplify Storage Product Line, Channel Program," *CRN*, February 1, 2013, www.crn.com/news/storage/240147697/actifio-looks-to-simplify-storage-product-line-channel-program.htm (Accessed February 23, 2015).

32. "Amazon Webstore," *Amazon*, http://webstore.amazon.com/ (Accessed February 23, 2015).

33. Sarah Nassuer, "If Your Fridge Could Talk..." *Wall Street Journal*, December 17, 2014, D1, D2.

34. Amy Ahlberg, "9 Shopping Sites for Every Type of Fashionista," *DailyWorth*, April 24, 2013, www.dailyworth.com/posts/1823-9-shopping-sites-worth-visiting/4 (Accessed February 24, 2015).

35. Janice Bitters, "Mpls. To Expand Car Sharing," *Minnesota Daily*, February 13, 2013, www.mndaily.com/2013/02/13/mpls-expand-car-sharing (Accessed February 25, 2015).

36. Erik Sherman, "Is iPad Mini Cannibalizing its Bigger Sibling?" *CBS*, January 18, 2013, www.cbsnews.com/8301-505124_162-57564708/is-ipad-mini-cannibalizing-its-bigger-sibling (Accessed February 25, 2015).

37. Laura Fagan, "How Birchbox Used CR to Successfully Scale Their Business," April 1, 2014, http://blogs.salesforce.com/company/2014/04/birchbox.html (Accessed February 24, 2015).

38. "All Brands," *Coca-Cola*, www.thecoca-colacompany.com/brands/brandlist.html (Accessed February 24, 2015).

39. Jeanine Poggi, "Can Esquire's Brand Make a TV Channel a Hit?" *Advertising Age*, http://adage.com/article/media/nbc-universal-rebrands-g4-esquire-network/239727/ (Accessed February 25, 2015).

40. "Nutrition Guide," *Kentucky Fried Chicken*, January 22, 2013, www.kfc.com/nutrition/pdf/kfc_nutrition.pdf (Accessed February 25, 2015).

41. "Our Brands," *Gap Inc.*, www.gapinc.com/content/gapinc/html/aboutus/ourbrands.html (Accessed February 24, 2015).

42. Lara O'Reilly, "Vertu Shifts from Bling to Emotional Positioning," *MarketingWeek*, February 12, 2013, www.marketingweek.co.uk/news/vertu-shifts-from-bling-to-emotional-positioning/4005671.article (Accessed February 23, 2015).

43. Susan Gunelius, "Kia Rolls Out Brand Repositioning Ad Campaign," *Corporate Eye*, January 9, 2015, www.corporate-eye.com/main/kia-rolls-out-brand-repositioning-ad-campaign (Accessed February 26, 2015).

9

1. "Internet of Things Study Highlights Our Conflicted Relationship with Privacy," *Quirk's Marketing Research Review*, October 2014, 10.

2. "The Auto Repair Process Needs an Overhaul," *Quirk's Marketing Research Review*, August 2014, 14–15.

3. "Report Identifies Auto Marques with Gabbiest Owners," *Quirk's Marketing Research Review*, January 2015, 19.

4. A Detailed Exploration," *Quirk's Marketing Research Review*, October 2014, 30–34.

5. "By the Numbers? 200+ Amazing Facebook Users Statistics," *Expanded Ramblings*, February 3, 2015, http://expandedramblings.com/index.php/by-the-numbers-17-amazing-facebook-stats/ (Accessed February 22, 2015).

6. "30+ # Twitter Marketing Stats: 2015 - #infographic," *Digital Information World*, January 24, 2015, www.digitalinformationworld.com/2015/01/twitter-marketing-stats-and-facts-you-should-know.html (Accessed February 22, 2015).

7. "Buy Signal: Facebook Widens Data Targeting," *Wall Street Journal*, April 10, 2013, B4.

8. "Zuckerberg's New Tools," *Marketing Insights*, Spring 2013, 5.

9. "Smile! Marketers Are Mining Selfies," *Wall Street Journal*, October 10, 2014, B1–B2.

10. Parmy Olson, "We Know Everything," *Forbes*, November 18, 2013, 68-70.

11. *Ibid.*

12. "Adopt the Industry Standard, For Free," *Flurry*, www.flurry.com/solutions/analytics (Accessed February 22, 2015).

13. "What is Apache Hadoop?" *Apache*, www.hadoop.apache.org/#What+Is+Apache+Hadoop%3F (Accessed February 23, 2015).

14. "Ten Big Data Case Studies in a Nutshell," *SearchCIO*, http://searchcio.techtarget.com/opinion/Ten-big-data-case-studies-in-a-nutshell (Accessed February 23, 2015).

15. "More of the Same Please, *Quirk's Marketing Research Review*, March 2014, 14.

16. Carl McDaniel and Roger Gates, *Marketing Research*, 10th ed., Wiley, 2015, 171.

17. "The Science of Shopping," *Indiana University*, http://Kelley.iu.edu/Marketing/Research/Labs/shopability1.htmp (Accessed February 24, 2015).

18. "Viva Vantage Named 2015 Product of the Year," *PR Newswire*, www.prnewswire.com/news-releases/viva-vantage-named-2015-product-of-the-year-30032887/html (Accessed February 25, 2015).

19. "Google Consumer Surveys," *Google*, www.google.com/insights/consumersurveys/how (Accessed February 25, 2015).

20. "Election Reopens Debate Over Online Polling," *National Journal*, www.nationaljournal.com/politics/election-reopens-debate-over-online-polling-10121130 (Accessed February 24, 2015).

21. "Character Counts, Characters Count," *Quirk's Marketing Research Review*, July 2013, 48–51.

22. "Brand + TV + iPad: The New Research Triangle," *Quirk's Marketing Research Review*, March 2014, 36–41.

23. "Screen Size Correlates with Completion Rates," *Quirk's Marketing Research Review*, April 2014, 8.

24. "Easy Answers," *Quirk's Marketing Research Review*, February 2015, 32–36.

25. "Instant Insight," *Marketing News*, February 2013, 46–49.

26. "That's the Spot" *Quirk's Marketing Research Review*, July 2014, 38–45.

27. *Ibid.*

28. "Behavior Scan CPG TV Ad Testing," *IRI Worldwide*, www.iriworldwide.com/ProductSolutions/AllProductsDetail/productID/29.aspx (Accessed February 25, 2015).

10

1. Jessica Whol, "Starbucks Rolling Out Upscale Teavana Tea Cafes," April 29, 2014, http://articles.chicagotribune.com/2014-04-29/business/ct-starbucks-teavana-0429-biz-20140429_1_tazo-ceo-howard-schultz-seattle-based-coffee-chain (Accessed March 19, 2015).

2. "Cat's Pride Launches Fresh & Light Ultimate Care – Performance Based Litter That is 'Light Done Right,'" *The Herald Online*, March 3, 2015, www.heraldonline.com/incoming/article12692651.html (Accessed March 19, 2015).

3. Stephanie Strom, "McDonald's Moves toward a Healthier Menu," *New York Times*, September 27, 2013, www.bostonglobe.com/business/2013/09/26/mcdonald-moves-toward-healthier-menu/6Ez4YH7zEOZCIK3oS31S1N/story.html (Accessed February 9, 2014).

4. Sarah Halzach, "Target's New Strategy: We Need More Than Just Minivan Moms," *Washington Post*, March 4, 2015, www.washingtonpost.com/news/business/wp/2015/03/04/targets-new-strategy-we-need-more-than-just-minivan-moms (Accessed March 19, 2015).

5. "Krispy Kreme Hopes Iced Beverages Bring Bigger Share of Coffee Market," *Journal Now*, February 18, 2014, www.journalnow.com/business

/business_news/local/article/f55f0020-8dc7-11e3 (Accessed March 19, 2015).

6. Sam Laird, "Yahoo Killing Message Boards Site and Other Products," *Mashable*, March 2, 2013, http://mashable.com/2013/03/01/yahoo-kills -properties (Accessed February 9, 2014).

7. Ashraf Eassa, "Google Stole Apple's Mojo," *Seeking Alpha*, March 3, 2013, http://seekingalpha .com/article/1242371-google-stole-apple-s-mojo (Accessed February 9, 2014); Darcy Travlos, "Is Apple Losing Its Brand Equity?" *Forbes*, January 19, 2013, www.Forbes.com/sites/darcytravlos /2013/01/19/is-apple-losing-its-brand-equity (Accessed February 9, 2015); Jordan Kahn, "Despite Declining Sales, Samsung Somehow Beats Apple in Cell Phone Customer Satisfaction," *9 to 5 Mac*, December 31, 2014, http://9to5mac .com/2014/12/31/samsung-vs-apple-customer -satisfaction (Accessed March 19, 2015).

8. Pat Reynolds, "Shoppers Believe Private Label = National Brands in Different Packaging," *Packaging World*, February 26, 2013, www.packworld.com /venue/private-label/shoppers-believe-private-label -national-brands-different-packaging (Accessed February 9, 2014).

9. Domenick Celentano, "Private Label 2013 Trends—Strong Growth—Affordable, High Quality," *About.com*, http://foodbeverage.about.com/od /StartingAFoodBusiness/a/Strong-Growth-In-Private -Label-Brands-Private-Label-Manufacturers -Association.htm (Accessed February 9, 2014).

10. Christine Birkner, "Losing the Label, August 2014, *Marketing News*, 10-11.

11. Keith Nunes, "Kroger Succeeding with Simple Truth," *Meat+Poultry*, March 9, 2015, www .meatpoultry.com/articles/news_home/Trends/2015 /03/Kroger_succeeding_with_Simple.aspx?ID =%7B45586455-1818-4988-A981-FEA683EF49DA %7D&cck=1 (Accessed match 19, 2015).

12. "Brands & Products: Brand Browser," *Church & Dwight*, www.churchdwight.com/brands-and -products/brand-browser.aspx (Accessed February 9, 2014).

13. "Bruegger's Bagels Co-branding with Jamba Juice," *Fast Casual*, February 12, 2014, www .fastcasual.com/article/227795/Bruegger-s-Bagels -co-branding-with-Jamba-Juice (Accessed February 17, 2014).

14. "Doc Popcorn, Dippin' Dots to Debut First Co-Brand Store," *Business Wire*, February 10, 2015, www.businesswire.com/news/home /20150210005273/en/Doc-Popcorn-Dippin'-Dots -Debut-Co-Brand-Store (Accessed match 19, 2015).

15. T. Thompson, "What Is the Difference between a Copyright, Trademark, and Patent?" *WiseGEEK*, February 9, 2013, www.wisegeek.com/what-is-the -difference-between-a-copyright-trademark-and -patent.htm (Accessed February 9, 2014).

16. Edward Wyatt, "F.C.C. Backs Consumers in Unlocking of Cellphones," *New York Times*, March 4, 2013, www.nytimes.com/2013/03/05/technology /fcc-urges-a-right-to-unlock-cellphones.html (Accessed February 9, 2014).

17. Monte Burke, "Under Armour Files Lawsuit against Nike for Trademark Infringement," *Forbes*, February 21, 2013, www.forbes.com/sites /monteburke/2013/02/21/under-armour-files -lawsuit-against-nike-for-trademark-infringement (Accessed February 9, 2014).

18. Chantal Fernandez, "Gucci Loses Trademark Infringement Case Against Guess in France," *Fashionista*, February 2, 2015, http://fashionista.com /2015/02/french-court-rejects-gucci-trademark -claims-against-guess-paris-france (Accessed

March 19, 2015); "Counterfeit Combat," *Inc.*, March 2015, 68–69.

19. "11 Ridiculous Fast Food Chain Ripoffs in China," *Hardware Zone*, http://forums.hardwarezone .com.sg/eat-drink-man-woman-16/11-ridiculous -fast-food-food-chain-ripoffs-china-4281444.html (Accessed February 9, 2014).

20. Molly Soat, "Misunderstood Measures," *Marketing News*, January 2015, 18-19.

21. Gemma Charles, "Brothers Cider Unveils Premium Packaging," *Marketing*, February 28, 2013, www.marketingmagazine.co.uk/news /1172938/Brothers-Cider-unveils-new-premium -packaging (Accessed February 9, 2014).

22. Nathan Rao, "'Wrap Rage' Soars Over Packaging We Can't Open," *Express*, January 28, 2014, www.express.co.uk/news/uk/456493/Wrap-Rage -soars-over-packaging-we-can-t-open (Accessed February 17, 2014).

23. "U.S. Consumers Increase 'Green' Purchases; But Are They Willing to Pay More?" *PR Newswire*, June 5, 2013, www.prnewswire.com/news-releases /us-consumers-increase-green-purchases-but -are-they-willing-to-pay-more-210221081.html (Accessed February 17, 2014).

24. "New Packaging to Monitor Food Freshness," *Health24*, February 28, 2013, www.health24.com /Diet-and-nutrition/News/New-packaging-to-monitor -food-freshness-20130228 (Accessed February 10, 2014).

25. Adele Peters, "The Disappearing Package: From Dissolving Wrappers to Products that Package Themselves," *GOOD*, January 31, 2013, www.good.is/posts/the-disappearing-package-from -dissolving-wrappers-to-products-that-package -themselves (Accessed February 10, 2014).

26. "About Green Seal," *Green Seal*, www .greenseal.org/AboutGreenSeal.aspx (Accessed February 10, 2014).

11

1. "The World's 50 Most Innovative Companies," *Fast Company*, www.fastcompany.com/section /most-innovative-companies-2015 (Accessed April 21, 2015).

2. "Phases of Development," *Pfizer*, www.pfizer .com/research/clinical_trials/phases_of_development (Accessed April 21, 2015).

3. "10 Companies Spending Most on R&D in the World," *Rediff*, March 15, 2013, www.rediff.com /business/slide-show/slide-show-1-10-companies -spending-most-on-r-and-d-in-the-world/20130315 .htm (Accessed April 21, 2015).

4. Dieter Bohn, "Hands-on With the new 12-inch MacBook with Retina Display," *The Verge*, March 9, 2015, www.theverge.com/2015/3/9/8173685 /macbook-retina-display-usb-type-c-hands-on -video (Accessed April 21, 2015).

5. Amar Toor. "Has the Transparent Smartphone Finally Arrived?" *The Verge*, February 15, 2013, www.theverge.com/2013/2/15/3966950/will-we-see -a-transparent-phone-polytron-prototype-display (Accessed April 21, 2015).

6. "Moleskine World," *Moleskine*, www.moleskine .com/moleskine_world (Accessed April 21, 2015).

7. Ben Popken, "Taco Bell's Cool Ranch Tacos: Co-branding Genius," *Today*, January 10, 2013, http://lifeinc.today.com/_news/2013/01/10/16430586 -taco-bells-cool-ranch-tacos-co-branding-genius (Accessed April 21, 2015).

8. Rick Armon, "Miller Lite Releases New Bottle in Bars and Restaurants," *Ohio Breweries*, May 11,

2013, www.ohio.com/blogs/the-beer-blog/the-beer -blog-1.273124/miller-lite-releases-new-bottle-in -bars-and-restaurants-1.396902 (Accessed April 21, 2015).

9. Steven J. Erwing, "Mercedes Renames Utility Vehicles, Repositions Maybach as Sub-brand," *Autoblog*, November 11, 2014, www.autoblog.com /2014/11/11/mercedes-name-changes-gl-maybach/ (Accessed April 21, 2015).

10. Jacob Morgan, "Five Uncommon Internal Innovation Examples," *Forbes*, April 8, 2015, www .forbes.com/sites/jacobmorgan/2015/04/08/five -uncommon-internal-innovation-examples/ (Accessed April 21 ,2015).

11. Rachel Emma Silverman, "For Bright Ideas, Ask the Staff," *Wall Street Journal*, October 17, 2011, B7.

12. Michelle Greenwald, "NikeID, Coca-Cola Freestyle and Other Brands Mastering Infinite Customization," *Forbes*, October 8, 2014, www .forbes.com/sites/michellegreenwald/2014/10/08 /infinite-customization-12-category-examples-6 -key-questions-to-ask/ (Accessed April 21, 2015).

13. Tyler Falk, "How Google's Secretive Lab Innovates: Rewarding Failure," *ZDNet*, January 27, 2014, www.zdnet.com/article/how-googles-secretive -lab-innovates-reward-failure/ (Accessed April 21, 2015).

14. "Fuld & Company Is the World's Preeminent Research and Consulting Firm in the Field of Competitive Intelligence," *Fuld & Company*, www.fuld.com/company (Accessed April 21, 2015).

15. Liz Welch, "Success, One Board at a Time," *Inc.*, March 2014, 24–25.

16. David Kramer, "US Seeing Its Lead in R&D Slipping Against Other Nations," *Physicstoday*, February 2014, http://scitation.aip.org/content/aip /magazine/physicstoday/news/10.1063/PT.5.1010 (Accessed April 21, 2015).

17. "Company Profile," *Continuum*, http:// continuuminnovation.com/about/company-profile (Accessed April 21, 2015).

18. Jen Hansegard, "Lego's Plan to Find the Next Big Hit: Crowdsource It," *Wall Street Journal*, February 25, 2015, http://blogs.wsj.com/digits /2015/02/25/legos-plan-to-find-the-next-big-hit -crowdsource-it/ (Accessed April 21, 2015).

19. Eddie Makuch, "Ubisoft's Open-world Racer The Crew Has Been in Development for Six Years," *Gamespot*, May 15, 2014, www.gamespot.com /articles/ubisoft-s-open-world-racer-the-crew-has -been-in-development-for-six-years/1100-6419658/ (Accessed April 21, 2015); Eddie Makuch, "Watch Dogs Sells 4 Million Copies in First Week, Needs 2 Million More to Match Assassin's Creed Lifetime Tally," *Gamespot*, June 3, 2014, www.gamespot .com/articles/watch-dogs-sells-4-million-copies-in -first-week-needs-2-million-more-to-match-assassin -s-creed-s-lifetime-tally/1100-6420059/ (Accessed April 21, 2015).

20. Michael D. Hutt and Thomas W. Speh, *Business Marketing Management*, 12th ed. (Cincinnati: Cengage Learning, 2015).

21. "Wheaties™ Fans Select Anthony Pettis as America's NEXT Bow Chanpion," *PR Newswire*, September 3, 2014, www.prnewswire.com/news -releases/wheaties-fans-select-anthony-pettis-as -americas-next-box-champion-273732841.html (Accessed April 21, 2015).

22. Mary Vanac, "Meet Wendy's Ciabatta Bacon Cheeseburger," *Columbus Dispatch*, January 27, 2014, www.dispatch.com/content/blogs/the-bottom -line/2014/01/wendys-bringing-bacon-cheeseburger -back-with-ciabatta-bun.html (Accessed April 21, 2015).

23. John Dodge, "Dark Barrel Latte: Starbucks Has No Immediate Plan To Serve Beer-Flavored Drink In Chicago," *CBS Chicago*, September 24, 2014, http://chicago.cbslocal.com/2014/09/24/dark-barrel-latte-starbucks-has-no-immediate-plan-to-serve-beer-flavored-drink-in-chicago/ (Accessed April 21, 2015).

24. "P&G Everyday," *Procter & Gamble*, www.pgeveryday.com/pgeds/index.jsp (Accessed April 21, 2015).

25. Copernicus Marketing Consulting and Research, "Top 10 Reasons for New Product Failure," *Green-Book*, www.greenbook.org/marketing-research.cfm/top-10-reasons-for-new-product-failure (Accessed April 21, 2015).

26. Sage McHugh, "8 Biggest Product Fails of 2014," *Alternet*, December 5, 2014 www.alternet.org/economy/8-biggest-product-fails-2014 (Accessed April 21, 2015).

27. Alex Pigliucci, "Wealth Management for China's Richest: An Industry with a Great Future," *Forbes*, January 28, 2013, www.Forbes.com/sites/Forbesleadershipforum/2013/01/28/wealth-management-for-chinas-richest-an-industry-with-a-great-future/ (Accessed April 21, 2015).

28. Susan Gunelius, "Data Proves Word-of-Mouth Marketing Works—Infographic," *Newstex*, February 12, 2014, http://newstex.com/2014/02/12/data-proves-word-of-mouth-marketing-works-infographic/ (Accessed April 21, 2015).

29. *Ibid*.

30. Mercedes Cardona, "Word-of-mouth Drives Teen Conversations," *Direct Marketing News*, July 1, 2012, www.dmnews.com/word-of-mouth-drives-teen-conversions/article/247170 (Accessed April 21, 2015).

31. *Ibid*.

32. "Millennials Depend on Word-of-Mouth More than Boomers," *RetailWire*, January 21, 2014, www.retailwire.com/discussion/17280/millennials-depend-on-word-of-mouth-more-than-boomers (Accessed April 21, 2015).

33. "Survey Reveals U.S. Consumers Feel Businesses Lead in Recognizing the Value of Listening to Feedback," *BusinessWire*, January 28, 2014, www.businesswire.com/news/home/20140128005598/en/Survey-Reveals-U.S.-Consumers-Feel-Businesses-Lead (Accessed April 21, 2015).

34. Rachael Feintzeig, "Boss's Next Demand: Make Lots of Friends," *Wall Street Journal*, February 12, 2014, B1.

35. Vivian Giang, "100 Fastest-Growing Companies," *Fortune*, http://fortune.com/100-fastest-growing-companies/on-assignment-3/ (Accessed April 21, 2015).

36. Robert Channick, "40% of Homes Now Without a Landline" *Chicago Tribune*, July 8, 2014, www.chicagotribune.com/business/breaking/chi-landlines-survey-20140708-story.html (Accessed April 21, 2015).

12

1. Aidan Smith, Roderick Asekhauno, Harold Laney, and Rebecca Hutchins, "Quarterly Estimates for Selected Service Industries 4th Quarter 2014," *U. S. Census Bureau*, www.census.gov/services/qss/qss-current (Accessed March 11, 2015); "Services," *Office of the United States Trade Representative*, August 28, 2014, https://ustr.gov/issue-areas/services-investment/services (Accessed March 11, 2015).

2. Flavio Martins, "Demystifying the Ritz-Carlton Secret of Legendary Customer Service," *Customer Think*, February 1, 2015, http://customerthink.com/demystifying-the-ritz-carlton-secret-of-legendary-customer-service (Accessed April 24, 2015).

3. Ed Jones, "Top 10 IT Certifications to Target in 2015," *Cloud Computing Intelligence*, January 5, 2015, www.cloudcomputingintelligence.com/item/1733-the-top-it-certifications-to-target-in-2015 (Accessed April 24, 2015).

4. Dwayne Gremler, Mary Jo Bitner, and Valarie Zeithaml, *Services Marketing* (New York: McGraw-Hill, 2012).

5. *Ibid*.

6. Simon Dumenco, "Venti, Venti Annoying: So How Does Starbucks Misspell Your Name?" *Advertising Age*, March 5, 2013, http://adage.com/article/the-media-guy/starbucks-pop-song-head/240104 (Accessed February 21, 2015).

7. Jim Harger, "New App Lets Fifth Third Bank Customers Deposit Checks via their Smartphones," *Michigan Live*, February 7, 2013, www.mlive.com/business/west-michigan/index.ssf/2013/02/new_app_lets_fifth_third_bank.html (Accessed February 24, 2015).

8. Douglas A. McIntyre, Alexander Kent, Alexander E.M. Hess, Thomas C. Frohlich, and Ashley C. Allen, "Customer Service Hall of Fame, http://247wallst.com/special-report/2014/07/18/customer-service-hall-of-fame, (Accessed March14, 2015).

9. Much of the material in this section is based on Christopher H. Lovelock and Jochen Wirtz, *Services Marketing*, 7th ed. (Upper Saddle River, NJ: Prentice Hall, 2011).

10. Zac Townsend, "Era of Mass Customization in Banking," *Bank Innovation*, April 17, 2014, http://bankinnovation.net/2014/04/era-of-mass-customization-in-banking (Accessed March 16, 2015).

11. Wendy Donahue, "Mac & Mia Trunk Club for Kids Makes Shopping Easy for Busy Moms," *The Charlotte Observer*, February 11, 2015, www.charlotteobserver.com/incoming/article10430567.html (Accessed April 24, 2015).

12. Lovelock and Wirtz, *Services Marketing*.

13. *Ibid*.

14. Much of the material in this section is based on Dwayne Gremler, Mary Jo Bitner, and Valarie Zeithaml, *Services Marketing*, (New York: McGraw-Hill), 2012.

15. Mia Taylor, "5 Hotels Opening in 2015 that Embody Latest Travel Trends," *MainStreet*, December 24, 2014, www.mainstreet.com/article/5-hotels-opening-in-2015-that-embody-latest-travel-trends (Accessed March 17, 2015).

16. "100 Best Companies to Work For 2015," *Fortune*, http://fortune.com/best-companies/ (Accessed April 14, 2015).

13

1. Hannah Elliott, "Rolls Royce's Bespoke Program Puts Virtually No Limits on Customization," *Pittsburgh Post-Gazette*, February 20, 2015.

2. Heather Clancy, "Kimberly-Clark Makes Sense of Demand," *Consumer Goods Technology*, October 11, 2012, http://consumergoods.edgl.com/case-studies/Kimberly-Clark-Makes-Sense-of-Demand82520 (Accessed February 2015).

3. Mark A. Moon, *Demand and Supply Integration: The Key to World-Class Demand Forecasting*. New York: Financial Times Press, 2013.

4. Much of this section is based on material adapted from Donald J. Bowersox, David J. Closs, and Theodore P. Stank, *21st Century Logistics: Making Supply Chain Integration a Reality*, Oak Brook, IL: Council of Logistics Management, 1999; Barbara Flynn, Michiya Morita, and Jose Machuca, *Managing Global Supply Chain Relationships: Operations, Strategies and Practices*, Business Science, Hershey, New York, 2010; and David Sims, "Integrated Supply Chains Maximize Efficiencies and Savings," *ThomasNet*, July 23, 2013, http://news.thomasnet.com/imt/2013/07/23/integrated-supply-chains-maximize-efficiencies-and-savings (Accessed March 2015).

5. Häagen-Dazs and General Mills to Help Smallholder Vanilla Farmers Increase Yields and Improve Sustainability Practices in Madagascar," *CSRwire*, February 20, 2013, www.csrwire.com/press_releases/35228-H-agen-Dazs-and-General-Mills-to-Help-Smallholder-Vanilla-Farmers-Increase-Yields-and-Improve-Sustainability-Practices-in-Madagascar (Accessed January 2015).

6. Much of this and the following sections are based on material adapted from the edited volume Douglas M. Lambert, ed., *Supply Chain Management: Processes, Partnerships and Performance*, Sarasota, FL: Supply Chain Management Institute, 2004; and "The Supply Chain Management Processes," *Supply Chain Management Institute*, www.ijlm.org/Our-Relationship-Based-Business-Model.htm (Accessed March 2015).

7. "C.H. Briggs Builds a Better Relationship with its Customers," *IBM*, October 16, 2012, www-01.ibm.com/software/success/cssdb.nsf/CS/STRD-8YWGWZ (Accessed March 2015).

8. James A. Cooke, "Inside Dell's Global Command Centers," *DC Velocity*, September 24, 2012, www.dcvelocity.com/articles/20120924-inside-dells-global-command-centers (Accessed January 2015).

9. Stephanie Grothe, "How They Did It: Red Wing Shoes' Journey to S&OP," *Supply Chain Management Review*, May/June 2014.

10. John Letzing, "Amazon Adds That Robotic Touch," *Wall Street Journal*, March 20, 2012, http://online.wsj.com/article/SB10001424052702304724404577291903244796214.htm (Accessed March 2015); Donna Tam, "Meet Amazon's Busiest Employee – The Kiva Robot," *CNET*, November 20, 2014, http://www.cnet.com/news/meet-amazons-busiest-employee-the-kiva-robot/ (Accessed March 2015).

11. Tony Hines, *Supply Chain Strategies: Demand Driven and Customer Focused*, 2nd ed., New York: Routledge, 2013.

12. "Bayer HealthCare to Purchase Pharmacy Supplier Steigerwald Arzneimittelwerk," *Zenopa*, May 17, 2013, www.zenopa.com/news/801587313/bayer-healthcare-to-purchase-pharmacy-supplier-steigerwald-arzneimittelwerk (Accessed March 3, 2015).

13. Kenneth J. Petersen, Robert Handfield, and Gary Ragatz, "Supplier Integration into New Product Development: Coordinating Product, Process, and Supply Chain Design," *Journal of Operations Management*, 23, no. 3-4, (2005): 371-388; and Stephen Trimble, "Analysis: US South Rises on Airbus, Boeing Expansion," *Flight Global*, www.flightglobal.com (Accessed February 2015).

14. Curtis Greve and Jerry Davis, "Recovering Lost Profits by Improving Reverse Logistics," *UPS*, www.ups.com/media/en/Reverse_Logistics_wp.pdf (Accessed February 2015).

15. UPS, "Logistics of Sustainability," *Compass*, Spring 2012, 10.

16. Steve Szilagyi, keynote address, *Warehousing Education and Research Council* Annual Conference, Atlanta GA, May 2012; and Judy Owen, "Lowe's Ramps Up Disability Inclusion," *Forbes*, April 2013.

17. Martin Christopher, *Logistics and Supply Chain Management*, 4th ed. (New York: Prentice Hall/Financial Times, 2010).

18. Kate Vitasek and Karl Manrodt, *Vested: How P&G, McDonalds, and Microsoft are Redefining Winning in Business Relationships* (New York: Palgrave MacMillan, 2012).

19. Dinah Wisenberg Brin, "Need Technology Experts? Try Rural America," *CNBC*, February 20, 2013, www.cnbc.com/id/100470457 (Accessed March 2015).

20. Wesley S. Randall, "Public-Private Partnerships in Supply Chain Management," *Journal of Business Logistics*, December 2013.

21. "Federal Highway Administration," *U.S. Department of Transportation*, www.fhwa.dot.gov/ (Accessed March 3, 2015).

22. "Printing Titanium Bicycle Parts. A Charge Bikes Collaboration with EADS," *Vimeo*, August 14, 2012, http://vimeo.com/47522348 (Accessed January 2015).

23. "Home," *3DLT*, www.3dlt.com_(Accessed March 2015).

24. Hans-Georg Kaltenbrunner, "How 3D Printing is Set to Shake Up Manufacturing Supply Chains," *The Guardian*, November 25, 2014.

25. J. Paul Dittmann, *Managing Risk in the Global Supply Chain*, Global Supply Chain Institute: Knoxville, TN, 2014.

26. John Markoff, "New Research Center Aims to Develop Second Generation of Surgical Robots," *The New York Times*, October 23, 2014.

27. Eric Savitz, "Apple Screens for iPad3 in Short Supply," *Forbes*, March 1, 2012, 9.

28. "Vera Bradley Strikes International Agreement," *Inside Indiana Business*, June 4, 2014, www.insideindianabusiness.com/newsitem.asp?id=65477 (Accessed March 3, 2015).

29. "Takeback Programs," *South Carolina Department of Health and Environmental Control*, www.scdhec.gov/environment/lwm/recycle/e-cycle/takeback_programs.htm (Accessed February 2015).

30. "Frequently Asked Questions About the Apple Recycling Program," *Apple*, www.apple.com/recycling/includes/recycling-faq.html (Accessed January 2015).

31. Aaron Strout, "Frictionless Mobile Commerce: 5 Examples of Companies that are Leading," *Marketing Land*, www.marketingland.com (Accessed January 2015).

32. Alex Hamilton, "M-Commerce Causing Sales Figures to Explode," *TechRadar*, www.techradar.com (Accessed February 2015).

33. "Retailers Leveraging Tablets to Elevate Brand, Boost Sales," *Retailing Insight*, http://retailinginsight.com/industrynews8.html, Accessed January 2015.

34. "What Is the Size of the M-Commerce Market In the US?" *Quora*, www.quora.com/Mobile-Commerce-1/What-is-the-size-of-the-m-commerce-market-in-the-US (Accessed January 2015).

35. Joanna Brenner, "Pew Internet: Mobile," *Pew Mobile*, September 13, 2013, http://pewinternet.org/Commentary/2012/February/Pew-Internet-Mobile.aspx (Accessed January 2015).

36. *Ibid*.

37. Aaron Smith, "In-store Mobile Commerce During the 2012 Holiday Shopping Season," *Pew Internet*, January 31, 2013, http://pewinternet.org/Reports/2013/in-store-mobile-commerce.aspx (Accessed January 2015).

38. *Ibid*.

39. Jack Uldrich, "The Future of Retail Isn't So Foreign," *Jump the Curve*, January 30, 2013, http://jumpthecurve.net/retail-marketing/the-future-of-retail-isnt-so-foreign/ (Accessed January 2015).

40. "Survey Finds Consumers Using Pinterest to Engage With Retailers More Than Facebook, Twitter," *Retailing Insight*, http://retailinginsight.com/industrynews9.html (Accessed January 2015).

41. Wang, J. J., Zhao, X., and Li, J. J. (2013). "Group Buying: A Strategic Form of Consumer Collective," *Journal of Retailing* 89(3), 338-351.

42. Taurn Kushwaha and Venkatesh Shankar, "Are multichannel customers really more valuable? The moderating role of product category characteristics," *Journal of Marketing*, 77, no. 4, 67-85.

43. Jennifer Lonoff Schiff, "Eight Ways to Create a Successful Multichannel Customer Experience," *CIO Magazine*, February 23, 2015.

14

1. "Monthly & Annual Retail Trade," *United States Census Bureau*, March 12, 2015, www.census.gov/retail (Accessed February 2015).

2. "Retail's Impact Report," *National Retail Federation*, www.nrf.com/advocacy/retails-impact (Accessed March 2015).

3. C. Brett Lockard and Michael Wolf, "Occupational Employment Projections to 2020," *Bureau of Labor Statistics Monthly Labor Review*, 135, no. 1, (2012): 84–108.

4. "Retail Firms by Employment Size," *National Retail Federation*, www.nrf.com (Accessed February 2015).

5. Jason Daley, "The 2015 Franchise 500," *Entrepreneur*, December 16, 2014.

6. Paul Tassi, "GTA 5 and the Ethics of Mass Murder," *Forbes*, December 11, 2014; "Toys R Us Pulls Breaking Bad Dolls After Florida Mom's Petition," *Tampa Bay Times*, October 21, 2014, www.tampabay.com/features/media/toys-r-us-pulls-breaking-bad-dolls-after-florida-moms-petition-w-video/2203155 (Accessed March 13, 2015).

7. Susan Johnston, "Beware These Online Retail Pricing Strategies," *US News and World Report*, June 24, 2013.

8. Alaric Dearment, "Target Tackles Movie Streaming," *Retailing Today*, September 25, 2013, http://retailingtoday.com/article/target-tackles-movie-streaming (Accessed February 2015).

9. "Man Cave – Home Parties for Men," *Man Cave*, www.mancaveworldwide.com (Accessed March 2015).

10. "Telemarketing in the 21st Century," *BusinessTM*, http://businesstm.com/home-based/telemarketing-in-the-21st-century.html (Accessed January 2015).

11. Tianyi Jiang and Alexander Tuzhilin, "Dynamic Microtargeting: Fitness-based Approach to Predicting Individual Preferences," *Knowledge and Information Systems* 19, no. 3, (2009): 337–60.

12. Al Urbanski, "Big Money for Big Data: Marketers will Spend $11.5B in 2015," *Direct Marketing News*, www.dmnews.com (Accessed February 2015).

13. "Market Research on Digital Media, Internet Marketing," *eMarketer*, www.emarketer.com (Accessed March 2015).

14. Ashley Lutz, "Zara's Genius Business Model Could Destroy JCPenney and Sears," *Business Insider*, March 4, 2013, www.businessinsider.com/zaras-genius-business-model-2013-3 (Accessed April 1, 2015).

15. Harry McCracken, "Amazon Holiday Delivery Woes: Send in the Drones," *Time*, December 26, 2013. http://techland.time.com/2013/12/26/amazon-holiday-delivery-woes-send-in-the-drones/ (Accessed March 2015).

16. Lydia Dishman, "The Entrepreneur Who Is Beating Amazon at Same-day Delivery," *Fast Company*, www.fastcompany.com/3042207/strong-female-lead/the-entrepreneur-who-is-beating-amazon-at-same-day-delivery (Accessed March 13, 2015).

17. Sarah Favot, "Two Build-your-own Pizza Restaurants Opening in Monrovia," *Pasadena Star-News*, March 21, 2014.

18. Gabrielle Karol, "TGI Fridays Offering $10 Unlimited Appetizers Promotion," *Fox Business*, July 7, 2014, www.foxbusiness.com/industries/2014/07/07/tgi-fridays-offering-10-unlimited-appetizers-promotion/ (Accessed January 2015).

19. Tiffany Hsu, "Toys R Us to Open Holiday Pop-up Shops in Macy's," *Los Angeles Times*, October 10, 2012, http://articles.latimes.com/2012/oct/10/business/la-fi-mo-toys-r-us-holiday-popup-macys-20121010 (Accessed January 2015).

20. Adam Blair, "The Drive to Localize," *RIS News*, May 7, 2011, http://risnews.edgl.com/retail-news/The-Drive-to-Localize72436 (Accessed March 2015).

21. Haithem Zourrig, Jean-Charles Chebat, and Roy Toffoli, "Consumer Revenge Behavior: A Cross-Cultural Perspective," *Journal of Business Research* 62, no. 10, (2009): 995–1001.

22. Christopher Ratcliff, "iBeacons: The Hunt for Stats," *Econsultancy.com*, August 26, 2014; Rachel Abrams, "Psst! It's Me, the Mannequin," *New York Times*, 2015, A8.

23. Ben Kersey, "Wal-Mart Tries a Blended Channel Approach to Survive in a Digital World," *The Verge*, November 23, 2012, www.theverge.com/2012/11/23/3681694/walmart-hybrid-model (Accessed January 2015).

24. Stuart Miller, "Customers Have High Expectations for Click and Collect," *Real Business*, November 28, 2013, http://realbusiness.co.uk/article/24866-customers-have-high-expectations-for-click-and-collect (Accessed March 2015).

15

1. McCarthy, Michael, "Sick of Ron Burgundy? Durango Certainly Isn't," *Advertising Age*, December 9, 2013, http://adage.com/article/news/sick-ron-burgundy-durango/245586/ (Accessed March 2015).

2. Michael Blaustein, "Watch: Ad for Colin Farrell Movie Goes Too Far with 'Elevator Murder' Video," *New York Post*, March 5, 2013, www.nypost.com/p/entertainment/movies/watch_marketing_elevator_collin_NOOBhxqXYHO3QXW8W4SjII (Accessed March 2015); Emily Verona, "True Detective Season 2 News: HBO Hit Giving Colin Farrell's Career A Boost?," *Enstarz*, January 19, 2015, www.enstarz.com/articles/60607/20150119/true-detective-season-2-news-hbo-hit-giving-colin-farrells-career-a-boost-video.htm (Accessed March 2015).

3. *Ibid*.

4. "Elevator Murder Experiment," *YouTube*, March 4, 2013, www.youtube.com/watch?v=qo6Jzh7SHRA (Accessed March 2015).

5. Steve Dent, "Google Glass' Now-like UI Finally Revealed, Just Accept and Say 'Ok,'" *Engadget*, February 20, 2013, www.engadget.com/2013/02/20/google-glass-how-it-feels-video (Accessed March 2015).

6. Jared Newman, "Ouya Ships March 28 to Kickstarter Backers, More Exclusives Coming," *TIME*, March 1, 2013, http://techland.time.com/2013/03/01/ouya-ships-march-28-to-kickstarter-backers-more-exclusives-coming (Accessed March 2015).

7. Ice Bucket Challenge, *ALS Association*, www.alsa.org/fight-als/ice-bucket-challenge.html (Accessed March 2015).

8. Andrew Johnson, "As Card Firms Try Social Media, Critics Keep Watch," *Wall Street Journal*, March 23, 2012, http://online.wsj.com/article/SB10001424052702304724404577297860607013698.html (Accessed March 2015); "Chase Freedom," *Facebook*, www.facebook.com/ChaseFreedom (Accessed March 2015).

9. The AIDA concept is based on the classic research of E. K. Strong Jr. as theorized in *The Psychology of Selling and Advertising* (New York: McGraw-Hill, 1925) and "Theories of Selling," *Journal of Applied Psychology*, 9, 1925, 75–86; "AIDA Communications Model Attention, Interest, Desire and Action," *Learn Marketing*, www.learnmarketing.net/AIDA.html (Accessed March 2015).

10. "How Many People in America Own an iPad?" *Answers*, http://wiki.answers.com/Q/How_many_people_in_America_own_an_iPad?#slide=2 (Accessed March 2015).

11. Thomas E. Barry and Daniel J. Howard, "A Review and Critique of the Hierarchy of Effects in Advertising," *International Journal of Advertising*, 9, 1990, 121–135.

12. Diana Reese, "Why Is Michelle Obama Praising Wal-Mart in Springfield, Mo.?" *Washington Post*, March 1, 2013, www.washingtonpost.com/blogs/she-the-people/wp/2013/03/01/why-is-michelle-obama-praising-walmart-in-springfield-mo (Accessed March 2015).

16

1. "Marketers" *Advertising Age 2015 Edition Marketing Fact Pack*, December 29, 2014, 6.

2. *Ibid.*

3. Darryl K. Taft, "IBM's Not-so-secret Weapon: Big Data," *eWeek*, February 26, 2013, www.eweek.com/database/ibms-not-so-secret-weapon-big-data-marketing (Accessed March 2015).

4. "The World's Most Valuable Brands," *Forbes*, www.forbes.com/powerful-brands/ (Accessed March 2015).

5. "How Americans Use Leisure Time," *Advertising Age 2015 Edition Marketing Fact Pack*, December 29, 2014, 31.

6. "Time Spent Using Media," *Advertising Age 2015 Edition Marketing Fact Pack*, December 29, 2014, 17.

7. Matthew Sparkes, "iPhone Owners Admit Having 'Blind Loyalty' to Apple," *Telegraph*, February 12, 2014, www.telegraph.co.uk/technology/apple/10632787/iPhone-owners-admit-having-blind-loyalty-to-Apple.html (Accessed February 18, 2014).

8. "25 largest US Advertisers," *Advertising Age 2015 Edition Marketing Fact Pack*, December 29, 2014, 8.

9. David Griner, "Oreo Surprises 26 Million Facebook Fans with Gay Pride Post," *Adweek*, June 25, 2012, www.adweek.com/adfreak/oreo-surprises-26-million-facebook-fans-gay-pride-post-141440 (Accessed March 2015).

10. Oussama Jebali, "First Interactive Print Ad Featuring LED Light and Battery by Motorola," *Esprit Mobile*, January 21, 2014, http://espritmobile.com/first-interactive-print-ad-featuring-led-light-and-battery-by-motorola/ (Accessed March 2015).

11. "'Shopping Carts' Commercial—21st Century Auto Insurance: Same Great Coverage for Less," *YouTube*, February 22, 2012, www.youtube.com/watch?v=CDoAmgIfj_U (Accessed March 2015).

12. *Ibid.*

13. John Babish, "Ithaca, NY Company, Bionexus, Introduces First Natural Skin Care Lotion for Dogs Containing Standardized Nigella Sativa Extracts," *PRNewswire*, April 17, 2012, www.facebook.com/permalink.php?id=118344488181338&story_fbid=419853818042564 (Accessed March 2015).

14. "Bag Designer Uses Video to Teach Counterfeiters," *Will Video For Food*, January 19, 2014, http://willvideoforfood.com/2014/01/19/bag-designer-uses-video-to-teach-counterfeiters/ (Accessed March 2015); "The Saddleback Story," *Saddleback Leather*, www.saddlebackleather.com/Saddleback-Story (Accessed March 2015).

15. Lauren Cleave, "What Do We Really Think about Humour in Advertising?" http://adgrad.co.uk/?author=4 (Accessed March 2015).

16. Neil King Jr., "Anti-Obama Ads Take Elegiac Tone," *Wall Street Journal*, May 4, 2012, http://online.wsj.com/article/SB10001424052702303877604577383950339656854.html (Accessed March 2015).

17. "The Best Ads of 2014," *Adweek*, www.adweek.com/news-gallery/advertising-branding/10-best-ads-2014-161692 (Accessed March 2015).

18. "Media – Share of Ad Spending by Medium," *Advertising Age 2015 Edition Marketing Fact Book*, December 29, 2014, 16.

19. *Ibid.*

20. Alex Kantrowitz, "$70 Billion TV Ad Market Easing into Digital Direction," *Advertising Age*, October 14, 2013, http://adage.com/article/media/70-billion-tv-ad-market-eases-digital-direction/244699/ (Accessed March 2015).

21. Jeanine Poggi, "TV Ad Prices: Football Is Still King," *Advertising Age*, October 20, 2013, http://adage.com/article/media/tv-ad-prices-football-king/244832/ (Accessed March 2015).

22. Jeanine Poggi, "Most Pricey TV Buy: A Spot in NFL," *Advertising Age*, February 28, 2015, http://gaia.adage.com/images/bin/pdf/TV_pricing_chart_for_web.pdf (Accessed March 19, 2015).

23. Ingrid Lunden, "Digital Ads Will Be 22% Of All U.S. Ad Spend In 2013, Mobile Ads 3.7%; Total Global Ad Spend In 2013 $503B," *TechCrunch*, September 30, 2013, http://www.convergemg.com/digital-ads-will-be-22-of-all-u-s-ad-spend-in-2013-mobile-ads-3-7-total-global-ad-spend-in-2013-503b/ (Accessed March 2015).

24. David Kaplan, "For Turner Digital, Audience Buying Risk Outweighs Reward," *AdExchanger*, October 9, 2012, www.adexchanger.com/online-advertising/for-turner-digital-audience-buying-risk-outweighs-reward (Accessed March 2015).

25. "IAB Internet Advertising Revenue Report: 2012 Full Year Results," *PricewaterhouseCoopers*, April 2013, www.iab.net/media/file/IAB_Internet_Advertising_Revenue_Report_FY_2012.pdf (Accessed March 2015).

26. "Most popular Facebook Games in February 2015," *Statista*, www.statista.com/statistics/267003/most-popular-social-games-on-facebook-based-on-daily-active-users/ (Accessed March 2015).

27. "Facebook vs. Non-Facebook Social Network Gaming Ecosystem and Market Analysis 2013 - 2018," *MarketWatch*, February 4, 2014, www.marketwatch.com/story/facebook-vs-non-facebook-social-network-gaming-ecosystem-and-market-analysis-2013-2018-2014-02-04 (Accessed March 2015).

28. Joanna Brenner, "Pew Internet: Mobile," *Pew Research Center*, January 31, 2013, http://pewinternet.org/Commentary/2012/February/Pew-Internet-Mobile.aspx (Accessed March 2015).

29. Alex Kantrowitz, "Mobile Ad Revenue Explodes, Finally," *Advertising Age*, December 16, 2013, 6.

30. Owen Thomas, "New Marissa Mayer's Complaint about Yahoo's Hold Music Has Turned into a Music Video," *Business Insider*, February 4, 2013, www.businessinsider.com/yahoo-earnings-hold-music-video-snow-rapper-2013-2 (Accessed March 2015).

31. John Moulding, "ABC Proves the Value of the Unified TV/Digital Ad Buy," *Videonet*, October 23, 2013, www.v-net.tv/abc-proves-the-value-of-the-unified-tvdigital-ad-buy/ (Accessed March 2015).

32. Kathy Crosett, "Online Product Placement to Increase," *Ad-ology*, January 10, 2013, www.marketingforecast.com/archives/22200 (Accessed March 2015).

33. "US Ad Spending Forecast from Zenith Optimedia," *Advertising Age 2015 Edition Marketing Fact Pack*, December 29, 2014, 14.

34. *Ibid.*

35. Jennifer Wang, "10 Marketing Masterworks," *Entrepreneur*, February 18, 2013, www.entrepreneur.com/article/225462 (Accessed March 2015).

36. Edmund Lawler, "The Rise of Experiential Marketing," *Advertising Age*, November 18, 2013, C1–C2.

37. Philip Caulfield, "Web Pranksters Hijack Restaurant's Mountain Dew Naming Contest," *New York Daily News*, August 15, 2012, www.nydailynews.com/news/national/web-pranksters-hijack-mountain-dew-online-crowdsourced-naming-effort-new-green-apple-flavored-soda-article-1.1136204 (Accessed March 2015).

38. "Inmar 2014 Coupon Trends – Year End 2013," *Inmar*, February 2014, http://go.inmar.com/rs/inmar/images/Inmar_2014_Coupon_Trends_Report.pdf (Accessed March 2015).

39. Caitlin McGarry, "Pay by Hashtag: Twitter Wants to Get Inside Your Wallet," *TechHive*, January 24, 2014, www.techhive.com/article/2090822/pay-by-hashtag-twitter-wants-to-get-inside-your-wallet.html (Accessed March 2015); Andrew R. Johnson, "@AmericanExpress Tries #Deals via Twitter," *Wall Street Journal*, March 7, 2012, www.wsj.com/articles/SB10001424052970204781804577267402969728444 (Accessed March 2015).

40. Donna L. Montaldo, "How to Avoid the Rebate Rip-off," *About.com*, http://couponing.about.com/od/bargainshoppingtips/a/hub_rebate.htm (Accessed March 2015).

41. Martin Moylan, "Retailers' Loyalty Programs Popular with Consumers," *Minnesota Public Radio*, January 2, 2013, http://minnesota.publicradio.org/display/web/2013/01/02/business/retail-rewards-programs (Accessed March 2015).

42. Elizabeth Holmes, "At Bloomies, Loyalty for All," *Wall Street Journal*, February 24, 2012, B5.

43. Kelly Short, "Study Shows In-store Sampling Events Outperform Other Top In-store Marketing Tactics," *Interactions*, February 28, 2013, www.interactionsmarketing.com/news/?p=352 (Accessed March 2015).

44. Jim Tierney, "Study Shows Most Customers Make Purchase Decisions In the Store," *Loyalty360*, November 11, 2013, http://loyalty360.org/resources/article/study-shows-most-customers-make-purchase-decisions-in-the-store (Accessed March 2015).

45. Don Davis, "Consumers Redeem 141% More Digital Coupons in 2013," *Internet Retailer*, January 16, 2014, www.internetretailer.com/2014/01/16/consumers-redeem-141-more-digital-coupons-2013 (Accessed March 2015).

46. Rachel King, "Google Trying out Real-time, Targeted Digital Coupons with Zavers," *ZDNet*, January 11, 2013, www.zdnet.com/google-trying-out-real-time-targeted-digital-coupons-with-zavers-7000009722/ (Accessed March 2015).

47. "Zero Moment of Truth (ZMOT)," *Google*, www.thinkwithgoogle.com/collections/zero-moment-truth.html (Accessed March 2015).

17

1. "Nordstrom Careers," *Nordstrom*, http://about.nordstrom.com/careers/ (Accessed March 2015).

2. "Personal Shoppers," *Bloomingdales*, www1.bloomingdales.com/about/shopping/personal.jsp (Accessed March 2015).

3. "What is LinkedIn?" *LinkedIn*, www.linkedin.com/static?key=what_is_linkedin&trk=hb_what (Accessed March 2015).

4. "Sales Navigator Product Datasheet," *LinkedIn*, https://business.linkedin.com/sales-solutions/site-forms/sales-navigator-datasheet (Accessed March 2015); "Featured Statistics – Brands," *Socialbakers*, www.socialbakers.com/statistics/facebook/pages/total/brands/ (Accessed April 7, 2015).

5. Alex Hisaka, "The 6-step Guide to Successful Social Selling on LinkedIn – Sales Solutions Blog," *LinkedIn*, January 22, 2015, http://sales.linkedin.com/blog/the-6-step-guide-to-successful-social-selling-on-linkedin/ (Accessed March 2015).

6. "Social Selling Tips: 10 Actionable Sale Tips LinkedIn Sales Solutions," *LinkedIn*, https://business.linkedin.com/sales-solutions/resources/social-selling/top-sales-tips (Accessed March 2015).

7. "Lead Qualification Response Management Teleservices," *Salesify*, www.salesify.com/lead-qualification (Accessed March 2015).

8. Kim Garst, "Find Prospects on Social Media and Turn Them into Customers," *Huffington Post*, February 18, 2014, www.huffingtonpost.com/kim-garst/find-prospects-on-social-_b_4785711.html (Accessed March 2015).

9. "Leadership Program," *General Electric*, www.ge.com/careers/students/clp/index.html(Accessed March 2015).

10. Linda Ray, "Examples of Cultural Differences in Business," *Demand Media*, http://smallbusiness.chron.com/examples-cultural-differences-business-21958.html (Accessed March 2015).

11. Weitz, B., Castleberry, S., and Tanner, J., *Selling*, Notebooks, 8th edition, 2014.

12. "Oracle PeopleSoft Applications," *Oracle*, www.oracle.com/us/products/applications/peoplesoft-enterprise/overview/index.htm (Accessed March 2015).

13. Peter Criscione, "Mary Kay's Top Salespeople are Pretty in Pink," *Brampton Guardian*, February 25, 2014, www.mississauga.com/news-story/4384280-mary-kay-s-top-salespeople-are-pretty-in (Accessed March 2015).

14. Paul Greenberg, "CRM Watchlist 2014 Winners: Upgraded to a Suite," *ZDNet*, February 17, 2014, www.zdnet.com/article/crm-watchlist-2014-winners-upgraded-to-a-suite-part-i/#! (Accessed March 2015).

15. "Revise Your Merchandising Strategy to Retain Customers in 2014," *Quantisense*, February 13, 2014, www.quantisense.com/blog/revise-your-merchandising-strategy-to-retain-customers-in-2014 (Accessed March 2015).

16. Heather Clancy, "7 Apps to Take Your Customer Loyalty Program Mobile," *ZDNet*, January 27, 2014, www.zdnet.com/7-apps-to-take-your-customer-loyalty-program-mobile-7000025654/ (Accessed February 19, 2014); Jessica Bruder, "A Customer Loyalty Program (From Some of the Folks Who Brought You Groupon)," *New York Times*, February 21, 2012, http://boss.blogs.nytimes.com/2012/02/21/a-customer-loyalty-program-from-some-of-the-folks-who-brought-you-groupon (Accessed March 2015).

17. Saul Perez, "Why Cross-Selling is Part of Wells Fargo's Strategy," *Market Realist*, October 10, 2014, http://finance.yahoo.com/news/why-cross-selling-part-wells-130018022.html;_ylt=aolevx (Accessed March 2015).

18. "About Recommendations," *Amazon*, www.amazon.com/gp/help/customer/display.html/ref=help_search_1-1?ie=UTF8&nodeId=16465251&qid=1426340118&sr=1-1 (Accessed March 2015).

18

1. "Social Media and the New Reality for Law Practice," *LegalWire*, February 24, 2013, www.legalwire.co.uk/?dt_portfolio=legal-profession-2-0-social-media-and-the-new-reality-for-law-firms (Accessed March 2015).

2. "Twitter: Most Followers," *FriendOrFollow*, http://friendorfollow.com/twitter/most-followers/ (Accessed March 2015).

3. Shanyndi Raice, Mike Ramsey, and Sam Schechner, "Facebook Gains Two Big Advertisers' Support," *Wall Street Journal*, June 20, 2012, B6.

4. "The 10 Most Liked Brands on Facebook; *Mashable*, September 6, 2013, http://mashable.com/2013/09/06/facebook-brands-likes/ (Accessed March 2015).

5. "Flo, the Progressive Girl," *Facebook*, www.facebook.com/flotheprogressivegirl (Accessed March 2015); Dale Buss, "Progressive Just Keeps Going with the Flo, Refreshing Its Effective Mascot," *Brandchannel*, November 5, 2013, www.brandchannel.com/home/post/2013/11/05/Progressive-Flo-110513.aspx (Accessed March 2015).

6. Lululemon Practiced Text Book Crisis PR During Yoga Pants Frenzy," *PR Daily*, www.prdaily.com/Main/Articles/Lululemon_practiced_textbook_crisis_PR_during_yoga_14137.aspx# (Accessed March 2015).

7. David Moth, "Six Brands that Have Been Busy Experimenting with Google Hangouts," *Econsultancy*, http://econsultancy.com/us/blog/62774-six-brands-that-have-been-busy-experimenting-with-google-hangouts (Accessed March 2015).

8. "5 Terrific Examples of Company Social Media Policies," *HireRabbit*, http://blog.hirerabbit.com/5-terrific-examples-of-company-social-media-policies/ (Accessed March 2015).

9. Tessa Stuart, "Secrets of a Celebrity Twitter Coach," *BuzzFeed*, February 19, 2013, www.buzzfeed.com/tessastuart/secrets-of-a-celebrity-twitter-coach (Accessed March 2015).

10. Cory Edwards, "A Shift in Social Media Training for Employees," *Adobe*, December 17, 2013, http://blogs.adobe.com/digitalmarketing/social-media/a-social-shift-in-social-media-training-for-employees/ (Accessed March 2015).

11. Parmy Olson, "Teenagers Say Goodbye to Facebook and Hello to Messenger Apps," *The Guardian*, November 9, 2013, www.theguardian.com/technology/2013/nov/10/teenagers-messenger-apps-facebook-exodus (Accessed March 2015).

12. "Useful Social Media Statistics for 2015," *Our Social Times*, December 22, 2014, http://oursocialtimes.com/8-useful-social-media-statistics-for-2015/ (Accessed April 7, 2015).

13. *Ibid.*

14. "SBANC Newsletter—June 5th, 2012," *International Council for Small Business*, June 5, 2012, www.icsb.org/article.asp?messageID=983 (Accessed March 2015).

15. Joanna Brenner, "Pew Internet: Mobile," *Pew Research Center*, January 31, 2013, http://pewinternet.org/Commentary/2012/February/Pew-Internet-Mobile.aspx (Accessed March 2015).

16. Steven Musil, "U.S. Tablet Usage Hits 'Critical Mass' ComScore Reports," *CNET*, June 10, 2012, http://news.cnet.com/8301-13579_3-57450079-37/u.s-tablet-usage-hits-critical-mass-comscore-reports (Accessed March 2015).

17. Sid Gandotra, "Why Social Commerce Matters," *Social Media Today*, November 6, 2012, http://socialmediatoday.com/sid-gandotra/974961/social-commerce-socialmedia-ecommerce (Accessed March 2015).

18. Janessa Rivera, "Gartner Says CRM Will Be at the Heart of Digital Initiatives for Years to Come," *Gartner*, February 12, 2014, www.gartner.com/newsroom/id/2665215 (Accessed March 2015).

19. Lauren Indvik, "7 Species of Social Commerce," *Mashable*, May 10, 2013, http://mashable.com/2013/05/10/social-commerce-definition/ (Accessed April 7, 2015).

20. "Giveaway!!! Pin it to Win it! An iPad Mini for Two Lucky Winners!!!" *Favorite Family Recipes*, March 10, 2013, www.favfamilyrecipes.com/2013/03/giveaway-pin-it-to-win-it-an-ipad-mini-for-two-lucky-winners.html (Accessed March 2015); Lauren Indvik, "How Brands Are Using Promotions to Market on Pinterest," *Mashable*, March 7, 2012, http://mashable.com/2012/03/07/pinterest-brand-marketing (Accessed March 2015).

21. *Ibid.*

22. "Complimentary White Paper: Forrester's US Interactive Marketing Forecast through 2016," *Adobe Marketing Cloud*, http://success.adobe.com/en/na/programs/products/digitalmarketing/migration12/1208_21408_forrester_interactive_marketing_forecast.html (Accessed March 2015).

23. Eric Mosley, "Crowdsource your Performance Reviews," *Harvard Business Review*, June 15, 2013, http://blogs.hbr.org/cs/2012/06/crowdsource_your_performance_r.html (Accessed March 2015).

24. "Photograph for Ellie Goulding with HP Connected Music," *Talenthouse*, www.talenthouse.com/photograph-for-ellie-goulding-and-hp-connected-music#description (Accessed March 2015).

25. "Paid Media Marketing," *Greenlight*, www.greenlightdigital.com/paid-media (Accessed March 2015).

26. *Ibid.*

27. Russell Working, "Most Unhappy with Social Media Measurement, Survey Says," *Ragan Communications*, www.ragan.com/Main/Articles/Most_unhappy_with_social_media_measurement_survey_45919.aspx (Accessed March 2015).

28. "Key Performance Indicators," *Intrafocus*, June 2013, www.intrafocus.com/wp-content/uploads/2014/06/Key-Performance-Indicators.docx (Accessed March 2015).

29. Andy Williams, "How Social Media Has Changed the Way We Complain," *Koozai*, February 25, 2013, www.koozai.com/blog/branding/reputation-management/how-social-media-has-changed-the-way-we-complain (Accessed March 2015); Bob Fine, "How Social Media Has Changed Politics: It's Not Just Tactics," *The Social Media Monthly*, January 18, 2013, http://thesocialmediamonthly

.com/how-social-media-has-changed-politics-its-not
-just-tactics (Accessed March 2015); "How Social
Media Has Changed the Way We Communicate,"
Information Gateway, January 24, 2013, www
.informationgateway.org/social-media-changed
-communicate (Accessed March 2015).

30. Charlene Li and Josh Bernoff, *Groundswell:
Winning in a World Transformed by Social Tech-
nologies*, revised ed. (Boston: Harvard Business
Press, 2011).

31. Gina Sverdlov, "Global Social Technographics
Update: US and EU Mature, Emerging Markets
Show Lots of Activity," *Forrester*, January 4, 2012,
http://blogs.forrester.com/gina_sverdlov/12-01-04
-global_social_technographics_update_2011_us
_and_eu_mature_emerging_markets_show_lots
_of_activity (Accessed March 2015); "What's the
Social Technographics Profile of Your Customer?"
Forrester Empowered, http://empowered.forrester
.com/tool_consumer.html (Accessed March 2015).

32. Paige ONeil, "Forrester: Social Media Use
in US and EU Maturing, More Passive Than
Emerging Markets," http://paigeoneill.com/2012
/01/05/forrester-social-media-use-in-us-and-eu
-maturing-more-passive-than-emerging-markets/
(Accessed March 2015).

33. Shanna Mallon, "Should Every Company Have
a Blog?" *The Media Revolution*, January 30, 2014,
www.blogworld.com/2014/01/30/should-every
-company-have-a-blog/ (Accessed March 2015).

34. Mark Schaefer, "The 10 Best Big Company
Blogs in the World," *Businesses Grow*, January 12,
2015, www.businessesgrow.com/2015/01/12/best
-company-blogs/ (Accessed March 2015).

35. Lauren Drell, "The Quick and Dirty Guide to
Tumblr for Small Business," *Mashable*, February 18,
2012, http://mashable.com/2012/02/18/tumblr-small
-biz-guide (Accessed March 2015).

36. Chris Erasmus, "The Voting Hub Facebook
Page," *Threadless*, February 16, 2014, www
.threadless.com/forum/post/990069/the_voting
_hub_facebook_page/ (Accessed March 2015).

37. Josh Bersin, "Facebook Vs. LinkedIn—What's
the Difference?" *Forbes*, May 21, 2012, www.forbes
.com/sites/joshbersin/2012/05/21/facebook-vs-linkedin
-whats-the-difference (Accessed March 2015).

38. "Top Sites," *Alexa*, www.alexa.com/topsites
(Accessed March 2015).

39. Rob Walker, "How Reddit's Ask Me Anything
Became Part of the Mainstream Media Circuit,"
Yahoo, March 13, 2013, http://news.yahoo.com
/how-reddit-s-ask-me-anything-became-part-of-the
-mainstream-media-circuit--130755591.html
(Accessed March 2015); "Top Scoring Links:
IAmA," *Reddit*, www.reddit.com/r/IAmA/top/
(Accessed March 2015).

40. Tony Nguyen, "The Importance of Social
Bookmarking and RSS in SEO," *Business Review
Center*, October 18, 2012, http://businessreviewcenter
.com/social-bookmarking-and-rss (Accessed
March 2015).

41. Jordan Slabaugh, "4 Ways to Get Customers on
Your Side," *iMedia Connection*, January 29, 2014,
www.imediaconnection.com/content/35808.asp
(Accessed March 2015).

42. "Yelp Elite Event: Tiki Beach Party at Le Lab"
Yelp, www.yelp.com/biz/yelp-elite-event-tiki-beach
-party-at-le-lab-montr%C3%A9al (Accessed
March 2015).

43. "Second Life Grid Survey—Economic
Metrics," *GridSurvey*, March 15, 2013, http://
gridsurvey.com/economy.php (Accessed
March 2015).

44. Emanuel Maiberg, "Top 25 Facebook Games
of May 2013," *Inside Social Games*, May 1, 2013,
www.insidesocialgames.com/2013/05/01/the-top
-25-facebook-games-of-may-2013/ (Accessed
March 2015).

45. Eddie Makuch, "93 Million People Play
Candy Crush Saga Daily—Do You?" *Gamespot*,
February 18, 2014, www.gamespot.com/articles
/93-million-people-play-candy-crush-saga-daily
-do-you/1100-6417819/ (Accessed March 2015).

46. Chelsea Stark, "Microtransactions and Digital
Sales Are Dominating Game Developers' Profits,"
Mashable, January 15, 2015, http://mashable.com
/2015/01/15/game-developer-survey-2015/ (Accessed
April 7, 2015).

47. Paul Tassl, "Kim Kardashian May Make $85
Million From Her Video Game," *Forbes*, July 17,
2014, www.forbes.com/sites/insertcoin/2014/07/17
/kim-kardashian-may-make-85-million-from-her
-video-game/ (Accessed April 7, 2015).

48. "Global Mobile Statistics 2013 Part A: Mobile
Subscribers; Handset Market Share; Mobile
Operators," *mobiThinking*, March 2013, http://
mobithinking.com/mobile-marketing-tools/latest
-mobile-stats/a (Accessed March 2015).

49. Ingrid Lunden, "Digital Ads Will Be 22%
Of All U.S. Ad Spend In 2013, Mobile Ads 3.7%;
Total Global Ad Spend In 2013 $503B," *Tech-
Crunch*, September 1, 2013, http://techcrunch
.com/2013/09/30/digital-ads-will-be-22-of-all-u-s
-ad-spend-in-2013-mobile-ads-3-7-total-gobal
-ad-spend-in-2013-503b-says-zenithoptimedia/
(Accessed March 2015).

50. "Modify QR Code Watch—Because Simply
Reading Time on Your Watch Is Soooo 2011,"
Modify Watches February 23, 2012, www
.modifywatches.com/blog/qr-code-watch (Accessed
March 2015).

51. "The Samsung Galaxy Tab 4 NOOK 7.0,"
Barnes and Noble, www.barnesandnoble.com/p
/samsung-galaxy-tab-4-nook-7-inch-barnes-noble
/1119732448 (Accessed March 2015).

52. "The Next Big Thing is Almost Here –
Samsung Galaxy S6," *T-Mobile*, www.t-mobile.com
/cell-phones/samsung-galaxy-s-6-edge.html
(Accessed March 2015).

53. Daniel Howley, "The Best iPhone Widgets
You're Not Using," January 24, 2015, www.yahoo
.com/tech/the-best-iphone-widgets-youre-not-using
-108954809304.html (Accessed March 2015).

19

1. "Hershey Price Hike Tests Theory That
Americans Love Chocolate at Any Price," *Wall
Street Journal*, July 18, 2014, http://blog.wsj.com
/moneybeat/2014/07/18/hershey-price-hike-tests
-theory-that-americans-love-chocolate-at-any-price
/html (Accessed February 26, 2015).

2. "Can You Trust That Web Price?" *Wall Street
Journal*, October 23, 2014, B1.

3. "Personalized Pricing," *Business Week*, January 2,
2014, 47–48; Koert van Ittersum, Brian Wansink,

Joost Pennings, and Daniel Sheehan, "Smart
Shopping Carts: How Real Time Feedback
Influences Spending," *Journal of Marketing*,
November 2013, 21–36.

4. "SFPark Called a Success, Will Expand
Throughout the City," June 21, 2014, *SFGate*,
www.sfgate.com/bayarea/article/SFpark-called
-a-success-willexpand-throughout-5568645.php
(Accessed February 26, 2015).

5. "How Much Did You Pay For That Lipstick?"
Forbes, April 14, 2015, 46–49.

6. "Best Buy Put Off By Showrooming, Guarantees
Low Price," *Market Realist*, January 19, 2015,
http://marketrealist.com/2015/01/best-buy-put-off
-by-showrooming-guarantees-low-price/ (Accessed
February 26, 2015).

7. Ryan Hamilton and Alexander Chernev, "Low
Prices Are Just the Beginning: Price Image in Retail
Management," *Journal of Marketing*, November
2013, 1–20.

8. *Ibid.*

9. Keith Coulter and Anne Roggeveen, "Price
Number Relationships and Deal Processing
Fluency: The Effects of Approximation Sequence
and Number Multiples," *Journal of Marketing
Research*, February 2014, 69–82.

10. "Developing a Sustainable Standard for
Products," *Walmart*, http://corporate.walmart.com
/global-responsibility/environment-sustainability
/sustainability-index (Accessed February 26, 2015).

11. Jennifer Chu, "Flying the Not-so-friendly
Skies" *MIT*, January 30, 2014, http://web.mit/edu
/newsoffice/2014/flying-the-not-so-friendly-skies
-0130.html (Accessed February 26, 2015).

12. Aylin Aydini, Marco Bertini, and Anja
Lambrecht, "Price Promotion for Emotional
Impact," *Journal of Marketing*, July 2014,
80–96.

13. Ayelet Eneezy, Uri Eneezy, and Dominique
Olié Lauga, "A Reference-Dependent Model of the
Price-Quality Heuristic," *Journal of Marketing
Research*, April 2014, 153–164.

14. "Future of Private Labels Looks Bright,"
McLoone, January 31, 2014, www.mccloone.com
/blog/future-of-private-labels-looks-bright/
(Accessed February 27, 2015).

15. "Spirit Airlines: The Power of a Clear Strategy,"
Strongbrands, February 2, 2015, http://timcalkins
.com/branding-insights/spirit-airlines-power-clear
-strategy/ (Accessed February 28, 2015).

16. "Free Shipping Is Getting More Expensive,"
Wall Street Journal, October 22, 2014, www.wsj
.com/articles/free-shipping-is-going-to-cost-you
-more-1414003507 (Accessed February 28, 2015).

17. *Ibid.*

18. Jan Wieseke, Sascha Alavi, and Johannes Habel,
"Willing to Pay More, Eager to Pay Less: The Role
of Consumer Loyalty in Price Negotiations," *Journal
of Marketing*, November 2014, 17–37.

19. "The Psychology Behind the Sweet Spots of
Pricing," *Fast Company*, www.fastcompany.com
/1826172/psychology-behind-sweet-spots-pricing
(Accessed February 28, 2015).

INDEX

B-to-C marketing. *See also* marketing
 comparison of with B-to-B
  marketing, 116
B2B marketing. *See* B-to-B marketing
Baby boomers, 54–55
 market segmentation and, 136
Back stock, 251
Bad Ad program (FDA), 63
Baidu Migrate, 156
Bait pricing, 359
Bakespace.com, 324
Bargain pricing, 8
Barnes & Noble, use of near field
  communication by, 338
Barter, 86
Base price, tactics for fine tuning,
  355–360
Basic research, 59
Basing-point pricing, 358
Baydin, 27
Bayer HealthCare, use of supplier
  relationship management process
  at, 224–225
Beacons, 258, 304, 337
Beats Electronics
 product development strategy of, 16
 strategic planning of, 19–20
Behavioral norms, 30
Behavioral targeting, 63, 161
BehaviorScan, 169
Belly, 319
Ben & Jerry's, 42
 mission of, 21–22
Benefit segmentation, 140
Best Buy, 249
 price match program of, 349
 social media policy of, 324
 use of reverse channels by, 237
Bidz, 350
Big data, 154–155
 analyzing, 155–156
 improving supply chain operations
  using, 231–232
 use of analytics by retailers, 258
Big Fish Games, 325
BlackBerry, 6
 strategic strategy of, 18
Blind loyalty, 282
Blitz, George, 23
Blogs, 331–332
Blue Bell ice cream, 24
Bluetooth marketing, 337
Boeing, 123
 competition and, 65
Boomerang, 27
BorgWarner, use of reciprocity by, 124

Boston Consulting Group model, 17–19
Botox, adjacent innovation, 17
Boycotts, 74
Brainstorming, 193
Brand, 178
Brand cannibalization, 253
Brand equity, 178–179
 power of, 179
Brand extensions, 94
Brand identity, 111
Brand loyalty, 56, 178–179, 282
Brand mark, 178
Brand name, 178
Branding, 178
 benefits of, 178–179
 global issues in, 185
 strategies for, 179–181
 trademarks, 181–182
Brazil, role of in global economy, 73
Break-even analysis, 347
Break-even pricing, 347–348
Bribery, 38
BRIC countries, role of in global
  economy, 73
Bristol-Myers Squibb, corporate social
  responsibility of, 43–44
Britannica, 11
Broadcast media, advertising on,
  289–290
Brokers, 233
Brothers Cider, packaging changes
  of, 183
Bruegger's Bagels, cooperative branding
  strategy of, 181
Buick, market orientation of, 5–6
Build, 19
Building relationships, 9
Building scenarios, 59–60
Bureau of Competition (FTC), 63
Bureau of Consumer Protection
  (FTC), 63
Bureau of Economics (FTC), 63
Burger King, global product
  adaptation, 83
Burton Snowboards, 192
Business
 cultural considerations, 72
 defining the mission, 21–22
 defining the primary goal, 12
 ethical behavior in, 34–38
 global marketing by individual
  firms, 80–82
 importance of marketing to, 13
 most ethical companies, 37–38
 organizational definition of, 10–11
 regulation of, 73

Business analysis, 193–194
 common questions, 194
Business buying behavior, 126–127
 business ethics, 129
 buying centers, 127–128
 buying situations, 128–129
 evaluative criteria, 128
Business customers
 governments, 120–121
 institutions, 121
 producers, 120
 resellers, 120
Business ethics
 B-to-B interactions, 129
 morality and, 35
Business marketing, 114. *See also*
  B-to-B marketing
Business markets, bases for
  segmenting, 141
Business position, 19
Business product distributors, 120
Business products, 114
 accessory equipment, 125
 business services, 126
 channels for, 235–236
 component parts, 126
 major equipment, 125
 processed materials, 126
 raw materials, 125
 supplies, 126
Business services, 126
Business *vs.* consumer markets, 122
 concentration of customers, 124
 demand, 122–123
 distribution structure, 124
 nature of buying in, 124
 negotiations, 124
 number of customers, 124
 primary promotion method, 125
 purchase volume, 123
 reciprocity, 124
 use of leasing, 124–125
Business-focused salespeople, 302–303
Business-to-business marketing. *See*
  B-to-B marketing
Buyer behavior
 defining the target market, 26
 values and, 49
Buyer for export, 81
Buying centers, 124, 127
 implications of for the marketing
  manager, 127–128
 roles in, 127–128
Buying decisions, types of and the
  promotional mix, 277
Buying power, 307

Personal interviews, 157
  computer-assisted, 158
Personal selling, 12, 270–271, 303–304
  comparison of with advertising/sales
    promotion, 304
  impact of technology on, 312
  sales process, 306–312
Personality, influence of on consumer
    buying decisions, 109
Personnel, retail operations, 256
Persuasive labeling, 183–184
Persuasive promotion, 267–268
  product life cycle and, 276–277
Pfizer, R&D spending at, 188
Philanthropic responsibility, 39–40
Philosophies of marketing, 4
  market orientation, 5–6
  production orientation, 4
  sales orientation, 4–5
  sales vs. market orientations, 7–12
  societal orientation, 6
Phones 4U, 119
Photo sharing sites, 334
Physical distribution strategies, 27
Physiological needs, 112
Piggybacking, 64
Pinterest, 50, 334
  gathering data from, 154
  social commerce using, 326
Pioneering advertising, 283–284
Place (distribution) strategies, 27
  adaptation for global markets, 84
  nonprofit organizations and decisions
    regarding, 215
  retail operations, 253–255
  services, 211
Place utility, 232–233
Planned obsolescence, 177
Planned purchases, 95
Planning, 20. See also Marketing plans;
    Strategic planning
Plurk, 332
Podcasts, 335
Point-of-purchase (P-O-P) display, 301
Point-of-sale interactions, 317
Police departments, use of big data
    analytics by, 155
Political factors, 22, 60–61
  consumer privacy, 63–64
  federal legislation, 61
  global marketing and, 73–79
  regulatory agencies, 62–63
  state and local laws, 61–62
Polytron Technologies, Switchable Glass
    technology of, 189
Pop-up shops, 255

Population, 52
  baby boomers, 54–55
  Generation X, 54
  Millennials, 54
  specifying for marketing research,
    162–163
  teenagers, 53
  tweens, 52–53
Porsche, concentrated targeting strategy
    of, 144
Portfolio matrix, 17–19
Positioning, 146–147
Positioning bases, 147–148
Possession processing, 209
Post-audit tasks, 28
Postconventional morality, 35
Postpurchase communication, 211–212
Preapproach, 308
Preconventional morality, 35
Predatory pricing, 355
Premiums, 299
Presentation, retail operations,
    255–256
Press relations, 295
Previous experience, purchase
    involvement and, 98
Price, 7
  cost determinant of, 346–348
  defining, 341
  demand determinant of, 344–345
  importance of, 340
  importance of in B-to-B
    interactions, 128
  importance of to marketing
    managers, 342
  relationship of to quality, 351–352
  retail operations, 255
  setting on products, 352
  tactics for fine tuning, 355–360
Price bundling, 359–360
Price discrimination, 355
Price fixing, 354–355
Price lining, 359
Price promotion, 351
Price skimming, 353
Price strategy, 353
PriceGrabber, 350
PricewaterhouseCoopers (PwC), iPlace
    employee innovation system, 191
Pricing
  break-even, 347–348
  demand of large customers, 351
  distribution strategy and, 350
  dynamic, 345–346
  establishing goals for, 352
  markup, 347

nonprofit organizational decisions,
    215–216
  objectives of, 342–344
  stages in product life cycle, 349
  status quo, 344
  strategies, 27
  strategies for global markets, 84–86
  strategy for services, 212
  unrealistic, 8
Primary data, 156–157
  ethnographic research, 161
  experiments, 162
  observation research, 160–161
  survey research, 157–159
  virtual shopping, 161–162
Primary membership groups,
    influence of on consumer buying
    decisions, 104
Pringles, product invention, 83
Print media, advertising in, 288–289
Privacy, online, 64
Private labels, 179–180
Private vs. manufacturers' brands,
    179–180
Privowny, 64
Probability samples, 163
Problem child strategic business units, 18
Processed materials, 126
Procter & Gamble (P&G)
  advertising spending by, 281
  consideration of economic factors
    by, 58
  global marketing standardization, 83
  individual branding practices of, 180
  market segmentation strategies,
    136–137
  mission of, 21
  multisegment targeting strategy
    of, 144
  R&D spending at, 188
  use of Internet to assess customer
    demand, 196
Producers
  factors affecting distribution channel
    choice, 240
  marketing to, 120
Product adaptation, global marketing
    and, 83
Product advertising, 283–284
Product benefits, identification of, 285
Product category, 200
Product decisions
  global marketing, 82–83
  nonprofit organizations, 215
Product design, cost competitive
    advantage and, 23

Product development, 16, 192. *See also*
New-product development process
Product development and
commercialization process, 225
Product differentiation, 77–78, 113,
146–147
Product factors, distribution channel
choice and, 239–240
Product failures, 257
Product identification, 178
Product invention, global marketing
and, 83
Product involvement, 99
Product items, 174
Product life cycle (PLC), 200
decline stage, 202
growth stage, 201–202
introductory stage, 200–201
maturity stage of, 202
stages of and pricing, 349
stages of and the promotional mix,
276–277
Product lines, 174–175
contraction of, 177–178
extensions of, 177
new, 189
width and depth of in retail, 246–247
Product mix, 175–176
width and depth of, 175–176
Product modification, 176–177
Product performance, 8
Product placement, 295
Product positioning, 146–147
Product publicity, 295
Product quality, global competition
and, 65
Product strategies, 27
services, 209–211
Product warranties, 185–186
Product/service differentiation, 23–24
Production innovations, cost
competitive advantage and, 23
Production orientation, 4
Products, 172
adjustments to, 176–178
characteristics of, 199
choosing for retail operations,
252–253
function of packaging of, 182–183
knowledge of, 308
nature of and promotional mix, 276
successful introduction of, 197
Professional services pricing, 358
Profiling, 319
Profit, 342
estimating, 352–353

Profit maximization, 342
Profit-oriented pricing, objectives of,
342–343
Progressive, Facebook presence,
323–324
Project Runway, 19
Promotion, 12, 262
adaptation of for global markets,
83–84
AIDA model, 273–275
ethics and small businesses,
37–38
goals of, 267–268, 273
point-of-purchase, 301
price as a strategy for, 351
product packaging, 183
resources for nonprofit
organizations, 215
retail, 253
role of in marketing mix, 263
strategies, 27
strategies for services, 211–212
strategy for in introductory stage of
PLC, 201
use of in B-to-B market, 125
Promotional allowance, 356
Promotional mix, 268–269
advertising, 269
AIDA model and, 274–275
characteristics of elements in, 272
communication process and,
271–273
content marketing and social
media, 271
factors affecting, 275–279
personal selling, 270–271
public relations, 269–270
sales promotion, 270
Promotional spending, 280
Promotional strategy, 262
Prospecting, 306–307
Protectionist movement, 78
Prototypes, 194
Prunier, Christy, 52
Psychographic segmentation, 139
variables of, 139
Psychographics, 109
defining the target market, 26
Psychological factors
influences of on consumer buying
decisions, 109–113
learning, 112–113
motivation, 111–112
perception, 110–111
Psychological pricing, 359
Public affairs, 295

Public relations, 269–270, 294
major tools, 294–296
managing unfavorable publicity,
296–297
Public relations departments, duties
of, 295
Public service advertisements
(PSAs), 215
Public-private partnerships (PPPs),
228–229
Publicity, 269–270, 294
Pull strategy, 279
Pulsing media schedule, 293
Purchase decisions, 94–95
Purchase involvement, levels of, 98–99
Purchase volume, 123
Purchasers, 106
Purchasing agents, exporters, 81
Purchasing power, 58
Pure research, 59
Purina, 25
Push money, 298
Push strategy, 278
Push *vs.* pull strategy, 279
Pyramid of corporate social
responsibility, 39–40

Q

Quaker Oats, cause-related marketing, 44
Qualifying leads, 307–308
Quality
importance of in B-to-B
interactions, 128
modification, 176
relationship of price to, 351–352
Quality of services, 205
evaluating, 206–207
Quantity discounts, 356
Question mark strategic business units, 18
Questionable practices, ethical decision
making and, 35
Questionnaire design, 159–160
types of questions used for national
market research, 160
Quick Response (QR) codes, 337–338
Quotas, 74
effect of protectionist movement on, 78
sales, 313
Qzone, 325

R

R&D, 192
spending on, 188
Radio, advertising on, 289–290

Target
  advertising campaigns of, 253
  pricing image of, 351
  use of big data analytics by, 258
Target customers, 11–12
Target market, 46, 142
  characteristics of and promotional mix, 277
  defining for retail operations, 252
  describing, 26
  nonprofit organizations, 214–215
  strategies for selecting, 142–145
Target marketing strategies, advantages and disadvantages of, 143
Target return on investment, 343
Targeted marketing communications, 320
Tariffs, 74
Teamwork, 10
Technological factors, 22, 59
  research, 59
  stimulating innovation, 59–60
Technology
  impact of on personal selling, 312
  planning integration and, 221
  use of for selling, 305
Technology products
  tarrifs on, 74
  use of to make purchase decisions, 95
Teenagers, 53
  word-of-mouth marketing by, 198
Telemarketing, 250
Television, advertising on, 290
Test marketing, 195–196
  alternatives to, 196
Text messaging, use of for marketing, 337
Text mining, 328
The Email Game, 27
Third-party logistics companies (3PLs), 227
Three-dimensional printing. *See* 3D printing
Threshold level of perception, 111
Tide detergent, core innovation, 17
Time, strategic alliance with Spring, 118
Time utility, 232–233
Tinder, 325
TinyCo, 31
Tobacco Control Act, 63
TOMS Shoes, 135
Top management
  actions on ethics, 35
  strategic planning at Google, 29
Touch points, 316
Toyota
  advertising spending by, 283
  R&D spending at, 188

Toyota Production System (TPS), 224
Trade agreements, 74–75
  CAFTA, 77
  Doha Round, 76
  European Union, 77–78
  NAFTA, 76–77
  Pacific Alliance, 76
  Trans-Pacific Partnership, 76
  Transatlantic Trade and Investment Partnership, 76
  Uruguay Round, 75–76
Trade allowances, 298, 356
Trade discounts, 356
Trade sales promotion, 297–298
  tools for, 298
Trademarks, 181–182
  violations of, 182
Trading up, 256
Traditional selling, comparison of with relationship selling, 305
Training
  ethics, 36–37
  role of in relationship building, 9
  sales force, 314
  social media, 325
Trans-Pacific Partnership, 76
Transactional functions, 234
Transatlantic Trade and Investment Partnership, 76
Transformational innovation, 17
Trialability, 199
Trust
  earning, 8
  importance of to strategic alliances, 119
Tuff, Geoff, 17
Tumblr, 50, 332
  consumer use of, 325
Tupperware, 249
Tweens, 52–53
  market segmentation and, 135
Twitch, 325
Twitter, 323, 332
  coaches, 325
  consumer use of, 325
  conversationalists, 331
  gathering data from, 154
  use of for B-to-B marketing, 117
  use of for marketing, 50–51
  Vine, 325, 334–335
Two-part pricing, 360

U

U.S. social classes, 103
Uber, 238
Ubid, 350

Ubisoft, new-product development at, 194–195
UCG, diversification strategy of, 16–17
Ultimate Fighting Championship (UFC), brand extensions, 94
Under Armour
  marketing campaign of, 107
  trademark suit of, 182
Undifferentiated targeting strategy, 143
Unfair trade practice acts, 354–355
Unfair trade practices, 354
Uniform delivered pricing, 357
Unilever
  promotion adaptation for global markets, 84
  societal marketing orientation of, 6
Uniqlo, product/service differentiation, 24
Unique selling proposition, 286
United Airlines, cooperative branding strategy of, 180–181
United Nations Global Compact (UNGC), 42
Universal product codes (UPCs), 184–185
Universe, specifying for marketing research, 162–163
Unmeasured media, 280
Unplanned purchases, 95
Unsought products, 174
Upper class, consumer buying behavior of, 102
UPS, environmental sustainability efforts of, 226
Upward mobility, 49
Urban Outfitters, store atmosphere, 255
Uruguay Round, 75–76
Usage-rate segmentation, 140
Used goods retailers, 249
User-curated shopping sites, 326
Utilitarian ethical theory, 33
Utilitarian value, 89–90

V

Value, 7
  consumer perception of, 89
  marketing for, 8
  perception of, 341
Value-based pricing, 255, 357
Values, 34
  American, 49
  global marketing and, 71–72
  influence of on consumer buying decisions, 101
Variable cost, 347

KEY CONCEPTS

1-1 Define the term *marketing*. Marketing is the activity, set of institutions, and processes for creating, communicating, delivering, and exchanging offerings that have value for customers, clients, partners, and society at large. Marketing also requires all facets of a company to work together to pool ideas and resources. One major goal of marketing is to create an exchange. An exchange has five conditions, as listed below. Even if all five conditions are met, however, an exchange might not occur. People engage in marketing whether or not an exchange happens.

Five conditions of exchange

1. There must be at least two parties.

2. Each party has something that might be of value to the other party.

3. Each party is capable of communication and delivery.

4. Each party is free to accept or reject the exchange offer.

5. Each party believes it is appropriate or desirable to deal with the other party.

Zuma Press, Inc./Alamy

Google offers many amenities to its employees, part of the reason Fortune ranked it as the best company to work for in 2012, 2013, and 2014.

1-2 Describe four marketing management philosophies. The role of marketing and the character of marketing activities within an organization are strongly influenced by the organization's marketing philosophy and orientation. A production-oriented organization focuses on the internal capabilities of the firm rather than on the desires and needs of the marketplace. A sales orientation is based on the beliefs that people will buy more products and services if aggressive sales techniques are used and that high sales volumes produce high profits. A market-oriented organization focuses on satisfying customer wants and needs while meeting organizational objectives. A societal marketing orientation goes beyond a market orientation to include the preservation or enhancement of individuals' and society's long-term best interests.

KEY TERMS

1-1
marketing the activity, set of institutions, and processes for creating, communicating, delivering, and exchanging offerings that have value for customers, clients, partners, and society at large

exchange people giving up something in order to receive something else they would rather have

1-2
production orientation a philosophy that focuses on the internal capabilities of the firm rather than on the desires and needs of the marketplace

sales orientation the belief that people will buy more goods and services if aggressive sales techniques are used and that high sales result in high profits

marketing concept the idea that the social and economic justification for an organization's existence is the satisfaction of customer wants and needs while meeting organizational objectives

market orientation a philosophy that assumes that a sale does not depend on an aggressive sales force but rather on a customer's decision to purchase a product; it is synonymous with the marketing concept

societal marketing orientation the idea that an organization exists not only to satisfy customer wants and needs and to meet organizational objectives but also to preserve or enhance individuals' and society's long-term best interests

1-3
customer value the relationship between benefits and the sacrifice necessary to obtain those benefits

customer satisfaction customers' evaluation of a good or service in terms of whether it has met their needs and expectations

relationship marketing a strategy that focuses on keeping and improving relationships with current customers

empowerment delegation of authority to solve customers' problems quickly—usually by the first person the customer notifies regarding a problem

teamwork collaborative efforts of people to accomplish common objectives

customer relationship management (CRM) a company-wide business strategy designed to optimize profitability, revenue, and customer satisfaction by focusing on highly defined and precise customer groups

on-demand marketing delivering relevant experiences, integrated across both physical and virtual environments, throughout the consumer's decision and buying process

1-3 Discuss the differences between sales and market orientations. First, sales-oriented firms focus on their own needs; market-oriented firms focus on customers' needs and preferences. Second, sales-oriented companies consider themselves to be deliverers of goods and services, whereas market-oriented companies view themselves as satisfiers of customers. Third, sales-oriented firms direct their products to everyone; market-oriented firms aim at specific segments of the population. Fourth, sales-oriented organizations place a higher premium on making a sale, while market-oriented businesses seek a long-term relationship with the customer. Finally, sales-oriented businesses pursue maximum sales volume through intensive promotion, whereas market-oriented businesses pursue customer satisfaction through coordinated activities.

AP Images/PRNewsFoto/Fairfield Inn & Suites by Marriott

Marriott's customer-oriented focus is evident in initiatives like the Fairfield Inn & Suites "Some Like It Hot" food truck, which serves hot, made-to-order breakfasts to customers for free.

1-4 Describe several reasons for studying marketing. First, marketing affects the allocation of goods and services that influence a nation's economy and standard of living. Second, an understanding of marketing is crucial to understanding most businesses. Third, career opportunities in marketing are diverse, profitable, and expected to increase significantly during the coming decade. Fourth, understanding marketing makes consumers more informed.

KEY CONCEPTS

2-1 Understand the importance of strategic planning. Strategic planning is the basis for all marketing strategies and decisions. These decisions affect the allocation of resources and ultimately the financial success of the company.

2-2 Define strategic business units (SBUs). Each SBU should have these characteristics: a distinct mission and a specific target market, control over its resources, its own competitors, a single business, and plans independent from other SBUs in the organization. Each SBU has its own rate of return on investment, growth potential, and associated risks, and requires its own strategies and funding.

2-3 Identify strategic alternatives and know a basic outline for a marketing plan. Ansoff's opportunity matrix presents four options to help management develop strategic alternatives: market penetration, market development, product development, and diversification. In selecting a strategic alternative, managers may use a portfolio matrix, which classifies strategic business units as stars, cash cows, problem children (or question marks), and dogs, depending on their present or projected growth and market share. Alternatively, the GE model suggests that companies determine strategic alternatives based on the comparisons between business position and market attractiveness.

A marketing plan should define the business mission, perform a situation analysis, define objectives, delineate a target market, and establish components of the marketing mix. Other elements that may be included in a plan are budgets, implementation timetables, required marketing research efforts, or elements of advanced strategic planning.

2-4 Develop an appropriate business mission statement. The firm's mission statement establishes boundaries for all subsequent decisions, objectives, and strategies. A mission statement should focus on the market(s) the organization is attempting to serve rather than on the good or service offered.

2-5 Describe the components of a situation analysis. In the situation (or SWOT) analysis, the firm should identify its internal strengths (S) and weaknesses (W) and also examine external opportunities (O) and threats (T). When examining external opportunities and threats, marketing managers must analyze aspects of the marketing environment in a process called environmental scanning. The six macroenvironmental forces studied most often are social, demographic, economic, technological, political and legal, and competitive.

2-6 Identify sources of competitive advantage. There are three types of competitive advantage: cost, product/service differentiation, and niche. Sources of cost competitive advantage include experience curves, efficient labor, no-frills goods and services, government subsidies, product design, reengineering, production innovations, and new methods of service delivery. A product/service differentiation competitive advantage exists when a firm provides something unique that is valuable to buyers beyond just low price. Niche competitive advantages come from targeting unique segments with specific needs and wants. The goal of all these sources of competitive advantage is to be sustainable.

2-7 Explain the criteria for stating good marketing objectives. Objectives should be realistic, measurable, time specific, and compared to a benchmark. They must also be consistent and indicate the priorities of the organization. Good marketing objectives communicate marketing management philosophies, provide management direction, motivate employees, force executives to think clearly, and form a basis for control.

KEY TERMS

2-1

strategic planning the managerial process of creating and maintaining a fit between the organization's objectives and resources and the evolving market opportunities

2-2

strategic business unit (SBU) a subgroup of a single business or collection of related businesses within the larger organization

2-3

market penetration a marketing strategy that tries to increase market share among existing customers

market development a marketing strategy that entails attracting new customers to existing products

product development a marketing strategy that entails the creation of new products for present markets

diversification a strategy of increasing sales by introducing new products into new markets

portfolio matrix a tool for allocating resources among products or strategic business units on the basis of relative market share and market growth rate

star in the portfolio matrix, a business unit that is a fast-growing market leader

cash cow in the portfolio matrix, a business unit that generates more cash than it needs to maintain its market share

problem child (question mark) in the portfolio matrix, a business unit that shows rapid growth but poor profit margins

dog in the portfolio matrix, a business unit that has low growth potential and a small market share

planning the process of anticipating future events and determining strategies to achieve organizational objectives in the future

marketing planning designing activities relating to marketing objectives and the changing marketing environment

marketing plan a written document that acts as a guidebook of marketing activities for the marketing manager

2-4

mission statement a statement of the firm's business based on a careful analysis of benefits sought by present and potential customers and an analysis of existing and anticipated environmental conditions

marketing myopia defining a business in terms of goods and services rather than in terms of the benefits customers seek

2-5

SWOT analysis identifying internal strengths (S) and weaknesses (W) and also examining external opportunities (O) and threats (T)

CHAPTER REVIEW 2

environmental scanning collection and interpretation of information about forces, events, and relationships in the external environment that may affect the future of the organization or the implementation of the marketing plan

2-6

competitive advantage a set of unique features of a company and its products that are perceived by the target market as significant and superior to those of the competition

cost competitive advantage being the low-cost competitor in an industry while maintaining satisfactory profit margins

experience curves curves that show costs declining at a predictable rate as experience with a product increases

product/service differentiation competitive advantage the provision of something that is unique and valuable to buyers beyond simply offering a lower price than that of the competition

niche competitive advantage the advantage achieved when a firm seeks to target and effectively serve a small segment of the market

sustainable competitive advantage an advantage that cannot be copied by the competition

2-7

marketing objective a statement of what is to be accomplished through marketing activities

2-8

marketing strategy the activities of selecting and describing one or more target markets and developing and maintaining a marketing mix that will produce mutually satisfying exchanges with target markets

market opportunity analysis (MOA) the description and estimation of the size and sales potential of market segments that are of interest to the firm and the assessment of key competitors in these market segments

2-9

marketing mix (four Ps) a unique blend of product, place (distribution), promotion, and pricing strategies designed to produce mutually satisfying exchanges with a target market

2-10

implementation the process that turns a marketing plan into action assignments and ensures that these assignments are executed in a way that accomplishes the plan's objectives

evaluation gauging the extent to which the marketing objectives have been achieved during the specified time period

control provides the mechanisms for evaluating marketing results in light of the plan's objectives and for correcting actions that do not help the organization reach those objectives within budget guidelines

marketing audit a thorough, systematic, periodic evaluation of the objectives, strategies, structure, and performance of the marketing organization

---

2-8 Discuss target market strategies. Targeting markets begins with a market opportunity analysis (MOA), which describes and estimates the size and sales potential of market segments that are of interest to the firm. In addition, an assessment of key competitors in these market segments is performed. After the market segments are described, one or more may be targeted by the firm.

2-9 Describe the elements of the marketing mix. The marketing mix is a blend of product, place, promotion, and pricing strategies (the four Ps) designed to produce mutually satisfying exchanges with a target market. The starting point of the marketing mix is the product offering—tangible goods, ideas, or services. Place (distribution) strategies are concerned with making products available when and where customers want them. Promotion includes advertising, public relations, sales promotion, and personal selling. Price is what a buyer must give up in order to obtain a product and is often the most flexible of the four marketing mix elements.

2-10 Explain why implementation, evaluation, and control of the marketing plan are necessary. Before a marketing plan can work, it must be implemented—that is, people must perform the actions in the plan. The plan should also be evaluated to see if it has achieved its objectives. Poor implementation can be a major factor in a plan's failure, but working to gain acceptance can be accomplished with task forces. Once implemented, one major aspect of control is the marketing audit and ultimately continuing to apply what the audit uncovered through post-audit tasks.

2-11 Identify several techniques that help make strategic planning effective. First, management must realize that strategic planning is an ongoing process and not a once-a-year exercise. Second, good strategic planning involves a high level of creativity. The last requirement is top management's support and participation.

CHAPTER REVIEW
Ethics and Social Responsibility

3

KEY CONCEPTS

3-1 Explain the determinants of a civil society. Societal order is created through the six modes of social control. Ethics are the moral principles or values that generally govern the conduct of an individual or a group. Laws come into being when ethical rules and guidelines are codified into law. Formal and informal groups have codes of conduct that prescribe acceptable and desired behaviors of their members. Self-regulation involves the voluntary acceptance of standards established by nongovernmental entities. The media play a key role in informing the public about the actions of individuals and organizations—both good and bad. An informed and engaged society can help mold individual and corporate behavior.

3-2 Explain the concept of ethical behavior. Ethics are the standards of behavior by which conduct is judged. Standards that are legal may not always be ethical. An ethics violation offends a person's sense of justice or fairness. Ethics basically constitute the unwritten rules developed to guide interactions. Many ethical questions arise from balancing a business's need to produce profit for shareholders against its desire to operate honestly and with concern for environmental and social issues.

Several ethical theories apply to marketing. Deontological theory states that people should adhere to their obligations and duties when analyzing an ethical dilemma. Utilitarian ethical theory says that the choice that yields the greatest benefit to the most people is the choice that is ethically correct. The casuist ethical theory compares a current ethical dilemma with examples of similar ethical dilemmas and their outcomes. Moral relativists believe in time-and-place ethics, that is, ethical truths depend on the individuals and groups holding them. Virtue ethics suggests that individuals become able to solve ethical dilemmas when they develop and nurture a set of virtues.

3-3 Describe ethical behavior in business. Business ethics may be viewed as a subset of the values of society as a whole, with a foundation based on the cultural values and norms that constitute a culture's morals. The ethical conduct of businesspeople is shaped by societal elements, including family, education, and religious institutions. Morals are the rules people develop as a result of cultural values and norms. As members of society, businesspeople are morally obligated to consider the ethical implications of their decisions. Ethical decision making can be grouped into three basic approaches. The first approach examines the consequences of decisions. The second approach relies on rules and laws to guide decision making. The third approach is based on a theory of moral development that places individuals or groups in one of three developmental stages: preconventional morality, conventional morality, or postconventional morality.

In addition to personal influences, there are many business influences on ethical decision making. Some of the most influential include the extent of ethical problems within the organization, top management's actions on ethics, potential magnitude of the consequences, social consensus, probability of a harmful outcome, length of time between the decision and the onset of consequences, and the number of people affected.

Many companies develop a code of ethics to help their employees make ethical decisions. A code of ethics can help employees identify acceptable business practices, be an effective internal control on behavior, help employees avoid confusion when determining whether decisions are ethical, and facilitate discussion about what is right and wrong.

Studies show that ethical beliefs vary little from country to country. However, there are enough cultural differences, such as the practice of bribery or gift giving, that laws such as the Foreign Corrupt Practices Act (FCPA) have been put in place to discourage and attempt to modify the current acceptance of such practices.

KEY TERMS

3-1
social control any means used to maintain behavioral norms and regulate conflict

behavioral norms standards of proper or acceptable behavior. Several modes of social control are important to marketing

ethics the moral principles or values that generally govern the conduct of an individual or a group

3-2
deontological theory ethical theory that states that people should adhere to their obligations and duties when analyzing an ethical dilemma

utilitarian ethical theory ethical theory that is founded on the ability to predict the consequences of an action

casuist ethical theory ethical theory that compares a current ethical dilemma with examples of similar ethical dilemmas and their outcomes

moral relativism an ethical theory of time-and-place ethics; that is, the belief that ethical truths depend on the individuals and groups holding them

virtue a character trait valued as being good

3-3
morals the rules people develop as a result of cultural values and norms

code of ethics a guideline to help marketing managers and other employees make better decisions

Foreign Corrupt Practices Act (FCPA) a law that prohibits U.S. corporations from making illegal payments to public officials of foreign governments to obtain business rights or to enhance their business dealings in those countries

3-4
corporate social responsibility (CSR) a business's concern for society's welfare

stakeholder theory ethical theory stating that social responsibility is paying attention to the interest of every affected stakeholder in every aspect of a firm's operation

pyramid of corporate social responsibility a model that suggests corporate social responsibility is composed of economic, legal, ethical, and philanthropic responsibilities and that a firm's economic performance supports the entire structure

3-5
sustainability the idea that socially responsible companies will outperform their peers by focusing on the world's social problems and viewing them as opportunities to build profits and help the world at the same time

CHAPTER REVIEW 3

green marketing the development and marketing of products designed to minimize negative effects on the physical environment or to improve the environment

3-6

cause-related marketing the cooperative marketing efforts between a for-profit firm and a nonprofit organization

3-4 Discuss corporate social responsibility. Corporate social responsibility (CSR) is a business's concern for society's welfare. Responsibility in business refers to a firm's concern for the way its decisions affect society. Stakeholder theory says that social responsibility means paying attention to the interest of every affected stakeholder in every aspect of a firm's operation, including employees, management, customers, the local community, suppliers, and owners. According to the pyramid of corporate social responsibility, CSR has four components: economic, legal, ethical, and philanthropic. These are intertwined, yet the most fundamental is earning a profit. If a firm does not earn a profit, the other three responsibilities are moot.

3-5 Describe the arguments for and against society responsibility. Most businesspeople believe they should do more than pursue profits. Although a company must consider its economic needs first, it must also operate within the law, do what is ethical and fair, and be a good corporate citizen. Sustainability is the concept that socially responsible companies will outperform their peers by focusing on the world's social problems and viewing them as an opportunity to earn profits and help the world at the same time. Social responsibility is growing, but it can be costly and the benefits are not always immediate. In addition, some surveys report that consumer desire to purchase responsible products does not always translate to actually purchasing those products. One branch of social responsibility is green marketing, which aids the environment and often the bottom line of a business.

3-6 Explain cause-related marketing. Cause-related marketing is the cooperative effort between a for-profit firm and a nonprofit organization. It is different from philanthropy, which is a specific, tax-deductible donation. Cause-related marketing is very popular because it can enhance the reputation of the corporation and also make additional profit for the company. However, consumers sometimes come to believe that every company is tied to a cause, resulting in consumer cause fatigue.

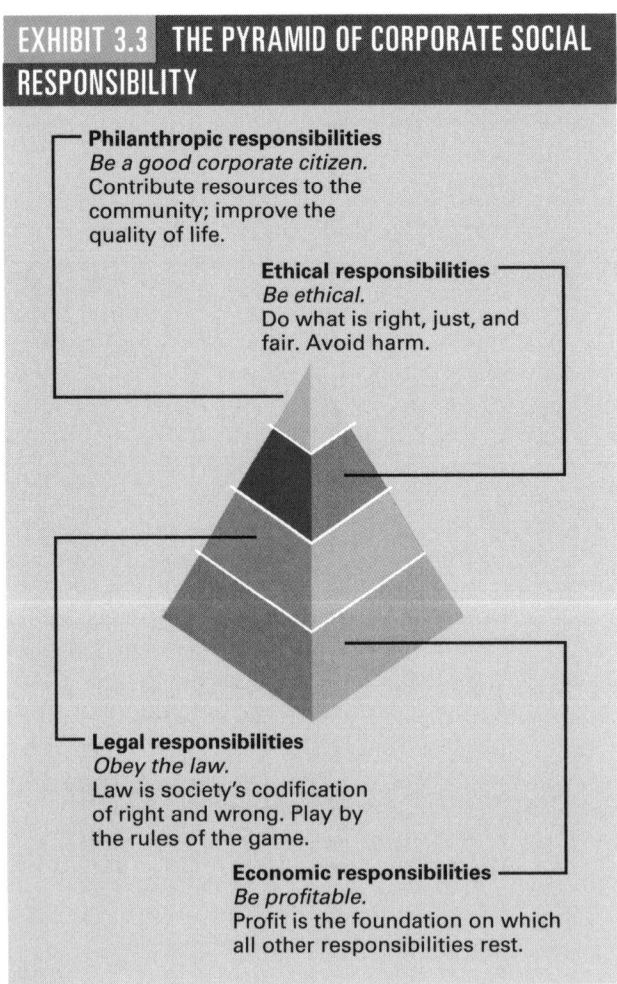

EXHIBIT 3.3 THE PYRAMID OF CORPORATE SOCIAL RESPONSIBILITY

Philanthropic responsibilities
Be a good corporate citizen.
Contribute resources to the community; improve the quality of life.

Ethical responsibilities
Be ethical.
Do what is right, just, and fair. Avoid harm.

Legal responsibilities
Obey the law.
Law is society's codification of right and wrong. Play by the rules of the game.

Economic responsibilities
Be profitable.
Profit is the foundation on which all other responsibilities rest.

KEY CONCEPTS

4-1 Discuss the external environment of marketing and explain how it affects a firm. The external marketing environment consists of social, demographic, economic, technological, political and legal, and competitive variables. Marketers generally cannot control the elements of the external environment. Instead, they must understand how the external environment is changing and the impact of that change on the target market. Then marketing managers can create a marketing mix to effectively meet the needs of target customers.

4-2 Describe the social factors that affect marketing. Within the external environment, social factors are perhaps the most difficult for marketers to anticipate. Several major social trends are currently shaping marketing strategies. First, people of all ages have a broader range of interests, defying traditional consumer profiles. Second, social media, Web-based, and mobile technology change how people and marketers interact by allowing one-to-one, one-to-many, and many-to-many communications. Because Facebook is about human-to-human interaction, companies are turning to it and other forms of social media with ever-increasing speed.

4-3 Explain the importance to marketing managers of current demographic trends. There are more than 7 billion people alive today. China has the largest population with 1.39 billion persons; India is second with 1.23 billion. Census data puts the U.S. population at more than 318 million, with metropolitan areas growing and rural areas shrinking in population. Marketers are faced with increasingly experienced consumers among the younger generations such as tweens and teens. And because the population is also growing older, marketers are offering more products that appeal to middle-aged and older consumers.

4-4 Explain the importance to marketing managers of growing ethnic markets. The minority population today is about 118 million. By 2050, around one in three U.S. residents will be Hispanic. The United States will flip completely to a majority-minority makeup in 2041. Many companies are creating departments and product lines to target multicultural market segments effectively. Companies have quickly found that ethnic markets are not homogeneous.

4-5 Identify consumer and marketer reactions to the state of the economy. The annual median household income in the United States in 2014 was approximately $52,000, though the median household income varies widely from state to state. During a time of inflation, marketers generally attempt to maintain level pricing to avoid losing customer brand loyalty. During times of recession, many marketers maintain or reduce prices to counter the effects of decreased demand; they also concentrate on increasing production efficiency and improving customer service. The Great Recession was the largest economic downturn since the Great Depression. While the causes of recession are very complex, this one began with the collapse of inflated housing prices.

4-6 Identify the impact of technology on a firm. Technological success is based upon innovation, and innovation requires imagination and risk taking. Monitoring new technology and encouraging research and development (R&D) of new technology are essential to keeping up with competitors in today's marketing environment. Innovation through R&D needs to be stimulated by upper management and fostered in creative environments. Although developing new technology internally is a key to creating and maintaining a long-term competitive advantage, external technology is also important to managers.

KEY TERMS

4-1

target market a group of people or organizations for which an organization designs, implements, and maintains a marketing mix intended to meet the need of that group, resulting in mutually satisfying exchanges

environmental management when a company implements strategies that attempt to shape the external environment within which it operates

4-2

component lifestyles the practice of choosing goods and services that meet one's diverse needs and interests rather than conforming to a single, traditional lifestyle

4-3

demography the study of people's vital statistics, such as age, race and ethnicity, and location

Millennials people born between 1979 and 1994

Generation X people born between 1965 and 1978

baby boomers people born between 1946 and 1964

4-5

purchasing power a comparison of income versus the relative cost of a standard set of goods and services in different geographic areas

inflation a measure of the decrease in the value of money, expressed as the percentage reduction in value since the previous year

recession a period of economic activity characterized by negative growth, which reduces demand for goods and services

4-6

basic research pure research that aims to confirm an existing theory or to learn more about a concept or phenomenon

applied research research that attempts to develop new or improved products

4-7

Consumer Product Safety Commission (CPSC) a federal agency established to protect the health and safety of consumers in and around their homes

Food and Drug Administration (FDA) a federal agency charged with enforcing regulations against selling and distributing adulterated, misbranded, or hazardous food and drug products

Federal Trade Commission (FTC) a federal agency empowered to prevent persons or corporations from using unfair methods of competition in commerce

4-7 Discuss the political and legal environment of marketing. All marketing activities are subject to state and federal laws and the rulings of regulatory agencies. Marketers are responsible for remaining aware of and abiding by such regulations. Some key federal agencies that affect marketing are the Consumer Product Safety Commission, the Food and Drug Administration, and the Federal Trade Commission. Many laws, including privacy laws, have been passed to protect the consumer as well. In 2012, the FTC called for online data collectors to adopt better privacy policies and asked Congress to pass comprehensive privacy legislation. Despite federal efforts, online tracking has become widespread and pervasive.

4-8 Explain the basics of foreign and domestic competition. The competitive environment encompasses the number of competitors a firm must face, the relative size of the competitors, and the degree of interdependence within the industry. Declining population growth, rising costs, and shortages of resources have heightened domestic competition.

EXHIBIT 4.2 PRIMARY U.S. LAWS PROTECTING CONSUMERS

Legislation	Impact on Marketing
Federal Food and Drug Act of 1906	Prohibits adulteration and misbranding of foods and drugs involved in interstate commerce; strengthened by the Food, Drug, and Cosmetic Act (1938) and the Kefauver-Harris Drug Amendment (1962).
Federal Hazardous Substances Act of 1960	Requires warning labels on hazardous household chemicals.
Kefauver-Harris Drug Amendment of 1962	Requires that manufacturers conduct tests to prove drug effectiveness and safety.
Consumer Credit Protection Act of 1968	Requires that lenders fully disclose true interest rates and all other charges to credit customers for loans and installment purchases.
Child Protection and Toy Safety Act of 1969	Prevents marketing of products so dangerous that adequate safety warnings cannot be given.
Public Health Smoking Act of 1970	Prohibits cigarette advertising on television and radio and revises the health hazard warning on cigarette packages.
Poison Prevention Labeling Act of 1970	Requires safety packaging for products that may be harmful to children.
National Environmental Policy Act of 1970	Established the Environmental Protection Agency to deal with various types of pollution and organizations that create pollution.
Public Health Cigarette Smoking Act of 1971	Prohibits tobacco advertising on radio and television.
Consumer Product Safety Act of 1972	Created the Consumer Product Safety Commission, which has authority to specify safety standards for most products.
Child Protection Act of 1990	Regulates the number of minutes of advertising on children's television.
Children's Online Privacy Protection Act of 1998	Empowers the FTC to set rules regarding how and when marketers must obtain parental permission before asking children marketing research questions.
Aviation Security Act of 2001	Requires airlines to take extra security measures to protect passengers, including the installation of stronger cockpit doors, improved baggage screening, and increased security training for airport personnel.
Homeland Security Act of 2002	Protects consumers against terrorist acts; created the Department of Homeland Security.
Do Not Call Law of 2003	Protects consumers against unwanted telemarketing calls.
CAN-SPAM Act of 2003	Protects consumers against unwanted e-mail, or spam.
Credit Card Act of 2009	Provides many credit card protections.
Restoring American Financial Stability Act of 2010	Created the Consumer Financial Protection Bureau to protect consumers against unfair, abusive, and deceptive financial practices.
Patient Protection and Affordable Care Act	Overhauled the U.S. healthcare system; mandated and subsidized health insurance for individuals.

KEY CONCEPTS

5-1 Discuss the importance of global marketing. Businesspeople who adopt a global vision are better able to identify global marketing opportunities, understand the nature of global networks, create effective global marketing strategies, and compete against foreign competition in domestic markets. Large corporations have traditionally been the major global competitors, but more and more small businesses are entering the global marketplace. Despite fears of job losses to other countries with cheaper labor, there are many benefits to globalization, including the reduction of poverty and increased standards of living.

5-2 Discuss the impact of multinational firms on the world economy. Multinational corporations are international traders that regularly operate across national borders. Because of their vast size and financial, technological, and material resources, multinational corporations have great influence on the world economy. They have the ability to overcome trade problems, save on labor costs, and tap new technology. There are critics and supporters of multinational corporations, and the critics question the actual benefits of bringing capital-intensive technology to impoverished nations. Many countries block foreign investment in factories, land, and companies to protect their economies.

Some companies presume that markets throughout the world are more and more similar, so some global products can be standardized across global markets.

5-3 Describe the external environment facing global marketers. Global marketers face the same environmental factors as they do domestically: culture, economic and technological development, the global economy, political structure and actions, demography, and natural resources. Cultural considerations include societal values, attitudes and beliefs, language, and customary business practices. A country's economic and technological status depends on its stage of industrial development, which, in turn, affects average family incomes. A global marketer today must be fully aware of the intertwined nature of the global economy. The political structure is shaped by political ideology and such policies as tariffs, quotas, boycotts, exchange controls, trade agreements, and market groupings. Demographic variables include the size of a population and its age and geographic distribution. A shortage of natural resources also affects the external environment by dictating what is available and at what price.

5-4 Identify the various ways of entering the global marketplace. Firms use the following strategies to enter global markets, in descending order of risk and profit: direct investment, joint venture, contract manufacturing, licensing and franchising, and exporting.

KEY TERMS

5-1

global marketing marketing that targets markets throughout the world

global vision recognizing and reacting to international marketing opportunities, using effective global marketing strategies, and being aware of threats from foreign competitors in all markets

gross domestic product (GDP) the total market value of all final goods and services produced in a country for a given time period

outsourcing sending U.S. jobs abroad

inshoring returning production jobs to the United States

5-2

multinational corporation a company that is heavily engaged in international trade, beyond exporting and importing

capital intensive using more capital than labor in the production process

global marketing standardization production of uniform products that can be sold the same way all over the world

multidomestic strategy when multinational firms enable individual subsidiaries to compete independently in domestic markets

5-3

Mercosur the largest Latin American trade agreement; includes Argentina, Bolivia, Brazil, Chile, Colombia, Ecuador, Paraguay, Peru, Uruguay, and Venezuela

Uruguay Round a trade agreement to dramatically lower trade barriers worldwide; created the World Trade Organization

World Trade Organization (WTO) a trade organization that replaced the old General Agreement on Tariffs and Trade (GATT)

General Agreement on Tariffs and Trade (GATT) a trade agreement that contained loopholes enabling countries to avoid trade-barrier reduction agreements

North American Free Trade Agreement (NAFTA) an agreement between Canada, the United States, and Mexico that created the world's then-largest free trade zone

CHAPTER REVIEW 5

Dominican Republic-Central America Free Trade Agreement (CAFTA-DR) a trade agreement instituted in 2005 that includes Costa Rica, the Dominican Republic, El Salvador, Guatemala, Honduras, Nicaragua, and the United States

European Union (EU) a free trade zone encompassing twenty-eight European countries

World Bank an international bank that offers low-interest loans, advice, and information to developing nations

International Monetary Fund (IMF) an international organization that acts as a lender of last resort, providing loans to troubled nations, and also works to promote trade through financial cooperation

Group of Twenty (G-20) a forum for international economic development that promotes discussion between industrial and emerging-market countries on key issues related to global economic stability

5-4

exporting selling domestically produced products to buyers in other countries

buyer for export an intermediary in the global market that assumes all ownership risks and sells globally for its own account

export broker an intermediary who plays the traditional broker's role by bringing buyer and seller together

export agent an intermediary who acts like a manufacturer's agent for the exporter; the export agent lives in the foreign market

licensing the legal process whereby a licensor allows another firm to use its manufacturing process, trademarks, patents, trade secrets, or other proprietary knowledge

contract manufacturing private label manufacturing by a foreign company

joint venture when a domestic firm buys part of a foreign company or joins with a foreign company to create a new entity

direct foreign investment active ownership of a foreign company or of overseas manufacturing or marketing facilities

5-5

exchange rate the price of one country's currency in terms of another country's currency

floating exchange rates a system in which prices of different currencies move up and down based on the demand for and the supply of each currency

dumping the sale of an exported product at a price lower than that charged for the same or a like product in the "home" market of the exporter

countertrade a form of trade in which all or part of the payment for goods or services is in the form of other goods or services

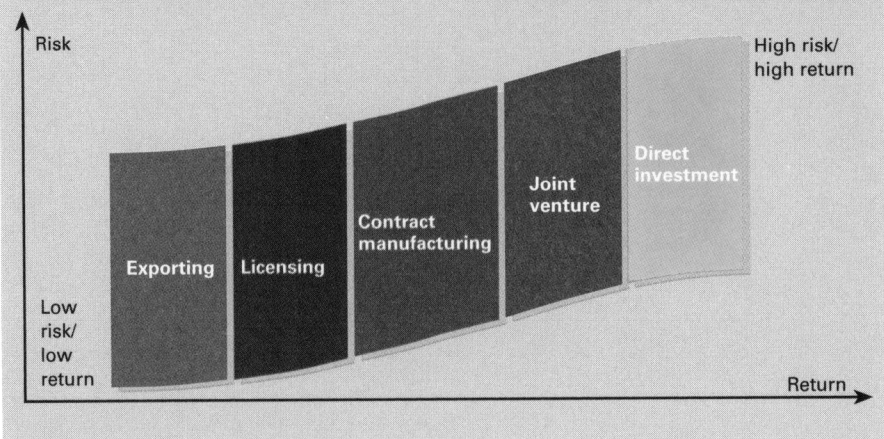

EXHIBIT 5.2 RISK LEVELS FOR FIVE METHODS OF ENTERING THE GLOBAL MARKETPLACE

5-5 List the basic elements involved in developing a global marketing mix. A firm's major consideration is how much it will adjust the four Ps—product, promotion, place (distribution), and price—within each country. One strategy is to use one product and one promotion message worldwide. A second strategy is to create new products for global markets. A third strategy is to keep the product basically the same but alter the promotional message. A fourth strategy is to slightly alter the product to meet local conditions.

5-6 Discover how the Internet is affecting global marketing. Simply opening an e-commerce site can open the door for international sales. International carriers, such as UPS, can help solve logistics problems. Language translation software can help an e-commerce business become multilingual. Yet cultural differences and old-line rules, regulations, and taxes hinder rapid development of e-commerce in many countries. Not only do global marketers use social media for understanding consumers. they also use social media to build their brands as they expand internationally.

KEY CONCEPTS

6-1 Explain why marketing managers should understand consumer behavior. An understanding of consumer behavior reduces marketing managers' uncertainty when they are defining a target market and designing a marketing mix.

6-2 Analyze the components of the consumer decision-making process. The consumer decision-making process begins with need recognition, when stimuli trigger awareness of an unfulfilled want. If additional information is required to make a purchase decision, the consumer may engage in an internal or external information search. The consumer then evaluates the alternatives using the additional information and establishes purchase guidelines. Finally, a purchase decision is made.

6-3 Explain the consumer's postpurchase evaluation process. Consumer postpurchase evaluation is influenced by prepurchase expectations, the prepurchase information search, and the consumer's general level of self-confidence. When a purchase creates cognitive dissonance, consumers tend to react by seeking positive reinforcement for the purchase decision, avoiding negative information about the purchase decision, or revoking the purchase decision by returning the product.

6-4 Identify the types of consumer buying decisions and discuss the significance of consumer involvement. Consumer decision making falls into three broad categories: routine response behavior, limited decision making, and extensive decision making. High-involvement decisions usually include an extensive information search and a thorough evaluation of alternatives. By contrast, low-involvement decisions are characterized by brand loyalty and a lack of personal identification with the product. The main factors affecting the level of consumer involvement are previous experience, interest, perceived risk of negative consequences (financial, social, and psychological), and social visibility. A purchase decision can be highly involved due to a wide range of factors, including product involvement, situational involvement, shopping involvement, enduring involvement, and emotional involvement.

6-5 Identify and understand the cultural factors that affect consumer buying decisions. Cultural influences on consumer buying decisions include culture and values, subculture, and social class. Culture is the essential character of a society that distinguishes it from other cultural groups. The underlying elements of every culture are the values, language, myths, customs, rituals, laws, and the artifacts, or products, that are transmitted from one generation to the next. The most defining element of a culture is its values. A culture can be divided into subcultures on the basis of demographic characteristics, geographic regions, national and ethnic background, political beliefs, and religious beliefs.

6-6 Identify and understand the social factors that affect consumer buying decisions. Social factors include such external influences as reference groups, opinion leaders, and family. Consumers seek out others' opinions for guidance on new products or services and products with image-related attributes or because attribute information is lacking or uninformative. Consumers may use products or brands to identify with or become a member of a reference group, or to follow an opinion leader. Family members also influence purchase decisions; children tend to shop in similar patterns as their parents.

6-7 Identify and understand the individual factors that affect consumer buying decisions. Individual factors that affect consumer buying decisions include gender; age and family life cycle stage; and personality, self-concept,

KEY TERMS

6-1

consumer behavior processes a consumer uses to make purchase decisions, as well as to use and dispose of purchased goods or services; also includes factors that influence purchase decisions and product use

value a personal assessment of the net worth one obtains from making a purchase, or the enduring belief that a specific mode of conduct is personally or socially preferable to another mode of conduct

perceived value the value a consumer *expects* to obtain from a purchase

utilitarian value a value derived from a product or service that helps the consumer solve problems and accomplish tasks

hedonic value a value that acts as an end in itself rather than as a means to an end

6-2

consumer decision-making process a five-step process used by consumers when buying goods or services

need recognition result of an imbalance between actual and desired states

want recognition of an unfulfilled need and a product that will satisfy it

stimulus any unit of input affecting one or more of the five senses: sight, smell, taste, touch, hearing

internal information search the process of recalling past information stored in the memory

external information search the process of seeking information in the outside environment

nonmarketing-controlled information source a product information source that is not associated with advertising or promotion

marketing-controlled information source a product information source that originates with marketers promoting the product

evoked set (consideration set) a group of brands resulting from an information search from which a buyer can choose

6-3

cognitive dissonance inner tension that a consumer experiences after recognizing an inconsistency between behavior and values or opinions

6-4

involvement the amount of time and effort a buyer invests in the search, evaluation, and decision processes of consumer behavior

CHAPTER REVIEW 6

routine response behavior the type of decision making exhibited by consumers buying frequently purchased, low-cost goods and services; requires little search and decision time

limited decision making the type of decision making that requires a moderate amount of time for gathering information and deliberating about an unfamiliar brand in a familiar product category

extensive decision making the most complex type of consumer decision making, used when buying an unfamiliar, expensive product or an infrequently bought item; requires use of several criteria for evaluating options and much time for seeking information

showrooming the practice of examining merchandise in a physical retail location without purchasing it, and then shopping online for a better deal on the same item

6-5

culture the set of values, norms, attitudes, and other meaningful symbols that shape human behavior and the artifacts, or products, of that behavior as they are transmitted from one generation to the next

subculture a homogeneous group of people who share elements of the overall culture as well as unique elements of their own group

social class a group of people in a society who are considered nearly equal in status or community esteem, who regularly socialize among themselves both formally and informally, and who share behavioral norms

6-6

reference group all of the formal and informal groups in society that influence an individual's purchasing behavior

primary membership group a reference group with which people interact regularly in an informal, face-to-face manner, such as family, friends, and coworkers

secondary membership group a reference group with which people associate less consistently and more formally than a primary membership group, such as a club, professional group, or religious group

aspirational reference group a group that someone would like to join

norm a value or attitude deemed acceptable by a group

nonaspirational reference group a group with which an individual does not want to associate

opinion leader an individual who influences the opinions of others

socialization process how cultural values and norms are passed down to children

separated self-schema a perspective whereby a consumer sees himself or herself as distinct and separate from others

and lifestyle. Beyond obvious physiological differences, men and women differ in their social and economic roles, and that affects consumer buying decisions. A consumer's age generally indicates what products he or she may be interested in purchasing. Marketers often define their target markets in terms of consumers' life cycle stage, following changes in consumers' attitudes and behavioral tendencies as they mature. Finally, certain products and brands reflect consumers' personality, self-concept, and lifestyle.

6-8 Identify and understand the psychological factors that affect consumer buying decisions. Psychological factors include perception, motivation, and learning. These factors allow consumers to interact with the world around them, recognize their feelings, gather and analyze information, formulate thoughts and opinions, and take action. Perception allows consumers to recognize their consumption problems. Motivation is what drives consumers to take action to satisfy specific consumption needs. Almost all consumer behavior results from learning, which is the process that creates changes in behavior through experience.

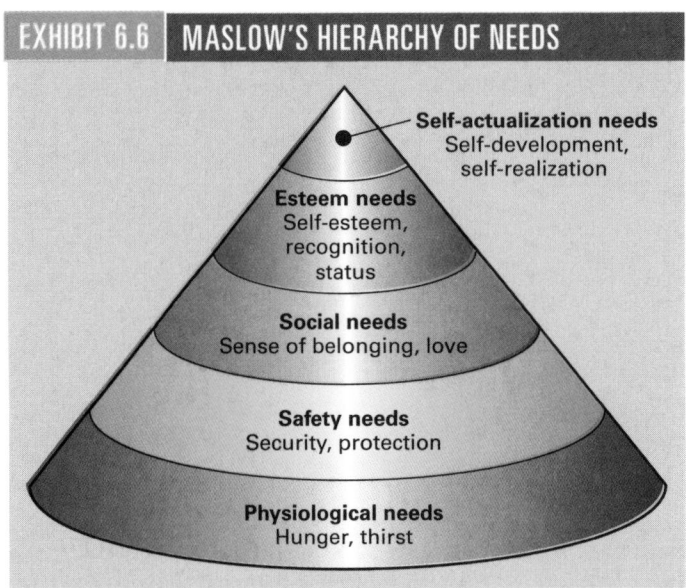

EXHIBIT 6.6 MASLOW'S HIERARCHY OF NEEDS

connected self-schema a perspective whereby a consumer sees himself or herself as an integral part of a group

6-7

personality a way of organizing and grouping the consistencies of an individual's reactions to situations

self-concept how consumers perceive themselves in terms of attitudes, perceptions, beliefs, and self-evaluations

ideal self-image the way an individual would like to be perceived

real self-image the way an individual actually perceives himself or herself

6-8

perception the process by which people select, organize, and interpret stimuli into a meaningful and coherent picture

selective exposure a process whereby a consumer notices certain stimuli and ignores others

selective distortion a process whereby a consumer changes or distorts information that conflicts with his or her feelings or beliefs

selective retention a process whereby a consumer remembers only that information that supports his or her personal beliefs

motive a driving force that causes a person to take action to satisfy specific needs

Maslow's hierarchy of needs a method of classifying human needs and motivations into five categories in ascending order of importance: physiological, safety, social, esteem, and self-actualization

learning a process that creates changes in behavior, immediate or expected, through experience and practice

stimulus generalization a form of learning that occurs when one response is extended to a second stimulus similar to the first

stimulus discrimination a learned ability to differentiate among similar products

KEY CONCEPTS

7-1 Describe business marketing. Business marketing provides goods and services that are bought for use in business rather than for personal consumption. Intended use, not physical characteristics, distinguishes a business product from a consumer product.

7-2 Describe trends in B-to-B Internet marketing. B-to-B companies use the Internet in three major ways. First, they use their Web sites to facilitate communication and orders. Second, they use digital marketing to increase brand awareness. Third, they use digital marketing—primarily in the form of content marketing—to position their businesses as thought leaders and therefore generate sales leads. Content marketing, a strategic marketing approach focused on creating and distributing valuable, relevant, and consistent content, has played an important role for B-to-B marketers. As they build reputations in their business areas, many B-to-B marketers use social media to share content, increase awareness, and build relationships and community. Some metrics that are particularly useful for increasing the success of a social media campaign are awareness, engagement, and conversion.

7-3 Discuss the role of relationship marketing and strategic alliances in business marketing. Relationship marketing entails seeking and establishing long-term alliances or partnerships with customers. A strategic alliance is a cooperative agreement between business firms. Firms form alliances to leverage what they do well by partnering with others that have complementary skills. Although the concepts of relationship marketing and strategic alliances are relatively new to American marketers, these ideas have long been used by marketers in other cultures.

7-4 Identify the four major categories of business market customers. Producer markets consist of for-profit individuals and organizations that buy products to use in producing other products, as components of other products, or in facilitating business operations. Reseller markets consist of wholesalers and retailers that buy finished products to resell for profit. Government markets include federal, state, county, and city governments that buy goods and services to support their own operations and serve the needs of citizens. Institutional markets consist of very diverse nonbusiness institutions whose main goals do not include profit.

7-5 Explain the North American Industry Classification System. The North American Industry Classification System (NAICS) provides a way to identify, analyze, segment, and target business and government markets. Organizations can be identified and compared by a numeric code indicating business sector, subsector, industry group, industry, and industry subdivision. NAICS is a valuable tool for analyzing, segmenting, and targeting business markets.

7-6 Explain the major differences between business and consumer markets. In business markets, demand is derived, inelastic, joint, and fluctuating. Purchase volume is much larger than in consumer markets, customers are fewer and more geographically concentrated, and distribution channels are more direct. Buying is approached more formally using professional purchasing agents, more people are involved in the buying process, negotiation is more complex, and reciprocity and leasing are more common. And, finally, selling strategy in business markets normally focuses on personal contact rather than on advertising.

KEY TERMS

7-1

business marketing (industrial, business-to-business, B-to-B, or B2B marketing) the marketing of goods and services to individuals and organizations for purposes other than personal consumption

business product (industrial product) a product used to manufacture other goods or services, to facilitate an organization's operations, or to resell to other customers

consumer product a product bought to satisfy an individual's personal wants or needs

7-2

Content marketing a strategic marketing approach that focuses on creating and distributing content that is valuable, relevant and consistent.

7-3

strategic alliance (strategic partnership) a cooperative agreement between business firms

relationship commitment a firm's belief that an ongoing relationship with another firm is so important that the relationship warrants maximum efforts at maintaining it indefinitely

trust the condition that exists when one party has confidence in an exchange partner's reliability and integrity

keiretsu a network of interlocking corporate affiliates

7-4

original equipment manufacturers (OEMs) individuals and organizations that buy business goods and incorporate them into the products they produce for eventual sale to other producers or to consumers

7-5

North American Industry Classification System (NAICS) a detailed numbering system developed by the United States, Canada, and Mexico to classify North American business establishments by their main production processes

7-6

derived demand the demand for business products

joint demand the demand for two or more items used together in a final product

multiplier effect (accelerator principle) phenomenon in which a small increase or decrease in consumer demand can produce a much larger change in demand for the facilities and equipment needed to make the consumer product

CHAPTER REVIEW 7

business-to-business online exchange an electronic trading floor that provides companies with integrated links to their customers and suppliers

reciprocity a practice whereby business purchasers choose to buy from their own customers

7-7

major equipment (installations) capital goods such as large or expensive machines, mainframe computers, blast furnaces, generators, airplanes, and buildings

accessory equipment goods, such as portable tools and office equipment, that are less expensive and shorter-lived than major equipment

raw materials unprocessed extractive or agricultural products, such as mineral ore, lumber, wheat, corn, fruits, vegetables, and fish

component parts either finished items ready for assembly or products that need very little processing before becoming part of some other product

processed materials products used directly in manufacturing other products

supplies consumable items that do not become part of the final product

business services expense items that do not become part of a final product

7-8

buying center all those people in an organization who become involved in the purchase decision

new buy a situation requiring the purchase of a product for the first time

modified rebuy a situation in which the purchaser wants some change in the original good or service

straight rebuy a situation in which the purchaser reorders the same goods or services without looking for new information or investigating other suppliers

7-7 Describe the seven types of business goods and services. Major equipment includes capital goods such as heavy machinery. Accessory equipment is typically less expensive and shorter lived than major equipment. Raw materials are extractive or agricultural products that have not been processed. Component parts are finished or near-finished items to be used as parts of other products. Processed materials are used to manufacture other products. Supplies are consumable and not used as part of a final product. Business services are intangible products that many companies use in their operations.

7-8 Discuss the unique aspects of business buying behavior. Business buying behavior is distinguished by five fundamental characteristics. First, buying is normally undertaken by a buying center consisting of many people who range widely in authority level. Second, business buyers typically evaluate alternative products and suppliers based on quality, service, and price—in that order. Third, business buying falls into three general categories: new buys, modified rebuys, and straight rebuys. Fourth, the ethics of business buyers and sellers are often scrutinized. Fifth, customer service before, during, and after the sale plays a big role in business purchase decisions.

KEY CONCEPTS

8-1 Describe the characteristics of markets and market segments.
A market is composed of individuals or organizations with the ability and willingness to make purchases to fulfill their needs or wants. A market segment is a group of individuals or organizations with similar product needs as a result of one or more common characteristics.

8-2 Explain the importance of market segmentation. Before the 1960s, few businesses targeted specific market segments. Today, segmentation is a crucial marketing strategy for nearly all successful organizations. Market segmentation enables marketers to tailor marketing mixes to meet the needs of particular population segments. Segmentation helps marketers identify consumer needs and preferences, areas of declining demand, and new marketing opportunities.

8-3 Discuss the criteria for successful market segmentation.
Successful market segmentation depends on four basic criteria: (1) a market segment must be substantial and have enough potential customers to be viable; (2) a market segment must be identifiable and measurable; (3) members of a market segment must be accessible to marketing efforts; and (4) a market segment must respond to particular marketing efforts in a way that distinguishes it from other segments.

8-4 Describe the bases commonly used to segment consumer markets. Five bases are commonly used for segmenting consumer markets. Geographic segmentation is based on region, size, density, and climate characteristics. Demographic segmentation is based on age, gender, income level, ethnicity, and family life cycle characteristics. Psychographic segmentation includes personality, motives, and lifestyle characteristics. Benefits sought is a type of segmentation that identifies customers according to the benefits they seek in a product. Finally, usage segmentation divides a market by the amount of product purchased or consumed.

8-5 Describe the bases for segmenting business markets. Business markets can be segmented on two general bases. First, businesses may segment markets based on company characteristics, such as customers' geographic location, type of company, company size, and product use. Second, companies may segment customers based on the buying processes those customers use.

8-6 List the steps involved in segmenting markets. Six steps are involved when segmenting markets: (1) selecting a market or product category for study; (2) choosing a basis or bases for segmenting the market; (3) selecting segmentation descriptors; (4) profiling and evaluating segments; (5) selecting target markets; and (6) designing, implementing, and maintaining appropriate marketing mixes.

8-7 Discuss alternative strategies for selecting target markets. Marketers select target markets using three different strategies: undifferentiated targeting, concentrated targeting, and multisegment targeting. An undifferentiated targeting strategy assumes that all members of a market have similar needs that can be met with a single marketing mix. A concentrated targeting strategy focuses all marketing efforts on a single market segment. Multisegment targeting is a strategy that uses two or more marketing mixes to target two or more market segments.

8-8 Explain how CRM can be used as a targeting tool. Companies that successfully implement CRM tend to customize the goods and services offered to their customers based on data generated through interactions between carefully defined groups of customers and the company. CRM relies on four things to be successful: personalization, time savings, loyalty, and technology. Although mass marketing will probably continue to be used, the advantages of CRM cannot be ignored.

KEY TERMS

8-1
market people or organizations with needs or wants and the ability and willingness to buy

market segment a subgroup of people or organizations sharing one or more characteristics that cause them to have similar product needs

market segmentation the process of dividing a market into meaningful, relatively similar, and identifiable segments or groups

8-4
segmentation bases (variables) characteristics of individuals, groups, or organizations

geographic segmentation segmenting markets by region of a country or the world, market size, market density, or climate

demographic segmentation segmenting markets by age, gender, income, ethnic background, and family life cycle

family life cycle (FLC) a series of stages determined by a combination of age, marital status, and the presence or absence of children

psychographic segmentation segmenting markets on the basis of personality, motives, lifestyles, and geodemographics

geodemographic segmentation segmenting potential customers into neighborhood lifestyle categories

benefit segmentation the process of grouping customers into market segments according to the benefits they seek from the product

usage-rate segmentation dividing a market by the amount of product bought or consumed

80/20 principle a principle holding that 20 percent of all customers generate 80 percent of the demand

8-5
satisficers business customers who place an order with the first familiar supplier to satisfy product and delivery requirements

optimizers business customers who consider numerous suppliers (both familiar and unfamiliar), solicit bids, and study all proposals carefully before selecting one

8-7
target market a group of people or organizations for which an organization designs, implements, and maintains a marketing mix intended to meet the needs of that group, resulting in mutually satisfying exchanges

undifferentiated targeting strategy a marketing approach that views the market as one big market with no individual segments and thus uses a single marketing mix

concentrated targeting strategy a strategy used to select one segment of a market for targeting marketing efforts

niche one segment of a market

multisegment targeting strategy a strategy that chooses two or more well-defined market segments and develops a distinct marketing mix for each

cannibalization a situation that occurs when sales of a new product cut into sales of a firm's existing products

8-9

positioning developing a specific marketing mix to influence potential customers' overall perception of a brand, product line, or organization in general

position the place a product, brand, or group of products occupies in consumers' minds relative to competing offerings

product differentiation a positioning strategy that some firms use to distinguish their products from those of competitors

perceptual mapping a means of displaying or graphing, in two or more dimensions, the location of products, brands, or groups of products in customers' minds

repositioning changing consumers' perceptions of a brand in relation to competing brands

8-9 Explain how and why firms implement positioning strategies and how product differentiation plays a role. Positioning is used to influence consumer perceptions of a particular brand, product line, or organization in relation to competitors. The term *position* refers to the place that the offering occupies in consumers' minds. To establish a unique position, many firms use product differentiation, emphasizing the real or perceived differences between competing offerings. Products may be differentiated on the basis of attribute, price and quality, use or application, product user, product class, competitor, or emotion. Some firms, instead of using product differentiation, position their products as being similar to competing products or brands. Sometimes products or companies are repositioned in order to sustain growth in slow markets or to correct positioning mistakes.

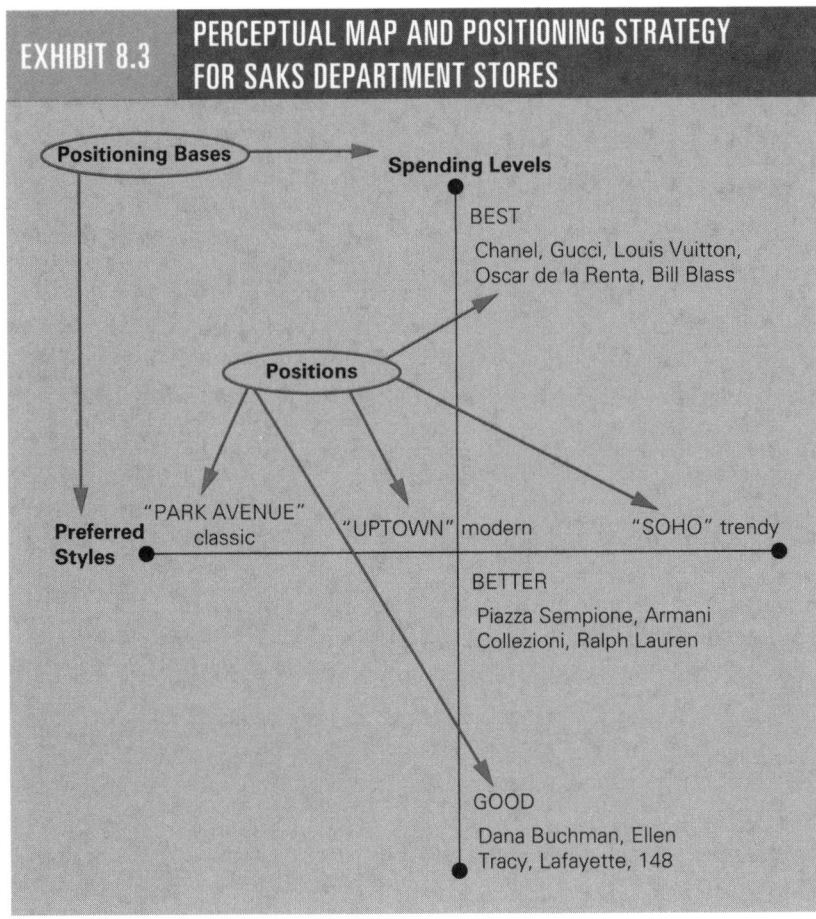

EXHIBIT 8.3 *PERCEPTUAL MAP AND POSITIONING STRATEGY FOR SAKS DEPARTMENT STORES*

KEY CONCEPTS

9-1 Define marketing research and explain its importance to marketing decision making. Marketing research is a process of collecting and analyzing data for the purpose of solving specific marketing problems. Practically speaking, marketers use marketing research to improve the decision-making process, trace problems, serve customers, gauge the value of goods and services, understand the marketplace, and measure customer service efforts.

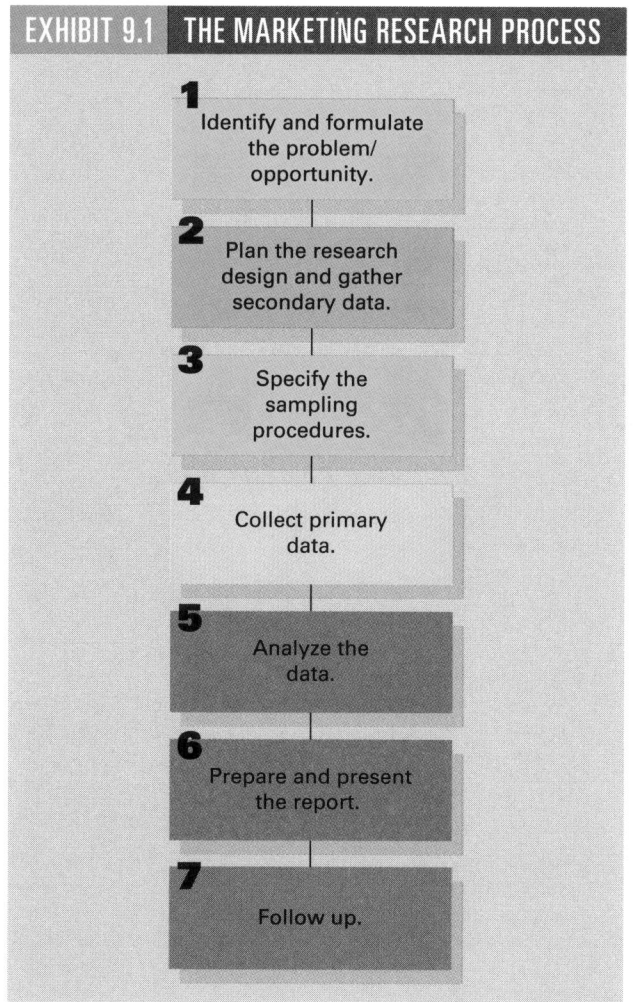

EXHIBIT 9.1 THE MARKETING RESEARCH PROCESS

1. Identify and formulate the problem/opportunity.
2. Plan the research design and gather secondary data.
3. Specify the sampling procedures.
4. Collect primary data.
5. Analyze the data.
6. Prepare and present the report.
7. Follow up.

9-2 Describe the steps involved in conducting a marketing research project. The marketing research process involves several basic steps. First, the researcher and the decision maker must agree on a problem statement or set of research objectives. Social media and big data may be helpful in this pursuit. The researcher then creates an overall research design to specify how primary data will be gathered and analyzed. Before collecting data, the researcher decides whether the group to be interviewed will be a probability or nonprobability sample. Field service firms are often hired to carry out data collection. Once data have been collected, the researcher analyzes them using statistical analysis. The researcher then prepares and presents oral and written reports, with

KEY TERMS

9-1

marketing research the process of planning, collecting, and analyzing data relevant to a marketing decision

9-2

marketing research problem determining what information is needed and how that information can be obtained efficiently and effectively

marketing research objective the specific information needed to solve a marketing research problem; the objective should be to provide insightful decision-making information

management decision problem a broad-based problem that uses marketing research in order for managers to take proper actions

secondary data data previously collected for any purpose other than the one at hand

big data the exponential growth in the volume, variety, and velocity of information and the development of complex, new tools to analyze and create meaning from such data

research design specifies which research questions must be answered, how and when the data will be gathered, and how the data will be analyzed

primary data information that is collected for the first time; used for solving the particular problem under investigation

survey research the most popular technique for gathering primary data, in which a researcher interacts with people to obtain facts, opinions, and attitudes

mall intercept interview a survey research method that involves interviewing people in the common areas of shopping malls

computer-assisted personal interviewing an interviewing method in which the interviewer reads questions from a computer screen and enters the respondent's data directly into the computer

computer-assisted self-interviewing an interviewing method in which a mall interviewer intercepts and directs willing respondents to nearby computers where each respondent reads questions off a computer screen and directly keys his or her answers into the computer

central-location telephone (CLT) facility a specially designed phone room used to conduct telephone interviewing

executive interview a type of survey that involves interviewing businesspeople at their offices concerning industrial products or services

focus group seven to ten people who participate in a group discussion led by a moderator

open-ended question an interview question that encourages an answer phrased in the respondent's own words

closed-ended question an interview question that asks the respondent to make a selection from a limited list of responses

scaled-response question a closed-ended question designed to measure the intensity of a respondent's answer

observation research a research method that relies on four types of observation: people watching people, people watching an activity, machines watching people, and machines watching an activity

mystery shoppers researchers posing as customers who gather observational data about a store

behavioral targeting (BT) a form of observation marketing research that combines a consumer's online activity with psychographic and demographic profiles compiled in databases

social media monitoring the use of automated tools to monitor online buzz, chatter, and conversations

ethnographic research the study of human behavior in its natural context; involves observation of behavior and physical setting

experiment a method of gathering primary data in which the researcher alters one or more variables while observing the effects of those alterations on another variable

sample a subset from a larger population

universe the population from which a sample will be drawn

probability sample a sample in which every element in the population has a known statistical likelihood of being selected

random sample a sample arranged in such a way that every element of the population has an equal chance of being selected as part of the sample

nonprobability sample any sample in which little or no attempt is made to get a representative cross section of the population

convenience sample a form of nonprobability sample using respondents who are convenient or readily accessible to the researcher—for example, employees, friends, or relatives

measurement error an error that occurs when there is a difference between the information desired by the researcher and the information provided by the measurement process

sampling error an error that occurs when a sample somehow does not represent the target population

frame error an error that occurs when a sample drawn from a population differs from the target population

random error an error that occurs when the selected sample is an imperfect representation of the overall population

conclusions and recommendations, to management. As a final step, the researcher determines whether the recommendations were implemented and what could have been done to make the project more successful.

9-3 Discuss the profound impact of the Internet on marketing research. The Internet has simplified the secondary data search process. Internet survey research is surging in popularity. Internet surveys can be created rapidly, are reported in real time, are relatively inexpensive, and are easily personalized. Often, researchers use the Internet to contact respondents who are difficult to reach by other means. The Internet can also be used to conduct focus groups, to distribute research proposals and reports, and to facilitate collaboration between the client and the research supplier.

9-4 Describe the growing importance of mobile research. Mobile survey traffic now accounts for approximately 30 percent of interview responses. Mobile surveys are designed to fit into the brief cracks of time that open up when a person waits for a plane, is early for an appointment, commutes to work on a train, or stands in a line. Marketers strive to engage respondents in the moment because mobile research provides immediate feedback when a consumer makes a decision to purchase, consumes a product, or experiences some form of promotion. Mobile research has also expanded into qualitative research. Using an app, respondents can participate in bulletin board and research community discussions.

9-5 Discuss the growing importance of scanner-based research. A scanner-based research system enables marketers to monitor a market panel's exposure and reaction to such variables as advertising, coupons, store displays, packaging, and price. By analyzing these variables in relation to the panel's subsequent buying behavior, marketers gain useful insight into sales and marketing strategies.

9-6 Explain when marketing research should be conducted. Because acquiring marketing information can be time-consuming and costly, deciding to acquire additional decision-making information depends on managers' perceptions of its quality, price, and timing. Research, therefore, should be undertaken only when the expected value of the information is greater than the cost of obtaining it. A customer relationship management system is integral to analyzing, transforming, and leveraging customer data.

9-7 Explain the concept of competitive intelligence. Intelligence is analyzed information, and it becomes decision-making intelligence when it has implications for the organization. By helping managers assess their competition and vendors, competitive intelligence (CI) leads to fewer surprises. CI is part of a sound marketing strategy, helps companies respond to competitive threats, and helps reduce unnecessary costs.

field service firm a firm that specializes in interviewing respondents on a subcontracted basis

cross-tabulation a method of analyzing data that lets the analyst look at the responses to one question in relation to the responses to one or more other questions

9-5

scanner-based research a system for gathering information from a single group of respondents by continuously monitoring the advertising, promotion, and pricing they are exposed to and the things they buy

BehaviorScan a scanner-based research program that tracks the purchases of 3,000 households through store scanners in each research market

InfoScan a scanner-based sales-tracking service for the consumer packaged-goods industry

neuromarketing a field of marketing that studies the body's responses to marketing stimuli

9-7

competitive intelligence (CI) an intelligence system that helps managers assess their competition and vendors in order to become more efficient and effective competitors

KEY CONCEPTS

10-1 Define the term _product_. A product is anything, desired or not, that a person or organization receives in an exchange. The basic goal of purchasing decisions is to receive the tangible and intangible benefits associated with a product. Tangible aspects include packaging, style, color, size, and features. Intangible qualities include service, the retailer's image, the manufacturer's reputation, and the social status associated with a product. An organization's product offering is the crucial element in any marketing mix.

10-2 Classify consumer products. Consumer products are classified into four categories: convenience products, shopping products, specialty products, and unsought products. Convenience products are relatively inexpensive and require limited shopping effort. Shopping products are of two types: homogeneous and heterogeneous. Because of the similarity of homogeneous products, they are differentiated mainly by price and features. In contrast, heterogeneous products appeal to consumers because of their distinct characteristics. Specialty products possess unique benefits that are highly desirable to certain customers. Finally, unsought products are either new products or products that require aggressive selling because they are generally avoided or overlooked by consumers.

10-3 Define the terms _product item, product line,_ and _product mix_. A product item is a specific version of a product that can be designated as a distinct offering among an organization's products. A product line is a group of closely related products offered by an organization. An organization's product mix includes all the products it sells. Product mix width refers to the number of product lines an organization offers. Product line depth is the number of product items in a product line. Firms modify existing products by changing their quality, functional characteristics, or style. Product line extension occurs when a firm adds new products to existing product lines.

10-4 Describe marketing uses of branding. A brand is a name, term, or symbol that identifies and differentiates a firm's products. Established brands encourage customer loyalty and help new products succeed. Branding strategies require decisions about individual, family, manufacturers', and private brands.

KEY TERMS

10-1

product everything, both favorable and unfavorable, that a person receives in an exchange

10-2

convenience product a relatively inexpensive item that merits little shopping effort

shopping product a product that requires comparison shopping because it is usually more expensive than a convenience product and is found in fewer stores

specialty product a particular item for which consumers search extensively and are very reluctant to accept substitutes

unsought product a product unknown to the potential buyer or a known product that the buyer does not actively seek

10-3

product item a specific version of a product that can be designated as a distinct offering among an organization's products

product line a group of closely related product items

product mix all products that an organization sells

product mix width the number of product lines an organization offers

product line depth the number of product items in a product line

product modification changing one or more of a product's characteristics

planned obsolescence the practice of modifying products so those that have already been sold become obsolete before they actually need replacement

EXHIBIT 10.3	COMPARISON OF MANUFACTURER'S AND PRIVATE BRANDS FROM THE RESELLERS PERSPECTIVE

Key Advantages of Carrying Manufacturers' Brands	Key Advantages of Carrying Private Brands
• Heavy advertising to the consumer by manufacturers such as Procter & Gamble helps develop strong consumer loyalties.	• A wholesaler or retailer can usually earn higher profits on its own brand. In addition, because the private brand is exclusive, there is less pressure to mark down the price to meet competition.
• Well-known manufacturers' brands, such as Kodak and Fisher-Price, can attract new customers and enhance the dealer's (wholesaler's or retailer's) prestige.	• A manufacturer can decide to drop a brand or a reseller at any time or even become a direct competitor to its dealers.
• Many manufacturers offer rapid delivery, enabling the dealer to carry less inventory.	• A private brand ties the customer to the wholesaler or retailer. A person who wants a DieHard battery must go to Sears.
• If a dealer happens to sell a manufacturer's brand of poor quality, the customer may simply switch brands and remain loyal to the dealer.	• Wholesalers and retailers have no control over the intensity of distribution of manufacturers' brands. Walmart store managers don't have to worry about competing with other sellers of Sam's American Choice products or Ol' Roy dog food. They know that these brands are sold only in Walmart and Sam's Club stores.

product line extension adding additional products to an existing product line in order to compete more broadly in the industry

10-4

brand a name, term, symbol, design, or combination thereof that identifies a seller's products and differentiates them from competitors' products

brand name that part of a brand that can be spoken, including letters, words, and numbers

brand mark the elements of a brand that cannot be spoken

brand equity the value of a company or brand name

global brand a brand that obtains at least a one-third of its earnings from outside its home country, is recognizable outside its home base of customers, and has publicly available marketing and financial data

brand loyalty consistent preference for one brand over all others

manufacturer's brand the brand name of a manufacturer

private brand a brand name owned by a wholesaler or a retailer

captive brand a brand manufactured by a third party for an exclusive retailer, without evidence of that retailer's affiliation

individual branding using different brand names for different products

family branding marketing several different products under the same brand name

co-branding placing two or more brand names on a product or its package

trademark the exclusive right to use a brand or part of a brand

service mark a trademark for a service

generic product name identifies a product by class or type and cannot be trademarked

10-5

persuasive labeling a type of package labeling that focuses on a promotional theme or logo, and consumer information is secondary

informational labeling a type of package labeling designed to help consumers make proper product selections and lower their cognitive dissonance after the purchase

universal product codes (UPCs) a series of thick and thin vertical lines (bar codes) readable by computerized optical scanners that represent numbers used to track products

10-7

warranty a confirmation of the quality or performance of a good or service

express warranty a written guarantee

implied warranty an unwritten guarantee that the good or service is fit for the purpose for which it was sold

10-5 Describe marketing uses of packaging and labeling. Packaging has four functions: containing and protecting products; promoting products; facilitating product storage, use, and convenience; and facilitating recycling and reducing environmental damage As a tool for promotion, packaging identifies the brand and its features. It also serves the critical function of differentiating a product from competing products and linking it with related products from the same manufacturer. The label is an integral part of the package, with persuasive and informational functions. In essence, the package is the marketer's last chance to influence buyers before they make a purchase decision.

10-6 Discuss global issues in branding and packaging. In addition to brand piracy, international marketers must address a variety of concerns regarding branding and packaging, including choosing a brand name policy, translating labels and meeting host-country labeling requirements, making packages aesthetically compatible with host-country cultures, and offering the sizes of packages preferred in host countries.

Global Branding Considerations	Global Packaging Considerations
One name	Labeling
Modify or adapt one name	Aesthetics
Different names in different markets	Climate

10-7 Describe how and why product warranties are important marketing tools. Just as a package is designed to protect the product, a warranty protects the buyer and gives essential information about the product. A warranty confirms the quality or performance of a good or service. An express warranty is a written guarantee. Express warranties range from simple statements—such as "100-percent cotton" (a guarantee of quality) and "complete satisfaction guaranteed" (a statement of performance)—to extensive documents written in technical language. In contrast, an implied warranty is an unwritten guarantee that the good or service is fit for the purpose for which it was sold. All sales have an implied warranty under the Uniform Commercial Code.

Express warranty = written guarantee

Implied warranty = unwritten guarantee

KEY CONCEPTS

11-1 Explain the importance of developing new products and describe the six categories of new products. New products are important to sustain growth and profits and to replace obsolete items. New products can be classified as new-to-the-world products (discontinuous innovations), new product lines, additions to existing product lines, improvements or revisions of existing products, repositioned products, or lower-priced products. To sustain or increase profits, a firm must innovate.

11-2 Explain the steps in the new-product development process. First, a firm forms a new-product strategy by outlining the characteristics and roles of future products. Then new-product ideas are generated by customers, employees, distributors, competitors, vendors, and internal research and development personnel. Once a product idea has survived initial screening by an appointed screening group, it undergoes business analysis to determine its potential profitability. If a product concept seems viable, it progresses into the development phase, in which the technical and economic feasibility of the manufacturing process is evaluated. The development phase also includes laboratory and use testing of a product for performance and safety. Following initial testing and refinement, most products are introduced in a test market to evaluate consumer response and marketing strategies. Finally, test market successes are propelled into full commercialization. The commercialization process involves starting up production, building inventories, shipping to distributors, training a sales force, announcing the product to the trade, and advertising to consumers.

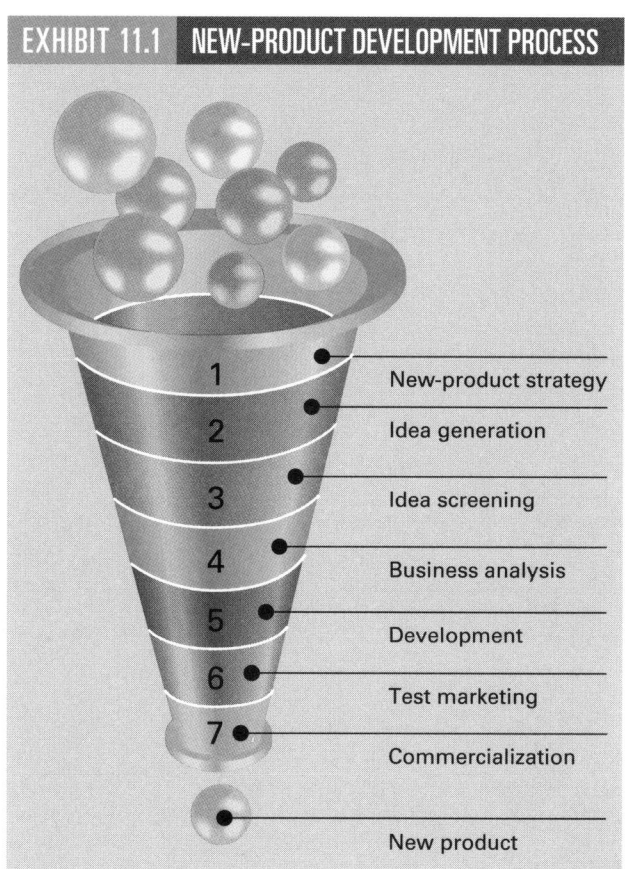

EXHIBIT 11.1 NEW-PRODUCT DEVELOPMENT PROCESS

1. New-product strategy
2. Idea generation
3. Idea screening
4. Business analysis
5. Development
6. Test marketing
7. Commercialization

New product

KEY TERMS

11-1

new product a product new to the world, the market, the producer, the seller, or some combination of these

11-2

new-product strategy a plan that links the new-product development process with the objectives of the marketing department, the business unit, and the corporation

product development a marketing strategy that entails the creation of marketable new products; the process of converting applications for new technologies into marketable products

brainstorming the process of getting a group to think of unlimited ways to vary a product or solve a problem

screening the first filter in the product development process, which eliminates ideas that are inconsistent with the organization's new-product strategy or are obviously inappropriate for some other reason

concept test a test to evaluate a new-product idea, usually before any prototype has been created

business analysis the second stage of the screening process where preliminary figures for demand, cost, sales, and profitability are calculated

development the stage in the product development process in which a prototype is developed and a marketing strategy is outlined

simultaneous product development a team-oriented approach to new-product development

test marketing the limited introduction of a product and a marketing program to determine the reactions of potential customers in a market situation

simulated (laboratory) market testing the presentation of advertising and other promotional materials for several products, including a test product, to members of the product's target market

commercialization the decision to market a product

11-5

innovation a product perceived as new by a potential adopter

diffusion the process by which the adoption of an innovation spreads

11-6

product life cycle (PLC) a concept that provides a way to trace the stages of a product's acceptance, from its introduction (birth) to its decline (death)

CHAPTER REVIEW 11

product category all brands that satisfy a particular type of need

introductory stage the full-scale launch of a new product into the marketplace

growth stage the second stage of the product life cycle when sales typically grow at an increasing rate, many competitors enter the market, large companies may start to acquire small pioneering firms, and profits are healthy

maturity stage a period during which sales increase at a decreasing rate

decline stage a long-run drop in sales

11-3 Understand why some products succeed and others fail. Despite the amount of time and money spent on developing and testing new products, a large proportion of new-product introductions fail. Products fail for a number of reasons. Failure can be a matter of degree—absolute failure occurs when a company cannot recoup its development, marketing, and production costs, while relative product failure occurs when the product returns a profit but fails to achieve sales, profit, or market share goals.

11-4 Discuss global issues in new-product development. A marketer with global vision seeks to develop products that can easily be adapted to suit local needs. The goal is not simply to develop a standard product that can be sold worldwide. Smart global marketers also look for good product ideas worldwide.

11-5 Explain the diffusion process through which new products are adopted. The diffusion process is the spread of a new product from its producer to ultimate adopters. Adopters in the diffusion process belong to five categories: innovators, early adopters, the early majority, the late majority, and laggards. Product characteristics that affect the rate of adoption include product complexity, compatibility with existing social values, relative advantage over existing substitutes, visibility, and "trialability." The diffusion process is facilitated by word-of-mouth communication and communication from marketers to consumers.

11-6 Explain the concept of product life cycles. All brands and product categories undergo a life cycle with four stages: introduction, growth, maturity, and decline. The rate at which products move through these stages varies dramatically. Marketing managers use the product life cycle concept as an analytical tool to forecast a product's future and devise effective marketing strategies.

EXHIBIT 11.2 FOUR STAGES OF THE PRODUCT LIFE CYCLE

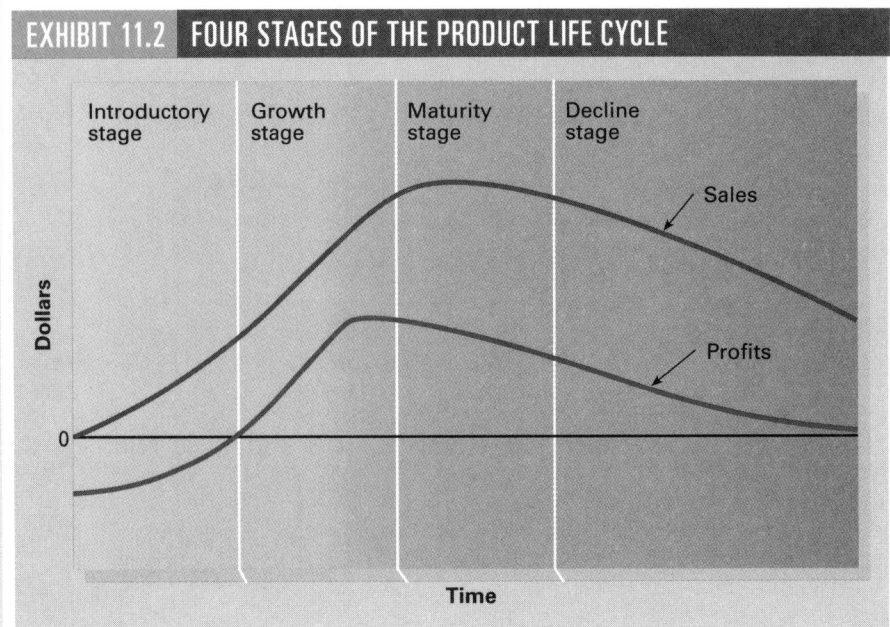

KEY CONCEPTS

12-1 Discuss the importance of services to the economy. The service sector plays a crucial role in the U.S. economy. In 2014, service industries accounted for 68 percent of U.S. GDP and four out of five U.S. jobs. Services have unique characteristics that distinguish them from goods, and marketing strategies need to be adjusted for these characteristics.

12-2 Discuss the differences between services and goods. Services are distinguished by four characteristics. Services are intangible performances in that they lack clearly identifiable physical characteristics, making it difficult for marketers to communicate their specific benefits to potential customers. The production and consumption of services occurs simultaneously. Services are heterogeneous because their quality depends on such elements as the service provider, individual consumer, location, and the like. Finally, services are perishable in the sense that they cannot be stored or saved. As a result, synchronizing supply with demand is particularly challenging in the service industry.

12-3 Describe the components of service quality and the gap model of service quality. Service quality has five components: reliability (ability to perform the service dependably, accurately, and consistently), responsiveness (providing prompt service), assurance (knowledge and courtesy of employees and their ability to convey trust), empathy (caring, individualized attention), and tangibles (physical evidence of the service).

The gap model identifies five key discrepancies that can influence customer evaluations of service quality. When the gaps are large, service quality is low. As the gaps shrink, service quality improves. Gap 1 is found between customers' expectations and management's perceptions of those expectations. Gap 2 is found between management's perception of what the customer wants and specifications for service quality. Gap 3 is found between service quality specifications and delivery of the service. Gap 4 is found between service delivery and what the company promises to the customer through external communication. Gap 5 is found between customers' service expectations and their perceptions of service performance.

12-4 Develop marketing mixes for services. "Product" (service) strategy issues include what is being processed (people, possessions, mental stimulus, information), core and supplementary services, customization versus standardization, and the service mix. Distribution (place) decisions involve convenience, number of outlets, direct versus indirect distribution, and scheduling. Stressing tangible cues, using personal sources of information, creating strong organizational images, and engaging in postpurchase communication are effective promotion strategies. Pricing objectives for services can be revenue oriented, operations oriented, patronage oriented, or any combination of the three.

12-5 Discuss relationship marketing in services. Relationship marketing in services involves attracting, developing, and retaining customer relationships. There are four levels of relationship marketing: level 1 focuses on pricing incentives; level 2 uses pricing incentives and social bonds with customers; level 3 focuses on customization; and level 4 uses pricing, social bonds, and structural bonds to build long-term relationships.

12-6 Explain internal marketing in services. Internal marketing means treating employees as customers and developing systems and benefits that satisfy their needs. Employees who like their jobs and are happy with the firm they work for are more likely to deliver good service.

KEY TERMS

12-1

service the result of applying human or mechanical efforts to people or objects

12-2

intangibility the inability of services to be touched, seen, tasted, heard, or felt in the same manner that goods can be sensed

search quality a characteristic that can be easily assessed before purchase

experience quality a characteristic that can be assessed only after use

credence quality a characteristic that consumers may have difficulty assessing even after purchase because they do not have the necessary knowledge or experience

inseparability the inability of the production and consumption of a service to be separated; consumers must be present during the production

heterogeneity the variability of the inputs and outputs of services, which causes services to tend to be less standardized and uniform than goods

perishability the inability of services to be stored, warehoused, or inventoried

12-3

reliability the ability to perform a service dependably, accurately, and consistently

responsiveness the ability to provide prompt service

assurance the knowledge and courtesy of employees and their ability to convey trust

empathy caring, individualized attention to customers

tangibles the physical evidence of a service, including the physical facilities, tools, and equipment used to provide the service

gap model a model identifying five gaps that can cause problems in service delivery and influence customer evaluations of service quality

12-4

core service the most basic benefit the consumer is buying

supplementary services a group of services that support or enhance the core service

mass customization a strategy that uses technology to deliver customized services on a mass basis

12-6

internal marketing treating employees as customers and developing systems and benefits that satisfy their needs

CHAPTER REVIEW 12

EXHIBIT 12.1   GAP MODEL OF SERVICE QUALITY

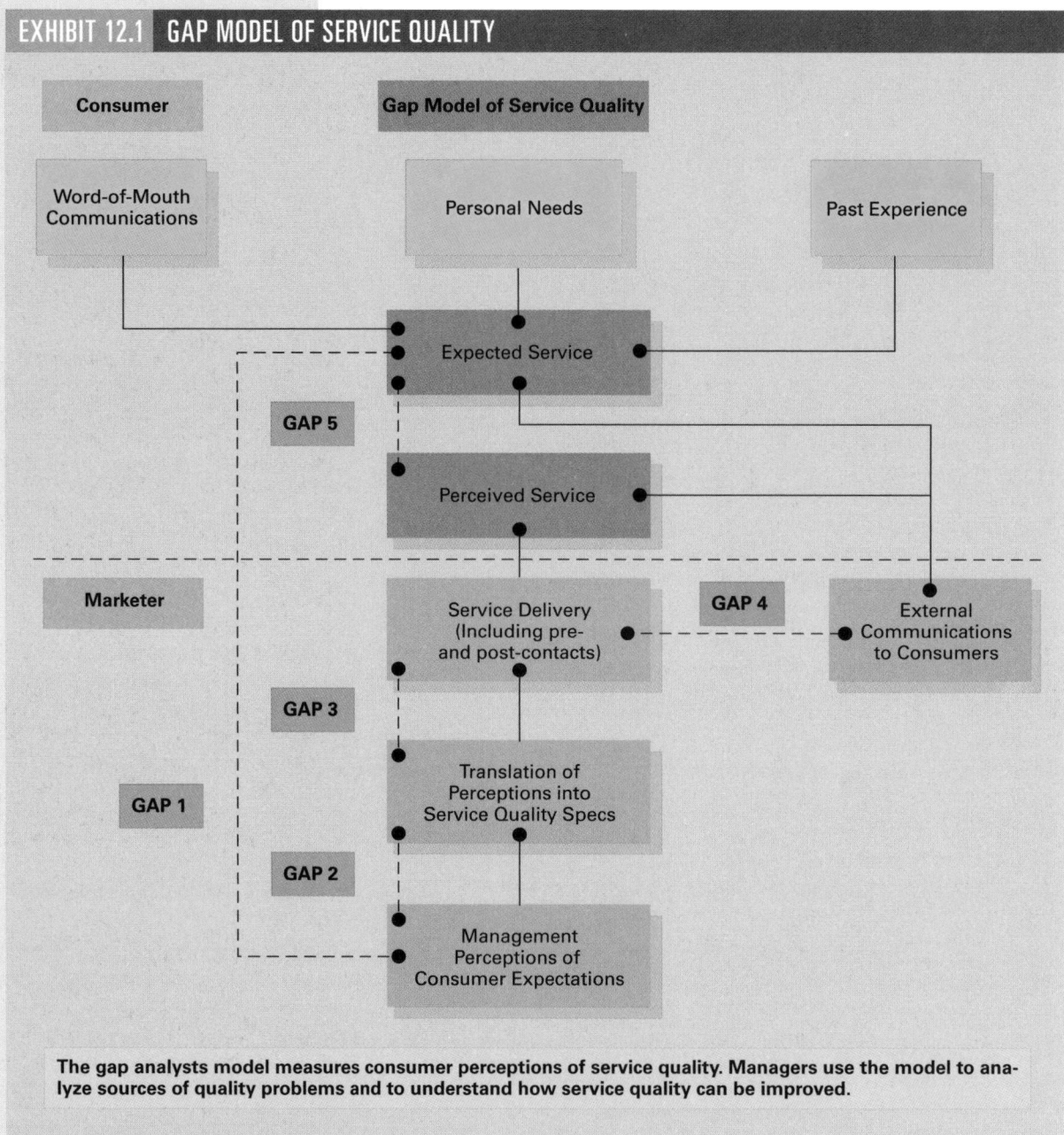

The gap analysts model measures consumer perceptions of service quality. Managers use the model to analyze sources of quality problems and to understand how service quality can be improved.

Based on Valarie A. Zeithaml, Mary Jo Bitner, and Dwayne Gremler, *Services Marketing*, 4/e, © 2006 (New York: McGraw-Hill, 2006).

12-7

nonprofit organization an organization that exists to achieve some goal other than the usual business goals of profit, market share, or return on investment

nonprofit organization marketing the effort by nonprofit organizations to bring about mutually satisfying exchanges with target markets

public service advertisement (PSA) an announcement that promotes a program of a federal, state, or local government or of a nonprofit organization

12-7 Describe nonprofit organization marketing. Nonprofit organizations pursue goals other than profit, market share, and return on investment. Nonprofit organization marketing facilitates mutually satisfying exchanges between nonprofit organizations and their target markets. Several unique characteristics distinguish nonbusiness marketing strategy, including a concern with services and social behaviors rather than manufactured goods and profit; a difficult, undifferentiated, and in some ways marginal target market; a complex product that may have only indirect benefits and elicit very low involvement; distribution that may or may not require special facilities depending on the service provided; a relative lack of resources for promotion; and prices only indirectly related to the exchange between the producer and the consumer of services.

12-8 Discuss global issues in services marketing. The United States has become the world's largest exporter of services. Although competition is keen, the United States has a competitive advantage because of its vast experience in many service industries. To be successful globally, service firms must adjust their marketing mix for the environment of each target country.

KEY CONCEPTS

13-1 Define the terms *supply chain* and *supply chain management* and discuss the benefits of supply chain management. Management coordinates and integrates all of the activities performed by supply chain members into a seamless process from the source to the point of consumption. The benefits of supply chain management include reduced inventory, transportation, warehousing, and packaging costs; greater supply chain flexibility; improved customer service; and higher revenues.

13-2 Discuss the concepts of internal and external supply chain integration and explain why each of these types of integration is important. In the modern supply chain, integration can be either internal or external. Internally, the very best companies develop a managerial orientation toward demand-supply integration. Externally, five types of integration are sought by firms interested in providing top-level service to customers: relationship integration, measurement integration, technology and planning integration, material and service supplier integration, and customer integration.

13-3 Identify the eight key processes of excellent supply chain management and discuss how each of these processes affects the end customer. The key processes that leading supply chain companies focus on are (1) customer relationship management, (2) customer service management, (3) demand management, (4) order fulfillment, (5) manufacturing flow management, (6) supplier relationship management, (7) product development and commercialization, and (8) returns management. When firms practice excellent supply chain management, each of these processes is integrated from end to end in the supply chain.

13-4 Understand the importance of sustainable supply chain management to modern business operations. Sustainable supply chain management involves the integration and balancing of environmental, social, and economic thinking into all phases of the supply chain management process.

13-5 Discuss how new technology and emerging trends are impacting the practice of supply chain management. Several emerging trends are changing the job of today's supply chain manager. Some of the business trends affecting supply chain management include outsourcing logistics, public-private partnerships, electronic distribution, maintaining a secure supply chain, and new analytics tools. While these changes exert pressure on managers to change the way their supply chains function, they also help make supply chain management more integrated and easier to track.

13-6 Explain what marketing channels and channel intermediaries are and describe their functions and activities. A marketing channel is a business structure of interdependent organizations that reach from the point of production to the consumer. Intermediaries negotiate with one another, buy and sell products, and facilitate the change of ownership between buyer and seller. Retailers are those firms in the channel that sell directly to consumers.

13-7 Describe common channel structures and strategies and the factors that influence their choice. When possible, producers use the direct channel to sell directly to consumers. When one or more channel members are small companies, an agent/broker channel may be the best solution. Most consumer products are sold through distribution channels similar to the retailer channel and the wholesaler channel. Dual distribution may be used to distribute the same product to target markets, and companies often form strategic channel alliances to use already-established channels.

KEY TERMS

13-1

supply chain the connected chain of all of the business entities, both internal and external to the company, that perform or support the logistics function

supply chain management a management system that coordinates and integrates all of the activities performed by supply chain members into a seamless process, from the source to the point of consumption, resulting in enhanced customer and economic value

supply chain agility an operational strategy focused on creating inventory velocity and operational flexibility simultaneously in the supply chain

13-2

supply chain orientation a system of management practices that are consistent with a "systems thinking" approach

supply chain integration when multiple firms or business functions in a supply chain coordinate their activities and processes so that they are seamlessly linked to one another in an effort to satisfy the customer

demand-supply integration (DSI) a supply chain operational philosophy focused on integrating the supply-management and demand-generating functions of an organization

13-3

business processes bundles of interconnected activities that stretch across firms in the supply chain

customer relationship management (CRM) process allows companies to prioritize their marketing focus on different customer groups according to each group's long-term value to the company or supply chain

customer service management process presents a multi-company, unified response system to the customer whenever complaints, concerns, questions, or comments are voiced

demand management process seeks to align supply and demand throughout the supply chain by anticipating customer requirements at each level and creating demand-related plans of action prior to actual customer purchasing behavior

order fulfillment process a highly integrated process, often requiring persons from multiple companies and multiple functions to come together and coordinate to create customer satisfaction at a given place and time

order cycle time the time delay between the placement of a customer's order and the customer's receipt of that order

manufacturing flow management process concerned with ensuring that firms in the supply chain have the needed resources to manufacture with flexibility and to move products through a multi-stage production process

CHAPTER REVIEW 13

supplier relationship management process supports manufacturing flow by identifying and maintaining relationships with highly valued suppliers

product development and commercialization process includes the group of activities that facilitates the joint development and marketing of new offerings among a group of supply chain partner firms

returns management process enables firms to manage volumes of returned product efficiently while minimizing returns-related costs and maximizing the value of the returned assets to the firms in the supply chain

13-4

sustainable supply chain management a supply chain management philosophy that embraces the need for optimizing social and environmental costs in addition to financial costs

13-5

outsourcing (contract logistics) a manufacturer's or supplier's use of an independent third party to manage an entire function of the logistics system, such as transportation, warehousing, or order processing

third-party logistics company (3PL) a firm that provides functional logistics services to others

fourth-party logistics company (4PL or logistics integrator) a consulting-based organization that assesses another's entire logistical service needs and provides integrated solutions, often drawing on multiple 3PLs for actual service

offshoring the outsourcing of a business process from one country to another for the purpose of gaining economic advantage

nearshoring the transfer of an offshored activity from a distant to a nearby country

public-private partnerships (PPPs) Critical to the satisfaction of both company and societal interests and provide a mechanism by which very-large scale problems or opportunities can be addressed

electronic distribution a distribution technique that includes any kind of product or service that can be distributed electronically, whether over traditional forms such as fiber-optic cable or through satellite transmission of electronic signals

three-dimensional printing (3DP) the creation of three-dimensional objects via an additive manufacturing (printing) technology that layers raw material into desired shapes

big data the rapidly collected and difficult-to-process large-scale datasets that have recently emerged, and which push the limits of current analytical capability

cloud computing the practice of using remote network servers to store, manage, and process data

supply chain analytics data analyses that support the improved design and management of the supply chain

Managers must decide what role distribution will play in the overall marketing strategy. In addition, they must be sure that the channel strategy chosen is consistent with market factors, product factors, and producer factors. Organizations have three options for intensity of distribution: intensive distribution, selective distribution, or exclusive distribution.

13-8 Discuss multichannel and omnichannel marketing in both B-to-B and B-to-C structures and explain why these concepts are important. Many companies have begun employing multichannel marketing strategies, whereby customers are offered information, goods, services, and/or support through one or more synchronized channels. While it can promote better consumer behavior, the multichannel design also creates redundancy and complexity in the firm's distribution system. Selling through multiple channels is typified by multiple parallel supply chains, each with its own inventory, processes, and performance metrics. Many companies are transitioning to omnichannel distribution operations that support their multichannel retail operations and unify their retail interfaces. With omnichannel operations, every customer receives equally efficient service.

13-6

marketing channel (channel of distribution) a set of interdependent organizations that eases the transfer of ownership as products move from producer to business user or consumer

channel members all parties in the marketing channel who negotiate with one another, buy and sell products, and facilitate the change of ownership between buyer and seller in the course of moving the product from the manufacturer into the hands of the final consumer

form utility the elements of the composition and appearance of a product that make it desirable

time utility the increase in customer satisfaction gained by making a good or service available at the appropriate time

place utility the usefulness of a good or service as a function of the location at which it is made available

exchange utility the increased value of a product that is created as its ownership is transferred

merchant wholesaler an institution that buys goods from manufacturers and resells them to businesses, government agencies, and other wholesalers or retailers and that receives and takes title to goods, stores them in its own warehouses, and later ships them

agents and brokers wholesaling intermediaries who do not take title to a product but facilitate its sale from producer to end user by representing retailers, wholesalers, or manufacturers

retailer a channel intermediary that sells mainly to consumers

13-7

direct channel a distribution channel in which producers sell directly to consumers

dual distribution (multiple distribution) the use of two or more channels to distribute the same product to target markets

nontraditional channels non-physical channels that facilitate the unique market access of products and services

strategic channel alliance a cooperative agreement between business firms to use the other's already established distribution channel

gray marketing channels secondary channels that are unintended to be used by the producer, and which often flow illegally obtained or counterfeit product toward customers

reverse channels channels that enable customers to return products or components for reuse or remanufacturing

drop and shop a system used by several retailers that allow customers to bring used products for return or donation at the entrance of the store

digital channels electronic pathways that allow products and related information to flow from producer to consumer

M-commerce the ability to conduct commerce using a mobile device for the purpose of buying or selling goods or services

intensive distribution a form of distribution aimed at having a product available in every outlet where target customers might want to buy it

selective distribution a form of distribution achieved by screening dealers to eliminate all but a few in any single area

exclusive distribution a form of distribution that establishes one or a few dealers within a given area

KEY CONCEPTS

14-1 Explain the importance of the retailer within the channel and the U.S. economy Retailing represents all the activities directly related to the sale of goods and services to the ultimate consumer for personal, nonbusiness use, and has enhanced the quality of our daily lives. When we shop for groceries, hair styling, clothes, books, and many other products and services, we are doing business with retailers. Retailing affects all people directly or indirectly. Trends and innovations relating to customer data, social media, and alternative forms of shopping are constantly developing, and retailers have no choice but to react.

14-2 List and understand the different types of retailers Retail establishments can be classified according to ownership, level of service, product assortment, and price. These variables can be combined in several ways to create various retail operating models. Retail ownership takes one of three forms: independent, part of a chain, or a franchise outlet. The service levels that retailers provide range from full-service to self-service. Retailers can also be categorized by the width and depth of their product lines. Price is the fourth way to position retail stores. Many stores fall into the basic types of retailers, but some companies have begun to experiment with alternative formats.

14-3 Explain why nonstore retailing is on the rise and list the advantages of its different forms Nonstore retailing enables customers to shop without visiting a physical store location. It adds a level of convenience for customers who wish to shop from their current locations. Due to broader changes in culture and society, nonstore retailing is currently growing faster than in-store retailing. The major forms of nonstore retailing are automatic vending, direct retailing, direct marketing, and Internet retailing.

KEY TERMS

14-1

retailing all the activities directly related to the sale of goods and services to the ultimate consumer for personal, nonbusiness use

retailer a channel intermediary that sells mainly to consumers

14-2

independent retailer a retailer owned by a single person or partnership and not operated as part of a larger retail institution

chain store a store that is part of a group of the same stores owned and operated by a single organization

franchise a relationship in which the business rights to operate and sell a product are granted by the franchisor to the franchisee

franchisor the originator of a trade name, product, methods of operation, and the like that grants operating rights to another party to sell its product

franchisee an individual or business that is granted the right to sell another party's product

gross margin the amount of money the retailer makes as a percentage of sales after the cost of goods sold is subtracted

EXHIBIT 14.1 TYPES OF STORES AND THEIR CHARACTERISTICS

Type of Retailer	Level of Service	Product Assortment	Price	Gross Margin
Department store	Moderately high to high	Broad	Moderate to high	Moderately high
Specialty store	High	Narrow	Moderate to high	High
Supermarket	Low	Broad	Moderate	Low
Drugstore	Low to moderate	Medium	Moderate	Low
Convenience store	Low	Medium to narrow	Moderately high	Moderately high
Full-line discount store	Moderate to low	Medium to broad	Moderately low	Moderately low
Specialty discount store	Moderate to low	Medium to broad	Moderately low to low	Moderately low
Warehouse club	Low	Broad	Low to very low	Low
Off-price retailer	Low	Medium to narrow	Low	Low
Restaurant	Low to high	Narrow	Low to high	Low to high

14-4 Discuss the different retail operations models and understand why they vary in strategy and format Retail formats are co-aligned with unique operating models that guide the decisions made by their managers. Each operating model can be summarized as a set of guiding principles. Today, most retail stores remain

department store a store housing several departments under one roof

specialty store a retail store specializing in a given type of merchandise

CHAPTER REVIEW 14

supermarket a large, departmentalized, self-service retailer that specializes in food and some nonfood items

drugstore a retail store that stocks pharmacy-related products and services as its main draw

convenience store a miniature supermarket, carrying only a limited line of high-turnover convenience goods

discount store a retailer that competes on the basis of low prices, high turnover, and high volume

full-line discount store a discount store that carries a vast depth and breadth of product within a single product category

supercenter a large retailer that stocks and sells a wide variety of merchandise including groceries, clothing, household goods, and other general merchandise

specialty discount store a retail store that offers a nearly complete selection of single-line merchandise and uses self-service, discount prices, high volume, and high turnover

category killer a large discount store that specializes in a single line of merchandise and becomes the dominant retailer in its category

warehouse club a large, no-frills retailer that sells bulk quantities of merchandise to customers at volume discount prices in exchange for a periodic membership fee

off-price retailer a retailer that sells at prices 25 percent or more below traditional department store prices because it pays cash for its stock and usually doesn't ask for return privileges

factory outlet an off-price retailer that is owned and operated by a manufacturer

used goods retailer a retailer whereby items purchased from one of the other types of retailers are resold to different customers

restaurant a retailer that provides both tangible products—food and drink—and valuable services—food preparation and presentation

14-3

nonstore retailing shopping without visiting a store

automatic vending the use of machines to offer goods for sale

self-service technologies (SST) technological interfaces that allow customers to provide themselves with products and/or services without the intervention of a service employee

direct retailing the selling of products by representatives who work door-to-door, office-to-office, or at home sales parties

direct marketing (DM) techniques used to get consumers to make a purchase from their home, office, or other nonretail setting

telemarketing the use of the telephone to sell directly to consumers

direct mail the delivery of advertising or marketing material to recipients of postal or electronic mail

operationally and tactically similar to those that have been in business for hundreds of years; with one or more physical locations that the customer must visit in order to purchase a stocked product, and with strategies in place to attract customers to visit.

14-5 Explain how retail marketing strategies are developed and executed Retail managers develop marketing strategies based on the goals established by stakeholders and the overall strategic plans developed by company leadership. Strategic retailing goals typically focus on increasing total sales, reducing costs of goods sold, and improving financial ratios such as return on assets or equity. The first and foremost task in developing a retail strategy is to define the target market. Then comes combining the elements of the retailing mix to come up with a single retailing method to attract that target market.

14-6 Discuss how services retailing differs from goods retailing The fastest-growing part of our economy is the service sector. Although distribution in the service sector is difficult to visualize, the same skills, techniques, and strategies used to manage inventory can also be used to manage service inventory, such as hospital beds, bank accounts, or airline seats. Because service industries are so customer oriented, service quality is a priority.

14-7 Understand how retailers address product/service failures and discuss the opportunities that service failures provide No retailer can be everything to every customer, and by making strategic decisions related to targeting, segmentation, and the retailing mix, retailers implicitly decide which customers will be delighted and which will probably leave the store unsatisfied. The best retailers have plans in place not only to recover from inevitable lapses in service but perhaps even to benefit from them.

14-8 Summarize current trends related to customer data, analytics, and technology Retailers are constantly innovating. They are always looking for new products and services (or ways to offer them) that will attract new customers or inspire current ones to buy in greater quantities or more frequently. Big data analytics, shopper marketing, mobile technology, and social media are at the front of this innovation. Some retailers have turned to channel omnification, while others have embraced click-and-collect.

microtargeting the use of direct marketing techniques that employ highly detailed data analytics in order to isolate potential customers with great precision

shop-at-home television network a specialized form of direct response marketing whereby television shows display merchandise, with the retail price, to home viewers

online retailing (e-tailing) a type of shopping available to consumers with personal computers and access to the Internet

14-4

floor stock inventory displayed for sale to customers

back stock inventory held in reserve for potential future sale in a retailer's storeroom or stockroom

14-5

retailing mix a combination of the six Ps—product, promotion, place, price, presentation, and personnel—to sell goods and services to the ultimate consumer

brand cannibalization the reduction of sales for one brand as the result of the introduction of a new product or promotion of a current product by another brand

destination store a store that consumers purposely plan to visit prior to shopping

atmosphere the overall impression conveyed by a store's physical layout, décor, and surroundings

layout the internal design and configuration of a store's fixtures and products

14-8

big data analytics the process of discovering patterns in large data sets for the purposes of extracting knowledge and understanding human behavior

beacon a device that sends out connecting signals to customers' smartphones and tablets in order to bring them into a retail store or improve their shopping experience

shopper marketing understanding how one's target consumers behave as shoppers, in different channels and formats, and leveraging this intelligence to generate sales or other positive outcomes

shopper analytics searching for and discovering meaningful patterns in shopper data for the purpose of fine-tuning, developing, or changing market offerings

retail channel omnification the reduction of multiple retail channel systems into a single, unified system for the purpose of creating efficiencies or saving costs

click-and-collect the practice of buying something online and then traveling to a physical store location to take delivery of the merchandise

KEY CONCEPTS

15-1 Discuss the role of promotion in the marketing mix. Promotional strategy is the plan for using the elements of promotion—advertising, public relations, sales promotion, personal selling, and social media—to meet the firm's overall objectives and marketing goals. Based on these objectives, the elements of the promotional strategy become a coordinated promotion plan. The promotion plan then becomes an integral part of the total marketing strategy for reaching the target market along with product, distribution, and price. Promotional strategies have changed a great deal over the years as many target customer segments have become harder and harder to reach.

15-2 Describe the communication process. The communication process has several steps. When an individual or organization has a message it wishes to convey to a target audience, it encodes that message using language and symbols familiar to the intended receiver and sends the message through a channel of communication. Noise in the transmission channel distorts the source's intended message. Reception occurs if the message falls within the receiver's frame of reference. The receiver decodes the message and usually provides feedback to the source. Normally, feedback is direct for interpersonal communication and indirect for mass communication. The Internet and social media have had an impact on the communication model in two major ways: consumers are now able to become senders, and marketers can personalize the feedback channel by initiating direct conversations with customers.

15-3 Explain the goals and tasks of promotion. The fundamental goals of promotion are to induce, modify, or reinforce behavior by informing, persuading, reminding, and connecting. Informative promotion explains a good's or service's purpose and benefits. Promotion that informs the consumer is typically used to increase demand for a general product category or to introduce a new good or service. Persuasive promotion is designed to stimulate a purchase or an action. Promotion that persuades the consumer to buy is essential during the growth stage of the product life cycle, when competition becomes fierce. Reminder promotion is used to keep the product and brand name in the public's mind. Promotions that remind are generally used during the maturity stage of the product life cycle. Connection promotion is designed to form relationships with customers and potential customers using social media. Connecting encourages customers to become brand advocates and share their experiences via social media.

15-4 Discuss the elements of the promotional mix. The elements of the promotional mix include advertising, public relations, sales promotion, personal selling, and social media. Advertising is a form of impersonal, one-way mass communication paid for by the source. Public relations is the function of promotion concerned with a firm's public image. Sales promotion is typically used to back up other components of the promotional mix by stimulating immediate demand. Personal selling typically involves direct communication, in person or by telephone; the seller tries to initiate a purchase by informing and persuading one or more potential buyers. Finally, social media are promotion tools used to facilitate conversations among people online.

15-5 Discuss the AIDA concept and its relationship to the promotional mix. The AIDA model outlines the four basic stages in the purchase decision-making process, which are initiated and propelled by promotional activities: (1) attention, (2) interest, (3) desire, and (4) action. The components of the promotional mix have varying levels of influence at each stage of the AIDA model. Advertising is a good tool for increasing awareness and knowledge of a good or service. Sales promotion is effective when consumers are at the purchase stage of the decision-making process. Personal selling is most effective in developing customer interest and desire.

KEY TERMS

15-1

promotion communication by marketers that informs, persuades, and reminds potential buyers of a product in order to influence an opinion or elicit a response

promotional strategy a plan for the optimal use of the elements of promotion: advertising, public relations, personal selling, sales promotion, and social media

competitive advantage one or more unique aspects of an organization that cause target consumers to patronize that firm rather than competitors

15-2

communication the process by which we exchange or share meaning through a common set of symbols

interpersonal communication direct, face-to-face communication between two or more people

mass communication the communication of a concept or message to large audiences

sender the originator of the message in the communication process

encoding the conversion of a sender's ideas and thoughts into a message, usually in the form of words or signs

channel a medium of communication—such as a voice, radio, or newspaper—for transmitting a message

noise anything that interferes with, distorts, or slows down the transmission of information

receiver the person who decodes a message

decoding interpretation of the language and symbols sent by the source through a channel

feedback the receiver's response to a message

15-4

promotional mix the combination of promotional tools—including advertising, public relations, personal selling, sales promotion, and social media—used to reach the target market and fulfill the organization's overall goals

advertising impersonal, one-way mass communication about a product or organization that is paid for by a marketer

public relations the marketing function that evaluates public attitudes, identifies areas within the organization the public may be interested in, and executes a program of action to earn public understanding and acceptance

publicity public information about a company, product, service, or issue appearing in the mass media as a news item

sales promotion marketing activities—other than personal selling, advertising, and public relations—that stimulate consumer buying and dealer effectiveness

personal selling a purchase situation involving a personal, paid-for communication between two people in an attempt to influence each other

paid media a category of promotional tactic based on the traditional advertising model, whereby a brand pays for media space

earned media a category of promotional tactic based on a public relations or publicity model that gets customers talking about products or services

owned media a new category of promotional tactic based on brands becoming publishers of their own content in order to maximize the brands' value to customers

15-5

AIDA concept a model that outlines the process for achieving promotional goals in terms of stages of consumer involvement with the message; the acronym stands for attention, interest, desire, and action

15-6

integrated marketing communications (IMC) the careful coordination of all promotional messages for a product or a service to ensure the consistency of messages at every contact point at which a company meets the consumer

15-7

push strategy a marketing strategy that uses aggressive personal selling and trade advertising to convince a wholesaler or a retailer to carry and sell particular merchandise

pull strategy a marketing strategy that stimulates consumer demand to obtain product distribution

15-6 Discuss the concept of integrated marketing communications.

Integrated marketing communications is the careful coordination of all promotional messages for a product or service to ensure the consistency of messages at every contact point where a company meets the consumer—advertising, sales promotion, personal selling, public relations, and social media, as well as direct marketing, packaging, and other forms of communication. Marketing managers carefully coordinate all promotional activities to ensure that consumers see and hear one message. Integrated marketing communications has received more attention in recent years due to the proliferation of media choices, the fragmentation of mass markets into more segmented niches, and the decrease in advertising spending in favor of promotional techniques that generate an immediate sales response.

15-7 Describe the factors that affect the promotional mix.

Promotion managers consider many factors when creating promotional mixes. These factors include the nature of the product, product life-cycle stage, target market characteristics, the type of buying decision involved, availability of funds, and feasibility of push or pull strategies. As products move through different stages of the product life cycle, marketers will choose to use different promotional elements. Characteristics of the target market, such as geographic location of potential buyers and brand loyalty, influence the promotional mix, as does whether the buying decision is complex or routine. The amount of funds a firm has to allocate to promotion may also help determine the promotional mix. Last, if a firm uses a push strategy to promote the product or service, the marketing manager might choose to use aggressive advertising and personal selling to wholesalers and retailers. If a pull strategy is chosen, then the manager often relies on aggressive mass promotion, such as advertising and sales promotion, to stimulate consumer demand.

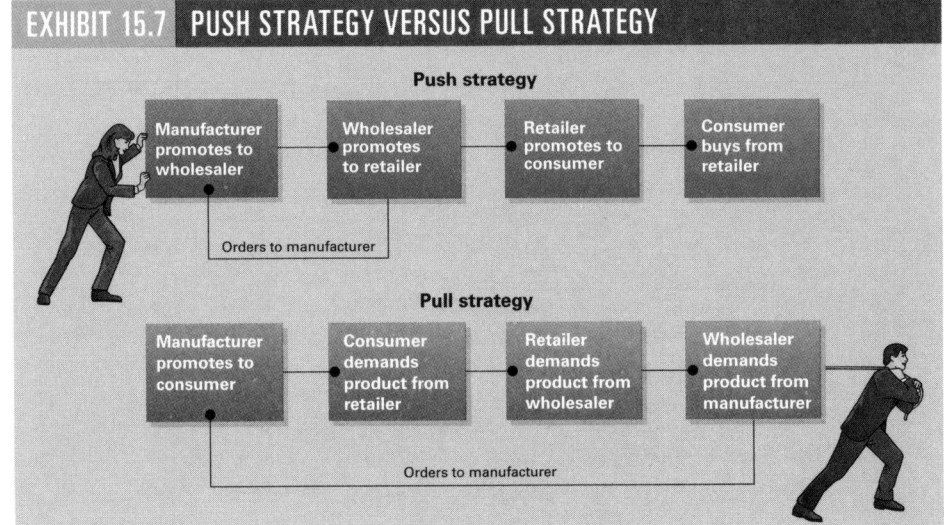

EXHIBIT 15.7 PUSH STRATEGY VERSUS PULL STRATEGY

KEY CONCEPTS

16-1 Discuss the effects of advertising on market share and consumers. Advertising helps marketers increase or maintain brand awareness and, subsequently, market share. Typically, more is spent to advertise new brands with a small market share than to advertise older brands. Brands with a large market share use advertising mainly to maintain their share of the market. Advertising affects consumers' daily lives as well as their purchases. Although advertising can seldom change strongly held consumer attitudes and values, it may transform a consumer's negative attitude toward a product into a positive one. Finally, advertising can also change the importance of a brand's attributes to consumers. By emphasizing different brand attributes, advertisers can change their appeal in response to consumers' changing needs or try to achieve an advantage over competing brands.

16-2 Identify the major types of advertising. Advertising is any form of nonpersonal, paid communication in which the sponsor or company is identified. The two major types of advertising are institutional advertising and product advertising. Institutional advertising is not product oriented; rather, its purpose is to foster a positive company image among the general public, investment community, customers, and employees. Product advertising is designed mainly to promote goods and services, and it is classified into three main categories: pioneering, competitive, and comparative. A product's place in the product life cycle is a major determinant of the type of advertising used to promote it.

16-3 Discuss the creative decisions in developing an advertising campaign. Before any creative work can begin on an advertising campaign, it is important to determine what goals or objectives the advertising should achieve. The objectives of a specific advertising campaign often depend on the overall corporate objectives and the product being advertised and are often determined using the DAGMAR approach. Once objectives are defined, creative work can begin (e.g., identifying the product's benefits, developing possible advertising appeals, evaluating and selecting the advertising appeals, executing the advertising message, and evaluating the effectiveness of the campaign).

16-4 Describe media evaluation and selection techniques. Media evaluation and selection make up a crucial step in the advertising campaign process. Major types of advertising media include newspapers, magazines, radio, television, the Internet, and outdoor media such as billboards and bus panels. Recent trends in advertising media include shopping carts, computer screen savers, interactive kiosks, advertisements run before movies, posters on bathroom stalls, and advertainments. Promotion managers choose the advertising campaign's media mix on the basis of the following variables: cost per contact, reach, frequency, characteristics of the target audience, flexibility of the medium, noise level, and the life span of the medium. After choosing the media mix, a media schedule designates when the advertisement will appear and the specific vehicles in which it will appear.

16-5 Discuss the role of public relations in the promotional mix. Public relations is a vital part of a firm's promotional mix. A company fosters good publicity to enhance its image and promote its products. Popular public relations tools include new-product publicity, product placement, consumer education, sponsorship, and company Web sites. An equally important aspect of public relations is managing unfavorable publicity in a way that is least damaging to a firm's image.

KEY TERMS

16-1

advertising response function a phenomenon in which spending for advertising and sales promotion increases sales or market share up to a certain level but then produces diminishing returns

16-2

institutional advertising a form of advertising designed to enhance a company's image rather than promote a particular product

product advertising a form of advertising that touts the benefits of a specific good or service

advocacy advertising a form of advertising in which an organization expresses its views on controversial issues or responds to media attacks

pioneering advertising a form of advertising designed to stimulate primary demand for a new product or product category

competitive advertising a form of advertising designed to influence demand for a specific brand

comparative advertising a form of advertising that compares two or more specifically named or shown competing brands on one or more specific attributes

16-3

advertising campaign a series of related advertisements focusing on a common theme, slogan, and set of advertising appeals

advertising objective a specific communication task that a campaign should accomplish for a specified target audience during a specified period

advertising appeal a reason for a person to buy a product

unique selling proposition a desirable, exclusive, and believable advertising appeal selected as the theme for a campaign

16-4

medium the channel used to convey a message to a target market

media planning the series of decisions advertisers make regarding the selection and use of media, allowing the marketer to optimally and cost-effectively communicate the message to the target audience

cooperative advertising an arrangement in which the manufacturer and the retailer split the costs of advertising the manufacturer's brand

infomercial a 30-minute or longer advertisement that looks more like a television talk show than a sales pitch

advergaming placing advertising messages in Web-based, mobile, console, or handheld video games to advertise or promote a product, service, organization, or issue

media mix the combination of media to be used for a promotional campaign

cost per contact (cost per thousand or CPM) the cost of reaching one member of the target market

cost per click the cost associated with a consumer clicking on a display or banner ad

reach the number of target consumers exposed to a commercial at least once during a specific period, usually four weeks

frequency the number of times an individual is exposed to a given message during a specific period

audience selectivity the ability of an advertising medium to reach a precisely defined market

media schedule designation of the media, the specific publications or programs, and the insertion dates of advertising

continuous media schedule a media scheduling strategy in which advertising is run steadily throughout the advertising period; used for products in the later stages of the product life cycle

flighted media schedule a media scheduling strategy in which ads are run heavily every other month or every two weeks to achieve a greater impact with an increased frequency and reach at those times

pulsing media schedule a media scheduling strategy that uses continuous scheduling throughout the year coupled with a flighted schedule during the best sales periods

seasonal media schedule a media scheduling strategy that runs advertising only during times of the year when the product is most likely to be used

EXHIBIT 16.3 ADVANTAGES AND DISADVANTAGES OF MAJOR ADVERTISING MEDIA

Medium	Advantages	Disadvantages
Newspapers	Geographic selectivity and flexibility; short-term advertiser commitments; news value and immediacy; year-round readership; high individual market coverage; co-op and local tie-in availability; short lead time	Little demographic selectivity; limited color capabilities; low pass-along rate; may be expensive
Magazines	Good reproduction, especially for color; demographic selectivity; regional selectivity; local market selectivity; relatively long advertising life; high pass-along rate	Long-term advertiser commitments; slow audience buildup; limited demonstration capabilities; lack of urgency; long lead time
Radio	Low cost; immediacy of message; can be scheduled on short notice; relatively no seasonal change in audience; highly portable; short-term advertiser commitments; entertainment carryover	No visual treatment; short advertising life of message; high frequency required to generate comprehension and retention; distractions from background sound; commercial clutter
Television	Ability to reach a wide, diverse audience; low cost per thousand; creative opportunities for demonstration; immediacy of messages; entertainment carryover; demographic selectivity with cable stations	Short life of message; some consumer skepticism about claims; high campaign cost; little demographic selectivity with network stations; long-term advertiser commitments; long lead times required for production; commercial clutter
Internet	Fastest-growing medium; ability to reach a narrow target audience; relatively short lead time required for creating Web-based advertising; moderate cost; ability to measure ad effectiveness; ability to engage consumers through search engine marketing, social media, display advertising, and mobile marketing	Most ad exposure relies on "click-through" from display ads; measurement for social media needs much improvement; not all consumers have access to the Internet, and many consumers are not using social media
Outdoor Media	Repetition; moderate cost; flexibility; geographic selectivity	Short message; lack of demographic selectivity; high "noise" level distracting audience

16-6 Define and state the objectives of sales promotion and the tools used to achieve them. Marketing managers can use sales promotion to increase the effectiveness of their promotional efforts. Sales promotion can target either trade or consumer markets. Trade promotions may push a product through the distribution channel using sales contests, premiums, P-O-P displays, trade allowances, push money, training, free merchandise, store demonstrations, and business meetings. Consumer promotions may push a product through the distribution channel using coupons, rebates, premiums, loyalty marketing programs or frequent buyer programs, contests, sweepstakes, sampling, and P-O-P displays. The biggest trend in sales promotion on both the trade and consumer sides has been the increased use of the Internet.

16-5

public relations the element in the promotional mix that evaluates public attitudes, identifies issues that may elicit public concern, and executes programs to gain public understanding and acceptance

publicity an effort to capture media attention, often initiated through press releases that further a corporation's public relations plans

product placement a public relations strategy that involves getting a product, service, or company name to appear in a movie, television show, radio program, magazine, newspaper, video game, video or audio clip, book, or commercial for another product; on the Internet; or at special events

sponsorship a public relations strategy in which a company spends money to support an issue, cause, or event that is consistent with corporate objectives, such as improving brand awareness or enhancing corporate image

crisis management a coordinated effort to handle all the effects of unfavorable publicity or another unexpected unfavorable event

16-6

sales promotion marketing communication activities other than advertising, personal selling, and public relations, in which a short-term incentive motivates consumers or members of the distribution channel to purchase a good or service immediately, either by lowering the price or by adding value

trade sales promotion promotion activities directed to members of the marketing channel, such as wholesalers and retailers

consumer sales promotion promotion activities targeted to the ultimate consumer market

trade allowance a price reduction offered by manufacturers to intermediaries such as wholesalers and retailers

push money money offered to channel intermediaries to encourage them to "push" products—that is, to encourage other members of the channel to sell the products

coupon a certificate that entitles consumers to an immediate price reduction when the product is purchased.

rebate a cash refund given for the purchase of a product during a specific period

premium an extra item offered to the consumer, usually in exchange for some proof of purchase of the promoted product

loyalty marketing program a promotional program designed to build long-term, mutually beneficial relationships between a company and its key customers

frequent buyer program a loyalty program in which loyal consumers are rewarded for making multiple purchases of a particular good or service

sampling a promotional program that allows the consumer the opportunity to try a product or service for free

point of purchase (P-O-P) display a promotional display set up at the retailer's location to build traffic, advertise the product, or induce impulse buying

KEY CONCEPTS

17-1 Understand the sales environment. Salespeople can be consumer-focused (as in the case of retail) or business-focused. The sales environment changes constantly as new competitors enter the market and old competitors leave. The ways that customers interact with salespeople and learn about products and suppliers are changing due to the rapid increase in new sales technologies. In order for companies to successfully sell products or services using a sales force, they must be very effective at personal selling, sales management, customer relationship management, and technology—all of which play critical roles in building strong long-term relationships with customers.

17-2 Describe personal selling. Personal selling is direct communication between a sales representative and one or more prospective buyers in an attempt to influence each other in a purchase situation. Broadly speaking, all businesspeople use personal selling to promote themselves and their ideas. Personal selling offers several advantages over other forms of promotion. Generally speaking, personal selling becomes more important as the number of potential customers decreases, as the complexity of the product increases, and as the value of the product grows. Technology plays an increasingly important role in personal selling. If salespeople do not stay well informed about the products they're selling, consumers may enter the store knowing even more than they do.

17-3 Discuss the key differences between relationship selling and traditional selling. Relationship selling is the practice of building, maintaining, and enhancing interactions with customers to develop long-term satisfaction through mutually beneficial partnerships. Traditional selling, on the other hand, is transaction focused. That is, the salesperson is most concerned with making a one-time sale and moving on to the next prospect. Salespeople practicing relationship selling spend more time understanding a prospect's needs and developing solutions to meet those needs.

17-4 List and explain the steps in the selling process. The selling process is composed of seven basic steps: (1) generating leads, (2) qualifying leads, (3) approaching the customer and probing needs, (4) developing and proposing solutions, (5) handling objections, (6) closing the sale, and (7) following up. The actual sales process depends on the features of the product or service, characteristics of customer segments, and internal processes in place within the firm (such as how leads are gathered). Some sales take only a few minutes to complete, but others may take much longer. Like other forms of promotion, the steps of selling follow the AIDA concept.

17-5 Understand the functions of sales management. The sales manager's basic job is to maximize sales at a reasonable cost while also maximizing profits. The sales manager's responsibilities include (1) defining sales goals and the sales process, (2) determining the sales force structure, (3) recruiting and training the sales force, (4) compensating and motivating the sales force, and (5) evaluating the sales force.

KEY TERMS

17-3

relationship selling (consultative selling) a sales practice that involves building, maintaining, and enhancing interactions with customers in order to develop long-term satisfaction through mutually beneficial partnerships

17-4

sales process (sales cycle) the set of steps a salesperson goes through in a particular organization to sell a particular product or service

lead generation (prospecting) identification of those firms and people most likely to buy the seller's offerings

cold calling a form of lead generation in which the salesperson approaches potential buyers without any prior knowledge of the prospects' needs or financial status

referral a recommendation to a salesperson from a customer or business associate

networking a process of finding out about potential clients from friends, business contacts, coworkers, acquaintances, and fellow members in professional and civic organizations

lead qualification determination of a sales prospect's (1) recognized need, (2) buying power, and (3) receptivity and accessibility

preapproach a process that describes the "homework" that must be done by a salesperson before he or she contacts a prospect

needs assessment a determination of the customer's specific needs and wants and the range of options the customer has for satisfying them

sales proposal a formal written document or professional presentation that outlines how the salesperson's product or service will meet or exceed the prospect's needs

sales presentation a formal meeting in which the salesperson presents a sales proposal to a prospective buyer

negotiation the process during which both the salesperson and the prospect offer special concessions in an attempt to arrive at a sales agreement

follow-up the final step of the selling process, in which the salesperson ensures delivery schedules are met, goods or services perform as promised, and the buyers' employees are properly trained to use the products

17-5

quota a statement of the salesperson's sales goals, usually based on sales volume

17-6

customer-centric a philosophy under which the company customizes its product and service offerings based on data generated through interactions between the customer and the company

knowledge management the process by which customer information is centralized and shared in order to enhance the relationship between customers and the organization

interaction the point at which a customer and a company representative exchange information and develop learning relationships

touch points areas of a business where customers have contact with the company and data might be gathered

point-of-sale interactions a touch point in stores or information kiosks that uses software to enable customers to easily provide information about themselves without feeling violated

campaign management developing product or service offerings customized for the appropriate customer segment and then pricing and communicating these offerings for the purpose of enhancing customer relationships

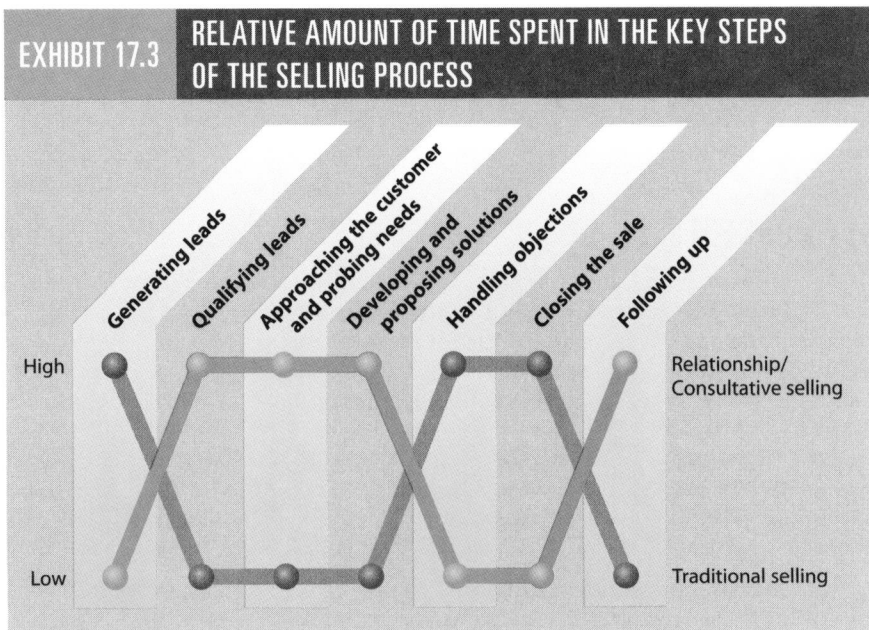

EXHIBIT 17.3 RELATIVE AMOUNT OF TIME SPENT IN THE KEY STEPS OF THE SELLING PROCESS

Source: Data from Robert M. Peterson, Patrick L. Schul, and George H. Lucas Jr., "Consultative Selling: Walking the Walk in the New Selling Environment," *National Conference on Sales Management Proceedings*, March 1996; and Mark Ellwood, *How Sales Reps Spend Their Time*, http://paceproductivity.com/files/How_Sales_Reps_Spend_Their_Time.pdf (Accessed March 2015).

17-6 Describe the use of customer relationship management in the selling process. Companies that have CRM systems follow a customer-centric focus or model. The interaction between the customer and the organization is the foundation on which a CRM system is built. Only through effective interactions can organizations learn about the expectations of their customers, generate and manage knowledge about them, negotiate mutually satisfying commitments, and build long-term relationships. If a company has identified its best customers, then it should make every effort to maintain and increase their loyalty.

KEY CONCEPTS

18-1 **Describe social media, how they are used, and their relation to integrated marketing communications.** Social media, commonly thought of as digital technology, offer a way for marketers to communicate one-on-one with consumers and measure the effects of those interactions. Social media include social networks, microblogs, and media sharing sites, all of which are used by the majority of adults. Smartphones and tablet computers have given consumers greater freedom to access social media on the go, which is likely to increase usage of social media sites. Many advertising budgets are allotting more money to online marketing, including social media, mobile marketing, and search marketing.

18-2 **Explain how to create a social media campaign.** A social media campaign should take advantage of owned media, earned media, and paid media. To use these types of media in a social media campaign, first implement an effective listening system. Marketers can interact with negative feedback, make changes, and effectively manage their online presence. Paying attention to the ways that competing brands attract and engage with their customers can be particularly enlightening for both small businesses and global brands. Second, develop a list of objectives that reflects how social media dynamically communicate with customers and build relationships.

18-3 **Evaluate the various methods of measurement for social media.** Most marketers have not been able to figure out how to measure the benefits of social media. Hundreds of metrics have been developed to measure social media's value, but these metrics are meaningless unless they are tied to key performance indicators. Some social media metrics to consider include buzz, interest, participation, search engine rank and results, influence, sentiment analysis, and Web site metrics.

18-4 **Explain consumer behavior on social media.** To effectively leverage social media, marketers must understand who uses social media and how they use it. If a brand's target market does not use social media, a social media campaign might not be useful. There are six categories of social media users: creators, critics, collectors, joiners, spectators, and inactives. A new category is emerging called "conversationalists," who post status updates on social networking sites or microblogs.

18-5 **Describe the social media tools in a marketer's toolbox and how they are useful.** A marketer has many tools to implement a social media campaign. However, new tools emerge daily, so these resources will change rapidly. Some of the strongest social media platforms are blogs, microblogs, social networks, media creation and sharing sites, social news sites, location-based social networking sites, and virtual worlds and online gaming. Blogs allow marketers and consumers to create content in the form of posts, which ideally build trust and a sense of authenticity in customers. Microblogs allow brands to follow, repost, respond to potential customers, and post content that inspires customers to engage the brand, laying a foundation for meaningful two-way conversation. Social networks allow marketers to increase awareness, target audiences, promote products, forge relationships, attract event participants, perform research, and generate new business. Media sharing sites give brands an interactive channel to disseminate content. Social news sites are useful to marketers to promote campaigns, create conversations, and build Web site traffic. Location-based social networking sites can forge lasting relationships and loyalty in customers. Review sites allow marketers to respond to customer reviews and comments about their brand. Online and mobile gaming are fertile grounds for branded content and advertising.

KEY TERMS

18-1

social media any tool or service that uses the Internet to facilitate conversations

social commerce a subset of e-commerce that involves the interaction and user contribution aspects of social online media to assist online buying and selling of products and services

crowdsourcing using consumers to develop and market products

18-2

social media monitoring the process of identifying and assessing what is being said about a company, individual, product, or brand

18-5

blog a publicly accessible Web page that functions as an interactive journal, whereby readers can post comments on the author's entries

corporate blogs blogs that are sponsored by a company or one of its brands and maintained by one or more of the company's employees

noncorporate blogs independent blogs that are not associated with the marketing efforts of any particular company or brand

microblogs blogs with strict post length limits

social networking sites Web sites that allow individuals to connect—or network—with friends, peers, and business associates

media sharing sites Web sites that allow users to upload and distribute multimedia content like videos and photos

social news sites Web sites that allow users to decide which content is promoted on a given Web site by voting that content up or down

location-based social networking sites Web sites that combine the fun of social networking with the utility of location-based GPS technology

review sites Web sites that allow consumers to post, read, rate, and comment on opinions regarding all kinds of products and services

CHAPTER REVIEW 18

18-6 Describe the impact of mobile technology on social media. The mobile platform is such an effective marketing tool—especially when targeting a younger audience. There are six reasons for the popularity of mobile marketing: (1) mobile platforms are standardized, (2) fewer consumers are concerned about privacy and pricing policies, (3) advertising can be done in real time, (4) mobile marketing is measurable, (5) in-store notification technology such as Apple's iBeacon can send promotional messages based on real-time interactions with customers, and (6) there is a higher response rate than with traditional advertising. Because of the rapid growth of smartphones, well-branded, integrated apps allow marketers to create buzz and generate customer engagement. Widgets allow customers to post a company's information to its site, are less expensive than apps, and broaden that company's exposure.

18-7 Understand the aspects of developing a social media plan. The social media plan should fit into the overall marketing plan and help marketers meet the organization's larger goals. There are six stages in creating an effective social media plan; (1) listening, (2) setting social media objectives, (3) defining strategies, (4) identifying the target audience, (5) selecting the appropriate tools and platforms, and (6) implementing and monitoring the strategy. Listening and revising the social media plan to accommodate changing market trends and needs is key to an effective social media plan.

EXHIBIT 18.2 SOCIAL MEDIA TRENDS

Trend	Change	Where Is It Now?
Yik Yak	Anonymous geolocated messaging	
Microsoft Office 365, Google Drive	Integration with file hosting	
Ello	Challengers to Facebook's dominance	
Bing	Rewards program offers prizes for using Bing Search	
The Internet of Things	Integration into wearables, appliances, apparel, and more	
Apple Pay, Google Wallet, Bitcoin, and NFC- enabled payment options	Replace credit cards with various forms of digital payment	
Loot Crate, Trunk Club, and NatureBox	Online and subscription-based personal shopping	
Twitch, Meerkat, and Periscope	Live video streaming for everybody	
Tinder and Grindr	The mainstreaming of geolocated dating apps	

KEY CONCEPTS

19-1 Discuss the importance of pricing decisions to the economy and to the individual firm. Pricing plays an integral role in the U.S. economy by allocating goods and services among consumers, governments, and businesses. Pricing is essential in business because it creates revenue, which is the basis of all business activity. In setting prices, marketing managers strive to find a level high enough to produce a satisfactory profit. Profit drives growth, salary increases, and corporate investment.

Price × Sales Units = Revenue

Revenue − Costs = Profit

19-2 List and explain a variety of pricing objectives. Establishing realistic and measurable pricing objectives is a critical part of any firm's marketing strategy. Pricing objectives are commonly classified into three categories: profit oriented, sales oriented, and status quo. Profit-oriented pricing is based on profit maximization, a satisfactory level of profit, or a target return on investment (ROI). The goal of profit maximization is to generate as much revenue as possible in relation to cost. Often, a more practical approach than profit maximization is setting prices to produce profits that will satisfy management and stockholders. The most common profit-oriented strategy is pricing for a specific ROI relative to a firm's assets. The second type of pricing objective is sales oriented, and it focuses on either maintaining a percentage share of the market or maximizing dollar or unit sales. The third type of pricing objective aims to maintain the status quo by matching competitors' prices.

19-3 Explain the role of demand in price determination. Demand is a key determinant of price. When establishing prices, a firm must first determine demand for its product. A typical demand schedule shows an inverse relationship between quantity demanded and price: when price is lowered, sales increase; when price is increased, the quantity demanded falls. For prestige products, however, there may be a direct relationship between demand and price: the quantity demanded will increase as price increases.

Marketing managers must also consider demand elasticity when setting prices. Elasticity of demand is the degree to which the quantity demanded fluctuates with changes in price. If consumers are sensitive to changes in price, demand is elastic; if they are insensitive to price changes, demand is inelastic. Thus, an increase in price will result in lower sales for an elastic product and little or no loss in sales for an inelastic product.

19-4 Understand the concepts of dynamic pricing and yield management systems. When competitive pressures are high, a company must know when it can raise prices to maximize its revenues. Dynamic pricing allows companies to adjust prices on the fly to meet demand. Yield management systems use complex mathematical software to fill unused capacity profitably. The software uses techniques such as discounting early purchases, limiting early sales at these discounted prices, and overbooking capacity. These systems are used in service and retail businesses and are substantially raising revenues.

19-5 Describe cost-oriented pricing strategies. The other major determinant of price is cost. Marketers use several cost-oriented pricing strategies. To cover their own expenses and obtain a profit, wholesalers and retailers commonly use markup pricing: they tack an extra amount on to the manufacturer's original price. Another pricing strategy determines how much a firm must sell to break even; this amount in turn is used as a reference point for adjusting price.

19-6 Demonstrate how the product life cycle, competition, distribution and promotion strategies, customer demands, the Internet and extranets, and perceptions of quality can affect price. The price of a product normally changes as it moves through the life cycle and as demand for the product and competitive conditions change. Management often sets a high price at

KEY TERMS

19-1
price that which is given up in an exchange to acquire a good or service
revenue the price charged to customers multiplied by the number of units sold
profit revenue minus expenses

19-2
return on investment (ROI) net profit after taxes divided by total assets
market share a company's product sales as a percentage of total sales for that industry
status quo pricing a pricing objective that maintains existing prices or meets the competition's prices

19-3
demand the quantity of a product that will be sold in the market at various prices for a specified period
supply the quantity of a product that will be offered to the market by a supplier at various prices for a specified period
elasticity of demand consumers' responsiveness or sensitivity to changes in price
elastic demand a situation in which consumer demand is sensitive to changes in price
inelastic demand a situation in which an increase or a decrease in price will not significantly affect demand for the product

19-4
dynamic pricing a strategy whereby prices are adjusted over time to maximize a company's revenues
yield management systems (YMS) a technique for adjusting prices that uses complex mathematical software to profitably fill unused capacity by discounting early purchases, limiting early sales at these discounted prices, and overbooking capacity

19-5
variable cost a cost that varies with changes in the level of output
fixed cost a cost that does not change as output is increased or decreased
markup pricing the cost of buying the product from the producer, plus amounts for profit and for expenses not otherwise accounted for
keystoning the practice of marking up prices by 100 percent, or doubling the cost
break-even analysis a method of determining what sales volume must be reached before total revenue equals total costs

19-6
extranet a private electronic network that links a company with its suppliers and customers

19-7
price strategy a basic, long-term pricing framework that establishes the initial price for a product and the intended direction for price movements over the product life cycle

price skimming a pricing policy whereby a firm charges a high introductory price, often coupled with heavy promotion

penetration pricing a pricing policy whereby a firm charges a relatively low price for a product when it is first rolled out as a way to reach the mass market

19-8

unfair trade practice acts laws that prohibit wholesalers and retailers from selling below cost

price fixing an agreement between two or more firms on the price they will charge for a product

predatory pricing the practice of charging a very low price for a product with the intent of driving competitors out of business or out of a market

19-9

base price the general price level at which the company expects to sell the good or service

quantity discount a price reduction offered to buyers buying in multiple units or above a specified dollar amount

cumulative quantity discount a deduction from list price that applies to the buyer's total purchases made during a specific period

noncumulative quantity discount a deduction from list price that applies to a single order rather than to the total volume of orders placed during a certain period

cash discount a price reduction offered to a consumer, an industrial user, or a marketing intermediary in return for prompt payment of a bill

functional discount (trade discount) a discount to wholesalers and retailers for performing channel functions

seasonal discount a price reduction for buying merchandise out of season

promotional allowance (trade allowance) a payment to a dealer for promoting the manufacturer's products

rebate a cash refund given for the purchase of a product during a specific period

value-based pricing setting the price at a level that seems to the customer to be a good price compared to the prices of other options

FOB origin pricing a price tactic that requires the buyer to absorb the freight costs from the shipping point ("free on board")

uniform delivered pricing a price tactic in which the seller pays the actual freight charges and bills every purchaser an identical, flat freight charge

zone pricing a modification of uniform delivered pricing that divides the United States (or the total market) into segments or zones and charges a flat freight rate to all customers in a given zone

freight absorption pricing a price tactic in which the seller pays all or part of the actual freight charges and does not pass them on to the buyer

basing-point pricing a price tactic that charges freight from a given (basing) point, regardless of the city from which the goods are shipped

single-price tactic a price tactic that offers all goods and services at the same price (or perhaps two or three prices)

flexible pricing (variable pricing) a price tactic in which different customers pay different prices for essentially the same merchandise bought in equal quantities

price lining the practice of offering a product line with several items at specific price points

leader pricing (loss-leader pricing) a price tactic in which a product is sold near or even below cost in the hope that shoppers will buy other items once they are in the store

bait pricing a price tactic that tries to get consumers into a store through false or misleading price advertising and then uses high-pressure selling to persuade consumers to buy more expensive merchandise

odd-even pricing (psychological pricing) a price tactic that uses odd-numbered prices to connote bargains and even-numbered prices to imply quality

price bundling marketing two or more products in a single package for a special price

two-part pricing a price tactic that charges two separate amounts to consume a single good or service

consumer penalty an extra fee paid by the consumer for violating the terms of the purchase agreement

---

the introductory stage, and the high price tends to attract competition. The competition usually drives prices down because individual competitors lower prices to gain market share. Adequate distribution for a new product can sometimes be obtained by offering a larger-than-usual profit margin to wholesalers and retailers. The Internet enables consumers to compare products and prices quickly and efficiently. Price is also used as a promotional tool to attract customers. Special low prices often attract new customers and entice existing customers to buy more. Large buyers can extract price concessions from vendors. Such demands can squeeze the profit margins of suppliers. Perceptions of quality can also influence pricing strategies.

19-7 Describe the procedure for setting the right price. The process of setting the right price on a product involves four major steps: (1) establishing pricing goals; (2) estimating demand, costs, and profits; (3) choosing a price policy to help determine a base price; and (4) fine-tuning the base price with pricing tactics. A price strategy establishes a long-term pricing framework for a good or service. The three main types of price policies are price skimming, penetration pricing, and status quo pricing.

19-8 Identify the legal constraints on pricing decisions. Government regulation helps monitor four major areas of pricing: unfair trade practices, price fixing, price discrimination, and predatory pricing. Many states have enacted unfair trade practice acts that protect small businesses from large firms that operate efficiently on extremely thin profit margins; the acts prohibit charging below-cost prices. The Sherman Act and the Federal Trade Commission Act prohibit both price fixing, which is an agreement between two or more firms on a particular price, and predatory pricing, in which a firm undercuts its competitors with extremely low prices to drive them out of business. Finally, the Robinson-Patman Act of 1936 makes it illegal for firms to discriminate between two or more buyers in terms of price. Predatory pricing is the practice of charging a very low price for a product with the intent of driving competitors out of business or out of a market.

19-9 Explain how discounts, geographic pricing, and other pricing tactics can be used to fine-tune a base price. Several techniques enable marketing managers to adjust prices within a general range in response to changes in competition, government regulation, consumer demand, and promotional and positioning goals. Techniques for fine-tuning a price can be divided into three main categories: discounts, allowances, rebates, and value-based pricing; geographic pricing; and other pricing tactics.

The first type of tactic gives lower prices to those who pay promptly, order a large quantity, or perform some function for the manufacturer. Additional tactics in this category include seasonal discounts, promotion allowances, and rebates (cash refunds).

Geographic pricing tactics—such as FOB origin pricing, uniform delivered pricing, zone pricing, freight absorption pricing, and basing-point pricing—are ways of moderating the impact of shipping costs on distant customers.

A variety of other pricing tactics stimulate demand for certain products, increase store patronage, and offer more merchandise at specific prices.

More and more customers are paying price penalties, which are extra fees for violating the terms of a purchase contract. The perceived fairness or unfairness of a penalty may affect some consumers' willingness to patronize a business in the future.

MKTG

ONLINE

REVIEW FLASHCARDS ANYTIME, ANYWHERE!

Create Flashcards from Your StudyBits

Review Key Term Flashcards Already Loaded on the StudyBoard

4LTR
PRESS

Access MKTG ONLINE at www.cengagebrain.com

LEARNING **YOUR** WAY

www.cengage.com/4ltrpress